The Dog Lover's Companion to California

5TH EDITION

Maria Goodavage

AVALON
TRAVEL

THE DOG LOVER'S COMPANION TO CALIFORNIA
THE INSIDE SCOOP ON WHERE TO TAKE YOUR DOG

Published by
Avalon Travel Publishing
1400 65th Street, Suite 250
Emeryville, CA 94608, USA

Avalon Travel Publishing
An Imprint of
Avalon Publishing Group, Inc.

AVALON
TRAVEL
publishing

Printing History
1st edition—1993
5th edition—May 2005
5 4 3 2 1

ISBN: 1-56691-696-8
ISSN: 1086-7856

Editor and Series Manager: Kathryn Ettinger
Acquisitions Manager: Rebecca K. Browning
Copy Editor: Karen Gaynor Bleske
Designer: Jacob Goolkasian
Graphics Coordinator: Tabitha Lahr
Production Coordinator: Jacob Goolkasian
Map Editors: Kevin Anglin, Olivia Solís
Cartographers: Kat Kalamaras, Mike Morgenfeld
Indexer: Greg Jewett

Cover and Interior Illustrations by Phil Frank

Printed in USA by Malloy Inc.

ABOUT THE AUTHOR

Maria Goodavage and Jake the Yellow-Lab-Sort-of-Dog have traveled throughout the state to check out some of the most dog-friendly parks, beaches, lodgings, and restaurants in the world. As part of their research, they've ridden on ferries, horse-drawn carriages, cable cars, and steam trains. They've visited drive-in movies, kitschy tourist attractions, and dog-friendly wineries. They've eaten at restaurants where dogs are

treated almost like people (except they never get the bill). They've stayed at the best hotels, the worst motels, and everything in between. Jake's favorite saying: "You're not really gonna leave the house without me, are ya?" (This is usually accompanied by all his extra folds of neck skin drooping forward into his face, his floppy ears hanging especially low, his tail sagging dejectedly, and his big brown eyes looking remarkably tearful.)

Since Jake is a dog without a driver's license (his furry feet don't reach the pedals), he relies on Maria, former longtime *USA Today* correspondent, to be his chauffeur. Maria is well qualified. She started chauffeuring dogs in 1989, when her intrepid Airedale, Joe, joined her during some of her travels for the newspaper. Joe and Maria sniffed out enough dog-friendly places that they came out with their first book, *The Dog Lover's Companion to the Bay Area*, shortly thereafter. *The Dog Lover's Companion to California* was born next. (Each book is now in its fifth edition!)

After 13 years of traveling with Maria, Joe recently left for Dog Heaven, where all the cats are slow and no one tells you not to eat horse manure. Jake says he's proud to be following in Joe's pawsteps.

Jake lives near the beach in San Francisco with Maria, her husband, and their daughter.

To get more information or offer a suggestion about dog-friendly travel in California, visit Maria's website, www.caldogtravel.com.

CONTENTS

CALIFORNIA

NORTHERN AREA COUNTIES

NORTHERN AREA COUNTIES — SIERRA COUNTIES — BAY AREA COUNTIES

SOUTH INLAND
COUNTIES

CENTRAL AREA
COUNTIES

SOUTH COAST
COUNTIES

Introduction

Now, Charley is a mind-reading dog. There have been many trips in his lifetime, and often he has to be left at home. He knows we are going long before the suitcases come out, and he paces and worries and whines and goes into a state of mild hysteria, old as he is.

John Steinbeck, *Travels with Charley*

There was a time when dogs could go just about anywhere they pleased. Well-dressed dogs with embarrassing names attended afternoon teas, while their less-kempt counterparts sauntered into saloons without anyone's blinking a bloodshot eye.

No one thought it strange to see a pug-nosed little snoochum-woochums of a dog snuggled on his mistress's lap on a long train journey. Equally accepted were dogs prancing through fine hotels, dogs at dining establishments, and dogs in almost any park they cared to visit.

But then there came a time (a period perhaps best referred to as the Doggy Dark Ages) when dogs came to be seen as beasts not fit for hotels, restaurants, or even many parks. The world was getting more crowded, patience growing thinner, there was only so much room, and dangit—four-legged varmints weren't going to be sharing it. They were just *dogs* after all—animals who eat from bowls on the floor and lick their heinies at unfortunate moments. Dogs were for the house, the backyard, sidewalks (with canines being "curbed"), and some tolerant parks. So we got used to leaving our dogs behind when we took off for an afternoon, or for a road trip. It hurt, oh, how it hurt, but what could you do?

Many of us know that guilt too well. The guilt that stabs at you as you push your dog's struggling body back inside the house and tug the door shut can be so painful that sometimes you just can't look back. Even a trip to the grocery store can become a heart-wrenching tale of woe. The most recent survey by the American Animal Hospital Association shows that the vast majority of us feel guilty when leaving pets at home. Thirty-nine percent of pet people call to talk to their pets when they're away. I've tried that, but it always made me feel even worse.

Joe, the Airedale terrier who inspired not only this book but the entire *Dog Lover's Companion* series, was born with an unparalleled gift for knowing how to make people feel guilty—and not your ordinary, run-of-the-mill guilt where you smart for a couple of hours after seeing your dog's moping eyes follow your car as you speed away. It's that deep-in-the-gut-for-days guilt, where the sight of that pouting snout, those drooping ears, and that tail lowered to half-mast hangs with you until you return home.

John Steinbeck's blue poodle, Charley, was a master of powerful pleas that were carefully designed to allow him to accompany his people on trips. Eventually, his hard work paid off and he won himself a seat in Steinbeck's brand-new truck/house on their epic journey across America. They sought and found the heart of this country in their adventures across 34 states.

Joe's guilt-inducing expertise won him a spot in my rusty, beat-up, hiccupping pickup truck in our sporadic little journeys throughout California. We sought and found thousands of dog-friendly places in our adventures and misadventures through California's 58 counties.

Joe and I were frequently joined by two other experts in the field of rating parks and sniffing out good dog attractions. Nisha, our old-lady springer spaniel, insisted on standing in the back of the truck, under the camper top, madly wagging her tail for hours on end as we drove and drove and drove. She was a real asset to have around when it came to checking out beaches, lakes, rivers, and ponds—any area with water. (Joe hated to get his paws wet, so he couldn't be impartial in his rating of watery attractions.)

Bill, a big, lovable galoot of a dog, was my other original canine researcher. I found him partway through my travels. He was trembling in the middle of a Northern California road, with a big chain tight around his neck. He'd evidently broken loose, because the last link of the thick chain was mauled. I came to find out that his owner beat him regularly. Bill went back to San

Francisco with me that afternoon. During the months when I was looking for the perfect home for him (oh, and did he ever get the perfect home!), he became one of the friendliest, most outgoing dogs I've ever had the pleasure to meet. His presence during my journeys was invaluable. He lifted my spirits when I was tired, and his 85 pounds of muscle kept away bad spirits when we visited questionable areas.

Time moves on. All journeys have to end someday. Bill is the only remaining dog from the original crew. Gregarious, loveable Nisha departed for Dog Heaven years ago. There, she can chew rocks and chase sticks to her heart's content.

And Joe, my most wonderful furry friend and constant traveling buddy for 13 years, joined her after the last edition of this book came out. He is dearly missed, but his legacy—that of helping other dogs lead better lives by sniffing out places they're allowed to go with their humans—lives on. I'm pretty sure that now he's chasing—and finally catching—cats (in Dog Heaven, in case you didn't know, all cats are slow), and eating all the horse manure he wants. And he *always* gets to go for rides in the car.

Before I choke up, I'd like to introduce you to a dog you'll be seeing plenty of throughout this book. His name is Jake, and we figure he's about 97 percent yellow Lab, leaving 3 percent for hound or Great Dane or some other big thing with short fur. When he was about six months old, we were asked to foster him for a week. That was well over a year ago. (We hear this happens when you foster a dog.)

Jake now weighs in at Bill's weight—85 pounds—and is one of the sweetest, most noodley dogs I've ever met. When we're home, he can usually be found reposing on the couch (despite our best attempts to keep him off it, the couch is now referred to as "Jake's couch"), jowls sprawled over the windowsill (which is half chewed away from his younger days, a very attractive sight), big brown eyes staring off into the distance as if longing for another road trip.

We've had some terrific trips together so far. Since traveling with a giant furry termite is a bad idea, I waited until his penchant for chewing furniture, windowsills, and floorboards had disappeared. Then we hit the road, enjoying dog-friendly lodgings, restaurants, and parks around the state.

As a water dog, he's wonderful at checking out liquidy attractions, from wading pools at dog parks to ponds, lakes, and beaches. Fortunately, I never have to worry about him going after ducks, per his breed's instinct. For some reason, when swimming ducks see him dog-paddling, they make a beeline right for him. This gives Jake the creeps, and he swims away, with the ducks fast on his tail. It's a sight that would make a duck hunter cry.

On a similar note, he's always glad when we visit a dog park that has a separate section for small dogs. Tiny dogs become giants with Jake, yapping a couple of times while giving him the chase. He tucks his tail between his legs and runs away, glancing nervously behind him to make sure he's escaped before relaxing enough to be his big doggy self again.

You'll be meeting Joe, Jake, Nisha, and Bill throughout this book. I think you'll find them fine representatives of the 6 million dogs (more dogs than in any other state) who live in California.

Many of the areas we've visited have higher elevations than populations. Those are often our favorite places. "The remoter, the better" seems to be the creed of dogs everywhere. People in relaxed, out-of-the-way communities sometimes call a leash a "leach." Or a "lease." No wonder dogs love the countryside.

These are some of the most polite folks I've come across. Sometimes people I met in urban areas would immediately ask me why I was traveling alone with a dog (or two or three)—was I running away from something, or just trying to find myself? The more rural folks would smile at me, nod at the dogs, and ask no pointed questions. They'd feel around in an indirect manner ("You don't see that brand of dog much anymore. Did you travel far with him?"), but they'd rarely come right out with a heat-seeking missile of a question.

I've spent a good deal of time in these less-populated areas, because during my research, I discovered an astounding statistic: Far from the reaches of most cities, 40 percent of California is open to dogs who are obedient enough to be off leash. That's 40 million acres. I normally jump for joy to find two acres that permit off-leash pooches, but 40 million acres? The thought is enough to make a grown dog swoon. This amazing acreage is part of two federal entities—the Bureau of Land Management and the U.S. Department of Agriculture's Forest Service. I've described many of these parcels throughout the book. If you have a good dog who longs to be a real off-leash explorer, try to take advantage of California's wealth of leash-free lands.

Jake and I are happy to announce that the fifth edition of the book finds the Doggy Dark Ages further behind us than ever. Dog travel is scorching hot. Everyone's getting in on it. For many reasons, dogs have become a real part of our families, and businesses have seen the golden opportunities.

Pet-travel agencies are starting to pop up. A pet-centered airline that transports dogs alongside their humans (Companion Air; www.companionair.com) is getting off the ground, with hopes business will soon take off. Iams pet food is producing handy little "Travel Meals" for "pets on the run" (www.travelmeals.com). Taxis that cater to pets and their people (such as San Diego's popular PETCAB Pet Taxi Service; www.petcabtaxi.com) are also starting to appear.

The hospitality industry, which has been lagging for a few years, is opening doors to dogs as never before. Motel 6, the first chain to allow dogs, has eliminated its policy of allowing only small dogs, and now most of its motel managers give the thumbs-up to any size good dog. Many upscale chains have taken the dog-friendly policy a step further. Loews has its "Loews Loves Pets" program. Kimpton hotels all welcome dogs and most provide them some sort of VIP package. And most recently, Starwood Hotels, one of the leading hotel companies in the world, started its Starwood LTD (Love That Dog) program in its Sheraton, Westin, and W hotels in the United States and Canada.

"Dog owners are a market niche that's been underserved by the travel industry," a Starwood press release announced. And Barry Sternlicht, Starwood's chairman and CEO, has lofty goals for Starwood. "We intend to become the most dog-friendly hotel company in the land, and not just allow dogs to stay, but actually pamper and spoil them," says Barry, who has two dogs of his own.

Many other lodgings, from the humblest cabins to the most regal luxury suites and chichi vacation rentals, are now allowing dog guests. "If we have a house that doesn't permit dogs, they're just not going to do very well," a vacation rental agent told me.

The vacation industry is truly going to the dogs. And California is rife with dog-friendly destinations.

We've tried to find the very best of everything you can do with your dog in California, so you'll never again have to face the prospect of shutting the door on your dog's nose. This book is crammed to the breaking point with descriptions of thousands of dog-friendly parks, restaurants with outdoor tables, and lodgings. The book also describes dozens of unusual adventures you and your dog can share in this crazy Golden State. You can ride on steam trains, gondolas, ferries, and surreys. You can sip chardonnay at a winery where dogs are adored, or watch a flick at a western film festival. You can pan for gold, attend a San Francisco Giants game, march in pet parades, visit small museums, go to drive-in movies, and shop at high-fashion stores. You can even get married, with your dog serving as ring bearer, flower girl, or best man.

The fifth edition of the book is the most fun-packed yet. We've added *hundreds* of new places to go with your dog. (And we've had to take away some of the less stellar listings to make room, but even longtime fans of the book shouldn't notice their loss.) We heard about many of these great finds through readers whose dogs insisted on writing to tell us about their favorite new park, cool eatery, or pooch-loving hotel. We're so grateful to these dogs that, whenever possible, we acknowledge them under the new listing. (See the imprint page for easy ways to get in touch with us with your hot dog tips. Or you can go to my website, www.caldogtravel.com, and click on the "contact" button.)

Dogs of California are lucky dogs indeed: Since the fourth edition, 62 brand-new dog parks and off-leash areas have popped up throughout the state! (Yes, 62. That is not a typo.) Dog parks are a huge trend, one that shows no signs of slowing. It doesn't make up for the great state beaches that have banned dogs since the last edition (yes, it's true—that snowy plover is at it again), but these parks do put a wag in many a dog's tail.

These dog parks run the gamut from areas that double as sumps and drainage basins to gorgeous, perfectly manicured, custom-designed doggy playgrounds. The prize for best-designed dog park goes to the new $300,000

Drigon Dog Park in Union City. (See the Union City section in the Alameda County chapter.) You've got to see it to believe it.

A traveling dog's life has changed significantly from the days when John Steinbeck and Charley traversed the country together. Dogs have less freedom, but ironically, more choices.

And you can pretty much rest assured that no one will look askance when he or she realizes that your traveling companion is none other than the furry beast at your side. "Used to be odd when someone wanted a room to stay in with their dog," says a rural innkeeper. "Now it doesn't even make us blink."

The Paws Scale

At some point, we've got to face the facts: Humans and dogs have different tastes. We like eating oranges and smelling lilacs and covering our bodies with soft clothes. They like eating roadkill and smelling each other's unmentionables and covering their bodies with horse manure.

The parks, beaches, and recreation areas in this book are rated with a dog in mind. Maybe your favorite park has lush gardens, a duck pond, a few acres of perfectly manicured lawns, and sweeping views of a nearby skyline. But unless your dog can run leash-free, swim in the pond, and roll in the grass, that park doesn't deserve a very high rating.

The very lowest rating you'll come across in this book is the fire hydrant symbol 🔥. This means the park is merely "worth a squat." Visit one of these parks only if your dog just can't hold it any longer. These parks have virtually no other redeeming qualities for canines.

Beyond that, the paws scale starts at one paw 🐾 and goes up to four paws 🐾🐾🐾🐾. A one-paw park isn't a dog's idea of a great time. Maybe it's a tiny park with few trees and too many kids running around. Or perhaps it's a magnificent-for-people national park that bans dogs from every inch of land except paved roads and a few campsites. Four-paw parks, on the other hand, are places your dog will drag you to visit. Some of these areas come as close to dog heaven as you can imagine. Many have lakes for swimming or zillions of acres for hiking. Some are small, fenced-in areas where leash-free dogs can tear around without danger of running into the road.

This book is *not* a comprehensive guide to all of the parks in California. If I included every single park, it would be larger than a multivolume set of the *Encyclopædia Britannica*. Instead, I tried to find the best, largest, and most convenient parks—and especially parks that allow dogs off leash. Some counties have so many wonderful parks that I had to make some tough choices in deciding which to include and which to leave out. Other counties have such a limited supply of parks that, for the sake of dogs living and visiting there, I ended up listing parks that wouldn't otherwise be worth mentioning.

If you're an astute, long-time reader of these books, you may notice some changes in paw ratings in this edition. Because of the tremendous increase in the number of dog parks, I've had to revise the criteria for their paws scale. Initially, almost anything off leash qualified for four paws—or three at the least. But with so many parks now, I have the luxury of truly looking at their amenities and sizes and not just their leash-free nature. In addition, some beaches have had paw changes. That's because so many beaches now ban dogs that Jake and I consider most dog-friendly beaches worthy of three or four paws. A final note: There are no longer half-paw ratings as in past editions.

I've provided specific directions to the major parks and parks near highways. Other parks are listed by their cross streets. I highly recommend checking an Internet map site such as Mapquest.com or picking up detailed street maps from the AAA—California State Automobile Association (maps are free for members)—before you and your dog set out on your adventures.

He, She, It

In this book, whether neutered, spayed, or au naturel, dogs are never referred to as "it." They are either "he" or "she." I alternate pronouns so no dog reading this book will feel left out.

To Leash or Not to Leash...

This is not a question that plagues dogs' minds. Ask just about any normal, red-blooded American dog whether she'd prefer to visit a park and be on leash or off, and she'll say, "Arf!" No question about it, most dogs would give their canine teeth to frolic about without a cumbersome leash.

Whenever you see the running dog symbol ![running dog] in this book, you'll know that under certain circumstances, your dog can run around in leash-free bliss. Fortunately, California is home to hundreds of such parks. The rest of the parks demand leashes. I wish I could write about the parks where dogs get away with being scofflaws. Unfortunately, those would be the first parks the animal control patrols would hit. I don't advocate breaking the law, but if you're going to, please follow your conscience and use common sense.

Also, just because dogs are permitted off leash in certain areas doesn't necessarily mean you should let your dog run free. In national forests and large tracts of wild land, unless you're sure your dog will come back when you call or will never stray more than a few yards from your side, you should probably keep her leashed. An otherwise docile homebody can turn into a savage hunter if the right prey is near. Or your curious dog could perturb a rattlesnake or dig up a rodent whose fleas carry bubonic plague. In pursuit of a strange scent, your dog could easily get lost in an unfamiliar area. (Some forest rangers recommend having your dog wear a bright orange collar, vest, or backpack when out in the wilderness.)

And there are many places where certain animals would love to have your dog for dinner—and not in a way Miss Manners would condone. One forest ranger told me about a bear at Yellowstone who now has the nickname "Poodlebreath" because of his dining on not one, but two poodles within a very short period.

Be careful out there. If your dog really needs leash-free exercise but can't be trusted off leash in remote areas, she'll be happy to know that a few beaches permit well-behaved, leashless pooches, as do a growing number of fenced-in dog exercise areas.

Fenced-in dog parks are the fastest-growing types of parks for pooches. In fact, back when this book was in its first edition, there were only six fenced-in dog parks in the state. Now there are more than 100! And more are in the works. Dogs with a disdain for leashes are applauding wildly. Aroooo!

There's No Business Like Dog Business

There's nothing appealing about bending down with a plastic bag or a piece of newspaper on a chilly morning and grabbing the steaming remnants of what your dog ate for dinner the night before. It's disgusting. Worse yet, you have to hang onto it until you can find a trash can. And how about when the newspaper doesn't endure before you can dispose of it? Yuck! It's enough to make you wish your dog could wear diapers. But as gross as it can be to scoop the poop, it's worse to step in it. It's really bad if a child falls in it, or—*gasp!*—starts eating it. And have you ever walked into a park where few people clean up after their dogs? The stench could make a hog want to hibernate.

Unscooped poop is one of a dog's worst enemies. Public policies banning dogs from parks are enacted because of it. And not all poop woes are outside. A dog-loving concierge at the U.S. Grant Hotel in San Diego told us that a guest came up to her and said there was some dirt beside the elevator. The concierge sent someone to clean it up. The dirt turned out to be dog poop. The U.S. Grant, which used to be one of the most elegant dog-friendly hotels in the state (it even had a Pampered Pet Program), now bans dogs. (There were other reasons, including a new boss, but the poop was the last straw.)

Just be responsible and clean up after your dog everywhere you go. (And obviously, if there's even a remote chance he'll relieve himself inside, don't even bring him into hotels or stores that permit dogs!) Anytime you take your dog out, stuff plastic bags in your jacket, purse, car, pants pockets—anywhere you might be able to pull one out when needed. Or, if plastic isn't your bag, newspapers will do the trick. If it makes it more palatable, bring along a paper bag, too, and put the used newspaper or plastic bag in it. That way you don't have to walk around with dripping paper or a plastic bag whose contents are visible to the world. If you don't enjoy the squishy sensation, try one of those cardboard or plastic bag pooper-scoopers sold at pet stores. If you don't feel like bending down, buy a long-handled scooper. There's a scooper for every taste.

This is the only lecture you'll get on scooping in this entire book. To help keep parks alive, I should harp on it in every park description, but that would take another 100 pages—and you'd start to ignore it anyway. And, if I mentioned it in some park listings but not others, it might imply that you don't have to clean up after your dog in the parks where it's not mentioned.

A final note: Don't pretend not to see your dog while he's doing his bit. Don't pretend to look for it without success. And don't fake scooping it up when you're really just covering it with sand. I know these tricks because I've been guilty of them myself—but no more. I've seen the light. I've been saved. I've been delivered from the depths of dog-doo depravity.

Etiquette Rex: The Well-Mannered Mutt

While cleaning up after your dog is your responsibility, a dog in a public place has his own responsibilities. Of course, it really boils down to your responsibility again, but the burden of action is on your dog. Etiquette for restaurants and hotels is covered in other sections of this chapter. What follows are some fundamental rules of dog etiquette. I'll go through it quickly, but if your dog's a slow reader, he can read it again: no vicious dogs; no jumping on people; no incessant barking; no leg lifts on surfboards, backpacks, human legs, or any other personal objects you'll find hanging around beaches and parks; dogs should come when they're called; dogs should stay on command.

Joe Dog managed to violate all but the first of these rules at one point or another. (Jake has followed in his pawsteps to an amazing extent, considering he never even met Joe.) Do your best to remedy any problems. It takes patience, and it's not always easy. For instance, there was a time during Joe's youth when he seemed to think that human legs were tree trunks. Rather than pretending I didn't know the beast, I strongly reprimanded him, apologized to the victim from the depths of my heart, and offered money for dry cleaning. Joe learned his lesson—many dry-cleaning bills later.

Safety First

A few essentials will keep your traveling dog happy and healthy.

Heat: If you must leave your dog alone in the car for a few minutes, do so only if it's cool out and if you can park in the shade. *Never, ever, ever* leave a dog in a car with the windows rolled up all the way. Even if it seems cool, the sun's heat passing through the window can kill a dog in a matter of minutes. Roll down the window enough so your dog gets air, but also so there's no danger of your dog's getting out or someone breaking in. Make sure your dog has plenty of water.

You also have to watch out for heat exposure when your car is in motion. Certain cars, such as hatchbacks, can make a dog in the backseat extra hot, even while you feel okay in the driver's seat.

Try to time your vacation so you don't visit a place when it's extremely warm. Dogs and heat don't get along, especially if the dog isn't used to heat. The opposite is also true. If your dog lives in a hot climate and you take him to a freezing place, it may not be a healthy shift. Check with your vet if you have any doubts. Spring and fall are usually the best times to travel.

Water: Water your dog frequently. Dogs on the road may drink even more than they do at home. Take regular water breaks, or bring a heavy bowl (the thick clay ones do nicely) and set it on the floor so your dog always has access to water. I use a nonspill bowl, which comes in really handy on curvy roads. When hiking, be sure to carry enough for you *and* a thirsty dog.

Rest Stops: Stop and unwater your dog. There's nothing more miserable than being stuck in a car when you can't find a rest stop. No matter how tightly you cross your legs and try to think of the desert, you're certain you'll burst within the next minute...so imagine how a dog feels when the urge strikes, and he can't tell you the problem. There are plenty of rest stops along the major California freeways. I've also included many parks close to freeways for dogs who need a good stretch with their bathroom break.

How frequently you stop depends on your dog's bladder. If your dog is constantly running out the doggy door at home to relieve himself, you may want to stop every hour. Others can go significantly longer without being uncomfortable. Watch for any signs of restlessness and gauge it for yourself.

Car Safety: Even the experts differ on how a dog should travel in a car. Some suggest doggy safety belts, available at pet-supply stores. Others firmly believe in keeping a dog kenneled. They say it's safer for the dog if there's an accident, and it's safer for the driver because there's no dog underfoot. Still others say you should just let your dog hang out without straps and boxes. They believe that if there's an accident, at least the dog isn't trapped in a cage. They say that dogs enjoy this more, anyway.

I'm a follower of the last school of thought. Jake loves sticking his snout out of the windows to smell the world go by. The danger is that if the car kicks up a pebble or angers a bee, his nose and eyes could be injured. So far, he's been okay, as has every other dog who has explored the Golden State with us, but I've seen dogs who needed to be treated for bee stings to the nose because of this practice. If in doubt, try opening the window just enough so your dog can't stick out much snout.

Whatever travel style you choose, your pet will be more comfortable if he has his own blanket with him. A veterinarian acquaintance brings a faux-sheepskin blanket for his dogs. At night in the hotel, the sheepskin doubles as the dog's bed.

Planes: Air travel is even more controversial. Personally, unless my dogs can fly with me in the passenger section (which very tiny dogs are sometimes allowed to do), I'd rather find a way to drive the distance or leave them at home with a friend. I've heard too many horror stories of dogs suffocating in what was supposed to be a pressurized cargo section, dying of heat exposure, or ending up in Miami while their people go to Seattle. There's just something unappealing about the idea of a dog's flying in the cargo hold, as if he's nothing more than a piece of luggage. Of course, many dogs survive just fine, but I'm not willing to take the chance. (That said, an airline called Companion Air is hoping to be the first to offer a way for humans and any size dog to be together during plane travel—and not in the cargo section! It's still in the planning stages, but you can visit the website at www.companionair.com for updates.)

If you need to transport your dog by plane, try to fly nonstop, and make sure you schedule takeoff and arrival times when the temperature is below 80°F (but not bitterly cold in winter). You'll want to consult the airline about regulations, required certificates, and fees. Be sure to check with your vet to make sure your pooch is healthy enough to fly.

The question of tranquilizing a dog for a plane journey is very controversial. Some vets think it's insane to give a dog a sedative before flying. They say a dog will be calmer and less fearful without a disorienting drug. Others think it's crazy not to afford your dog the little relaxation he might not otherwise get without a tranquilizer. Discuss the issue with your vet, who will take into account the trip length and your dog's personality.

Many websites deal with air-bound pooches. I highly recommend checking them out for further info on safe air travel with your dog. (Most of the web pages have long and cumbersome names, so you're best off searching for keywords such as "Traveling Airlines Pets.")

The Ultimate Doggy Bag

Your dog can't pack his own bags, and even if he could, he'd probably fill them with dog biscuits and chew toys. It's important to stash some of those in your dog's vacation kit, but here are other handy items to bring along: bowls, bedding, a brush, towels (for those muddy days), a first-aid kit, pooper-scoopers, water, food, prescription drugs, tags, treats, toys, and—of course—this book.

Make sure your dog is wearing his license, identification tag, and rabies tag. Bringing along your dog's up-to-date vaccination records is a good idea, too. If you should find yourself at a park or campground that requires the actual rabies certificate, you'll be set. In addition, you may unexpectedly end up needing to leave your dog in a doggy day care for a few hours so you can go somewhere you just can't bring your dog. A record of his shots is imperative. (You'll also have to get him a kennel-cough shot if boarding is a possibility.)

It's a good idea to snap a disposable ID on your dog's collar, too, showing a cell phone number or the name, address, and phone number either of where you'll be vacationing, or of a friend who'll be home to field calls. That way, if your dog should get lost, at least the finder won't be calling your empty house. Paper key-chain tags you buy at hardware stores offer a cheap way to change your dog's contact info as often as needed when on vacation. Dog-book author and pet columnist Gina Spadafori advises always listing a local number on the tag. "You'd be surprised how many people don't want to make a long-distance phone call," she writes in her book *Dogs for Dummies*.

Some people think dogs should drink only water brought from home, so their bodies don't have to get used to too many new things. I've never had a problem giving my dogs tap water from other parts of the state, nor has anyone else I know. Most vets think your dog will be fine drinking tap water in most U.S. cities.

"Think of it this way," says Pete Beeman, a longtime San Francisco veterinarian. "Your dog's probably going to eat poop if he can get hold of some, and even that's probably not going to harm him. I really don't think that drinking water that's okay for people is going to be bad for dogs." (Jake can attest to the poop part. But let's not talk about that.)

Bone Appétit

In some European countries, dogs enter restaurants and dine alongside their folks as if they were people, too. (Or at least they sit and watch and drool while their people dine.) Not so in the United States. Rightly or wrongly, dogs are considered a health threat here. But many health inspectors I've spoken with say they see no reason why clean, well-behaved dogs shouldn't be permitted inside a restaurant. "Aesthetically, it may not appeal to Americans," an environmental specialist with the state Department of Health told me. "But the truth is, there's no harm in this practice."

Ernest Hemingway made an expatriate of his dog, Black Dog (aka Blackie), partly because of America's restrictive views on dogs in dining establishments. In "The Christmas Gift," a story published in *Look* magazine in 1954, he describes how he made the decision to take Black Dog to Cuba, rather than leave him behind in Ketchum, Idaho.

> This was a town where a man was once not regarded as respectable unless he was accompanied by his dog. But a reform movement had set in, led by several local religionists, and gambling had been abolished and there was even a movement on foot to forbid a dog from entering a public eating place with his master. Blackie had always tugged me by the trouser leg as we passed a combination gambling and eating place called the Alpine where they served the finest sizzling steak in the West. Blackie wanted me to order the giant sizzling steak and it was difficult to pass the Alpine.... We decided to make a command decision and take Blackie to Cuba.

Fortunately, you don't have to take your dog to a foreign country to eat together at a restaurant. California is full of restaurants with outdoor tables, and hundreds of them welcome dogs to join their people for an alfresco experience. The law on outdoor dining is somewhat vague, and each county has different versions of it. In general, as long as your dog doesn't go inside a restaurant (even to get to outdoor tables in the back) and isn't near the food preparation areas, it's probably legal. The decision is then up to the restaurant proprietor.

The restaurants listed in this book have given us permission to tout them as dog-friendly eateries. But keep in mind that rules can change and restaurants can close, so I highly recommend phoning before you set your stomach on a particular kind of cuisine. Since some restaurants close during colder months, phoning ahead is a doubly wise thing to do. (Of course, you can assume that where there's snow or ultracold temperatures, the outdoor tables will move indoors for a while each year.) If you can't call first, be sure to ask the manager of the restaurant for permission before you sit down with your sidekick. Remember, it's the restaurant proprietor, not you, who will be in trouble if someone complains to the health department.

Some basic rules of restaurant etiquette: Dogs shouldn't beg from other diners, no matter how delicious their steaks look. They should not attempt to get their snouts (or their entire bodies) up on the table. They should be clean, quiet, and as unobtrusive as possible. If your dog leaves a good impression with the management and other customers, it will help pave the way for all the other dogs who want to dine alongside their best friends in the future.

A Room at the Inn

Good dogs make great hotel guests. They don't steal towels, and they don't get drunk and keep the neighbors up all night. California is full of lodgings whose owners welcome dogs. This book lists dog-friendly accommodations of all types, from motels to bed-and-breakfast inns to elegant hotels—but the basic dog etiquette rules are the same everywhere.

Dogs should never be left alone in your room. Leaving a dog alone in a strange place invites serious trouble. Scared, nervous dogs may tear apart

DIVERSION

Ch-Ch-Chains: An increasing number of stores permit pooches these days, including many within chains such as Borders, Saks Fifth Avenue, REI, Nordstrom, Big Dogs Sportwear, and Restoration Hardware. Not all stores within these chains welcome dogs, but most do. If your dog is longing to do more than just window shop, she'll likely be in luck if one of these stores is on your shopping list.

drapes, carpeting, and furniture. They may even injure themselves. They might also bark nonstop and scare the daylights out of the housekeeper. Just don't do it.

Only bring a house-trained dog to a lodging. How would you like a house-guest to go to the bathroom in the middle of your bedroom?

Make sure your pooch is flea-free. Otherwise, future guests will be itching to leave.

It helps to bring your dog's bed or blanket along for the night. Your dog will feel more at home and won't be tempted to jump on the hotel bed. If your dog sleeps on the bed with you at home (as 47 percent do, according to the American Animal Hospital Association survey), bring a sheet and put it on top of the bed so the hotel's bedspread won't get furry or dirty.

Don't wash your dog in the hotel tub. "It's very yucky," I was told by one motel manager who has seen so many furry tubs that she's thinking about banning dogs.

Likewise, refrain from using the ice bucket as a water or food bowl. Bring your own bowls, or stay in a hotel that provides them, as many of the nicer ones do these days.

After a few days in a hotel, some dogs come to think of it as home. They get territorial. When another hotel guest walks by, it's "Bark! Bark!" When the housekeeper knocks, it's "Bark! Snarl! Bark! Gnash!" Keep your dog quiet, or you'll both find yourselves looking for a new home away from home.

For some strange reason, many lodgings prefer small dogs as guests. All I can say is, "Yip! Yap!" It's really ridiculous. Large dogs are often much calmer and quieter than their tiny, high-energy cousins.

If you're in a location where you can't find a hotel that will accept you and your big brute (a growing rarity these days), it's time to try a sell job. Let the manager know how good and quiet your dog is (if he is). Promise he won't eat the bathtub or run around and shake all over the hotel. Offer a deposit or sign a waiver, even if they're not required for small dogs. It helps if your sweet, soppy-eyed dog is at your side to convince the decision-maker.

I've sneaked dogs into hotels, but I don't recommend it. The lodging might have a good reason for its rules. Besides, you always feel as if you're going to be caught and thrown out on your hindquarters. You race in and out of your room with your dog as if ducking sniper fire. It's better to avoid feeling like a criminal and move on to a more dog-friendly location. With the numbers of lodgings that welcome dogs these days, you won't have to go far.

The lodgings described in this book are for dogs who obey all the rules. I list a range of rates for each lodging, from the least expensive room during low season to the priciest room during high season. Most of the rooms are doubles, so there's not usually a huge variation. But when a room price gets into the thousands of dollars, you know we're looking at royal suites.

Many lodgings charge extra for your dog. If you see "Dogs are $10 (or whatever amount) extra," that means $10 extra per night. Some charge a fee for the length of a dog's stay, and others ask for a deposit. These details are also noted in the lodging description. A few places still ask for nothing more than your dog's promise that she'll be on her best behavior. So, if no extra charge is mentioned in a listing, it means your dog can stay with you for free.

Natural Troubles

Chances are your adventuring will go without a hitch, but you should always be prepared to deal with trouble. Make sure you know the basics of animal first aid before you embark on a long journey with your dog.

The more common woes—ticks, foxtails, poison oak, and skunks—can make life with a traveling dog a somewhat trying experience. Ticks are hard to avoid in many parts of California. They can carry Lyme disease, so you should always check yourself and your dog all over after a day in tick country. Don't forget to check ears and between the toes. If you see a tick, just pull it straight out with tweezers, not with your bare hands.

The tiny deer ticks that carry Lyme disease are difficult to find. Consult your veterinarian if your dog is lethargic for a few days, has a fever, loses her appetite, or becomes lame. These symptoms could indicate Lyme disease. Some vets recommend a new vaccine that is supposed to prevent the onset of the disease.

Foxtails—those arrow-shaped pieces of dry grass that attach to your socks, your sweater, and your dog—are an everyday annoyance. In certain cases, they can also be lethal. They may stick in your dog's eyes, nose, ears, or mouth and work their way in. Check every nook and cranny of your dog after a walk if you've been anywhere near dry grass. Despite my constant effort to find these things in Joe's curly tan fur, I missed several and they beat a path through his foot and into his leg. Be vigilant.

Poison oak is also a common California menace. Get familiar with it through a friend who knows nature or through a guided nature walk. Dogs don't generally have reactions to poison oak, but they can easily pass its oils on to people. If you think your dog has made contact with some poison oak, avoid petting her until you can get home and bathe her (preferably with rubber gloves). If you do pet her before you can wash her, don't touch your eyes and be sure to wash your hands immediately.

If your dog loses a contest with a skunk (and she *always* will), rinse her eyes first with plain warm water and then forget the old tomato-juice remedy. All that does is make a dog itchy—and if she starts out white, she can turn a creepy shade of orange.

I've had the fortune of being handed the best-ever recipe for de-skunking by Jamie Ray, an expert in the field. She's the founder of the San Francisco Rescued Orphan Mammal Program (SF ROMP), an urban wildlife rescue group.

foxtail

poison oak

And it just so happens that some of the urban wildlife her group rescues is black and white and furry and occasionally whiffy, if you get my drift.

I phoned her one day after Jake had a much-too-close encounter of the skunky kind. The fumes were so bad I could barely breathe. Tomato juice wasn't an option, as it had never worked for our other dogs. I figured if anyone could help, Jamie could. And did she ever. Jake was left with barely any eau d'skunk, and you had to get very close to smell it. On two subsequent occasions, the recipe also worked magic.

I suggest you write down the recipe and keep it handy. You may also want to keep an extra bottle or two of hydrogen peroxide around so you'll always be ready. The other ingredients are in just about any household.

Make a mixture with the ratio of one cup hydrogen peroxide, two tablespoons of baking soda, and one tablespoon of dishwashing soap—Dawn works best. (For Jake, we multiplied this recipe times six, since he is so big and was so stinky.) Stir, and apply it all over your dog. Don't hold back. Use plenty, being careful to keep it away from the eyes. Rub it in, wait a couple of minutes, and rinse. You may need to do it again to really eradicate the stink. Rinse well. I've followed up each de-skunking with some gentle dog shampoo.

(If you ever use this recipe, you might want to consider sending a small thank-you to SF ROMP, which always needs donations. You can find info on SF ROMP at www.sfwildlifeservices.org.)

Ruffing It Together

Whenever we went camping, Joe insisted on sleeping in the tent. He sprawled out and wouldn't budge. At the first hint of dawn, he'd tiptoe outside (sometimes right through the bug screen) as if he'd been standing vigil all night. He tried not to look shamefaced, but under all that curly hair lurked an embarrassed grin.

Actually, Joe might have had the right idea. Some outdoor experts say it's dangerous to leave even a tethered dog outside your tent at night. The dog can escape or become a late dinner for some hungry creature.

All state parks require dogs to be kept in a tent or vehicle at night. Some county parks follow suit. Other policies are more lenient. Use good judgment.

If you're camping with your dog, chances are you're also hiking with him. Even if you're not hiking for long, watch out for your dog's paws, especially the paws of those who are fair of foot. Rough terrain can cause a dog's pads to become raw and painful, making it almost impossible for him to walk. Several types of dog boots are available for such feet. It's easier to carry the booties than to carry your dog home.

Be sure to bring plenty of water for you and your pooch. Stop frequently to wet your whistles. Some veterinarians warn against letting your dog drink out of a stream because of the chance of ingesting giardia and other internal parasites, but it's not always easy to stop a thirsty dog.

A Dog in Need

If you don't have a dog but could provide a good home for one, I'd like to make a plea on behalf of all the unwanted dogs who will be euthanized tomorrow—and the day after that and the day after that. Animal shelters and humane organizations are overflowing with dogs who would devote their lives to being your best buddy, your faithful traveling companion, and a dedicated listener to all your tales of bliss and woe.

Need a nudge? Remember the oft-quoted words of Samuel Butler:

> "The great pleasure of a dog is that you may make a fool of yourself with him and not only will he not scold you, but he will make a fool of himself, too."

Keep in Touch

Our readers mean everything to us. We explore California so you and your dogs can spend true quality time together. Your input to this book is very important. In the last few years, we've heard from many wonderful dogs and their people about new dog-friendly places or old dog-friendly places we didn't know about. If you have any suggestions or insights to offer, please contact us using the information listed in the front of this book, or via my website, www.caldogtravel.com.

NORTHERN AREA COUNTIES

CHAPTER 1
Del Norte County

Don't call this beautiful coastal redwood empire "Del Nort-ay" County, as many Californians do because of all the Spanish influence in this state. It's as much of a giveaway that you're from out of town as pronouncing the next state north "Or-ih-gohn" instead of "Or-ih-ghin." Pronounce this county "Del Nort," even if it reminds you of something Ralph Kramden would say.

If you want a real coastal getaway, you couldn't ask for a more beautiful, remote area. Part of the reason so few Californians know the local pronunciation of this county is because it's so out of the way that we don't often hear about the place.

As one of the state's best-kept secrets, it's a gem for people vacationing with a dog. While there are plenty of leash laws, there are also many places where civilization hasn't yet encroached sufficiently to make leashes a mandatory part of a dog's attire. The 305,000-acre Smith River National Recreation Area in the Six Rivers National Forest makes up the majority of this county and allows dogs off leash everywhere except in campgrounds!

PICK OF THE LITTER—DEL NORTE COUNTY

BEST WILD AREA
Six Rivers National Forest (page 22)

BEST HOMEMADE JAM
Glen's Bakery, Crescent City (page 26)

BEST KITSCHY ATTRACTION
Trees of Mystery, Crescent City/Klamath (page 25)

The climate in Del Norte County is very mild, with coastal temperatures generally ranging 65–75°F. That's good news for dogs who don't like temperature extremes. But this region is also known for its rain. One hundred inches a year here is common, making outdoor cafés almost nonexistent. The forests here are actually rain forests. They're lush and verdant. They're also often wet. Some dogs and people prefer this to the desert scenarios in other parts of the state. With a slicker, a dog towel, and a love of the outdoors, you and your dog could be very happy here. (While here, be sure to catch up with Paul Bunyan and ride a gondola 571 feet up a mountain—with your dog! See the Diversion Have a Great Big Time.)

NATIONAL FORESTS

The National Forests and Wilderness Areas resource at the back of this book has important information and safety tips on visiting national forests with your dog and has more background on the Six Rivers National Forest.

Six Rivers National Forest

This county is green thanks in great part to the lush 305,000-acre Smith River National Recreation Area, which is part of Six Rivers National Forest. The U.S. Forest Service has been designated as the steward of this fairly new national recreation area, and that's fantastic for dogs. The Wild and Scenic River, the 65 miles of trails, and the seven distinct plant communities can all be enjoyed by off-leash dogs, as long as they're obedient.

Smith River

PARKS, BEACHES, AND RECREATION AREAS

❶ Pelican State Beach

🐾🐾🐾🐾 (See Del Norte County map on page 20)

It's only five acres, but that's plenty of running room for a dog who's been cooped up in the car all day. Pelican State Beach is actually a few miles northwest of Smith River, the closest California city to the Oregon border. It seems to be a popular stop for folks who've just come from or are about to go over to visit our northern neighbor. Dogs are supposed to be leashed, but they love sniffing around the beach for the driftwood that's so plentiful here.

The beach is just west of U.S. 101, five miles south of the Oregon border. 707/464-6101.

❷ Mouth of the Smith River

🐾🐾🐾🐾 (See Del Norte County map on page 20)

This beautiful park, right on the mouth of the Smith River, is part of the state's Wild and Scenic River system. It's a great place to relax on the pebbly beach and take in the sights, or walk to Pyramid Point and do a little bird-watching with your leashed dog. It's also a popular backdrop for photographs. If your dog wants to be in pictures, this might be the place to snap away.

The park is at the end of Smith River Road. 707/464-7230.

PLACES TO STAY

Clifford Kamph Memorial Park: Camp at the ocean in one of nine sites at this two-acre county-run campground. One site is on the beach, a couple are on a bluff, and the rest are set just a bone's throw inland. Sites are a mere $5. Keep in mind there are no showers here. Your dog will enjoy this, but you may not. The park is about 1.5 miles south of the Oregon border, just west of U.S. 101. 707/462-7230.

Ship Ashore Best Western: If yours is a teeny-weeny dog, she can stay here with you. The weight limit for pets is 10 pounds. Fortunately, there is no weight limit for human guests. But in case you need the exercise, there's a pooch path on the premises. Rates are $60–69. 12370 U.S. 101 North 95567; 707/487-3141 or 800/528-1234.

Crescent City

This 1.25-square-mile coastal city was devastated by a giant tsunami in 1964. A series of waves about 12 feet high rushed inland as far as 1,600 feet, destroying 29 downtown blocks and killing 11 people. The city has since rebuilt, and the beach that the tsunami washed over is now awash with happy dogs (see Beachfront Park under Parks, Beaches, and Recreation Areas). Although the city itself has no leash law, it follows the county's leash law, so pooches must be appropriately attired.

PARKS, BEACHES, AND RECREATION AREAS

🐾 Florence Keller Regional Park

🐾🐾🐾 (See Del Norte County map on page 20)

This 30-acre county park is one big redwood grove with space carved out for trails, playing fields, and playgrounds. It's a good balance of wild and civilized, if you need that kind of balance. Dogs have to be leashed. There are no showers here, so bring extra deodorant, or all the dogs in camp may follow you home. Camping at any of the 50 sites costs $10 a night.

Exit U.S. 101 at Cunningham Lane and follow the signs to the park. 707/464-7230.

🐾 Beachfront Park

🐾🐾🐾🐾 (See Del Norte County map on page 20)

Pooches are supposed to be leashed at this often empty 80-acre beach/grassy park, but that doesn't stop them from having a ball here. They run and roll and do some mighty fine beachcombing. They stretch out beside their people in the charming gazebo, and they even manage to do the dog paddle when the surf is down. (Watch out for Elk Creek, which empties into the harbor here. Occasionally it can be too swift for even the strongest canine swimmer.)

If dogs aren't the only people in your life, this is an especially fun park to visit. Children can check out the playground, while anglers can make the acquaintance of fish at the 850-foot public fishing pier.

From U.S. 101, go west on Front Street. The park is at Front Street between B and F Streets. 707/464-9507; www.crescentcity.org.

PLACES TO EAT

Beacon Burger: This place truly is a beacon for dogs and their people. People often place food orders for their dogs, who get a big bowl of water if they're thirsty. If you want to make your dog very happy, try the namesake burger, which is a half-pounder with bacon and cheese. The view from the outdoor tables is terrific. 160 Anchor Way; 707/464-6565.

DIVERSION

Have a Great Big Time!: A visit to the campy but fascinating **Trees of Mystery** between Crescent City and the next town along U.S. 101, Klamath, will be a visit you and your canine buddy will never forget. This is the most dog-friendly, fun roadside-type attraction we've ever come across.

From the moment you step out of your car, your kitschy adventure begins. A 50-foot-tall statue of Paul Bunyan greets patrons in the parking lot. He really talks to you. He'll greet your dog by name, too. This literally scares the pee out of a few dogs, but usually dogs just look at the giant wooden man as if he's just a big weird tree with a voice—and what's so unusual about that?

When you pay your admission fee, you'll have access to a nature trail that takes you through some of the world's oldest and largest trees. But these are no ordinary trees! These are the Trees of Mystery. We won't ruin the many surprises that await you, but let's just say you'll definitely want a camera with a wide-angle lens. Boy dogs are especially fond of the trees here.

You can also go on a terrific 10-minute gondola ride 571 feet up the mountain. Although the altitude at the top is only 742 feet, you get a stunning view of the Pacific on one side and mountains on the other. You can sniff around once you disembark at the top and either ride or walk back down. (Those afraid of heights might want to walk.) The rides are included in your entry fee, and you can go up and down as many times as you want.

Our dog friend Fergus wasn't into the views up there but was very interested in the Trees of Mystery gift store. The people who work here adore dogs. Four Great Pyrenees pooches strolled in one day and "we just about went crazy over them," says Joan, one of the dog-lovers who works here. "They better be prepared to spend extra time here getting lots of love." Not only do they get love, but they also get a free dog biscuit. Humans get a free sample of delectable fudge. (They make 30 pounds of the stuff here daily.) The gift shop is also the place where you can borrow a leash if your dog is normally the naked type.

And finally, your dog can join you at The End of the Trail Museum, which adjoins the gift shop. The fascinating museum houses one of the largest private collections of Native American artifacts in the United States. We applaud the museum for welcoming well-behaved dogs.

Admission to the museum is free. The entry fee to the Trees trails and gondola is $12 for adults, $10 for seniors, and $5 for children ages 4–10. Dogs get in free, as do kids under four. 15500 U.S. 101, Klamath; 707/482-5613 or 800/638-3389; www.treesofmystery.net.

Glen's Bakery: The folks here make their own jam at this bakery. Add it to the fresh-baked bread, and you and your dog can feast. Try the clam chowder if you're in the mood for something hot. Dine with doggy at the outdoor bench. 722 3rd Street; 707/464-2914.

PLACES TO STAY

Best Value Inn: Good news for some dogs: No cats allowed! Bad news for some dogs: No cats allowed. Rates are $40–85. Dogs are $5 extra. 440 U.S. 101 North 95531; 707/464-4141.

Florence Keller Regional Park: See Florence Keller Regional Park, above, for camping information.

Gardenia Motel: This is your typical decent little motel. Dogs are allowed in some rooms. Rates are $50–55. Dogs are $5 extra. 119 L Street 95531; 707/464-2181.

Redwoods State Park: Dogs aren't allowed on the trails here, but they can sleep in one of the 245 campsites under a grove of redwoods. Rates are $19. The campground is about 10 miles southeast of Crescent City, just off U.S. 101. For reservations, call 800/444-PARK (800/444-7275). For information on the park, phone 707/464-6101.

Klamath

If you and your dog are sniffing out the marvelous Trees of Mystery (see the Diversion Have a Great Big Time!) and need a place to spend the night, Klamath offers a couple of good lodging choices.

PLACES TO STAY

Camp Marigold Garden Cottages: The cottages here were built in 1939 and are rustic, but not too much so: A poodle we know who recently stayed here gives it two paws up. Camp Marigold's cottages are set on four acres of grass and gardens, but it's the cottages' proximity to the Six Rivers National Forest that's the biggest hit with dogs. The place backs up right to the national forest, with plenty of excellent hiking trails to explore together.

Rates are $48–65. If you're throwing a big bash and want to rent Camp Marigold's large lodge, which sleeps up to 15 and is also dog-friendly, you'll pay $215 per night. 16101 U.S. 101 95548; 707/482-3585 or 800/621-8513.

Motel Trees: If the talking Paul Bunyan at the Trees of Mystery made your dog's hair stand on end, you might want to choose another lodging: Motel Trees is directly opposite the Trees of Mystery, and there's no escaping the scary giant man. Most dogs do just fine here and enjoy being able to look at the Trees of Mystery from their motel window. Rates are $48–60. Dogs are $5 extra. 15495 U.S. 101 North 95548; 707/482-3152.

28

CHAPTER 2

Siskiyou County

Siskiyou County is home to some of the least creative names for parks that we've ever seen. Dogs tend to yawn when they find out that three towns here have parks called "City Park." But fortunately, two of the City Parks are really outstanding—as are many of the parks and recreation areas in this huge and wild county.

The visual highlight of Siskiyou County is towering Mt. Shasta, but there's so much beauty here that almost anywhere you go, something's bound to impress your senses. Two national forests make up a big part of the county. As you travel on Highway 96, you'll find dozens of places to pull off and explore the Klamath River in the Klamath National Forest. If you stop at a wide river access point that's far from the road, your dog can trot around off leash while you fish or soak your weary legs. Be careful, though. The current can really whip in some spots.

Two of the best places to spend the night and have howling good views of Mt. Shasta are former fire lookouts in the Shasta-Trinity National Forest. (See Girard Ridge Lookout in the Dunsmuir section.) The price is right and the

PICK OF THE LITTER—SISKIYOU COUNTY

BEST FRESH DRINKING WATER
City Park's Sacramento River headwaters, Mount Shasta
(page 33)

BEST HIGH-ALTITUDE DIGS
Girard Ridge Lookout/Little Mt. Hoffman Lookout,
Dunsmuir area (page 36)

BEST CHOO-CHOOS FOR POOCHOOS
Blue Goose Steam Train, Yreka (page 32)

experience is one you and your dog won't soon forget. (Plus you get to bond, because, like your dog, you also must go outside when you have to go to the bathroom. At least you'll have an outhouse.)

NATIONAL FORESTS

The National Forests and Wilderness Areas resource at the back of this book has important information and safety tips on visiting national forests with your dog and has more background on the national forests listed below.

Klamath National Forest

Shasta-Trinity National Forest

Dorris

PARKS, BEACHES, AND RECREATION AREAS

■ Lower Klamath National Wildlife Refuge
(See Siskiyou County map on page 28)
This 54,000-acre waterfowl haven is home to what may be the largest wintering concentration of bald eagles in the lower 48 states. Dogs are allowed off leash only if they're helping you during waterfowl and pheasant hunting seasons. Otherwise, they have to be leashed at all times to protect this important nesting and migration area.

Lower Klamath Lake and the surrounding marshy area and uplands are a bird-watcher's paradise. During summer you'll see avocets, grebes, herons, white pelicans, black-necked stilts, and killdeers. Nearly one million waterfowl use this and nearby Tule Lake during fall migration. Keep those binoculars peeled.

The refuge has many entrances. From U.S. 97 at the Oregon border, head east on Highway 161. The refuge's entrances will be on your right in a few miles. Call 530/667-2231 for information and directions to other areas of the refuge.

Yreka

Yreka, Eureka, Ukiah, Arcata. Traveling in Northern California can be confusing, with cities whose names sound like bad Scrabble hands. But here's an easy way to have Yreka (why-REE-kuh) stick out in your mind: When you're here, just look south. See spectacular, snowy Mt. Shasta in the distance? *Yreka* is an Indian word for "white mountain." The "Y" in Yreka sounds sort of like the "white" in white mountain. Got it?

This is the county seat of Siskiyou County, and it's an attractive, historic place on the eastern edge of a huge section of the Klamath National Forest. Dogs prefer to run around unleashed in the forest, but there's a city park in town where they can enjoy a more civilized walk. And if your dog is small, he can have a roaring good time aboard the Blue Goose Steam Train (see the Diversion Choo Choo with Your Poochoo).

PARKS, BEACHES, AND RECREATION AREAS

🏁 City Park
😺😺 (See Siskiyou County map on page 28)

This small city park is conveniently located near the historic district of Yreka. Dogs like it just fine, as long as they don't mind a leash. The grass is green and the shade trees are big. There's also a playground and a ball field so the kids can work off their energy while the dog explores.

From Highway 3, drive west about six blocks on West Miner Street. The park is on your left, at Gold and West Miner Streets. 530/841-2386.

PLACES TO STAY

Best Western Miner's Inn: Small- and medium-sized dogs are invited to sleep here. Rates are $68–108. 122 East Miner Street 96097; 530/842-4355.

Economy Inn: There's plenty of land around here for a little romping with your pooch. Rates are $53–58. Dogs are $5 extra. 526 South Main Street 96097; 530/842-4404.

DIVERSION

Choo Choo with Your Poochoo: Put on your engineer caps and get ready to ride along a short-line railroad that's been in continuous operation since 1889. Dogs who stay out of the aisle, whether on your lap or at your feet, are allowed to accompany you on the **Blue Goose Steam Train** for a magical three-hour tour from Yreka east through Shasta Valley. You'll pass lumber mills, cross the Shasta River, and chug along through beautiful cattle country—all with majestic Mt. Shasta in the background.

The 1915 Baldwin steam engine stops for 1.5 hours in the old cattle town of Montague, where you can picnic in the park and afterward visit the old-fashioned soda fountain or take a wagon ride.

You can choose from an open car, two 1920s cars, and a couple of vintage 1948 passenger cars. Unless your dog doesn't like the wind in his face or the sound of steam rushing skyward, the open cars are the best ones for canines. Just keep hold of that leash.

The train runs from Memorial Day weekend through the last Sunday of October. Rates are $14 adults, $11 seniors, $7 kids, and dogs travel free. If your dog is too big, ask if she can stay in the manager's office. Railway manager Larry Bacon says he occasionally allows good doggies to stay with him, which is sure nice of him. Dogs take a liking to Bacon. With a name like that, they can't help themselves.

Exit I-5 at the Central Yreka exit. The depot is just east of the freeway. 530/842-4146; www.yrekawesternrr.com.

Wayside Inn: This bright inn has interesting knotty pine furniture. Rates are $35–38. Dogs are $4 extra. 1235 South Main Street 96097; 530/842-4412.

Weed

At times, the name Weed has been a stumbling block in public relations, but it doesn't stop people from visiting this old town nestled in the western slopes of Mt. Shasta. Today it's a sleepy place with breathtaking views of the mountain. But between the 1900s and the 1940s, it was considered to be the Sodom and Gomorrah of Siskiyou County. Because of its remote location, the law was barely enforced. Things sometimes would get so out of hand that train conductors would warn people not to disembark here.

PARKS, BEACHES, AND RECREATION AREAS

We were disappointed in Lake Shastina, the beautiful lake that was turned into a golf resort just outside town. It used to be much wilder, but now about the wildest areas the public has access to are the sand traps. And since dogs aren't permitted on the courses, it's not much fun.

Fortunately, just to the east of Weed is the Shasta Wilderness Area in Shasta-Trinity National Forest, complete with magnificent 14,162-foot Mt. Shasta and even a few fairly nonstrenuous trails.

3 Bel Air Park

 (See Siskiyou County map on page 28)

The park finally changed its name from City Park! Much of Bel Air is taken up by ball fields, but there's still some room for leashed dogs to roam and a few trees for them to mark. It's a convenient stop if your dog is crossing his legs while you're driving on I-5. Exit at the College of the Siskiyous turnoff and take South Weed Boulevard south one block, and then go right on College Avenue. The park is on your left after three blocks. 530/926-2494.

PLACES TO EAT

Pizza Factory: Jake's favorite food here is the juicy calzone, which he enjoys smelling at a table under the awning. 132 North Weed Boulevard; 530/938-3088.

PLACES TO STAY

Motel 6: Rates are $44–56 for the first adult, $6 for the second. 466 North Weed Boulevard 96094; 530/938-4101.

Mount Shasta

This small town sits under the watchful eye of the mighty mountain that goes by the same name. It can provide a quick highway rest stop for the weary or an enchanting place to unwind for days. Some who have come for a few days end up spending the rest of their lives here. Mount Shasta has the best of all worlds—it's remote and wildly natural, yet civilized to the point of being the area's cultural hub. Even dogs like the combination.

PARKS, BEACHES, AND RECREATION AREAS

4 City Park

(See Siskiyou County map on page 28)

We have to stop here every time we pass Mt. Shasta. We bring a couple of empty water bottles and a big thirst, since this fairly small city park is actually home to the headwaters of the Sacramento River. The crystal-clear, cold water comes bubbling down the rocks of a couple of small streams that become the Sacramento. It's the best water we've ever tasted, and it's free! There are no rules yet on how much water people can take, but there may be in the future if people abuse the privilege. Don't be a glutton and you'll be dipping your cup into eternity.

Dogs have to be leashed at this shady park, but they don't seem to mind. This is a relaxing place, where you have the chance to sit under a tree in a green meadow or under the gazebo and tune out the world for a while. Bring a picnic and toast your favorite dog with your favorite water at one of the riverside picnic tables. If your dog needs to stretch his legs more, there's a wide trail that starts in the area behind the stream. But do keep him out of the water. Dog hair doesn't go well with bottled water.

From I-5, take the Mount Shasta Boulevard exit and head southeast. Turn right within a half mile at Nixon Road and bear right into the park. 530/926-2494.

5 Lake Siskiyou

🐾🐾🐾 (See Siskiyou County map on page 28)

This man-made reservoir, created solely for recreational use, sits in the morning shadow of awesome Mt. Shasta. Trout fishing is one of the big draws—the lake is stocked with 20,000 trout each year! But you can also have a great vacation just camping and hiking in the area surrounding this 437-acre lake. Leashed dogs may go pretty much everywhere except the swimming beach and the picnic area.

Several trails wind through the ponderosa pines and cedars that encircle much of the lake. You can actually leave the campground and walk around the entire lake with your dog, as long as you don't mind hoofing it across a small section of the Sacramento River.

The day-use fee is $1 per human, but since dogs have to stay out of the water and away from the picnic tables, rangers tend to discourage day use with doggies. Too many people have left dogs in cars on warm days. Rangers here are so adamantly against people leaving dogs in their cars during the day that they'll flat out turn you back if they catch you. It's a good, lifesaving policy. Dogs don't pay anything during the day, but it costs $2 extra per night if your dog camps with you. There are 367 sites with fees ranging $18–25. From I-5, take the Central Mount Shasta exit, turn left at the stop sign, and follow the signs west on W. A. Barr Road to the lake. 530/926-2610; www.lakesis.com.

PLACES TO EAT

Mountain View Cafe: Dogs love to watch you dine on salads and sandwiches at the many outdoor, umbrella-covered tables. 401 North Mount Shasta Boulevard; 530/926-4998.

PLACES TO STAY

Dream Inn Bed and Breakfast: You and your dog have a choice of rooms in two very different houses when you stay here: a 1904 Victorian home or 1938 Spanish-style home. The Victorian home frightens Jake the Dog with all its breakable old lamps, plates, glassware, and frilly doodads. (Less waggy and klutzy dogs will do fine here.) Dogs of Jake's ilk might feel more comfortable in the Spanish-style home, just next door. It's got a kind of Spanish/American West/1970s thing going on, without all the antiques and breakables. The homes are surrounded by 160 rose bushes, myriad flower beds, and even a couple of big apple trees. If you're lucky, you'll be greeted by Noel, a sweet little 11-year-old black Lab with a graying chin. Rates are $70–190. 326 Chestnut Street 96067; 530/926-1536 or 877/375-4744; www.dreaminnshastacity.com.

Econo Lodge: Rates are $49–89. There's a $7 one-time fee for dogs. 908 South Mount Shasta Boulevard 96067; 530/926-3145; www.mtshasta-econolodge.com.

Lake Siskiyou: See Lake Siskiyou, above, for camping information.

Mountain Air Lodge: If your dog likes a little grass around his lodgings, he'll enjoy a night or two here. Rates are $59–79. Dogs are $7 extra. 1121 South Mount Shasta Boulevard 96067; 530/926-3411.

Mount Shasta Ranch Bed and Breakfast: A stay at this elegant two-story ranch house puts you up close and personal with Mt. Shasta. This historic inn offers spacious suites, a quaint vacation cottage, a large fireplace, an outdoor spa, and a tasty country-style breakfast. Dogs will enjoy the good dog-walking trails nearby. Your dog's requirement: He has to be flea-free to stay. Rooms are furnished with Oriental rugs and antiques, and a flea infestation would not be a good thing. And even squeaky-clean dogs are not allowed on the beds, so be sure to bring a bed your dog can call her own. Rates are $60–115. Dogs are $10 extra. 1008 W. A. Barr Road 96067; 530/926-3870; www.best-staysinshasta.com.

Swiss Holiday Lodge: Sleep here and watch the sun rise on Mt. Shasta right from your window. Rates are $55–75. Dogs are $5 extra. 2400 South Mount Shasta Boulevard 96067; 530/926-3448.

Tree House Best Western: There's no tree house here, but at least some of the rooms have views of Mt. Shasta. The maximum dog size allowed is 60 pounds, which is a generous improvement from the previous weight limit of 25 pounds. Rates are $101–113. Dogs are $10 extra. 111 Morgan Way 96067; 530/926-3101.

Dunsmuir

When I first visited this old town on the Sacramento River, it was July of 1991 and I was covering the toxic metam sodium spill that wiped out river life and made residents ill. The sign at the town's entrance boasting "Dunsmuir—home of the best water on earth" was nothing but a sad irony and a good line for an article.

But these days, the river is clean and burgeoning with life again. The sign at the town's entrance is no longer incongruous. Check out the crystal-clear water from City Park (below) while you and your leashed dog picnic along the river. It's so nice not to have bright green clouds of toxic pesticides floating by while you're trying to eat.

PARKS, BEACHES, AND RECREATION AREAS

6 City Park

🐾🐾🐾 (See Siskiyou County map on page 28)

This is not your typical, well-groomed city park. It's wild, woodsy, and full of trails winding up and down hills surrounding the Sacramento River. It's almost completely shaded here, keeping it cool during all but the hottest days of summer. If it's a particularly sticky day, you and your panting pooch can dip your toes in the always-cool river. If your dog is a landlubber like Joe was, he may want to hang out near the shaded picnic tables, so be sure to pack a little snack. "Make mine mignon," was Joe's favorite saying.

Take the Central Dunsmuir exit off I-5 and go north on Dunsmuir Avenue. The park will be on your left. 530/235-4740.

PLACES TO EAT

Café Maddalena: The best way to characterize the cuisine at this upscale-yet-casual restaurant in the heart of Dunsmuir's historic district is Italian/Spanish/North African/Southern French. Actually, the best way to describe it takes only one word: delicious. If you've got a vegetarian in you just hankering to come out, this is a good place to start. Try the butternut squash risotto or the spiced lentils with roasted veggies. If meat is your dish, Jake the Dog swears by the café's ribeye steak with shallot butter. Actually, he swears at it, because anytime a waiter brings one to the outdoor eating area, it's never for our table. 5801 Sacramento Avenue; 530/235-2725.

Cornerstone Bakery and Cafe: Everything here is made fresh. Enjoy the veggie focaccia bread or a roasted turkey breast sandwich at the umbrella-topped tables outside. 5759 Dunsmuir Avenue; 530/235-4677.

PLACES TO STAY

Girard Ridge Lookout: You and your dog may have stayed at fancy hotels, rustic cabins, and cute inns, but you've probably never seen a lodging quite like this. Imagine sleeping in a place that has only one room, and that room is perched on a 12-foot-tall base, and is walled by glass, with crystal-clear views of Mt. Shasta and Castle Crags. There are no neighbors to keep you up at night, no managers watching over you to make sure your dog behaves himself.

On the flipside, there are no bathrooms (just an outhouse), you have to bring your own sleeping bags, and you can't head downstairs to an antique-festooned dining room for a piping hot breakfast in the morning.

But spending the night in a U.S. Forest Service lookout such as Girard Ridge is an experience not to be missed if you don't mind roughing it a little. You bring everything you'd bring if you were going camping (except for the tent), but you're protected from the elements, and you'll have plenty of privacy at night.

At Girard Ridge, you get to drive right up to the lookout (as do other people who will undoubtedly think you're a fire-watch ranger and ask you how you get such a magnificent job), so there's no lugging of equipment. But—joy of joys!—you're in the middle of the Shasta-Trinity National Forest, and the Pacific Crest Trail runs right by here, so you and your dog can explore from dawn 'til dusk.

The rate is $35. Girard Ridge is about 10 miles from Dunsmuir. Another lookout, Little Mt. Hoffman Lookout, is truly in the middle of nowhere, at an elevation of 7,000 feet, on the border of Siskiyou and Modoc Counties. It has magnificent 360-degree views that include Mt. Shasta and Mt. Lassen. It's so high on a peak that it doesn't have to be on a high manmade perch. The rate is also $35. Call 530/964-2184 to reserve either and to find out how to go about getting to them.

Oak Tree Inn: "This is the way the world is supposed to be," says Dorcas, who owns this 1950s-era motel with her husband. "Children ride their bikes and scooters here, we sit around and talk with guests and just welcome them like family." Dogs are just as welcome as humans at this motel, as long as humans clean up after their dogs. You can even let them do their business on the little lawns here, as long as you scoop the poop. "One thing makes me real unhappy, and that's having to clean up after someone's dog," says Dorcas. With two dogs of her own (one was left here by a guest), two cats, and a couple of human children, she wipes up after enough critters. Rates are $52–58. Dogs are $8 extra. 6604 Dunsmuir Avenue 96025; 530/235-2884 or 877/235-2884; www.oaktreeinn.com.

Railroad Park Resort/Caboose Motel: Stay here in a caboose that was once an important part of any of several major rail lines, including the Santa Fe. These restored caboose cars are intriguing places to hang your leash with your good dog, who is welcome as long as you call ahead and get the OK. The owners prefer dogs to bring their own beds. Humans get comfy brass beds and cushy armchairs. If you stay in the deluxe boxcar, you'll get your own wet bar and your tub will have claw feet (dogs can relate). The rooms have no kitchens, but a terrific restaurant in the dining car makes up for this (no dogs, though). You can also stay at one of the resort's cabins. The grounds of the resort are like a park, with plenty of places to walk a dog. Pooches have to stay off landscaped areas. Rates are $85–95. Dogs are $10 extra. 100 Railroad Park Road 96025; 530/235-4440; www.rrpark.com.

CHAPTER 3

Modoc County

Not too many people or dogs venture to the far northeast reaches of the state, but those who do find dog heaven. About 90 percent of this county is made up of Modoc National Forest and other public lands. That means years of off-leash walks for you and your pooch.

Many folks travel through here on U.S. 395 on the way from the Pacific Northwest to Reno. Alturas is a popular stopping point. But check out the numerous entrances to the eastern chunk of Modoc National Forest. Just north of Alturas you can follow Highway 299 east into the Cedar Mountain area, where there are a couple of primitive campgrounds. Closer to the town of Likely, you can head east and enter the South Warner Wilderness for access to numerous lakes, streams, and trails.

Alturas, the county seat and the only town of notable size, has a population of 3,000. That should tell you all you need to know about this get-away-from-it-all county.

PICK OF THE LITTER—MODOC COUNTY

BEST PEACEFUL LAKES
Cave Lake/Lily Lake, New Pine Creek (page 40)

NATIONAL FORESTS

The National Forests and Wilderness Areas resource at the back of this book has important information and safety tips on visiting national forests with your dog and has more background on the Modoc National Forest.

Modoc National Forest
🐾🐾🐾🐾🐕

The South Warner Wilderness, about 14 miles east of the town of Likely in the Modoc National Forest, is a serene place to visit. Clear little lakes abound, as do the creeks that feed them.

New Pine Creek

PARKS, BEACHES, AND RECREATION AREAS

1 Cave Lake/Lily Lake
🐾🐾🐾🐾🐕 (See Modoc County map on page 38)

You can't get much more remote than this in California. These small, trout-filled lakes are on the Oregon border, and it takes a six-mile drive up a fairly steep gravel road to get there. You probably won't find any people here, but you'll find all the peace you need. The world is truly hushed at this 6,600-foot elevation.

Dogs love it because they're allowed to hike leash-free. The campground at Cave Lake has six sites, each available on a first-come, first-served basis. Leash your dog if anyone else is camping here. The campground is free and is open July–October.

From U.S. 395 in New Pine Creek, take unpaved Forest Service Road 2 east about six long, uphill miles. The campsites are just after the Lily Lake picnic area. 530/233-5811.

PLACES TO STAY

Cave Lake/Lily Lake: See Cave Lake/Lily Lake, above, for camping information.

Alturas

PARKS, BEACHES, AND RECREATION AREAS

🐾 Modoc National Wildlife Refuge

🐾🐾🐾🐕 (See Modoc County map on page 38)

The only dogs who are allowed off leash here are bird hunters, and only during the appropriate seasons. Otherwise, dogs have to wear leashes in the Dorris Reservoir area of the refuge. Sections of the reservoir are closed during nesting season, but you can usually take your leashed dog on a hike on the horse trail that goes across the top of the dam and down to the surrounding land. The bird-watching is excellent in the late fall and early winter. Bring your binoculars and get up close and personal with tundra swans, Canada geese, and cinnamon teal. Earthbound residents include coyotes, antelope, and rabbits. It's hard to hold binoculars while your dog is tugging at the leash, but make sure your pooch doesn't get away.

From Alturas, drive about three miles east on Parker Creek Road. Call 530/233-3572 for dates and restrictions.

🐾 Veteran's Memorial Park

🐾🐾 (See Modoc County map on page 38)

About the size of a city block, this park is chock-full of trees on one side and covered with grass on the other. Picnic tables dot the grounds. Since there are no restaurants with outdoor tables for dogs and their people in Alturas, this is a good place to bring your lunch so you can break bread with your pooch. Dogs must be leashed.

The park is on County Road 56 and U.S. 395. 530/233-6403.

PLACES TO STAY

It may seem as though Alturas has an incongruously high number of motels per capita, but when you consider how many people pass through here, it makes sense. The dogs sure appreciate the small-town hospitality.

Best Western Trailside Inn: Rates are $63–67. Dogs are $5 extra per visit. 343 North Main Street 96101; 530/233-4111.

Drifters Inn: This one's on lots of property. Rates are $37–40. Dogs are $3 extra. 395 Lake View Road 96101; 530/233-2428.

Essex Motel: Rates are $36–55. If you're a hunting dog, you'll have to look for a room elsewhere: "They're too dirty to be in the rooms," says a manager. 1216 North Main Street 96101; 530/233-2821.

Frontier Motel: There's a big backyard behind the motel, and good dogs are allowed to check it out. Rates are $35–45. 1033 North Main Street 96101; 530/233-3383.

Hacienda Motel: Rates are $35–55. Dogs are $5 extra. 201 East 12th Street 96101; 530/233-3459.

Wagon Wheel Motel: Rates are $40. 308 West 12th Street 96101; 530/233-5866.

CHAPTER 4

Humboldt County

Bigfoot. Giant redwoods. Fog. Off-leash beaches. Humboldt County is home to the magical, mythical wonders of Northern California. Dogs love them all, with the possible exception of Bigfoot. Jake, however, would undoubtedly adore getting a whiff of the enormous hairy creature's reputedly rotten body odor. But so far, the only big, smelly, hairy creature he's seen up this way has been in a mirror.

The coast here is one of the best in the state, as far as dogs are concerned. A few beaches and one 62,000-acre coastal park allow your dog to strip and go leashless. (Many of the county beaches are leashes-optional, but the rules are complex and vary by beach; don't assume that when you see a county beach you can let your dog run free.)

Sun worshipers won't share a dog's excitement about the coast. If fog is a four-letter word to you, try another county, or at least drive inland a bit. The fog can be so thick in Arcata that you'll have a hard time seeing your dog on the beach. But then as you drive east on mountainous Highway 299, the fog gives way a little at a time. As you reach higher elevations, white mist

PICK OF THE LITTER—HUMBOLDT COUNTY

BEST BEACHES
Mad River County Park, Arcata (page 46)
Samoa Dunes Recreation Area, Eureka (page 48)

BEST SWEEPING COASTAL PARK
King Range National Conservation Area, Shelter Cove (page 55)

MOST DOG-FRIENDLY PLACE TO STAY
Collingwood Inn Bed and Breakfast, Ferndale (page 52)

BEST GIANT TREES
Eternal Tree House, Redcrest (page 53)
Shrine Drive-Thru Tree, Myers Flat (page 55)

swirls around the taller trees, and on the way downhill on the other side, it's suddenly gone. You're free to frolic in the sun, but your beaches will be far behind.

No visit to Humboldt County is complete without a drive down the Avenue of the Giants. This world-famous 31-mile scenic drive between Redway and Pepperwood will take you past some of the biggest and most magnificent redwoods in the world. Just about all the adjectives for "really old" have been used to name the giants in this area. You can visit the Grandfather Tree, the Eternal Tree, and the Immortal Tree, to name a few of the elderly stars appearing on The Strip.

NATIONAL FORESTS

The National Forests and Wilderness Areas resource at the back of this book has important information and safety tips on visiting national forests with your dog and has more background on the national forests listed below.

Shasta-Trinity National Forest

Six Rivers National Forest

Trinidad

This small coastal town, complete with its own white lighthouse and rocky outcroppings, is like a Mendocino that hasn't been taken over by tourists and artists. Visit before your dog spreads the word about this well-kept secret spot.

PARKS, BEACHES, AND RECREATION AREAS

1 Moonstone Beach

🐾🐾🐾🐾 🐕 (See Humboldt County map on page 42)

Well-behaved dogs can throw their leashes to the wind when they visit this popular county-run beach. Jake loves the surf here (as do the many surfers who were riding the waves when we visited). But wanna-be water dogs can also enjoy Moonstone Beach's wet stuff: Creek waters flow out to sea, making a decent swimming hole for more landlubbing breeds. We've seen dogs who were petrified of swimming in the ocean delight in splashing through the calm waters of the creek.

On sunny days, this is one of the more popular beaches in the area, so if your pooch has a proclivity toward poaching picnics, chasing horses, or sniffing toddlers' diapers, you may want to try a more isolated beach. Note that between March 1 and September 15, dogs must be on leash from the parking area to the high-tide line, because this is a prime nesting ground of the snowy plover. (A big thanks to Woody and Katy Dog, and their human, Debra Roby, for helping us sniff out this gem.)

From Trinidad's Main Street, turn left on Scenic Road and follow it to Moonstone Beach Road, which will take you to the beach's free parking lot. 707/455-7651.

PLACES TO STAY

Bishop Pine Lodge: Most of the rustic, wood-paneled cottages here have kitchens, but does your dog care? Not unless you happen to be cooking a burger with his name on it. Dogs care much more about what's outside the cozy cabins at this very dog-friendly lodge. And what's outside is sure to put a smile on even the most somber snout. The lodge is on eight acres of tree-studded land where well-behaved pooches may walk leash-free with you. Rates are $80–120. Dogs are $10 extra. 1481 Patrick's Point 95570; 707/677-3314; www.bishoppinelodge.com.

Trinidad Inn: At this small, pleasant motel, you and your dog can walk right outside your door and find a trail leading to the woods nearby. Rates are $80–130. Dogs are $10 extra and require a $20 deposit. 1170 Patrick's Point 95570; 707/677-3349; www.trinidadinn.com.

Arcata

For a university town, Arcata is a mellow place. But dogs who want to have a wild time have ample opportunity. Although canines are not permitted in the lush green park in the old town square, they're allowed off leash at a couple of really prime areas, and on leash in a few more magical spots. For added dog pleasure, it's usually cool and foggy here, so it's a wonderful place to visit when the rest of the state is broiling.

PARKS, BEACHES, AND RECREATION AREAS

🛂 Clam Beach County Park

🐾🐾🐾🐾🐕 (See Humboldt County map on page 42)

The winds of leash-law change have blown in again, and under limited circumstances, dogs under voice control are once more permitted off leash. Here's the deal: Dogs can be leash-free only on the "wave slope" area. This is the area wetted by the last high tide. In other words, you're up a creek if you come at high tide. If you want to visit and walk on the biggest swatch of sand possible, get yourself a tidebook for the area and look for a major high tide and a major low tide on the same day. Get here at low tide on one of those days, and the beach is your oyster!

Speaking of mollusks, Clam Beach is a good clamming area, as even your dog might have guessed from the park's name. Some dogs like to help you dig for your bivalve supper, which you can cook at the campground here. (Note that between March 1 and September 15, dogs must be on leash from the parking/camping area to the high-tide line, because this area is a prime nesting ground of the snowy plover.) There are 12 tent sites in sand dunes, available on a first-come, first-served basis. Sites are $10. Dogs are $1 extra.

From U.S. 101, about seven miles north of Arcata, take the Clam Beach Park exit west a couple of miles. 707/445-7651.

🛂 Mad River County Park

🐾🐾🐾🐾🐕 (See Humboldt County map on page 42)

As you drive to this park past old barns and huge green fields full of grazing cows, you'll feel as though you're in the English countryside, especially if it's foggy. Dogs are delirious about the rural five-mile drive from Arcata.

Better yet is that once you get to this magnificent beach, leashes are no longer the law for dogs under voice control! The beach is wide, long, and desolate. Beachcombing is fun, and there's plenty of driftwood to keep your dog intrigued. The only other people we've ever seen here have been old men with metal detectors, hippies who sometimes spend the night, and dedicated dog owners willing to make the labyrinthine drive from town. Here, unlike Clam Beach, dogs aren't relegated to a narrow strip of beach. (However, between

March 1 and September 15, dogs must be on leash from the parking area to the high-tide line, because that's a prime nesting ground of the snowy plover.)

From U.S. 101, exit west on Giuntoli Lane and go right almost immediately onto Heindon Road. Follow the signs to the park. On the way, you'll pass one end of the Hammond Trail, a 2.2-mile hiking/biking coastal trail between Arcata and McKinleyville. It's an invigorating walk. Once at the Mad River, you'll see a sign leading you to the right for fishing access. That's where you can launch your boat on the river, but chances are your dog would prefer to run on the beach, so keep going straight until you hit the small parking lot at the end of the road. 707/445-7651.

4 Arcata Community Forest/Redwood Park

🐾🐾🐾🐾 (See Humboldt County map on page 42)

Just a couple of minutes away from the quaint old downtown area of Arcata, this 575-acre park offers 17 trails with 10 miles of hiking for you and your leashed dog. Mornings are enchanting here. Songbirds come to life, and the earth and the redwoods smell fresh in the damp, foggy air.

From U.S. 101, exit at Samoa Boulevard and drive east. At Union Street, go north a few blocks and make a right onto 14th Street. Drive into the forest and park in the large lot. Several trailheads start here. 707/822-7091.

5 Arcata Marsh and Wildlife Sanctuary

🐾🐾🐾 (See Humboldt County map on page 42)

Formerly a sanitary landfill, this 174-acre model restoration project has three freshwater marshes, a brackish lake, and one saltwater marsh. Together, they attract about 200 species of birds, as well as critters such as river otters and muskrats. To add to your dog's joy, treated wastewater helps in wetlands restoration here.

Dogs must be leashed, for obvious reasons. Bird-watchers come from all over the state to view a vast array of fine-feathered friends, including Iceland gulls, old-squaws, bald eagles, and endangered brown pelicans. Despite Joe's exemplary behavior on his last visit, he got the evil eye from a couple of people who were chirping to some birds hidden in a tree. I found that walking around with binoculars helps these avid folks realize you're just like them, except you have a dog who shares in the wonders of our winged friends. If you've got a yapper dog, take him somewhere else.

Exit U.S. 101 at Samoa Boulevard and drive west, following the coastal access signs. Turn left on I Street and drive about a mile. The parking lot is on your right. Once in the marsh area, bear right at the wood-chip trail for the best walk possible. You can get a map and guide to the area by calling 707/822-7091.

PLACES TO EAT

Hole in the Wall: This is a popular pooch hangout. Dogs enjoy intermingling and catching sandwich crusts in the semienclosed outdoor area. 590 G Street; 707/822-7407.

Los Bagels: Denise Selleck, one of my wonderful fact checkers, highly recommends this bagelry. She says she's eaten at the outdoor tables here several times "with various beasts." (This includes at least a few dogs and her husband.) 1061 I Street; 707/822-3150.

PLACES TO STAY

Best Western Arcata Inn: Rates are $69–75. Dogs are $10 extra. 4827 Valley West Boulevard 95521; 707/826-0313.

Clam Beach County Park: See Clam Beach County Park, above, for camping information.

Hotel Arcata: Dogs seem to sense the history at this refurbished 1915 hotel. When Joe visited, all he could do was stick his snout around the baseboards and snort in the scents. Rates are $84–150. Dogs are $5 extra, plus there's a $50 pooch deposit. 708 9th Street 95521; 707/826-0217; www.hotelarcata.com.

Motel 6: This one is right beside U.S. 101, and the staff will often put dogs and their human companions in the rooms closest to the highway because there's a little on-leash dog-relief area there. The constant drone of cars can actually be soothing at 3 A.M. when your dog decides to start scratching himself. Rates are $51–56. 4755 Valley West Boulevard 95521; 707/822-7061.

Quality Inn–Mad River: There's a pretty beach next door where leashed dogs like to roam. Rates are $55–75. Dogs are $10 extra and require a $100 deposit. 3535 Janes Road 95521; 707/822-0409.

Eureka

This is the county seat of Humboldt, and it's a bustling small city. Fortunately, it also has some Victorian charm, as well as the ocean and Humboldt Bay, so it's not a typical center of commerce.

PARKS, BEACHES, AND RECREATION AREAS

Dogs aren't allowed in Eureka's best city park, Sequoia Park, but that's OK. We found a couple of areas that more than make up for the loss.

⑥ Samoa Dunes Recreation Area

🐾🐾🐾🐾🐾 (See Humboldt County map on page 42)

Does your dog like sand, sand, and more sand? How does 300 acres of coastal dunes between the Pacific and Humboldt Bay sound? How about boundless, fairly calm ocean? Cool breezes year-round?

If your dog isn't salivating about this park yet, here's the clincher: Well-behaved dogs can run off leash everywhere except the established trails at this Bureau of Land Management park! While you cast for surfperch, hunt for driftwood, or just relax and listen to the foghorns and gulls, your dog is free to run around, as long as he'll come when you call.

We learned about the vital importance of voice control when we spotted an injured duck waddling along the shore. Another dog, a retriever type, scooped up the bird in her mouth and brought it back to her owner. Fortunately, Joe was well leashed by the time he decided he'd like to look into a duck dinner. And even more luckily, once the bird overcame its fear, it got up and continued waddling down the beach as if nothing had happened.

The retriever's owner was shocked that her dog had taken off. "She's so obedient. She always comes when I call," she explained after severely reprimanding her dog. It just goes to show that even the most obedient dogs can get out of hand in tempting situations, so even if you've got a voice-control champ, keep a close eye on him when he's off leash.

This area is actually for off-highway vehicles to peruse, but we saw none on our visits. The place was deserted, except for a few beachcombers, a couple of dogs, and a kayaker. But keep in mind that your peace might be shattered by the roar of engines. The drivers of these noisy vehicles may not always be aware of dogs, so make sure you and your dog are aware of them. Also be aware that cars are allowed on the beach, but they generally tend to drive very slowly. There's ample room for vehicles, people, and dogs.

From Eureka, turn west on Highway 255 and cross the Samoa Bridge. Once on the Samoa Peninsula, turn left on New Navy Base Road. The park is about five miles south of the bridge, on the right side of the street. There are also several small access points along the road, but it's best to start from the main lot here. 707/825-2300.

7 Samoa Boat Ramp County Park

🐾🐾🐾 🏃 (See Humboldt County map on page 42)

If you own a boat and a dog, and you've got them both with you, you'll be glad to know about this small park. Not only is there a launch ramp into the south end of Humboldt Bay, but there's also a small beach here so your dog can run around (leash free!) and stretch his legs before he becomes your crewmate during a cruise on the bay. (Be sure to keep your dog leashed from the parking area to the high-tide line March 1–September 15. This is snowy plover nesting land, and dogs need to steer clear in spring and summer.)

From Eureka, turn west on Highway 255 and cross the Samoa Bridge. Once on the Samoa Peninsula, turn left on New Navy Base Road. The park is about five miles south of the bridge, on the left side of the street. 707/445-7651.

PLACES TO EAT

This often foggy city does not exactly abound with outdoor eateries.

Fresh Freeze Drive-In: Like burgers and ice cream? Tell your dog to make sure you visit this decadent place. At Harris and F Streets; 707/442-6967.

PLACES TO STAY

Best Western Bayshore Inn: It's clean, it's comfortable, and, for people who like to eat in the room with their dogs, it's convenient: Each room has a fridge and a microwave. Some rooms even come with a fireplace and a whirlpool tub, should you hanker for extra relaxation. Rates are $88–119. There's a $100 deposit for dogs. 3500 Broadway 95503; 707/268-8005 or 888/268-8005; www.bwbayshoreinn.com.

Eureka Inn: Dogs don't often get to stay in a national historic landmark, so take advantage of the dog-friendly attitude here. From the Tudor architecture and lobby with high beam ceilings and a fireplace, to the rooms with Queen Anne–style furnishings, the place exemplifies casual elegance. Dogs are asked to stay in the ground-floor rooms. It's usually cooler there in the summer, anyway. (Note: At press time for the latest edition, the inn was under new ownership and was closed for extensive refurbishing. We hope it's as dog-friendly as it used to be when it reopens.)

Rates for these rooms, at least prerefurbishing: $109–169. The phone had been disconnected during the refurbishing, so your best bet for updates is to check out the inn's website. 518 7th Street 95501; www.eurekainn.com.

Eureka KOA: The "Kamping Kabins" here, with their cozy wood interiors and Old West bunk-style bed arrangements, are great fun for dogs, and the price is right. Rates are $45–65. Dogs are $5 extra, and are allowed in four of the 10 cabins. 4050 North U.S. 101 95503; 707/822-4243 or 800/562-3136; www.koa.com.

Halcyon Inn Bed and Breakfast: Dogs traveling with their people are allowed to stay at the Rose Room in this 1920s home that's been converted into a lovely inn. The furnishings here are antique but not in a kitschy or dark way. They're simple, tasteful, and attractive. The Rose Room even has a restored bathroom with an antique tub, fir floors, and some bath salts thrown in for good measure. (Not for your dog, should she read this and panic about the "b" word.) The innkeepers, Mary and Ike Floyd, adore having dogs as guests and even have a rescued greyhound of their own. "We love dogs," says Mary, who is one of the nicest innkeepers you'll ever meet and who makes a scrumptious breakfast to boot. Rates are $105–115. Dogs are $20 extra the first night and $10 per night after that. (They steam clean the rug after each doggy visitor.) 1420 C Street 95501; 707/444-1310 or 888/882-1310; www.halcyoninn.com.

Old Town Bed and Breakfast Inn: This sweet old house, built in 1871, is about as welcoming as inns get. Since it's often cool and overcast in Eureka, a cozy breakfast is served near a blazing fireplace, with added light from oil lanterns. The house itself is cheery and airy and offers four nicely appointed guest rooms. Jake's favorite is the Lavender Room, which comes with its own wood stove.

Dogs feel at home here and are allowed to stay with you in any of the guest rooms. "Everybody that travels with dogs is very, very good," says innkeeper Karen Albright, who has two dogs of her own. The inn has a wide front porch where dogs are welcome to repose while their people eat breakfast. They can also run around the fenced front yard, although the fence is only three feet high, which may be too tempting for escape artists. I can picture Jake thinking to himself, "Hey, I'm not getting any French toast from this place. Lemme see if I can find another joint that'll give me some," and hopping neatly over the white-washed wood to pursue his doggy dreams. Rates are $120–140. Dogs pay a $15 one-time charge. 1521 3rd Street 95501; 707/443-5235; www.oldtownbnb.com.

Red Lion Inn: Rates are $94–149. Dogs are $15 extra. 1929 4th Street 95501; 707/445-0844; www.redlion.com.

TraveLodge: Rates at this basic motel are $54–64. Dogs are $10 extra. 4 4th Street 95501; 707/443-6345 or 800/758-7878; www.travelodge.com.

Ferndale

This sweet Victorian town is so historically and architecturally authentic that the entire village is a state historic landmark. You and your dog can savor a walk down Main Street, where you're sure to pass at least a few other dogs with their people. It's so old and refined that it looks as if it could be the model for Disneyland's Main Street.

PARKS, BEACHES, AND RECREATION AREAS

8 Centerville County Beach

😻😻😻😻 🐆 (See Humboldt County map on page 42)

This beach isn't exactly right in the middle of downtown Ferndale. In fact, it's not exactly right in the middle of anywhere, which is why Jake's tail wags nonstop when we visit. "The remoter the better" is his mantra. His favorite activity here is beachcombing: He's known for trotting merrily down the beach with pieces of driftwood longer than our car.

The county section of this desolate beach is miles long and comfortably wide at low tide. You'll want to get here during a fairly low tide, because dogs are allowed off leash here only on the "wave slope," which is the area that got wet from the last high tide. Come here at high tide and your dog will give you a look you won't soon forget. (Note that March 1–September 15, dogs must be on leash from the parking area to the high-tide line, because this is a prime nesting ground of the snowy plover.)

Head west on Main Street and take a right at Centerville Road. The beach is in about four miles. 707/445-7651.

PLACES TO EAT

Ferndale is filled with great places to eat. Most of them didn't want to publicize that they allow dogs at their outdoor tables, but here are two that didn't mind:

No Brand Burger Stand: The logo is a steer skull. The place is right behind the Yancey Feed Company. Is there any connection here? Eat big burgers at the picnic table. 1400 Main Street; 707/786-9474.

Red Front Store: This is a convenience store with a little bench where you and your dog can eat the little hot dogs made inside. 577 Main Street; 707/786-9611.

PLACES TO STAY

Collingwood Inn Bed and Breakfast: This grand, elegant Victorian manor is one of the most beautiful and dog-friendly inns we've come across. If you're venturing anywhere near Ferndale with your dog, this is a must-stay kind of place. (You should actually be willing to drive well out of your way to stay here. It's that wonderful.)

The inn was built in 1885, and both the exterior and interior still have the look and grace of long ago, but with updates that make it charming, relaxing, and perfect for a 21st-century guest. Three of the inn's five guest rooms are pet-friendly. Our favorite is the Hart Room, with its plush red drapes that frame the room's large windows, and its elegant featherbed, fireplace, claw-foot tub for two (and we're not talking you and your dog), sunny stained glass, wide-board hardwood floors, and private sitting porch with a garden view.

All the inn's rooms come with featherbeds, house-made soaps and bubble bath, a fruit basket, and fresh flowers. There's a wonderful full breakfast buffet each morning, and an English tea every afternoon, complete with tea (yup, it's true), cookies, scones, and little cakes.

These features are delectable for humans, but what about dogs? Innkeepers Chris and Peter make sure that dogs who lead their humans to the inn here get treated very well indeed. "We like our four-legged guests to be as happy as our two-legged guests," says Chris. He and Peter supply dogs who stay here with dishes for food and water, doggy blankets, special treats, and poop bags. (The dishes and blankets are loaners. The poop bags you can keep.)

Rates for all this are $99–203. Dogs are $25 extra each. (That's a per-night charge, not per visit.) 831 Main Street 95536; 707/786-9219 or 800/469-1632; www.collingwoodinn.com.

Fortuna

We don't normally list just one chain lodging under a town, but this one's so close to the popular redwood attractions, and one of the few with more modern amenities, that we're making an exception.

PLACES TO STAY

Holiday Inn Express: It's somewhat disconcerting to find this clean, modern "luxury motor inn" so close to some of the biggest, oldest redwoods in the world. But we can't complain. It's a fun place to stay, and the staff is friendly to our canine friends. The indoor heated pool is especially comfy in the cooler months. Rates are $92–98. Dogs are $10 extra. 1859 Alamar Way 95540; 707/725-5500 or 800/483-9446; www.hiexpress.com.

Redcrest

You want redwood gifts? This is your town. The few stores in this tiny community along the Avenue of the Giants carry every redwood gift imaginable, most of no practical value. From redwood burl wall clocks to giant redwood Indians, they've got it all.

PLACES TO EAT

Eternal Tree Cafe: Dine on big old redwood tables under the shade of big old redwoods. (Is this like eating a hamburger in front of a cow?) Then visit the Eternal Tree House giant redwood, just behind the building (see the Diversion Survive the Ultimate Temptation). 26510 Avenue of the Giants; 707/722-4247.

DIVERSION

Survive the Ultimate Temptation: Your boy dog won't believe his eyes when he visits the **Eternal Tree House,** along the Avenue of the Giants in Redcrest. When Joe Dog saw this 2,500-year-old giant redwood, he tugged on his leash incessantly so he could get a closer sniff and decide what part of this tree he wanted to claim. It took all my strength to convince him not to desecrate this natural wonder. It's just one of many reasons your dog should be leashed here. The tree (there's no actual "tree house") is at 26510 Avenue of the Giants, Redcrest; 707/722-4262.

PLACES TO STAY

Redcrest Motor Inn Resort: Dog guests and their people who used to stay here were always greeted by Mandy, an affable golden retriever who was so thrilled to see you that her tail was often in danger of wagging off. She was so beloved she was even listed as one of the owners on Redcrest's brochure. Sadly, she has gone to Dog Heaven. But her spirit lives on: "We LOVE dogs!" exclaims one of the human owners of the lodging. The owners here can't wag their tails, but they'll be thrilled to see you step out of your car with a pooch at your side. Cabins are $45–110, with kitchens available in some cabins. Dogs are $5 extra. 26459 Avenue of the Giants 95569; 707/722-4208.

Petrolia

If you plan to get lost on the Lost Coast, this little hamlet offers an interesting place to spend a night or a week.

PLACES TO STAY

Mattole River Organic Farm's Country Cabins: The name doesn't exactly roll off the tongue, but dogs don't care: How often does a pooch get to stay at a remote mountain getaway that specializes in organic pickled peppers and pears, and not have to worry about a guy named Peter Piper?

The small working farm here has a veggie garden, plenty of peppers, a pear and apple orchard, and chickens who donate eggs to the cause. Guests who stay at the cabins can sample some of the pickings with the OK of the owners.

Big trees surround the five cabins, which are simple and rustic. (They have TVs and little kitchens, so you're not exactly camping.) The cabins are just a little hike to the Mattole River, where the swimming is mighty refreshing on a hot summer afternoon. Rates are $65–100. 42354 Mattole Road 95558; 707/629-3445 or 800/845-4607.

Miranda

PLACES TO STAY

Miranda Gardens Resort: Trees, trees, trees. Trees, trees, trees. That's what your boy dog will see when you stay at this resort's quaint, attractive cottages. After all, the resort is on the Avenue of the Giants, and there's no shortage of old-growth redwoods on the property.

But while the trees are the high point for pooches and many people (for different reasons, fortunately), there's much more to ogle here than the arbors. The flowering gardens around the cottages are lush. The gazebos are lovely. The cottages are homey and comfortable—a bit more upscale than most typi-

DIVERSION

Give Him the Ultimate Tree Experience: Most dogs love to relax in the shade of trees or sniff at trees for hints of other dogs. But how many dogs know they can actually drive smack through the center of a tree? Few trees oblige such a fantasy, so the **Shrine Drive-Thru Tree** in Myers Flat north of Miranda is a real find. Dogs seem to enjoy riding through the car-sized hole in the 275-foot-tall redwood's 21-foot-diameter base. But, to be honest, they seem to prefer the adjacent picnic area, where sticky droplets of ice cream from the kitschy but fun gift shop hide in the grass.

A sign says the tree is 5,000 years old, but the folks around here say that it's more like 2,000 years. It doesn't really matter. It's big and it's old and it's dog-friendly. "We get lots of dogs coming through here. They like the whole tree thing," says a Shrine Drive-Thru Tree employee.

It costs $1.50 per person for folks over nine years old. Dogs, regardless of age, go free, but they must be leashed. 13078 Avenue of the Giants, Myers Flat; 707/943-1658.

cal California rural resorts. Dogs can't do the dog paddle in the heated swimming pool here, but well-behaved leashed dogs are welcome to attend the nightly campfires hosted by the resort in the summer.

Note: Dogs need to bring their own beds (and to sleep in them) to be allowed to stay here. Rates are $95–225. There's a $150 deposit for dogs, and a $15 charge per pooch for the length of your stay. 6766 Avenue of the Giants, P.O. Box 186 95553; 707/943-3011; www.mirandagardens.com.

Shelter Cove

This coastal community is in the heart of the Lost Coast area of California. It's known for its pristine beauty and prime fishing. But dogs like it because it's surrounded by the King Range National Conservation Area (see below). Three areas of this preplanned, privately owned community provide ocean access. We like the Little Black Sand Beach, just off Dolphin Drive.

PARKS, BEACHES, AND RECREATION AREAS

🄈 King Range National Conservation Area

🐾🐾🐾🐾🦴 (See Humboldt County map on page 42)

We came upon this magnificent 62,000-acre coastal area by accident, and all Joe Dog could do was thank the Great Dog in the Sky. This primitive region, which constitutes a good chunk of the Lost Coast, has everything a dog desires deep in his heart: ocean, grassy flats, sandy beaches, trees galore, and best of all, leash-free living.

In less than a three-mile stretch, the King Range rises from sea level to 4,087 feet. The topography is rugged but far from impassable. Several trails take you across some of the most unspoiled coastal territory in California.

A few Indiana Jones–like dogs can handle the 35-mile wilderness trek along the Lost Coast Trail. Most of the trail is along the beach, and in the mornings you'll likely come to know one of the reasons this area is called the Lost Coast. The fog sometimes gets so thick that even the gulls are silent. But when it lifts, what spectacular sights you'll see! You and your dog will traverse green meadows, Douglas fir groves, and many streams. The terrain is fairly flat, so the real challenge is its length—don't forget, there's always the walk back! Most people prefer to leave a car at one end to make the round-trip easier. You should also keep in mind that this trail can be tough on "house dog" paws. Rangers advise dog booties for parts of the trail.

Joe was the kind of soft-pawed pooch who preferred trails such as the Lightning Trail. It's the shortest and shadiest route to King's Peak. Joe approved of the sparkling mountain streams, the shade from the firs, and the brushy meadowland where he could roll like a fool. He especially liked the trail's length—a mere 2.5 miles. The view from the top is hard to beat.

During your hikes, you may run into deer, cattle, sheep, horses, rattlesnakes, and poison oak, so if you let your dog off leash, do so only if she's under excellent voice control. And be sure to keep your pooch very far away from the marine mammals who clamber onto the beaches and rocks. This is a popular rookery, and dogs and sea critters do not mix.

You may camp anywhere you please for no fee, but you need a permit for campfires. Dogs must be leashed in designated campgrounds. It's a good idea to leash your dog at night anyway. Many dogs feel even safer in your tent. You'll pay $5–8 to camp in a designated campground.

Exit U.S. 101 at Redway and follow Briceland Thorne Road west to this Bureau of Land Management area. For more specific directions to your exact destination in this sprawling conservation area, contact the Bureau of Land Management, Arcata Resource Area, 1125 16th Street, P.O. Box 1112, Arcata, CA 95521; 707/825-2300.

PLACES TO EAT

Lost Coast Coffee Company: This dog-friendly café has several outdoor tables, some where you can look right out at the Pacific Ocean. For breakfast, try the organic oatmeal. It's nourishing, warming, and a great way to start your day of dog adventures. The café is on the ground floor of the Inn of the Lost Coast (see below), at 205 Wave Drive; 707/986-7888.

PLACES TO STAY

Inn of the Lost Coast: Stay here and you'll be atop a cliff overlooking the beautiful Pacific Ocean. All rooms at this two-building lodging have direct ocean views. You might even be able to see a gray whale passing by from your own patio, so don't forget the binoculars. Dogs enjoy going outside here, where the salty breeze ruffles their hair as they explore the bluffs. "Loads of dogs were just wandering around the property with me," writes Fergus, a well-informed canine correspondent. The inn, formerly known as the Shelter Cove Motor Inn, even has its own dog-friendly restaurant. (See above.) Room rates are $90–120. Dogs are $10 for the length of their stay. 205 Wave Drive 95589; 707/986-7521 or 888/570-9676; www.innofthelostcoast.com.

King Range National Conservation Area: See King Range National Conservation Area, above, for camping information.

Garberville

PLACES TO STAY

Benbow Lake State Recreation Area: Of the 975 acres here, dogs are relegated to the campground areas. We've seen some people fishing with their dogs down by the South Fork of the Eel River, but rangers differ about whether or not that's OK. The park is just off U.S. 101, about two miles south of Garberville. Follow the signs. Campsites are $15–20. To reserve one of the 75 sites, call 800/444-PARK (800/444-7275). For park information, phone 707/923-3238 in summer or 707/247-3318 in winter.

Best Western Humboldt House Inn: This is one of the better places to spend the night around here. It has limited availability for the doggy set, so book early. Rates are $85–105. 701 Redwood Drive 95542; 707/923-2771.

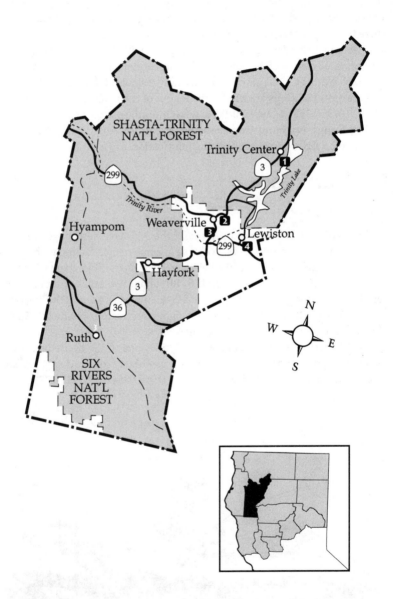

SHASTA-TRINITY
NAT'L FOREST

Trinity Center

299

Trinity River

Hyampom

Weaverville

Lewiston

299

Hayfork

36

Ruth

SIX
RIVERS
NAT'L
FOREST

N
W   E
S

CHAPTER 5
Trinity County

Think about this place we call dog heaven. What are some of the ingredients your dog would desire in his elysian ideal? Besides having you at his side without a leash, he'd want lots of trees, that's for sure. Rivers. Lakes. The scents of nature and rich earth. And maybe some decaying woodland critter to roll on.

Trinity County has all a dog could ever want in heaven or on earth. Joe even managed to find a decaying woodland critter when we last visited, and he rolled all over it and then came running up to me to spread the good news all over my jeans. When I walked into a store to buy some supplies later that day, the clerk and all the customers started asking each other if they smelled a mighty bad stench. I joined them in wrinkling my nose and nodding my head, praying no one would figure out my guilt until I was long gone.

The county has a couple of charming old towns, but the real charm here for dogs and their people is that more than 90 percent of the land is part of the national forest system. When driving from just about any location to just about any other location in the county (other than the few main towns on the

PICK OF THE LITTER—TRINITY COUNTY

MOST ALPINE LAKE
Trinity Lake, Trinity Center (page 61)

MEATIEST RESTAURANT
Bear's Breath Bar and Grill, Lewiston (page 66)

LODGING WITH MOST LAND
Old Garrett Ranch, Hyampom (page 63)

MOST DOG-FRIENDLY PLACE TO STAY
Barker Valley Doghouse, Hayfork (page 67)

BEST WATER ADVENTURE
Trinity Lake houseboats, Trinity Center (page 62)

east side), there are countless places where you can pull your car over and take your obedient dog for a leash-free hike. As long as you're in a national forest and away from houses and developed areas, it's generally OK.

While here, you mustn't miss the magnificent Trinity Alps. You'll feel as if you're in Switzerland, only your dog won't have to deal with plane tickets and passports! The only paper you'll need to hike the Trinity Alps Wilderness is a permit from the U.S. Forest Service.

NATIONAL FORESTS

The National Forests and Wilderness Areas resource at the back of this book has important information and safety tips on visiting national forests with your dog and has more background on the national forests listed below.

Shasta-Trinity National Forest
🐾🐾🐾🐾🐕

Six Rivers National Forest
🐾🐾🐾🐾🐕

Trinity Center

This tiny community is the home, in spirit if nothing else, of the giant and breathtaking Trinity Lake. It's also quite close to the breathtaking Trinity Alps Wilderness, where dogs can hoof it off leash.

PARKS, BEACHES, AND RECREATION AREAS

🐾 Trinity Lake

😋😋😋😋 🐕 (See Trinity County map on page 58)

Even the national forest staff here call this place dog heaven. One dog-friendly ranger told me, "You just take your boat, pull up to just about any bank, and say, 'Okay, Fido, let's get a little exercise. No leashes required!'"

Your best bet is to take your dog to the more remote parts of the lake. And the best way to get there is by boat. If you don't have one, why not rent one? And what better boat to rent than a houseboat?

Mid-June to mid-July is the best time of year to come here. Snow still covers the peaks of the glorious Trinity Alps (which you can see in all their glory from almost anywhere on the lake), but the weather at the lake is great. So is the fishing. It's not nearly as crowded as Lake Shasta to the east, so you can fish without worrying about too many loud personal watercraft or fast boats.

The south end of the lake is 14 miles north of Weaverville on Highway 3. Call the Shasta-Trinity National Forest District Office at 530/623-2121 for more details and suggestions on which area would best suit your purposes.

PLACES TO STAY

There are campgrounds all around Trinity Lake. Most are concentrated on the lake's south side, but a couple of the more secluded ones are toward the north. Below we've listed one on each side of the lake. Dogs must be leashed at all campgrounds. Call the Shasta-Cascade Wonderland Association at 800/326-6944 for more information on cabins and other lakeside lodgings.

Cedar Stock Resort: This is a great place to enjoy a vacation at Trinity Lake. The cabins are rented by the week, with costs ranging $550–1,300. Dogs are $40 extra per week each. And if you're in the mood for a nautical stay, call for information on houseboat rentals. The resort is 15 miles north of Weaverville. 45810 State Highway 3 96091; 530/286-2225 or 800/982-2279.

Clark Springs Campground: There are two lakeside sites here to make everyone happy. An added bonus for boaters is a boat ramp that's just a stick's throw away. Sites are $10, available on a first-come, first-served basis. Dogs must be leashed. From Weaverville, drive 18 miles north on Highway 3. The campground is at Mule Creek Station in the Shasta-Trinity National Forest. 530/623-2121.

DIVERSION

Float in a Houseboat: Renting a houseboat is the ultimate human-dog vacation. Houseboats can be small and simple or large and fairly luxurious. (OK, OK, they usually do look like mobile homes, but they are comfortable.) As long as you pull up to shore enough for her to exercise and do her thing, she's going to be one happy pooch. The lake is pretty much surrounded by national forestland, where your dog can exercise leash-free. Make sure you keep an eye on her, though, and don't forget about her while you're inside making a soufflé.

One of the largest and most dog-friendly houseboat rental companies is **Cedar Stock Resort.** "Dogs are just as much a part of the family as everyone else. They can't miss a vacation like this," says Steve, one of the resort's managers. Bringing a dog along will cost you $40 extra per week. The houseboats here run $1,100–3,495 weekly, with big off-season discounts. The smaller ones fit up to six, and the larger ones can stash all your relatives.

The Cedar Stock Resort's houseboat headquarters is 15 miles north of Weaverville on Highway 3. The mailing address is HCR 1, Box 510, Lewiston, CA 96052; 530/286-2225 or 800/982-2279. For other companies, call the Trinity County Visitor's Center at 530/623-6101. Be sure to reserve early. Sometimes summer rentals are completely booked by April! Houseboat "high season" is usually April–November.

Jackass Springs Campground: This one's a rustic and fairly secluded U.S. Forest Service campground with 21 sites on the northeast section of the lake. There's no fee, so you can buy your leashed pooch a bone with the money you save. All sites are available on a first-come, first-served basis. Be sure to bring plenty of water, because there's no drinking water supplied. This is not the kind of place you want to visit for just one night. The ride itself may make you want to stay for the rest of your life or be airlifted out. From Highway 299, turn north on Trinity Mountain Road (west of Whiskeytown Lake) and drive about 12 miles to the Trinity Mountain Station. Turn right and drive about 12 miles on East Side Road—it's gravel, so be ready for some hopping around. At Delta Road (it's dirt), go left and drive about three more miles to the campground. It's actually worth the drive to get away from the more crowded southeast side of the lake. 530/623-2121.

Ripple Creek Cabins: The Trinity River runs right by these cozy, homey housekeeping cabins. You'll have no shortage of outdoor adventures to share with your dog here. Each cabin has a woodstove and electric heat. This is helpful, because unlike most other resorts in the area, Ripple Creek is open year-round. If he's around, the friendly owner, Jim Coleman, will make you and your pup feel right at home. Rates are $75–145. Dogs are charged a $10 per-stay fee. The address is Box 4020, Route 2 96091; 530/266-3505 or 510/531-5315; www.ripplecreekcabins.com.

Trinity Alps Resort: The 43 housekeeping cabins here were built in the 1920s, and they're clean and comfy, with real wood paneling and large sleeping verandas overlooking the Stuart Fork of the Trinity River. The resort is on 90 acres and is surrounded by 500,000 acres of Shasta-Trinity National Forest. The folks here welcome dogs. "We consider dogs part of the family," says a manager. There's even a dog-friendly eatery on the premises. (See Bear's Breath Bar and Grill in the Lewiston section.)

The weekly rate is $550 for a cabin for up to four people. If you're feeling very social, you can rent a cabin for 10 people for $1,150 per week. 1750 Trinity Alps Road 96091; 530/286-2205; www.trinityalpsresort.com.

Hyampom

Don't worry if you're a native Californian and you've never heard of Hyampom. Some folks in adjacent towns have never heard of it either. Hyampomeranians (OK, that's not what they call themselves, but Jake forced me to write this) identify their location by telling you they're "about 20 miles west of Hayfork." Well, now, that certainly settles things. Dogs like it because there's plenty of national forest land around the area, and the people who live here (250 on a very good day) seem to have a big place in their hearts for dogs.

PLACES TO STAY

Old Garrett Ranch: Dogs, sit down when you read this: If you talk your folks into coming here, you'll get to stay in an old cowboy cabin on 225 acres! And those 225 acres are bordered on three sides by the Shasta-Trinity National Forest! And it's on the banks of the South Fork Trinity River! We can't say it's all yours, because there's also a dog-friendly rentable duplex at the ranch, plus horses, chickens, dogs, and the ranch's owners, Ebbe and Uschi Schneider.

And as the Schneiders are fond of reminding guests, this beautiful property is also where bear and mountain lion meet. Please remember this if you plan to let your dog roam leash-free with you. That's absolutely allowed here, but your dog really must be under excellent voice control if you don't want to end up giving a new meaning to dog food.

The one-bedroom cowboy cabin, officially known as the Birdwatcher's Cabin, isn't fancy, but it's cozy, with an open-beam ceiling and a woodstove, which is the cabin's only heat source. It also has a living room, a little kitchen, a deck, and in case you were wondering just how rustic it is—a bathroom. The two two-bedroom units in the duplex are more modern, and the bottom unit is wheelchair-accessible.

The Schneiders also run a dog-boarding service and train dogs, so if you're in need of either, it's right here in your own very large backyard.

Please bring a blanket or bed for your dog. Rates are $75–80. Weekly rates are available. The mailing address is P.O. Box 155 96046; 530/628-4569.

RiverSong Village: The seven wooden housekeeping cabins at this little resort are somewhat rustic, but quite affordable and very clean. Most dogs don't really give a hang about interior decoration anyway: What really sets their tails to wagging here is the natural splendor outside the cabins. The resort is set on some beautifully landscaped land along the South Fork of the Trinity River. Apple, peach, and pear trees abound, as do brilliant flowers.

This property, formerly Ziegler's Trails End, has something for everyone: Water dogs and their soggy people can head for the relaxing beach and swimming area. (Well-behaved dogs can be leash-free on most of the property.) Anglers will drool over the great steelhead and trout fishing. Bird-watchers can take a gander at great blue herons, ospreys, and bald eagles. Folks who enjoy working the land can pick blackberries all spring. And anyone who relishes wholesome country foods will love the fresh eggs (from Lee and Thora Ziegler's very own brood) and fresh-baked bread available here for a very reasonable rate.

Rates are $55 for up to two people. Each additional guest is $10. Dog rates are $10 for the first dog, $6 for each extra dog. Weekly rates are available. The resort is off Highway 3. The mailing address is P.O. Box 150 96046; 530/628-5616 or 800/566-5266; www.riversongvillage.com.

Weaverville

This is the gateway to the Trinity Alps, and what a gateway it is. It's a former boomtown with a Main Street that's almost unchanged from the 1850s, complete with spiral staircases and brick facades.

About 2,500 Chinese immigrants were among the miners who came here during the Gold Rush. The Joss House State Historic Park contains the oldest active Chinese temple in California. Dogs aren't allowed inside, but as you're driving to the adjacent Lee Fong Park on Main Street, you can take a gander at it.

Work continues on the Weaverville Basin Trail System, a trail around the periphery of the Weaverville area. About 40 miles are done, with another 10 or so to go. Even now, in its unfinished state, it offers an excellent way to explore the area with your leashed dog. A couple of trailheads are near town. For a brochure and trail map, call the Trinity County Chamber of Commerce at 530/623-6101, the Trinity County Resource Conservation District at 530/623-6004, or the U.S. Forest Service at 530/623-2121. For updates on the Internet: www.tcrd.net.

PARKS, BEACHES, AND RECREATION AREAS

🐾 Lowden Park

🐾🐾 (See Trinity County map on page 58)

Dogs who like big pine trees like Lowden Park. The park has playing fields, playgrounds, and an area where you don't have to do anything at all. Its edges are lined by pines and a tall fence. Dogs have to be leashed, but it's good to know that if they pull the leash from your hands, they'll still be pretty safe from traffic.

From Highway 3 in the north part of town, go south on Washington Street. The park will be on your left in about a block. 530/623-1319.

🐾 Lee Fong Park

🐾🐾🐾 (See Trinity County map on page 58)

Set on the land once owned and farmed by a prominent local Chinese family, this magnificent park still has the appeal of an old-time farm. It even has several apple and pear trees that still bear fruit—but don't steal from the branches. (We were told that it's OK to pick up a piece of fruit from the ground, though.)

The park is undeveloped and fairly large. It's far from the paved road, but leashes are the law here anyway. A dirt path will take you around the park's perimeter in about 10 minutes if you want a fast walk, but most people who come here like to stop and smell the fresh and fruity air. You can pretend it's your own orchard, and chances are good that no other park user will stop by and ruin your fantasy. For some reason, the place gets very little use.

Dogs seem to love this park. Joe and Bill had a field day sniffing the freshly fallen fruit and checking out what was lurking in the tall grass. Each walked away with a fairly mushy apple in his mouth.

The park is on Main Street/Highway 299 just south of the historic part of town. It will be on your right as you're driving south. Although a small sign points to the park, the bigger farmer's market sign is actually a better landmark. Turn right and drive a few hundred feet to the dirt parking lot. When you see the bathroom in front of you and the old ranch house on your left beyond some trees, you'll know you're in the right place. 530/623-5925 or 530/623-6101.

PLACES TO EAT

Alan's Oak Pit: Come and get just about anything that can possibly be barbecued. Eat at the picnic benches out back. They come complete with grass and trees. 1324 Nugget Lane; 530/623-2182.

Miller's Drive-In: Eat at the outdoor tables, or get served in your car. Jake likes the idea of the latter, but I think he's just hoping to see a waitress in a poodle skirt. 796 Main Street; 530/623-4585.

PLACES TO STAY

Best Western Weaverville Victorian Inn: This is a modern, nice-looking motel. We haven't stayed there, but we've heard from a couple of people who have had problems with the management, so make sure you know what you're getting into when you reserve your room with a credit card deposit. 1709 Main Street 299 West, P.O. Box 2400 96093; 530/623-4432.

49er Gold Country Inn: The innkeepers have had some trouble with dogs here, so they ask that canine friends be kept in "a container" at night. The mind reels with interesting container possibilities, but stick with a kennel. Rates are $50–68. 718 Main Street 96093; 530/623-4937; www.49ermotel.com.

Lewiston

This is a tiny, historic mining town that has so few tourists, you'll think you're in a time warp. What's really great about a visit to Lewiston is that there's plenty of access to the Trinity River. Just look around and it's there. The area off Rush Creek Road at Lewiston Road is a popular access point.

PARKS, BEACHES, AND RECREATION AREAS

🛂 Community Park

 (See Trinity County map on page 58)

You may as well take your dog on a walking tour of this quaint town, because you'll definitely cover more land, and you'll surely see more grass, trees, and bushes than you will in this small park. It's a pretty spot for humans, but only about one of its two acres is accessible right now. Dogs may find it a little restricting, but if your leashed dog just needs to stretch her legs, it's not a bad place to set a spell.

On Lewiston Road at Viola Lane, the park is run entirely through volunteer efforts by the residents of this small community, so there's no phone number for it.

PLACES TO EAT

Bear's Breath Bar and Grill: Well, that name sure leaves you hankering for a big chunk o' beef, doesn't it? What it lacks in romanticism, the Bear's Breath makes up for in pure charm and dog-friendly atmosphere. The restaurant has a patio and outdoor tables overlooking the Trinity River, and dogs are welcome to join you for some prime rib, steaks, chicken, tasty pasta dishes, or salad. (Jake says I should strike that last item.) The Bear's Breath is at the Trinity Alps Resort, 1750 Trinity Alps Road; 530/286-2205.

PLACES TO STAY

Lakeview Terrace Resort: If you ever wanted a place to call your own right on fishable, swimmable Lewiston Lake, this is about as close as you'll come (unless you call the local real estate agent). You and the dog of your choice get to stay in your very own, very clean, air-conditioned housekeeping cabin. The owners of the cabins are sweet people who love dogs. They'll be happy to point you to some good on-leash walking areas around the grounds. Boat rentals are available.

Rates are $66–173. Dogs are $10 extra. RVs can stay here for $18–21. The resort's mailing address is HCI Box 250 96052; 530/778-3803; www.lakeviewterraceresort.com.

Hayfork

This valley town in the Trinity Alps was at the heart of the state's logging culture for nearly a century. Doggy visitors checking out the trees can stay in a most wonderful lodging.

PLACES TO STAY

Barker Valley Doghouse: Michael Richman, owner of this charming vacation home in remote Barker Valley, loves his flat-coated retriever so much he did something very special for him: "I bought this place for him," he says.

Bodie is a very lucky dog indeed. When he makes the occasional sojourn from his home in San Francisco to Barker Valley (a most apt name for his country home's location), he gets to stay on seven pretty acres with a year-round creek running through the property. The house is on a little dirt road with just a few cars going by each day, but since Bodie is a car-chaser, there's now not one, but two solid fences that keep him in the yard and off the road. This is great news for visiting dogs, because their people can let them out the door with nary a worry about cars. (Note: If you do venture beyond the fences, just make sure your dog is under voice control if you let him off leash: There's a sheep farm nearby, and deer frequent the area. You don't want to take a chance that your dog will chase either.)

The 800-square-foot home, which sports a kind of Ikea-meets-Southwest decor, comes with conveniences such as a fully equipped kitchen, a washer and dryer, and satellite TV with VCR. (The latter luxury is for those who only kind of want to get away from it all.) The deck is a terrific spot for looking out at the surrounding mountain scenery. "It's a great place to relax and have a drink with your dog at your feet," says Joe Hague, a San Francisco dog-walker who visited with his wife and dog.

Dogs who stay here get to use the Doghouse's water and food bowls and doggy blankets. They can even munch some treats Bodie leaves for fellow canine guests. This is the kind of doghouse most dogs can only dream of.

The Barker Valley Doghouse is rented by the week, for $495. Arrangements can be made for shorter visits. It's about five miles from Hayfork, the nearest town, and you can get directions and the address when you make your reservation. For reservations, phone 415/252-9590 or email michael .richman@mindspring.com.

CHAPTER 6
Shasta County

If you and your dog are aching to get away from city life, have we got a county for you! See that leash draped over your banister? You'll have to bring it, but you won't have to use it much.

Between the national forests, a state forest, and even a small city park, your obedient pooch can get all the leash-free exercise she needs. She'll go home with a wide grin on her snout. Your snout will be smiling, too.

NATIONAL FORESTS

The National Forests and Wilderness Areas resource at the back of this book has important information and safety tips on visiting national forests with your dog and has more background on the national forests listed below.

PICK OF THE LITTER—SHASTA COUNTY

BEST SWIMMING HOLE
Shasta Lake, Lakehead (page 70)

BEST FOREST HIKING
Latour Demonstration State Forest, Burney (page 74)

BEST WATER ADVENTURE
Shasta Lake houseboats, Lakehead (page 72)

Lassen National Forest
🐾🐾🐾🐾 🐕

Shasta-Trinity National Forest
🐾🐾🐾🐾 🐕

The forest pretty much surrounds beautiful, fish-filled Shasta Lake. If it's not too snowy before Christmas, you and your dog can pay $10 and go find yourselves a Christmas tree. Not many people have hundreds of thousands of acres of Christmas tree lots.

NATIONAL PARKS

Lassen Volcanic National Park

Dogs are barely allowed to set paw in this fascinating park. (For more details on what you and your dog are not missing if you stay away from this national park, see the description in the Lassen County chapter.)

Lakehead

PARKS, BEACHES, AND RECREATION AREAS

🄵 Shasta Lake
🐾🐾🐾🐾 🐕 (See Shasta County map on page 68)

At 29,500 acres, this is California's largest man-made lake. If you and your dog fish, swim, or watch waterfowl, you'll be in heaven here. When full, it has 370 miles of shoreline—more than San Francisco Bay.

The lake is surrounded by national forest land. More than 30 miles of trails travel into the nearby forest, and once you're away from civilization and campsites, your dog can throw his leash to the wind. Depending on where you hike, you'll pass all kinds of natural wonders, from wooded flats and secluded creeks to rocky mountains and gushing waterfalls. Keep in mind that even though this is a northern lake, it can still get mighty toasty in the summer, so try to bring your dog here at some cooler time of year.

The U.S. Forest Service manages 380 sites at 21 campgrounds. Some are very primitive, while others seem like minimotels. Sites cost $8–16. The lake is one of the few in California where you and your dog can camp along the shore. If your pooch has been extra good, he deserves to "ruff" it at one of these sites. About a quarter of the sites are available on a first-come, first-served basis, the rest must be reserved.

A first visit to Shasta Lake can be a confusing experience. The lake has so many arms and so many trails that it's hard to know where to go. The trails at Jones Valley, Packers Bay, Bailey Cove, Shasta Dam, and Hirz Bay not only make for excellent woodland hiking, but they provide good access to shoreline fishing. (The lake can get very crowded during the summer, so be prepared to sacrifice solitude for the sounds of loud boats and personal watercraft, too many of which sound like mosquitoes on steroids.)

There's also such a variety of campsites that it can make your head ache just thinking about the possibilities. And who needs that just before a four-paw vacation?

Here's a suggestion: Get a map or a brochure of the lake and a little advice from a ranger. The folks at the visitor center are very helpful, but you may find them insisting that your dog must be leashed everywhere in the forest. As of this printing, that's just not true. To get to the visitor center, take the Mountain Gate–Wonderland Boulevard exit off I-5 about four miles south of the lake. Follow the signs. The phone number is 530/275-1587. Call the U.S. Forest Service supervisor's office at 530/226-2500 for the latest on the leash/leashless law. (As of now, dogs can be off leash in all but developed lands, campsites, and the like. And they aren't allowed at all in the Mt. Shasta Wilderness.) Call 877/444-6777 for reservations.

PLACES TO STAY

Lakeshore Inn: The 10 cabins here are lined up one after another, and they have a sort of motel feeling to them inside, but dogs and their people enjoy staying here. The resort's pool is graced by tall pines and old oaks, and it has a killer view of Shasta Lake. Rates are $85–120. You can also camp here for $25–29. Camping dogs are $1 extra. 20483 Lakeshore Drive 96051; 530/238-2003; www.shastacamping.com.

Shasta Lake: See Shasta Lake, above, for camping information.

DIVERSION

Leave the Doggone Dramamine Behind: Shasta Lake is bliss for anyone of the seasick persuasion. The best way to experience this calm lake is to **rent a houseboat** for a few days. The only thing that may make you nauseated is having to go home at the end of your floating vacation.

Imagine waking up in a secluded cove, taking your dog for a lakeside hike and a brief swim, and then sitting down to a big breakfast cooked in your boat's well-equipped kitchen before setting off to cruise around the lake. (Joe, the landlubbing Airedale, would say pass the bacon but forget about the swim.)

Several local houseboat outfitters permit pooches on their boats. Weekly rates are $1,750–4,565. You can rent some for just two or three days, if that's more in your budget. Although houseboats are meant to be shared with friends, you won't want to fill the boat to capacity if you're bringing your dog along. Two big people, one or two kids, and a dog on a boat that sleeps six gives you plenty of paw room.

Four dog-friendly outfitters are Seven Crown Resorts, 800/752-9669, www.sevencrown.com; Antlers Resort, 530/238-2553 or 800/238-3924, www.shastalakevacations.com/rent_houseboat; Holiday Harbor, 800/776-BOAT (800/776-2628), www.lakeshasta.com; and Jones Valley Resort, 530/275-7950, www.houseboats.com/shasta/other_rentals.

Sugarloaf Cottages Resort: The comfortably furnished cottages are just a Frisbee's throw from the lake. We've really enjoyed our sojourns to these modern but cozy cabins. If you visit at the right time, you'll be stunned at the peace and quiet. We stayed here once in April, and boy, was it ever quiet. Of course, it was freezing cold and pouring rain, so maybe that had something to do with it. But the comfy cabins were sure good to come home to after a long day of wet outdoor fun.

The folks who run this place have two wonderful dogs of their own, and they have the run of the place. Don't be surprised to see Bailey or Indiana's big, friendly yellow Lab faces at your front door for a pat on the head.

Daily rates Labor Day–Memorial Day are $90–160. During the rest of the year, the cabins must be rented by the week, and they cost $1,000–2,000. 19667 Lakeshore Drive 96051; 530/238-2448; www.shastalakecabins.com.

Tsasdi Resort: David, the owner of this attractive resort, loves animals. He has two golden retrievers himself. But he isn't fond of people who aren't responsible about their dogs, and because of a few of these people in recent years, he is reconsidering his dog-friendly policy. (It's no fun for him, for instance, when canine guests eat furniture when their humans leave them alone—a big no-no at almost every lodging, as it should be.) But for now, he's leaving the dogs-welcome policy in place, in hopes that it will work out.

Many of the 20 housekeeping cabins at Tsasdi (SAUZ-dee, which David says is a Wintu Indian word meaning "white mountain") have decks overlooking Shasta Lake, which is just a long staircase down the hill. The cabins, built in the 1960s, are attractive and comfortable, and a forest of black oaks surround them—a big plus on a hot summer day.

Rates are $85–185. Dogs are $12 extra. During summer, rentals are by the week only. 19990 Lakeshore Drive 96051; 530/238-2575 or 800/995-0291; www.shastalakecabins.com.

Burney

This scenic mountain community is an excellent place to get away from urban life without getting carried away with the idea. There's enough civilization here to please even the primmest poodle.

PARKS, BEACHES, AND RECREATION AREAS

You won't find many community-style parks in these parts. What you will find are forests everywhere—many thousands of acres. Much of the surrounding land is public land, and people and their pooches just have to pull off the road for a fun little hike. But make sure you're not treading on private property first. Just ask around town and you'll get so much help from the dog-friendly folks here that you'll have a hard time deciding which piece of dog heaven to visit.

For a great hiking experience in a place with well-defined dog rules (off leash!) and boundaries, take your dog to the Latour Demonstration State Forest.

🛂 McArthur–Burney Falls Memorial State Park
🐾🐾🐾 (See Shasta County map on page 68)

This park is home to breathtaking 129-foot Burney Falls, which Theodore Roosevelt once dubbed "the eighth wonder of the world." Dogs can get a glimpse of this wonder from "The Overlook" at the top of the falls, next to the parking lot. Don't be surprised if your pooch gets that "I gotta go to the bathroom" look while gazing at the falls. About 100 million gallons of icy water cascade daily. It's enough to make a grown dog cross his legs.

And there's some great news, especially since this is a state park: A new one-mile trail allows leashed dogs to walk down to the lake! Water dogs can even swim in the lake near the dirt parking lot where the boat trailers are parked. (But not at Swim Beach.)

You can camp at one of the park's 128 sites with your pooch. Rates are $20. The day-use rate is $6 per car. From Burney, drive about five miles northeast on Highway 299, then go north on Highway 89 about another six miles to the park. Call 800/444-PARK (800/444-7275) for reservations. For park information, call 530/335-2777.

🐾 Latour Demonstration State Forest

🐾🐾🐾🐾🐕 (See Shasta County map on page 68)

This 9,033-acre forest provides sweeping vistas of the Cascade Range. The 67 miles of logging roads are open to people and their leash-free pooches. But don't take your dog off leash unless she's 101 percent obedient, since the park is home to bobcats and mountain lions, who can get revenge on dogs on behalf of their city cat cousins. "Be careful, because dogs are real tasty tidbits," warned Dan Higgins, assistant manager of the forest.

Firs, pines, mountain shrubs, and delicate wildflowers abound. You don't have to stay on the logging roads to enjoy the forest. Because of the sustainable-yield forestry practiced here, it's not a dense forest. "You can just pick out a creek and follow it all day and have a magnificent time," says Higgins.

Camping is terrific and fairly primitive. Eight campsites, available on a first-come, first-served basis, are spread throughout the forest. Better yet, there's no fee. The forest is off-limits through the winter, unless your dog knows how to use a snowmobile.

From Highway 299 just west of Burney, drive south on Tamarack Road. In about 10 miles, Tamarack will fork. Take the road that keeps going straight, Jack's Backbone Road/Road 16. In about six more miles, you'll see a sign for the forest. Turn right and drive to the forest headquarters to pick up a map. The park is also accessible from Redding. Call 530/225-2418 for directions or information.

PLACES TO EAT

Alpine Drive-In: The beef is here. Eat a hamburger at the outdoor tables with your pooch. 37148 Main Street; 530/335-2211.

PLACES TO STAY

Charm Motel: Rates are $61–67. Dogs are $5–10 extra, depending on size. (Eighty-five-pound Jake Dog thinks the big dogs should pay less than the tiny ones.) 37363 Main Street 96013; 530/335-2254; www.charmmotel.com.

Green Gables Motel: You won't find Anne (of Green Gables) around here, but you will find yourself feeling at home at this little motel nestled in pine-studded surroundings. It's conveniently situated for fishing. All rooms come with coffeepots and refrigerators. Rates are $47–98. Dogs are $5–10 extra, depending on their size. (Big Jake is starting to get impatient with this popular local policy.) 37385 Main Street 96013; 530/335-2264; www.greengablesmotel.com.

Latour Demonstration State Forest: See the Latour Demonstration State Forest, above, for camping information.

McArthur–Burney Falls Memorial State Park: See McArthur–Burney Falls Memorial State Park, above, for camping information.

Fall River Mills

PLACES TO STAY

Fall River Hotel: As long as dogs go in through the side door (there's a good, flea-free restaurant and bar in the front) and they're not too big, they're very welcome at this historic, friendly 12-room hotel. Between the brass beds, antique furnishings (including quaint Victorian lampshades for dogs who are Martha Stewart fans), and handmade quilts, a stay at this lodging, built in 1935, makes you feel as if you've stepped back in time. Some rooms have private baths, and one even has its own kitchen. The hotel also offers a "fun package," which includes a gourmet dinner and a terrific country breakfast.

The cost is $65–75. Dogs are $5. The hotel is near a PGA-rated golf course and some world-class fishing, and it's about halfway between Lassen Volcanic National Park and Mt. Shasta. 24860 Main Street, P.O. Box 718 96028; 530/336-5550; www.fallriverhotel.com.

Whiskeytown

PARKS, BEACHES, AND RECREATION AREAS

🐾 Whiskeytown Lake

🐾🐾🐾🐾 (See Shasta County map on page 68)

Many miles of trails await you and your leashed, four-legged beast at this 42,500-acre segment of the Whiskeytown-Shasta-Trinity National Recreation unit. The lake has 36 miles of shoreline for great fishing and pooch swimming (as long as the dog-paddling isn't at designated beaches), but most dogs seem to like to hang out here with all four feet planted on terra firma.

Dogs are allowed on 90 percent of the trails here. You can get a map and a little advice from a ranger about your hiking options.

For pooches who like to sleep in all day, the camping is divine. Sites are on a first-come, first-served basis Labor Day–Memorial Day, but reservations are needed during the busy summer months. Call 800/365-CAMP (800/365-2267). Sites are $16–18. There's a $5 day-use fee per vehicle.

From Redding, drive about eight miles west on Highway 299. The information center and overlook is at Highway 299 and Kennedy Memorial Drive. It's not far from Dog Gulch, in case your dog was asking. 530/246-1225.

PLACES TO STAY

Whiskeytown Lake: See Whiskeytown Lake, above, for camping information.

Redding

It may be full of franchise motels and restaurant chains, but this city is the hub of the northern reaches of California. It's an excellent base for exploring the surrounding wildlands.

PARKS, BEACHES, AND RECREATION AREAS

Dogs have their own park here and they're allowed to hike on the Sacramento River Trail. Other than that, city parks are off-limits to pooches.

5 Sacramento River Trail

🐾🐾🐾 (See Shasta County map on page 68)

This 5.7-mile paved trail follows the wide and wonderful Sacramento River, leading you and your leashed dog through riparian terrain and rolling hills. It's best to visit on weekdays or uncrowded weekends, because on some days your dog can get the feeling of being mighty squished with the masses who like to hike and bike through here.

Bill Dog loved to take a dip in the water when we visited. He could lie in the Sacramento all day, but he hated the idea that he was missing out on sniffing the scents left by other dogs. When he was in the river, he was constantly looking to see who passed on the trail. When he was on the trail, he always kept one eye on the beckoning river. It was a real doggy dilemma, but he managed.

From Market Street/Highway 273, go west on Riverside Drive (just south of the river). Head west to the parking area. There are many other access points. Call 530/225-4095 for details.

6 Benton Airpark Park

🐾🐾🐾🐕 (See Shasta County map on page 68)

Joe's eyes opened wide and he stood utterly still for a few moments when he first saw this park. Somehow, although there were no dogs in it at the time, it seemed he could tell that this was a place of great dog happiness. He sniffed that joyous dog smell in the air, his tail started twitching, and he began pawing the gate to get in.

Once inside this large, completely fenced dog park, he rolled for several minutes. He rolled underneath the cold aluminum picnic table. He rolled on the mud around the water fountain. He rolled in the grass on the park's east side, and then in the grass on the west side. He stopped rolling only when another dog came in to share the park with him. They chased each other around like fiends for 30 seconds. Then he started rolling again, this time on the grass in the north side of the park. He was in heaven.

The fact that there are only a couple of small trees here doesn't seem to bother dogs. If they want shade, they can go under the picnic tables. If they need to lift a leg, there's always a fence post.

From I-5, exit at Highway 299 and go west for about two miles, following Highway 299 through a couple of turns in central Redding. At Walnut Street, turn left. Drive five blocks and turn right on Placer Street. You'll see the park in one block, at the corner of Placer Street and Airpark Drive, adjacent to the Benton Airpark (where the airplane activity provides amusement for bird dogs here). 530/225-4095.

PLACES TO EAT

Hamburger: Sit on the patio with your favorite well-behaved dog and eat the classic burgers. The place has been here since 1938. 1320 Placer Street; 530/241-0136.

Wall Street Pizza: The pizza is tasty here, but the garlic rolls are decadently delicious. Share one with your pooch at the picnic tables outside. 1165 Hartnell Avenue; 530/221-7100.

PLACES TO STAY

Thanks to the very dog-friendly new manager of several motels around town, Redding is an easy, convenient place to spend the night with your traveling pooch.

Best Western Hospitality House: Rates are $80–90. Dogs are $10 extra. 532 North Market Street 96003; 530/241-6464 or 800/700-3019.

Best Western Ponderosa Inn: Rates are $40–65. Dogs under 25 pounds require a $15 one-time fee. Larger dogs cost $25 per stay. "The extra charge is for the extra cleaning large dogs require," we're told. (Jake says, "No fair!" He makes no more mess than his Chihuahua friend Noodle.) 2220 Pine Street 96001; 530/241-6300.

Capri Motel: Rates are $48–54. Dogs are $10 extra per night or $25 extra per week. 4620 Westside Road 96001; 530/241-1156.

Comfort Inn: Rates are $70–106. Dogs are $15 extra for the length of their stay. 2059 Hilltop Drive 96002; 530/221-6530 or 800/228-5150; www.choicehotels.com.

Hilltop Lodge: Rates are $55. Dogs are $10 extra per stay and may require a $100 deposit. 2240 Hilltop Drive 96002; 530/221-5432 or 800/626-1900.

Motel 6 Redding Central: One pooch per room is permitted. Rates are $46–66. 1640 Hilltop Drive 96002; 530/221-1800.

Red Lion Hotel: The folks here identify this pleasant hotel as "a pet-friendly establishment." Dogs can stay here if they're under 50 pounds. Rates are $89–119. Dogs require a $50 deposit. 1830 Hilltop Drive 96002; 530/221-8700; www.redlion.com.

River Inn: This sweet motel backs up to a little lagoon where you and your leashed dog can try to catch some fish. (The management will even lend you a fishing rod!) And if your angling is successful, you can grill your catch at the motel's barbecues and eat it at the picnic tables. Then the human people in your group can go for a swim in the motel's heated pool. (Dog people can't go in the pool.) 1835 Park Marina Drive 96001; 530/241-9500 or 800/995-4341.

Anderson

PARKS, BEACHES, AND RECREATION AREAS

7 Anderson River Park

🐾🐾🐾 (See Shasta County map on page 68)

This 425-acre park has plenty of trees for boy dogs with bottomless bladders. Dogs seem to like the one-mile nature trail better than anything, except for the sweet little pond full of ducks. The ducks would like to remind you that dogs must be leashed here. For the humans in the crowd, the park has picnic tables and a playground.

The park is on Rupert Road at the Sacramento River. Driving south on I-5, exit at the North Street off-ramp and follow North Street north a few blocks to Stingy Lane. Turn right and drive a few blocks to Rupert Road, then turn left. Drive to the end and you'll be at the park. 530/378-6656.

PLACES TO STAY

Best Western Knights Inn: The room rate is $62. 2688 Gateway Drive 96007; 530/365-2753.

CHAPTER 7

Lassen County

There's not much civilization around here, so you and your dog may have to be content with hiking, camping, and spending quality time at the Lassen and Modoc National Forests. Most dogs could think of worse things to do.

NATIONAL FORESTS

The National Forests and Wilderness Areas resource at the back of this book has important information and safety tips on visiting national forests with your dog and has more background on the national forests listed below.

Lassen National Forest

🐾🐾🐾🐾🐾 🐕

They're a little more sticky about off-leash dogs here than at most national forests. Dogs are allowed sans leash, but rangers say they're quick to bow to the county leash law if there's any complaint. This could be because the forest surrounds Lassen Volcanic National Park, which has extremely strict dog laws.

PICK OF THE LITTER—LASSEN COUNTY

BEST LAKE
Eagle Lake, Susanville (page 83)

MOST INTERESTING HIKE
Biz Johnson Rail Trail, Susanville (page 83)

Modoc National Forest

NATIONAL PARKS

Lassen Volcanic National Park

Don't get your hopes up about enjoying this astounding national park with your dog. Pooches are all but banned from this geological wonderland. Here's the long and exciting list of places they're allowed to visit: parking lots, paved main roads, and campgrounds.

Since walking in a parking lot or along a heavily used road probably isn't your dog's idea of a good time, we'll just describe the camping. Dogs are permitted, on leash, at the four campgrounds that are accessible by car. There are a total of 357 campsites, many on a first-come, first-served basis, but some are reservable. Sites are $10–16, and are in both Shasta and Lassen Counties. Call 530/595-4444 for directions to the campground most convenient to you. For reservations: 877/444-6777.

Susanville

Susanville is the second-oldest town in the western Great Basin, and a stroll through the historic uptown area with the city's free "Come Walk with Us" guide will fill you with all the historical knowledge you and your dog could ever need. But quite frankly, your dog will probably enjoy romping outdoors in this area much better than boning up on the local lore.

PARKS, BEACHES, AND RECREATION AREAS

1 Eagle Lake

🐾🐾🐾🐾 (See Lassen County map on page 80)

Tired of all those look-alike man-made reservoirs and lakes? Here's a lake that's large and natural. In fact, at 42 square miles, Eagle Lake is the second-largest natural lake in California. Better yet, it's also one of the state's cleanest and least crowded lakes.

If you like trout fishing, you and your dog will enjoy angling for Eagle Lake trout, which are found nowhere else in the world. In the cold fall months, you can fish from the north shore and land some big ones. But don't forget that even though your dog is wearing a coat, he's going to freeze if you don't occasionally get up and walk around with him.

The northern end of this clear blue lake is characteristic of high desert country, with sage and juniper, rocky shoreline, and reed patches. There's plenty of open land where you and your dog can dillydally the day away. The land leading down to the south shore is a drastic contrast, with lush pine forests and mountains of green.

Dogs should be leashed, because critters as various as deer, pronghorn antelope, and bald eagles are quite common here.

The U.S. Forest Service runs four campgrounds here, with a total of 325 sites. Fees range $15–17. Call 877/444-6777 for reservations. The Bureau of Land Management's North Eagle Lake Campground has some rugged sites on the north end of the lake. BLM sites are $8 per night, and they're available on a first-come, first-served basis. Call 530/257-0456 for BLM camping information.

From Susanville, drive 2.5 miles west on Highway 44, and then turn north at County Road A1. After about 16 miles, you'll reach the south shore campgrounds. Watch for signs. For more information, call Lassen National Forest at 530/257-2151, or the Eagle Lake ranger district at 530/257-4188.

2 Biz Johnson Rail Trail

🐾🐾🐾🐾🐾 (See Lassen County map on page 80)

Whether your dog is a couch poochtato or a super athlete, this trail is bound to become a favorite. The wide trail winds more than 25 miles from Susanville to Mason Station and then follows existing roads another 4.5 miles into Westwood. You'll know you're there when you see the 25-foot carved redwood statue of Paul Bunyan and Babe the Blue Ox. (Boy dogs, please have some respect for this folklore hero and fight the temptation to do leg lifts on him and his bovine buddy. This is his "birthplace," and they say his ghost doesn't take kindly to such indiscretions.)

With 11 bridges and two tunnels, the trail follows the Fernley and Lassen Railway line, which was built in 1914 to serve the world's largest pine mill. As you hike, you'll find signs marking the locations of a 300-man logging camp, freight and passenger stations, and logging spur lines. The place is popular in the warmer months. Obedient dogs are allowed off leash, but beware of fast mountain bikes. In winter, it's a cross-country skier's heaven. Leashless dogs love charging through the white powder at your side.

If your dog prefers his hikes or ski jaunts to be short, you can use any of six trailheads and flip around when he's looking bored or bedraggled. If he's a rugged outdoor kind of guy, you'll want to consider hiking longer sections of the trail and camping along the way. Primitive sites are open year-round along the very scenic Susan River, and there's no fee. It's advisable to pack your own water or treat the river water before you drink it.

From Susanville, follow Highway 36 to South Lassen Street at the western end of town. Go left on South Lassen Street for four blocks to the trail. Call the Bureau of Land Management's Eagle Lake Resource Area at 530/257-0456 for directions to other trailheads and for pocket-sized trail guides and plant identification keys. Some of the land here is also under the management of Lassen National Forest. Call its headquarters at 530/257-2151.

PLACES TO STAY

America's Best Inns: It's your basic one-story type of motel, but it serves fresh-baked muffins in the morning, which makes the place smell most inviting. Rates are $46–60. Dogs are $10 extra. 2705 Main Street 96103; 530/257-4522.

Biz Johnson Rail Trail: See Biz Johnson Rail Trail, above, for camping information.

Eagle Lake: See Eagle Lake, above, for camping information.

River Inn Motel: Rates are $51–60. Dogs are $10.80 extra. (Only $5.40 with AAA! We've never heard of a doggy AAA discount.) 1710 Main Street 96130; 530/257-6051.

Super 8 Motel: Rates are $58–67. Dogs are $10 extra. 2975 Johnstonville Road 96130; 530/257-2782.

Westwood

PARKS, BEACHES, AND RECREATION AREAS

◙ Biz Johnson Rail Trail

🐾🐾🐾🐾🐾 (See Lassen County map on page 80)

See the Susanville section for trail information. The Westwood section of the trail starts at Ash Street near 3rd Street and follows Ash Street and County Road A21 four miles to the Mason Station trailhead. That's where the main part of the trail begins.

Phil Frank

CHAPTER 8
Mendocino County

When people from out of town think of Mendocino County, they often think of quaint inns, sweeping seascapes, and perfect little coastal villages teeming with artists and tourists. But there's one vital image missing, that of a nosy dog sniffing about, exploring forests and fields, oceans and rivers, and some of the most dog-friendly inns in the state.

Several unbelievably wonderful lodgings have recently started welcoming dogs, and at one renowned vegetarian restaurant in the village of Mendocino, dogs can actually dine inside. (For more on this, see The Ravens, below.) This more European (and legal) dining setup is a first in the state, and we hope it's not the last. (However, Jake the Dog would appreciate it if the next restaurant that does this could be a steak restaurant, not a vegetarian one.)

Because of these new developments, we're giving Mendocino County, which was already a terrific place to be a dog, our "Most Improved" award. Take a bow, Mendocino.

While the coast of Mendocino County attracts most visitors, dogs have much more freedom inland, where they're allowed to run off leash in three

PICK OF THE LITTER—MENDOCINO COUNTY

BEST COASTAL WALKIES
Mendocino Headlands State Park/Big River Beach,
Mendocino (page 96)

BEST (ONLY) INDOOR DOGGY DINING IN THE STATE
The Ravens, Mendocino (page 97)

MOST DOG-FRIENDLY PLACES TO STAY
Delamere Cottages, Fort Bragg (page 94)
MacCallum House, Mendocino (page 98)
Stanford Inn by the Sea, Mendocino (page 100)
Inn at Schoolhouse Creek, Little River (page 102)
Little River Inn, Little River (page 102)
Highland Ranch, Philo (page 104)
Point Arena Lighthouse lodging, Point Arena (page 108)
Sheep Dung Estates, Yorkville (page 111)

BEST WINE ADVENTURE
Mendo Wine Tours, Mendocino (page 109)

very large parcels of land. But there's still something magical about the Mendocino coast. Although it offers no leash-free areas, dogs thrive on the ever-cool climate and the salty air. Joe once perched himself on a Mendocino bluff top for a solid hour and sat utterly still, except for his flaring nostrils. For Mr. Mobility to have such patience and fascination, there must be magic in the air (or at least the smell of a few deceased fish).

NATIONAL FORESTS

The National Forests and Wilderness Areas resource at the back of this book has important information and safety tips on visiting national forests with your dog and has more background on the Mendocino National Forest.

Mendocino National Forest

Only a tiny section of this national forest rests in its namesake county. Some rangers prefer to have dogs off leash only in the two wilderness areas, neither of which is in Mendocino County. Others say it's OK for dogs to be leash-free everywhere but in camping areas.

Westport

Here's another New England look-alike. Westport is a tiny coastal town with a couple of inns and restaurants and a whole lot of charm. It's a wonderful place to visit if you like the appeal of Mendocino but prefer your sidewalks tourist-free and your beaches isolated.

PARKS, BEACHES, AND RECREATION AREAS

🐾 Westport–Union Landing State Beach

🐾🐾🐾🐾 (See Mendocino County map on page 86)

On one of the busiest weekends of the year, not a soul was using this beach. Only one of the 100 campsites was occupied. This is the kind of place you can pretend is your own almost year-round. You and your dog may well find yourself alone in the campgrounds and along the sandy beaches, but pooches are still supposed to be leashed.

One of the best times to visit is during the gray whale migration January–April. There are several good spots on the bluff tops where you can watch whales in comfort. Just set up a lawn chair, sit back with your binoculars, and wait. Even if you don't see a leviathan, at least you and your dog will have spent some good outdoor hanging-out time together. To make it even better, have a picnic.

DIVERSION

Hang Around a Chandelier: The **Chandelier Tree** beckons all dogs and people who have ever stood with mouths agape at nature's awesome work. Sure, the 315-foot-high, 2,400-year-old tree has a painful-looking gaping hole in the center of its 21-foot-diameter base so cars can pass through. But of all the drive-through trees on California's north coast, this is the most spectacular: The thick limbs (some of which are eight feet in diameter) branch out about 100 feet above the ground in a most fascinating, chandelier-like way.

Dogs dig the tree, but they generally prefer the little nature trail that starts near the gift shop. It winds through a small section of fern-carpeted redwood forest. The short hike hits the spot after a long car ride.

The entry fee for the park is $3 per car. It's just south of Leggett, near the junction of U.S. 101 and Highway 1. Follow the signs. 707/925-6363.

Campsites are $15 and are first-come, first-served. The sites are all on the bluff tops, near the park road, and not far from Highway 1. You'll have no shade and no privacy unless you're the only camper (you camp just off the parking lots), but plenty of quiet. At night, it's easy to fall asleep to the gentle churning of the Pacific. The park has three entrances. We hear that the farther north you go, the better your chances of finding people. The beach is about 2.5 miles north of the town of Westport. You can't miss the empty parking lots, but if you do, you'll still see the signs. 707/937-5804.

PLACES TO STAY

Howard Creek Ranch: This rustic and historic redwood inn, built in 1867, offers privacy, quiet, and 40 acres of coastal beauty. Each room at this working ranch is unique, with features so special it's hard to decide where to stay. Joe liked the old boat, which is now a miniature cabin, complete with wood-burning stoves and low wooden ceilings. He didn't have to duck here like his human companions often did, and he seemed to get a real kick out of hearing the thwack of a *Homo sapien*'s head against a thick beam. The redwood cabin is in the woods next to a stream that runs through the property, and it's oh so private.

For a truly relaxing weekend, stay in a room with a hot tub or sauna. After your own personalized spa treatment, take your best bud for a romp at the ocean, which is only about 300 yards away.

Rooms are $75–160 a night. Dogs are $10 extra and are permitted only by prior arrangement. 40501 North Highway 1 95488; 707/964-6725; www.howardcreekranch.com.

Westport–Union Landing State Beach: See Westport–Union Landing State Beach, above, for camping information.

Fort Bragg

While Fort Bragg is now the commercial hub of the Mendocino coast, it once served as a fort built to maintain order for the Pomo Indian Reservation. The fort was abandoned in 1864, and it wasn't until 20 years later that Fort Bragg found its calling as a lumber town.

You and your dog can visit the Chamber of Commerce and pick up a walking-tour map of historic Fort Bragg. This won't substitute for a visit to the many wonderful beaches in the area, but it's a good way to learn about history while your dog puts his nose to the ground and learns who's been walking on the city's sidewalks. Sadly, one of the best activities here, a trip on the Skunk Train, won't be on canine agendas any more because a dog passenger bit the conductor. Understandably, the easygoing dog rule changed. The only way to take a dog on the train now is in a carrier. (The conductor is OK, thank goodness.)

DOG-EAR YOUR CALENDAR

Dogs not only get to witness four days of people showing off their strength and logging skills when they attend Fort Bragg's **Paul Bunyan Days,** they actually get to participate. They can't take part in the ax throwing or the power-saw bucking. But if your dog is ugly—so ugly that cats laugh at him and babies scream when he walks by—he can enter the annual Ugly Dog Contest. It usually takes place on the Saturday of this four-day Labor Day weekend event. There are also contests for the largest dog, the smallest dog, the smartest dog, the prettiest dog, and the Frisbee-est dog.

The dog part of the festival takes place at the middle school fields, at the corner of Harold and Laurel Streets. Phone the Chamber of Commerce for more information: 707/961-6300.

Our favorite part of town is the Noyo fishing village. Fishing fleets come in here with their catches and unload them at restaurants and processing plants. This is the real thing, not a San Francisco Fisherman's Wharf facade where selling T-shirts has come to replace the real business of fishing. And mmmm, it smells so fishy. Dogs are exhilarated just breathing the air.

PARKS, BEACHES, AND RECREATION AREAS

◨ MacKerricher State Park

🐾🐾🐾🐾 (See Mendocino County map on page 86)

This eight-mile beach encompasses a few smaller beaches, including the secluded Pudding Creek Beach at MacKerricher's southern end. Unfortunately, dogs are forbidden at the strip of beach near the main parking lot, but all you have to do is walk north or south a few hundred yards and miles of beach are all yours.

Jake the Water Dog adores this seaweed-strewn beach, although his species is supposed to be leashed. There's a little of everything here, from headlands to forests to a small lake. For dog exercise, it's best to stick to the beach. You'll run into fewer people and horses than you will in other park areas. Near the northern section of the beach, it gets so wide that you feel as though you and your dog are walking with Lawrence of Arabia. It may be tempting to walk on for what seems like eternity, but keep an eye on the time: It's tough walking back when it's dark.

Wildlife is everywhere. More than 100 species of birds inhabit the park, including the snowy plover. Because of the plover (who is endangered or threatened or maybe neither, but we'll leave that to the experts), certain areas are off-limits to doggies, but there are still plenty of places for our furry friends. Tidepools are rich with life. And harbor seals bask and breed on secluded rock outcroppings, sometimes even in the beach areas. But don't go anywhere near them, with or without your dog! They're shy creatures and will balk at the slightest disturbance, sometimes diving for long periods to avoid the possible threat.

It's fun to camp with your dog here. The 142 campsites are roomy and many are surrounded by trees. Sites are $15–20. Phone 800/444-PARK (800/444-7275) for reservations.

The best place for doggy access to the beach is at the Ward Avenue entrance, about a half mile north of the main park entrance. This is also where the beach starts becoming an enormous sandy mass. But if you're camping in the main section, beach access is just a short walk north or south. If you're unsure of where you and the pooch can walk on the beach, ask a ranger. The areas are not clearly marked.

The day use fee is $6. The main entrance is on the west side of Highway 1, about three miles north of Fort Bragg. It's marked by a large sign. You'll pass by a ranger kiosk, but there's no fee for day use. 707/937-5804.

▋ Noyo Beach

🐾🐾🐾 (See Mendocino County map on page 86)

A better name would be Solitude Beach. We've never seen anyone here, although we've seen footprints, so someone else must know about this place. This small, sandy beach on the mouth of the Noyo River has a leash law, but dogs enjoy trekking around and watching the boats come in with the catch of the day. This is also a good place to pick up the Coastal Trail. For great views, follow it northwest to the entrance to Noyo Bay.

Heading north on Highway 1, go right on North Harbor Drive and loop around down to the beach. An important note: At press time there was construction going on overhead on a bridge. The project was to continue through 2006. It may be impossible, difficult, or dangerous to get down to the beach at times. Phone first for beach access status. 707/964-4719.

▋ Jackson State Forest

🐾🐾🐾🐾 (See Mendocino County map on page 86)

Dogs are no longer allowed off leash at this 50,000-acre park. It's still a great place to visit with your dog, but it just isn't the same on a tether.

This is a demonstration area for forest management practices, with several self-guided educational nature trails and many miles of hiking available on old logging roads. One of the more popular trails is the Tree Identification Trail, just off Highway 20, about 11 miles east of Highway 1. It's one of the few areas of the forest that's actually marked from the highway, and it's a great place for you and your dog to learn the difference between madrone, hemlock, redwood, fir, and any other varieties that confuse you (including the oft-ignored wax myrtle). Dogs probably already know all about these trees, since the males of the species have made intimate acquaintances with so many in their lives. But they won't mind going along for the walk.

Critters abound, so leashes do make some sense. We've run into only the occasional quail and salamander during our sojourns, but we hear there are black bears and mountain lions around as well.

Sadly, the budget for the state forests has been cut so drastically that the forest is open to the public only from Memorial Day through Labor Day for now, and some trails might become neglected and some campgrounds may have to close. Call the forest before you visit to find out the status and obtain maps. As of press time, the forest had 44 campsites, available at no fee. You'll need to bring your own water (and don't forget your dog's) because the sites don't runneth over with amenities. You'll also need a camping permit and a campground map, which you can get from the camp host on site. Call 707/964-5674.

The forest stretches along Highway 20 from just east of Mendocino and Fort Bragg to about nine miles west of Willits.

PLACES TO EAT

Jenny's Giant Burger: Dogs love to smell the fries frying, the burgers grilling, the milk shakes shaking. It may not be healthy food, but it's good. Dine with doggy at the outdoor seating. 940 North Main Street; 707/964-2235.

PLACES TO STAY

Beachcomber Motel: Dogs love this place just a pinecone's throw from the beach and MacKerricher State Park. Rates are $59–109. Dogs are $20 extra the first night, $10 extra each additional night. 111 North Main Street 95437; 707/964-2402 or 800/400-7873; www.beachcombermotel.com.

Cleone Gardens Inn: It's hard to define Cleone Gardens: It has an older motel feel, but some of the rooms have a fireplace, some have a kitchen, and one dog-friendly "room"—Grandpa's Cottage—is actually a cute little house with wood-paneled walls and a cozy old kitchen. Jake likes this accommodation the best, because he has ample room to stretch his ample body. There's even a pasture beside the cottage, which makes it extra special for canine visitors. Wherever you stay at Cleone, you're welcome to stroll around the inn's well-maintained five acres with your leashed pooch. (Bring a "doggy bag," of course.) Rates are $89–140. Dogs are $6 extra. 24600 North U.S. 1 95437; 707/964-2788; www.cleonegardensinn.com.

Coast Motel: Who needs a dog park with this place around? The owner permits dogs to run leashless on five tree-filled acres of land behind the motel! It's pretty safe from traffic. Rates are $39–104. Dogs are $10 extra. 18661 Highway 1 95437; 707/964-2852; www.coast-motel.com.

Delamere Cottages: If you're looking to combine a romantic getaway with a blissful vacation for your dog, look no further. Admittedly, dogs and romance don't necessarily go hand-in-paw. Dogs somehow inevitably start chewing on their private parts or making strange noises during romantic moments. But at Delamere's two cozy oceanfront cottages, the combination somehow works.

The cottages are roomy enough so your dog can give you privacy, should you request it. Each cottage has a living room with fireplace, a kitchen, a dining area, and of course, a bathroom and bedroom. Beautiful gardens and gorgeous landscapes surround the cottages.

Two items Jake thought your dog should know: 1) There's a private path that leads down to a quiet beach and cove. It's gorgeous. 2) Dogs who stay here always get dog cookies.

Rates are $150 nightly, and there's a two-night minimum. Cash only, please. 16821 Ocean Drive 95437; 707/964-3175; www.delamerecottages.com.

MacKerricher State Park: See MacKerricher State Park, above, for camping information.

Caspar

PARKS, BEACHES, AND RECREATION AREAS

5 Caspar State Beach

😊😊😊 (See Mendocino County map on page 86)

The beach here is small, but it's a good place to walk your dog if you're between Mendocino and Fort Bragg and your dog starts getting that desperate look. You won't find many people here, but dogs still have to be leashed.

The beach is at Doyle Creek, off Point Cabrillo Drive (Old Highway 1). 707/937-5804.

PLACES TO STAY

Caspar Beach RV Park: A minicity, this RV park is for people who want to get away from civilization while not getting *too* far from it. About 25 tent sites are available, but you might feel lost among the mobile homes. In addition to hiking with your on-leash dog at the adjacent beach, you can also rent a video or play your favorite game in the video arcade. It's not exactly roughing it, but some people and their dogs are in heaven here.

Rates are $25. Dogs are $2 extra. From Mendocino, drive three miles north and take the Point Cabrillo Drive exit to Russian Gulch State Park. Take Point Cabrillo Drive west to the campground. 707/964-3306; www.casparbeachrvpark.com.

Mendocino

Take your dog to New England and never leave the Golden State! Visiting this quaint village, which stood in as Angela Lansbury's hometown in *Murder, She Wrote*, is like stepping across the country and back in time. (Dogs can actually stay in the inn that was supposed to be her home—the Blair House Inn.)

Mendocino is no stranger to the limelight; it's been cast in many movies and TV shows (usually as a New England town). Credits include *East of Eden* (1955), *The Russians Are Coming! The Russians Are Coming!* (1966), and even *Humanoids from the Deep* (1980). Take a stroll with your dog and see if anything looks familiar. If you're a James Dean fan, stop at the corner of Main and Kasten to see where Dean brooded while sitting on a curb in the beginning of *East of Eden*. Dogs may not enjoy this part of your stay too much, because no *Lassie* or *Rin Tin Tin* episodes were shot here. But they don't mind going along for the exercise.

The art galleries that give Mendocino its flavor generally don't allow dogs. But at least you can window-shop with your favorite canine critic. If you see something you like, the artists and gallery owners tend to be very accommodating. One art collector we know ended up having tea and toast in a gallery where she was buying several small prints. Her mutt, Rosy, got her own piece of toast and was offered a pot of tea, which she couldn't drink because it was too warm. The artist obligingly found some ice.

DIVERSION

Take Your Pooch for a Paddle: Here's a sure-fire way to get some vacation photos your friends will actually *want* to see: Take your dog for a canoe ride on the Big River. The Catch-a-Canoe rental shop is home to what's affectionately known around here as **"the dog canoe."** It's a bit wider and shorter than most canoes, thus a bit more stable. If your dog promises not to rock the boat too much, a canoe ride on the river can be a spectacular way to share your vacation time with him. The shop will supply your dog with a doggy life vest, just in case. Be sure to call in advance to find out about tides and to reserve the dog canoe.

The rate for the doggy canoe is $18 an hour, or $54 for the day. There's a two-hour minimum, so you may as well make a day of it. Other canoes are available for super calm dogs. You can call or go in and chat with the folks who run this place to figure out what's right for you. They're really friendly here. Catch-a-Canoe is part of the Stanford Inn by the Sea, so it's convenient for guests there. 44850 Comptche-Ukiah Road, Mendocino; 707/937-0273.

PARKS, BEACHES, AND RECREATION AREAS

6 Russian Gulch State Park

🐾🐾🐾 (See Mendocino County map on page 86)

Your dog will enjoy this small, wild park whose streams drain Russian Gulch. You must leash up, though, and stay off some of the back trails here. But you can still enjoy exploring among the trees of the deciduous forest. And dogs of the leg-lifting persuasion like the fact that huge groves of willows line the gulch. In wet season, you'll have to wade across the gulch to reach the beach, a small one with cliffs at each end. The surf is ferocious; don't let your dog near it. Swimming in the fresh creeks is much more fun for her, anyway.

The day-use fee is $6. You and your dog can pitch a tent at the 30-site campground here for $15–20.

As you continue on Highway 1, about two miles north of Mendocino, watch for a small brown sign marking the turnoff. There's a dirt parking lot at the entrance. 707/937-5804.

7 Friendship Park

🐾🐾 (See Mendocino County map on page 86)

If your dog is bursting at the seams, this is a decent place to pull off Highway 1. Otherwise, the Mendocino Headlands is a much better deal for dogs. The park is small, but friendly to leashed dogs. You'll find green grass, a playing field, and even some picnic tables in case your dog doesn't want to visit the local eateries after taking care of essential business here. Friendship Park is at Little Lake Road and School Street. 707/937-4133.

8 Mendocino Headlands State Park/Big River Beach

🐾🐾🐾🐾 (See Mendocino County map on page 86)

Mendocino's sculpted shoreline is a spectacular place for you and your dog to enjoy the sights, scents, and sounds of the Mendocino coast. Unlike most state parks, this one allows leashed dogs on the trails, which wind around the rocky bluffs and provide good views of wave tunnels and arched rocks. Fields extend along the cliff tops, so there's plenty of room for dogs who don't like to hover over the edge of promontories. It's cool year-round, so even malamutes can enjoy an August romp. A sandy beach at the mouth of the Big River near the southern headlands is a tempting place to let your dog off her leash, but watch out—the place can be heavily patrolled.

It's difficult to explore the tiny town of Mendocino without running into the headlands at every turn. Exit Highway 1 at Lansing Street and drive west. The park actually surrounds the little Mendocino peninsula, so just stop at any part that looks appealing. Parking won't be far away. To get to the sandy beach, exit Highway 1 at the sign for Mendocino Headlands State Park and Big River Beach. Follow the signs east. 707/937-5804.

PLACES TO EAT

Gray Whale Bar and Café: The beautiful porch that wraps around the Mac-Callum House inn's main Victorian (see below) is a fun place to dine with your dog. The cuisine features seasonal vegetables (organic when possible), fresh fish, and organic meats, and the wine list showcases some excellent choices from wineries in the nearby Anderson Valley. Despite the epicurean cuisine, this is a very casual restaurant. Humans without dogs can eat inside, but on nice days, they prefer the porch tables, too. 45020 Albion Street; 800/609-0492.

Mendocino Bakery: The food here is scrumptious and often even good for you. The bakery concentrates on vegetarian meals, and the pizza is out of this world. Dine with your dog at the many outdoor tables alongside the restaurant. 10483 Lansing Street; 707/937-0836.

Mendocino Burgers: Tucked right behind the Mendocino Bakery is this down-to-earth eatery offering beef burgers, turkey burgers, and even veggie burgers. In warmer months, there's usually a bowl of water near the outdoor picnic tables. If not, the folks who work here will be happy to get your thirsty pooch a bowl. 10483 Lansing Street; 707/937-1111.

Mendocino Cafe: Dogs love coming here. They get treated beautifully, with a bowl of fresh water and lots of love (if it's not too busy). Reader Melissa Miller, and her German shepherd, Lassy, wrote and told us that a waitress gave Lassy "a lovely plate of cooked beef chunks." Now that's one lucky Lassy! (Actually, Lassy lived the first part of her life in Hong Kong, and Miller says her life there was less than perfect, so she deserves this kind of beefy luck, doesn't she?) Oh, the food for humans is good, too, with a wide range of choices, from light and healthful to sticky and sinful. Dine with your dog on the deck overlooking the water and a garden. 10451 Lansing Street; 707/937-2422.

Patterson's Pub: You have a choice of 100 (yes, one hundred) beers here, as well as tasty and hearty pub food such as fish-and-chips, burgers, and sandwiches. Sip a cold brew and get a hot meal with your pooch at the picnic tables in the enclosed grassy outdoor garden area. Lassy Dog and Melissa Miller turned us on to this great place, too, and we thank them for another terrific tip. 10485 Lansing Street; 707/937-4782.

The Ravens: Here's a first: Dogs who accompany their people to this outstanding organic vegetarian restaurant actually get to eat indoors. We all know that health departments ban all but assistance dogs from being inside restaurants, so how can this work? Since the restaurant is part of the magnificent Stanford Inn by the Sea (see below), and the inn allows dogs in its lobby, innkeepers have simply set up some little tables in the lobby, next to the main restaurant dining area. You will be served there just as graciously as you would be in the main restaurant. "We don't eat animals here, so it's an appropriate place for animals to be," says owner Jeff Stanford.

Eating with your dog at indoor tables is an exciting idea whose time has come in California. Who knows, maybe one day restaurant patrons around the state will be asked "dog, or no dog?" the same way they used to be asked "smoking, or nonsmoking?"

The cuisine here is delicious. Even nonvegetarians enjoy eating at the Ravens, although your dog may be left scratching her head about where all those normal meaty smells have gone. Breakfasts are terrific, with the usual breakfast fare (although from happy hens and with top-rate ingredients: no Mrs. Butterworth here.) Dinner choices include a delectable assortment of pizzas and salads and a long list of creative and tasty entrées. (Try the seapalm strudel if it's on the menu when you visit.) Many vegan dishes are available, too.

Important note: If your dog is a cat-chaser, you should take your appetites elsewhere: A few of the Stanford Inn's cats make their living reposing around here.

The Ravens is at the Coast Highway and Comptche-Ukiah Road; 707/331-8884; www.stanfordinn.com/ravens.html.

PLACES TO STAY

Abigail's: Stay here if you're on a budget but want to stay in town: Rooms at this house-turned-inn start at a mere $89—chicken feed for this area. The rooms and suites here are spacious and attractive, with big windows, wood blinds, and very comfy beds. Rooms are $89–129. At $199–299, suites are not quite as easy on the wallet. 951 Ukiah Street 95460; 800/962-0934; www.abigailsmendocino.com.

Blair House Inn: The Blair House is one of the most well-known houses in Mendocino. If this Victorian mansion looks familiar to you and your dog, it's probably because it starred as the exterior of Jessica Fletcher's (played by Angela Lansbury) home in the TV series *Murder, She Wrote.* (And you thought she lived in Cabot Cove, Maine.)

The house really does make you feel as if you're in old New England. The simple, clean elegance here is rare these days. It's full of Swedish and American antiques, Oriental rugs, and all kinds of nifty things. But since you're staying here with your pooch, you can't actually stay in the house itself. That's OK, though, because you and your dog get to stay in your very own carriage house. The one-room carriage house is more rustic than the main house, but it's still a charmer, with a queen bed, a little kitchen, a bathroom (with shower), and a small loft area up top.

The inn is a very short walk from the Mendocino Headlands. Rates for the carriage house are $150–175. Dogs are $10 extra. 45110 Little Lake Street, P.O. Box 1608 95460; 707/937-1800 or 800/699-9296; www.blairhouse.com.

MacCallum House: This is one of the most special, fun, welcoming, exquisite, first-rate places you'll ever stay with your dog. But don't let that scare you away: The prices are reasonable, and any size dog is warmly welcome—even large, drooling specimens such as Jake. "We've never, ever had any problems with dogs," says dog-loving owner Jed Ayres. "They are a joy to have around."

Just about any dog may end up drooling here: The dog-friendly attitude is so deep and firmly entrenched that even the dog-loving chef at the renowned MacCallum House Restaurant (see above) gets in on the dog-welcoming bandwagon with his delectable doggy treats made from organic goose livers. Dogs who stay here get these treats as part as a terrific dog package, which includes a fluffy plush dog bed, a towel, a sheet, soft bedding, and dog bowls. (Everything but the treats is a loaner.)

The MacCallum House itself—a Victorian mansion built in 1882—is about the only place dogs can't stay. But there are myriad rooms, suites, cottages, and even houses on the property and on nearby MacCallum property for dogs and their people. They're tastefully appointed—some could grace the best interior design magazines—and have a warm-yet-airy ambiance.

The barn, built in the 1880s, now houses several rooms with features that include decks, ocean views, hot tubs, and sumptuous riverstone fireplaces. A handful of dog-friendly cottages dot the property. The most fabulous (and the most expensive) is the Water Tower, built in the late 1800s. It's a three-story vertical suite with to-die-for ocean views, a two-person tub, a dry sauna, and plenty of room. Water is still stored in a tank up top and you can see a real working well below the tower via glass on the first floor. The tower has been lovingly restored, and it is one of the most attractive of these old structures in the area. Slightly less expensive is the Greenhouse cottage, with a beautiful trellised back dining area next to a hot tub.

As if these choices weren't enough, every suite in the four-star luxury MacCallum Suites, on a hill overlooking the village, is dog-friendly and stunning. The MacCallum-run vacation homes are also hits with people and their dogs: The Oceansong house is even fenced in, for extra-fun dog frolicking.

Prices for the range of accommodations are $110–395. The price includes a gourmet breakfast and a wine hour. (Dogs can join you on the wraparound porch of the main MacCallum House for these.) Dogs are $25 extra nightly. 45020 Albion Street 95460; 707/937-0289 or 800/609-0492; www.maccallum-house.com.

Mendocino Seaside Cottage: Don't be fooled by the name: This is no little cottage, but a large oceanside inn with four spacious suites and a separate cottage that's almost exclusively for pets and their people. How's this for a rule reversal: "People without pets may be able to stay, but only by special arrangement," says inn owner Linda. Dogs wag their tails hard when they stay here: They get a gift basket with treats, a food bowl, and other goodies. Is it your dog's birthday? You get a 10 percent discount on your stay. (Now you can wag your tail.)

Perhaps the best feature for dogs is that Mendocino Headlands State Park (see above) is pretty much the front yard here. It's a terrific place to explore with your leashed dog.

If you like an inn that caters to Romance (yes, with a capital R), this is the place for you: "You are a Special Valentine 365 Days a Year," touts the inn's aptly named website, www.romancebythesea.com. The phone number even has the word "heart" in it. The suites have a honeymoon bent and a pretty feel that might not go well with a certain large yellow Lab I know (I shall mention no names, Jake), but dogs of the toy variety look perfect here. Actually, any size well-behaved dog is welcome at the inn. "We love all pets," says Linda. "As long as their people are well behaved."

Humans also get the royal treatment, with chocolates, fresh flowers, and champagne or sparkling cider waiting in the guest rooms. Suites and the cottage have a featherbed, fireplace/wood stove, spa tubs, and ocean or park views.

Rates are $145–292. (A discount for human birthdays is also offered.) Reservations must be made with a check, since the innkeepers don't accept credit cards. The inn is a few blocks from the village of Mendocino, at 10940 Lansing Street, but correspondence should be sent to the inn's business address: 1050 Wallace Drive, Redwood Valley, CA 95470; 800/94-HEART (that's 800/443-2728). Besides the website mentioned above, the inn has a site that tells about its special amenities for your furry friend. It couldn't have a romance-inspired name, could it? Oh yes: www.specialvalentine.com.

Russian Gulch State Park: See Russian Gulch State Park, above, for information on camping.

Stanford Inn by the Sea: Do you and your pooch love luxury, rustic surroundings, and the ocean? Have we got a place for you!

The Stanford Inn by the Sea has plenty of all three. There's luxury: The beds are big, comfortable antiques, and the rooms all have fireplaces and French doors leading to private decks. There's rustic scenery: The redwood inn is nestled in a grove of pines, surrounded by 11 acres. There's water: On one side of the property is the Pacific, on the other is the Big River.

What more could you want? Red-carpet treatment for your dog? How's this: Dogs are provided doggy sheets so they can relax anywhere in your room and not leave it covered with their dogginess. Not enough? Okay, we'll tell all: Dogs get the canine equivalent of a pillow chocolate—dog biscuits wrapped with ribbons. (And humans get the real gourmet deal.) The inn also supplies pooches with Frisbees, bowls for water and food, and poop bags. The staff here also will take your dog's photo for a Very Important Pet photo album in the lobby. Speaking of the lobby, dogs are even allowed to join you at the indoor lobby tables of the inn's superb vegetarian restaurant, The Ravens. (See above.)

Humans get the royal treatment at the inn, too. Guests all get to use plush white terry robes, swim in the beautiful greenhouse's heated pool or indulge in a spa or sauna there, start the day with a gourmet breakfast, and partake of wine and tasty snacks at the end of a day of adventuring. Several different styles of massage are also available, from standard Swedish style to a hot rock massage (this is not done to the tunes of the Rolling Stones, by the way) or raindrop therapy. You can also take a yoga class here. Try the downward-dog posture. You and your pooch will have something to talk about when you get back from class.

Rates are $235–465. Your dog's entire stay will cost him $25. Additional pooches are $12.50 each. The inn is at Comptche-Ukiah Road and Highway 1. The mailing address is P.O. Box 487 95460; 707/937-5615 or 800/331-8884; www.stanfordinn.com.

Sweetwater Spa and Inn: The Sweetwater is even more dog-friendly than it was in its former incarnation as the Sears House Inn. The new owner says dogs have been such great guests that he couldn't help but open up some new areas to them. Dogs are welcome to lounge around with you at the four small cottages (complete with fireplaces or Franklin stoves) that surround this Victorian inn in the heart of Mendocino, and one water tower.

Joe Dog's top choice of places to stay was the smaller of the two water towers, where he could watch tourists and local cats stroll by in three directions. The tower has a spiral staircase leading up to a wonderful loft-bedroom area. Downstairs is another bedroom and a skylighted sitting room with a Franklin stove. The cottages and water tower all come with yards, so if your dog feels the urge to visit the WC at 3 A.M., you don't have to trudge to the parks. Of course, don't forget to scoop the poop.

The Sweetwater also includes beautiful ocean-view lodging in Little River. Pooches are permitted in four rooms there.

The best part of the Sweetwater, in this human's opinion, is its spa. Yummy professional massages and an oh-so-relaxing atmosphere will melt the tension out of any visitor. Another feature that makes it an ideal place to stay is its proximity to the ocean and town—and especially its proximity to the terrific Cafe Beaujolais. Dogs aren't allowed there, but there's nothing wrong with take-out.

Rates are $70–175. Dogs are $15 extra. 955 Ukiah Street, 95460; 707/937-4076 or 800/300-4140; www.sweetwaterspa.com.

Whitegate Inn vacation rental: Got a bunch of friends who want to stay in a beautiful Mendocino Victorian home but don't want to pay the prices of a bed-and-breakfast or inn? You can rent this sweet, spacious three-bedroom, two-bathroom house and its charming one-bedroom, one-bath cottage for a very affordable price. (Split four ways, it can be as low as $55 per room nightly, during slow season—not including taxes or a rather steep cleaning fee.)

The main house has a living room, dining room, and full kitchen. The master bedroom offers ocean views, so whoever gets to stay there might want to consider forking over a little extra. There's also a sauna and an indoor hot tub, for that pleasant sensation of home far away from home.

The retreat's pretty yard is fenced, but keep an eye on your dog, because it's definitely jumpable for pooches bent on escape. (Why a dog would want to escape from here is a mystery. Oh wait: Mendocino Burgers. See above.)

Don't confuse the Whitegate Inn vacation rental with the Whitegate Inn Bed and Breakfast. They're owned by the same folks, but the latter doesn't allow dogs. Rates for the vacation rental are $220–295. Dogs are $50 extra for the length of their stay, and there's a $150 cleaning fee. (This fee is for both the dogged and the dogless.) 45130 Calpella Street 95460; 800/531-7282; www.whitegateinn.com/mendocino-retreat.html.

Little River

PLACES TO STAY

Inn at Schoolhouse Creek: You and your dog can hunker down in one of the cozy cottages here, or at a room in a small lodge reminiscent of a 1950s motel. It's a fun place to stay, and more of a bed-and-breakfast at heart than anything else. The inn, set on eight acres of meadows, gardens, and forest, provides a mouthwatering breakfast, and wine and hors d'oeuvres in the late afternoon. If your dog promises to watch, not participate, you can even head to the top of the meadow with her to soak in the inn's hot tub while you watch the sunset over the ocean.

On the more active side, you and the pooch can walk to Schoolhouse Creek, which runs through the eight-acre property, or cross the street and take a five-minute walk to a secluded ocean cove. This is most dogs' favorite thing to do, but here's one that comes in a close second: investigating the wonderful dog goodies they get upon arrival. Dog guests receive gourmet biscuits, a Frisbee, a towel, sheet, bowl, and poop bags. Such hospitality makes dogs feel utterly at home here.

Rates are $87–275. There's a $25–75 dog fee per stay, depending on your accommodation. The inn is at 7051 North Highway 1 in Little River. The mailing address is P.O. Box 1637 95460; 707/937-5525 or 800/731-5525; www.schoolhousecreek.com.

Little River Inn: Dogs who like deep dog-friendliness and wonderful lodgings with sumptuous views adore this seaside retreat. The inn rests on a hillside, and it is made up of many small buildings, most of which resemble elongated cottages. Dogs can stay in the inn's oceanview rooms (many have a fireplace or a whirlpool bath) or the two rooms in the Rose Cottage (this one's a very good deal for the money). Dogs aren't allowed in the rooms at the inn's main building, built in the 1850s, but that's OK because they won't have to doggyfoot around all the antiques.

The ocean is right across the road, and wonderful romping room is all around. The innkeepers will point you in the right direction. They love dogs. In fact, lucky dogs who stay here get a basket of pet treats, a food-and-water dish, poop bags, and special sheets to cover bedding and towels for muddy coats. If you'd like to go out for a while without your furry friend, the innkeepers will supply you with local pet-sitter referrals.

Rates are $125–265. Dogs are $25 extra. 7901 North Highway 1 95456; 707/937-5942 or 888/466-5683 (which spells INN-LOVE, in case you were wondering); www.littleriverinn.com.

S.S. Seafoam Lodge: If your dog is a water dog, she'll take to this place in a snap. Each room has a nautical motif, and some provide views of the shoreline in the distance. You'll even have access to a secluded little beach. The cottages and small buildings are set in big tree territory, just a few miles south of Mendocino. With all this going for it, who could ask for anything more? OK, since you asked: The owners of the S.S. Seafoam Lodge love dogs, so your pooch will be a most welcome guest here. Rates are $110–195. Special winter rates are available. Dogs are $10 extra. The lodge is at 6751 North Highway 1 in Little River. The mailing address is P.O. Box 68 95460; 707/937-1827 or 800/606-1827; www.seafoamlodge.com.

Sweetwater Inn: This is the cute little sibling of the terrific Sweetwater Inn in Mendocino (see the Mendocino section). The inn is set on a sunny hill above Buckhorn Cove. You and your leashed pooch can saunter on down to that sheltered cove for some fine dog ambles along the water. Dogs are allowed in four of the six rooms here. Each has a fireplace and a fridge. Rates are $70–175. Dogs are $15 extra. You'll have to write to or call Mendocino's Sweetwater (aka The Big Sister) for reservations and more information. You check in at the Mendocino Inn and get directions to this one while you're there. The Mendocino Sweetwater is at 955 Ukiah Street 95460; 707/937-4076 or 800/300-4140.

Elk

PARKS, BEACHES, AND RECREATION AREAS

⊡ Greenwood State Park

😺😺😺 (See Mendocino County map on page 86)

Leashed dogs enjoy a romp on the quarter-mile-long beach here just about as much as their people do. The sea stacks alone are worth checking out, but with 47 acres of park set along coastal bluffs, there's more to do than just gawk. Admission is free. The park is conveniently situated beside the divine Greenwood Pier Inn (see below). You'll see the signs for the park once you're in the area. 707/937-5804.

PLACES TO EAT

Greenwood Pier Cafe: Dogs and their guests can sit at the outdoor tables among lettuce, herbs, and other plants growing for the scrumptious salads served here. Fresh local seafood is the specialty, but the place will tickle your taste buds no matter what you choose. The café is a new addition to the four-paw Greenwood Pier Inn (see below). 5928 South Highway 1; 707/877-9997 or 707/877-3423.

PLACES TO STAY

Greenwood Pier Inn: I drool when I think of the Greenwood Pier Inn. It can't be helped. The place is a peaceful, spectacular work of art with one of the best locations of any inn we've ever come across. It's at the top of a magnificent ocean bluff. The views of the ocean are amazing, there's easy beach access, and the food is to die for (see Greenwood Pier Cafe, above). There's even a big outdoor hot tub perched on a bluff. (Sorry, water dogs, but the tub is for humans only.) The inn's cozy rooms are adorned with fireplaces, handmade quilts, and original, unique artwork. Rates are $130–195. Dogs and extra people (more than two) are an additional $15 each. 5928 South Highway 1, P.O. Box 336 95432; 707/877-9997, 707/877-3423, or 800/807-3423; www.greenwoodpierinn.com.

Philo

PLACES TO STAY

Highland Ranch: If you and your little dawgie (or big dawgie, though that doesn't really go with the old song) are hankering to git along out to the country and have a real ranch experience, complete with 20 horses and an Old West–style ranch dining area, you'll find no more beautiful or hospitable locale than the Highland Ranch.

Ranch owner George Gaines, a dapper and worldly rancher if ever there was one (he ran the international division of General Mills in Europe for many years, among his varied careers), has gone out of his way to make his 300-acre ranch super-welcoming for dogs and their dudes. (It is kind of a dude ranch, albeit an upscale one.) Dogs who stay here get a Doggy Pack with two towels, a doggy bedspread, chew toys, and a couple of dog biscuits. "We have several people who come here to give their dogs a vacation," he says without a wink.

Each of the eight large, homey guest cabins has a wood-burning fireplace, plenty of books to thumb through, vaulted beamed ceilings, and a big red-wood deck. Dogs are welcome to explore the property off leash. And what property it is: The ranch has four ponds, stocked with all kinds of fish for your angling pleasure. Water dogs love the ponds, especially on warm afternoons. There's plenty of shade from redwoods and firs, and, thanks to the ranch's land being adjacent to lumber company land, more than 100 miles of bridle trails. If you like to ride, you may have bow legs by the end of your stay.

Human guests eat all their meals in the large dining room at the ranch's spacious, airy main house. With its high, beamed ceilings and simple Western decor, you wouldn't be surprised to see Hoss Cartwright ambling in for some chow. The food is fresh and tasty and always accompanied by a selection of Anderson Valley wines and locally brewed beers. (Hard to picture Hoss with a glass of chardonnay.) Cocktails are served in the living room. On cool evenings, you can sip beside a crackling fire.

At $300 per adult and $200 per child, the rates aren't cheap, but they include your cabin, all meals, wine, beer, cocktails, riding, and taxes. (Extra charges apply only for private riding lessons, long-distance phone calls, and equipment if you want to shoot clay pigeons—a popular pastime here.) And if you stay for five nights, you may as well stay two more, because they'll be free. P.O. Box 150 95466; 707/895-3660; www.highlandranch.com.

Ukiah

PARKS, BEACHES, AND RECREATION AREAS

🔟 Mendocino Lake Recreation Area

🐾🐾🐾 (See Mendocino County map on page 86)

Next time there's a full moon rising at sunset, this is the place to take your dog. He probably won't become a werewolf, or even a weredog, but there's something magical here when the moon rises over the mountains and lake. It starts its lunar journey as an enormous, orange disk on the horizon, almost as grand as the moon Mrs. Moore saw in *A Passage to India*. As it rises through the fading sky, its face stares into eternity and glows whiter with each degree it ascends. The white cuts a gossamer streak through the lake, and the chorus of serenading crickets becomes almost deafening. You'll want to stay all night, but this is when you should exit, because park gates close shortly after sunset. While the moon provides a wondrous show, it's not worth staying late and having to sleep in your car until the next day. Doggy morning breath can be atrocious.

For all those other days of the year when there's not a full moon rising at sunset, this huge area is still a fun place for a dog who doesn't mind a leash. A couple of trails wind around about half of the lake and frequently take you right down to the lake's edge. It's very quiet here, barring personal watercraft. You can throw a line into the lake and come up with dinner in the form of bass or trout. Or just take time out from your hike to watch the deer and the buffleheads play.

If you camp here, you get to watch the moon all night, if you want. There are three campgrounds with 216 sites. Rates are $10–22. You can make a reservation by calling 877/444-6777, or in slow times of year, go the first-come, first-served route. Please note that the cheapest campground, Chekaka, is also closest to town, and that the homeless call this place home sometimes.

From U.S. 101, take Lake Mendocino Drive and follow it east to the lake. You'll have to make a short jog north on North State Road, but you'll catch up with Lake Mendocino Drive in 30 seconds. Then veer east again. The best place to enter with your dog is at the Joe Riley Area, past the boat-launching ramp. This is a grassy picnic area, perfect for lunch before a hike. The trailhead starts just beyond the picnic area. 707/462-7581.

11 Cow Mountain Recreation Area

🐾🐾🐾🐾 🐕 (See Mendocino County map on page 86)

How does 27,000 acres of leashless bliss sound? This rugged recreation area, run by the Bureau of Land Management, is heaven for dogs who need real, off-leash exercise. With elevations ranging 800–4,000 feet, a good-sized section of this land is probably off-limits for couch-potato dogs. But there are plenty of trails that even the most sedentary dog/human pair can enjoy.

Dogs can be off leash everywhere but in developed areas such as the two small designated campgrounds, where pitching a tent at one of the 12 designated, first-come, first-served sites won't cost you a cent. Make sure that your dog is under voice control when he's off leash. Many mountain lions, deer, and bears (as well as human hunters in the right season) call Cow Mountain their home, and you don't want your dog tangling with any of them.

If you like nature-watching, you'll really enjoy it here. Quail, doves, rabbits, and feral pigs are common sights. Hunters also like it here for the same reasons. Anglers can fish the entire area, including the cold-water streams, which often brim with rainbow trout. Several of the small reservoirs have been stocked with sunfish.

The park is actually 50,000 acres, but 23,000 of those acres in the South Cow Mountain Recreation Area are devoted to off-highway vehicles. If you venture on that acreage with your dog, do keep him on leash. But why go there when you can stay to the north, where the only forms of transportation you have to watch out for are horses and bicycles?

Other than Jackson State Forest and little bits of Mendocino National Forest that sneak into this county, this is the only public land that allows dogs off leash in all of Mendocino County. Use it well, tread lightly, and pack out what you pack in.

Exit U.S. 101 at Talmage Road and drive east until you come to the City of 10,000 Buddhas (a Buddhist temple), where the road ends. Make a right onto East Side Road, and in about a half mile, go left on Mill Creek Road. The entrance to Cow Mountain will be on your left. For information and maps, call 707/468-4000.

🐾 Mill Creek Park

🐾🐾🐾🐾 (See Mendocino County map on page 86)

This 400-acre park directly across from Cow Mountain has everything dogs could want, except off-leash freedom. They can hike, splash in streams, picnic, relax in the shade of bay trees, and draw deep dog breaths on ridge tops.

Exit U.S. 101 at Talmage Road and drive east until you come to the City of 10,000 Buddhas, where the road ends. Make a right onto East Side Road, and in about a half mile, go left on Mill Creek Road. After you pass the pond, you'll see signs for the park. Go right almost immediately, into a group picnic/playground area. Your dog can frolic in the meadow or hike with you on the trail that starts on the west end of the group picnic area. That trail branches off into several different trails, including a nature trail that follows the creek and a trail that leads you to the top of the southernmost ridge, where the views are unbeatable. Alternate entrances, in case the gate to the picnic area is shut, are available around the creek and pond, near the small, strategically situated parking lots. 707/463-4267.

PLACES TO STAY

Cow Mountain Recreation Area: See Cow Mountain Recreation Area, above, for camping information.

Long Valley Ranch: Want dog heaven? Rent this charming four-bedroom, two-bath house on 800 acres. That's no typo. Yes, 800 acres! It's leash-free pooch paradise here. There's a two-night minimum stay. Up to eight people and four dogs can stay here for $325–400 nightly. Because we're slim on space, and because the same great folks who own Sheep Dung Estates (see the Yorkville section) and The Other Place (see the Boonville section) own this, we'll leave the rest of your investigations to checking their website or phoning. 707/894-5322; www.sheepdung.com.

Mendocino Lake Recreation Area campgrounds: See Mendocino Lake Recreation Area, above, for camping information.

Motel 6: Rates are $45 for the first adult, $6 for the second. 1208 South State Street 95482; 707/468-5404.

Point Arena

This little town that juts into the Pacific is best known for its historic lighthouse. With the great increase in ship traffic after the Gold Rush, mariners needed something to mark this significant point. The lighthouse, built in 1869, has served as a vital marker for mariners ever since. It's also recently become a beacon for dogs everywhere. (See below.)

PLACES TO STAY

Point Arena Lighthouse lodging: It used to take four men to keep the historic Point Arena lighthouse (see above) going, and these four men were each provided a good-sized home next to the lighthouse. Since there's no longer the need for this kind of upkeep, the homes, which have been rebuilt, are now rented out as vacation homes. And not just any vacation homes—very dog-friendly ones. Dogs who stay here get treats and lots of pats if the manager is around. A couple of cute dog photos grace the lodging's website, with the words "PET FRIENDLY!" emblazoned underneath.

"I love animals," says Jeff Gales, managing director of the nonprofit organization that now maintains the lighthouse. (Money from the house rentals is a major source of funding for the ongoing preservation of the lighthouse.) "I've never had a problem with any dog that's stayed here."

As far as I know, this is the only lighthouse in California where you can stay with your dog. Gales says it's also the only lighthouse where humans can rent a whole house, as opposed to a bed in a hostel or a room in a bed-and-breakfast.

The houses, and the lighthouse, are set toward the end of a long, thin spit of land. The spit, being a spit, is surrounded by ocean on three sides. There's nothing like being lulled to sleep by the sound of the crashing ocean. The views are to drool for, as are the tastefully furnished homes, which all have three bedrooms, two bathrooms, wood-burning fireplaces (wood is supplied), full kitchens, and satellite TV, should you want to look at something other than some of the world's most stunning ocean scenery. Leashed dogs can join you to sniff out the land near the houses.

Rates are $175–190, plus a one-time cleaning fee of $35. (This fee is for people without dogs, too.) Dog guests have to sign a pet agreement. 45500 Lighthouse Road 95468; 707/882-2777; www.pointarenalighthouse.com.

Boonville

Fewer than 1,000 people live in this scenic Anderson Valley enclave. It's a low-key town that's home to a wonderfully eclectic bunch. You and your dog can imbibe the laid-back feel by staying at one of a couple of terrific lodgings that welcome dogs.

PARKS, BEACHES, AND RECREATION AREAS

13 Faulkner County Park

😾 😾 (See Mendocino County map on page 86)

Since you and your dog probably each enjoy flowering shrubs for your own reasons, you'll have a pleasant stroll here. Of the two trails that wind through this 40-acre park, the Azalea Discovery Trail is the one nosy dogs like best.

DIVERSION

Get Whisked Through Wine Country: Few people (and fewer dogs) know that Mendocino County has its own highly acclaimed wine country, in the beautiful Anderson Valley. You and your dog can sniff out the wineries on your own, but then your dog would have to be the designated driver, and this gets messy.

That's where **Mendo Wine Tours** comes in. In the morning, a luxury stretch SUV limo will pick you up in the village of Mendocino and drive you about a half-hour away to Anderson Valley. On the drive, you and the others in the limo can sip sparkling wine or other beverages that come with the tour. You'll visit several outstanding wineries and be given the VIP treatment wherever you go. You can sample handcrafted breads and cheeses in the tasting rooms, try wine straight from the barrels, and enjoy a gourmet picnic basket lunch usually served at a scenic alfresco location.

The tours run Friday–Sunday. Your well-behaved dog can go along for no extra charge, but humans pay $125 each. For reservations, phone 888/805-TOUR (888/805-8687).

This is a 12-stop nature trail through a stand of azalea shrubs and redwoods. Difficult as it may be, try to prevent your dog from doing one-leg salutes to the azaleas.

The park also features a hiking trail to the top of the ridge. It's a short trail, but it gets the blood flowing after a long car trip. Kids enjoy the small playground near the entrance.

The park is on Mountain View Road, two miles west of Boonville. 707/463-4267.

PLACES TO EAT

Boont Berry Farm: The food at this quaint yet rustic restaurant is healthful and delicious. Most of the produce is organic, and most of the deli food is vegetarian. Pick up goodies for a picnic or dine with your dog at one of two wooden benches outside the attractive storefront. 13981 Highway 128; 707/895-3576.

PLACES TO STAY

The Boonville Hotel: This beautiful hotel was built in the 1860s, and from the outside you'd swear you were on a Hollywood backlot for old Westerns. But inside it's another story. It's up to date with clean lines, natural materials, and a very cozy-yet-hip feel. Local artisans created everything from the natural wood blinds in each room to various beds and armoires. As the people who run the lodging say, the Boonville Hotel celebrates the past without dwelling on it. (And in that spirit, rooms are free from phones and TVs.)

Dogs can't actually stay in the main hotel, but they're welcome to overnight in one of two rooms in an enchanting creekside building. Each room has a little yard and private entrance. At $250 per night, plus another $15 per pooch, these are the most expensive rooms, but they're also the largest. The hotel is on Highway 128 at Lambert Lane, P.O. Box 326, 95415; 707/895-2210; www.boonvillehotel.com.

The Other Place: Welcome to canine nirvana, dog heaven, pooch paradise! There are few other places like The Other Place (except for its nearby sister, Sheep Dung Estates—see the Yorkville section for details on that gem).

When you stay at The Other Place, you get 550 acres almost to yourself. The only folks you'll share the property with are the guests of the four cottages here. Your dog gets to be leash-free when you go for walks on all this rural gem! There's just one place you may want to consider leashing—around the few cows who live in the upper reaches of the property, should your hike take you that far. If you have any doubts about what your dog may do in a bovine encounter, please do leash up before you get to cow country.

Even if you choose to forego exploring to stay in the comfort of your gorgeous cottage, your dog will still have the equivalent of a very, very large dog park in her own backyard. Each cottage is surrounded by three or four fenced acres. You can just let your dog out the door and not worry about her escaping! This amazing feature is the brainchild of owners Anne and Aaron Bennett, who also own the blissful Sheep Dung Estates in Yorkville. They created The Other Place for people who really want to get away from it all, and who want to do so with their dogs. The dogs of California salute you, Anne and Aaron.

Actually, you don't have to get away from it all at The Other Place, because unlike Sheep Dung, the cottages have TVs (with discreetly placed satellite dishes) and phones. You don't have to use them, but they're there. Speaking of cottages, they're exquisite. They all have kitchens, wood-burning stoves, and are beautifully furnished and designed. The interiors should be featured in a magazine article on elegant simplicity. They're airy, with clean lines and a cozy, upscale feel. The cottages are good-sized, with one having two bedrooms. Our favorite is The Oaks, a one-bedroom studio under a canopy of very old oak trees. The view is to pant for. You can see vineyards in the valley, mountains in the distance, and Boonville. As with Sheep Dung, cottages are stocked with a few dog essentials such as water bowls, a canine first-aid kit, and tomato juice. Humans get fixings for a healthful breakfast—and then some: Cottages are stocked with coffee, tea, milk, granola, organic apple juice, and wine.

Enough slobbering. Onto business. There's a two-night minimum stay. Rates at the one-bedroom cottages for up to two people and two dogs are $175 midweek, $250 weekends and holidays. Rates at the two-bedroom cottage for up to four people and four dogs are $225 midweek, $300 weekends and holidays. Additional people or pooches are $25 each. Please note that the Bennetts don't do credit cards, so you can't put your vacation on plastic. Although The Other Place is in Boonville, the mailing address is the same as Sheep Dung: P.O. Box 49 95494; 707/894-5322; www.sheepdung.com.

Yorkville

PLACES TO STAY

Sheep Dung Estates: People often ask about staying somewhere really dog-friendly. You won't find many better places than the four cottages and one guesthouse on 320 acres in this rustic haven near Boonville. To attest to this, 80 percent of the visitors here bring dogs!

The place looks much better than its name implies. From the huge windows of the homey, airy cottages, you and your dog can enjoy sweeping vistas of the Anderson Valley and surrounding forests. The secluded cottages all have private roads, wood-burning stoves, down comforters, minikitchens stocked with breakfast fixings, and covered porches. The cottages are also stocked with some mighty handy items for dogs and their people, including water bowls, dog brushes, and some excellent doggy first-aid items (with many things for foxtail encounters). People get a wonderful assortment of goodies, including coffee, tea, milk, granola, and wine.

The newest cottage, the Hill House, actually has its own small guest-house, called the Tree Top. It's ideal for couples traveling together. Owners Anne and Aaron Bennett ask that you bring a sheet if your dog insists on sleeping on the bed with you, because the luxurious bedding can't take the beating dogs give.

Your pooch need not look farther than his own front door for a place to run around and just be a dog, since voice-controlled dogs are free to run and explore the huge property. The Bennetts recently made a 1.5-mile trail that goes to the top of the ridge. "We call it Big Rock Trail," says charming, dog-adoring, and vivacious Anne Bennett. "But guests call it Cardiac Hill."

If you and your dog like your walks a little less sweaty, there's a gorgeous 40-acre area with gently rolling hills dotted with firs and oaks. Guests call that one Geriatric Park, but young-at-heart (and body) dogs and people love it. There's even a very large pond where water dogs can practice the dog paddle. Anne says many dogs have learned to swim here because they wanted to be with their swimming humans. Plus, it's nice and safe and quiet, with no personal watercraft, no waves, none of the stuff that dogs balk at in most areas where they can swim.

The Bennetts recently opened another huge swath of dog heaven. (Please see The Other Place, in the Boonville section.)

There's a two-night minimum stay at Sheep Dung, and credit cards aren't accepted. Rates for this magnificent chunk of dog heaven are $105–135 nightly during the week and $125–175 per night on weekends and holidays. The Hill House/Tree Top cottages are rented together and cost $175 on weekdays and $250 per night on weekends. Sheep Dung Estates is about 40 miles southeast of Mendocino, near Highway 128. The Bennetts will give you directions when you make your reservation. (Say, isn't that your dog behind you, handing you the phone?) The mailing address is P.O. Box 49 95494; 707/894-5322; www.sheepdung.com.

Gualala

Gualala (gwa-LA-la for some, wa-LA-la for those who know) is a funny-sounding name for a cute little seaside town. The southernmost coastal town in Mendocino County, Gualala is the perfect place to visit if you're staying in Sea Ranch, just down the road in Sonoma County, and are getting tired of all that uninterrupted tranquility.

PARKS, BEACHES, AND RECREATION AREAS

14 Gualala Point Regional Park

🐾🐾🐾 (See Mendocino County map on page 86)

This is the pristine, driftwood-strewn beach you can see from the town of Gualala, just over the Mendocino/Sonoma County border. The small, friendly visitor center offers displays of shore life, Pomo Indian artifacts, and old machinery. Outside is a sandstone replica of a bull sea lion. From there, it's a half-mile walk to the beach on a smoothly paved trail, where you and your leashed dog will stroll through mixed grasses, ferns, berries, dunes, and rows of pines and cypresses. At the beach, you can take a trail through a marsh or along a coastal bluff. On the beach you'll find driftwood and piles of kelp bulbs, good for jumping on for their satisfying *pop*.

The day-use fee is $4. Campsites are $17 (for up to two vehicles), with overnight dogs costing $1. There are 26 sites. For reservations, call 707/565-2267. From U.S. 101, turn just south of Gualala at the sign announcing the park and the Sea Ranch Golf Links. 707/565-2041.

PLACES TO STAY

Gualala Point Regional Park: See Gualala Point Regional Park, above, for camping information.

Mar Vista Cottages: On a typical weekend at these 12 rustic cottages overlooking beautiful Anchor Bay, 10 or so dog guests cavort merrily around the property, sniffing each other and generally enjoying life. In addition, there's the resident goat, and a couple of pooch proprietors. "It's as much of a dog lover's paradise as you can get," says Suzanne Samuel, who flagged us to Mar Vista's wonders after she visited with Aleph Dog.

Humans love Mar Vista as much as their dog companions. Mar Vista owners Renata and Tom Dorn bought these 1930s and 1940s cottages in 2000 and are improving them all the time. Some still need work, but it's still a charming retreat. The cottages are far enough from each other so there's privacy and quiet. Some of the cottages have fireplaces or wood-burning stoves, and all have full kitchens, hardwood floors, and country-style furniture. In addition, all are stocked with a big basket of dog towels, to keep pooches dry after a jaunt to the beach. The Dorns also offer bowls, dog rugs, and pooch beds upon request.

A note: It turns out that one of the Dorns' dogs, Maggie, sometimes has issues with other dogs. They let guests with dogs know about this, and they have a system where Maggie doesn't interact with dog guests. Rates are $140–200, but the Dorns offer deep discounts for two-night stays November–March. Dogs are $25 per stay for the first dog, $10 for a second. No more than two pooches per cottage, please. 35101 South Highway 1 95445; 707/884-3522 or 877/855-3522; www.marvistamendocino.com. (Be sure to check out the "Pet Friendly" section of their website.)

Serenisea: Want to rent an attractive cottage or house on the exquisite Mendocino coast? Want good rates, a fireplace or woodstove, a full kitchen, and a hot tub? How about easy access to little beaches and tidepools? If your dog answered yes to any of these questions, check out the cottages and eight vacation homes offered to dogs and their people through Serenisea cottages and vacation rentals.

A couple of Jake's favorite homes are Colt Cottage and the Anchor Bay house. The cozy wooden Colt Cottage has great views of the ocean and is on an acre of land, but it doesn't have beach access. The Anchor Bay house is very attractive, with excellent beach access, although less of its own land, which is really no big deal around here.

Rates for the vacation rentals are $140–210. The three cottages owned by Serenisea start at $95 and have tidepool access. 36100 Highway 1 South 95445; 707/884-3836 or 800/331-3836; www.serenisea.com.

CHAPTER 9

Tehama County

This county can be described as a green sandwich. It has a little bit of Lassen National Forest on one side, a touch of Mendocino National Forest on the other, and lots of farmland in between. If you feel like doing your dog a favor, stop in Red Bluff and visit lush and lovely Dog Island. If it weren't for the leash thing—few off-leash opportunities—dogs would probably never want to go home.

NATIONAL FORESTS

The National Forests and Wilderness Areas resource at the back of this book has important information and safety tips on visiting national forests with your dog and has more background on the national forests listed below.

PICK OF THE LITTER—TEHAMA COUNTY

BEST WOODSY WALKS

Dog Island Park/Samuel Ayer Park, Red Bluff (page 116)

Woodson Bridge State Recreation Area,
Corning (page 120)

Lassen National Forest

Mendocino National Forest

The Mendocino National Forest is full of campgrounds in the southwest part of the county.

Mill Creek

PLACES TO STAY

Mill Creek Resort: The nine housekeeping cabins here aren't terribly fancy, but they sit along Mill Creek, a catch-and-release trout stream, near Lassen Volcanic National Park. No dogs are allowed at Lassen unless they want to walk along paved roads or camp. The elevation is 4,800 feet, which means lots of fresh air and some cold mountain streams. Keep your dog leashed, because chaseable creatures (deer, raccoons, squirrels) abound. Rates are $60–95. 1 Highway 172 96061; 530/595-4449; www.millcreekresort.net.

Red Bluff

PARKS, BEACHES, AND RECREATION AREAS

◼ Dog Island Park/Samuel Ayer Park

(See Tehama County map on page 114)

Wow! A park named for the very creatures who most enjoy being here! Now if only dogs could legally run off leash, someone would have to change the name of this place to Dog Heaven Park.

This is a terrific place to take a dog. The park is lush, wild, and alive with riparian vegetation. You almost feel that somehow it's too verdant to be part of California.

Numerous nature trails wind throughout the park. One of them leads to a footbridge that takes you over to Dog Island, a big chunk of land nestled securely in the crook of a Sacramento River bend. The island is enchanting, but not super-quiet. I-5 crosses over the river close by.

From I-5, take the Red Bluff/Highway 36 exit west, cross the river, and turn right on Main Street. Follow Main Street to the sign for Dog Island Park, which will be on your right in a few blocks. 530/527-8133.

� William B. Ide Adobe State Historic Park

😊😊 (See Tehama County map on page 114)

This is a fun and historically interesting park to set paw in, but pooches can visit only under very restricted conditions—they're not allowed to visit the historic zone or the area where the animals hang out. (The chickens here are frequently mauled by marauding pooches, and the donkey was once attacked by three pit bulls, so the park's rangers are understandably protective.)

Until recently, dogs were pretty much relegated to the picnic area overlooking the Sacramento River. (That was OK with most dogs, since it's more fun to sniff the ground for fallen macaroni salad than to stare blankly at the adobe memorial to a man who was president for 22 days during the infamous Bear Flag Revolt.) But now there's a 1.5-mile trail down by the Sacramento River Discovery Center that leashed pooches can peruse with you.

The entry fee is $4 per vehicle. From northbound I-5, take the Antelope Boulevard exit and drive west a few blocks to Main Street. Turn right, drive about a mile to Adobe Road, and go right again. The park will be on your right in about one mile. 530/529-8599.

🐾 Red Bluff Diversion Dam Recreation Area

🐾🐾 (See Tehama County map on page 114)

Don't be fooled. On a map, this area looks as if it must be dog heaven. It's on the water (called Lake Red Bluff here, but it's actually just a wider, dammed section of the Sacramento River), it's fairly big, and it's got several campsites perched over the river. It's almost barren, slightly industrial, and can smell a little funky at times.

A couple of trails take you and your leashed dog short distances, but at least there's plenty of parking. You won't be excited about the fishing, but you can fish-watch from a platform set up next to the dam.

Camping at the 29 sites is on a first-come, first-served basis and costs $10 per site. Each campsite has a pretty good tree next to it, so you'll be buffered from the hot summer afternoons a little.

Exit I-5 at Highway 36 and head east. Take the first right turn, Sale Lane, and follow it to the end. That's where you'll find the camping and the visitors' kiosk. Call the Corning Ranger District of Mendocino National Forest for the best times of year to watch the fish: 530/527-2813.

PLACES TO STAY

Cinderella Riverview Motel: You really can see the river from here, and there are plenty of balconies to prove it. Rates are $50–60. Dogs ae $5 extra. 600 Rio Street 96080; 530/527-5490.

Red Bluff Diversion Dam Recreation Area: See Red Bluff Diversion Dam Recreation Area, above, for camping information.

Sportsman's Lodge: This motel is so doggone animal-friendly that someone's pet camel stayed here one fine night. If you're heading for a dog show at the fairgrounds, this is a close, convenient place to stay with your pooch. Rates are $55–60. Dogs are $7 extra. 768 Antelope Boulevard 96080; 530/527-2888.

Los Molinos

PARKS, BEACHES, AND RECREATION AREAS

◪ Mill Creek Park

🐾🐾🐾 (See Tehama County map on page 114)

This park has great access to the Sacramento River for dogs who like to help you catch dinner or like to screw up your chances of catching it by wading in all the fishy water. Since dogs are supposed to be leashed, you can usually control the situation.

Landlubbing pooches prefer the shaded meadows and the fenced-in ball fields. All in all, this is a peaceful, relaxing place to come with a dog.

From Highway 99, take Tehama Vina Road west, toward the Sacramento River. In a little under a mile, you'll start paralleling railroad tracks. You'll see River Road on your right, and immediately after that an unnamed road with a sign leading to Mill Creek Park. Turn right and follow it to the park. 530/528-1111.

PLACES TO STAY

Hidden Harbor RV Park and Fishing Resort: This is the closest an RV park can come to being a serene place to stay. It must have something to do with all the water around here. The park is on the Sacramento River and bordered by Mill Creek, and it has a harbor with slips for your boat. This is a great place to stay in the fall if you like to fish for salmon. Many folks use the park as their salmon-fishing homebase. Pooches like it here because there's a nearby field for walks. Tent camping and RV camping both cost $23. 24680 Hidden Harbor Drive 96055; 530/384-1800; www.hiddenharborrv.com.

Corning

PARKS, BEACHES, AND RECREATION AREAS

5 Woodson Bridge State Recreation Area

🐾🐾🐾🐾 (See Tehama County map on page 114)

You're in the middle of giant valley oak country here—a fact that sends many dogs into fits of happiness. Between all the oaks (*and* poison oak, so watch it!), walnuts, cottonwoods, elderberries, and willows, your boy dog will hardly be able to contain himself.

Wildflowers are abundant in this 428-acre park. With its location, flanking both sides of the Sacramento River, there's plenty of beauty, especially in spring. Autumn is also a spectacular and colorful sight. Just get on the nature trail and hike your city woes away.

During your visit, some of your neighbors may include Columbian blacktailed deer, bats, muskrats, hares, river otters, and skunks. If you're a birdwatcher, you'll love this place. If you're lucky, you may even spot the rare and endangered yellow-billed cuckoo. You'll know it when you see it.

The law requires that you keep your dog on a leash here and not use any unpaved trails. The day-use fee is $4. You can camp at any of the 46 campsites for $9–14. From I-5, take the South Avenue exit and drive about eight miles east to the park. 530/839-2112.

6 Tehama County River Park

🐾🐾🐾 (See Tehama County map on page 114)

This park is almost directly across from the Woodson Bridge State Recreation Area. While it's not as large as the state park, there's no fee to use it, which makes it a very attractive alternative.

South Avenue bisects the park. The north side is grassy and fairly undeveloped, with great fishing access. When we visited, each of the three people fishing in the Sacramento had at least one dog. All the dogs were in and out of the river constantly. Of course, if the ranger had stopped by, everyone would have been fined for allowing their dogs off leash.

The section to the south of South Avenue is more developed, with playgrounds, a little store, and a picnic area. You can go back and forth between the two sections via a very short tunnel under the road.

From I-5, take the South Avenue exit and drive about eight miles east to the park. 530/527-4630.

7 Black Butte Lake

🐾🐾🐾🐾🦮 (See Tehama County map on page 114)

See the Glenn County chapter.

PLACES TO STAY

Best Western Inn Corning: There's a big area to walk your pooch here. Rates are $55–66. Dogs are $10 per day, and that fee will cover as many as you care to bring. "If they want five or six animals in their room, it's totally their choice," says management. 2165 Solano Street 96021; 530/824-2468.

Days Inn: Rates are $55. Dogs are $5 extra and require a $50 deposit if you're paying cash. 3475 Highway 99W 96021; 530/824-2735.

Holiday Inn Express: This is a quiet place, with a good continental breakfast and a relaxing steam room, sauna, pool, and whirlpool bath. Rates are $79–85. Dogs are $10 extra. 3350 Sunrise Way 96021; 530/824-2940; www.hiexcorning.com.

Woodson Bridge State Recreation Area: See Woodson Bridge State Recreation Area, above, for camping information.

CHAPTER 10
Glenn County

There's not much in Glenn County that people or dogs would drive hundreds of miles to see. But several big wildlife areas can provide you and your dog with many memorable nature-watching hikes. Don't come here if you're seeking the bohemian café society life.

NATIONAL FORESTS

The National Forests and Wilderness Areas resource at the back of this book has important information and safety tips on visiting national forests with your dog and has more background on the Mendocino National Forest.

Mendocino National Forest
🐾🐾🐾🐾🐕

You'll find many rugged, attractive camping areas in the northwest corner of the county, where the land is about a mile above sea level.

PICK OF THE LITTER—GLENN COUNTY

WILDEST WALKS
Black Butte Lake, Orland (page 124)
Sacramento National Wildlife Refuge, Willows (page 127)

Orland

PARKS, BEACHES, AND RECREATION AREAS

❶ Black Butte Lake

🐾🐾🐾🐾🐾 (See Glenn County map on page 122)

It's mighty secluded out here in the undeveloped parts of this big reservoir area run by the U.S. Army Corps of Engineers—so secluded, in fact, that you can hunt, if that's what you like to do. And if you hunt for birds, you can bring your dog along leash-free during the appropriate seasons.

Dogs don't have to be leashed in undeveloped areas, but they have to be under your control, even in the most remote acreage. The deer and rabbits appreciate it. If you're not going to be hunting, you might want to stay away from the very roughest land and enjoy any of three self-guided nature trails. You'll find nature at its best on these trails, without the brambles and burrs that take hours to pull out of your dog's coat. The Buckhorn Trail, an easy 1.5-hour walk, is at its freshest and most vibrant in the spring. You can pick up trail guides at the park headquarters or at the trailhead at the Buckhorn Campground.

The fishing at the lake is excellent in the spring and early summer. If some folks in your party aren't the angling types, they can hang out on land and picnic, visit the playground, or hike the nature trails. There are 40 miles of shoreline, and while dogs aren't allowed to swim at the Buckhorn Day-Use Beach, they can practice the dog paddle in most other places.

Camping with your dog is loads of fun, especially when the full moon slips over the lake and turns it a ghostly white. The 100 developed Class A campsites are $14; make reservations. Dogs must be leashed in camping areas. 877/444-6777.

Exit I-5 at the Highway 32/Black Butte Lake exit at Orland and drive west (the road will turn into Road 200) for about six miles. You'll come to a fork in the road. To get to the park headquarters, continue straight another couple of miles. That's also the way to the Buckhorn Recreation Area, with its nature trail and plenty of camping. To get to the other two nature trails, go left at the fork in the road, onto County Road 206. The Paul Thomas Trail is in the Orland Buttes Recreation Area. The Big Oak Trail is on County Road 200A, which continues from County Road 206. (Definitely bring a map.)

The most remote area is Grizzly Flat, which is barely accessible by car. Drive around the southernmost point of the lake on County Road 200A and you'll soon come to a rough gravel road, and then no road at all. You'll know you're there when you're still bouncing even though your car has stopped. For more info, you can write or call: Park Manager, 19225 Newville Road, Orland, CA 95963-8901; 530/865-4781.

❷ Library Park

🐾🐾 (See Glenn County map on page 122)

Library Park may occupy only one city block, but the landscapers have made the very best of that one block. The grass is more perfect than AstroTurf, and there are so many tall trees that the place is shaded during much of the day, making for a refreshing summertime outing for you and your hot dog.

From I-5, exit at Newville Road/County Road 200 and drive southeast one-third of a mile to County Road 200. The road becomes Swift Street. Continue on Swift Street for three blocks, then turn right at 4th Street. Drive two blocks south. The park is on the corner of 4th and Mill Streets. 530/865-1616.

PLACES TO STAY

Amber Light Inn Motel: Dogs are allowed, but only at the manager's discretion. Rates are $54. Dogs are $5 extra. 828 Newville Road 95963; 530/865-7655.

Black Butte Lake: See Black Butte Lake, above, for camping information.

Orland Inn: Rates are $52–$60. Dogs are $5 extra for the length of their stay. 1052 South Street 95963; 530/865-7632; www.orlandinn.com.

Hamilton City

PARKS, BEACHES, AND RECREATION AREAS

❸ Bidwell Sacramento River State Park

🐾🐾🐾 (See Glenn County map on page 122)

Sacramento River access at this 180-acre park is easy as one, two, wade. Fishing along the four miles of riverfront here is popular, but chances are you won't find too many people on the hiking trail. That's good news if you want to exercise your leashed dog before a day of angling together.

For a state park, the rules here are pretty laid-back—probably because until recently this was a state recreation area. At least for now, dogs can still go on unpaved trails. Be sure to check with a ranger before you set off on a hike with your dog, because this can change.

Dogs aren't allowed at the Chico Creek Day-Use Area. Your best bet is to stop at the first section of park you come to, the Indian Fishery Day-Use Area, where there's a small picnic setting and an attractive wooded trail leading down to the river. It's usually very quiet here.

From Highway 32, go south on River Road. It's about 4.5 miles to the Indian Fishery Day-Use Area. 530/342-5185.

Willows

PARKS, BEACHES, AND RECREATION AREAS

◳ Sycamore Park

😾😾 (See Glenn County map on page 122)

This is a pretty big park for Willows. It's green, grassy, and groovy for dogs who like to roam around open fields wearing a leash. A paved path runs through the park and passes by medium-sized trees and several picnic tables.

The park is on the corner of Sycamore Street and Culver Avenue, right next to downtown Willows. 530/934-7041.

5 Sacramento National Wildlife Refuge

🐾🐾🐾🐾 🐕 (See Glenn County map on page 122)

Only hunting dogs are allowed off leash here, and only in specified areas during hunting season. But plain old average everyday pooches are allowed to explore along the 10,700 acres of marshy waterfowl territory, as long as they're leashed and stay on the walking trails.

More than 300 species of birds and mammals use the refuge throughout the year. It's a phenomenal place for wildlife observation. Bring your binoculars and a field guidebook, and you and your dog can learn all about the birds and the beasts here.

The refuge is open year-round. The entrance is about eight miles south of Willows. From Willows, take the Road 57 exit and drive south along the frontage road, Highway 99W (old Highway 99), about six miles to the entrance. 530/934-2801.

PLACES TO STAY

Best Value Inn: All you Saint Bernard owners, rejoice. The folks here have absolutely no compunctions at all about the size of the dogs who stay here. They even had an elephant as a guest once! (Although he didn't stay in a room.) Rates are $44–68. Dogs are $7 extra. Call ahead for the fee for elephants. 452 North Humboldt Avenue 95988; 530/934-7026.

Best Western Golden Pheasant: Springer spaniels and pointers drool at the name of this hotel. There's plenty of room on the hotel's grounds for your pooch to stretch her legs. Rates are $65–88. Dogs are $10 extra. 249 North Humboldt Avenue 95988; 530/934-4603 or 800/528-1234.

CHAPTER 11

Butte County

A couple of large off-leash parks, as well as the off-leash Plumas National Forest, make Butte County a fine place to take the four-footed beast in your life.

NATIONAL FORESTS

The National Forests and Wilderness Areas resource at the back of this book has important information and safety tips on visiting national forests with your dog and has more background on the Plumas National Forest.

Plumas National Forest
🐾🐾🐾🐾🐾🐕

A good-sized chunk of the northeast corner of the county is made up of this magical forest.

PICK OF THE LITTER—BUTTE COUNTY

BEST LEASH-FREE CITY PARK
Bidwell Park, Chico (page 131)

BEST LEASH-FREE HIKE
Oroville State Wildlife Area/Thermalito Afterbay,
Oroville (page 136)

MOST DOG-FRIENDLY PLACES TO EAT
Beachfront Deli, Chico (page 131)
Shubert's Ice Cream, Chico (page 132)

MOST DOG-FRIENDLY PLACES TO STAY
Chico Oxford Suites and Inn, Chico (page 132)
Lake Oroville Bed and Breakfast, Berry Creek (page 135)

Chico

The laid-back atmosphere of California State University, Chico, helps make this community a relaxed, dog-friendly place. There's even a sweeping section of a large park that begins near campus where dogs can run around off leash (see Bidwell Park).

PARKS, BEACHES, AND RECREATION AREAS

◻ Chico City Plaza

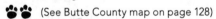

(See Butte County map on page 128)

This is a sweet little park tucked in between municipal buildings in the center of town. Leashed dogs can hang out on the lawn area or near the benches. The park is in the heart of the old downtown area of Chico, so if you're going café-hopping or window-shopping with your pooch, you'll have a green spot for resting all your weary bones.

Concerts are held here during the summer, and as long as your dog doesn't disturb the peace, she's welcome to accompany you.

The park is on Main Street between East 4th and East 5th Streets. 530/895-4972.

☑ Bidwell Park

😊😊😊😊🐕 (See Butte County map on page 128)

Some city brochures claim this is the third-largest municipal park in the United States. Others step the claim down a notch and call it the fourth-largest. Dogs don't care about such distinctions. They just know this 3,670-acre park is a happening place for dogs to trot around, do leg lifts, and get back to nature.

Most dogs we know prefer the rougher, untamed sections of the Upper Park segment. And guess what? That's exactly where they're allowed to run around off leash. The entire huge area north of Upper Park Road is a leash-free swath of dog heaven. You can explore the terrain via miles of trails that run through here or just kick up your heels in a grassy field. Only the lakes are off-limits.

If you want your dog to be leashless in a more developed area, you'll have to get up early. The large section of park west of Manzanita Avenue permits leashless dogs from half an hour before sunrise through 8:30 A.M. You have to stay away from playgrounds, picnic areas, and swimming holes, but your dog can still have a great run here. There are plenty of trails and wooded sections that are well protected from traffic.

A fun addition to the park is a 37-acre parcel that was once a U.S. Forest Service tree nursery. A newly renovated half-mile trail, called the World of Trees Independence Trail, runs through the property. Dogs like the name, but they have to be leashed. In the 1890s, 16,000 trees from around the world were planted here to see which would do well in the climate. Many of those trees survived, and the trail has 20 "stops" where you can read about various trees. It's educational for humans and a good romp for dogs. It's even an excellent place for working companion and guide dogs, since the trail is accessible to the physically and visually challenged. Signs are in English and Braille. The trail is off Cedar Grove Road, near East 8th Street.

The park stretches 10 miles, from the university area all the way east to the rugged crags of Big Chico Creek Canyon. From Highway 99, exit at Highway 32 and head east to Bruce Road. Turn left on Bruce Road and drive north. The road will curve sharply to the right and become Chico Canyon Drive. Stay straight (Bruce Road becomes Manzanita Avenue) and drive on Manzanita about a half mile to Upper Park Road. Turn right and you'll be in the park. Watch for the dog area signs on your left. For the limited leash-free area, a good way to find a place with trails is to make a left turn from Manzanita Avenue onto Vallombrosa Avenue. Park on the road and walk in at any of several open areas in the wood fence. 530/895-4972.

PLACES TO EAT

Beachfront Deli: Try the Beach Bacon Blues Burger. It not only goes with the restaurant's theme, but it's got a tasty reputation. Dine at the covered patio or at the tables on the large lawn. Dogs who come here get treats and water, and they're very happy. 160 Convair Avenue; 530/898-1020.

Moxie's Café and Gallery: Too bad dogs can't go inside restaurants; there's a nifty bone-shaped table in Moxie's. But at least pooches can join you at the three outdoor tables. Moxie's is known for its vegetarian and vegan dishes. 128 Broadway; 530/345-0601.

Shubert's Ice Cream: If your dog comes here at the right time, he'll be in for a snout-licking treat. Shubert's owners, Chuck and Kay Pullian, hate to see ice cream go to waste, and they love dogs, so when someone's ice cream falls off the cone and onto the floor here, the Pullians put it in a container, pop it in a special section of a freezer, and save it for the next dog customer. Same for ice cream that a customer licked but didn't like. These mishaps don't happen often, so you do have to be somewhat lucky to get one of these free dog delights. (Don't get the idea that this is a swell way to provide yourself with a free scoop of ice cream. A few bargain-hunting humans with little concern about prelicked ice cream already tried this trick, and the Pullians now require you to show a dog when you get the free ice cream.)

If you don't luck out, your dog can still enjoy Shubert's delicious ice cream at the outdoor benches here. "Lots of people buy their dog their own cone," says Kay. "Some people even buy one and share it with their dog. The person licks it, then their dog licks it, and they take turns. I don't know about that." Blech! I don't either, but Jake Dog says he's not so sure he wants to share a cone with me anyway.

Shubert's opened in 1938 and has been owned by the same family all these years, with the fourth generation now slinging the scoops. That alone makes it worth a visit. 178 East 7th Street; 530/342-7163.

PLACES TO STAY

Chico Oxford Suites and Inn: If you have to visit Chico, this is a terrific place to stay. Dogs love it here, but not just because of the clean and pleasant nature of the lodging, the refreshing pool, and the free breakfast and afternoon drinks and hors d'oeuvres. More likely it's because of the treats dogs get upon checking in, and because of the small outdoor swatch that's set aside for leashed dogs: It's only about 120 square feet, but it has a small tree, a fire hydrant, water, and poop bags. There's a fence, but it wouldn't keep even a baby mouse in: It's six inches high, just enough to set off the area. Another big draw: Burt, a manager here, has been described to me as "maybe the friendliest person on earth." Rates are $90–169. Dogs are $25 for the length of their stay. (There may be a propensity toward allowing smaller dogs here, but if you have a good big dog, you probably won't have a problem.) 2035 Business Lane 95928; 530/899-9090 or 800/870-7848; www.oxfordsuites.com.

Holiday Inn of Chico: As long as your dog is "no bigger than a polar bear or a desk clerk," says the desk clerk, you and he (your dog, not the clerk) can cozy up together and watch satellite TV. Rates are $85–114. There's a $25 pooch fee per visit. 685 Manzanita Court 95926; 530/345-2491; www.holiday-inn.com.

Matador Motel: There are no bullfighters here, but an affable 140-pound bull mastiff named Chewy lives at the Matador with the motel's sweet manager, Irene. But Chewy is not behind the motel's name, either. The name probably comes from the 1930s Mission Revival style of the building. There are still wonderful painted tiles on the building facade and in the bathrooms. The rooms that allow dogs all have red-tile floors.

The Matador is nothing fancy, but it's a clean, interesting, inexpensive place to stay. What makes it an excellent place to bring a dog is Irene's love of dogs (if you have time, she'll gladly sit down and show you a photo album of her previous bull mastiff, and listen to stories about your own dog), and the motel's proximity to decent dog-walking areas. It's on a frontage road where lots of other dogs stroll, and it's 10 minutes from Upper Bidwell Park (see above).

A big tail-wag to Tapper the Traveling Dog and his chauffeur, Suzanne, for letting us know about the Matador. Rates are $38–60. 1934 Esplanade 95926; 530/342-7543.

Motel 6: Rates are $46–51 for the first adult, $6 for the second. 665 Manzanita Court 95926; 530/345-5500.

Music Express Inn: This bed-and-breakfast inn consists of two 1970s ranch-style houses on four acres. The houses have nine rooms, all available to dogs and their people. All rooms have private baths, and most have private entrances and little fridges. Some have whirlpool baths. The inn gets its name from the children's music school on the premises. Rates (for rooms, not lessons) are $76–106. Dogs are $5 extra. 1145 El Monte Avenue 95928; 530/891-9833.

Safari Garden Motel: If you and your pooch stay here, you'll be only a mile from wonderful Bidwell Park (see above). One dog per room, and they're $10 extra. Rates are $43–60. 2352 Esplanade 95926; 530/343-3201.

Super 8 Motel: Rates are $60–66. Dogs are $4 extra. 655 Manzanita Court 95926; 530/345-2533 or 877/345-2533; www.super8chico.com.

Vagabond Inn: This is a convenient place to stop for a night with a pooch; it's not far from dog-lovin' Bidwell Park (see above), and one block from another city park. The pool here makes hot humans happy. Rates are $69–79. Dogs are $10 extra. 630 Main Street 95928; 530/895-1323 or 800/522-1555.

Magalia

PARKS, BEACHES, AND RECREATION AREAS

❸ Upper Ridge Nature Preserve

🐾 🐾 🐾 (See Butte County map on page 128)

The soft dirt trails here are covered with pine needles, making this one of the cushiest parks around. Dogs enjoy winding along these nature trails while you stop at the numbered stations and learn all about this piece of pine and oak forest.

When you arrive at the preserve, go to the kiosk near the parking area, pick up a wonderfully detailed nature-trail map, and get your bearings. You can follow one of two mile-long trails. Both are lovely and will take you and your leashed pooch past streams, springs, and a whopping variety of trees. Dogs who like tranquility prefer the trail across the street from the parking area. It's a little more secluded.

The 80-acre park is leased from the Bureau of Land Management by a group of energetic, wilderness-loving retired men and women. They created the trails so people could learn about the natural environment here. Says Tom Rodgers, who helped get the group started in his mid-80s, "It's such a pleasure knowing that nature is a little better for what we've done, and that so are the people who nature helps educate."

From the Magalia area, follow Skyway to Ponderosa Way and turn left. Drive a little more than a mile and follow the signs to the preserve, which is just down the road on a gravel drive. The lessees have no phone number, but you can contact them by writing to Upper Ridge Wilderness Areas, P.O. Box 154, Magalia, CA 95945. The Bureau of Land Management may be able to help with questions. Call the office at 530/224-2100.

Paradise

As you enter town, a big wooden sign announces "PARADISE." To be all its name implies.

Sorry, Paradise. You failed the dog test. The Happy Hunting Grounds you are not. Dogs are banned at all municipal parks, and that gets their fur standing on end. (Besides, if you're going to have a sign like that, maybe you should put it in a place where the next thing you see is not a sign advertising duplexes, and then a Burger King, and then a tire shop and a wig store. It kind of takes the oomph out of a heavenly idea.)

Fortunately, the beautiful Upper Ridge Nature Preserve just north of town in Magalia (see above), has everything a leashed dog could want. And some of the scenery in the less-populated parts of Paradise really is beautiful. The town is surrounded by mountains, spectacular canyons, and tall pines.

PLACES TO EAT

Dolly O Donuts: The last name here may be "Donuts," but the middle name is "O," as in "O! My dog and I had no idea you also serve homemade soup and decent sandwiches." Dine at the outdoor benches. 591 Pearson Road; 530/877-4331.

PLACES TO STAY

Lantern Inn: This cozy 15-room motel is nestled in the pines, with a big vacant lot behind it. Dogs dig the location. There's even a great walking trail for leashed dogs and their people within a bone's throw. Water dogs quiver at the sight of the inn's attractive pool, but paws need to stay on terra firma. All the rooms have minifridges and come with continental breakfast.

We found out about the Lantern Inn from Chewy, a 35-pound shepherd mix who had an extended stay here with his people. The motel's owners, Eric and Wendy, and their dog, Murphy, apparently went out of their way to make Chewy and his people feel at home. Rates are $55–75. Dogs are $5–10 extra, depending on their size. 5799 Wildwood Lane 95969; 530/877-5553.

Ponderosa Gardens Motel: Rates are $68–80. Dogs are $6 extra. 7010 Skyway 95969; 530/872-9094 or 888/727-3423.

Berry Creek

PLACES TO STAY

Lake Oroville Bed and Breakfast: This romantic, charming, cozy country inn is a treasure for pooches and their people. The six airy, antique-furnished bedrooms are so sweet that your dog's mouth might gape in awe that he's welcome here. Dogs are so welcome, in fact, that owners Ron and Cheryl Damberger provide tasty homemade dog biscuits wrapped in ribbon upon arrival of your pooch.

All the bedrooms come with private baths, and five have whirlpool tubs. Adding to the enchantment is an inviting parlor with a fireplace, a sunroom/reading room, a children's playroom, a warmly hued old-style billiard room, a wraparound porch, a barbecue area with great views, and a spectacular breakfast. Cheryl uses organically grown foods as much as possible and can cater to people with special diets, such as vegans or diabetics.

Dogs think all this is just keen, but most care much more about what's outside the big white doors. The inn is set on 40 acres of private property in the rolling hills overlooking Lake Oroville. Birds, butterflies, and wildflowers abound. Well-behaved pooches are even allowed to go leashless (which is a real blessing, especially considering that the nearby town of Oroville doesn't even allow dogs in its parks). But if your dog might chase deer or skunks, keep him leashed for everyone's sake.

The resident yellow Lab, Abby, is at least as enchanting as the inn itself. When we visited, we could have sworn she was smiling as she followed us around the grounds.

Rates are $125–165. Dogs are $10 extra. 240 Sunday Drive 95916; 530/589-0700 or 800/455-5253; www.lakeorovillebedandbreakfast.com.

Oroville

PARKS, BEACHES, AND RECREATION AREAS

Dogs are not allowed in any Oroville city parks, nor in any Feather River Recreation and Park District parks. Oh boy, party on, dogs! The saving grace is the Oroville State Wildlife Area/Thermalito Afterbay.

🞜 Oroville State Wildlife Area/Thermalito Afterbay

🐾🐾🐾🐾🐕 (See Butte County map on page 128)

Unlike at many other wildlife areas, if your dog isn't a hunting companion, she can still be off leash here as long as she's under voice control. There are about 5,000 acres of grasslands, marshlands, and riparian forests for you and your dog to explore. Where it's too wet to walk, take a levee.

Be sure to bring your binoculars if you enjoy bird-watching. More than 140 kinds of songbirds have been seen here. As you wander through the forests of cottonwoods, willows, and valley oaks, you may also spot other interesting fauna. If you're not certain your dog will stay close by, do the animals a favor and leash her.

From Highway 162, go south on Larkin Road (just east of the Oroville Airport). Follow the road a few miles to Vance Avenue and turn left. In three-quarters of a mile, you'll be at the wildlife area. Maps are usually available at the entry stations. 530/538-2236.

PLACES TO STAY

Lake Oroville State Recreation Area: This is a state park and it's one of the strict ones. Although it's a 30,000-acre park with 20 miles of trails, dogs can't go on the trails or the picnic areas or far off a paved road. In essence, all they can really do here is hang out with you on your boat or go camping with you.

There are 300 sites available. Campsites are $13–18. If you choose to stay on and around the paved roadways with your leashed pooch, you can enter the park for a $2 day-use fee. From Montgomery Street in the main part of Oroville, follow the green line down the road to the lake. For park information, call 530/538-2200 or 530/538-2219. For camping reservations, phone 800/444-7275.

Motel 6: Rates are $43 for the first adult, $6 for the second. Montgomery Street 95965; 530/532-9400 or 800/466-8356.

Gridley

PARKS, BEACHES, AND RECREATION AREAS

5 Grey Lodge State Wildlife Area

🐾🐾🐾🐾🐕 (See Butte County map on page 128)

Hunting dogs are the only ones who can be off leash in this spectacular wetland, and only during certain times of year. But this 8,400-acre wildlife area is a wonderful place to take well-behaved, leashed dogs the rest of the year. Barkers and yappers should be left at home, especially during waterfowl season. Many of the birds have flown thousands of miles, and if they're disturbed, it could be detrimental to their health.

For most of the year, you can walk around on about 60 miles of hiking trails and levees. During waterfowl and nesting seasons, the hiking is very limited—to about four miles. But you don't have to walk a marathon to see amazing wildlife. Among some of the critters you may run into are sandhill cranes, hawks, river otters, egrets, waterfowl, deer, beavers, orioles, and black-shouldered kites.

From Highway 99, turn west on Sycamore Road and go six miles to Pennington Road. Turn left and continue three miles to the entrance on the right. The main parking lot is two miles to the west. The California Department of Fish and Game provides a handy little brochure with a decent trail map. You may be able to pick one up at the wildlife area, or order one by calling 530/846-7500.

PLACES TO STAY

Pacific Motel: "We take pains to make guests comfy, even dog guests," a friendly manager here told us. Nothing special here, just the basics conveniently situated on Highway 99. Three units at this small motel have kitchenettes, which is mighty handy given the dearth of dog-friendly eateries in the neighborhood. Rates are $53–60. 1308 Highway 99 95948; 530/846-4580.

CHAPTER 12
Plumas County

Hidden between the ever-popular vacationlands of Shasta and Tahoe, Plumas County lives up to its publicity slogan, "California's Best Kept Secret." Even people in the next county asked, "Where's that?" when I told them where we'd just visited.

This county is 67 percent Plumas National Forest, which means there's natural beauty and off-leash dog heaven at almost every turn. It's Feather River Country here, with dozens of lakes and hundreds of miles of streams and rivers. That translates into endless good times hiking, fishing, swimming, wading, and cross-country skiing for you and your pooch.

Plumas is one of those counties so untouched by tourists that you can still find the best of rural life. The towns of Quincy and Portola have some of the most delicious country-style cooking we've ever tasted. And the country-style humor (watch for yellow roadside deer warning signs with the deers sporting big red noses) isn't bad either.

PICK OF THE LITTER—PLUMAS COUNTY

BEST LEASH-FREE HIKES
Plumas National Forest (page 140)
Collins-Almanor Forest, Chester/Lake Almanor
(page 140)
Bucks Lake, Bucks Lake (page 142)

MOST DOG-FRIENDLY PLACE TO STAY
Gray Eagle Lodge, Blairsden (page 146)

NATIONAL FORESTS

The National Forests and Wilderness Areas resource at the back of this book has important information and safety tips on visiting national forests with your dog and has more background on the national forests listed below.

Lassen National Forest

Only a tiny part of this national forest falls in Plumas County. See the National Forests and Wilderness Areas resource for a more complete description of this magnificent forest.

Plumas National Forest

Chester/Lake Almanor

PARKS, BEACHES, AND RECREATION AREAS

◼ Collins-Almanor Forest

🐾🐾🐾🐾🐾 (See Plumas County map on page 138)

"Dogs love trees, and we love dogs," says dog-loving forester Dan Howell. That's why the Collins Pine Company rolls out the pine needle carpet for pooches in its 91,000-acre mixed conifer forest. Leashes can be shoved in your backpack, and you and your dog can hike unattached throughout this glorious working forest.

This is one of the most environmentally correct timber companies in the country, so you won't be seeing clear-cut patches that make the landscape look like a dog with mange. The family-owned company has been logging this forest since 1941, but with such a commitment to long-term sustainable forestry that they even win accolades from environmentalists.

You'll love this place so much that you may want to spend a few days here. That means spending a few nights here. Many camping areas are available and the ones near streams are the best. There's no fee for any of this.

You'll want to stop in at the Chester office to get additional information about the best access routes for your level of hiking and to find out what areas of the forest are open. The office is at 500 Main Street. It's the one with the big green lawn (at least in the spring and summer). The phone number is 530/258-2111 or 530/258-4401.

2 Lake Almanor

🐾🐾🐾 (See Plumas County map on page 138)

The azure waters of this idyllic lake make a beautiful centerpiece for an adventurous canine time. The lake is big (52 square miles), and sections of the surrounding areas are controlled by many different entities, both public and private. It can be confusing, and you can get yourself into trouble if you stumble onto the wrong land parcel with a dog.

Although parts of the lake are surrounded by both the Plumas and Lassen National Forests, neither of these areas is set up for hiking around the lake. They're geared more toward camping. Dogs should remain on leash in the sections of forest immediately around the lake. That will also keep them from bounding onto the privately owned land that weaves throughout the public lands here.

If you stay at the resorts along Lake Almanor, keep in mind that most have their own land, which you can explore with a leashed dog. Some even have views of magnificent snowcapped Mt. Lassen rising in the distance.

A fun stop with your pooch comes just after the dam at the south end of the lake as you're driving north on Highway 89. You can pull off to the right, near the Canyon Dam Boat Launch, and trot along the flats near the lake. Bring your fishing equipment and make a few casts as you meander along. The lake, actually a reservoir, is known for its salmon, trout, and even small-mouth bass.

For general lake and camping information, contact the Almanor Ranger District of Lassen National Forest at 530/258-2141. Campsites are $10–15, with reservations necessary for some. Phone 877/444-6777 for reservations. When in Chester, you can visit the ranger station and pick up maps and advice. It's at 900 East Highway 36. The Chester/Lake Almanor Chamber of Commerce can also provide you good information. Call at 530/258-2426.

PLACES TO STAY

Cedar Lodge Motel: The owner here loves dogs, so you'll feel mighty welcome. That is, unless you're a rottie or a pit bull; then you'll have to go elsewhere to feel welcome, as these dogs aren't allowed here. The motel, which has a swimming pool, barbecue area, and play area, is a good place for families. All rooms have a minifridge and microwave. Rates are $50–57. Junction Highway 36 and Highway 89, Box 677, Chester, CA 96020; 530/258-2904.

Collins-Almanor Forest: See Collins-Almanor Forest, above, for camping information.

Lake Almanor Resort: The cozy cabins here are set among the trees, a little way back from the lake. The resort is open May–mid-October. Rates are $80–93. Dogs are $10 extra per day or $55 per week. 2706 Big Springs Road, Lake Almanor, CA 96137; 530/596-3337; www.lakealmanorresort.com.

Lassen View Resort: The housekeeping cabins here range $86–92. You'll get slapped with an extra charge if you don't pick up after your pooch, so, as you should everywhere, scoop the poop. The 94 RV sites are $27. Dogs are $5 extra wherever they stay. The resort is open May–November. 7457 Highway 147, Lake Almanor, CA 96137; 530/596-3437.

Little Norway Resort: Dogs enjoy the lakeside housekeeping cabins almost as much as they dislike the loud personal watercraft the resort rents out. It usually is quiet here, though. The resort has enough land around it so dogs and their people can get some good exercise. There's been a bit of a problem here lately with people's dogs sleeping on the beds. Resort owner Linda and an employee have spent up to four hours removing dog hair from a wool blanket. (They went through rolls of duct tape.) If your dog likes to sleep on your bed, please be sure to bring a sheet to throw over the bedding. Linda may soon be providing dog bedding herself. Rates are $80–105. Pooches are $10 extra. 432 Peninsula Drive, Lake Almanor, CA 96137; 530/596-3225; www.littlenorway.net.

Timber House: The folks here say they don't want Shetland ponies or Saint Bernards at this motel, but just about any other size pooch is OK. Rates are $50–60. Dogs are $5 extra. Chester Park is nearby. 1st and Main Streets, P.O. Box 1010, Chester, CA 96020; 530/258-2729.

Bucks Lake

PARKS, BEACHES, AND RECREATION AREAS

🛑 Bucks Lake

🐾🐾🐾🐾🦴 (See Plumas County map on page 138)

During warmer months, you and your dog can hike, swim, and fish till you drop. Campgrounds here are good places to drop, and the 49 sites in Plumas National Forest are free. (They're also undeveloped.) Twenty-nine of these sites are right along the lake's 14-mile shoreline, making for exquisite views. Sites are $16–18. All are first-come, first-served.

If trout fishing is your fancy, you'll have a hard time finding a much troutier lake. The lake is stocked annually with rainbow trout, so it's a great place to take young anglers and dogs who are entertained by fishing activity.

The lake is almost completely surrounded by Plumas National Forest, where dogs can run free in undeveloped areas. On the northeast side is the beautiful Bucks Lake Wilderness, where your obedient dog may also accompany you without a leash. From some of the peaks in this wilderness, you can see forever—or at least as far as Mt. Lassen.

During winter, the Bucks Lake area is a great spot for cross-country skiing. Dogs love going along for a little exercise, as long as the snow isn't too high.

From Highway 70 in Quincy, take Bucks Lake Road west about 12 miles to the lake. For information on campgrounds and the lake, call 530/283-0555.

PLACES TO STAY

Bucks Lake: See Bucks Lake, above, for camping information.

Bucks Lake Lodge: You and your pooch can stay at any of a dozen rustic housekeeping cabins at this lakeside resort. There's plenty of wilderness and open space around for you and your dog to explore on leash. The lodge has a restaurant, bar, and small store, so you can stay here for a while and never have to get into your car.

The road to the lodge is closed in winter, so plan ahead. If you really want to stay here in the cold months, you have to use a snowmobile or cross-country skis. (And unless your dog is bipedal, the ski option just isn't going to cut it.) Rates are $77–115. (The $115 cabins sleep up to 10 people. You can really get your money's worth with these if you're visiting with a big happy group.) Dogs are $10 extra. 16525 Bucks Lake Road, P.O. Box 236, Quincy, CA 95791; 530/283-2262; www.buckslakelodge.com.

Quincy

This is a Main Street community with restored and preserved buildings dating to the town's roots in the mid-1800s. If you whiz through town heading west, you'll barely get a glimpse of the downtown area, which is home to a couple of good, dog-friendly restaurants. Main Street goes only east and it's worth a gander.

PARKS, BEACHES, AND RECREATION AREAS

4 Gansner Park

🐾🐾🐾 (See Plumas County map on page 138)

Dogs enjoy bouncing around this long and luscious park. They're supposed to bounce around on leash, but if your dog happens to escape from your grasp, there's little danger: The park is almost entirely fenced. Generally, where there aren't fences, trees and brush are so thick that dogs would have a difficult time getting out. The grass is very green, the pines are very large, and the park generally is very uninhabited. You can picnic, barbecue, play tennis, or watch the kids at the park's small playground.

From Highway 70/89 just north of town, turn east on Gansner Park Road (there will be signs for the park). 530/283-3278.

PLACES TO EAT

Stoney's Country Burger: "Dogs? They're my favorite animals," says the kindly owner of this burger café. Try the Stoney burger. You'll love it, and if you don't, your dog will. 11 Lindan Avenue; 530/283-3911.

Cromberg

PLACES TO STAY

Long Valley Resort: Dogs are more than welcome to stay at this sweet resort's cottages. They're of the no-frills modern ilk with basic furniture, and they all have decent kitchens. (Some of the cottages have more charm than others.) But what dogs like best is what surrounds the cottages: trees, meadows, and pastures. A few cottages have views of the resort's horses, who graze contentedly in the adjacent meadow. "Our horses are amused by visiting dogs and their carrot-bearing friends," writes innkeeper Stephanie Sprague, who has two friendly dogs of her own.

Dogs aren't allowed in the resort's motel, but that's OK. The cottages are better for pooches anyway. A continental breakfast of homemade muffins and other baked goodies plus the usual breakfast beverages comes with your stay. Cottage rates are $85–125. Dogs are $7 extra. Weekly rates are available. 59532 Highway 70; 530/836-0754 or 800/887-6653; www.longvalleyresort.com.

Portola

This old town is right on the Middle Fork Feather River, which is very accessible from many parts of town. Just bring your rod, reel, hiking shoes, and dog, and you can create a canine's dream day. Sadly, the wonderful Portola Railroad Museum no longer allows dogs on its trains.

PARKS, BEACHES, AND RECREATION AREAS

5 Lake Davis

🐾🐾🐾 🐕 (See Plumas County map on page 138)

This is the largest of the three Upper Feather River lakes, with 32 miles of shoreline, most of it in Plumas National Forest. The hiking right at the lake is limited, but you can manage to get in some exercise on trails and dirt roads that extend into the national forest from the lake area.

It's the perfect spot if you're vacationing with an avid angler. The hiking is excellent and off leash once you're out of the campgrounds and adjacent state game refuge and into the undeveloped areas of the Plumas National Forest. And there's plenty of nature to watch: Waterfowl, bald eagles, and bats are easy to see at various times of year.

Leashed dogs can choose from a total of 165 campsites. About half are available on a first-come, first-served basis. You'll need a reservation for the rest. Call 877/444-6777 to reserve a site. Sites are $14, except for a few undeveloped sites, which are free. From Highway 70, take Grizzly Road or Lake Davis Road about seven miles north to the lake. For information on Lake Davis or to get maps of the forest near the other two Upper Feather River lakes, call 530/836-2575.

6 Portola City Park

🐾🐾🐾 🐕 (See Plumas County map on page 138)

Much more space is devoted to human activities than dog activities here, but there's still a decent little field, some trees, and a gazebo that leashed dogs seem to enjoy. The great news is that if your dog is under voice control, he can be leash-free here, as long as you keep him from the more developed spots. It's not far from the street, so think twice before you unleash. Either way, this is a nice little place to take a break with your dog.

From Highway 70, go south on South Gulling Street. The park will be on your left, across from City Hall, shortly after you cross over the bridge. 530/832-4216.

PLACES TO STAY

Lake Davis: See Lake Davis, above, for camping information.

Sleepy Pines Motel: The owners of this homey motel have their own dog, and they'll often allow dogs as guests, but they want "nothing huge or dangerous." The lodging is very close to the Feather River. The owners can point you to the best fishing spots. Rates are $66–71. 74631 Highway 70 96122; 530/832-4291; www.sleepypines.com.

Blairsden

PLACES TO STAY

Gray Eagle Lodge: Many regulars say this is the pooch paradise, human heaven. Glowing elysian comparisons are only natural when you stay at this extraordinary Sierra lodge, set in the middle of some of the best national forest land in the state. Reader Cynthia Harris says she and her then-new hubby brought their two basset hounds, Otis and Monroe, along on their honeymoon and had the time of their lives. "Our cabin had a deck that descended down to a stream, which was ideal for swimming bassets!" she wrote. Joe Dog (aka Mr. Water Is to Drink, Not to Swim In) was curious about how they wring all that water from their hush-puppy ears. (He was just jealous that they could float and he couldn't.)

A dozen Plumas National Forest trailheads start at the property. Well-behaved pooches can go leash-free on the trails, which lead to meadows, peaceful ponds, streams, and 40 alpine lakes where the fishing can be so good that the angler in you may never want to leave. If you catch a fish and clean it, the chef here will cook it for your breakfast. But the brochure admonishes, "Keep in mind, Chef's largest frying pan is ONLY 24 inches wide!" Those guests who tell a good fish story will be rewarded with a glass of champagne, so if you err on the side of exaggeration, this is your kind of place.

You can really get away from it all at the cozy TV- and phone-free wood cabins. But don't leave your taste buds behind, because the gourmet meals here (full breakfast and a four-course dinner are included in the room price) are wonderful. Picnic lunches are available for an additional charge. The ever-changing dinner menu includes terrific chicken, meat, fish, and vegetarian dishes, plus a notched-up comfort-food selection such as veal meatloaf with caramelized onion sauce.

Dogs can't go in the restaurant, but they can enjoy munching on their own delectable taste treats: The staff here provides pooch guests gourmet dog biscuits upon arrival!

After a long day of exploring and eating, relax by the big fireplace in the main lodge. (Dogs can no longer curl up beside that hearth. It's a health-code thing.) The lodge is open May–October. Rates are $195–235 per couple and include the sumptuous meals. Dogs are $20 extra. 5000 Gold Lake Road 96103; 530/836-2511 or 800/635-8778; www.grayeaglelodge.com.

Graeagle

PARKS, BEACHES, AND RECREATION AREAS

7 Plumas-Eureka State Park

😊😊😊😊 (See Plumas County map on page 138)

Your dog isn't going to believe his pointy ears when you tell him the following news. (Before you tell him, make sure he's sitting.) Here it is: Dogs are actually allowed on a trail in this park. State parks pretty much ban pooches from trails, but because this is such a short trail and it leads to a very long and wonderful national forest trail, it's A-OK.

Dogs have to be leashed on the state park end of the trail. But it may be a wise idea to keep your dog leashed when you hit national forest land—even though leashes aren't mandatory—since there are bears in dem dar hills. We know this firsthand, because on our camping honeymoon, Mr. Bear visited our secluded campsite at Rock Lake. He hung out from midnight until about 3 A.M., when he probably realized he wasn't going to enjoy our dehydrated camping food any more than we did.

Back to state park grounds: Dogs are very limited in their activities in the historic 5,000-acre park surrounding the old mining town of Johnsville. But one thing they can do is camp with you at one of the 67 sites here. The fee is $20 a night. The campground can get crowded, and sites are first-come, first-served, so arrive early in the day during summer.

If you want to skip the more heavily used part of the park and get right to the Jameson Creek Trail (which leads to several isolated, pristine lakes), look for a sign for the trail on the left, about one-eighth of a mile before the park entrance. Follow the dirt road to the trailhead. You can also pick up the trail from the main part of the park. Just ask a ranger where it starts.

From Highway 89, take County Road A14 west a few miles to the park. 530/836-2380.

PLACES TO STAY

Plumas-Eureka State Park: See Plumas-Eureka State Park, above, for camping information.

CHAPTER 13

Lake County

This is a county with an attitude about dogs—a bad attitude, with the exception of the Edgewater Resort in Kelseyville. Dogs aren't allowed in any county parks. Since parks in the small towns are county parks, that's a double dose of bad news. The major cities (Clearlake and Lakeport) also ban dogs from their parks, and dogs aren't permitted at public beaches around Clear Lake.

Signs throughout the county shout that dogs must be licensed and leashed and will be shot if they're caught molesting farm critters. Even the trash barrels in county parks are painted with big white "No Dogs" warnings. Looks as if you can't even walk your dog in a garbage can around here.

Welcome to Lake County, a major disappointment for our fine four-legged friends. The county slogan that occasionally pops up here is "Lake County: Dare to Explore." But that's a cruel joke for the canines in our midst. If they dare to explore too much, they're going to get socked with a big fine. And guess who has to pay?

PICK OF THE LITTER—LAKE COUNTY

BEST LEASH-FREE HIKES

Cache Creek Recreation Area, Clearlake Oaks (page 153)

Boggs Mountain Demonstration State Forest, Cobb Mountain (page 154)

MOST DOG-FRIENDLY PLACE TO STAY

Edgewater Resort, Kelseyville (page 151)

What's a dog to do? She could start by thanking the Big Dog in the Sky for the national forests, the Bureau of Land Management, the California Department of Forestry, and (I never thought I'd say this) the state park system. If not for these, dogs would have to sneak around everywhere.

If your dog wants to hang out near the lake, you'll have to stay in one of the private resorts that has lakeside access. The Edgewater Resort is the best of these, at least from a dog's point of view. But there are plenty of others, should you follow the county's slogan and "Dare to Explore."

NATIONAL FORESTS

The National Forests and Wilderness Areas resource at the back of this book has important information and safety tips on visiting national forests with your dog and has more background on the Mendocino National Forest.

Mendocino National Forest

A huge section of this forest is in Lake County. It's a relief to dogs who aren't even permitted to set paw in county parks.

Lakeport

PARKS, BEACHES, AND RECREATION AREAS

🚩 Cow Mountain Recreation Area
 (See Lake County map on page 148)

This is a great place to visit with your dog, who can run leash-free in many areas. The main entrance is on the other side of the county border, near

Ukiah. Enter at Younce Road (Old Toll Road) from Lake County. (See the Ukiah section of the Mendocino County chapter for more details on this recreation area.)

PLACES TO EAT

Park Place: The fresh-made pasta here is delightful. Wash it down with your favorite local wine while you and your dog relax at the outdoor tables. The restaurant is next to a lakeside park, but since dogs aren't permitted at the park, all they can do is watch the ducks go by. 50 3rd Street; 707/263-0444.

PLACES TO STAY

Rainbow Lodge: The inn has recently been remodeled and no longer has the 1960s look. Instead of carpet, Mexican tiles grace the floor. It has log furniture and an intimate atmosphere, with only 12 rooms. Rates are $75–85. Dogs are $5–10, depending on their size. 2569 Lakeshore Boulevard 95453; 707/263-4309.

Kelseyville

Kelseyville calls itself "a friendly little country town." (It also calls itself "pear capital of the world.") The Main Street area does, indeed, look a little like something out of *The Andy Griffith Show*—at least if you don't have your glasses on. Your happy hound will fit right in here.

PLACES TO STAY

Clear Lake State Park: Dogs enjoy spending the night under the oaks at one of the 147 sites at this lakeside park. Since they're not permitted on trails or in the water, they can't do much else here anyway. Rates are $19. From Highway 29, take the Kelseyville exit and turn north on Main Street. The road will turn into State Street, then Gaddy Lane. In about two miles, go right on Soda Bay Road. The park will be on your left in about a half mile. For reservations, phone 800/444-7275. For park information, call 707/279-4293.

Creekside Lodge: Rates are $52–62. Dogs are $10 extra, and you have to sign a waiver taking responsibility for dog damage. In addition, great big dogs aren't allowed. Even Labs are banned. (That's Jake you hear sulking in the background.) 7990 Highway 29 95451; 707/279-9258 or 800/279-1380; www.kitscorner.com.

Edgewater Resort: Wanna make your dog happy? Come here. The Edgewater Resort is one of the most hot-diggety-doggone dog-friendly places we've run across. How dog friendly is it? (Warning: This will be like Rodney Dangerfield without the humor.) It's so dog-friendly that one of its brochures shows a big photo of a fluffy white dog inspecting a black bass caught by her human. It's so dog-friendly that another of its brochures beckons obedient dogs to run off leash on its beach and swim in the lake. It's so dog-friendly that there's even a doggy hitching post outside the resort's store, and a pooch rinse-off station for postswim cleanup.

The friendly and kindly resort owners, Sandra West and Lora Tell, adore dogs, if you couldn't already figure that out. They'll greet your dog with loving hugs and a dog biscuit if they're here when you check in. You and poochface can stay in a cozy cabin by the lake or camp in your tent or RV. The cabins aren't the Taj Mahal, but they have real wood paneling and kitchens, and they're surrounded by lawn and big old trees. You can fish off a 230-foot fishing pier here or swim at the beach (humans can swim at the pool). Keep in mind that at the end of summer, heat and low water levels can lead to algae growth, which can turn the still water green.

Rates at the resort are $28–38 for tent or RV camping and $125–400 for a cabin. Dogs are $2.50 extra in tents or RVs, and $10 extra in the cabins. 6420 Soda Bay Road 95451; 707/279-0208 or 800/396-6224; www.edgewaterresort.net.

Glenhaven

PLACES TO STAY

Indian Beach Resort: Stay at any of nine cottages on the lake. All have kitchenettes. There's plenty of room to walk your leashed pooch. Rates are $78–125. Dogs are $7 extra. 9945 East Highway 20, P.O. Box 648 95443; 707/998-3760; www.ngl.net/indianbeach.

Clearlake Oaks

PARKS, BEACHES, AND RECREATION AREAS

2 Cache Creek Recreation Area

🐾🐾🐾🐾🦮 (See Lake County map on page 148)

This 70,000-acre Bureau of Land Management area is a very welcome sight for dogs, who are banned from most parks in the county. Not only can they explore this huge and wild area, they can do so off leash, as long as they're obedient sorts. If you can't trust your dog not to wander away and get eaten, or not to wander away and eat another animal, then please keep him leashed.

Bring your binoculars, because you'll need them. You may see bald eagles, blue herons, tule elk, or even a black bear. A seven-mile trail (steep at times) provides you and the dog in your life with ample room to start an adventure. We like to visit in the spring, when the wildflowers open their blazing petals to a new year.

You can also camp here in primitive, fee-free sites. You'll need to get a campfire permit from any California Department of Forestry, Bureau of Land Management, or U.S. Forest Service office. The entrance to this patch of dog heaven is about eight miles east of town, on the south side of Highway 20. You'll see the signs. 707/468-4000.

PLACES TO STAY

Cache Creek Recreation Area: See Cache Creek Recreation Area, above, for camping information.

Lake Haven Motel: This motel on a sheltered canal is owned by folks who love dogs and welcome leashed pooches (except rotties and pit bulls) to sniff out the surrounding area. Rates are $60–80. Dogs are $5 extra. 100 Short Street 95423; 707/998-3908 or 800/998-0106.

Lower Lake

PARKS, BEACHES, AND RECREATION AREAS

3 Anderson Marsh State Historic Park

🐾 🐾 (See Lake County map on page 148)

For humans without dogs, this 870-acre park is a terrific adventure. Several miles of trails lead to remote bird-watching areas far from any roads.

But if you're lucky enough to be traveling with a dog, this park is just a leg-stretching zone. Dogs are not permitted on trails, but they're allowed at the picnic area at the ranch house. This is a pleasant place to plop down for a while. They're also permitted in the open fields behind the old Anderson barn. Since only the area adjacent to the barn is mowed, there's not much room to roam. The tall grass beyond the lawn can be full of ticks. At least your leashed dog will get to sniff an old outhouse or sit patiently outside the portable toilet while you explore its inner realms.

Open Wednesday–Sunday. The fee is $2 per car. The ranger is usually in the form of an iron post with a box on it, so if you'll be here only a few minutes, you might not need to pay. But real human rangers can come out of the woodwork (and there's quite a lot of wood around the barn), so be careful.

From Highway 53 just north of Lower Lake, turn west at Anderson Ranch Parkway and make an immediate right into the park. 707/994-0688 or 707/279-2267.

Cobb Mountain

PARKS, BEACHES, AND RECREATION AREAS

4 Boggs Mountain Demonstration State Forest

🐾 🐾 🐾 🐾 🐕 (See Lake County map on page 148)

You and your blissfully leash-free dog can hike for days in a 3,500-acre forestry experiment. The forest is being studied as an example of how a forest that was nearly stripped by someone else can be brought back and managed for continuous forest production, public recreation, wildlife habitat, and a watershed.

It's working. You'll hike on miles of trails that wander through mixed conifer forests and grasslands. As long as your dog is obedient, you can let her off leash. But if she can't be trusted around deer and other critters of the woods, keep her leashed.

From Highway 175 about a mile north of Cobb Mountain, watch for a blue-and-white sign for the state fire station. At the first intersection past it, go east for about a quarter of a mile to the park's entrance. 707/928-4378.

PLACES TO STAY

Beaver Creek Campground: You can stay with your dog in your own tent or RV, or try one of the resort's tepees for a unique experience. It won't be a deep wilderness experience (tent sites have their own sink, water, and electricity), but there's a pond with rental kayaks and canoes, and enough room to stretch your paws. Rates are $20–25. If you like having a hard roof over your head, you can rent a simple cabin for $44–49. 14417 Bottle Rock Road, P.O. Box 49 95426; 707/928-4322 or 800/307-CAMP (800/307-2267); www.campbeavercreek.com.

CHAPTER 14

Colusa County

This is a county of refuge. Actually, it's a county of a few refuges. Birds see the refuges on their little bird maps and flock here by the millions. It's an amazing sight to see with your leashed pooch during the winter.

Maxwell

PARKS, BEACHES, AND RECREATION AREAS

The Delevan National Wildlife Refuge is not open to the public, but the Sacramento National Wildlife Refuge is quite a special place to visit with a dog.

🐾 Sacramento National Wildlife Refuge

🐾🐾🐾🐾 🐕 (See Colusa County map on page 156)

The southern end of this magnificent refuge extends into northern Colusa County. (See Willows in the Glenn County chapter for an in-depth description.)

PICK OF THE LITTER—COLUSA COUNTY

WILDEST WALKIES
Colusa-Sacramento River State Recreation Area, Colusa
(page 158)

BEST PLACE TO EAT
Granzella's, Williams (page 159)

Colusa

PARKS, BEACHES, AND RECREATION AREAS

🛂 Colusa-Sacramento River State Recreation Area
🐾🐾🐾 (See Colusa County map on page 156)

Primitive trails and mucky riverbeds are begging to be explored here. Dogs adore this place, but they're supposed to be leashed.

Our favorite trail starts right next to the boat-launch area. If you ignore some of the smaller trails that branch off it, the main trail will take you down to the sandy/muddy "beach" area along the Sacramento River. Some folks like to fish here, so if you want to get away, just head left and walk down the riverbed. You'll likely see dozens of beasty footprints from the night's activities. Dogs love to sniff at raccoon, deer, and bird prints.

The day-use fee is $6. It costs $15 to camp at one of the 14 sites. Campsite reservations are accepted from the middle of April through September. Highway 20 will take you directly to the park. Coming from I-5, Highway 20 changes its name to 10th Street once you enter Colusa. Follow 10th Street through town and into the park. For camping reservations, call ParkNet at 800/444-7275. For park information, call 530/458-4927.

🛃 Memorial Park
🐾🐾🐾 (See Colusa County map on page 156)

The park is in a really beautiful old section of town. It fits in well here, with graceful palms, stately trees, ultragreen grass, and plenty of places to sit. It's only a square block in area, but leashed dogs get plenty of fulfilment. Humans also enjoy the posh and relaxing surroundings.

The park is between Market and Jay Streets and 9th and 10th Streets. 530/458-5622.

PLACES TO EAT

Rick's Burgers and Shakes: They like dogs at this place and will probably give your pooch some water if she's thirsty. 854 10th Street; 530/458-2831.

PLACES TO STAY

Colusa-Sacramento River State Recreation Area: See the Colusa-Sacramento River State Recreation Area, above, for camping information.

Williams

Guys who wear cowboy hats for real hang out in Williams. So do oodles of people traveling on I-5. The latter folks don't stop because of any tourist attraction. They stop for gas and food. Fortunately, this town has much more ambience than most pit stops on the interstate.

PARKS, BEACHES, AND RECREATION AREAS

🏅 City Park

🐾 (See Colusa County map on page 156)

If you're stopping in Williams for gas, you may as well come here and give your pooch a quick walk. A few trees and a bit of grass will be welcome sights to the dog in your life, and a tiny playground seems to please any tots tagging along.

Exit I-5 at the main Williams exit, drive west to 9th Street, and turn left. The park will be on your left in a couple of blocks. 530/473-5389.

PLACES TO EAT

Granzella's: The food here is mahhvelous. Joe always drooled when he saw anyone eating the special hot turkey and gravy sandwich. Best of all, the restaurant folks love dogs as much as dogs love the restaurant. "We're real animal lovers," says owner Linda Granzella. "We'll even go around the restaurant and find people who left their dogs in the cars with the windows rolled up." They're even happy to give your dog water. Eat at the very long wood picnic table on the porch. 451 6th Street; 530/473-5583.

La Fortuna Bakery: Eat fattening bakery food at two picnic tables. 669 F Street; 530/473-2023.

PLACES TO STAY

Comfort Inn: Rates are $68–76, and that includes a continental breakfast. Dogs are $5 extra. 400 C Street 95987; 530/473-2381 or 800/228-5150.

Motel 6: Rates are $50–54 for the first adult, $6 for the second. 455 4th Street 95987; 530/473-5337.

Stage Stop Motel: There's a fridge in every room here. It's not quite like a chicken in every pot, but it's not bad. The room rate is $45. Dogs are $5 extra. 330 7th Street 95987; 530/473-2281.

SIERRA COUNTIES

CHAPTER 15

Sutter County

There's not much to do here with a dog, but where there's a full bladder, there's a way.

Live Oak

PARKS, BEACHES, AND RECREATION AREAS

❶ Live Oak Recreation Park

🐾🐾🐾 (See Sutter County map on page 162)

This park doesn't have any big trails, but you and your leashed dog can hike around the dirt roads that wind through the park or just walk around the grassy fields. Feather River fans will appreciate the decent boat launch. People with pooches like to picnic under the oaks and willows before turning in for the night at the county's only campground. Small trails lead to the river, but it's a little rough at times and swimming is not allowed.

PICK OF THE LITTER—SUTTER COUNTY

BEST PARK
Live Oak Recreation Park, Live Oak (page 163)

The day-use fee is $3 per car. Camping at one of the 25 sites is $7 a night. Seniors get a cut rate of $3 for camping. You might be able to drive in and get a site, but if you don't want to take a chance that they'll all be gone, call 530/695-3823 for reservations. Exit Highway 99 at Pennington Road and drive east about a mile to the end of the road, where you'll find the park. 530/695-3823.

PLACES TO STAY

Live Oak Recreation Park: See Live Oak Recreation Park, above, for camping information.

Sutter

PARKS, BEACHES, AND RECREATION AREAS

2 Vera Carroll Park

🐾 (See Sutter County map on page 162)

The huge orchard across from this tiny park may be tempting to visit with your dog, but if you don't own it or work on it, you can't set foot on it. The park has a fenced-in playing field, a few shaded picnic tables, and a swimming pool. As long as your dog is leashed and stays out of the pool, he'll be welcome here.

From Highway 20, go north on Acacia Avenue for about two miles. The park will be on your right, at College Avenue. It's run by the Sutter Youth Organization. 530/673-2495.

Yuba City

PARKS, BEACHES, AND RECREATION AREAS

"Our parks are for the people, not for the animals. We'd rather not be put in that book," a parks department staffer told me. But since dogs are permitted at all city parks on an eight-foot leash, we thought it would be nice for dogs to know their rights.

◼ Sam Brannan Park

:paw::paw: (See Sutter County map on page 162)

The back area of this park is nicely fenced, so if your leashed dog makes a break for it, she'll be relatively safe. Otherwise, peruse the big grassy area, let your dog sniff the trees, or have a relaxing picnic at the many tables here.

From Highway 99, turn east on Bridge Street, drive a few blocks, and go left on Gray Avenue. The park is on your left in a few more blocks. 530/822-4626.

PLACES TO EAT

Pizza Pizzazz: You and the pooch can share pizza, pasta, and sandwiches at the outdoor tables. 1190 Bridge Street; 530/671-2323.

CHAPTER 16

Yuba County

If you're just passing through with a dog, you're doing the right thing. With the exception of a small piece of national forest land, Yuba County isn't exactly dog heaven. Besides, if you want to spend the night, you'll have to either camp, knock on a friend's door, or find the one lodging in the entire county where dogs are allowed.

NATIONAL FORESTS

The National Forests and Wilderness Areas resource at the back of this book has important information and safety tips on visiting national forests with your dog and has more background on the Tahoe National Forest.

Tahoe National Forest

A tiny section of this forest creeps into the eastern edge of Yuba County.

PICK OF THE LITTER—YUBA COUNTY

BEST SWIMMING HOLES
Bullard's Bar Reservoir, Dobbins (page 168)
Collins Lake, Oregon House (page 169)

Dobbins

PARKS, BEACHES, AND RECREATION AREAS

🔟 Bullard's Bar Reservoir

🐾🐾🐾🐾🐕 (See Yuba County map on page 166)

This 16-mile-long crystal-clear lake is heaven to anglers and paradise to pooches. "You betcha, the fishing's the best and we like well-behaved dogs a lot," says a manager of the Emerald Cove Resort and Marina, the full-service concession at the southern tip of the lake.

While dogs must be leashed in campgrounds, developed areas, and at the Emerald Cove facilities, they're permitted to be leash-free in much of the land surrounding the eastern part of the lake. That's because the land is part of the mighty dog-friendly Tahoe National Forest. The Sierra foothills here are full of pine, manzanita, and oak. This makes boy dogs happy and also makes for some good-looking scenery.

The lake has 60 miles of shoreline and contains such goodies as black bass, kokanee salmon, and rainbow trout. If you've got the urge to wet a line, Bullard's Bar is a wise choice. If you need a boat to tote you around, Emerald Cove rents all kinds of fun water vehicles (see the Diversion Get Soggy with Your Doggy).

Camping is available at three main campgrounds, and there's even some shoreline camping. Sites are $14. A $5 reservation fee may be charged. The good news is that if you camp October–March, you'll camp for free.

From Highway 20 about 12 miles east of Marysville, turn north on Marysville Road/County Road E21. Drive north about 15 miles on the narrow, winding road to Bullard's Bar Reservoir. When you pass by the tiny town of Dobbins (the closest town to the main resort area), you and your potentially carsick passengers will be glad to know you've got less than a mile to go. 530/692-3200; www.bullardsbar.com.

PLACES TO STAY

Bullard's Bar Reservoir: See Bullard's Bar Reservoir, above, for camping information.

Oregon House

PARKS, BEACHES, AND RECREATION AREAS

2 Collins Lake

🐾🐾🐾🐾🦴 (See Yuba County map on page 166)

Good dogs who won't chase deer, skunks, and other critters are welcome to strip off their leashes and trot naked around the 600 acres of oaks and pines that surround 1,000-acre Collins Lake. Dog paddling is a popular pastime with unleashed pooches, so if you have a water dog, you couldn't ask for a more dog-friendly swimming hole. Dogs can't go swimming at the official swim beach, but there are plenty of other places to dip a paw. The fishing is terrific, too. Make sure your dog is leashed when you go anywhere near anglers or the developed area of the lake.

The lake has one developed campground and one undeveloped one. The latter is dog heaven. There are no barbecues or tables, but you won't have any neighbors, either. You'll be surrounded by trees and plenty of land. It's a first-rate way to get away from noise, loud kids, radios, and just about everything that reminds you of civilization.

DIVERSION

Get Soggy with Your Doggy: So, you're visiting **Bullard's Bar Reservoir** near Dobbins and you're overcome with the urge to make like Cap'n Crunch and hang out at the helm of a boat? If the closest thing you have to a water vehicle is your set of water wings, fret not. You're in luck: **Emerald Cove Resort and Marina** rents just about any kind of lake boat you and your dog may desire. You can rent patio boats, houseboats, pontoon boats, paddleboats, and even fishing boats for competitive prices. Call for a price list and brochure. When making a reservation, be sure to say you're bringing a pooch, because there are certain upholstered boats that need to stay dog-free. 530/692-3200; www.bullardsbar.com.

You'll find 155 sites here, with nightly fees ranging $19–38. Reservations are recommended in spring and summer. Dogs are $2 extra. The park's day-use fee is $7 per vehicle, $13 per boat. From Marysville, take Highway 20 east for 12 miles and turn north on Marysville Road. The lake entrance will be on your right in about 10 miles. 530/692-1600 or 800/286-0576; www.collinslake.com.

PLACES TO STAY

Collins Lake: See Collins Lake, above, for camping information.

Marysville

The historic district in Marysville is a real charmer—quite different from anything else you'll find in this sprawling, suburban-style county.

PARKS, BEACHES, AND RECREATION AREAS

🐾 Ellis Lake Park

🐾🐾🐾 (See Yuba County map on page 166)

Swans, ducks, and geese enjoy this quaint park at least as much as people and their dogs do. Most of the park's 30 acres is taken up by a decent-sized lake, which was once a sprawling swamp. The swamp disappeared in 1924, when John McLaren, designer of San Francisco's Golden Gate Park, presented a local women's civic group with plans for transforming the muddy soup to its present pleasant state.

An attractive path encircles the lake, but you and your leashed pooch can also spend time at an old stone footbridge, a gazebo, and picnic tables. Dogs who like grass and dirt (and what dog doesn't?) enjoy lounging in the shade of the maples that dot the park.

Ellis Lake Park is between 9th and 14th Streets and B and D Streets. You won't want to hang out at the B Street side, because that's where all the car shops and convenience stores are. 530/749-3902.

🐾 Plaza Park

🐾🐾 (See Yuba County map on page 166)

This park is very tiny, but it's green, close to the Yuba River, and in the historic district next to the Chinese Bok Kai Temple, home of Bok Kai, the river god of good fortune. Peace-loving pooches like to picnic at the park's lone table. It's a very tranquil setting and it's usually quite lush. Dogs must be leashed. The park is at the foot of D Street, at 1st Street. 530/749-3902.

PLACES TO EAT

Silver Dollar Saloon: This is a wonderful place with a big side patio for you and your dog. It's right next to Plaza Park's Chinese Bok Kai Temple. Just sit at the edge of the patio, near the gate, to keep your dog out of the bustle of this busy spot. The saloon has a pretty substantial menu, including steaks, sandwiches, and salads. 330 1/2 B Street; 530/743-1558.

PLACES TO STAY

Best Value Inn: Rates are $45–85. Dogs are $5 extra. 904 E Street 95901; 530/743-1531.

CHAPTER 17

CHAPTER 17
Sierra County

Tahoe National Forest makes up a huge part of this mountainous county, causing dogs to give almost the entire county a four-paw rating. Peaks stretch to 9,000 feet above sea level and plunge into gigantic, serene meadows carpeted with wildflowers in the spring and snow in the colder months.

The North Fork of the Yuba River cuts through big rocks and mountains of tall pines and oaks. In summer, you and your dog can pull off Highway 49 and swim, fish (the fly-fishing is exceptional here), or pan for gold in the river. In autumn, bask in bright colors as the water maples and aspens prepare for winter.

Campgrounds are plentiful along Highway 49. They can be good places to start hikes, but there are actually only a few trailheads that begin near the road. Part of the Pacific Crest Trail passes between Bassett's Station and Sierra City. It's a great place to hike with an off-leash dog, because this section is on dog-friendly national forest land.

PICK OF THE LITTER—SIERRA COUNTY

BEST WAY FOR DOGS TO GET RICH QUICK
Gold panning, Downieville (page 175)

BEST EDUCATIONAL WALKIES
Sierra County Historical Park, Sierra City (page 177)

LODGING WITH MOST LAND
Herrington's Sierra Pines Resort, Sierra City (page 178)

NATIONAL FORESTS

The National Forests and Wilderness Areas resource at the back of this book has important information and safety tips on visiting national forests with your dog and has more background on the Tahoe National Forest.

Tahoe National Forest

Calpine

PLACES TO STAY

Sierra Valley Lodge: Dogs who like their vacations far from the hubbub of humans enjoy coming to the historic Sierra Valley Lodge. It's the only public-oriented business in this logging town of 200 people, and you won't get a TV or telephone in your room. A rustic lounge with a large rock fireplace adds to the peaceful flavor of this old-timey place—although on some weekends there's live music. If your dog's fur stands on end at the thought of this, please ask before booking a reservation. Dogs are allowed in two of the lodge's rooms. Rates are $59–64. Dogs are $10 extra. 151 Main Street 96124; 530/994-3367.

Loyalton

PLACES TO STAY

Country Cookin' Restaurant and Inn: This little lodging has six units that share one common kitchen and three bathrooms. It's fun to stay here with your dog because it's like a home away from home. You can bring your own groceries and never worry about searching out a dog-friendly restaurant. But should you decide to search, you won't have to look much beyond your own front door. The inn's restaurant, Country Cookin', has an outdoor patio area that welcomes good dogs. And dogs and humans think the Old West, country-style cooking is the cat's meow. You want hearty? Try the biscuits and gravy or one of the special omelets whipped up here. The restaurant is open for breakfast and lunch. Room rates are $45. 820 Main Street 96118; 530/993-1162.

Golden West Saloon: This inn's lobby and bar date from about 100 years ago, but the room where you and your pooch are allowed to stay is merely a throwback to the 1970s. That's OK with Jake, who says any place that specializes in prime rib (served at the inn's restaurant, where the rule is no dogs) has got to be OK. A room here is $57. The mailing address is just Highway 49 (Main Street) 96118; 530/993-4467.

Downieville

While visiting this Old West gold town, you and your dog may feel as if some old miner might come running up behind you screaming he's hit the Mother Lode. It could happen. A while back, Joe and I ran into a prospector who was selling a chunk of gold big enough to pay his bills for two years. Granted, his bills were minimal since he lived out of a camper truck, but it was still impressive. He bought a drink for everyone within 100 feet and treated Joe to a piece of pizza.

Authentic is not the word for Downieville. Authentic implies that something has changed over time and then has been restored to be more like the original. But Downieville has barely changed since its heyday in the 1850s. Wood planks still serve as sidewalks and many buildings still have walls made of thick stones. The streets are narrow and jagged, just wide enough for a few stagecoaches (although cars do manage here nowadays). Ghastly green gallows stand next to the county jail, a grim reminder of the town's rowdy past. And gold miners still gather at the local assay office at dusk to weigh and sell the gold flecks and chunks they find in the North Fork of the Yuba River.

Inspired by this gold, Joe and I bought a $4 gold pan and a little red book that tells you how to pan for the stuff. (You can get panning supplies at at least a couple of stores in town.) We drove west of town a few miles on Highway 49 and stopped when we found what looked like a lucky spot on the Yuba River in Tahoe National Forest. We could feel our fortune in the air. We knew that after we spent a couple of hours sifting gravel and dirt, we'd find something that would let us retire early, or at least buy a bag of dog food. It was one of those things you could just sense.

Two hours later, I was still trying to get Joe to stop digging holes and covering up my freshly shaken gold pan with his freshly dug river dirt. It was bad enough that we had to watch the little red instruction booklet float away, then sink, after Joe crashed into me and knocked me into the river in a fit of canine glee within minutes of getting to our spot.

We left with soggy coats and unfulfilled dreams. That night, we bought a lottery ticket, won $5, and felt much better.

PARKS, BEACHES, AND RECREATION AREAS

◼ Lion's Memorial Park

🐾🐾 (See Sierra County map on page 172)

If you like looking at old mining equipment, you'll enjoy this park. Several old, rusty gold mining relics are constantly on display here. The park is also a decent place to take a break from exploring town and relax on a bench with your dog.

The best part of this small, on-leash park is that it provides easy access to the Downie River, which runs right through town. Just watch out for the pair of geese who seem to run the place. Whenever we've visited, they've honked us right off the beach. The park is just next to Courthouse Bridge. 530/289-3201.

PLACES TO EAT

Indian Valley Outpost: Step inside and order a good home-cooked meal. While you wait (with someone staying by the picnic tables outside with your dog), shop the little store here for things such as handmade earrings and other local crafts. It's a fun place to spend a few extra dollars. Highway 49, about 12 miles west of Downieville; 530/289-3630.

River View Pizzeria: Dine at any of several rugged picnic tables in the front of the restaurant, or take your pizza out back to Lion's Memorial Park (see above) and eat at the picnic tables overlooking the Downie River. 103 Nevada Street; 530/289-3540.

PLACES TO STAY

Camp Yuba: The three rustic cabins and five RV spaces here are nestled in the Tahoe National Forest on the north fork of the Yuba River. The camp is about five miles east of downtown Downieville, so there's plenty of space for walking around with your best buddy. The owners here love dogs but have had a couple of bad experiences, so make sure your dog is really good here. And please keep him off the furniture. RV spaces are $22 nightly. Cabin rates are $500–550 per week. The cabins can be rented nightly only when available. 21792 Highway 49 95936; 530/289-2779; www.campyuba.com.

Downieville Carriage House Inn: The folks here like to see your dog before they OK a stay here, but they'll settle for talking to you on the phone about your dog. "We just need to make sure a dog is well mannered," says John, who owns the inn. Your dog doesn't need to know which side of the plate the wine glass goes on; she needs only to be your basic good dog who won't tear the place apart or eat other guests or furniture. The inn, built in 1938, is a simple nine-room lodging. Dogs love that it's a bone's throw to the Downie River. On weekends, your room comes with fresh hot bread or muffins, and something to sip on, too. Rates are $50–100. 110 Commercial Street 95936; 530/289-3573 or 800/296-2289; www.downievillecarriagehouse.com.

Downieville Inn: Dogs who like to eat home-cooked food like this motel—rooms with kitchenettes are available at no extra cost. The motel is across the street from the north fork of the Yuba River. Rates are $50–89. Dogs pay a $10 fee per stay. 117 Main Street 95936; 530/289-3243; www.downievilleinn.com.

Downieville River Inn and Resort: This beautiful Old West inn makes dogs feel mighty welcome, thanks to its owners, Lancelot and Guenivere, two friendly Australian cattle dogs. Their person, Crystal, also loves to see dog guests. Cats Pixie, Dixie, and Grace are a little less joyous about dog guests, but they tolerate them. Humans like the inn's sauna and heated pool. Dogs have to be content with a dunk in the river. Rates are $79–195. 121 River Street 95936; 530/289-3308 or 800/696-3308; www.downievilleriverinn.com.

The Lure Resort: Dogs love to stay in the charming housekeeping cottages and the cozy log camping cabins at this riverside resort. But mostly, dogs love to be outside here. The resort is set on 14 acres along a half-mile stretch of the north fork of the Yuba River. Dogs are crazy about swimming in the river and hiking (on leash) around the property. People enjoy the outdoors too; the fishing is great, the gold panning is good, and the air smells oh-so-fresh. All well-behaved dogs are welcome except for rottweilers and pit bulls, no matter how nice they are. (Sorry, I don't make the rules, I just report 'em.) Rates are $55–220. Dogs are $20 extra. 100 Lure Bridge Lane, P.O. Box 95 95936; 530/289-3465 or 800/671-4084; www.lureresort.com.

Riverside Inn: Stay here and stay at the confluence of the Yuba and Downie Rivers. Joe (aka "Mr. Don't Get Me Wet") wouldn't have given a hoot, but it's Jake's dream come true. The 1940s-style motel has knotty-pine rooms with balconies overlooking the water below. It's a peaceful place to snooze the night away, since the sounds of the river can cover up the sounds of your snoring dog. Rates are $70–80. Dogs are $10 for the length of their stay. 206 Commercial Street 95936; 530/289-1000 or 888/883-5100; www.downieville.us.

Sierra City

PARKS, BEACHES, AND RECREATION AREAS

🐾 Sierra County Historical Park

🐾🐾 (See Sierra County map on page 172)

A restored hard-rock gold mine and stamp mill are the main attractions at this hilly, forested park a mile east of Sierra City. It's fascinating to learn about how gold ore is mined, crushed, and has its gold extracted. While dogs are not allowed in the museum, they are sometimes permitted to go on a guided tour of the Kentucky Mine with you. Or you can take your own tour, looking into a restored miner's cabin or down a deep hole into the mine.

Leashed dogs enjoy the paved paths that lead to the attractions and the amphitheater. But they seem to like the smaller dirt paths above the amphitheater even more. If you continue on those paths, eventually you'll be in national forest jurisdiction. But it's best to start one of those magical off-leash romps at designated sites within the forest.

The park is just east of the main part of Sierra City, on Highway 49. It's open Memorial Day–September or October, depending on what's going on. Hours vary. For more information phone 530/862-1310.

PLACES TO EAT

Sierra Country Store: Eat grocery-store cuisine with your dog at the outside benches. 213 Main Street; 530/862-1560.

PLACES TO STAY

Buttes Resort: Outdoorsy dogs will enjoy this lodge just off the Yuba River. The Pacific Crest Trail and some quiet lakes aren't too far away either. Some of the units in this attractive wood-shingled lodge have kitchens. Many have decks overlooking the Yuba. Rates are $80–125. Dogs are $10 per stay. 230 Main Street (Highway 49) 96125; 530/862-1170 or 800/991-1170; www.sierracity.com.

Herrington's Sierra Pines Resort: This pretty, old resort is on the Yuba River, which is great for a good night's sleep. But it's even better for a good day's walk with your best pal, because well-behaved dogs are allowed off leash at the river's edge. And better yet, obedient dogs are allowed leash-free on the 55 acres of land surrounding the resort. For dogs whose people like to fish, there's a pond stocked with 3,000 rainbow trout. If the fish outwit you, you can enjoy a scrumptious meal at the resort's beautiful dining room, which has a cozy, log-cabin feel. The rooms are mostly motel-style, with wood paneling, and there are a few housekeeping units. The resort is closed Thanksgiving–March. Rates are $64–125. 104 Main Street (Highway 49) 96125; 530/862-1151 or 800/862-9848; www.herringtonssierrapines.com.

Kokanee Kabins: These rustic buildings are in Tahoe National Forest, and just across the road is river access to the Yuba. Dogs dig it here because the

DOG-EAR YOUR CALENDAR

The **Kentucky Mine Concert Series,** at Sierra County Historical Park, provides a summer of musical entertainment for you and your extraordinarily well-behaved dog. The concerts feature a wide variety of music, from Broadway to Celtic to Old West. Dogs who promise not to bark, howl, or stamp their feet are allowed to sit with you in the intimate outdoor amphitheater. For schedules and price information, write P.O. Box 368, Sierra City, CA 96125, or call 530/862-1310.

land in the back of the cabins is great for doggy hikes and comes complete with fragrant pines and cedars. It also comes with bears, coyotes, foxes, and raccoons, so it's a good idea to keep your pooch leashed. Cabins are $65. The address is just Highway 49 96125; 530/862-1287; www.kokaneekabins.com.

Sattley

PLACES TO STAY

Yuba Pass Campground: Stay here and your dog can brag to his buddies that he slept right on Yuba Pass, at an elevation of 6,708 feet. With only 20 campsites, it's fairly private and quiet. Dogs have to be leashed in the camping areas, but if you go on a hike in surrounding Tahoe National Forest, obedient dogs can go off leash. Sites are $18, and they're available on a first-come, first-served basis. The campground is about seven miles west of Sattley, off Highway 49 at Yuba Pass; 530/993-1410.

Sierraville

This charming old town is just down the road from the amazing Sierra Hot Springs (formerly Campbell Hot Springs). Dogs aren't allowed there, so we offer some good camping alternatives. At worst, you and a friend can take turns dog-sitting and visiting the hot springs.

PLACES TO STAY

Cottonwood Creek Campground: Surrounded by big forests and set along Cottonwood Creek at an elevation of 5,600 feet, this campground with 48 sites is an enchanting one. It's not a typical remote national forest camp, but it's not exactly bustling either. Leashed dogs are welcome to peruse the area. They especially enjoy the three miles of trails that start at the main trailhead. Water dogs go gaga for the Fisherman's Trail, which runs alongside the creek. Sites are $15. From Sierraville, take Highway 89 about four miles southeast. The campground will be on your left. For reservations, call 877/444-6777. For more information, call 530/994-3401.

Stampede Reservoir Campground: This is a huge and popular campground on the huge and popular Stampede Reservoir. The reservoir has 25 miles of shoreline. Fishing is great, and hiking is even better. When you get away from people, you can even let your dog off leash, since it's all part of Tahoe National Forest. You'll have your choice of 252 campsites on the south side of the reservoir. Sites are $15. The campground opens Memorial Day weekend and usually closes in September or October. From I-80, take the Boca-Hirschdale/Stampede Meadows Road exit about eight miles north. At the reservoir's dam, turn left and drive a mile to the campground. Call 800/280-CAMP (800/280-2267) for campsite reservations. For more information, phone 530/587-3558.

CHAPTER 18

Nevada County

Do you have a digging dog? Buy yourself a plot of land and start scooping that dirt. Locals boast that more than half the gold that came out of California during the Gold Rush was found in Nevada City, Grass Valley, and other foothill areas of this county. Your hot-digged-y dog probably won't come up with much, but it's always fun to dream.

If you want to see where the riches really were, your best bet is to visit the Empire Mine State Historic Park (see the Grass Valley section), where hole-digging dogs can ooh and ahh at the mouth of the mine shaft that winds 5,000 feet below the surface.

Autumn in Nevada County is about as beautiful as autumn in New England. Much of the county, especially Tahoe National Forest in the east, shows its true colors in the winter, when mountains are a crispy white. In Spanish, the very name *nevada* means "snow-covered." If you've always wanted a white Christmas, this is a spectacular place to watch the flurries fly.

PICK OF THE LITTER—NEVADA COUNTY

BEST LEASH-FREE RIVER WALK
Truckee River access, Truckee (page 189)

MOST DOG-FRIENDLY PLACE TO EAT
Cousin Jack's Pasties, Grass Valley (page 185)

MOST DOG-FRIENDLY PLACES TO STAY
Grass Valley Courtyard Suites, Grass Valley (page 186)
Grinnin' Bear Cabin, Truckee (page 190)

BEST DOG SCENTS
Nevada City Carriage Company carriage ride,
Nevada City (page 187)

COOLEST VIEWS
Northstar-at-Tahoe's gondolas, Truckee area (page 189)

NATIONAL FORESTS

The National Forests and Wilderness Areas resource at the back of this book has important information and safety tips on visiting national forests with your dog and has more information on the Tahoe National Forest.

Tahoe National Forest

North Bloomfield

PLACES TO STAY

Malakoff Diggins State Historic Park: If only dogs could explore this fascinating park with you, they'd get to see what the world's richest and largest hydraulic gold mine was like in its heyday. Fortunately, dogs don't care about such things. But they do generally enjoy a good night of camping. And while dogs aren't allowed on the trails or in the Blair Lake area, they are permitted to join you in certain spots in the park. In case you're interested in a very limited day excursion with your dog, the day-use fee is $6.

There are 30 campsites. Sites are $15. Take Highway 49 from Nevada City and go right at Tyler Foote Crossing Road. Drive 16 miles to the park on this sometimes paved, sometimes precipitous, gravelly road. For camping reservations, call 800/444-7275. For park information, phone 530/265-2740. (We extend a thank-you to Wendell Kallenberger for helping us figure out exactly what town the park should be listed under.)

Penn Valley

PARKS, BEACHES, AND RECREATION AREAS

🐾 South Yuba River State Park

🐾🐾🐾 (See Nevada County map on page 180)

This is one of the most interesting units in the state park system. For now, at least, leashed dogs are allowed to peruse the place. This is great news for pooches who like nature at its finest. The park is a patchwork of lands spread over a 20-mile length along the South Yuba River Canyon, from the top of Englebright Lake at Bridgeport to Tahoe National Forest above Malakoff Diggins State Historic Park (see the North Bloomfield section).

The park has many access points, but our favorites are in the western section. For seclusion and serene beauty, try the westernmost access area. Driving north from Lake Wildwood on Pleasant Valley Road, you'll see a sign for the park and a small parking/pullout area on your left (there's space for only a few cars). If you're coming from Grass Valley or the town of Penn Valley, take Highway 20 west, turn right (north) on Pleasant Valley Road, and drive about six miles to the park.

As soon as you get out of the car, you and your leashed dog will hear the flowing river. Hike down the wide dirt path and when you come to a gravel section, go left. A few yards in, you'll come to one of the most beautiful sections of the South Yuba. The beach around it is sandy and the water in the river is a clear tropical blue (during nonrainy times of year). You'll want to stay forever.

If you're going to run into any people in this part of the park, it's going to be here. The maximum number of humans we've seen at one time at this beachy area has been two. If you want real privacy, you can always ford the river. If the river is high, the current is slow, and your dog's a swimmer, just do the dog paddle across. You're almost guaranteed that no one will be on the other side. Or if you're looking for exercise, continue along the first dirt trail and you can hike your heart out.

Just a few hundred feet up Pleasant Valley Road is the Bridgeport Recreation Area, a much more widely used part of the park with bigger parking lots. Here's where you and your leashed dog can walk across the longest (243 feet) single-span covered bridge in existence. It's been around since 1862! Back then, it cost a whopping $5.50 to get across, but the fee included you, a loaded wagon, and six mules, oxen, or horses. These days, it's free.

You can also relax and picnic at a riverside table, swim in the crystal-clear Yuba, or hike a number of trails. One of the most rugged and scenic trails starts to the left of the covered bridge as you cross from the parking lot. The narrow trail takes you to Englebright Lake, about a mile away.

Please note that May 1–September 30, a couple of busy areas are off-limits to dogs (thanks to some negligent dog people in the past). You'll see the signs. And if you come in rainy season, be aware that this place can be tick heaven. 530/432-2546.

❷ Western Gateway Regional Park

🐾🐾🐾🐕 (See Nevada County map on page 180)

One of the favorite summertime activities at this park is for kids to lie face down on the big water pipes over the creek and watch the water gurgle by. Dogs love to watch the water, too, but it's best if they do it downstream a little. Just walk down the bank to a more secluded spot, where your splashing dog won't frighten or dampen kids.

The park has wide meadows, a miniforest area with small dirt trails, and lots of shrubs for dogs. Leashed dogs love all that. For kids, the place is loaded with playgrounds, ball fields, and basketball courts. Dogs are banned from the playing fields, but they are free to walk on leash around the rest of the park. The big news here is that there's now a fenced dog park next to the creek by the graveyard. (Fear not, it's not creepy.) It's a little under an acre, and it has shade, benches, and trash cans. Bring your own water and you'll have a heavenly time here.

From Highway 20, go south about a half block on Indian Springs Road, then turn left on Penn Valley Drive. The park is on the left. 530/432-1990.

Grass Valley

Like Nevada City a few miles up the road, Grass Valley is a classic Old West town, only older and wester. But danged if it didn't ban dogs from city parks recently. Horsefeathers!

PARKS, BEACHES, AND RECREATION AREAS

🐾 Empire Mine State Historic Park

🐾🐾🐾 (See Nevada County map on page 180)

At one time, miners descended in cagelike trains deep into the earth here and rumbled the ground searching for gold in 350 miles of tunnels. The place was alive 24 hours a day—dirty, dusty, and dancing with gold. Miners extracted more than six million ounces of the precious ore during the mine's century of use.

Now, it's a quiet, calm 800-acre park with lush gardens and green meadows. While the mine and surrounding buildings are inactive, they're still fascinating to inspect. On hot summer days, a dog's favorite place is the shaft viewing area. It's a few dozen feet below ground, and the earthy scents are almost as relaxing as the cool, damp air. Leashed dogs are allowed on most trails, but not in the buildings.

The fee for adults is $3. From Highway 49, drive east on Highway 20/Empire Street about 1.5 miles. The park is on the right. 530/273-8522.

PLACES TO EAT

Cousin Jack's Pasties: British dogs go wild when they smell the Cornish pasties (yummy meat-and-potato pies) you can eat on the porch here. "Dogs are very welcome, and may even get an extra snack," says a dog-loving manager. "Everything's homemade here, including the dog treats." 100 South Auburn Street; 530/272-9230.

PLACES TO STAY

Alta Sierra Village Inn: Your dog will like the views of the small lake you can see from your roomside deck. The lodging is on four acres, and no matter where you are, you'll have a view of the lake or the golf course. Rates are $79. Dogs are $10 extra. 11858 Tammy Way 95949; 530/273-9102 or 800/992-5300.

Best Western Gold Country Inn: If you want your motel to be nestled in the pines, this is a good choice. If you want a pool and spa, it's a great choice. A continental breakfast comes with your room. Rates are $99–129. Dogs are $10 extra. 11972 Sutton Way 95945; 530/273-1393.

Golden Chain Resort Motel: If it's hot, this is a cool place to stay—shady trees abound on the property. Rates are $49–79. Dogs are $10 extra for the length of their stay. 13363 Highway 49 95949; 530/273-7279.

Grass Valley Courtyard Suites: You may not have thought of coming to Grass Valley for luxury accommodations, but that's what you and your lucky dog will get if you choose to stay here. The rooms and suites are spacious and attractive, with featherbeds, robes, and other niceties. The suites boast full kitchens and wonderful layouts. Humans can also use the heated pool, spa, and a decent little exercise area. By now your dog is probably looking at you and saying, "Yah, yah, but what's in it for me?" Good question, you clever canine. Waiting in the room or suite for your dog will be goodies such as tasty treats, a blanket, a dog bowl, and poop bags. "We love dogs staying with us," a late-night clerk told us. "They brighten our day—or night."

Rates are $115–270. Dogs are $25 extra for the length of their stay. The inn is conveniently situated within a block of historic Main Street, at 210 North Auburn Street 95945; 530/272-7696; www.gvcourtyardsuites.com.

Holiday Lodge: This is a popular accommodation for dogs on the show circuit. The hotel even has a little area for walking pooches. Rates are $75–85. Dogs require a $25 deposit. 1221 East Main Street 95949; 530/273-4406 or 800/742-7125; www.holidaylodge.biz.

Swan-Levine House: This big, airy house was built in 1880 and soon after was transformed into a small hospital. Now it's a magical inn, complete with an art studio (where you can try your hand at printmaking), brightly colored rooms furnished with antiques, and cozy fireplaces. Dogs who stay here should like cats—there are plenty of these critters on the property. In fact, if you're planning to visit with your pooch, call first and tell the owner about any cat-munching idiosyncrasies your dog may or may not have. Pooches stay at the discretion of the owner, so you'll need to have a chat first anyway. Rates are $95–110. Dogs are $15 extra. 328 South Church Street 95945; 530/272-1873; www.swanlevinehouse.com.

Nevada City

Dogs are everywhere in this colorful Gold Rush town in the Sierra foothills. They dine with their owners, frolic off leash in Pioneer Park, and hang out with human friends on historic Broad Street. They sometimes even get to go shopping in some of the cutesy tourist-oriented stores.

The entire Old West/Victorian downtown is registered as a national historic landmark. On winter nights, when snow falls around the gaslit lamps in the narrow streets, it's classic Currier and Ives. Your dog trotting along will only add to the sweet scene.

DIVERSION

Get the Drift of a Draft Horse: Dogs think being drawn along the historic streets of Nevada City in a carriage pulled by a hunky Percheron draft horse is one of the most riveting olfactory experiences ever. They thrill at the scent of horse heinie, their noses quivering perchance the horse does his horse business. And it's almost inevitable the horse will provide such canine entertainment—these big, calm beauties eat 20 pounds of grain and 30 pounds of hay daily. Fortunately for the carriage driver, no pooper-scooper is necessary.

The **Nevada City Carriage Company** offers terrific rides through historic downtown and the Victorian district. Rides for up to four people (and a dog) start at $30 for 15 minutes, and go up to $95 for the one-hour grand tour. Dave, the dog-friendly manager, also offers special rides in more elaborate horse-drawn vehicles. Hours for regular rides vary by season, but the horses are out there daily year-round, weather permitting. Stable tours are also available.

You'll often find the carriages until 6 P.M. in front of the National Hotel downtown. In the evening, they'll be in front of Friar Tuck's Restaurant, at 111 North Pine Street. Look for the "Carriage for Hire" sign. For an information card, write 431 Uren Street (not Urine Street, tempting as that may be), Nevada City, CA 95959, or call 530/265-8778. The folks here are out and about on weekends, so you should phone during the week.

PARKS, BEACHES, AND RECREATION AREAS

◼ Pioneer Park

🐾🐾🐾 (See Nevada County map on page 180)

Dogs love the tall pines that edge the park. These trees provide both shade and places for dogs to do their thing. Ball fields, a playground, a pool, and a shed with old firewagons are the major human interests here.

From northbound I-80, exit at Sacramento Street and go right immediately on Nile Street (at the sign for Pioneer Park). When the road comes to a T, go right. The park is on your left. You can either drive all the way in and park near the fountain, or park on Nimrod Street and walk down a paved road into the park's largest open field. 530/265-8223.

PLACES TO EAT

Walking Dog: The hot dogs at this stand are quite tasty, but the Walking Dog logo looks more like Mr. Peanut on a bad hair day than an ambulatory wiener. Jake the Dog thinks it should look more like a walking canine, but the implications of that idea might make you think twice before biting that frankfurter. 408 Broad Street; there's no phone number.

PLACES TO STAY

Outside Inn: What do you get when you take a 1940s-era motel and renovate it using loads of imagination and a love of the outdoors? You get the Outside Inn, situated under some sweet-smelling pines a short walk from downtown Nevada City. Most of the rooms at this fun inn have an outdoor theme. The Angler's Room is a fishing-fan's fantasy, while the Wildlife Room puts you in the company of critters who call Nevada County home (fear not, the critters are not real). The inn's staff is well-versed in directing people and their pooches to some wonderful nearby hikes. (In addition, the outdoor-oriented staff can set up bike rentals, kayak lessons, and point you to some choice swimming holes.) Rates are $65–140. Dogs are $10 extra. 575 East Broad Street 95959; 530/265-2233; www.outsideinn.com.

Truckee

If you want a preview of just what you're going to see when you visit this colorful old city, rent the silent Charlie Chaplin flick *The Gold Rush.* Some of the late-1800s architecture along Truckee's main street, Commercial Row, appears in the film. This enchanting old street hasn't changed much since then.

Your dog will enjoy the rough, Old West–feel of the historic part of town, and you'll like the myriad enchanting shops and restaurants. But sadly for people with dogs, Commercial Row is so old-style that it doesn't have room for outdoor tables for human and doggy dining.

Truckee is home to Donner Lake, where many in the ill-fated Donner Party died in the winter of 1846 after running out of provisions during a "shortcut" leg of their journey from the Midwest. Their tragic tale is recounted at Donner Memorial State Park (see below).

A more upbeat way to experience Truckee's freshwater wonders is to go hiking or trout fishing at the Truckee River. You'll find an access point just outside downtown (see below). It's a great location if someone you're traveling with wants to shop while you and the dog get your paws wet.

PARKS, BEACHES, AND RECREATION AREAS

Truckee has a perfectly manicured regional park, but dogs don't feel welcome there. We prefer to drive another mile down the road and enjoy the wonders of Martis Creek Lake. The recreation area surrounding the lake straddles two counties (it's described in detail in the Northstar section of the Placer County chapter).

DIVERSION

Make Like a Venetian: You won't have to sing "O Sole Mio" to climb aboard the high-speed **gondola at Northstar-at-Tahoe** ski resort in the summer and fall. The 2004 season was the first time dogs were allowed on the comfortable, large gondola that zips up to midmountain. The year before that, if dogs wanted a boost up the mountain, they had to be hoisted into a kennel on an actual chairlift—not always an easy feat. And before that, they had to hoof it up the mountain to have the pleasure of hiking down. (You're still allowed to hike up. It's free, and great exercise!)

Once at midmountain, you and your dog can hike on any of several trails and fire roads. If dogs are truly under voice control, and kept close to their people, they can be off leash. Mountain bike trails aren't far away, so be careful.

At the base of the mountain, you and your dog can grab a bite at the Northstar village restaurant's outdoor tables, or enjoy your own picnic lunch.

The gondola fee is $10 per day for dogs, $15 for humans. 100 Northstar Drive, in Truckee; 800/GONORTH (800/466-6784); www.skinorthstar.com.

5 Truckee River

😊😊😊😊🐾 (See Nevada County map on page 180)

This beautiful, trout-filled river beckons hikers and anglers and their adventurous canines. The really good news is that dogs are allowed off leash along the river, since it's in Tahoe National Forest! Your pup can frolic while you catch and release all day. Use artificial lures and barbless hooks only.

Once you get past the first couple of hundred feet along the riverbank, the trail can be narrow and rocky. If your dog is a klutz or has thin-skinned paws, you may not want to go any farther. She can still have plenty of fun sniffing around while you cast all day for the big one hiding behind the boulder.

From central Truckee, drive northeast on Highway 267 and go right on Glenshire Drive (it's about halfway between downtown and I-80). After 4.5 miles, you'll come to the Glenshire Bridge. Make a sharp right onto a dirt road after the bridge, and park in the flat, dirt area near the river. When choosing a fishing spot, be sure to head to the left as you face the river. If you walk to the right, you'll be in very private fishing grounds very quickly.

The folks at Mountain Hardware can give you fishing tips and updated regulations. Call them at 530/587-4844. The Truckee Ranger District of Tahoe National Forest wasn't very knowledgeable about this part of the river when we called, but they can be helpful with other information. 530/587-3558.

PLACES TO EAT

Gateway Deli: Eat tasty deli fare with your favorite dog at the outdoor tables here. 11012 Donner Pass Road; 530/587-3106.

PLACES TO STAY

Donner Memorial State Park: Dogs aren't allowed on the trails or in the museum that tells the tragic story of the Donner Party, trapped here for the winter of 1846. But they can stay with you at any of the park's 150 campsites. And they can also accompany you to pay homage to the dozens of pioneers who perished here. A 22-foot-high monument rests on a stone base that's 16 feet high; 22 feet was the depth of the snow during that desperate winter. It's within doggy access. Sites are $20. The park is about two miles west of the town of Truckee, on Donner Pass Road. Phone 800/444-7275 for reservations, or call the park at 530/582-7892 for more information.

    Grinnin' Bear Cabin: Stay at this cute vacation rental and here's what you get: a very dog-friendly three-bedroom, two-bathroom house that sleeps up to 15 people for a most reasonable price, nearby hikes, a securely fenced yard with a huge doghouse ("It's a mansion," says the house's owner, Andrea), a doggy door leading to the backyard, a wood-burning stove, big-screen TV, and most of the other creature comforts. (The garage also sports a large kennel inside, in case you opt to go skiing or out on the town and don't want to bring your dog, but you also don't want to take the chance that he'll eat the house.) Because the home is in a planned community, you'll also have access to a large, private lake that allows dogs to do the dog paddle, and to a swimming pool, playground, and tennis courts.

Andrea says she decided to welcome dogs because she doesn't think people should have to leave their best buddy in a kennel when they go on vacation. "I have a terrific place for dogs. Why not invite them to stay, too?" she says.

Rates are $195–350. The house is four miles east of the historic part of Truckee. The mailing address: Box 10799 96162; 530/582-8703 or 800/289-1522; www.sierraviews.com.

Inn at Truckee: This is an attractive and comfortable place to stay—kind of a hybrid of hotel-motel, featuring a continental breakfast, in-room fridges, and a relaxing spa and sauna. The folks here love dogs (the manager comes to work with her German shepherd) and will direct you to a few secret dog areas, including some ponds that will put a smile on your water dog's snout. Actually, your dog won't have to go far to stretch her legs: There's a grassy fenced area and a creek just behind the inn.

A big thanks to Boomer and Bridget, the intrepid snow dogs, for having their human, Marcia (aka Dogma), write us about the inn. Rates are $70–133. It costs $11 extra for as many dogs as you bring—a refreshing change from the usual per-pet charge. (Someone brought four dogs once, and that was pushing the limit a little. The only pack you should bring should be a backpack.) 11506 Deerfield Drive 96161; 530/587-8888 or 888/733-6888; www.innattruckee.com.

CHAPTER 19

Placer County

If your dog likes fresh mountain air, world-class ski resorts, and rivers rushing over hidden gold, Placer County is her kind of place. The county has a little of everything, and dogs should experience its diversity.

Most dogs think the county gets better as they go from its more populated western end past the Mother Lode and into the magnificent mountains. Unless your dog likes to shop 'til she drops, the western valley region of Placer County probably won't be nearly as appealing to her as the high country.

Part of the appeal of the eastern half is that much of it is Tahoe National Forest land, where dogs can shed their leashes everywhere except in campgrounds and developed recreation areas. Keep in mind that the northwest corner of the Granite Chief Wilderness bans dogs May 15–July 15 during deer fawning.

The western half of the county is far from a suburban slumberland. In fact, a good part of it is heavily agricultural. You and your dog can experience the farming life firsthand by driving the '49er Fruit Trail. The trail passes by 100 farms, where you (and often your dog) can stop, look around, and buy very

PICK OF THE LITTER—PLACER COUNTY

BEST HIKING
Tahoe National Forest (page 195)
Auburn State Recreation Area, Auburn (page 204)

MOST DOG-FRIENDLY PLACES TO EAT
Char Pit, Kings Beach (page 196)
Mother Barclay's Cafe, Squaw Valley (page 196)

MOST DOG-FRIENDLY PLACES TO STAY
Rustic Cottages, Tahoe Vista (page 198)
Tahoe Moon Properties, Tahoe City (page 201)
Tahoma Meadows B & B Cottages, Tahoma (page 203)

BEST NATURAL HIGH
Squaw Valley Ski Resort cable car/gondola ride,
Squaw Valley (page 197)

COOLEST SKIING
Tahoe Cross Country Ski Area, Tahoe City (page 199)

fresh farm goods—everything from apples to grapes to walnuts. There are even places to buy trout, sheep, and catfish! Before you let your dog out of the car, ask the farmer if it's OK. If it's not, and it's hot, drive on. Don't leave your dog in the car in warm weather even for a few minutes. For a map and list of all the farms, go to www.sacramentogardening.com/49erFruitTrails.html.

If you want to hit the slopes but can't figure out what to do with your dog, check out the numerous phone book listings for pet-sitting services. A favorite of tourists around here is Doggie Love Daycare and Sleepovers. Owner Lisa and her sweet dog, Bodie (aka Juicy Lips), will host your dog in their house, which is full of toys and dog beds and all the creature comforts. Lisa has a huge fenced backyard where dogs, six at the maximum, can run around and have a ball. She's also known for taking dogs hiking and swimming every day, although in winter she steers clear of the water/ ice. In the summer, she fills a kiddie pool with water and lets dogs take a dip. Day care goes 7 A.M.–5 P.M. and costs $40. Sleepovers are $50. She'll even pick up your dog if you're not too far away from her Tahoma home base. 530/525-6189; www.doggielovedaycare.com.

NATIONAL FORESTS

The National Forests and Wilderness Areas resource at the back of this book has important information and safety tips on visiting national forests with your dog and has more information on the Tahoe National Forest.

Tahoe National Forest

Northstar

PARKS, BEACHES, AND RECREATION AREAS

🄴 Martis Creek Lake

🐾🐾🐾 (See Placer County map on page 192)

This is a prime wildlife-viewing area, with great catch-and-release trout fishing and more than 1,400 acres of meadows, rolling sagebrush hills, and dense conifer forests. There's very little shade around the lake itself, so in hot weather don't plan to paddle around the lake all day while a friend and your dog watch from shore.

You and your leashed dog will have a chance to gawk at all kinds of wildlife, including red-tailed hawks, mule deer, and chickadees. In spring, you can lie back in the meadows full of alpine wildflowers and watch life unfold.

Dogs and their friends enjoy the lake's campground. It's set in a prime wildlife-viewing area and is fairly quiet. The 25 sites are often filled with early-rising anglers or bird-watchers. Sites are $10. All sites but the two for campers with disabilities are available on a first-come, first-served basis.

The lake is halfway between Truckee and Northstar. From Northstar, travel about two miles northwest on Highway 267 to the park entrance. The campground is open May–September. Call 530/639-2342 to reserve the barrier-free sites for disabled campers or for more information on the lake.

PLACES TO STAY

Martis Creek Lake: See Martis Creek Lake, above, for camping information.

Kings Beach

A stinky law has dogs bumming out here. Dogs are no longer allowed at Coon's Beach. Granted, it wasn't exactly poochy paradise, but it was good for a little paw stretching. The problem? Poop. Or to be exact, the lack of scooping. You'd think dog people would learn....

PLACES TO EAT

Brockway Bakery: Got a hungry dog? Order her an organic dog biscuit while you order your own baked goods. Got a thirsty dog? There's a faucet where you can fill 'er up outside. Dine at the umbrella-topped tables. 8710 North Lake Boulevard; 530/546-2431.

Char Pit: No longer do dogs have to sit and wait and pray that you'll drop a bit of your lunch while dining with you at the outdoor tables here: Char Pit now sells a "Dog Burger." I did a double take when I first heard about the menu item, because "beef burger" means made from beef, "turkey burger" means made from turkey meat, so therefore "dog burger" means... But fortunately, all it means is the owners love dogs, and for $1.50 your dog can enjoy a lovely beefy burger patty. 8732 North Lake Boulevard; 530/546-3171.

PLACES TO STAY

North Shore Lodge: The cabins and even the motel rooms here are comfy and quiet. Better yet, the lodge sports a small, mostly fenced area dotted with pines. Dogs dig it. They also like the shaded picnic area in back of the lodge. The new owners have been making many improvements, so it's only bound to get better. Rates are $50–90. Dogs are $10 extra. 8755 North Lake Boulevard 96143; 530/546-4833.

Squaw Valley

PLACES TO EAT

Mother Barclay's Cafe: Gorgeous golden retriever Miles and his people, Russ and Jean Glines, wrote to give us the heads-up about this wonderfully dog-friendly café. "The owners have two goldens and the walls are adorned with picture after picture of their beloved dogs (Barclay and Berger). This was a true find. They literally hovered over Miles, offering biscuits, water, and hugs," wrote Jean.

Turns out restaurant owners Jay and Pat love all dogs, not just goldens. Pooch customers really do feel welcomed by lots of attention and pats and hugs (when it's not too busy), and they also get free doggy biscuits. Even the café's logo is dog-loving—a dog (Barclay, we presume) in a chef's hat surrounded by mixing bowls and spoons. I frankly wouldn't feel comfortable with Jake the yellow Lab preparing *my* meal, but goldens are another matter all together. On the menu, in small print: "We accept Visa, MasterCard, and 50-lb. bags of Eukanuba." You've gotta love this place, whether you're a human or a dog.

The food is delicious, hearty breakfast and lunch cuisine. The menu breaks it down into cute sections such as "traditional stuff" and "not so traditional stuff." Several of the dishes have Barclay's and Berger's names on them, including Barclay's Bad Boy Burrito, Famous Barclay Burger, and Berger's Lox

DIVERSION

Get High with Your Dog: During summer and autumn, you and the dog of your choice can be whisked halfway to the stars by cable cars/gondolas at **Squaw Valley Ski Resort.** You'll dangle high above the mountains on the way up, so if you've ever felt like James Stewart in *Vertigo,* here's some advice: Don't look down, not even at your dog, who will probably be smiling and sniffing everyone's feet anyway.

Once the gondola drops you off, you can hike down the mountain on any number of trails. If you're just visiting for the view, you can turn around and go back on the next cable car. Dogs and their people think the hike is the best way to go, especially in early summer when it's still cool and the wildflowers are blooming.

The Squaw Valley Ski Resort gondola ride costs $17 per adult. After 5 P.M., it's $8. Dogs go for free. Hours can vary but are usually around 9:30 A.M.–9:30 P.M. Nighttime hikes down the mountain trails can be tricky. 530/583-6985.

and Bagel. There's something for everyone here. Health-conscious folks can order the Newport Nine-Grain Cereal (served hot with brown sugar and raisins), and those in need of extra carbohydrates for the slopes can order Powder Day Potatoes. (It's such a big baked, stuffed potato that the menu exclaims that "show dogs jump over them.")

The café is in Squaw Valley, USA, at 1900 Squaw Valley Road; 530/581-3251.

Tahoe Vista

PARKS, BEACHES, AND RECREATION AREAS

The Tahoe National Forest is right in your backyard here, but a local regional park makes for a more civilized outing.

🐾 North Tahoe Regional Park

🐾🐾🐾 (See Placer County map on page 192)

This kind of land is very rare in these parts. Leashed dogs are allowed everywhere except on the playing fields and bleachers in this 108-acre park. That means four miles of hiking trails are at their disposal. Better yet, some of those trails lead to Tahoe National Forest, where your dog can run untethered. The regional park is even fun in the winter because of its popular snow-play hill.

If you're shopping around for a companion for your dog, stop in at the county animal shelter, just a Frisbee's throw from the park. You can't miss the signs for it. The shelter has many sweet dogs who would much rather be romping around in parks with you than caged up and worrying about their fate. They're at 849 Shelter Road. 530/546-4269.

The park is at the corner of Donner Road and National Avenue. From Highway 28, drive inland a few blocks past the scenic cinderblock manufacturer and its neighboring mobile home park. Turn left at the sign for the park. 530/546-4212.

PLACES TO STAY

Rustic Cottages: This resort has been dog-friendly since 1925! It's a great place for a poochy vacation, and with plans for further improvements (the cottages are continually upgraded), it's going to be a doggone dynamite place. The owners, Janet and Marshall, are very nice folks, but they did a lot of work on the place, and they're a little wary about allowing dogs, so please let your dog inspire them to have confidence in their ilk.

The beds here are one of the biggest draws. One of the resort's owners handcrafts wrought iron and brass beds for a living, so his talent was put to use in each of the 18 cottages here. The linens are also first-rate, so the owners ask you not to let your dog on the bed unless you bring your own sheet to cover up the bed first.

The cottages even have TVs, which get a whopping 30 channels each, not that you want to be a couch 'tater when you're vacationing in Tahoe. But just in case, each TV has a VCR, so you can bring your own videos or borrow one of the hundred or so the resort lends out to guests. Reggie Dog, a boxer friend, told us he recently checked out the *Dog Babysitter* video here. He found it a bore, but one of his chauffeurs, Denise Selleck, was mesmerized. In the morning, you can pick up homemade muffins in the main cottage. (You can nab homemade cookies there all day.)

Better yet, though, is that the place is on two acres, with a small, semienclosed lot where your pooch can run leash-free if you stay with him and have a little faith that he won't escape. The lot isn't anything fancy, but dogs don't mind a little overgrown grass and a tree stump. In fact, most dogs prefer this decor to a perfectly manicured lawn. If you want quaint scenery, just look around the cottages. In the warmer months, fresh flowers adorn most cottage fronts. Lake Tahoe is across the street, though there's no beach access there for dogs. But some Tahoe National Forest land is behind the resort, and it's a four-paw adventure for dogs and their people. Reggie Dog and his people got rather lost on a trail here one day, but they eventually made it back to civilization.

Rates are $59–149. Dogs are $15 extra. 7449 North Lake Boulevard 96148; 530/546-3523 or 888/778-7842; www.rusticcottages.com.

Woodvista Lodge: All rooms at this motel have a small fridge, and there are a pool and hot tub. Rates are $70–125. Dogs are $10 extra. No aggressive breeds, please. (Call if in doubt.) 7699 North Lake Boulevard 96148; 530/546-3839.

Tahoe City

Tahoe City is a fun and scenic place to go for a bite to eat with your dog. During summer, there are so many eateries with outdoor tables in this lakeside village that you and your dog will drool just making the choice. It's an ideal place to bring your appetites after a long day of hiking in nearby Tahoe National Forest.

PARKS, BEACHES, AND RECREATION AREAS

🟦 William B. Layton Park

🐾🐾 (See Placer County map on page 192)

While dogs have to stay out of the park's most interesting feature, the Gatekeeper's Cabin Museum, they may stroll the 3.5 green acres of park on the shores of Lake Tahoe as long as they're leashed. Because of the park's picturesque gardens and ancient conifers, the place is often rented out for weddings and private parties. If your dog isn't invited, he has to stay away.

The park has picnic tables in the shade, but it's so close to many of the city's dog dining joints that you probably won't be hungry by the time you arrive here. The park is at 130 West Lake Boulevard. 530/583-1762.

DIVERSION

Dashing Through the Snow: While you ski at the **Tahoe Cross Country Ski Area,** your happy, leash-free dog can trot along beside you on five miles of beautifully groomed dog-friendly trails. (Leashes are required only at the trailhead and parking lot.) It's a blissful experience for most dogs. In fact, Jake is so happy when he gets to ski with us that he leaves lots of cheery yellow marks all over the place.

For obvious reasons, dogs must be under voice control. The two dog-friendly trails are open to dogs 8:30 A.M.–5 P.M. Monday–Friday and limited hours on weekends and holidays. Humans pay $19 for a day of skiing. Dogs pay $3. Season passes are available. In fact, your dog's season pass will have his photo emblazoned on it!

The ski lodge is just as welcoming as the trails. Inside the cozy lounge you'll find plenty of dog biscuits. For humans, you'll find hot chocolate and cookies.

The ski area is at 925 Country Club Drive in Tahoe City; 530/583-5475; www.tahoexc.org. (A big woof of thanks goes to Alexandra, Deuce, and Jasper for letting us know about this terrific place.)

DIVERSION

Say Your Nuptials While Your Pup Chills: Calm, well-behaved, flea-free dogs are welcome to join you and your future spouse when you launch your lifetime of togetherness at **A Chapel at Lake Tahoe.** And fear not: The interior of the chapel is not gauche. "There's nothing plastic, glitzy, or Elvis about it," says a chapel owner. In fact, it's simple, with wrought-iron and wood benches and real live plants.

The basic wedding ceremony package is $295, which includes your wedding license. For more information, write to 3080 North Lake Boulevard, Tahoe City, CA 96154, or call 530/581-2757 or 800/581-2758; www.chapelatlaketahoe.com.

PLACES TO EAT

Here's a sampling of the dog-friendly restaurants in Tahoe City:

Fiamma Cucina Rustica: This is a beautiful, romantic restaurant with some scrumptious pastas, chicken dishes, and pizzas. The smoked mozzarella and roasted eggplant pizza is out of this world. Dogs are allowed to dine with you at the lovely wooden tables outside, as long as it's not too busy. 521 North Lake Boulevard; 530/581-1416.

Rosie's Cafe: Eat steaks, burgers, and pasta on the charming porch. 571 North Lake Boulevard; 530/583-8504.

Sierra Vista: Dine with your dog on cuisine from around the world at this fine lakeside restaurant's patio tables. It's got everything from Hungarian goulash to Japanese sea bass. Thirsty dogs get water. 700 North Lake Boulevard; 530/583-0233.

Sunnyside Market: It's not exactly the most elegant dining experience, but you and your pooch may eat on benches outside this little convenience store. 1780 West Lake Boulevard; 530/583-7626.

Tahoe House Bakery and Gourmet Store: You and your dog can cool your paws under the awning-covered outdoor eating area here. Dogs can get water from a dog water station here, and in keeping with the theme of your doggy vacation, you (the human) can order a dog-paw–shaped cookie. The sandwiches and pastries are tasty, too. This is also where you can buy some quality gourmet meals that you can simply heat up when you get back to your lodging. 625 West Lake Boulevard; 530/583-1377.

PLACES TO STAY

Hauserman Rental Group: This is a very dog-friendly vacation rental agency, with many of the 300 rentals welcoming dogs. You can rent a condo, cabin, or luxurious lakeview home with your dog. You name the amenity, the agency will find it for you. Rates are $105–650, depending on the location and size of the rental. 475 North Lake Boulevard 96145; 800/20-TAHOE (800/208-2463); www.enjoytahoe.com.

Tahoe Moon Properties: Of the 50 rental properties managed by this vacation rental agency, 47 permit pooches. "When I went into this business, I found that dog people are much better guests than nondog people," says Jill, who runs the agency. "Except for cleaning poop. Some aren't fantastic about that." (Picture a snowblower. Picture poop jettisoning through the snow blower. Not a pretty sight. Scoop the poop!)

Despite the poop problem, she decided that dog people are such good guests that the vacation rentals should offer something special. Now all dog-friendly rentals come with a bottle of wine for the humans, and a dog bowl, dog bed, dog biscuits, and even dog tags for canine friends. Many of the rentals have fenced yards, which make a dog's vacation even more heavenly.

Jill offers rentals throughout the Lake Tahoe area. Rates vary greatly, from $125 nightly for a modest one-bedroom home to $750 a night for a stunning and luxurious four-bedroom home. Tahoe Moon Properties' mailing address is P.O. Box 7521 96145; 866/581-2771; www.tahoemoonproperties.com.

Homewood

PLACES TO EAT

West Shore Cafe: This lovely lakefront restaurant formerly was an all-outdoor affair with tons of tables along the lake and a pier. Recently, however, the owners enclosed a section of the restaurant, though leashed dogs are still allowed at the remaining outdoor seating.

The lunch and dinner menus are to drool for: Appetizers include smoked salmon, escargot phyllo, and ahi tuna sashimi. The lunch entrée menu is basic, with tasty burgers, pastas, and sandwiches. Dinner entrées tend toward the meaty side, but there's usually an equally delicious veggie pasta if you're watching your consumption of rack of lamb and filet mignon.

The café is open only in summer and is right across the street from the Homewood Mountain Resort. 5180 West Lake Boulevard; 530/525-5200.

Tahoma

PLACES TO EAT

Brian's: This is the name of the Norfolk Woods Inn's excellent, dog-friendly restaurant. (See below for details.)

PLACES TO STAY

Norfolk Woods Inn: Dogs are "very welcome" to stay at the rustic cabins of this sweet bed-and-breakfast inn. "We love dogs," says a friendly manager. The cabins have two bedrooms upstairs and a kitchen downstairs. Fireplaces make the cabins extra cozy in the winter. A heated pool makes for a refreshing dip during the warmer months.

The inn also has a restaurant, Brian's, complete with a veranda for you and your dog. Brian was just opening the restaurant when we last sniffed it out, and he promised to "serve sexy American food and make insane vegetables." Sounds like a must-visit kind of place.

Rates for the cabins are $110–190. The price includes breakfast. Dogs are $10 extra. 6941 West Lake Boulevard 96142; 530/525-5000.

Tahoe Lake Cottages: Dogs think this place is tops, but not necessarily because of the cozy cottages with full kitchens, knotty-pine interiors, and "old Tahoe" shingled exteriors. More likely it's because of the old-growth cedars and sugar pines that surround those cottages. "They get my leg a-twitchin'," says Jake Dog.

The owners, the Lafferty family, adore dogs and kids. They have a dog of their own. Brody's his name, but Mike Lafferty prefers to call him "Brody, the World-Famous Tree-Climbing Dog." You'll see why when you visit. He's

110 pounds of fun. The cottages also have a pool and a hot tub, but no dogs, please, lest their fur gunk up the works.

Rates for the cottages are $140–225. Dogs are $10 extra. Be sure to ask for the dog-lover's special discounts. They're available much of the time in off-season. 7030 Highway 89 96142; 530/525-4411 or 800/852-8246; www .tahoelakecottages.com.

Tahoma Lodge: Boyce, who owns these cabins, puts it simply: "I've been allowing dogs here for 19 years. Let's say they're quite welcome." Cabins come with a woodstove or fireplace. A pool is on the premises and so is a hot tub, but only for critters of the human persuasion. Pets are welcome with prior approval. Rates are $60–355. Dogs are $10 extra. 7018 West Lake Boulevard 96142; 530/525-7721; www.tahomalodge.com.

Tahoma Meadows B & B Cottages: Seven of the 15 wonderful cottages here welcome dogs—and I do mean welcome. Lucky dogs who visit get biscuits, a couple of tennis balls, a dog bowl (just a loaner, not a keeper), and a list of favorite doggy hikes and outings in the area. "We really enjoy our dog guests," says Dick, your host. Shasta, his big white Lab (perfect for camouflage in the snow), likes to greet new visitors when possible.

The cozy cottages are surrounded by towering pines, with plenty of room to roam around. Many cottages have fireplaces, most have kitchens. Those that don't have kitchens are called bed-and-breakfast cottages, and your stay includes a full breakfast at the main building. Guests of all the cottages can head to the main building for a fun, relaxing wine-and-cheese hour every afternoon. You'll enjoy an excellent lake view from the upper floor here.

Rates are $119–295. Dogs are $10 extra. If you stay for more than three nights, you just pay a $25 dog fee for the length of your stay. 6821 West Lake Boulevard 96142; 530/525-1553 or 866/525-1553; www.tahomameadows.com.

Auburn

While this city has sprawled in so many directions that it looks like a giant mall, there's still a fairly large, very historic downtown that looks like a big old valuable antique. It's a great place to sniff out with your dog.

PARKS, BEACHES, AND RECREATION AREAS

4 Auburn District Regional Park

🐾🐾 (See Placer County map on page 192)

You can roll up your overalls and fish in the park's willow-shaded pond and feel remarkably like Tom Sawyer. Except for the sports fields and playground, this 62-acre park is a quiet one. Dogs may feel a little intimidated by the perfect green meadows, but if you look hard, there are a couple of scruffier sections around the edges. Leashes are a must.

Take the Dry Creek Road exit from Highway 49 and go west a few blocks to Richardson Drive. 530/885-8461.

5 Ashford Park

🐾🐾 (See Placer County map on page 192)

This city park is convenient to I-80 travelers whose leashed dogs like their restroom breaks nice and pretty. While the park is only seven acres, it has a little pond and is full of trees and picnic tables on well-manicured grass. Kids like the playground, so it's an ideal rest stop for your whole carload.

From I-80, exit at Foresthill Road and go west for a couple of blocks. When you cross over railroad tracks, the entrance will be coming up on your left. Park on the street. 530/885-8461.

6 Auburn State Recreation Area

🐾🐾🐾🐾 (See Placer County map on page 192)

This 30,000-acre park lies along 30 miles of the North and Middle Forks of the American River. A few of the activities (and inactivities) available include fishing, gold panning, rafting, swimming, hiking, biking, horseback riding, sunbathing, picnicking, and camping. Since dogs are supposed to stay out of the rivers and they don't ride bikes or horses, their selection is more limited.

On a quiet day when it's just you, your leashed dog, and the river, try to imagine 10,000 miners crowded into this area in hot pursuit of gold. It makes the occasional passerby seem less obtrusive.

If you and your dog have good hiking paws, 57 miles of trails await you. There are several trailheads. For an easy-to-find, quick hike to break up a long I-80 trip, take the Foresthill Road exit off I-80 and drive east. As soon as you pass over the Foresthill Bridge (it's the one that's 750 feet above the North Fork of the American River and a little more than a mile from the highway), pull over in the tiny off-road parking area to the right. Walk back toward the bridge and bear left when you see a little dirt area with signs that ban motorcycles from the trails.

Not only is this a superb area to view the lands around the north fork of the river, it's also the starting point for several trails that wind their way down toward the river. Some are very steep and attract mountain bikers. From the trailhead you can see which trails have a gentler grade—it's better for everyone if you choose one of the less precarious ones.

If you want a longer hike, a very popular starting point is behind the Auburn Fairgrounds, at Pleasant Avenue. Park in the large lot. If you're planning on hiking the whole trail, you'd better bring a few horses to carry your gear: The trail goes to the confluence of the Middle and North Forks of the American River, and then continues through national forests all the way to Squaw Valley.

Dogs are allowed at all areas and campsites in the Auburn State Recreation Area except around Lake Clementine and its campsites. Supervising Ranger Mike Van Hook says that area was closed to canines because inconsiderate owners didn't clean up after them and let them wreak general havoc. It's rare to find a state park that allows dogs on the trails, so let's be careful. You also have to watch out for mountain lions. This is the area where a woman was killed by a lion a few years ago. If you don't know how to handle a mountain lion encounter, contact the ranger. Chances are you'll never see one of these wild cats, but it's better to be on the safe side.

The recreation area has 50 campsites. They are first-come, first-served and cost $9 a night. A favorite for people who like to get away from the crowds is the Ruck-A-Chucky Campground. It's a quiet, primitive campground next to the Ruck-A-Chucky rapids on the Middle Fork of the American River. Ruck-A-Chucky has only seven campsites, but it has a pleasant day-use area with picnic tables. 530/885-4527.

PLACES TO EAT

Awful Annie's: The name doesn't reflect the cuisine here, according to Reggie Dog, who stopped in with his folks, Denise and Kevin, and called to tell us about it. The food is good breakfast and lunch cuisine, with omelettes, soups, and salads. Vegetarians get to choose from a few dishes. Reggie Dog got a bowl of fresh water when he visited and was very impressed. Dine with your dog at two "dogs-allowed" tables on the attractive deck in Oldtown Auburn. 160 Sacramento Street; 530/888-9857.

Ikeda's Tasty Burgers: "A lot of people bring dogs. They have good taste," says Steve, Ikeda's co-owner. A local sheriff's official tells us Ikeda's has the "best burgers for a long ways," and we believe him. You can see Ikeda's from I-80, so it's a good place to come when you get the road-hungries. 13500 Lincoln Way; 530/885-4243.

La Bou: Eat yummy baked goods, sip stimulating coffee. Do it all under the shade of La Bou's canopy. 2150 Grass Valley Highway; 530/823-2303.

PLACES TO STAY

Auburn State Recreation Area: See Auburn State Recreation Area, above, for camping information.

Best Western Golden Key: This is a rosy place to stay: More than 120 rose bushes grace the gardens around the motel. There's plenty of lawn area for your dog to sniff out. Humans enjoy swimming in the year-round pool and relaxing in the spa. Rates are $75–115. Dogs are $15 extra. 13450 Lincoln Way 95603; 530/885-8611 or 888/201-0121.

Holiday Inn Auburn: Stay at this comfy, clean Holiday Inn and you'll get use of the heated outdoor pool, a spa, and little exercise facility. Rates are $114–165. Dogs are $20 extra. 120 Grass Valley Highway 95603; 530/887-8787 or 800/814-8787.

TraveLodge: Rates are $59–99. Dogs are $10 extra. 13480 Lincoln Way 95603; 530/885-7025 or 877/885-7025.

Roseville

PARKS, BEACHES, AND RECREATION AREAS

For many years, dogs were banned from all Roseville parks. They couldn't set paw in them, even on leash. Eventually, this led dogs to convince their people that something should be done, so their people did something. They talked the city into giving dogs a park of their very own! Dogs are still verboten in all city parks except this one, but that's OK with them. When you have a slice of poochy paradise, who needs a people park?

Another chunk of dog heaven is scheduled to open in 2005, probably by the time you read this. Bear Dog Park (hmm, does this mean that it's for dogs who hunt bears? Dogs who look like bears? Dogs who run around bear, er, bare?) will be within Mahany Park, at 1545 Pleasant Grove Boulevard, at the corner of Woodcreek Oaks and Pleasant Grove Boulevards. It sounds like it'll be a winner, with a grassy area and a natural preserve with a creek. A huge thanks to Donna Treibel, president of the Roseville Dog Owners' Group (RDOG), for this info. For more info on RDOG, check out www.rosevilledog.org.

7 Marco Dog Park

🐾🐾🐾🐾🐕 (See Placer County map on page 192)

Doggone it, this is one great place to be a dog. The park is a tail-waggin', leash-free kind of place. It consists of four fenced acres, with hills, flatlands, some shade trees, a doggy/human water fountain, and some small wading pools where your pooch can stay cool.

The park is immensely popular with dogs and their folks. Marco Dog Park would be a perfect park, except for one little problem: It was built on property that's used as flood control land during the rainy months. That means that during much of the winter, the flat area is under about three feet of water and it's closed to dogs. But ducks love it, if that's any consolation. Thousands come to dip their little webbed toes and bob around for a bit. Duck Park is what locals call it then.

The park, like Petaluma's Rocky Memorial Dog Park (see the Sonoma County chapter), was named after a police dog who was killed in the line of duty during a drug raid. Maybe Rocky and Marco are romping around together in Dog Heaven right now with big grins on their snouts, comparing the parks that bear their names. (Joe Dog is probably trying to get their autographs. He loved these parks.)

The park is closed dawn–3:30 P.M. Wednesdays for weekly maintenance. Marco Dog Park is at Sierra Gardens Drive just north of Douglas Boulevard. It's in a ravine, several feet lower than the street and surrounding properties, so it's possible you might miss it if you're not looking carefully. 916/774-5242.

Granite Bay

PARKS, BEACHES, AND RECREATION AREAS

8 Folsom Lake State Recreation Area

🐾🐾🐾🐾 (See Placer County map on page 192)

An important entrance to this popular lake is in Granite Bay, just south of Folsom Road. Although most of this large park is in Placer County, we've listed it in Sacramento County, under its namesake, the town of Folsom.

CHAPTER 20
El Dorado County

From Lake Tahoe to the lands east of the Mother Lode vein, this county is as attractive to people as it is to their dogs. The Eldorado National Forest is in your backyard almost everywhere you go. It's as scenic as it is dog-friendly. Lodgings that welcome dogs abound. Nevada's casinos are a bone's throw away. Wineries are plentiful, and many allow dogs in their picnic areas. Apple farms, Christmas tree farms, and even some fishing boats think well-behaved dogs make fine visitors.

When Jake first visited, he got to swim in Lake Tahoe, have a picnic at a winery, sleep at a dog-loving lodging, and run, run, run on many miles of National Forest trails. His tongue constantly hung out of his mouth like a slab of bologna, and he always had a huge smile on his snout. "That's one happy dog," someone observed. "Looks like he belongs in one of those dog food commercials." That's what this county can do to a dog.

PICK OF THE LITTER—EL DORADO COUNTY

BEST OFF-LEASH HIKING
Eldorado National Forest (page 210)

MOST DOG-FRIENDLY PLACES TO STAY
Alder Inn and Cottages, South Lake Tahoe (page 214)
Fireside Lodge, South Lake Tahoe (page 215)
Sandor's Chateau Motel, South Lake Tahoe (page 216)

MOST LUXURIOUS VACATION RENTALS
Stonehenge at Tahoe, South Lake Tahoe (page 217)

BEST CHARTER FISHING
Tahoe Sport Fishing, South Lake Tahoe (page 212)

NATIONAL FORESTS

The National Forests and Wilderness Areas resource at the back of this book has important information and safety tips on visiting national forests with your dog and has more information on the Eldorado National Forest.

Eldorado National Forest

The major part of Eldorado National Forest is in its namesake county. An exception to the off-leash policy of the national forests is in the Desolation Wilderness, where dogs are supposed to be leashed at all times.

South Lake Tahoe

With all its recreational opportunities, South Lake Tahoe can be a terrific place to be a dog. The biggest problem is when a dog's humans head for the ski slopes or casinos and leave their canine friends behind in their lodgings. As we've mentioned more than once, this is a big no-no. (A refreshing exception: At the Fireside Lodge, dogs are allowed to be in a kennel in your room if you're not there. That's a big plus, as long as your dog is used to being crated.) What's a dog to do? If dogs had opposable thumbs they could pick up the phone and ring up a pet-sitter. But since they can't, you should. Pet-sitters are plentiful around here and are usually found under Pet Sitting Services in the Yellow Pages.

DIVERSION

Here Comes the Bride...and the Groom...and the Dog:
They've seen it all at the **Chapel of the Bells.** Dogs have worn tuxedos to weddings. They've been the best man, the maid of honor, the ring bearer, or the flower girl. They've given away the bride. "They've even cried," says employee Carolyn Lewis.

The chapel has both a pooch-friendly indoor and outdoor facility in the heart of a woodsy but suburban neighborhood. The basic wedding costs $175, including the license but excluding the donation for the minister. For that kind of price, you can afford to bring the dog along on the honeymoon.

If you're in the Tahoe area and want to get married fast but this chapel doesn't ring your bells, just pick up a phone book and look in the Yellow Pages under Weddings. You're sure to find something the bride, groom, and pooch will all remember happily ever after.

The Chapel of the Bells is at 2700 U.S. 50. Its mailing address is P.O. Box 18410, South Lake Tahoe, CA 96151. 530/544-1112 or 800/247-4333; www.weddingtahoe.com.

One service we've heard terrific things about is KYPSAH (Keep Your Pet Safe and Happy). Pet-sitter Jessie Riggs offers day care for $40 a day, and she takes her tourist dogs everywhere her "regulars" go, including hikes, errands, and her home. She also offers in-home overnight sitting, should you want to burn the midnight oil at the casinos. Her number is 530/867-6727, and her website is www.kypsah.com. Casinos have their own kennels, but they're usually for guests only, and they're often found in places such as the garage. Not a dog's dream vacation.

PARKS, BEACHES, AND RECREATION AREAS

South Lake Tahoe has very few places to walk with your dog. Pooches are banned from city beaches and even from those federal beaches and federal parks that charge entrance fees. State parks here allow dogs only in camping and picnic areas. But there are a couple of places (both run by the folks who run the national forests) that dogs will be as excited to visit as humans.

DIVERSION

Give Your Dog His Lake Legs: If you want to fish, sail, or motor around Lake Tahoe but don't want to leave your furry friend behind, there's good news: A few **boat-rental** businesses and **sport-fishing charters** allow well-behaved dogs who promise not to get the decks wetter than the lake will get them (if ya know what I mean).

You'll want a fairly calm dog who isn't so enticed by water that he'll jump in and paddle wherever his webbed paws will take him. Jake the Water Dog has been known to belly-flop out of a slow boat and swim oh-so-joyously around the lake, oblivious to the calls and enticements we were using to try to lure him back. I could just picture him thinking, "Hmm, swimming or stale crust of peanut butter sandwich? See ya later, Maria!"

Tahoe Keys Boat and Charter Rentals offers several types of boats, including sailboats, pontoon boats, and regular old fast motorboats. Rates are $95–150 per hour. Half-day and full-day rates are significantly discounted. 2345 Venice Drive East, South Lake Tahoe; 530/544-8888; www.tahoesports.com.

Dogs who wish for fish can join you in a chartered trout-fishing boat run by Tahoe Sport Fishing as long as the boat isn't crowded. Rates are $85 per person for a five-hour trip. 900 Ski Run Boulevard, South Lake Tahoe; 530/541-5448; www.tahoesportfishing.com.

⬛ The Forest Service Taylor Creek Visitor's Center

🐾🐾🐾🐾 (See El Dorado County map on page 208)

This is among the most fascinating and well-developed wildlife-viewing areas in the state. You and your dog can spend the whole day here agog at Mother Nature while learning about this wet meadow area and the abundant life it supports.

A half-dozen trails with interpretive displays lead you over creeks, through aspen forests and grassy wetlands, and among wildlife you never dreamed you'd see so close to Harrah's and Caesars Tahoe. Among some of the critters you might spot are ospreys, beavers, Canada geese, kokanee salmon, trout, and, yes, hairy woodpeckers. There's even the possibility you'll see some deer and coyotes, so keep a tight hold of that leash.

The park may have the only aquarium in the world that welcomes dogs. It's not exactly the Monterey Bay Aquarium, but it is an underwater building where you can see native fish in their native stream.

The beach and undeveloped forestlands around the visitor center provide ample room to get away from the heavy summer crowds. If you plan to make a day of it, pack a lunch to eat at the comfortable picnic areas here.

From the junction of U.S. 50 and Highway 89, the center is about three miles north on Highway 89. The entrance is on your right. 530/543-2674.

🐾 Tallac Historic Picnic Site/Kiva Beach

🐾🐾🐾 (See El Dorado County map on page 208)

The huge swath of scattered pine trees that greets you as you enter this area is just as enticing for your leashed dog as the shoreline itself. There's some sage undergrowth, but it's fairly easy to navigate.

If you want to go directly to the water, just park and take the long dirt trail. The water's edge is a large and sandy area and provides a great panorama of Lake Tahoe. Apparently there have been some problems with off-leash dogs of late, so the pooch patrol is out in force. If you don't want a citation, don't forget to leash up and scoop up.

You can also have a picnic with your dog in the shady picnic area, or take him on a hike up the Tallac Historic Trail, which starts near the east end of the beach. There he'll be shaded from the sun and inundated with fascinating tidbits about the area's past.

From the junction of U.S. 50 and Highway 89, take Highway 89 north about 2.5 miles. The entrance is on your right. 530/573-2674.

PLACES TO EAT

Colombo's Burgers A-Go-Go: You and your hungry dog can dine on burgers, chicken nuggets, and the like at the outdoor tables here. 841 Emerald Bay Road; 530/541-4646.

Dixon's: Dixon's has got the usual burger and fries cuisine here, but you can also get a good veggie lasagna and some tasty homemade desserts. And if you're in the mood for a tall, cold one, Dixon's boasts the largest beer selection on the lake. Enjoy it all with your pooch at your side at the shaded outdoor tables. "We are pet lovers here!" exclaimed a friendly server. 646 Emerald Bay Road; 530/542-3389.

Grass Roots Natural Foods: This is a great place to visit for healthful, wholesome food. It even tastes delicious! Your dog can join you at the benches outside the big old blue house/store. If you want to make it an extra special dog day, buy some natural dog treats inside so your dog can eat with you. There's even a large grassy area to sniff around. 2040 Dunlap Drive; 530/541-7788.

J&J Pizza: At J&J's, you and your dog can have your calzone and eat it too, thanks to the dog-friendly outdoor tables here. The pizzas are also snout-lickin' good. "Just don't let your dog do nothing on my sidewalk," requests a manager. 2660 Lake Tahoe Boulevard; 530/542-2780.

Shoreline Cafe: This one's mighty close to the lake. The mahi-mahi sandwich is delectable. The vegan food is great, too. Thirsty dogs get water. 3310 Lake Tahoe Boulevard; 530/541-7858.

Sprouts: As the name might imply, fresh natural foods, not greasy onion rings and shakes, are the forte here. Eat at the picnic tables with your pooch. 3125 Harrison Avenue; 530/541-6969.

PLACES TO STAY

Please don't leave your dog alone in your room and go gamble across the state line! (See the introduction to the South Lake Tahoe section for more on this.)

Alder Inn and Cottages: If you feel like hitting the slopes but your dog just doesn't have the urge to don her skis, the inn, set on four wooded acres, can supply you with a dog-sitter and/or dog-walker for a decent fee. If you have more than one pooch, it will cost you a little extra. We've never used the service, but we've heard dogs get lots of tender loving care. In addition, the folks at the motel provide pooches with dog treats. Jake thinks that's a doggone decent thing to do. Rates are $42–125. Dogs are $10 extra. 1072 Ski Run Boulevard 96150; 530/544-4485 or 800/544-0056; www.alderinn.com.

Best Western Timber Cove Lodge: Dogs enjoy the courtyard here. Room rates are $69–145. Dogs are $25 extra, and a $100 doggy deposit is required. 3411 Lake Tahoe Boulevard 96150; 800/972-8558; www.timbercovetahoe.com.

Cedar Lodge: Rates are $40–100. Dogs are $20 extra for the length of their stay. 4081 Cedar Avenue 96150; 530/541-5004; www.cedarlodgetahoe.com.

Days Inn: Bosco, a Mill Valley dog of the half-beagle persuasion, heartily recommends this Days Inn. "It's a great place, for a Days Inn," he writes. Rates are $54–169. Pooches are $10 extra, and must be a year old before visiting here. Be sure to let the staff know ahead of time that you're bringing a pooch; otherwise the pooch-designated rooms might be booked with nondog people. 968 Park Avenue 96157; 530/541-4800; www.hotellaketahoe.com.

Emerald Bay State Park: Camping is available only in the summer. Although dogs are not allowed on the trails or the beaches, it's worth it to camp here just to be in this park's splendor. About 100 campsites are on the south side of the tranquil bay. Sites are $20. The park is on Highway 89, about eight miles north of the junction of Highway 89 and U.S. 50. Call park headquarters at 530/525-7277 for information. For reservations, call 800/444-7275.

Fallen Leaf Lake: This is a good place for dogs who enjoy socializing. In summer, chances are good that you'll be in close proximity to dozens of campers in this popular recreational lake area on U.S. Forest Service land. Anglers with dogs like to come here to take advantage of the hot bite the lake has in the summer.

There are 205 campsites. Fees are $20 a night. From the junction of Highway 89 and U.S. 50, go north about two miles on Highway 89 to the Fallen Leaf Lake turnoff. Go left and drive 1.5 miles to the camping area. Call 530/543-2600 for park information. For reservations, call 877/444-6777.

If you prefer to be away from the madding crowd, the Desolation Wilderness is accessible from here. There you can camp in peace, except for the occasional twittering of songbirds. Camping here costs $5 per person per night for the first two nights. After that, there's no charge. You must have a permit. And unlike in many other wilderness areas, dogs must be leashed.

Fireside Lodge: What used to be an old rundown motel is now a sparkling, fun, super-dog-friendly lodging. The rooms all sport a unique country mountain theme, with names such as the True West Room, the Angler Room, and the Bear's Den Suite (our favorite). The rooms are all cheery log-cabin style, with beautiful river-rock gas fireplaces and decor that lives up to the room's name. Each room also has a microwave and little fridge.

But wait! That's not all. Stay here and you get to go to the lodge's super-cozy Emerald Gathering Room for a wonderful cocktail hour and an expanded continental breakfast. In winter, you'll find big pots of homemade soup and bread there for your enjoyment.

But there's still more! And this is the part your dog has been waiting for: The property backs up to national forest land, and you know how joyous national forests make dogs. In addition, use of the lodge's kayaks comes free with your room, and dogs are more than welcome to ride along. It's a 15-minute walk to the lake, so either someone at the lodge will drive the kayak to the lake for you, or you can do it yourself. (The staff will also tell you about some terrific paddling spots and beaches that swimming dogs adore.) And to top it off, all dogs who visit get dog cookies. Their people get doggy sheets to put on the beds and poop bags for those less-scenic moments.

Your dog can stay in your room while you're skiing or gambling as long as she's in a crate. This dogs-allowed-alone rule is a rarity in the area. Rooms are $69–195. Dogs are $20 extra, and require a $100 deposit. 515 Emerald Bay Road 96150; 530/544-5515 or 800/MYCABIN (800/692-2246); www.tahoefiresidelodge.com.

Holly's Place: The wonderfully cozy cabins on this 2.5-acre property are nestled under fragrant pines, and the property is completely enclosed by a six-foot-high wall of stacked firewood. That means well-behaved dogs can be off leash here! And children enjoy the place too: Kids get to use the sandbox in summer, play outdoor games, glide on sleds in winter, and even get to watch movies while eating hot popcorn. Please note that there are no in-room phones, and that maid service is available only by request during your stay. This is advertised as promoting much-sought privacy. Rates are $140–495. Dogs are $15 extra, and must get prior approval. The mailing address is P.O. Box 13197, South Lake Tahoe, CA 96151; the street address is 1201 Rufus Allen Boulevard 96150; 530/544-7040 or 800/745-7041; www.hollysplace.com.

Inn at Heavenly B&B Lodge: If you like mountains, trees, steam baths, saunas, and bed-and-breakfast inns, and if you really like your dog, come here! Dogs are welcome at this cozy bed-and-breakfast lodge, which is surrounded by a lovely wooded park. Most rooms have attractive river-rock gas fireplaces, patchwork quilts, and even log furniture. And unlike many other bed-and-breakfasts, each of the 14 rooms has its own bathroom and cable TV. (None of that business of sharing the WC with the neighbors while pining away for ESPN.) Rooms also have their own minifridges and microwaves. Human guests get to use the spa room (hot tub, steam bath, and sauna) privately for one hour per day. Rates are $69–160. Dogs are $20 extra. 1261 Ski Run Boulevard 96150; 530/544-4244 or 800/692-2246; www.innatheavenly.com.

Motel 6: Too many people have left their dogs alone in their rooms here. This is a huge no-no. The motel has kennel and dog-sitter info available now to help eliminate this problem. Rates are $45–65. 2375 Lake Tahoe Boulevard 95731; 530/542-1400.

Ridgewood Inn: Montana the Dog wrote to tell us about this cute, slightly upscale motel, with each room featuring a river-rock gas fireplace. The lodging's owners have a big, friendly yellow Lab (friendly, of course, is excess verbiage when describing a yellow Lab) who might greet you on your arrival. Rates are $62–89. Dogs are $10 extra. 1341 Emerald Bay Road 96150; 530/541-8589; www.ridgewoodinn.com.

Sandor's Chateau Motel: Sure, humans often get to use an exercise room when they stay at a hotel or motel. But what about dogs? Lucky dogs who stay at this chateau-style motel get their own version of an exercise room: a quarter-acre fenced dog-exercise area, where dogs can run around leash-free! There's also plenty of room for leashed dogs to explore around the motel grounds. If dogs are really lucky, they'll get to pal around there with Bear, the owner's aptly named jovial St. Bernard. "We want dogs to have fun here," says the owner. Dogs who help their people check in at the office get to partake in the equivalent of a candy jar: a little bowl of treats just for them. Rates are $55–95. 1137 Emerald Bay Road 96150; 530/541-6312 or 877/726-3677; www.tahoemotel.com.

South Lake Tahoe Reservation Bureau: Tired of motel roulette? Sick of toilet bowls with banners bragging about their sanitary conditions? You and your dog should consider phoning this reputable vacation rental bureau, where you can choose from dozens of dog-friendly cabins, condos, and houses. Many of the rentals even come with fenced-in yards. Rentals vary from studios to four-bedroom homes. Rates are $150–1,000. Dogs are $25 for the length of your stay. The agency works hand-in-hand with the Tahoe Keys Resort (see below), but these rentals are in areas other than the Keys'. 599 Tahoe Keys Boulevard 96151; 530/544-5397 or 800/462-5397; www.tahoevacationguide.com.

Spruce Grove: The cabins and suites here are really fun places to stay with a dog. All cabins are decorated in a vintage Tahoe-type theme. You'll find Field and Stream, which is billed as "the ultimate hideaway for the American angler," and the Bear's Den cabin, complete with a large river-rock fireplace. In addition, you and your pooch can stay at El Snowshoe, The Pioneer, and The Prospector, to name a few of the other theme cabins. While your dog may not give an arf about the decor, he'll be mighty happy to know that the whole property is fenced in. That means you can feel pretty secure in letting your pooch off leash if he's under voice control. Each cabin has a fully equipped kitchen and a gas fireplace. Gourmet coffee and tasty muffins are up for grabs in the morning. Rates are $150–295. 3597 Spruce Avenue 96150; 530/544-0549 or 800/777-0914; www.sprucegrovetahoe.com.

Stonehenge at Tahoe: Seven of the nine super-luxurious vacation rental homes offered by this agency welcome dogs. In one of the more unusual houses, guests have to enter a big stone cavern with a sod roof to get to the front door. Then there's another huge boulder in one end of the very large living room. (This one is aptly named Stonehenge, the agency's namesake.) The houses are so different and uniquely designed that it's hard to find any common words to describe them, except spacious and upscale. Rates range $400–1,000 nightly. For the budget-conscious, the agency offers a stunning cottage (really a house) on the Nevada section of the lake, for $175–250 nightly. The agency's mailing address is P.O. Box 9541 96158; 530/577-0732 or 800/822-1460; www.tahoestonehenge.com.

Tahoe Keys Resort: Dogs who like to have a home away from home, as opposed to a motel room away from home, will drool for joy when you spend your vacation here. And if your dog is a water dog, get out the drool bucket. The resort is a 750-acre community laced with 11 miles of inland waterways, right on the southern edge of Lake Tahoe. Each house is a waterfront home, situated on one of numerous lagoons. Rentals vary from studio condos to four-bedroom homes. Pooches are permitted in a bunch of the homes. Rates are $95–1,700 per night. Dogs require a $25 fee, which covers the length of your stay. 599 Tahoe Keys Boulevard 96151; 530/544-5397 or 800/462-5397; www.tahoevacationguide.com.

Tahoe Tropicana Lodge: You won't find Ricky Ricardo at this Tropicana, but at least your dog will be welcomed here. Rooms are $40–90. Dogs are $25 extra per stay. 4132 Cedar Avenue 96150; 530/541-3911; www.tahoetropicana.com.

Tahoe Valley Campground: This is an attractive campground for such a large one, with a total of 413 camping and RV sites gracing the place. You'll find a rec room, a heated pool, laundry facilities, a tennis court, and a playground, to name a few of the amenities. There's even a free casino shuttle bus that will shuffle you off to the wonders on the other side of the state border. (No dogs allowed, but that's OK since most dogs don't understand crapshooting or blackjack.) The Truckee River is about a quarter of a mile from the park, and there are plenty of trees surrounding the campground. A big surprise is that it's open year-round these days. Rates are $24–42. 1175 Melba Street 96158; 530/541-2222; www.rvonthego.com.

3 Peaks Resort and Beach Club: Ask for a remodeled room if you stay at this motel-like resort whose logo is an adorable St. Bernard dog wearing Hawaiian shorts. These rooms are reminiscent of cozy cabins, with pine paneling and pine furniture. A few have gas fireplaces, and some suites with kitchens are available. You'll pay the same price for a room that hasn't been remodeled, and unless you want your dog to think you have no taste, you don't want one of these rooms. One bizarre feature is the carpeting that's not only on the floor, but also on the walls. (At least it's not shag.) The grounds of the resort are a treat for dogs, with lots of grass and big trees to sniff out. Humans love the heated outdoor swimming pool and hot tub. People who stay here also get to enjoy a private gated beach nearby. Dogs have to remain on terra firma. Rates are $49–109, with suites running up to $229. Pets are $15 extra. 931 Park Avenue 96150; 800/331-3951; www.lake-tahoe-hotels.com.

Cool

By virtue of its name alone, this town southeast of Auburn is worth a stop. Unfortunately, Cool doesn't have many amenities for pooches who are just visiting. For this reason, we think the town should be renamed Kinda Cool. So far, residents aren't buying the idea.

PARKS, BEACHES, AND RECREATION AREAS

❸ Auburn State Recreation Area

🐾🐾🐾🐾 (See El Dorado County map on page 208)

This 30,000-acre park is just a couple of miles up Highway 49 from the main part of Cool. (Most of it is in Placer County, and it's described more fully in that chapter.) But there is a section you can hike with your dog that starts less than a half mile before the first bridge you come to after leaving Cool (going toward Auburn). The parking area and trailhead are unmarked, so be on the lookout for a dirt road that veers off sharply to the right. If you miss it, just turn around at the bridge and come back almost a half mile and you'll be there. 530/885-4527.

Pilot Hill

PARKS, BEACHES, AND RECREATION AREAS

❹ Folsom Lake State Recreation Area

🐾🐾🐾🐾 (See El Dorado County map on page 208)

A big part of this 12,000-acre lake is in El Dorado County, but it's listed under Folsom in Sacramento County.

Coloma

PARKS, BEACHES, AND RECREATION AREAS

❺ Marshall Gold Discovery State Historic Park

🐾🐾🐾 (See El Dorado County map on page 208)

James Marshall, whose discovery of gold in John Sutter's mill here started the Gold Rush, died a penniless recluse. But at least he had a dog-friendly state park dedicated to him.

Dogs are allowed in more places here than at most state parks. While they're banned from American River beaches and most trails, they can hang out with you at picnic areas and walk with you in the meadow behind the visitor center. They can stroll along Main Street and peer at historic buildings, including a replica of Sutter's Mill. Dogs are even permitted to accompany you to the Munroe Orchard, where you can pick a piece of fruit and sit under a tree to while away the afternoon while your friends pan for gold in the river.

Rates are $5 per car, and a dog fee may soon be instituted. (They called it a "nuisance fee." Jake would growl about that if he had a growling bone in his body.) The park is on Highway 49 between Placerville and Auburn. 530/622-3470.

Placerville

When this city was one of the great camps of Gold Country, it was first known as Dry Diggins. The name lasted about a year. In 1849, after a number of lynchings, the place became known as Hangtown.

People had it tough back then. But dogs may have it even tougher here today, since there are very few parks. Open land has been replaced by strip shopping centers and new housing. The name Placerville may have been good for welcoming suburbia, but dogs should be sorely disappointed at the changes the decades have brought to this city on the east side of the famous Mother Lode vein.

DIVERSION

Wine, Wine Everywhere: When you think of quality California wine, El Dorado County probably isn't the first vine-covered area that pops into your head. But the county's **vineyards and wineries,** small and family-operated, produce some surprisingly excellent wines. And the good news for your dog is that he doesn't have to be human to set paw on winery property: The majority of the 19 El Dorado Winery Association members permit well-behaved, leashed dogs to join you at their picnic areas. There's nothing like doing a little tasting (you'll have to split up your party so someone is always outside with the pooch), then a little buying, then a little picnicking.

Among the older and better-known wineries is the Boeger Winery, 1709 Carson Road, Placerville; 530/622-8094. Dogs are welcome at the picnic area here, as well as at several other Placerville wineries, including Holly's Hill Vineyards, 3680 Leisure Lane, 530/344-0227; Gold Hill Vineyard, 5660 Vineyard Lane, 530/626-6522; Lava Cap Winery, 2221 Fruitridge Road; 530/621-0175. Dog-friendly wineries can also be found in Camino, Fair Play, and Somerset. See www.eldoradowines.org for a list of area wineries.

Still, the historic downtown is a fun place to stroll with your dog. And you can even learn something about the old Gold Rush days if you visit Hangtown's Gold Bug Park.

PARKS, BEACHES, AND RECREATION AREAS

⑥ Hangtown's Gold Bug Park

🐾🐾🐾 (See El Dorado County map on page 208)

Dogs dig it here. But it's not the gold they dig (lucrative as they may be, such terrierlike habits are discouraged). It's the park itself. Gold Bug is the city's largest park. While dogs aren't allowed to run around without a leash, it's a great place for them to stretch their legs while they explore a park that was once home to 250 mines.

If you're traveling with another human, one of you can walk around the park's dirt paths with the dog or picnic in the shade of oaks and pines while the other visits the Gold Bug Mine, which bans dogs. The mine is an educational experience for anyone who ever wondered what it was like inside one of these places. Admission to the mine is $3 for adults. Half-pints are a buck. Quarter-pints (under five) are free. An additional $1 will rent you a fascinating audiotape-guided tour.

DIVERSION

To the Trees, If You Please: El Dorado County is home to dozens of **Christmas tree farms** and **apple growers** that welcome dogs. (Please, no leg lifts on the host trees.)

Some farms do double duty as Christmas tree farms and apple farms. Your dog can help you sniff out a tasty apple pie or fresh bag of apples at the Harris Tree Farm fruit stand and picnic area starting in August, and toward Christmas, he can watch as you choose and cut your own Christmas tree. (Dogs get all the easy jobs.) Harris is at 2640 Blair Road, in Pollock Pines; 530/644-2194. For a full listing of El Dorado County Christmas Tree Growers farms, see www.visit-eldorado.com/christmas.asp. Most permit leashed pooches.

Mother Lode Orchards has a big friendly black dog who welcomes visitors to the picnic tables, where you can feast on the 30 acres of orchards' peaches, plums, and apples. (You buy these already picked.) 4341 North Canyon Road, in Camino; 530/644-5101. A dog-friendly U-pick option is Hangtown Kid Apple Orchards, 2598 Mace Road, in Camino; 530/647-1810. A list of the county's many apple growers can be found at www.applehill.com.

The park is easily accessible from U.S. 50. Take the Bedford Avenue exit north for almost a mile and you're there. 530/642-5207; www.goldbug.org.

PLACES TO EAT

Noah's Ark: "Everybody should allow dogs!" exclaimed a dog-lovin' employee at the aptly named Noah's Ark. Buy your food inside this natural food market (doggy needs to stay outside) and eat it at the outdoor tables with your furry friend. You can buy soups, sandwiches, and all kinds of organic goodies. 535 Placerville Drive; 530/621-3663.

Sweetie Pie's: The owners describe themselves as "major dog lovers," so your dog will feel right at home at the umbrella-topped tables here. The muffins, fresh fruit, sandwiches, quiche, and homemade soups taste extra good when you know you're not getting the evil eye from the management. 577 Main Street; 530/642-0128.

PLACES TO STAY

Best Western Placerville Inn: You get a filling breakfast with your stay here. You also get to dip your paws in the heated outdoor pool. Dogs have no such luck, and they're $10–20 extra, depending on their size. Rates are $89–109. 6850 Green Leaf Drive 95667; 530/622-9100 or 800/854-9100.

Gold Trail Motor Lodge: There's plenty of shade on the well-landscaped grounds of this motel, a real plus in the hot summer months. Rates are $38–68. Dogs are $7–10 extra. 1970 Broadway 95667; 530/622-2906.

Mother Lode Motel: Rates are $54–78. Dogs are $10 extra. 1940 Broadway 95667; 530/622-0895.

Pollock Pines

PARKS, BEACHES, AND RECREATION AREAS

7 Sly Park Recreation Area

🐾🐾🐾 (See El Dorado County map on page 208)

Does your leashed dog like fun boating, terrific hiking, and watching people ride by on horses? Does she like camping, but prefer to do it in a somewhat civilized fashion? If so, the Jenkinson Lake camping area is for her. There are 190 sites in this year-round campground, so she'll never feel alone. Alas, she'll feel very dry here: No dogs are allowed to set paw in the lake. (Thanks to Dina Savoroski's dog for letting us know this sad fact. Jake the Water Dog sobbed when he read her letter.)

Reservations are accepted March–September Otherwise, sites are first-come, first-served. Sites are $20–25 a night. Dogs are an additional $2 nightly for the first two pooches. More dogs than two? They're free. If you come here only for the day, the entry fee is $8. From U.S. 50, go south on Sly Park Road for about five miles. 530/644-2545.

PLACES TO STAY

Sly Park Recreation Area: See Sly Park Recreation Area, above, for camping information.

TOIYABE NAT'L FOREST

88

Carson Pass EL. 8,573 ft.

88

Hope Valley

Markleeville

1 Kirkwood

ELDORADO NAT'L FOR.

Lower Blue Lake

TOIYABE NAT'L FOREST

2

89

Upper Blue Lake

Twin Lake

Meadow Lake

4

TOIYABE NAT'L FOREST

Molelumne R.

Ebbetts Pass EL. 8,730 ft.

Alpine Lake

STANISLAUS NAT'L FOREST

N. Fork Stanislaus

Carson River

Carson Fork Stanislaus River

N

W E

S

CHAPTER 21
Alpine County

More people live in one Los Angeles high-rise than in this entire county! With a population of only 1,200, Alpine County has plenty of room for a few good dogs. More than 90 percent of the land is public, most of it in the form of very dog-friendly national forests.

You'll find trailheads into the Eldorado, Stanislaus, and Toiyabe National Forests along Highways 88, 89, and 4. You can just pull over into a safe zone and hike with your dog if you know it's national forest land. As soon as you're away from roads and campgrounds, your dog can go leashless in nearly 800 square miles of meadows, alpine forests, and rocky mountains. There's one exception to this, just east of the county line in the Mokelumne Wilderness of Eldorado National Forest off Highway 88.

A drive along Highway 4 can be exciting as well as very scenic. The highway gets so narrow that eventually the stripes in the middle of the road disappear. It's steep and winding in parts, so tell your dog to look up if he's scared of heights. As you ascend to nearly 9,000 feet, the scenery becomes otherworldly.

PICK OF THE LITTER—ALPINE COUNTY

BEST DOGGY PHOTO ID
Kirkwood Ski and Summer Resort hikes,
Kirkwood (page 227)

BEST HOT WATER YOU CAN GET INTO
Grover Hot Springs State Park, Markleeville (page 230)

BEST PLACE TO STAY
Sorensen's Resort, Hope Valley (page 229)

BEST KIT-BUILT LODGING
Carson River Resort's 1940s Sears and Roebuck cabins,
Markleeville (page 231)

BEST MUSHY TIME
Kirkwood Ski Resort skijoring lessons,
Kirkwood (page 228)

Huge rock formations are everywhere. They're rounded from the passage of time and some are stacked in impossible configurations.

Since the road is so winding, it's a good idea to make frequent stops, especially if your dog starts turning green. At Ebbett's Pass (elevation 8,730 feet), you can pull over and take him out to a large meadow on your left or to the rocky hill on your right. Because it's part of the Stanislaus National Forest, he can go leashless. There are several campgrounds and limitless backcountry camping in the national forests along the way, so there's no shortage of places to pitch a tent.

Dogs also like to visit Mosquito Lake and Lake Alpine. Since there can be many other visitors, dogs should be leashed in these areas of Stanislaus National Forest.

The four seasons are magical in Alpine County. Springtime brings an incomparable carpet of wildflowers. Summer days rarely get too warm. When we last visited, it was mid-August. During the day, people were wearing sweaters. Dogs, even those sporting thick coats, weren't panting. In autumn, aspen and cottonwoods burst into magnificent oranges, yellows, and reds. Dogs who claim to have black-and-white vision may not appreciate it, but the seasonal change can be a bit of a thrill for their caretakers. During winter, Alpine County is a wonderland of white, but some of the mountain roads can be impassable. It's a good idea to call your destination to check road conditions before setting paw out of your front door.

NATIONAL FORESTS

The National Forests and Wilderness Areas resource at the back of this book has important information and safety tips on visiting national forests with your dog and has more information on the national forests listed below.

Eldorado National Forest
🐾🐾🐾🐾🐕

Stanislaus National Forest
🐾🐾🐾🐾🐕

Toiyabe National Forest
🐾🐾🐾🐾🐕

Kirkwood

Kirkwood, one of the best ski and summer recreation areas in California, is also quite accommodating to dogs. The town is split among three counties, but most people here consider Alpine County home.

PARKS, BEACHES, AND RECREATION AREAS

❶ Kirkwood Ski and Summer Resort
🐾🐾🐾🐾 (See Alpine County map on page 224)

During summer and these days, winter, you can't help but see dog after dog romping around this serene high Sierra playground. In summer, most of them have smiles on their slobbery faces because they're welcome to explore the resort's 12 miles of trails through meadows and up slopes and back bowl areas. They're supposed to be on leash, but it's a small price for your dog to pay to be able to tell his friends he vacationed here. In addition to wearing smiles, summer canine visitors can end up wearing a special mini-ski tag that serves as a hiking pass and doggy ID. "It's so cute!" says the dog-loving Shawna, who answers the phone here. And beyond cute, Shawna says the passes are functional: Kirkwood takes a photo of any dog who gets a pass and keeps the photo on file for reference if your dog should get lost. (Of course, this won't likely happen if your dog is leashed, but...) The pass/ID is $5.

In winter, you can learn how to cross-country ski with your pooch! (Please see the Diversion Get Mushy for more on this very cool way to spend a vacation with your dog.)

DIVERSION

Get Mushy: If you want to bone up on how to cross-country ski, you don't have to leave your pooch behind. Kirkwood Ski Resort actually hosts cross-country ski clinics for people who have dogs! You'll learn about the sport of **skijoring**, in which a rope is attached to a waist belt you wear and to your dog. It's a combination of cross-country skiing and mushing. You'll learn how to pick the right speed so you don't run over your dog or drag him along, or vice versa. You won't encounter real hills, so it doesn't get messy. When you're comfortable, you can take to the resort's skijoring trail! Call for prices and schedule. 209/258-6000; www.kirkwood.com.

The resort is about 60 miles northeast of Jackson, on Highway 88. You can't miss the signs for it. Once there, ask for a map of the trails from the general store/reservations desk. 209/258-6000; www.kirkwood.com.

PLACES TO EAT

Kirkwood Inn: This place has barely changed since it was built in 1864 by early settlers Zachary and Eliza Kirkwood. You'll still find bullet holes in the thick wood ceiling when you walk inside to order your down-home cooking, and the bar is the original one (except for a section a drunken woman crushed while dancing on it in the winter of 1992). Dogs like it here, but despite the place's wild and woolly past, they're relegated to the outdoor tables when they're not covered with snow. If you like burgers and steak, this is an excellent place to visit. The restaurant is at Highway 88, across from the entrance to Kirkwood Ski and Summer Resort (six miles west of Carson Pass); 209/258-7304.

PLACES TO STAY

Kirkwood Accommodations: From June through September, lucky dogs are allowed to stay in some of the lodges and condominiums at the Kirkwood Ski and Summer Resort. They're right across from the ski lifts, which won't matter to you in the summer. There's tons of hiking in the area, in addition to fishing, swimming, and general reposing in this peaceful Sierra setting. For more civilized relaxation, there are a pool and hot tub in the community center. Rates for the condos are $130–185 a night during summer. There's also a dog-friendly three-bedroom house available in summer. Rates are $450–600. Weekly and monthly rates are available for the condos and the house. Pooches require a $100 cash deposit and a $35 fee for their stay. The resort is about 60 miles northeast of Jackson, on Highway 88. You can't miss the signs. P.O. Box 1 95646; 209/258-8575 or 869/471-3932; www.kirkwoodaccommodations.com.

Hope Valley

PLACES TO EAT

Sorensen's Resort Cafe: See Sorensen's Resort (below) for more on this dog-friendly café.

PLACES TO STAY

Sorensen's Resort: This is a magical place to come with your dog. Six of the 33 cozy, nicely appointed cabins permit pooches, and some have gas log fireplaces for your happy dog to curl up in front of on a cold winter night. Several trails that start around the Sorensen property are ideal for hiking or cross-country skiing with your dog. You can just about ski right out your front door. There's an on-site café that's open for breakfast, lunch, and dinner, and in all but the most chilly months, the patio is open and welcomes dogs. Sorensen's is one-stop shopping for you and your smiling dog. Rates for the dog cabins vary seasonally, $95–400. Since not many places around here take dogs, these cabins are in high demand, so reserve well in advance of your stay. 14255 Highway 88 96120; 530/694-2203 or 800/423-9949; www.sorensensresort.com.

Markleeville

Jacob Marklee founded this Old West town in 1861 and spent the rest of his years—all three of them—here. In 1864, he was dead, the loser in a shoot-out with a fellow named H. W. Tuttle. Today, Markleeville has the distinction of being the county seat of the least-populous county in California.

PARKS, BEACHES, AND RECREATION AREAS

🐾 Grover Hot Springs State Park

🐾🐾🐾🐾 (See Alpine County map on page 224)

This is a rare bird for a state park—dogs are actually allowed to walk with you on trails. Leashed dogs can hike through ponderosa pine, incense cedars, and quaking aspen year-round. They're also allowed to camp with you in all four seasons. About the only thing they can't do is bask in the 105°F water in the pools or refresh themselves in the cold plunge area.

But that doesn't mean you have to deprive yourself of the possibly therapeutic effects of the waters. You and a friend can take turns. One can soak in the hot mineral water (it actually comes out of the ground at 148°F!) while the other takes the dog for a walk or on a minifishing trip at the creeks and lakes here. Then switch. This way, everyone gets to enjoy the best this park has to offer.

The day-use fee, which covers pool use, is $5 per adult, $2 per child. Sleeping at one of the 76 campsites costs $15–20. The park is three miles west of Markleeville, off Highway 88 on Hot Springs Road. Call 530/694-2248 for information. For reservations, call 800/444-7275.

PLACES TO STAY

Carson River Resort: Dogs and their people are welcome to stay in five of the seven rustic, clean cabins set among the big pines by the east fork of the Carson River. One is an old miner's cabin, and the rest were built from Sears and Roebuck cabin kits from the 1940s. They're real classics. Most have kitchens, and all have a picnic table and barbecue grill. They like dogs here. "The manager was incredibly friendly to Lucky," writes Sara Peterson, who helped us sniff out this place. She also loved the "lovely quilts and warm blankets." The River Cabin has a woodstove, to add to the comfy feel. (If you're a fan of old, little-known novels, stay in this cabin. It's the backdrop for the 1927 romantic novel *The Looted Bonanza*.) Rates are $70–140. Dogs are $15 extra. P.O. Box 457 96120; 877/694-2229; www.carsonriverresort.com.

Grover Hot Springs State Park: See Grover Hot Springs State Park, above, for camping information.

CHAPTER 22

Amador County

Amador County is a place too many people drive through without stopping to take a look around. Highway 88 makes it easy to cruise through this narrow county on the way to another destination. But if you drive past here with blinders on, not only are you missing some quaint old Gold Rush towns, you're also bypassing some of the most unusual vista points in California.

Among the sights you should try to take in is the rocky terrain of the Devil's Garden in the eastern part of the county along Highway 88 in Eldorado National Forest. Nearby are several trailheads leading into sections of this vast forest where dogs can usually prance about leashless. Eldorado National Forest is the only swath of public land in Amador County where dogs can experience this blissful freedom.

NATIONAL FORESTS

The National Forests and Wilderness Areas resource at the back of this book has important information and safety tips on visiting national forests with your dog and has more information on Eldorado National Forest.

PICK OF THE LITTER—AMADOR COUNTY

BEST LEASH-FREE HIKING
Eldorado National Forest (page 234)

BEST DIGS IN A QUASI-GHOST TOWN
St. George Hotel, Volcano (page 235)

BEST POOCHY POOL PARTY
At the Three Dog Bakery, Sutter Creek (page 236)

Eldorado National Forest

Sutter Creek

John Sutter, who owned the mill where gold was first discovered in the Mother Lode, also had his Midas-touch hand in a nearby creek. The creek was named after him, and the town came next.

PARKS, BEACHES, AND RECREATION AREAS

🟦 Minnie Provis Park

🐾🐾 (See Amador County map on page 232)

How often does a dog get to visit a park named after a city clerk? Minnie Provis Park, set in the heart of historic Sutter Creek, may be the only one with such a namesake. Minnie was Sutter Creek's first city clerk. She must have been a good one.

This small, green park is ideally situated if you and your leashed dog happen to be exploring the old downtown section of Sutter Creek. The park, which has its own poop-bag dispenser, is just behind City Hall. Exit Highway 49 at Church Street and go east a half block. Park on the street. 209/267-5647.

PLACES TO EAT

Three Dog Bakery: While walking down the streets of historic Sutter Creek, stop in this for-dogs-only bakery. Any baked treat your dog could wish for is available here. The goodies look so much like human food that you'll be hard-pressed not to sneak one for yourself. (See the Diversion Party with Your Pooch for info on the bakery's fun year-round dog events.) 16 Eureka Street; 209/267-1500.

Volcano

The '49er miners thought a volcano had formed the bowl-shaped valley here, thus the name. But there is no volcano in Volcano. There is, however, a very picturesque semighost town with some fine remnants of the Mother Lode days. Visit in early spring to view Daffodil Hill, which becomes a resplendent sea of yellow—a sight that may be lost on your dog if she really does see in only black and white.

PLACES TO STAY

St. George Hotel: Dogs come really close to staying in a National Historic Landmark hotel when they visit here. The main building of the hotel is a three-story brick structure built during the Gold Rush. Alas, dogs can't sleep there, but they're welcome to stay at the beautiful bungalow garden room annex, in an elegant room with hardwood floors, lace curtains, and an antique sewing cabinet. It'll remind your dog of Grandma's house. The bungalow is set behind the hotel and overlooks the inn's beautiful gardens. Thanks to Fergie the Traveling Boxer for sniffing out this gem for us. Rates are $97–102. Dogs are $20 extra. 16104 Main Street 95689; 209/296-4458; www.stgeorgehotel.com.

Pine Grove

PARKS, BEACHES, AND RECREATION AREAS

🐾🐾 Indian Grinding Rock State Historic Park

🐾🐾 (See Amador County map on page 232)

Dogs aren't permitted on trails here, but they are allowed on paved walkways and can visit bits of the reconstructed Miwok village and sniff at the old grinding rock. Leashed dogs can even read some of the petroglyphs around the park if they're of the erudite ilk.

Day-use visits cost $6 per carload. There are 23 campsites, available on a first-come, first-served basis. Sites are $18. The park is about halfway between Pine Grove and Volcano, on Pine Grove-Volcano Road. 209/296-7488.

PLACES TO STAY

Indian Grinding Rock State Historic Park: See Indian Grinding Rock State Historic Park, above, for camping information.

Jackson

Jackson is one Old West town where there's still plenty of evidence of a rich and colorful heritage. The streets of downtown look as if they were pulled from a Hollywood back lot. You can even hear lively piano music pouring out of the classic old National Hotel (no dogs allowed).

DIVERSION

Party with Your Pooch: The **Three Dog Bakery** in historic Sutter Creek offers yummy, fresh-baked dog treats, so it's worth a stop during your trip to this cute town. But what sets a dog's tail to wagging even harder is that the bakery is pooch-party central during the warmer months. Typical warm-weather activities at the little outdoor "yard" area (normally paved, but covered with artificial turf for special events) include pool parties (OK, wading pool parties), barbecues, and doggy ice cream socials. In addition, there are celebrations and photo ops at Halloween, Christmas, and Easter. You don't need an invitation to attend, just a pooch with a penchant for parties. The bakery is just off Highway 49 at 16 Eureka Street; 209/267-1500.

Dogs are welcome to stroll through the historic downtown district with you. A couple of stores that sell goods reminiscent of the Gold Rush era might allow you in with your dog. These shop owners asked Joe not to tell anyone he shopped there, and we've yet to divulge the names.

The city has only a couple of parks, but there's no shortage of restaurants that will let your dog dine outside with you during good weather.

PARKS, BEACHES, AND RECREATION AREAS

🐾 Kennedy Tailing Wheels Park

🐾🐾 (See Amador County map on page 232)

This is the less lovely of the two larger city parks. Instead of grass, there's usually dirt underfoot. But there's plenty of shade from large oak trees, so your leashed dog will be comfortable as you walk around learning about the history of the gold mines from the kiosks and placards here. The park is famous for its huge tailing wheels, built to carry nongold waste away to nearby ponds. (Boy dogs: Keep your legs down. These are antiques!)

Follow North Main Street to the northern part of the city, where the name of the street changes to Jackson Gate Road. Big signs mark the park on the east side of the street. 209/223-1646.

🐾 Detert Park

🐾🐾 (See Amador County map on page 232)

Does your pup like square dancing? Then dog-si-do on over to this pleasant community park's bandstand. Two local square dancing clubs practice here some enchanted evenings, and if you're lucky, you might get to watch (or take part in) some of the finest square dancing around.

If your dog prefers to stroll (on leash), the park has lush lawns and many shady trees. For the kids, there's a swimming pool and a unique playground. The park is an ideal stop if you're visiting the historic part of town. It's just east of Highway 49/88, north of Hoffman Street. 209/223-1646.

PLACES TO EAT

Mel and Faye's Diner: Down a burger and fries while at the "to go" patio with your dog. 205 North Highway 49; 209/223-0853.

PLACES TO STAY

Amador Motel: Dogs, if you want to feel mighty welcome, trot on over to this motel. "I'd rather have dogs here than children," says Mary, the owner. She'll even let pooches run free in the big backyard area here. All this made me realize Mary is a smart woman, but when she told me "your book is my favorite book," I realized she also has very good taste. Rates are $42–58. 12408 Kennedy Flat Road 95642; 209/223-0970.

Jackson Gold Lodge: Even though this lodge is just a bone's throw from Highway 49, it's tucked away on a steep incline so it's fairly well sheltered from traffic noise. Dogs feel perfectly at home in the basic motel rooms and duplex-style cottages here, and the pool provides welcome relief after a hot day of exploring in Gold Country. The lawn here is advertised as "perfect for letting your pets run around, or your kids." Rates are $55–110. Dogs are $10 extra. 850 North Highway 49 95642; 209/223-0486.

Ione

PARKS, BEACHES, AND RECREATION AREAS

5 Charles Howard Park

😊😊 (See Amador County map on page 232)

This is your basic community park. Nice trees, nice grass, nice cemetery. Keep in shape together by jogging on the track that goes around the park. It's at Brickyard Road and Church Street. 209/274-2412.

6 Lake Camanche

😊😊😊 (See Amador County map on page 232)

See the listing for Lake Camanche in the Valley Springs section of the Calaveras County chapter for details. Camanche Village is just north of Lake Camanche's north shore.

PLACES TO EAT

Erma's Diner: Burgers are the specialty of the house at Erma's. Eat lunch with your pooch at the two picnic tables out front. 4 Plymouth Highway; 209/274-4116.

CHAPTER 23

Calaveras County

There are only four traffic lights in this entire Mother Lode county, and they're very new. Only one town (Angels Camp) is incorporated. If you want to mall-hop, you have to drive at least 70 miles. And just about every pickup truck has a dog.

"This is where dogs are still dogs, and there may be more of them than of us people," explained Pat Mulgrew, the resident caretaker of a park in the "town" of Murphys. "It's very old California. There's a leash law and it should be obeyed. But local dogs often choose to walk on their own, visit the park, and hang out with their friends. It's just that kind of place."

At least it's that way until the rest of the world moves in with all its ugly baggage. The folks at the Calaveras Lodging and Visitors Association boast that this is one of the fastest-growing counties in California. They're trying to attract more and more companies so they can bring in more residents. The real-estate business is booming. Visit while you can, before this historic land succumbs to suburban sprawl.

PICK OF THE LITTER—CALAVERAS COUNTY

BEST OFF-LEASH HIKING
Stanislaus National Forest (page 240)

BEST BONES TO PICK
Stories in Stones, Angels Camp (page 244)

NATIONAL FORESTS

The National Forests and Wilderness Areas resource at the back of this book has important information and safety tips on visiting national forests with your dog and has more information on the Stanislaus National Forest.

Stanislaus National Forest

🐾🐾🐾🐾🏃

About one-third of Calaveras County has the privilege of being part of Stanislaus National Forest.

Arnold

This is a fun Old West town that shares its name with the pig on *Green Acres.* Joe Dog discovered that it's not mere coincidence. If you're good and hungry, visit the dog-friendly restaurants he scouted out and you'll discover why.

PARKS, BEACHES, AND RECREATION AREAS

1 Calaveras Big Trees State Park

🐾🐾🐾 (See Calaveras County map on page 238)

Dogs aren't permitted on the trails here, but nothing's stopping them from hiking along the fire roads and paved roads. "You and your dog might see more wilderness on these fire roads than you would on the regular trails," says interpretive ranger Joe Von Herrman.

The giant sequoias aren't accessible from the fire roads, but you'll probably pass by some of the largest sugar pines in existence. Depending on which roads you take, you could hike close to the Stanislaus River, pass by a historic logging railroad, or walk through chaparral-covered slopes and fir-filled forests.

For $1 you can buy a map of the fire roads and trails at the entry kiosk. The day-use fee is $6. There are 129 campsites. Sites are $19. The park is four miles northeast of Arnold, on Highway 4. Follow the signs. For camping reservations, call 800/444-7275. For park information, phone 209/795-2334.

PLACES TO EAT

Blue Coyote Cafe: Dogs feel a kinship with this place. Is it the water the servers give to dog visitors, or is it all in the name? Bring along your poochy dining companion and find out while eating great Southwest grub at the four outdoor tables. 1224 Oak Circle; 209/795-2872.

Giant Burger: Forget about restaurants such as Stars and Chez Panisse. Dogs like it plain and simple. And big. And beefy. Jake gives the food here his top rating: four paws and the big drool. Check it out with your dog at the 10 outdoor tables. 846 Highway 4; 209/795-1594.

PLACES TO STAY

Calaveras Big Trees State Park: See Calaveras Big Trees State Park, above, for camping information.

Ebbett's Pass Lodge: Rates for family cabins are $42–115. Dogs are $5 extra. 1173 Highway 4 95223; 209/795-1563.

Meadowmont Lodge: Huge dogs can't stay here, nor can dogs who shed a lot, but all others are welcome. (Big, shedding Jake had better look elsewhere.) Actually, if you bring a kennel or your dog's bed, you'll have a better chance of staying here with your large or shed-prone dog, especially if she's clean. Rates are $69–99. Dogs are $10 extra. It's at Country Club Drive and Highway 4. The mailing address is P.O. Box E 95223; 209/795-1394.

Sierra Vacation Rentals: Rent a cabin or mountain chalet to take your favorite canine companion and a few friends for an extra-special vacation getaway. All of the rentals have fireplaces or wood-burning stoves for those cold winter nights. Rates for up to eight people and a dog are $165–250 for the first night and $100–175 for each additional night. Dogs require a $200 deposit. P.O. Box 1080 CA 95223; 209/795-2422 or 800/995-2422; www.sierravacationrentals.com.

Valley Springs

PARKS, BEACHES, AND RECREATION AREAS

❷ Lake Camanche

🐾🐾🐾 (See Calaveras County map on page 238)

Come here during the off-season, when it's not too hot or too inundated by water-skiers, and your dog will have a delightful visit. Pooches aren't allowed on trails here, but the land is very open, with scattered oaks on rolling hills and lakeside flats. Dogs can walk anywhere you do, as long as you stay off the trails.

Your dog can dip her paws in the water, but since she's supposed to be leashed, she can't pull an Esther Williams. The fishing is fantastic in the spring and early summer. If thoughts of catching bass, bluegill, or trout keep you awake at night, come here, fulfill your dreams, and rest easy.

There are 300 campsites, with rates of $21 a night. Dogs are $12 extra. Sites are open year-round on a first-come, first-served basis, although reservations are available for holiday weekends. The day-use fee is $7.50 per car, with that extra $2 charge for hairy beasts. The lake is north of Highway 12 in the easternmost part of the county. Follow the signs seven miles to the entrance. 209/763-5178.

🔳 New Hogan Reservoir
🐾🐾🐾 (See Calaveras County map on page 238)

It's cheaper (free, in fact) to visit here than Lake Camanche, and leashed dogs actually get to romp around on the trails. The terrain is about the same, with open land, rolling hills, rocks, dirt, and some oaks. Dogs can dip their paws in the lake, and they can even join you in your boat as the two of you pursue supper.

Water-skiers can make it noisy in the summer, but there are still plenty of places to escape most of the madness. The lake has 50 miles of shoreline, and partiers can't overtake every inch of it.

There are 182 campsites. Nightly rates range $10–16. For reservations phone 877/444-6444. From Highway 26 in the Valley Springs area, you can't miss the signs for the lake. It's about three miles to the entrance. 209/772-1343.

PLACES TO STAY

Lake Camanche: See Lake Camanche, above, for camping information.

New Hogan Reservoir: See New Hogan Reservoir, above, for camping information.

San Andreas

PARKS, BEACHES, AND RECREATION AREAS

🔳 Nielsen Park
🐾🐾 (See Calaveras County map on page 238)

This is a fine place to stop with your leashed pooch during your Gold Country explorations. It's grassy, shady, and set along the refreshing San Andreas Creek.

The park is on Main Street, just east of Highway 49 and close to the local visitor center. There's no official phone number.

PLACES TO STAY

Courtyard Bed and Breakfast: This is a truly enchanting inn. Dogs, don't tell a soul about it. It's our little secret. One of the two rooms here is so romantic it could make a grown dog blush. It's the honeymoon suite, complete with a baby grand piano, private access, a private deck, and a fireplace. There's even a stained glass window over the bath, for those who like to watch Mr. Bubble in living color. The other room is also enchanting, with French blue highlights and oak and wicker furniture.

Hungry travelers like the fact that refreshments are served upon arrival. In the morning, fresh-brewed coffee is delivered to your room. Then you can amble down to the inn's cheery breakfast room, or in good weather, outside to the deck, where you can eat a big breakfast under the shade of a walnut tree. (Dogs prefer the latter option.) If your muscles are aching after a long drive, soak in the outdoor hot tub here. No dogs in the hot tub, though; they have to settle for a good back rub.

The rate for the suite is a mere $100. The other room is $90. 334 West Saint Charles Street 95249; 209/754-1518.

Murphys

PARKS, BEACHES, AND RECREATION AREAS

5 Murphys Park

🐾🐾🐾 (See Calaveras County map on page 238)

This is where the local dogs hang out. They like the shade, they enjoy the creek that flows through here year-round, and they appreciate each other's company. Many of them don't even wait for their owners to leash them up and walk them here. They head over by themselves. "It's breaking the rules, but they don't get themselves in trouble and they have real street smarts," says Pat Mulgrew, a park caretaker.

They also have good taste. The creek here is large, with a wooden footbridge you can cross to walk on the shadier, more secluded side of the park. It's at Main and South Algiers Streets. For more info, call Ron at Murphy's Silver Company (that's how things like parks departments work in this neck of the woods). 209/728-2126.

Angels Camp

You can still check out the saloon in the Angels Hotel, on Main Street, where a barkeep told 29-year-old Mark Twain the tale that inspired his first published short story, "The Notorious Jumping Frog of Calaveras County."

DIVERSION

Sniff Out Some Old Bones: Stories in Stones is an earth-science store that feels almost like a small museum. Fossils, rocks, shells, and minerals are labeled in a scientific way and set in cabinets. But unlike in a museum, you can buy almost anything you see here. You'll also find jewelry, educational books and kits, beads, and gift items, should old rocks not light your fire.

The owners and staff here adore dog visitors and welcome them inside. Even with all the tempting, ancient, crunchy items sitting around on the shelves, there haven't been many doggy faux pas here. Once, a little cocker spaniel came in, grabbed a preserved alligator head from a cabinet, and proudly paraded it around the store. When he finally spit out the gator head, it was undamaged, except for a little drool. "It was very funny," says a long-time employee.

The store is in the heart of old Angels Camp, at 1249 South Main Street; 209/736-1300; www.stories-in-stones.com.

Since the story was set in this dog-friendly land, it wouldn't have been complete without an interlude about a dog. The one in Twain's story was named Andrew Jackson, and he was apparently a bulldog. Twain's narrative could easily have been called "The Notorious Fighting Dog of Calaveras County," but publishers may not have jumped at it.

Fighting dogs aren't welcome here, but jumping frogs have never been forgotten. Each year, the town hosts the world-famous Jumping Frog Jubilee. As you may have guessed, dogs are not particularly welcome.

PARKS, BEACHES, AND RECREATION AREAS

⑥ Tryon Park

🐾🐾 (See Calaveras County map on page 238)

You and your gold-digging canine can pan for gold at Angels Creek, which runs right through this small park. It's a good place to take a rest if you're traveling on Highway 4. The park is on Highway 4 at Booster Way. 209/736-2181.

⑦ Utica Park

🐾🐾 (See Calaveras County map on page 238)

Mark Twain's statue is here, and your leashed dog is welcome if he promises not to do leg lifts on it. (Twain may have been amused, but it's just not a respectful way to treat the memory of someone who wrote so much good stuff about dog beasts.)

The park covers only 2.63 acres (you can afford to measure land that's this small by the hundredth of an acre), but it seems a good deal bigger. There's plenty of grass for rolling on and plenty of trees for shading you on warmer days. During the summer, you and your dog can attend a few free concerts here. The park is conveniently situated on Highway 49/Main Street at Sam's Way. 209/736-2181.

🐾 New Melones Reservoir

🐾🐾🐾 (See Calaveras County map on page 238)

When the lake is full, the five-mile trail that meanders around part of it may actually come close to the shore. But usually you and your leashed dog will have to be content wandering around the rolling foothills, among small scrub oaks that provide little shade. In the summer, it's probably not worth the visit. But the rest of the year, the hiking is pleasant—and the scenery is quite breathtaking in the spring.

Fishing isn't the best in the area, but in the spring the bass bite isn't bad, especially at the lake's northern arms. Your dog is welcome to wet his paws while you fish from shore or to join you on your fishing boat.

There are 300 campsites. They cost $16 a night. (Walk-ins are $12.) For reservations phone 877/444-6777. There's no day-use fee. From Angels Camp, head south on Highway 49 and follow the signs to the lake's north end. 209/536-9094.

PLACES TO EAT

Mr. B's Frosty: Share a shake with your pooch on the patio of this fast-food eatery. 22 North Main Street; 209/736-4312.

PLACES TO STAY

Best Western Cedar Inn and Suites: "This is one of those places where the room is bigger than your house," wrote an impressed dog and his human. "You should check it out." Indeed we did, and it's a modern-yet-homey, clean place to stay when visiting this historic area. (The room size is impressive, and the suites could rival the size of some small houses. Some suites even have a gas fireplace.) People like the outdoor pool and whirlpool, and dogs like getting the crumbs from your continental breakfast. Rates are $99–169. Dogs are $10 extra. 444 South Main Street 95222; 209/736-4000 or 800/767-1127; www.bestwesternangelscamp.com.

New Melones Reservoir: See New Melones Reservoir, above, for camping information.

CHAPTER 24

Tuolumne County

For any dogs who don't know how to pronounce the name of this county, think of what you'd say if someone asked you, "To whom should I give this huge, rare steak?" You'd probably pipe up and shout, "To all o' me!" or something like that. And that's close enough.

Tuolumne is a colorful Mother Lode county, with many exciting adventures awaiting dogs and their people. Be sure not to miss Jamestown or the Columbia State Historic Park. Dogs adore these places (during off-season when they're not so crowded).

NATIONAL FORESTS

The National Forests and Wilderness Areas resource at the back of this book has important information and safety tips on visiting national forests with your dog and has more information on the Stanislaus National Forest.

PICK OF THE LITTER—TUOLUMNE COUNTY

BEST LIVING GHOST TOWN
Columbia State Historic Park, Columbia (page 249)

MOST HISTORIC INN
National Hotel, Jamestown (page 251)

MOST DOG-FRIENDLY PLACE TO STAY
Groveland Hotel, Groveland (page 256)

BEST EYEFUL FOR DOGS
Tom Fraser's Carriage Tours horse heinies,
Jamestown (page 252)

BEST GOLD-COUNTRY ADVENTURE
Gold Prospecting Expeditions, Jamestown (page 253)

Stanislaus National Forest

There are plenty of places in this stunning forest where you can pull off along the northeast section of Highway 108 to hike or camp.

NATIONAL PARKS

Yosemite National Park
😊😊😊

Yosemite has a bad reputation among dogs. Some of it's deserved, some isn't. (See the full listing in the Mariposa County chapter.)

Strawberry

PLACES TO STAY

Cabins at Strawberry: Chocolate Lab Reina loves to greet fellow canines as they arrive for their stay at these very upscale cabins. "She thinks she owns the place," says Mary, who really does.

Three of the 10 cabins allow dogs. They're actually not so much cabins as two-story houses with an airy cabin ambience. Each has three bedrooms, two bathrooms, a gas fireplace, very tasteful decor, a fully equipped kitchen, and a large fenced deck. Most overlook the river, which can be a deliciously tortuous view for water dogs such as Jake, who sit there staring in anticipation at the flowing water, riveted…waiting…trembling. Normal dogs (sorry, Jake) simply enjoy the earthy scents and the surrounding pines, cedars, and firs.

Rates are $129–190. There's a $100 pooch deposit. 31888 Highway 108 95375; 209/965-0885 or 888/965-0885; www.strawberrycabins.com.

Rivers Resort: If you and your dog want to stay in cabins right on the Stanislaus River, rent one of the 14 very cozy cabins here. The cabins were recently upgraded (the place was formerly the Sparrow Resort), and they're better than ever. Humans drool over the large fireplaces in some cottages, and they love the quality wood interiors and the heated pool that's available in warmer months. Dogs go gaga over the fact that the national forest surrounds this resort. Joe Dog loved to fall asleep to the sound of the river. If you don't want to get away from it all, fear not—there's cable TV.

Cottages range in size 1–4 bedrooms, and rates are $90–275. Weekly rates are available. There's a $150 deposit for dogs. The deposit smarts, but you can use your credit card. There's no street address, but the resort is one of a few businesses on Highway 108 in Strawberry. The mailing address is P.O. Box 81 95375; 209/965-3278 for information, or 800/514-6777; www.gorr.com.

Mi-Wuk Village

PLACES TO STAY

Mi-Wuk Village Inn and Resort: The country-style rooms at this nice little motel have VCRs, so if all the nature around here is just too natural for you, snuggle up with your dog in front of a campy old flick. Rates are $79–145. Pooches are $10 extra. 24680 Highway 108 95346; 209/586-3031 or 800/549-7886; www.miwukvillageinn.com.

Columbia

PARKS, BEACHES, AND RECREATION AREAS

■ Columbia State Historic Park

🐾🐾🐾🐾 (See Tuolumne County map on page 246)

This park is actually a ghost town from the Gold Rush. But it's preserved in such a manner that it still has a pulse. It's alive. You can get a haircut at the state's oldest barbershop, sip sarsaparilla at a saloon, and buy old-style dry goods at one of the 1850s stores.

Be sure to bring a friend if you want to enter these establishments, because dogs have to stay outside (and be leashed), and you shouldn't leave them tied up, even for a few minutes. Just take turns dog-sitting.

But you don't have to go into the buildings to enjoy this town. The dogs and I like to saunter down the streets (no cars allowed!), kicking up dust as we amble along. We can stop and look inside these wonderful old buildings, but we get along fine without having to actually go inside. No shopping means no cash outflow. Since there's no admission fee at this "living museum," it's a very cheap date.

To give a dog a break from all the history here, go to the old schoolhouse and find the adjacent Karen Bakersville Smith Memorial Trail (named after a local teacher who died in a car crash). It's only a little over a half mile long, but it's wonderful to spy on nature as you hike through meadows and oak woodlands.

Please don't bring a dog here during the summer, unless it's raining or at least threatening to. It gets torturously crowded. We last visited in late fall, when the weather was perfect and the park almost empty.

Stop by the park headquarters and pick up a brochure outlining a 1.5-hour tour. From Highway 49, drive north on Parrott's Ferry Road/County Road E18. The entrance is in just over 1.5 miles, and it's on your right. 209/532-3184 or 209/588-9128; www.columbiacalifornia.com.

PLACES TO EAT

The Lickskillet: OK, we promise the name has nothing to do with the fact that this excellent restaurant welcomes dogs to dine at its outdoor tables. Dogs don't get to lick the skillets, but they do lick their chops over the unique cuisine and dog-friendly attitude here. "Dogs get water before their owners get a menu," says Peg, one of the dog-lovin' owners. The Lickskillet's 35 outdoor tables are a favorite hangout for local dogs and their people. The restaurant is open Wednesday–Sunday for dinner, and Thursday–Sunday for lunch. As with most other local eateries, the outdoor tables go south in the winter, so dogs are wise to come here in the warmer eight or nine months of the year. 11256 State Street; 209/536-9599.

PLACES TO STAY

Columbia Gem Motel: The "motel" name of this little gem, tucked under a canopy of pines and sequoias a bone's throw from Columbia State Historic Park, doesn't really do it justice. Only four units are of the motel persuasion. Seven are log cabins, with warm and cozy interiors (which, fortunately, are cool and cozy in summer).

The Gem (I can't in good conscience write "motel") is set on an acre of lovely manicured land, which leashed dogs are free to peruse as long as their humans promise to scoop the poop. Be aware that Baby, the owner's friendly cat, may be wandering around the property while you are. If your dog is like Jake, keep a tight hold of that leash.

Rates are $69–129, or $158 for a cabin that sleeps up to eight. 22131 Parrott's Ferry Road 95310; 209/532-4508 or 866/436-6685; www.columbiagem.com.

Jamestown

Jamestown was one of Bill Dog's favorite places to visit. During off-season, it's so uncrowded that he felt like one of the locals in this small Mother Lode town. That's when the town stops being quaint and becomes a real Old West hangout. Bill liked to sit on a bench outside one of the dusty buildings and listen to a couple of old natives tell their stories. But more than anything else, he enjoyed wearing his rust-colored bandanna around his shiny black neck. He knew he looked devastating.

Dogs can really have fun here. Between panning for gold, riding in a horse-drawn carriage, and exploring this colorful old town, they'll have enough entertainment to last them until their next vacation.

PARKS, BEACHES, AND RECREATION AREAS

🖻 New Melones Reservoir

🐾🐾🐾 (See Tuolumne County map on page 246)

Since the bulk of the lake (and the best fishing) is on the Calaveras County side, you'll find its description in the Angels Camp section of that chapter.

PLACES TO EAT

Jimtown Frostie: Joan, the manager here, will be glad to give your pooch a drink of water and maybe even a meat patty or a dab of Frostie ice cream. Humans can eat here, too. Pooches and their people get to eat at the patio seating. The restaurant is at the corner of Main Street and Highway 108; 209/984-3444.

Motherlode Coffee Shop: Dogs like it here because the people are so pleasant. We didn't go to this one in person, but Fergus the intrepid canine correspondent told us about it, and he knows a dog-friendly place when he sees one. Dine at the benches out front or the tables on the patio. 18169 Main Street; 209/984-3386.

PLACES TO STAY

National Hotel: Want some luxury with your history? Try this enchanting place. Built in 1859, it's one of the oldest continuously running hotels in California. Your dog can't wet his whistle at the old-fashioned saloon downstairs,

DIVERSION

Get Hot to Trot: Want a terrific way to experience Jamestown with your well-behaved pooch? Try **Tom Fraser's Carriage Tours.** You and your dog will ride in an antique carriage while a beautiful horse pulls you along the historic streets. But when you talk with your dog after your trip, you'll realize that the two of you had completely different experiences.

What humans see: antique shops, wooden sidewalks, great Old West buildings, old trains, and tourists taking pictures.

What dogs see: a horse's butt, a horse's butt, a horse's butt, a passing cat, and a horse's butt.

Co-owner Jan Fraser says she and her husband, Tom, love having quiet dogs as riders. "For most travelers, their pets are like their kids. How can we say no?"

The price is right. A 20-minute ride is $6 per adult, $4 per child. Dogs have to sit on the floor, and they ride free. The carriages load at the park on Main Street. Rides are by reservation. 209/984-3125.

---

but he'll probably be too busy admiring the simple antique decor in your room to notice. Unlike in the old days, the hotel now provides private bathrooms. Rates are $90–140. Dogs are $10 extra. 77 Main Street 95327; 209/984-3446 or 800/894-3446; www.national-hotel.com.

Royal Carriage Inn: This Victorian/Western-style inn was built by a man named Royal H. Rushing, thus the name. ("Rushing Carriage Inn" would have created a rather odd image.) The main building here looks like something you'd see on a Hollywood backlot, but it's not where dogs get to stay. In back of the hotel's lovely garden are a few cute cottages. Dogs are welcome at one of these, which is actually half of a duplex. It's not a historic building like its tall, stately sister up front, and no one would ever want to shoot a scene for a Western here. But there is a Hollywood/Western link: According to the inn's owner, Dennis, Clint Eastwood once stayed in that very cottage. Who knows…your dog may still be able to detect his scent.

The humans in your party can enjoy the sumptuous parlor in the main building, because that's where continental breakfast is served. (You should probably take turns dining, because dogs mustn't be left alone in the cottage.) The cottage rate is $125 –150. 18239 Main Street 95327; 209/984-5271; www.royalcarriageinn.com.

DIVERSION

Hit the Mother Lode: Cowabunga! No, er, Eureka! Aroooo! You and your dog will be hopping around like Yosemite Sam if you find a few specks of gold around here.

The folks at **Gold Prospecting Expeditions** say they've never met a dog who didn't like helping his owner pan for gold. You and your dog can take a walking tour guided by a prospector, and then get down to the business of panning. You keep what you find—and the folks here say you'll always find something in their special section of the Mother Lode.

If your dog can pan like Twinkles, the company's former resident poodle, you'll be rich. Twinkles used to stick her head underwater in a panning trough and come up with a gold nugget every time. Of course, she'd been trained, and the nugget was always there, so don't be too disappointed if your dog doesn't scoop up the down payment for your new house. (Sweet Twinkles is now panning for gold in Dog Heaven.)

Prices start at $30 per adult for a nearby 1–2-hour session. Kids 13–17 are half price. Under that, they're free, as are their dog friends. Reservations are appreciated, even if just a day ahead of time, to ensure having enough guides. Prospecting Expeditions is at 18170 Main Street, Jamestown, CA 95327; 209/984-GOLD (209/984-4653) or 800/596-0009; www.goldprospecting.com.

Sonora

This is the county seat of Tuolumne County and it's a real charmer. A stroll through the colorful downtown area with your leashed dog is a fun way to feel out the town's history of bullfights, bear fights, and gold camp justice. If you like an Old West town with an attitude, you'll enjoy Sonora.

PARKS, BEACHES, AND RECREATION AREAS

3 Woods Creek Rotary Park

🐾🐾🐾 (See Tuolumne County map on page 246)

Woods Creek runs through this pretty, shaded park. Dogs love to wet their paws in it on warm summer afternoons. Joe, the consummate landlubber, prefered to picnic at the tables set under shade trees, but Jake's preference would be to actually eat in the water. It's a great place to come to sample the tasty gourmet items you just bought downtown.

The park is just southwest of town, on Stockton Street and Woods Creek Drive (across from the Mother Lode Fairgrounds). 209/532-4541.

DIVERSION

Tools of the Trail: When I met Tonja Peterson, co-owner of the **Sierra Nevada Adventure Company,** she was running around the winter woods on snowshoes with her dog, Avery Mae, at her side. (Avery was sans snowshoes. "Too awkward," claimed the rottie-Australian shepherd mix.) We got to talking about Peterson's terrific outdoor store. "All genders, shapes, and sizes of dogs are welcome. We'd rate it four paws for dogs," Peterson said, taking her cue from a terrific California dog guidebook she stocks.

So we checked it out, and sure enough, it's doggone great. Dogs who visit here will get water, a dog treat, and some serious ear rubs if the place isn't too busy. Dogs can also pick from lots of dog bowls, dog books, collars, leashes, and dog backpacks. Alas, Avery Mae has gone on to the big dog store in the sky, but her sweet friend, Choco, will likely come over to say hi.

Peterson also owns a new, larger branch of the store in Arnold, and she says it's just as dog-friendly. If Choco isn't there, Al "the Pal" and his gal pal, Sammie, probably will be. The Arnold address is 2293 Highway 4; 209/795-9310. The Sonora store is at 173 South Washington Street; 209/532-5621.

PLACES TO EAT

Schnoog's Espresso and Smoothie Bar: Enjoy imported espresso, locally produced coffee (coffee plantations in Sonora?), and fresh baked goods from the house kitchen at the eight outdoor tables here. The manager here loves dogs, so your pooch will feel right at home. 1005 Mono Way; 209/533-2486.

PLACES TO STAY

Best Western Sonora Oaks: This is one of the more attractive, newer motels in the area. The outdoor pool is a big plus on hot summer afternoons. (It's a big covered ice patch on cold winter afternoons.) Rates are $94–116. Dogs are $20 extra. 19551 Hess Avenue 95370; 209/533-4400.

Sonora Aladdin Motor Inn: Dogs are welcome at this clean, modern motel. But they need to stay out of the refreshing pool and spa. The fur gunks up the plumbing. Rates are $70–110. Dogs are $5 extra. 14260 Mono Way 95370; 209/533-4971 or 800/696-3969; www.aladdininn.com.

Sonora Days Inn: Dogs can stay only in the more modern, motel section of this partly historic inn. And the lobby in the historic part of the inn is no longer off-limits: "Small house dogs" can join you here. Rates are $79–83. Dogs are $10 extra for the length of their stay. 160 South Washington Street 95370; 209/532-2400 or 800/580-4667; www.sonoradaysinn.com.

Sonora Gold Lodge: This is a decent little motel not far from the main drag of Sonora. The rooms are clean, the pool is cool in the warm months, and you can even get a room with a little fridge and microwave for those home-away-from-home eats. Rates are $69–79. Dogs are $10 extra for the length of their stay. 480 West Stockton Street 95370; 209/532-3952 or 800/863-2154; www.goldlodge.com.

Twain Harte

Dogs enjoy strolling along the sidewalks of this charming little town, especially if they're of the literary persuasion. The town was named for writers Mark Twain and Bret Harte. It's a good thing that Aleksandr Solzhenitsyn and Michel Eyquem de Montaigne weren't big in the area when the place was named.

It's a very dog-friendly place. You never know where your dog will be invited in or given a treat. The Ace hardware store here allows well-behaved dogs inside and provides them little biscuits. Tellers at a bank's drive-up window have been known to slip a dog a treat in the little metal drawer. (Jake wants me to switch banks.)

PLACES TO STAY

El Dorado Motel: This is a decent place to stay, especially if you'd like a microwave and a fridge in your room. (This comes in handy when traveling with a dog.) Rates are $55–65. Dogs are $10 per visit. 22678 Black Hawk Drive 95383; 209/586-4479.

Gables Cedar Creek Inn: The eight enchanting cabins here have fireplaces/wood-burning stoves, antique furniture, and comfy beds with down comforters. Most have little kitchens. This is all just peachy with dogs, but what really gets their tails wagging is the setting: a lush grassy area surrounded by tall pines and cedars. Jake's favorite cabin is the Hideaway, a spacious, creekside log cabin. Since it's across the creek from the other cabins (you have to cross a stone bridge to get there), it's quite secluded, really living up to its name.

The owners have enforced a 30-pound size limit for dogs for some time. But this policy seems to be getting much less strict of late, with a few big galoot dogs (well behaved, of course) having been given the OK. (A note: If you phone for reservations while dog-loving Emma is on duty, you'll have a better chance. "I really push for dogs," she says.) The beef against dogs has primarily been their fur getting on everything. And the bigger the dog, the more fur is likely to be left behind. If you promise to use your cabin's vacuum well, and bring a lint brush, Emma says your chances of staying here will improve.

Rates are $79–110. A beautiful vacation home with storybook charm is also available, with rates starting at $210. 22560 Twain Harte Drive 95383; 209/586-3008 or 888/900-4224; www.gocedarcreek.com.

Groveland

In 1849, when the town was founded, it was a rough-and-ready gold mining center. Today it's smoother around the edges, but you can't miss that Old West ambience.

PLACES TO STAY

Groveland Hotel: The suites at this Gold Rush–era inn come with a fireplace and a whirlpool bath so that you can have an evening of romantic relaxation. The place was chosen as one of the "12 Best Country Inns" by *Country Inns* magazine. The hotel was originally built in 1849 but has subsequently been restored and refined. (You have use of a white terry robe with your room. It's that kind of place.) The Groveland Hotel is a top-notch inn as far as dogs are concerned and not because of the robes. Dogs who stay here get a treat, a snuggly quilt, and a dish. Lucky dogs! Rates are $135–275. Dogs are $10 per visit. 18767 Main Street 95321; 209/962-4000 or 800/273-3314; www.groveland.com.

Sunset Inn: The three sweet housekeeping cabins here are set in a quiet meadow surrounded by the Stanislaus National Forest (dog heaven). The cabins are very cozy, comfy, and attractive. "This is really an ideal place for dogs," says friendly cabin owner Lauren. "We can't not have dogs here!" Each cabin has a kitchen and very useable porch/deck. If you want to visit Yosemite National Park, the cabins provide a fine place to start your adventure, since they're just two miles from the park's west gate. Rates are $110–150 for the double cabin, and up to $200 for the larger family cabin. Dogs are $10 extra. 33569 Hardin Flat Road 95321; 209/962-4360.

Yosemite Westgate Motel: Enjoy a splash in the pool (humans only, please) before driving to nearby Yosemite. Rates are $69–169. Pooches are $10 extra. 7647 Highway 120 95321; 209/962-5281 or 800/253-9673.

CHAPTER 25

Mono County

This is raw and rugged eastern Sierra country, where the cows graze amid such spectacular scenery that it's hard to believe they don't moo and ahh whenever we turn our backs.

When you contemplate the origins of the word "mono," you'll probably think of words such as "alone," "one," or "single." Certainly they capture the feel of this unique land. But in this case, the meaning of the word isn't so romantic. *Mono* is the Yokut Indian word for flies. Brine flies, abundant on the shores of salty Mono Lake, were an important source of protein for the Yokut, and they're still the most visible insect at Mono Lake. Fortunately, the flies don't bite, eat your picnic, or otherwise act tempestuously toward humans and their dogs.

In "Fly County," you can often just pull off the road into open public land and hike your heart out, especially in the county's northern reaches. As you drive along U.S. 395, you'll see so many signs for camping, fishing, and other outdoor recreation that you won't know where to turn first. This chapter describes a few of the more dog-friendly areas, but know that when you see

PICK OF THE LITTER—MONO COUNTY

BEST GHOST TOWN
Bodie State Historic Park, Bodie (page 263)

MOST OTHERWORLDLY PLACE
Mono Lake, Lee Vining (page 264)

BEST OFF-LEASH HIKES NEAR CIVILIZATION
Trails at Lake Mary and Horseshoe Lake,
Mammoth Lakes (page 270)

BEST DOGGY DINING
Tailwaggers, Mammoth Lakes (page 272)

BEST LUXURY TREATMENT
Double Eagle Resort and Spa, June Lake (page 266).

STEAMIEST SHOWERS
Convict Lake Resort, Mammoth Lakes (page 272)

MOST DOG-FRIENDLY PLACE TO STAY
Edelweiss Lodge, Mammoth Lakes (page 273)

EASIEST WAY TO RISE ABOVE IT ALL
Mammoth Mountain Ski Area gondolas,
Mammoth Lakes (page 269)

signs for places such as Convict Lake, Crowley Lake, and Bridgeport Lake, generally you and your leashed dog will be welcome.

Lucky dogs who visit Mono County now get to stay at dozens of remarkable cabins in gorgeous settings. Some of these cabins are extremely luxurious, and some don't even have warm water. Most are somewhere between. "It's becoming doggy heaven in Mono County," writes canine correspondent Rexall, of West Hollywood. "I drag my human driver up here as often as I can."

A note to dogs: Don't get too excited when you see signs for the Dogtown State Historic Landmark on U.S. 395 just south of Willow Springs. It's interesting, but it's not what you think.

NATIONAL FORESTS

The National Forests and Wilderness Areas resource at the back of this book has important information and safety tips on visiting national forests with your dog and has more information on the national forests listed below.

Inyo National Forest

Toiyabe National Forest

Bridgeport

If you and your dog are film noir fans, you'll want to stop at this quiet little village and see if it looks familiar. Remember the movie *Out of the Past,* starring Robert Mitchum? Much of it was set right here in Bridgeport.

PARKS, BEACHES, AND RECREATION AREAS

❶ Bridgeport Park

🐾 (See Mono County map on page 258)

This tiny county park is just a bunch of picnic tables on grass in the midst of a few pieces of old mining equipment. It's right next to the Mono County Museum, in case you're with someone who wants a little culture.

From U.S. 395, go east on School Street and left on Middle Street. 760/932-5248.

PLACES TO STAY

Best Western Ruby Inn: Stay here and you get a small area to walk your leashless pooch! Rates are $80–160. 33 Main Street 93517; 760/932-7241.

Mono Village Fisherman's Resort and Family Vacation Hideaway: What this resort lacks in name brevity it makes up for in scenic beauty. Actually, it's the surrounding scenery that's exquisite, with Upper Twin Lake in the front yard and mountains and glorious trees everywhere else. The resort itself varies from very tinny (several dozen RV sites) to very campy (many tent sites) to very rustic (many attractive log cabins). Dogs are relegated to the tent and RV sites.

Autumn here is especially beautiful. And if you're an angler, that's definitely the time to visit, since fishing is at its best then. The resort has a grocery store, café, cocktail lounge, and boathouse.

Sites are $12–14. There's no real street address, but the mailing address is Annett's Mono Village, P.O. Box 455 93517; 760/932-7071.

Silver Maple Inn: This place is very pet-friendly. People have brought pet goats and pet pigs. "We take just about any pet!" exclaimed a pet-loving manager. Rates are $75–95. 310 Main Street 93517; 760/932-7383.

Twin Lakes Resort: The eight remodeled cabins here are set on a football field–sized lawn, and the lawn is surrounded by beautiful pine, aspen, silver maple, and cottonwood trees. It's enough to make a boy dog cry with joy. In summer, the trees of the surrounding Toiyabe National Forest are so lush that you may not be able to see nearby Lower Twin Lake. But it's still there. And it's very inviting for dogs and their people to take a swim, or even rent a boat and motor around the lake. (Boat rentals are available at the resort's marina and cost $55–130 per day. Dogs are welcome to join you.)

Winter is also a fun time to visit with a dog. "Dogs have so much fun in the snow here," says the very pleasant owner, Lori. "I watch dogs that have never seen snow before. They don't even know how to take a step in it at first. By the end of the visit, their owners can't even get them into the car they love the snow so much."

The cabins are basic, but attractive. There are no phones and no TVs. "We've got lotsa nothin'" says Lori. Rates are $131–168. Dogs are $25 per stay. The two-night rates are a bit lower. The resort is 11 miles south of Bridgeport, but Bridgeport is the official address. P.O. Box 248 93517; 877/932-7751; www.lowertwinlakesresort.com.

Virginia Creek Settlement: This is a fun place to stay if you like casual Old West style and a friendly lot of people. It's part motel (the rooms look like the inside of a sparkling-clean log cabin), part campground, part housekeeping cabins, and part tent cabins. But the coolest part of all is the two old covered wagons. You and your dog can actually bunk overnight in them. You just provide the sleeping bag. The mattresses are already there. The wagons are kind of well worn, but that's part of their charm. (And they make for great photo ops with the pooch.) Much of this is set up as an old-fashioned Camp Town, which harkens to Gold Rush days. The folks here will even point you in the right direction to try some gold panning.

The Virginia Creek Settlement features its own cozy Italian/American-style restaurant. I don't know how many Italian restaurants were around during the Gold Rush, but I'm glad this one is. The food is most fulfilling after a day of adventuring.

Motel rooms are $60–75, cabins are about $99, and tent cabins and covered wagons are $20, plus $6 per bed. Bring your own towels and soap for the more rustic accommodations, or pay an extra $1.50 per person. Tent sites are $14. You'll find it on U.S. 395 about five miles south of town, but the official address is still Bridgeport. It's one of the closest lodgings to Bodie State Historic Park (see the Bodie section). H.C.R. 62, Box 1050 93517; 707/932-7780; www.virginiacreeksettlement.com.

Virginia Lakes Resort: Some of the 19 housekeeping cabins at this very popular resort have views of beautiful Little Virginia Lake. The rest are on Virginia Creek. It's water, water everywhere, which makes Jake tremble with anticipation. (My fisherman husband trembles right along with Jake; trout fishing is hot here and at adjacent Big Virginia Lake.) The cabins vary from rustic to modern condo style, and our favorites have a fireplace and sundeck overlooking the lake.

The owners adore dogs. Their own dear dog, a wolf hybrid, died in 2003, and they probably won't be getting another one anytime soon. "It's too hard, but we love seeing our dog guests. It helps," says Carolyn. She'll provide you with info on local hikes and let you know when it's super-important to leash up on hikes. (Fawning season, for instance.)

The resort is open around May 20–October 15. It's about 13 miles south of Bridgeport, off U.S. 395 at Conway Summit. The mailing address: H.C. 62, Box 1065 93517; 707/647-6484; www.virginialakesresort.com.

Walker River Lodge: This is a very dog-friendly motel. The kind owners here will show you a nearby little hike you can do with your furry friend. The lodge is right on the Walker River, a big-time trout area. Rates are $70–155. 1 Main Street 93517; 760/932-7021; www.walkerriverlodge.com.

Bodie

PARKS, BEACHES, AND RECREATION AREAS

🐾 Bodie State Historic Park

🐾🐾🐾 (See Mono County map on page 258)

This ghost town looks so much like *Gunsmoke*-land on a really bad day that it's hard to picture it as a thriving, raunchy, pulsating boomtown. But that's exactly what it was back in the 1870s during this area's gold rush. Dozens of saloons, a burgeoning red-light district, and murders nearly every day kept this lawless mining camp hopping.

These days, dogs can enjoy the 486 acres of this town-turned-historic park as long as they're law-abiding citizens on a leash. They're allowed to walk down the dusty streets with you and sniff at the 170 dilapidated buildings that remain, or they can kick up their heels in the more open areas of the park. Dogs seem to appreciate the wild and woolly luster that still shines through the educational veneer here.

From U.S. 395 just south of Willow Springs, take Highway 270/Bodie Road east about 13 miles. The last three miles are unpaved and can be impassable in winter. You'll pay $3 per adult, $1 per child. Dogs are free. 760/647-6445. A great website has lots of info on Bodie. It's not an official park service site, but it's well worth checking out: www.bodie.com.

Lee Vining

PARKS, BEACHES, AND RECREATION AREAS

🐾 Mono Lake

🐾🐾🐾🐾 (See Mono County map on page 258)

Spending the day at this strange and ancient lake is about the closest you and your dog will come to visiting another planet. You'll want to check your map and make sure you're still on Earth when you see the eerie volcanic formations, the old lake, and the tufa spires that look like giant, oozy sand castles.

This 700,000-year-old lake covers 60 square miles, but it's just a shadow of its former self. Since Los Angeles started using the fresh streams that fill Mono Lake, the lake has dropped 40 feet and its salinity has doubled. These days, the lake is nearly three times as salty and 80 times as alkaline as seawater. The salinity increase in this already salty lake seems to be creating some problems for the local environment, and studies on its effects are ongoing. But on the upside, it does make for buoyant swimming.

The alkaline water isn't a new phenomenon. Mark Twain wrote of Mono: "Its sluggish waters are so strong with alkali that if you only dip the most hopelessly soiled garment into them once or twice, and wring it out, it will be found as clean as if it had been through the ablest of washerwoman's hands." You may be tempted to toss your dirty dog in for a little cleansing splash, but the water can be irritating to the eyes.

The land surrounding the lake is run by different agencies. Fortunately, these agencies all have the same rules, which makes it easy to traipse from one part of the lake to the other without getting busted for a dog violation. Dogs are permitted, but they have to be on a leash, even in the Mono Basin National Forest Scenic Area. It's that simple.

Drive on U.S. 395 to the Mono Lake Visitors Center in Lee Vining and pick up some brochures about the geology of this fascinating area. Then look for signs for areas such as the Mono Lake Tufa State Reserve (there are areas on either side of the lake and the one on the south side is best) or the Mono Basin National Forest Scenic Area. Drive east until you're either in the middle of a dormant, pumice-covered volcano or standing on the shores of one of the oldest lakes in North America. It's ideal dog territory, with few souls venturing on the longer hikes.

The fee is $3 in the South Tufa area; the rest of the state reserve and the national forest are free. Call the reserve at 760/647-6331 or the national forest at 760/647-3044. You may actually have better luck reaching a real person at the Mono Lake Committee Information Center. 760/647-6595; www.monolake.org.

PLACES TO STAY

Aspen Campground: A creek runs through this 56-site county-run campground, and if you're lucky, you can catch your supper of brookies and browns and cook 'em over the campfire. Aspen trees dot the grounds. There's a decent-sized meadow on the side. Sites are $7 and are available on a first-come, first-served basis. From U.S. 395, take Highway 120 west for 4.7 miles. 760/647-3044 or 760/647-6595.

Lundy Canyon Campground: This county-run campground is set at 8,000 feet near Lundy Lake, just across the highway from Mono Lake. It's a barren, otherworldly dreamscape. Leashed dogs love it. They also seem to enjoy the county park where the campsites are. But if you want to take your dog for a long and fascinating hike, just take a quick ride to nearby Mono Lake. There are 60 sites, all first-come, first-served. Sites are $7. From U.S. 395 about five miles north of Lee Vining, look for the signs for the campground, which is on the west side of the highway. 760/647-3044 or 760/647-6595.

Murphey's Motel: The attitude toward dogs at this fine little motel: "We love them!" Rates are $53–108. Dogs are $5 extra. The motel is directly on U.S. 395 in Lee Vining. You can't miss it. 51493 Highway 395 93541; 760/647-6316.

June Lake

PARKS, BEACHES, AND RECREATION AREAS

The June Lake Loop consists of four lakes west of U.S. 395. Dogs are permitted at all of them. Here we'll discuss only the two smaller lakes.

❹ Gull Lake

🐾 🐾 🐾 (See Mono County map on page 258)

As the smallest lake of the June Lake Loop chain, Gull Lake also tends to be the quietest. People are apt to miss this stunning 64-acre lake while on the prowl for its three bigger sisters. That's what dogs like about this place. Very few people get underfoot.

Nonetheless, pooches should be leashed here, and they're not supposed to swim, so watch those slippery water dogs. But they do have a good time watching you fish from shore for all those planted trout. They even seem to enjoy the scenery, or at least the smellery. The lake is set in what could be called "the Sierra Bowl," a dramatic, rocky expanse with all kinds of critters running around.

Camping is good here during the warmer months. There are 11 sites that go for $13 a night, first-come, first-served. From U.S. 395 about 13 miles north of Mammoth Lakes, exit at the June Lake junction and drive southwest about three miles to the lake. 760/647-3045 or 760/647-6595.

5 Silver Lake

🐾🐾🐾🐾🐕 (See Mono County map on page 258)

Leashed dogs may wag a tail or two when you catch trout after trout here. This 80-acre lake is stocked with many thousands of rainbows each year. But what really sets dogs off is that when you take them for a long hike up the magnificent trail that takes you far, far away from the bait store, the full-service resort, and the boat rental facility, they can be leash-free!

The trailhead is near the camping area ($13 per site, dogs must be leashed). Once you start hiking, you and your leash-free dog may never want to return. The trail actually can loop you into Yosemite National Park, so you have to watch how long you tread, because dogs are banned from Yosemite's trails. But an exciting and not too strenuous hike will take you along the Rush Creek drainage, past Gem Lake and Agnew Lake and into the pristine Ansel Adams Wilderness. Bring a big lunch and lots of water, and you'll have a vacation your dog will remember into her old age.

The lake is about halfway on the June Lake Loop, so you can exit U.S. 395 at the north or south end of the loop (Highway 158), depending on the direction you're traveling. The campground, which has about 63 sites, is open May–September. All sites are first-come, first-served. 760/647-3045 or 760/647-6595.

PLACES TO STAY

Double Eagle Resort and Spa: So you think you'll be roughing it just because you're staying in the eastern Sierra Nevada? 'Tis to laugh! This is not a resort in the classic California lakeside sense of the word. It's a resort in the "ooh" and "ahhh" sense of the word. The Double Eagle was recently listed by Forbes. com as being one of the top 10 spas in world. It's an outstanding, upscale place, with amenities that will leave you and your dog drooling.

The two-bedroom cabins are new, luxurious, and exquisitely furnished. Wood-burning fireplaces and stoves, big decks, and fully equipped kitchens make you feel right at home in the quiet forest setting here. The resort is on 14 acres and bordered on two sides by National Forest land. This makes for some wonderful hikes. Nanda Devi, a lovely golden retriever, gave us the heads up about this place. She enjoyed hikes by the lake and swimming, while her mom reveled in spa treatments.

The spa offers more than 50 specialty massages. One involves stones. It's somehow supposed to be pretty relaxing. A few treatment rooms have fireplaces. It's worth the extra money if you want the ultimate in relaxation during winter. Humans love the indoor swimming pool, whirlpool, and excellent fitness center. The resort's restaurant offers healthful, delicious cuisine. None of this interests dogs, but that's OK. It gets you there, which gets them there, and that's what counts.

Dogs are allowed at five of the cottages. Rates are $287–319, with dogs costing $15 extra. 5587 Highway 158 93529; 760/648-7004; www.doubleeagleresort.com.

Fern Creek Lodge: It's kind of like a little village here. You've got 10 cabins (some are like big, two-story houses), four apartment units, a store that sells everything from groceries to fishing gear, and a large barbecue area. All the buildings are arranged in a semicirclular fashion, with the main lodge and store in the center. Fern Creek has a very dog-friendly atmosphere, with many people either visiting with dogs or wanting to pet yours. Rates are $55–130. The biggest cabins sleep up to 16 people and cost $210. Dogs are $10 extra. 4628 Highway 158 93529; 760/648-7722 or 800/621-9146; www.ferncreek-lodge.com.

Gull Lake: See Gull Lake, above, for camping information.

Gull Lake Lodge: You're surrounded by forest at this *very* dog-friendly lodge. Owner Vikki Magee loves dogs and has a great theory about traveling pooches: "No bad dogs make it as far as the car," she says. It's been her experience that dogs who get to vacation with their people must be pretty darned special. And she's right. "Besides," she says, "they don't steal towels." Upon your arrival, you'll likely be greeted by her own two fabulously friendly pooches, Taco and Maggie. The entire lodge was recently remodeled. All units now have kitchens and are looking very nice. Rates are $70–165, and that includes fish-cleaning facilities. The lodge is between June and Gull Lakes. Some rooms have lake views. 132 Leonard Street 93529; 760/648-7516 or 800/631-4081; www.gulllakelodge.com.

Silver Lake: See Silver Lake, above, for camping information.

Mammoth Lakes

This charming resort town is a magical ski haven in the winter and an angler's dream in the summer. It's an excellent base for exploring the 200,000 surrounding acres known as Mammoth Lakes Recreational Area.

The lakes in this region are numerous and abound with great fishing and camping opportunities. The mountains and forests are rife with hiking and cross-country skiing areas for you and the pooch of your dreams. You can ski just about anywhere in the national forest, as long as you keep your dog off the groomed cross-country trails. And once you get away from people, you can unleash your obedient dog and bound through nature together.

Dog-friendly lodgings abound, but if you need extra help watching your dog (should you want to ski with your human traveling partner, for instance), check out Tailwaggers Too, which offers excellent doggy day care and overnight boarding. (It's right upstairs from Tailwaggers dog bakery, at the Sierra Center

Mall, 924 Old Mammoth Road, 760/924-2800.) Another place your dog can hang out while you ski or dine or shop is Marta's Doggie Day Care. (See description under Edelweiss Lodge, below.) At either day care, your dog will probably have as good a time as you will. (And if you ski like I do, a better time.)

PARKS, BEACHES, AND RECREATION AREAS

6 Mammoth Mountain

🐾🐾 (See Mono County map on page 258)

You and your calm dog can take an exciting gondola ride up the hill to reach great hiking trails during the summer. (See the Diversion Up, Up, and Away.) The walk down is a bit precarious, or at least unnerving, with bare pumicey trails and sometimes steep mountain slips, er, slopes. (I speak from personal experience.) You and your dog will want to be sure-pawed to attempt this feat. Some lower trails provide better footing.

To get here, exit U.S. 395 at the Mammoth Junction exit and drive west along Highway 203/Main Street, through the town of Mammoth Lakes. Once past town, turn right at Minaret Summit/Minaret Road and drive about four miles. The mountain, with the big gondola, will be on your left. You can't miss it. 760/934-2571.

7 Shady Rest Trail

🐾🐾🐾 (See Mono County map on page 258)

This national forest trail is on the edge of the town of Mammoth Lakes, making it as convenient as it is splendid. Unfortunately, since the city officially runs this trail, leashes are the law.

During the summer, you and your pooch can walk or run on the six-mile forested trail that loops around Shady Rest Park (a Mammoth Lakes recreation park, where leashes are also the law).

In winter, it's a stunning place to take your dog on a little cross-country ski trip. Leashes can come in handy here. We've seen some people leash their dogs to their belts while skiing. When there's a little uphill slope, guess who's the engine? Most dogs wouldn't appreciate this and are happier gamboling through the woods than playing mush dog. Dogs aren't allowed on the groomed trails (there's nothing like paw holes to dampen a smooth cross-country adventure), but they can usually trot along on the left side of the trail.

From U.S. 395, exit at Mammoth Junction and drive west along Highway 203/Main Street until the U.S. Forest Service Visitors Center, which will be before town on your right. You can stop in here and ask for additional trail information or proceed west on Highway 203 another quarter of a mile to Old Sawmill Road. Turn right and follow the road to Shady Rest Park. You'll see parts of the trail weaving around the park's perimeter and even along the entry road. Call 760/924-5500 for more information.

DIVERSION

Up, Up, and Away: If the idea of dangling 11,000 feet above sea level doesn't faze you or your dog, hop aboard the **Mammoth Mountain Ski Area gondolas** for a lofty adventure.

Actually, during your 12-minute ascent from 9,000 feet to 11,000 feet on the Scenic Gondola Ride, you'll glide only a few dozen feet above the ground—spectacular views make it seem as though you're higher. You can sniff out a scenic spot about .2 mile away, or try your paw at descending the mountain. It's rather barren, and the trails aren't for the faint of heart: They're narrow and seem precipitous at times. (One very windy afternoon, I got several hundred yards down and decided that I'd better turn around. I felt as if I were going to blow off the mountainside. The gondola ride down was much less hair-raising, despite the high winds that made it feel like an amusement park ride.) The hike all the way down takes about 1.5–2 hours, depending on how you handle the trails.

The fee for adults is $16. Older children are $8, and kids six and under go for free. Dogs of all ages go for free, too. To get here, exit U.S. 395 at the Mammoth Junction exit and drive west along Highway 203/Main Street through the town of Mammoth Lakes. Go right on Minaret Summit/Minaret Road. In about four miles you'll see the gondola station on your right. 760/934-2571 or 888/4-MAMMOTH (888/462-6668).

🖥 Devil's Postpile National Monument

🐾🐾🐾🐾 (See Mono County map on page 258)

Although Devil's Postpile is actually just over the border in Madera County, it is accessible only via its neighbor, Mammoth Lakes. If you're in the area with your dog, take advantage of this great exception to the national park system—dogs are allowed just about everywhere people can go, as long as they're leashed.

And what a place it is. If the devil ever did have a pile of posts, this would be it. The 60-foot wall of columnar basalt "posts" is truly awe-inspiring. Pick up a brochure and find out the fascinating geology behind these geometric (and geologic) wonders.

In addition to the postpile, this 800-acre park is also home to Rainbow Falls, where the Middle Fork of the San Joaquin River drops 101 feet over a cliff of volcanic lava. It's a remarkable sight. You can also get to some great backcountry trails from here: The Pacific Crest Trail and John Muir Trail are among the trails dogs love to sniff out.

Unless you plan on going up very early in the morning or after 8 P.M., or unless you're going to be camping or fishing one of the area's lakes with a boat, you'll have to take a fun shuttle bus a few miles down to the valley. On a recent trip, we met up with a little tiny mutt in a front carrier and a giant German shepherd from San Diego. The shepherd befriended my human child and shared a seat with her. (She said it was the best part of the trip. So much for Mother Nature.)

A great place to catch the shuttle is in front of the Mammoth Mountain Inn. Exit U.S. 395 at Mammoth Junction and drive west along Highway 203/Main Street through the town of Mammoth Lakes. Turn right at Minaret Summit/Minaret Road and drive about four miles. You can buy your ticket in the gondola building. The cost is $7 round-trip for adults, $4 for children. Dogs go free. The road is impassable in the winter, so the park is closed during snowy months (which can sometimes last into June, so call first). Call the U.S. Forest Service at 760/924-5500 for bus schedules and pickup locations. Phone 760/934-2289 for Devil's Postpile information.

☑ Lake Mary
🐾🐾🐾🐾 🐕 (See Mono County map on page 258)

Dogs have to be leashed around developed and heavily used Lake Mary, but they can trot around leashless when they accompany you on the scenic trail that starts on the east side of the lake. Rangers ask that you wait until you're far from the lake to let your dog run free, and to do so only if she's under good control.

Lots of folks like to take their dogs on an early morning walk on the trail and then turn around and fish for dinner. The trout are planted, and it's hard not to catch one while trolling, or even fishing from shore. Most dogs seem to enjoy watching people fish, even if nothing is being caught. Some people don't even mind just walking around the lake with a leashed dog. There's also a gold mine at the very end of Coldwater Campground, next to the trailhead parking. You'll see the signs.

Other folks come here just for the off-leash hiking. The trail takes you many miles away. If your dog is a water dog, she'll love it. You pass by several quiet little lakes and one big one on the way to the Pacific Crest Trail. Consult an Inyo National Forest ranger at 760/873-2400 for maps and guidance.

June–November, 48 campsites are available here for $16 a night, first-come, first-served. Dogs must be leashed, but with the great views of the lake they get, they just don't seem to mind.

To reach the lake, exit U.S. 395 at Mammoth Junction and drive west along Highway 203/Main Street, through the town of Mammoth Lakes. The road curves to the left and becomes Lake Mary Road. Follow it about three miles to the lake. 760/924-5500.

🔟 Horseshoe Lake

🐾🐾🐾🐾🐾 (See Mono County map on page 258)

Most of the lakes in this part of the eastern Sierra are developed and popular among humankind. But although Horseshoe Lake is just a stick's throw from civilization, it's a refreshing exception. Not only is it breathtaking, it's quiet.

You really can get away from folks here. In summer, it's not as heavily fished as other local lakes, partly because it's not stocked with trout. But if you visit with a dog, chances are you'll have more on your mind than fishing anyway. And that's where this lake is a little piece of dog heaven. While your dog has to be leashed around the lake, he's allowed to romp leashless once he hits the connecting trails.

At the north end of the lake, you'll find a trailhead that leads you through magnificent landscapes, all set around 9,000 feet. The air is so clean you can almost feel yourself getting healthier with each step. Jake thinks it's the cat's pajamas. Eventually, the trail runs into the Pacific Crest Trail, where you can choose to venture off on longer or shorter treks. Consult an Inyo National Forest ranger at 760/934-2505 for maps and guidance.

To reach the lake, exit U.S. 395 at Mammoth Junction and drive west along Highway 203/Main Street, through the town of Mammoth Lakes. The road curves to the left and becomes Lake Mary Road. Follow it about seven miles. It loops by Lake Mary and eventually ends at Horseshoe Lake. 760/924-5500.

PLACES TO EAT

Alpenrose: Your dog can be just on the other side of the rail on the Swiss-style patio here when you eat the delicious, homemade continental cuisine served by the Alpenrose's owners, a dog-friendly Swiss-German family. Try the Wiener schnitzel or the apple strudel. Just about everything is homemade. 343 Old Mammoth Road; 760/934-3077.

Giovanni's Restaurant and Lounge: Order a pizza to go and bring it to the outdoor tables to share with your dog. One of our favorite combos is the Gio special, with pesto, artichokes, mushrooms, and feta cheese. (Jake spits out the veggies oh, so delicately, but wolfs down the cheese and crust.) 437 Old Mammoth Road; 760/934-7563.

Schat's Bakery: This is a great place to grab a coffee and warm pastry before a morning hike. Relax at the outdoor chairs here. 3305 Main Street; 760/934-6055.

Tailwaggers: Here's a dog's ideal alternative to Schat's Bakery. Tailwaggers is a gourmet dog bakery, with cookies featuring items such as beef puree. Hmm, I think I'll still get my cookies at Schat's. Dogs love visiting here when they come for treats and dog boutique items, but they're not always so keen on visiting the other part of the Tailwaggers business: the self-service dog bath. The tubs are a great place to come after a messy day at a lake or a muddy trail. In addition, Tailwaggers now offers wonderful pooch massages. The massage therapist, Andrea Baldwin, is known for her wonderful human massages at a nearby highly acclaimed spa. The dogs we've spoken with tell us she also has a magic touch with canines. Call for her hours, fees, or to book an appointment. Tailwaggers is at the Sierra Center Mall, at 924 Old Mammoth Road; 760/924-3400; www.tailwaggersbakery.com.

PLACES TO STAY

Convict Lake Resort: Dogs love coming to this terrific resort. Jake Dog thinks it's because they feel so welcome here. Says the owner: "We love all pets, even ostriches and tarantulas." Psst: The resort even takes cats.

Pets can stay at several deluxe cabins. The owners recently built four super-luxurious cabins, which come with fireplaces, double spa baths, and even steam showers. (A steam shower, should you be in the dark ages of pampery bathroom fixtures as I am, is a regular shower with a control that makes steam billow out any time you want. You don't even have to take a shower to get a steam. It's kind of like a spa steambath in your own cabin. Take that, Davy Crockett.)

In summer, dogs and their people can go out on the lake in a boat, help fish for supper, watch you ride a horse, or just hike around the wilderness on the other side of the lake. Dogs like Jake have plenty of swimming options. The resort also has a wonderful restaurant, but you'll have to get takeout if you want your dog to partake.

The regular cabins are cute and are only $99. The new cabins are $210–250. There's even a cabin that sleeps up to 34 people. That's $960. Dogs are $15 for the length of their stay. Route 1, Box 204 93546; 760/934-3800 or 800/992-2260; www.convictlake.com.

Crystal Crag Lodge: Stay at this charming mountain resort on the shores of Lake Mary and you can wander around many acres of beautiful land with your leashed dog. But you'd better visit May–mid-October, because the lodge is closed in the winter. The rustic wood cabins are attractive and have full kitchens and baths. Most come with living rooms and fireplaces, too. Dogs like all that, but water dogs think it's truly the cat's meow that you can rent a small aluminum boat here and meander around the lake. Rates are $85–170. Dogs are $9 extra. 307 Crystal Crag Drive 93546; 760/934-2436; www.mammothweb.com.

Edelweiss Lodge: Has your dog been very good this year? If so, she deserves a visit to the rustic, cozy, super-dog-friendly cabins and apartments that comprise the Edelweiss Lodge. The lodgings all have kitchenettes, wood-burning stoves, and access to a whirlpool bath.

"Yada, yada, yada," your dog may be saying right about now. OK, we'll cut to the chase: Edelweiss has everything a dog could dream of (except cats). Dog-adoring managers Keith and Marta want to make every dog feel at home, and they start out by providing pooches a Doggie Welcome Basket. This includes a dog bed/pad, blankets to protect the human bedding, gourmet dog biscuits, temporary ID tags, water and food bowls, and poop bags. "We even provide a dumpster to put the poop bags in, but you can't take it to your room," says Keith. (Whew!)

Marta even has her own doggy side business, Marta's Doggie Day Care. She'll walk your dog for you if you're off for a while and need to leave your dog in a kennel in your room. (This is allowed here.) If you want complete day care, your lucky dog gets to go to her home, where day-care dogs cavort about as if it's their home. She takes the dogs for walks and hikes and brings them on errands with her. She also houses dogs overnight, but that's probably not necessary given the breadth of dog-friendly lodgings here. Sometimes guests ask Marta and Keith if their dogs can just hang out with them at the lodge office for a while, and that can be worked out, too. Rates are about $25 daily for full day care, $15 for a good walk.

Lodging rates are $115–325. Dogs are $10 extra. 1872 Old Mammoth Road 93546; 760/934-2445 or 877/233-3593; www.edelweiss-lodge.com.

Lake Mary: See Lake Mary, above, for camping information.

Motel 6: Rates are $50–87. This one looks more like a giant ski lodge than a roadside motel. 3372 Main Street 93546; 760/934-6660.

Old Shady Rest Campground: Believe it or not, you're pretty much in town when you camp here, though you'd never know it by the scenery. You're in the woods, without a trace of civilization. Dogs are permitted on leash. There are 46 sites. Fees are $15. For reservations, phone 877/444-6777. Sites are open year-round. From U.S. 395, drive west on Highway 203 for three miles to the Mammoth Visitor Center. Turn right and follow the signs to the campground. 760/924-5500. (There's also a New Shady Rest Campground nearby, with 87 sites. The same phone numbers apply for info and reservations.)

Rockcreek Lodge: If you like modern cabins, the lodge has got some attractive small and large ones. If you like your cabins rustic and old, it's got those, too. And if you like your rustic cabins with only cold running water, you can even get a couple of those here. (From the 1920s!) Dogs love coming here because the lodge is set on seven acres of lodgepole pines, with several trails leading from the property. The trails can take you on some magnificent hikes to lakes, remote forests, and peaceful meadows. A fishable creek is a quick walk from the lodge. (Come in the summer for a stunning wildflower display.) Stay here and you're on the edge of the John Muir Wilderness. After a long day of outdoor fun, settle back in with a delicious meal from the lodge's restaurant. Rates are $85–150. Dogs are $15 extra. Route 1, Box 12 93546; 877/935-4170; www.rockcreeklodge.com.

Shilo Inn: Don't worry about your large dog's being allowed to stay here—the manager *prefers* big dogs! All the rooms are minisuites, and they're air-conditioned, which is a rare feature up here. Unnecessary in the winter, but it can be a real blessing in August. The very sweet dog-friendly owners ask to know ahead of time if you'll be bringing a dog so they can plan a room strategy (perhaps to avoid having a cat as your next-door neighbor). They also work with a nearby veterinarian who boards pets for people who will be skiing during the day and don't know what to do with the pooch. They'll be happy to give you the info you need. Rates are $89–150. Dogs pay a $10 fee for the length of their stay. The motel is a half block east of Old Mammoth Road, on Highway 203. 2963 Main Street CA 93546; 760/934-4500; www.shiloinns.com.

Sierra Nevada Rodeway Inn: Some rooms here have fireplaces and kitchens, for that home-away-from-home feeling. Most are just basic rooms. Rates are $79–169. 164 Old Mammoth Road 93546; 760/934-2515; www.mammothsnri.com.

Crowley Lake

PLACES TO STAY

Mono Sierra Lodge: This Eastern Sierra–style lodge (think a fusion of Western and Alpine) is surrounded by plenty of dog-friendly hiking areas. The folks here will be glad to point you and your pooch in the right direction. Stay at a comfortable motel room, a small housekeeping unit, or a deluxe housekeeping unit with a fireplace. Open year-round, it gets mighty pretty here when the nearby mountains are covered with snow. Rates are $75–150. Dogs are $10 extra. The lodge is on Crowley Lake Drive, just off Highway 395; the mailing address is Route 1, Box 88 93546; 800/723-5387; www.monosierralodge.com.

CHAPTER 26

Mariposa County

I've learned something about Yosemite National Park since the first edition of this book: While it's not a poochy paradise, it's not dog hell, either. When I first visited with Joe the Dog many moons ago, it seemed so restrictive, with its "dogs on pavement only and certain campgrounds" rules. But I've since discovered that pavement doesn't have to be Doggy Enemy Number 1, especially when there's so much of it. A bane for the natural beauty of Yosemite turns out to be a bonus for dogs. Paved paths and roads ribbon their way through the entire breathtaking valley, and you can see a great deal from them. In fact, if it makes your dog feel any better, let her know that many dog-free people spend almost their entire Yosemite vacation on asphalt. (See National Parks for more on Yosemite.)

At least Yosemite is clearcut about its rules and the rangers have a good attitude about dogs when they're in the right place. The county parks system is another story: It's enough to make a grown dog growl.

PICK OF THE LITTER—MARIPOSA COUNTY

BEST OFF-LEASH HIKES
Sierra and Stanislaus National Forests (page 278)

BEST PLACE TO STAY
The Redwoods in Yosemite, Yosemite National Park
(page 280)

BEST RIDE
Sugar Pine Railroad, Fish Camp (page 283)

"Yep," said a razor-voiced woman on the other end of the phone. "We allow leashed dogs. But we don't like 'em." A voice in the background started cackling with sadistic laughter. "You tell her!" her cohort chortled. "Nope, we don't like them at all." Click.

Don't pay any attention to those people, dogs. You've got the law on your side. It's a leash law, but just the same, it's the law. Exercise your right to exercise your legs. Don't let the snarling civil servants get you down.

NATIONAL FORESTS

The National Forests and Wilderness Areas resource at the back of this book has important information and safety tips on visiting national forests with your dog and has more information on the national forests listed below.

Sierra National Forest

Stanislaus National Forest
😺😺😺😺🐾

NATIONAL PARKS

Yosemite National Park
😺😺😺

Ask just about everyone who's ever visited this park about what they've seen, and they'll gush about the impossibly beautiful geography, the dramatic waterfalls, the magnificent trails, the sheer cliffs, the pristine wildlife, and every other detail they can dredge up. It's not hyperbole. This fantastic park is bigger than the imagination, bigger than life. It inspires even the most jaded parkgoer to sing its praises.

Then ask the same question of people who've visited with dogs. They'll be able to tell you all about the lovely car campsites here. They can even expound on the glories of the commercialization of Yosemite Village, the clever way the parking lots are set up, and how toasty the blacktop gets at 2 P.M. in August.

But it turns out that Yosemite is not really such a doggy drag. You just have to know where to go. While dogs are not allowed on any trails, in meadows, or in the backcountry of Yosemite, they are permitted to explore the beautiful Yosemite Valley area via paved roads and paths. And for better or worse, there's a lot of pavement here. That means you and your leashed dog can peruse some absolutely stunning scenery from miles of flat, easy terrain. (More silver lining: The pavement will help keep your dog's nails trimmed.)

If you want to hit the real trails, you can have your dog stay at the park's kennel Memorial Day–Labor Day. (No, not the whole time. You know what we mean.) And we're not talking luxury suites here. We're talking your basic cagelike contraptions that make you feel incredibly guilty for leaving the little guy behind. The kennel costs $8 per day, and space is limited. It's first-come, first-served, so get there early during busy times. Dogs are required to have all their shots, be more than 16 weeks old, and to be more than 10 pounds. (Sorry, teacup poodles!) The kennel phone is 209/372-8348.

Some folks think they can get away with leaving their dog tied up to their campsite for a few hours while they go exploring. But remember, if the ranger doesn't catch up with you, there's always the chance that a mountain lion or other cunning critter might catch up with your tethered dog. "We call one of these camping areas Coyote Point," a park employee told me. "You'd be a fool to leave your dog behind even for a little bit."

One clever reader wrote to us and told us how she and her husband get away with taking their smallish dogs through Yosemite. They tote them along on little doggy trailers attached to their bikes. Sometimes they strap a dog carrier to their chests and away they go. It probably isn't legal, so I won't use their names. But their truck's license plate is so wonderfully appropriate to the theme of this book that I can't help but mention it: CAB4K9S. (It sure be.)

Here are the campgrounds that permit pooches: In the valley, there's the Upper Pines Campground. Along Highway 120, you can stay at Hodgdon Meadow Campground, Crane Flat Campground (section A), White Wolf Campground (section C), Yosemite Creek Campground (front section), and the west end of the Tuolumne Meadows Campground. Along Glacier Point Road and Highway 41, you can stay at the Bridalveil Creek Campground (section A) and the Wawona Campground.

The campsites cost $14–18. Some are first-come, first-served; others are by reservation only. Call 800/436-7275 for reservation information, or 209/372-0299 for park information. Rates to enter Yosemite are $20 per car, and the pass you'll get is good for one week; www.nps.gov/yose.

PLACES TO STAY

The Redwoods in Yosemite: This group of lovely, privately owned mountain homes is by far the best thing that's ever happened to dogs in Yosemite. The Redwoods is nestled in the forest at 4,000 feet, where the air is so clean you can smell it. The homes range in size from cozy one-bedroom cottages to big five-bedroom spreads. They're all different, but they're attractive and woodsy, and most have decks and fireplaces.

General manager Pamela Kornell is a very dog-friendly person. She's trying to get as many homes as possible to open their doors to dogs. So far, 30 of the Redwoods' 125 homes say yes. Some are really magical, with wide picture windows and huge stone fireplaces.

Dogs who stay here get to peruse the surrounding area on leash. They can sniff at trees and cruise by streams. This is much more than they can do in the rest of the park. There's even a little market, the Pine Tree, where dogs can often be seen waiting for their people to finish shopping.

Homes rent for a minimum of 2–3 days. Rates are $115–616 a night. Dogs are $10 extra. P.O. Box 2085, Wawona, Yosemite National Park, CA 95389; 209/375-6666 or 888/225-6666; www.redwoodsinyosemite.com.

Yosemite National Park: See Yosemite National Park, above, for camping information.

Coulterville

Dogs, listen up. Without your kind, this tiny Old West town may never have even made it onto the map. Here's why. Back in 1850, a certain George Coulter started a tent store here to keep roofs over the heads of the local gold miners. This fellow also built the first hotel, which helped attract a more civilized sort. But the place needed water. So Coulter convinced a couple of Newfoundland dogs to pump water from the well. The hotel is now home to the Northern Mariposa History Center. You'll have to stop in for a visit to learn the rest of this shaggy-dog tale.

PARKS, BEACHES, AND RECREATION AREAS

1 Coulterville County Park

🐾🐾 (See Mariposa County map on page 276)

Dogs like rolling in the grass and cooling off under the picnic tables. The park, which isn't very big, is conveniently situated just off Highway 49, in the center of "town." Just pull off the highway and park, or take Highway 49 to Main Street, head east, and make an immediate left onto Park Lane. 209/966-2498.

2 Lake McClure

🐾🐾🐾 (See Mariposa County map on page 276)

With 7,100 surface acres of water, this beautiful lake is a water dog's dream. But it's not bad for landlubbers either. The lake is surrounded by the kind of perfect green land you see only around model-train sets and in picture puzzles your old aunt used to give you.

The lake has several recreation areas with decent places to walk a leashed dog and even better campsites. The 110 sites at the Horseshoe Bend Recreation Area at the northeast corner of the lake are filled with trees and provide plenty of privacy. During the off-season, you might even have the place to yourselves. The ranger here recommends walking your dog by the hang-gliding area when no one else is around. It's far from cars and has ample acreage.

The Bagby Recreation Area, on the Merced River section of the lake, has a pretty good trail along the river, across from the camping spots. The 30 campsites get more secluded the farther you drive down the winding road.

The day-use fee for the recreation areas is $6.50 per car. Campsites are $15–24. Reservations are advised. Dogs are $2 extra, day or night. To get to the Horseshoe Bend Recreation Area from Highway 49 just south of Coulterville, go west on Highway 132 for about three miles. The entrance will be on your left. Call 800/468-8889 for reservations. Call 209/378-2521 for a brochure or directions to other parts of the lake.

PLACES TO STAY

Lake McClure: See Lake McClure, above, for camping information.

Midpines

PLACES TO STAY

Homestead Guest Ranch: When you stay here, the house is all yours. It comes with a fireplace, a barbecue, and a well-stocked kitchen. Rates are $120 per couple plus $45 for each additional person. This is a wonderful place to stay, and the owners are sweet, dog-loving folks. They're happy to give you the good news that your dog can be leash-free on the ranch's 13 acres. Aroo! The ranch is about a half mile off Highway 140. The mailing address is P.O. Box 13 95345; 209/966-2820.

Mariposa

If you're on your way to Yosemite with your dog, take time to stop at this historic town. It's the county seat, but it looks nothing like most governmental centers we've seen. It's full of historic Gold Rush–era buildings and antique shops. The restaurants aren't bad either.

PARKS, BEACHES, AND RECREATION AREAS

🐾 Mariposa County Park

🐾🐾🐾 (See Mariposa County map on page 276)

This tiered park is like a wedding cake, with something delectable on every layer. Your dog will want to sink her teeth into it.

The top of the park is green and grassy, with picnic tables, a small playground, and excellent views of the town of Mariposa. A dirt road leads you to the lower levels, which have plenty of shade, picnic tables, and a decent walking path. Dogs must be leashed.

From Highway 49/140 going south, turn right on 6th Street. In one block, jog right on Strong Street and make a quick left onto County Parks Road. 209/966-2498.

PLACES TO EAT

Frost Shop: Your dog may find canine company at the outdoor tables— plenty of dogs bring their people here for a bite of burger. In fact, photos of dog customers eating ice cream grace part of a wall. "We love, love, love dogs!" says Kay Mickel, one of the owners. Dogs are treated to bowls of fresh water. 5087 Highway 140; 209/966-5557.

DIVERSION

Take a Sentimental Journey: If you're hankering to ride the old Logger Steam Train through some of Sierra National Forest's most magnificent scenery, you don't have to worry about waving good-bye to your dog. Leashed, calm dogs who can fit on your lap are welcome aboard the quaint old trains of the **Sugar Pine Railroad.** (In other words, 85-pound wiggly Jake Dog is not a good candidate.) Rates for the hour-long Logger ride are $14 for adults, $7 for kids. Dogs don't pay a cent.

If your dog is shy of loud noises, get as far back from the engine as possible, or simply take the railroad's "Model A"–powered trip. It's quieter, shorter (30 minutes), and cheaper ($10 per adult, $5 per child) than the Logger train.

For fairly obvious reasons, no dogs are allowed on the evening dinner ride. The train station is at 56001 Highway 41. It's about 12 miles past Oakhurst, two miles before the town of Fish Camp. And there's a terrific fringe benefit: It's right next to a couple of trailheads into dog-friendly Sierra National Forest. 559/683-7273; www.ymsprr.com.

PLACES TO STAY

Motherlode Lodge: Lucky dogs are allowed to be off leash in the back area here. That's great news for dogs who are weary of dainty little leashed walks while on a road trip. The owner, Lisa, adores dogs, and will make your dog feel at home. Rates are $38–149. The physical address is 5051 Highway 140, and the mailing address is P.O. Box 986 95338; 209/966-2521 or 800/398-9770.

Fish Camp

PLACES TO STAY

Apple Tree Inn: Towering sugar pines surround the 18 new townhouselike cabins that make up the Apple Tree Inn. It's tree city here, which is excellent news for dogs of the male persuasion. The Sierra National Forest is right across the street, and that's wonderful for all dogs. Yosemite National Park (see National Parks in this chapter) is just two miles down the road. This is a very peaceful place to stay, and the cabin rooms are beautifully designed. Dogs can't stay in the upstairs rooms (which are actually suites), but they're welcome at all the first-floor rooms. Surprisingly, this serene resort is home to a delightfully unserene racquetball court, as well as an indoor pool and spa.

Rates are $99–179. Dogs are $50 per visit. 1110 Highway 41 93623; 559/683-5111 or 888/683-5111; www.appletreeinn-yosemite.com.

Narrow Gauge Inn: Stay here and you're just a bone's throw from the dog-friendly Sugar Pine Railroad (see the Diversion Take a Sentimental Journey) and four miles from Yosemite National Park. This is an old-fashioned country-style inn. Most of the 26 guest rooms are on the small side, but they sport terrific mountain views, making them feel larger. The dog rooms are on the first level of the three-story inn, and all have balcony entrances. Dogs enjoy the property's tall trees, short trail, and seasonal creek. People like taking a dip in the heated outdoor pool or soaking in the hot tub. (Dogs would too, but they have to stick to the creek.) Rates are $79–149. Dogs are $25 extra per visit. 48571 Highway 41 93623; 559/683-7720; www.narrowgaugeinn.com.

BAY AREA COUNTIES

CHAPTER 27

Sonoma County

The horticulturist Luther Burbank, who made his home in Santa Rosa and Sebastopol from 1875 to 1926, called Sonoma County "the chosen spot of all the Earth as far as nature is concerned." Practically anything will grow in Sonoma County. It's the Bay Area capital for trees, flowers, and vegetables, as well as goats, sheep, cattle, chickens, pigs, and probably a few farm animals that are just now being invented.

Unfortunately, dogs and farm animals don't mix. Some Sonoma sheep ranchers have been known to impose the ultimate penalty on loose dogs that they see near their livestock: They shoot them. They're not acting under the law of the Wild West, either. It's a county ordinance that dogs harassing livestock in unincorporated areas or on private property may be shot by the property owner.

But fear not. Sonoma County has many enchanting places where the only shot your dog will experience is a shot of adrenaline when he lays eyes on the stunning scenery and some mesmerizing, dog-friendly hangouts. The off-leash doggy areas in Sonoma County are increasing every year. Oh joy of

PICK OF THE LITTER—SONOMA COUNTY

BIGGEST AND BEST DOG PARK
Rocky Memorial Dog Park, Petaluma (page 313)

BEST BEACH
Sonoma Coast State Beaches, Jenner (page 298)

MOST DOG-FRIENDLY PLACE TO EAT
Garden Court Cafe, Glen Ellen (page 309)

MOST BEAUTIFUL OCEANFRONT HOUSE
Robinsong, rented through Sea Ranch Vacation Homes, Sea Ranch (page 289)

MOST DOG-FRIENDLY PLACES TO STAY
Creekside Inn and Resort, Guerneville (page 294)
Fern Grove Cottages, Guerneville (page 295)
Larissa's House, rented through Russian River Vacation Homes, Guerneville (page 296)
Sheraton Sonoma County, Petaluma (page 316)

BEST SECLUDED INN
Stone Grove Inn, Sonoma (page 317)

MOST DOG-FRIENDLY WINE TASTING
The Wine Room, Kenwood (page 292)

joys! It's hard to find a Sonoma County dog whose tail isn't wagging a little faster these days.

Sea Ranch

PARKS, BEACHES, AND RECREATION AREAS

🚩 Sea Ranch Beach Trails

🐾🐾🐾 (See Sonoma County map on page 286)

Sea Ranch is a private development, but seven public foot trails cross the property leading to the beach, which is also public property. The smooth, wide dirt trails are managed by Sonoma County Regional Parks, and they offer incomparable solitary walks through unspoiled grassy hills.

All the trails are clearly marked on Highway 1. Each trailhead has restrooms and a box where you are asked to deposit $4 for parking. No motorcycles, bicycles, or horses are allowed. Keep your dog on leash.

Here are the distances to the beach, listing trails from north to south: Salal Trail, .6 mile; Bluff-Top Trail, 3.5 miles; Walk-On Beach Trail, .4 mile; Shell Beach Trail, .6 mile; Stengel Beach Trail, .2 mile; Pebble Beach Trail, .3 mile; Black Point Trail, .3 mile. 707/785-2377.

PLACES TO STAY

Sea Ranch Vacation Homes beach rentals: The Sea Ranch Vacation Homes rental agency offers 14 beautiful, dog-friendly homes for rent in the glorious oceanfront community of Sea Ranch. Some homes are almost on the water, some are set in wooded areas. All are attractive, but our favorite is Robinsong, a stellar example of how a seaside home can live up to its landscape. The fireplace flanked by smartly cushioned "window seats" is worth the price of admission. You will love reading there, and your dog will adore snoozing on a blanket beside you. The look of the interior is clean and crisp, yet amazingly cozy. The spacious kitchen, which boasts an island, is set up for the chef in you.

Rates for the Robinsong are $240 nightly (there's a two-night minimum) and $1,440 for the week. It's one of the more expensive dog-friendly homes, but if you have it in your budget, it's worth it. Rates for the variety of dog-friendly homes are $130–240. Weekly rates are $780–1440. Dogs are $10 extra nightly. For reservations and information, call 707/884-4235; www.searanchrentals.com.

Cloverdale

PARKS, BEACHES, AND RECREATION AREAS

🐾 Lake Sonoma Recreation Area

🐾🐾🐾 (See Sonoma County map on page 286)

This is the only recreation site in the nine counties of the Bay Area run by the U.S. Army Corps of Engineers, and it's too bad. The Corps has a liberal attitude toward dogs, and this park is beautifully developed and managed, not to mention clean. It's also free. You must keep your dog on a six-foot leash, and he's not allowed on the swimming beach at the north end, but rangers told us there's no rule against dogs swimming anywhere else.

If you're the type who doesn't clean up after your dog, here's a warning: Change your act, or stay far from here. Rangers have been known to charge a cleanup fee for owners who ignore the deposits of their dogs.

A large lawn with picnic tables, some shaded, is at the visitor center. You can rent a boat from the private concession on the lake, which allows leashed dogs on all boats. Follow signs from the visitor center. To reserve a boat, call 707/433-2200. Waterskiing and camping are also popular here.

For a good dog hike, pick up a map at the visitor center and drive west on Dry Creek Road to the trailheads, which have their own parking lots. There are 40 miles of trails. Here are two of our favorites: There's a bit of shade at the Gray Pine Flat Trailhead. This smooth foot trail goes down to the lake through an unusual forest of foothill pines, madrone, manzanita, and blooming desert brush. The buzz of motorboats on the lake blends with the hammering of woodpeckers. You get a good view of the lake fairly quickly. If you'd prefer less of a climb back to the trailhead, take the Little Flat Trail, which starts lower down.

Horses are allowed on these trails, but bikes aren't—a plus for your dog's safety. Unfortunately, it gets bone-dry here in summer, and poison oak is common.

Camping is available at 113 sites at Liberty Glen Campground and several primitive boat-in sites on the lake. None of these sites has water. (Campers at Liberty Glen can stock up nearby.) Rates are $10–14. For reservations (advised in summer), phone 877/444-6777.

Take U.S. 101 to the Canyon Road exit. Go west to Dry Creek Road and turn right into the entrance. Take a right at the only fork. 707/433-9483.

PLACES TO STAY

Lake Sonoma Recreation Area: See the Lake Sonoma Recreation Area, above, for camping information.

Timber Cove

PARKS, BEACHES, AND RECREATION AREAS

🐾 Salt Point State Park

🐾🐾🐾 (See Sonoma County map on page 286)

Dogs are allowed only on South Gerstle Cove Beach—south of the rocky tidepool area, which is an underwater reserve—and in the Gerstle Cove, Woodside, and Fisk Mill Cove picnic areas and campsites. Gerstle Cove picnic area is right above the section of the beach where dogs are allowed, so that's your best bet. The surf is usually gentle here, but if in doubt, you can call for an ocean-conditions recording at 707/847-3222. As far as walking around, dogs get to do it only on paved roads. They must be leashed everywhere.

The parking fee is $6. Dogs are allowed at all campsites here except the walk-in and group sites. The park has about 30 tents in the upland part of the park. East of Highway 1 are 80 family sites. Sites are $15–20 per night. Call 800/444-7275 for reservations.

The park is about five miles north of Timber Cove and six miles south of Stewarts Point, off Highway 1. For park info, call 707/847-3221.

◪ Stillwater Cove Regional Park

🐾🐾🐾 (See Sonoma County map on page 286)

This is a tiny but delightful beach at the foot of spectacular pine-covered cliffs. Park in the small lot beside Highway 1, leash your dog, and walk down. There is a larger picnic area above the highway, where a $4 day-use fee is charged. From here, you have to cross the highway to get to the cove. Look both ways!

There are 23 campsites, available on a first-come, first-served basis. If you want to make a reservation, they're available through park headquarters. Sites are $17 per night. The turnout is about one mile north of Fort Ross State Park (where dogs are banned). 707/847-3245.

PLACES TO STAY

Salt Point State Park: See Salt Point State Park, above, for camping information.

Stillwater Cove Regional Park: See Stillwater Cove Regional Park, above, for camping information.

Healdsburg

PARKS, BEACHES, AND RECREATION AREAS

◪ Villa Chanticleer Dog Park

🐾🐾🐾🐾🐕 (See Sonoma County map on page 286)

This 1.5-acre fenced dog park is a great place to take your dog whether you live here or you're just visiting. It's within a beautiful oak grove setting, so it's easy on the eyes, plus there's plenty of shade. Lucky dogs who come here have it all: trees, enough room to romp, and the smells of nature. It has all the good dog-park amenities, including benches and water. The ground cover is wood chips, which adds to the woodsy feeling here, but Jake thinks each wood chip is a delicacy and is content to plop himself down and gnaw away until an interesting dog or errant tennis ball catches his eye.

The park is set within the larger Villa Chanticleer Park, which has buildings and backdrops that are popular for weddings. Be sure your dog is on leash if you explore beyond the dog area: You don't want your dog interfering with any nuptials. The address is 1248 Chanticleer Way.

DIVERSION

Merlot Over and Play Dead: I didn't make up this pun. (Mine are usually worse.) It's the name of a wine made by a Healdsburg vintner who owns the Mutt Lynch Winery. Other "doggone good wines," as Brenda Lynch calls them, are Canis Major and Portrait of a Mutt.

Sonoma County wineries are going to the dogs. Two have their own lines of dog-labeled wines. Many allow well-behaved dogs in their tasting rooms and at their picnic areas. Below is a sampling of some of Sonoma's more dog-friendly wineries, listed by area. Phone the individual wineries for hours, prices, and dog-friendly specifics.

GUERNEVILLE:
Korbel Champagne Cellars, 13250 River Road; 707/824-7000.

HEALDSBURG:
Foppiano Vineyards, 12707 Old Redwood Highway; 707/433-7272.
Lambert Bridge Winery, 4085 West Dry Creek Road; 707/431-9600.
Mutt Lynch Winery, 1960 Dry Creek Road; 707/942-6180. Open by appointment only. Dog-labeled wines abound.

KENWOOD:
The Wine Room, 9575 Sonoma Highway; 707/833-6131. Dogs get dog treats at this multiwinery co-op tasting room. A new wine line, The Family Dog, has rolled out its first label, Barney. The dog wine line is seeking more dogs for its labels.

SANTA ROSA:
De Loach Vineyards, 1791 Olivet Road; 707/526-9111.
Martini and Prati Winery, 2191 Laguna Road; 707/823-2404.

SONOMA:
Sebastiani Vineyards and Winery, 389 4th Street East; 707/933-3230. Visiting dogs get to drink fresh water from the outside dog bowls. Leashes are available, lest you forget yours.

WINDSOR:
Martinelli Vineyards and Winery, 3360 River Road; 707/525-0570.

6 Badger Park Dog Park

🐾🐾🐾🐕 (See Sonoma County map on page 286)

If only this park were bigger than a quarter acre we could give it an extra paw. It's a lovely little fenced park, with one gorgeous large oak that people tend to congregate under. The ground is grassy, which dog paws appreciate. The park is set within Badger Park, which is at 750 Heron Drive. 707/431-3384.

PLACES TO EAT

Costeaux French Bakery: Stroll around Healdsburg's good-looking town square, with its old buildings and benches for shady rest stops, and then drop in here for dinner or a wonderful pastry snack at an outdoor table. The bakery sells delicious homemade dog bones, should your dog inquire. 417 Healdsburg Avenue; 707/433-1913.

Oakville Grocery: This gourmet grocer is the home of a terrific alfresco café where dogs are welcome. The outdoor café features a wood-burning fireplace, which makes for cozy evenings. Jake loves sniffing the rotisserie chicken, and the pizzas are to drool for. Wine is big here, too, but dogs should stick with water, which is plentiful: There's always a doggy bowl here for thirsty pooches. 124 Matheson Street; 707/433-3200.

PLACES TO STAY

Best Western Dry Creek Inn: Rates are $69–129. Dogs are $20 extra. 198 Dry Creek Road 95448; 707/433-0300.

Windsor

Until 1992, Windsor wasn't anything but an unincorporated county area. Then it became a town, thanks to the "d" word (development). In 1997, it spawned its very first park, and with that park came a fenced-in dog park. Dogs think Windsor's movers and shakers are very smart people, indeed.

PARKS, BEACHES, AND RECREATION AREAS

7 Pleasant Oak Park

🐾🐾🐕 (See Sonoma County map on page 286)

This is a fine example of how a fenced-in dog park can become a decent place, despite a rather austere start. In the park's early days, it was little more than a dirt lot surrounded by a very high fence with double gates. But now it's really something to wag about. It has water, grass, and enough trees to cast a cooling shade in the summer. Dogs from miles around come to socialize. Their humans have been known to follow suit. The park is at Old Redwood Highway and Pleasant Avenue. 707/838-1260.

Guerneville

PARKS, BEACHES, AND RECREATION AREAS

🔢 Armstrong Redwoods State Reserve

🐾🐾 (See Sonoma County map on page 286)

As is usual in state parks, you can take a dog only on paved roads and into picnic areas. But here you can give your dog and yourself an exceptional treat. The picnic grounds are a cool, hushed redwood cathedral. You can walk on Armstrong Woods Road, which winds along Fife Creek (usually lush, but dry in the heart of summer) all the way to the top of McCray Mountain, about three miles.

The drive is fairly terrifying, so you may prefer to walk anyway. Hikers, bicycles, and autos all share the road, so be very careful. Your dog must be leashed everywhere in the park. From Guerneville, go about 2.5 miles north on Armstrong Woods Road. The day-use fee is $6, but if you park out front you can walk in for free. 707/869-2015 or 707/865-2391.

🔢 Vacation Beach

🐾🐾🐾 (See Sonoma County map on page 286)

Vacation Beach is not really a beach, but an access point where the Russian River is dammed by two roads across it. It's one of several public spots where you and your dog used to be able to legally jump into the drink, but leashes seem to be the law here now. It's still fun. People and pooches picnic, swim, put in canoes, and cool their feet and paws in the cool river.

From Highway 116 between Guerneville and Monte Rio, turn south at the unmarked road where you see Old Cazadero Road veering north. You can park at the approaches to the dams but not on the crossing itself. 707/869-9000.

PLACES TO STAY

Creekside Inn and Resort: Dogs get to stay at three of several cottages and rooms at this fun inn near the Russian River. Bird dogs enjoy lounging in the Quail Cottage, a small, bright cottage with a fireplace. The Deck House, another poochy haven, is a little larger, with a sunny deck. The sweet one-bedroom Apple House is separated from the inn by a very old apple tree.

The real apple of your dog's eyes will be the Dog Days Package. You and your dog will each get a tasty treat (gourmet chocolate for you, liver goody for your dog, and aren't you glad it's not vice-versa?) You'll also receive a coupon for a little doggy gift and discounts on a grooming for your dog and a massage for you. The package entails staying a few nights, but it ends up being less expensive than doing a night-by-night tally. Other packages, such as the popular Gay Honeymoon package, are also available.

The inn's land is dotted with several large redwoods. The property spans three acres, and dogs are welcome to cruise around on leash. Human guests may hang out in the inn's main dining room and lounge, both of which have fireplaces. Humans can also swim in the pool here. Dogs have to be content to do the dog paddle in the Russian River, not too far away.

Rates are $105–165. Weekly rates are available. If you'd like to stay in a larger house, you can also rent the Summer Crossing, a small vacation home here. It goes for $285 nightly and sleeps up to four. 16180 Neeley Road, P.O. Box 2185 95446; 707/869-3623 or 800/776-6586; www.creeksideinn.com.

Fern Grove Cottages: Sleep in one of 20 charming cabins under 200-foot redwoods here! The friendly owners, Mike and Margaret Kennett, will even point you and your pooch toward their favorite (secret) dog hike, which includes a dip in a pristine creek. It's a dog's idea of a perfect vacation.

The Kennetts welcome good pooches. "We've had some great dogs stay here," says Margaret, who doles out biscuits at check-in and provides old blankets for your dog's sleeping pleasure.

The cottages are simple, but cozy, with tasteful decor. Most have fireplaces, and some have kitchens. A delicious continental breakfast comes with your stay. The homemade granola and scones are divine. Rates are $89–209. Dogs are $15 extra. 16650 Highway 116 95446; 707/869-8105; www.ferngrove.com.

Fifes Guest Ranch: The cottages on this 15-acre redwood-festooned property will melt your heart if you like older abodes. These were built in 1905, and they still have the charm of their day, updated with a simple, light, airy decor. They're super comfy, too. Dogs think they're the cat's meow, but truth be told, they really like walking around the ranch better. The meadows, the trees, the river, all speak to a dog's soul.

If you like camping, you can pitch your tent at one of 85 tents-only sites, some of which are along the river. Camping rates are $19–50 for one-tent sites. Cottages are $65–305. Dogs are $25 for the length of their stay while camping or in the cottages.

The ranch hosts many events throughout the year. Recent events included a food and wine fest; the LeatherSIR and Leatherboy outdoor-themed weekend (the event tied up many guests); and Liquid, a pool party for women. 16467 Highway 116, P.O. Box 45 95446; 707/869-0656 or 800/734-3371; www.fifes.com.

Highlands Resort: If your dog has never been to a bar, ask to stay in the Highland's studio: The large room not only has a cozy fireplace and love seat, but it has its own wet bar. Teetotaling dogs might prefer the five larger cabins that allow dogs. The cabins have fireplaces, and some have kitchenettes, but no bar.

The Highlands, known as "a straight-friendly gay resort," is set on three wooded acres (which dogs can explore on leash) and has the feel of a country retreat. It has a swimming pool and outdoor hot tub—both clothing-optional. In the resort's brochure there's a bird's-eye–view picture of a fellow standing in the hot tub, with just a bit of bun showing. Joe Dog blushed and came back for another look. The owner asked us to mention that people with diverse lifestyles feel right at home here.

Rates are $85–135. Dogs are $25 extra for the length of their stay. 14000 Woodland Drive 95446; 707/869-0333; www.highlandsresort.com.

Russian River Getaways: If you and your dog want a home away from home while you vacation in the Russian River area, you've hit the jackpot. Russian River Getaways has about 50 beautiful dog-friendly homes for rent on a nightly or weekly basis. The homes are generally quite upscale, but the prices are fairly down to earth. (An aside that will put a smile on your dog's snout: Only six of the 56 homes rented through Russian River Getaways don't permit dogs. "We tell them that if they don't allow dogs, they're not going to do such good business," says an employee. "They really can't compete.")

Most of the homes are very attractive, with wonderfully creative touches. Just the names of some of the homes make you and your dog friend want to check them out: Bellagio, Bohemian Rhapsody, Jujube, The Bird Cage/La Cage aux Folles, the Luv Shack, and the Grand Prix (please don't pronounce the "x." You'll embarrass your dog.) are not your typical vacation home rental names. If you're looking to drop some dollars, check out Grandma's House (let's just say this must be some grandma with a billiard table in her 31-foot living room and a hot tub in her gazebo) and the River Queen, a fabulous manse on the river.

Rates for the homes range $175–975 nightly. Weekly rates are $1,050–5,850. For a brochure describing the homes, write Russian River Getaways at 14075 Mill Street, P.O. Box 1673 95446, or phone 707/869-4560 or 800/433-6673. The best way to check out the rentals is at www.rrgetaways.com.

Russian River Vacation Homes: Spend your Russian River–area vacation in your own charming private house. This is an ideal way to vacation with your pooch. Russian River Vacation Homes offers two dozen beautiful, quaint houses for pets and their people. From a one-bedroom rustic log cabin on the river to a three-bedroom riverside home complete with hot tub, you and your holiday hound will find the home of your dreams.

One of Joe's favorites was Larissa's House, a sweet one-bedroom home with a flowery, fenced-in yard on the river. Larissa, the owner, lives next door and adores dogs. In fact, you pretty much have to have a dog to stay here. It's so doggone dog-friendly that the shower is designed so that you and your dog can shower at the same time. (Joe was shy, so he didn't care for this arrangement.) If Larissa has time, she'll make sure your pooch has a welcoming bag of treats when she arrives. Dogs fall instantly in love when they meet Larissa, and the love-fest often continues year-round, because she sends them (note: *them*, not *you*) Christmas cards.

Rates are $145–535. Weekly rates are $700–2,400. For a brochure describing all the dog-friendly properties, write Russian River Vacation Homes at 14080 Mill Street 95446; 707/869-9030, 800/310-0804 (California only), or 800/997-3312 (nationwide); www.riverhomes.com.

Forestville

This beautiful town's motto is: "Where wine country meets the redwoods." This is Russian River country, and dogs love sniffing around some terrific beaches here. Be sure to visit the historic community's little "downtown." It's an eclectic charmer.

PARKS, BEACHES, AND RECREATION AREAS

If you have a dog who likes splashing in water, prepare for a very happy pooch: Forestville is home to three county beaches that permit leashed dogs. They're all Russian River havens, with good river access, old black walnut forests, German ivy, and lots of birds. Dogs need to be leashed, but there's plenty to enjoy, even tethered together. Since this pretty much describes all three river access locales, below we'll just list the pertinent info for each.

10 Steelhead Beach

🐾🐾🐾 (See Sonoma County map on page 286)

At 50 acres, with lots of picnic areas and flat grassy territory, this is the largest and most developed of the three county beach access areas in Forestville. If you drive in, you pay $4. Walk in and it's free. For info on the park's natural features, see the introduction to the Parks section, above. The park is at 9000 River Road. 707/565-2041.

11 Forestville River Access/Mom's Beach

🐾🐾🐾 (See Sonoma County map on page 286)

It's 10-acres of on-leash fun here. This is a totally undeveloped area, at 10584 River Drive, off River Road. For info on the park's natural features, see the introduction to the Parks section, above. 707/565-2041.

12 Sunset Beach

🐾🐾🐾 (See Sonoma County map on page 286)

This is a wild and lovely river access location, with about 10 acres to explore with your leashed dog. For info on the park's natural features, see the introduction to the Parks section, above. 11057 Sunset Drive. 707/565-2041.

Jenner

PARKS, BEACHES, AND RECREATION AREAS

13 Sonoma Coast State Beaches

🐾🐾🐾🐾 (See Sonoma County map on page 286)

A string of beautiful, clean beaches runs south from Jenner to Bodega Bay, and you can't go wrong from Goat Rock Beach south to Salmon Creek Beach: Gorgeous bluff views, stretches of brown sand, gnarled rocks, and grassy dunes welcome you. Always keep an eye on the surf and a leash on your dog.

Dogs are not allowed on any of the trails that run on the bluffs above the beaches, on Bodega Head, in the Willow Creek area east of Bridgehaven, or in the seal rookery upriver from Goat Rock Beach. (Watch for the warning sign.) No camping is permitted on any of the beaches, except Bodega Dunes and Wright's Beach, which have campgrounds. These two also charge a $6 day-use fee. Day use of all other beaches is free. 707/875-3483.

The Bodega Dunes Campground has 99 developed sites, and Wright's Beach Campground has 27 developed sites. Sites are $20 at Bodega, and $30 at Wright's. Reservations are highly recommended. Call 800/444-7275. For general beach info, call 707/875-3483.

PLACES TO EAT

Seagull Deli: Don't look up when you eat at the outdoor tables here! Hah. It's an old joke, apparently, based on the deli's name. You and your dog can dine on creamy clam chowder while overlooking the mouth of the Russian River from one of the picnic tables. It's a tasty way to spend part of a crisp autumn afternoon. 10439 North Coast Highway (Highway 1); 707/865-2594.

PLACES TO STAY

Jenner Inn: This area is a black hole for cell phones, and only a few of the rooms and cottages have phones, and none have TVs, so this is a great place to visit if you really want to get away from it all. (That said, they're considering getting high-speed Internet access in the main inn.)

There's so much relaxing to be done here that you'll scarcely notice that you're not doing anything. The early-20th-century rooms and cottages are comfy and furnished with antiques. Some have fireplaces, some have kitchens, some have river views. The Russian River is just a bone's throw away, and it's a fairly quick walk to the ocean, should you want to see big water. The best part of staying here with a dog is the big three-acre meadow in the back: Pooches are welcome to trot around off leash! You won't need to worry about finding a local dog park if you stay here.

Rates are $138–188. A wonderful vacation home is available for $288. Highway 1, Box 69 95450; 707/865-2377; www.jennerinn.com.

Sonoma Coast State Beaches: See Sonoma Coast State Beaches, above, for camping information.

Occidental

If you become an accidental Occidental tourist, you and your leashed pooch can enjoy a stroll through this historic landmark town, with its interesting assortment of shops and galleries. If you want to spend the night, here's a dog-friendly lodging.

PLACES TO STAY

Negri's Occidental Hotel: This is a very basic, although decent, motel. It's close to the village, and there's a pool, should you feel like doing the dog paddle. (Your dog needs to stay dry here.) Rates are $59–139. Dogs are $8.70 extra. 3610 Bohemian Highway 95465; 707/874-3623 or 877/867-6084; www.occidentalhotel.com.

Sebastopol

Dogs enjoy sniffing out this sweet semirural community. It's got oodles of little Farm Trails farms (see the Sniff Out the Farm Trail Diversion), should you be drooling for some fresh produce. (Some sell meat, too, should that interest your dog.)

PARKS, BEACHES, AND RECREATION AREAS

14 Ragle Ranch Regional Park

🐾🐾🐾 (See Sonoma County map on page 286)

While some of this 156-acre park is developed with sports fields and courts, much of it is devoted to being its good old natural self. A lovely nature trail will take you and your leashed dog to Atascadero Creek. Hang onto that leash, because this is a primo bird-watching area. Boy dogs love the oak grove that shades this area.

It costs $5 to park inside the park. From Highway 12, drive north on Ragle Road. The park will be on your left in several blocks. 707/565-2041.

PLACES TO EAT

Pasta Bella: The linguine with tomatoes is to drool for. Jake likes the bowl of water provided for thirsty dogs. 796 Gravenstein Highway South; 707/824-8191.

DIVERSION

Sniff Out the Farm Trail: This area is replete with fun little farms, selling everything from apples to wine to Christmas trees to meat and cheese. Well-behaved leashed dogs are often invited to join you at the many different farms that are part of the **Sonoma County Farm Trails.** Phone ahead to make sure it's OK. You can get a Farm Trails map and booklet with descriptions and phone numbers by contacting Sonoma County Farm Trails, P.O. Box 6032, Santa Rosa, CA 95406; 800/207-9464; or from the local Chamber of Commerce, P.O. Box 178, Sebastopol, CA 95473; 707/823-3032. Better yet, check out www.farmtrails.org.

Santa Rosa

PARKS, BEACHES, AND RECREATION AREAS

This sprawling city has gone to the dogs in the last few years, and dogs and their people couldn't be happier. It used to be that if you wanted to give your pooch a little off-leash exercise, you'd go out of town or sneak out to a park at night and hope no one was watching. But now the city has five very attractive off-leash dog parks and four parks that aren't fenced and have limited off-leash hours. That sound you hear is the sound of tails thumping. Hard. (Children's tails aren't wagging quite as quickly: Kids under 10 aren't allowed in any of the dog parks—not even on leash.)

For the most part, the dog parks are wonderful. And if you don't mind getting up early, the parks with limited off-leash hours offer even more room and more doggy-heaven scents. Dogs who visit these parks are allowed to run off leash 6–8 A.M. every day. The hours are strictly enforced, so be sure to wind your watch. Dogs have to be under voice control, nonaggressive, spayed or neutered, and more than four months old. As always, be sure to scoop the poop. The highest fine for poop lawbreakers could buy you a round-trip ticket to Hawaii, and then some: up to $500.

We like the philosophy of the parks department people here. In a nutshell, if there's a rough part of a park where people are afraid to go, they put in a dog park because they believe "it brings positive activities into the parks. It makes it much safer and more comfortable for kids and others," according to Bill Montgomery, the department's now-retired deputy director. We hope other communities look to Santa Rosa as an example of how to incorporate dogs into the park scene so that it makes life better for everyone.

15 DeTurk Round Barn Park

🐾🐾🐾🐕 (See Sonoma County map on page 286)

This is one of the more interesting parks to peruse with your pooch. It's a smallish park in the historic westside district of town, and it's home to a wonderful rare round barn that was built in the 1870s. Dogs have to be leashed to explore around the barn area.

What dogs like best about this park is a relatively small (9,000 square feet) dog park where they can throw their leashes to the wind. It's fenced with attractive white wood and has some young trees working to become shade trees. The dog park is actually called Maverick Park, in honor of a valuable member of the K-9 Corps of the Sonoma County Sheriff's Department who was killed in the line of duty in Santa Rosa. We won't forget you, Maverick.

The park is at Donahue and 8th Streets. 707/543-3292 or 707/539-5979.

16 Doyle Park

🐾🐾🐾🐾🐕 (See Sonoma County map on page 286)

Doyle Park is a very stately place to take a pooch. A little stone bridge takes you over a stream and into the park's main entry area. The trees here have an elegant, deep-rooted look. The grass is like a cool, plush green carpet. At Doyle, even the squirrels don't look squirrelly.

Dogs think it's all grand. But what they think is even better is the fact that they can run around all this splendor without a leash 6–8 A.M., thanks to a great program run by the city. Dogs who can't make these hours don't have to mope around on leash, though: Doyle Park is graced not only with the off-leash program, but it has its very own fenced doggy park. It's not as riveting as the rest of the park, but it's got water and some trees, and it's a very safe place to take even an escape artist. Unlike Rincon Park's dog run, Doyle's dog run doesn't close during the winter rains.

In addition to the rules mentioned in the beginning of this section, there's one that's a little tough if you're a parent of a dog and a youngish child: No children under 10 years old are allowed in the dog run, whether accompanied by a parent or not. The park users devised this rule, which was apparently meant to protect kids from getting mowed over by herds of dogs, and also to protect herds of dogs from lawsuits.

For the main entrance, take Sonoma Avenue to Doyle Park Drive and turn south, driving a few hundred feet over insufferable speed bumps to the parking area. The dog run will be way over to the left. To park closer to the dog run, take Sonoma Avenue to Hoen Avenue and turn south. The parking lot is on the right, and the dog run is on the other side of the ball field. 707/543-3292 or 707/539-5979.

17 Franklin Park

😺 😺 🐕 (See Sonoma County map on page 286)

Franklin is the smallest of the four parks that allow dogs off leash 6–8 A.M. It's green and slopey, with enough trees to make any boy dog happy. Be careful, because it's not as safe from traffic as some of the other parks (though it's not exactly Indy 500 territory around here).

The park is at Franklin Avenue and Gay Street. 707/543-3292 or 707/539-5979.

18 Galvin Community Park

😺 😺 😺 🐕 (See Sonoma County map on page 286)

Yahoo! This is yet another addition to Santa Rosa's growing legion of dog parks. The fenced dog park is where your pooch can run free here. It's about three-quarters of an acre. Amenities include benches for your tired tush and water for your thirsty pooch. The ground cover is mostly wood chips. And it smells so good when it's first brought in. Sometimes it can be a little hard to tell the poop from the wood chips, but you get used to it. Jake always poops in the grass, which is easy to see, but so hard to clean up. (This is more than you needed to know about Jake.)

The park is at Yulupa Avenue and Bennett Valley Road. 707/543-3292 or 707/539-5979.

19 Hood Mountain Regional Park

😺 😺 😺 (See Sonoma County map on page 286)

Dogs and people love the trails in this 1,450-acre park, but the hiking isn't a walk in the park, so to speak. You'll end up going up, up, up if you expect to get to any of the best spots here. From Gunsight Rock, you can see the Golden Gate Bridge on a clear day.

To get to the only entrance, from Highway 12 turn east on Los Alamos Road—not Adobe Canyon Road, which leads only to Sugarloaf Ridge State Park, where dogs aren't allowed on trails. (If a sign appears at the Los Alamos Road turnoff saying that the park is closed, believe it: The park is subject to closures when there's danger of mudslides or fire.) The road is long, winding, steep, and narrow for the last two miles. It's not for nervous drivers or carsick pooches, but it's a beautiful four-mile drive, with a good close-up of Hood Mountain's bare rock outcropping "hood."

A machine in the parking lot will ask you to pay $4. Call to make sure the park is open before driving here. A final note: Watch out for ticks. They're rampant. 707/565-2041.

20 Northwest Community Park

🐾🐾🐾🐕 (See Sonoma County map on page 286)

The fenced dog park within Northwest Park has doubled in size since its inception, and is once again up and running—and so are the neighborhood dogs. (No, smarty, the dogs haven't actually doubled in size.)

The dog area is now an acre and has two sections, grass, some shade, and at press time water and benches were about to go in. The dog park is just northwest of Northwest Park's soccer fields. The park is on Marlow Road, behind Comstock Junior High School, north of Guerneville Road. 707/543-3292 or 707/539-5979.

21 Rincon Valley Community Park

🐾🐾🐾🐾🐕 (See Sonoma County map on page 286)

The fenced dog park here is one of the more attractive dog parks in these parts. That's mostly because it has grass. Real grass. Not just a few green sprigs fighting their way through the tough dirt, but good ol' carpety grass. That's not because the dogs here pussyfoot around. In fact, dogs are so happy to be here that they tear around with great gusto. We're not exactly sure why there's so much grass, but we do know that the dog run closes during the rainy winter months, so that could have something to do with it.

A few trees grace the dog-run area, and the views of the surrounding hills make it seem as if it's in the middle of the countryside. As of this writing, it's actually on the edge of the countryside.

The dogs who come to Rincon's dog run are a friendly lot, running to the fence and sniffing all newcomers, tails wagging exuberantly. The people who come here are much the same, except they chat rather than sniff. An interesting rule: No little kiddies under 10 allowed, even if they're with their parents. A parks department spokesman says the park users made up the rule. So apparently if you've got a kid and a dog, you'll have to hire a sitter to bring your dog here. Boo!

But now here's something to cheer about: The dog park includes a little wading pond! This puts some big wag in a water dog's tail. There's also a separate section for large and small dogs. The park is on Montecito Boulevard, west of Calistoga Road. Don't forget that it's closed during the rainy months. 707/543-3292 or 707/539-5979.

22 Southwest Community Park
🐾🐾🐾🐾 (See Sonoma County map on page 286)

If your dog doesn't need a park in the hoity-toitiest part of town, this is a mighty convenient and friendly place to take him. First of all, it's relatively close to the freeway, so it's easy to get to if you're on the road. But better than that, it's big and green, with neatly paved paths that meander by cascading willows. It's also far enough from the road that the traffic danger is minimal. Why care about traffic? Because your dog can be off leash here 6–8 A.M., thanks to a program that's got dogs at its very heart.

From U.S. 101, take the Hearn Avenue exit and drive west for nearly a mile. The park is on the left, across from Westland Drive. 707/543-3292 or 707/539-5979.

23 Spring Lake Regional Park
🐾🐾🐾 (See Sonoma County map on page 286)

In winter, this county park doesn't offer dogs much more than a leashed trot around the lake. But in summer, it's leafy and full of the sounds of kids yelling and thumping oars. It's more fun here for people than dogs, who must be leashed. This is a good spot for a picnic, blading, working out on a parcourse fitness trail, a boat ride, or human swimming (no dogs allowed in the swim area). The path around the lake is paved for skaters, strollers, and bicyclists, and there are short dirt paths off into the open oak and brush woods. You can fish from the banks, where they're cleared of tules and willows.

The parking fee is $4 in winter, $5 in summer; the large lot has some shady spots. Campsites are $17, plus $1 extra for a dog. Most of the 30 sites are reservable, and a few are first-come, first-served. For reservations phone 707/565-2267. Dogs must have proof of a rabies vaccination. The campground is open daily May 1–September 30, weekends and holidays the rest of the year.

From Highway 12, on the Farmer's Lane section in Santa Rosa, turn east on Hoen Avenue. Take Hoen four stoplights to Newanga Avenue. Turn left on Newanga, which goes straight to the entrance. 707/539-8092.

■24 Youth Community Park

🐾🐾🐾🐾🐾 (See Sonoma County map on page 286)

If you like oak trees, come here. Big oaks hang out all over the park. Some really big, really old oaks even have their own fences, so no one can do leg lifts or initial carving on their trunks.

The main attraction for dogs is the big green meadowy lawn area. Pooches love rolling on it and cantering over it. Your dog can be off leash here 6–8 A.M. thanks to a dog-friendly program.

A word of warning: Skateboarders abound here. A little skateboard area is in front of the park, and kids love skateboarding around the parking lot, too. Some dogs don't even notice them; others get nervous about the sound of board crashing on pavement.

The park is in the far west reaches of the city, on the west side of Fulton Road, about a quarter of a mile south of Piner Road. 707/543-3292.

PLACES TO EAT

Flying Goat Coffee: Want to justify eating a doughnut from this fun Railroad Square eatery? You can get organic ones here! Dine with your dog at the four umbrella-topped tables outside. There's usually a bowl of water out here, too. (For your dog, not your feet.) 10 4th Street; 707/575-1202.

Juice Shack: In the summer, come here with your hot pooch and cool off with a creamy smoothie or a fresh organic juice. In cooler months, you can enjoy hot juices here. Hmm. I'd rather go for the hot soup served here, or the wrap sandwiches. Dine with your dog at the outdoor area under the big pine tree. Thirsty dogs will get water on request. 1810 Mendocino Avenue; 707/528-6131.

PLACES TO STAY

Best Western Garden Inn: Dogs should be under 50 pounds to stay here. Rates are $72–185. Dogs are $15 extra. 1500 Santa Rosa Avenue 95404; 707/546-4031.

Los Robles Lodge: Rates are $60–129. Dogs are $15 extra. 1985 Cleveland Avenue 95401; 707/545-6330 or 800/255-6330; www.losrobleslodge.com.

Spring Lake Regional Park: See Spring Lake Regional Park, above, for camping information.

Vineyard Lodge: Rates at this former TraveLodge are $55–89. Dogs are $20 extra. 1815 Santa Rosa Avenue 95407; 707/542-3472.

Bodega Bay

PARKS, BEACHES, AND RECREATION AREAS

🐾 Westside Regional Park

🐾🐾 (See Sonoma County map on page 286)

This is an undistinguished but handy park and campground built on landfill right on the water, with picnic tables and barbecues. Spud Point Marina, just to the north, also allows leashed dogs.

The fee for day use is $4 most of the year, and $5 Memorial Day to Labor Day. There are 47 campsites, costing $17, plus $1 for each dog. It's first-come, first-served. The park is on Westshore Road, a westward turn off Highway 1 in town. Phone 707/875-3540 for more info, or 707/565-2267 for camping reservations.

🐾 Doran Beach Regional Park

🐾🐾🐾 (See Sonoma County map on page 286)

This Sonoma County regional park offers leashed dogs access to marshland full of egrets, herons, and deer, as well as to the Pinnacle Gulch Trail. The plain but serviceable beach has almost no surf (which is great for dog swims), and there are picnic tables near the beach.

The fee for day use is $4 most of the year, and $5 Memorial Day to Labor Day. Campsites are $17 plus $1 for each dog. The campground, which has 134 sites, is on a first-come, first-served basis. The park is on Highway 1, one mile south of Bodega Bay. Phone 707/875-3540 for more info, or 707/565-2267 for camping reservations.

PLACES TO EAT

The Boat House: This restaurant in downtown Bodega Bay will allow you to sit with your dog as you eat fish-and-chips, oysters, and calamari at one of the six unshaded tables on its patio. If fish isn't your dog's wish, he can order a burger. 1445 Highway 1; 707/875-3495.

The Dog House: The name of the restaurant says it all. But if you need more, here are the words of one of the servers: "Dogs are treated better than people here." The Dog House is indeed a very dog-friendly place to dine. The food is unpretentious (hot dogs, burgers, etc.), and the servers love seeing a dog come to one of the eight outdoor tables. They often offer a bowl of water before the pooch even gets a chance to peruse the menu. 537 Highway 1; 707/875-2441.

Lucas Wharf: Your dog's nose will flare and drip with excitement as you dine at the outdoor tables here. That's partly because of the tasty deli specials, but it's mostly because your dog will be getting high on sea smells at this place right on the water. Speaking of water, the folks here love dogs and will provide your pooch with water, should she need to wet her whistle. 595 Highway 1; 707/875-3522.

PLACES TO STAY

Bodega Bay RV Park: If you have an RV and want to stay in this wonderful area, park 'er here. The managers will point you to some nearby property where you can run your good dog without a leash. Rates are $25–39. 2000 Highway 1 94923; 707/875-3701 or 800/201-6864.

Doran Beach Regional Park: See Doran Beach Regional Park, above, for camping information.

Westside Regional Park: See Westside Regional Park, above, for camping information.

Rohnert Park

PARKS, BEACHES, AND RECREATION AREAS

27 Crane Creek Regional Park

🐾🐾🐾 (See Sonoma County map on page 286)

For years, this 128-acre patch of grazing land in the middle of nowhere has been undeveloped open space for your dog's pleasure. Recent improvements include an upgraded parking lot, the addition of picnic tables, and the widening of 2.6 miles of hiking trails. Unfortunately, the leash law is enforced here, and a sign tells you why: "Dogs Caught in Livestock May Be Shot." Carry water; you may get thirsty just trying to find the place in your car.

From Rohnert Park, drive east on the Rohnert Park Expressway to Petaluma Hill Road. Turn south on Petaluma Hill Road to Roberts Road, and go east for two miles on Roberts Road. You'll find the park shortly after Roberts turns into Pressley Road. A machine is there to collect a $4 parking fee from you. 707/565-2041 or 707/823-7262.

PLACES TO STAY

Best Western Rohnert Park: This hotel is right next door to a huge veterinary center that is nationally renowned for its neurology department. If you find yourself taking your dog there, stay here. The manager, Johnny, loves dogs and brings his own pooch to work with him. According to Baron, a quesadilla-loving German shorthaired pointer who wrote to me, Johnny and the staff bent over backward making his stay as comfortable as possible when Baron was getting MRIs next door. Rates are $95–105. 6500 Redwood Drive 94928; 707/584-7435.

Glen Ellen

PARKS, BEACHES, AND RECREATION AREAS

28 Jack London State Historic Park

😺😺😺 (See Sonoma County map on page 286)

The extensive backcountry trails here are off-limits to dogs, but the parts of historic interest are not. You're free to take your leashed dog the half mile to Wolf House, visiting Jack London's grave en route, and around the stone house containing the museum of Londoniana (open 10 A.M.–5 P.M., no pets inside). The trail is paved and smooth up to the museum, but then it becomes dirt and narrow.

Oaks, pines, laurels, and madrones cast dappled light, and the ups and downs are gentle. Signs warn of poison oak and rattlesnakes. The ruins of the huge stone lodge that was London's dream Wolf House are impressive and sad. A fire of unknown origin destroyed it in 1913. London planned to rebuild it, but he died three years later.

Dogs are also allowed in the picnic areas by the parking lot and the museum. From Highway 12, follow signs to the park. Turn west on Arnold Drive, then west again on London Ranch Road. The fee is $6 for day use. 707/938-5216.

29 Sonoma Valley Regional Park/
Elizabeth Anne Perrone Dog Park

😺😺😺😺🐕 (See Sonoma County map on page 286)

This large, welcoming park has a paved, level trail that winds alongside a branch of Sonoma Creek. Better yet for dogs who like to roll, it sports many dirt trails that head off into the oak woodlands above. Varied grasses, wildflowers, madrones, and moss-hung oaks make this a scenic walk. Dogs like to chew some of the grasses, roll on the wildflowers (don't let them do this!), and do leg lifts on the madrones and oaks. They may enjoy the park even more than you. If you start at the park entrance off Highway 12 and walk westward across the park to Glen Ellen for about a mile, you'll end up at Sonoma Creek and the old mill, with its huge working waterwheel.

Dogs need to be on leash for all that fun. But the big fenced dog park within the park is an exception. The Elizabeth Anne Perrone Dog Park is only about an acre, but it feels like more. It's totally landscaped, with grass and trees. "A dog lover's paradise," as reader Robin Domer and her furry children, Max and Oliver, wrote us. Pooper-scoopers, poop bags, and fresh water are supplied. As if this weren't enough, the super-dog-friendly Garden Court Cafe is right across the street.

The park is just south of Glen Ellen between Arnold Drive and Highway 12. The entrance is off Highway 12. The parking fee is $4. 707/539-8092.

PLACES TO EAT

Garden Court Cafe: This sweet café, right across the street from the leash-free Elizabeth Anne Perrone Dog Park (see above), is just as dog-friendly as the park! Dogs may join you on the patio (open only on weekends), where they can drink from dog water bowls and even choose from a few items on a dog menu. Jake likes the Blue Plate Special, a kind of egg scramble with burger, zucchini, and garlic. (His dog breath is rather interesting after such a meal.) If your dog hankers for something Italian, try the "Babaloo" pizza, which is a biscuit crust topped with ketchup, jack cheese, and fresh herbs. It's good-looking enough that you might be tempted to share it with your dog, but the human food here is tasty, too, and your dog will like you better if you order your own. If your dog doesn't feel like paying for one of these dishes, he can get a free house-made pooch biscuit. (Far from a consolation prize, judging by the blissful expression on Jake's face.) 13875 Highway 12; 707/935-1565.

Petaluma

Petaluma is a captivating Sunday afternoon stroll, with its tree-lined streets and pocket parks for your dog's pleasure. Victorian buildings, old feed mills, and a riverfront that remains mostly original, but not dilapidated, complete the charming picture. And let's not forget an added canine bonus: Depending on the wind direction, you can often smell fresh cow manure wafting in from the surrounding hills. Dogs thrive on this.

Best of all, dogs get to run leashless during set (if early) hours in a whopping 13 parks, and all day at their very own pooch park! No wonder they call this place PET-aluma.

PARKS, BEACHES, AND RECREATION AREAS

Dogs who live in Petaluma are lucky dogs indeed. A few years back, the enlightened Parks and Recreation Department decided that dogs needed places to run off leash and gave dogs who are under voice control the OK to be leash-free in a dozen parks during certain hours. Most of those hours have increased since then, but you should still watch your off-leash hours like a hawk—the fine for a first offense is up to $100! Better to invest that money in a good watch.

Dogs also have their very own park, called Rocky Memorial Dog Park. It's one of the largest dog parks in the state. Dogs are singing its praises ("Howl-elujah!").

30 Arroyo Park

🐾🐾🐾🐕 (See Sonoma County map on page 286)

Most of Arroyo Park is very well groomed, with golf course–like green grass and a perfectly paved walking path running through its three acres. However, it seems many dogs prefer the seedier side of the park—the weedier, uncut area on the right as you face the park. We hope that area remains like this for dogs who like to walk a little on the wild side.

Dogs are allowed off leash here 6–11 A.M. weekdays and 6–8 A.M. weekends, and 8–10 P.M. every night. It's just a bone's throw from Wiseman Airport Park (listed below), though, which is a much safer place to run a dog, since you can get farther from the road. The park is at Garfield and Village East Drives. 707/778-4380.

31 Bond Park

🐾🐾🐾🐕 (See Sonoma County map on page 286)

It's green here, so green that Joe couldn't help but run out of the car and throw himself down on the grass and start wriggling and writhing in ecstasy. I thought for sure he'd found something odious to roll in, but underneath him was just clean, green grass. He rolled for about 10 minutes, got up, and heaved himself down in another spot, rolling and groaning and making the children in the playground giggle. The park is pleasant, with some shade from medium-sized trees. With six acres, it's a good size for dogs. And it's set in a quiet area, on Banff Way just south of Maria Drive, so traffic is minimal. Dogs are allowed off leash here 6–11 A.M. weekdays and 6–8 A.M. weekends, and 8–10 P.M. every night. 707/778-4380.

32 Del Oro Park

🐾🐾🐾🐕 (See Sonoma County map on page 286)

Del Oro is very suburban. It's got a nice little play area for kids. It's got green grass. It's surrounded by not-too-old suburban homes. It's got soccer goal posts. When we last visited, there were even two old Suburban sport utility vehicles parked in front.

Something not terribly suburban, a fire hydrant in one of the grassy areas, is probably the most coveted part of the park—at least for boy dogs. Well-behaved pooches can be off leash here 6–11 A.M. weekdays and 6–8 A.M. weekends, and 8–10 P.M. every night. The park is at Sartori Drive and Del Oro Circle. 707/778-4380.

33 Glenbrook Park

🐾🐾🐕 (See Sonoma County map on page 286)

Who'd believe it? When we last visited, a great blue heron landed in this narrow park, which is surrounded by newish homes. This was a wonderful sight, because the land around here looks as if it's still in shock from all the development of the past decade.

The park is nearly four acres and is much longer than it is wide. It's directly across the street from Sunrise Park (listed below), but it's a little quieter and more attractive, with some medium-sized trees here and there. Its off-leash hours are generous on the hind end: 6–10 A.M. and 6–10 P.M. daily. The park is at Maria Drive and Sunrise Parkway. 707/778-4380.

34 Helen Putnam Regional Park

🐾🐾🐾 (See Sonoma County map on page 286)

This 216-acre county regional park is, and will remain, a minimally developed stretch of converted cow pasture with oak trees. A wide paved trail shared by hikers and bicyclists runs between the main entrance and the Victoria housing development (to enter from that end, go to the end of Oxford Court). Dogs must be leashed. There's no shade from the scrub oaks, and it can get mighty windy. The paved trail has gentle ups and downs. Some other dirt trails give you steeper hill climbs. About a quarter of a mile in from the main entrance is an old cattle pond good for a dog swim (if the dog stays on a leash—quite a feat).

Parking is $4. Next to the lot is a kids' playground and a picnic gazebo, set by a creek that's only a gully in summer. Drive south on Western Avenue and turn left on Chileno Valley Road. After a half mile, you'll see the turnoff to the park. 707/565-2041.

35 Lucchesi Park

🐾🐾🐾🐕 (See Sonoma County map on page 286)

This is a well-kept, popular city park with a postmodern community center that impresses people but doesn't stir dogs much. Dogs prefer strolling through empty sports fields, picnicking at shaded tables, lounging under the weepy willows, watching ducks and the spewing fountain at the large pond, and trotting along the paved paths here. No dog swimming is allowed in the pond. It's a rule that makes it impossible to take Jake Dog near the pond, because he can't contain his excitement at the idea of being in the water. We've met other water dogs with the same affliction here.

Dogs are allowed off leash here 6–11 A.M. weekdays and 6–8 A.M. weekends, and 8–10 P.M. every night. Be sure to keep dogs away from the ducks and geese who like to lounge beside their pond, because feathers should not fly as a result of the city's kindly off-leash allowances. The park is at North McDowell Boulevard and Madison Street. 707/778-4386.

🐾 McNear Park

🐾🐾🐾 🐕 (See Sonoma County map on page 286)

McNear is an attractive seven-acre park, with green, green grass, plenty of shade, picnic tables, and a playground. But the part of the park dogs like best is the enclosed athletic field, where they're allowed to romp off leash 6–11 A.M. weekdays and 6–8 A.M. weekends, and 8–10 P.M. every night. The field is usually green and almost entirely fenced, but there are a couple of spots where a clever escape artist could slip out, so heads up. It's at F and 9th Streets. 707/778-4380.

🐾 Oak Hill Park

🐾🐾🐾🐾 🐕 (See Sonoma County map on page 286)

Dogs love running up and down the gently rolling hills on this five-acre park set in the midst of beautiful old Victorian homes near downtown Petaluma. Oak Hill Park is hilly and oaky (surprise!), qualities dogs enjoy. Some good-sized oaks make their home in various parts of the park, and dogs appreciate their shade-giving arms.

Dogs are permitted to run off leash on the east side of the creek from Sunnyslope to Westridge Drive 6 A.M.–10 P.M. Monday–Friday. That's a lotta hours. But wait, that's not all! They can also visit the park off leash 6–11 A.M. and 5–10 P.M. on weekends. These are magnificent hours. The park is at Howard and Oak Streets. 707/778-4380.

🐾 Petaluma Adobe State Historic Park

🐾🐾 (See Sonoma County map on page 286)

Leashed dogs are welcome here, if they behave well around goats and such, and if you avoid the farm animal courtyard. From the parking lot, walk across a wooden bridge over a wide, willow-lined creek (dry in summer) to the house, built in 1836 as headquarters for General Mariano Vallejo's 66,600-acre Rancho Petaluma. Clustered around the house are tempting displays of animal hides, saddles, and tallow makings, as well as sheep, chickens, and a donkey. Dogs must use their best manners. If you see them starting to think of lamb chops for dinner, make sure you hang on hard to that leash.

The park is southeast of Petaluma at Adobe Road and Casa Grande Road. From U.S. 101, you'll see an exit sign for the Petaluma Adobe. Admission is $2 for adults. 707/762-4871.

🐾 Petaluma City Hall Lawn

🐾🐾 🐕 (See Sonoma County map on page 286)

If you have business to conduct at city hall, your dog can conduct his own kind of business outside. (Unlike your business, your dog's will have to be scooped.)

The west lawn area permits off-leash dogs 6–8 A.M. every day, with evening hours 8–10 P.M. August–October, and 6–10 P.M. November–July. Petaluma City Hall is at 11 English Street. 707/778-4380.

40 Prince Park

😊😊😊😊🐕 (See Sonoma County map on page 286)

Dogs are permitted off leash at this attractive 20-acre park during longer hours than they are at most other parks in the city, and they think this is just swell. On a recent visit, a springer-shepherd mix was running around drooling and panting and smiling like a dog in love. His person said when he comes here, he's ecstatic. "Willie loves the grass and the trees. I love the hours for off leash, and I love its safety from traffic," she said. (The park is set back quite far from street traffic.) Off-leash hours are rather confusing at first glance, but they're actually quite simple at second glance: 6 A.M.–3 P.M. weekdays September–May, 6–8 A.M. weekdays June–August, 6–8 A.M. weekends, and 8–10 P.M. every night. The park is across East Washington Street from the airport, just a little north of the airport sign. 707/778-4380.

41 Rocky Memorial Dog Park

😊😊😊😊🐕 (See Sonoma County map on page 286)

The scenery isn't great, and the land has nary a tree on it, but it's one of the biggest dog parks we've ever encountered. And size does matter, at least when it comes to fenced dog parks.

This flat nine-acre piece of land is the best thing that's happened to Petaluma's dogs since the park system began allowing them off leash at certain parks during limited hours a few years back. Dogs enjoy the smell that can pervade the land; it's beside a marshy area next to the Petaluma River. Fortunately, it's well fenced so dogs can't chase the marsh birds or roll in the marsh muck. The fencing keeps the dogs from escaping to all areas but the parking lot, which leads to the park entrance, which eventually leads a busy road. So if you have a pooch who's prone to running away, be aware the place is safe, but it isn't foolproof.

Because it's so barren here, it can really roast on hot days. Be sure to bring water. A sign at the entrance says "No dogs in heat," and I thought it was nice of them to be so concerned about the temperature for dog walking. It took me a few seconds and an eye roll from my husband to realize the sign's true intent.

On our first visit, Joe searched in vain for something to lift a leg on. He found only some garbage cans and a few big weeds, and they were right next to the parking lot. The next visit he just succumbed to the lack of leg-lift targets and took to relieving his bladder like a girl dog. But not, of course, until looking around to make sure no one was watching.

Rocky Park was named after a big-hearted police dog who died at the too-young age of 10 during a narcotics search. It was kidney failure that got him, not the wrong end of a dealer's pistol. Rocky had helped seize a few million dollars of narcotics in his career, but his greatest act came in 1992 when he saved the life of his beloved handler one night. A felon had escaped and the officer chased him to a creek, where the felon got the upper hand and was holding the officer's head underwater. The officer managed to hit a remote control button that opened the windows of the patrol car and released Rocky, who'd seen his friend in trouble. Rocky bolted to the creek and got the upper paw. He saved his friend and helped bag the bad guy. "It was the beginning of the era of Rocky," said Officer Jeff Hasty, a dog handler with the Petaluma Police Department. A bust of Rocky now graces the front lobby of the police department.

This is an easy park to visit if you're on U.S. 101 and your pooch is hankering to stretch his gams. Take the Highway 116 east (*not* west)/Lakeville exit and follow the street just over a half mile to Casa Grande Road, where you'll take a sharp right. Drive a few hundred feet past ugly storage bins and trucks and you'll soon hit the entrance to the park. Unlike most of the other city parks with off-leash times, this one has great hours: 6 A.M.–10 P.M. 707/778-4380.

42 Sunrise Park

🐾 🐕 (See Sonoma County map on page 286)

If you're a real estate developer, there's a chance you might enjoy this park. It's very, very narrow, squeezed like an old tube of toothpaste by cookie-cutter condos and townhouses. It's too close to traffic. It's not terribly attractive. But in its defense, it does have decent grassy areas and fun (for dogs) weedy patches. Another plus: Dogs can be off leash 6–10 A.M. and 6–10 P.M. daily. Those are some pretty long hours for a pretty slim park. It's at Marina Drive and Sunrise Parkway. 707/778-4380.

43 Westridge Open Space

🐾 🐾 🐾 🐕 (See Sonoma County map on page 286)

Dogs get to peruse the east side of this three-acre park off leash 6–10 A.M. and 6–10 P.M. daily. The park is long and narrow, with plenty of medium-sized trees, which turn a warm red in autumn. When we visited, a fluffy black cat teased Joe from the middle of the road. Another kitty was there when we recently sniffed out the park with Jake. Cat-chasers, exercise caution when off leash. The park is on Westridge Drive, near its intersection with Westridge Place. 707/778-4380.

44 Wiseman Airport Park

😺😺😺😺 🐾 (See Sonoma County map on page 286)

Plenty of pooches visit this park, and for good reason. Wiseman is 32 acres of well-kept playing fields, uncut grass, many shade trees, and comfortably wide walking paths. It's also a good place to watch little planes land and take off, because of its proximity to the airport. (They don't call it Airport Park for nothing.) Best of all, dogs can run off leash in the athletic fields during these hours: 6–11 A.M. weekdays and 6–8 A.M. weekends, and 8–10 P.M. every night. The best access is at St. Augustine Circle. 707/778-4380.

PLACES TO EAT

Apple Box: A store of antiques and housewares, this charmer also serves good desserts, teas, and coffee. There are 10 tables outside, right by the river. It's real olfactory bliss for your dog. 224 B Street; 707/762-5222.

Aram's Cafe: Dine on really good Mediterranean and Armenian food at the five outdoor tables. Aram's is in downtown Petaluma. 131 Kentucky Street; 707/765-9775.

Dempseys Restaurant and Brewery: There's always a dog water bowl here, and it's kept filled to the brim. The menu here is terrific. Jake drools over our neighbors' chicken and chops. (Fortunately not right over it.) Thank you to John Flynn and his dogs for sniffing this place out for us. 50 East Washington Street; 707/765-9694.

PLACES TO STAY

Motel 6: Rates are $44–70 for the first adult, $3 for the second. 1368 North McDowell Boulevard 94954; 707/765-0333.

San Francisco North KOA: This is Jake's kind of camping. Upon arrival at this family camping resort, dogs get a little treat attached to a card that lists the doggy rules. The 60-acre campground is more attractive than most KOAs we've visited. The setting is rural, and there are trees everywhere. Like other KOAs, the campsites are drive-up and pretty doggone close to each other, but it's still a fun place to pitch a tent, especially if you like hot showers and cool pools as part of your camping experience. Better yet, try one of the cute log "Kamping Kabins." They're cozy, with a bunk bed and a queen bed. (You provide the bedding.)

Adding to its rural charm, this KOA even has a pen that houses several goats. Visit in the spring to see some adorable furry kids.

The managers here ask that you walk your dog on leash, either on camping roads or the designated field (which has poop bags!). The rule here, as it is at many KOAs, is no pit bulls. Rates are $29–47 for camping. Kamping Kabins are $49–69. 20 Rainsville Road 94952; 707/763-1492 or 800/992-2267; www.sanfranciscokoa.com.

Sheraton Sonoma County: Dogs are welcome to stay at this attractive hotel, as long as they weigh no more than 80 pounds. They're so welcome, in fact, that they'll get use of a big dog bed and doggy bowls. "We like to make their stay nice, too," says a hotelier. The hotel has a heated outdoor pool and a hot tub for the humans in your crew. It's close to a popular jogging trail that permits pooches on leashes. Dogs must stay in first-floor rooms, and they mustn't smoke. (The entire hotel is nonsmoking.) Rates are $129–269. 745 Baywood Drive 94954; 707/283-2888.

Sonoma

Downtown Sonoma is a treat for people, and until the last few years, dogs had been banned from all the good spots—most city parks, Sonoma plaza, and the state historic park. But there's finally something to wag about: a new park just two blocks from the plaza.

PARKS, BEACHES, AND RECREATION AREAS

45 Ernest Holman Dog Park

🐾🐾🐾🐕 (See Sonoma County map on page 286)

Ernest was a good dog. So good that his person, Sue Holman, donated enough money for a dog park in his name. (Most of my human friends don't even have such formal-sounding names.) Opened in 1999, Ernest Holman Dog Park is a welcome addition to downtown Sonoma. It's small—a little under an acre—and the turf can be mushy in the wet season, but it's incredibly popular. Happy dogs of every ilk tear around this fenced area. When they need to catch their doggy breaths, they repose in the shade of the park's enormous redwood trees. People enjoy sitting on benches and chatting with other dog folks while watching their panting pooches. (There's water for when they—the dogs, not the people—need to wet their whistles.)

The park is two blocks north of the plaza, on 1st Street West, next to the police station. It's part of the Field of Dreams sporting field complex. 707/938-3681.

46 Maxwell Farms Regional Park

🐾🐾 (See Sonoma County map on page 286)

This park offers playing fields, picnic tables, a generous kids' playground, smooth paths, and a large undeveloped area where paths follow Sonoma Creek under huge laurels wound with wild grapevines. The creek is dry in summer, but leashed dogs like to sniff it anyway.

The entrance is off Verano Avenue, west of Highway 12. The day-use fee is $2. 707/565-2041.

PLACES TO EAT

Coffee Garden: This is a peaceful haven for dogs and their people. The magnificent garden patio has a fountain that fascinates some dogs and makes others look as if they need to head to the nearest tree fast. Actually, a big, 160-year-old fig tree is in the middle of the patio area, but leg lifts are definitely not permitted.

The café is housed in the historic Captain Salvador Vallejo Adobe, which was built in the late 1830s. A brochure you can pick up at the café explains its history and suggests carefully examining its architecture for various details. Most dogs would rather not have to closely explore the unique adobe brick construction of the walls, as suggested by the brochure, unless there happened to be a little chicken salad splattered on it.

Brandon Dog, pooch extraordinaire of Forest Service spokesman extraordinaire Matt Mathes and his wife (also extraordinaire, says Matt), loves this place. When Brandon visited recently, a guitar player was strumming out some gentle melodies. "Brandon seemed to enjoy the guitar. But he was more interested in the food," says Matt.

The food here is light and very tasty. Try the smoked salmon sandwich or the zesty Chinese chicken sandwich. There's a good espresso menu and a small selection of beers and wines. The Coffee Garden is on the Sonoma Plaza, at 415-421 1st Street West; 707/996-6645.

PLACES TO STAY

Best Western Sonoma Valley Inn: If you want to stay close to the town plaza, this hotel is just a little more than a block away. Rates are $114–354. One dog is $30 extra. Two are $45 extra. 550 2nd Street West 95476; 707/938-9200 or 800/334-5784; www.sonomavalleyinn.com.

Stone Grove Inn: Dogs think they've died and gone to Greece when they stay at this rustic, charming inn. That's because owner Charles Papanteles has a flair for decorating with the old-world Mediterranean flair of his ancestors.

But what really makes dogs say *"Opa!"* is that the inn is surrounded by acres of gorgeous meadows, pastures, and organic veggie gardens. There's plenty of room for leashed walking. ("A dog walk path is one cornfield away," we're told.) The stone cottage, where dogs are permitted (they aren't allowed in the red barn studio), is really made of stone, and it's small, private, and secluded. It had better be secluded, because it has a detached bathroom and an outdoor shower. We found this kind of fun, but if your bladder is the size of a peanut, this may not be the place for you. Bathrooms aside, the stone cottage, which is more than 100 years old, can be mighty cozy with the potbellied stove blazing.

Rates are $95–125. Dogs are $10–20 extra. The cottage is just a bone's throw from Sonoma's town square, at 240 2nd Street 95476; 707/939-8249; www.stonegrovebb.com.

CHAPTER 28

Napa County

Napa dogs don't whine. They wine. And since there are plenty of dog-friendly restaurants here, they often wine and dine.

This is the home of California's most famous wine-making valley, and dogs get to experience some of the fringe benefits of this productive area. A few attractive wineries invite well-behaved dogs to relax and sniff around with their owners (our favorite is the Dutch Henry Winery in the Calistoga area; see the Diversions Grape Expectations for this and others), but most don't want to publicize their dog policy. When you do find a dog-friendly winery, don't let your dog do leg lifts on inappropriate items, because Bacchus will get you. And your little dog, too.

Since the book's last edition, a few more terrific inns in Napa have opened their doors to dogs, who would give this a thumbs-up if only they had opposable ones.

PICK OF THE LITTER—NAPA COUNTY

BEST DOG PARK
Alston Park/Canine Commons, Napa (page 330)

PRETTIEST RESTAURANT
Ristorante Tra Vigne, St. Helena (page 327)

MOST DOG-FRIENDLY PLACE TO EAT
Angele Restaurant, Napa (page 331)

MOST DOG-FRIENDLY PLACES TO STAY
Washington Street Lodging, Calistoga (page 325)
Napa River Inn, Napa (page 332)
Napa Valley Country Cottage, Napa (page 333)

BEST FUNKY ATTRACTIONS
Old Faithful Geyser, Calistoga (page 322)
Petrified Forest, Calistoga (page 324)

BEST PLACE TO TRY SOME BUBBLY
Mumm Napa Valley, Rutherford (page 326)

The county's parks come up a little on the dry side. With the county's lush, fertile, and inviting vineyards, it seems as if there's so much land that dogs would be in heaven here. Jake and I only wish the parks could follow in the pawsteps of three Calistoga lodgings that have land from 11 to 40 acres: Dogs with well-behaved humans can not only sniff around the acreage, but they can do so off leash!

Only about a dozen public parks and a few miscellaneous sites in Napa County allow dogs. The city of Napa has four parks where dogs are allowed, and all four permit them off leash in certain sections. You may incur the grapes of your dog's wrath if you don't take her to visit one of these leash-free lands next time you're in town.

Calistoga

PARKS, BEACHES, AND RECREATION AREAS

❶ Pioneer Park

🐾🐾 (See Napa County map on page 318)

This is a small park, but its location so close to the heart of Calistoga makes it a great place to stop for a relaxing picnic with your leashed pooch. The two-acre park has plenty of shade trees and enough open area so your canine won't feel claustrophobic.

Going north on Foothill Boulevard, turn right on Lincoln Avenue. In two blocks, turn left on Cedar Street. The park will be on your right within a block. 707/942-2800.

❷ Bothe-Napa State Park

🐾🐾 (See Napa County map on page 318)

Dogs are relegated to paved roads and campgrounds here, and it's a crime because of all the alluring trails. Hiking the asphalt can be fun, though. Joe seemed especially captivated by a man who was burning bacon over the campfire, his wife yelling that this was some vacation.

A wilderness haven this park is not, at least for you and your dog. Dogs must be leashed at all times. One of the two roads they're allowed on parallels Highway 29 and is so close you can see the drivers' eyes, often bloodshot from too much wine-tasting.

On the positive end, the roads are stunning in autumn when the leaves change color. And dogs are allowed to camp with you, on leash. Dogs are also allowed in some of the picnic areas just off the roads.

The day-use fee is $6. There are 50 campsites. Fees are $20. Call 800/444-7275 for reservations. The park is on Highway 29, halfway between St. Helena and Calistoga, just north of Bale Lane. The entrance is on the west side of the road. 3801 North St. Helena Highway (Highway 29). 707/942-4575.

PLACES TO EAT

Home Plate: Far from the tourist parking woes in town, this inexpensive, unassuming short-order restaurant makes some of the best grilled-cheese sandwiches that ever melted in a mouth. Dine at one of three big outdoor tables. If your dog is thirsty, you can get a bowl of water here. 2448 Foothill Boulevard (Highway 128); 707/942-5646.

PLACES TO STAY

Hillcrest II Bed and Breakfast: On the outside it's a good-looking, large, modern house. But on the inside, it's filled with antiques and other family

DIVERSION

See Old Faithful in Your Own Backyard: You know you're in for a treat when a big sign greets you at the entry to **Old Faithful Geyser:** "Many Notable People Have Come to SEE HEAR AND LEARN the mysteries of this WONDER OF NATURE which captures the imagination. IT'S AMAZING."

And indeed, when dogs see the 350°F plume of water gushing 50 to 70 feet into the air, they generally stare for a few seconds with their mouths agape. But the sight of tourists jumping in front of the geyser for a quick photo before the eruption subsides quickly bores them. Dogs then try to wander to the snack bar and persuade the person on the other end of the leash to buy a couple of hot dogs. But even more fascinating is the scent of goat and pig in nearby pens.

If your dog is the brave sort, don't hesitate to bring him to visit Clow, the fainting goat. Clow butts her head against her fence at first, but she's only playing. After a few minutes, she was calming Joe's fears by licking him on the nose. Soon he was in love. Valentino, the Vietnamese potbellied pig who scared the heck out of Joe, is no longer here. (I hope he didn't go the way of so many of his oversized brethren.)

Old Faithful erupts every 40 minutes, and the eruptions last about two to three minutes. Picnic tables are plentiful, so bring a snack or buy one here between eruptions. A sign at the site warns that dogs aren't allowed in the geyser viewing area, but you can bring your dog—securely leashed—within a safe distance of the geyser and not get scolded or scalded.

The geyser and goats are between Highways 128 and 29 on Tubbs Lane in Calistoga and are open 9 A.M.–6 P.M. in summer, 9 A.M.–5 P.M. in winter. Admission is $8 for adults. 707/942-6463.

heirlooms of the locally famed Tubbs family. Debbie O'Gorman, owner of Hillcrest II, is the last of the Tubbs family to live in the Napa area, and she's tastefully stocked the house with items from the family mansion, which burned down in 1964. There's even an old Steinway grand piano waiting to be played in the sitting room (which also has a fireplace).

All this is well and good with dog guests, but what they *really* adore is that the house is set on 40 acres where they're allowed to romp on terrific trails without a leash if their humans are well behaved. This is a dog's dream come true, because there just aren't leash-free stomping grounds like these in Napa County, unless you own big property. Fisherfolks and their dogs love it here, too, because there's a fishing pond on the property stocked with all kinds of fishies, including catfish and bluegill. The property is at the base of Mt. St. Helena, and the house is on a hilltop (thus the name), so the views are breathtaking.

Humans enjoy using the gorgeous 40-foot-long pool. Dogs enjoy dipping their paws in the pond. Humans can also use the kitchen and barbecue areas, which is convenient if you don't want to go out to eat every day. A delectable continental breakfast is served on weekends.

Debbie, who has two friendly dogs of her own, asks that you bring a bed for your dog, if he sleeps on the floor, or a blanket to place under him if he sleeps on human furniture. She also provides a large outdoor kennel should you want to head out for a little bit and have a dog who doesn't mind kennels. In addition—and better yet for many dogs—Debbie can sometimes pet-sit while you go out. Dogs love her and are happy in her care.

Rates are $69–175. Dogs are $10 extra. 3225 Lake County Highway 94515; 707/942-6334; www.bnbweb.com/hillcrest.

Meadowlark Country House: The simple elegance of this secluded 20-acre estate makes guests feel right at home. The house where dogs with people get to stay has a light and airy feel and attractive decor, but it's really the surrounding property that makes this place so special. Beware, though. Cats and guinea hens also make their home around the house, so if your dog is a chaser, hang on to that leash.

You and your pooch can hike on the estate's trails, past pastured horses, ancient oaks, and fields replete with wildflowers (and meadowlarks, thus the name). It's quiet here—a perfect place for a hilltop picnic with the pooch. If your dog can be trusted off leash, he can hike naked. It's "leashes optional" here, and that's a perfect match for the pool. If it's warm, the humans in your party can cool their heels (and knees and shoulders) in the beautiful swimming pool, which is surrounded by a cobblestone walk. The pool is clothing-optional, so if your dog blushes when he sees tushies, best wear your clothes. If all this isn't enough to fill your day, take a quick drive down the road and spend some time at the Petrified Forest.

Rates are $195–265. A delicious, large breakfast is included in the price. 601 Petrified Forest Road 94515; 707/942-5651 or 800/942-5651; www.meadowlarkinn.com.

Napa County Fairgrounds: A far cry from the great outdoors, this flat landscape with few trees is at least a good, fair-priced campground if all the inns and motels are booked. There are 70 sites, mostly decent places to park your recreational vehicle. Some tents sites are available in a grassy area. Sites are $22–25. 1435 Oak Street 94515; for info: 707/942-5221; for reservations: 707/942-5111.

Pink Mansion: This enchanting old place is an 1875 Victorian—very picturesque and very pink. It's a frequent recipient of numerous awards for its charm and beauty.

Dogs are allowed in only one room—the Wine Suite (not the Whine Sweet, as some dogs may do to stay here)—so book ahead lest another dog beats you to the phone. It has a fireplace, a private entrance that leads to the garden, and a private sitting room with an extra bed upstairs. Dogs must be of the nonbarking, clean, well-behaved variety, and they need to keep off the furniture and the beds.

If you have a bird dog, think twice about staying here, since also in residence are some doves and a chicken. Water dogs will enjoy watching you splash around in the comfy heated indoor pool and adjacent hot tub, but they mustn't set paw in the water. Rates are $185. Pooches are $30 extra. 1415 Foothill Boulevard (Highway 128) 94515; 707/942-0558 or 800/238-7465; www.pinkmansion.com.

Triple S Ranch: Once a working ranch, this hidden 11-acre spread in the hills above Calistoga still retains that old ranch feel. The nine rustic yet cozy cabins have only one large room each, so they feel like bunkhouses. But each comes

DIVERSION

Sniff Out a Petrified Forest: You and your leashed dog can roam among trees entombed by a volcanic explosion 3.4 million years ago. During a summertime visit, Joe found out why they call it the **Petrified Forest.** The sign announced in big bold letters, "Once Towering Redwoods—Now the Rock of Ages." But Joe didn't know the true meaning of petrified until we encountered—the elves.

The Elves of Ages, that is. The ceramic kind you find on suburban lawns. They appeared everywhere Joe looked and at eye level for an Airedale. Every time he saw a new one, he backed away with his tail between his legs, checking periodically to make sure it wasn't following him.

Then came the petrifying elf. It didn't look any different from the others. But as soon as Joe laid eyes on it and its donkey companion, his tail went down. For about two minutes, he was too frightened to look at the elf, growling instead at a tree. Then, suddenly he decided enough was enough and bolted—leash and all. He was waiting by the wishing well when I finally caught up to him. He would have left the park if he could have negotiated the turnstile by himself. I couldn't help wondering how Airedales have remained so popular for frontline duty during wars.

The Petrified Forest is at 4100 Petrified Forest Road, off Highway 128. It's actually in the outskirts of Sonoma County, but its address is in Calistoga. The unpaved trail is a quarter-mile loop. Admission is $6 for adults. Dozens of tables are around the gift shop, so pack a picnic. The forest is open 9 A.M.–7 P.M. in summer, 9 A.M.–6 P.M. in winter. 707/942-6667.

with a private bathroom, so you won't have to wander out to the outhouse in the middle of the night. They're pretty basic, and definitely for those with a macaroni-and-cheese budget for touring Napa, but they fill the budget bill.

What really sets dogs' tails to wagging is that if they're obedient, they get to run around the ranch's property without a leash. That's right, a leash-free doggy haven. (Watch out for foxtails.) Don't be surprised if your dog doesn't want to leave this place. You'll probably be feeling much the same yourself. It's hard to kiss all this—and a pool, and a fun restaurant (in the converted barn) with some of the best onion rings around—good-bye. The fried frog legs, on the other hand...

Rates are $85–95. 4600 Mountain Home Ranch Road 94515; 707/942-6730.

Washington Street Lodging: Relax in any of several cabins, each with its own little kitchen. You're just a couple of blocks from Calistoga's main drag here. Joan, the animal-loving owner, has cats, but she says if they don't like your pooch, or vice versa, they'll make themselves scarce. She also has a happy basset hound who will probably become your fast friend when you visit. Your stay here includes a continental breakfast and a doggy treat or two. Cabins are $90–130, and dogs are charged a $15 fee per visit. 1605 Washington Street 94515; 707/942-6968 or 877/214-3869; www.washingtonstreetlodging.com.

St. Helena

PARKS, BEACHES, AND RECREATION AREAS

🔢 Lyman Park

🐾🐾 (See Napa County map on page 318)

You'll think you're on a movie set for some old-time village scene when you and your dog wander into this small, cozy park on historic Main Street. Leashes are mandatory, but the park has a gazebo, lots of trees and benches, a flower garden, and—best of all for dogs—an antique horse/dog water fountain. The top part is for horses, the lower bowl for dogs. Horses aren't allowed here anymore, so if your dog is huge, he might as well sip from the equine bowl.

The park is nestled snugly between the police station and a funeral home, at 1400 Main Street, and is open dawn–dusk. 707/963-5706.

🔢 Baldwin Park

🐾🐾 (See Napa County map on page 318)

Baldwin Park has everything you could want in a park, except size. But what it lacks in acreage, it makes up for in dog appeal. Set off a small road, it's almost entirely fenced and full of flowering trees, oaks, and big pines. A dirt path winds through green grass from one end of the park to the other, passing by a water fountain and a conveniently placed garbage can.

DIVERSION

Grape Expectations: Dogs are welcome at so many wineries in Napa Valley these days that you may start wishing your dog could be your designated driver. (Don't try it: Dogs just don't have the opposable thumbs to operate those pesky steering wheels.)

Many of the wineries listed below allow dogs in their tasting rooms, but since health department officials aren't sure what to think about this, we're not going to point them out specifically. Most welcome dogs at their picnic areas. Some even allow pooches on vineyard tours. Phone the individual wineries for hours, prices, and dog-friendly specifics.

Here's a taste of some of Napa's most dog-friendly wineries, listed by area:

CALISTOGA:
Cuvaison, 4550 Silverado Trail North; 707/942-6266.
Dutch Henry Winery, 4310 Silverado Trail North; 707/942-5771. Winery Airedale Buggsy and her occasional city-cousin sidekick, Teddy, greet dog guests. Check out the website www.dutchhenry.com for a page dedicated to the winery pets.
Graeser Winery, 255 Petrified Forest Road; 707/942-4437. Graeser has a new line of dog-labeled wines named after various winery dogs.

RUTHERFORD:
Mumm Napa Valley, 8445 Silverado Trail North; 707/967-7700. Dogs get royal treatment, with dog treats and water. Mumm Napa Valley even has its own line of logo doggy products.
Sullivan Vineyards, 1090 Galleron Road; 707/963-9646. Open by appointment only.

ST. HELENA:
Casa Nuestra, 3451 Silverado Trail North; 707/963-5783. A most mellow winery where dogs can stare at the resident goats who have a nonvintage table wine named after them. Dogs get tasty biscuits, too.
Markham Vineyards, 2812 St. Helena Highway North; 707/963-5292.
RustRidge Winery, 2910 Lower Chiles Valley Road; 707/965-2871. Open by appointment only. Two big, friendly resident dogs welcome you and yours.
V. Sattui Winery, 1111 White Lane; 707/963-7774.

YOUNTVILLE:
Domaine Chandon, 1 California Drive; 707/944-2280.

Unfortunately, dogs must be leashed, but it's still a pleasant place to stretch all your legs after a tour through the wine country. The park is on Spring Street between Stockton Street and North Crane Avenue and is open dawn–dusk. 707/963-5706.

PLACES TO EAT

Pizzeria Tra Vigne: The little sister of the more expensive and upscale Tra Vigne Ristorante (see below), this pizzeria is just what the vet ordered if you have a pooch and a pedigreed palate but a more paltry pocketbook. Lots of families come here. The pastas, pizzas, and salads are delicious. Munch with your dog at the four tables on the patio. Got a thirsty dog? The staff will provide her a bowl of water. 1016 Main Street; 707/967-9999.

Ristorante Tra Vigne: This is one of the most attractive restaurants with some of the best food in the Bay Area. The wood-burning oven gives even the most simple pasta, pizza, and meat dishes a taste that's out of this world. Your dog can dine with you at the 20 tables in the large, garden-like lower courtyard. (The terrace is out because you have to go through the restaurant to get there, and that's a no-no.) The two of you are sure to drool over the gourmet cuisine. Thirsty dogs get a bowl of water. 1050 Charter Oak Avenue (you'll see the restaurant from Main Street, though); 707/963-4444.

PLACES TO STAY

El Bonita Motel: This little motel provides decent lodging at fairly reasonable prices for this area. Rates are $90–229. Dogs are $5 extra. 195 Main Street 94574; 707/963-3216 or 800/541-3284; www.elbonita.com.

Lake Berryessa

PARKS, BEACHES, AND RECREATION AREAS

5 Lake Berryessa
😼😼 (See Napa County map on page 318)

Lake Berryessa, one of the largest man-made lakes in Northern California, offers 165 miles of shoreline for human and canine enjoyment. Most of the resort areas on the lake allow leashed dogs. Better yet, they allow them off leash to swim. The summer heat is stifling here, so your dog will want to take advantage of the water.

Most resorts rent fishing boats and allow dogs to go along on your angling adventure. The fishing is fantastic, especially for trout in the fall and black bass in the spring. It's cooler then, too, so you won't have to contend with so many folks riding personal watercraft, and your dog won't roast.

If you just want to hike and swim for an afternoon, explore the Smittle Creek Trail. The entrance is just north of the lake's visitor center, on Knoxville Road. The trail takes you up and down the fingers of the lake. Dogs must be leashed, except when swimming. In the future there may be much more romping room for dogs—even some off-leash areas—if plans for a 150-mile shoreline trail go through, as lobbyists are hoping it will. (See www.berryessatrails.org for more. A link will take you to a page called The Dog Owner's Vision for Lake Berryessa.)

To get to Lake Berryessa from the Rutherford area, take Highway 128 and turn left at the Lake Berryessa/Spanish Flat sign. It's a very curvy route, so take it easy if you or your dog tend toward car sickness. For more information about the lake, call the Bureau of Reclamation Visitor Information Center at 707/966-2111. For questions about lakeside businesses, call the Lake Berryessa Chamber of Commerce at 800/726-1256.

PLACES TO STAY

Here are a few places to pitch a tent, park an RV, or stay in a yurt (Spanish Flat only) on Lake Berryessa.

Rancho Monticello Resort: Stay in a tent or in your RV with your pooch. There are 56 tent sites and 20 RV sites. Rates are $24–31. Dogs are $2. The day-use fee, should you not want to camp, is $11. 707/966-2188.

Spanish Flat Resort: Camping will cost you $24–32. Dogs are $2 extra and love sniffing around the waterfront and walking on the meandering roads on leash. The very cool yurts are $45 nightly. Day-use fee is $12. 707/966-7700; www.spanishflatresort.com.

Steele Park Resort: Dogs can go only RV camping here. Rates are $32–40. Dogs are $2 extra. Day-use fee is $15. 707/966-2123 or 800/522-2123; www.steelepark.com.

Rutherford

PLACES TO EAT

Rutherford Grill: The outdoor area is *the* place to eat at this wonderful restaurant (and of course, the only place to eat with a dog). It features a wood-burning fireplace, a fountain, and several attractive umbrella-topped tables. Try the "Knife and Fork Baby Back Barbecue Ribs," one of the most requested entrées. (Fear not: If you're not of the carnivorous persuasion, the restaurant offers several tasty dishes without meat.) The only time dogs aren't allowed is when there's live music outside—usually Thursday nights. 1180 Rutherford Road; 707/963-1792.

Yountville

Unlike the Yountville town government, which bans dogs from its parks, restaurateurs here have the right idea. Several exquisite restaurants welcome dogs to their patios, which are generally shaded and very accommodating to people and their canines. The only word of warning is to avoid these restaurants when they're packed with people from the tour buses that occasionally descend upon the town. It's just too crowded for dogs, who usually get tripped on and later photographed as tourist souvenirs.

PLACES TO EAT

Compadres Mexican Bar and Grill: Tropical landscaping, intoxicating jasmine and honeysuckle, and umbrellas over tables make this one of the most pleasant restaurants for spending a few hours with your dog. Try the *pollo borracho,* a whole chicken cooked with white wine and tequila. 6539 Washington Street, at the Vintage 1870 complex; 707/944-2406.

Napa Valley Grill: California cuisine reigns here, with fresh seafood as the focal point. Several outdoor tables with oversized umbrellas keep you and your dog cool. 6795 Washington Street; 707/944-2330.

Piatti Restaurant: The atmosphere at the 10-table semienclosed patio is enchanting, and the food is just as wonderful. Choose from a couple of dozen house-made pastas, rotisserie-cooked chicken, fresh-caught fish, pizzas from a wood-burning oven, and many other delectable items. As long as it's not too crowded, your dog is welcome to dine at your side. Thirsty pooches get a bowl of water. 6480 Washington Street; 707/944-2070.

PLACES TO STAY

Vintage Inn: Dogs who get to stay here are lucky dogs indeed. This inn ("inn" is an understated description of this place) puts dogs and their people in the lap of luxury, with a perfect blend of old-world charm and new-world design. The airy, beautiful, multilevel villas have fireplaces, and many have views of nearby vineyards. Dogs swoon over the grounds, which have pools, gardens, courtyards, and even a fountain.

This is a great place to stay if you're checking out the wineries on warm days and don't want to bring your dog along. The staff here can arrange for a pet-sitter to watch your pooch so he can keep cool and comfy while you sip your way through wine country.

Rates are $215–455 and include a "California Champagne breakfast." Dogs pay a $30 fee per visit. 6541 Washington Street 94599; 707/944-1112 or 800/351-1133; www.vintageinn.com.

Napa

The city of Napa has about 40 parks. Dogs are allowed in a whopping four, each of which has an off-leash section. You'll see dogs in some of the bigger parks, such as the Lake Hennessey Recreation Area, but they're not officially sanctioned, so we can't officially mention them.

PARKS, BEACHES, AND RECREATION AREAS

6 Alston Park/Canine Commons

🐾🐾🐾🐾 🐕 (See Napa County map on page 318)

With 157 acres of rolling hills surrounded by vineyards, Alston Park seems to stretch out forever. The lower part of the land used to be a prune orchard, and these prunes are just about the only trees you'll find here.

From there on up, the park is wide-open land with a lone tree here and there. Without shade, dogs and people can fry on hot summer days. But the park is magical during early summer mornings or any cooler time of year.

Miles of trails take you and your dog to places far from the road and the sound of traffic. Dogs are supposed to be off leash only in the lower, flat section of the park, known as Canine Commons. There's now a decent-sized fenced dog park there, complete with poop bags and drinking water.

From Highway 29, take Trower Avenue southwest to the end, at Dry Creek Road. The parking lot for the park is a short jog to your right on Dry Creek Road and across the street. It's open dawn–dusk. 707/257-9529.

7 Century Oaks Park

🧍🐕 (See Napa County map on page 318)

This park is a cruel hoax on canines. Dogs are restricted to a dangerous dog run—a tiny postage stamp of an area without fences, just off a busy street. And as for the park's name, which promises granddaddy oak trees, we're talking saplings here—maybe a dozen in the whole dog-run area. We don't know how many are in the rest of the park, because dogs aren't allowed there even on leash.

The dog-run area (we suggest keeping all but the most highly trained dogs on leash here) is on Brown's Valley Road, just off Westview Drive. Park on Westview Drive and walk around the corner to the dog run. The short walk to the park, with its shade and shrubs, is more enjoyable than the park itself. It's open dawn–dusk. 707/257-9529.

🖲 John F. Kennedy Memorial Park

🐾🐾🐾🐾 (See Napa County map on page 318)

Throw your dog's leash to the wind here and ramble along the Napa River. Dogs are allowed in the undeveloped areas near the park's boat marina. The only spot to avoid is a marshland that's more land than marsh during dry times.

Dogs enjoy chasing each other around the flat, grassy area beside the parking lot. There's also a dirt trail that runs along the river. You can take it from either side of the marina, although as of this writing, the signs designate only the south side as a dog-exercise area. The scenery isn't terrific—radio towers and construction cranes dot the horizon—but dogs without a sense of decor don't seem to mind.

Dogs like to amble by the river, which is down a fair incline from the trail. But be careful if you've got a water dog, because riders of personal watercraft and motor-boaters have been known to mow over anything in their path. There's no drinking water in the dog area and it gets mighty hot in the summer, so bring your own.

Take Highway 221 to Streblow Drive, and follow the signs past the Napa Municipal Golf Course and Napa Valley College to the boat marina/launch area. Park in the lot and look for the trail by the river. The park is open dawn–dusk. 707/257-9529.

🖲 Shurtleff Park

🐾🐾🐾🐾 (See Napa County map on page 318)

The farther away from the road you go, the better it is in this long, narrow park. It gets shadier and thicker with large firs and eucalyptus trees. Dogs are allowed off leash as soon as you think they're safe from the road.

The park is almost entirely fenced, but there are a few escape hatches. Two are at the entrance and two others are along the side that lead you into the schoolyard of Phillips Elementary School. This isn't normally a problem, unless your dog runs into the day-care center at lunchtime, as Joe once did. A teacher escorted him out by the scruff of his neck before he could steal someone's peanut butter sandwich.

You'll find the park on Shelter Street at Shurtleff, beside Phillips Elementary School. It's open dawn–dusk. 707/257-9529.

PLACES TO EAT

Angele Restaurant: Doggies who dine at this restaurant's riverfront tables get treats and water! "We love dogs!" says a server. The food is excellent—French with a Napa Valley flair. The restaurant is just a couple of blocks from the wonderful Napa River Inn. A big thanks to the aptly named Bacchus, a personable traveling rottie, for sniffing this one out for us. 540 Main Street; 707/252-8115.

Brown's Valley Yogurt and Espresso Bar: Cool off with a cold frozen one at the outside tables shaded by a wooden awning. 3265 Brown's Valley Road; 707/252-4977.

Downtown Joe's: This microbrewery is housed in a 100-year-old landmark building on the Napa River. Dogs get to sit with you at the edge of the area with outdoor tables (not in the covered section, though), or they can stretch out beside you on the comfy lawn. Dogs get to drink water in doggy bowls while you get to sip good beers made right on the premises. The brewery even makes a red ale called Tail Waggin' Ale. Our first time here I thought Joe was foaming at the mouth with enthusiasm for the place, but I soon discovered he'd just dipped his snout into a near-empty, still-foamy glass of Tail Waggin' someone had left behind. Hungry? The food's as good as the beers. 902 Main Street; 707/258-2337.

Napa Valley Traditions: Enjoy fresh baked goods and cappuccino at four outside tables shaded by two trees and an awning. Your dog will find as much to enjoy here as you will—inside, the shop also sells dog biscuits. 1202 Main Street; 707/226-2044.

PLACES TO STAY

The Chablis Inn: Don't be fooled by the name of this place: It's not a darling wine-country bed-and-breakfast inn. It's simply a decent motel with an enticing moniker. But it's striving to be more innlike, with some rooms offering down comforters and whirlpool tubs. All rooms come with bottled water, too. The motel has a couple of features that most charming inns don't, namely a pool and cable TV. Rates are $89–235. (The high-end price is for the fancier rooms in high season.) Dogs are $10–15 extra, depending on their size. 3360 Solano Avenue 94558; 707/257-1944 or 800/443-3490; www.chablisinn.com.

The Napa Inn: If Queen Anne–style Victorians are your dog's cup of tea, sniff out this terrific 1899 bed-and-breakfast. Dogs are allowed to stay in a pretty garden guest room and a separate cottage here. Angelina's Garden Room has 12-foot-high ceilings, a whirlpool bath for two (your dog can't be one of the two), a shower for two (ditto about the dog), a fireplace, and even a private garden area. The Garden Cottage has a fireplace, minikitchen, and French doors that look out on a private flower garden. Dogs mustn't sleep on the beds in either accommodation. If the inn is really busy the innkeepers prefer small dogs, but they're open to well-behaved larger pooches at other times.

Your stay includes breakfast for two (humans) in the inn's sumptuous dining area. On cooler evenings, the humans in your party can sidle up to a fire in the relaxing parlor. Rates are $195–255. Dogs are $20 extra. 1137 Warren Street 94559; 707/257-1444 or 800/435-1144; www.napainn.com.

Napa River Inn: This dog-friendly full-service luxury hotel doesn't just permit pooches: It showers them with goodies and services.

But before I gush further, you need to know that dogs have to weigh less than 50 pounds to stay here. If your dog is on the medium-large side or larger, don't read on, because it'll break your heart.

If you're still reading, you're one of the lucky ones with a lighter dog (or else you're a sucker for punishment). You won't believe what this upscale boutique hotel offers dogs. Upon check-in, your dog gets use of a pet blanket embroidered with the inn's logo, a matching placemat, and attractive food and water bowls to put on the placemat. (If you want to buy these items, the gift shop sells them. The ones that come with your room are just loaners.) In addition, dogs get poop bags and locally made gourmet dog biscuits. As you may have guessed, unlike the aforementioned goodies, you don't have to give these items back when you're done with them. If you need a little assistance with dog duties, the bell staff here is often available to take your dog for a little walk along the inn's namesake, the Napa River. Dog-sitting can also be arranged through an outside service.

One of the three buildings that make up the inn dates from 1887. Its rooms are opulent but unpretentious, with fireplaces, claw-foot tubs, and canopy king-sized beds. Rooms at the other two lovely buildings feature nautical themes or "contemporary wine country design." Included in your stay is a delicious breakfast at any of the wonderful restaurants on the 2.5-acre property. Rates are $179–499. Dogs are $25 extra. 500 Main Street 94559; 707/251-8500 or 877/251-8500; www.na.pariverinn.com.

Napa Valley Country Cottage: A sweet patch of pooch paradise awaits you and the dog of your life here. This cozy cottage is surrounded by 12 acres of gardens, woods, walking paths, and open areas that are perfect for throwing a stick. Some of the acreage is fenced and gated, for that extra-secure leash-free romp. There's even a little vineyard, should you want some real wine-country ambience. A wooded area with a seasonal creek separates the cottage from the cottage-owners' house, so there's plenty of privacy.

The wood cottage itself is a very cute one-bedroom affair with a little kitchen and dining area, and a living room. (The futon in the living room folds out, should you be traveling with extra humans.) The large, sunny deck makes great setting for dining alfresco with your dog friend. The cottage is perfect for pooches: It has Italian tile floors and is well stocked with doggy treats, doggy dishes, and a pooch bed.

Rates are $950 for one week, plus a $50 cleaning fee (even for nondog people). Dogs are $50 extra for the length of their stay; two dogs will cost you $75. During slow times you can rent the cottage for four nights, for $575 plus the cleaning and dog fees. The cottage is on beautiful Mount Veeder. When you make your reservation you'll get the address. 707/226-6621; www.napa-valleycasa.com.

Redwood Inn: Rates are $67–139. Dogs are $10 extra. 3380 Solano Avenue 94558; 707/257-6111 or 877/872-6272; www.napavalleyredwoodinn.net.

CHAPTER 29
Yolo County

The little towns along the winding Sacramento River haven't changed much since the early 1900s. That's good news for you, but it's not necessarily what your dog wants to hear. Restaurants with outdoor dining are rare, and dog-friendly parks are equally uncommon. You'll see mile after mile of wide-open land and dense forests, but most of it is privately owned and off-limits. For information on the one state wildlife area here (the Sacramento Bypass), call the California Department of Fish and Game at 530/355-0978.

The Sacramento River is so integral to life here that many of the county's parks are formed around public boat ramps that charge nominal launching fees. If you have a dog who loves to go angling for salmon, stripers, or shad, this is a great place to bring her to show off your fishing skills.

Davis is the only city with off-leash dog areas and a fair number of outdoor dining establishments. Some of the parks are close to major highways, so they're a blessing when your dog starts moaning and getting that bulgy-eyed look on a long trip.

PICK OF THE LITTER—YOLO COUNTY

BEST HIKING
Cache Creek Canyon Regional Park, Rumsey (page 336)

BEST LEASH-FREE PARK
Slide Hill Park, Davis (page 339)

Rumsey

PARKS, BEACHES, AND RECREATION AREAS

🟫 Cache Creek Canyon Regional Park

🐾🐾🐾 (See Yolo County map on page 334)

This 700-acre park is flat in the developed sections and very hilly when you get away from people. Couch-potato canines enjoy picnicking at any of three car-accessible sites, as well as "ruffing" it at the campground. More adventurous dogs prefer hiking over the creek and into the woods with their human friends on a self-guided nature walk.

We've found that some park hosts don't know about the trails, so it's best to get a map of the nature walk before you go. Write for one from the Yolo County Parks Division at 292 West Beamer Street, Woodland, CA 95695.

Very feisty dogs may want to continue their treks onto federal land, where they're allowed to be off leash. More than 15,000 acres—some of it inaccessible because of the steep terrain—is out there for your leashless bliss. It can be tricky to find. Contact the Bureau of Land Management, Clear Lake Resource Area, 555 Leslie Street, Ukiah, CA 95482; 707/462-3873.

Camping at Cache Creek Canyon Regional Park costs $17–19. Dogs are $2 extra. There are 45 sites, all first-come, first-served. The day-use fee is $6. The first of the three park turnoffs is about six miles west of Rumsey on Highway 16. All sites are on the south side of the road. 530/666-8115.

PLACES TO STAY

Cache Creek Canyon Regional Park: See Cache Creek Canyon Regional Park, above, for camping information.

Esparto

You could get your hopes up if you're hungry when entering the main street to this tiny old-time town. A sign bigger than most around here announces that the Dogtown Diner is dead ahead. When we arrived late one Monday afternoon, it was indeed dead. In fact, all three of the town's eateries were closed.

It turns out that even when they're open, only the Burger Barn has outdoor seating. About the only place to get hot food around here after 5 P.M. is at the Cache Creek Indian Bingo and Casino center, a few miles west on Highway 16. There are no outdoor tables, but if you're traveling with another human companion, one of you can walk the dog around the area outside the incongruously large building while the other goes inside and orders a three-piece fried chicken dinner with beans and mashed potatoes and gravy for a mighty reasonable price. Be sure to order an extra mashed potato cup for your dog. While you're in there, you can take your change and try your luck at the video slot machines on the other side of bingoland. (Whatever you do, don't leave your dog alone in the car here. It is often mortally hot.)

PARKS, BEACHES, AND RECREATION AREAS

◨ Esparto Community Park

🐾 🐾 (See Yolo County map on page 334)

A brochure announces that this four-acre park is "mainly used for passive recreation." That suits most dogs just fine, since they have to be on leash here anyway. It's a convenient stop on the long and scenic Highway 116.

The park, which is loaded with shade trees, is about five miles west of I-505, on Highway 16. 530/666-8115.

PLACES TO EAT

Burger Barn: Eat big burgers at this eatery's lone, shaded picnic table. If you bring your dog's bowl, the folks here will gladly provide water. 7090 Yolo Avenue; 530/787-3720.

Woodland

This little city has churches and saloons in unusually high numbers. You can do the sin-forgiveness-sin-forgiveness theme all week long here and barely walk (stumble?) a couple of blocks.

PARKS, BEACHES, AND RECREATION AREAS

The parks here used to allow dogs off-leash with a permit. Now leashes are the law for everyone.

Phil Frank

❸ Woodside Park

🐾🐾 (See Yolo County map on page 334)

There's plenty of green, flat open space here for your dog's jogging pleasure. The park also has several shaded picnic tables for your dog's dining pleasure. The park is on the corner of Cottonwood Street and El Dorado Drive, just six blocks west of Crawford Park (see below). 530/661-5880.

❹ Crawford Park

🐾🐾 (See Yolo County map on page 334)

You and your dog will enjoy the year-round green grass and the abundance of shade trees here. This park is a great place to come to exercise your human and canine children at the same time. There's a pint-sized railroad village in the middle of the playground. Kids love it.

Exit I-5 at East Street and go south for several blocks. Turn right on Gibson Road. After a few blocks, go left on College Street and you'll find the park at the corner of College Street and El Dorado Drive. 530/661-5880.

Davis

Davis is home to a large University of California campus and a laid-back collegiate crowd. Many of the students miss their dogs and want to pet yours. It's also home to six parks that have sections for leashless dogs. Davis is a nice place to be a dog.

PARKS, BEACHES, AND RECREATION AREAS

We describe four of the city's six leash-free areas below. Of the other two, one is a quarter-acre unfenced section of Walnut Park (the leash-free section is closest to Lillard Drive, just east of Cowell Boulevard). It's marked by signs. The other is a small section of the Aspen Greenbelt. It's on the north end of the greenbelt, near Glacier and Denali Drives. (Ooh, sounds cold!). It's hard to see because it runs 100 feet from the quiet road and is separated by brush.

5 Community Park Dog Park

🐾🐾🐕 (See Yolo County map on page 334)

This is Davis's only fenced dog park. It's just a quarter acre, so it's truly a post-age stamp–sized park, but it's a triangular stamp, so it's an interesting one. And it's not entirely flat, which is also a fairly unusual concept in dog parks. The park is a grassy area that's gently sloped, with a smaller flat area for dogs who prefer a more couch-potato approach. It has a green vinyl fence to match the grass (No, the grass isn't vinyl, smarty!) and a lot of shade from Chinese tallow trees. Davis is considering implementing a real-deal two-acre fenced dog park within Community Park at some point, so maybe this tiny park is just a precursor. The park is on F Street between 14th Street and Covell Boulevard. 530/757-5626.

6 Sycamore Park

🐾🐾🐕 (See Yolo County map on page 334)

If your dog won't be tempted to join in the fun and games of the playground on her right and the sports field on her left, the off-leash section of this park will suit her just fine. It's green, grassy, and fairly safe from traffic.

Park along Sycamore Lane between Villanova and Bucknell Drives, not in the parking lot of West Davis Intermediate School. Go into the park's grassy field to the right of the school as you face it from Sycamore Lane. The dog-exercise area is to the left of the playground and is clearly marked. 530/757-5626.

7 Slide Hill Park

🐾🐾🐾🐕 (See Yolo County map on page 334)

The off-leash part of this diverse community park is toward the back, pro-tected from most traffic. It's also partly shaded and it has green grass, even in the middle of summer! What more could a city dog want? More room? Pos-sibly, but this off-leash area is Davis's largest (although at a half-acre, it's not exactly a Goliath), so why be picky?

The park is also a great place to take kids. There are playgrounds and tennis courts, and there's even a decent-sized swimming pool in the front.

To get to the dog area, park in the lot at Temple Drive and walk into the park on the paved path, heading left past the tennis courts until you reach the back. The dog spot, under a small grove of trees, is marked by a garbage can and a sign. 530/757-5626.

8 Pioneer Park

🐾🐾🐕 (See Yolo County map on page 334)

This park is good for kids, with playgrounds and basketball hoops, but the dog-exercise area is a little too close to the road for our comfort. It's also very small. If you have a very obedient dog who needs to stretch his legs off leash, but doesn't need to stretch them very far, this will do. It's clean, green, and has some shade. Fortunately, it's on a quiet road, so the danger from cars is low.

Pioneer Park is convenient for dogs traveling through on the freeway. Heading east on I-80, take the Mace Boulevard exit and go left on Chiles Road. Take a right on El Cemonte Avenue. Go left on Swingle Drive and you'll be at the park. The dog-walk area is just to the right, about halfway down the block on Hamel Street. 530/757-5626.

PLACES TO EAT

Most of the city's best restaurants are downtown. Unfortunately, according to dog owners in Davis, many students have let their dogs run loose around here—there's a backlash going on against dogs in the downtown area, though we've never seen evidence of it. A few restaurants still allow dogs to eat at their outdoor tables, but they prefer not to be listed. Here are two that don't mind.

London Fish 'n' Chips: The fish-and-chips are a favorite of many a UC Davis student. Dine with your dog at the shaded outdoor tables. 129 E Street; 530/753-7210.

Subway: Eat subs at a couple of outdoor tables. 130 G Street; 530/756-1440.

PLACES TO STAY

Best Western University Lodge: When your dog needs to go see someone graduate or consult with a professor on some "arcanine" matter, this motel one block off campus (and a couple of blocks from Central Park, a good spot for leashed dogs) is a convenient place to stay. Rates are $99–175. Dogs are $5 extra. 123 B Street 95616; 530/756-7890.

Econo Lodge: Rates are $57–70. Dogs are $5 extra. 221 D Street 95616; 530/756-1040 or 800/533-2666.

Howard Johnson Hotel: Reserve early: The normal doggy fee for pooch-designated rooms is $10 per night. But that fee goes up to $25 if the hotel has no dog rooms available. (The staff has to deep-clean in case someone with allergies should stay there.) Room rates are $79–109. 4100 Chiles Road 95616; 530/792-0800.

Motel 6: Rates are $37–48 for the first adult, $3 for the second. There's a little grass on the premises for a wee stroll. 4835 Chiles Road 95616; 530/753-3777.

GRRRRR

CHAPTER 30

Solano County

Solano County is slowly going to the dogs. The marvelous 2,070-acre Rush Ranch Open Space now permits leash-free pooches on a two-mile trail with views that are to drool for. This alone makes it absolutely worth the trip to Solano County. So does the Grizzly Island Wildlife Area, in the thick of the Suisun Marsh. As long as you visit when dogs can be off leash, your pooch will think she's in heaven. It's mud heaven. Bring a towel.

Smaller leash-free areas (much smaller!) include dog parks in Vacaville and Benicia. Two parks in Dixon allow off-leash dogs, but if your dog isn't at perfect heel when you're at the parks, leash him fast, or you could find yourself paying a fine old fine. The county is growing so rapidly that there's a real need for more leash-free areas.

If you find yourself at the famed Jelly Belly jelly bean factory in Fairfield, you'll be happy to know that while you wait for the rest of your crew to take the tour inside, you and your dog can have a decent time at the teeny little dog "relief" area beside the parking lot. You'll find some very green grass, some pretty ivy, poop bags, water, and a red fire hydrant ("This hydrant is here for

PICK OF THE LITTER—SOLANO COUNTY

MOST TEMPTING HYDRANT
Jelly Belly dog "relief" area, Fairfield (page 343)

BEST POOCH PARK FOR A BARBECUE
Phenix Community Dog Park, Benicia (page 349)

BEST OFF-LEASH HIKING
Rush Ranch Open Space, Suisun City (page 351)

MOST DOG-FRIENDLY PLACES TO EAT
Java Point, Benicia (page 350)
Valley Cafe, Suisun City (page 352)

your dog's pleasure," a big sign says. "Not a working hydrant." If God forbid the Jelly Belly factory goes up in flames, at least the firefighters won't be fooled by the doggy decor.) It's not exactly Rush Ranch, but it's better than sitting in your car the whole time watching tired, jelly bean–stuffed children having sugar-induced meltdowns on the asphalt.

Vacaville

PARKS, BEACHES, AND RECREATION AREAS

Vacaville finally has its very own dog park.

1 Janine Jordan Park for Dogs

🐾🐾🐾🐕 (See Solano County map on page 342)

Jake gives this park three paws despite its relatively small size of two-thirds of an acre. That's because it has friendly people, grass (although not always of the green variety), shade trees, and best of all: a golden fire hydrant (most dogs probably only dream of such idols) and a doggy drinking fountain made out of a decommissioned fire hydrant. The golden hydrant is a memorial to Panto, a dearly departed Vacaville Police K-9 partner. The fountain hydrant is an homage to all dogs.

The dog park is within Lagoon Valley Regional Park. If you're going to become a park regular, you should join its organizational group, P.A.W.S. The $25 membership fee goes toward park upkeep and supplies. (From what a visitor tells us, the park looks as if it's in need of some TLC lately. It wasn't when we saw it, though. Either way, your membership dollars will be put to good use.) Plus your membership will get you into the park without having to pay the $3 entry fee for the regional park. But if you're just passing through and want to check it out, it's worth the $3. (You'll also have to sign a waiver. They're available at the kiosk, or you can download one by going to the dog park's website, www.ourdogpark.org.)

Exit I-80 at Pena Adobe Road/Lagoon Valley Regional Park. Go right at the stop sign (this is Riviera Road), and go left onto Pena Adobe. Follow the signs to Lagoon Valley Regional Park, which will be on your right. Drive .2 more miles and you'll come to the dog park. Lagoon Valley's number is 707/449-6122. The number to contact P.A.W.S. is 866/510-3681.

❷ Andrews Park

😸 😸 (See Solano County map on page 342)

If you need a shopping cart, try this park first. For some reason, the creek that cuts through the west end of the park contains more shopping carts than most supermarkets.

The chunk of park to the east of the creek is graced with gentle rolling hills, picnic areas, barbecues, deciduous trees, and a lawn as green and smooth as a golf course. But dogs must be leashed.

The west side of the creek is just a shady trail that officially stops at the first overpass and can get pretty seedy if you continue.

The best parking for the east side is on School Street, near Davis Street. For the west side of the creek, park in a lot at Kendal Street, off Dobbins Street. 707/449-6122.

PLACES TO STAY

Best Western Heritage Inn: Small to medium dogs are allowed here. Don't try to pass your Saint Bernard off as a lapdog, even if he is your lapdog. Rates are $70–90. Pooches are $10–20 extra. 1420 East Monte Vista Avenue 95688; 707/448-8453.

Motel 6: If you want to shop at the famous outlet mall in Vacaville and you're traveling with someone who will watch your pooch, this is a convenient place to stay—it's about 1,000 feet from the mall. Shop 'til you drop, then drag yourself back here. Rates are $55–60 for the first adult, $6 for the second. 107 Lawrence Drive 95687; 707/447-5550.

Dixon

Although it's no more stringent than most, the pooper-scooper law in Dixon has such a formidable name that we had to pass it on. It's called the "Canine Defecation Ordinance." Yowza! It doesn't sound like anything we want to break.

Here's the good news: If your dog is super-obedient and stays really close to you (actually, he'd need to stay at your heel), he can be off leash in the parks here!

PARKS, BEACHES, AND RECREATION AREAS

🖪 Northwest Park

😺😺🐾 (See Solano County map on page 342)

If your dog will stay very close at heel without a leash, she may go leashless at this grassy, 20-acre park. Otherwise, use your leash. With these fairly stringent rules, she probably wouldn't notice her freedom anyway.

The park is on West H and North Lincoln Streets. 707/678-7000.

🖪 Hall Memorial Park

😺😺🐾 (See Solano County map on page 342)

If you have to conduct business with city government and you want your dog to conduct business, too, you couldn't have asked for a better location for a park. It's right behind City Hall.

There's not much in the way of shade here, but on cooler days this park proves a decent stroll for dogs, provided they're leashed or at very firm heel. The park also has a playground, a swimming pool, tennis courts, and picnic areas with barbecues, so it's even better for people. The park is at Hall Park Drive and East Mayes Street. 707/678-7000.

PLACES TO STAY

Best Western Inn: This is a convenient place to stay if you have to attend a packed University of California event and no rooms are available in Davis. It's just eight miles away, and a swift drive. The staff prefers to have small dogs here but doesn't always demand it. Rates are $90–100. Dogs are $10 extra. 1345 Commercial Way 95620; 707/678-1400 or 800/528-1234.

Fairfield

PARKS, BEACHES, AND RECREATION AREAS

City park ranger Teri Geiger has been longing to get a group of locals together to try to implement a fairly large dog park at one of the larger park parcels. If you're interested in her mission (if you have a dog, you should be), phone her at 707/428-7614.

🖪 Rockville Hills Regional Park

😺😺😺 (See Solano County map on page 342)

Hike, fish, and enjoy nature in this 630-acre park filled with trees and trails. The main trail is fairly steep and takes you to the top of the park, where you'll find two small ponds for fishing. After this hike on a summer afternoon, many dogs jump in when they reach the summit. A man told me that a small beagle once disappeared for several seconds and came up with a tiny fish flailing in her mouth. Could this be just another flagrant flailing fish story?

Once you enter the park, you're safe from traffic. But dogs are supposed to be leashed anyway, since the park is officially run by the city of Fairfield, which has a strict leash law. Check out the nature trail that a local Eagle Scout troop has created. A favorite of many dogs is the Mystic Trail. The 25 miles of trails are arranged in sort of stacked loop formations, so it's easy to get lost. No brochures or trail maps are available at the entrance. Phone the number below for both, or for advice, before you visit.

For the most vigorous workout, try the main trail. It's the one that bends slightly to the left and up a steep hill as you enter from the parking lot. The park is often desolate, so use judgment about hiking alone.

Exit Highway 80 at Suisun Valley Road and drive 1.5 miles (in the opposite direction from the myriad fast-food outlets) to Rockville Road. Go left on Rockville. In about .7 mile you'll come to a small brown sign for the park. In 1,500 feet you'll find a small parking area. At press time there was no entrance fee, but by the time you read this, you may have to drop some cash into the iron ranger, so bring a few bucks. (The fee could be $3 for humans, $1 for dog.) 707/428-7614.

Vallejo

PARKS, BEACHES, AND RECREATION AREAS

Jake Dog and I are crossing our fingers that by the next edition we'll have a real dog park to describe. At press time, the city's dog people were hoping to convince the city to establish a five-acre leash-free area at Wardlow Park. Phone 707/648-4600 for updates.

⬛ River Park

🐾🐾🐾 (See Solano County map on page 342)

With goldenrod as high as an elephant's eye and a preponderance of low brush, this waterfront park looks like a huge abandoned lot. That's actually one of its charms—you don't have to worry about your dog's mowing over children in a playground or digging up a plug of green grass. The only park-like features here are a couple of benches along the Mare Island Strait.

A wide dirt path leads you toward the water and far from traffic danger. Unfortunately, the leash law is in effect here, and unless your dog is inclined to wade through several yards of mucky marsh to get to the water, he's not going to go swimming. It's still fun to walk along the water and look at the now-defunct Mare Island Naval Shipyard.

DIVERSION

Seize the Bay from Vallejo: Lucky dogs! You get to take a ferry ride to San Francisco on the **Blue and Gold Fleet.** Fares are $9.50 one-way for adults. Additional destinations are available through San Francisco. The ferry terminal is at 495 Mare Island Way in Vallejo. Phone 415/705-8200 for schedules and more information, or 415/705-5555 for tickets; www.blueandgoldfleet.com.

There are two entry points. If you're driving, use the south entrance on Wilson Avenue, just north of Hichborn Street, which has a small parking lot. Otherwise, you can enter at Wilson Avenue just across the street from Sims Avenue. 707/648-4600.

7 Dan Foley Park

😊😊 (See Solano County map on page 342)

You won't often see this at Marine World–Africa USA—professional water-skiers practicing their acts over sloping jumps, then landing headfirst in the water when everything doesn't work out perfectly.

But you and your dog will be treated to this unpolished spectacle if you visit this park on the right day. The park is directly across Lake Chabot from Marine World, so you get to witness a good chunk of the goings-on there. Since dogs aren't allowed at Marine World, this is an ideal place to walk them if your kids are spending a few hours with more exotic animals. You still get to hear the sound of jazz bands and the roar of amazed crowds.

Dan Foley Park is so well maintained we initially were afraid it was a golf course. Willows and pines on rolling hills provide cooling shade, and there's usually a breeze from the lake. Leashed dogs are invited everywhere but the water. Even humans aren't supposed to swim in it. Picnic tables are right across from the water-ski practice area, so if your dog wants entertainment with his sandwich, this is the place.

The park is on Camino Alto North just east of Tuolumne Street. There is a $3 parking fee, $4 for nonresidents. 707/648-4600.

8 The Wharf

😊😊😊 (See Solano County map on page 342)

This is the place for hip Vallejo dogs, and it's not even an official park. The paved path along the Mare Island Strait looks toward the old Mare Island Naval Shipyard on the other side of the strait, providing a real nautical atmosphere.

It's also the perfect place to take your dog while you're waiting for your ship to come in, since this is where the Vallejo–San Francisco ferry stops.

There's a substantial strip of grass beside the path where dogs like to take frequent breaks. Here, they can socialize without getting under joggers' sneakers. Leashes are a must.

The wharf area covers almost the entire length of Mare Island Way, starting around the Vallejo Yacht Club. Your best bet is to park at the public parking area of the ferry terminal. 707/648-4600.

PLACES TO EAT

Sardine Can: Get a view of the strait while you eat some of the freshest seafood available. Dogs get great treatment here, including a big bowl of water. Dine at the two outdoor tables. It's at 0 (as in zero) Harbor Way; 707/553-9492.

PLACES TO STAY

Holiday Inn: While the kids are busy turning upside-down at unnerving speeds at the nearby Six Flags Marine World, you and your small dog (the only pooches allowed) can curl up, read a book, and enjoy the peace. Rates are $109–149. Dogs are charged a $25 fee per visit. 1000 Fairgrounds Drive 94590; 707/644-1200.

Motel 6: This one's a mere two blocks from Six Flags Marine World. Rates are $40–56 for the first adult, $6 for the second. 458 Fairgrounds Drive 94589; 707/642-7781.

Quality Inn: Rates are $59–79. Dogs are $10 extra. 44 Admiral Callaghan Lane 94591; 707/643-1061.

Ramada Inn: Rates are $68–150. Dogs are charged a $50 fee per visit. 1000 Admiral Callaghan Lane 94591; 707/643-2700.

Benicia

PARKS, BEACHES, AND RECREATION AREAS

🐾 Phenix Community Dog Park

🐾🐾🐾🐾🐕 (See Solano County map on page 342)

Phenix Community Dog Park, named after a brave retired police dog, is a swell place for dogs. It's got a little more than an acre of grassy leash-free running room, and it's fenced, with water, picnic tables (which little dogs love to dodge under during chase games), poop bags, and small trees that are growing into shade-givers.

And here's a first—this pooch park comes with its own barbecue grills! And you can use them! Of course, you have to be prepared to fend off burger-minded dogs, but if you don't mind, the park people don't mind either. I love this happy, relaxed attitude. Some dog parks I've visited won't even let you bring in a graham cracker for fear you'll be mauled. Those are generally the same parks that ban children. The attitude at Phenix toward children: "You have to allow kids. Kids need to have these friendly interactions with dogs," says Gretchen Burgess, who was behind the park's founding. I like this woman's attitude.

The park is in the northwest corner of the 50-acre Benicia Community Park. Enter the parking lot at Rose and Kearny Drives and drive to the far west end. Then just follow the wide asphalt path with the painted paw prints (I love it!) to the dog park. Keep in mind that the rest of the park prohibits dogs, so don't let your dog talk you into visiting anywhere but the pooch park. If you enter the park elsewhere, the paw prints will still lead to Phenix. 707/746-4285.

10 Point Benicia Fishing Pier Area

 (See Solano County map on page 342)

Park and fish at this big drive-on pier at the end of 1st Street that juts into the Carquinez Strait. It's a popular spot among local anglers. If you're not up for fishing, bring a lunch from a nearby restaurant and park yourself on one of the benches near the old train station. You'll be amazed at the numbers of gulls vying for your crusts.

Dogs enjoy the smells of the strait. While the pier itself isn't conducive to dog exercise, there's an area of undeveloped land nearby where they can cut loose as much as their leashes will allow.

This area also happens to be along the Waterfront Trail that winds through the city. The trail is a fun walk for you and your leashed dog, but make sure that when the trail passes through city parks, you and your dog take a detour.

The pier is at the southern end of 1st Street, just past A Street. 707/746-4285.

PLACES TO EAT

Java Point: You and the dog of your choice are sure to enjoy the soups, sandwiches, bagels, and jammin' good java served here. This would be a terrific place to bring the pooch even if the food was just so-so. The folks here bring pooches organic dog treats and a fresh bowl of water. Dine with your smiling dog at the umbrella-topped patio. 366 1st Street; 707/745-1449.

Pacifica Pizza: Choose from a large selection of pizzas to eat at tables shaded by umbrellas. 915 1st Street; 707/746-1790.

PLACES TO STAY

Best Western Heritage Inn: Rates are $89–120. Dogs pay a $25 fee for the length of their stay. 1955 East 2nd Street 94510; 707/746-0401.

Suisun City

PARKS, BEACHES, AND RECREATION AREAS

🐾 Grizzly Island Wildlife Area

🐾🐾🐾🐾 🐕 (See Solano County map on page 342)

This is what dogs have been praying for since they started living in cities: 8,600 acres of wide-open land where they can run—leashless—among the sort of wildlife you see only in PBS specials.

This sprawling wetland, in the heart of the Suisun Marsh, is home to an amazing array of fauna, including tule elk, river otters, waterfowl of every type, jackrabbits, white pelicans, and peregrine falcons.

Of course, walking in marshy areas has its pros and cons. But you don't have to get muddy feet here; the landscapes are as varied as the animal life. Dry upland fields are plentiful. You can also canoe down a slough with your steady dog or hike on dozens of dirt trails. Many folks bring dogs here to train them for hunting, which brings us to the unfortunate subject of the park's schedule.

Because of hunting and bird-nesting seasons, Grizzly Island Wildlife Area is closed during fairly large chunks of the year. Be sure to phone first!

If your dog helps you hunt for ducks or pheasant, she's allowed to join you during some of the hunting seasons. Department of Fish and Game staff also occasionally open small sections to people during the off-season, but it's unpredictable from one year to another when and if they'll do it. Even when the park is open, certain sections may be off-limits to dogs. Check with staff when you come in.

To get to the Grizzly Island Wildlife Area, exit I-80 at Highway 12 heading toward Rio Vista. Turn onto Grizzly Island Road at the stoplight for the Sunset Shopping Center. Drive 10 miles, past farms, sloughs, and marshes, until you get to the headquarters. You'll have to check in here and pay a $2.50 fee unless you have a hunting or fishing license. Then continue driving to the parking lot nearest the area that you want to explore (staff can advise you). Don't forget your binoculars. 707/425-3828.

🐾 Rush Ranch Open Space

🐾🐾🐾🐾 🐕 (See Solano County map on page 342)

From freshwater and saltwater marshes to rolling grass-covered hills and meadowlike pastures, this 2,070-acre open-space parcel is home to some wonderfully diverse landscapes.

The to-wag-for news for dogs is that they're allowed to be off-leash on one of the three trails here if they're under voice control. (They're not allowed to even set paw on the other two.) Suisun Hill Trail is a big hit among canines. The two-mile trail takes you into hills with killer 360-degree views of the

Suisun Marsh and the hills and mountains to the north. Rangers tell us that on a clear day, you can see the Sierra Nevada.

Cattle are in these here hills, so if your dog is a chaser, or a herder with an uncontrollable urge to do his job, keep him leashed. (Cattle dogs have been known to try to herd bevies of bovines. The cattle don't think this is cute. Neither do Rush Ranch rangers.) Plenty of wildlife is here, too. If in doubt, leash. (Bikes and horses aren't allowed, so those are two fewer distractions to worry about.)

This is a special place, run by the Solano Land Trust. If you'd like to help support the educational and interpretive activities of the Rush Ranch Educational Council, or if you want more information, phone 707/432-0150. For details on Rush Ranch's history, flora and fauna, and other park info, see www.rushranch.org.

From Highway 12, exit at Grizzly Island Road and drive south for a couple of miles. To get to the trail, park near the entrance sign and cross Grizzly Island Road to the gate. Walk to the left and follow the trail markers.

PLACES TO EAT

Valley Cafe: Your dog will have a hard time forgiving you if you're on your way to Lake Berryessa and you don't stop at this cute eatery. That's because the owner loves dogs and makes 'em feel right at home. Next to the register is a jar of pooch treats that calls dogs from far and wide. If you cock your head just right, you can almost hear it in the breeze. "Oh dogggggyyyyy! Come eat us!!!! We're really yummmmmyyyyyy!!" Dogs also can wet their whistles with bowls of fresh water here. By the way, humans enjoy the café/diner cuisine. The BLT on grainy artisan bread is to drool for. Dine with your dog at the seven umbrella-covered tables outside. 4171 Suisun Valley Road; 707/864-2507.

Rio Vista

Humphrey the humpback whale visited this Delta town, and so should your dog. For now, this is a real, dusty Old West town—not one of those cute villages loaded with boutiques and "shoppes." It's refreshing to find a town with more bait shops than banks. However, in the name of "progress," Rio Vista is slowly becoming home to some major housing developments and all the shopping centers and other unsightly amenities that go with them. Get here now, and take some photos on the old streets with your smiling dog. In a few years, they could be collector's items.

Rio Vista isn't bursting with dog amenities. In fact, it's really appropriate to visit with your dog only if you're on a fishing holiday. Then you and your pooch can slip your boat into the water and take off on the Delta for a few hours. Come back with your catch and eat dinner at the county park as the sun goes down on another Delta day.

DIVERSION

Hire a Houseboat: There's nothing like cruising around the Delta in your very own house. Your dog can feel right at home, and nothing makes her happier than having you home all the time. Just remember that, as on land, you have to walk your dog—only you have to dock to do it. Call the Rio Vista Chamber of Commerce at 707/374-2700 for information on houseboat rentals in the Delta.

PARKS, BEACHES, AND RECREATION AREAS

13 Sandy Beach County Park

🐾🐾🐾🐾 (See Solano County map on page 342)

Take your dog to the very back of the park, and he can run around off leash and even do the dog paddle in the Sacramento River! It's not a huge area, but it's all you'll need to show your dog a good time. The closer day-use section is completely off-limits to dogs, so be sure you end up in the right area.

Your dog has another chance of getting wet if he follows you into the showers at the campground. Dogs are allowed at the campground. It's not terribly scenic and can get mighty dry at times, but hey, it's a place to stay on the river. There are 42 sites. Fees are $14–21 a night. Dogs are $1 extra. Half the sites are first-come, first-served. Reservations are recommended during summer.

Take Highway 12 all the way to Rio Vista; follow Main Street to 2nd Street, and go right. When the street bears left and becomes Beach Drive, the park is within a quarter mile. Bring proof of a rabies vaccination. 707/374-2097.

PLACES TO EAT

Shelby's Drive-In: Shelby's has got every kind of fast food you could ever want and several picnic tables for your feast. The staff will bring your dog water if he needs to wet his snout. 650 Highway 12; 707/374-2020.

PLACES TO STAY

Sandy Beach County Park: See Sandy Beach County Park, above, for camping information.

CHAPTER 31

Sacramento County

Capitol dogs are having a capital time these days. Sacramento County's dog parks are sprouting like foxtails on a warm summer's day. At last count, there were nine, with a few more in the works. (The Wild West is back, judging by the names of a couple of them: The Canine Corral and C-Bar-C Dog Park.)

On the on-leash front, the American River Parkway is one of the finest county park systems we've come across. This riverside greenbelt extends 23 miles from Discovery Regional Park to Folsom Lake, encompassing 20 recreation areas and 5,000 acres. A bike trail connects it all. If your dog were a bike, you'd be all set.

Unfortunately, dogs aren't allowed on the bike trails here. They're also banned from the numerous horse trails. That leaves them with a few small hiking trails, plenty of open land, and the riverbank. It's not a bad fate, but it could be much better. In fact, local dogs are in the middle of a battle with the county about obtaining some leash-free areas around the parkway. We'll keep you posted. Three of the American River Parkway recreation areas are

PICK OF THE LITTER—SACRAMENTO COUNTY

BEST HIKING
Folsom Lake State Recreation Area, Folsom (page 358)

BEST DOG PARKS
Phoenix Dog Park, Fair Oaks (page 360)
Partner Park, Sacramento (page 365)

MOST TEMPTING TREES
Capitol Park, Sacramento (page 367)

MOST DOG-FRIENDLY PLACE TO EAT
Bella Bru Cafe, Carmichael (page 360)

BEST DOGGY MUNCHIES
My Best Friend's Barkery, Sacramento (page 367)

MOST DOG-FRIENDLY PLACE TO STAY
Sheraton Grand Sacramento Hotel, Sacramento (page 368)

BEST RIDES
Mini steam trains, Rancho Cordova (page 362)
Top Hand Ranch Carriage Company carriage rides,
Sacramento (page 363)

described in this chapter. For more information, call the county parks department at 916/875-6961.

If you and your dog have a hankering to visit the state capitol building together, you'll get as close as the front door before you're ushered away. But it's more attractive from the outside anyway.

The park surrounding the capitol (called Capitol Park, strangely enough) is an exquisite place, with hundreds of trees from around the world. If you're tired of high taxes and crooked politicians, you'll get vicarious pleasure watching your he-dog do leg lifts here.

Rio Linda

PARKS, BEACHES, AND RECREATION AREAS

🔟 Westside Park Dog Park

🐾🐾🐾🐕 (See Sacramento County map on page 354)

Here's the Westside story: It's your basic, decent fenced one-acre dog park with water, some small trees, and an attempt at grass. It's a popular place (you can tell by the condition of the grass) and gets a good workout with the after-5 pooch set. The park is at West 2nd Street and M Street. 916/991-5929.

Citrus Heights

PARKS, BEACHES, AND RECREATION AREAS

🔟 C-Bar-C Dog Park

🐾🐾🐾🐾🐕 (See Sacramento County map on page 354)

If your dog's a cattle dog, how could you not bring her here? C-Bar-C isn't a ranch, but it sure sounds as if it is. Here's what it looks like: More than two big, fenced acres with grass. (See? It could be a cattle stomping ground!) You won't find anyone mooing around here, but you will find some oohing and aahing by dog people who haven't seen it before. The trees here really set the park apart from so many; they're big, and they're plentiful. Oaks and pines predominate. Boy dogs keep very busy here.

The park has picnic tables, restrooms, water, and good parking. It's on Oak Avenue, a little less than a mile east of Sunrise Boulevard. It's on the north side of Oak. 8275 Oak Avenue; 916/725-1585.

Folsom

Thanks in part to Johnny Cash, most folks who aren't from the area know of Folsom because of the imposing Folsom State Prison. But this is a charming Gold Rush town, which boasts in its motto that it's "Where the West Came and Stayed." A walk down historic Sutter Street will prove this slogan right. The wealth of antique shops, art galleries, and restaurants makes it a popular place for tourists. And we're keeping our paws crossed that soon it may be a more popular place for pooches: Dog people here have been working for years to get a dog park. Just when it looks as if it's going to happen, it doesn't. Phone the city parks department at 916/355-7285 for updates, or check www.fidoinc.org (the website of Folsom Independent Dog Owners).

PARKS, BEACHES, AND RECREATION AREAS

🛈 Folsom Lake State Recreation Area

🐾🐾🐾🐾 (See Sacramento County map on page 354)

The bulk of this 12,000-acre reservoir is in Placer and El Dorado Counties, but its Folsom entrance is popular and easy to find. With four million visitors every year, this park is one of the busiest recreational lakes in the state park system.

Fortunately, that doesn't stop the rangers from permitting leashed pooches on the 80 miles of trails here. The farther you get from the water, the better, at least during crowded months. It can get really crazy around the lake. The operative word here is *party*. But the hiking and horse trails that meander through the recreation area should give you and your dog a little peace.

You'll wander through valley oaks, oracle oaks, foothill pines, and toyon here. In the spring, wildflowers are everywhere. You'll see Indian paintbrush, California poppy, and countless other colorful varieties. It's the best time to visit this park, because it's usually not too crowded or hot.

Bring your binoculars. You and your keen-eyed dog may come across such winged beauties as quail, grebes, red-tailed hawks, and eagles. Many are visible from the lake's edge. Dogs aren't allowed on the swimming beaches here, but with the lake's 75 miles of shoreline (when full), you're bound to find a few lakeside spots. You might even want to try your paw at fishing, which can be mighty good here.

The day-use fee is $7 per vehicle. Camping at one of the 182 sites costs $20. Sites are available on a first-come, first-served basis, except in summer, when reservations are highly recommended. Call 800/444-7275 to reserve a site. There are many ways to reach the park. To get to the park headquarters from the town of Folsom, go a couple of miles north on Folsom-Auburn Road. 916/988-0205.

🛈 Folsom City Park

🐾🐾 (See Sacramento County map on page 354)

If you and your dog are with a friend who's visiting the unusual gift shop (or an inmate) at the Folsom State Prison, this is the perfect place to wait. It's next door to the maximum-security prison grounds. Even though your dog must be leashed, she'll feel free compared with the folks inside that gray granite structure.

The park is flat and grassy, with ball fields, playgrounds, picnic areas, and a zoo (which is not the most appealing place, if the sight of wild animals in small cages bothers you). Dogs can't go to the zoo, but they revel in sniffing the air that wafts out of it. The park is at East Natoma and Stafford Streets. 916/355-7285.

PLACES TO STAY

Folsom Lake State Recreation Area: See Folsom Lake State Recreation Area, above, for camping information.

Lake Natoma Inn: This large, attractive hotel nestles among the big trees that flank Lake Natoma and the American River. The location is enough to put the wag in any dog's tail. From here you can embark on some great hikes along the American River Parkway (see the introduction to this chapter). Rates are $99–245. Dogs require a $45 fee, plus they're $15 extra (per night). 702 Gold Lake Drive 95630; 916/351-1500 or 800/808-5253; www.lakenatomainn.com.

Carmichael

PARKS, BEACHES, AND RECREATION AREAS

🖪 Carmichael Park Canine Corral

😻😻😻🐾 (See Sacramento County map on page 354)

There's a showdown at the Canine Corral! At press time for this book, it was the big dogs versus the little dogs. Actually, it's the big-dog people versus the little-dog people. Some people with small dogs have been requesting a separate fenced section within this one-acre park. All they want is one-tenth of the park space so their more delicate dogs don't get mowed down. But a few big-dog folks are baring their teeth over losing a chunk of land to the poochettes. Stay tuned for the next edition to find out if the little dogs win the land grab.

The park is about half grass, half dirt, with water, lights, and lots of shade from big oaks. It also has a concrete wash station for muddy paws, and there's even a delightful little wading pool. It's at Fair Oaks Boulevard and Grant Avenue. 916/485-5322.

🖪 Ancil Hoffman Park

😻😻😻 (See Sacramento County map on page 354)

This 393-acre park is part of the grand American River Parkway. It has plenty of wooded areas for dogs who like to sniff trees and dozens of acres of open grassy land.

Our favorite part is toward the back of the park, near the picnic area. This section is full of shade trees and sports a wonderful dirt trail along the upper banks of the American River. It's also where you have easy access to the river. When we visited, a few folks were picnicking at the tables above, but not a soul (canine or human) was down by the river. If you don't mind walking on small, smooth rocks, you can have a good riverside hike. Dogs are supposed to be leashed, but water dogs have no problem taking a short dip. And as with all county parks, dogs are not permitted on any bike or horse trails.

A $4 vehicle entry fee is usually charged. You can park at an outside street and walk in fee-free if you don't mind a bit of a hike. From Fair Oaks Boulevard, drive east on Kenneth Avenue a few blocks, south on California Avenue one block, then east again on Tarshes Drive, into the park. 916/875-6961.

PLACES TO EAT

Bella Bru Cafe: Bring your dog to dine with you at umbrella-topped outdoor tables, and the folks here will throw in some pooch treats for your dog. 5038 Fair Oaks Boulevard; 916/485-2883.

Fair Oaks

PARKS, BEACHES, AND RECREATION AREAS

7 Phoenix Dog Park

🐾🐾🐾🐾🐾🐕 (See Sacramento County map on page 354)

Dogs adore this 2.5-acre patch of pooch paradise. It has everything a dog could want, from a separate area for small or shy dogs to a swimming pool. Yes, a swimming pool. It's really a very sturdy, decent-sized wading pool, but it has water and it's a hit with dogs. (The littlest dogs can actually get a decent dog paddle going in it.) A hit with dog people is the paw-wash area—a concrete pad with a water faucet, which comes in mighty handy on muddy winter days. The park also has drinking water, poop bags, and benches.

This is the kind of park you get when dog people and park people work well together. "The people in the dog group have been wonderful to deal with," says Lorne Prescott, the park department's very nice dog park liaison. The dog people say the same about the park department. Check out the dog people website, www.fordog.org, for more on the park, or phone the city at 916/966-1036. The dog park is in the southwest corner of Phoenix Park. The main entrance to the park is at 9050 Sunset Avenue, a few blocks east of Hazel Avenue, but a good entry point for the dog park location is on Kruitof Way (about a block south of Sunset), just east of Hazel.

PLACES TO EAT

Sunflower Drive-In Restaurant: We love this natural foods drive-in. So do many other people, judging by the crowds it attracts. You and your dog can eat a variety of healthful, tasty dishes at the two picnic tables here, but watch out for the chickens who like to hang out. If the tables aren't available, just walk next door to Village Park and eat at one of the picnic tables there. At least the chickens won't be henpecking you. The people who work at the Sunflower adore dogs, and yours will feel very welcome. 10344 Fair Oaks Boulevard; 916/967-4331.

Rancho Cordova

PARKS, BEACHES, AND RECREATION AREAS

Rancho Cordova has 20 city parks, all of which permit leashed pooches. We list the best one below. For the last few years, dogs have been keeping their toes crossed about the possibility of having a little dog park to call their own in Rancho Cordova. So far, the city's decision-makers have just been discussing the idea. Nothing concrete (or grassy) yet. Dogs' toes are getting cramped. For information on the progress of the talks, or to find out how you can help the canine cause, call the city parks department at 916/362-1841.

Meanwhile, the huge new Mather Regional Park is the newest dog-friendly county park around. And soon it too may become home to a large off-leash dog park. This is a historic time for dogs in these parts.

8 Hagan Community Park

🐾🐾🐾 (See Sacramento County map on page 354)

Leashed dogs adore visiting this grassy 61-acre park, which adjoins the American River Parkway. Dogs can get their paws wet in the river or they can stare longingly at the ducks in the park's serene pond.

Dogs have to stay away from the park's fun little petting zoo, which contains such cuties as goats, rabbits, chickens, a sheep, a pig, and a very friendly turkey. But they'll soon forget their disappointment when they learn that well-behaved pooches are permitted on the hand-built miniature train that travels on a quarter mile of track in the park. (See the Diversion Train Your Dog for more on this fun ride.)

A $4 vehicle entrance fee is in effect early April–Labor Day. From U.S. 50, exit at Mather Field Road and drive north a few blocks to Folsom Boulevard. Turn right at Folsom and in a few more blocks, head left on Coloma Road. In a few more blocks, go left on Chase Drive and follow it another nine blocks to the park. 916/362-1841.

9 Mather Regional Park

🐾🐾🐾 (See Sacramento County map on page 354)

This community is still bruised from the closure of Mather Air Force Base, but there's a silver lining: There's now a thriving 1,440-acre park on part of the former base's site.

At this point, Mather Regional Park is slowly being developed, but there's still plenty of undeveloped land, with lots of knee-level weeds, dry grass, and no trees to speak of. Dogs like it this way. Fortunately, because much of the acreage is home to vernal pools and other fragile environments, up to a third of the land could be protected against development.

DIVERSION

Train Your Dog: No, not that kind of train. This is a diversion—it's supposed to be fun! Well-behaved dogs who aren't too big are welcome to ride the wonderful **miniature steam train** (and I do mean miniature—it's the smallest of all the rideable minitrains I've seen) with you at Hagan Community Park in Rancho Cordova. Their ears flap in the breeze, their nostrils flutter with delight at scents from the nearby petting zoo. The ride is a quarter-mile and costs $0.00. That's right! The good folks with the Sacramento Valley Live Steamers Club run the choo-choo and have a 30-year tradition of never charging. That said, donations are most gratefully accepted. "They keep the train running," one Steamer told us. (For directions, see the listing for Hagan Community Park.) Phone the park at 916/362-1841 for this year's train schedule, or better yet, check out the Steamers' website: www.svls.org.

From U.S. 50, exit at Mather Field Road, drive south, and follow the signs to the golf course, which is adjacent to the park's main entrance. 916/875-6961.

PLACES TO STAY

AmeriSuites: Oh, there's no place like home, Toto. Actually, if your home is very clean, comfortable, quiet, roomy, and dog-friendly, there *is* a place like home: the AmeriSuites hotel.

Every "room" at this hotel is actually a suite, with a living room (complete with sofa sleeper, easy chair, and desk area), separate bedroom, fridge, microwave, wet bar, and cable TV with VCR player. It's a real boon to have all this space and all these amenities when traveling with a dog. If you're in town on business, you may want to request a "TCB Suite" (don't ask us, the brochure, or the front desk person what this stands for...), which is even more deluxe on the office end of things. These suites include an oversized work desk, great office chair, high-speed Internet access, office supplies, and even snacks to keep you going.

The hotel also has a free, extensive breakfast buffet, a heated outdoor pool, and a fitness center. Your dog can't take advantage of these features, but he'll be happy to know he's welcome to peruse the big field in back of the hotel. The dog-loving director of sales, Christine Rakela, says even sheriff's dogs stay here during special events.

Unlike the majority of other hotels, the best rates here are on weekends and in summer. Rates are $69–139. 10744 Gold Center Drive 95670; 916/635-4799; www.amerisuites.com.

DIVERSION

A Moveable Beast: If you and your dog want to get a feel for Sacramento before you start exploring on your own, Jake highly recommends a carriage ride through the charming old part of town.

The folks who run the **Top Hand Ranch Carriage Company** are more than happy to take you and your well-behaved dog on a carriage tour around the more quaint section of Sacramento. As long as your dog doesn't interfere with the horse who's pulling this old-style carriage, he'll be welcome on any of the rides offered by Top Hand Ranch.

You'll find the carriage somewhere on the streets of Old Sacramento just about every day and on weekend nights. The price for a 10–15-minute ride is $10 for a small family (including a dog). A river park ride is $35 and lasts about a half hour. For a higher fee, you can arrange to go just about anywhere in the carriage. The capitol building is a frequent request. That tour takes roughly one hour and will cost you about $50. Call 916/655-3444 for locations and prices.

Economy Inns of America: The rooms that are set aside for pets are on the ground floor, face the highway, and are for smokers. If your dog smokes and likes to watch traffic, you'll be all set. This inn is about a mile from the American River. Rates are $75. 12249 Folsom Boulevard 95670; 916/351-1213.

Quality Inn and Suites: Rates are $69–79. A $100 pooch deposit is required. 3240 Mather Field Road 95670; 916/363-3344.

Sacramento

This is a capital place to be a dog.

PARKS, BEACHES, AND RECREATION AREAS

10 Discovery Regional Park

🐾🐾🐾 (See Sacramento County map on page 354)

Lots of leashed urban dogs stroll down here for their early evening walks, dragging their work-weary people behind them. The park has 275 acres of green open space, and although much of it is devoted to human activities such as archery and softball, there's more than enough room for your average dog to take an average walk. It's nothing your dog will write home about, but since he can't write anyway, it's no fur off his back.

Unfortunately, because it's a county park, dogs are not permitted on the equestrian trails or the bike path here. That cuts down on easy walking. But the park is well manicured, so there aren't any bushes or dense tree groves to get in your way. You won't want to let that leash slip out of your hand, as roads wind throughout the park.

Water dogs enjoy Discovery Regional Park because it's at the confluence of the American and Sacramento Rivers. The banks are steep, so it's hard to reach out and touch the rivers. But they sure do look good.

Many people walk here with their dogs and avoid the $4 entry fee that is occasionally charged. If you're driving from the north end of the city, take I-5 to the Garden Highway, drive east, and take the first road to the right, Discovery Park Road. 916/875-6961.

🐾 Howe About Dogs Park

🐾🐾🐾🦮 (See Sacramento County map on page 354)

This was the very first dog park in Sacramento, and it helped pave the way for the others in the city. The park is on Howe Avenue, thus the name (actually, it's a longer story, but you can ask the folks there), and it has trees, a picnic table, benches, and quite a bit of grass.

Unfortunately it's relatively small—a little over a quarter acre—which can make it a bit of a menagerie on weekends.

The park is within Howe Community Park, at Howe Avenue and Cottage Way (a few blocks north of Arden Way). 916/264-5200.

🐾 Goethe Park

🐾🐾🐾 (See Sacramento County map on page 354)

Even though it's spelled just like the name of the famed German poet and author, don't do what I've done for years and call this park "GER-tuh." It's pronounced "GA-tey," as in "You forgot to close the gatey, matey." It's an appropriate pronunciation, because the man for whom the park is named was in the navy. It makes sense: navy, matey, gatey.

But dogs don't care about pronunciation; they're just happy to be allowed to jingle-jangle along a trail here. This chunk of the American River Parkway has a dirt trail that runs along a segment of bank above the American River—and it's one of the few trails here where dogs are actually permitted. All county parks ban dogs from bike trails and equestrian trails—and this one has both in abundance. In fact, it's not easy to get around here without them. You'll find some very well shaded picnic areas here, but they don't make up for the lack of legally walkable places.

The vehicle fee is $4. You can park on the street a few blocks from the entrance and get in for free. If you have a boat you can carry to the water, it will cost you $8 to launch it here. Canoeing canines think this is grand. Exit U.S. 50 at Bradshaw Road, head north, then go right on Folsom Boulevard (just after the railroad tracks), and left on Rod Beaudry Road. Beaudry will take you straight into the park in about a mile. 916/875-6961.

13 Bannon Creek Park Dog Park

🐾🐾🐾🐾 (See Sacramento County map on page 354)

At just over a half acre, Bannon Creek Park is the smallest of the city's new fenced dog parks. But it's a lovely one, with grass and mature shade-giving trees. Amenities include benches, a pooch drinking fountain, and poop bags. We like the comfortable, lush setting. (At least it was lush when we visited.) It's in Bannon Creek Park, on Bannon Creek Drive off Azevedo Drive. 916/264-5200.

14 Granite Park Dog Park

🐾🐾🐾🐾 (See Sacramento County map on page 354)

Dogs enjoy chasing each other around this two-acre fenced park almost as much as their people enjoy chatting with each other. This is a very social place to bring a pooch. The park's trees are in the sapling stage, so they don't give much shade, but there's water if your pooch gets thirsty. The park is in the new Granite Regional Park, on Ramona Avenue off Power Inn Road. 916/264-5200.

15 Miller Park/Sacramento Marina

🐾🐾🐾🐾 (See Sacramento County map on page 354)

You and your leashed dog can stroll along a path overlooking the marina here or picnic under big shade trees while you watch the mighty Sacramento River flow by. You can dip your paws in or even do some casting for your supper. It's a very relaxing way to spend a dog-day afternoon.

Drive west to the end of Broadway (past all the lovely refinery tanks) and turn left on Marina View Drive. 916/264-5200.

16 Partner Park

🐾🐾🐾🐾 (See Sacramento County map on page 354)

You and your pooch partner are sure to enjoy a romp at this 2.5-acre fenced park. It's an extremely popular place among people with pooches. The park is gorgeous, with rolling hills, green grass, and mature trees that are wonderful at giving shade—definitely a cut above most fenced dog parks. A pathway wanders out to the hills, so if you want to get away from the cluster of dogs and people in the well-used part of the park, you can take a little hike. Amenities include water, poop bags, benches, and lights.

Partner Park is behind Belle Cooledge Community Center at 5699 South Land Park Drive, off South Land Park Drive. Parking is behind the center. 916/264-5200.

🔟🔟 William Land Park

🐾🐾🐾 (See Sacramento County map on page 354)

As you enter this 236-acre park, you may be struck by the thought that it looks just like a golf course. Now hold on to that thought and look around very carefully. See those shiny sticks glimmering in the background and those people in white-and-green outfits walking forward at a determined pace or standing around scratching their heads? Those are golfers. Joe Dog, Nisha Dog, and I learned this the hard way one day when we bounded out of our car and directly into the line of fire of a golfer quite some distance away. Nisha immediately tried to eat the ball. It was not a walk I care to remember, nor, I'm sure, was it a game the golfer remembers fondly.

The golf course is not fenced off from most of the rest of the park, so you really do have to be careful here. A safe, shaded section of the park is at the north end. Since dogs must be leashed, it doesn't matter that a couple of little roads run fairly close. If you brought along the kids and someone to watch them, they can go explore the zoo and the amusement park on the other side of the park.

You can reach the park's north side by taking Riverside Boulevard (parallel to I-5) to 12th Avenue and turning east. 916/264-5200.

🔟🔟 Chorley Park

🐾🐾🐾 (See Sacramento County map on page 354)

If you and your dog are waiting to pick up a loved one at Sacramento's Executive Airport, a visit to this nearby park is a wonderful way for your dog to expend some energy so she won't maul the homecomer with jumps of adulation.

This park is a real find. At first it looks just like so many other neighborhood parks, with a small playground and a little grassy area. But as you walk in, you'll see that it has the potential to be Land of the Dogs. The back of the park is extremely wide, far from traffic, and fenced from the adjacent golf course. Tall firs provide some shade. During wet months, there's even a tiny creek back here.

Even when we've visited on beautiful Saturday mornings, the place has been empty. If it stays this way, it's actually a better place to visit than many of the sprawling county parks, which get heavier use and charge a fee. Dogs are supposed to be leashed here.

Exit I-5 at Florin Road and drive east just a little more than a mile to 20th Street and turn left. Drive to the end and park on the street just outside the park. 916/264-5200.

19 Capitol Park

🐾🐾🐾 (See Sacramento County map on page 354)

Your boy dog will be overwhelmed if you bring him here for the Capitol Park Tree Tour, a self-guided tour of this 40-acre park's magnificent assemblage of trees, which represent the continents and climates of the world. On the tour brochure, each tree is numbered and its scientific and common names are given. So when your leashed dog sniffs at or does a leg lift on a dawn redwood tree, you can impress him by saying, "That's quite a *Metasequoia glyptostroboides*, eh, Spot?"

The park extends from the front of the state capitol building to several blocks behind it. It's a great excuse to get up close and personal with the capitol. Take a picnic and relax under the shade of a *Calocedrus decurrens* (incense cedar).

Warning: If your dog has any hint of terrier in him, you may not want to bring him here. Squirrels are everywhere. Joe Dog once pulled my arm so hard I thought I wouldn't be able to drive home. And the squirrels are probably still talking about the loud howling shrieks that emanated from this refined-looking Airedale's face.

The park runs from the capitol back to 15th Street, between L and N Streets. Call 916/324-0333 to receive a tree-tour brochure.

PLACES TO EAT

Look around Old Town Sacramento, and you'll find some good restaurants that permit pooches. Here are a few others nearby:

My Best Friend's Barkery: This dog bakery is just what the doggy ordered after a morning of exploring Old Town Sacramento or hiking along the American River Parkway. It features freshly baked cookies and cakes just for canines. Dine at the tables and benches next to the bakery. It's in Old Town, in front of the American River. 1050 Front Street, Suite 120; 916/448-3436.

A Shot of Class: Dine on fine continental cuisine at the outdoor tables, right in the heart of Sacramento. 1120 11th Street; 916/447-5340.

Vallejo's Mexican Cafe: The Mexican food here is tasty. Share it with your dog at the sidewalk tables. It's at the corner of O and 14th Streets. 916/444-2837.

PLACES TO STAY

Many hotels in neighboring towns welcome dogs. One of our favorites is the AmeriSuites in nearby Rancho Cordova. Here are some capital inns:

Bradshaw Inn: Rates are $49–59. Dogs are $5 extra. 3343 Bradshaw Road 95827; 916/366-1266.

Canterbury Inn: Rates are $59–69. Pooches pay $10 extra. 1900 Canterbury Road 95815; 916/927-3492.

Doubletree Hotel: Dogs under 50 pounds are welcome here. Rates are $99–395. Dogs are $50 for the length of their stay. 2001 Point West Way 95815; 916/929-8855.

Motel 6: Rates are $44–58 for the first adult, $6 for the second. 1415 30th Street 95816; 916/457-0777.

Radisson Hotel: "We're very dog-friendly here!" says a front desk person, and she's right. During a recent stay, there were dogs walking up and down the lovely paths as if they owned the place. The rooms here are pleasant and clean, and it's nice because although the hotel has lots of rooms, it's only two levels (it's very spread out). Some rooms provide a water dog with views of the ultimate temptation—a little lake on the hotel's property. But sorry, dogs. No dog paddling is allowed here, or in the hotel's pool. Rates are $139–169. Dogs pay a $50 flat fee for their stay, and require a $50 deposit. 500 Leisure Lane 95815; 916/922-2020.

Red Roof Inn: Dogs who are under 45 pounds are welcome here. Rates for humans are $50–70. One dog is free, but if you bring a second, he'll be $20. Be sure to declare your dog (as in "I have a dog with me," not "My dog is the best in the world, I do declare!") because if you sneak him in and get caught, you'll be charged $250. 3796 Northgate Boulevard 95834; 916/927-7117.

Sheraton Grand Sacramento Hotel: If you've never stayed in a restored Public Market Building, this is your chance. This historic marketplace has become a very attractive, dog-friendly hotel. Dogs under 80 pounds are welcome, and get treats upon arrival and use of a comfy dog bed and doggy bowls. Humans get use of the heated outdoor pool and decent fitness center. Rates are $99–150. Dogs require a $100 deposit. 1230 J Street 95814; 916/447-1700.

Elk Grove

This 130-square-mile service area (it's not really a city) has its first dog run and is working on another.

PARKS, BEACHES, AND RECREATION AREAS

20 Laguna Community Park Dog Park

😊😊🐕 (See Sacramento County map on page 354)

Dogs are loving this half-acre fenced park almost to death. "It's getting worn out," says a park worker. "It's overused, and we need a second one to take the burden off this one." The grass is a bit on the worn-out side, and it's not the largest dog park in the world, but it's still a fine place to take a dog in need of leash-free romping room. The park has water, poop bags, a little shade, and benches. It's at Big Horn Boulevard and Bruceville Road. 916/685-3917.

Isleton

PARKS, BEACHES, AND RECREATION AREAS

21 Brannan Island State Recreation Area

😊😊😊 (See Sacramento County map on page 354)

Most people come to this Delta haven to fish or sailboard. Those activities may not be among your dog's favorites, but even if your dog isn't the sporting sort, this park is pleasing enough. You and your dog can dip your paws in a cool slough, walk around open grassy land (on leash), or picnic in the shade of a eucalyptus. If you get tired, you can just saunter back to your tent and take a nap. It's a dog's life.

The day-use fee is $5. The recreation area has 102 campsites that go for $20 nightly. Reservations are recommended in summer and on holiday weekends. From Highway 160 a few miles south of Isleton, go east at the signs for the park. Call 800/444-7275 to reserve a campsite. For park info, call 916/777-6671.

PLACES TO STAY

Brannan Island State Recreation Area: See Brannan Island State Recreation Area, above, for camping information.

CHAPTER 32

Contra Costa County

Although much of Contra Costa County is considered a sleepy bedroom community for San Francisco, it's a rip-roaring frontierland of fun for dogs. From the renowned off-leash dog haven of the Point Isabel Regional Shoreline to the leash-free inland nirvanas of the East Bay Regional Park District (such as the Morgan Territory, in Clayton), this county enables every dog to have her day, day after day. (For more on the wonders of the East Bay Regional Park District, see the introduction to the Alameda County chapter.)

For dogs who like long hikes through highly diverse lands, 10 long regional trails lace Lafayette, Walnut Creek, and the other urban areas of the Diablo Valley. There are 60 miles of trails in all, linking a dozen towns and many beautiful parklands. Dogs must be leashed, but with all the horses and bikes that can visit here, it's a sensible rule.

The Briones to Diablo Regional Trail is one of the more popular trails. It's about 12 miles long and it snakes through some terrific parkland, including the off-leash wonderlands of the Acalanes Ridge Open Space Recreation Area and the Shell Ridge Open Space Recreation Area (both described in the Walnut Creek

PICK OF THE LITTER—CONTRA COSTA COUNTY

BEST OFF-LEASH HIKING

Sobrante Ridge Regional Preserve, El Sobrante (page 372)

Black Diamond Mines Regional Preserve,
Antioch (page 375)

Morgan Territory Regional Preserve, Clayton (page 378)

Briones Regional Park, Lafayette (page 385)

Las Trampas Regional Wilderness, Danville (page 387)

BEST DOG PARK

The Paw Patch, Concord (page 377)

BEST OFF-LEASH BEACH

Point Isabel Regional Shoreline, Richmond (page 382)

BEST CHURCH

**First Presbyterian Church of Richmond car church
services,** Pinole (page 375)

section). The trail, which is part paved/part dirt, starts at Briones Regional Park's Lafayette Ridge Staging Area, on Pleasant Hill Road just north of Highway 24.

The Contra Costa Canal Regional Trail is a good one for dogs who like to look at water but not set foot in it. We love this 12-mile trail that follows the off-limits canal. For information and a trail map of all 10 regional trails, call 510/635-0135.

Dogs who like more civilized settings will be happy to know that since this book's last edition, eight dog parks have sprouted up around the county. If it seems a little breezier around here lately, it could be from all the wagging tails.

El Sobrante

PARKS, BEACHES, AND RECREATION AREAS

1 Sobrante Ridge Regional Preserve

🐾🐾🐾🐾🐾 (See Contra Costa County map on page 370)

Dogs love visiting this quiet preserve, but Sobrante Ridge hasn't always been a place where animals smile. In the 1970s, the property belonged to Cutter Laboratories, which raised horses and cattle and used their blood to produce various vaccines. That breeze you may feel while visiting is just an equine and bovine sigh of relief that Cutter is outta here.

These days, Sobrante is a happy place, full of deer, coyotes, salamanders, and oodles of birds. Unless your dog is under perfect voice control, it's a good idea to use a leash here. From the Coach Way entrance, follow the dirt trail branching back to the left 100 feet from the entrance. This is the Sobrante Ridge Trail, which will take you through grass, dwarf manzanita, oaks, and coyote brush, up a half mile to views of both Mt. Tam and the top of Mt. Diablo. Branch off on the short loop, Broken Oaks Trail, for a picnic at one of the tables under cool oaks.

This 277-acre preserve is the habitat of the extremely rare Alameda manzanita. So that your dog knows what to watch out for, this manzanita is a gnarled, red-barked shrub that may have sprays of urn-shaped blossoms or clusters of red berries, depending on the time of year. The manzanitas cling to the hillsides. Don't let your boy dog do anything the manzanitas wouldn't want him to do.

From I-80 in Richmond, exit at San Pablo Dam Road and drive south to Castro Ranch Road. Turn left on Castro Ranch, then left at Conestoga Way, going into the Carriage Hills housing development. Take another left on Carriage Drive and a right on Coach Way. Park at the end of Coach and walk into the preserve. 510/635-0135 or 510/223-7840.

Port Costa

Port Costa is a sleepy, picturesque town of Victorian cottages. In the 19th century, it was a booming wheat export dock. Of course, if your dog remembers Frank Norris's book *The Octopus,* he already knows this.

PARKS, BEACHES, AND RECREATION AREAS

🖥 Carquinez Strait Regional Shoreline

🐾🐾🐾🐾🐾 (See Contra Costa County map on page 370)

This regional shoreline, run by East Bay Regional Parks, lies just east of Crockett. From the Bull Valley Staging Area, on Carquinez Scenic Drive, you can choose one of two leash-free hillside trails. The Carquinez Overlook Loop, to the right, gives better views of Port Costa, the Carquinez Bridge, and Benicia. We once surprised a deer here sleeping in the shade of a clump of eucalyptus.

The eastern part of the park, east of Port Costa, is contiguous with Martinez Regional Shoreline. But beware: You can't get there from here. (Carquinez Scenic Drive is closed at a spot between Port Costa and Martinez. You must turn south on twisty McEwen Road to Highway 4 instead.)

To get to the Carquinez Strait Regional Shoreline from I-80, exit at Crockett and drive east on Pomona Street through town. Pomona turns into Carquinez Scenic Drive, from which you'll see the staging area. 510/635-0135 or 925/228-0112.

Pinole

PARKS, BEACHES, AND RECREATION AREAS

🐾 Pinole Valley Park

🐾🐾🐾🐕 (See Contra Costa County map on page 370)

This city park is fortunate enough to be contiguous with Sobrante Ridge Regional Preserve (see the El Sobrante section). The paved bike path off to the right past the children's playground leads to Alhambra Creek—a good plunge for your dog if he can negotiate the banks wearing a leash. The path then becomes a fire trail and ambles through brush, oaks, and nicely varied deciduous trees. This trail is quite wild and litter-free. It ends at an outlet on Alhambra Road.

And joy of joys! There's now a dog park within the park, between the baseball field and the barbecue pits. It's about an acre, with grass, benches, poop bags, and water. It's fun to mix a little off-leash romp with a leashed walk around the rest of the attractive park.

The entrance to the main park is at Pinole Valley Road and Simas Avenue. 510/724-9002.

PLACES TO STAY

Motel 6: Rates are $49 for the first adult and $6 for the second. 1501 Fitzgerald Drive 94564; 510/222-8174.

Martinez

Martinez has a charming historic district right off the entrance to its regional shoreline park, so spend some time walking with your dog around the Amtrak station and antique shops. You'll see plenty of fellow strollers taking a break from the train.

PARKS, BEACHES, AND RECREATION AREAS

🐾 Hidden Lakes Open Space

🐾🐾🐾🐾🐕 (See Contra Costa County map on page 370)

Although the city park called Hidden Valley Park doesn't allow dogs, the open space to the south of it does. It's crossed by one of the East Bay Regional Parks' trails (the California Riding and Hiking Trail) on its way from the Carquinez Strait Regional Shoreline to where it connects with the Contra Costa Canal Trail. Call 510/635-0135 or see www.ebparks.org for maps of the Contra Costa Regional Trails.

One entrance to Hidden Lakes is off Morello Avenue, where it intersects with Chilpancingo Parkway.

DIVERSION

Drive Your Pooch to the Pulpit: Want to take your dog to church? If you don't think he's ready to pray in a pew, you can bring him along to attend a service in the comfort of your car. Since 1975, the **First Presbyterian Church of Richmond** has offered a drive-in service in a shopping mall parking lot. Held at 8:30 A.M. every Sunday outside the Appian 80 shopping center in Pinole, the ceremony attracts a few dozen worshippers every week.

Pastors David and Ruth Sandberg transmit the service over short-wave radio from a mobile pulpit, complete with a sermon and choral music. Church elders bring communion around to each car on a silver platter and parishioners honk and flash their headlights at the pastors to say "Amen." It's quite a scene—and afterward you can go shopping. Dogs are as welcome to attend as anyone. (In fact, you may see Marty the Poodle in one of the cars there. The dapper dog has become a regular since reading about services in this book.) Other animals are also welcome: Peepers the Duck usually makes a weekly appearance as well. (Lucky for Peepers that Marty is a poodle and not a Lab.)

Exit I-80 at Appian Way. The shopping center is just north of the freeway, on the west side of Appian Way, Pinole. For more information, call 510/234-0954.

Antioch

Antioch is pretty much a desert for dogs, but south of town are two charming spots of relief.

PARKS, BEACHES, AND RECREATION AREAS

5 Black Diamond Mines Regional Preserve

😃😃😃😃 🦴 (See Contra Costa County map on page 370)

Leash-free dogs, especially leash-free dogs of the male persuasion, think this park is an excellent place to visit. The coal miners who worked and lived here in the 1860s and 1870s planted a variety of drought-tolerant trees not usually found in the East Bay, including something called "trees of heaven." Dogs who sniff these trees seem to know why they're called trees of heaven. Their noses just can't get enough as they press them deep into the bark.

The hills of Black Diamond Mines are jumbled and ragged, looking a lot like the Sierra foothills. From the parking lot, it's a moderate climb to the Rose Hill Cemetery, where Protestant Welsh miners (the tombstones bear the names

Davis, Evans, and Jenkins) buried victims of mine accidents and many of their children, who died of diphtheria, typhoid, and scarlet fever.

Plenty of tunnel openings and piles of tailings have been preserved by the park for walkers to examine. A brochure marks mine sites. You should be alert for rattlers during warm seasons, although any rattler not actually snoozing will probably get out of your way before you even know he's near.

You can walk into this East Bay regional preserve from the Contra Loma Regional Park just below it (see below). But from that direction, the trails are too hot and dry for a dog in summer. Instead, enter from the north by car via Somersville Road and park in the last lot, which has some shady trees.

It's $4 to park here. Dogs are $1 extra. Backpack camping is available for $5. Phone 510/636-1684 for camp info. From Highway 4 at Antioch, exit at Somersville Road and drive south to the park entrance. Keep driving for a bit more than one mile if you want to park in the lot farthest in. You'll pass wonderful old mining-era houses and barns, now used as park headquarters and offices. 510/635-0135 or 925/757-2620.

6 Contra Loma Regional Park

🐾🐾🐾🐾🐕 (See Contra Costa County map on page 370)

This 776-acre park is so well hidden amid the barren hills north of Black Diamond Mines that you might not ever know it was here. A few attractive trails, including a trail leading into Black Diamond Mines Regional Preserve, rise into the surrounding hills for you and your leash-free dog to explore. Dogs can be off leash in the back country. You'll know it when you see it.

Unfortunately, as in all regional parks, your dog may not accompany you in the swimming area. Nor can he take an informal swim himself in the fishing areas, since the park managers want to protect his feet from stray fishhooks. It's probably better not to bring your dog here on a hot day. Instead, save the trip for winter or spring, when the wildflowers burst open.

From Highway 4, take the Lone Tree Way exit. Go south on Lone Tree for a little more than a half mile, then turn right onto Bluerock Drive. Follow Bluerock along the park's east side to the entrance. The fee for parking is $4. The dog fee is $1. 510/635-0135.

Hercules

PARKS, BEACHES, AND RECREATION AREAS

7 San Pablo Bay Shoreline Park

🐾🐾🐾🐕 (See Contra Costa County map on page 370)

This tiny, undeveloped East Bay Regional Park shoreline is just right if you happen to be in Hercules exploring the old Santa Fe Railroad yard. A paved trail runs about one-eighth of a mile along the tracks. New housing developments and interesting restored Victorian railroad workers' housing surround a small but pretty area of grass, swamp, and eucalyptus trees. Best of all, you and your dog can check it all out without a leash.

If you follow Railroad Avenue to its end, across the line into Pinole, there's a very small and beautifully landscaped city park behind the wastewater treatment plant (which smells fresh as a rose). You must keep your dog on leash here.

From I-80, exit at Pinole Valley Road and travel north. Pinole Valley Road becomes Tennent Avenue, then Railroad Avenue. Park somewhere around the Civic Arts Facility, a cluster of Victorian buildings in a grove of palms and eucalyptus. Call 510/724-9004 or 510/635-0135.

Pleasant Hill

PARKS, BEACHES, AND RECREATION AREAS

🐾 Paso Nogal Park

🐾🐾🐾🐾 🐕 (See Contra Costa County map on page 370)

This large open-space park has the best of both worlds: smooth dirt trails along gentle oak-dotted slopes, where leashed dogs can hike to their hearts' content, and a fenced park where they can throw off their leashes and run like the wind. The dog park has benches, tables, water, and good parking. It's grassy and surrounded by trees. The trees within the park are nothing but glorified sticks right now, but they'll grow.

The dog park is open Monday–Saturday and is closed Sunday for maintenance. To help preserve the lush grass, it's also closed when the ground is wet. (This can be weeks at a time during rainy season.) The park is at Morello Avenue and Paso Nogal Road. 925/682-0896.

Concord

PARKS, BEACHES, AND RECREATION AREAS

🐾 The Paw Patch

🐾🐾🐾🐾 🐕 (See Contra Costa County map on page 370)

The grass truly is always greener on the other side of the fence at this wonderful 2.5-acre dog park. It's so green and lush that it has other dog parks green with envy. Dog parks with grass (aka turf) often struggle in vain against a tide of pounding paws. The grass can end up anything but green and rather downtrodden. But not the grass here. The park district folks work hard to maintain it. In fact, they recently won a coveted award for their turf management from the California Parks and Recreation Society.

There's more to this park than grass, though. It's got benches, water, poop bags, a smaller fenced area for small dogs, and lots of toys. The lucky dogs who come here get to sniff through a toy box and pick out a favorite toy to play with here. Or they find them scattered around the grass.

The park is within the lovely 126-acre Newhall Community Park. You can take your dog around the park on a leash. From the top of the hill you're rewarded with great views of everything from Mount Diablo to the Carquinez Straits. (This is where you'll also find a Vietnam War memorial.) The park is at Turtle Creek Road and Ayres Road. 925/671-3444.

10 Lime Ridge Open Space Recreation Area

🐾🐾🐾🐾🐕 (See Contra Costa County map on page 370)

This open space reserve is huge, sprawling across parts of both Walnut Creek and Concord. It's undeveloped and open to lucky leash-free dogs. You can sometimes find a creek, depending on the time of year and status of drought, and that's a real relief during the long, hot summers.

The only entry point from Concord is from the parking lot on Treat Boulevard west of Cowell Road. 925/671-3270.

PLACES TO STAY

Holiday Inn Concord: Rates are $79–133. Dogs require a $100 deposit. 1050 Burnett Avenue 94520; 925/687-5500.

Clayton

PARKS, BEACHES, AND RECREATION AREAS

11 Clayton Dog Park

🐾🐾🐕 (See Contra Costa County map on page 370)

Big oaks are adjacent to this dog park, but there's very little shade within. It has a water meter but no water (yet). A dirt lot has wood chips, but dog people pine for grass. Yet for all its little foibles, this is a perfectly decent place to take a dog for an off-leash romp. It may not be the Ritz, but it's not a dive either. It has a picnic table, two benches, and poop bags, and it's along the Creek Trail, which makes for a fine leashed dog walk. The park is on Marsh Creek Road and Regency Drive, across from Clayton Park. 925/673-7300.

12 Morgan Territory Regional Preserve

🐾🐾🐾🐾🐕 (See Contra Costa County map on page 370)

Morgan Territory, named after a farmer who owned the land long before it became part of the East Bay Regional Parks system, is as far away from the Bay Area as you can get while still being in the Bay Area. From its heights, on a rim above the Central Valley, you see the San Joaquin River, the Delta, the valley, and, on a clear day, the peaks of the Sierra. Eagles and hawks soar above as you and your leash-free pooch explore ancient twisted giant oaks and lichen-covered sandstone outcrops below. Morgan Territory is close to the end of the earth and well worth the journey.

As the crow flies, Morgan Territory is equidistant from Clayton, Danville, San Ramon, Livermore, Byron, and Brentwood. And "distant" is the key word.

This 4,147-acre preserve has miles of hiking and riding trails. If you don't want to climb much but want great views of the Central Valley, try the Blue Oak Trail, which starts at the entrance. You'll even see the "backside" of Mt. Diablo. It's an unusual vantage point for Bay Area folks.

Most of the creeks are dry in the summer, though your dog can splash into cattle ponds, if he's so inclined. Watch for wicked foxtails in these grasses. These are the sticky wickets that help make veterinarians a well-off breed.

The easiest access is from Livermore in Alameda County. From I-580, take the North Livermore Avenue exit and drive north on North Livermore Avenue. Shortly after the road curves left (west), turn right, onto Morgan Territory Road, and follow it 10.7 miles to the entrance. From the Walnut Creek/Concord area, take Clayton Road to Marsh Creek Road, then turn right onto Morgan Territory Road. The entrance is 9.4 miles from Marsh Creek Road. 510/635-0135 or 925/757-2620.

PLACES TO EAT

Skipolini's Pizza: The folks here serve New York–style pizza, as well as salads and sandwiches. They welcome dogs at their outdoor tables. 1033 Diablo Street; 925/672-5555.

Richmond

Point Richmond, the Richmond neighborhood tucked between the Richmond-San Rafael Bridge and Miller-Knox Regional Shoreline, is a cheerful small-town hangout for you and your dog. Consider stopping by for a snack on your way to some of the magical, four-paw shoreline here.

Sit on a bench in the Point Richmond Triangle, the town center. You'll be surrounded by nicely preserved Victorian buildings, the Hotel Mac, and many delis and bakeries, some with outdoor tables. We were asked not to mention one by name because it welcomes cats as well as dogs. Grrrr. The Santa Fe Railroad rattles past periodically, blowing the first two notes of "Here Comes the Bride."

From I-580, on the Richmond end of the Richmond–San Rafael Bridge, exit at Cutting Boulevard and drive west to town. Bear right on Richmond Avenue. The Triangle is at the intersection of Richmond and Washington Avenues and Park Place.

PARKS, BEACHES, AND RECREATION AREAS

13 Point Pinole Regional Shoreline

🐾🐾🐾🐾🐕 (See Contra Costa County map on page 370)

Of all the East Bay Regional Parks' shorelines, this is the farthest from civilization and its discontents, and thus the cleanest and least spoiled. It's also huge and a heavenly walk for dog or owner, with its views of Mt. Tamalpais across San Pablo Bay, and its docks, salt marsh, beaches, eucalyptus groves, and expanses of wild grassland waving in the breeze. Some of the eucalyptus trees are so wind-carved they could be mistaken for cypresses.

The park has fine bike paths, and your dog should be leashed for safety on these, but he's free on the unpaved trails—even on the dirt paths through marshes, such as the Marsh Trail. Just make sure he stays on the trail and doesn't go into the marsh itself. Dogs may not go on the fishing pier or on the shuttle bus to the pier.

From I-80, exit at Hilltop Drive, go west and take a right on San Pablo Avenue, then left on Atlas Road to the park entrance. There's a $4 parking fee and a $1 dog fee. 510/635-0135.

14 Wildcat Canyon Regional Park

🐾🐾🐾🐾🐕 (See Contra Costa County map on page 370)

This is Tilden Regional Park's northern twin. Tilden (see the Berkeley section of the Alameda County chapter) has its attractive spots, but it's designed for people. Wildcat seems made for dogs, because not much goes on here. Dogs really dig this. Who needs all those human feet passing by anyway? (Unless, of course, they're tracking eau du cow patty or some other savory scent.) Best of all, you can leave your dog's leash tucked away in your pocket.

Large coast live oaks, madrones, bay laurels, and all kinds of chaparral thrive on the east side. And since the area was ranchland from the days of Spanish land grants and traces of house foundations remain, it isn't surprising that a lot of exotic plants flourish here alongside the expected ones. You'll find berries, nasturtiums, and cardoon thistle, which looks like an artichoke allowed to grow up. All kinds of grasses and wildflowers cover the western hillsides.

At the entrance parking lot is Wildcat Creek, which gets low but usually not entirely dry in summer. Then you can follow the Wildcat Creek Trail (actually an abandoned paved road); it travels gently uphill and then follows the southern ridge of the park. Or follow any of the nameless side trails, which are wonderfully wild and solitary. You can hear train whistles all the way up from Emeryville and the dull roar of civilization below, but somehow it doesn't bother you up here.

Other trails lead through groves of pines or follow Wildcat Creek. The park is roughly three miles long. If you come to the boundary with Tilden, remember that dogs aren't allowed in the nature area across the line. You can get on the East Bay Skyline National Recreation Trail (Nimitz Way), running along the park's north side. Don't branch off onto the Eagle's Nest Trail, however; it belongs to the East Bay Municipal Utility District, which requires a permit and frowns on dogs. But there's plenty of room here. You and your dog could spend several blissful days in Wildcat.

From I-80, southbound, take the McBryde exit and turn left on McBryde Avenue to the park entrance. If you're northbound, take the Amador/Solano exit. Go three blocks north on Amador Street and turn right (east) on McBryde to the entrance. 510/635-0135 or 510/236-1262.

15 Kennedy Grove Regional Recreation Area

🐾🐾🐾 (See Contra Costa County map on page 370)

This is a large picnic and play area for folks who like softball, volleyball, and horseshoes. Dogs must be leashed. The best part of this park is that you can get to the Bay Area Ridge Trail from here from a gate to the right as you enter the park, or from a trailhead at the Senior Parking Area. You'll cross some East Bay Municipal Utility District land (no permits necessary in this section) and San Pablo Dam Road. The trail ascends and soon becomes the Eagle's Nest Trail. If you're really inspired and your pooch isn't pooped, you can then climb all the way to Inspiration Point in Tilden Regional Park (see the Berkeley section of the Alameda County chapter). Dogs like Joe firmly put their paw down when it comes to such rigorous tasks. Whenever we visited, he would just sit there riveted to the ground like a fire hydrant. You could almost see him shaking his head "no way."

From I-80, take the San Pablo Dam Road exit and go south; the entrance is a quarter mile past the intersection of Castro Ranch Road. The parking fee is $4 and there's a $1 dog fee. 510/635-0135 or 510/223-7840.

16 Miller-Knox Regional Shoreline

🐾🐾🐾🐾 🐕 (See Contra Costa County map on page 370)

Hooray! Wooooof! Yap! Although your dog must be leashed in developed areas, she can run free on the hillside trails east of Dornan Drive in this 259-acre park.

West of Dornan is a generous expanse of grass, pine, and eucalyptus trees with picnic tables, a lagoon with egrets (so there's no swimming), and Keller Beach (dogs are prohibited). It's breezy here and prettier than most shoreline parks by virtue of its protecting gentle hills, whose trails offer terrific views of the Richmond-San Rafael Bridge, Mt. Tamalpais, Angel Island, and San Francisco. Ground squirrels stand right by their holes and pipe their alarms. Although you can't bring your dog onto Keller Beach, there's a paved path above it along riprap shoreline, where your dog can reach the water if he's so inclined. In the picnic areas, watch for discarded chicken bones!

You can also tour the Richmond Yacht Harbor by continuing on Dornan Drive south to Brickyard Cove Road, a left turn past the railroad tracks. Or, from Garrard Boulevard, drive south till you see the Brickyard Cove housing development. The paved paths lining the harbor offer views of yachts, San Francisco, Oakland, and the Bay Bridge.

From either I-80 or I-580, exit at Cutting Boulevard and go west to Garrard Boulevard. Go left, pass through a tunnel, and park in one of two lots off Dornan Drive. 510/635-0135.

17 Point Isabel Regional Shoreline

🐾🐾🐾🐾🐕 (See Contra Costa County map on page 370)

With so many Bay Area beaches either outright banning dogs or enforcing new leash demands, it not easy being a water dog around here these days. Thank goodness for this 21-acre patch of utter water-dog heaven! Dogs are so happy when they come here that some howl as they arrive in their cars. (Some owners do, too, but they're another story.)

Point Isabel is an exception to the East Bay Regional Parks' rule that dogs must be on leash in "developed" areas. This is a decidedly unwild but terrific shoreline park with plenty of grass and paw-friendly paved paths. It's swarming with dogs. In a recent census by the park district, 558,930 people and 784,370 pooches visited in one year. Fortunately, people here are generally very responsible, and the park looks pretty good, despite being accosted by more than four million feet and paws annually.

The large lawn area is perfect for fetching, Frisbee throwing, and chasing each other around. And the bay and the sand—ahh: These are a water dog's delight. The surf here is usually very tame, making dog paddling a joy.

There are benches, picnic tables, restrooms, a water fountain for people and dogs, and many racks full of bags for scooping. Cinder paths run along the riprap waterfront, where you can watch sailboarders against a backdrop of the Golden Gate and Bay Bridges, San Francisco, the Marin Headlands, and Mt. Tamalpais. On a brisk day, a little surf even splashes against the rocks.

After a wet and wonderful walk, you may want to take your pooch to Mudpuppy's Tub and Scrub, which is right here, for a little cleaning up. And after that, if you've been a very good human, you can treat yourself to a cuppa joe and some café cuisine at the new Mudpuppy's Sit and Stay Café. Talk about a people and pooch paradise. (See the Diversion Foof 'Er Up.)

From I-80 in Richmond, exit at Central Avenue and go west to the park entrance, next to the U.S. Postal Service Bulk Mail Center. For more info on the park or its wonderful doggy user group, PIDO (Point Isabel Dog Owners and Friends—why isn't it called PIDOF?), see www.pido.org. 510/635-0135.

DIVERSION

Foof 'Er Up: Is your pooch starting to smell like a dog? If you go to Point Isabel, you can give your dog both the walk of his life and a bath. **Mudpuppy's Tub and Scrub,** the park's very own dog wash, offers full- or self-service scrubbings in several elevated tubs. The cost is very reasonable, considering it includes shampoo, drying, and someone else to clean the tub afterward. And not only can your dog get unmuddy and downright gorgeous here, he can go home with some pretty doggone nice pooch items, too. Mudpuppy's offers a full line of dog toys, treats, and gifts. Owners Eddie Lundeen and Daniel Bergerac provide a fun, clean atmosphere. Call or stop by before your walk in the park to reserve your tub. (The earlier you do so, the better, especially on weekends.)

And here's some great news for your dog's best friend. (That would be you.) Mudpuppy's now has a café just down the road: It's called Mudpuppy's Sit and Stay Café. It has a walk-up window so you and your dog can go and get some delectable goodies for humans, including espresso, tasty pastries, warming soups (usually featuring one veggie variety and something hearty), great sandwiches, salads, and ice cream. The café makes this area one of the most dog-friendly and dog-person–friendly around. Eat, drink, walk, talk, buy, suds, scrub, enjoy.

Mudpuppy's is in the first parking lot inside the park, off Isabel Road, Richmond. 510/559-8899; www.mudpuppys.com.

El Cerrito

PARKS, BEACHES, AND RECREATION AREAS

18 Hillside Park

😺 (See Contra Costa County map on page 370)

This is not the prettiest park around; the southern end is mostly an eroded hillside of scrubby grass with power lines. But off Schmidt Lane is the much more attractive El Cerrito Foundation Memorial Grove. A bumpy dirt path leads up through coyote brush to eucalyptus groves at the hilltop, overlooking El Cerrito, the Golden Gate and Bay Bridges, and Mt. Tamalpais. The trail doesn't go far into the open space.

Enter off Schmidt Lane, which runs north off San Pablo Avenue. 510/215-4300.

Orinda

PARKS, BEACHES, AND RECREATION AREAS

🐾🐾 San Pablo Dam Reservoir

🐾🐾🐾 (See Contra Costa County map on page 370)

This reservoir is a top fishing spot in the Bay Area. It's stocked with more trout than any lake in California. That's great news for humans, but dogs could not care less. They're not allowed to set paw in this magnificent body of water (and neither are people), so hanging out alongside a human angler is out of the question. You can't even take your pooch out on your own boat.

The paved and dirt trails around the reservoir are lovely and often empty once you and your leashed dog wind into the hills. The dirt trails get rougher as you leave the popular fishing areas. You'll have to ford some creek beds or streams, and there's too much poison oak for comfort if your dog doesn't step daintily right down the middle of the trail. The trails are wild and woodsy, though, and dogs recommend them highly.

The entrance fee is $6.50 for parking and $1 for dogs. You can buy a season ticket for $88 a car or $85 a boat. Fishing is $4, and you'll need your fishing license, of course. The lake itself is open mid-February–mid-November.

From I-80, exit at San Pablo Dam Road and drive east about six miles. From Highway 24, exit at Camino Pablo/San Pablo Dam Road and go north about 5.5 miles. 510/223-1661.

🐾🐾 Robert Sibley Volcanic Regional Preserve

🐾🐾🐾🐾🦮 (See Contra Costa County map on page 370)

We're not exactly talking Mt. St. Helens here, but this 371-acre park has some pretty interesting volcanic history. Geologically inclined dogs can wander leashless as you explore volcanic dikes, mudflows, lava flows, and other evidence of extinct volcanoes.

The preserve is actually closer to Oakland than Orinda, but it lies in Contra Costa County. From the entrance on Skyline Boulevard, you can get on the East Bay Skyline National Recreation Trail and walk north to Tilden Regional Park (see the Berkeley section of the Alameda County chapter) or south to Redwood Regional Park (see the Oakland section of the Alameda County chapter). Or, for a shorter stroll, take the road to Round Top, the highest peak in the Berkeley Hills, made of volcanic debris left over from a 10-million-year-old volcano.

More attractive and less steep is the road to the quarries. It's partly paved and smooth enough for a wheelchair or stroller, but it becomes smooth dirt about halfway to the quarries. Both trails are labeled for geological features. (Pick up a brochure at the visitor center.) At the quarry pits, there's a good view of Mt. Diablo. This is a dry, scrubby, cattle-grazed area, but in the rainy season your dog may be lucky enough to find swimming in a pit near the quarries. In the spring, look for poppies and lupines.

From Highway 24 east of the Caldecott Tunnel, exit on Fish Ranch Road, drive north to Grizzly Peak Boulevard, and then take a left. Go south on Grizzly Peak to the intersection with Skyline Boulevard. Go left on Skyline. The entrance is just to the east of the intersection. 510/635-0135.

PLACES TO EAT

High Tech Burrito: The burritos and fajitas here are really, really good. The ingredients are fresh and combined in very interesting ways. Try the veggie burrito. It's *muy bueno*. Dogs can dine with you (no spicy scraps, please!) at the many courtyard tables at Theatre Square. 2 Theatre Square; 925/254-8884.

Lafayette

PARKS, BEACHES, AND RECREATION AREAS

21 Briones Regional Park

🐾🐾🐾🐾🐾 (See Contra Costa County map on page 370)

From both main entrances to this park, you can walk one-quarter of a mile and be lost in sunny, rolling hills or cool oak woodlands. Unless you stick to the stream areas, it's not a good park for hot summer days. But with a good supply of your own water, you and your dog, who may run blissfully leashless, can walk gentle ups and downs all day on fire roads or foot trails.

The north entrance requires an immediate uphill climb into the hills, but you're rewarded with a quick view of Mt. Diablo and the piping of ground squirrels, all of whom are long gone safely into their burrows by the time your dog realizes they might be fun to chase. If your dog is a self-starter, this end of the park is fine for you. The Alhambra Creek Trail, which follows Alhambra Creek, does offer water in the rainy season. Stay away from the John Muir Nature Area (shaded on your brochure map), where dogs aren't allowed.

When we're feeling lazy, we prefer the south entrance at Bear Creek, just east of the inaccessible (to dogs) Briones Reservoir. Here you have an immediate choice of open hills or woodsy canyons, and the land is level for a few miles. The Homestead Valley Trail leads gently up and down through cool, sharp-scented bay and oak woodlands.

Watch for deer, horses, and cattle. Some dogs near and dear to me love rolling in fresh cow patties—an additional hazard of the beasts existing in close proximity.

From Highway 24, take the Orinda exit; go north on Camino Pablo, then right on Bear Creek Road to Briones Road, to the park entrance. The parking fee is $4 and the dog fee is $1. 510/635-0135.

Walnut Creek

Walnut Creek's big secret is its beautiful creeks and canals, former irrigation ditches that now adorn golf courses and housing developments. Walnut Creek, San Ramon Creek, the Contra Costa Canal, and the Ygnacio Canal all pass through town. Dogs must be leashed everywhere, except in a new dog park and the undeveloped areas of city-owned open spaces, as we describe below.

PARKS, BEACHES, AND RECREATION AREAS

22 Acalanes Ridge Open Space Recreation Area

🐾🐾🐾🐾🐕 (See Contra Costa County map on page 370)

In 1974, the city of Walnut Creek set aside a few open spaces for a limited-use "land bank." Dogs must be "under voice or sight command" (translation: off leash if obedient). Hoo boy! The trails are open to hikers, dogs, horses, and bicycles, however, so on a fine day, your dog may have some competition.

Acalanes Ridge, close to Briones Regional Park (see the Lafayette section), is crossed by the Briones to Diablo Regional Trail. Like the others, it lacks water.

A good entry point is from Camino Verde Circle, reached by driving south on Camino Verde from the intersection of Pleasant Hill and Geary Roads. For information on any of the open spaces, call 925/943-5899.

23 San Miguel Park

🐾🐾🐾🐾🐕 (See Contra Costa County map on page 370)

Dogs who are early risers love waking up, throwing on their leashes, coming to this park, and then throwing off their leashes. From 6–9 A.M. daily, this grassy four-acre park goes to the dogs. It's positively poochy here during the morning canine commute. It's not a fenced area, and that's fine with dogs. Boy dogs and shade-seekers like the park's trees.

The park is a few minutes northeast of the I-680/Highway 24 interchange. From northbound I-680, take the exit toward Ygnacio Valley Road and turn right in a little over a half mile onto Ygnacio Valley Road. In about two miles, turn right on San Carlos Drive and in .3 mile, go left at San Jose Court. The park is at San Jose Court, off Los Cerros Avenue. 925/943-5855.

24 Shell Ridge Open Space Recreation Area

🐾🐾🐾🐾🐕 (See Contra Costa County map on page 370)

Dogs may run off leash everywhere but in the developed areas (parking lots, picnic grounds), but "must be under positive voice and sight command." The people who write these rules must be retired military document writers or part-time computer-manual writers.

Within the Shell Ridge Open Space is the Old Borges Ranch, a demonstration farm staffed irregularly by rangers. The ranch house is sometimes open noon–4 P.M. on Sunday. Call first to check. For information or to make a reservation to visit, call 925/943-5860.

You can enter by the Sugarloaf-Shell Ridge Trail at the north edge. From I-680, take the Ignacio Valley Road exit, go east on Ignacio Valley Road to Walnut Avenue (not Boulevard), turn right and right again on Castle Rock Road. Go past the high school, turn right, and follow the signs. 925/943-5899.

PLACES TO EAT

Walnut Creek's "downtown," your respite from mallsville, is Main Street. Here, you'll find several welcoming outdoor restaurants, benches for just sitting, and good weather. One of our favorites follows.

Original Hot Dog Place: Every kind of hot dog is served in this tiny shop with a neat hot dog mural on the wall and a wooden Indian outside next to the tables. 1420 Lincoln Avenue at Main Street; 925/256-7302.

PLACES TO STAY

Holiday Inn: A few months before I originally wrote about this, I got a letter from Daniel Fevre, then the general manager of this hotel. "My first question (when I took this job) was—you guessed it—'Do we take pets?' The answer was 'No.' My reply was 'We do now!' To test the program, I stayed with my two dogs (and one cat) for several days until the movers arrived, and the staff was great."

Fevre is no longer with the hotel, but his legacy—the dog-friendly policy—is intact. It has a pool, which humans enjoy, but what's really special about this place is its proximity to a hiking trail. The staff will tell you about it at the front desk. Rates are $79–169. There's a $25 fee for the length of your dog's stay. 2730 North Main Street 94598; 925/932-3332.

Walnut Creek Motor Lodge: Very small dogs only, please (15 pounds or under). Rates are $70–85. 1960 North Main Street 94596; 925/932-2811.

Danville

PARKS, BEACHES, AND RECREATION AREAS

🐾🐾🐾🐾 Las Trampas Regional Wilderness

🐾🐾🐾🐾🐾🐕 (See Contra Costa County map on page 370)

This regional wilderness is remarkable for its sense of isolation from the rest of the Bay Area. You can experience utter silence at this 3,298-acre park, and the views from the ridge tops are breathtaking.

Rocky Ridge Trail (from the parking lot at the end of Bollinger Canyon Road) takes you and your leash-free pooch on a fairly steep .75-mile ascent to the top of the ridge, where you'll enter the East Bay Municipal Utility District watershed. Since dogs aren't allowed here and permits are required even for humans, it's better to head west on any of several trails climbing the sunny southern flanks of Las Trampas Ridge.

Creeks run low or dry during the summer, so bring plenty of water. Your dog should know how to behave around cattle, deer, and horses.

From I-680 about six miles north of the intersection with I-580, take the Bollinger Canyon Road exit and head north on Bollinger Canyon Road to the entrance. (Go past the entrance to Little Hills Ranch Recreation Area, where dogs aren't allowed.) 510/635-0135 or 925/837-3145.

26 Oak Hill Park

🐾🐾🐾 (See Contra Costa County map on page 370)

Here's a very clean, beautiful park run by the city of Danville. It's about as good as a park designed for people can get, offering picnic tables, a pond with ducks and geese and waterfalls, volleyball and tennis courts, and an unusually attractive children's play area with swings, a slide, and its own waterfall. The rest of the park is natural oak-studded hillside laced by an equestrian/hiking/exercise dirt trail, from which there is a fine view of Mt. Diablo. Dogs will enjoy this path, but they must remain on leash. No wading in the pond, either. The park is at Stone Valley Road and Glenwood Court. 925/314-3400.

27 Hap Magee Ranch Canine Corral

🐾🐾🐾🐕 (See Contra Costa County map on page 370)

In the summer of 2004, this 1.5-acre park had been opened just three weeks when it was hit by a doggy tragedy. A big dog and a Jack Russell terrier blind-sided each other while running around, and the Jack Russell died. The accident immediately resulted in a "time share" arrangement, where big dogs were allowed at odd hours, small dogs at even hours. There are plans for a separate area for smaller dogs to be constructed so that all dogs will be able to use the park at the same time.

The park is a pretty mix of grass and wood chips, with a little shade. From I-680 going north, exit at El Cerro Boulevard and turn right onto El Cerro at the light. At the second light, go right at La Gonda Way. The park is on the left after the stop sign. Park in the paved lot. 925/314-3400.

San Ramon

PARKS, BEACHES, AND RECREATION AREAS

28 Memorial Park Dog Park

🐾🐾🐾🐕 (See Contra Costa County map on page 370)

Once a dog's paws get used to the decomposed granite that's on the surface of this park, this place is a positively peachy for poochies. It's 1.3 acres, with a separate section within for dogs under 20 pounds. (These are the ones Jake would pick up and carry around a park in his mouth ever so gently when we first adopted him at six months.) There will be shade trees here one day, but until the saplings grow, manmade shade structures do the trick. The park has water, poop bags, benches, and picnic tables.

The park is on the northwest side of town. Exit I-680 at Bollinger Canyon Road and drive west less than a quarter mile to San Ramon Valley Boulevard, where you'll find parking straight ahead on the south side of Bollinger. 925/973-3200.

29 Del Mar Dog Park

🐾🐾🐾🐕 (See Contra Costa County map on page 370)

This one-acre fenced park is covered with cedar wood chips. Jake, unfortunately, is content to trot around a little and then settle down to see how many wood chips he can chew to smithereens before I can get him to start acting more like a dog, less like a termite. But normal dogs love gallivanting around here. The park has all the usual amenities, including water, benches, and shade structures (no shade trees yet). The park is on the south side of town, at Del Mar Drive and Pine Valley Road. 925/973-3200.

PLACES TO STAY

San Ramon Marriott at Bishop Ranch: The folks who run this attractive hotel are very friendly to creatures of the doggy persuasion. Rates are $79–199. Dogs pay a $75 fee for the length of their stay. 2600 Bishop Drive 94583; 925/867-9200.

CHAPTER 33
Alameda County

From the hallowed hippie havens of Berkeley's Telegraph Avenue to the pleasing suburban pleasantries of Pleasanton, Alameda County is like California in miniature: It has nearly every level of population density and type, and nearly every temperate natural environment. Somehow, it all works.

Dogs dig it here, whether they're rasta dogs or shaved shih tzus. The county is like the creek it's named after—it's been lined with concrete, filled with trash, and dammed into oblivion, yet it still manages to gush joyfully onward. Some of the wildest country in the Bay Area is in this county, full of hidden gems of nature. So many of these parks are off-leash havens that your dog may think he's dreaming.

The 12-mile Alameda Creek Regional Trail (see Fremont section) is a favorite among dogs. They can run off leash on most of the trail, but where signs say leashes are required, heed the message.

As if all this weren't enough good news, your dog's hair will stand on end when he learns that unless he's a pit bull, he's allowed to run leashless on thousands of acres of parkland within the East Bay Regional Park District.

PICK OF THE LITTER—ALAMEDA COUNTY

BEST BAYSIDE OFF-LEASH AREA
César Chávez Park, Berkeley (page 394)

BEST LEASH-FREE HIKES
Tilden Regional Park, Berkeley (page 395)
Redwood Regional Park, Oakland (page 404)
Chabot Regional Park, Castro Valley (page 409)
Sunol Regional Wilderness, Fremont (page 415)

COOLEST DOG PARK
Drigon Dog Park, Union City (page 412)

MOST DOG-FRIENDLY PLACES TO EAT
Flippers, Montclair District, Oakland (page 407)
Montclair Malt Shop, Montclair District, Oakland (page 407)
Noah's Bagels, Montclair District, Oakland (page 408)
Café Paradiso, Livermore (page 419)

BEST HIKING BUDDIES
Sierra Club's Canine Hike Unit (page 397)

Some 59 parks and recreation areas and 29 regional interpark trails—95,000 acres in all—fall under the district's jurisdiction. Poop-bag dispensers are installed at the most heavily used areas, such as Point Isabel Regional Shoreline in Richmond (Contra Costa County).

The only places where dogs must be leashed within the district's parks are in developed areas, parking lots, picnic sites, lawns, and in posted Nature Areas. They aren't permitted on beaches (Point Isabel Regional Shoreline is a major exception), wetlands, marshes, or in the Tilden Nature Area. In addition, the district was deciding whether dogs have to be leashed along Redwood Regional Park's Stream Trail. Call 510/635-0135 for more information on the East Bay Regional Park District. You can also check out more details about the dog rules and hiking tips by going to www.ebparks.org and looking for the "Dogs" section. (Special rules and permits apply to anyone bringing more than three dogs. This was primarily designed for dog walkers, but if you have a gaggle of dogs yourself, you should check out the info on the site.)

All this is great, but Alameda County dogs are waggier than ever these days: They've got a few wonderful new parks that are devoted to their off-leash selves! In fact, the county is home to the very best fenced dog park in the state. It's in Union City and well worth a visit. (See Drigon Dog Park in the Union City section.)

A final note: Berkeley is the home of *The Bark*, the best dog magazine on dog's green earth. It doesn't even seem right to call it a dog magazine. *The Bark* bills itself as "the magazine of the modern dog culture," and "the magazine about life with dogs." It's smart, hip, beautifully designed, and a joy to read. *The Bark* grew out of a regional newsletter, *The Berkeley Bark*, created by Claudia Kawczynska. At the time I called it "the best regional dog newsletter I've ever seen." Its grown-up form is even better. If you appreciate good writing, gorgeous design, and you love dogs, check out *The Bark*'s website: www.thebark.com.

Berkeley

Berkeley, well known for its tolerance of eccentricity, is equally eccentric when it comes to dogs. Like most of Alameda County, it features strict leash laws: You break the law, you pay the price—which can be above $100 for the second offense.

But there is a unique loophole. If your dog is obedience-trained, Berkeley doesn't require him to be leashed. If an animal control officer sees you with your unleashed dog, you'll be asked to demonstrate that your dog is under absolute voice control. If the officer is not persuaded, you'll be cited and asked to appear in court with your dog, where you'll have another chance to prove it. (I can just picture Jake sitting, lying down, and rolling over in court. Well, maybe if a treat were involved. Nahhh.)

Whether they're all under absolute voice control or not, you'll see a lot more unleashed dogs in Berkeley than in any other Bay Area city. The University of California at Berkeley also has a leash law, but the campus is swarming with loose dogs, too.

Berkeley created the country's first official dog park, Ohlone Dog Park. Still, it was a big battle recently when it came to opening a 17-acre chunk of dog heaven at César Chávez Park at the Berkeley Marina. Foes included the Sierra Club and a blind woman. (Fortunately, the Girl Scouts and the pope stayed out of the melee.) The dogs triumphed, and the park just keeps getting better.

DIVERSION

Sniff Out a Good Book: Just try leaving your dog tied up outside when you visit either of the two **Cody's bookstores** in Berkeley. As soon as you're immersed in a dog-eared volume, you will be jolted back to reality by an announcement: "Will the guardian of the small yellow dog who is tied up outside please go get him and bring him in the store? Dogs are welcome in Cody's." Indeed they are. In fact, on some weekends the number of dogs here equals the number of humans at other bookstores. And the workers here can't remember the last time a dog gave a book a one-leg salute. Good work, dogs.

Cody's bookstores are known for having the best selection of books in the Bay Area. You can get almost anything you want here. And if you and your dog can't sniff out a title you're seeking, the staff here will be happy to help you track it down. The two store locations and phone numbers: 2454 Telegraph Avenue, Berkeley, 510/845-7852; 1730 4th Street, Berkeley, 510/559-9500.

PARKS, BEACHES, AND RECREATION AREAS

1 César Chávez Park

🐾🐾🐾🐾 🐕 (See Alameda County map on page 390)

Urban pooch paradise doesn't get much better than this. Dogs who come here get to feel the bay breeze blowing through their fur as they frolic with their friends on 17 acres of prime land on the San Francisco Bay. Trails meander up and down the rolling hills and wind through a couple of quiet meadows. There's grass, grass everywhere.

The views of San Francisco, the Golden Gate Bridge, and the Bay Bridge are some of the best around. The park is equipped with plenty of poop-bag stations crammed to the gills. Use them. In fact, while you're at it, pick up an "orphan" poop if you see one lying around. Many people worked very hard for a very long time to get this park established, and the goal is to keep it beautiful and dog-friendly.

This is also a great place to fly a kite, and there are plenty of instructions posted on how to do it safely around here.

Take University Avenue west past the I-80 interchange and follow the signs to the Berkeley Marina and César Chávez Park. 510/981-5150.

2 Ohlone Dog Park

🐾🐾 🐕 (See Alameda County map on page 390)

For years after it opened as the first leash-free dog park in America in 1979, Ohlone provided a model for other cities considering opening a dog park. But

DIVERSION

Go Shopping in 1969: You and your dog can shop in the autumn of love when you stroll through the sidewalks of **Telegraph Avenue** near the UC Berkeley campus. Street vendors sell tie-dyed clothes, crystals, pottery, and T-shirts airbrushed with clouds. Street performers sing, juggle, beg for money, or do whatever else comes naturally. Incense and other herbaceous odors waft through the air, but dogs prefer the scents of all the nondeodorized humans.

Dogs who reminisce about the 1960s really dig it here. They're perceived as totally cool dudes and given major amounts of love from people who like to hug dogs hard. When we last visited, Jake was wearing his favorite psychedelic bandana, and he received a few "duuuudes" per block.

Some dogs—and humans—may find the weekend crowds a sensory overload. If your schedule allows, try a cool afternoon. From I-80, take the Ashby exit, go about two miles east to Telegraph, and turn left (north). The street-merchant part begins around the intersection of Dwight Way.

---

sadly, the park is often in pretty bad shape these days, with mud happening before rainy season and in winter overtaking everything, including the mulch and woodchips used for covering the mud.

Still, it's a decent place for an off-leash romp in a safely fenced area. You'll find a water faucet, complete with a dog bowl set in concrete, and two picnic tables for owners who want to relax while their dogs socialize. The grass isn't always green here, but it's definitely better than what's on the other side of the fence. (Speaking of which, some of the park's neighbors have been making moves to limit hours or even to move the park out of the neighborhood. We'll update you about this sad situation in the next edition. This should not be happening to the nation's first dog park.)

The park is at Martin Luther King Jr. Way and Hearst Street. 510/981-5150.

⑧ Tilden Regional Park

🐾🐾🐾🐾 🦴 (See Alameda County map on page 390)

Humans and dogs alike give Tilden a big thumbs-up (dewclaws-up). Leash-free dogs find the scents from its western ridge delectable and humans find the ridge's breathtaking views of the entire San Francisco Bay equally enticing.

Escapes from civilization are everywhere in this 2,078-acre park. Try the trails leading east from South Park Drive. They connect with the East Bay Skyline National Recreation Trail.

You can pick up the Arroyo Trail at the Big Springs sign and take it all the way to the ridge top. There's a great stream at the trailhead that you can follow through laurel, pine, toyon, and scrub on your low-grade ascent. Your dog may want to take a dip in the stream for refreshment.

After the trail veers from the stream, it steepens and leads into cypress-studded meadows and eucalyptus groves. Eventually it feeds into the Skyline National Recreation Trail, also known as the Sea View Trail, offering vistas over the bay along the way.

Dogs aren't allowed in the large nature area at the northern end or in the Lake Anza swimming area. Leashes are required in all the developed areas, including picnic grounds and ball fields. Remember to watch your step in the areas frequented by dogs, as some owners neglect to clean up after their furry friends. There's nothing like stepping in a steaming pile of dog dung to put a damper on a day of exploring nature.

Speaking of steaming, be sure to check out Tilden's miniature steam train for a riveting good time.

From Highway 24, take the Fish Ranch Road exit north (at the eastern end of the Caldecott Tunnel). At the intersection of Fish Ranch, Grizzly Peak Boulevard, and Claremont Avenue, take a right on Grizzly Peak and con-

DIVERSION

Ride a Dog-Sized Train: If your dog's not an escape artist or the nervous type, he's welcome to ride with you on **Tilden Regional Park's miniature train.** The open-car train takes you for a 12-minute ride through woods and past stunning views of the surrounding area. Adventurous dogs like it when the train toots its whistle as it rumbles past a miniature water tower, a car barn, and other such train accessories. When Joe Dog appeared on KRON-TV's *Bay Area Backroads* riding the train, he was fine until we hit the little tunnel—then he decided he wanted to go home. He was relieved that part ended up on the cutting-room floor.

The Redwood Valley Railway Company runs trains 11 A.M.–6 P.M. weekends and holidays (not Thanksgiving or Christmas) only, except during spring and summer school vacations, when it also runs weekdays noon–5 P.M. and weekends until 6 P.M. Tickets are $1.75; kids under two and dogs ride free. You must keep the dog on a tight leash and make sure he doesn't jump out. It's in the southeast corner of Tilden Regional Park in Berkeley. From the intersection of Grizzly Peak Boulevard and Lomas Cantadas, follow the signs. 510/548-6100.

tinue north to South Park Drive. One more mile north brings you to Big Springs Trail. During peak season, continue on Grizzly Peak to the Shasta Gate. 510/635-0135.

4 Aquatic Park

😺 😺 (See Alameda County map on page 390)

Take advantage of this city park for a quick stroll by the water. Conveniently situated off I-80, it's fairly tranquil, even with the lagoon's powerboats and water-skiers whizzing by. The lagoon's banks are planted with a mixture of grass, willows, cypress, and eucalyptus. Boy dogs have lifted many a leg in homage here.

Thanks to its greenery, birds are plentiful. Dogs like to bird-watch from the paved paths and the parcourse fitness trail. The pooch paddle is banned, and wading dogs are frowned upon, too.

Should you choose to walk to greener pastures, there's now a grand pedestrian crossing that takes you and your pooch over the freeway and lets you off within walking distance of César Chávez Park. (It's at least a half-hour walk to get to Chávez from here via the walkway, but it's a beautiful walk.) You can't miss it.

From I-80, take the Ashby exit and turn north on Bay Street. There's a small parking lot. If you come from the north side of the park, you can park at a couple of areas on Bolivar Drive, along the park's east side. 510/981-5150.

DIVERSION

Take a Hike!: East Bay dogs who enjoy the great outdoors are very lucky indeed. Berkeley is the home base for the San Francisco Bay chapter of the **Sierra Club.** The club holds dozens of fun hikes for dogs each year, via its Canine Hike unit, and most of the hikes are in the East Bay. Dogs get to hike and play off leash, as long as they're well behaved and under voice control. Hikes are of varying difficulties and lengths. Some involve easy swimming (Jake is drooling), some involve camping, some even involve meeting the love of your life (when Sierra Singles and their dogs come out to play). The folks who participate in the canine hikes are almost as friendly and fun-loving as their dogs. Phone 510/848-0800 for info on the dog hikes, or to find out how to join the Sierra Club. You don't have to be a member to do the hikes, but one of the benefits of membership is that you'll receive a schedule of all Sierra Club events—including doggy hikes—every two months.

🗷 Claremont Canyon Regional Preserve

🐾🐾🐾🐾🐕 (See Alameda County map on page 390)

This large park is full of steep hillside trails that lead to crests with stunning views of the university and the surrounding hills and valleys. If your dog likes eucalyptus trees and doesn't like leashes, take him here. It's one of those tree-filled, leashes-optional parks.

From Highway 13 (Ashby Avenue), drive north on College Avenue. Turn right on Derby Street, past the Clark Kerr Campus of UC Berkeley. The trailhead is at the southeast corner of the school grounds, near the beginning of Stonewall Road. 510/635-0135.

PLACES TO EAT

So many restaurants here have outdoor tables where dogs are welcome. Because of space, we list just a handful.

Bel Forno: Dine with your doggy under a shade-giving awning and next to a couple of trees. The turkey pesto sandwiches are tasty. Thirsty dogs get water. 1400 Shattuck Avenue; 510/644-1601.

Fontina Caffe Italiana: Dogs like dining with their people at the five umbrella-topped tables here. The food is snout-licking good. But what they like even better is that Fontina is right next door to the Shattuck Cat Clinic. Poor Joe Dog never knew the pleasures of Fontina, because he knew too well the pleasures of cats. 1730 Shattuck Avenue; 510/649-8090.

La Mediterranée: This delicious and inexpensive Middle Eastern restaurant has built up quite a following; there's usually a line on weekends when Cal is midsemester. The folks here will let your dog sit quietly at your feet at the outdoor tables, which have the added benefit of an outdoor heater on cool nights. You might want to tie your dog up on the sidewalk outside the fence separating the tables if it's especially crowded. 2936 College Avenue; 510/540-7773.

NeFeli: The light Greek cuisine at NeFeli really hits the spot. Try the Athenian panini if you like your Greek sans meat. It's a real treat. Dogs get to join you at tables under the awning in front. 1854 Euclid Avenue; 510/841-6374.

Rick and Ann's Restaurant: Dogs feel really at home here, because Rick and Ann and their staff love dogs. There's always a bowl of water for your thirsty pooch. This is also a popular place among people. The food is delicious and all-American. Joe's favorites were meatloaf and creamy macaroni and cheese. It may take you a while to choose something from the imaginative menu, but just about anything you select will be great. 2922 Domingo Avenue; 510/649-8538.

Sea Breeze Market and Deli: Smack in the middle of the I-80 interchange, you won't even notice the traffic as you and your dog bask at sunny picnic tables, where crab claws crunch underfoot and begging is outstanding. Dogs are perfectly welcome so long as they don't wander into the store itself. You can buy groceries, beer, wine, classy ice cream, or a meal from the deli: fresh fish-and-chips, calamari, prawns, scallops, chicken, and quiche. The deli serves croissants and coffee early; if you live in the East Bay, you can zip in for a quick croissant and a dog walk at César Chávez Park before work. It's at the foot of University Avenue, past the I-80 entrance. 598 University Avenue; 510/486-0802.

PLACES TO STAY

Golden Bear Inn: Rates are $89–99. Dogs pay a $15 fee for the length of their stay. 1620 San Pablo Avenue, 94702; 510/525-6770; www.goldenbearinn.com.

Emeryville

PARKS, BEACHES, AND RECREATION AREAS

6 Emeryville Marina Park

🐾🐾 (See Alameda County map on page 390)

If you're a human, this is a fine park. If you're a leashed dog, it's just so-so. A concrete path follows the riprap shoreline past cypress trees and through manicured grass. A quick and scenic stroll down the north side will give you a fine view of the marina and a miniature bird refuge where egrets, sandpipers, blackbirds, and doves inhabit a tiny marsh. Dogs who like to bird-watch think it's cool here.

Dogs who like to fish don't have it so easy. Pooches aren't allowed on the fishing pier. But if you console them with an offer to picnic at tables with grand views of the Bay Bridge, they usually snap out of their funk.

From I-80, take the Powell Street exit at Emeryville and go west on Powell to the end of the marina. It has lots of free parking. 510/577-6080.

PLACES TO STAY

Woodfin Suite Hotel: This is a big, friendly hotel for people, who get a full hot and cold breakfast buffet in the morning, and drinks and hors d'oeuvres in the evening, plus a pool, spa, and fitness center. Dogs just get to stay in an all-suites hotel, and only if they're not too big. "About 50 to 60 pounds" is the limit, says a front-desk clerk. Rates are $145. Dogs are $5 extra and require a $150 deposit. 5800 Shellmound 94608; 510/601-5880 or 888/433-9042.

Alameda

PARKS, BEACHES, AND RECREATION AREAS

7 Alameda Point Dog Run

🐾 🐕 (See Alameda County map on page 390)

While this fenced park encompasses two acres along the Oakland Estuary, it's not much to look at—or to be in, for that matter. There are no trees. The ground is pretty much rock-hard, having baked in the sun and weathered through the years. Being just 100 feet back from this part of the estuary does provide a breeze, but the super-nice park supervisor, Fred, says the breeze tends to be a bit strong here. Your dog's ears may flap in the breeze, but more likely they'll just stream straight back. There's no water, either. It's a good place to take a dog if you're near the ferry terminal, because it's on Main Street, adjacent to the terminal. It's better than nothing. 510/748-4568.

8 Alameda Dog Exercise Area

🐾 🐾 🐾 🐾 🐕 (See Alameda County map on page 390)

Wahoo! This is one of the bigger fenced-in dog parks we've encountered. It's nearly six acres, shaded here and there by some wonderful big cypress and pine trees. The ground wants to be grass, but it's pretty much packed dirt at this point. Dogs have a howling good time chasing each other around big brush patches here and there. Among the amenities: benches, a separate section for small dogs, water, and poop bags. But the best amenity here is a natural one: a fresh bay breeze. The park is right off the bay. You can see the masts of the boats in the harbor from the dog park.

The park is set beside Crown Memorial Beach, which bans dogs. The dog park is actually part of Alameda's largest park, Washington Park. That park has lots of great amenities for people, including wonderful playgrounds and

DIVERSION

Seize the Bay from Oakland and Alameda: Water-loving dogs just about swoon when they learn they're allowed on the **Blue and Gold Fleet's ferries** that run between Oakland/Alameda and San Francisco. Fares are $5.25 one-way for adults. The Oakland ferry terminal is at the foot of Clay Street in Jack London Square. The Alameda dock is at the Gateway Center, 2991 Main Street. Phone 415/705-8200 for schedules and more information, or 415/705-5555 for tickets; www.blueandgoldfleet.com.

ball fields. Leashed dogs enjoy the wide green expanses, the bike path, and the edge of the marsh here. Unfortunately for hungry dogs, pooches aren't permitted at the picnic areas. Your best bet is to stick to the dog exercise area. They're more than welcome at the picnic tables there. The dog park is at 8th Street and Central Avenue. It's to the left of Washington Park's tennis courts. 510/748-4568.

PLACES TO EAT

Aroma Restaurant: Any restaurant that has something about smell in its name is a sure-fire winner in a dog's book. And this places smells mahhh-velous! It looks pretty terrific, too. It's right on a narrow bit of the Oakland Estuary, just a bone's throw from the Park Street Bridge. The outdoor dining area (where dogs can join their humans) looks like something you'd see in a wedding banquet, with lots of tables under white awnings. The food? A wonderful cuisine defies a succinct description. There's a little of everything—Italian, French, Asian-Pacific—and it all has a California twist. The seafood is fresh, and the weekend brunches are eggy and tasty. 2237 Blanding Avenue; 510/337-0333.

Good and Plenty Cafe de Ballena: This wonderful café is a veritable Noah's Ark. Animals of all kinds come to the outdoor tables here with their people. It's not uncommon to see cats on laps and birds on shoulders. But dogs are by far the best—er, most common—critters who visit while their people dine on delicious deli food. Kira, a 100-pound malamute who moved here from Arizona to live on a boat, convinced her "dad" to write and tell us that the food servers "welcome pets with open arms and have been known to get suckered out of a snack or two by the appropriate big, brown-eyed doggy look.... Kira gives this place a four-paw rating with no hesitation." The café is near the Ballena Isle Marina at 1132 Ballena Boulevard; 510/769-2132.

Piedmont

Piedmont is almost entirely residential, and very proper and clean. This means you won't be able to find a stray scrap of paper to scoop with, so be prepared. Its quiet streets are delightful for walking, offering views from the hills.

The parks below allow dogs off leash—but only if they have a permit from the city's police department. Licensed dogs from any city can get one, but it'll cost you more if you don't live in Piedmont, and more still if your dog is not spayed or neutered. The police department's animal services division issues these permits during limited hours on Thursdays only. Phone 510/420-3000 for details.

PARKS, BEACHES, AND RECREATION AREAS

9 Linda Off-Leash Area

😺 🐕 (See Alameda County map on page 390)

This is just a strip of pavement running down a dirt area (formerly grass) about the length of one city block. There's some shade. The "park" is set along a hill, but it's too close to a couple of roads for true off-leash comfort as far as my dogs are concerned. For some reason it gets tremendous use.

Beach Park is across from Beach School, at Linda and Lake Avenues. You'll see the little doggy signs. A permit is required for your off-leash use. Please see above for more information. 510/420-3050.

10 Dracena Park

😺😺😺😺 🐕 (See Alameda County map on page 390)

Parts of this park are grassy, with tall shade trees here and there. But the part dogs long for is the off-leash section. It's a lovely area, with a paved path up and down a wooded, secluded hill. Tall firs and eucalyptus provide plenty of shade, and sometimes it's so quiet here you can hear several kinds of birds. The area isn't fenced, and at the top and bottom there's potential for escape artists to run into the road, so be careful and leash up at these points if you have any doggy doubts.

Poop bags are provided. The trail takes about 15 minutes round-trip, if you assume a very leisurely pace. We like to enter on Artuna Avenue at Ricardo Avenue, because it's safest from traffic and parking's plentiful on the park side of the street. But lots of folks enter at Blair and Dracena Avenues. A permit is required for off-leash use. Please see above for more information. 510/420-3050.

11 Piedmont Park

😺😺😺😺 🐕 (See Alameda County map on page 390)

The huge off-leash section (by permit only; see above) of this beautiful park is one of the best examples of a leash-free dog area in the state. A few salmon-pink concrete pathways lead you and your happy dog alongside a gurgling stream and up and down the hills around the stream. It's absolutely gorgeous and serene back here. (On our last visit, a hummingbird greeted us at the entrance and was back again when we left.) The park smells like heaven, with eucalyptus, redwood, acacia, pine, and deep, earthy scents wafting around everywhere. It reminds me of a serene Japanese garden, minus the Japanese plants.

The stream is fed year-round by a spring higher in the hills. This is pure bliss for dogs during the summer. The trails for dogs and their people run on the cooler side anyway, with all the tall trees. Almost the entire leash-free section is set in a deep canyon, so it's very safe from traffic. A leisurely round-trip stroll will take you about an hour, if you want it to. Poop bags are supplied at a few strategically located stations along the paths. Use them.

A hint if you want your walk to be as peaceful as possible: Don't come here during the school year around lunchtime or quittin' time for school. The high school at the top of a hill on the other side of the stream can spew some very loud students at those times. On one ill-timed visit, a couple of them were throwing glass bottles into the stream. Joe Dog almost got thwacked right in the ol' kisser.

To get to the leash-free section of this elegant park, come in through the main entrance at Highland and Magnolia Avenues. You'll see a willow tree just as you enter. Continue on the path past the willow tree and follow it down to the left side of the stream. You'll see signs for the dog area. Be sure to leash up in other parts of the park, should you explore beyond the stream area. 510/420-3050.

Oakland

Oakland, the most urban city in the East Bay, is also blessed with a collection of generous and tolerant city parks. Unfortunately, what we call the "white gloves" part of Oakland—the parklands ringing Lake Merritt and the Oakland Museum—is off-limits to dogs. But read on. Pooches who enjoy the bay are thrilled to learn that they're allowed on the Blue and Gold Fleet's ferries that run between Oakland and San Francisco. Fares are $5.25 one-way for adults. The ferry terminal is at the foot of Clay Street at Jack London Square. Phone 415/773-1188 for schedules and more information; www.blueandgold-fleet.com. The city now even has a leash-free dog park, and a few more were in the early planning stages.

If you're looking for a super dog-friendly neighborhood, look no further than Montclair. The bookstore, the florist, the pet store, and the hardware store have all been very kind to four-legged friends, including an anonymous doggy tipster who emailed me about this dog-loving community. In addition, the three dog-friendly Montclair eateries listed below really go all out for dogs.

PARKS, BEACHES, AND RECREATION AREAS

12 Joaquin Miller Park
🐾🐾🐾 (See Alameda County map on page 390)

This large, beautiful city park is nestled at the western edge of the huge Redwood Regional Park. If it weren't for the Oakland city parks' rule that dogs must always be leashed, Joaquin Miller would be dog heaven.

Dogs can't enter some of the landscaped areas, such as around Woodminster Amphitheater. On the deliciously cool and damp creek trails below, however, you and your dog will feel as if you own the place.

The West Ridge Trail, reachable from Skyline Boulevard, is popular with mountain bikers. It's waterless, but it's still a good run. The best trails can be entered from the ranger station off Joaquin Miller Road. The Sunset Trail descends about one-eighth of a mile to a cool, ferny stream winding through second- and third-growth redwoods, pines, oak, and laurel. It then ascends to a ridge overlooking cities and the bay. In spring, the ridge is peppered with wildflowers. Plenty of picnic tables and water fountains are scattered throughout the park.

From Highway 13 in Oakland, take the Joaquin Miller Road exit and go one-half mile east to the ranger station. 510/238-7275.

13 Redwood Regional Park

🐾🐾🐾🐾🐕 (See Alameda County map on page 390)

Although it's just a few miles over the ridge from downtown Oakland, Redwood Regional Park is about as far as you can get from urbanity while still within the scope of the Bay Area. Dogs who love nature at its best, and love it even more off leash, adore the 1,836-acre park. People who need to get far from the madding crowd also go gaga over the place.

The park is delectable year-round, but it's a particularly wonderful spot to visit when you need to cool off from hot summer weather. Much of the park is a majestic forest of 150-foot coast redwoods (known to those with scientific tongues as *Sequoia sempervirens*). The redwoods provide drippy cool shade most of the time, which is a real boon for dogs with hefty coats. Back in the mid-1800s, this area was heavily logged for building supplies for San Francisco, and it wasn't a pretty sight. But fortunately, sometimes progress progresses backward, and the fallen trees have some splendid replacements.

There's something for every dog's tastes here. In addition to the redwoods, the park is also home to pine, eucalyptus, madrone, flowering fruit trees, chaparral, and grasslands. Wild critters like the park, too, so leash up immediately if there's any hint of a deer, rabbit, or other woodland creatures around. Many dogs, even "good" dogs, aren't able to withstand the temptation to chase.

Dogs have to leash up along the beautiful Stream Trail, which runs along the environmentally sensitive stream. You'll see the leash signage if this "trial" is still going on during your visit. On or off leash, mud is inevitable if you follow the Stream Trail, so be sure to keep a towel in the car. Water dogs may try to dip their paws in Redwood Creek, which runs through the park. But please don't let them. This is a very sensitive area. Rainbow trout spawn here after migrating from a reservoir downstream, and it's not an easy trip for them. If you and your dog need to splash around somewhere, try the ocean, the bay, or your bathtub.

No parking fee is charged at Skyline Gate at the north end (in Contra Costa County—the park straddles Contra Costa and Alameda Counties). Entering here also lets you avoid the tempting smells of picnic tables at the south end.

The Stream Trail leads steadily downhill, and then takes a steep plunge to the canyon bottom. It's uphill all the way back, but it's worth it. From Highway 13, exit at Joaquin Miller Road and head east to Skyline Boulevard. Turn left on Skyline and go four miles to the Skyline Gate.

If you prefer to go to the main entrance on Redwood Road, exit Highway 13 at Carson/Redwood Road and drive east on Redwood Road. Once you pass Skyline Boulevard, continue two miles on Redwood. The park and parking will be on your left. The Redwood Road entrance charges a $4 parking fee and a $1 dog fee. 510/635-0135.

14 Dimond Park

🐾🐾🐾 (See Alameda County map on page 390)

Dimond Park is a small jewel of a canyon, dense and wild in the midst of the city. Your leashed dog's eyes will sparkle when she sees this lush place. The Dimond Canyon Hiking Trail begins to the east of El Centro Avenue. There's a small parking lot at El Centro where it bisects the park. A short foot trail goes off west of El Centro, ending quickly at the Dimond Recreation Center and an attractive jungle gym for children.

The main trail is wide and of smooth dirt. It starts on the east side and follows Sausal Creek about a quarter of a mile up the canyon. At that point, the trail becomes the creek bed, so you can continue only in dry season. But what a quarter mile! The deciduous tangle of trees and ivy makes the canyon into a hushed, cool bower, and the creek is wide and accessible to dogs longing for a splash. When the water level is high enough, there are falls and, except in the driest months, there's enough for a dog pool or two. After the trail goes into the creek bed, the going is a little rougher, but you can follow it all the way to the ridge at the eastern end.

From I-580, take the Fruitvale Avenue exit north to the corner of Fruitvale and Lyman Road, the eastern entrance. Or, to park at the trailhead, take the Park Boulevard exit from Highway 13 and turn left (south) on El Centro Avenue. 510/482-7831.

15 Hardy Dog Park

🐾🐾🐾🐕 (See Alameda County map on page 390)

This two-acre park in the Rockridge district has easy freeway access and plenty of shade. That's because it's under the freeway. But that's OK. It's a huge improvement from its previous incarnation as a fenced quarter-acre patch of dirt. Now it's big and grassy, with benches, water, and poop bags.

To get to the park from Highway 24, take the Claremont exit and follow Claremont Avenue back under the freeway. The park is under the freeway, at Claremont and Hudson Street. 510/238-3791.

16 Leona Heights Regional Open Space

🐾🐾🐾🐕 (See Alameda County map on page 390)

Unmarked on most maps, and devoid of most amenities (water and restrooms, for instance) this 271-acre open space is good for dogs who like to get away from the crowd. You won't find many bikes or horses here. Since it's part of the East Bay Regional Park District, your dog need not be on leash.

The open space stretches from Merritt College south to Oak Knoll, and from I-580 east to Chabot Regional Park. A bumpy fire trail goes from Merritt College downhill to the southern entrance, just north of Oak Knoll. The best way to enter is to park at a lot off Canyon Oaks Drive, next to a condominium parking lot. Right at this entrance is a pond, but you won't see any more water as you ascend. It's a dry hike in warm weather.

The 2.7-mile fire trail leads gently uphill all the way to Merritt, through coyote brush and oak woodland. In spring, it's full of wildflowers and abuzz with the loud hum of bees. Watch out for poison oak.

From I-580, exit at Keller Avenue and drive east to Campus Drive. Take a left (north), then a left on Canyon Oaks Drive. 510/635-0135.

17 Martin Luther King Jr. Regional Shoreline

🐾🐾 (See Alameda County map on page 390)

The Oakland shoreline doesn't have much to offer a dog besides this park (formerly known as the San Leandro Bay Regional Shoreline), which is well maintained by the East Bay Regional Park District. And it has a major flaw: The district classifies the whole thing as a developed area, so you must leash. The kind of fun a dog most wants—running full-out across grass or swimming in the bay—is illegal.

But you can have a genteel good time on a sunny day that's not too windy, ambling together along the extensive paved bayside trails. Amenities for people are plentiful: picnic tables, a few trees, fountains, a parcourse fitness trail, a tiny beach, and a huge playing field.

A wooden walkway crosses over some mudflats for watching shorebirds and terns fishing. For bird-watching, go at low tide. Keep your dog firmly leashed and held close to you and hike along the San Leandro Creek Channel to Arrowhead Marsh. If you enter from Doolittle Drive, walk along the Doolittle Trail. There's a small sandy beach here, but dogs aren't allowed to swim. (The usual East Bay Regional Park rules apply: No dogs allowed on beaches.)

From I-880, exit at Hegenberger Road in Oakland. Go west on Hegenberger and turn on Edgewater Drive, Pardee Drive, or Doolittle Drive. Parking is free at each of these entry points. 510/635-0135.

PLACES TO EAT

Oakland's College Avenue, in the Rockridge district, has a tolerant family atmosphere. Lawyers with briefcases buy flowers on the way home from the BART station, and students flirt over ice cream. I've never seen anyone in this neighborhood who didn't love dogs.

The avenue is known to be a food lover's paradise, and among the attractions are a string of restaurants with outdoor tables, several of which follow. The Montclair district also has a couple of hits with the dog crowd.

Cafe Rustica: The pizza here is elegant. Eat it at the outdoor tables with your drooling dog. 5422 College Avenue; 510/654-1601.

Crepevine: This popular café serves yummy sweet and savory crepes, pastas, salads, and all-day breakfast. The patio and street tables are available year-round and sometimes the overhead heaters will warm you and your pooch as you enjoy the exotic crepe concoctions. 5600 College Avenue, two blocks from Rockville BART; 510/658-2026.

Flippers: The servers at this Montclair-district eatery are very dog-friendly. They'll bring your dog water, and when possible, they manage to find a meaty treat to "sneak" to your pet (with your permission, of course). Flippers serves breakfast all day here, but it's really known for its burgers. 2080 Mountain Boulevard; 510/339-2082.

Montclair Malt Shop: Don'tcha just hate it when you go to an ice cream parlor and your dog's eyes almost tear up with the anticipation of a single drop of yummy cold cream falling from your cone to the ground so he can lap it off the sidewalk? You won't have to deal with those pleading eyes if you visit this delightful ice creamery: Dogs can order their very own special brew of pooch-friendly ice cream, known as Frosty Paws. Then you can dine together at the bench outside, or just stand around and talk with other dog people while your dog inhales his frozen treat. The place is known for its dog business; on a recent hot summer afternoon, 17 dogs were outside, downing their ice creams with delight. "We love dogs here," says super-friendly Diane, who makes the best malt this side of the bay. (She will be the first to tell you this, and she speaks the truth.) 2066 Mountain Boulevard; 510/339-1886.

Noah's Bagels: We initially learned about this dog-friendly Montclair-district bagelry from a letter to the editor in the *San Francisco Chronicle*. The author of the letter wrote that she finds dogs in public offensive, which is why it gives such pleasure to offer her "tip." In her own words, "If you're not a dog lover, don't go to Noah's Bagels in Montclair on any weekend morning. I've even seen dog dishes outside the store. I avoid this area altogether now...." Sounds like our kind of place. Not only do dogs get water in doggy bowls, but they also get "floor bagels" when available. These are bagels that have been dropped on the floor, either by customers or employees. Do dogs care that their bagel has taken a little roll on terra firma? No! They're still snout-licking good anyway. Dine with your dog at several outdoor tables here. 2060 Mountain Boulevard; 510/339-6663.

Oliveto Cafe: This café and Peaberry's, next door, share a building with the Market Hall, God's own food emporium. The food's the best, but for a dog, the atmosphere is congested. It's not for nervous dogs. Oliveto serves very classy pizza, tapas, bar food, desserts, coffees, and drinks, but alcohol is not allowed at the sidewalk tables. 5655 College Avenue, just south of Rockridge BART; 510/547-5356.

Peaberry's: Enjoy coffees, pastries, and desserts at the outdoor tables here. This is a favorite with BART commuters. 5655 College Avenue; 510/653-0450.

Royal Coffee: This is a cheery and popular place with very good coffee (in the bean or in the cup), tea, and supplies. On weekend mornings, it's dog central. 307 63rd Street at College Avenue; 510/653-5458.

PLACES TO STAY

Oakland Airport Hilton: Dogs have to be under 30 pounds to stay here. Rates are $169–189. Dogs require a $300 deposit. 1 Hegenberger Road 94614; 510/635-5000; www.hilton.com.

San Lorenzo

PARKS, BEACHES, AND RECREATION AREAS

18 San Lorenzo Dog Park

🐾🐾🐾🐕 (See Alameda County map on page 390)

It's just ducky with your dog if you want to take him to this pretty dog park: Part of it curves around a duck pond. The quackers sometimes waddle right by, somehow knowing that their canine friends can't get to them through the fence. It's almost like a cartoon at times, with a duck strutting his stuff while a dog looks on with almost embarrassed disbelief that there's no way on dog's green earth that he'll be having duck for dinner that night.

The dog park is only about two-thirds of an acre, but it has all the good pooch-park amenities, including water, benches, and poop bags. It's grassy with some decomposed granite. There's not much shade, although the back end has some big trees on the outside perimeter, and they can provide shade at times.

The dog park is toward the back of San Lorenzo Community Park, at the very west end of Via Buena Vista. The address is 1970 Via Buena Vista. 510/881-6700.

Castro Valley

PARKS, BEACHES, AND RECREATION AREAS

19 Chabot Regional Park

🐾🐾🐾🐾🐕 (See Alameda County map on page 390)

You and your leash-free dog can throw your urban cares to the wind when you visit this 4,972-acre park filled with magnificent trails and enchanting woodlands. Except for the occasional sounds of gunfire, you'll scarcely believe you're in the hills east of metropolitan Oakland. But fear not—the guns you'll hear are merely being used for target practice at the park's marksmanship range.

The trails at Chabot (sha-BO) are so secluded that if no one is firing a gun, the only sounds you may hear are those of your panting dog and the singing birds. Adventure-loving dogs like to take the Goldenrod Trail, starting at the southern terminus of Skyline Boulevard and Grass Valley Road. It connects with the East Bay Skyline National Recreation Trail, which winds through Grass Valley and climbs through eucalyptus forests. Lucky dogs can be off leash everywhere but in developed areas.

Campsites are $16–20. Dogs are $1 extra. Reserve by phoning 925/373-0144. No reservations are taken October 1–March 31, when the 23 sites are first-come, first-served.

From the intersection of Redwood Road and Castro Valley Boulevard in Castro Valley, go north on Redwood about 4.5 miles to Marciel Gate. (The campground is about two miles inside the gate.) From Oakland at the intersection of Redwood Road and Skyline Boulevard, go about 6.5 miles east on Redwood to Marciel Gate. For general park info, call 510/635-0135.

20 Castro Valley Dog Park

🐾🐾🐾🐕 (See Alameda County map on page 390)

This is a fun place to take a dog for some leash-free exercise. It's about two-thirds of an acre and has water, poop bags, and benches. It's set within the beautiful Earl Warren Park, whose walking path is worth sniffing out despite the on-leash requirement. The park is at 4660 Crow Canyon Road. Exit I-580 at Crow Canyon Road and head north several blocks. 510/881-6700.

21 Cull Canyon Regional Recreation Area

🐾🐾🐾🐕 (See Alameda County map on page 390)

Dogs may be off leash up on the grassy slopes laced with eucalyptus stands, but they have to wear their leashes in the areas designed for human fun. It's not such a bad fate, considering that there are plenty of grassy slopes away from developed areas.

In summer, fishing and swimming are popular here. But pooches may not go near the swimming complex, which includes an attractive pavilion and sandy beach. Leashed dogs may visit picnic areas, the Cull Creek area, and the willow-lined reservoir that sports a wooden bridge and a handful of ducks and coots.

From I-580, take the Center Street/Crow Canyon Road exit. Go left on Center Street and take a right on Castro Valley Boulevard. Follow it to Crow Canyon Road and take a left. Take another left on Cull Canyon Road. It's a half mile to the park entrance. 510/635-0135.

PLACES TO STAY

Chabot Regional Park: See Chabot Regional Park, above, for camping information.

Hayward

PARKS, BEACHES, AND RECREATION AREAS

🐾🐾 Hayward Memorial Park Hiking and Riding Trails

🐾🐾🐾 (See Alameda County map on page 390)

For humans, Memorial Park offers all kinds of amenities, including an indoor pool, tennis courts, kids' swings and slides, picnic tables, a band shell, and even a slightly funky cage full of doves. But really, if you're a dog, the big question is, "Who cares?"

The fun for dogs begins when you get on the Wally Wickander (poor guy) Memorial Trail and enter the greenbelt part of the park, laced with dirt fire trails designed for hikers and horses. Dogs must remain leashed, but the trail is so beautiful that it doesn't seem to matter. It follows a steep-sided creek lined with a thick tangle of oak, laurel, maple, and lots of noisy birds. The trash pickup is a little lax, but if you're looking for solitude in a city park, you'll find it here.

You can enter through Hayward Memorial Park, at Mission Boulevard (Highway 238) just south of the intersection of Highway 92. You can also enter at the parking lots on East Avenue through East Avenue Park on the north end, or on Highland Boulevard through Old Highland Park on the south end. 510/881-6715.

🐾🐾 Garin Regional Park and Dry Creek Regional Park

🐾🐾🐾🐾🐾 (See Alameda County map on page 390)

Garin Regional Park is about one mile and one century away from one of the busiest streets in Hayward. It's a fascinating place for you and your dog to learn about Alameda County farming and ranching. The parking lot next to Garin Barn—an actual barn, blacksmith's shop, and tool shed that is also Garin's visitor center—is strewn with antique farm machinery.

A total of 20 miles of trails, looping among the sweeps of grassy hills, beckon you and your dog. Off-leash dogs are fine on the trails once you've left the visitor center. Dogs seem to like to think they're on their own farm here, looking for all the world as if they're strutting down their very own property and watching out for evil feline intruders.

Dry Creek, which runs near the visitor center, was a delightful small torrent one day when we were there after a March storm. There isn't much shade on hot days, though. That's when you might want to try cooling your paws at tiny Jordan Pond. It's stocked with catfish, should your dog care to join you on his kind of fishing excursion.

From Highway 238 (Mission Boulevard), Tamarack Drive takes you quickly up the hill to Dry Creek Regional Park. Garin Avenue takes you to Garin, or you can enter Garin from the California State University, Hayward campus. The parking fee is $4. Dogs are $1 extra. 510/635-0135.

PLACES TO STAY

Motel 6: Rates are $46–62 for the first adult, $6 for the second. 30155 Industrial Parkway Southwest 94544; 510/489-8333.

Vagabond Inn: Rates are $80–100. Dogs are $10 extra. 20455 Hesperian Boulevard 94541; 510/785-5480.

Union City

PARKS, BEACHES, AND RECREATION AREAS

24 Drigon Dog Park

😊😊😊😊 🐕 (See Alameda County map on page 390)

A dogbone-shaped walkway dotted with pawprints? Doggy tunnels, hoops, jumps, and other fun agility toys? Fire hydrants galore? A gated entrance featuring a giant dog bone and big concrete pillars with huge paw prints? What is this—dog heaven or something?

Yes! Drigon (DRY-ghin) Dog Park is pooch paradise that happens to be firmly planted on grassy terra firma. It is paws down the most well designed of California's fenced dog parks. The design is the brainchild of two dog-loving park district planners—a $300,000 shining gem that's utterly to drool for. You drive by, you see it, you can't help but smile, even if you don't have a dog. It's like real-world-meets-cartoon-fantasy—something you could find around the corner if you lived in Toontown.

The park is 1.5 acres, with a small section for wee dogs. It has water, poop bags, nicely designed benches, and shade in the form of a permanent awning. Everything here is doggy: The concrete around the newly planted trees has embedded paw prints. The hydrants are concrete (they can't rust or corrode from boy dog bladder activities) and have drainage. This helps keep the grassy area pretty green.

The park, named for a heroic police dog who is in a more ethereal dog heaven now, is closed Mondays for maintenance. It's in the middle of a residential suburban neighborhood, at 7th Street and Mission Boulevard. 510/471-3232.

Pleasanton

PARKS, BEACHES, AND RECREATION AREAS

🐾🐾🐾🐕 Muirwood Park Dog Exercise Area

🐾🐾🐾🐕 (See Alameda County map on page 390)

Dogs enjoy galloping around this very long, narrow park in part because it's so easy on their paws. The ground cover is affectionately known as "forest floor material," which is basically degraded wood chips mixed with leaf and branch litter. Much as you'd find in the real Muir Woods in Marin, the stuff makes for cushy walks and runs—it's great for the joints of older dogs.

If your dog likes chasing far-flung balls, this is a perfect place for it. The park is about 300 feet long by 40 feet wide, which means there's plenty of room to use your tennis ball launcher to its full capacity. The park has all the usual dog-park amenities, including benches, water, and poop-bag dispensers. There's ample shade from evergreen acacias—a popular food with giraffes. (You won't likely see any giraffes wandering through the dog park, but park workers have been known to collect leaves and branches for the giraffes at the Oakland Zoo.)

The park is at 4701 Muirwood Drive. The cross street is Las Positas Boulevard. 925/931-5340.

🐾🐾🐾🐾🐕 Pleasanton Ridge Regional Park

🐾🐾🐾🐾🐕 (See Alameda County map on page 390)

This fairly recent and beautiful addition to the East Bay Regional Parks system is an isolated treat. Dogs may run off leash on all the secluded trails here as soon as you leave the staging area.

You can reach Pleasanton Ridge from either Foothill or Golden Eagle Roads. At the Foothill Staging Area, there are fine picnic sites at the trailhead. Climb up on the Oak Tree fire trail to the ridgeline, where a looping set of trails goes off to the right. The incline is gentle, through pasture (you share this park with cattle) dotted with oak and—careful—poison oak. Wildflowers riot in spring. It's a hot place in summer. At the bottom of the park, however, is a beautiful streamside stretch along Arroyo de la Laguna. There's no water above the entrance, so be sure to carry plenty.

From I-680, take the Castlewood Drive exit and go left (west) on Foothill Road to the staging area. 510/635-0135.

PLACES TO STAY

Crown Plaza: Rates are $69–179. Dogs pay a $50 fee for length of their stay, and may stay only in ground-floor rooms, which are also smoking rooms. 11950 Dublin Canyon Road 94588; 925/847-6000.

Fremont

PARKS, BEACHES, AND RECREATION AREAS

27 Coyote Hills Regional Park

🐾🐾🐾 (See Alameda County map on page 390)

This park is a paradox. It's a working research project on Ohlone Indian history, a teeming wildlife sanctuary, and a family picnic and bicycling mecca—all rolled into 966 acres.

Dogs used to be able to run leashless in the small hills that give the park its name, but leashes are now the law. We understand. (Waaah.) Wildlife is abundant here. You'll see red-tailed hawks, vultures, and white-tailed kites that swoop down on unsuspecting squirrels.

The beautiful Bayview Trail climbs quickly behind the visitor center. From the crest of Red Hill—green even in the dry season because its ground cover is drought-tolerant—you look down on varied colors of marsh grasses, waterfowl, and wading birds, and the shallow salt ponds in the bay. Most of the park is a fragile sanctuary, and dogs must stay on the little hills or at the picnic area by the visitor center.

From I-880, take the Decoto Road/Highway 84 exit in Fremont. Go west on Highway 84 to the Thornton Avenue/Paseo Padre Parkway exit. Go north on Paseo Padre about one mile to Patterson Ranch Road/Commerce. A left on Patterson Ranch Road brings you to the entrance. When the kiosk is staffed, the parking fee is $4. The dog fee is $1. For information on tours and activities, call 510/795-9385. For general information, call 510/635-0135.

28 Alameda Creek Regional Trail

🐾🐾🐾🐕 (See Alameda County map on page 390)

This 12.4-mile trail runs from the bayshore to the East Bay hills, and dogs can actually be off leash in many sections. But they may be disappointed when they discover that it's not as pristine a trail as the name might imply. First of all, the trail is paved. Second of all, the creek is paved. (You'll see what I mean.) But more important, the trail doesn't just pass through farmland and greenbelt areas. It also runs alongside railyards, industrial lots, and quarries. Junkyard dogs like it. Wilderness dogs just shrug their hairy shoulders. A scenic stretch of this paved trail is at the Niles Canyon end. Dogs find it especially interesting in winter after a storm, when there's actually water in the concrete-lined creek and ducks and coots splash around.

Although the East Bay Regional Park District's usual liberal leash rules apply here, it has posted a good many areas with "leash up" symbols. If you see one, do so. On this trail, as on any you share with other hikers, horses, and bicycles, just use common sense.

You may enter this trail at many points near the creek's mouth—in the salt flats of the bay by Coyote Hills Regional Park. The trail officially begins in Fremont's Niles district, at the intersection of Mission Boulevard (Highway 238) and Niles Canyon Road (Highway 84). 510/635-0135.

29 Fremont Dog Park

🐾 🐾 🐕 (See Alameda County map on page 390)

A park with male-pattern baldness? That's what you get when you visit this fenced one-acre park. The surface is grass, but in the middle, there's a big bald patch. But dogs don't care about the aesthetics. They're just happy to be able to cruise around off leash. The park has benches, poop bags, and water. There's no shade, so it can get toasty at times.

The park is within the beautiful, 450-acre Central Park, which leashed dogs are welcome to explore. The dog section is on Stevenson Boulevard, just west of Gallaudet Drive, near the softball fields. 510/790-5541.

30 Mission Peak Regional Preserve

🐾 🐾 🐾 🐾 🐕 (See Alameda County map on page 390)

Smart Fremont dwellers take their dogs to this 2,596-acre park. It's a huge expanse of grass, dotted with occasional oak groves and scrub. Unfortunately for humans who get short of breath, the foot trails head straight up. Trails to the top rise 2,500 feet in three miles. (Pant, pant.)

Leash-free dogs love this place. The entrance at Stanford Avenue offers a gentler climb than the entrance from the Ohlone College campus. You'll pass Caliente Creek if you take the Peak Meadow Trail, but in hot weather, there won't be much relief from the sun. Be sure to carry water for yourself and your dog. The main point of puffing up Mission Peak is the renowned view stretching from Mt. Tamalpais to Mt. Hamilton. (On very clear days, you can see to the Sierra's snowy crest.) Your dog may not care much for the scenery, but she'll probably appreciate the complete freedom of the expanse of pasture here.

From I-680, take the southern Mission Boulevard exit in Fremont (there are two exits; the one you want is in the Warm Springs district). Go east on Mission to Stanford Avenue, turn right (east), and in less than a mile, you'll be at the entrance. 510/635-0135.

31 Sunol Regional Wilderness

🐾 🐾 🐾 🐾 🐕 (See Alameda County map on page 390)

You and your leash-free dog will howl for joy when you visit this large and deserted wilderness treasure. It's like going to a national park without having to leave your poor pooch behind.

One of the best treats for canines and their companions is a hike along the Camp Ohlone Trail, which you reach via the main park entrance, on Geary Road. The trail takes you to an area called Little Yosemite. Like its namesake,

Little Yosemite is magnificent. It's a steep-sided gorge with a creek at the bottom, lofty crags, and outcrops of greenstone and basalt that reveal a turbulent geological history. Its huge boulders throw Alameda Creek into gurgling eddies and falls. There's no swimming allowed here, much to Jake's dismay.

You can return via the higher Canyon View Trail or head for several other destinations: wooded canyons, grassy slopes, peaks with peeks of Calaveras Reservoir or Mt. Diablo. The park brochure offers useful descriptions of each trail. Dogs may run leashless on trails except for on the Backpack Loop.

Dogs are allowed only at the Family Campground site at headquarters and not at the backpacking campsites farther in. Sites are $12. The dog fee is $1. Dogs must be leashed in the campground or confined to your tent. (Anyone whose dog has ever chased off after a wild boar in the middle of the night understands the reason for this rule, and this park has plenty of boars.) Call 510/636-1684 to reserve. Reserved sites are held until 5 P.M. The day-use parking fee is $4, plus $1 extra for your dog.

From I-680, take the Calaveras Road exit, then go left (east) on Geary Road to the park entrance. The park may be closed or restricted during fire season, June–October. 925/862-2244.

PLACES TO STAY

Best Western Garden Court: Rates are $59–99. Dogs are $10 extra. 5400 Mowry Avenue 94538; 510/792-4300.

Sunol Regional Wilderness: See the Sunol Regional Wilderness, above, for camping information.

Livermore

PARKS, BEACHES, AND RECREATION AREAS

Livermore is barking up the right tree: Plans are in the works for two more dog parks. Meanwhile, dogs are greatly enjoying the current three.

3 2 May Nissen Dog Park

🐾🐾🐾 (See Alameda County map on page 390)

At one-third of an acre, this is the smallest of Livermore's dog parks. But there's still enough room for dogs to have a decent time. There's water, some grass, and shade-providing trees. A double-gated entry helps prevent escape artist pooches from bolting when someone leaves or enters the park.

The dog park is set within May Nissen Park. It's on Rincon Avenue, just south of Pine Street. 925/373-5700.

3 3 Vista Meadows Park

🐾🐾🐾🐾 (See Alameda County map on page 390)

Your dog can't quite live out a favorite nursery rhyme and go 'round the mulberry bush here, but he can go under a mulberry tree (or do a leg lift on it, which is a popular pastime with some dogs here). This .75-acre fenced park has some mulberry trees on its back end. There's even a bench under them, should you feel like relaxing in their shade. The grass here is pretty worn down, but it can come back again with the help of the wonderful parks department. Amenities include water, poop bags, and a double-gated entry. The park is at Westminster and Lambeth Road. 925/373-5700.

3 4 Max Baer Dog Park

🐾🐾🐾🐾 (See Alameda County map on page 390)

This .6-acre, fenced-in dog park is level and grassy, with lots of shady trees. It's double-gated, for your dog's safety. Inside the park are poop bags, a water fountain and bowls, and chairs where people can hang out while their dogs romp. On summer evenings, as many as 25–30 dogs enjoy the park. "Everybody loves it," says veterinarian Martin Plone, who was behind the park's birth in 1993. "It's become a meeting place for people. While their dogs are playing, people form friendships."

The dog park is part of the popular Max Baer Park. It's at Murdell Lane and Stanley Boulevard. 925/373-5700.

3 5 Sycamore Grove Park

🐾🐾🐾 (See Alameda County map on page 390)

Sycamore Grove is an unusual and attractive streamside park. In rainy times, it can look semiswampy, as most of the Central Valley used to look. In fact, it is Lake Del Valle's floodplain, and federal flood controllers occasionally send runoff into this park's stream, Arroyo Del Valle, when Lake Del Valle rises too high.

With its low hills, tall grass, and loud sounds of birds and squirrels, it's almost an African savanna. Blackbirds and swallows swoop over the stream and marshy spots, grabbing insects. Poppies are plentiful in spring. Kids, dogs, miniature horses, potbellied pigs, and llamas live in harmony here, mostly because everyone obeys the leash law. Water dogs and their kin love wading in the stream pools near the picnic tables. Follow the paths far enough and the place becomes satisfyingly wild.

The park is quite flat, perfect for dogs who don't do well in low gear. Take I-580 to Livermore; exit to Portola Avenue. Go east to North Livermore Avenue and turn right. After 2.5 miles, North Livermore turns into Arroyo Road. Turn right on Wetmore Road. There's a $2 fee. 925/373-5700.

36 Del Valle Regional Park

🐾🐾🐾🐾🐕 (See Alameda County map on page 390)

This popular reservoir is best known for swimming, boating, fishing, and camping. Like Chabot Regional Park (see the Castro Valley section), it's primarily a manicured and popular human recreation area, with neat lawns and picnic tables (where dogs must be leashed).

But, glory be to dog, the park sports several unspoiled trails for leash-free hiking in the surrounding hills. And, unlike at Lake Chabot, here you're permitted to take a dog on a rented boat. Every dog can have his day here.

From this recreation area, you can enter the Ohlone Wilderness Trail—29 miles of gorgeous trail through four regional parks. (See Ohlone Regional Wilderness, below.)

The 150 sites at Family Camp allow dogs, but only on leash or confined to your tent. Sites are $15–20. Reserve by calling 510/636-1684.

From I-580, take North Livermore Avenue from downtown Livermore. It will become South Livermore Avenue, then Tesla Road. Take a right (south) on Mines Road, and then turn right on Del Valle Road. The parking fee is $6. The dog fee is $1. 510/635-0135.

37 Ohlone Wilderness Trail

🐾🐾🐾🐾🐕 (See Alameda County map on page 390)

Some of the area's most remote and peaceful wilderness areas are accessible only by way of this 29-mile trail. The trail stretches from Mission Peak, east of Fremont, through Sunol Regional Wilderness and Ohlone Regional Wilderness to Del Valle Regional Park, south of Livermore. You and your occasionally leash-free dog (signs tell you when it's allowed) will hike through oak and bay woods and grassy uplands that are carpeted with wildflowers in spring.

You'll also see abundant wildlife—if you're quiet and lucky, you might even see an endangered bald eagle. If your dog can't take the pressure of merely watching as tule elk and deer pass by, you should keep him leashed.

A permit is required. (See Ohlone Regional Wilderness, below, for permit details.) Because of some restrictions, you won't be able to do all 29 miles at once with your dog. That's OK. In fact, that's probably just fine with your dog. 510/635-0135.

🛭🛭 Ohlone Regional Wilderness

🐾🐾🐾🐾🐾 (See Alameda County map on page 390)

The centerpiece of this magnificent parkland is the 3,817-foot Rose Peak—only 32 feet lower than Mt. Diablo. Leash-free dogs are in heaven on earth as they explore the surrounding 6,758 acres of grassy ridges. Wildlife is abundant, so if your dog isn't obedient, it's best to keep her leashed. The tule elk appreciate it, and your dog will appreciate it, too, should you run into a mountain lion.

The regional parks system shares the wilderness with the San Francisco Water District, which wants to limit the human presence here. Dogs may not stay overnight in the campgrounds.

To enter this wild and breathtaking area east of Sunol Regional Wilderness, you must pick up a permit (which includes a detailed trail map and camping information) for $2 at the East Bay Regional Park District headquarters or at the Del Valle and Sunol kiosks, and at the Coyote Hills Visitors Center (Fremont). 510/635-0135.

PLACES TO EAT

Café Paradiso: "Start your day in paradise," says a manager here. And the food here is heavenly. Try the Bird of Paradise sandwich for a real taste treat. The lucky dogs who dine at the umbrella-topped outdoor tables get not only water, but treats! 53 Wright Brothers Avenue; 925/371-2233.

PLACES TO STAY

Del Valle Regional Park: See Del Valle Regional Park, above, for camping information.

Residence Inn Livermore: These are convenient little apartments/suites if you need more than just a room. Rates are $169–224, and there's a $75 fee per doggy visit, so you might want to stay a while. 1000 Airway Boulevard 94550; 925/373-1800.

CHAPTER 34

Marin County

This is a good place to be a dog or a well-heeled human. For four-legged friends, it's got it all, from the bay to the ocean to the redwoods and hilly parklands in between. Throw in some dog-friendly restaurants, inns, and cottages, and you've got the makings of a pooch paradise.

Unfortunately, the once-leash-free Golden Gate National Recreation Area lands require leashes these days. It's a huge loss to dogs, who could once gallavant buck-naked on dozens of trails and a couple of beaches. It's enough to make a dog want to take off his bandanna and cry into it. (Try not to let him blow his nose into it, though. That's always a bit of a mess.) This rule is being evaluated, and we hope that by the next edition of this book we'll have good news.

One large park entity still allows dogs off leash, but this may not be forever, either. Marin County operates 33 Open Space District lands. The landscapes include grassy expanses, wooded trails, redwood groves, marshes, and steep mountainsides. The idea is to set aside bits of land so that Marin never ends up looking like Santa Clara Valley. The Open Space parks are free and completely

PICK OF THE LITTER—MARIN COUNTY

BEST OFF-LEASH BEACH
Dillon Beach Resort, Dillon Beach (page 423)

BEST REMOTE BEACH
Kehoe Beach, Inverness (page 424)

PLACE TO HIKE OFF LEASH IN THE HEAT
Indian Tree Open Space Preserve, Novato (page 431)

BEST BREAD
Bovine Bakery, Point Reyes Station (page 428)

MOST DOG-FRIENDLY PLACE TO EAT
Fish, Sausalito (page 455)

MOST MAGICAL LODGINGS
The Ark, Inverness (page 425)
Manka's Inverness Lodge, Inverness (page 426)
Rosemary Cottages, Inverness (page 426)
The Old Point Reyes Schoolhouse Compound, Point Reyes Station (page 428)
The Olema Inn, Olema (page 430)

undeveloped. Until fairly recently, dogs were permitted off leash just about everywhere on these lands. But now they can run leashless only on designated fire roads. They must be leashed on trails. It's still a pretty good deal, since most dogs don't mind the wide berth. Speaking of wide berth, you're not allowed to bring more than three dogs at a time to open space lands. This rule keeps commercial dog walking at bay. See www.marinopenspace.org for more park info, or phone 415/499-6387.

Life on a leash isn't the same as the untethered life. But it's not always a drag. Marin offers some real gems to leashed pooches. Most dogs are surprised to discover that if they wear a leash, they're permitted to explore a bit of beautiful Mt. Tamalpais (see Mount Tamalpais State Park and Mount Tamalpais–Marin Municipal Water District Land in the Mill Valley section).

Dogs' mouths also tend to drop open when you mention they can visit parts of the 65,000-acre Point Reyes National Seashore. Because it's a delicate ecosystem and a national treasure, dogs are banned from campgrounds, most trails, and several beaches. Point Reyes National Seashore is home to 350 species of birds and 72 species of mammals (not including dogs). Where dogs are permitted, they must be on leash. It's a small price to pay to be able to peruse the place with the pooch at all. Kehoe Beach, Point Reyes Beach South, and Point Reyes Beach North are the seashore's most dog-friendly areas.

I don't normally mention doggy day-care facilities (after all, the book is about places you can go with your dog), but Camp K-9 of Marin is worthy of a little rule-breaking. It offers training, day care, and overnight boarding, but it also has a do-it-yourself dog wash and even a "campground rental," which is a large, enclosed outdoor area with everything you'll need for a private dog park for that special event, or simply to work on training. If you do nothing else, check out Camp K-9's fun, hip, very retro website, www.campk-9ofmarin.com. (It makes me want to sip a neat cocktail while wearing a little apron and listening to 1960s smooth lounge music.) Phone 415/924-CAMP (415/924-2267) for more info.

Dillon Beach

PARKS, BEACHES, AND RECREATION AREAS

◩ Dillon Beach Resort

🐾🐾🐾🐾🐕 (See Marin County map on page 420)

Don't let the name fool you: This is a beach, not a high-end hotel with dozens of spa treatments. What really gets dogs excited is that not only are they allowed on the beach, but at a certain point that seems to confuse everyone we've spoken with there, they can throw their leashes to the wind. The rule says something to the effect that from the parking lot to the high tide line, dogs must be leashed, and from the tide line and into the water, dogs can be leash free. Check with the person at the kiosk when you drive in. Please make super-sure your dog is truly under voice control before letting her go, because this a rare privilege these days. (The next leash-free beach to the north is in Humboldt County; to the south it's in Pacifica.)

The beach is privately run and very well maintained. If you notice broken glass or anything that's not in keeping with a clean, safe beach, the staff asks you to report it.

There's a $5 fee per vehicle. It's worth the price. The beach is the northernmost beach in Marin County. So far north, in fact, that it has the Sonoma County area code. The address is One Beach Avenue; 707/878-2696.

PLACES TO STAY

Lawson's Landing and Resort: When you camp here, you camp in a grassy meadow along the sand dunes. There are no set campsites, just the open meadow. That's great, because sometimes you can have the whole place to yourself. Other times you have to share the meadow with lots of other out-doorsy sorts of folks. Camping is $17. Weekly rates are available. Lawson's Landing is easy to find once you're in Dillon Beach. The address is 137 Marine View Drive, P.O. Box 67, Dillon Beach, CA 94929; 707/878-2443; www.lawsonslanding.com.

Inverness

This sweet, quiet village on Tomales Bay is one of the most attractive in Marin. The dog-friendly beaches, cafés, and lodgings are to drool for. What's not to love about this place?

PARKS, BEACHES, AND RECREATION AREAS

⧉ Kehoe Beach

🐾🐾🐾🐾 (See Marin County map on page 420)

This is our favorite of the Point Reyes National Seashore beaches that allow dogs, since it's both the most beautiful and the least accessible. The only parking is at roadside. You take a half-mile cinder path through wildflowers and thistles, with marsh on one side and hill on the other. In the morning, you may see some mule deer. Then, you come out on medium-brown sand that stretches forever. Since the water is shallow, the surf repeats its crests in multiple white rows, as in Hawai'i. Behind you are limestone cliffs. Scattered rocks offer tidepools filled with mussels, crabs, anemones, barnacles, snails, and sea flora.

In such a paradise of shore life, the leash rule makes sense. The chief reasons for leashing dogs (or banning them altogether) at the Point Reyes National Seashore beaches are the harbor seals that haul out onto the beaches. They're in no position to get away fast from a charging dog. The snowy plover, a threatened shorebird that nests on the ground, also appreciates your dog obeying the leash law. In fact, sections of this beach and the other Point Reyes beaches may become closed long-term because of these birds. Restricted areas will be posted so tell your dog to keep her eyes peeled.

From Inverness, follow Sir Francis Drake Boulevard to the fork. Bear right on Pierce Point Road and go about four miles; park beside the road where you see the sign and walk about a half mile to the beach. 415/464-5100.

🕄 Point Reyes Beach North

😾😾😾😾 (See Marin County map on page 420)

Point Reyes Beach North is a generous, functional beach. There's no long trail from the parking lot, no special tidepools or rocks, just a long, clean, beautiful running beach for the two of you. Officially, however, dogs must be leashed.

From Inverness, take Sir Francis Drake Boulevard. Follow signs for the lighthouse. Go about 10 miles. The turnoff for the beach is well marked. 415/464-5100.

🕄 Point Reyes Beach South

😾😾😾 (See Marin County map on page 420)

Point Reyes Beach South is a little narrower and steeper than Point Reyes Beach North, and it has a few interesting sandstone outcrops with wind-carved holes. It has a bit less of that wide-open feeling. Leash the dog.

Follow the directions for Point Reyes Beach North; it's the next beach southward. 415/464-5100.

PLACES TO EAT

Inverness Store: Lots of dogs visit this little grocery store, which has been around for more than 80 years. The folks here are kind to doggies and welcome them to munch a lunch at the picnic table at the dike here. They even invite dogs and their people to bring a blanket and make it a real picnic. (No ants, though.) 12784 Sir Francis Drake Boulevard; 415/669-1041.

Manka's Inverness Lodge: This magnificent lodge is home to a mouth-watering restaurant, if wild game is the type of dish that makes your mouth water. (See Places to Stay for more information.)

Priscilla's Pizza and Cafe: The salads, pizzas, pastas, and sandwiches here are a delight. Dine with doggy at the large side patio. 12781 Sir Francis Drake Boulevard; 415/669-1244.

PLACES TO STAY

The Ark: Don't expect 40 days and 40 nights of rain during your stay at The Ark. But be assured that even if it's raining cats and dogs, you'll still have a wonderful time here. That's because this two-room cottage is cozy and charming, with vast skylights, a soaring ceiling, a nifty loft, and the down-home comfort of a woodstove. It's furnished with lovely wood pieces and locally handcrafted items. The Ark is far removed from the hustle and bustle of downtown Inverness, and it is adjacent to a wildlife preserve, replete with trees. If you enjoy singing birds, open a window and let the songs stream in. Or walk outside to the beautiful, private area surrounding the cottage.

The Ark was built in 1971 by a class of UC Berkeley architecture students under the guidance of maverick architect Sim Van der Ryn. The class was called "Making a Place in the Country." If you took a class in the result of this project, it would probably be called "Making a Place in Your Heart." Your dog won't soon forget a vacation here, and neither will you. As long as your dog doesn't take a stab at the subjects of "Making a Hole in the Yard" or "Making Pee-Pee on the Floor," he'll be as welcome here as the humans in his party.

The Ark sleeps up to six people. Rates are $215 for two people, $25 per additional person. Dogs pay a flat fee for their visit: $25 for one dog, $35 for two dogs. Healthful, delicious, organic breakfast fixings (described below in mouthwatering detail in the listing for the Ark's sister property, Rosemary Cottages) are $20 extra. You'll get the address when you make your reservation; 415/663-9338 or 800/808-9338; www.rosemarybb.com (click on The Ark).

Manka's Inverness Lodge: Often, humans and their dogs spend the night here, eat breakfast, and decide never to return home. It's an old hunting lodge, surrounded by woods and the beaches and mudflats of Tomales Bay—and the owners love dogs.

The lodgings are super-cozy, fun, and funky. Features vary from one to the other, and include fireplaces, huge tubs, antiques, and a variety of surprising decorative touches. Views are either of Tomales Bay or the surrounding woods.

Dogs can stay in the cabins or one suite. Rates for dog-friendly accommodations are $265–385. Dogs are $50 extra for the length of their stay.

The food here is exceptional. The lodge's restaurant has received many an award. The vegetarian and fish dishes are exotic and mouthwatering. But it's all the wild game dishes that make dogs vote it a four-paw restaurant. If dogs accompany you for a meal at the outdoor tables here, they'll drool over every mouthful you eat.

Look for the uphill turn off Sir Francis Drake Boulevard and take Argyle Way about 400 yards to the lodge. P.O. Box 1110, Inverness, CA 94937; 415/669-1034 or 800/58-LODGE (800/585-6343); www.mankas.com.

Rosemary Cottages: The two gorgeous cottages that share this spacious, wooded property are the kind of places you and your dog will not leave easily. The Fir Tree Inn and The Rosemary Cottage are set in a secluded spot, each with a wall of windows looking out at the stunning forest scenery of the Point Reyes National Seashore. A deck overlooks a sweet-smelling herb garden. The inside of the cottages are cozy and beautifully crafted, with a full kitchen and many homey details. Snuggle up near the wood-burning stove on chilly evenings after a day of whale-watching and dog-walking at nearby beaches. Hearth-type dogs love it here.

There's plenty of privacy: Although the cottages share the garden and hot tub (which uses chemicals other than chlorine and its harsh brethren), many guests spend their vacation here and never even know just where the other cottage is.

Owner Suzanne Storch wants your stay to be as restful and healthful as possible, and she provides a "green" environment (only more-natural cleansers are used) and the most delectable organic breakfast fixings, including a basket of oranges and other fruit, granola, yogurt, pancake mix, maple syrup, homemade jam (made by Suzanne), and eggs from her chickens. You don't have to have these amazing organic foods, and it'll be $20 less if you don't, but where else can you find a deal like this for such a sumptuous feast?

The Rosemary Cottage is $245 for up to two people, and The Fir Tree is $265. If you want the breakfast fixings at either cottage, add $20. If you have one dog, you'll pay a $25 flat fee. For two dogs you'll pay a $35 flat fee. You'll get the address when you make your reservation. 415/663-9338 or 800/808-9338; www.rosemarybb.com.

Point Reyes Station

This community is the commercial hub of West Marin. But that's not saying much, because it's not exactly Development Central out here. In fact, there are probably more cows than people. You'll find some terrific places to eat and to spend the night with your dog. We list some below, but a great resource for information on the entire West Marin area, and additional places to stay with a dog, is Bobbi, who runs the West Marin Network, a lodging service. Give her a jingle at 415/663-9543.

DIVERSION

If Only Dogs Could Read: Point Reyes Books once sent me a letter that ended like this: "We welcome genteel canines, whether a reading rover or a browsing bowser—or just a patiently waiting companion. *Se habla* milkbone." So of course, next time we found ourselves pawing around for a good book, Joe hounded me to drive with him to this wonderful little bookstore. He immediately fell in love with the place. Dogs get lots of loving and a crunchy biscuit. After a recent visit, his protégé, Jake, decided that instead of chewing books, he'd simply make dog-eared pages. Anything to go back.

This store really is a treat—for dogs and humans. It has a big selection of new and used books, with a strong outdoor book section. Combine a visit here with a hike and a lunch, and you've got yourselves a doggone great day. 11315 Highway 1, Point Reyes Station; 415/663-1542; www.ptreyesbooks.com.

PLACES TO EAT

Bovine Bakery: The bread here will make you drool, which will make your dog embarrassed. Dine on bread or pizza or "killer monster cookies" at the bench in front. 11315 Highway 1; 415/663-9420.

Cafe Reyes: The patio on the café's side is big and very attractive, with excellent views of local scenery. Even dogs seem to enjoy its ambience. The food is great, too. Bring it to the 15 umbrella-topped tables and wolf it down with your pooch at your side. The cuisine is best described as Tex-Mex with a California leaning. Try one of the Thai burritos for a true international experience. You can also get baked goodies and strong coffee, for those lazy, foggy days here. There's not really a street address. It's on Highway 1 and is big and wooden. You can't miss it. 415/663-9493.

PLACES TO STAY

The Berry Patch Cottage: This delightful garden cottage is surrounded by trees and has a private yard with plenty of berries (thus the name), fruit trees, and nut trees. The cottage owners live next door, and they invite guests to share their vegetable garden. Some times of the year, it's pretty much food city here. It's a terrific getaway from the urban lifestyle. The cottage is a charmer, with a full kitchen that opens to a redwood deck, a living room with a wonderful little reading nook (and books to read in that nook), and a bedroom that's warmed by an old Sears & Roebuck potbelly stove. Rates are $100 to $150. Dogs are $5 extra. The mailing address is P.O. Box 712 94956. You'll get the physical address when you make a reservation. 415/663-1942 or 888/663-1942; www.berrypatchcottage.com.

The Old Point Reyes Schoolhouse Compound: The three glorious getaway cottages that make up the old schoolhouse area are the cat's meow for dogs and their people. On a serene stretch of rolling pastureland in Point Reyes Station, the cottages have a sweet country theme and seem perfectly at home in their surroundings. Dogs love it here, because each cottage is adorned with its own private enclosed patio and garden. They're wonderful places to relax outside with your pooch.

The cottages also have fully equipped kitchens that come with a real bonus: a lovely picnic basket and all the gear that goes with it (excluding the food). Now there's no excuse for not taking your pooch on a picnic. In addition, each cottage has access to a wonderful organic garden and a secluded garden hot tub. The larger two have fireplaces and full kitchens.

Jasmine Cottage is the smaller of the two romantic hideaways. It's sequestered in a country garden at the top of a hill and has small flower gardens, vegetable gardens, and even a flock of chickens, who provide guests with their morning eggs. A full, simple breakfast is included in your stay at this cottage. The chickens are in a protected area, but if your dog has a hankering for KFC, best keep her away. When we visited, Joe Dog went cuckoo over the cock-a-doodle-doos. We had to drag him kicking and screaming back inside the cottage for fear he would give a hen a heart attack.

Gray's Retreat is just as enchanting, but chicken-free and bigger. It's more geared toward families, since it sleeps up to six and comes with a high chair and a portable crib. Breakfast is not provided, but the kitchen is stocked with enough basic dry goods (including organic breakfast goodies) that with a few groceries, you can have yourself a feast. The newest addition, the Barn Loft, is the smallest, but it offers the best views and the best price. (No breakfast here, either.)

Rates for the cottages: Jasmine, $220; Gray's, $245; Barn Loft, $185. Stay seven days, and get the seventh night free. Dogs are $50 extra for the length of their stay. The cottages are on the historic Old Point Reyes Schoolhouse Compound. The mailing address is P.O. Box 56, Point Reyes Station, CA 94956; 415/663-1166; www.oldpointreyesschoolhouse.com.

Point Reyes Station Inn: Dogs are welcome to stay in one room at this recently built inn. It's a first-floor room with a private entrance, its own patio, a fireplace, and a whirlpool tub for two (that would be two humans, lest your water dog gets any ideas). Rates are $135–165. 11591 Highway 1 94956; www.pointreyesstationinn.com.

Seven Grey Foxes Bed and Bath: These two sweet apartments are tucked away on a quiet country road in a cozy neighborhood just outside the village. It's very peaceful here. The two-room apartment (aka the cottage) is very attractive, with huge windows overlooking beautiful gardens, and a Franklin fireplace. The one-room apartment is just a smaller version of the other, and it doesn't have the wall of windows. Rates are $95 for the smaller, $150 for the larger. You'll get the address when you make your reservation. 415/663-9543; www.sevengreyfoxes.com.

Olema

PARKS, BEACHES, AND RECREATION AREAS

5 Limantour Beach

🐾🐾🐾🐾 (See Marin County map on page 420)

This bountiful beach at Point Reyes National Seashore is most people's favorite, so it's often crowded. From the main parking lot, walk a quarter of a mile through tule marsh, grasses and brush, and scattered pines, past Limantour Estero. Dogs are prohibited on the side trails south of the parking lot.

Rules for leashed dogs are clearly marked—a refreshing exception to the obscure and contradictory rules in so many parks. For example, approaching Limantour Beach on the path, you'll see a sign that says dogs are prohibited to your right, allowed to your left. This beach is plenty big, so it's an excellent arrangement that keeps dog owners and dog avoiders equally happy. You may walk with your dog to Santa Maria Beach.

From Highway 1, look for the turnoff to Bear Valley Road, which runs between Olema and Inverness Park. Take Bear Valley from either direction to Limantour Road; turn south on Limantour all the way to the beach. 415/464-5100.

6 Bolinas Ridge Trail

🐾 🐾 🐾 🐾 (See Marin County map on page 420)

This Golden Gate National Recreation Area trail, part of the Bay Area Ridge Trail, is not for sissies—canine or human. It climbs steadily for 11 miles from the Olema end, giving you gorgeous views of Tomales Bay, Bolinas, and the ocean, and ends up at the Bolinas-Fairfax Road below Alpine Lake.

You must keep your dog leashed. One good reason for this is that there are cattle roaming unfenced along the trail. And the trail is very popular with nonsissy mountain bikers. (The trail is wide, but made of dirt and rock.) From the western end, you'll walk through rolling grassland with cypress clumps. Rock outcrops sport crowns of poison oak, so watch it.

You may be able to cope with 11 miles of this, but remember your dog's bare pads and don't overdo it. Also, it isn't much fun for man or beast to walk 11 miles attached by a leash.

Unfortunately, only the Bolinas Ridge Trail is open to dogs; you can't take any of the spur trails going south.

The western end begins about one mile north of Olema on Sir Francis Drake Boulevard. There's roadside parking only. 415/556-0560 or 415/663-1092.

PLACES TO STAY

The Olema Inn: This absolutely enchanting inn is exactly 100 years younger than our nation. It opened on July 4, 1876. That's a long, long time ago by California standards. The inn has obviously been revamped a bit since then, but it still retains the elegant charm of the era. The six beautiful rooms feature antique furniture mingling with up-to-date luxuries such as super-comfortable European Sleepworks mattresses topped with down comforters. (No dogs on the bedding, please.) A fresh breakfast of croissants, local artisan cheeses, fruit, and beverages comes with your stay. Eat it in the dining room or enjoy it in the pretty garden, the lush green grounds, or the big porch out front. Rates are $145–185. 10,000 Sir Francis Drake Boulevard 94950; 415/663-9559; www.theolemainn.com.

Olema Ranch Campground: It's hard to find a campground that's decent for both RVs and tent campers, so we were mighty pleased to find Olema Ranch. RV folks get all the hookups they need, and tenters get a choice of scenic meadow or forest campsites. Many sites come with water. The campground features amenities such as a kitchen, laundry facilities, and a supply store, so we're not exactly talking the big wilderness adventure here. But still, it's a terrific spot to set up a tent with a dog who doesn't mind a little civilized camping. Rates are $23–35. Dogs are $1 extra. 10155 Highway 1, P.O. Box 175, Olema, CA 94950; 415/663-8001 or 800/655-CAMP (800/655-2267); www.olemaranch.com.

Novato

PARKS, BEACHES, AND RECREATION AREAS

🐾 Mount Burdell Open Space Preserve

🐾🐾🐾🐾🐕 (See Marin County map on page 420)

Mount Burdell is the largest of Marin's open space preserves. You'll share it with cattle, but there's plenty of room. There are several miles of trails, including part of the Bay Area Ridge Trail, that wind through its oak-dotted grasslands. (Dogs have to be leashed on trails, but are permitted to run leashless on fire roads here.)

A creek is about one-eighth of a mile up the trail starting at San Andreas Drive, but it's dry in summer. In winter, you might find the preserve's Hidden Lake. In summer, there are lots of foxtails and fire danger is high. No fires are ever allowed. Camping is allowed by permit, but there are no facilities.

From San Marin Drive, turn north on San Andreas Drive. Park on the street. 415/499-6387.

🐾 Miwuk Park

🐾🐾🐾 (See Marin County map on page 420)

This is one of the best city parks we've visited. Dogs must be on leash, but it offers a great combination of dog pleasures and human amenities. Paved paths, good for strollers, wind through pine trees. You will find boccie ball courts, horseshoes, a kids' gym, and a lovely shaded picnic area with grills.

Outside the Museum of the American Indian in this park is an intriguing display of California native plants that the coastal Miwuk used for food, clothing, and shelter.

Best of all for canines, Novato Creek flows deep and 30–40 feet wide (even in summer). A woman we encountered with a golden retriever told us that the muddy bottom can sometimes be soft and treacherous, so keep a close eye on your dog if he goes swimming. The park is at Novato Boulevard and San Miguel Drive. 415/897-4323.

🐾 Indian Tree Open Space Preserve

🐾🐾🐾🐾🐕 (See Marin County map on page 420)

This is a great choice for a hike if the weather is hot: Your ascent to the top (and to terrific views) takes you through cool, shaded woodlands of oak, madrone, and bay. You'll also encounter redwoods and ferns along the way. At the top, the open area isn't parched and sun-baked like so many areas around here in summer: It's often cool and drippy with fog. Jake the dog, who lives in a foggy area of the city and can't take the heat, is very happy here. You needn't leash on fire roads here, but watch out for horses. Leashes are the law on the preserve's trails.

From U.S. 101, exit at San Marin Drive/Atherton Avenue; drive west on San Marin. After San Marin turns into Sutro Avenue, take a right onto Vineyard Road. Park along the dirt county road that begins at the trailhead. 415/499-6387.

🔟 Dogbone Meadow Dog Park

🐾🐾🐾🐾🦮 (See Marin County map on page 420)

Lucky dogs who visit here have two fenced acres of off-leash running room and all the "playground equipment" they could want. The park sports tunnels, ramps, jumps, hanging tires, and other fun agility equipment. Big dogs have big toys, and little dogs have littler toys. Everyone's happy here.

The park is a pretty combination of grass and landscaping bark, with the rolling hills of O'Hair Park in the background. (You can walk your dog on leash in this 100-acre city park.) The volunteers who worked so hard to make this park a reality have planted 35 trees, but it will take many years before they're shade-giving. Until then, people gather under shade structures on hot, sunny days. If your dog is dirty from all the romping around, you can use the dog-wash station near the entrance/exit. The park is at San Marin Drive and Novato Boulevard, on the left as you're heading west. 415/897-4323.

🔟🔟 Deer Island Open Space Preserve

🐾🐾🐾🐾🦮 (See Marin County map on page 420)

This preserve is called an island because it's a high point in the floodplain of the Petaluma River, an oak-crowned hill surrounded by miles of dock and tules. You can easily imagine it surrounded by shallow-water Miwuk canoes slipping through rafts of ducks. The trail is a 1.8-mile loop of gentle ups and downs above ponds and marshy fields. There are some sturdy old oaks among the mixed deciduous groves, and lots of laurels. The trail is partly shaded and bans bikes. Dogs have to be leashed on the trails but are permitted off leash on fire roads here.

From U.S. 101, exit at San Marin Drive/Atherton Avenue; drive east about 1.5 miles and take a right on Olive Avenue, then a left on Deer Island Lane. Park in a small lot at the trailhead, by a small engineering company building. 415/499-6387.

12 Indian Valley Open Space Preserve

😊😊😊😊🐾 (See Marin County map on page 420)

Lots of dogs come here to trot around in leashless ecstasy on the fire road. On hiking trails, they have to trot around in leashed ecstasy. The hiking trails and fire roads are partly sunny, partly shaded by laurels, and much-revered by canines. Take the Waterfall Trail if you love waterfalls and don't mind leashes. You'll be rewarded at the end, unless of course it's dry season.

From U.S. 101, exit at DeLong Avenue and go west on DeLong, which becomes Diablo Avenue. Take a left on Hill Road and a right on Indian Valley Road. Drive all the way to the end; park on this road before you walk left at the spur road marked "Not a Through Street," just south of Old Ranch Road. Cross Arroyo Avichi Creek right at the entrance (dry in summer). 415/499-6387.

13 Lucas Valley Open Space Preserve

😊😊😊😊🐾 (See Marin County map on page 420)

This space of rolling, oak-dotted hills affords great views of Novato and Lucas Valley developments. The summit here is 1,825 feet—the second-highest in Marin. We like to take the scenic Big Rock Trail up to the Big Rock Fire Road. It's a gentle grade for beasts and their people.

The preserve has a dozen access points, most from Lucas Valley and Marinwood. One access point is reached by turning left (north) off Lucas Valley Road on Mount Shasta Drive, followed by a brief right turn on Vogelsang Drive. Park near this dead end and walk in. Keep in mind that all Marin Open Space Preserves require pooches to be on leash except on fire roads. 415/499-6387.

14 Loma Verde Open Space Preserve

😊😊😊🐾 (See Marin County map on page 420)

This rugged open space connects to a couple of others, which makes for a vigorous hike if you and your dog aren't fair of paw. There are two access points to this open space, where dogs are allowed off leash on fire roads. One, south of the Marin Country Club, is a waterless, tree-covered hillside with a fire road. Bikes are allowed, so be sure to keep your leash-free dog under voice control. It's a good road if you like easily reachable high spots; there are fine views of San Pablo Bay. Exit U.S. 101 at Ignacio Boulevard. Go west to Fairway Drive and turn left (south), then left on Alameda de la Loma, then right on Pebble Beach Drive. Access is at the end of Pebble Beach.

The second access point is through the Posada West housing development. From Alameda del Prado, turn south on Posada del Sol. The trail opening is at the end of this street. 415/499-6387.

PLACES TO STAY

Inn Marin: Any lodging that boasts three "dog pot stations" on the property has got to be doggone dog-friendly (and doggone clean, too). These stations are actually just waste cans coupled with plastic bag dispensers, but we appreciate the inn's discreet name for them. The 70-room inn is stylish, clean, and convenient to U.S. 101. It features excellent amenities for people traveling on business (data ports, two-line speaker phones, large desks) and people with disabilities (seven rooms have special features for wheelchairs, and for sight- or hearing-impaired guests). Rates are $99–169. Dogs are $20 total for the first six days, and then $40 per week after. (And get this: "You can have up to four per room!") 250 Entrada Drive 94949; 415/883-5952 or 800/652-6565; www.innmarin.com.

TraveLodge: Rates are $59–99. Dogs are $10 extra. 7600 Redwood Boulevard 94945; 415/892-7500.

Lagunitas

PARKS, BEACHES, AND RECREATION AREAS

15 Samuel P. Taylor State Park

🐾🐾🐾 (See Marin County map on page 420)

An exception among the state parks: Dog access is generous. You can take a dog into the picnic areas, and that's worth doing here. The main picnic area right off Sir Francis Drake Boulevard is cool and often lively with the grinding call of jays. It's an easy place to bring out-of-state visitors who may just want to eat a sandwich, hug a redwood, and go home. The park has hollow trees stretching 20 feet across that you can actually stand inside.

But best of all, you and your dog may spend a whole day on the wide fire trails—roughly 10 miles of them—clearly differentiated on the map you get at the entrance. Dogs may not go on the foot trails, but the fire trails are delightful enough. You can take the bicycle/horse trail from near the entrance along Papermill Creek, rising for four miles to Barnabe Peak, at 1,466 feet. Unfortunately, your dog must stay leashed, but you may actually appreciate that when you see the excellent artist's drawing of a poison oak cluster on the park's map—it's everywhere.

The park has 60 campsites. Sites are $18–20. From April through October, call for reservations: 800/444-7275. The park's day-use fee is $6. The entrance is on Sir Francis Drake Boulevard about two miles west of Lagunitas. 415/488-9897.

PLACES TO EAT

Lagunitas Grocery: Grab a sandwich at the deli inside and feast on it at the outdoor tables with your dog. Thirsty dogs can ask for a bowl of water. 7890 Sir Francis Drake Boulevard; 415/488-4844.

PLACES TO STAY

Samuel P. Taylor State Park: See Samuel P. Taylor State Park, above, for camping information.

Woodacre

PARKS, BEACHES, AND RECREATION AREAS

🟥 Gary Giacomini Open Space Preserve

🐾🐾🐾🐾🐾 (See Marin County map on page 420)

The most recent addition to Marin's open-space lands is this 1,600-acre gem. The preserve stretches for seven miles along the southern edge of the San Geronimo Valley. Stands of old-growth redwoods shade the ferny lower regions of the park. The higher you go, the more grassy it gets. Dogs such as Jake (i.e., male) prefer the trees, but they can get the best of both worlds by following one of the wide fire trails and sniffing out various areas along the way.

Pooches may go leashless on the fire roads but not on the more narrow hiking trails. Come visit before the rest of the doggone world finds out about this hidden treasure.

From U.S. 101, take Sir Francis Drake Boulevard west to San Geronimo Valley Drive and turn left. You can park at the intersection of Redwood Canyon Drive, just west of Woodacre, and begin your hike at the nearby trailhead. This is a fun route to take with your dog, since it brings you from thick forest to the top of the ridge. 415/499-6387.

Fairfax

This small, friendly, progressive town is known as the birthplace of the mountain bike. That's not news that will put a wag in your dog's tail, but this will: Secret Agent Dog, a pooch with impeccable taste, had his person write to tell me that "Fairfax is...one of the most dog-friendly places we've ever lived." Mutt Mitt dispensers are placed strategically through town, and there are two drinking fountains (one by the baseball field, one by town hall) for both humans and dogs. People here love to see dogs with their people; some stores will welcome your dog if it's not busy, but we'll leave that on a case-by-case basis.

PARKS, BEACHES, AND RECREATION AREAS

⓱ Cascade Canyon Open Space Preserve

🐾🐾🐾🐾🐕 (See Marin County map on page 420)

As on all of Marin's open space lands, dogs can cavort about off leash on the fire roads. The fire road here is vehicle-free except for rangers. It's a pleasant walk that leads all the way into the Marin Municipal Water District lands of Mt. Tamalpais. (Once you enter these, you must leash.)

These days, dogs must be leashed on all open-space hiking trails. But the trails are so enticing that they're actually worth trying despite the new leash law. The main trail sticks close to San Anselmo Creek, which is reduced to a dry creek bed in summer. A no-bicycles trail branches off to the right and disappears into the creek; the left branch fords the creek. When the water's high, you may be stopped right here. But in summer, you can walk a long way. Side trails lead you into shady glens of laurel and other deciduous trees, but there's lots of poison oak, too.

The park is at the end of Cascade Drive. There's a Town of Fairfax sign saying "Elliott Nature Preserve," but it's official open space. Please don't park at the end of Cascade. Spread out so the folks who live at the end of Cascade don't get so inundated with dogs. Pooches have been a problem for some residents, whose beautiful flowers and lawns have succumbed to dog feet and pooch poop. Be courteous, and think how you'd feel if the shoe were on the other paw. 415/499-6387.

San Anselmo

San Anselmo Avenue provides you and your mellow pooch a laid-back stroll, and you can both cool your paws in San Anselmo Creek, which runs through town. Your well-behaved pooch can even be off leash, provided she's under voice control. A group has been trying for years to get a dog park at Red Hill Park, behind the Red Hill Shopping Center at the end of Shaw Drive. For more information on this noble effort, call 415/258-4645.

PARKS, BEACHES, AND RECREATION AREAS

⓲ Creek Park

🐾🐾🐾 (See Marin County map on page 420)

San Anselmo Creek runs between Sir Francis Drake Boulevard—which has a wide variety of antique shops—and San Anselmo Avenue, the main shopping street. A bridge connects the two streets.

Creek Park is small, but handy and clean. It's next to a free public lot with some shady spaces. Along the creek banks on the Sir Francis Drake side are picnic tables on a lawn with beautiful willows and maples. Lots of people lounge on the grass. Wooden steps lead down to the water. You'll find plenty of shade in which to picnic or lie on the grass while resting between shopping binges for antiques.

Turn into the parking lot from Sir Francis Drake Boulevard, near "The Hub" (intersection of Sir Francis Drake and Red Hill Avenue). 415/258-4645.

19 Loma Alta Open Space Preserve

🐾🐾🐾🐾🐕 (See Marin County map on page 420)

A little canyon amid bare hills, lined with oaks, bay laurel, and buckeye, this is an exceptional open-space preserve. Shade is plentiful. The trail follows White Hill Creek, which is dry in the summer. Leashes are required on the trails, but obedient dogs can throw their leashes to the wind on the fire road.

You can park at the trailhead at the end of Glen Avenue, a turn north off Sir Francis Drake Boulevard. 415/499-6387.

20 Memorial Park

🐾🐾🐾🐕 (See Marin County map on page 420)

This pleasant and popular city park has tennis courts, three baseball diamonds, and a children's play area. Next to the diamonds is a dog-exercise area, where leash-free dogs romp joyfully, fetching, chasing Frisbees, or socializing. Even a creek runs nearby. There's a hitch—dogs can be off leash only before 8 A.M. and from one hour before sunset to, well, sunset. The park is at Veterans Place, a quick jog east from San Francisco Boulevard. 415/258-4645.

21 Sorich Ranch Park

🐾🐾🐾🐾🐕 (See Marin County map on page 420)

The biggest and by far the wildest city park in San Anselmo is Sorich Ranch Park, an undeveloped open space soaring to a ridge top from which you can see a distant make-believe San Francisco skyline across the bay. From the very top of the ridge, you also can see Mt. Tamalpais and most of San Rafael, including the one-of-a-kind turquoise and salmon Marin County Civic Center, designed by Frank Lloyd Wright. (Some Marinites are glad there's only one.)

The entrance from the San Anselmo side is at the end of San Francisco Boulevard, and the path is pretty much straight up. But if you aren't up to a 10-minute puffing ascent, you can just stroll in the meadows at the bottom. No leash is required, and the park is uncrowded and often pleasantly breezy. No water is available, and it can be scorching in summer. 415/258-4645.

PLACES TO EAT

Bubba's Diner: If you found an eatery by this name in many other towns, you might be inclined to stride by with nary a glance, lest you absorb grease and saturated fat just by looking at it. But being that this Bubba's Diner is in San

Anselmo, grease is not the main ingredient of most dishes, and the saturated fat is at least upscale saturated fat.

Bubba's is a really fun, unpretentious place to bring a dog for some extra-tasty American-style eats. The cheery owner, Beth, likes to see well-behaved dogs dining at the two awning-shaded tables and benches in front of the restaurant. But she warns people not to tie dogs to the benches, lest the dog drag away the bench. (One small pooch actually went exploring the neighborhood, pulling the hefty pine bench behind him!) Take Beth's advice and hook your dog to the pay phone if you're dining alone and need to run in to place your order.

Choose from dozens of yummy dishes here. The food varies from healthful and delicious (oyster salad, grilled salmon with asparagus and sautéed spinach) to decadent and delicious (pot roast, fried chicken, burgers, mashed potato pancakes). If you're pining for some fried green tomatoes, look no further. Bubba's is famous for them. Thirsty doggies can get water here. 566 San Anselmo Avenue; 415/459-6862.

San Rafael

PARKS, BEACHES, AND RECREATION AREAS

We can't officially recommend Red Hill Park, behind the Red Hill Shopping center, because it's still not a real dog park. One of these days.... Meanwhile, there are plenty of other places for pooch paws to be happy.

22 Terra Linda–Sleepy Hollow Divide Open Space Preserve

😺😺😺😺 🐕 (See Marin County map on page 420)

This ridgeline preserve has many entrances, but generally the best are the highest on the ridge. We'll describe the one that starts you at a good high point, so that you don't have to climb. From the entrance at the end of Ridgewood Drive, you can walk into Sorich Ranch Park (see the San Anselmo section).

From this ridge, you can see the city of San Rafael, U.S. 101, the wonderful turquoise-roofed Marin County Civic Center, the bay, and the hills of Solano County. No leash is necessary on fire roads, unless you're worried about your dog's tangling with deer. But pooches must be leashed on trails.

Park near the very end of Ridgewood Drive. The entrance is unmarked, and you have to step over a low locked gate. 415/499-6387.

23 Field of Dogs

😺😺😺😺 🐕 (See Marin County map on page 420)

We love the name, love the park. The people behind Field of Dogs worked really hard to make the park a reality. It took about six years. It's not only real now, but it's a great place to take a dog for off-leash exercise.

The one-acre park has little trees, big trees, a double-gated entry, benches, picnic tables, poop bags, and very nice park-goers—of both the pooch and people variety. Some trees are in the middle of the park, and we've heard about more than one head-on canine collision with a tree during chase games. After the swirling stars and tweeting birds wear off, the dogs are just fine.

The park is behind the civic center, at 3540 Civic Center Drive. It's an easy jaunt from U.S. 101. Exit U.S. 101 and continue east to Civic Center Drive, which is the first light.Turn left and the park will be on your right just past the post office and firehouse. 415/485-3333.

24 John F. McInnis County Park

🐾🐾🐾🐕 (See Marin County map on page 420)

This is an all-around, got-everything park for people. Among its riches are two softball fields, two soccer fields, tennis courts, a picnic area, a scale-model car track, a nine-hole golf course, miniature golf, batting cages, and a dirt creekside nature trail.

Best of all for trustworthy dogs, they can be off leash, so long as they're under verbal command and out of the golf course. This park isn't particularly pretty, but it's very utilitarian. From U.S. 101, exit at Smith Ranch Road. 415/499-6387.

25 San Pedro Mountain Open Space Preserve

🐾🐾🐾🐾🐕 (See Marin County map on page 420)

A narrow footpath rises moderately but inexorably upward through a madrone forest. But if you make it up far enough, you'll be rewarded with terrific views of the bay and Marin's peaks. Deer are plentiful, so it's kind to leash your dog if you don't trust him completely to stay by your side.

Park at the entrance at the end of Woodoaks Drive, a short street off North Point San Pedro Road just north of the Jewish Community Center of Marin. 415/499-6387.

26 Santa Margarita Island Open Space Preserve

🐾🐾🐾 (See Marin County map on page 420)

What a wonderful, secret place this is. Gallinas Creek, fortified by levees, is lined with rickety piers and small boats, like a bit of the Delta. You can cross to a tiny island via a footbridge and climb the hill you'll find here, covered with oaks and boulders, or walk around the edge on a dirt path. Watch for poison oak on the hill. Though of course it isn't true, you can feel as if no one has been here before you except Coast Miwuks. Dogs are supposed to be leashed at this open space.

From North Point San Pedro Road, turn west on Meadow Drive. Where it ends, at the western end of Vendola Drive, is the footbridge. You can park on the street. Carry water if you plan to stay long. 415/499-6387.

27 Santa Venetia Marsh Open Space Preserve

🐾🐾🐾🐾 (See Marin County map on page 420)

Dogs are very lucky to be able to visit this saltwater marsh. Only leashed pooches on their best behavior should come here, because the preserve is home to an endangered bird, the California clapper rail. Keep your eyes peeled: It looks like a chicken (and apparently tastes something like one, too—it was heavily hunted during the Gold Rush, when its meat was considered a delightful delicacy), but it has a long beak.

Mmm, doggy, the scents can be mighty strong here sometimes. They're so doggone nose-flaring good your dog may not even notice he's wearing a leash. You may not feel the same about the odor, but hey, just keep saying to yourself "it's a natural smell."

It's cool and breezy here, but gentler than any San Francisco Bay shore park. The grasses and pickleweed make a pretty mixture of colors, and swallows dart above the ground hunting insects.

Vendola Drive has two distinct parts, and you can get to the marsh from the end of either. At the western end of the creekside segment of Vendola, at the corner of Meadow Drive, is a footbridge leading to Santa Margarita Island (see above). 415/499-6387.

28 Boyd Park

🐾🐾 (See Marin County map on page 420)

This is not a very doggy park, until you drive past the Dollar mansion (now the Falkirk Community Cultural Center) into the hills on Robert Dollar Scenic Drive to the undeveloped section. The only parking is at a turnout off the drive, but at that spot, the drive becomes a dirt fire trail, closed to autos, that mounts the ridgecrest in a steady uphill climb through brush, oak, and madrone.

Leash your pup and start walking. You'll get a breathtaking view of the Richmond–San Rafael Bridge, the Bay Bridge, the Oakland skyline, and Mt. Tam. Robert Dollar Scenic Drive begins at the end of Laurel Place. 415/485-3333.

29 China Camp State Park

🐾🐾🐾 (See Marin County map on page 420)

You shouldn't miss a drive through this lovely park, although it's not terribly hospitable to dogs except at Village Beach, the site of the 1890s Chinese fishing village for which the park is named. As you drive in, you'll see a rare piece of bay, marsh, and oak-covered hills as the Miwuks saw it. The hills, like islands, rise from salt-marsh seas of pickleweed and cordgrass. You'll see the "No Dogs" symbol at every trailhead, in case you're tempted. However, with your dog you may visit any of three picnic grounds on the way, via North Point

San Pedro Road. Buckeye Point and Weber Point both have tables in shade or sun overlooking San Pablo Bay, mudflats at low tide, and the hills beyond the bay. Bullhead Flat lets you get right next to the water, but there's no shade at the tables.

Watch for the sign to China Camp Village, a left turn into a lot, where there's some shade. You'll see the rickety old pier and the wood-and-tin village. Park, leash your dog, and walk down to the village and the beach. On weekdays, this park is much less crowded. There are more picnic tables overlooking the water by the parking lot, an interpretive exhibit and, on weekends, a refreshment stand serving shrimp, crab, and beer. You can eat at picnic tables right on the beach—small, but pleasantly sheltered by hillsides, with gentle surf.

Swimming is encouraged here, and it's often warm enough. Derelict fishing boats and shacks are preserved on the beach. You can walk all the way to a rocky point at the south end, but watch out for the luxuriant poison oak in the brush along the beach. You may occasionally find broken glass.

There are 31 primitive walk-in campsites here. As in all state parks, dogs must always be leashed or confined to your tent. Sites are $15–20. To reserve (recommended April–October), call 800/444-7275. From U.S. 101, take the North Point San Pedro Road exit and follow it all the way into the park. (Don't go near McNears Beach County Park just south of China Camp. Dogs are strictly forbidden.) 415/456-0766.

PLACES TO EAT

Cento Stelle: We really enjoy eating at Cento Stelle, which in Italian means 100 stars. Besides being in love with the name, we're also in love with the very good Italian food. Dine with dog at the four sidewalk tables. 901 Lincoln Avenue; 415/485-4422.

Phyllis' Giant Burgers: Dogs dig this drive-in burger joint. Order your meat-eater one of the giant burgers. Or if your pooch is in a no-beef mode, try a veggie burger. 2202 4th Street; 415/456-0866.

Shaky Grounds: The shaky grounds here refer to coffee, not earthquakes (we think). If coffee isn't your cup of tea, you can order pastries, smoothies, soups, salads, and sandwiches. 1800 4th Street; 415/256-2420.

PLACES TO STAY

China Camp State Park: See China Camp State Park, above, for camping information.

Villa Inn: This place recently got much more dog-friendly: There are no more dog fees, and dogs don't have to be shrimps to stay here; any size dog is welcome. Rates are $69–125. 1600 Lincoln Avenue 94901; 415/456-4975 or 888/845-5246.

Ross

PARKS, BEACHES, AND RECREATION AREAS

🐾 Natalie Coffin Greene Park

🐾🐾🐾 (See Marin County map on page 420)

Leashed dogs are welcome at this enchanted mixed forest of redwood and deciduous trees. The picnic area has an old-fashioned shelter built of logs and stone.

The park borders generic Marin Municipal Water District land, and from the park, you can pick up the wide cinder fire road leading to Phoenix Lake, a five-minute walk. Bikers, hikers, and leashed dogs are all welcome on this road, but the lake is a reservoir, so no body contact is allowed—for man or beast.

The road continues, depending how far you want to walk, to Lagunitas Lake, Bon Tempe Lake, Alpine Lake, and Kent Lake. (No swimming in any of them; sorry, dogs.) Combined, the water district offers 94 miles of road and 44 miles of trail in this area, meandering through hillsides, densely forested with pine, oak, madrone, and a variety of other trees. For a trail map, send a self-addressed, stamped envelope to Sky Oaks Ranger Station, P.O. Box 865, Fairfax, CA 94978, Attention: Trail Map.

At the corner of Sir Francis Drake Boulevard and Lagunitas Road, go west on Lagunitas all the way to the end, past the country club. You'll find a parking lot and some portable toilets. 415/453-1453.

Kentfield

PARKS, BEACHES, AND RECREATION AREAS

🐾 Baltimore Canyon Open Space Preserve

🐾🐾🐾🐾🐾 (See Marin County map on page 420)

If you don't like heat, this 175-acre open space is a fine place to come for a summer stroll. You have less chance of getting roasty-toasty here than at many other nearby parks: The big oaks, madrones, bays, firs, and even redwoods tend to keep things cool in the canyon. It even has a year-round creek and a seasonal 30-foot waterfall. It's worth the hike to the end of the canyon to see this cascade.

From this open space you have good access to a lot of fire roads through the ridges connecting with Mt. Tamalpais and water-district lands. Leashes aren't required on the fire roads, but bikes are also allowed on these trails, so be careful. Dogs must be leashed on regular hiking trails.

Two access points are at the ends of Crown Road and Evergreen Drive. 415/499-6387.

Larkspur

PARKS, BEACHES, AND RECREATION AREAS

🐾 Blithedale Summit Open Space Preserve

🐾🐾🐾🐾🐕 (See Marin County map on page 420)

The access point at the end of Madrone Avenue—the north end of this open space—is a delightful walk in hot weather, through cool redwoods that let some light filter through. This isn't one of those really dark, drippy canyons; you're at a medium-high altitude on the slopes of Mt. Tamalpais. The trail follows Larkspur Creek, which retains some pools in summer. Cross the footbridge and follow the slightly rough foot trail. Unfortunately, leashes are now the law on these trails. But you can let your dog off his leash once you hit the fire road.

The drive up narrow Madrone Avenue is an adventure in itself; redwoods grow right in the street. According to a sign at the entrance, the part of this space belonging to the city of Larkspur requires dogs to be leashed. 415/499-6387.

🐾 Creekside Park

🐾🐾🐾 (See Marin County map on page 420)

This is the small, attractive park where the multipurpose Bon Air Path starts. The 1.8-mile paved trail goes from Bon Air Road, following Corte Madera Creek, westward to the town of Ross and eastward to the Larkspur Landing shopping center, near the ferry terminal. There are lots of paths by Corte Madera Creek, and a kids' gym. You must leash your dog and be sure to keep him out of marshy areas. A bulletin board displays excellent bike-trail maps and descriptions of local flora and fauna.

From Sir Francis Drake Boulevard, turn south on Bon Air Road; from Magnolia Drive, turn north. The park entrance is across from Marin General Hospital. You can get more information on the county's bike trails from the Bicycle Trails Council of Marin at 415/456-7512. For more park information, call 415/499-6387.

🐾 Canine Commons

🐾🐾🐾🐕 (See Marin County map on page 420)

Canine Commons is popular with common canines. It isn't a very big dog park, but it was the first in Marin, opening its doggy gates in 1989. That's ancient history in the annals of dog parkdom. It's a basic dog park, with water, poop bags, and tennis balls.

Canine Commons is set within Piper Park, where you can play or watch softball, volleyball, tennis, and even cricket. Outside Canine Commons, dogs must be leashed. The park is between Doherty Drive and Corte Madera Creek. Canine Commons is at the west end of the park. Note: At press time, the dog park was closed while some work was being done there. There's a chance it may end up being moved to a new location. (Jake Dog says he hopes not many dogs are in it on moving day. That could get pretty interesting for the movers.) 415/927-5110.

PLACES TO EAT

The Left Bank: Your dog doesn't have to be a poodle to enjoy dining at this terrific French restaurant. Because it's a French place, management knows that dogs and restaurants really do mix. But because they're in America, they have to abide by local health regulations and keep doggies from dining inside. That's OK, though, because there are plenty of outside tables. When it's crowded, managers ask that you tie your dog to the railing that surrounds the outdoor area. You can still dine right beside your pooch. Thirsty pooches can get a bowl of water. 507 Magnolia Avenue; 415/927-3331.

Marin Brewing Company: The brewery makes its own beer here, and it's really good. Swig some with your dog and your sandwich at the nine outdoor tables. 1809 Larkspur Circle; 415/461-4677.

Bolinas

Bolinas is famous for trying to hide from curious visitors—thereby drawing hordes of them. They keep coming, even though town citizens regularly take down the turnoff sign on Highway 1. So if you're coming from the east (San Francisco area), turn left at the unmarked road where Bolinas Lagoon ends. If you're coming from the west, turn right where the lagoon begins.

Sometimes it seems as if half the inhabitants of Bolinas are dogs, most of them black. They stand guard outside bars, curl at shop owners' feet, snooze in the middle of the road. You'll find no city hall in Bolinas, an unincorporated area, and no chamber of commerce. Dogs are always welcome here, but cars, horses, bicycles, and too many unleashed dogs compete for space. Be thoughtful and keep your pooch leashed in town.

PARKS, BEACHES, AND RECREATION AREAS

Alas, dogs are no longer officially allowed on beautiful Agate Beach.

35 Bolinas Beach

🐾🐾🐾🐾 (See Marin County map on page 420)

At the end of the main street, Wharf Road, is a sand-and-pebble beach at the foot of a bluff. Dogs are free to run off leash. But watch for horses—with riders and without—thundering past without warning. It's animal anarchy here, and it's not the cleanest beach in Marin. We give it points for fun, though. 415/499-6387.

PLACES TO EAT

Coast Cafe: This is a very dog-friendly spot for breakfast, lunch, and dinner, beer, wine, and ice cream. "Dogs are great!" has been the mantra of more than one waiter we've met here through the years. Dogs can dine with you at the street tables and sometimes the patio tables (ask first). A bowl of water is available on request, and in the morning, a coffee kiosk sells dog biscuits. Yum! 46 Wharf Road; 415/868-2298.

Stinson Beach

It's fun to poke around Stinson, which is swarming with surfers and tourists on beautiful days. You'll find a relaxed attitude toward dogs at the outdoor snack-shop tables. Bolinas Lagoon, stretching along Highway 1 between Stinson Beach and Bolinas, is tempting but environmentally fragile, so you should picnic along the water only if your dog is controllable. You'll also be taking a chance with muddy paws in your car. Don't go near Audubon Canyon Ranch, where herons and egrets nest.

PARKS, BEACHES, AND RECREATION AREAS

3 6 Stinson Beach ("Dog Beach")

🐾🐾🐾🐾 (See Marin County map on page 420)

Highway 1 to Stinson and Bolinas is worth the curves you'll negotiate. Don't be in a hurry. On sunny weekends, traffic will be heavy. Try it on a foggy day—it's otherworldly. Anyway, dogs often don't care whether or not the sun is shining.

Before setting out, we asked around. "Go to Stinson," said a friend. "There are dogs everywhere." "Dogs aren't allowed on Stinson Beach," said a Golden Gate National Recreation Area ranger. "Stinson is swarming with dogs," said another friend.

A kind woman in the Muir Woods bookstore solved the mystery. "No dogs on Stinson," she said sternly, "but there's this little part at the north end that isn't Stinson. We call it 'Dog Beach.'"

Indeed, the county-managed stretch where private houses are built at the north end does allow dogs on leash. This is itself a bit of a contradiction, because as you walk along with your obediently leashed dog, dogs who live in the houses lining the county stretch, and who don't have to wear leashes, come prancing out like the local law enforcement to check out the new kid. Leashed and leashless, dogs are indeed everywhere at Stinson. It's merry and there's plenty of room for them.

You and your dog will be equally happy on Stinson Beach, with its backdrop of low hills and lining of dunes. Keep the dog off the dunes where they're roped off, being "repaired" by the forces of nature. Dogs are allowed in Stinson Beach's picnic area by Eskoot Creek, a pretty setting redolent with tantalizing smells.

Take the beach turnoff from Highway 1. Turn right at the parking lot and park at the far north end. Walk right by the sign that says, "No Pets on Beach"—you can't avoid it—and turn right. Where the houses start is the county beach. You'll see a sign dividing the two jurisdictions saying, "End of Guarded Beach." 415/868-0942.

PLACES TO STAY

Beachtime Beach House: This wonderful three-bedroom vacation rental puts the "Oh!!!" in ocean views. It's right on the dog-friendly beach, with sand truly just in front of the house. (The owners try to keep it there, and not inside, which is why they have an outdoor shower and hose, plus slate tile floors and hardwood floors—no carpeting.) It's an airy, attractive house, with three decks, a hot tub on the back deck, a great fireplace stove in the living room, and windows with views that are beyond droolworthy. Rates are $280 per night, and $1,860–2,260 weekly. There's a $60 cleaning fee for the length of your stay. During winter you can rent the house on a monthly basis for a greatly reduced price. You'll get the address when you book the house. 415/383-7870; www.beachtime.org.

Redwoods Haus Bed and Breakfast: It's hard to categorize this place. It's funky, it's a little odd, it's clean, it's super-friendly, it's comfy, and it's cheap compared to most other West Marin lodgings. A very masculine boxer friend of Jake (a boxer dog, not the Muhammad Ali variety) stayed in what's called The Pink Room. With its pink bedspread, pink floral curtains, pink lamp, and other pink decorative touches and white girly furniture, it looks rather dollhousey. He didn't mind a bit, mostly because his people promised not to let anyone know that he stayed there. "Fergus would be so embarrassed," says Denise, his person. (Oops...Sorry, Fergus.)

Jake's favorite of the four guestrooms is The Crows Nest, which has soft but more masculine hues than The Pink Room, and sports excellent ocean views. It's the biggest room, too, with a queen bed, a day bed, and a queen futon.

Here's an example of the funky nature of the Redwoods Haus: "All rooms come with...access to our piano, acoustic guitars, video library, charcoal barbecue, biergarten, and buffet area," its literature announces. That's quite a combination of amenities. It continues, "Cats are OK—purrr. Dogs are OK—wooof."

Rooms come with breakfast. It's not gourmet, but with eggs, ham, cereal, fruit, bread, and beverages, it hits the spot. Rates are $55–165. The Redwood Haus is at 1 Belvedere Street (at Highway 1) 94970; 415/868-9828; www.stinson-beach.com.

Mill Valley

PARKS, BEACHES, AND RECREATION AREAS

🐾🐾 Mount Tamalpais State Park

🐾🐾🐾 (See Marin County map on page 420)

Generally, dogs are restricted to paved roads here. But dogs may stay in one of the campgrounds, and there are also a few spots near the summit where you can take your dog. The views from here are something you'll certainly appreciate on a clear day.

Stop for lunch at the Bootjack Picnic Area, west of the Mountain Home Inn on Panoramic Highway and about a quarter mile east of the turnoff to the summit, Pantoll Road. The tables are attractively sited on the hillside under oak trees. This picnic ground is an access point for the Bootjack Trail and Matt Davis Trail. The Matt Davis Trail is off-limits, but you and your dog may—howl-elujah!—use the 100 feet of Bootjack Trail that leads you into Marin Municipal Water District land, where leashed dogs are allowed. (You must travel north on the Bootjack Trail, though, not south; it's all state park in that direction.)

Heading northward, you can hook up with the Old Stage Fire Road and the Old Railroad Grade Fire Road, which are water district roads going almost the whole distance to the summit. You can also enter the Old Stage Fire Road right across from the Pantoll Ranger Station, at the intersection of Panoramic Highway and Pantoll Road. Pooches have special permission to cross the 100 feet or so of state park trail approaching water district trail.

The Bootjack Picnic Area parking lot charges $6 to park. (Once you pay in any state park lot, your receipt is good for any other spot that you hit that day.) The park has 16 developed walk-in campsites that allow dogs. They're at the Pantoll Station Campground. Sites are $15. All sites are first-come, first-served. 415/388-2070.

🐾🐾 Mount Tamalpais Summit

🐾🐾🐾 (See Marin County map on page 420)

The summit of Mt. Tam is worth the $6 fee that you're charged merely to drive here. But in addition to appreciating the magnificent views, you may also take your dog on one trail up here.

You'll find a small refreshment stand, restrooms, a visitor center, and viewing platforms. On clear days, you can see nine counties, whether you want to or not. In summer, white fingers of fog obscure a good part of your view as they creep between the "knuckles" of Marin's ridges.

It's too bad if your leashed dog doesn't care about views. But he will take eagerly to the smoothly paved Verna Dunshee Trail, about one mile long, running almost level around the summit. About three-quarters of this trail is also wheelchair-accessible.

From U.S. 101, take the Stinson Beach/Highway 1 exit. Follow Highway 1 to Panoramic Highway, which will be a right turn. Continue on Panoramic to the right turnoff to Pantoll Road; Pantoll soon becomes East Ridgecrest Road and goes to the summit, and then loops back for your trip down. 415/945-1455.

🐾🐾 Mount Tamalpais–Marin Municipal Water District Land

🐾🐾🐾 (See Marin County map on page 420)

Your very best bet for a dog walk high on the mountain is to find one of the water district fire roads near the summit. Your dog must be leashed, but at least she can go on the trails with you, and you both can experience the greenness of this wonderful mountain. At this elevation, the green comes from chaparral, pine, and madrone.

Just below the summit on East Ridgecrest Boulevard, watch for the water district's gate and sign. This is the Old Railroad Grade Fire Road, which descends 1,785 feet from the entry point just west of the summit. On the way it intersects Old Stage Fire Road, then emerges at the Bootjack Picnic Area. En route, you'll cross three creeks. For obvious reasons, you'll be happier in warm weather taking this road down, not up; get someone to meet you in a car at the Bootjack Picnic Area.

Another spot to pick up a water district trail is off Panoramic Highway just west of the Mountain Home Inn. Look for the Marin Municipal Water District sign by the fire station. Park at the state park parking lot west of Mountain Home Inn and walk east along this fire road, called Gravity Car Road (though it's unmarked), through mixed pines, redwoods, fir, madrone, and scrub. Keep your eyes open for fast-moving mountain bikes. 415/945-1400.

🐾 Old Mill Park

🐾🐾🐾 (See Marin County map on page 420)

Refresh your dog under cool redwoods right in the town of Mill Valley. The old mill, built in 1834, was recently restored. A wooden bridge over Old Mill Creek leads to well-maintained paths that run along the creek. The creek is dog-accessible, though pooches are supposed to be leashed.

One picnic table here sits within the hugest "fairy ring" we've ever seen— 40 feet across. Boy dogs like to imagine the size of the mother tree whose stump engendered this ring of saplings. The park is on Throckmorton Avenue at Olive Street, near the public library. 415/383-1370.

🐾 Camino Alto Open Space Preserve

🐾🐾🐾🐕 (See Marin County map on page 420)

In this accessible open space, your dog may run free on a wide fire trail along a ridge connecting with Mt. Tamalpais. You'll walk through bay laurels, madrones, and chaparral, looking down on soaring vultures and the bay, Highway 1, the hills, and the headlands. A small imperfection is that you can hear the whoosh of traffic. Just pretend it's the wind. Dogs must be leashed on the regular hiking trails here. Park at the end of Escalon Drive, just west of Camino Alto. 415/499-6387.

42 Bayfront Park

🐾🐾🐾🐾 🐕 (See Marin County map on page 420)

This good-looking park is well designed for every kind of family activity and for dogs. It has an exercise course, lawns are green and silky, and picnic areas are clean and attractive. The multiuse trails for bicycles, strollers, and whatnot may be used only by leashed dogs (there are bikes galore). But here's the canine payoff: It has a special dog run next to an estuary, where dogs are free to dip their paws.

The dog-use area starts where you see the signs and all the other dogs. Beware, owners of escape artists: The area is a big three acres, but it's not fenced. No scoops or water are furnished, but the Richardson Bay Estuary is right there to jump into.

At the end of the run there's even a marsh that dogs can explore, if you're willing to put a very mucky friend back into the car with you. Luckily, this marsh is all organic muck, free from the dangerous trash that fills many unprotected bay marshes.

For a dog park, this one offers an unparalleled view of Mt. Tam. Horses and bikes pass by harmlessly on their own separate trail in the foreground, and mockingbirds sing in the bushes.

There had been a heap o' controversy over whether this should continue to be a dog-run area. Some people thought soccer players of the young human persuasion should have the area, and that dogs should have to be leashed. But hooray, the dogs won! The city council approved a permanent dog run here. That's thanks to the work of a magnificent, high-energy group called Park People and Dogs. If you want to find out how you can help Park People and Dogs in its continuing efforts to make this park dog heaven, call Barbara Berlenbach at 415/388-0071. Unfortunately, Barbara tells us that there's been more friction between dog people and nondog people of late. She implores dog-park users to keep dogs on leash until they get to the off-leash area, and to be certain to scoop the poop.

The parking lot is on Sycamore Avenue, just after you cross Camino Alto, next to the wastewater treatment plant. Keep your dog leashed near the steepsided sewage ponds; dogs have drowned in them. Also, be sure to keep your dog leashed until you've reached the grassy dog-run area; there's a $50 ticket if you're caught unleashed. 415/383-1370.

PLACES TO STAY

Mount Tamalpais State Park: See Mount Tamalpais State Park, above, for camping information.

Corte Madera

Dogs are banned from all parks here. But mope not, pooches, because at least you get to munch on café cuisine.

PLACES TO EAT

Book Passage Cafe: Whether your dog is illiterate or erudite, he's welcome to join you at the many shaded tables outside this bookstore/café. You can dine on sandwiches, muffins, and a few assorted hot entrées, as well as tasty coffees and healthful smoothies. Dogs aren't allowed inside the bookstore, so if you want to peruse (and who wouldn't—the bookstore is one of the best we've seen), bring a friend and take turns dog-sitting. 51 Tamal Vista Boulevard; 415/927-1503.

Twin Cities Market: Pick up a fresh deli sandwich (with your dog's favorite cold cuts, of course) and eat it with your pooch at the three tables outside. It's casual, but that's how most dogs like it. 118 Corte Madera Avenue; 415/924-7372.

PLACES TO STAY

Marin Suites Hotel: The guest accommodations here are mostly of the spacious suite variety, which works out great when traveling with a dog. (Too bad your dog has to be small to stay here. The rule is 20 pounds or less. Spacious suites call for spacious dogs, in my opinion.) You'll get a fully equipped kitchen and separate living room and bedroom. Traditional hotel rooms, with kitchenettes, are also available. Rates are $154–204. Dogs are $10 extra. 45 Tamal Vista Boulevard 94925; 415/924-3608 or 800/362-3372; www.marinsuites.com.

Tiburon

The town of Tiburon is almost too Disneyland-perfect, with its green lawns and fountains, brick sidewalks, and lack of smells. On a sunny day you can't beat the clean, safe street atmosphere for eating and strolling. Dogs, of course, must be as polite and well behaved as their owners. Tiburon did a good job of planning for parking: There's almost none except for one large lot with reasonable prices, which means that cars aren't driving around searching for a spot. Just give up and park there.

PARKS, BEACHES, AND RECREATION AREAS

43 Richardson Bay Park

🐾🐾🐾 (See Marin County map on page 420)

Generally known as the Tiburon Bike Path, this is a terrific multiuse park, unusual because it can be safely enjoyed by both bicyclists and dogs. It stretches two-thirds the length of Tiburon's peninsula and has parking at both ends. The larger lot is at the northern end. A dirt road, Brunini Way (no vehicles), leads into the park at the north end. You'll find a quiet, natural bay shoreline with a bit of marsh. There's some flotsam and jetsam, but only the highest quality, of course.

Keep walking and you'll enter McKegney Green, the wide bike path that runs for two miles along Tiburon Boulevard toward downtown. (It doesn't go all the way, though.) Your dog must be leashed. The path, marked for running trainers, swings past benches overlooking the bay and a kids' jungle gym.

Soon the path splits and goes past both sides of a stretch of soccer fields, fenced wildlife ponds (no dogs), and a parcourse fitness trail. You can take your dog on either side, but be aware that bicyclists use both. You'll also share this path, on a fair weekend day, with roller skaters and parents pushing strollers. On the green are sunbathers and kite fliers.

The view: Mt. Tamalpais and Belvedere, with the Bay Bridge, San Francisco, and the Golden Gate Bridge peeking out from behind. Bring a jacket—it can be breezy here—and carry water for your dog if you're walking far. The only fountains are for people. Going toward town on Tiburon Boulevard, turn right at the sign that says Blackie's Pasture Road. It leads to the parking lot. 415/435-7373.

PLACES TO EAT

Boudins Bakery: Dine on delectable baked goods and café food at the four outdoor tables here. Dogs get water. 221 Main Street; 415/913-1849.

  Paradise Hamburgers and Ice Cream: This place furnishes bike racks and lots of outdoor tables. There's always a Fido bowl of water outside the door. The owners adore dogs and occasionally give a pooch a special treat. 1694 Tiburon Boulevard; 415/435-8823.

Muir Beach

PARKS, BEACHES, AND RECREATION AREAS

44 Muir Beach

🐾🐾🐾🐾 (See Marin County map on page 420)

This beach is small, but a real gem, with rugged sand dunes spotted with plants, a parking lot and large picnic area, a small lagoon with tules, and its share of wind. Redwood Creek empties into the ocean here.

  You can reach Muir Beach the long way, hiking about five miles from the Marin Headlands Visitors Center (see Rodeo Beach and Lagoon in the Sausalito section), or the easy way, via Highway 1. From Highway 1, watch for the turnoff for the beach. 415/388-2596.

Sausalito

Even if you live here, you should play tourist and stroll around Sausalito's harbor in the brilliant sea light (or luminous sea fog). On weekends, it's especially pleasant early in the day, before the ferries disgorge their passengers. The city's attitude toward dogs is relaxed. It's the perfect place to stop and sniff around for awhile. If you have your sea legs, board the Blue and Gold Fleet's ferry. You and your dog can go from Sausalito to San Francisco for a mere $7.25. That's cheaper than admission to a bad movie, and there are no commercials.

PARKS, BEACHES, AND RECREATION AREAS

45 Dunphy Park

🐾🐾🐾 (See Marin County map on page 420)

This is a small but accessible park by the bay, and it comes complete with grass, willows, picnic tables, and a volleyball court. Best of all, there's a small beach, and canine swimming is fine. You can watch sailing and sailboarding from here, too. Dogs officially must be on leash. The parking lot is at Bridgeway and Bee Streets. 415/289-4100.

DIVERSION

Seize the Bay from Sausalito: Ahoy, dogs, if you love the Bay, then *carpe diem* and take a ride on a **Blue and Gold Fleet** ferry. Lucky dogs get to sail from Sausalito to San Francisco and Tiburon. The one-way fare from Sausalito to San Francisco is $7.25. Dogs pay nothing. The Sausalito ferry dock is at the foot of El Portal, east of Bridgeway. Phone 415/705-8200 for schedules and more information, or 415/705-5555 for tickets; www.blueandgoldfleet.com.

46 Remington Dog Park

🐾🐾🐾🐾🐕 (See Marin County map on page 420)

Your leash-free dog can exercise his paws while you both exercise your social skills at this delightful park. Remington Park is named after the dog whose owner, Dianne Chute, helped raise the money to put the park together a few years back. It's more than an acre, all fenced, on a grassy slope with trees. Dogs have the time of their lives tearing around chasing each other, and humans have a great time chatting. The park comes complete with an informative bulletin board, a leash rack, benches, poop bags, and water. It even has a tent you can hide under in foul weather! Everything is cozy here.

Best of all, on Friday evening, about 100 human patrons and their dogs gather for cocktail hour, with wine, cheese, bread, and of course, doggy treats. It sounds very Marin, but it's really just very civilized. On a recent summer evening, the park was host to a Mexican happy hour. Margaritas, chips, and salsa made the atmosphere even more festive than the usual Friday night gathering.

From the day it was finished, Remington and his dog friends have made terrific use of this place. "It's the social hub of Sausalito," says cartoonist Phil Frank, "where the elite with four feet meet." What a boon to freedom-loving Sausalito dogs, who otherwise must be leashed everywhere in town.

From U.S. 101, take the Sausalito/Marin City exit, driving west to Bridgeway. Turn right on Bridgeway and drive south the equivalent of a long city block. Turn right at Ebbtide Avenue and park in the large lot at the end of Ebbtide.

47 Rodeo Beach and Lagoon

🐾🐾🐾🐾 (See Marin County map on page 420)

Rodeo Beach is small but majestic, made of the dark sand common in Marin. Large rocks on shore are covered with "whitewash," birders' polite name for guano. Voice-controlled dogs used to be able to go off leash here, but no more. Leashes are now mandatory. Water dogs enjoy this beach, but letting your dog swim in Marin County surf is always risky—currents are strong, and trying to rescue a dog who is being swept away is to risk your own life. With that mandatory leash, he probably won't be doing the pooch paddle anyway. Don't turn your back on the surf here. Especially in winter, a "sneaker" wave can sweep you and your dog away.

If your dog promises not to bark and disturb wildlife, he can join you on an interesting walk around Rodeo Lagoon. The lagoon is lined with tules and pickleweed. Ocean water splashes into the lagoon in winter and rainfall swells it until it overflows, continually mixing salt and fresh water. Birds love this fecund lagoon. It can be almost too much for a bird dog to take. An attractive wooden walkway leads across the lagoon to the beach.

From the Marin Headlands Visitors Center, follow the signs west. 415/331-1540.

48 Marin Headlands Trails

🐾🐾🐾🐾 (See Marin County map on page 420)

From Rodeo Beach (above), you can circle the lagoon or head up into the hills, as long as your pooch is leashed. You're in for a gorgeous walk—or a gorgeous and challenging walk, depending on the weather. Look at a map of the Bay Area, and it will be obvious why the headlands' trees all grow at an eastward slant. In summer especially, cold ocean air funnels through the Golden Gate, sucked in by the Central Valley's heat—chilling the headlands and the inhabitants of western San Francisco with fog and wind. The Bay Area may be "air-conditioned by God," but the headlands sit right at the air inflow, and it's set on "high." Never come here without at least one jacket.

Your dog will love the wind. The combination of fishy breeze and aromatic brush from the hillsides sends many into olfactory ecstasy. What looks from a distance like green fuzz on these headlands is a profusion of wildflowers and low brush. Indian paintbrush, hemlock, sticky monkeyflower, ferns, dock, morning glory, blackberry, sage, and thousands more species grow here—even some stunted but effective poison oak on the windward sides. (On the lee of the hills, it's not stunted.) Groves of eucalyptus grow on the crests. You hear a lovely low rustle and roar of wind, surf, birds, and insects—and the squeak and groan of eucalyptuses rubbing against each other. Pinch some sage between your fingers and sniff; if you can ever leave California again after that, you're a strong person.

From the beach and lagoon, you can hike the circle formed by the Miwuk Trail starting at the eastern end of the lagoon, meeting the Wolf Ridge Trail, then meeting the Coastal Trail (à la the Pacific Coast Trail), back to where you started. Or you can pick up the Coastal Trail off Bunker Road near Rodeo Beach. Look for the trailhead signs.

Sights along these trails include World War II gun emplacements, the Golden Gate Bridge, and San Francisco. As the trail rises and falls, you will discover a blessing: You'll be intermittently sheltered from the wind, and in these pockets, if the sun warms your back, you'll think you've died and gone to heaven.

Dogs used to be able to legally run off leash on most of these trails, but no longer. The Golden Gate National Recreation Area (GGNRA), which oversees this 12,000-acre chunk of heaven, has become much stricter of late. The "company" line now is that all dogs must be leashed on all Marin GGNRA lands. It's a howling shame.

If you want to hike from Rodeo Beach to Muir Beach (see the Muir Beach section), remember that dogs have to be leashed the entire way now. And sadly, once you get there, leashes are also now the law. This is tick country, so search carefully when you get home. 415/331-1540.

PLACES TO EAT

Just a few of Sausalito's pooch-friendly restaurants:

Fish: This new eatery on the Sausalito waterfront is one of the most fun restaurants around. The fish is fresh, the harborside tables are to drool for, and the servers love dogs. Dogs get big bowls of water and samples of dog treats made with salmon! If your dog likes the treats (and she will), you can buy them here. The website is worth checking out: It's www.331fish.com. You can get the latest fish news and local bay and ocean-related activity schedules there, too. You can even click on the "fish.cam" to see what's happening at the restaurant at any given minute. What we especially love about the restaurant's location is that it's next to a dog-friendly point of land at Clipper Yacht Harbor. You'll see the Mutt Mitt dispenser. Dogs enjoy the bay views and the scents and sounds of the nearby harbor seals. The restaurant is at 350 Harbor Drive; 415/331-FISH (415/331-3474).

Scoma's: Want fresh salmon and a magnificent view of the bay? Come to this waterfront eatery and dine with your dog on the deck. 588 Bridgeway; 415/332-9551.

Tommy's Wok: This fun Chinese restaurant is just a bone's throw from Remington Park, so it's a great place to dine after your dog burns up all his energy. The food is delicious, leaning more toward Szechuan dishes, but accommodating Cantonese-loving palates as well. Dine with your good doggy at the four outdoor tables. 3001 Bridgeway; 415/332-5818.

Treviso Restaurant: Dogs can join you at the four sidewalk tables at this lovely restaurant that serves delectable Mediterranean cuisine. 39 Caledonia Street; 415/332-4500.

Winship's Restaurant: Dogs like coming to the two outdoor tables here for a big breakfast, but the fare later in the day is good, too. It's the usual tasty soup, salad, sandwich, pasta menu, but this stuff always tastes even better with your dog at your side. 670 Bridgeway; 415/332-1454.

CHAPTER 35

San Francisco County

For the first three editions of this book, I described San Francisco as being "possibly the most dog-friendly large city on earth." Then the last edition saw Joe Dog weeping into his kibble because of the threats to the oodles of leash-free parks here. But with the fifth edition, life is looking brighter for San Francisco dogs. All of the threatened leash-free areas managed by the city are up and running again, and the city has more leash-free areas than ever. (Dear old Joe went to Dog Heaven—where the cats are slow and all parks are leash-free—before this good news. But he still managed to have one doggone great off-leash life on earth.)

The situation with the formerly off-leash Golden Gate National Recreation Area parklands isn't quite so rosy, but there is some hope. (See the introduction to the Parks, Beaches, and Recreation Areas section for more details on these developments.)

Even with all the roller-coaster events surrounding leash-free areas here, other city attractions have always made dogs feel at home. (Look at Jake Dog. He feels so at home here. Oh, that's right. San Francisco is his home.)

PICK OF THE LITTER—SAN FRANCISCO COUNTY

OFF-LEASH PARK WITH BEST VIEWS
Buena Vista Park (page 472)

PARKS POOCHES ARE PRAYING FOR
Crissy Field (page 461)
Fort Funston (page 479)

CREAMIEST CANINE CANNOLI
Bella and Daisy's (page 481)

MOST DOG-FRIENDLY PLACE TO EAT
Cool Beans (page 483)

MOST DOG-FRIENDLY PLACES TO STAY
Hotel Cosmo (page 489)
Hotel Monaco (page 489)
Hotel Palomar (page 490)
Westin St. Francis (page 493)

BEST WALK WITH/AS A TOURIST
Golden Gate Bridge walk (page 460)

BEST RIDES
Blue and Gold Fleet ferries (page 465)
San Francisco cable cars (page 482)

BEST DAYS TO HAVE A BALL
San Francisco Giants' Dog Days of Summer (page 475)
Bark and Whine Ball (page 481)

No public transportation anywhere compares with San Francisco's, where canines can ride cable cars, streetcars, ferries, and buses. And the finest hotels here permit dogs, as do some of the most popular tourist spots, including Fisherman's Wharf and the Golden Gate Bridge.

Now if we can just get the GGNRA lands to be legally leash-free again, San Francisco will once more be an unparalleled urban paradise for pooches and their people. It would make Joe proud.

San Francisco

San Francisco is the only city in San Francisco County. When you have a city like this, who could ask for anything more?

PARKS, BEACHES, AND RECREATION AREAS

As I mentioned in the beginning of the chapter, the situation with city parks is back on track. This is excellent news for dogs who live here, and for tourist dogs, too. Some dog people would like to see even broader access to city parks. If you would too, contact SFDOG (San Francisco Dog Owner's Group; www.sfdog.org), whose support, in part, is to thank for keeping access to city parks.

The wonderful GGNRA beaches and parks, which had been off-leash heaven on earth until a few years ago, are still sporting signs that say, "Pets on Leash" with a symbol of such underneath (the latter is obviously for dogs who can't read). This is a huge blow to any dog who has ever had the pleasure of running around some of the nation's finest leash-free lands. This sweeping ban on leashless recreation includes the magnificent Fort Funston, Crissy Field, Land's End, Ocean Beach, the Presidio, and Baker Beach. I won't spend time on the reasons in this edition. Suffice it to say that the GGNRA is part of the National Park Service, which maintains a not-so-dog-friendly policy, and that the leash-free lifestyle of GGNRA lands came to the attention of the NPS.

At press time, the GGNRA had received the OK from a federal panel to enter an assessment phase to help determine the leash-free future of its lands. The GGNRA has handed over control of the process to an environmental conflict-resolution organization. User groups from all walks of life—dog people, bikers, equestrians, parents, and environmentalists—will be interviewed during an evaluation phase called negotiated rule-making. It's the beginning of a long and complex process. It could take years before the fate of dogs on GGNRA parklands is determined.

Meanwhile, if you visit GGNRA parks, you may still see other dogs running sans leash. But their people are playing ranger roulette. Citations are inevitable in the areas that had been popular off-leash spots. Legally, dogs are to be leashed until a ruling changes things. Citations start at $50 per pooch. We know a few pups whose people had received tickets at Fort Funston and Ocean Beach. My dog scouts tell me that Crissy Field is the area that's been hardest hit with tickets.

For updates or to find out what you can do to help win back the leash-free lifestyle, go to the SFDOG website, www.sfdog.org. For official updates, check out the GGNRA's website at www.nps.gov/goga. The main page will provide a link to the dog issues pages. You can also phone the GGNRA dog-policy liaisons at 415/561-4732.

DIVERSION

Saunter Across the Golden Gate: Like their people, dogs are thrilled to walk San Francisco's most famous landmark, spanning 1.9 miles from the city to Marin County. It's open 5 A.M.–9 P.M. daily to human and canine pedestrians, no fee.

The **Golden Gate Bridge** folks ask only that 1) if your dog can't contain his excitement over the views, you *please* pick up his poop (even if he's not so keen on the scenery and does his number, you'll need to scoop); and 2) your dog wear a leash. You both probably will want to wear sweaters, too—it can be a little nippy when making your way across.

You'll find vista points with parking lots on the northeast (Marin County) and southeast (San Francisco) sides of the bridge. These are the best embarkation points for your walk. The San Francisco side has meters that charge $.25 for 15 minutes. On the Marin side you can park for free for up to four hours. (Ah, but they get you with the $5 bridge toll when you come back to the city.) For more info, call 415/921-5858.

❶ Baker Beach

🐾🐾🐾🐾 (See San Francisco County map on page 456)

This beach brings your dog almost within a bone's throw of the Golden Gate Bridge. And what a sight it is. Though in summer you shouldn't hold out much hope for a sunny day here, this sandy shoreline is ideal for a romp in the misty air. And dogs really appreciate Baker Beach in the summer. It's almost always cool and breezy.

If you like to sunbathe without a bathing suit and want to take your dog along, the very north end of the beach (closest to the bridge) is perfect. It's the only official nude beach in Northern California where dogs are welcome. But just make sure he doesn't get too up close and personal with your exposed cobathers.

The south end is also intriguing, with trails meandering through wooded areas and lots of picnic tables for leisurely lunches. Battery Chamberlain, with its 95,000-pound cannon aimed toward the sea, looms nearby.

Leashes have become the law here, but we're hopeful this could change. From either direction, take Lincoln Boulevard to Bowley Street, and then make the first turn into the two parking lots. 415/556-8371.

🐾 Fort Point National Historical Site

🐾🐾 (See San Francisco County map on page 456)

Beneath the Golden Gate Bridge, this mid–19th-century brick fortification stands as a reminder of the strategic military significance San Francisco once had. Now it serves as a tourist attraction and one of the best places to view the skyline, Alcatraz, and the bridge. It's also a magnificent spot for your dog to stand mesmerized by the crashing surf.

By itself, Fort Point doesn't offer much for dogs. They must be leashed and there's only a small patch of grass. We recommend Fort Point as the goal of a long hike that starts at Crissy Field. On this jaunt, you'll come to an old pier. There are actually two piers, but the one you're allowed on is closer to the bridge. Stroll to the end for a close-up view of sailboats being tossed about on the bay. When you finally reach Fort Point, it's a tradition among dog people to continue to the westernmost point and touch the fence. There's no telling why, but you may as well try it.

To get to Fort Point without a long hike, follow the signs from Lincoln Avenue as you approach the Golden Gate Bridge. 415/556-8371.

🐾 Crissy Field

🐾🐾🐾🐾 (See San Francisco County map on page 456)

There's nothing quite like Crissy Field at sunset. As the orange sun disappears behind the Golden Gate Bridge, you'll be viewing one of the most stunning blends of natural and man-made wonders in the world.

Crissy Field, part of the Golden Gate National Recreation Area, is a jewel of a park any time of day. In the past, and perhaps one day again, obedient, leash-free dogs could chase and cavort up and down the beach and jump into the bay whenever they feel like it. But as with other GGNRA lands, leashes are now the law here. (Please see the intro to the Parks, Beaches, and Recreation Areas section for more on this situation.) Rangers do routinely patrol the area and aren't shy about issuing citations.

Leashed or not, your dog will find the views here are to drool for. As you walk westward, you'll see the Golden Gate Bridge before you, Alcatraz and bits of the city skyline behind you. Sailboats sometimes glide so close you can hear the sails flapping in the wind. A newly restored 20-acre marsh lends a satisfying air of swampiness. (For more than $25 million, it should lend something.)

Enter on Mason Street in the Marina district and drive past the warehouses. Go right on Mitchell Street and through the parking lot. If you go too far to the east, you'll run into a sea of sailboarders, so try starting your walk close to the western edge of the parking lot. The beach is bordered by delicate dunes that are undergoing restoration in many places, including the entrance, so keep canines off. 415/556-8371.

DIVERSION

Take Me Out to the Ballgame: Can't make it to the San Francisco Giants' Dog Days of Summer? Try a stroll around the outside of SBC Park. A wide promenade flanks right field along **McCovey Cove.** At game time, you and the pooch can get a dog's-eye view of the game alongside other nonticketed folks.

Or make a day of it and walk the entire waterfront of San Francisco with your dog from here. Head west along the promenade, which turns into a sidewalk. You'll come to a grassy marina, complete with a poop-bag station. Continuing west, you'll pass the Embarcadero, Fisherman's Wharf, the Marina District, and, finally, beautiful Crissy Field. Keep walking west and you'll be under the Golden Gate Bridge. SBC Park is at 24 Willie Mays Plaza. Call 415/972-2000 or visit the SF Giants' website: www.sfgiants.com.

◪ Presidio National Park

🐾🐾🐾🐾 (See San Francisco County map on page 456)

Dogs and their people like to pretend that the Presidio is their very own country estate, complete with acre after rolling acre (1,480 in all!) of secret pathways, open meadows, and dense groves of eucalyptus and pine. It's truly a magnificent spread.

Now that the Presidio is a park, and not a military base, it's expected to draw more visitors than either Yosemite or Yellowstone National Parks. But there are still some out-of-the-way areas that even the most adventurous tourists will have a difficult time finding. A fun tour starts when you park at the golf course parking lot just inside the Arguello Boulevard gate. Cross the street (carefully—it can get busy on this road), and follow the path down the hill. It will quickly widen and loop past wildflowers and seasonal sweet peas. Bear left at the first major fork and hike through a thick forest area, then bear right when that path gives you a choice. You'll hike up and down a gentle sequence of hills. Pull over and enjoy the larger hills to the west. Dogs thrill at dragging their people up and down them for no apparent reason. You'll run into a few more side trails along the way.

A more tame walk starts to the west of the playground on West Pacific Avenue. Again enter on Arguello, but immediately bear right. Parking will be on your right on the bottom of the hill. Cross the street and you'll see a plastic-bag dispenser for scooping the poop. That's where you want to start.

Leashes are now the law throughout the Presidio, but at some point, this could change so that at least some of segments are once again their good old leash-free selves. (Please see the intro the Parks, Beaches, and Recreation Areas section for more on this situation.) 415/556-8371.

5 Palace of Fine Arts

🐾🐾🐾 (See San Francisco County map on page 456)

The glory of ancient Rome embraces you even as you approach this relic of the 1915 Panama-Pacific Exposition. From the huge colonnaded rotunda to the serene reflecting pool, the place drips with Romanesque splendor.

The Palace is especially grand under its night lighting. It's also an ideal place to take your dog while the kids go to the Exploratorium inside. Walk around the paved path that winds through the grand columns and around the pond. But keep your eyes peeled for people feeding the multitudes of pigeons, ducks, and geese. Dogs like to break up the feeding frenzy with an abrupt tug on the mandatory leash. Feathers fly and dried bread scatters everywhere.

The best place to enter for the full Roman effect is on Baker Street, between North Point and Jefferson Streets. Dogs are not allowed inside the buildings, although Joe did sneak into the Exploratorium one fine afternoon. (It's a long story.) He got as far as the tornado demonstration machine when he was nabbed and whisked away. 415/831-2700.

6 Marina Green

🐾🐾🐾 (See San Francisco County map on page 456)

The clang of halyards against masts creates a magical symphony from the nearby marinas here on windy days. Your dog's first reaction may be a puzzled 30-degree head tilt.

Most of us know the Marina Green for its high-flying kites and hard-running joggers. But it's also a decent place to take your dog, as long as he's leashed. It's too close to the rush of cars on Marina Boulevard to be comfortable off leash, anyway.

The grass is always green here, as the park's name indicates. It's a treat for eyes overdosed on dry yellow grass and paws laden with foxtails. There's also an attractive heart parcourse fitness trail and a great view of Alcatraz.

Enter on Marina Boulevard, anywhere between Scott and Buchanan Streets. 415/556-0560.

7 Fort Mason

🐾🐾🐾 (See San Francisco County map on page 456)

This park, perched high above the bay, is full of surprises. Depending on the disposition of your dog, some of the surprises are great fun. One can be downright frightening.

The best stands right in the middle of the wide-open field that constitutes the main part of the park. It's a fire hydrant, and it sticks out like a sore yellow thumb from its flat green surroundings. Joyous male dogs bound up and pay it homage time and time again.

The object that seems to take dogs aback, although people find it riveting, is a gigantic bronze statue of Phillip Burton, who helped secure the national park system, including the GGNRA. Several feet taller and broader than life (although even when alive, Burton was larger than life), with outstretched hand, it can send a dog fleeing as far as his mandatory leash will allow.

Lower Fort Mason is also interesting to investigate. You can walk alongside the piers and sniff the bay, or peer at the liberty ship *Jeremiah O'Brien.*

Enter the lower Fort Mason parking lot at Buchanan Street and take the stairs all the way up to upper Fort Mason. (Huff, puff.) Or park along Bay Street or Laguna Street and walk in. 415/556-0560.

🐾 Aquatic Park

🐾🐾 (See San Francisco County map on page 456)

You've got tourist friends in town and don't feel like taking them for the usual amble through Fisherman's Wharf? Here's a great plan that lets you be semi-sporting about the whole thing while you take your dog for a jaunt. Drop off your friends at Aquatic Park, point them toward the tourist attractions, and walk your dog right there.

Aquatic Park is just a few minutes from Ghirardelli Square, Fisherman's Wharf, a cable-car line, and the Hyde Street Pier. It's also a decent place for a leashed dog to romp, with its large grassy field and plenty of pine trees, benches, and flowers. But stay away from the little beach—dogs aren't allowed. If you feel like shopping for T-shirts, jewelry, or arts and crafts, you can take your dog along Beach Street, where dozens of sidewalk vendors sell their wares (see the Diversion These Stores Are for the Dogs!).

The park is on Beach Street between Hyde and Polk Streets. 415/556-8371.

🐾 Land's End/Lincoln Park

🐾🐾🐾🐾 (See San Francisco County map on page 456)

This is probably the most spectacular park in San Francisco. You won't believe your eyes and your leashed dog won't believe his nose. And neither of you will believe your ears—it's so far removed from traffic that all you hear are foghorns, the calls of birds, and the wind whistling through the pines and eucalyptus.

The towering cliffs, high above the crashing tide below, overlook virtually no civilization. For miles, all you can see is ocean, cliffs, trees, wildflowers, and boats. It looks more like Mendocino did 100 years ago—at least until you round one final bend and the Golden Gate Bridge jars your senses back to semiurban reality.

If you want to venture the entire length of the dirt trail, keep two things in mind: 1) Don't wear tight pants—you'll have to do some high stepping in some spots, and you don't want your legs packed into your Levi's; and 2) don't bring a young puppy or an out-of-control dog. The cliffs here can be danger-ous, especially where the trail becomes narrow.

DIVERSION

Seize the Bay: Salty sea dogs wag their tails hard and fast when they learn that the **Blue and Gold Fleet** ferry system permits pooches on most of its runs. That means well-behaved, leashed dogs can go by ferry from San Francisco to all these destinations: Sausalito, Tiburon, Oakland, Alameda, and Vallejo. And they don't have to pay a dime! Just two places are forbidden: Angel Island and Alcatraz, both state parks that don't allow dogs.

Most dogs are enraptured when cruising on the bay. Jake the yellow Lab is a huge fan of ferrydom. He's in ecstasy when his ears flap in the chilly, fishy breeze, his eyes slightly shut as his nose greedily takes in the scents of the bay. (This is in huge contrast to poor ol' Joe, the landlubbing Airedale, who would turn green at the gills at even the sight of a boat.)

Fares range $5.25–9.50 one-way for adults, depending on your destination. Jake's favorite trip, from San Francisco to Sausalito, is $7.25 one-way. From San Francisco, the ferry leaves from Pier 41, just west of the dog-friendly tourist attraction Pier 39, in the Fisherman's Wharf area. Some routes also leave from the Ferry Building, at Market and Embarcadero Streets. Phone 415/705-8200 for schedules and more information, or 415/705-5555 for tickets; www.blueandgoldfleet.com.

There are many entrance points, but we like to start from the parking lot at the end of Camino del Mar. Go down the wooden steps to the wide dirt trail and turn right. As you hike, you'll come to occasional wood benches overlooking wildly beautiful seascapes. Take a moment to sit down. Your dog will appreciate the chance to contemplate the wondrous odors coming through her bulbous olfactory sensor.

As you continue, you'll pass a sign that makes its point efficiently and effectively: "Caution! Cliff and surf are extremely dangerous. People have been swept from the rocks and drowned." You'll have no problem if you proceed on the main trail and ignore the temptation to follow the dozens of tiny paths down the cliff face. (Naked men often hang out at a beach or two down there, so if your dog blushes easily, you'll have extra reason to stay on the wider paths.) A new, very long wooden stairway leads from the main path all the way down to a beautiful rock-strewn beach with great views of the Golden Gate. The trip down is worth the rather vigorous hike back up.

Leashes are now the law here, but in the future, this could change so that Lands End one day returns to its glorious leash-free self. (Please see the intro to the Parks, Beaches, and Recreation Areas section for more on this situation.)

A very convenient entry point is at the parking lot on Point Lobos (which is what Geary Street turns into toward the ocean) just above the Cliff House and Louie's. But we like to park in the lot at the end of Camino del Mar, a little street just above that lot. You'll pass a sign for Fort Miley on your right just after you enter Camino del Mar. Leashed dogs are allowed on this large patch of trees on a hill, and the views are stunning. It's a good place to visit to get away from the weekend crowds who can descend on Land's End. 415/556-8371.

10 Mountain Lake Park

🐾🐾🐾 🐕 (See San Francisco County map on page 456)

In this sociable park, your dog can cavort with other dogs while you shoot the breeze with other dog people. The off-leash area is between two signs on the east side of the park. You'll find a bench for humans and a pretty good safety net of trees and grass between dogs and the outside world.

The favorite game among dogs here involves a big green bush. One dog usually starts running around it for no apparent reason. Circle after circle, he'll attract more and more dogs into chasing him until almost every dog is swirling around in a dizzying loop. Watch too closely and you can get seasick.

Dogs find the rest of the park mildly entertaining, although they have to be leashed. The lake that's the park's namesake is little more than a pond. Ducks and a couple of swans live here, and the temptation may be too much for your dog. We've seen dogs drag their owners ankle-deep into the muddy pond in pursuit of a duck dinner. The park is also home to an attractive playground and a decent heart parcourse fitness trail.

To reach the dog-run area, enter on 8th Avenue at Lake Street. 415/831-2700.

11 Alta Plaza Park

🐾🐾🐾 🐕 (See San Francisco County map on page 456)

Smack in the middle of Pacific Heights, this park is where all the best breeds and most magnificent mutts gather daily. They flock to the hill on the north side of the park and conduct their dog business in the most discriminating fashion. It's not uncommon to see 25 dogs trotting around the park. Owners often address each other by their dogs' names—"Shane's mom! How are you?"

The park's off-leash run is actually on the other side of the playground and tennis courts, on the second level up from Clay Street. Bushes line the paved walkway, and it's far enough from traffic that you don't have to worry too much about cars.

The park is bordered by Jackson, Clay, Steiner, and Scott Streets. 415/831-2700.

12 Lafayette Park

🐾🐾🐕 (See San Francisco County map on page 456)

This four-square-block park gets lots of dog traffic. The park is hilly and green and studded with palm trees, pines, and well-trimmed bushes. The official dog-run area is near Sacramento Street, between Octavia and Gough Streets. As you enter the park from the main Sacramento Street entrance, it's on your right. But most dogs gather atop the hill to the left, around two huge, smelly garbage cans.

The park is bounded by Laguna, Gough, Sacramento, and Washington Streets. 415/831-2700.

13 Washington Square

🐾🐾 (See San Francisco County map on page 456)

Grab a gelato, leash your dog, and relax in this park in the middle of North Beach. There are plenty of benches and enough trees to make your dog comfortable with his surroundings. The park is only about one block square, but it's great for a stroll when you're hitting the cafés of San Francisco's Little Italy. And if you have a child with you, so much the better. There's a small playground that's popular with local parents.

Washington Square is right across from the ornate Saints Peter and Paul Catholic Church, and the Transamerica pyramid looks close enough to reach out and touch.

Enter the park at any of its four borders: Columbus, Union, Stockton, or Filbert Streets. Try not to drive to North Beach. Even during the day, parking's a bear. 415/831-2700.

14 Ocean Beach

🐾🐾🐾🐾 (See San Francisco County map on page 456)

This broad, four-mile-long beach with a crashing surf isn't exactly Palm Beach. It's usually cold and windy and full of seaweed, jellyfish, jagged bits of shells, and less savory deposits from the Pacific. In other words, dogs think it's grand.

Unfortunately, this is no longer a leash-free poochy paradise. Rangers regularly patrol the beach in their trucks, so it's not easy to sneak around without a leash. But the breathtaking view and salty air still provide a good romp. (See the intro to the Parks, Beaches, and Recreation Areas section for information on potential changes to the leashes-only law.)

You can park along the ocean, between the Cliff House and Balboa Street. Walk south on the sidewalk until you hit the beach. Or park in the spaces between Fulton Street and Lincoln Way. A parking lot is also at Sloat Boulevard, but beach access is limited because of erosion. 415/556-8371.

DIVERSION

These Stores Are for the Dogs!: Dogs who enjoy shopping with their people love San Francisco. Following are a few of the more pooch-friendly retail spots for the leashed and well-behaved.

Beach Street: This isn't a store but a kind of outdoor tourist market where you can shop for baubles, bangles, and T-shirts with your leashed dog at any of dozens of little stands up and down this Fisherman's Wharf area street. The bulk of the stands on Beach Street are between Hyde and Polk Streets.

Neiman Marcus: Even jaded dogs can be agog when they visit this upscale store's beautiful atrium lobby. 150 Stockton Street; 415/362-3900.

Saks Fifth Avenue: Keep your dog under tight rein and she's welcome here. 384 Post Street; 415/986-4300.

Wilkes Bashford Company: Pooches of any size are welcome to peruse this upscale, Union Square store (it's to drool for), as long as they're clean and don't conduct any dog business. "I'm a nut about dogs," says Wilkes Bashford, the store's owner. "Dogs are a vital part of life." And he says all the dogs who've visited his store have been very well behaved. Bashford has been bringing his dogs to the store since 1968. Little Callie goes to work with Bashford just about every day. And even when Bashford is out of town on business, Callie makes her rounds at the store. Bashford's driver takes her there in the morning and drives her home in the afternoon. 375 Sutter Street; 415/986-4380.

15 Golden Gate Park

🐾🐾🐾 🐕 (See San Francisco County map on page 456)

This famed city park provides much dog bliss, but only in the places where dogs are supposed to be leashed. Four areas are set aside for leashless dogs (see below), but dogs in the know like to avoid those places, for good reason. The following listings are for both leash and off-leash areas, from west to east, and north to south. For information about any area in the park, call 415/831-2700.

16 Golden Gate Park (Beach Chalet)

🐾 (See San Francisco County map on page 456)

The paths in back of the Beach Chalet (near the soccer fields between the windmills near the ocean) run along the edge of the fields and can be a little unsavory at times. But to leashed dogs, they're full of good smells and interesting characters. There's also the hilly, piney area up behind the archery field. We haven't heard of any impalements up there, but be careful.

DIVERSION

Wash That Sand Right Outta Her Hair: Soggy day at Ocean Beach? You need **Bill's Doggie Bath-O-Mat.** The beauty of Bill's is that you can bathe your dog without cleaning the waist-high tub afterward (or, worse yet, having to bathe in the tub yourself afterward!). A $12 fee includes use of shampoo, combs, brushes, towels, a doggy blow-dryer, and a cute doggy apron. Bill's a nice guy who gives good grooming advice if needed, and he gives away great puppy calendars in January. 3928 Irving Street (about 10 blocks inland); 415/661-6950.

17 Golden Gate Park Dog Run

🐾 🐾 🐕 (See San Francisco County map on page 456)

This fenced-in dog exercise area has the dubious distinction of being right next to a field full of buffalo. Some dogs adore the location, especially when the wind is blowing in just the right direction. It's the only fenced-in dog run in the city, so it's really the only game in town for escape artists. But the park's fans aren't just dogs who walk on the wild side. All sizes and shapes of dogs come here for playtime. So many dogs use it that much of it is grassless and dusty.

The place can sometimes get a little rough around the edges when the usual dog crowd isn't around. People who like their dogs tough will occasionally drop in and hang out with something to swig while their dogs strut around. It's not usually a problem, though, especially during the normal dog rush hours (before work and after work for 9-to-5ers, and all day on weekends).

We've found more amorous dogs here than in any other park, so if your dog isn't in the mood (or you don't want her to be), this isn't the place to take her. For some reason, Jake, like dear Joe before him, gets accosted at almost every visit, so it's not one of his favorite places. He's flattered, but he's not that kind of dog.

The Dog Run is at 38th Avenue and Fulton Street. Park on Fulton Street and walk in, or take 36th Avenue into the park and go right at the first paved road. Drive all the way to the end, and there it is.

18 Golden Gate Park (by the Polo Field)

🐾 🐾 🐾 (See San Francisco County map on page 456)

Dogs who prefer playing Frisbee (on a mandatory leash) go to the meadow just east of the polo field. It's known for wide-open dells, good bushes, and plenty of gopher holes for old sports. Your best bet here is to come early in the morning.

19 Golden Gate Park (horse paths)

🐾🐾🐾 (See San Francisco County map on page 456)

Dogs who like to promenade take to the horse paths that radiate from the now unused stables. Alas, with all the horses gone from this area (except for the police horses), there's a lot less poop to sniff out. If you don't mind walking in circles, you can simply walk along the track that circles the field. You'll pass joggers and bicyclists (or more likely, they'll pass you) and other people with happy dogs.

20 Golden Gate Park (south side)

🐾🐾🐕 (See San Francisco County map on page 456)

Two areas set aside for leash-free dogs are slivers along the south end of the park. One is between 2nd and 7th Avenues and bounded on the north and south by Lincoln Way and Martin Luther King Jr. Drive. It's a good length, but it's not terribly wide. The other is on the south side of the polo field, between 34th and 38th Avenues and Middle and Martin Luther King Jr. Drives. Bring your dog to these sections if he's very good off leash. They're too close to busy traffic for less disciplined dogs.

21 Golden Gate Park (Stow Lake/Strawberry Hill)

🐾🐾🐾 (See San Francisco County map on page 456)

The summit of the man-made mountain at Stow Lake is truly a sniffer's paradise. Dogs who like to look at ducks will also enjoy the lake area. The path winds up Strawberry Hill to a breathtaking 360-degree view of the city. Unfortunately, dogs are not supposed to be off leash. It's best to avoid this walk on weekends, when bikers and hikers and wee ones are everywhere.

Stow Lake is between 15th and 19th Avenues. From John F. Kennedy or Martin Luther King Jr. Drives, follow the Stow Lake signs.

DOG-EAR YOUR CALENDAR

Pet Pride Day, sponsored by the San Francisco Department of Animal Care and Control, is a day filled with pets on parade, pets in costumes (if the event falls near Halloween, the costumes get especially interesting), pets "pawditioning" for prizes, and many pet-oriented exhibits. Donations go directly to the department's adoption and outreach programs. Pet Pride Day is held in Golden Gate Park's Sharon Meadow the last Sunday in October. For more information, call 415/554-9414.

22 Golden Gate Park (northeast corner)

😊 🐕 (See San Francisco County map on page 456)

Dogs are allowed off-leash on one of the narrow fields at the northeast corner of the park, up by the horseshoe courts. It's a strange little area with hills and dales and dirt paths. Homeless people live here, and some don't keep good house. You'll see the campfire remains, old sleeping bags, and trash of every type. It's best to avoid this place, except in the middle of the day. Enter at Stanyan and Grove Streets.

23 Golden Gate Park (The Panhandle)

😊😊😊 (See San Francisco County map on page 456)

That long, thin strip of park that extends eight blocks from the east end of the park to Baker Street is a great hangout for cool dogs. It's got a real Haight-Ashbury influence in parts, and although dogs must be leashed, they love to saunter around visiting other dogs wearing bandannas.

24 Alamo Square Park

😊😊😊 🐕 (See San Francisco County map on page 456)

A postcard comes to life in this park for you and your leashed dog. This is where the famed Painted Ladies hold court over the city. These six brightly colored Victorian homes are even better in person than they are on a postcard.

Walk up the east side of the park, near Steiner Street, to enjoy the view of the old houses with the modern city skyline in the background. (Dogs need to be leashed in this half of the park.) Even if your dog doesn't care about architecture, she'll love the grassy hills that make up this park.

Dogs who like to run around all nudey (sans leash) are joyful these days because the city has given the OK to an official leash-free area on the park's west half. Hooray! (This had been a de facto leash-free area forever. Now it has the city's seal of approval.)

The park is bordered by Fulton, Hayes, Scott, and Steiner Streets. 415/831-2700.

25 Duboce Park

😊😊 (See San Francisco County map on page 456)

If peering into people's windows is your dog's idea of fun, this urban park is his kind of place. A couple of large buildings have ground-floor windows that seem to fascinate dogs. Perhaps there's a cat colony inside.

Your dog will probably find other dogs to play with here. They're supposed to be leashed, since they're never more than a few fast steps from the nearest street. The park is grassy and has pines and a variety of smaller trees around some of its borders. A children's playground is at the west end.

The park is at Duboce Avenue between Steiner and Scott Streets. 415/831-2700.

DIVERSIONS

Cruise the Castro: Your well-behaved dog is welcome to join you on a fascinating four-hour walking tour focusing on the gay and lesbian history of the **Castro district.** Tour leader Trevor Hailey will guide you and a small group to historically significant Castro settings while giving a superb narrative of how the Castro came to be what it is today. Trevor starts with the Lavender Cowboys of the 1849 Gold Rush and takes you through the impact of the 1906 earthquake, World War II, and the Summer of Love.

Dogs may not attend the brunch/lunch, included in the tour's $45 fee. Brunch is inside a restaurant, and pooches are not permitted. Trevor suggests coming with a friend and taking turns eating brunch and walking the dog. You'll miss out on a little of the history Trevor relates at mealtime, but at least you won't miss out on the tasty brunch.

All tour-takers, including dogs, get a miniature rainbow flag as part of the deal. Tours are given Tuesday–Saturday, May–November; 415/550-8110; www.webcastro.com/castrotour.

Say Yippie for Hippies: The **Flower Power Haight Ashbury Walking Tour** is a delight for humans and dogs, and you don't have to be flower children/puppies to enjoy it. This riveting tour guides you through the history of the Haight, from the Victorian era to the Human Be-in, the Digger feeds, the free Grateful Dead concerts, and of course, the Summer of Love. Dogs don't dig the history much, but they revel in the smell of old hippies who sit on the sidewalks.

Humans of all ages and leashed, well-behaved dogs are welcome. A 2.5-hour tour is $15. Dogs are free. For more information or reservations, write The Flower Power Haight Ashbury Walking Tour, 520 Shrader Street, #1, San Francisco, CA 94117; 415/863-1621.

26 Buena Vista Park

😊😊😊😊🐾 (See San Francisco County map on page 456)

The presence of vagrants who sometimes congregate at the front of the park has scared off lots of would-be park users, but it shouldn't. They're generally a friendly lot, posing no threat to folks exploring the park's upper limits with a dog.

This park is a real find for anyone living near the Haight-Ashbury district. Hike along the myriad dirt and paved trails winding through the hills, enveloped by eucalyptus and redwood trees. Some of the gutters are lined with pieces of tombstone from a nearby cemetery. The cemetery's occupants, who died in the 1800s, were moved to the oh-so-quiet town of Colma. The gutters give the park a historical, haunted feeling.

From the top of the park, you can see the ocean, the bay, the Marin headlands, and both the Golden Gate and Bay Bridges. Birds sing everywhere, and there are lots of benches to rest on. Dogs are allowed off leash at the woodsy west side of the park, near Central Street.

A note: Sometimes people meet for assignations at the top of the park. Concealing shrubs and bushes have gotten haircuts of late, but this area is still a "hot spot," so to speak. If this bothers you or your dog, avoid this lovers' lane.

Enter at Buena Vista Avenue West and Central Street, or from Haight Street. 415/831-2700.

27 Corona Heights Park/Red Rock Park

🐾🐾🐾🐕 (See San Francisco County map on page 456)

The rust-colored boulders atop this park cast long, surreal shadows at dawn. If you and your dog are early risers, it's worth the hike to the summit to witness this. And there's a fine view any time of day of downtown and the Castro district.

Unfortunately, dogs aren't allowed off leash on hikes up the hill. Until recently, the off-leash area was a roomy square of grass at the foot of the park. The leash-free section has now been made smaller (about three-quarters of an acre) and is completely fenced. It was a compromise between the dog people and the folks who like to sunbathe there without getting stomped upon and sniffed at. Because of heavy use, the fenced dog park is no longer grassy, but the surrounding area—leashes mandatory—is lush. (The grass truly is greener on the other side of this fence.)

After a bit of leashless playing, you can don a leash and take your pooch up the hill. Fences keep dogs and people from falling down the steep cliffs and from treading on native habitat. Keep in mind that there's virtually no shade, so if you have a black rug of a dog, think twice about climbing the hill on hot, sunny days.

The park is at Museum Way and Roosevelt Avenue. 415/831-2700.

28 Mission Dolores Park

🐾🐾🐕 (See San Francisco County map on page 456)

You can get a little history lesson while walking your dog here. A statue of Miguel Hidalgo overlooks the park, and Mexico's liberty bell hangs at the Dolores Street entrance.

History may not impress your dog, but a wide-open space for running off leash will. It's behind the tennis courts.

There are two problems with this area, though: 1) It's easy for your dog to run into the road—even if she's the voice control type, she could find herself in Church Street traffic just by running a little too far to catch a ball; and 2) you have to be on the lookout that your dog doesn't run over people who live in the park. Joe once slid into a sleeping homeless woman and scared her so badly she screamed and ran away.

Enter anywhere on Dolores or Church Streets, between 18th and 20th Streets. The off-leash area is south of the tennis courts and north of the soccer field. 415/831-2700.

29 McKinley Square

🐾 🐾 🐕 (See San Francisco County map on page 456)

The view from this little patch of land is, shall we say, interesting. You can see for miles and miles, and the view includes several other leash-free parks, such as Buena Vista, Corona Heights, Mission Dolores, and Bernal Heights Parks. But you can also see such lovely sights as U.S. 101, with its cars rushing madcap-fashion just a couple of hundred feet down the hill from you. And if you ever craved a view of San Francisco General Hospital's most austere, Dickensian brick buildings, this is the place to come. If you had really long arms, you could almost reach out and touch them. Actually, depending on the direction of the wind, on some days they reach out and touch you—the steam from the hospital's huge chimneys has been known to slip right up to this hilltop park.

Dogs are permitted off leash in the back section of the park, between the playground and the community gardens. Signs will point you in the right direction. It's nothing beautiful, just a wide path with a little running room on a hillside dotted with brush and occasional trees.

The off-leash section is on 20th Street and San Bruno Avenue, just a few blocks from the heart of the Potrero Hill business district. 415/831-2700.

30 Twin Peaks

🐾 🐾 (See San Francisco County map on page 456)

So dogs aren't allowed at the Top of the Mark. So what! The view from up here will put all those "No Dogs Allowed" establishments to shame, and it's cheaper to entertain guests up here—it's free, in fact.

The summits of the Twin Peaks are higher than 900 feet. It's usually cold up here, so bundle up. You can drive to the northern peak and park in the lot. It's very touristy, and on this peak, signs tell you what you're looking at—Tiburon, Nob Hill, Mt. Diablo, Japantown, and Mt. Tamalpais. Your dog won't get much exercise, though, since all he can do is walk around the paved viewing area on leash. And frankly, many dogs are bored by the marvelous vistas.

For your dog's sake, try exploring the other peak. It's a bare hill with wooden stairs up one side. While dogs must be on leash, it's not bad exercise. And the view—at almost 20 feet higher than the first peak—is *magnificent*. From here you can see other potential walks for you and your dog on the lower hills,

DOG-EAR YOUR CALENDAR

You won't strike out with your dog if you bring her to the **Dog Days of Summer** at SBC Park. In fact, you'll score a home run. If you thought hot dogs and baseball go together, you should see just plain dog dogs and baseball. It's a match made in dog heaven!

At Dog Days of Summer, your pooch gets to join you for a baseball game on a set day in August. You'll sit together in "The Dog Zone" (aka the bleachers) and watch the San Francisco Giants pound the heck out of the visiting team (we hope). But that's not all. Before the game, you and your dog can take part in a poochy parade around the field! Not many dogs (or humans) can say they've cruised around a pro ball park. There's also a dog costume contest, should your dog be feeling creative. Cost for the day is $37 for one human, and you can bring one dog. Additional humans in your party (sans dogs) are $18. Dogs have to wear ID and rabies tags. 415/972-2000; www.sfgiants.com.

where the views are almost as dynamic and the air is a little warmer. Be sure to keep him on leash, because the road is never far away.

The Twin Peaks are on Twin Peaks Boulevard, just north of Portola Drive. 415/831-2700.

31 Douglass Park

🐾🐾🐾🐾🐕 (See San Francisco County map on page 456)

The leash-free section at Douglass Park used to be a steep hillside with fences that were falling apart. It was so bad and difficult to get to (and to stay on!) that I decided not to waste space on it in previous editions. But now the city has changed the locale, and it's a completely different animal: a big, attractive, grassy field flanked by tall trees. It's actually a barely used softball field, so your dog can make like Barry Bonds and run the bases and then go out for a fly ball (of the lobbed tennis variety) to right field. There's plenty of room for dogs to run and play, and boy do they.

Escape artist dogs are pretty safe here, although the park is not totally enclosed. The area near the entrance has no barrier. But the park is so big that you can keep your activities to a far-flung section of the field if escape is a concern.

The park has good views of downtown from the back fence area (it has some very tall fences in back from its softball days). If you want to sit and sip your coffee while your dog gallops around, you'll have to be a bump on a log: The only place to repose is a big log bordering the outfield. The leash-free part of the park is all the way at the top, on Douglass at 27th Street. 415/831-2700.

😊 Glen Canyon Park

😊😊😊 (See San Francisco County map on page 456)

From the cypress forests to the streams and grassy hills, this park was made for you and your dog. The nature trail in the middle of the park follows a muddy creek and is so overgrown with brush and bramble that at times you nearly have to crawl. It's as though the trail were blazed for dogs. There are so many dragonflies of all colors and sizes near the creek, and so much lush vegetation, that you may wonder if you've stepped back to the age of the dinosaurs.

Park at Bosworth Street and O'Shaughnessy Boulevard and walk down a dirt trail past a recreation center, through the redwoods and loud birds. Stay away from the paved road—it can look deserted for hours on end, and then a car suddenly whizzes by. Your dog is supposed to be leashed, but you should still be aware of the road. In a few minutes, you'll come to a long, low building. At this point, you can go left and up a hill for some secluded picnic spots or keep going and take the nature trail. When you finally emerge from the dragonflies and dense greenery, take any of several trails up the open, rolling hills and enjoy a panorama of the park.

The park is at Bosworth Street and O'Shaughnessy Boulevard. 415/831-2700.

😊 Mount Davidson

😊😊😊 (See San Francisco County map on page 456)

Hiking to the peak of this park can be a religious experience—literally. As you emerge from the tall pine and eucalyptus trees leading to the 927-foot summit, a concrete structure looms in the distance. As you get closer you'll see that it's a gigantic cross, 103 feet tall. It's so huge, and in such a prominent spot—at the end of a long, wide path surrounded by trees—that it can be a startling sight. On his first encounter, Joe backed out of his collar and collided with a tree. Since leashes are the law here, we had to quickly put him back together.

In 1934, President Franklin Delano Roosevelt became the first person to flick the switch and light the cross. It's visible for miles, especially vivid under its nighttime floodlighting. On a night hike up Mt. Davidson, you can follow the glow to the top. Recently there was lots of controversy about keeping the cross (a religious symbol) in the park (a city-run property). That church and state-mixing thing just wasn't making some folks happy. Thank God (so to speak), an Armenian group bought the property surrounding the cross. The cross, an intriguing landmark for generations—much more than a religious icon—will remain.

Since you enter the park at such a high altitude, it's only about a 10-minute pilgrimage to the peak. But you can make it a much longer walk by experimenting with different trails.

Enter at Dalewood Way and Lansdale Avenue. 415/831-2700.

34 Upper Noe Park

(See San Francisco County map on page 456)

At last sniff, the leash-free section of this park was a tiny little area of compacted dirt. It was fenced and had water and two benches but no shade and no real appeal other than being an off-leash area. At press time the city was considering redoing it and redefining its borders, so it may warrant another paw or two in the future. (To be fair, regular users say it's better than it used to be when the ground was a sandy, dusty mess.) The off-leash section is on Day and Sanchez Streets, east of the ballfield. (You can enter only on Day Street at this point.) 415/831-2700.

35 Potrero Hill Mini Park

(See San Francisco County map on page 456)

If you value your safety, don't go to the designated off-leash part of this park, even if your dog is crossing her legs in need of an off-leash romp. A friend was mugged twice at gunpoint when she used to play tennis at the courts adjacent to the dog run. (For some reason she no longer plays tennis there.) The leash-free section of this tiny park is a postage-stamp-sized lawn next to a tiny, ancient playground. A steep, uncleared patch of land that stretches from the nearby housing projects to the lawn is also supposed to be part of the dog run. The city needs to rethink this whole setup. The park is at 22nd and Arkansas Streets. 415/831-2700.

36 Pine Lake Park

(See San Francisco County map on page 456)

Adjacent to its more famous cousin, Stern Grove (below), Pine Lake Park can be even more fun for dogs because it has Laguna Puerca, a small lake at the west end of the park. Swimming isn't allowed, but there's always the muddy shore for wallowing.

The lake is in a valley at the bottom of steep slopes, so there's not much need to worry about traffic. Leashes are supposed to be on at all times, in any case. At the lake's east end, there's a big field where dogs can really cut loose—as far as leashes allow.

Enter at Crestlake Drive and Wawona Street and follow the paved path, which quickly turns into a dirt trail. 415/831-2700.

37 Stern Grove

(See San Francisco County map on page 456)

If your dog wants to hear some hot music this summer, bring her to the Stern Grove Festival concerts. Dogs can't enjoy the opera, ballet, jazz, classical, or world music performances from the meadow, but they're tolerated around the peripheral hills, on leash. Bring a picnic, a bottle of wine, a rawhide bone, and, of course, a poop bag.

Stern Grove is a treasure of trees, hills, meadows, and birds. There's even a spot where dogs are allowed off leash. Unfortunately, it's one of the least attractive areas in the park—very close to the street—although trees act as an effective barrier. And if you perch on the inner edge, the dog-run area isn't a bad place to listen to a concert. The violins get a little tinny at that distance, but your dog won't care.

City parks officials are considering allowing some of the trails here to be leash-free. But for now, the only legal leash-free area is on Stern Grove's north side, on Wawona Street between 21st and 23rd Avenues. 415/831-2700.

🐾 Bernal Heights Park

🐾🐾🐾🐾 (See San Francisco County map on page 456)

On one visit to this park, a dozen wolf-shepherds were the only dogs atop the amber hill. They ran and played in such pure wolf fashion that it was hard to believe they weren't the genuine item. The icy wind hit the power lines overhead and made a low, arctic whistle. The scene left an indelible impression that even in the middle of a city such as San Francisco, the wild is just beneath the surface.

The rugged hills here are fairly rigorous for bipeds, but dogs have a magnificent time bolting up and down. Humans can enjoy the view of the Golden Gate and Bay Bridges. The vista makes up for the austere look of the treeless park. Dogs are allowed off leash on the hills bordered by Bernal Heights Boulevard. It can be very windy and cold, so bundle up.

Enter at Carver Street and Bernal Heights Boulevard, or keep going on Bernal Heights Boulevard until just past Anderson Street. 415/831-2700.

🐾 St. Mary's Park

🐾🐾🐾 (See San Francisco County map on page 456)

If it weren't for its teeny size, St. Mary's dog park would score three paws. It's an attractive place with friendly people and well-manicured grass that somehow withstands the pounding of paws day after day. It's totally enclosed and has three picnic tables and occasional shade from trees on a steep adjacent hillside. The leash-free section of St. Mary's is very close to I-280 (and the constant drone of traffic). From the park's main entrance on Murray Street at Justin Drive, walk immediately to the right and follow a paved path downhill past a playground and to the dog park, which will be on your left. A closer entrance is a block south, on Benton Avenue at Justin Drive. 415/831-2700.

🐾 McLaren Park/Crocker Amazon Playground

🐾🐾🐾 (See San Francisco County map on page 456)

You and your dog can enter this large park anywhere and find a trail within seconds. The surprise is that most of McLaren's trails run through remote wooded areas and windswept hills with sweeping views. At press time, leashes were required on the trails, but the city parks department may soon be experimenting with leash-free trail access.

If you drive to the northeast part of the park, to the section bounded by John F. Shelley Drive and Mansell Street, you'll find a leash-free area far from traffic. Certain parts can be crowded with schoolchildren or company picnickers or ne'er-do-wells, so watch where you wander. There's another leash-free section in the park's south section, which is really known as Crocker Amazon Playground. You get there via the 1600 block of Geneva Avenue or the 1600 block of Sunnydale. It's in the upper part of the park. You'll have to walk through some of the park to get there, since you can't get a car too close. 415/831-2700.

41 Fort Funston

🐾🐾🐾🐾 (See San Francisco County map on page 456)

Get a hanky ready: After decades of dogs' being allowed to run around in their birthday suits (no leashes), leashes have become the law—at least temporarily. Some future decision-making offers a glimmer of hope for Fort Funston to once again be one of the world's best areas for leash-free dogs, but it may be some time before that happens again. (See the intro to the Parks, Beaches, and Recreation Areas section for more on this.) In the meantime, know that rangers do occasionally come through and issue citations to some people whose dogs aren't attached to them.

It just isn't the same here on leash, but "Fort Fun" still gets high marks for natural beauty. This scenic park set on seaside cliffs still will make your jaw drop with awe the first (and second and third) time you see it. Trails will still wind through magnificent bluffs overlooking the mighty Pacific. And dogs will still slobber with giddiness to be part of all this.

There are a few areas where you can start your walk, but the easiest access is from the main parking lot, next to the take-off cliff for hang gliders. Before you begin, walk your dog to the watering hole—actually a bowl underneath a drinking fountain—and fill her up.

Now that you're all watered and ready for adventure, turn around and take the first trail to the north of the parking lot, the Sunset Trail. You'll meander through dunes and ice plant, encountering every kind of dog imaginable. You'll soon come to the main entrance to Battery Davis, which was built in 1939 to protect San Francisco from enemy ship bombardment. It was sealed shut in recent years because of some rotten sorts who hung out there, but you can still get a good feel for the place.

Continue on trails on either side of the battery. Both eventually end up in the same place. If you take the trail at the rear of the battery, you'll quickly be able to see the Golden Gate Bridge and the Cliff House. At that point, you'll also see a trail that takes you back into a miniforest. Don't go all the way down, though, or you'll end up on a busy road.

If you visit frequently, expand your explorations. Many trails wander throughout Fort Funston, and you and your dog will want to sniff out every inch of this place that you're allowed to. (Be careful to avoid poison oak and areas marked as off-limits. A 12-acre area is now untreadable by dogs and humans because of some delicate habitat. Please heed the signs.)

To get to Fort Funston, follow the brown signs on the Great Highway. It's about one-half mile south of the turnoff to John Muir Drive. (If you get to the Daly City limits, you've gone too far south.) There's also some roadside parking near that intersection. Once on the main drive into the park, bear right (going left will take you to the interesting new Fort Funston Visitors Center, but dogs have no desire to visit, since they're not allowed). Continue past a little building with paintings of hang gliders, and drive into the main parking lot. 415/556-8371.

42 Lake Merced

🐾 🐾 🐕 (See San Francisco County map on page 456)

As the city's largest body of water, Lake Merced is favored by Labrador retrievers, Irish setters, and the like. An ideal spot to explore is the footbridge area near the south end of the lake. A couple of sandy beaches there are safe from traffic, but dogs are supposed to be leashed anyway. Once you cross the bridge, you'll find an inviting area with lots of little trees. This is where you'll find one of two double-decker drinking fountains for humans and their best friends. Lap up if you're going to hike around the entire lake: It's about a five-mile walk on paved trails and can be heavily used on weekends.

The off-leash section of Lake Merced is at the north lake area, at Lake Merced Boulevard and Middlefield Drive. Park on Middlefield and cross Lake Merced Boulevard at the light. You'll enter a small grassy/weedy section and come to a narrow dirt trail overlooking the lake's northeast bowl. We don't recommend letting dogs off leash until you're at least a couple of hundred feet into the park, because menacing traffic is so close by. There are birds galore and purple wildflowers in spring. The park is a tease, though, because there's no way to get to the lake from here—it's down a very formidable slope covered with impenetrable brush. 415/831-2700.

PLACES TO EAT

For a city that's known for its cool, foggy weather, San Francisco sure has a lot of sidewalk cafés. Here's just a smattering:

Angelina's Caffe: Conveniently situated one-half block from Cal's Discount Pet Supply, Angelina's is a good place for you and your dog to take a break from shopping. It's got everything from soup to pine nuts, plus a large variety of coffees. Enjoy them at one of six sidewalk tables. You can also stock on up on Italian souvenirs here, but watch out for the red, white, and green hats. 6000 California Street; 415/221-7801.

Asqew Grill: The name may be spelled all askew, but I ask you, have you ever eaten at a restaurant where almost everything is cooked and served on a skewer? Jake Dog would like to recommend any of the meat kabobs, but there are some mighty tasty veggie skewers awaiting the herbivore in your life. The restaurant serves lunch and dinner. Breakfast would be disastrous. (There's a reason you've never heard of a scrambled egg kabob or skewered pancakes.) 3348 Steiner Street; 415/931-9201.

Bella and Daisy's: If your dog has been very good, get her a canine cannoli at this fun pooch bakery and boutique. Or order some doggy donuts, cupcakes, or brownies. (All made for dogs, so no chocolate, no sugar.) If it's her birthday, let her eat cake. Bella's knows no bounds. What's unique about Bella's, compared with some other dog bakeries, is that the bakery owners provide coffee and indoor seating for dog people, so you can actually hang out here while your dog eats. Of course, a dog does not usually take very long to eat a cupcake or what have you, so the seating is really for the benefit of humans who want to meet and chat about this and that (this usually being their dog, and that being your dog). Bella's has a 1,300-square-foot party area in the back, and a small little turf area in front for dogs to sniff out. Nonbakery boutique items such as doggy cashmere and fancy bowls and carriers are big here, too. And so is the healing center, where dogs can get acupuncture, massage, and other body treatments. 1750 Union Street; 415/440-7007.

Bistro Yoffi: It seems there's always a happy dog hanging out at the sidewalk tables in front of this colorful Marina district restaurant. The international and California-style cuisine here is marvelous. Jake Dog sends a thank-you to Matt Golden and his smiling dog for the tip. 2231 Chestnut Street; 415/885-5133.

Blue Danube Coffee House: Have your cake and eat soup and sandwiches, too, at five tables outside this charming café. You can even indulge in a wide selection of beer or wine, but you'll have to drink alone if your dog is under 21. On sunny days, it may be hard to find an empty spot. 306 Clement Street; 415/221-9041.

DOG-EAR YOUR CALENDAR

The dog's version of the famous Black and White Ball is truly a spectacle to behold. At the **Bark and Whine Ball,** well-heeled dogs and their people shine. This is definitely one of those events to see and be seen. No one even shrugs when they see someone dancing with his or her dog. The ball features good music, passed hors d'oeuvres (dogs love this, but it's really for humans), and wine (ditto). It's held in late February. Tickets are $75–125. Dogs are $20. Go to www.sfspca.org/barkandwhine for this year's date or phone 415/522-3535.

DIVERSIONS

Hop on a Bus: It's good to be a dog in San Francisco. Dogs are allowed on **Muni buses** and streetcars as long as it's not commute time (dog hours are 9 A.M.–3 P.M. and 7 P.M.–5 A.M.). Only one dog is permitted per vehicle. Dogs must be on a short leash and muzzled, no matter how little or how sweet. (There are many muzzles dogs barely notice. Shop around 'til you find one your dog doesn't despise.) Bus driver Tom Brown told us about the creative, but ineffective, ways some people muzzle their dogs. "This one man had a part pit-bull dog, and he put a little rubber band around its mouth," said Brown. "No way that dog was getting on my bus."

Dogs pay the same fare as owners. If you're an adult, you pay $1.25, and your dog does, too. Dogs of seniors pay the senior rate. Lap-sized dogs can stay on your lap, but all others are consigned to the floor. Keep your dog from getting underfoot and be sure he's well walked before he gets on. Call 415/673-MUNI (415/673-6864) for more information.

Ride Halfway to the Stars: Not many world-famous tourist attractions permit pooches. Can dogs ascend the Eiffel Tower? No. Can they visit the Vatican? No. Can they ride in a beautiful old **San Francisco cable car?** They sure can! (They can also go on the Golden Gate Bridge. See the Diversion for details.)

Jake the Dog has mixed feelings about the cable car privilege. He doesn't mind the clanging of the bells, as his predecessor Joe did. But he's not too keen on wearing a muzzle (a requirement, along with a leash; the muzzle can be a gentle nylon one that most dogs, not including Jake, barely notice), but what he really doesn't care for are the hills. On a recent descent to Fisherman's Wharf, he tried to scramble from the floor to my lap, and we both slid down the bench and smack into the open newspaper of a surprised commuter. "Welcome to the sports section," he said with a bemused grin.

Opinions vary about whether dogs should ride inside or outside. Some drivers think the outside is better because the cable noise isn't so amplified, and dogs don't get so nervous. Others say the outside is too dangerous—that a dog could panic and jump off. I opt for inside, but if you have a small dog and can hold her securely on your lap, riding outside is the best way to get the full San Francisco experience.

Only one dog is permitted per cable car. Dogs aren't allowed during peak commute times (see above for hours), and you should never take your dog on a crowded cable car. Off-season and away from touristy areas are your best bets. Dogs pay the same fare as their person. If you pay the full $3 adult rate, your dog does too. For more information, call 415/673-MUNI (415/673-6864).

Cafe Niebaum Coppola: Dogs are welcome to join their people at any of 12 white-cloth–covered tables outside this upscale North Beach/Financial District restaurant owned by Francis Ford Coppola. Apparently if you come here enough, you're bound to run into the famous bearded director himself. 916 Kearney Street; 415/291-1700.

Caffe Centro: The bistro dinners are so good you'll wish you could afford to come here with your dog every night to dine at the eight outdoor tables. Try the seared tuna Niçoise or the saffron fettuccine with grilled prawns. You can also get gourmet breakfasts and lunches at this South of Market café. 102 South Park; 415/882-1500.

Calzone's Pizza Cucina: You and your dog can dine on wonderful pastas, pizzas, calzones, seafood, and steak at this North Beach restaurant. It has about a trillion outdoor tables to choose from. 430 Columbus Avenue; 415/397-3600.

The Cannery: This old Del Monte packing plant is home to three delightful restaurants with courtyard tables for you and your dog, and there's often entertainment here. The restaurants usually don't have courtyard service after dark because it's too cold, so call first to find out. The Cannery is at 2801 Leavenworth Street. One of its dog-friendly restaurants is **Las Margaritas Restaurant.** Seven kinds of margaritas, mesquite-grilled shark, and a great view of the courtyard below make this one of the more popular Mexican restaurants this side of the Mission district. 415/776-6996.

The Canvas Gallery: There's always a water bowl for dogs on the patio of this progressive art gallery that doubles as a very popular café and lounge. It's where the hip dogs go in the Inner Sunset district. The California cuisine is tasty, and even if you can't go inside with your dog to see the art, you can always peek in. 1200 9th Avenue (at Lincoln Way); 415/504-0060.

Cioppino's: Dogs love coming to this well-known Fisherman's Wharf seafood restaurant because they know they're more than welcome. The folks here always provide water to thirsty pooches. You can dine at any of oodles of plastic sidewalk tables here. 400 Jefferson Street; 415/775-9311.

Cool Beans: The owners of this delightful café adore dogs and keep a treat jar by the front door, near the tiny outdoor eating area. You can dine on tasty homemade soups, sandwiches, and sweets while your dog munches and crunches and drools on her biscuits. The coffee is delectable, but if you're not a coffee drinker, try the yummy chai. Thanks to Riko and her dog for the heads-up about this little gem. 4342 California Street; 415/750-1955.

Crepevine: Mmmm. MMMMMmmm. MMMMMM. That's the way Jake groans with desire when he comes here and looks at all the happy folks sitting at the outdoor tables dining on their steaming hot crepes. You can choose from a variety of delicious crepes or create your own concoction. Crepevine has a cozy, bohemian feel, even outside. 624 Irving Street; 415/681-5858.

Curbside Cafe: The servers here are very dog-friendly, and the continental cuisine is top-notch. Try not to let your dog block the sidewalk, since it's a tight squeeze here. 2417 California Street; 415/929-9030.

Curbside Too: Want to have your dog at your side while you dine on tasty French cuisine? He'll lick his lips as you down your escargot at the attractive outdoor tables here. It's casual, but high quality. Just a bone's throw from the Presidio's western entrance. 2769 Lombard Street; 415/921-4442.

Extreme Pizza: Dine on delicious gourmet pizzas and tasty salads with your happy dog at your side. The outdoor area features fun 1950s soda fountain–type stools and several tables. 1980 Union Street; 415/929-8234.

Fisherman's Pizzeria: If you and your salty mutt are sniffing around Fisherman's Wharf for pizza, you'll get a decent meal here. A sign above the entrance features a fisherman and his dog in a little boat, so you'll know you and your canine crew are welcome. Dine at the seven sidewalk tables. 2800 Leavenworth; 415/928-2998.

Ghirardelli Square: What was once a chocolate factory is now one of the classiest tourist shopping centers in the country. More important than that, it's got a lot to offer residents and their dogs. Ghirardelli Square is at 900 North Point Street. Two restaurants with outdoor cafés are: **Boudin Sourdough Bakery and Cafe:** Dine on pastries, croissants, cheesecake, or huge sandwiches as you gaze across Beach Street at the bay, 415/928-7404; and **Ghirardelli Fountain and Candy:** Here's where you can get some of that famous rich Ghirardelli ice cream with all the fixings. Just remember: The more your dog gets, the fewer sit-ups you have to do. Stay away from chocolate, though. It can be very bad for dogs, 415/474-3938.

Grove Cafe: This coffeehouse is so popular you might need a shoehorn to find room at the plentiful outdoor tables here. But if you and your dog like the Chestnut Street coffee scene, you'll enjoy sipping your joe among the Marina District masses. You can wash down your coffee with some fine sandwiches, salads, and pastries. 2250 Chestnut Street, 415/474-4843.

Horse Shoe Coffeehouse: Enjoy good coffee and pastries at a down-to-earth café with two sidewalk tables. 566 Haight Street; 415/626-8852.

Java Beach: After a morning of combing Ocean Beach, you can catch some rays and eat some lunch on one of the benches outside this mellow soup, sandwich, and salad shop. 1396 La Playa at the Great Highway; 415/665-5282.

La Mediterranée: Dog owners are lucky—there are two of these top Mideast/Greek restaurants in the city; each puts tables outside in decent weather and has a dog-loving staff. Try the vegetarian Middle-East plate. Even meateaters enjoy it. The restaurant at 2210 Fillmore Street, 415/921-2956, has only a couple of tiny outdoor tables. (The area inside is fairly tiny, too.) The restaurant at 288 Noe Street, 415/431-7210, has several roomy sidewalk tables, some of which are covered by an awning.

Left at Albuquerque: The Southwest comes to San Francisco at this fun Union Street eatery. For an appetizer, try the cilantro-lime shrimp quesadilla. And if you want to make your dog very happy, order the Cowboy Mix Grill, a heaping plateful of ribs, chicken, and steak, with mashed potatoes. Your drooling dog may join you at the very attractive street-side dining area. 2140 Union Street; 415/749-6700.

Liverpool Lil's: You can see two wonderful sights from this fun English pub: 1) the Golden Gate Bridge; and 2) the western end of the Presidio. Enjoy a drink and fish-and-chips with your dog at your side at the six pleasant outdoor tables. 2942 Lyon Street; 415/921-6664.

Mocca on Maiden Lane: Now your dog can dine in one of the most posh streets of the Union Square area. Just a bone's throw from the finest stores in San Francisco, Mocca is a European-style café famed for its many types of salads. Dine at the zillions of umbrella-topped tables right on the street, which is closed to traffic. 174 Maiden Lane; 415/956-1188.

Mona Lisa Restaurant: This family-owned and operated North Beach restaurant is our little secret, OK? We discovered it one day while roaming around without Joe Dog and had a most sumptuous feast inside. Everything we ordered, from salad to pasta to main dish to dessert, was wonderful. Plenty of insiders know about the Mona Lisa, but it's off the radar screen for most. We like that. But of course, after this appears, it will be on many a dog's radar. The pizza here has been called the best in North Beach by many a patron. Pooches get to join their people at four outdoor tables. 353 Columbus Avenue; 415/989-4917.

Pasta Pomodoro: San Francisco is home to eight Pasta Pomodoro restaurants, and they all have the same tasty Italian cuisine. (Don't come here for pizza, as they don't do pizza. The polenta dish is a winner, though.) Several have plenty of outdoor seating and welcome good pooches. The one we've checked out personally is in Noe Valley, at 4000 24th Street; 415/920-9904.

Pier 39: If your dog doesn't mind flocks of tourists, you'll find a wide selection of decent eateries with outdoor tables for the two of you here. Your dog gets to smell the bay and sniff at the sea lions below. Pier 39 is off the Embarcadero, near Jefferson Street. Here are a couple of the restaurants where you and your dog are allowed (and they're not allowed at all restaurants' outdoor tables, so ask before settling in with your dog): **Chowder's:** Fried seafood and several types of chowder make Pier 39 really feel like a pier, 415/391-4737; **Sal's Pizzeria:** You and your dog can get a real taste of San Francisco by biting into any of Sal's special pizzas, 415/398-1198. Sometimes it's fun to just grab a snack at one of a few walk-up windows on the pier as you stroll around. Jake highly recommends ordering a little bagful of hot and crispy-yet-gooey doughnuts from Trish's Mini Donuts, and then accidentally dropping one right in front of your dog.

Pompei's Grotto: If your dog likes the smell of seafood, he probably won't mind joining you at an outdoor table at this famous restaurant on the main drag at Fisherman's Wharf. The fish is fresh and the pasta delicious. And if your dog is thirsty, one of the friendly servers will probably offer her a cup of water. 340 Jefferson Street; 415/776-9265.

Primo Patio Cafe: If you and the pooch need sustenance before or after a good sniff around SBC Park, this casual Caribbean restaurant is a primo place to visit. It's just a block or so away from the San Francisco Giants' home, and the food is mouthwatering. Dine with your dugout dog at the two sidewalk tables here. (Sorry, no dogs in the garden section of the restaurant, since they would have to walk through the indoor section and past the kitchen.) 214 Townsend Street; 415/957-1129.

Rose's Cafe: As soon as you sit down to dine with your dog at this elegant Italian-Californian restaurant's lovely side patio, you'll know you've come to the most dog-friendly restaurant in the city. Your dog will almost immediately be greeted by someone from the staff (often the dog-loving manager, Matthew) and given a big bowl of water. Then comes the gourmet house-made dog biscuit, available for a fairly good price. Throughout the meal comes plenty of attention, often from other diners, sometimes from the folks who run Rose's.

My introduction to Rose's came a few years back, when I got a letter from reader Carol Copsey, and her dog, Bella, a flirty American Eskimo. She was a frequent patron and wanted to let Joe and me know about Bella's favorite restaurant. I phoned her, and we got together one cool summer evening for dinner at Rose's. Joe was immediately smitten by Bella's fluffy good looks, but he fell asleep somewhere between the second and third gourmet dog biscuit. Bella didn't know what to make of Joe's snoozing on their date, but she pulled through after another nibble of dog treat. We had a wonderful time dining under the cream-colored awning, heat lamps getting us warm enough to take off our wraps.

The food here is superb. The menu changes frequently, but here are a few dishes to be sure to order if you see them listed: bruschetta with fresh tomatoes, garlic and basil; peaches, kadota figs, and prosciutto; crescenza-stuffed focaccia; soft polenta with gorgonzola; sautéed sweet white corn; local albacore with tomato, fennel, romano beans, and tapenade. The desserts are every bit as delicious.

It can get pretty busy here at times, so try to come when it's less hectic, for your dog's sake as well as other patrons'. A good bet is to phone for reservations and mention that you'll be bringing your well-behaved furry friend along. There are also a few tables along the front of the restaurant, but if you have a choice, the side area is the best. 2298 Union Street; 415/775-2200.

Rustico: This eatery in Potrero Hill features pizza, pasta, panini, soup, and salads. It has lots of outside tables. 300 DeHaro Street; 415/252-0180.

Sea Breeze Café: Come here for delicious comfort food with a European twist. If you're here for weekend brunch, try the brown sugar and vanilla cream oatmeal; the weather in the Outer Sunset district is usually just right for this kind of cozy dish. But what dogs like best is that the café owners love dogs and welcome them at the sidewalk tables with a bowl of fresh water. (You can get tasty, natural dog treats at the natural food store next door.) 3940 Judah Street; 415/242-6022.

Squat and Gobble: Dogs love visiting the Castro's Squat and Gobble café and crepery. Not only are the servers really friendly, but the sidewalk alfresco dining area is spacious and there's always a bowl of water for thirsty dogs. Try the Zorba the Greek crepe. It's to drool for. (Jake urges any dogs reading this to convince their people to order the Gobble Burger instead.) 3600 16th Street (at Market and Noe); 415/552-2125.

Steps of Rome: "Of course we allow dogs!" exclaimed a manager on a recent visit. "We love dogs!" This big and bustling North Beach restaurant is a really fun place for a meal or just coffee and people-watching. The staff is friendly, and the atmosphere is very Italian, in a modern kind of way. And the food—*delicioso!* I love it here because I'm a big risotto fan, and Steps features a different risotto daily. The sidewalk tables for you and your dog are plentiful and popular. 348 Columbus Avenue; 415/397-0435.

Toy Boat Dessert Cafe: You may not be able to say it 10 times fast, but you and your dog won't feel a need to speak when you're at the outside bench eating rich and creamy desserts. 401 Clement Street; 415/751-7505.

Universal Cafe: This charming little Potrero Hill restaurant is very popular with the pooch set. The very friendly staffers here love dogs and provide them water and kind words. The restaurant features a variety of magnificent dishes with a California twist. If it's on the menu, be sure to try the caramelized onion pizza with prosciutto, fontina, and ricotta. Dine with your happy dog at the five outdoor tables. (A big thank-you to Rosie Dog and her people, Melanie and Sandra, for letting us know about this gem.) 2814 19th Street; 415/821-4608.

DIVERSION

Sniff Out an Apartment with Your Dog: Looking for some digs with your dog? It's not always easy in San Francisco. But thanks to a wonderful program of the San Francisco SPCA, dog people are finding it easier to rent in the city. The **Open Door Program** helps landlords and potential tenants come together. This program has helped hundreds of canines and their people find housing since its inception a few years back. To see listings, and to get tips about how to make you and your dog more viable candidates for tenanthood, go to www.sfspca.org and click on Open Door.

PLACES TO STAY

The City by the Bay has some of the most wonderful dog-friendly hotels anywhere.

Campton Place: The European ambience and superb service make this a luxury hotel your dog will never forget. The rooms are magnificently comfortable, gorgeous, and filled with extra touches that really make your stay here stand out. Some of the king rooms even feature sweet window seats with roman shades. A sample photo of such a room on Campton's website shows a border collie striking a pose on the cushions of the seat. That pretty much speaks to the dog-friendly attitude: "Any size dog is welcome!" says a dog-loving hotelier. (It used to be that only dogs 25 pounds or less—no larger than a respectable Thanksgiving turkey—were allowed. The smart management here decided that just didn't make sense. We hope other hotels with size limits follow suit.)

The hotel is just a half-block away from Union Square. Rates are $335–2,000. Dogs are $35 extra per day. 340 Stockton Street 94108; 415/781-5555; www.camptonplace.com.

Castro Suites: The owners of the two gorgeous apartments in this 1890s Italianate Victorian home advertise that they cater to gay, lesbian, and straight clientele. What they don't say right off is that they also cater to dog clientele. They welcome dogs. Dogs who dig gardens (not in the literal sense of the word, please) should stay at the delectable garden suite, with its open airy feel and its beautiful garden. Urban-oriented dogs enjoy the apartment with its views of downtown and the bay. Rates are $200. Weekly rates are available. You'll get the address when you make your reservation. 415/437-1783; www.castrosuites.com.

Hotel Beresford: This Union Square–area hotel bills itself as "the friendliest hotel in San Francisco." Is it true? We don't know, as we haven't done a personality survey of the city's hotel employees. But we can say that the staff members we've encountered here have been very friendly and helpful. When asked if there's a size limit on pet guests, a chipper front desk manager replied, "No, as long as you don't bring an elephant." We like the attitude.

The family-owned hotel features attractive rooms—nothing fancy, but comfortable and clean. You'll get a decent continental breakfast with your stay. Humans get to eat at the hotel's adjacent restaurant, the White Horse Tavern. It has a real English pub feel, but the food is actually delicious—and even healthful, if you order right.

Dogs need to stay in the hotel's first-floor smoking rooms. Rates are $89–139. 635 Sutter Street 94102; 415/673-9900 or 800/533-6533; www.beresford.com.

Hotel Beresford Arms: The sister hotel of the Hotel Beresford, this one is bigger and more elegant, with a few extra amenities. The lobby, complete with pillars and a chandelier, is a bit grander. You and the pooch can stay in a standard room or a suite with a kitchen. A continental breakfast and a fun afternoon tea and wine social comes with your stay. As an added attraction, the hotel advertises that its rooms feature whirlpool baths and bidets. (We aren't sure of the lure of the latter and assume that these bidets are not of the whirlpool bath variety.)

While this hotel is the prettier of the two, it's a little tougher on dogs. Pooches need to be in the smallish range (the front desk clerk will help you decide if your dog is smallish), must stay on the third (smoking) floor, and are not allowed in the elevator. (In fairness, we really like that neither of these hotels charges an extra fee for dogs.)

On the outside, the hotel looks like any of the many decent old brick-facade apartment buildings in the slightly-off-Union-Square neighborhood. It's not the Ritz, but it is a comfy place to stay with your wee dog. Rates are $99–199. 701 Post Street 94109; 415/673-2600 or 800/533-6533; www.beresford.com.

Hotel Cosmo: Dogs love this hip hotel. The views are cool and the room are cosmopolitan yet comfy (the beds have cushy pillowtops). The hotel is artsy without being pretentious. Dogs hate pretentiousness. But what dogs like most at this hotel is that they're treated like welcome guests here. Upon arrival, every dog gets a Tails of the City Kit, which includes a pet blanket, a food and water bowl, a mat to put those on, a treat, and "Yip Yap" breath fresheners (for your dog, not you, unless of course you forgot your toothpaste). Dogs who stay here also get access to the hotel's open-air patio. Rates are $79–179. 761 Post Street 94109; 415/673-6040; www.hotel-cosmo.com.

Hotel Monaco: You and your dog will have *so* much fun at this upscale, sophisticated, whimsical hotel near Union Square. Upon entering the main lobby, you'll be wowed by the gorgeous two-story-tall French-style fireplace. (It's like the famed fireplace in *Citizen Kane*, only without the austere emotional surroundings.) Louis Armstrong hits and other sumptuous music floats around the high ceilings, which sport wonderful, light-hearted murals of the sky and hot-air balloons.

The rooms here are sumptuous, with opulent decor. You'll find a variety of furnishings, including canopied beds (with thick, rich material for the canopy), Chinese-style armoires, and cushy ottomans. If you need more room, you can stay in a gorgeous suite that comes with a big whirlpool tub and entertainment center with VCR.

The hotel's mission is to seduce and pamper, and dogs are not excluded from this noble cause. The Monaco offers something called the Bone A Petit Pet Package. It includes bottled water, clean-up bags, dog towels, quality chew toys, gourmet dog cookies, and temporary pooch ID tags. You can also ask the front desk for Lassie, Babe, or Dr. Doolittle videos. The price for all this: $0! Yes, free! But you have to mention the Pet Package when you make your reservation. In addition, so that your furry friend won't be lonely if you need to step out, dog-walking or sitting services are available for a fee.

Rates are $179–350. Don't forget to ask for the Pet Package when making your reservation. The Monaco, a Kimpton hotel (see Kimpton Hotels, below, for more on these beauties) is directly across from the Curran Theater. 501 Geary Street 94102; 415/292-0100 or 800/214-4220; www.monaco-sf.com.

Hotel Nikko: Small dogs are welcome to spend the night with you at this lovely contemporary Japanese-style hotel located three blocks west of Union Square. Rates are $179–3,000. 222 Mason Street 94102; 415/394-1111; www.nikkohotels.com.

Hotel Triton: If you're hankering for a wonderfully unique, creative, fun, intimate, whimsical, sophisticated place to stay, hanker no more, and book yourself any of the 140 rooms at the Hotel Triton. It's as if Betty Boop, Salvador Dali, Pee Wee Herman, and UB Iwerks somehow came together to create their dream lodging.

I normally consider it a sign of laziness when guidebook authors lift material straight out of a brochure, but I shall do this here with the noble purpose of letting the creative Triton folks speak for themselves: "Totally hip without the attitude, the Hotel Triton is not for your average Joe…" (I pause for a moment to say that Joe Dog tried hard not to take offense at this statement) "…but for guests with imagination and style. A tarot reading during nightly wine hour, whimsical sculptured furniture, and a twinkly-eyed staff" (I pause again to attest to the fact that their eyes do, indeed, seem to sparkle a little more than those of most other hotel staffers') "await you at this fun and funky gem. Stay in one of the celebrity suites designed by the likes of Jerry Garcia, Santana, or Graham Nash. If you're feeling environmentally correct, try an Eco-Room. For a little more yin in your yang, a Zen Den might help you attain harmony."

The hotel offers a number of special packages, but the most unusual is the "So Hip It Hurts" package: For $289, you get a deluxe guestroom and a $65 tattoo or piercing at Mom's Body Shop on Haight Street. Well, that's one way for a hotel to leave an impression on you.

Room rates are $150–389. The Triton, a Kimpton hotel (see Kimpton Hotels, below, for other dog-friendly Kimptons) is right across the street from the Dragon Gate entrance to Chinatown. 342 Grant Avenue 94108; 415/394-0500 or 800/433-6611; www.hotel-tritonsf.com.

Kimpton Hotels: There are 13 of these delightful, super-dog-friendly boutique hotels in San Francisco. Alas, there's not room to write about them all in detail. I've described three in my usual fashion in this section, but I don't want to ignore the others, so here's a synopsis of each. They charge no dog fee except when a special dog package is offered. If you want to save money, you don't have to take the package, no matter how pleading your dogs' eyes.

Union Square area
Hotel Monaco: See full listing, above.

Hotel Palomar: It's sophisticated, it's luxurious, it's South of Market, and it's got an amazing dog package called the Lap of Luxury, which includes a visit from a pet stylist to do your dog's nails and hair, a pet massage, a pet robe (it's true, it's true!), a leopard print dog bed, bottled water, treats, a Palomar signature collar and leash, doggy breath mints, and a toy. 12 4th Street 94103; 415/348-1111 or 877/294-9711; www.hotelpalomar.com.

Monticello Inn: The only thing missing in this grand colonial-style hotel is Thomas Jefferson. The hotel is housed in a landmark 1906 building. 127 Ellis Street 94102; 415/392-8800 or 866/778-6169; www.monticelloinn.com.

The Prescott Hotel: Enjoy quiet luxury at this beautiful hotel. The rich color schemes in each room are perfect for a relaxing evening with your quiet dog. 545 Post Street 94102; 415/563-0303 or 866/271-3632; www.prescotthotel.com.

The Serrano Hotel: Dogs enjoy staying at this Spanish-revival hotel not because of the interesting architecture but because of the Pet Palace Package. It includes designer mineral water, gourmet dog treats, and poopy bags. For an extra fee, dogs can get a little walk, dog food, a dog bed, or a leash. 405 Taylor Street 94102; 415/885-2500 or 866/289-6561; www.serranohotel.com.

The Sir Francis Drake Hotel: See full listing, below.

Villa Florence Hotel: You like Italy? Stay at this lovely Italian-themed little hotel. 225 Powell Street 94102; 415/397-7700 or 866/823-4669; www.villaflorence.com.

Nob Hill
Hotel Juliana: The pillowtop beds at this contemporary, stylish hotel are great for humans, but dogs who stay here can get the Man's Best Friend package, which includes dog treats, a park map for finding a good spot for "walkies," a chew toy, and bottled water. Humans get a number of goodies in this package, including a box of chocolates and free parking. 590 Bush Street 94108; 415/392-2540 or 866/325-9457; www.julianahotel.com.

Fisherman's Wharf
Argonaut Hotel: This luxurious, historic waterfront hotel provides great views of the Golden Gate Bridge, Alcatraz, and Ghirardelli Square. 495 Jefferson Street at Hyde Street 94109; 415/563-0800 or 800/790-1415; www.argonauthotel.com.

Best Western Tuscan Inn: Yes, Kimpton runs this Best Western, and you can tell by the nice touches, including a big fireplace in the lobby. Opt for the special Wag and Stay package and you'll get dog bedding, biscuits, toys, poop bags, and a CD of music created especially for pets. (I have no idea what this sounds like.) 425 Northpoint Street 94133; 415/561-1100 or 800/648-4626; www.tuscaninn.com.

Financial District
Galleria Park Hotel: You'll find an urban oasis at this 1911 Art Nouveau–style hotel. Choose the Something to Bark About package and your dog will get a "doggy bag" filled with treats, a plush toy, bottled water, a bowl,

and poop bags. 191 Sutter Street 94104; 415/781-3060 or 866/756-3036; www.galleriapark.com.

Harbor Court Hotel: The Harbor Court is homey and restful at the same time it's a happening place. Dogs who stay here can get the Pet Retreat package, which features a pet bed and pad, a rawhide bone, water and food bowls, bottled water, and poop bags. 165 Steuart Street 94105; 415/882-1300 or 866/792-6283; www.harborcourthotel.com.

Hotel Triton: See full listing, above.

Laurel Motor Inn: The owners love dogs, so many visiting dogs choose to stay here. It's conveniently situated in a lovely neighborhood just far enough from downtown to be able to get great views of it from some of the rooms. It's also just a bone's throw from the magnificent Presidio National Park (see Parks, Beaches, and Recreation Areas). Rates are $145–190. 444 Presidio Avenue 94115; 415/567-8467; www.thelaurelinn.com.

The Marina Motel: This charming 1930s motel is a few blocks from two great places to walk your dog—Crissy Field and the Presidio (see Parks, Beaches, and Recreation Areas). It has a bougainvillea and fuschia-festooned courtyard and little wrought iron balconies, which makes it feel less motelly and more Mediterranean. Some rooms have kitchens, and every room comes with free parking for one car. This alone is worth the room price in this neighborhood! Rates are $79–125. Dogs are $10 extra. 2576 Lombard Street 94123; 800/346-6118; www.marinamotel.com.

Ocean Park Motel: This art deco gem is San Francisco's very first motel. It was completed in 1937, one month before the Golden Gate Bridge. "When we took the place over (in 1977), deco was pretty much a lost art," says owner Marc Duffett. "But my wife and I put everything into this place to preserve the deco flair and at the same time make it homey."

Conveniently situated just a long block from Ocean Beach (above) and the San Francisco Zoo, this pleasant motel provides a quiet, safe atmosphere away from the hectic pace (and price) of downtown. You can hear the foghorns from the motel's relaxing hot tub. You can also hear the trolley cars, but it's not bad. And there's a special little play area for kids (the Duffetts have two and know the importance of playgrounds). Rates are $75–115. Two-room suites with three queen-sized beds and a kitchen are $160–195. Dogs are $10 extra. 2690 46th Avenue; 415/566-7020; www.oceanparkmotel.citysearch.com.

The Palace Hotel: Dogs at the Palace? I know what you're thinking: These must be those itsy-bitsy dogs you can't see until you step on them and they shriek, right? Wrong! This four-diamond luxury hotel welcomes dogs up to 80 pounds to stay here (as long as they're not pit bulls or rotties). Eighty pounds is a lot of dog, and it's thrilling to me that they're able to hunker down at this gorgeous old downtown hotel. Today the Palace, tomorrow the White House! Dogs can't have tea with you in the gorgeous tea room, but if you want a version of the infamous Tea at the Palace, you can simply order room service. Rates are $149–550. 2 New Montgomery Street 94105; 415/512-1111; www.sfpalace.com.

San Francisco Marriott Fisherman's Wharf: Stay here and you and your pooch are just two blocks from all the T-shirt and souvenir shops that have taken over Fisherman's Wharf. Actually, some fishing boats still live at the Wharf, and some local crabs still frequent the restaurants, so it's not as commercialized as it looks at first (and second) glance. The rooms are decent, and your stay includes use of the hotel's health club and sauna. Dogs need to be under 50 pounds to stay here. Rates are $159–279. 1250 Columbus Avenue 94133; 415/775-7555 or 800/228-9290.

The Sir Francis Drake Hotel: This luxurious old Union Square hotel is famous for its Beefeater doorman who helps tourists and hotel guests alike. Jake likes the Beefeater almost as much as he likes beef. So do other doggy visitors, who tend to get excited about this man in plush red and a cool hat.

This hotel has been a stylin' place since 1928, and since it's become a Kimpton hotel (see above for more on the dog-friendly Kimptons), it's also become a little more mod and super-dog-friendly. If you opt for the Bowzer Buddy Package during your stay, you can get a dog bowl with "in-room water service daily," a Sir Francis Drake Hotel chew toy, and a few other goodies. Rates for the package start at $189. You can choose a plain old stay at the hotel and it'll run you $139–429. Should you care to dance, the concierge will help you find a dog-sitter so you can cut a rug or two at the marvelous Harry Denton's Starlight Lounge, at the top of the hotel. 450 Powell Street 94102; 415/392-7755 or 800/795-7129; www.sirfrancisdrake.com.

TraveLodge by the Bay: Some rooms here have private patios. A few even have extra-length beds, should you find that you're tall. This motel is just three blocks from the part of Lombard Street that's known as "the crookedest street in the world." Rates are $65–135. Dogs are $20 extra and are relegated to the smoking rooms. 1450 Lombard Street 94123; 415/673-0691.

Westin St. Francis: The cable car stops in front of this historic landmark, so there's no excuse for not taking your dog on it. (See the Diversion Ride Halfway to the Stars for more about dogs on cable cars.) After a day of sniffing around San Francisco, your medium to small dog (40 pounds is the max allowed here) can crash on the Heavenly Pet Bed supplied by the St. Francis. It's a miniature version of the delectably comfortable Heavenly Bed that humans get to sleep on here. Dogs love this, but they're also grateful that humans get one Heavenly item dogs don't: The Heavenly Bath. Rates are $219–1,850. 335 Powell Street 94102; 415/397-7000; www.westinstfrancis.com.

CHAPTER 36

San Mateo County

From the cool and foggy beaches of the coast to the warm and sunny inland communities, there's something for every dog's taste in San Mateo County. Sadly, the 15,000 acres of county parklands still ban dogs, and some state beaches recently followed suit. But don't let your dog cry in her kibble. A few beaches (including one off-leash beauty in Pacifica) and plenty of parks still welcome your dog. And a couple of off-leash parks were born here since the last edition.

The Midpeninsula Regional Open Space District has become one of a dog's best friends, with four preserves in San Mateo County that allow dogs. One even has a 16-acre off-leash area (see Pulgas Ridge Open Space Preserve in the San Carlos section). Be sure to follow extremely good doggy etiquette at all the district's preserves, because there are a lot of antidoggers out there who would love to get the district to take away our privileges.

PICK OF THE LITTER—SAN MATEO COUNTY

BEST OFF-LEASH BEACH
Esplanade Beach, Pacifica (page 499)

MOST PRIM AND TRIM DOG PARK
Foster City Dog Playground, Foster City (page 506)

BEST CHUNK OF LEASH-FREE LAND
16 acres within Pulgas Ridge Open Space Preserve,
San Carlos (page 514)

MOST DOG-FRIENDLY PLACES TO EAT
Beach Cafe, Pacifica (page 500)
Cameron's Inn, Half Moon Bay (page 512)
Moon Juice Cafe, Half Moon Bay (page 513)

MOST DOG-FRIENDLY PLACE TO STAY
Westin San Francisco Airport, Millbrae (page 501)

BEST SEAVIEW COTTAGES
Estancia del Mar Cottages, Pescadero (page 520)

FRIENDLIEST BOOKSTORE
Kepler's Books, Menlo Park (page 516)

The district has unique rules about poop-scooping and six-foot leashes. Scooping the poop is required in places, but because of limited trash disposal sites, if you kick the poop off the trail, that's usually considered OK. (Helpful hint: Don't wear open-toed sandals.) And retractable leashes are allowed to go beyond the six-foot mark in many instances, which is a rare thing indeed. The exceptions: when you're within 100 feet of parking lots, roads, trailheads, picnic areas, and restrooms, and when you're within 50 feet of other people or any body of water, including creeks. It's a great policy—one other park districts should implement.

The district provides excellent park brochures and a comprehensive flyer about dog rules. When we received the most recent packet, it came in an attractive translucent green vellum envelope and had everything we needed, and then some. Phone 650/691-1200 for doggy details.

Daly City

PARKS, BEACHES, AND RECREATION AREAS

Daly City isn't flush with great places to take a dog. In fact, some city parks don't even permit pooches. Here are two that do.

❶ Palisades Park Dog Area

🐾 🐕 (See San Mateo County map on page 494)

This is the smallest dog park I've ever seen. It's about 3,600 square feet—not much bigger than many backyards in the area. It's fenced and has double gates for dog safety, but it's not signed, and there's nothing in it at all except for some petrified poops scattered around the thick grass. The grass is so lush here's because it's not doggy Grand Central Station, as so many dog parks are. Without the stampeding paws, the grass will grow. If you have a dog who will chase a tennis ball, bring him here and he could get a decent workout. (Just don't throw the ball too far, or it could land in the ocean, which is just behind some tall shrubs and way down a cliff.)

The park is conveniently situated if you're on Highway 35/Skyline Boulevard and your dog starts crossing his legs. Turn west on Westridge Avenue and you'll see Palisades Park at the end of the road. Look to the right of the playground and you'll see the teeny dog park. 650/991-8006.

❷ Gellert Park

🐾 (See San Mateo County map on page 494)

The best feature of this flat, square park is that it's right behind the Serramonte Library. It's also conveniently situated if you are going to pay homage to someone at the Chinese Cemetery, right across the street. The park is made up of a few sports fields—watch out for flying baseballs, soccer balls, and softballs. The park's trees, which grow on two sides, aren't accessible—they're on top of a very steep little ridge. Your dog may become frustrated, especially since he must wear a leash through all this.

The park is on Wembley Drive at Gellert Boulevard. 650/991-8006.

South San Francisco

PARKS, BEACHES, AND RECREATION AREAS

❸ Orange Memorial Park

🐾 🐾 (See San Mateo County map on page 494)

Hidden behind the park's large baseball field is a big square of land surrounded on all sides by tall trees. It's good for a quick on-leash romp. There seem to be all kinds of sniffs around the large weeping willow tree in the middle of the field. It's on Orange Avenue at Tennis Drive. 650/829-3800.

🐾 Westborough Park

🐾🐾 (See San Mateo County map on page 494)

This is a hilly little park with many picnic tables, a tennis court, and a children's playground. Your best bet is to take the narrow, paved path along the back of the park. It's lined with trees and far from the madding baseball field below. Leashes are required. It's on Westborough Avenue at Galway Drive, just west of I-280. 650/829-3800.

PLACES TO STAY

La Quinta Inn San Francisco Airport: Rates are $119–129. 20 Airport Boulevard 94080; 650/583-2223; www.laquinta.com.

San Bruno

PARKS, BEACHES, AND RECREATION AREAS

🐾 San Bruno Dog Exercise Area/Sandberg Field

🐾🐾🐾🐾🐕 (See San Mateo County map on page 494)

This is a gem of a fenced-in park, where dogs can run their tails off—without a leash. The grass always seems to be green. There's plenty of water, poop bags galore, and benches for two-legged beasts. As an extra bonus, it has a great view of the bay. And for those who can't get enough of it while driving north on U.S. 101, there's an unparalleled view of that strange sign: "South San Francisco—The Industrial City."

The park opened in 1989 after local dog trainer Mal Lightfoot was fined for walking his notoriously obedient dogs off leash. "I spend all my life training dogs to be good citizens, and I was treated like a criminal," says Lightfoot, who runs the San Bruno Dog Training School. "It was the last straw." It took him and dozens of other frustrated dog owners nearly two years of working with—and against—city officials to get the park of their dreams.

Some detailed directions are necessary for finding this out-of-the-way park, even for locals. From El Camino Real, take Sneath Lane west. Just past I-280, turn right on Rollingwood Drive. Go right again at the first possible right, Crestwood Drive. Go left on Valleywood Drive and take a sharp right at Evergreen Drive. The park is in a few blocks, at Maywood and Evergreen Drives in back of the old Carl Sandburg School. Once at the school driveway, take the first road to the right and drive until you see the dog park. 650/738-7381.

6 Sweeney Ridge

🐾🐾🐾🐾 (See San Mateo County map on page 494)

If your dog appreciates breathtaking vistas of the Bay Area, with a rainbow assortment of wildflowers in the foreground, this 1,000-acre park is a rare treat. But if your canine is like most, he can take or leave such a magnificent panorama.

Still, if you like stunning views and a vigorous uphill climb, take the Sneath Lane entrance. It may be toasty when you start, but bring a couple of thick wool sweaters if you plan to hike along the ridge—it's cold and often foggy up there. The furrier your dog, the more she'll take to the invigorating conditions.

The Skyline College entrance is ideal if you want a more moderate grade, but both trailheads will take you to the same place. The leash law here can come in handy if your dog is of the pulling mentality. Just say "mush" on those steep slopes.

From different parts of the ridge, you'll be able to see the ocean (and the Farallon Islands, on a good day), as well as Mt. Tamalpais in Marin, Mt. Diablo to the east, and Montara Mountain to the south. Judging by all the canines with flaring nostrils, the scents from all four directions must be as enticing as the views.

For the Sneath Lane entrance, take San Bruno's Sneath Lane all the way to the end. There's usually plenty of parking. The Skyline College entrance, off College Drive, is in the southeast corner of campus, near Lot 2. 415/239-2366 or 415/556-8371.

Pacifica

PARKS, BEACHES, AND RECREATION AREAS

Tails are wagging fast around here these days. This coastal community now has a leash-free beach! (See Esplanade Beach.)

7 Esplanade Beach

🐾🐾🐾🐾🐕 (See San Mateo County map on page 494)

This is the only beach between Humboldt County and Santa Cruz where dogs can legally trot around off leash these days (with the exception of two small beaches in Marin), so it's a really big deal that they're permitted to enjoy a leash-free walk if they're under voice control. The beach is fairly wide (if it's not high tide) and long enough for a very good walk. Many people who come here bring tennis-ball launchers so their dogs can really go out for a fly ball.

At the top of the long staircase that leads to the beach you'll find an attractive grassy area right in front of some long, low apartments. Leashed dogs are welcome to sniff around this area. To get to the beach, exit Highway 1 at Manor Drive and head west on Manor toward the ocean. It will dead-end at Esplanade Drive. Turn right and follow Esplanade about a third of a mile to where it makes almost a 90-degree curve to the right. (You'll see a large sign for the Land's End apartments.) The green park will be on your left, as will the staircase leading down the cliff to the beach. Park anywhere along the street. 650/738-7381.

🛭 Pacifica State Beach/Linda Mar Beach

🐾🐾🐾 (See San Mateo County map on page 494)

Even though this is a state beach, leashed dogs are welcome here. It's run by the city of Pacifica, so it doesn't have to follow the more stringent "no dogs" rules being enforced by most other state beaches in coastal San Mateo County. The setting alone warrants a visit. With green rolling hills in the distance behind you and the pounding sea before you, you and your dog won't regret stopping here. This is Surfer Heaven, so if your dog likes to see surfers doing their thing, this is the place to come. On Highway 1, park between Crespi Drive and Linda Mar Boulevard. 415/561-4700.

🛭 Milagra Ridge

🐾🐾🐾🐾 (See San Mateo County map on page 494)

Follow the trail up to the top of the tallest hill and you'll end up with both an incredible view of the Pacific and a perfect plateau for a picnic. You'll see hillsides covered with ice plant and even a few Monterey pines along the way. Visit in the spring if you want to be wowed by wildflowers.

Despite the leash law, dogs really seem to enjoy this park. Make sure to keep them on the trail, as the environment here is fragile. And keep your eyes peeled for the Mission Blue butterfly. This park is one of its last habitats. Milagra Ridge is especially magical at night. You've never seen the full moon until you've seen it from here.

Enter on Sharp Park Road in Pacifica, between Highway 1 and Skyline Boulevard. 415/239-2366 or 415/556-8371.

🔟 Sweeney Ridge

🐾🐾🐾🐾 (See San Mateo County map on page 494)

See San Bruno section.

PLACES TO EAT

Beach Cafe: After a walk on the chilly beach, there's nothing like a hot espresso and homemade croissant at the outdoor tables here. Owner Paula Thomson loves dogs, so lucky dogs who visit get a treat or two. Highway 1 at Rockaway Beach Avenue, at 4430 Highway 1; 650/355-4532.

Sam's Deli: Sam's is a refreshing spot to hit after an afternoon at Pacifica State Beach. It has good sandwiches at low prices and two outdoor tables. It's at the Linda Mar Shopping Center, just behind the beach, on the same side as Denny's and the shoe stores, about halfway down the row of shops. 1261 Linda Mar Shopping Center; 650/359-5330.

Millbrae

Now that dogs aren't allowed on trails surrounding Crystal Springs Reservoir, they are howling. But they can still grab a bite and spend the night.

PLACES TO EAT

Leonardo's Delicatessen: This truly Italian deli has plenty of outdoor tables, all comfortably far from sidewalk traffic. 540 Broadway Avenue; 650/697-9779.

PLACES TO STAY

Clarion Hotel: Rates are $89–249. Dogs are $30 extra. 401 East Millbrae Avenue 94030; 650/692-6363; www.clarionhotels.com.

Westin San Francisco Airport: If you're traveling by air and need to stay somewhere with your dog, this is about the most convenient and luxurious place you can stay. It's only two minutes from the airport. Each of the 390 rooms is well appointed and has a very comfortable bed, known as the Heavenly Bed. So that dogs don't feel left out, dogs who stay here get their own Heavenly Pet Bed. Pooches we've talked with say the beds are dreamy. For humans, there are mutt mitts (not exciting, but very handy) and better yet, there's a fitness center and a yummy Mediterranean-style bistro. Rates are $99–379. 1 Old Bayshore Highway 94030; 650/692-3500 or 800/228-3000; www.starwood.com.

Burlingame

PARKS, BEACHES, AND RECREATION AREAS

🔟 Burlingame Dog Exercise Park

🐾🐾🐾🐆 (See San Mateo County map on page 494)

Hooray! Burlingame's dog park is finally a reality. The half-grass, half–fine gravel park is a popular place, with a very different shape than most dog parks. It's very long, almost as long as two football fields end to end, and not extremely wide (anywhere from 30 feet to 70 feet). This lends itself very well to the park's name: It's a dog *exercise* park. With a shape like this, forward movement beckons. You and your dog can stand around and chat and sniff (as most do here), or you can really walk in this fenced park. In more typical squarish dog parks, you'd look kind of foolish taking a hike.

There are no decent-sized trees here yet. All are in the sapling stage, about waist-high at last check. But boy dogs still manage to do plenty of leg lifts on other spots they seem to find fascinating. Speaking of bodily functions, the one drawback to this park is that it's right next to a sewage treatment plant. This can make the park a little whiffy at times, depending on which way the wind is blowing, but it's usually not a problem. In fact, as far as dogs are concerned, the stinkier the better.

A nice bonus if you use this park: There's a great path you can follow. You can pick up the path behind the dog park. You have to leash up to use it, but it's a good walk. It's within Bayside Park, on the Old Bayshore Freeway between Anza Boulevard and Broadway. 650/558-7300.

12 Washington Park

😺😺 (See San Mateo County map on page 494)

This relatively small park has the look of an old college campus. Its trees are big and old and mostly deciduous, making autumn a particularly brilliant time. Bring a lunch and eat it on the thick, knotty old redwood picnic tables. They're something out of the Enchanted Forest. Joe Dog was always intrigued by the abundance of squirrels, but he never got too far with his pursuits, since leashes have been the law forever, and since the police station is around the corner.

The park is at 850 Burlingame Avenue below Carolan Avenue. 650/558-7300.

PLACES TO EAT

Cafe La Scala: The outdoor area at this exquisite Italian restaurant has dozens of tables, but it's still very romantic, with beautiful flowers, soft music, and pastoral murals. It's all very Florentine. Dogs need to sit at the edge of the patio area. In cooler months, the area is warmed by heat lamps. 1219 Burlingame Avenue; 650/347-3035.

PLACES TO STAY

San Francisco Airport Marriott: If you need to stay near the airport, and your dog appreciates good views of San Francisco Bay, you couldn't ask for a better hotel. Rates are $89–245. 1800 Old Bayshore Highway 94010; 650/692-9100.

Vagabond Inn: With these prices, it's a wonder they still call it Vagabond Inn. Rates are $92–120. Dogs are $10 extra. 1640 Bayshore Highway 94010; 650/692-4040.

Montara

PARKS, BEACHES, AND RECREATION AREAS

🔳🔳 McNee Ranch State Park

🐾🐾🐾🐾 (See San Mateo County map on page 494)

State parks usually ban dogs completely, or at least from all but paved roadways. But McNee is a refreshing exception to the rule. At McNee, you can hike at the same level as the soaring gulls and watch the gem-blue ocean below. The higher you go up Montara Mountain, the more magnificent the view. Hardly a soul knows about this park, so if it's peace you want, it's peace you'll get.

And if it's a workout you want, you'll get that, too. Just strap on a day pack and bring lots of water for you and your dog. If you do the full hike, you'll ascend from sea level to 1,898 feet in a couple of hours. As you hike up and away from the ocean and the road, you lose all sounds of civilization, and Highway 1 fades into a thin ribbon and disappears below.

As soon as you go through the gate at the bottom of the park, follow the narrow trails to the left up the hills. You may be tempted to take the wide and winding paved road from the start, but to avoid any bikers, take the little trails. Besides, they lead to much better vistas.

Eventually, you'll come to a point where you have a choice of going left or right on a wider part of the trail. It's a choice between paradise and heaven. Left will lead you to a stunning view of the Golden Gate Bridge and the Farallon Islands. Right will bring you to the top of the ridge, where you see Mt. Diablo and the rest of San Francisco Bay.

This was one of Joe's favorite parks, despite the leash law. Still, he always managed to slide down several steep grassy hills on his back, wriggling and moaning in ecstasy all the way.

It's easy to miss this park since there aren't any signs and there's no official parking lot. From Highway 1 in Montara, park at the far northern end of the Montara State Beach parking lot and walk across the road. Be careful as you walk along Highway 1, because there's hardly any room on the shoulder. You'll see a gate on a dirt road just north of you and a small state property sign. That's where you go in. A few cars can also park next to the gate on the sides of the dirt road. But don't block the gate or your car probably won't be there when you get back. 415/726-8819.

🔳🔳 Montara State Beach

🐾🐾🐾🐾 (See San Mateo County map on page 494)

This long, wide beach has more nooks and crannies than your dog will be able to investigate. Around midbeach, you'll find several little inlets carved into the minicliffs. Take your dog back there at low tide and you'll find all sorts of water, grass, mud, and beach flotsam. It's a good place for her to get her paws wet while obeying the leash law. The water at the inlets is as calm as pond water. This is where Joe first dared to walk in water. It was only a centimeter deep, but he licked his paws in triumph all the way home.

With the recent banning of dogs at other state beaches in the area, this one has been taking a pounding of late. I know it's hard, but please keep your dog on leash, or this beach could go the way of so many others.

Off Highway 1, park in the little lot behind the Chart House restaurant. There's also a parking area on the north side of the beach, off Highway 1. 415/726-8819.

PLACES TO STAY

Farallone Bed and Breakfast Inn: Two of the nine rooms in this homey Victorian inn have a private balcony and a small whirlpool bath. Some rooms have ocean views. A basic breakfast comes with your room. Rooms are $65–130. Dogs require a $25 deposit and are charged a $25 fee for the length of their stay. 1410 Main Street 94037; 650/728-8200 or 800/818-7319; www.faralloneinn.com.

Hillsborough

PARKS, BEACHES, AND RECREATION AREAS

15 Vista Park

🐾 (See San Mateo County map on page 494)

You can visit this park only if you live here, unless you choose to walk miles to get to it—there's no street parking for blocks, and no parking lot. And chances are that if you live in this town, your backyard is bigger anyway. A little section in the back has several tall eucalyptus trees that leashed neighborhood dogs call their own. It's good for sniffs when you can't get to a better park.

The park is at Vista and Culebra Roads. 650/579-3800.

San Mateo

PARKS, BEACHES, AND RECREATION AREAS

16 Central Park

🐾🐾🐾 (See San Mateo County map on page 494)

Bring plenty of quarters if you want to fully experience this strange park on the edge of downtown. It costs a quarter to park in the underground lot; a quarter to put your finger in the pulse machine; a quarter to watch the chicken lay a plastic prize egg; a quarter for the Pen Vendorama; it even costs a quarter for a cup of water at the refreshment stand, although smart shoppers know there's a water fountain within 20 feet.

As you enter the park from the 5th Avenue side, you immediately encounter the concession stand and surrounding dispensers that rival any at state fairs. The stand has good ice cream and tolerable pizza.

The rest of the park is a lush, green, miniature version of Golden Gate Park. There's a Japanese garden, and although no dogs are allowed inside, the Japanese ambience spills outside. The days we've visited, there was always something going on at the outdoor stage in back of the recreation center. A couple of large meadows are bordered by big shady redwoods. There's even a pint-sized railroad that takes up part of a small field. Someone told us that dogs have been known to chase the cars as they chug along the track. Leashes are a must, a rule you'd be well advised to follow: The fine for loose dogs is not a quarter.

The park is on East 5th Avenue at El Camino Real. 650/522-7420.

🐾🐾 Bayside-Joinville Park

🐾🐾 (See San Mateo County map on page 494)

Human olfactory senses may be mildly offended by the scents in this park, but dogs seem to thrive on them. Depending on which way the wind is blowing, the odor is bound to hit you at some point. It's a stale smell, like a dishrag that's still in the sink a week after Thanksgiving. Sometimes it's even worse. The alleged culprit is an old compost site across the street, where Shoreline Park will be built in the future. When it's potent, dogs tend to stand noses to the wind, tails slightly trembling, glued in homage.

But the park has some notable qualities. It's just across the street from San Francisco Bay, it's on Marina Lagoon (sorry, no swimming allowed), and it's well maintained.

The park has two sections. If you're the type who likes the bad news first, start at the Anchor Road entrance and take the path along the lagoon, over a guano-covered footbridge, past the big gray pump station, and onto a little dirt path on the edge of the lagoon. Then go left and take the second, cleaner footbridge over to the better half of the park. It's got a decent-sized field, young trees, and tennis courts. Or you can enter at Kehoe Avenue and Roberta Drive and reverse the path. 650/522-7420.

🐾🐾🐾 Laurelwood Park

🐾🐾🐾 (See San Mateo County map on page 494)

A small, clear stream winds the length of this rural park in the suburbs. Joe Dog never wanted anything to do with the water and jumped from one side to the other without getting a toenail damp. But Jake, aka Mr. Water, delights in its fresh scents and enticing sounds. Follow the bike trail—heeding the leash law, as this is a popular spot for bikers—along the stream, and enjoy tree-covered hillsides in a virtually suburb-free environment. Only a few blocks from the Laurelwood Shopping Center, this park is an ideal getaway after a quick shopping trip. The kids can use the playground at the foot of the bike trail.

The park is at Glendora and Cedarwood Drives. 650/522-7420.

19 Beresford Park

🐾🐾 (See San Mateo County map on page 494)

The bulk of this park is made up of sports fields. But venture behind the garden center and you and your pooch can enjoy a pleasant little leashed romp on a large grassy field. Many youthful-but-shady pine trees are growing well despite dozens of daily assaults from male dogs. Several picnic tables and a large children's play area near the field make this an adequate spot for a weekend afternoon with the family. People are friendly here—we were twice offered soda and beer by locals, who wanted Joe to "hang" with them.

The park is on Parkside Way at Alameda de las Pulgas. 650/522-7420.

PLACES TO EAT

Borel's Deli: You have your choice of deli food or hot food here. "Order the baked, hot turkey. Get extra gravy. Then drop it so your dog can eat it," Joe Dog would advise. Dine with your pooch outside at two tables. 59 Bovet Road; 650/573-7710.

PLACES TO STAY

Residence Inn by Marriott: There's a walking path not far from here, so it's a good place to stay with your pooch. Besides, it's a comfy lodging—not quite home, but it tries to come close. Rates are $89–179. Dogs are $10 extra, plus a $75 fee per visit. 2000 Winward Way 94404; 650/574-4700; www.marriott.com.

Foster City

PARKS, BEACHES, AND RECREATION AREAS

20 Foster City Dog Playground

🐾🐾🐾🦴 (See San Mateo County map on page 494)

This tidy, neat, petite fenced park with artificial grass is a little like a Stepford Wife: Lovely to look at, but perfect to the point of being scary. When I visited with Jake, I spent the whole time silently praying that he'd poop on the refined gravel ground cover (formally known as decomposed granite), not on the carpetlike Field Turf. The turf is the modern version of Astroturf, and it's like a green rug that aspires to be golf-course grass. I asked a nice gent there what happens if a dog does go to the bathroom on it, and he pointed to a poop-bag dispenser (no problem), and also to a scrub brush and bucket of water near the water fountain (ah, the Cinderella routine).

In the end, Jake didn't poop anywhere. He was having too much fun playing chase games with his new friends and learning to run through an agility tire and over an agility jump. Big dogs have their own section, which is great, because the small-dog section had really tiny, breakable dogs when we visited. (The small-dog section had the air of a casual country club, with the well-dressed dog people reposing on a variety of lawn chairs.) The entire park is less than a half acre, but dogs greatly enjoy themselves. There's shade from two large green shade structures, and water, scoops, picnic tables, and benches. A couple of very cute rusted-metal dog sculptures grace one end of the park.

Exit eastbound Highway 92 at Foster City Boulevard, go left at the offramp, and then right within a block at Foster City Boulevard. Travel about .7 mile and go right on Bounty Drive, and then left almost immediately into the parking lot. 650/286-3382.

PLACES TO EAT

Dogs dig dining at Foster City's lagoon-side restaurants. Here's one that welcomes dogs. Others do, too, but don't jump at the chance to advertise it.

Plaza Gourmet: Good dogs can dine with you on the attractive wood-planked deck. If your dog is thirsty, a fresh bowl of water is hers for the asking. 929C Edgewater Boulevard; 650/638-0214.

Redwood City

PARKS, BEACHES, AND RECREATION AREAS

21 Shore Dogs Park

🐾🐾🐾🐕 (See San Mateo County map on page 494)

This park is only three-quarters of an acre, but it doesn't matter. Dogs and their people are simply overjoyed just to have some legal off-leash romping room after so many years of being banned from all city parks. (It can get might windy here, and it's quite a sight to see dogs joyously running around with their ears flapping, and then standing still only to have their ears continue to flap.)

As its name may tell you, Shore Dogs Park is near the water. And what dog doesn't dig being able to sniff the odors wafting off of San Francisco Bay? During winter and fall, the park's location gives you and your dog a front-row seat to the shorebird migration. Your dog's jaw will drop as she watches an egret flap its gigantic wings. The birds have nothing to fear, as the park is fenced, and dogs can't fly.

Speaking of fear, the park is a good place to bring a small dog who feels intimidated by big beefy canines; there's a special fenced grassy area just for the little guys. Small dogs are welcome to join their bigger cousins at the main dog run, but sometimes it can be a little intimidating if your head doesn't even reach the knee of a giant who's running full out. (I know dogs don't have knees, but you get the picture.) The park is off Redwood Shores Parkway, near the end of Radio Road, in Redwood Shores. 650/654-6538.

PLACES TO EAT

Curly, Harmony, and Brittney are Redwood City dogs with great taste in dining. Here are their tried-and-true recommendations.

City Pub: Like pub food? Dine at the outdoor tables here at this charming hangout. If your dog is thirsty, the staff will happily provide a big bowl of water. 2620 Broadway; 650/363-2620.

Milagro's: The outdoor tables at this upscale Mexican restaurant are warm and cozy year-round, thanks to some effective heat lamps. Got a thirsty dog? The friendly servers bring out bowls of water for pooch diners. "I just sat a table of dogs and people yesterday!" said a vivacious host. "They were so well behaved and fun." 1099 Middlefield Road; 650/369-4730.

Mulligan's: There are lots of tables here for you and your dog. The dining, while not fine, will make your dog put on her best begging eyes. (Hot dogs, burgers, pizza, and fries tend to do that to even the most stoic pooch.) 2650 Broadway; 650/364-5600.

Belmont

PARKS, BEACHES, AND RECREATION AREAS

🐾 Water Dog Lake Park

🐾🐾🐾 (See San Mateo County map on page 494)

Dogs and their people seem magically drawn to this large, wooded park with a little lake in the middle. Maybe it's the way the moss drips off the trees at the bottom of this mountainous area, or the way the lake seems to create a refreshing breeze on the hottest days.

Or maybe it's got something to do with the name. We asked several dog owners how the park came to be called Water Dog Lake Park.

"I think the lake is kind of shaped like a dog. Actually, it's more like a kangaroo, isn't it?" said the proud owner of a beagle/terrier mix.

"It would be a good place to water your dog, if that were allowed," said a woman with a black Lab.

"When dogs and people were allowed to swim here, you couldn't get the Labs and all those water dogs out of this lake," explained a man with an Irish setter.

We hate to burst the romantic fantasy that a park as alluring as this one is named after man's best friend. But after some searching through historical records, we discovered the biting truth: Water Dog Lake Park was named after salamanders. A colloquial name for a salamander is "water dog," and apparently the little critters used to wriggle all over the place around here. We still think the park is great. Too bad dogs have to be leashed.

One other thing that we discovered about this park: If people would follow their dogs, perhaps a lot fewer would stumble onto the wrong trail. The one that goes up to the top of the park never comes near the lake and leads you more than a mile away from where you started. Joe tried tugging in the other direction, but I ignored him. We got a ride back to the entrance from a teenage boy who felt sorry for us.

Upon entering the park from the Lake Road entrance, take the wide path that goes straight in front of you. It will lead you down to the lake. Neither you nor your dog can go in the water, but you can have a great picnic there, or even go fishing off the little wooden pier.

If you start off taking the smaller trail that veers to the right, you'll get good exercise and a great view of the bay, but we don't recommend it, unless you enjoy getting lost and suffering heat fatigue in the summer. A final word of warning: Watch out for bikers. They're fast here.

Enter on Lake Road, just off Carlmont Drive. Try to come back to the same place. 650/595-7441.

🐾 Cipriani Park Dog Exercise Area

🐾🐾🐾🐕 (See San Mateo County map on page 494)

At press time for the book's latest edition, the big trees here had just been cut down, much to the dismay of dogs and their people. And the grass and wood-chip carpet had given way to decomposed granite. But this three-quarter-acre fenced park is still a treat for leash-free pooches and their chauffeurs. That's partly because of all the social events that take place here: There are frequent potlucks, seminars on topics such as canine first aid, and even a couple of fairs a year. In addition, the park has all good dog-park amenities, including poop bags, water, picnic tables, and attractive surroundings.

The park is at 2525 Buena Vista Avenue, behind the Cipriani School. It's a little hard to find. From El Camino Real, go west on Ralston Avenue. In about 1.5 miles, you'll pass Alameda de las Pulgas. Drive about another three-quarters of a mile, and be on the lookout for Cipriani Boulevard. It's a small street you can easily miss. Turn right on Cipriani and follow it a few blocks to Buena Vista. Turn left on Buena Vista and park near the school. You won't see the dog run from the street, but if you walk west and enter through the main park entrance, you'll soon see it. Whatever you do, don't take your dog through the school's playground when kids are present. The school really frowns on this. 650/595-7441.

24 Twin Pines Park

🐾🐾🐾 (See San Mateo County map on page 494)

This park is a hidden treasure, nestled among eucalyptus trees just outside the business district of Belmont. You'd never guess the dog wonders that await within. Your dog may hardly notice she's leashed. The main trail is paved and winds through sweet-smelling trees and brush. A clear stream runs below. In dry seasons, it's only about two feet deep, but in good years it swells to several feet. Dogs love to go down to the stream and wet their whistles. Past the picnic area are numerous small, quiet dirt trails that can take you up the woodsy hill or alongside the stream.

It's at 1225 Ralston Avenue, behind the police department. 650/595-7441.

El Granada

PLACES TO STAY

Harbor View Inn: Each of the 17 comfortable rooms at this upscale motel features a wonderful bay window seat, where you can get a very good view of the ocean and the harbor. You'll have to look over Highway 1, since you're on the east side of the road, but it's a nice touch you don't usually find at motels. The owners, Bob and Judy, have a little Yorkie, Joey, and they're mighty dog-friendly folks. They'll point you in the direction of a couple of hush-hush dog-walking spots nearby. Rates are $85–180. 51 Avenue Alhambra 94018; 650/726-2329; www.harbor-view-inn.com.

Half Moon Bay

This is a delightful place to come for a day of sniffing around the enchanting old "downtown" and checking out the beautiful ocean views. It's a real treat on days that are scorching elsewhere: This area is air-conditioned by the god of woolly sheepdogs. No matter how steaming hot it is elsewhere, you can almost always count on cool weather here. It's often chilly and foggy in the summer, wet and windy in the winter, and moderate in the fall and spring.

PARKS, BEACHES, AND RECREATION AREAS

Dogs are no longer allowed on the sand at any of the four Half Moon Bay State Beach areas, but they're still welcome to take a stroll on the scenic blufftop paths that stretch almost from one end of Half Moon Bay to the other. (See Surfer's Beach, Half Moon Bay State Beach, and Bluff Top Park for areas of easy trail access.)

Fortunately for sand-loving hounds, two city beaches permit leashed beasts.

25 Surfer's Beach

🐾🐾 (See San Mateo County map on page 494)

Water dogs dig being able to dip their paws in the water here. On almost any day, no matter how cold and gray it is, you'll find loads of surfers waiting for the perfect wave. The beach isn't big or wide, and it can be crowded at times, but it's a fun place to take a little stroll with your leashed dog. A trail that starts here takes you miles down the shore. It's a terrific, flat, easy, and very scenic hike. Jake highly recommends it.

Surfer's Beach is on Highway 1 and Coronado Street, just south of Pillar Point Harbor. 650/726-8297.

26 Half Moon Bay State Beach Trail

🐾🐾🐾 (See San Mateo County map on page 494)

This name is a misnomer. Thanks to the threatened snowy plover bird, and to people who abused the leashed-dog privilege, dogs are no longer allowed on the beach, even if they promise to wear their leashes and behave perfectly. But they are welcome on the paved blufftop trail here. The views are excellent, the sea air uplifting.

You can hook up with the trail here at several points. There's signage along different spots of Highway 1. At the very west end of Kelly Avenue you'll find Francis Beach and the entrance for the campground. (More on camping below.) At the west end of Venice Boulevard is Venice Beach (not to be confused with its radically different counterpart in Los Angeles County), and at the west end of Young Avenue you'll find both Dunes Beach and Roosevelt Beach.

This isn't the place to come for a 15-minute romp: If you park in the lots, it costs $6. You can park a little away on the street, or take your car down to the city-run Bluff Top Park, which has not only a paved trail, but a leashed-dog-friendly sandy beach—for free! (See below.)

If you can ignore all the RVs and crowds of tents, the area above Francis Beach is a stunning camping spot. Perched on ice plant–covered dunes above the Pacific, it's one of the most accessible beach camping areas in the Bay Area. All of the 52 campsites are available on a first-come, first-served basis. Sites are $20–25.

From Highway 1, follow the brown and white signs to the appropriate beach. 650/726-8820.

27 Bluff Top Park

🐾🐾🐾 (See San Mateo County map on page 494)

This is a splendid area to visit with a leashed dog. The beach is beautiful, long, and fairly wide, and the bluff top has a couple of fun and scenic trails. If you're hankering for a great walk, you can hoof it through other park and beach areas for several miles—almost all the way to the Half Moon Bay harbor.

From Highway 1, take Poplar Avenue west all the way to the end. A parking lot will be on your left. 650/726-8297.

28 Half Moon Bay Dog Park

🐾🐾🐕 (See San Mateo County map on page 494)

This 15,000-square-foot dog park is just temporary until the long-awaited Coastside Dog Park is up and running. (That one's been years in the planning and debating stages, so don't let your dog hold his dog breath. In fact, when I asked a former dog park coordinator about when the park might become a reality, he asked me if I was over 30. I said yes. "Not in your lifetime," he replied. Apparently there's been a lot of frustration about how the city has handled some issues.)

The park is a disheveled mass of landscaping bark and scattered dog toys surrounded by temporary and not terribly attractive fencing. In other words, dogs love it here! Jake goes kooky when he arrives at this park, running around with every dog toy in his smiling face until we have to leave. And he never wants to leave. It goes to show that a dog park doesn't have to be fancy to be a hit with the canine crowd.

From Highway 1, turn west on Wavecrest Street (the intersection is where you'll find the super-dog-friendly eatery, Cameron's; see below) and continue down the bumpy old road about .3 mile almost to the end. You'll see a brown sign that says all dogs must be on a leash. Immediately after that is a little dirt road to the right. Follow that past the horseshoe pits and you'll be there. For an update on the park situation, check out www.coastdogs .org. 650/726-8297.

PLACES TO EAT

Cameron's Inn: English pub grub and rich and creamy fountain treats are the specialty here, but burgers, pizza, and salads are big sellers, too. Dine with your pooch at the big outdoor patio. Dogs who are lucky enough to come to this funky, charming, British treasure get to sniff out a double-decker bus out front. (It makes for a very cute photo.) The folks here love dogs and provide them treats and water. Cameron's is a bone's throw from Half Moon Bay's temporary dog park. (See above.) 1410 South Cabrillo Highway/Highway 1; 650/726-5705.

Casey's Cafe: The outdoor seating here is attractive, with several umbrella-topped tables in a pretty plaza. If you like to play games other than fetch, come here on game nights, which are usually Friday and Saturday. On warmer evenings you can play your favorite board game at the outdoor tables while snacking with your dog at your side. (If he's a border collie you can even use him as your game partner.) Casey's is right next to the Zaballa House (see Places to Stay), 328 Main Street; 650/560-4880.

Half Moon Bay Brewing Company: Good beer, good food, good dog-friendly ambience, and good sniffs from the waterfront. What else could a dog want? A bowl of water? It's yours for the asking. This fun eatery and drinkery is in nearby Princeton's Pillar Point Harbor, at 390 Capistrano Road; 650/728-BREW (650/728-2739).

Moon Juice Cafe: Vicki, who owns this delightful smoothie-juicey-sandwichey café, adores dogs and welcomes them to dine with their people at the two outdoor tables in this off-street area. If she knows you have a dog with you, she'll be sure to provide a big treat and ask if your dog would like some water. If you like bacon but want to convince yourself you're being at least somewhat healthy, order the BLT wrap. It's delicious. The café is just off the north end of Main Street, at 20 Stone Pine Road; 650/712-1635.

Moonside Bakery: All the delicious treats here are baked daily, except for the soup, which generally isn't baked. (But it's still made fresh daily.) This is truly an exceptional bakery, featuring all kinds of crusty breads and delectable sweets but specializing in German baked goods. Dine with dog at the many attractive, wooden, umbrella-topped tables outside. 604 Main Street; 650/726-9070.

Pasta Moon: This restaurant offers several sidewalk tables and every type of pasta imaginable. A *San Francisco Chronicle* food critic calls the house-made pastas here "addictive." Jake Dog suggests ordering the tagliatelle bathed in cream and surrounded by sliced sausage and prosciutto. It's a big plateful that you probably can't finish yourself, so your baleful-eyed canine might get lucky. 315 Main Street; 650/726-5125.

PLACES TO STAY

Half Moon Bay State Beach: See Half Moon Bay State Beach, above, for camping information.

Holiday Inn Express: Just five blocks from Half Moon Bay State Beach, and a few blocks from downtown, this dog-friendly hotel is conveniently situated for adventure-seeking pooches and their people. Rates are $93–179. Dogs are $10 extra. 230 Cabrillo Highway 94019; 650/726-3400; www.hiexpress .com/halfmoonbay.

Zaballa House: Dogs and their human roommates get to stay in the attractive rooms and suites in back of this Victorian inn's main building—the oldest standing house in Half Moon Bay, built in 1859. Dogs don't mind the more modern digs. The rooms are spacious and very attractive, and all have fireplaces. Suites come with fireplaces, kitchenettes, whirlpool tubs, and private decks.

The owners of the inn really enjoy dog guests. "A lot of pets are nicer than their people," says one of the innkeepers. If you visit at the right time, the front-desk person might take a photo of you and your dog to put in the VIP Dog Guest photo album. The album is tucked away, and sometimes employees don't seem to know of its existence, but it's there.

The inn is right in beautiful downtown Half Moon Bay, next to some mighty dog-friendly eateries. Rates are $99–279. Dogs pay $10 extra. 324 Main Street 94019; 650/726-9123; www.zaballahouse.net.

San Carlos

PARKS, BEACHES, AND RECREATION AREAS

29 Heather Park

🐾🐾🐕 (See San Mateo County map on page 494)

This is one of the few fenced-in dog parks we've ever seen that comes complete with rolling hills, wildflowers, old gnarled trees, and singing birds. Your dog will have the time of his life here, bounding up and down hills or trotting down the winding paved path to the bottom of the park—sans leash. You may be tempted to take some of the tiny dirt trails up the steep hills, but they tend to end abruptly, leaving you and your dog teetering precariously. The only thing the park lacks is water, usually a given at dog parks.

If you have a dog who likes to wander, watch out. There are a couple of potential escape routes near the two gates at the far ends of the park. Also, some dog people have not been scooping the poop as they should be, and the city of San Carlos is trying to get them to clean up their acts. The city is publicizing the problem to increase public awareness and is also increasing enforcement. City folks sent us a fax with the poop on scooping. Please, folks, it's not a fun job, but you've gotta do it.

The park is at Melendy and Portofino Drives. 650/593-8011.

30 Pulgas Ridge Open Space Preserve

🐾🐾🐾🐕 (See San Mateo County map on page 494)

Dogs were happy when the Midpeninsula Regional Open Space District opened this 293-acre preserve to leashed pooches a few years back. But now that 16 acres in the middle of the preserve has been designated OK for leash-free dogs, dogs are downright delirious.

The off-leash area is only for dogs under excellent voice control. That's always the case in off-leash, unenclosed areas, but it's particularly important here because of wildlife—and because of some vociferous folks who would love nothing better than to see leashes be mandatory here again. You know, those kind of people. The off-leash area is oak woodland and grassland, so dogs can explore a variety of landscapes. It's in the middle of the preserve and accessible via the Blue Oak Trail or the Cordilleras Trail.

Leashed dogs can explore the rest of this fairly flat, oak-chaparral area via three miles of trails that wind throughout. The best time to visit is in the spring, when the wildflowers come to life everywhere.

During your hike, you might see what you think looks like remnants of buildings. You'd be right. The preserve is on land that was once the site of the Hassler Health Home, a tuberculosis sanatorium owned by San Francisco. In the 1980s, the district bought the land and demolished the sanatorium, but you can still see rock retaining walls and steps here and there. Humans like this kind of trivia. Dogs could give a bark.

Exit I-280 at Edgewood Road and drive east almost a mile. Turn left at Crestview Drive and make an immediate left onto Edmonds Road. You'll see signs for the preserve. Roadside parking is limited here, but it's usually enough. 650/691-1200.

PLACES TO EAT

Cafe La Tosca: Dogs sing the praises of this lovely Italian café. Dine on tasty pastas and a sumptuous risotto at the four outdoor tables. 777 Laurel Street; 650/592-7749.

Menlo Park

PARKS, BEACHES, AND RECREATION AREAS

🐾 Bayfront Park

🐾🐾🐾 (See San Mateo County map on page 494)

This place used to be a dump—literally. It was the regional landfill site until it reached capacity in 1984. Then the city sealed the huge mounds of garbage under a two-foot clay barrier and covered it with four feet of soil, planted grass and trees, and voilà—instant 160-acre park!

Now it's a land of rolling hills with a distinctly Native American flavor. The packed dirt trails take you up to majestic views of the bay and surrounding marshes. There's no sign of garbage anywhere, unless you look down from the top of a hill and spot the methane extraction plant. Fortunately, very few vista points include that.

Our favorite part of the park is a trail studded with large, dark rocks arranged to form symbols, which in series make up a poem. The concept was inspired by Native American pictographs—a visual language system for recording daily events. At the trailhead, you'll find a sign quoting part of the poem and giving a map of the trail, showing the meaning of each rock arrangement as it corresponds to the poem.

Although leashes are required, dogs seem really fond of this park, sniffing everywhere, their tails wagging constantly. Perhaps they can sense the park's less picturesque days deep underground. Or they may be touched by the Native American magic that imbues these hills.

DIVERSION

Sniff Out a Good Book: Your dog doesn't have to be Mr. Peabody to appreciate fine books. In fact, even if your dog doesn't know his assonance from his alliteration, he could have fun accompanying you to **Kepler's Books.** Kepler's, one of the largest and very best independent bookstores around, permits clean, leashed, well-behaved dogs to cruise the aisles with you. In fact, dogs who visit even get a tasty treat! Common sense and good manners apply. Please, no leg lifts on the merchandise; Kepler's frowns on yellow journalism. Dogs who lean toward the literary are welcome. Those who *jump* on the literature are not. 1010 El Camino Real, Menlo Park; 650/324-4321.

The park starts at the end of Marsh Road, just on the other side of the Bayfront Expressway. To get to the beginning of the rock poem trail, continue past the entrance on Marsh Road to the second parking lot on the right. 650/858-3470.

PLACES TO EAT

Flea Street Cafe: Dogs would normally flee from a restaurant with the word "flea" in it, but not from this dog-friendly eatery. You can get upscale organic food here, including Niman Ranch meats. Drooling Jake recommends the Niman Ranch rib eye steak with wild mushroom wine au jus. The restaurant serves dinner only these days. Dine with doggy at the outdoor tables. 3607 Alameda de las Pulgas; 650/854-1226.

Iberia Restaurant: This restaurant is among the finest dog-friendly restaurants in the state. It's so elegant you can eat like a Spanish king. Dine with your dog in a stately garden under the canopy of an enormous 400-year-old oak tree. Flaming dishes are big here, so if your furry friend fears fire, try ordering something a little less dramatic. (Fans of the Garden Grill, which occupied this space until 2000, will be happy to know that the owners, Jose Luis Relinque and his wife, Jessica, are the same—and so is the impeccable service and top-notch food.) 1026 Alma Street; 650/325-8981.

Rock of Gibraltar Comestibles: If you like what you've eaten at Iberia Restaurant next door, check out the gourmet Spanish food fixin's at this store/café. *Perros* need to stay outside while you shop, but they're welcome to join you at the outdoor tables for coffee and pastries in the morning or a variety of delicious sandwiches at lunch. The Rock is owned by the Relinques, who also own the Iberia Restaurant. 1022 Alma Street; 650/327-0413.

Atherton

PARKS, BEACHES, AND RECREATION AREAS

🐾🐾 Holbrook-Palmer Park

🐾🐾 (See San Mateo County map on page 494)

Roses. Gazebos. Bathrooms that look like saunas. Trellises. Jasmine plots. Tennis courts. Buildings that belong in a country club. People in white linen love it here; dogs are often just plain intimidated. Joe didn't lift his leg once last time we visited.

"Don't put it in your book that we allow dogs," a woman with the Atherton Parks and Recreation Department told us. "We have too many weddings and banquets going on here, and the people don't want to be disturbed."

Don't forget a leash.

Holbrook-Palmer Park is on Watkins Avenue, between El Camino Real and Middlefield Road. Leave your car at one of several lots in the park. 650/688-6534.

Woodside

PARKS, BEACHES, AND RECREATION AREAS

🐾🐾🐾 Thornewood Open Space Preserve

🐾🐾🐾 (See San Mateo County map on page 494)

This 141-acre preserve is a former estate, and the views of the valley from parts of this land are magnificent. Dogs can peruse the preserve on leash. Thornewood is the smallest of the Midpeninsula Regional Open Space District's preserves, but dogs dig the one-mile trail that runs through the oak woodland, chaparral, and redwoods here.

Dogs have to stay away from Schilling Pond because swans call it home, and dogs and swans don't mix. In fact, although the pond is almost entirely surrounded by dense vegetation, rangers have spotted dogs swimming after these beautiful birds. If this happens very much, the entire preserve could be off-limits to all dogs, so let's be careful out there.

From I-280, exit at Highway 84/Woodside Road and drive west into the hills, about five miles. The road will make several sharp turns, but keep following Highway 84. Go left at the narrow, signed driveway. It winds through the woods for a third of a mile before reaching the small parking lot on the west side of the driveway. 650/691-1200.

PLACES TO EAT

Alice's Restaurant: You can get almost anything you want at this restaurant, including a table for you and your dog on the large porch. Weekends here are packed with bikers, especially for Alice's colossal breakfasts. If your dog rides in your motorcycle sidecar, this is the place for you. It's at 17288 Skyline Boulevard, on the corner of Highways 35 and 84, just two miles north of Portola Valley's Windy Hill Open Space Preserve; 650/851-0303.

Portola Valley

PARKS, BEACHES, AND RECREATION AREAS

🐾🐾 Windy Hill Open Space Preserve

🐾🐾🐾🐾 (See San Mateo County map on page 494)

You can look out from the top of the first big hill you come to and see for miles all around—and though you're on the edge of the suburbs, you'll see hardly a house. This 1,130-acre preserve of the Midpeninsula Regional Open Space District has as many different terrains as it has views, including grassland ridges and lush wooded ravines with serene creeks and drippy redwoods.

There are more than three miles of trails that allow you and your leashed canine companion. But watch out for foxtails. The park is so dry that foxtails seem to proliferate all year.

Start at the Anniversary Trail, to the left of the entrance. The hike is a vigorous three-quarters of a mile uphill, and that may be enough, especially when it's baking. But you can continue down the other side of the hill and loop right, onto the Spring Ridge Trail. Near the end of this 2.5-mile path, you'll come to a wooded area with a small, very refreshing creek. This is a good place to sit a spell before heading back. These two trails are the only ones that permit pooches, so don't try your paw at any others.

Park at the lot on Highway 35 (Skyline Boulevard), 2.3 miles south of Highway 84 and five miles north of Alpine Road. You'll see the big sign for the preserve and three picnic tables. 650/691-1200.

🐾🐾 Coal Creek Open Space Preserve

🐾🐾🐾🐾 (See San Mateo County map on page 494)

Jake loves visiting this 493-acre preserve in the winter because of the little waterfalls that gurgle along a couple of creeks. In fact, year-round, this is one of the best of the Midpeninsula Regional Open Space District preserves for dogs, because it's generally cooler than most. The dense oak and madrone forests offer a real respite from the hot summer weather.

Banana slugs like this climate as much as dogs do, so don't be surprised to see a few lurking on the trails. When Joe Dog happened upon a banana slug here, at first he looked disgusted. Then he barked at it a couple of times and sat down and moaned at it when it didn't respond. I tugged hard on his leash to get him away, because I knew his next move would be to make a banana slug appetizer out of it.

If rolling meadows are more your dog's style, this preserve has those, too. The five miles of trails will take you through all kinds of landscapes. Let your dog choose his favorite, but make sure he's leashed.

The preserve has two entry points along Skyline Boulevard (Highway 35) in the southernmost part of the county (south of Portola Valley). One is about 1.2 miles north of Page Mill Road, at the Caltrans vista point, on the east side of the road. The other is at Skyline and Crazy Pete's Road, about two miles north of Page Mill Road, also on the east side of Skyline. This one has the closest access to the preserve, but there's only room for about three cars, and you'll need to walk down a fairly steep residential road to get to the trails. 650/691-1200.

Pescadero

PARKS, BEACHES, AND RECREATION AREAS

Once upon a time, long ago (OK, actually in the last edition of this book), dogs who came here were so happy their tails almost wagged off. But no more. The wonderful Pescadero State Beach no longer allows pooches, even those with leashes and shamelessly pleading eyes. And Butano State Park, which had allowed dogs on its myriad fire trails, is now just like other state parks and permits them only in the camping area and on paved roads. At least dogs still have Bean Hollow. And they've also got the magnificent Estancia del Mar Cottages, which your dog will surely want to move into after visiting. (See below.)

36 Bean Hollow State Beach

🐾🐾🐾 (See San Mateo County map on page 494)

This isn't a big sandy beach. In fact, it can be hard to find sand here at all. It's rocks, rocks everywhere, which is kind of fun. The rocky intertidal zone here is terrific for tidepooling, but only if you and your dog are surefooted. To get to the best tidepools, you must perform an amazing feat of team coordination—climbing down 70-million-year-old rock formations while attached to each other by leash. It's not that steep, just awkward. The pitted rocks can be slippery. This maneuver is not recommended for dogs like Jake, who goes deaf and senseless when the alluring ocean beckons him to swim. Besides, the surf can be treacherous in this area.

If you reach the tidepools, you're in for a real treat. But make sure your canine companion doesn't go fishing—we've seen a dog stick his entire head in a tidepool to capture a little crab. Fur and fangs aren't natural in the delicate balance of this wet habitat, so please keep dogs out of the tidepools. The mussels will thank you.

If you decide to play it safe and stay on flat land, you can still see the harbor seal rookery on the rocks below the coastal bluffs. Bring binoculars and you can really get a view of them up close and personal.

The beach is off Highway 1 at Bean Hollow Road. 415/330-6300.

37 Butano State Park

😺 (See San Mateo County map on page 494)

This is one of the last state parks to succumb to the mandate that dogs must only be on paved roads, campgrounds, and other developed areas. It's very sad indeed, because until recently, much of this 2,200-acre state park was open to them via 11 miles of fire trails.

This park, nestled in the Santa Cruz Mountains, is resplendent with coastal scrub and redwoods. The ocean views from higher spots are breathtaking, but since tar doesn't go thar, your dog can't either.

Dogs can even camp at the 39 sites here. Sites are $20. The day-use fee is $6 if you park inside the park. Butano is five miles south of Pescadero on Cloverdale Road, and off Highway 1 from Gazos Creek Road. 650/879-2040 or 650/879-2044.

PLACES TO EAT

Arcangeli Grocery Company: There's always fresh-baked bread here—still hot—waiting for you after a cold day at the beach. We like to buy a loaf of steaming herb-garlic bread and eat it at the picnic tables on the lawn in the back of the store. 287 Stage Road; 650/879-0147.

PLACES TO STAY

Butano State Park: See Butano State Park, above, for camping information.

Estancia del Mar Cottages: The pooch-friendly cottages here are a true doggy delight. They're set on a beautiful five-acre horse farm, and that's surrounded by 30,000 acres (!) of farmland and protected open space. Dogs need to be leashed at Estancia because of the horses and the proximity to the road, but it's a small price to pay for the privilege of guesthood here.

Three of the six immaculate, cozy one-bedroom cottages welcome dogs. Two of them have great ocean views (the ocean is about 500 yards away, across Highway 1), and one looks out at the glorious Pigeon Point Lighthouse. The Lighthouse-View cottage also comes with a loft that has a queen futon, a small wood-burning stove, and a whirlpool tub. The cottage without the ocean view gets good sea scenery from its private outside yard and patio. (Many dogs prefer this one because of the yard.) All have full kitchens, which is handy if the idea of eating out for every meal turns your dog's stomach.

Rates are $125–175, and a multinight stay makes the nightly rate less expensive. Weekly rates are $650–1,100. Dogs fees are $50 for the first night, and $10 for each additional night. (The owners keep these places super-clean, doing deep cleansings and even changing the comforters after only a single night with a dog, so their cleaning expenses are high for "one-night stands.") You'll get the address once you make your reservation; 650/879-1500; www.estanciadelmar.com.

CHAPTER 37

Santa Clara County

While some parts of Santa Clara County are quite scenic, dogs have to face the facts: The place still revolves around Silicon Valley, and it's not a pretty sight. Cookie-cutter duplexes and town houses abound. So do suburban-style office buildings, strip shopping centers, and low-lying metal warehouses. Even dogs with questionable taste wince.

But if you get your dog out of the more populated areas and into the quieter county parks, you'll scarcely know you're in the middle of a megabyting, microchipping mecca. Some of the larger, wilder county parks may put your dog back in touch with the wolf inside herself. One dog we met on a trail at one park was sitting and howling every few hundred feet. Her person said she was just happy to be there. Joe Dog thought maybe the dog was just saying, "Get this leash off me!"

A few leash-free dog parks now grace the area. The newest two, San Jose's Watson Dog Park and the Milpitas Dog Park, are cause for canine celebration.

PICK OF THE LITTER—SANTA CLARA COUNTY

BEST DOG PARK
Milpitas Dog Park, Milpitas (page 530)

COOLEST HIKE
Mount Madonna County Park, Gilroy (page 545)

TASTIEST DOG TREATS
Five Paw Bakery, Los Altos (page 531)

MOST DOG-FRIENDLY PLACES TO EAT
Bill's Cafe, San Jose (page 539)
Rock Bottom Restaurant and Brewery,
Campbell (page 540)
Classic Burgers of Los Gatos, Los Gatos (page 544)

MOST DOG-FRIENDLY PLACE TO STAY
Cypress Hotel, Cupertino (page 534)

BEST SHOPPING
Stanford Shopping Center, Palo Alto (page 526)
Santana Row, San Jose (page 526)

FRIENDLIEST PLACE TO BUY A PLANT
Yamagami's Nursery, Cupertino (page 533)

BEST SOCIAL GATHERINGS
Society Dog (page 542)

The Midpeninsula Regional Open Space District is popular with pooches of late, with three dog-friendly open-space preserves in the county. The district has unique rules about poop-scooping and six-foot leashes. (See the San Mateo County chapter for more on these rules.)

Palo Alto

For dogs, this town is the county's garden spot. Here, you'll find lots of other dog lovers and well-behaved dogs, enticing city parks—all of which allow dogs—and no fewer than three leash-free dog runs. At the Baylands, you and your leashed dog can watch birds and get a good workout at the same time. And many student-oriented restaurants with outdoor seating welcome your dog. If you're lucky enough to have a Palo Alto address, or a friend with one, you may bring your dog to the glorious Foothills Park on weekdays.

PARKS, BEACHES, AND RECREATION AREAS

Unless you have a working dog (and no, this does *not* mean a dog who is working on getting the dog treats out of your coat pocket—we're talking guide dogs and their ilk), you and your pooch can no longer walk together at the Stanford Dish. We know a good many dogs who have cried into their kibble because of this pooch ban. Fortunately, other pleasant Palo Alto areas still permit pooches to paw around.

1 Palo Alto Baylands

🐾🐾🐾 (See Santa Clara County map on page 522)

This is the best-developed wetlands park in the Bay Area for adults, children, and dogs. It's laced with paved bike trails and levee trails. Along the pretty levee paths, benches face the mudflats. Don't forget your binoculars on a walk here. A cacophony of mewling gulls, mumbling pigeons, and clucking blackbirds fills the air. Small planes putt-putt into the nearby airport, and your dog will love the fishy smells coming from the marshes. This seems to be a popular spot for dog exercise. Keep your pooch leashed and on the trails.

Dogs shouldn't go near the well-marked waterfowl nesting area, but they're welcome to watch children feed the noisy ducks and Canada geese in the duck pond, as long as they don't think about snacks à l'orange.

From U.S. 101, exit at Embarcadero Road East and go all the way to the end. At the entrance, turn left for the trails, ranger station, and duck pond. A right turn takes you to a recycling center. 650/329-2423.

2 Greer Park

🐾🐾🐕 (See Santa Clara County map on page 522)

This is one of Palo Alto's parks with an off-leash dog run, but it isn't the largest (see Mitchell Park, below). The park is green and pleasant, as are all the city's parks, but it's somewhat noisy because of nearby Bayshore Road. Dogs have to be leashed outside the dog run. There are athletic fields, picnic tables, and two playground areas. The dog run, near the Bayshore side, is small and treeless, but it's entirely fenced, if that's what your dog needs.

The park is at Amarillo Street and West Bayshore Road. The parking lot is off Bayshore, conveniently near the dog run. 650/496-5928.

DIVERSION

Stop and Smell the Shopping Centers: Dogs are welcome to join you at **Stanford Shopping Center,** a 70-acre open-air mall that's disguised as a park. The grounds are home to 1,300 trees of 35 species, plus hundreds of hanging baskets and planters dripping with flowers. If a dog has to go shopping, this is one of the more pleasant places she could go. Many of the 120 stores allow dogs inside. Nordstrom and Neiman Marcus, two of the nation's most dog-friendly department stores, welcome dogs here. Rules at some of the others change frequently, so if you're interested in going inside with your dog, poke your head in and see if you can find someone to give your dog the thumbs-up. Chances are that not only will you end up sniffing out plenty of dog-friendly stores, but your dog will be offered some treats along the way. At El Camino Real and Sand Hill Road, in Palo Alto; 650/617-8200.

An intimate, slightly more trendy shopping center is the new **Santana Row** in San Jose. Charro, a San Jose pooch, wrote to tell us how much fun it is to be a dog there, and even though Jake isn't a shopping kind of dog, he enjoyed a trip there because he got so many pats from shopkeepers and fellow shoppers. (Plus there were plenty of palms and oaks to explore.) He was particularly interested in some leather shoes at Diesel (which only sometimes allows dogs), although he wasn't particular about which ones. Selecting shoes to chew is apparently a much quicker process than selecting shoes to wear. I quickly shooed him out of there and we made our way to Mutts, an amusing upscale dog boutique. Santana Row is at Winchester Boulevard and Stevens Creek Boulevard, just off I-880 in San Jose. 408/551-4600.

❸ Hoover Park

🐾🐾🐕 (See Santa Clara County map on page 522)

This park may be small, but dogs don't really care. It's home to a little-known dog park that's not as popular as the run at Mitchell Park (see below), but that's part of the charm. There've been some improvements here recently, so if you haven't checked it out lately, it's worth a sniff.

The park is at Cowper Street between Colorado and Loma Verde Avenues. 650/496-5928.

❹ Mitchell Park

🐾🐾🐾🐕 (See Santa Clara County map on page 522)

This generous, green park has some unusual amenities, including two human-sized chessboards and a roller-skating rink. The park is also a standout in the canine book: It has its own dog park that's completely fenced and has a row of pine trees on one side, water dishes on the other, and scrappy tennis balls everywhere. When we last visited, there were a couple of beat-up old office-style chairs just waiting to be sat upon, knocked over, or at least marked by a leg-lifting varmint.

The park has plenty of shade to delight a dog. Remember to leash outside the dog run. For kids, the playground area has sculptured bears for climbing and a water play area (sorry, no dogs). The dog park is a short walk from the parking lot.

The park is on East Meadow Drive just south of Middlefield Road. 650/496-5928.

5 Arastradero Nature Preserve
🐾🐾🐾 (See Santa Clara County map on page 522)

With 613 acres of rolling savanna grassland and broadleaf evergreen forest, Arastradero Preserve is one of the more peaceful and attractive parks in the area. Dogs dig it, but they have to be leashed. It's a good rule, because mountain lions, rattlesnakes, poison oak, and coyotes can be part of the scene here. And so can bikers.

Anglers are right at home in the preserve. A hike to Arastradero Lake takes only about 20 minutes from the main parking lot, and the fishing can be very good. (Sorry, no swimming, boats, or flotation devices.)

There are 6.25 miles of hiking trails. Jake Dog enjoys the hilly 2.8-mile Acorn Trail when he's in the mood to pant. Bring plenty of water; it can get toasty here.

From I-280, exit at Page Mill Road and go south. Turn right (west) on Arastradero Road (Refuge Road on some maps) and drive into the parking lot. 650/329-2423.

6 Esther Clark Park
🐾🐾🐾 (See Santa Clara County map on page 522)

This is a beautiful piece of undeveloped land with some dirt paths, right on the border of Los Altos Hills. There are no facilities but plenty of meadow and eucalyptus trees. A creek bed promises water in the wet season.

Where Old Adobe Road bends to the left and makes a cul-de-sac, the park is the undeveloped land on your right. 650/617-3156.

7 Foothills Park
🐾🐾🐾 (See Santa Clara County map on page 522)

To use this 1,400-acre park, privately owned by the city of Palo Alto, you must prove you're a resident or be the guest of one. Dogs are allowed only on weekdays (no holidays, though) and must be on leash, but they can go on all the trails.

The park has a large lake surrounded by unspoiled foothills, plus 15 miles of hiking trails of varying difficulty. At sundown, deer are plentiful. It's a beautiful sight, but be sure to keep tight hold of that leash. This park is heaven on Earth for dogs and people alike. If you don't already live in Palo Alto, it could make you consider moving.

To find Foothills Park from I-280, exit at Page Mill Road and drive about 2.5 miles south. As usual, when you're searching for a really good Santa Clara County park, the road will become impossibly narrow and winding, and you'll think you're lost. But you aren't. Probably. 650/329-2423.

PLACES TO EAT

Downtown Palo Alto is a walker-friendly and dog-adoring kind of place. It's full of benches and plazas for sitting, and quite a few restaurants will serve both of you out on the sidewalk or patio. Here are a few snout-licking options there and elsewhere.

Fratelli Deli: Hungry for a quick salad, pasta, or sandwich? Pop over to Fratelli and grab a bite. Eat with your pooch at the two outdoor tables. 405 University Avenue; 650/323-0423.

Palo Alto Sol: The friendly staff here will bring your thirsty pooch some water while he's drooling over your tasty Mexican food. The mole sauce is a must-order. 408 California Avenue; 650/328-8840.

Taxi's Hamburger: Taxi's burgers are award-winning (yes, there apparently are awards for hamburgers) and 100 percent beef. Just passing by makes dogs drool. But you don't have to pass by. Dogs are welcome here. Many patrons of this upscale American-style grill order burgers for their dogs. Dine at the half-dozen tables outside. 403 University Avenue; 650/322-8294.

Torrefazione: All the coffees and pastries at this café are served in hand-painted Italian china. Dogs with a keen sense of aesthetics appreciate this. Coffee fans love the whole-bean coffee, but I'm not even sure what that is. Doesn't sound like Taster's Choice to me, though. Sit outside the historic building that houses the café and dine with your dog at the two tables. Thirsty dogs get a bowl of water. 419 University Avenue; 650/325-7731.

World Wrapps: The cooks here take anything that's delicious and slightly exotic and put it in wraps. To them, the world is a burrito, just waiting to be enveloped. We had a really good Thai wrap when we visited. Jake Dog wants to know when they're going to have a dog food wrap. The smoothies are tasty, too. Dine with doggy at the 10 outdoor tables, some of which are shaded by trees. 201 University Avenue; 650/327-9777.

PLACES TO STAY

Sheraton Palo Alto: Rates are $132–329. Dogs must be under 80 pounds—a significant improvement over the former 20-pound pooch limit. 625 El Camino Real 94301; 650/328-2800; www.sheraton.com.

TraveLodge Palo Alto: Rates are $79–95. Dogs pay a $50 flat fee. 3255 El Camino Real 94306; 650/493-6340.

Mountain View

PARKS, BEACHES, AND RECREATION AREAS

🐾🐾🦴 Rengstorff Park

🐾🐾🦴 **(with permit)** (See Santa Clara County map on page 522)

This park is typically neat, green, and interesting for people, and it has another excellent feature: A sign reads, "Dogs must be on leash (except by permit)." This means that you can get a permit from the city that allows you to train a dog off leash, with the understanding that he'll be under control. Be fore-warned, though: If you don't bring the permit along with you when training, you will be ticketed.

Rengstorff Park is at Rengstorff Avenue between California Street and Central Expressway. Call for details on getting a permit. 650/903-6331.

🐾🐾🐾🦴 Mountain View Dog Park

🐾🐾🐾🦴 (See Santa Clara County map on page 522)

Ahh, this fenced park has redwood trees. They're Jake's favorite arbors. Other amenities in this .75-acre park include benches and a separate area for smaller or more timid dogs. The ground cover is mostly grass, so it's easy on the paws. It's an off-leash oasis, and dogs seem mighty happy to be here.

The park is on North Shoreline Boulevard at North Road. 650/903-6392.

PLACES TO STAY

Best Western Tropicana Lodge: No Ricky Ricardo band here, but it's a decent place to stay with your pup-a-loo. Rates are $70–110. 1720 West El Camino Real 94040; 650/961-0220; www.tropicanalodge.com.

   Residence Inn by Marriott: You and your dog will feel right at home at the suites at this attractive hotel. They have kitchens and lots of other extras you won't find in a regular hotel. But better than that is the very dog-friendly attitude here. "We take all pets, from snakes to rabbits. We see them as part of the family and try to accommodate the owner's needs," one manager told us. The place even has a little fenced area for exercising dogs, and the staff is happy to point you to nearby trails. Rates are $99–249. There's a $75 doggy fee per visit, so it's best to stay for a while to get the most bang for your buck. Dogs are $15 extra per night. 1854 West El Camino Real 94040; 650/940-1300.

Milpitas

PARKS, BEACHES, AND RECREATION AREAS

10 Milpitas Dog Park

🐾🐾🐾🐾🐕 (See Santa Clara County map on page 522)

The big-dog side of this terrific two-acre park has smallish trees. And the small-dog section has big trees. Go figure! But some of that small-dog shade leaks over to the large-dog side, so it's a win-win situation.

This is a great place to bring a dog who longs to run like the wind. It's mostly grassy, and it's a very generous size. Dogs can really work up a sweat while chasing each other or running after lobbed tennis balls. The dog park is flanked by the scenic rolling hills of the surrounding 1,539-acre Ed Levin County Park. (Dogs are allowed only on one short segment of the Bay Area Ridge Trail there, and in the picnic areas, so don't be too tempted to sniff out Ed Levin.)

The dog park has all the usual pooch amenities, from water to picnic tables to poop bags. And it has an interesting extra one: A tiny concrete-floored fenced area with a bench. No one was using it when we visited, but it looks like a decent place for a child who wants to feel protected from the pounding paws.

There's an entrance fee to get into the county park, and therefore to get into the dog park. It's a steep $5 per car. But annual passes are available for $65, should you want to make this a regular stomping ground. The dog park is at the very end of the county park. (If you're not confident you'll find it, just ask the park ranger at the fee gate.) The county park is at 3100 Calaveras Road, about 2.5 miles east of I-680. For dog-park inquiries, phone the City of Milpitas at 408/586-3210. For questions about Ed Levin, phone 408/262-6980 or 408/355-2200.

PLACES TO STAY

Best Western Brookside Inn: Rates are $79–129. Dogs are $15 extra. 400 Valley Way 95035; 408/263-5566; www.bestwestern.com.

Los Altos

Los Altos, like Saratoga and Los Gatos, is a clean town with civic pride, great for strolling. The hand-painted benches and spotless lawns look as if no dog has ever passed through, but in fact dogs are here in force. They're just mannerly.

PLACES TO EAT

Five Paw Bakery: If you want your dog to enjoy fresh, all-natural pooch pastries and treats, trot over to this terrific bakery. It's exclusively for dogs (and the occasional cat), so if you're a human with a hankering for a baked good, try the bakery next door. The cuisine at Five Paw Bakery is to drool for, and Paul, the owner, is super-friendly and truly loves what he does. The bakery also features an upscale pet boutique, should you really want to treat your best friend to something special. You can wet your dog's whistle at the ever-present water bowl outside. The bakery is conveniently situated a bone's throw from a very large, popular veterinary hospital, at 315 Main Street; 650/941-5729; www.fivepaw.com.

Italian Delicatessen: Drop by for great salami smells. Better yet, order one of the delicious specialty sandwiches and dine at the outdoor tables with your pooch. If you have a drop of Italian blood in you, the Godfather sandwich, which is loaded with mortadella, prosciutto, provolone, and lots of other great Italian ingredients, will make you drool. (But you can blame the drool on your dog.) 139 Main Street; 408/948-6745.

Santa Clara

PARKS, BEACHES, AND RECREATION AREAS

11 Santa Clara Dog Park

🐾🐾🐾 🐕 (See Santa Clara County map on page 522)

It's not huge, but this 200-by-200-foot fenced dog run is the only leash-free option in Santa Clara. On the grounds of what used to be Curtis Intermediate School, it's a flat stretch of grass bordered by stands of shady trees. Inside, you'll find water, poop bags, and benches. It's your basic dog park, and Santa Clara dogs are very happy to have it.

It's at the corner of Pomeroy Avenue and Lochinvar Street, near Lawrence Expressway and Homestead Road. 408/615-2260.

12 Central Park

🐾🐾 (See Santa Clara County map on page 522)

This Santa Clara city park, like most of the others, has a sign that reveals a certain slant: "No Dogs Allowed Except on Leash." If you can get past that, the park is big and has a wide assortment of trees. The creek here is large and deep, but dry in summer. A beautiful round picnic pavilion has tables fully shaded by wisteria vines, the most we've ever seen in one place.

The park is on Kiely Boulevard between Homestead Road and Benton Street. 408/615-2260.

DIVERSION

Go on a Pilgrimage: Mission Santa Clara, on the Santa Clara University campus, allows leashed dogs on its grounds. You might make it part of your walk if you're exploring the campus. The building, dating from 1929, is a replica of one version of the old mission, which was first built in 1777 but was destroyed five times by earthquake, flood, and fire. Preserved fragments of the original mission and the old adobe Faculty Club are the oldest college buildings standing in the western United States. The mission is on campus, off El Camino Real, Santa Clara. 408/554-4023.

PLACES TO STAY

Guest House Inn and Suites: Rates are $79–129. Dogs are $10 extra. 2930 El Camino Real 95051; 408/241-3010.

The Vagabond Inn: Rates are $69–99. Dogs are $10 extra. 3580 El Camino Real 95051; 408/241-0771.

Sunnyvale

PARKS, BEACHES, AND RECREATION AREAS

13 Las Palmas Park

🐾🐾🐾🐾🐾✖ (See Santa Clara County map on page 522)

With its paved paths, green grass, and beautiful pond, this park used to be the best in town for a walk among rolling hills. Now it's really terrific, because of its recently opened dog run. The two-acre run has everything a dog could possibly desire—shade, water, poop bags, and even a fire hydrant. It's a kind of fenced-in nirvana. Dogs get deliriously happy when they visit. Some spend so much time rolling in the cool grass that they miss out on hanging with their fellow canines. But do they care? A look at their smiling snouts and flaring nostrils will answer that question.

A quick note about that fire hydrant. Enough dogs have run headlong into it that there was some thought about removing it. So far, it's still here. Doggies, keep your eyes open!

The park is at Danforth and Russet Drives. 408/730-7350.

PLACES TO STAY

Summerfield Suites: There's supposed to be a 50-pound pooch limit, but so many of the employees here have and/or love dogs that this rule is often bent.

DIVERSION

Nursery Tail Wag: Dogs love visiting **Yamagami's Nursery.** Not only do they get to help you sniff out some great plants and flowers for your home, but just for setting paw inside, they get a dog treat. "We're very friendly with dogs," says a Yamagami plant doctor at this old and popular family business. 1361 South DeAnza Boulevard, Cupertino; 408/252-3347.

The suites are large and very livable, with kitchens and most of the amenities of home. Rates are $79–189. There's a $150 pooch fee per visit (this place is used to longish-term visitors). 900 Hamlin Court 94089, 408/745-1515 or 800/833-4353; www.wyndham.com.

The Vagabond Inn: Rates are $65–149. Dogs are $10 extra, and must be under 20 pounds. This seems a bit on the picky side for a Vagabond Inn. 816 Ahwanee Avenue 94086; 408/734-4607; www.vagabondinn.com.

Cupertino

PARKS, BEACHES, AND RECREATION AREAS

🔟 Fremont Older Open Space Preserve

🐾🐾🐾 (See Santa Clara County map on page 522)

This 739-acre preserve smells sweet and clean, but that doesn't disappoint dogs. Pooches have enough trees and ground-level odors to keep them happily trotting along on their mandatory leashes.

Once you park in the small lot, you'll walk several hundred feet on a paved roadway, but be sure to turn right at the first sign for hikers. Otherwise you'll find yourself in the middle of a bicycle freeway. The narrow dirt trail to the right takes you on a three-mile loop through cool woodlands and rolling open hills up to Hunters Point via the Seven Springs Loop Trail. The view of Santa Clara Valley from the top of the 900-foot hill is incomparable. More trails may be open soon, so your dog's feet will be able to explore as never before.

Signs at the entrance warn of ticks, so be sure to give your dog (and yourself) a thorough inspection after your hike.

From U.S. 101 or I-280, take Highway 85 (Saratoga-Sunnyvale Road) south to Prospect Road. Turn right and follow the road to the park entrance. 650/691-1200.

PLACES TO EAT

Bobbi's Coffee Shop: Charro the Dog told us about this eatery, where every dog gets a bowl of water upon arrival at the outdoor tables. It's a convenient place to stop for a bite before or after a visit to the dog-friendly Yamagami's Nursery (see the Diversion Nursery Tail Wag), right next door. 1361 De Anza Boulevard; 408/257-4040.

PLACES TO STAY

Cypress Hotel: The word "Cypress" in a hotel name seems to confer ultra-dog-friendliness. Witness Doris Day's Cypress Inn in Carmel. The Cupertino Cypress, while larger and more hotelly than Doris Day's inn, makes dogs feel equally at home. They're not only welcome to join you at this fun boutique hotel, but they're encouraged to do so. There's even a package designed especially for pooches. It's called "See Spot at the Cypress." Included in your deluxe guestroom or executive suite is a pet area with a dog bowl, biscuits, bottled water, chew toys, and a dog bed. Your dog will also get a dog tag stating, "I was pampered at the Cypress Hotel," and some other goodies, including free valet parking—something that comes in handy when you're traveling with luggage and a dog. The rate for the package is $129–299. If you want to simply stay here without the package but with your dog, your room will run you $89–229.

For a little more money, the concierge will arrange a pet massage, a grooming session, or even some time with a doggy psychic. (If a pet psychic were to read Jake's brain, she'd be hard-pressed to get beyond his ever-present thoughts of food, food, food.) 10050 South DeAnza Boulevard 95014; 408/253-8900; www.thecypresshotel.com.

San Jose

If you think San Jose offers little for dogs, think again. Okay, it's not dog heaven, but it does permit pooches in some decent parks, and now it even has three parks where dogs can say good riddance to their leashes.

PARKS, BEACHES, AND RECREATION AREAS

San Jose's parks still have the issue of being under the shadow of the freeways (some literally) and air traffic, but some are slowly going to the dogs—in the best sense of the word. The mantra here is that each of the city's 10 districts will have at least one dog park. Now that's something to bark about.

15 Watson Dog Park

🐾🐾🐾🐾🐕 (See Santa Clara County map on page 522)

The glorious centerpiece of this grassy, 1.25-acre park is an enormous Tree of Heaven, known among more scientific dogs as an *Ailanthus altissima*. It truly is a heavenly tree. It's where people and dogs congregate, which is a refreshing change from the common crowd-near-the-park-gate syndrome. While the park looks ethereal, the sound is that of the nearby freeway. Ah well, now your dog has a great excuse not to hear you when you call her to go home. The park has all the usual amenities, from benches and picnic tables to water and poop bags. As a bonus, it has a separate section for small dogs.

The dog park is in the northeast corner of Watson Park, at Jackson and North 22nd Streets. It's just off U.S. 101. From northbound U.S. 101, exit at Julian Street/McKee Road, and turn left onto Julian Street. In a half mile, turn right onto North 21st Street, and in another half mile, make another right onto Jackson Street. The park will be within a block. 408/277-4661.

16 William Street Park

🐾🐾🐾 (See Santa Clara County map on page 522)

This park is a boy dog's dream come true. It's only about 15 acres, but it has 200 trees and 400 shrubs. The acreage-to-trees/shrubs ratio makes it easy for boy dogs to sniff out just about every arbor. The trees make it a really pleasant, attractive place to visit, even in the armpits of summer. Head for the shade and let your happy, leashed pooch loll and roll in the green grass.

The park is at 16th Street and East William Street. 408/277-4661.

DOG-EAR YOUR CALENDAR

Bark in the Park—that's the name of a fun, incredibly popular dog day that takes place at the William Street Park in San Jose every summer. Bark in the park is also what your dog may do because he's so happy to be here. He'll be able to sniff out scads of doggy activities, such as musical dog chairs, obstacle courses, and pooch "beauty" contests. There are vendors galore, selling all the things dogs love, and there's even a misting tent, complete with little wading pools, for dogs who need to cool their paws. The event is sponsored by the Beautification Committee of the Campus Community Association, a nonprofit neighborhood organization. For info about this year's event, call 408/793-5125.

🐾 Joseph D. Grant County Park

🐾🐾🐾 (See Santa Clara County map on page 522)

Here's another huge, gorgeous, wild park that your dog can barely set foot in. Dogs are limited to the campgrounds, picnic areas, Edwards Field Hill, and the Edwards Trail. But if you don't mind a long, winding drive for one short—albeit satisfying—trail hike, by all means try this park. Stop in at the homey old ranch house that's now the visitor center for directions to the Edwards Trail, which isn't easy to find.

Or try these directions: On Mount Hamilton Road midway between the intersection with Quimby Road and the park border is a white barn on your right as you're heading out of the park. Just past the white barn is an unmarked pedestrian gate on the left, which is the trailhead. This trail is a fine walk through a deciduous forest.

There's a $5 parking fee. The park has 22 campsites, available on a first-come, first-served basis. Sites are $9–18. To get to the park from I-680, exit at the Capitol Expressway and drive south to Quimby Road. Turn left (east) on Quimby and wind tortuously to the park entrance. It's a long six miles and the road is often a one-lane cliffhanger. Alternatively, you can get to the park from I-680 via Highway 130 (Mount Hamilton Road). It's similar, but at least it's a two-laner. 408/274-6121 or 408/355-2200.

🐾 Emma Prusch Park

🐾🐾🐾 (See Santa Clara County map on page 522)

This park, one of San Jose's most attractive working farms, is a museum. Like a symbol of the county, it lies in the shadow of the intersection of three freeways. Yet it's a charming place and, surprisingly, it allows your leashed dog to wander around the farm with you so long as he stays out of the farm-animal areas. A smooth paved path, good for strollers and wheelchairs, winds among a Victorian farmhouse (which serves as the visitor center), a multicultural arts center, farm machinery, a barn, an orchard, and gardens. Picnic tables are on an expanse of lawn with trees.

The entrance is on South King Road, near the intersection of U.S. 101 and I-680/280. 408/277-4567.

🐾 Coyote Creek Multiple-Use Trail

🐾🐾🐾 (See Santa Clara County map on page 522)

When this trail is completely paved, it will furnish your dog with 13 miles of trail, if she doesn't mind sharing space with bicycles. You'll find poop-bag dispensers along the way. You may take your dog, leashed, on any section between the Hellyer County Park end and Parkway Lakes, a private fishing concession at the south end, close to Morgan Hill. (Your only reason to go there would be to pull in some of the club's stocked trout or to enter one of its fishing derbies.)

See the directions to Coyote-Hellyer County Park (below). 408/255-0225.

20 Coyote-Hellyer County Park

🐾🐾🐾🐕 (See Santa Clara County map on page 522)

This county park, which surrounds the one-acre Shadowbluff Dog Run (see below), is a generous, rustic area, popular with bicyclists. The best deal for dogs is the El Arroyo del Coyote Nature Trail, which by some miracle allows dogs. Walk to the left at the entrance kiosk and cross under Hellyer Avenue on the bike trail to find the entrance to the nature trail. Cross the creek on a pedestrian bridge to your right; once across, take the dirt path to your left. Bikes aren't allowed, making it all the better for dogs.

Willows and cottonwoods are luxuriant here, and in spring, poppies bloom. Eucalyptus groves provide occasional shade. Watch out for bees and poison oak. Otherwise, this is heavenly territory for your dog.

The park is closed Wednesdays for maintenance. Access is very easy from U.S. 101. Exit U.S. 101 at Hellyer Avenue and follow prominent signs to the park. The dog area is about 100 yards past the entry kiosk. A parking fee of $5 is charged, and that can add up fast, since there's really no good parking nearby. So if you're planning to be a regular, your best bet would be to buy a $65 park pass for the year. It's a small investment to make for your dog's happiness. 408/255-0225 or 408/355-2200.

21 Shadowbluff Dog Run

😊😊😊😊🐕 (See Santa Clara County map on page 522)

The one-acre enclosure within the large Coyote-Hellyer County Park has just about anything a pooch could desire. You'll find shade from a few trees, water to slurp up, and lots of green grass. For humans, there are benches, poop bags, and garbage cans. (Seems the dogs get the better end of the deal.) For more information, see Coyote-Hellyer County Park, above.

22 Guadalupe Oak Grove Park

😊😊😊 (See Santa Clara County map on page 522)

This park is a pleasant exception to most of the others in San Jose—it's undeveloped, beautiful, and doesn't allow bicycles—and sure enough, it may not be open to dogs forever. For years we've been hearing it may "soon" be declared an oak woodlands preserve. It hasn't been yet, so go and enjoy it.

Dirt trails wind through hills, alternately semiopen and covered with thick groves of oaks. Birds are plentiful and noisy. Be aware of high fire danger in the dry season, and don't even think of letting your dog off leash. The park ranger loves dogs, but she'll ticket you, and she's heard all the excuses—from "He just slipped out of his collar for a moment..." to "I couldn't get my dog through the gate with his leash on..."

Guadalupe Oak Grove Park is at Golden Oak Way and Vargas Drive. 408/277-2821.

23 Miyuki Dog Park

😊😊🐕 (See Santa Clara County map on page 522)

Dogs are happy to be at this tiny (three-eighths-acre) park without their leashes, even though the park isn't quite what it could be. The ground is covered with crushed granite, which can get a little dusty when everyone is running around. There's no water. The trees are small, but that will change. Meanwhile, many dogs enjoy sniffing and running around here. (Perhaps they haven't visited Watson Dog Park yet; see above.)

The park is at Miyuki Drive and Santa Theresa Boulevard. 408/277-4661.

24 Almaden Quicksilver County Park

😊😊😊 (See Santa Clara County map on page 522)

This rustic, 3,600-acre park allows dogs on about half of its 30 miles of trails. Some of these trails are popular for horseback riding, so watch out; although leashes are the law here, they don't always stop dogs who like to chase hooves.

In the spring, the hills explode with wildlife and wildflowers. Any of the trails will take you through a wonderland of colorful flowers and butterflies who like to tease safely leashed dogs. Speaking of insects, there's a downside to this park: Ticks seem to hang out here. "We got 20 off our dog, then three more when big welts developed," a poor San Jose resident writes. Keep your pooch in the center of trails, and the bloodsucking pests will have to go elsewhere for dinner.

Dogs are allowed on the Guadalupe Trail, the Hacienda Trail, parts of the Mine Hill Trail, the Mockingbird Picnic Area, the No Name Trail, and the Senator Mine Trail. Call the park for more information about the trails and the locations of their trailheads.

You can enter the park at several points. We prefer the main park entrance, where New Almaden Road turns into Alamitos Road, near Almaden Way. 408/268-3883 or 408/355-2200.

PLACES TO EAT

Bill's Cafe: You and your favorite dog can munch on simple café cuisine at this bistro with umbrella-topped tables. Lucky dogs who visit get water and a biscuit! 1115 Willow Street; 408/294-1125.

Maggiano's Little Italy: Dogs delight in joining their people at this Southern Italian–style restaurant's large outdoor section. The portions are big, the selection is huge, and the food is delicious. Dogs get a bowl of water if they're thirsty. Maggiano's is in the Santana Row shopping center (see the Diversion Stop and Smell the Shopping Centers), 3055 Olin Avenue. (Santana Row is at Stevens Creek Boulevard and Winchester Boulevard.) 408/423-8973.

PLACES TO STAY

Doubletree Hotel: Rates are $89–179. A $100 dog deposit is required. 2050 Gateway Place 95110; 408/453-4000.

Homewood Suites: The suites here are comfy and much more like home than traditional hotels. Rates are $229. Dogs must be under 30 pounds to stay here, and they pay a $75 fee for the length of their stay, plus a deposit of $275. 10 West Trimble Road 95131; 408/428-9900.

Joseph D. Grant County Park: See Joseph D. Grant County Park, above, for camping information.

Staybridge Suites Hotel: The hotel has only suites, which makes for a comfy stay. All suites are equipped with a kitchen. It's convenient for people traveling with pooches. Rates are $89–189. Dogs have to pay a $150 fee per visit, so you'd better stay a while to make it worth that fee. 1602 Crane Court 95112; 408/436-1600.

Campbell

At press time this lovely town was in the final stages of creating its very own dog park. Check back next edition for the details.

PARKS, BEACHES, AND RECREATION AREAS

25 Los Gatos Creek County Park

🐾 🐾 🐾 (See Santa Clara County map on page 522)

Here your leashed dog can romp on grass, have a picnic with you in the shade of Los Gatos Creek's medium-sized trees, and watch ducks and geese in the percolation ponds of Los Gatos Creek, which are good for fishing. Jake's Labrador retriever genes make him quiver with excitement when he sees these birds, but he just watches and doesn't ruffle any feathers. The Los Gatos Creek Trail runs through here, should you care to take a jaunt.

From Highway 17, exit at Camden Avenue; go west on San Tomas Expressway, south on Winchester Boulevard, and left on Hacienda Avenue to the park. A $5 parking fee is charged in summer and on weekends and holidays. 408/356-2729 or 408/355-2200.

PLACES TO EAT

The King's Head Pub and Restaurant: Want British food and drink, with a super-dog-friendly atmosphere? Come here for some fine brews and interesting food. Your dog can join you on the shady deck, and she'll get a big bowl of water if she's thirsty. On Sunday afternoons, there's live music here. It's of the slow-jazzy-hip variety. Dogs dig it. Speaking of jazz, we owe thanks to Jaz Dog and Trevor Dog for letting us know about this eatery. (They're the lucky dogs of the founders of Society Dog, a social group if ever there was one. See the Diversion Drink Wine, Get Naked, Hop on a Bus.) 201 Orchard City Drive; 408/871-2499.

Orchard Valley Coffee: Enjoy coffee, snacks, and pastries, and nighttime live music, at one of five tables right on the sidewalk at this dog-friendly place. 349 East Campbell Avenue; 408/374-2115.

Rock Bottom Restaurant and Brewery: The restaurant used to have a dog menu here, but most people were just ordering things such as bunless burgers for their dogs off the human menu (even before the low-carb craze), so it went back to human menus only. If you don't want to invest in your dog's carnivorous desires, you should know that the friendly servers here provide treats and water for pooches. For people, the signature microbrews are a big draw, as are tasty salads and interesting concoctions such as alder-smoked fish-and-chips. Dine at the full-service patio with your dog (it's even heated in the chilly months). It's at 1875 South Bascom Road, in the Pruneyard Shopping Center; 408/377-0707.

PLACES TO STAY

Residence Inn by Marriott: This is a convenient, comfortable place to stay when traveling with a dog. Residence Inns have only suites and apartments,

DIVERSION

You Doity Dog: Even if your dog hates a bath more than anything, he'll surely like it a bit better if it's you working him over and not some stranger. Campbell's **Shampoo Chez** (sham-POO-ches) is a wash-him-yourself dog-grooming establishment, and the current owners say they've hosted about a zillion self-service washes since they began. That's a lot of shampoo and fleas down the drain. A shampoo for any size dog is $12 for 30 minutes of wash time and an additional $1 for each five minutes after that. (There's another branch in Santa Cruz; for more information, see the Diversion Get All Dolled Up and Catch a Movie in the Santa Cruz chapter.) 523 East Campbell Avenue, Campbell; 408/379-WASH (408/379-9274).

and they all come with kitchens. Rates are $129–179. Extended stays get a discounted rate. Dogs have to pay a $75 cleaning fee. 2761 South Bascom Avenue 95008; 408/559-1551.

Saratoga

PLACES TO EAT

Bella Saratoga: The slogan of this Italian date spot is, "It's Romantic," and it is, even at the front sidewalk tables next to a short stone wall right on the street. Dogs have to be tied up on the other side of the wall, but they're close enough for your handouts. Plus, the dog-friendly staff gives pooch guests a big bowl of filtered water. (None of that straight tap stuff!) If it's crowded, dogs aren't allowed, so be sure to visit during "off" times. Sit at one of the three tables by the wall. 14503 Big Basin Way; 408/741-5115.

International Coffee Exchange: This very dog-friendly café serves the best mochas around. They're made with Ghirardelli chocolate and fresh, house-made whipped cream. The café also serves pastries and sandwiches, should you want a little nosh with your pooch. Dine together at the outdoor area's umbrella-topped tables. 14471 Big Basin Way; 408/741-1185.

Vienna Woods Restaurant and Deli: If you have an appetite for Austrian food, bring your dog here. You can get bratwurst, potato pancakes, and even apple strudel. The restaurant also serves sandwiches, quiches, lasagna, and other non-Austrian items. Dine with your pooch at the sheltered outdoor tables. 14567 Big Basin Way; 408/867-2410.

Los Gatos

Dogs like Los Gatos, but they think it needs a name change. Jake suggests "Los Perros."

PARKS, BEACHES, AND RECREATION AREAS

2.6 Vasona Lake County Park

🐾🐾🐾 (See Santa Clara County map on page 522)

This is a perfectly manicured park, with grass like that of a golf course. Dogs find it tailor-made for rolling, although they tend to get tangled in their leashes—which the county demands they wear here.

Several pathways take you through this 151-acre park and down to the lake's edge. But no swimming is allowed. And dogs aren't allowed to visit the children's playground either. You can picnic in the shade of one of the large willows or lead your dog up to the groves of pines and firs for a relief session.

From Highway 17, take Highway 9 (Saratoga-Los Gatos Road) west to University Avenue. Go right and continue to Blossom Hill Road. The park will be on your left. Enter at Garden Hill Drive. The parking fee is $5. 408/356-2729 or 408/355-2200.

DIVERSION

Drink Wine, Get Naked, Hop on a Bus: If you and your dog like to socialize, have we got a group for you: **Society Dog.** It bills itself as "a social club for dogs and their people," and boy, is it social. When we attended a doggy Easter egg hunt at a Saratoga winery, people were sipping wine and making new friends, and dogs were sniffing each others' heinies and making new friends too.

It's just one of many gatherings throughout the year for this South Bay group. It has monthly "naked" dog walks where dogs can be leash-free, and "bark in the dark" walks on Tuesday and Thursday evenings. Some get-togethers culminate in hanging out at an alfresco restaurant together. Special events include winery tours, group sojourns via bus to fabulously dog-friendly destinations such as Carmel, and a field trip to the San Francisco Giants' Dog Days of Summer event (see Dog-Ear Your Calendar in the San Francisco chapter), also via bus. A regular "Yappy Hour" was in the planning stages. Membership is free, but you pay for special events. See www.societydog.com for more info and a schedule of upcoming events.

27 St. Joseph's Hill Open Space Preserve

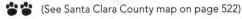 (See Santa Clara County map on page 522)

Want a quick escape from urban life? Visit this scenic, 173-acre preserve with your leashed pooch. Dogs are allowed on all four miles of trails here, but beware, it can get steep. The trails wind through oak woodlands and open grassland, and at the top of the 1,250-foot St. Joseph's Hill, you'll get magnificent views of the surrounding parklands. Joe used to love to sit here and let his nostrils flare.

From Highway 17, take the Alma Bridge Road exit and go across the dam. Public parking is available at Lexington Reservoir County Park. The trail to St. Joseph's Hill starts opposite the boat-launching area at the north end of the reservoir. 650/691-1200.

28 Lexington Reservoir County Park

(See Santa Clara County map on page 522)

When the reservoir is full, this park is full of life. Birds sing and the foliage is bright green. But in drought years, everything here—trees, grass, brush—is covered with silt. This death mask must frighten birds away to better nesting areas, because it's utterly silent, except for a few cars kicking up dust on a nearby road.

It can really bake during summer, too. And since there's no swimming allowed, dogs get miserable fast. (To cool himself off here, Joe would roll on the dusty ground until his entire body was coated with ash-colored silt. He looked like some kind of moving statue on a mandatory leash.)

Exit Highway 17 at Montevina Road and drive east a quarter of a mile. You can stop at any of several parking areas along the road. There is no entrance fee, except for the Miller Picnic Site, where you'll pay $5. 408/358-3741 or 408/355-2200.

29 Sierra Azul Open Space Preserve (Kennedy-Limekiln area)

(See Santa Clara County map on page 522)

The wildlife at this 5,000-acre preserve has it pretty good. There's so much steep, rugged terrain and dense chaparral that humans and their leashed doggy interlopers are pretty much forced to stay on the trails, out of critters' ways. Unfortunately for dogs and their people, mountain bikes seem to be everywhere on these trails, and they can go really fast. So on weekends especially, keep your eyes and ears peeled and be ready to dodge the traffic.

This is not a park for the fair of paw. A hike to the 2,000-foot ridge top can make even the most fit dog sweat. But the views from here or from the 1,700-foot Priest Rock are worth a little panting, at least on your part. Take it easy on your dog, though, and don't let him pant too much. It can get very, very hot here in the summer, and there's virtually no decent shade. The folks at the

Midpeninsula Regional Open Space District beg you not to take your pooch here on summer afternoons.

Parking here is a real problem. More on that in the next paragraph, but if you visit on a busy day, have a contingency plan in case you don't get one of the coveted spaces. Also note that the two other sections of the Sierra Azul Preserve (Cathedral Oaks and Mt. Umunhum) don't permit pooches.

From Highway 85, exit at Los Gatos Boulevard and drive west a little more than two miles. At Kennedy Road, turn left and follow the road about two more miles to the parking spot at the trailhead. There's room for only two cars here. This is utterly inadequate, and the district is working to do something about this. In the meantime, there's room for about seven cars across Kennedy, on Top of the Hill Road. Please be considerate of the residents here, and keep noise to a minimum and don't litter. 650/691-1200.

PLACES TO EAT

Classic Burgers of Los Gatos: This dog-friendly eatery has fine burgers. Dogs drool over them at the four tables on the patio. In fact, they've drooled so much that the café's proprietors now offer dogs their very own bunless patties for $1. Dogs, even those not caught up in the low-carb trend, adore this place. They can get water if thirsty, too. 15737 Los Gatos Boulevard; 408/356-6910.

Dolce Spazio Gelato: On warm days, this is the place to come. The homemade gelato is creamy and delicious. When there's a chill in the air, try something from the café's espresso bar. The good-sized patio has heat lamps, which helps dogs and their people cozy up to a winter visit. Thirsty dogs get water on request. 221 North Santa Cruz Avenue; 408/395-1335.

Morgan Hill

PARKS, BEACHES, AND RECREATION AREAS

30 Anderson Lake County Park

🐾🐾 (See Santa Clara County map on page 522)

When there's enough water to keep the reservoir open to the public, dogs love to go along on fishing trips. But when it's low, dogs take solace in dipping their paws in the shady, secluded stream that runs between picnic areas. Call the rangers to find out if the reservoir is open, because if it isn't, it may not be worth a trip. You can't get anywhere near the lake if it's too low.

The only trail connects picnic areas, and it isn't even a half mile long. Plenty of picnic tables have lots of shade, but dogs tend to get bored unless hunks of hamburger happen to fall from the grills. The picnic areas can be rowdy, with lots of beer and loud music, so if your dog doesn't like rap, take him somewhere else.

From U.S. 101, follow Cochrane Road east to the park. 408/779-3634 or 408/355-2200.

🐾 Uvas Canyon County Park

🐾 🐾 🐾 (See Santa Clara County map on page 522)

This is a pretty, clean park of oak, madrone, and Douglas fir trees in cool canyons. The Uvas Creek Trail is a favorite trail. Dogs always appreciate a creek on a warm summer day, and this one doesn't dry up in hot weather. You might also try the wide, dirt Alec Canyon Trail, 1.5 miles long, within sight of Alec Creek, or the Nature Trail Loop, about one mile long, beside Swanson Creek. You may see some waterfalls in late winter and early spring. Dogs aren't allowed on one trail: the Knibbs Knob Trail. There's a $5 day-use fee.

Dogs are allowed in the campgrounds and picnic areas of Uvas Canyon. The park has 25 campsites, available on a first-come, first-served basis, for $9–18 a night. The campground is open daily April 15–October 31, and Friday and Saturday November–March. It's crowded on weekends during late spring and summer, so arrive early or camp during the week. Phone 408/355-2201 for reservations.

From U.S. 101, exit at Cochrane Road; go south on Business 101 to Watsonville Road, then right (west) on Watsonville to McKean-Uvas Road. Turn right on Uvas (past Uvas Reservoir) to Croy Road. Go left on Croy to the park. The last four miles on Croy are fairly tortuous. 408/779-9232 or 408/355-2200.

PLACES TO STAY

Best Western Country Inn: Rates are $78–139. Dogs are allowed in smoking rooms only and are $10 extra. 16525 Condit Road, 95037; 408/779-0447.

Uvas Canyon County Park: See Uvas Canyon County Park, above, for camping information.

Gilroy

PARKS, BEACHES, AND RECREATION AREAS

🐾 Mount Madonna County Park

🐾 🐾 🐾 🐾 (See Santa Clara County map on page 522)

This magnificent 3,700-acre park is midway between Gilroy and Watsonville (in Santa Cruz County). No matter where you're coming from, it's worth the drive. The mountain, covered with mixed conifers, oak, madrone, and bay and sword ferns, is wonderfully quiet and cool—which is especially appreciated by San Jose dwellers, whose parks are almost never far from the roar of freeways. You may hear the screech of jays and little else.

Try driving on Valley View Road (to the right from the ranger station) to the Giant Twins Trail, where you can park in the shady campsite of the same name—at least when no one is camping there. (When we were there on a perfect Indian summer day in late September, the park was deserted.) Two huge old redwoods, green with lichen, give the trail its name. After half a mile, the trail becomes Sprig Lake Trail and continues for another two miles. Sprig Lake, really a pond, is empty in summer, but in spring it's stocked for children's fishing.

This walk isn't much of a strain. If you'd like more exercise, there are plenty of longer and steeper trails—18 miles in all, and as of this writing, your dog may enjoy every one of them. From the Redwood Trail or the Blackhawk Canyon Trail, you'll be rewarded with views of the Santa Clara Valley, the Salinas Valley, and Monterey Bay. For a walk almost completely around the park, try the Merry-Go-Round Trail.

The park's deer are only one of many reasons you should keep your dog securely leashed, tempting as it might be to let her off. "Dogs have instincts," a friendly ranger said.

Your dog might enjoy a camping vacation here. There are 113 large, private campsites. Sites are $12–20 per night. Phone 408/355-2201 for reservations. A $5 day-use fee is always charged on weekends and daily Memorial Day–Labor Day.

From U.S. 101, exit at Highway 152 west to Gilroy. Continue on 152 (Hecker Pass Highway) through part of the park. The entrance is a right (north) turn at Pole Line Road. 408/842-2341 or 408/355-2200.

🐾🐾 Coyote Lake Park

🐾🐾🐾 (See Santa Clara County map on page 522)

This county park is full of wildlife no matter how high or low the lake. In fact, when we last visited, we saw foxes, wild turkeys, and a grazing deer—and there wasn't a drop of water in the reservoir. The reservoir had been bone dry for so long that it looked like an enormous open field. Brush and a few trees were starting to emerge from the hard, dry ground.

When it's in this drought condition, the lake bed is a favorite stomping ground for leashed canines—who are usually relegated to picnic areas, the campground, and the one-mile trail connecting them.

The campsites are roomy, and several are shaded by large oak trees. Others look out on the lake—or field, depending on the water level. We like to visit the nearby picnic areas after stopping at one of Gilroy's garlic stores for lunch supplies.

There are 74 sites here, and they're $9–18. County parks allow two dogs per site. Phone 408/355-2201 for reservations. The day-use fee is $5. From U.S. 101, exit at Leavesley Road and follow the signs to the park. 408/842-7800 or 408/355-2200.

PLACES TO STAY

Coyote Lake Park: See Coyote Lake Park, above, for camping information.

Leavesley Inn: Rates are $63–73. Dogs are charged a $20 fee per visit. 8430 Murray Avenue 95020; 408/847-5500.

Mount Madonna County Park: See Mount Madonna County Park, above, for camping information.

CHAPTER 38

Santa Cruz County

If you have a beach-loving dog, Santa Cruz County is a great place to take him. The beaches here rarely get too warm, and while some are packed beyond belief (dogs are generally not allowed at the popular beaches), most are on the quieter side.

Jake, who is the ultimate Beach Dog Dude, is very happy whenever we visit Santa Cruz County. On a recent sojourn, though, after a satisfying romp at It's Beach, we took him up to see a surfer statue, which is along the walkway there. After all, Jake is a dude. But the statue, a large and beautiful homage to surfers who have caught their last wave, scared the brave boy and he fluffed up and wouldn't go near it. In his attempt to escape, he even collided with a real surfer who was on his way down to the beach. It wasn't one of Jake's finer Beach Dog Dude moments.

Beach Dog Dudes have a couple of options for getting to the sand. They can convince you to drive or walk, of course. But if you're in midcounty, a far more interesting way to get to the beach is to take the turn-of-the-20th-century steam train run by the Roaring Camp and Big Trees Narrow-Gauge Railroad. The

PICK OF THE LITTER—SANTA CRUZ COUNTY

BEST DOG PARK
Scotts Valley Dog Park, Scotts Valley (page 551)

BEST LEASH-FREE BEACH
West Lighthouse Beach/It's Beach, Santa Cruz (page 558)

BEST BET FOR A DOG HOUSE
A House in Santa Cruz owner-managed rentals (pages 556, 560)

MOST DOG-FRIENDLY PLACE TO STAY
Seashell Cottage Oceanfront Vacation Rental,
Santa Cruz (page 560)

MOST FUN ROOM
The Wine Cellar, *at the Apple Lane Inn,* Aptos (page 562)

BEST RIDES
Roaring Camp and Big Trees Narrow-Gauge Railroad,
Felton (page 552)
Santa Cruz Harbor water taxi, Santa Cruz (page 559)

MOST FUN FLICKS
Video Video, Santa Cruz (page 557)
Skyview Drive-In Theatre, Santa Cruz (page 558)

same company runs an 1880s narrow-gauge railroad through the redwoods. Both trips can be the thrill of a dog's life. (See the Diversion Choo on This.)

Jake's favorite beaches are the more desolate ones along the northernmost coast of Santa Cruz County. Only one, Bonnie Doon Beach, is detailed later in this chapter because there are so many of them and they're relatively small, with parking only on the shoulder of the road. But they're wonderful for getting away from the crowds, especially if you're also looking at getting away from day-use fees.

These beaches run from Scott Creek in the north to Wilder Ranch State Park in the south. Davenport is the midpoint. Many of the beaches are hidden from Highway 1, so sometimes the only way to tell if there's a beach at all is to look for a few other cars parked on the roadside.

A word of warning about those big green patches you'll see when you look at a map of the county: They're mostly state parks and they ban dogs from doing everything but camping with you and hanging out on the paved sections of road (not the chosen path of most dogs). But for an exciting exception, check out the beautiful Henry Cowell Redwoods State Park—one of the most dog-friendly state parks we've seen.

A couple of new off-leash parks help put a wag in a dog's tail. One of them even has its own rendition of an off-leash beach: an off-leash wading pool. Your dog can be a Dog Beach Dude even if he never sets paw on sand. The only thing missing is the surfer statue. (Lucky for Jake. See the Scott's Valley section for more on this dog park.)

Ben Lomond

PARKS, BEACHES, AND RECREATION AREAS

1 Quail Hollow Ranch

🐾🐾🐾 (See Santa Cruz County map on page 548)

This 300-acre ranch-style park is the largest county park in Santa Cruz. It's also one of the least developed, making it a good area for a dog. There's plenty of wildlife around, so bring your binoculars and hold on tight to that leash. Deer and coyotes abound certain times of year. You'll also see a few quail, but don't get any ideas about dinner: No hunting is allowed.

From Highway 9, go east on Graham Hill Road and then north (left) on East Zayante Road. Turn left at Quail Hollow Road. The park is on the right. The official address is 800 Quail Hollow Road. 831/454-7900.

Scotts Valley

PARKS, BEACHES, AND RECREATION AREAS

2 Scotts Valley Dog Park

🐾🐾🐾🐾🐕 (See Santa Cruz County map on page 548)

It's only natural that, being in Santa Cruz County, there would be something in this park for water dogs: a little wading pool—and sometimes two, from what I hear. When Jake visited on a warm afternoon, he walked up to it as if he were going to take a drink, and then he suddenly plopped in and sat down, his blond tail wagging as fast as the water would allow.

The park is 1.2 fenced acres, with a smaller section for small or shy dogs. There are tennis balls galore, and water, poop bags, and plenty of seating. In summer, a temporary awning provides shade. The ground cover is a slightly softer version of the common wood-chip material found in many dog parks. Jake prefers grass, but this stuff makes scooping the poop a breeze and park maintenance pretty easy, too.

DIVERSION

Choo on This: Riding on the antique **Roaring Camp and Big Trees Narrow-Gauge Railroad** was one of Joe's favorite adventures ever—except whenever the engineer released loud bellows of steam. And whenever the railroad car moved.

Eventually he did get used to the chug-a-lug motion. Toward the end of the 1.5 hours, he was thoroughly enjoying himself, nose in the air, sucking in the smells of the primeval redwood forest from our open train car. But he still wouldn't leave my lap.

Most dogs are ecstatic on the train. Joe smiled the whole time and his tail never stopped wagging. When the steam let loose, he followed it with his eyes as if it were a beautiful white bird. He alternated between fascination, napping, and staring blankly at the sky, trying to sort out what had happened to him.

The railroad company offers another trip to the Santa Cruz city beach. But since dogs aren't allowed in that area, we recommend the excursion through the redwoods. Besides, halfway through the redwood trip, dogs and their people get to walk around the ancient forest a little before clambering back aboard.

At the end of either train journey, nothing beats spreading out a picnic at the old-fashioned depot's picnic tables. There's plenty of room for walking your leashed dog around the grounds. And humans have fun shopping at the antique general store. It's hard to leave the little shop without buying the kids a miniature train car, so if you don't want to spend extra money, you'd better not even go in.

Rates for the redwood trip are $18 for adults and $12 for children ages 3–12. Rates for the Santa Cruz beach excursion are $20 for adults and $15 for kids. Dogs get a free ride on both. Please note that dogs are now required to wear muzzles. It's not as bad as it sounds. We're not talking one of those Spanish Inquisition leather contraptions; just a simple nylon and Velcro muzzle will do. (When Joe Dog had to wear one, he didn't even seem to notice it was there.) If you don't have your own muzzle, it's likely there's one here you can borrow.

From Highway 1 in the Santa Cruz area, take Highway 17 north toward San Jose. Exit at the Scotts Valley/Big Basin exit and drive west on Mount Hermon Road 3.5 miles to Graham Hill Road. Turn left onto Graham Hill Road. Roaring Camp is one-half mile ahead on the right. Call for schedules and alternate excursions. 831/335-4484.

From Highway 17 in Santa Cruz, take the Mount Hermon Road exit and drive straight. You'll pass Scotts Valley Drive. Continue to the next street, Kings Village Road, and go right. The road ends in a T; go left (it's still Kings

Village Road) and you'll quickly see the park and the parking lot. The address is 361 Kings Village Road. 831/438-3251.

PLACES TO STAY

Hilton Santa Cruz/Scotts Valley: Stay here and you and your dog can watch free movies from your spacious, comfortable room: Each room comes with a VCR and free access to the hotel's video library. Busy humans can work in a 24-hour business center and then work out in a 24-hour fitness center, or just take to the pool. Rates are $129–229. Dogs are $25 extra. 6001 La Madrona Drive 95066; 831/440-1000.

Felton

PARKS, BEACHES, AND RECREATION AREAS

🖪 Henry Cowell Redwoods State Park

🐾🐾🐾🐾 (See Santa Cruz County map on page 548)

Dogs are actually allowed on three trails here! This is a huge deal because state parks are not exactly known for their dog-friendliness. The main section of the park is 1,750 acres, and it's filled with things dogs love best: trees. Big trees. Redwoods. The largest is 250 feet tall and 16 feet wide. The oldest trees are between 1,400 and 1,800 years old. They've seen a lot in their lifetimes.

Dogs are permitted on Graham Hill Trail, Meadow Trail, and Pipeline Road. They can also dine with you at the picnic areas and camp at the 100-plus campsites. Dogs adore this, because the sites are surrounded by big old trees. The day-use fee is $6. Camping is $20. From Felton, take Graham Hill Road southeast about two miles to the park. The entrance is on the right. Phone 831/335-4598 for park information or call 800/444-7275 for campsite reservations.

PLACES TO STAY

Henry Cowell Redwoods State Park: See Henry Cowell Redwoods State Park, above, for camping information.

Bonnie Doon

PARKS, BEACHES, AND RECREATION AREAS

🖪 Bonnie Doon Beach

🐾🐾🐾🐾 (See Santa Cruz County map on page 548)

This beach, just north of Santa Cruz, is hidden from Highway 1 by bluffs, so few people know it exists. That's good news for dogs, even though they're still supposed to be leashed. Some days, you won't find a soul here. Other times, the crowd will consist of a couple of dozen folks picnicking and strolling. Still other times (sunny, warm days, usually), the crowd will consist of quite a few naked people. Naked men, to be exact. If your dog is an incorrigible sniffer of private places, it's best to steer clear of here on pleasant days. (Joe flunked the sniff test on two other nudie beaches, so we visited here in fog only.)

(See the introduction to this chapter for information on other small beaches along the north coast of Santa Cruz County.) Bonnie Doon Beach is at Highway 1 and Bonnie Doon Road. There's a small dirt parking lot on the side of the road. 831/454-7900.

PLACES TO STAY

Redwood Croft Bed and Breakfast: Stay in this beautiful country home with your dog and you'll feel as if you've gone to grandma's house—only grandma is very hip with a good eye for arts, antiques, and hot tubs. One of the two guest rooms here has a rock fireplace and a totally enclosed little yard with its own hot tub. You can soak while your dog sniffs around the place, and you won't have to worry about her wandering off. The house has big decks all around it, and it's sunny, even though it's surrounded by redwoods. The gardens here are to drool for. So are the breakfasts. Rates are $145–195. You'll get the address when you make reservations. 831/458-1939.

Davenport

This fun little coastal community is just a bone's throw from Bonnie Doon and its wonderful beach and dog-friendly lodging. The bakery below is a fun place to make a road stop.

PLACES TO EAT

Whale City Bakery, Bar and Grill: This is a fun and convenient place to stop on a trip between San Francisco and some far-flung destination to the south. The name of this restaurant tells you just about everything you need to know about the cuisine. (Jake would like to add, however, that while the burgers here are to drool for, the fried calamari are truly a greaser-dog's dream come true.) Drink and dine at the tables out front, facing the ocean and Highway 1. They're wonderful in the cliffside fog or the bright sun. 490 Highway 1; 831/423-9803.

Capitola

This beautiful resort area's main beach, Capitola City Beach, is off-limits to dogs. But just down the road, New Brighton State Beach more than makes up for the loss.

If you feel like a beautiful stroll by Soquel Creek, take your leashed dog to the Esplanade, just off Opal Cliff Drive. It's the paved walk that usually has flowers at the entrance, east and inland of the Capitola Wharf (which also doesn't allow dogs).

PARKS, BEACHES, AND RECREATION AREAS

5 New Brighton State Beach

🐾🐾🐾🐾 (See Santa Cruz County map on page 548)

Feel that breeze? It's the breeze of so many dog tails wagging on this beach lately. Yes, ON the beach! Dogs and their people did very well during a trial period of beach access, and now it's officially OK to bring your dog down to the sand. Dogs have to be leashed, but it's a far howl better than the previous rule banning dogs entirely.

Dogs are also permitted on the little trails above the beach. If your dog is tiring of all the sand and surf on the beach, take her on the trail that leads up to big pines and eucalyptus trees. It starts to the left of the main beach entrance. If you walk along the forest/dune area, you'll be able to see Capitola as birds see it. Dogs like to sit up here and let their nostrils quiver over scents drifting in from around the world.

From Highway 1, take the New Brighton Beach exit west. Day-use fees are $6 per car. You'll find 112 campsites set on bluffs and surrounded by trees. Rates are $12 per night. For campground reservations (strongly recommended, as this is a mighty popular place), phone 800/444-7275. Call 831/464-6329 for beach information.

PLACES TO EAT

Caffe Lido: It's a smallish outdoor area, but if you keep your dog from getting underfoot, you'll enjoy a relaxed California-Italian meal. 110 Monterey Avenue; 831/475-6544.

Souza Cones Ice Cream and Candy: "Dogs are our best customers," a dog-loving staffer told us on our most recent visit. Dine on dripping waffle cones with your drooling dog at the outside bench here. If he's thirsty, the staffers will give you a bowl of water for him. 200 Monterey Avenue; 831/475-9339.

PLACES TO STAY

Best Western Capitola by-the-Sea Inn and Suites: The list of amenities here is actually longer than the hotel's name. They include breakfast, heated pool, morning paper, and some rooms with whirlpools, fireplaces, microwaves, and fridges. Rates are $125–189. Dogs are $10 extra. 1435 41st Avenue 95010; 831/477-0607; www.bestwestern.com.

A House in Santa Cruz: The pickings are kind of slim when it comes to dog-friendly Capitola hotels, so if you can't find a room, why not try a vacation rental? This directory of owner-managed rentals features some fabulous homes and cottages at or near the coast in Capitola. Our favorite is the Opal Ocean Front House. Everything about it is top-notch. I don't describe it in detail because it's a dream house and I can't afford the $595 nightly or $3,995 weekly. It makes Jake and me queasy to think of something so close and enchanting, yet so out of reach, so we'll let you check out the website for this house and many other charmers: www.ahouseinsantacruz.com/dogfriendly. It features excellent photos and descriptions of each rental, plus phone numbers and rates for each.

New Brighton State Beach: See New Brighton State Beach, above, for camping information.

Santa Cruz

Hey dogs, I'll bet you think this is a way laid-back town, don't you? You probably imagine you could roam around just about anywhere in this cool place, and that leashes would be viewed by city officials as a ridiculous contrivance, and that restaurants everywhere would welcome you with open, tattooed arms. Well, get that bandanna off your neck and get ready to wipe your doggy tears: The reality of Santa Cruz doesn't live up to the fantasy.

Forget the leash-free dream: Leashes can come off at just a couple of beach areas, and only then during limited hours. As far as being allowed everywhere, that's another doggy disappointment. Dogs are banned from the main alfresco restaurant–filled street on the downtown mall area, and at such hangouts as Santa Cruz Beach, the Boardwalk, and the Municipal Wharf.

If this were any other city, it wouldn't be such a disappointment. But this is Santa Cruz, land of the free, home of the unusual. Still, we've managed to sniff out some fun spots for dogs.

PARKS, BEACHES, AND RECREATION AREAS

One beach and one open area allow dogs off leash during limited hours. Most city parks permit leashed dogs. San Lorenzo Park is a notable exception. So is Nearys Lagoon City Park, a popular wildlife sanctuary you may be tempted to visit with your canine friend. But since dogs aren't part of the natural scenery here, they're not allowed.

6 Lighthouse Field

🐾🐾🐕 (See Santa Cruz County map on page 548)

This is officially part of Lighthouse Field State Beach, but even though it's state parkland, dogs may run off-leash during certain hours. It's a great dog privilege, but the area itself is no prize. It's not large enough for escape art-

DIVERSIONS

Get All Dolled Up and Catch a Movie: It's Friday afternoon. Your dog reeks and is scratching at his resident fleas again. And you're itching to do something tonight other than watch bad TV. With the following Santa Cruz businesses so close to each other, you'll be able to take care of both problems in one fell swoop:

Shampoo Chez: Shampoo Chez (sham-POO-ches) has a wonderful self-service **pooch wash** for doity dogs. You provide the elbow grease and the shampoo (or you can buy shampoo here), it provides the tub and all the fixin's. The tubs are at waist level, so there's no back strain, but the best part is that you don't have to make the tub immaculate afterward. After all, you're not going to be sitting your naked body down in this tub! It's a lovely, comfortable place to clean up your dog. The products sold here, from shampoos to biscuits, are natural and good for your dog. Shampoo Chez even sells doggy homeopathics. Self-serve wash rates are $14 for the first 20 minutes, and $1 for every five minutes after that. Full grooming is also available. (There's another branch in Campbell; for more information, see the Diversion You Doity Dog in the Santa Clara chapter.) 1380 Soquel Avenue; 831/427-BATH (831/427-2284); www.shampoo-chez.com.

Video Video: Dogs are welcome to browse through this fun **video store** with you. Pooches have even been known to get treats here, but that's not a guarantee because the folks here often don't have them in stock. That's OK. They've got plenty of videos: At least 12,000 titles are in stock. If you want an offbeat video, chances are good that you'll find it here. A big thanks to Chloe the Jack Russell terrier, for telling us about Video Video. 1376 Soquel Avenue; 831/427-2282; www.videovideo.com.

---

ist dogs to be safe from traffic, and there's not much shade. But the view of the ocean is a winner. Unless your dog likes traipsing through eye-high dry grass, which is what this place has most of the year, you're better off taking him to West Lighthouse Beach/It's Beach on the other side of West Cliff Drive (see below).

Dogs can run off leash here sunrise–10 A.M. and 4 P.M.–sunset. The rest of the time they need to be leashed. Don't worry if signs tell you only that dogs must always be leashed, without mentioning the off-leash hours. The Lighthouse Field is on the nonocean side of West Cliff Drive, west of Point Santa Cruz. 831/420-5270.

DIVERSION

Go to the Movies: Santa Cruz's **Skyview Drive-In Theatre** is one of those rare drive-in joints that dares to call itself a theater. In fact, these days, it's one of those rare drive-ins, period. We're thrilled it's still around. You'll need an FM radio to receive the soundtrack, and $8 per adult. Kids under 12, and dogs of all ages, are free. 2260 Soquel Drive. 831/475-3405.

7 West Lighthouse Beach/It's Beach

🐾🐾🐾🐾🐾 (See Santa Cruz County map on page 548)

The beach is narrow and not nearly as heavily used as other beaches in the area. This is surfer heaven here. Dogs seem to enjoy sniffing at surfers' neoprene-clad bodies as they jog toward the ocean with their boards. Jake once swam after a surfer and stayed near him until I was able to get his attention to call him back in. On his way back, a wave went over his head, scaring me to death and knocking some sense into him about safe swimming practices. He hasn't followed a surfer out since.

Even though this is part of Lighthouse Field State Beach, dogs are allowed to run leashless sunrise–10 A.M. and 4 P.M.–sunset. The rest of the time they're not supposed to even set paw on the sand, leashed or not. A big ticket can ensue. The beach is on the ocean side (duh) of West Cliff Drive, west of Point Santa Cruz and just west of the infamous Santa Cruz Surfing Museum. 831/420-5370.

8 Twin Lakes State Beach

🐾🐾🐾 (See Santa Cruz County map on page 548)

The beach here is wide and inviting for leashed dogs and their people. But unfortunately, even more inviting is a section that dogs should stay away from: Schwan Lagoon, a wildfowl refuge full of ducksch and geesch and, they say, even a few schwans.

Twin Lakes State Beach is on both sides of the Santa Cruz Small Craft Harbor, on East Cliff Drive and 7th Avenue. 831/427-4870.

PLACES TO EAT

Santa Cruz has many, many restaurants with outdoor tables. Here's a sampling of a few dog-friendly ones. You'll be able to sniff out plenty more on your own while you're exploring with your pooch. Just stay away from the myriad alfresco restaurants on Pacific Avenue, the main drag downtown. It's a drag in more than one sense of the word: Dogs are banned from the entire strip. (So are skateboards, if that makes your dog feel any better.)

DIVERSION

Hail a Water Taxi: Want that seafaring experience without the rolling waves or the expense? If it's Saturday or Sunday, and it's summer, and you're in Santa Cruz, you and your salty dog are in luck. The port district here runs free water taxis that motor around the **Santa Cruz Harbor,** making several stops to pick up and drop off passengers. The price? Zippo. Yes, a free taxi, and no crazy city taxi driver either. Such a deal. Even if your dog is prone to turning green at the mere sight of any water that's not in his bowl, he should be just fine on the water taxi. These flat-bottomed boats are stable, plus the harbor isn't exactly the Bering Sea. We're talking flat.

You can catch the taxi at several harbor spots. Our favorite is at Aldo's Restaurant, because there's decent parking around here and because there's nothing like waiting for a water taxi at a bustling, friendly dockside fish restaurant. (It's located at 616 Atlantic Avenue.) For more water taxi info, phone 831/475-6161.

Harbor Deli: The Mexican food and burgers are satisfying. 460 7th Avenue; 831/479-1366.

Pleasure Pizza: Pop over here with your pooch for some primo pizza at Pleasure's outdoor tables. 4000 Portola Drive; 831/475-4999.

Tony and Alba's Pizza: Dogs like hanging out under the shade of a cool umbrella-covered table while you enjoy pizza and pasta. 817 Soquel Avenue; 831/425-8669.

Walnut Avenue Cafe: You can sit next to your pooch at this café, but he must be tied to the other side of the railing. It serves a good breakfast. Joe once mooched some eggs Benedict from a toddler here. She started crying when he wouldn't eat the green garnishy thing that came with the eggs, so he ate that, too. Such a softy. 106 Walnut Avenue; 831/457-2307.

Westside Coffee Company: If you're in the mood for a light but tasty snack with your pooch, stop here and dine at the six tables nestled under an overhang. 849 Almar Street; 831/427-1300.

PLACES TO STAY

Continental Inn: This one's about five blocks from the water. Rates are $45–280. Dogs are $10 extra. 414 Ocean Street 95060; 831/429-1221; www.continentalinn.net.

Edgewater Beach Motel: No two rooms are alike at this attractive, dog-friendly haunt. Four of the rooms were built in 1886, although 1955 was the year a big chunk of the motel came into existence. You can get a room adorned with mahogany, redwood, or even a sunken fireplace, or a basic room with less character, but just as much comfort. (Face it. If you're traveling with your dog, you've probably got all the character you can handle anyway.)

Outside is a flower garden, a lawn area for kids, a picnic area with gas barbecues, and best for dogs, a big lot where they can do things doggies like to do. (Do clean up.) The lot is across the street from the wharf, where dogs are banned.

The owners love dogs and have three pooches themselves. "Pets make great guests. I'm more reluctant about having some people stay here than I am about dogs," says owner Win Alexander. Dog guests are supplied a dog bowl and a dog sheet while they're here. Rates are $89–299. Dogs are $10–30 extra, depending on their size. 525 2nd Street, 95060; 831/423-0440; www.edgewaterbeachmotel.com.

A House in Santa Cruz: Looking for a pooch-friendly vacation rental by the ocean? This directory of owner-managed rentals features wonderful homes and cottages. Some are right across the street from the ocean, some are tucked away in quiet neighborhoods, and some have enclosed backyards for your dog friend. There's no agent to contact, so there's no one phone number. The website, www.ahouseinsantacruz.com/dogfriendly, has excellent photos and descriptions of each rental, plus phone numbers and rates for each.

Ocean Pacific Lodge: You're just a couple of blocks from beach action when you stay here. This is a clean, decent-looking place, with minifridges and nukers in all the rooms, which makes traveling with your canine troupe a bit easier. Humans enjoy the heated pool and continental breakfast. Rates are $59–145. Dogs must be under 25 pounds and pay a $20 fee for the length of their stay. 120 Washington Street 95060; 831/457-1234 or 800/995-0289.

Pacific Inn: The rooms all have little fridges, so you and your dog can have some cool midnight snacks. The motel also has a heated indoor pool, but no paw-dipping, please. Rates are $80–200. Dogs are $10 extra. 330 Ocean Street 95060; 831/425-3722.

Seashell Cottage Oceanfront Vacation Rental: "I give first priority to people with dogs," says friendly rental manager Susanna Eaton. "They make the best guests." The Seashell Cottage is the most popular of her five beach rentals. It's an utterly enchanting one-room cottage perched over a secluded beach near the edge of a cliff. (Don't worry, it won't fall.) Enjoy a book on the window seat that faces the ocean. Or relax in the small yard or deck, keeping off the chill with the outdoor fireplace.

Dogs truly feel welcome here. Treats are waiting for them when they arrive, and there's even a water dish and a spare leash, should you forget yours.

Rates are $250 nightly, or $1,500 weekly. For more on Seashell or Susan's other rentals, see www.beachnest.com, or phone 831/722-0202. You'll get the address of your rental when you make your reservation.

Aptos

If all suburbs could be like Aptos, this country would be a much better-looking place. While Aptos is falling victim to the suburban sprawl of its neighbors to the north, it still retains a core of grace in its old village section. Check out the rustic Redwood Village, whose quaint stores were originally built in 1928 with redwood hewn from trees on the property.

While exploring Aptos, if you run into Loma Prieta Drive, don't sit around with your dog and wonder why someone would name a street after the deadly 1989 earthquake. This is the area of the epicenter of that quake, which measured 7.1 on the Richter scale. If your dog starts acting restless, you may want to move on. It could be fleas. It could be boredom. It could even be gas. But why take a chance? Actually, people around here say the pressure along the fault line was relieved by the quake, so there's probably little chance that another big one could be centered here again for a while.

PARKS, BEACHES, AND RECREATION AREAS

⛏ Aptos Polo Grounds Dog Park

🐾🐾🐾🦮 (See Santa Cruz County map on page 548)

This one-acre fenced park seems bigger than it really is. It could be because it's a super-flat park with a wood-chip ground cover that blends in with the brownish grass (most of the year) behind it, creating the illusion of grandness. Jake seems to have fallen pray to the illusion, becoming exhausted after a few quick passes from one side to the other while being chased by a friendly boxer.

The park is flanked on two sides by tall, beautiful trees, but no trees grace the park, so shade is limited to times when the sun is just right. The park has water, poop bags, benches, and a portable toilet right outside, in case you're hankering to do a leg lift yourself.

It's a quick trip from Highway 1 to the park, so it's handy if you need an exercise stop on a road trip. From Santa Cruz, take Highway 1 to the Rio Del Mar exit. Go left after the freeway and turn right on Monroe Avenue (the second traffic light). Monroe turns into Wallace Avenue. You'll come to a fork in the road, where you'll bear left onto Huntington Drive. The park entrance will be on your left after an area of houses. Drive in and you'll find the fenced doggy park. Please note that dogs are banned from the playing fields at Polo Grounds Park, but they're welcome to peruse a fun trail near the dog park as long as they're leashed. A big thanks to Joan Fuhry for giving us the first heads-up about the park. 831/454-7900.

PLACES TO EAT

Britannia Arms: We wouldn't characterize this restaurant and pub as English, as it serves mostly American-style food (plenty of barbecued dishes and burgers). But it's as dog-friendly as any English springer spaniel or Airedale could hope. When you step inside to order your food, you can attach your dog's leash to a dog hitch made specially for this situation. There's usually water for dogs, but if there isn't, it's yours for the asking. We've heard dogs get occasional treats, but it's not the official policy. Dine with your dog at several umbrella-topped patio tables. 8017 Soquel Drive; 831/688-1233.

Café Rio: If you wish for fish, try a dish from Café Rio. It's a primo fish restaurant with everything from abalone to smoked salmon. If your dog prefers aged beef, it's got that, too. The outdoor patio area here is big and leafy and welcomes well-behaved dogs. Café Rio is close to the Polo Grounds Dog Park. 131 Esplanade; 831/688-8917.

Cafe Sparrow: Eat your croissant sandwich on the bench in front of this little restaurant. 8042 Soquel Drive; 831/688-6238.

PLACES TO STAY

Apple Lane Inn: If you and your dog are hankering for simpler times—times when you could stroll out to the barn, collect a few eggs, pat the horses, mosey back to your Victorian farmhouse and have someone cook a gourmet breakfast for you, read a book under blooming wisteria on a pretty patio, pick a few apples from your trees, visit the geese and rabbits, go back inside and listen to the player piano while you play cards or games with your friends inside the parlor—you've found your nirvana. You can do all this and more—or much less, if you really want to take it really easy—when you stay at this historic inn built on more than two acres. (Okay, it's not exactly a Tara spread, but then again, that wouldn't be a simple life, would it?)

Dogs can stay with their people in the large room called the Wine Cellar. It's a great place to stay with a dog, because it has its own private garden entrance. The Wine Cellar is actually more than a room, since it has a very attractive dining area and a sofa (which can become a bed if needed). Many inns would consider this a suite. The stained-glass windows, the cooler air from its ground-floor location, and the full wine bottles that live in built-in wine racks on the walls impart a kind of winery feel (or if you were raised Catholic, a churchlike feel). But don't drink that wine! It's old, and not in a good old kind of way, apparently. But it sure looks pretty.

The inn's dog-loving manager, Lori, loves to see people visit with their pooches. But for several reasons (the inn's chickens, pheasants, turkey, rabbits, and geese are a few that come to mind), dogs need to be leashed anytime they're outside your room. Rates are $100–200. Dogs are $25 extra. Oh, and if you bring a horse, he's $25 extra too, but he'll need to stay in the big barn or the field here, not in your room. 6265 Soquel Drive, 95003; 831/475-6868 or 800/649-8988; www.applelaneinn.com.

Seacliff

PARKS, BEACHES, AND RECREATION AREAS

🐾 Seacliff State Beach
🐾🐾🐾🐾 (See Santa Cruz County map on page 548)

Want to make your dog happy, even though he's officially supposed to be on a leash? Bring him here. A yearlong trial period showed that dogs and their well-behaved people should be allowed here. Before, the closest dogs could get to Seacliff State Beach was the RV campground perched above the beach. Somehow, looking down at a beach from your RV's picnic table isn't quite the same as trotting merrily down the beach with the breeze blowing through your fur.

The beach is about a mile long, so even though it can get pretty packed with pooches at the popular south end, there's plenty of space for some good exercise. And if you and your dog get hungry from all your beach activity, you can settle yourselves at the beach's picnic area. You can even nab one with a barbecue pit, if you feel like sharing a burger with your drooling canine.

Please remember to scoop the poop. Although there are plenty of garbage cans in which to toss your furry friend's feces (I couldn't help the alliteration), a park ranger tells us there's way too much poop left lying around. If this continues, things could go back to the way they used to be, and that wouldn't be fun for anyone. The day-use fee here is $6, if you park in the lot. Exit Highway 1 at State Park Drive and head toward the ocean. 831/685-6442.

Watsonville

PARKS, BEACHES, AND RECREATION AREAS

At press time, Watsonville was in the "considering" stages of dog a park. Let's hope the powers that be consider it a good idea, and we have a new park to visit for the book's next edition.

🐾 Palm Beach
🐾🐾🐾🐾 (See Santa Cruz County map on page 548)

Dahling! What a mahvelous place! And not a sign of anyone rich and famous for miles!

This may not be the Palm Beach of rich Southern Floridians' fame, but it's a heavenly, remote place that has considerably more to offer down-to-earth dogs and their people. A trail takes you through a large eucalyptus grove where you and your dog can stop for a cool, relaxing picnic. Then it's onward to the large beach, where your dog has to remain leashed, but he can still have a jolly old time sniffing and walking and walking and sniffing. Even on perfect summer afternoons, this beach gets very little use, probably because of its location at the end of the county.

Fees are $6 per car. Exit Highway 1 at Riverside Drive/Highway 129 and follow the signs to Beach Road, past huge farms. The beach is at the end of the road. 831/429-2850 or 831/763-7064.

PLACES TO STAY

Motel 6: This one's only a couple of miles from Palm Beach. Rates are $57–77 for one adult, $6 for the second adult. The owners ask that you let them know ahead of time if you'll be bringing a dog. 125 Silver Leaf Drive 95076; 831/728-4144.

Santa Cruz KOA Kampground: Does your dog's idea of roughing it entail sleeping at the foot of your bed? The Kamping Kabins at this KOA resort are the answer to the prayers of dogs who wince at the notion of spending the night in a tent in the woods. The rustic log cabins have no bathrooms (they're nearby), but they do have plenty of space. You bring the linens and blankets, and the cabins supply the mattresses. One-room cabins sleep four; two-room cabins sleep six. There's some land around outside where you and your dog can stretch your gams.

The secluded seaside road that leads to this campground is enough to put a smile on any dog's snout. The road isn't actually right next to the ocean, but it's separated by expanses of farm fields, which are often covered with expanses of fertilizer. Joe would always get intoxicated by the blend of fresh sea air and cow poop.

Alas, the smell of manure never gets as far as this KOA, but that's just fine with the humans in the party. The Santa Cruz KOA Kampground is one of the more attractive ones, since it's set under big pines so close to the water. If you prefer to camp in the great outdoors (OK, it's outdoors, although not necessarily great. In the tradition of KOAs everywhere, your campsite is up close and personal with your neighbor's), you can pitch a tent with your dog here too.

The KOA is a family-oriented place, with miniature golf, volleyball courts, a hot tub, swimming pools, and horseshoes. This is the priciest KOA in California, in large part because of the real estate values around here. Kamping Kabin rates are $66–75. (The upper end is for two-room Kabins.) Rates for the tent sites are $32–42. If you have an RV, you'll pay $45–58. The KOA is one mile from the coast, at 1186 San Andreas Road 95076; 831/722-0551 or 800/562-7701.

Sunset State Beach: The main unit of Sunset State Beach allows dogs to camp, but it doesn't allow them on the beach. Water-loving dogs should cruise down to Palm Beach (see above). This campground is a good one, though, with 90 sites set back on a bluff over the Pacific. It has a decent amount of exercise area for your dog to survive without trying to sneak down to the beach. Sites are $20 per night. From Santa Cruz, exit Highway 1 at San Andreas Road and go right at Sunset Beach Road. For campsite reservations, call 800/444-7275. For beach information, call 831/429-2850 or 831/763-7064.

CENTRAL AREA COUNTIES

CHAPTER 39
San Joaquin County

Chances are you won't be driving a few hundred miles just to vacation here with your dog. That's good. In fact, your dog is probably reading over your shoulder right now and slobbering in gratitude.

It's not that San Joaquin County is a terrible place for dogs. It certainly has its share of attractive parks. But since dogs aren't permitted off leash around here, and since this isn't exactly the wilderness capital of California, it's just not a great doggy destination.

Here's a good rule of thumb to remember if you don't want to come away with a ticket for a dog offense: Tempting as it may be, don't let your dog walk on the paths and trails in the county-run parks. It's an offense punishable by a few dollars out of your dog bone fund. It's a ridiculous rule. What would have happened to Toto if he hadn't been permitted to walk on the Yellow Brick Road?

PICK OF THE LITTER—SAN JOAQUIN COUNTY

BEST PLACE FOR THE DOG PADDLE
Lodi Lake, Lodi (page 568)

BIGGEST OFF-LEASH DOG AREA
Vinewood Park, Lodi (page 569)

BEST SPOT TO COOL YOUR HEELS
Woodbridge Regional Park, Woodbridge (page 569)

BEST WATERY ADVENTURE
Delta houseboat rentals, Stockton (page 570)

Lodi

PARKS, BEACHES, AND RECREATION AREAS

Lodi doesn't have dog parks, per se. "They're called Designated Dog Areas," a parks rep tells us. "They're not dog parks." And they're really not, in the traditional sense. (But a rose by any other name would smell as sweet.) Lodi has four not-dog parks. We write about our favorite two here.

🔳 Lodi Lake

🐾🐾🐾🐾 (See San Joaquin County map on page 566)

Water dogs love this 114-acre city park: They actually get to do the dog paddle—leash-free—in one section of the park's seven-acre lake. The swim area is only about 80 feet long, but that's plenty of splashing room. The park also features a very small fenced dog run. It has lots of trees, which boy dogs enjoy, and it's adjacent to the Mokelumne River. Dogs can take a stroll on paved paths around the rest of the park, but they must be leashed.

The doggy swim area is on the west bank of the lake, north of the dam, and bordered by the cemetery (which is fenced off; have no fear of your terrier going into dig mode). You'll see the signs. The dog run is on the lake's north side. The park address is 1101 West Turner Road, at Mills Avenue. 209/333-6742.

❷ Vinewood Park

🐾🐾🐾🐕 (See San Joaquin County map on page 566)

The off-leash area within Vinewood Park is actually part of a retention basin/ sump area. This means that it can close during rain or even threat of rain. But with four big acres of grassy, semifenced leash-free bliss, it's still a hot-diggety-dog place to go. The entire park itself is fenced, but the dog area is not separated by anything but signs and a wide strip of dirt. Pay attention to the signs: The dog area is the south basin. Whatever you do, don't let your dog wander to the north basin off leash. There's a $270 fine for this offense. (That's a lotta dog food money.) Dog people here would like to see the dog area fenced off so this kind of thing doesn't happen.

The dog area has benches, poop-bag dispensers, lots of trees, and is wheelchair-accessible. Water is just outside the area. The park is at 1824 West Tokay Street, at Mills Avenue. From Highway 12, go north on Mills Avenue and drive about three stop signs. Go right on Virginia Street. 209/333-6742.

Woodbridge

PARKS, BEACHES, AND RECREATION AREAS

❸ Woodbridge Regional Park

🐾🐾🐾 (See San Joaquin County map on page 566)

A quarter-mile stretch of the Mokelumne River is yours at this undeveloped riparian park. It's good for fishing or for dipping your paws on a warm day. It gets much less use than other county parks and it's free. Just keep your dog on a leash, and keep him off the trail here. It's the law. We don't like it, but what can you do?

The park is on East River Meadows Drive at the Mokelumne River, just north of Woodbridge Road. 209/953-8800.

Stockton

PARKS, BEACHES, AND RECREATION AREAS

❹ Oak Grove Regional County Park

🐾🐾🐾 (See San Joaquin County map on page 566)

This 180-acre park has more than 1,500 oak trees. If you want shade, or your boy dog wants a target for leg lifts, you've come to the right place.

You can easily get around the park without use of the wonderful 1.5-mile nature trail, and it's a good thing, because dogs aren't allowed to set paw on it. As with all San Joaquin County parks, dogs aren't permitted on trails or paths. But this park has enough open land so it won't matter much except on muddy days.

DIVERSION

Doggy Does Delta: There's really no better way to explore the Delta than on a houseboat. As your first mate steers the boat through the Delta's snaking waterways, you can prepare dinner, take a snooze on one of the boat's beds, catch some rays (and some fish), or just sit on the deck with your dog and sniff the brackish breeze. Just remember to park the boat occasionally (there's plenty of isolated, parkable land around) to let your pooch stretch his legs and tend to his business.

A dog-friendly **houseboat rental** company, Herman and Helen's Marina, rents the boats by the weekend or week, depending on the time of year. Weekly rates start at $1,195 for a houseboat that sleeps six, and go up to $4,895 for a week on an ultraswank houseboat that sleeps 14. For information, contact Herman and Helen's Marina, Venice Island Ferry, Stockton, CA 95219; 209/951-4634 or 800/676-4841. Another houseboat rental company, Seven Crown Resorts, will rent you and your dog and some friends a houseboat for $550 for three days/two nights to $1,900 for a week. Phone 800/752-9669 for more information; www.houseboat.com.

Dogs must be leashed. There's a $2 vehicle entry fee on weekdays, $5 on weekends and holidays. Dogs are $1. 209/953-8800.

5 Louis Park

😊😊😊 (See San Joaquin County map on page 566)

The address of this park is the intersection of the San Joaquin River and Smiths Canal. It's where the whole watery world converges—where freighters move their bulk alongside water-skiers, where tugboat captains wave to shoreline anglers.

You and your leashed dog will enjoy watching all the action from the comfort of this 70-acre park. It's slightly contoured, so some sections provide better views than others. Because the park was established in the 1920s, it has plenty of large trees for shade. Conifers, cottonwoods, native valley oaks, and broadleafs abound.

The park is also home to softball diamonds, tennis courts, a free boat ramp, and Pixie Woods, a children's play area complete with carousels and a miniature train. Louis Park is at the western end of Monte Diablo Avenue, at Occidental Avenue. 209/937-8206.

⑥ Victory Park

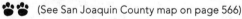 (See San Joaquin County map on page 566)

Local dogs come to mingle at this attractive park, which is full of large oaks and conifers. There's a paved walkway around the park's 27 acres. A hike around it makes for an excellent exercise routine.

Weekdays after work are the best times to visit if you want your leashed dog to hang out with other leashed dogs. Too bad the city couldn't set aside a couple of acres as a fenced-in dog-exercise area so dogs could play as they really want to—sans leash.

The park is at Pershing Avenue and Picardy Drive. 209/937-8206.

PLACES TO STAY

La Quinta Inn: Rates are $79–119. 2710 West March Lane 95219; 209/952-7800.

Tiki Lagun Resort and Marina: This is kind of a fun place to come camping with your canine, especially if you're not into a big wilderness adventure. The 30 soft-grass campsites are set under tall shade trees, just a bone's throw from the Delta. Dogs dig it here. If you visit in an RV, there's a separate RV park, with 30 spaces and complete hookups. Compared to most RV/camp areas, it's small and secluded. Tiki Lagun even has launch ramps, should you bring a boat. Rates are $25. 12988 West McDonald Road 95206; 209/941-8975 or 800/338-7176; www.tikimarina.com.

Manteca

PARKS, BEACHES, AND RECREATION AREAS

⑦ Northgate Park

 (See San Joaquin County map on page 566)

If your dog wants to meet the hounds of Manteca, come to Northgate Park, where Manteca dogs gather for long afternoons of leisure. The setting is grassy and fairly flat, with softball fields and picnic tables. It's not exactly Yosemite National Park, but dogs have more fun here.

Dogs are supposed to be leashed. The park is at Northgate Drive and Hoyt Lane. 209/239-8470.

Tracy

PARKS, BEACHES, AND RECREATION AREAS

🔟 El Pescadero Dog Park

🐾🐾🐾🐕 (See San Joaquin County map on page 566)

Wow! A dog park in this neck of the woods! This surprised even Joe Dog, who was more than happy to visit on a long road trip. Local canines are crazy for this fenced dog park. It's about an acre, with lots of grass for happy dogs to run around on. Park amenities include benches, water, and poop bags. The park is within El Pescadero Park, which is at Kavanagh and Louise Avenues. The dog park is on the Kavanagh side. 209/831-4200.

🔟 Lincoln Park

🐾🐾 (See San Joaquin County map on page 566)

The trees are big and the walkways are flat here, just how lazy leashed dogs like it. The park is an old, attractive one in the downtown area. It's at Eaton Avenue and East Street. 209/831-4200.

PLACES TO EAT

Banta Inn: Dogs are welcome at the patio tables while you dine on char-broiled sandwiches, steaks, and fish. 22563 South 7th Street; 209/835-1311.

PLACES TO STAY

Motel 6: This one's a trucker haven but it has plenty of dog guests. Rates are $40–49 for one adult, $6 extra for the second. 3810 North Tracy Boulevard 95376; 209/836-4900.

Woodward Res.

4

Knights Ferry

1

3

2

108 120

Riverbank

Oakdale

Stanislaus R.

108

Hetch Hetchy Aqueduct

Modesto Res.

La Grange

6

132

4

Modesto

5

Tuolumne River

Turlock Lake

33

99

5

7

Patterson

8

Turlock

J17

San Joaquin R.

Calif. Aqueduct

N

W — E

S

CHAPTER 40

Stanislaus County

Chambers of Commerce in these parts boast that "Summer Lasts Longer" here. Longer than what? When we asked, they weren't too sure. But when it's late September and your dog's tongue is unfurled just as long and bologna-like as it was in July, you may find the answer yourself: Summer lasts longer than hell here.

Fortunately, there are plenty of decent parks near the county's rivers. Dogs like to cool their fuzzy heels in the water.

Director George Lucas grew up here, surviving one sweltering summer after another. In his film *American Graffiti* (inspired by his younger years in Modesto, but not set there), a drive-in diner played a key role in the lives of his characters. It was a cool place to go on hot summer nights. If you and your dog want to dine alfresco here, you'll find a respectable number of outdoor restaurants. The most fitting is Modesto's very own A&W Root Beer drive-in restaurant, where carhops on roller skates will take your dog's order lickety-split. Just don't let your dog do naughty things to any passing poodle skirts.

PICK OF THE LITTER—STANISLAUS COUNTY

BEST HIKES
La Grange Regional Park, La Grange (page 579)
Frank Raines Regional Park, Patterson (page 580)

Oakdale

PARKS, BEACHES, AND RECREATION AREAS

■ Woodward Reservoir Regional Park

🐾🐾🐾 (See Stanislaus County map on page 574)

Although this is the largest county park in the system, dogs generally prefer Frank Raines Regional Park (see the Patterson section). Raines Park is 1,800 acres smaller, but it's got a lot more of the natural stuff that some dogs need.

Woodward is more barren and yet much more developed. By virtue of its 3,800 acres of land (not including the 2,900-acre reservoir), it's a fine place to take the leashed dog in your life. If someone in your family has the urge to water-ski or fish, you and your dog can dip your paws in the reservoir and stroll around the park's rolling hills while you wait.

Since there are no official trails here, most people walk around on the small dirt roads. But when the park gets extremely crowded, as it's wont to be on some weekends, you and your dog won't feel safe on these roads. Stick to the meadowy sections of the park.

The day-use fee is $8 per vehicle. Camping fees range $15–23 per site. Dogs are $2 extra day or night. There are 152 sites available on a first-come, first-served basis. If you want to launch your boat here, you'll pay an additional $7. From Highway 108/120, drive north on 26 Mile Road for about six miles to the park's entrance, which will be on your right. 209/525-6750.

■ Valley Oak Recreation Area

🐾🐾🐾 (See Stanislaus County map on page 574)

Some of the most pristine river woodland left in California lies along the Stanislaus River, and you should be able to see a sampling when you and your leashed dog visit this park. A hiking trail here offers a short tour of the lush river woodland. Moisture-loving trees such as cottonwoods, alders, and willows will keep you shaded while you dip your toes in the cool river.

This isn't a well-known park, so it doesn't get as crowded as some of the other riverside parks in the area. There are 10 boat-in campsites available for $8 per site. There is also one group site available, for $38. Reservations are required. From Highway 108/120, go north on County Road J9 and cross the river. Turn right at Rodden Road and follow it east to the park. 209/881-3517.

PLACES TO STAY

Valley Oak Recreation Area: See Valley Oak Recreation Area, above, for camping information.

Woodward Reservoir Regional Park: See Woodward Reservoir Regional Park, above, for camping information.

Knights Ferry

PARKS, BEACHES, AND RECREATION AREAS

🐾 Knights Ferry Recreation Area

🐾🐾🐾 (See Stanislaus County map on page 574)

You and your leashed dog can swim, fish, hike, or just relax under a big oak tree at this popular riverside park. A historic covered bridge takes you from one side of the Stanislaus River to the other. You'll find picnic tables and room for a little walking on either side. It's crowded on weekends, but during weekdays, it's a relaxing getaway.

From Highway 108/120, head north on Kennedy Road to the river. 209/881-3517.

Modesto

PARKS, BEACHES, AND RECREATION AREAS

🐾 Dry Creek Regional Park

🐾🐾🐾 (See Stanislaus County map on page 574)

A well-maintained bike/pedestrian trail leads you and the leashed dog in your life for more than three miles along the south side of Dry Creek. This park is actually a few parks strung together, so you'll find different terrain as you stroll merrily along. If your dog likes sniffing big trees or meditating at a riverside, he'll be happy here.

The park runs between La Loma Avenue and Claus Road. The section from El Vista Avenue east to Claus Road is not used much because it's very undeveloped. You may want to stick with the western part of the park. 209/577-5344.

5 Tuolumne River Regional Park

🐾🐾🐾 (See Stanislaus County map on page 574)

It's rare to find a city park that's even a couple of miles long, but here's one that spans six miles. Dogs think it's the cat's meow.

It has just about everything a dog could want, except permission to run around off leash. It's mostly undeveloped, meaning few softball fields or playgrounds to get in the way of a dog's endeavors. It's on the banks of the Tuolumne River, so water-loving dogs can cool their paws where they're able to reach the river. And it has an appealing blend of wide-open meadows, oak knolls, and natural riparian land.

The park is on the north side of the Tuolumne River and runs from Ohio Avenue on the west to Mitchell Road on the east. It has a golf course where dogs are verboten. It's also broken up by the occasional road and some sections of parkland that aren't too appealing. Try the area east of Tioga Drive. 209/577-5344.

PLACES TO EAT

A&W Root Beer: It's not the same diner as the one in *American Graffiti*, but the carhops still come by on roller skates, and poodle skirts are still in. Come here on a summer afternoon and slurp down a root beer served in a frosted mug. Your dog can join you at the shaded patio. In the winter, the patio is heated. That's the time to try two piping-hot cheeseburgers, one for you, one for you-know-who. 1404 G Street; 209/522-7700.

Piccadilly Deli: You and your dog will enjoy the deli fare, and you'll be grateful for the covered patio area during Modesto's long, hot summers. 941 10th Street; 209/523-0748.

PLACES TO STAY

Best Western Town House Lodge: Rates are $62–85. Dogs are $10 extra. 909 16th Street 95354; 209/524-7261 or 800/772-7261.

Doubletree Hotel: Rates at this comfortable hotel are $89–169. Dogs pay a $20 flat fee per visit. 1150 9th Street 95354; 209/526-6000; www.modesto .doubletree.com.

La Grange

PARKS, BEACHES, AND RECREATION AREAS

☑ La Grange Regional Park

🐾🐾🐾🐾 (See Stanislaus County map on page 574)

This 750-acre park has an undeveloped trail system that takes you along the Tuolumne River and through a delicate wilderness area. Woodpeckers, eagles, bobcats, deer, and all their friends make the park their home at different times of the year. Bring your binoculars and keep your dog leashed. (It's a real trick to bird-watch with a dog who's tugging on your arm to visit a nearby tree, but it can be done.)

The park is in the historic town of La Grange and contains ancient adobe buildings, an old jail, a schoolhouse, a cemetery, and an abandoned gold dredge. It makes for an interesting pit stop.

There are several parcels of La Grange Park, which has a $8 day-use fee. Dogs are $3 extra. We like to start at the Basso Bridge Fishing Access. Exit Highway 132 at Lake Road and follow the signs. You'll be there in a snap. Park in the lot and head upriver. You can continue walking for a few miles and have a pleasant riverside hike. Or you can cross the street when you see a sign for the wilderness area and pay a visit to a more pristine setting. La Grange even offers camping. The sites are undeveloped and cost $14. 209/525-6750.

PLACES TO STAY

La Grange Regional Park: See La Grange Regional Park, above, for camping information.

Patterson

PARKS, BEACHES, AND RECREATION AREAS

7 Frank Raines Regional Park

🐾🐾🐾🐾 (See Stanislaus County map on page 574)

This 2,000-acre county park is remote, mountainous, and full of wildlife you don't see much around these parts anymore. Leashed dogs love to hike among junipers, oaks, and foothill pines on the many dirt trails that wind through the park.

Springtime is the best season for a visit. The wildflowers are fantastic and the creek looks splendid when it's full.

About 640 acres of parkland are set aside for off-highway vehicle use. There are signs to steer you away from this area, but if you hear a roar that's not your dog's stomach, hike to another area. You may have accidentally stumbled into OHV land. There are also 43 acres of lawn with barbecues, a baseball diamond, and a playground. Dogs actually seem to like this manicured section because of the enchanting little nature trail here.

Tempting as it may be to slip your dog's leash off in the backcountry, you really shouldn't. If I can't inspire you to listen to the law, perhaps the tarantulas, rattlesnakes, bobcats, and occasional mountain lions can.

The day-use fee is $8. Campsite fees range $14–16. Dogs are $3 extra. There are 54 sites available on a first-come, first-served basis. From I-5, exit at Del Puerto Canyon Road and head west. You'll reach the park in about 18 winding miles. Follow the signs. 209/525-6750.

PLACES TO STAY

Frank Raines Regional Park: See Frank Raines Regional Park, above, for camping information.

Turlock

PARKS, BEACHES, AND RECREATION AREAS

8 Donnelly Park

🐾🐾 (See Stanislaus County map on page 574)

One day, the adolescent trees here will be massive and shady, but for now, your dog will have to bring his own umbrella if he wants shelter from the sun. A pond takes up about half of the park. Ducks like it, and so do water dogs. But the latter aren't allowed in the water.

The park is conveniently situated in the middle of town. From Highway 99, exit at Fulkerth Road and drive east about 1.5 miles. (Fulkerth Road turns into Hawkeye Avenue, but keep going.) The park will be on your left, between Del's Lane and Donnelly Drive. 209/668-5550.

PLACES TO STAY

Best Western Orchard Inn: The rate here is $78. There's also a $50 doggy deposit. 5025 North Golden State Boulevard 95382; 209/667-2827.

Turlock TraveLodge: Rates are $60–75. 201 West Glenwood Avenue 95380; 209/668-3400.

N
W · E
S

CHAPTER 41
Merced County

The county parks here ban dogs. The national wildlife refuges ban dogs. Even some of the smaller cities ban dogs from their parks. It can make a dog howling mad.

But clench not thine paws, canines. Merced County is rescued from the recesses of rottendom by the state wildlife areas here. Most are huge and permit off-leash pooches for at least a few months of the year. Two of these areas, Los Banos and O'Neill Forebay, are discussed in this chapter. For information on the others, call 209/826-0463.

Atwater

PARKS, BEACHES, AND RECREATION AREAS

🐾 Ralston Park
🐾🐾 (See Merced County map on page 582)

If you're window-shopping in the antique stores a few blocks away and need to rest your weary paws, try Ralston Park. It's got lots of lawn and plenty of trees.

PICK OF THE LITTER—MERCED COUNTY

BEST WALKS ON THE WILDLIFE SIDE
O'Neill Forebay Wildlife Area, Santa Nella (page 586)
Los Banos Wildlife Area, Los Banos (page 587)

MOST DOG-FRIENDLY PLACE TO EAT
Out to Lunch, Atwater (page 584)

LODGING WITH COOLEST ARCHITECTURE
Ramada Inn Mission de Oro, Santa Nella (page 586)

Ralston Park is between Grove and Fir Avenues, on 3rd Street. 209/357-6320.

PLACES TO EAT

Out to Lunch: Owners Ken and Michelle love dogs. And dogs love sitting around the covered porch while their people eat tasty quiche or mouthwatering sandwiches. Try the zucchini bread sandwich with cream cheese and veggies. Got a sweet tooth? Ken and Michelle make their own cheesecake. Or order a slice of Kahlua cake. And stop drooling.

Ken and Michelle have played host to small doggy birthday parties. You provide the party hats and dog gifts, and they'll provide the roast beef sandwiches on paper plates (or whatever else your dog desires that's fairly healthful). It costs no more than the food you buy here, and they might even throw in a little scoop of vanilla ice cream for the partying pooches. 1301 Winton Way; 209/357-1170.

Merced

Dogs of the male persuasion, rejoice! Merced is designated as a Tree City U.S.A. by the National Arbor Association. It's not exactly a forest, but the city does have an abundance of trees. It gives a dog plenty to sniff at, even if he's just accompanying you on a short walk.

PARKS, BEACHES, AND RECREATION AREAS

A Class-A bike path runs through town and passes many of the city's tree-shaded parks. You and your leashed dog are welcome to use the path, as long as you stay out of the way of things that could run you over. It's a great way to check out the various parks around the city.

If you get a chance, swing by the Courthouse Museum. It's a striking Italian Renaissance–style structure with columns, sculpted window frames, and a magnificent cupola. Dogs can't hang out in the museum, but the park just outside is fine for leashed dogs.

2 Applegate Park

🐾🐾🐾 (See Merced County map on page 582)

More than 60 varieties of trees grace this lovely 23-acre park that borders Bear Creek. Boy, oh boy, do boy dogs adore Applegate Park! Kids like it, too. The park is home to a small zoo, as well as the Kiwanis Kiddieland mini-amusement park.

The city's 12-mile bike path runs through Applegate Park, so if you and your leashed dog want to saunter off to other parks, just follow the path to the next clump of greenery. Applegate is between M and R Streets, on the south side of Bear Creek. 209/385-6855.

PLACES TO STAY

Merced Yosemite TraveLodge: Some of the spacious rooms here have tub spas, and you can swim in the motel's decent little pool, too. Water dogs have to be content to watch. Rates are $42–90. Dogs are $10 extra and require a $25 deposit. 1260 Yosemite Parkway 95340; 209/722-6224.

Motel 6: Rates are $42 for the first adult, $6 for the second. 1410 V Street 95340; 209/384-2181.

Santa Nella

This town is alive because of I-5, which spews visitors into and out of town as quickly as they can get some gas and a bowl of Andersen's Split Pea Soup (which, in turn, can give folks enough of a different type of gas to last them clear to the Oregon border). If you want your pooch to have a sip of the delectable soup, go easy on it. Remember, you may be traveling in an enclosed vehicle together for many hours.

PARKS, BEACHES, AND RECREATION AREAS

3 San Luis Reservoir State Recreation Area

🐾🐾🐾 (See Merced County map on page 582)

The San Luis Reservoir is a water dog's dream. It's made up of three man-made lakes, and pooches have permission to do the dog paddle in all areas of the reservoir. In addition, part of the O'Neill Forebay (see below) is within the recreation area's borders. While dogs aren't permitted on the beaches of the forebay, they can jump into the drink just about anywhere else there.

This park focuses on water activities, including fishing, swimming, and plenty of boating. It can get loud and crowded in the hot summer months, which always seem to attract fast boats. A better bet is in the spring, when it's cool and the fish are hungry. If you and the pooch are landlubbers at heart, you should probably find another park, since there's not much acreage outside of the picnic areas and campgrounds.

There are approximately 130 developed campsites and 400 primitive sites, many of which are along the water. Primitive sites are first-come, first-served and are free. Developed sites are $12. Exit I-5 at Highway 152 and drive west about four miles to the entrance road on the left. Call 800/444-7275 for reservations, or phone the park at 209/826-1197 for more information.

◪ O'Neill Forebay Wildlife Area

🐾🐾🐾🐾🐾 (See Merced County map on page 582)

If your dog's just aching to get out of the car and have a really good stretch, try this 700-acre grassland just to the west of I-5. It's a terrific place if your obedient dog needs to run around without her leash for a while. As long as she's an obedient pooch, during certain times of year she can gambol at your side as you hike on trails and levees through the wetlands and grasslands.

You'll find some marshy sections, but you'll be able to reach most of the wildlife area by fire roads and levees. The wildlife-viewing from here is wonderful.

An important note: Dogs must be on leash April 1–June 30 because of nesting season. It's also closed two weekends a year in November/December. Phone the number below for exact dates if you'll be visiting that time of year. Also, if you don't want to bring your dog here during hunting seasons, phone to find out a good time to visit.

Exit I-5 at Highway 33 and drive about two miles south to the entrance, which will be on your right. 209/826-0463.

PLACES TO STAY

Motel 6: Rates are $40 for the first adult, $6 for the second. 12733 South Highway 33 95322; 209/826-6644.

Ramada Inn Mission de Oro: This hotel looks more like a Spanish mission than a place to spend the night with your dog. It's set on five acres of land that's terrific for leashed dog walks. Enjoy the fun outdoor pool here, but paws must stay on dry land. If you're here on a Sunday, you can attend a service at the on-site church. Your dog will have to say her prayers alone, because it's a church for human animals only. Rates are $64–85. Dogs are $10 extra. 13070 Highway 33 South 95322; 209/826-4444.

San Luis Reservoir State Recreation Area: See San Luis Reservoir State Recreation Area, above, for camping information.

Los Banos

PARKS, BEACHES, AND RECREATION AREAS

5 Los Banos Wildlife Area

🐾🐾🐾🐾🐕 (See Merced County map on page 582)

Dogs are allowed to roam leash-free here during certain times of the year, and the terrific news is that they don't have to be hunters' companions to do it. Unlike so many other state wildlife areas, even dogs who just like to walk around and watch the birds fly by are permitted to experience this leash-free bliss.

The wildlife area is 5,568 acres of flat, grassy land with intermittent marshlands and ponds. You and your dog can walk just about anywhere on the dirt roads and levees here. With more than 200 species of birds, plenty of reptiles (including the rare giant garter snake), and many mammals, you'll have plenty to watch. Bring your binoculars and a good pair of walking shoes. Don't forget a towel for your dog. It can get muddy.

Camping is available February–mid-September. While there are no developed campsites, the Department of Fish and Game can suggest areas where you might find a good, very primitive site. There's no fee for camping. The day-use fee is $2.50, but that's waived if you have a valid hunting or fishing license or a California Wildlands Pass.

An important note: Dogs must be on leash April 1–June 30 because of nesting season. In addition, Los Banos is closed a few days every week in fall and winter, so be sure to phone the number below before venturing out here. From Highway 152, exit at Mercey Springs Road/Highway 165 and drive north for three miles to the wildlife area. 209/826-0463.

PLACES TO STAY

Best Western Executive Inn: This hotel looks more like a Federalist mansion than a Best Western. Some rooms even have a fireplace. Stay here and enjoy a pool, whirlpool, exercise room, and continental breakfast. Rates are $60–95. Dogs are $10 extra. 301 West Pecheco Boulevard 93635; 209/827-0954.

Los Banos Wildlife Area: See Los Banos Wildlife Area, above, for camping information.

CHAPTER 42

Madera County

A farm that looks like a pizza is one of the most dog-friendly places we've encountered in our travels through California. Dogs have to be leashed, but it's worth a stop to watch their jaws drop when the cows start mooing up-close and personal.

Between the Pizza Farm, Sierra National Forest, and a couple of lakes where dogs can go leashless, Madera County is a hidden gem for dogs and their people. OK, so it's more like a tourmaline than a diamond. It still outshines many of the nearby areas.

NATIONAL FORESTS

The National Forests and Wilderness Areas resource at the back of this book has important information and safety tips on visiting national forests with your dog and has more information on the Sierra National Forest.

PICK OF THE LITTER—MADERA COUNTY

BEST OFF-LEASH HIKE AND SWIM
Hensley Lake, Madera (page 592)

MOST BEAST-FRIENDLY PLACE TO STAY
Pine Rose Inn, Oakhurst (page 592)

BEST SLICE OF FARM LIFE
Pizza Farm, Madera (page 591)

Sierra National Forest

NATIONAL MONUMENTS

Devil's Postpile National Monument

See the Mammoth Lakes section of the Mono County chapter for a description of Devil's Postpile. You can't get there from here, even though it's officially in Madera County.

NATIONAL PARKS

Yosemite National Park

See the Mariposa County chapter for a detailed account of all the things dogs can and can't do at this wonderland.

Oakhurst

Many who live in this busy little foothills town consider Oakhurst the gateway to Yosemite. At about 15 miles from the south gateway to Yosemite National Park, it's certainly the closest town that has lots of amenities. Oakhurst is a good place to load up on dog treats, local crafts, fast food, and gasoline. It's also home to a couple of dog-friendly lodgings, should you care to spend the night here before (or after) your Yosemite adventure.

DIVERSION

One Half-Acre Pizza, Please: As long as your leashed dog doesn't poop on this gigantic pizza or try to terrorize the pepperoni pigs, she'll be welcome at the **Pizza Farm.**

The point of the Pizza Farm is to show how integral farming is to the food we eat. The half-acre, circular Pizza Farm is divided into eight "slices." Each slice contains something that's growing (or grazing for) the ingredients of a pizza. One slice has tomatoes. Another has cows who supply the milk for the cheese. Another has piggies for pepperoni. Other slices vary seasonally. But there will never be any anchovies, says pizza farmer Darren Schmall: "They have to be planted too deep."

The Pizza Farm is surrounded by more land, where your dog may stretch her legs. And get this: You can actually buy pizza here! A pizza lunch of two slices and a soft drink will run you only $3. You can choose either cheese or pepperoni. The pigs here implore you to choose wisely.

The farm, in Madera, is open seven days a week March–September. The best time to visit is in the growing season, in late spring and summer. The fee is $5 per person, and it includes a 1.5-hour tour. The pizza farm recently moved from the Madera County Fairgrounds to Cobb Ranch, at Highway 41 and the San Joaquin River. (Jake wonders if they just put it all in a pizza box and delivered it within 30 minutes.) Call 559/674-2391 for more information; www.cobbranch.com.

PARKS, BEACHES, AND RECREATION AREAS

1 Oakhurst Community Park

🐾🐾 (See Madera County map on page 588)

This is a really green, meadowy park that you can get to by crossing over a wooden footbridge from the Chamber of Commerce parking lot. It's very convenient for people on the go with a dog who's got to go.

A little dirt path encircles the park. You can walk around the park a few times to stretch all of your legs or relax in the gazebo or at a picnic table.

The park is just off Road 426 on Civic Circle. Follow the signs for the Chamber of Commerce. 559/683-7766.

PLACES TO EAT

Subway Sandwiches and Salads: Eat subs at the outdoor tables here. 425A Stagecoach Road; 559/683-3066.

PLACES TO STAY

Best Western Yosemite Gateway Inn: This inn is 17 miles from the south gate of Yosemite. Rates are $49–152. 40530 Highway 41 93644; 559/683-2378.

Pine Rose Inn: This bed-and-breakfast inn welcomes dogs as guests. "We love doggies and the people that come with them," says owner Anita Griffin. It's a beautiful place in a quiet mountain countryside setting just 12 miles from the south gate of Yosemite and two miles from Bass Lake. There's also plenty of hiking even closer to the inn.

Griffin has had some unusual guests. She once played hostess to a baby leopard who was so young his spots hadn't come out yet. A chimpanzee also made the inn his home for a few days while acting in a movie filmed in the area. "Obviously, good dogs are no problem at all," says Griffin.

You and your dog can stay in the main house or in one of five cottages. The rooms are full of country antiques, and some rooms even have fireplaces for those cold, wintry nights. A few rooms also have whirlpool tubs. This is the perfect place to get away from it all. If the "it all" of the previous sentence means your dog for a while, the staff will be happy to arrange for a pet-sitter.

Rates are $79–169. The price includes a country breakfast. Dogs are $10 extra. 41703 Road 222 93644; 559/642-2800; www.basslakeca.com/pineroseinn.

Madera

PARKS, BEACHES, AND RECREATION AREAS

As you'll note by the names of the two smaller parks, this is a very civic-minded area. I just want to know where the Shriners' park is—and what about those Masons?

❷ Hensley Lake

🐾🐾🐾🐾 🐕 (See Madera County map on page 588)

This 1,500-acre lake provides some choice fishing opportunities for you and your angling dog. With a launch fee of only $4, you can't lose, even if the bass aren't biting.

If you're the types who prefer to stick around terra firma, you'll be happy to know that the lake is surrounded by 1,500 acres of hilly land that you and your well-behaved dog can roam without a leash.

Visit in the springtime during the wildflower bloom if you really want a piece of paradise. If it's a tad warm, you'll find refreshing shade under the many oaks here. If it's still too warm for you, take a dip in the lake. Dogs are permitted to swim here, as long as they're not on the official beach areas. The day-use fee is $4. If you plan to go boating, the launch fee is $4. There's camping here, but no dogs allowed. (Maybe it's their snoring?)

From Madera, drive northeast on Highway 145 for about six miles. Turn left on County Road 400 and drive 10 miles north to the lake. 559/673-5151.

For information on Eastman Lake, just northwest of Hensley Lake, call 559/689-3255. The setting, prices, and rules are pretty much the same as Hensley's, but hydrilla weeds can prevent swimming.

🐾 Lions Town and Country Regional Park

🐾🐾🐾 (See Madera County map on page 588)

This charming park has lots of places to roam. The rolling hills and shaded meadows make it a fine park for an afternoon walk with your leashed dog.

A little canal runs through the park. Arched wooden footbridges take you over the waterway to more romping room. As long as there's not a baseball game going on, you won't have to worry about crowds.

The park is in the southwest part of town, at Howard Road, just east of Granada Drive. 559/661-5495.

🐾 Rotary Park

🐾🐾 (See Madera County map on page 588)

If you're cruising along Highway 99 and your dog starts crossing his legs and humming an unintelligible tune while avoiding direct eye contact with the bottle of water you've wedged between the seats, pull over here. The park has plenty of trees and lots of grass, even for the most discriminating dog's needs.

Exit Highway 99 at Cleveland Avenue and drive east about a block to Gateway Drive (just before the railroad tracks). Turn right. The park will be on your right almost immediately. Snap on that leash and trot, don't walk, to the nearest tree. 559/661-5495.

PLACES TO STAY

Best Western Madera Valley Inn: Humans can enjoy the good-sized outdoor pool, the exercise room, and the continental breakfast here. Rooms come with a minifridge, and some have a microwave. Rates are $56–85. Dogs are $15 extra. 317 North G Street 93637; 559/673-5164.

Days Inn: Dogs are welcome to stay here "as long as they don't shed too much," says the manager. Jake the Dog will probably have to look for a room elsewhere. Rates are $50–55. Dogs are $5 extra. 25327 Avenue 16 93637; 559/674-8817.

Hensley Lake: See Hensley Lake, above, for camping information.

CHAPTER 43

Fresno County

At first glance, Fresno County seems like both an agricultural wonderland and a doggy wasteland. But your dog doesn't have to bite his toenails when he hears you're going to be spending some time exploring the area. The county has something for just about every dog's taste.

Rugged canines will enjoy the leashless freedom they'll experience in the national forest and the Bureau of Land Management areas. And those who prefer their toenails painted and their bouffants fluffed will enjoy the tinier, well-manicured city parks.

Dogs with a taste for olfactory offenses will appreciate visits to the pungent section near the zoo at Fresno's Roeding Park and to the stinky creek at Coalinga Mineral Springs. You may not be crazy about the odors, but it's worth a few moments of holding your breath to see that enraptured expression on your dog's quivering snout. Dogs who like the sweet smell of success must visit Fresno's two off-leash parks. It was a bit of a battle to get these parks, but dogs are now basking in the victory.

PICK OF THE LITTER—FRESNO COUNTY

BEST PLACE TO DOG-PADDLE
Shaver Lake, Shaver Lake (page 597)

BEST OFF-LEASH WILDFLOWER HIKE
Panoche Hills, Mercey Hot Springs (page 598)

BEST DOG PARK
El Capitan Dog Park, Fresno (page 601)

BEST STINKY PARK
Coalinga Mineral Springs Recreation Area,
Coalinga (page 602)

NATIONAL FORESTS

The National Forests and Wilderness Areas resource at the back of this book
has important information and safety tips on visiting national forests with
your dog and has more information on the Sierra National Forest.

Sierra National Forest

The cross-country skiing in some areas of this forest is first-rate. Leashless
dogs love to bound along beside you as you slice through the snow.

NATIONAL PARKS

Kings Canyon National Park

See Sequoia and Kings Canyon National Parks in the Tulare County chapter
for information on this not-so-dog-friendly park.

Lakeshore

A visit here will put you right on the shores of beautiful Huntington Lake.
At an elevation of 7,000 feet, the lake is a great place to visit when it's roasty-
toasty in the other parts of the state. It rarely gets too sizzling here. That helps
make fishing pretty decent in the summer when the trout in lower lakes are
hiding out and praying for underwater air conditioning.

PLACES TO STAY

Cedar Crest Resort: Depending on your style and mood, you and the pooch can stay at the resort's housekeeping cabins or floored tent cottages (concrete or wood floors with canvas sides and top, bed inside). Joe Dog, who was not into roughing it, preferred the resort's higher-end cabins, which overlook Huntington Lake and have fireplaces and porches. Big pines surround most cabins here, and that was plenty of nature for a dog such as he was. You can even rent a "nonsinkable" boat here and putter around the lake with your pooch! Most dogs (unlike Joe the Landlubber) seem to enjoy a little cruise. Rates for the cabins are $95–150. The tent cottages are $35–40. Dogs are $10 extra. 61011 Cedar Crest Lane 93634; 559/893-3233; www.cedarcrestresort.com.

Lakeshore Resort: The managers at this 1920s-style mountain resort at Huntington Lake are a little gun-shy about allowing dogs. They've had people leave destructive pooches alone in the rooms only to find ruined furniture and torn-apart curtains and rugs. But more responsible dogs and their people might renew their faith in the canine species. And if you have a pup-sitter and want to party, there's a saloon and dance hall on the premises. Rates are $70–150. Dogs are $10 extra. During certain times of year, the managers may ask that you sign a pooch release. 61953 Huntington Lake Road 93634; 559/893-3193; www.lakeshoreresort.com.

Shaver Lake

PARKS, BEACHES, AND RECREATION AREAS

1 Shaver Lake

🐾🐾🐾🐾 🐕 (See Fresno County map on page 594)

Although some of the land immediately surrounding this attractive lake is run by the county, even more of it is administered by the U.S. Forest Service. In fact, Sierra National Forest pretty much surrounds the lake. And you know what that means for dogs: No mandatory leashes on national forest land! (But be sure to leash up on county land.)

The lake is set at an elevation of 5,000 feet. There are 252 camping sites (at an area called Camp Edison), ranging $20–40 per site. Dogs are $4 extra. Reservations are highly recommended mid-June–mid-September. From the town of Shaver Lake, follow Highway 168 north to the lake. 559/297-0706.

PLACES TO STAY

Shaver Lake: See Shaver Lake, above, for camping information.

Mercey Hot Springs

PARKS, BEACHES, AND RECREATION AREAS

🔟 Panoche Hills

🐾🐾🐾🐾🐕 (See Fresno County map on page 594)

Panoche has panache! These 30,000 acres of rolling hills and grasslands are heaven to dogs who need more than just your average community park to make them feel like real dogs. Because the Bureau of Land Management operates it, obedient dogs are allowed to run around leashless. Keep a close eye on your dog, though, because the hills are home to endangered species such as the San Joaquin kit fox and the blunt-nosed leopard lizard.

Hilltops, some of which are more than 2,500 feet tall, give you great views of the lush San Joaquin Valley and the dramatic Sierra Nevada. And if you visit in the spring (by far the best time of year to come), you'll be treated to a spectacular wildflower bloom. The hilltops are also excellent for setting up a telescope and watching other worlds go by. Bring a hearty dinner and a blanket for your dog, and you couldn't ask for a better viewing station.

The hills are near Mercey Hot Springs, off County Road J1. You'll see the signs. Call before you visit so you can find out about any hunting that might be going on or closures due to fire danger. 831/630-5000.

Mendota

PARKS, BEACHES, AND RECREATION AREAS

🔟 Mendota Wildlife Area

🐾🐾🐾🐾🐕 (See Fresno County map on page 594)

Your dog doesn't have to be a hunter to enjoy off-leash privileges at this 11,802-acre wildlife haven. As long as she's an obedient pooch, during certain times of year she can gambol at your side as you hike on trails and levees through the wetlands and grasslands. (An important note: Dogs must be on leash April 1–June 30 because of nesting season. In addition, Mendota is closed a few days every week in fall and winter, so be sure to phone the number below before venturing out here.)

Bring your binoculars if you want to get up close and personal with the waterfowl and shorebirds who hang around the area. And watch out for skunks. We know one dog who got blasted here and who has never quite smelled the same. From Highway 180, follow the signs to Mendota. Call 559/655-4645.

Fresno

In the midst of the region's raisin growers and cattle rustlers lies Fresno, the heart of the Central Valley. And like all hearts that are anatomically correct (not like the kind you get on a Valentine's Day card), it's functional and essential but not too attractive.

Rest assured, there are some pretty good-looking parks in the midst of the malls and the cookie-cutter developments. If you have time to visit the charming Tower District, you may even start looking at Fresno in a different way. Or at least you'll start looking at Fresno. And with this new edition, dogs can look at the city with grateful eyes. They now have two leash-free parks to call their own!

PARKS, BEACHES, AND RECREATION AREAS

◪ Woodward Dog Park and Woodward Park

🐾🐾🐾🐾 (See Fresno County map on page 594)

Situated within the beautiful and somewhat wild Woodward Park, this fenced one-acre dog park is a boon to dogs who want the best of both worlds. They need to be leashed when exploring regular park land, but they can throw their leashes to the wind upon entering the dog park. When we last saw the park, it had just been reseeded with grass, so there was hope of greenery in the future. A couple of big trees provide some shade and some good aiming spots for boy dogs.

If you're going to pay the $3 parking fee to get into Woodward Park to get to the dog park, you might want to take advantage of Woodward Park itself. (Once again, leashes are the law outside the dog park.) With 299 acres of grassy meadows, rolling hills, big trees, trails, streams, lakes, and ponds, the park provides a much-needed refuge from life in Fresnoland. The park actually started out as a bird refuge. The sanctuary remains virtually untouched, but the surrounding parklands can be packed with people. It's not the kind of place your dog will want to visit on a weekend or just about any decent summer day. That's one reason the dog park is so handy—freedom from the masses and the leashes.

The parking fee February–October is $3 per car, but the rest of the year it's free. During the fee season, you can arrive before 9 A.M. to avoid the fee. You can also walk in and not have to pay. Driving north on Highway 41, exit at North Friant Road and drive northeast to East Audubon Drive. You'll be at the southeast corner of the park. Turn left and follow East Audubon Drive to the main entrance. You'll see signs for the dog park. 559/621-2900.

5 Kearney Park

😺😺😺 (See Fresno County map on page 594)

People who visit this tree-filled 225-acre park may well think that the man for whom this park is named was a philanthropic sweetheart. After all, his huge mansion is in the middle of the park, and the land for the park was essentially his yard, surrounded by thousands of acres of his farmland. Anyone who would give that kind of property to the city must be a kindly gent, right?

But according to Dave Caglia, head of parks and grounds operations for the county, English-born Martin Kearney was an ornery, racist farmer who acquired his land through crooked deals. He was jilted by the love of his life and became richer and more bitter through the years. The raisin mogul turned into a woman-hating recluse and built this mansion, complete with 18-inch-thick walls.

When he died in the early 1900s (on a transatlantic ocean crossing, no less), he left some of the land to the University of California. In 1949, the university gave it to the county. It was the start of the Fresno County Park System.

The old guy may have been mean, but he sure knew how to make a pretty park. It's very popular—too popular for a dog's taste, at times. Don't come here with your dog on beautiful weekend afternoons unless you want to share it with the masses.

The park is filled with 100-year-old trees, including maples, palms, oaks, and eucalyptus trees that are seven feet across and 200 feet tall! Boy dogs can barely contain themselves. But they can't go too wild, because leashes are the law here.

There's a $4 day-use fee. The park is on Kearney Boulevard, seven miles west of Fresno. 559/488-3004.

6 Roeding Park

😺😺😺 (See Fresno County map on page 594)

Before you and your dog look at your map and start drooling over this 157-acre chunk of land, you should know that it's much better for humans than for dogs. That's not to say dogs don't have a good time here. They have to be leashed, but they do enjoy the grass and trees in the sections where they're actually allowed.

Dogs are fairly restricted because of all the fun activities for humans. Between such dog-banning attractions as the Fresno Zoo, Storyland, Playland, and the park's numerous tennis courts and playgrounds, a dog could get to feeling as if he's not a real person. But when he walks near the zoo and gets a whiff of the elephant and zebra poop, he'll be so enraptured that he'll probably forget all about his dejection.

There's a $1 parking fee February–October. You can walk in free. The rest of the year, there's no fee for parking. Exit Highway 99 at Belmont or Olive Avenue and drive east to the park's main entrance. 559/621-2900.

7 El Capitan Dog Park

🐾🐾🐾🐾🐕 (See Fresno County map on page 594)

This is the kind of park dogs just drool to visit. It's fenced and tree-lined, with nearly 2.5 acres of grass. Dogs here have big smiles on their snouts as they run around and around and around.

On hot summer days, some folks bring plastic wading pools so dogs can cool their paws. The folks here are friendly, donating chairs to put under shade trees and making newcomers feel welcome. The park has wheelchair access, double gates for pooch security, lights, tables, poop bags, and water.

Please note that the park is actually built on land the city uses as an overflow area during heavy rains. The park can be closed at times during winter because of flooding. When in doubt, phone the park department at the number below. The park is at El Capitan and Alamos Streets, just off Shaw Avenue. 559/621-2900.

8 Einstein Park

🐾🐾 (See Fresno County map on page 594)

There's a completely fenced-in section in the southwest part of this grassy park, and you don't have to be a genius to figure out why dogs and their people like it. We can say no more here. Go visit for yourself. Just a word of warning: There really is a leash law.

The park is at East Dakota Avenue, just west of North Millerbrook Avenue. 559/621-2900.

PLACES TO EAT

City Cafe: Sometimes customers with canines order plain meat for their dogs while they dine on the tasty sandwiches served at the patio. Dogs also get a bowl of water here. 5048 North Blackstone Avenue, Suite 108; 559/224-4399.

PLACES TO STAY

Best Western Garden Court: Rates are $58–80. Pooches are $10 extra per day. 2141 North Parkway Drive 93705; 559/237-1881.

Days Inn: At last check, leashed dogs were welcome to use the large, grassy area on the premises, as long as their human cleaned up after them. Rates are $48–85. Dogs are $5 extra. 1101 North Parkway Drive 93728; 559/268-6211 or 800/329-7466.

Executive Suites of Fresno: If you and your dog find yourself facing a long stay in Fresno, check out the pooch-friendly condos and apartments available through Executive Suites. Dallas Debatin, who manages the service, says he "would rather have dogs, cats, or snakes than smokers." Hiss, say the smokers (and the snakes), but howlelujah say the dogs. Rates are $550–1,250 per month. There's a $150 pooch deposit. There's no street address, since the suites are in various locations. P.O. Box 42 93707; 559/237-7444.

Quality Inn: "Of course dogs are allowed. They are man's best friend!" exclaimed inn employee Richard, a dog owner himself. The inn doesn't have room, though, for "huge" dogs. Rates are $57–84. Dogs pay a $20 flat fee. 4278 West Ashlan Avenue 93722; 559/275-2727.

Radisson Hotel: Swim in the heated pool here or relax in the sauna and whirlpool. Dogs can't do the spa thing but they enjoy staying here just the same. Rates are $109–139. Dogs pay a $50 flat fee. 2233 Ventura Street 93721; 559/268-1000; www.radisson.com.

Sanger

PARKS, BEACHES, AND RECREATION AREAS

To walk your leashed dog in Sanger parks, you used to have to get written permission from the city. Fortunately that's no longer the case.

9 Greenwood Park

🐾🐾 (See Fresno County map on page 594)

This is a green, grassy, somewhat hilly community park with picnic tables and plenty of trees. It can get crowded on nice weekends, so you may want to steer your dog elsewhere. The park is at 5th Street and Academy Avenue. 559/875-7513.

Coalinga

PARKS, BEACHES, AND RECREATION AREAS

10 Coalinga Mineral Springs Recreation Area

🐾🐾🐾 (See Fresno County map on page 594)

Question: What smells like rotten eggs and attracts both man and beast? *Answer:* This park.

Leashed dogs love to come here because of the sulfur stench given off by the mineral-laden creek that runs through the park. Whenever Jake Dog starts staring at the ground as if he's just had an epiphany, I know we're either getting near one of these sulfur heavens or approaching a piece of roadkill.

Humans enjoy this flat 35-acre park because it's full of pines and surrounded by mountains. There are warnings against drinking the stinky creek water, but a local woman in her 80s has been drinking it for decades and at our last visit she looked mahhhvelous.

Camping here is very secluded, primitive, and cheap (free). It's used mostly by hunters during wild boar season. You have to bring your own water and get prior written permission from the county parks department. You could stay back in the campground for a few days and never see a soul.

The day-use fee is $4. From Coalinga, drive northwest on Highway 198 for about 18 miles and turn right on Coalinga Mineral Springs Road. Continue five more miles to the park. 559/488-3004.

11 Coalinga Mineral Springs Scenic Trail

🐾🐾🐾🐾🦮 (See Fresno County map on page 594)

Adjoining the county park (see above) are 9,000 acres of open land run by the dog-friendly Bureau of Land Management. If the 35-acre county park doesn't satisfy you or your dog, continue to the adjacent BLM land and let the good times roll you through the grasslands. Just watch out for the occasional rocky outcropping.

The best part of this adventure is that if your dog is very obedient, you can let him run around leashless. But the 2.5-mile trail is also an equestrian trail, so if your dog thinks horses are giant dogs just waiting to be chased, keep him on his leash. Also be aware that deer live in the area surrounding the trail. If you aren't absolutely certain that your dog won't bound off after one, do everyone a favor and don't unleash him.

The hike is not for the fair of paw, since it can be steep. But if you and your dog are in good shape, it's worth the exertion. The trail leads you to Kreyenhagen Peak, where you'll have wonderful views of the southern Diablo Mountains. Come in the spring and watch the wildflowers go wild. In the warmer months, it can be mighty toasty and parched here.

We've heard that ticks can be a real problem at times. Call 831/630-5000 for information, advice, and a schedule of when hunters might be shooting at the deer and other critters you and your dog are trying to avoid. The trail starts where the county park leaves off. See Coalinga Mineral Springs Recreation Area, above, for directions to the county park.

PLACES TO STAY

Coalinga Mineral Springs: See Coalinga Mineral Springs Recreation Area, above, for camping information.

The Inn at Harris Ranch: Ahh, Spanish-style architecture and the smell of broiling beef wafting into your room from the famed steak-o-rama next door. What more could a dog want? The only smell that could make this place more appealing to dogs is that of the very whiffy Harris Ranch feedlot, but it's eight miles away. Unless the wind is just right, dogs are out of luck. Rates are $119–250. Dogs are $10 extra. It's just off I-5 at the Highway 198/Hanford-Lemoore exit. The location is 24505 West Dorris Street, and the mailing address is Route 1, P.O. Box 777 93210; 559/935-0717; www.harrisranch.com.

CHAPTER 44
San Benito County

If you look at a map of this county, you may wonder, "What's a dog to do here?" Joe Dog looked as if he were being sent to purgatory the first time I told him we were going to visit San Benito County. He sat at the front door of the house and wouldn't budge. When I tried pulling him, he tugged back and slipped out of his collar. But since I had longer legs, a stronger body, and a box of desiccated liver treats, I won the battle. He gulped down the bait, frowned, and succumbed to his fate.

He must have remembered those vast stretches of privately owned nothingness we once drove across on the way from nowhere to not-much-of-anyplace-else. Even *I* wanted to be anywhere but there. But our last visit was different. It wasn't heaven, but it wasn't hell either. At the end of our time in this county, even Joe had a smile on his boxy snout.

PICK OF THE LITTER—SAN BENITO COUNTY

BEST EARLY CALIFORNIA LORE
San Juan Bautista State Historic Park, San Juan Bautista
(page 606)

BEST OFF-LEASH HIKE
Griswold Hills Recreation Area, New Idria (page 608)

San Juan Bautista

Be sure to swing by the Mission San Juan Bautista when you visit this town, especially if you or your dog are fans of Alfred Hitchcock. The mission (the largest of the old California missions) starred in the Hitchcock classic *Vertigo*. It's worth a peek, but dogs have to stay firmly planted on the ground outside. Jimmy Stewart would have envied the stance.

If you're hungry, don't let all the restaurants with outdoor tables fool you. We couldn't find any eateries that would permit pooches. But as the pendulum swings, we don't expect that to last for long.

PARKS, BEACHES, AND RECREATION AREAS

1 San Juan Bautista State Historic Park

🐾🐾🐾 (See San Benito County map on page 604)

Leashed dogs who like local history are welcome to accompany you as you tour this small state park. You'll see buildings such as the old Plaza Hotel, which was a popular stagecoach stop, and the Castro House, at one time the administrative headquarters of Mexican California. But since dogs must stay outside such buildings, they prefer to tour the livery stables, gardens, and orchards.

The park is on the plaza in the center of town. Admission is $2 per adult. Call 831/623-4881.

PLACES TO STAY

San Juan Inn: If you and your pooch are looking for a quiet spot to spend the night, stay here. Rates are $67–89. Dogs are $10 extra. 410 Alameda Street 95045; 408/831-4380.

Hollister

PARKS, BEACHES, AND RECREATION AREAS

🐾 Vista Park Hill

🐾🐾🐾 (See San Benito County map on page 604)

This hilltop park overlooks town and has plenty of undeveloped acres for your leashed dog to explore. In this case, though, undeveloped means dry grass, weeds, and, yes, foxtails in the wrong time of year. Be careful out there. You may want to stick with the green open spaces and the eucalyptus-lined walkways that are also in this park.

From Highway 156, go west on Hill Street for a long block to the park's entrance. The Bureau of Land Management's local office is also here. It's a good place to stop in and pick up information on the nearby BLM lands (see Griswold Hills Recreation Area in the New Idria section for information on one of these off-leash areas). The city park department's phone number is 831/636-4390.

🐾 San Justo Reservoir County Park

🐾🐾🐾 (See San Benito County map on page 604)

You and your leashed dog are free to hike on the dirt trail/fire road that encircles this 580-acre park. Many folks like to come here to fish at the 200-acre reservoir, but dogs generally prefer to amble through the open land. It's not the most attractive place in the world, but it beats the backyard.

The day-use fee is $5 per vehicle. You can launch your boat from here for a mere $2–3. The park is west of town. Exit Highway 156 at Union Road and drive south. The park will be on your right in a little less than a mile, at 2265 Union Road. Hours are limited, so call 831/638-3300 for a schedule.

Bitterwater

PLACES TO STAY

Pinnacles National Monument: Dogs are permitted only in picnic areas, parking lots, paved roads, and the campground here, so they miss exploring all the fascinating pinnacle-shaped volcanic rock formations within. It's not much fun for your pooch, but you can console her with a good camping experience.

A privately operated campground, Pinnacles Campground, permits pooches, although it also discourages them, because the area is a wildlife preserve. The staff is diligent about dogs' being on leash at all times. You can get to this 90-site campground from San Benito County, which leads into the east end of the park. Campsites are $7. Dogs have to pay a $10 deposit, which they can get back if they've never been off leash. Reservations are required for groups of 10 or more. To get to this campground: From Highway 25 about 13 miles north of Bitterwater (32 miles south of Hollister), take Highway 146 southwest to the park. The Pinnacle Campground phone number is 831/389-4462. The Pinnacles National Monument campground is no longer open. The number at the Pinnacles National Monument headquarters is 831/389-4485.

New Idria

PARKS, BEACHES, AND RECREATION AREAS

4 Griswold Hills Recreation Area

🐾🐾🐾🐾 🐕 (See San Benito County map on page 604)

Some small city parks I've explored are run by departments that tell you the parks' acreage down to the hundredth of an acre. When you're dealing with parks that are 3.21 acres, you want to count every square inch.

But then along comes the Bureau of Land Management. In its written material, it says Griswold Hills is "several thousand acres." We're not talking exact measurements here. But that's the charm of these off-leash BLM havens. Precision and rules are left at the gate (when there is a gate). Rules exist, but few restrict a well-behaved dog's good time.

This recreation area is made up of rugged canyons of scrub oak, juniper, and chaparral. Some trails take you to ridge tops for good views of the surrounding valleys. Others take you to the riparian zone at Griswold Creek. Not many people know about this area, so if you and your dog need to get away from it all, there's a good chance you can.

The park isn't as big or as scenic as the BLM's nearby 50,000-acre Clear Creek Management Area. But we don't recommend that area for people who worry about things such as asbestosis, mesothelioma, or cancer. Because of naturally occurring asbestos, you and your dog are supposed to wear protective clothing and respirators when setting paw on much of the land. It's not worth it.

The main entrance to Griswold Hills is three miles south of Panoche Road on New Idria Road. Watch out for hunters during deer and quail seasons. Call 831/630-5000 for hunting dates and more information on local BLM lands.

CHAPTER 45

Monterey County

Native son John Steinbeck and his fearless blue poodle, Charley, visited here during their cross-country journey recorded in the 1961 classic, *Travels with Charley*. The Gentle Reader is never sure what Charley did while his master paid homage to old bars and old memories in Monterey and Salinas, but wherever Charley went in this county, he probably felt as accepted as his human friend. Monterey County is as warm and welcoming as an old Italian aunt.

The county is a wonderland for dogs and their drivers. People get part of the vast agricultural sweeps in the east part of the county and the rugged mountain coast along the mighty Pacific in the west. Dogs get the pungent odor of fresh fertilizer in the east and the tantalizing scents carried miles by the Pacific winds in the west.

The Carmel area is one of the most dog-friendly places on Earth. In fact, dogs are almost de rigueur here. With each edition of this book, it just keeps getting better. Dog-loving restaurants and inns abound. Three terrific restaurants now have dog menus. There's even Papillon, a human day spa where

PICK OF THE LITTER—MONTEREY COUNTY

pooches can lounge on dog blankets and eat dog treats while their human friends get rubbed, scrubbed, and coiffed. And there's Rodrigue Studio, which welcomes dogs by giving them biscuits in a crystal dish and letting them peruse the artwork.

If going leashless is your dog's fantasy, Carmel, Carmel Valley, and Pacific Grove are ideal stopping points. Their designated off-leash romping grounds are as picturesque as their cozy inns. And your dog would never forgive you if you forgot the northern segment of the magnificent Los Padres National Forest for a hearty leashless hike.

In addition, a two-hour walking tour welcomes dogs on its stroll through Carmel. Your dog will have a doggone great time, because part of the tour is devoted to the dogginess here.

I'm sad to report that dogs are now banned from several state beaches in the county. (The entire town of Moss Landing was wiped out of this book because the three beaches there now ban dogs. It's a sweet seaside community and worth sniffing out; just don't expect to be able to beach it there.) The blame has been placed squarely on the feathered shoulders of the questionably threatened bird, the snowy plover, but I've also heard it may have had something to do with other beach users getting annoyed at dogs whose people let them run around leashless despite the leash laws. Fortunately, enough beaches welcome dogs that you won't have to see yours cry in his kibble during your visit to magnificent Monterey County.

NATIONAL FORESTS

The National Forests and Wilderness Areas resource at the back of this book has important information and safety tips on visiting national forests with your dog and has more information on the Los Padres National Forest.

Los Padres National Forest
🐾🐾🐾🐾🐕

This spectacular, rugged terrain in the Big Sur area is great for an outing with a spectacular, rugged dog. Actually, even spectacular couch-potato dogs can enjoy some of the hikes here in the Ventana Wilderness.

Pacific Grove

This quaint town on the rocky coast is a good place to get away from the crowds that can sometimes smother you and your dog during the peak tourist season in its neighboring city, Monterey. And if you like Monarch butterflies, Pacific Grove is your kind of town: It's known as "Butterfly City, USA" because of the millions of Monarch butterflies that winter here every year.

PARKS, BEACHES, AND RECREATION AREAS

▮ Asilomar State Beach
🐾🐾🐾 (See Monterey County map on page 610)

The beach here is great fun for leashed dogs. Not only do they get to romp on prime beach land, but they also can watch whales in the fall and winter and see what real tidepooling is all about year-round.

Tucked in and around this rugged shoreline are a vast variety of marine critters representative of the Central Coast. I've seen dogs try to eat the contents of tidepools—a dining activity that should be strictly forbidden. And for your dog's safety, don't take him on slippery rocks or let him get too close to the surf, where there can be hazardous rip currents.

Park along the shore on Sunset Drive, across from the Asilomar Conference Grounds. For sandy beach, park along the south end of Sunset Drive. 831/649-2836 or 831/372-4076.

❷ George Washington Park

🐾🐾🐾🐕 (See Monterey County map on page 610)

If you're dining at any of Pacific Grove's many outdoor eateries in the village center and your dog starts crossing his legs, have no fear, this park is near. And better yet, part of the park is devoted to off-leash dogs during certain times of the day.

Dogs may run leashless sunrise–9 A.M. and 4 P.M.–sunset. During winter, those hours can be a little restrictive, but it's better than nothing.

The segment of the park for leash-free canines is bounded by Short Street, Melrose Avenue, Alder Street, and Pine Avenue. Dogs are allowed on leash in the entire park at any time during the day. 831/648-3100.

❸ Lynn "Rip" Van Winkle Open Space

🐾🐾🐾🐾🐕 (See Monterey County map on page 610)

This scrub oak haven near Pebble Beach is large enough so that even dogs who tend to wander out of sight aren't in much danger of wandering into the road. Dogs may be leashless sunrise–9 A.M. and 4 P.M.–sunset.

You'll find many a dog and many a dog person here during the off-leash hours. They tend to congregate near the park's entrance, but if your dog would prefer walking to talking, there are plenty of trails leading through the twisted scrub oaks and the small clear areas of the park.

The entrance can be hard to find. Follow the nontoll section of 17 Mile Drive south and go left on Sunset Drive, then right on Congress Avenue. Pass Forest Grove Elementary School on your left. Within a few hundred yards, you'll see a dirt parking area on your right. There's no sign, but this is the main entrance to the open space. 831/648-3100.

PLACES TO EAT

Bagel Bakery: It's bagels, bagels, bagels at this dog-friendly eatery. Get some bagel bones (twice-baked, extra hard bagels) for your dog while you nosh on a bagel sandwich, a bagel with shmear, or a plain old naked bagel. Dine together at the outdoor tables. 1132 Forest Avenue; 831/649-6272.

Goodies: The food here is fresh and tasty. Choose from any of about 10,000 sandwiches. (OK, 30 sandwiches, but what a variety—my favorite is the Mediterraneo, with feta, olives, spinach, cukes, and their ilk.) Thanks to Tracy and her dog, Chewbacca, for recommending Goodies to us. They have good taste. Dine with your pooch at several tables on the sunny patio. 518 Lighthouse Avenue; 831/655-3663.

Rocky Coast Ice Cream Company: Share a cold, creamy cone while chilling with your pooch at the little benches out front. 708 Lighthouse Avenue; 831/373-0587.

PLACES TO STAY

Andril Fireplace Cottages: In these homey cottages, it's easy to get away from it all or to be on top of it all: All the separate cottages in this quiet area have cable TV, with VCRs for the asking. They also have wood-burning fireplaces, perfect for snuggling up with a human friend and a dog friend after a long day exploring the nearby beach. Rates are $80–190. Dogs are $14 extra. 569 Asilomar Boulevard 93950; 831/375-0994; www.andrilcottages.com.

Lighthouse Lodge and Suites: This used to be a Best Western, but now it's quite a lovely hotel, with upgraded rooms and a cool website. You'll get luxury (and very comfy beds) on a semibudget. Humans get to enjoy the pool, spa, and breakfast. Dogs get to enjoy sniffing the surrounding Monterey Pines. Rates are $89–189. Dogs are $25 extra. 1150 Lighthouse Avenue 93950; 831/655-2111 or 800/858-1249; www.lhls.com.

Olympia Motor Lodge: Dogs are allowed here only November–March. Then you and your dog can sit on your private balcony and contemplate life while staring at the ocean. Rates are $88–180. Dogs are $20 extra. 1140 Lighthouse Avenue 93950; 831/373-2777.

Salinas

The "Salad Bowl of the World" was one of Joe Dog's favorite places to visit on a Sunday drive. Most other city dogs we've talked to agree that it's a grand olfactory experience. When Joe smelled the chicken manure spread across great fields of green and saw horses readying for the rodeo, his nostrils shivered and his eyes bugged out, making him look very cartoony.

PARKS, BEACHES, AND RECREATION AREAS

❹ Toro Regional Park

🐾🐾🐾🐾 (See Monterey County map on page 610)

This is the only park in the Salinas area where you and your dog can really take a hike. More than 4,500 acres of wilderness await leashed pooches. About 12 miles of hiking and horse trails are etched into the rolling foothills of Mt. Toro. As you climb, you'll occasionally be rewarded with shade from oak trees. It can be very hot in the summer, so be sure to bring extra water for you and your dog.

The views up high are spectacular. You can see both the Salinas Valley and the Monterey Bay, depending on where you hike. The park also features a self-guided nature trail adjacent to a gentle creek, as well as many picnic sites and play areas in the flat green valley near the parking lots.

Remember, as always when you travel with your dog, to have him wear his rabies tag or to bring along other proof of his rabies vaccination. This is one of those places where the staff is going to ask to see it before letting him in. From Salinas, follow Highway 68 west about five miles to the signs for the park. The park's entrance is just a few hundred yards from the highway. Fees are $4 per vehicle on weekdays, $6 on weekends. Dogs must show proof of rabies vaccination. 831/755-4899.

PLACES TO STAY

The lodgings that accommodate dogs here may not be fancy, but they're excellent places to relax and watch bad TV with your dog after a day of traveling.

Motel 6: Rates are $44–55 for the first adult, $6 for the second. 1257 De La Torre Boulevard 93905; 831/757-3077.

Vagabond Inn: Close to U.S. 101, this is where Joe and I once stayed and encountered at least five other dogs who were also guests. Rates are $55–75. Dogs are $10 extra. 131 Kern Street 93905; 831/758-4693.

Pebble Beach

PLACES TO STAY

The Lodge at Pebble Beach: Jack Lemmon brought his poodle here. Joe Pesci brings his pooch here, too. This magnificent lodge, adjacent to the Pebble Beach Golf Links, is as dog-friendly as it is distinguished.

The place is beautiful on the outside and like home (if your home is gorgeous and has spectacular views) on the inside. Most rooms have a fireplace, and all are lovely, with a wet bar, an honor-stocked fridge, and a patio or deck with to-drool-for views. In your bathroom you'll find an extra phone and a plush terry robe.

All this is fine with dogs, but what they really love about The Lodge is that it's a dog-adoring place. "We love doggies!" says the concierge, and she means it. The staff stocks treats at several strategically located points in the lobby, including the concierge desk, the bell desk, and the front desk. And even better than this, dogs get to explore the large, wooded area surrounding the inn. If they're really well-behaved, you can let them be leashless! The paths here are splendid. Be forewarned, though, that you might be sharing the paths with horses, so if your dog is a chaser, keep that leash on.

Rates are $475–1,700. The lodge is on 17 Mile Drive. When you call for reservations, you can get directions. The address is simply 17 Mile Drive 93953; 831/647-7500 or 800/654-9300; www.pebblebeach.com.

Monterey

Although there's nowhere to legally let your dog off leash here, Monterey is still a grand stomping ground for dogs and their people. A few activities you can enjoy with your dog include taking in the sights of old/new Cannery Row, fishing off Municipal Wharf No. 2, and watching sea otters frolic about Monterey Bay.

Alas, dogs are not allowed on Fisherman's Wharf, home to some of the world's most dog-friendly scents. Joe Dog visited a few times before we learned of the rule and he never got into trouble, except when he tried to eat the calamari out of somebody's carry-out cup. And then there was the time he stuck his nose in a kid's cotton candy and set the kid to wailing so hard that her parents rushed over thinking Joe had taken a bite out of her.

Another dog rule you should be aware of: Pooches aren't allowed to be tied up on public property. That means not even for a couple of minutes while you run inside a café to grab a cup of coffee. We learned about this law from an upset judge in the Sierra Nevada who had tied her dog Billy (a cocker–Lhasa apso mix) outside a restaurant while she went in to use the phone. When she came out, her dog was gone. In his place was a note to call the SPCA. Turns out a policeman had turned in Billy on the basis of this law. Getting Billy back proved to be a logistical nightmare, with events that included Billy's mom's being sent to the County Corporation Yard, where she was promised Billy would be after she'd paid a fine (he wasn't).

DIVERSION

Take Someone Furry on a Surrey: Chicks and ducks and geese better scurry when you take your dog on a bicycle-powered surrey from **Bay Bikes,** on the famous Cannery Row. The surreys come complete with a fringe at the top. And so what if the dashboard isn't genuine leather? These surreys have baskets in the front, perfect for small- or medium-sized dogs. You and a friend can pedal up and down Monterey's scenic Recreation Trail while your dog just sits back and takes in the scents and sights. Folks who know recommend bringing a jacket or something soft and comfy for your dog to sit on. Wire baskets and dog tushies just don't mix.

Large surreys fit six adults and two children and cost $26 per hour. Smaller surreys fit fewer people, but they're only $16 per hour. 640 Wave Street (under the carousel); 831/646-9090.

DIVERSION

Tie the Knot, Bring Spot: If, while saying your wedding vows at the enchanting **Monterey Stone Chapel,** you begin to feel someone's cold nose nuzzling your ankle, don't blame a fresh guest or an eager spouse. It's just your dog. Probably.

The Monterey Stone Chapel is a terrific place to get hitched with your favorite pooch at your side. Owner Patt O'Brien loves dogs, especially dogs who don't mistake the green carpeting in the chapel for grass. The only dog who ever did that was her three-pound Yorkie, and he did it when he was only a puppy. When something that small does his business, you almost need a magnifying glass to clean it up.

O'Brien has been through it all with dogs at weddings. One time, a dapper Lab in a bow tie threw up all over his master's shiny shoes in the middle of the ceremony. But most of O'Brien's dog weddings go without a hitch (so to speak).

The chapel itself is a real looker. Unlike so many of its brethren, it's completely unkitschy, with a big stone fireplace, white lace curtains, and handmade wrought-iron candelabras. If you prefer to hold your ceremony outside, the setting in front of the chapel is a photographer's dream, complete with a little lake, redwoods (a boy dog's dream), and a wrought-iron archway. O'Brien can even set up your ceremony at one of many breathtaking outdoor coastal locations. Her business is called A By-the-Sea Wedding, and once you check out her favorite spots, you'll know why. Another real plus about getting hitched here: The terrific Tarpy's Roadhouse is right next door. It's a superb place to unwind after tying the knot.

The price is right, too. O'Brien will marry you with your dogs and a couple of friends at your side outside the chapel for $200. Add $150 to $300 more for 10 or more (but not that many more) guests. For an additional $75, she can supply you the required license so you can get married as quickly as California law allows—and in some cases, that means lickety-split.

For more information, write to O'Brien at A By-the-Sea Wedding, 2999 Monterey-Salinas Highway, Suite 3, Monterey, CA 93940, or call 831/375-8574.

When I called about the statute, a police officer told me it's in place for public safety and dog safety. I agree heartily that for a dog's sake, he shouldn't be tied up, especially anywhere you can't see him the few minutes you're shopping or noshing. Too many dogs have been stolen this way. Others have torn themselves loose and gotten lost. But I hope that in the future in Monterey, such situations are handled with a little more finesse than in Billy's case.

One last note. It's against this book's philosophy to include kennels, but in cases where people may be too tempted to leave a dog in the car or a hotel room, we bend the rule a little. I've seen too many dogs panting away in cars while their people are ogling the octopi and otters at the Monterey Bay Aquarium, so here goes the rule bending:

For a true home-away-from-home experience, dogs can stay at the **Home Away from Home** day care. Dogs get to play all day, or to go off and rest. No kennels! Dogs are carefully screened, and they get lots of TLC. The dropoff fee is $20 for the day. Phone ahead to reserve a space; 1231 10th Street, 831/375-1215. A traditional kennel, the **Casa De Amigos Animal Hotel,** conveniently situated just two blocks from the aquarium, is a decent place for your pooch to spend a few hours, if need be. The accommodations are nothing fancy (kennels and some indoor runs), but dogs are treated well and get three short walks a day. Rates are $15–18 for the day, depending on your dog's size. Be sure to call first, because it can get full fast. The "hotel" is at 715 Foam Street; 831/373-0482. Both doggy digs require proof of various vaccinations. Be sure to ask when you call for reservations.

PARKS, BEACHES, AND RECREATION AREAS

The only city park that allows dogs is El Estero Park. Keep that in mind while strolling past the small parks along the Recreation Trail. Leashed dogs are welcome on city beaches and county parks near Monterey.

5 El Estero Park

🐾🐾🐾 (See Monterey County map on page 610)

Dogs are advised to stay away from this park's best feature, Dennis the Menace Playground (designed by the comic's creator, Hank Ketcham). But while the kids frolic on the playground's steam engine, roller slide, and giant swing ride, you and the dog can walk around El Estero Lake.

It's a fun walk for leashed dogs and their people. If you like bird-watching (and what dog doesn't?), you'll enjoy the ducks and migrating birds who hang out on the lake. Benches and picnic tables are scattered around this well-manicured park, so you can really make an afternoon of it.

If you're heading from Highway 1 to the Cannery Row area of Monterey, you'll run right into the park. Exit Highway 1 at the Central Monterey exit. Stay in the right lane and go right on Camino Aguajito. The park will be immediately on your left. You'll get to the best parking area by going left on 3rd Street. 831/646-3866.

6 Jack's Peak Regional Park

🐾🐾🐾🐾 (See Monterey County map on page 610)

Some of the most stunning views of the Monterey Bay, Carmel Valley, and Santa Lucia Mountain Range can be seen from 1,068-foot Jack's Peak, the highest point on the Monterey Peninsula. You and your leashed dog will love the cool Pacific Ocean breezes that sweep through the pine-covered ridges and cathedral-like forests.

On the 8.5 miles of intersecting trails (including a self-guided nature trail), you and your dog can make a day of it or just take in a little fresh air for a half hour. Jake enjoys the Pine Trail, which starts at the Jack's Peak parking area. This is also where you'll find one of the last three remaining native stands of Monterey pine in the world.

The best time to visit here is the spring, when the meadows are blanketed with wildflowers. But this park is worth a visit any time of year.

Fees are $3 on weekdays and $4 on weekends. From Monterey, take Highway 68 east a couple of miles and go right on Olmstead Road. Then turn left on Jack's Peak Road and follow the signs to the park. 831/755-4899.

🐾 Monterey State Beach

🐾🐾🐾 (See Monterey County map on page 610)

The entire state beach is actually made up of three segments spanning a few miles. But these days, dogs are permitted only at one section. If you're strolling along the Recreation Trail (see below) and your dog needs to go roll in some sand, hit the beach at Del Monte Avenue, at the foot of Park Avenue. The official "dogs OK" area runs from just east of the Municpial Wharf to Seaside State Beach. 831/649-2836.

🐾 Recreation Trail

🐾🐾🐾 (See Monterey County map on page 610)

Stretching five miles from Lover's Point in Pacific Grove (no dogs allowed in the little Lover's Point Park) past Cannery Row and into Seaside, this paved bike and walking path is a great way to see Monterey.

You and your leashed dog can get your fill of sightseeing and exercise here. You can sit on one of the many benches that dot the trail and watch some of the world's most fascinating marine life. Jake the Dog likes to check out the mama otters wrapping their babes in kelp before they swim off to forage for food. He could stare for hours at the bobbing babes, but fortunately, the mothers return pretty quickly.

You can start the trail anywhere, but many folks like to start at Fisherman's Wharf. Although dogs aren't allowed on the wharf, this is where smaller dogs get to embark on one of the most fun adventures known to canines: riding on a bike, while you pedal.

PLACES TO EAT

Captain's Gig Restaurant: Ahoy, matie! Got a thirsty dog? Take him to the outdoor tables at this Fisherman's Wharf restaurant. Water is available upon request, as are some scrumptious fish burgers. 6 Fisherman's Wharf #1; 831/373-5559.

Tarpy's Roadhouse: When you and your good dog dine at the courtyard tables at this turn-of-the-last-century roadhouse, you'll know why this is such a popular place. The wonderful food, understated elegance, and beautiful gardens make it special indeed. If you're a fan of grilled food, your mouth will water over any food that comes from Tarpy's wood-burning grill. Try the grilled turkey breast with roasted garlic mashed potatoes. Jake Dog gets weak in the knees even thinking about it. Tarpy's is right next door to the dog-friendly Monterey Stone Chapel, which makes Tarpy's a perfect place to visit after saying your nuptials there. 2999 Monterey-Salinas Highway; 831/647-1444.

Trailside Cafe: Tired of the crowds on Cannery Row, but hungry too? Come here! It's just a short jog off the main drag, and the patio is a peaceful place to eat with a pooch. Dogs get treated like canine kings at the Trailside Cafe. The friendly folks here always give dogs a treat or two and make them feel right at home. Doggy water is always available for the asking. There's even a sign on the adjacent Recreation Trail (see above) that says "Dogs Welcome on Patio." You can get breakfast or lunch here. Vegetarians like the grilled portabella burger. Meat eaters and their dogs slobber over the New York steak sandwich. And if you're in the mood to eat something whose cousin you've visited at the Monterey Bay Aquarium, try the Monterey sand dabs, which are lightly sautéed in a caper-lemon sauce. The café is a short walk from the Best Western Victorian Inn (below), at 550 Wave Street; 831/649-8600.

PLACES TO STAY

Bay Park Hotel: Plenty of trees surround this lodging, so dogs who like shade or leg lifts enjoy a stay here. Humans get use of the attractive pool and hot tub. Rates are $99–169. Dogs are $10 extra. 1425 Munras Avenue 93940; 831/649-1020 or 800/338-3564; www.bayparkhotel.com.

The Beach Resort: This Best Western is one of Jake's favorites. From his first-floor room (dogs are restricted to ground level) he can see the beach, gulls walking around, and girls in bikinis. But what he likes even more is the easy access to Monterey State Beach (see above). Rates are $99–369. Dogs are $25 extra. 2600 Sand Dunes Drive 93940; 831/394-3321 or 800/242-8627; www.montereybeachresort.com.

Best Western Victorian Inn: Dogs and their people are welcome to stay in the first-floor rooms of this charming hotel. You can't actually stay in the main beautiful Victorian house here. (That's for curling up with your dog in front of the marble fireplace and other such cozy activities.) But the simple country Victorian-style rooms in the more modern part of the hotel are just fine with the inn's happy dog and human guests. Many of the rooms have fireplaces, too, should you like to curl up in the comfort of your own room.

The best part of the deal for your furry roommate is that dogs who stay here get a Pooch Package with a dog bowl (with the inn's logo), tasty dog cookies, and bottled water for your dog. It's the dog's meow! People get to enjoy a good continental breakfast, and in the evening, a wine and cheese reception. All this is included with your room. Rates are $159–219. Dogs are $35 extra for the length of their stay. 487 Foam Street 93940; 831/373-8000 or 800/232-4141; www.coastalhotel.com.

El Adobe Inn: Rates are $49–199. Dogs are $10 extra. 936 Munras Avenue 93940; 831/372-5409; www.el-adobe-inn.com.

Hyatt Regency Monterey: Dogs who like golf will enjoy staying at this luxurious hotel; it's flush up against a huge, well-known golf course. While dogs can't romp on the course, they can watch the balls go flying by from the hotel's spacious, well-manicured grounds. The hotel is made up of 26 three-story buildings with 30 rooms each. It takes 10 minutes to walk from one end of the hotel property to the other, so it's not exactly an intimate place. Dogs are relegated to Building 16, which isn't known for its great views. But they don't care: The rooms are comfortable, and right outside the building is a big, grassy, tree-dotted area set aside for dogs. It's not fenced, and dogs need to be leashed, but they don't have to feel guilty going to the bathroom there, as they might in other parts of the hotel's landscaping. (Of course, scoop no matter where the poop happens.)

If golf isn't your bag, you can choose from a full-service racquet club with several tennis courts, two outdoor pools with whirlpools, and a pretty decent poolside fitness center. Or you can just take your dog for a stroll on some nearby paths. (Your dog wants you to choose this exercise option.) Rates are $139–350. There's also an unusual $10 resort fee per night. Dogs are $50 extra for the length of their stay. 1 Old Golf Course Road 93490; 831/372-1234 or 800/824-2196; www.monterey.hyatt.com.

Monterey Bay Lodge: Dogs like staying here because it's relatively close to Monterey Bay (less than two blocks). They can wake up and sniff the crabby breezes. Dogs of most sizes are welcome but the lodge staff prefers no "really huge dogs." Rates are $79–229. Dogs require a $100 deposit and are $15 extra. 55 Camino Aguajito Road 93940; 831/372-8057 or 800/558-1900; www.montereybaylodge.com.

Monterey Fireside Lodge: Stay here and your dog gets a treat that's almost as good as a dog biscuit: "I'll pet them and give them lots of love," says Steve, the innkeeper. The only other stipulation for dogs who stay here (besides being clean, well behaved, and never being left alone in the room or let on the beds): "The dog has to be cute," says Steve, who luckily thinks every dog is just the best.

The lodge is really a motel with pretty clothes. Every room has a gas fireplace, and some of the suites have a sort of garden ambience. Many rooms come with a fridge and microwave. Rates are $59–359. Dogs under 20 pounds are $10 extra. Dogs over 20 pounds are $20. There's no scale at the front desk, so if your dog weighs in at 23 pounds, you may be able to get in at the cheaper rate, especially if your dog sucks in his gut. 1131 10th Street 93940; 831/373-4172 or 800/722-2624; www.montereyfireside.com.

Motel 6: This is one of the most attractive Motel 6s we've ever seen: There's no trucker area, which makes for quieter nights, and the place has some tenderly cared-for landscaping, even around the little pool. It's very close to the heart of Monterey (albeit on cheapy motel row) so although it's one of the more pricey Motel 6s, it's a real deal. Rates are $76–92 for the first adult, $3 for the second. 2124 North Fremont Street 93940; 831/646-8585.

Carmel

Dogs feel more welcome in this picturesque village than almost anywhere in the world. Maybe there's an aura emanating from dog-lover Doris Day's Cypress Inn or the other gorgeous, super-dog-friendly inns here. Or perhaps it's the tantalizing dog burgers (that's burgers for dogs, lest a gruesome image flashed through your head) served at the wonderful Le Coq d'Or, or the dog burgers on pooch plates and the water served to dogs in champagne buckets at the delightful Portabella restaurant, or the biscuits offered to art-loving pooches at the Rodrigue Studio (formerly known as Galerie Blue Dog), or the dog menu offered at the Forge in the Forest, the Plaza Café and Grill, and Lenny's Deli. Of course, that welcome feeling could well come from knowing that Carmel City Beach, one of the most enticing beaches in California, lets pooches run leashless, as does the Mission Trail Park. And more well-read dogs might somehow know that the two local weekly papers have gone to the dogs—they feature regular columns about Carmel's canines.

Whatever the case, your dog can't help but be happy in Carmel, which in these busy times still shuns the idea of street addresses. You won't have a problem finding your destinations, though, because the village is small enough and the people are friendly enough that it's very hard to stay lost for long—especially with a dog at your side.

PARKS, BEACHES, AND RECREATION AREAS

🐾 Carmel River State Beach

🐾🐾🐾 (See Monterey County map on page 610)

Dogs can enjoy this large stretch of beach as far as their leashes will allow. It's convenient if you're stuck south of Carmel, but most dogs prefer Carmel City Beach because of its leash-free policy.

The state beach is accessible from many points, including Ribera Road, off Highway 1. 831/649-2836.

DIVERSION

Shop with Class (Yes, and with Your Dog): Big dogs, little dogs, foo-foo dogs, and noodle-head dogs are welcome to join you as you shop at the high-end stores of **Carmel Plaza.** The motto here: Top of the Ocean, Top of the Line. It's strictly upscale, with stores such as Luis Vuitton, Saks Fifth Avenue, and Georgiou. (Dogs with a more casual bent can sniff around the likes of Banana Republic and Chico's and The Sharper Image.)

They don't just tolerate dogs here. They welcome them with open, tennis bracelet–clad arms. Most of the stores have a canister with dog biscuits. Your dog can eat 'til he plops as you shop 'til you drop. Two of the restaurants here (Lenny's Deli and Plaza Café and Grill—see Places to Eat in the Carmel section) even feature dog menus, in case the biscuits aren't fortification enough.

Be sure to stop by The Fountain of Woof, a wonderful creation that features a dog with water pouring out of his mouth and into a fountain base with a couple of little pools. Stop by and give your dog a guzzle. Every August, the plaza celebrates the anniversary of the fountain with a big fund-raising bash for the local SPCA. A recent guest of honor was none other than Betty White. Check the Carmel Plaza website for info on future dog parties.

Carmel Plaza is on Ocean Avenue between Junipero and Mission Streets. 831/624-0137; www.carmelplaza.com.

🔟 Carmel City Beach

🐾🐾🐾🐾🦮 (See Monterey County map on page 610)

The fine white sand crunches underfoot as you and your leash-free dog explore this pristine beach. It's the only beach for many, many miles that allows dogs off their leashes, so it's a real gem for dog travelers. Bordered by cypress trees and a walking trail, the beach is also popular among humans, especially on weekends. So if your dog is the type to mark beach blankets and eat things out of other peoples' picnic baskets, you may want to leash him until you find a less crowded part of the beach.

Poop bags are available at dispensers here, but it's a good idea to bring your own just in case doggy demand is high and they run out. From Highway 1, take the Ocean Avenue exit all the way to the end, where you'll find a large parking area that's not large enough on summer weekends. 831/624-3543.

DIVERSION

Take a Walk on the Dog Side: You and your pooch can learn all about Carmel, its history, its art, and its dogs—yes, its *dogs*—on a very entertaining, educational stroll given by **Carmel Walks.** The walk lasts about two hours, and Gale, who runs the company, always includes a segment on Carmel's dogs. You'll go to a couple of dog-friendly haunts and you'll meet a couple of the town's famous pooches. Gale is a real dog-lover; it turns out Joe and I knew her Airedale, Heidi, way back when they lived in San Francisco. (Of course, being dog people, we don't remember each other, just each other's dogs.) Heidi is now in Airedale heaven with Joe, where the cats are always fat and the gophers always slow, but her spirit lives on through Gale's dog-friendly tours. These days Gale is accompanied on tours by Heidi's Airedale protege, Squirt.

The tours are $20 per human. Dogs go for free, but they must be leashed. 831/642-2700; www.carmelwalks.com.

11 Mission Trail Park

🐾🐾🐾🐾🐾 🐕 (See Monterey County map on page 610)

This 37-acre park, also known as the Mission Trail Nature Preserve, is lush with oaks, pines, toyon, willows, and other native vegetation, including various shrubs and wildflowers. There's really nothing else like this around here. The preserve's keepers say the park is actually the last remaining refuge of Carmel's natural flora. (Watch out for one of the natives—poison oak. It's abundant, so stick to the trails.)

It's a very appealing park, with five miles of trails for hiking and pleasant benches along the way for resting your weary paws or just relaxing while listening to the sounds of nature. What's particularly wonderful for the dog crowd is that dogs under voice control can be off leash here. Again, try to keep your dog on the trail to protect the native plants and protect yourself from poison oak. (Your dog can't get it, but if it gets on his coat and you touch him, you sure can get it!) During your visit, be sure to paw it over to the wooden footbridge here. It's a great spot for a photo opportunity.

There are several entrances to the park, but the most popular one is right across the street from the historic Carmel Mission, on Rio Road, a little east of Junipero Street. You won't miss the mission, and there's plenty of parking there. You'll find poop bag stations at the entrance. 831/624-3543.

DIVERSION

Get a Spa Treatment, Bring Spot: Need your nails done, your hair coiffed, your lashes tinted, your legs waxed, your face facialed, or your body massaged? Come to the **Papillon Salon,** and you can get every one of these services while your dog rests comfortably at your side. Tracy Carey, owner of the salon, is a dog-lover through and through. Not only does she let your pet in with you, but she provides pooches comfy dog blankets (she calls them "guest blankets") and even treats. Now that's what we call a full-service salon! Papillon is on Mission Street between 5th and 6th Avenues, Carmel. 831/624-7900.

12 Garrapata State Park

🐾🐾🐾🐾 (See Monterey County map on page 610)

This 3,000-acre state park has a mile-long sandy beach. It's the only part of the park that allows dogs, but leashed dogs are thrilled with the chance to trot around the sand. The surf can be quite rough here, so dog paddling is strongly discouraged. Even though the park is just seven miles south of Carmel, it's very Big Sur. The rugged scenery is to drool for.

Speaking of scenery, you should know that the beach draws its share of naturists. (No, not naturalists. We're talking naked people, not experts on wildlife, although I suppose they're not mutually exclusive.) They're not officially supposed to be here, but they're usually off at the far north end, out of the way of curious dogs and their people. If you need a tangible reason to keep your dog's leash on, remember that dogs like to sniff, and, well, a dog run amok in a clothing-optional area can get pretty embarrassing for everyone but the dog. (I speak from experience. Joe the Dog was a notorious nudey-sniffer-outer.)

The two beach access entrances are along Highway 1, between nine and 10 miles south of Rio Road in Carmel. Look for the numbered placards for Gate 18 or 19. (The number system for the state park starts at the north end of the park with Gate 1. Gate 19 is the southernmost gate.) 831/624-4909.

PLACES TO EAT

There are so many dog-friendly restaurants these days that we may have to create a book just for them! Carmel definitely takes the cake (or rather, the Milk-Bone) for pooch-pleasing dining. (Thanks to Sophie the Dog and her person, Kerry, for giving us the heads-up about several of these fabulous eateries.)

Allegro Gourmet Pizzeria: If you like a pizza with a real Mediterranean taste, be sure to order pizza with goat cheese, garlic, and tomatoes. It's liplickin' good. Dine with your dog at the outdoor tables here. 3770 The Barnyard; 831/626-5454.

Anton and Michel: Dine "fountainside" with your dog at the outdoor area of this yummy continental-style restaurant. The atmosphere is casual and elegant (these two adjectives pretty much define most of Carmel, by the way). The Italian and French food is delicious. Dogs get a big bowl of water here. The restaurant is at Mission Street and 7th Avenue. 831/624-2406.

Cafe Gringo: You and your dog will have a great time at this very dog-friendly, casual Mexican restaurant. Dogs get a bowl of water and dog biscuits on the house! Humans get a menu full of traditional Mexican dishes (burritos et al.) and nontraditional delights. (Try the chicken breast cooked with tequila under a brick. It melts in your mouth, and you can still drive.) Dine with your doggy at the outdoor tables. The restaurant is on San Carlos Street between Ocean and 7th Avenues. 831/626-8226.

Cafe Stravaganza: This is an excellent place to stop for a bite if you're on Highway 1 with a dog who is hungering for something different. The food here is eclectic, with everything from American comfort food to good Italian and Greek dishes. Try the primavera potatoes (garlic mashed potatoes topped with sautéed vegetables) for a taste that'll make you want seconds. Your dog might prod you to get the lamb marsala, too. We're told it's a winner. You and your dog can dine together at the outdoor tables. The café is at the Crossroads Shopping Center, at Highway 1 and Rio Road. 831/625-3733.

Caffe Cardinale Coffee Roasting: Even if your dog doesn't have a taste for coffee, quiches, or tasty sandwiches, he'll like joining you at this dog-loving café. There's just one hitch. Really. There's a doggy hitch outside the café, so you can safely hitch your dog while you place your order. Then come back outside and dine with your pooch at the outdoor tables. Doggy diners get little biscuits for visiting. The café is on Ocean Avenue between San Carlos and Dolores Streets. 831/626-2095.

Casanova Restaurant: Known around these parts as Carmel's most romantic restaurant, Casanova's is also surprisingly dog-friendly. It may take a little of the romance out of your evening when your dog starts grinding his chin into your date's lap in pursuit of a handout, but hey, it could also provide a much-needed icebreaker. Well-behaved pooches are welcome on the lovely front patio. The country French and Italian cuisine is superb. Casanova's is at 5th Avenue between San Carlos and Mission Streets; 831/625-0501.

The Forge in the Forest: Dogs would give this wonderful restaurant five paws up if they had five paws. They get to dine with their humans at a delightful outdoor area, which is warmed by an outdoor fireplace when a chill sets in. Better yet, lucky dogs get to order from their very own dog menu! They get to choose from several dishes, including the Quarter Hounder (a burger patty, $3.95), Hot Diggity Dog (all-beef kosher hot dog, $3.95), and the Good Dog, which the menu announces is "for the very, very good dog. The Good

DIVERSION

Sniff Out an Art Gallery: The **Rodrigue Studio** (formerly known as Blue Dog Galerie) is one of those places your dog just won't be able to believe he's allowed to set paw in. After all, it's the California home of the art of George Rodrigue. The paintings start at $18,000, but hey, you can get a silk-screen print for as little as $750. One leg lift in the wrong place—some of the art is within aiming distance—and you've got yourself a wet masterpiece. (And yes, an excited pooch did make a little puddle here once, but no harm was done. Still, if you have any doubts about your dog, you may want to visit the beach instead.)

If any art gallery were to invite dogs in, it would be this one, and there are two reasons for this. One is that the gallery is devoted to Rodrigue's Blue Dog series. The blue dog (you may have seen the paintings in ads for Absolut vodka, or in numerous stories about Rodrigue) is the "ghost" of the artist's dog Tiffany, who watched him paint his Cajun people all her life. Tiffany's "ghost" is light blue with yellow eyes and a face that you can't get out of your head. There's a great story behind the evolution of this series, but I don't have space to tell it here. You'll learn about it when you visit the gallery.

The other reason your dog is welcome here is because gallery director Sandra Crake loves dogs. She has dog biscuits ready for any dog who visits. At Christmas, she sometimes even bakes special biscuits for poochy visitors. The gallery is at 6th Avenue and Dolores Street, and the mailing address is P.O. Box S-3214, Carmel, CA 93923; 831/626-4444; www.georgerodrigue.com.

Dog is six ounces of grilled juicy New York steak. The cost: $12.95. Several dogs have been treated to the Good Dog, according to dog-loving co-owner Donna. It's generally bought as a birthday treat, or when the dog's person is celebrating something special. If you don't feel like spending any money for your dog's dining, that's OK too. All dogs get dog treats here. The price: The wag of a tail. Oh, did we mention that that food for humans is delicious too? You can choose from a very wide array of seafood, pastas, gourmet pizzas, sandwiches, soups, and salads. This heavenly eatery is on the southwest corner of 5th Avenue and Junipero Street; 831/624-2233.

Grasing's Coastal Cuisine: The seafood is so fresh here you'd swear it just jumped onto your plate from the ocean. The pastas and salads are tops, too. If your dog is thirsty, the staff will make sure she gets a snootful of water. It's at 6th Avenue and Mission Street. 831/624-6562.

Jack London's Bar and Grill: Dine on ribs, steaks, and other hearty foods while relaxing in the shade of the canvas canopy. Dogs may drool while watching you chow down on the meaty fare, but if you don't feel like sharing, don't feel too bad: The folks here make sure all dog diners get dog biscuits. The outdoor tables here are actually part of a shared courtyard, but dogs are more than welcome. At 6th Avenue and Dolores Street; 831/624-2336.

Le Coq d'Or: This intimate, delightful European country-style restaurant that serves only dinner is a paws-down favorite among dogs: Pooches who come here get a burger to call their own. The dog-loving restaurant owner, Annelore, serves her own special dog burgers, which consist of ground beef, rice, and garlic, with a dash of salt and pepper. "They smell so good I could eat one myself," she says. The burger comes with a dog bowl filled with fresh water. The cost for all this: $0. "I do it because I love dogs and I think customers like seeing their dogs eat at a restaurant," says Annelore, who also doles out cookies to dogs who are just passing by. (Jake the Dog will never forget the way he was greeted with a big dog biscuit when we were just poking our heads in to say hi one day. Whenever we've walked by since, he pulls hard to steer me to the restaurant.) The people food here is out of this world. Try the coq au vin or the Alsatian onion tart. We hear the sweetbreads are tasty, but you'll never get a firsthand review of them in this book unless Jake Dog takes over authorship. It's on the east side of Mission Street, between 4th and 5th Avenues; 831/626-9319.

Lenny's Deli: Get yourself some fine New York/California deli food (try the lox), and let your dog choose her lunch from her very own menu. Lucky dogs here can get anything from dog food to steak. If your dog can't read, just get whatever her nose points to when she sniffs her menu. Dog menu prices are just a tad above the prices on the kid's menu. (And kids don't get to choose kibble.) Dine at the umbrella-topped courtyard tables here. Lenny's is in Carmel Plaza, at the corner of Ocean Avenue and Junipero Street; 831/624-5265.

Nico: You and your dog can get excellent burgers here. Nico also makes a couple of good sandwiches for nonmeat eaters. Enjoy the bistro cuisine at the outdoor tables. The restaurant is at San Carlos Street and Ocean Avenue; 831/624-6545.

Plaza Café and Grill: The café has got everything a human could want, from fresh fish to pizza. But more important, it's got everything a dog could want, including fresh water and a menu with the things dogs usually only dream about. Canine cuisine includes steak, chicken, hamburgers, and dog food. (Jake says yes, yes, yes, no!) "We love it when people bring their dogs to eat with them," says café owner Ken. "The dog menu is just our way of making sure everyone is happy." Judging by the wagging tails of people and their pooches dining at the umbrella-shaded tables outside the restaurant, Ken's mission is accomplished. The Plaza Café is in Carmel Plaza, at the corner of Ocean Avenue and Junipero Street; 831/624-4433.

Portabella: If you love unique French, Italian, and Spanish food, and if your dog loves being treated like the toast of the town, come to this elegant, yet casual, *ristorante*. Among the mouthwatering dishes are ravioli with pan-fried goat cheese and sun-dried tomatoes (my personal favorite). It's truly to drool for. You can get all kinds of Mediterranean-style dishes and fresh seafood here, but you can also get ye ol' basic hamburger. Dogs think that's very cool. And they think it's even cooler that they're given water, and that the water comes not in a bowl but in a champagne bucket. It's enough to make even the most earthy mutt feel just a bit classy. Jake the Dog's first time with the champagne bucket was an embarrassingly noisy affair. The sound of his giant slurps echoed loudly off the walls of the semienclosed back patio, causing a bit of a titter among the patient diners. "Your dog was so good," said a fellow diner when we passed in the street later. "And so quiet, except when he drank." Many dogs come here and order from the children's menu. Portabella is on Ocean Avenue between Lincoln and Monte Verde Streets; 831/624-4395.

Sherlock Holmes Pub and Restaurant: Dogs enjoy being surrounded by such English goodies as fish-and-chips, bangers, English pies, and Yorkshire pudding while sitting at the patio here. If you and the pooch aren't Anglophiles, Sherlock Holmes also serves good hot turkey sandwiches, Reubens, fajitas, tacos, and even filet mignon. You'll find it at 3772 The Barnyard; 831/625-0340.

Tita's Cafe: The homestyle Mexican food at Tita's is *muy, muy bueno.* With choices from soup to flan, your tastebuds will be very happy here. And so will your canine bud: Dogs get biscuits and a bowl of cold water when they dine with you at the comfy outdoor tables. At San Carlos Street and Ocean Avenue; 831/626-8226.

PLACES TO STAY

The ever-growing number of wonderful dog-friendly lodgings here is a testament to Carmel's dog-friendly lifestyle.

Best Western Carmel Mission Inn: Want a comfortable, attractive, and reasonably priced place to stay in Carmel? With rates that start as low as $79, this Best Western is a good place to bed down in this pricey village if budget is a consideration. The rooms are fairly well appointed, and the folks here are friendly. If you like to wallow in water, check out the heated pool and two spas. (Dogs have to wait until they're at the Carmel City Beach to wet their paws.) Rates are $79–369. (The more expensive rooms are suites.) Dogs are $35 extra for the length of their stay. 3665 Rio Road 93923; 831/624-1841 or 800/348-9090; www.carmelmissioninn.com.

Carmel Country Inn: If you and your dog feel like a cozy room in a quiet setting, you'll enjoy a stay at this pretty 12-room inn. Fresh flowers adorn the rooms, which have a serene country feel. Suites have a balcony, a sitting room, and a fireplace. The inn is set around a cheerful garden, which dogs love to sniff around. But no doggy business there, please! Rates are $150–295. Dogs pay $20 extra. The inn is at 3rd Avenue and Dolores Street, and the mailing address is P.O. Box 3756 93921; 831/625-3263 or 800/215-6343; www.carmel-countryinn.com.

Carmel Garden Court Inn: The rooms here are light and airy, and the kind of "pretty" that beckons you to have a tea party. While you may not be able to get the Alice in Wonderland thing going, you can revel in another English tradition: evening port and sherry served by the fire at the inn's cozy little lobby. It's a great way to wind down after an active day of taking in the sights and smells with your dog.

Your day at the Garden Court starts with a yummy and fairly bounteous continental breakfast, complete with champagne (do we notice a little imbibement theme here?), which is brought to your room with the day's local newspaper. You can eat it (the breakfast, not the paper) in your PJs in your room or patio with poochy at your side. Or you can saunter out to the radiant fountain garden to partake in your eats.

Many of the rooms have fireplaces. Jake prefers the patio suites, which feature beautiful breakfast nooks and patios where he can sniff at life in Carmel. Rates are $150–245. There's a $50 charge for your dog for the length of his stay. The inn is at 4th Avenue and Torres Street. The mailing address is P.O. Box 6226 93921; 831/624-6926; www.carmelgardencourtinn.com.

Carmel River Inn: Lucky dogs who stay here get treated to some biscuits and a water bowl when they check in. And that's just the start: The 24 attractively furnished cottages here are sprinkled around 10 acres of lush, peaceful gardens. Dogs like it so much that many somehow convince their humans to keep coming here year after year. "We get lots of return guests with dogs," says an innkeeper. A few cottages are tiny; others are very generously sized. Many have fireplaces, which makes for a cozy picture if your dog likes to curl up in front of the hearth at night (as opposed to the sprawled-out-like-he's-been-shot-in-a-bad-Western-movie position Jake assumes in front of a crackling fire). Rates are $125–$350. Dogs are $10 extra. The inn is at Highway 1 at the Carmel River Bridge. The mailing address: P.O. Box 221609 93922; 831/624-1575 or 800/882-8142; www.carmelriverinn.com.

Carmel Tradewinds Inn: At press time this sumptuous four-star luxury hotel was getting set for a visit from *Architectural Digest* because of a $4 million renovation that catapulted it from the ho-hum to the stunning. The Pacific Rim–style hotel has an upscale but casual elegance, and its rooms and courtyard are so peaceful and perfect that your dog may scratch her head in wonder that the hotel allows dogs here at all. (As long as she's not scratching her head from fleas, you're all set.)

If your dog promises to be very quiet, you can take her to visit the secret garden, where you'll find a statue of Buddha. It's a very meditative garden, so don't bring a dog like Jake there. Water dogs tend to be mesmerized by the waterfall that cascades down one side of the plant-filled courtyard.

Rates are $195–450. (Some dog-friendly rooms are available with a fireplace and whirlpool tub.) Dogs are $25 extra. The inn is at Mission Street and 3rd Avenue. The mailing address: P.O. Box 3403 93921; 831/624-2776 or 800/624-6665; www.tradewindsinn.com.

Casa de Carmel: If you like wicker decor, light and cheery rooms, and a convenient location in the heart of the village, knock on the door of the Casa de Carmel. The exterior is an attractive blend of Spanish mission style and upscale motel. The rooms aren't terribly roomy, but do you really want to stay in your room very much when visiting one of the most dog-friendly places in the world? The rates are hard to beat around here: $135–165. The dog rate is $20 extra for the first pooch, $10 thereafter. On Monte Verde Street between Ocean and 7th Avenues. The mailing address is P.O. Box 2747 93921; 831/624-7738 or 800/262-1262; www.casadecarmel.com.

Coachman's Inn: This is a warm and fuzzy place to stay with your warm and furry friend. There's an air of Olde England here, with the inn's timbered stucco walls and comfortable decor. In the morning you'll get a danish (not an English, but that's OK), and in the late afternoon you can partake in sherry hour. Rates are $125–250. Dogs are $20 extra, and they must stay in one of the six rooms on the ground floor. The inn is on San Carlos Street at 7th Avenue. The mailing address is P.O. Box C-1 93921; 831/624-6421; www.coachmansinn.com.

Cypress Inn: Dogs get the royal treatment here, in part because actress and animal activist Doris Day owns this sumptuous hotel. The stately Moorish Mediterranean–style inn is very elegant, with fine oak floors and delicate antiques, but you never feel out of place with your dog. Day's staff makes sure your dog feels especially welcome, right down to offering pet beds and pet food for your four-legged friend. The hotel staff will help get you a pet-sitter, should you decide to venture out on your own without your dog. (We doubt your pooch will say *"que sera, sera"* to this idea. Carmel is so dog-friendly you can easily do the whole scene with him. But some very friendly, excellent pet-sitters are available through the hotel if you can stand your dog's hound-dog look when you leave.)

No two rooms are the same here, but they're all enchanting, relaxing, and first-rate. The rooms come with extras not offered by most hotels, including fresh flowers, bottled water, fresh fruit, your very own decanter of sherry, and occasional chocolates. In addition, for an extra fee you can partake in a delightful afternoon tea in the inn's gorgeous library bar. Dogs are even welcome to join you for cocktails there.

Rates are $125–500. It's $25 extra for one pooch, $40 for two. The inn is at Lincoln Street and 7th Avenue, and the mailing address is P.O. Box Y 93921; 831/624-3871; www.cypress-inn.com.

The Forest Lodge: You may feel as though you're in an enchanting forest cabin when you stay here, even though you're just a bone's throw from the center of Carmel. The Forest Lodge consists of four delightful wooden cottages surrounded by lovely gardens and an assortment of good-sized trees. The cottages vary from small and cozy to large and, well, cozy. Two have wood-burning fireplaces, three have featherbeds, one has marble floors in the bathroom, and one even has a peek of the ocean.

The place is as dog-friendly as it is attractive. Your pooch is sure to get a treat or two when he stays here. To make matters even better for dogs, the Forest Lodge is seven short blocks from dog-friendly Carmel City Beach and Mission Trail Park.

We've heard from several happy dogs and their people about how much they've enjoyed their stays here. The Forest Lodge gets plenty of repeat customers. In fact, half of the guests here are of the canine variety. It's not as upscale as the Cypress Inn, but it's friendly and down to earth. Things may be changing, though, because the lodge was recently purchased by the people who own the Vagabond's House Inn, and they've already ripped out the miniature golf area and are "classing it up."

Rates are $125–300. Dogs are $20 extra for one, $30 for two. The Forest Lodge is at Ocean Avenue and Torres Street, and the mailing address is P.O. Box 1316 93921; 831/624-7023.

Hofsas House Hotel: This lovely boutique hotel has the intimate feeling of a bed-and-breakfast inn with the privacy afforded by a small hotel. The rooms are all decorated differently. One sports a beautiful Asian theme, while some have a light and airy upscale alpine cottage feel. Many of the 38 spacious rooms have excellent ocean views and fireplaces. There are also a refreshing outdoor heated swimming pool and two dry saunas. Rates are $89–180. Suites run up to $250. Dogs are $20 extra, but if you travel with more than one dog, the second one is a mere $5 extra. Such a deal! Bring the pack! (No, don't.) The hotel is on San Carlos Street between 3rd and 4th Avenues, and the mailing address is P.O. Box 1195 93921; 831/624-2745; www.hofsashouse.com.

Lamp Lighter Inn: The two cottages and four guest rooms here are some of the most enchanting lodgings around. When you see them on your jaunts down Ocean Avenue you feel as if you're looking at something straight out of a sweet old storybook. The accommodations are airy yet very cozy (and not at all cutesy), with an understated luxury. Dogs don't really care about all this, however. What they like is that it's just a bone's throw (about four short blocks) to the leash-free Carmel City Beach. They also think it's neat that a light, healthy breakfast is brought to your room each morning. (Jake likes the hard-boiled eggs, and since I don't, it's a match made in heaven.) Alternatively, you may ask for it to be served in the lovely garden area. Rates are $175–285. Dogs are $20 extra for one, $30 for two. The inn is at Ocean Avenue and Camino Real, and the mailing address is P.O. Box AF 93291; 831/624-7372; www.carmellamplighter.com.

Lincoln Green Inn: We love the four gorgeous, classy, old English–style cottages that make up this inn. Each white cottage, set in the inn's lush English country garden, is like its own little England, from the steep-pitched roofs to the forest-green shutters to the airy and cozy interiors with beautiful furnishings. Fireplaces are the rule here. The three one-bedroom cottages have kitchens, too, in case you feel like playing chef during your visit. (The fourth cottage, which has two bedrooms, sports an efficiency kitchen.) If you're longing for quiet, the Lincoln Green is for you. It's set in a restful part of town, far enough from the not-so-madding crowds in Carmel to afford real tranquility. The inn is just a short walk to the Carmel River State Beach.

Rates are $225–285. The dog rate is $20 extra for the first pooch, $10 for the second. The cottages are at on Carmello Street between 15th and 16th Avenues, but since there's no office at the cottages, and since they're owned by the folks who own the Vagabond's House Inn (see below), their contact info is the same as Vagabond's: P.O. Box 2747 93921; 831/624-7738 or 800/262-1262; www.vagabondshouseinn.com.

Sunset House: It's hard to know where to start a description of this attractive, romantic, extremely dog- and people-friendly inn. The wonderful former owners, the Pikes, have moved on, but the new owners, Ray and Diane Roeder, are following in their footsteps with their hospitality and wonderful service.

First, a little about the Sunset House itself. The house was built in the 1960s to be a bed-and-breakfast inn, so all four of the rooms are large (600 square feet), with real brick wood-burning fireplaces that are match-ready, and private bathrooms. The rooms are airy, yet cozy, and are furnished beautifully with a mixture of antiques and classic contemporary furniture. The two dog-friendly rooms have private entrances. Our favorite, the Porpoise Suite, has a whirlpool tub and canopy bed. The inn is in an attractive residential neighborhood, where it's a very short, two-minute walk to leash-free Carmel City Beach and the quaint shops of Carmel.

Now a little about the service: The staff welcomes canine and human guests with gift baskets. Humans get a smallish bottle of wine, some crackers, and other tasty treats. Dogs get treats of a different ilk, toys, and towels (for après-beach). In the morning fresh fruit, juice, coffee, and yogurt are delivered to your room. In addition, you'll get a breakfast certificate to be redeemed at one of four premiere restaurants nearby. By the time you read this, there should be an evening cordials hour, too.

There's so much here that you might be tempted to stick close by. But here's something that may lure you back to the road: At press time, the Roeders were working out a system in which dogs and their people could get use of one of their shiny classic cars from the '50s or early '60s. Can't you just picture driving down the beautiful Pacific Coast Highway in one of these timeless machines, top down (or up if your pooch prefers), just enjoying the sunshine and the breeze off the ocean?

Rates for the dog-friendly rooms are $210–230. Dogs pay a $25 fee for the length of their stay. The inn is on Camino Real, between Ocean and 7th Avenues, and the mailing address is P.O. Box 1925 93921; 831/626-7100 or 877/966-9100; www.sunsethousecarmel.com.

Vagabond's House Inn: This is not a Vagabond Inn! Not by a lonnnng shot. Your dog will drool over this inn's beautiful courtyard with its ancient oak tree, little waterfall, and magical garden. (You may drool, too, but don't let your dog catch you or you'll never hear the end of it.) The humans in your party will fall in love with this English Tudor country inn. It's right in town, but you feel as though you're in merry old England here. When you sip the cream sherry that's brought to your room in the afternoon, you may think you've died and gone to the British Isles.

The rooms have fresh flowers and are furnished with antiques. Most have fireplaces and Ralph Lauren bedding. Yummy! In the morning, continental breakfast is brought to the room. And Sally, the dog-loving owner of the inn, is not one to forget your pooch: He gets his very own doggy biscuits with breakfast! (At least you won't have to share your pastries.) Evening sherry is also offered here. Dogs don't get to drink the stuff, though. It makes them too silly.

Rates are $145–225. Dogs are $25 extra. (A second dog is $10 extra.) In case you have any nondog children, you should know that human children under 12 aren't allowed. (Now there's a twist.) The inn is at 4th Avenue and Dolores Street, P.O. Box 2747, 92921; 831/624-7738 or 800/262-1262; www.vagabondshouseinn.com.

Wayside Inn: Part inn, part motel, this is a charming old ivy-covered brick building well off the beaten path. What it lacks in divine exterior grace it makes up for inside, with comfortable country-style surroundings. Some rooms come with kitchenettes or fireplaces. Rates are $99–300. The inn is at Mission Street and 7th Avenue, and the mailing address is P.O. Box 1900 93921; 831/624-5336; www.innsbythesea.com.

Carmel Valley

Only 10 miles inland from Highway 1, this is one of the hidden jewels of the Central Coast. Carmel Valley boasts an average of 283 sunny days a year—quite a feat for any place so close to the ocean. The peaceful country setting isn't marred by the little Carmel Valley Village, the "city center" that's chock full of outdoor cafés that put out the welcome mat for dogs.

Jake, like Joe before him, was disappointed to learn that when Charley and John Steinbeck reached Carmel Valley in their travels, the human half of the team wasn't happy. In *Travels with Charley,* Steinbeck wrote of a conversation he had with his old friend Johnny Garcia in a Monterey bar: "I went to the Carmel Valley where once we could shoot a thirty-thirty in any direction. Now you couldn't shoot a marble knuckles down without wounding a foreigner. And Johnny, I don't mind people, you know that. But these are rich people. They plant geraniums in big pots. Swimming pools where frogs and crayfish used to wait for us."

Jake the Water Dog begs to differ about Steinbeck's comment about too many swimming pools. And he'll be the first to tell you that frogs and their friends still make Carmel Valley their home. You just have to visit Garland Ranch Regional Park to get a sampling of what was once wild and wonderful about the entire Carmel Valley area.

PARKS, BEACHES, AND RECREATION AREAS

🐾🐾🐾🐾🐆 Garland Ranch Regional Park

(See Monterey County map on page 610)

This 4,500-acre park is heaven for any dog who has ever dreamed of living in the country. From the maple-filled canyons to the dense oak woodlands to the willow-covered banks of the Carmel River, you can find almost any environment you and your dog like.

Nine miles of trails can take you and your leash-free dog from just above sea level to 2,000 feet. The wildlife here is plentiful. At the visitor center, you can pick up trail maps as well as species lists of common birds, mammals, and plants to look for while on the trails. Make sure your dog is kind to nature and doesn't disturb the creatures of the woods. Your dog should also know that this is horse country, so if he's thinking of spooking any equines, he'd better be leashed.

While the park has its wild side, it also can be downright civilized. You'll find restrooms and oodles of picnic tables near the visitor center.

Take Carmel Valley Road about 10 miles east from Highway 1. The park will be on your right. Park in one of the lots and follow any of the narrow trails over the Carmel River and to the visitor center, which is the convenient trailhead for all the park's trails. 831/659-4488.

PLACES TO EAT

The Corkscrew Café: This is a wonderful restaurant with a lovely outdoor seating area that has trees, a grape awning, and umbrella-topped tables. Dogs may not only join you there, but they also get treats and water. Try the cornmeal trout or the organic cheeseburger. 55 West Carmel Valley Road; 831/659-8888.

PLACES TO STAY

Blue Sky Lodge: The people who run this lodge/motel are super-friendly to humans and dogs. We've received rave reviews about the Blue Sky from a few of our readers, including Kerry Davis and her travel-lovin' dog, Sophie. It's not so much that it's a fancy place—it's really not. It's actually more of a basic motel from the 1950s. You can get anything from a motel room with patio to a little townhouse. The friendly folks here and the nice spots to exercise Spot (they'll point you to an attractive nearby field, or you can take a short drive to Garland Park), combined with the lodge's very reasonable prices, make it an easy place to stay. Dogs are welcome just about anywhere at the lodge. They can even hang out with you beside the heated swimming pool (not in it, though), or in the lodge's attractive and spacious lodge, complete with big fireplace and comfy old chairs. Rates are $89–139. P.O. Box 233, 10 Flight Road 93924; 831/659-2256 or 800/549-2256; www.blueskylodge.com.

Carmel Valley Lodge: This quiet, secluded country inn is a great place for dogs to get away from city life. The redwood buildings and cottages, some with fireplaces, kitchenettes, and private decks, are the perfect place to relax after a long day of hiking at Garland Ranch Regional Park. Humans get to enjoy the lodge's beautiful heated pool, sauna, hot spa, and fitness center. The place is as dog-friendly as it is beautiful. Its brochure and website feature a picture of "Lucky, the Lodge Dog," and some lodge literature states in bold: "Children and dogs are welcome as long as the kids are on a leash and the dogs are at least 12." The people who work here adore dogs and will point you and yours to some very nearby areas where your dog can get lots of exercise. In addition, dogs who stay here get treats upon arrival. Rates are $149–339. Dogs are $10 extra. A hearty continental breakfast is included in the price. The lodge is at Carmel Valley and Ford Roads. The mailing address is P.O. Box 93 93924; 831/659-2261 or 800/641-4646; www.valleylodge.com.

Los Laureles Lodge: What's good enough for a horse is good enough for you and your dog, right? Back in the 1930s, many of the 10 one-story buildings here were stables housing happy thoroughbreds owned by a wealthy family. Today they've been converted into comfortable guest rooms with knotty-pine paneling and simple country decor. There's no lingering equine odor, much to Jake's chagrin. Other rooms in other buildings are even older and have no horsey history. If you can afford a little extra, the king suite with a big stone fireplace and a white picket-fenced yard is a great place to stay with a dog. Dogs are happy staying anywhere at the lodge, because they get to trot around (leashed) on the property's 10 acres. People who like older saloons and newer pools enjoy the lodge's version of each of these, but dogs need to stay dry, in more ways than one. (No dogs in the drink or near the drinks.) Rates are $75–280. 313 West Carmel Valley Road 93924; 831/659-2233 or 800/533-4404; www.loslaureles.com.

Big Sur Area

As the two-lane ribbon of Highway 1 winds 90 miles up and down what many think is the most spectacular coastal scenery in the world, your dog may be praying for the end of the trip—or at least wishing for a dose of Dramamine.

Carsick dogs are not uncommon as mountains shoot up 1,000 feet over the crashing Pacific, only to curve and slope down again, roller-coaster fashion. It's a good idea to take your time and stop at as many vista points as you can along the road. Your dog will thank you for it, and you'll get to breathe the exhilarating Pacific air and study the rugged shoreline.

A must-stop vista point is at the Bixby Creek Bridge, 260 feet high and more than 700 feet long. There are pullouts on either side.

Whatever you do when you're making these stops along Big Sur, make sure your dog is securely leashed and in no danger of stepping too close to the edge of the world. There's usually not much room between Highway 1 and the hazardous cliffs.

PARKS, BEACHES, AND RECREATION AREAS

14 Pfeiffer Beach

🐾🐾🐾🐾 (See Monterey County map on page 610)

You and your leashed dog will be stunned at the natural beauty of this white, sandy beach. Surrounded by sea caves, steep cliffs, and natural arches, you won't know what to marvel at first. Your dog will be so thrilled that he won't even notice he's leashed.

From the north, take the second right turn (Sycamore Canyon Road) off Highway 1 south of Big Sur State Park. It's a sharp turn. At the end of the narrow, two-mile road is a sandy trail under a canopy of cypress trees. It leads to the beach. The beach is dog-friendly because it's run by the good old U.S. Forest Service. 831/385-5434.

15 Sand Dollar Picnic Area and Beach

🐾🐾🐾 (See Monterey County map on page 610)

Your dog will enjoy the romance of a picnic among the cypress trees here. After downing your French bread, brie, and white wine, take one of the trails across the field and follow it down to the beach. Although dogs must be leashed, it's a terrific spot. It's toward the southern end of Big Sur, so it's at a perfect place to take a break from driving.

The picnic area is about 11 miles south of Lucia, west of Highway 1. This is another beach run by the U.S. Forest Service, which explains its dog-friendly rules. 831/385-5454.

PLACES TO STAY

Here are just a few of the private and public campgrounds along the Big Sur coast.

Big Sur Campground: If you're into family-oriented camping, this is your kind of place. This privately owned campground in the redwoods along the Big Sur River features basketball courts and a playground for the kids. Tent campsites are $27, and dogs are $4 extra. The campground is on Highway 1, about 24 miles south of Carmel. For reservations (taken up to a year in advance, and it's a good idea to make one), contact the campground at Highway 1, Big Sur, CA 93920; 831/667-2322; www.bigsurcampgroundandcabins.com.

China Camp: It's fun to camp here if you're planning on hiking in the Ventana Wilderness (see the Los Padres National Forest in the Resources section) but you're not quite sure about camping in the wilderness itself. A trail leads directly from the camp into the Ventana Wilderness. Dogs must be on leash at the campsite, but they can put their leashes in their doggy backpacks as soon as they're in the wilderness area. Six sites are available on a first-come, first-served basis. There's no charge for the sites, but you can't get out of the red tape that easily: You need a wilderness permit to come here. There's a two-dog maximum, and pooches must show proof of rabies vaccine. It's good for day adventuring, camping, or both. Keep in mind that there's no piped-in water, so bring plenty, or be ready to filter any you find in streams along the way. The campground is inland, about 20 miles southwest of Carmel Valley, on Tassajara Road. Call the Los Padres National Forest main office at 831/385-5434.

Fernwood Resort: Dogs enjoy a stay here because they have access to the Big Sur River. You and the pooch can stay only at the resort's campground, not the motel. It's conveniently situated right off Highway 1, but it's set back enough so you don't feel as if the cars are right in your backyard. Tent sites are $24–27, and RVs get to stay here for $29. Dogs are $3 extra. There's no street address. It's just Highway 1, Big Sur CA 93920; 831/667-2422.

Kirk Creek Campground: You'll love the view from the bluffs above the beach here, and your dog will appreciate the cool Pacific breezes. You can bring your leashed dog down to the beach on a couple of steep trails, or you can take a trail from here that leads into the Ventana Wilderness. That's where your dog can legally remove his leash. Kirk Creek has 33 campsites, costing $18. The campground is west of Highway 1, about four miles south of Lucia. Call the Los Padres National Forest main office at 831/385-5434.

Pfeiffer Big Sur State Park: Though this state park has 821 acres of redwoods, some near Big Sur River, dogs are permitted only in the camping area. It's not so bad—each of the 218 campsites has a picnic table where your dog can join you for gourmet outdoor cooking, or he can sleep under it when the shade of the redwoods isn't enough. Sites are $20–25. The park is east of Highway 1, about 26 miles south of Carmel. Call park headquarters at 831/667-2315 for information. For reservations, call 800/444-7275.

Ventana Campground: This privately owned campground set in a redwood canyon is ideal for getting away from motor-home campers without getting too primitive. No reservations are necessary for the 70 campsites, but they are recommended for summer weekends. It's more rustic than many campgrounds you'll find around here, which is something Jake appreciates. Sites are $27. Dogs are an extra $5. The campground is about 2.5 miles south of Pfeiffer Big Sur State Park. The mailing address is P.O. Box 206, Big Sur, CA 93920; 831/667-2712; www.ventanawilderness.com.

King City

This is a fine place to stop with your dog, but a word of warning: It's also a good place to get caught speeding. The California Highway Patrol seems omnipresent on this stretch of U.S. 101, so watch yourself. The troopers don't take kindly to the old "my dog really has to go to the bathroom" excuse.

PARKS, BEACHES, AND RECREATION AREAS

16 San Lorenzo Regional Park

🐾🐾🐾 (See Monterey County map on page 610)

Conveniently situated just off U.S. 101 almost midway between San Francisco and Los Angeles, this is a great park for your dog to get out and stretch his legs on a long journey. The park is home to the intriguing Agricultural and Rural Life Museum, which tells the story of Salinas Valley agriculture. Although dogs aren't welcome in the buildings, humans are invited to enter a one-room schoolhouse and farmhouse. Day use is $4 per vehicle on weekdays, $6 weekends.

If you want to make a night of it, you can camp at any of the park's 190 campsites. Reservations are necessary only for group sites but are available for regular sites, too. Sites are $20–25. Dogs are $4 extra. Your dog must have proof of rabies vaccination. Exit U.S. 101 at Broadway and follow the signs. 831/385-5964.

PLACES TO STAY

Motel 6: Rates are $38–53 for the first adult, $6 for the second. 3 Broadway Circle 93930; 831/385-5000.

    San Lorenzo Regional Park: See San Lorenzo Regional Park, above, for camping information.

CHAPTER 46

Kings County

This is farm country, the kind of land that drives dogs crazy around the time the fertilizer's being spread. But despite all the open fields and rural surroundings, it's tough to find a place to take a dog for a good time. Dogs would love to roll in the cow patties, but between your objections, the farmers' objections, and that killer look on Bessie's face, they quickly realize it's not the best idea in the world.

Ironically, the most appealing areas for dogs are in the small cities, especially Lemoore and historic Hanford. Off-leash parks are nonexistent, but pooches still manage to stretch their legs a little.

PICK OF THE LITTER—KINGS COUNTY

BEST OLD-FASHIONED PARK
Civic Center Park, Hanford (page 644)

Hanford

Anyone looking for a set for *The Music Man?* You couldn't find a more perfect one than the turn-of-the-last-century town square in the middle of the old part of Hanford. It's got all the charm and permanence of River City, Iowa, and you won't have to put up with a freckle-faced kid with a bad lisp. The city has some of the grandest old buildings in California. Most of them are in or around Civic Center Park, where your leashed dog can enjoy green grass and big, stately trees.

Dogs also seem to enjoy walking down China Alley, the center of an area that in its heyday boasted one of the largest populations of Chinese immigrants in the United States. The Taoist Temple, built in 1893, still retains its position as the centerpiece of China Alley. It's now a theater, and dogs have to stay outside, but it's still amazing to see something like this in the middle of the San Joaquin Valley.

If you stray out of the old core of town, you'll be transported to Wal-Mart world—not a pretty sight. A hefty chunk of Hanford is a fairly major suburban-style shopping area, complete with the biggest chains and fast-food restaurants. Dogs highly recommend staying in the historic district, especially since members of their kind aren't always appreciated in department stores.

PARKS, BEACHES, AND RECREATION AREAS

🖘 Civic Center Park

🐾🐾🐾 (See Kings County map on page 642)

If you were to find yourself in the middle of a park with huge shade trees, flowers, an antique carousel, a fire engine from 1911, and a neoclassical courthouse building, in what year do you think you'd be? 1920? 1930? It's hard to believe, but this old charmer exists today.

It must be something about the clock on the front of the Civic Auditorium across the street. The impressive classical revival building's big clock actually works. The whole thing is reminiscent of *Back to the Future*—clock, columns, and all. But the title of this ideal town square would have to be *Back to the Past.*

The place is very friendly to leashed dogs. The courthouse has been converted into quaint shops and offices. There's even a deli with outdoor tables (see below).

Exit Highway 198 at 11th Avenue, drive north a few blocks, and go right on 7th Street. The park is at Irwin and 7th Streets. 559/585-2500.

PLACES TO EAT

Port of Subs: Munch good deli food outside with your pooch. 729 West Lacey Boulevard; 559/582-7651.

PLACES TO STAY

Sequoia Inn: This is one of the nicest lodgings around these parts, and dogs are thrilled that they're welcome here. The decor is attractive, the rooms and suites comfortable, and the pool, spa, exercise room, and sauna are wonderful bonuses for the humans in your party. An expanded continental breakfast comes with your room. Rates are $60–110. Dogs require a $100 deposit. 1655 Mall Drive 93230; 559/582-0338.

Lemoore

Besides the gigantic Harris Ranch (a must-smell for dogs, described in the Coalinga section of the Fresno County chapter), Lemoore is the first civilization you come to driving east on Highway 198 from I-5. It's got a cute town center, lined with trees and antique stores.

PARKS, BEACHES, AND RECREATION AREAS

2 City Park

🐾🐾 (See Kings County map on page 642)

This square-block park is usually green and grassy, which makes it ideal for dogs who like to roll. Willows and palms abound, so even in the heat of summer, you and your dog can survive. Kids like it here because of the special playground.

Take the Lemoore/Fresno exit (Highway 41) from Highway 198 and go north to West Bush Street. Go right on West Bush Street and drive for about 12 blocks. The park is on your left. 559/924-6767.

Corcoran

You'll see plenty of dogs here, but they're usually in the backs of big pickup trucks parked at local bars and convenience stores. The dogs like to bark, especially at each other.

To want to drive all the way out here with your dog, you probably have to have a loved one at the maximum-security Corcoran State Prison. Dogs aren't allowed to visit any of the prison's 5,500 inmates, so they'll be sorely disappointed if that's the only reason they came with you.

PARKS, BEACHES, AND RECREATION AREAS

3 Community Park

🐾🐾 (See Kings County map on page 642)

This is exactly what it sounds like—a park for the community, featuring picnic tables, ball fields, and children's playgrounds. It's the only game in town if your dog needs to relieve her bladder, and it can be quite crowded with local kids. The park is at Dairy and Patterson Avenues. 559/992-2151.

Kettleman City

What can we say about Kettleman City, except that it's a good place to take a break while traversing the state on I-5?

PLACES TO STAY

Best Western Kettleman Inn and Suites: Stay here if you want comfort, an expanded breakfast, a little pool, and a whirlpool. The suites here are very roomy and well designed, and the rooms are spacious. Some of the rooms have whirlpools. It's the perfect place to stretch your legs during a long I-5 car trip. Rates are $70–169. Dogs are $4 extra. 33410 Powers Drive 93239; 559/386-0804.

Super 8 Motel: Rates are $55–65. Dogs pay $10 for the length of their stay. There's a $40 deposit for dogs. 33415 Powers Drive 93239; 559/386-9530.

CHAPTER 47
Tulare County

Some people come here from other parts of the state and call this place "Tool-air" County. Others call it "Tool-ahh-ray." Don't do dat! You'll be pegged as an outsider immediately and your dog's credentials as a real dog will be questioned. When you're trying to remember how to say the name of this place, just think about the personality of a late-night CNN talk show host. If you say he's just too, too, "Too-larry" (King), you'll fit right in.

Don't worry if you don't find your thrills in the civilized parts of Tulare. About one-third of the county belongs to the U.S. Forest Service, the Bureau of Land Management (BLM), and the California Department of Forestry. In dog-speak, that translates to "Look, Ma, no leash!"

The BLM's dog-friendly Chimney Peak Recreation Area is split between Tulare County and its southern neighbor, Kern County. While Tulare County contains the best part of the recreation area, it's more easily reached from Kern County. (Please see the Inyokern section in the Kern County chapter for a description.)

PICK OF THE LITTER—TULARE COUNTY

BEST DOG PARK
Cody Kelly Bark Park, Visalia (page 651)

BEST HIKE AMONG THE TREES
Mountain Home State Forest, Springville (page 653)

NATIONAL FORESTS

The National Forests and Wilderness Areas resource at the back of this book has important information and safety tips on visiting national forests with your dog and has more information on the national forests listed below.

Inyo National Forest

Sequoia National Forest

NATIONAL PARKS

Sequoia and Kings Canyon National Parks

If you were a chocoholic, your idea of hell would probably include being chained to the middle of a small island surrounded by a sea of unreachable, creamy Ghirardelli, Godiva, and Guittard chocolates. If you were an ice skater, purgatory might include being relegated to gravel driveways for the rest of your life, never being able to set a blade on the ice that's all around you. And if you were a dog, your idea of hell would probably involve a visit to these two exquisite national parks.

Sequoia National Park contains the thickest concentration (and the biggest individual specimens) of giant sequoia trees in the world. And while Kings Canyon doesn't have the huge trees, it's wild and untamed, just begging to be sniffed at by an inquisitive dog snout. Dogs, however, must be cloistered in the car-camping areas and the little villages here, far from the trails and the madding trees. This is bad news. This makes boy dogs moan. This is hell.

A day-use pass is $10 per car, and this is good for a week. Fees for sites where dogs can camp are $8–14. There are approximately 1,300 sites available on a first-come, first-served basis. The parks are connected and stretch for almost 60 miles from north to south. Because of their sizes, we can't provide specific directions here. Call the parks at 559/565-3134 for information on what areas might be best for you and your traveling dog. And if no one in your traveling party is going to be around to hang out with your dog while you explore the parks, leave him home with a friend. Too many dogs get stuck in cars here, and that can be dangerous as well as a crashing bore.

Dinuba

PARKS, BEACHES, AND RECREATION AREAS

1 Rose Ann Vuich Park

🐾🐾 (See Tulare County map on page 648)

Leashed dogs are welcome to stroll through this grassy, tree-filled park. It's in the middle of town, so if you've got business to attend to, you can take your dog here for some doggy business afterward.

The park is at East El Monte Way at McKinley Avenue. 559/591-5921.

Visalia

PARKS, BEACHES, AND RECREATION AREAS

This relatively small community is now home to two pooch parks! Let that be an example to you larger towns that won't even consider them.

2 Cody Kelly Bark Park

🐾🐾🐾🐾🐕 (See Tulare County map on page 648)

This is one of the more attractive dog parks we've come across, and it's got just about every possible dog-park amenity on its two acres, including separate areas for large and small dogs, double gates, benches, poop-bag dispensers, doggy water fountains, faux fire hydrants, and plenty of trees. The park is named after a West Highland terrier who has a generous human who helped make the park possible. Thank you for inspiring your human, Cody. And thanks to chocolate Labs Molly and Godiva for giving us the woof about this place.

The park is within Plaza Park, where you and your leashed dog can hike on a trail, relax under a big shade tree, or watch kids fish in a little pond. It's west of town, at Highway 198 and Plaza Drive, just east of Highway 99. If you know where the Visalia Airport is, you can't miss the park. (It's very conveniently situated if you're staying at the Holiday Inn Plaza Park, which is a bone's throw away. See below.) For the official city word on the park, phone 559/713-4365. For info from the dog-park people, phone Amy at 559/280-3054.

3 Seven Oaks Bark Park

🐾🐾🐾🐕 (See Tulare County map on page 648)

This one is the younger, smaller, more diminutive sibling of Cody Kelly Bark Park. (See above.) It's about an acre, and it has a bench, water, a picnic table, and poop-bag dispenser. There's not much shade, so it can be a scorcher on hot days. The park is on Tulare Avenue, just south of Ben Maddox Way. For the official city word on the park, phone 559/713-4365. For info from the dog-park people, phone Amy at 559/280-3054.

PLACES TO STAY

Best Western Visalia Inn Motel: Rates are $79–96. Dogs must be under 25 pounds, and they're $10 extra. 623 West Main Street 93291; 559/732-4561.

Holiday Inn Plaza Park: Stay at this comfy, clean hotel and you're almost within Cody Kelly Bark Park. (See above.) Rates are $95–109. Dogs pay a $25 deposit. 9000 West Airport Drive 93277; 559/651-5000 or 800/465-4329.

Tulare

PARKS, BEACHES, AND RECREATION AREAS

4 Live Oak Park

😾😾 (See Tulare County map on page 648)

If you happen to be passing through town, this green park is worth sniffing out. Dogs like the combination of trees and fitness course.

The park is close to Highway 99. Take the Tulare Avenue exit east a few blocks and turn left on Laspina Street. In a few more blocks, you'll be at the park. It's right beside the Live Oak Middle School. 559/685-2380.

PLACES TO STAY

Best Western: Rates are $67–82. Dogs pay a flat $20 fee. 1051 North Blackstone Avenue 93274; 559/688-7537.

Days Inn: There's a little lot just a bone's throw away where you can walk your leashed pooch. The rate here is $49–59. Dogs are $5 extra. 1183 Blackstone Street 93274; 559/686-0985.

Porterville

PARKS, BEACHES, AND RECREATION AREAS

5 Veterans Park

😾😾😾 (See Tulare County map on page 648)

This L-shaped park has a nature trail that leashed dogs are welcome to sniff out. It runs the length of the park, so you get to hike a total of almost two miles in one direction. You'll walk by cottonwoods and huge oaks. If you get tired, you can relax at the picnic tables or under the shade trees here.

The really interesting part of this park is the big HU1B dust-off helicopter that's mounted about 20 feet up in the air on the park's north side. It's in a landing position, and it's meant to symbolize the end of the Vietnam War.

This town was hard-hit by the war. A local veteran told me that the Porterville area is home to the highest number of men per capita killed in Vietnam. In addition to the chopper, the memorial is encircled by several young redwood trees—one per local hero killed in the war. This end of the park is at Henderson Avenue and Newcomb Street. 559/782-7536.

Springville

PARKS, BEACHES, AND RECREATION AREAS

6 Mountain Home State Forest

😊😊😊😊🐾 (See Tulare County map on page 648)

If you and your leash-free pooch want to see the seventh-largest tree in the world, you'd better make nice with the rangers here. The tree isn't on any maps, and rangers prefer to point it out only to the folks they like.

If the ranger just doesn't dig you or your dog enough to let you check out that tree, don't worry. Plenty of other trees can make up for your loss. The forest's 4,800 acres are filled with trails that take you past other giant sequoias in addition to ponderosa pines, sugar pines, cedars, and firs.

Some of the rangers aren't keen on the forest's leash-free policy, and they recommend it only for the best-trained dogs. They say they've seen too many dogs get lost or chase down critters that are best left alone. But chances are if you and your dog aren't used to elevations around 6,500 feet, neither of you will be in the mood to run far. In the words of one ranger: "People just suck for oxygen until they get accustomed to the air up here."

Campsites are free, but dogs must be leashed. Sites are available June–October and are on a first-come, first-served basis. From Highway 190 in Springville, drive north on Balch Park Drive for three miles and then head east on Bear Creek Road for 15–21 miles, depending on your destination within the forest. Mobile homes should take an alternate route, continuing up Balch Park Drive for about 30 more miles to the park. Be sure to get a trail map and some ranger advice before venturing into the forest. 559/539-2855 in summer, 559/539-2321 in winter.

PLACES TO STAY

Mountain Home State Forest: See Mountain Home State Forest, above, for camping information.

CHAPTER 48

San Luis Obispo County

Home of Hearst Castle, spectacular beaches, quaint seaside hamlets, and the mighty Pismo clam, this county is one of the state's most popular getaways. Dogs appreciate the olfactory beauty—the fishy piers, the farm-fresh soil, the suntan lotion—as much as their drivers enjoy the scenery and the history.

Dog activities are numerous. Your dog can dine with you at countless restaurants with outdoor tables. She can camp with you, fish with you, and tour wineries with you. She can stay with you at some decent digs, two of which are exceptionally dog-friendly. (Dogs aren't allowed in Hearst Castle, or on its grounds, but that's no big surprise. See the Cambria section for an idea of how you can get to see the castle and not worry about your dog.)

Ocean-loving dogs are going through a bit of a dry spell here these days: They're no longer allowed at most beaches throughout the county. It's a very sorry state of affairs for dogs, and it makes for a skinnier chapter than in the past. The ban is supposed to be for the good of snowy plovers and

PICK OF THE LITTER—SAN LUIS OBISPO COUNTY

BEST BEACHES
Cayucos State Beach, Cayucos (page 664)
Oceano Dunes/Pismo State Beach, Pismo Beach (page 673)

BEST DOG PARK
El Chorro Regional Park Dog Park, San Luis Obispo
(page 668)

RESTAURANT WITH BEST VIEWS
San Simeon Beach Bar and Grill, San Simeon (page 659)

MOST DOG-FRIENDLY PLACE TO EAT
Mustache Pete's, Cambria (page 661)

LODGING WITH BEST BEACH ACCESS
Best Western Cavalier Oceanfront Resort, San Simeon
(page 659)

MOST DOG-FRIENDLY PLACES TO STAY
Cambria Shores Inn, Cambria (page 662)
Fogcatcher Inn, Cambria (page 662)
Cayucos Beach Inn, Cayucos (page 664)
Cottage Inn by the Sea, Pismo Beach (page 674)

BEST WINERIES
Paso Robles wineries (page 658)

other birds—and even little fish in some areas. Fortunately, one beach in San Simeon still allows leashed dogs (see Best Western Cavalier Oceanfront Resort in the San Simeon section), as do Cayucos State Beach, a little area near Morro Rock, and some beaches in the Pismo area.

NATIONAL FORESTS

The National Forests and Wilderness Areas resource at the back of this book has important information and safety tips on visiting national forests with your dog and has more information on the Los Padres National Forest.

Los Padres National Forest

Both the Santa Lucia Wilderness and the Manchesna Mountain Wilderness, east of the city of San Luis Obispo, are ideal for dogs who like their wilderness spelled with a capital W.

Paso Robles

PARKS, BEACHES, AND RECREATION AREAS

Dogs are not allowed at any Paso Robles city park unless there's an event that includes them (training or a show, to be more specific). Let's hear it, dogs: Hissssss. Booooooo.

Fortunately, Lake Nacimiento is around to help dogs get over their disappointment. It's not very close and there is a fee, but it's pooch-friendly.

1 Lake Nacimiento

🐾🐾 (See San Luis Obispo County map on page 654)

While this oak-lined lake has 165 miles of shoreline, only the section run by Lake Nacimiento Resort is open to the public. And with the resort's limited dog areas, that means just a so-so vacation for canines. Dogs are allowed on leash in the meadows and picnic areas. They're also allowed to camp with you at any of the resort's 350 sites. But unless your dog enjoys helping you fish for white bass and smallmouth bass from your boat, a visit here probably won't be the highlight of her year.

Dogs need to show proof of rabies vaccine. (I love the way rangers everywhere often state this: "They need to show proof of rabies." I've been tempted to answer, "Well, sir, he has been getting a little foamy around the mouth of late. Is that proof enough?" But I refrain, because I want to get into the park.) The day-use fee is $10 for the first two people, and $3 per additional adult. Kids are free. Dogs are $2–6 extra. Campsites are $25 per night per vehicle. Reservations are needed for RV sites. From U.S. 101, exit at Highway 46 and go west at the off-ramp. Follow this road, known for most of its span as Nacimiento Lake Road, for eight miles. When you get to County Road G-14, make a hard right and drive another eight miles. The resort is on the left. 805/238-3256.

PLACES TO EAT

DK's Donuts: Eat your way out of your New Year's resolutions at the sidewalk tables. Your dog can be at your side to witness the downing of the doughnuts. 1740 Spring Street; 805/238-9371.

DIVERSION

A Loaf of Bread, a Glass of Wine, and Thy Dog: When you think of wine country, Paso Robles may not be the first place that comes to mind. But there are some fine wineries east of town, and a few allow your dog to hang out with you at their serene picnic areas while you sip your newly bought wine. **Eberle Winery** and **Meridian Vineyards,** both east of town on Highway 46, welcome dogs in their picnic areas. Eberle has the added advantage of a water spigot handy for your dog. Call Eberle at 805/238-9607. Meridian's number is 805/237-6000.

Good Ol' Burgers: Dogs and their people have to sit at the farthest possible rugged wood tables, but that's OK. You can smell the charbroiled beef from hundreds of yards away. 1145 24th Street; 805/238-0655.

21st Street Drive-In: If you're on the road and want to stop for some quick eats with your pooch, this is a fine place to grab a bite, if you don't mind burger cuisine. The shakes here are as close to "real" as any fast-food shake can get. Dine with doggy at the outdoor tables. 2110 Spring Street; 805/238-0360.

PLACES TO STAY

Hampton Inn and Suites: The rooms here are spacious and clean, and they come with a little fridge, microwave, and access to the hotel's heated outdoor pool and whirlpool. Start your day with some good eats from the inn's breakfast bar. (Your dog must be content with her dog food, though.)

The official size limit for dog guests is 45 pounds, but if you have a big, good Lab who's looking for a room at the inn, don't sweat it. "We've even had Great Danes. We just don't want horses," says a manager. Rates are $99–169. There's a credit card deposit against doggy damage. 212 Alexa Court 93446; 805/226-9988.

Lake Nacimiento Resort: See Lake Nacimiento, above, for camping information.

Motel 6: Rates are $42–52 for the first adult, $6 for the second. "As long as your dog can fit through the door," you can bring him, says a hotelier. In other words, the former "small dogs only" rule no longer applies. 1134 Black Oak Drive 93446; 805/239-9090.

TraveLodge: Rates are $59–159. The inn used to advertise that only small dogs were allowed, but now "We're more dog-friendly. As long as your dog's not an elephant," he's allowed, says the manager. Dogs are $10 extra. 2701 Spring Street 93446; 805/238-0078 or 800/578-7878.

San Simeon

Dogs aren't trusted anywhere near the gilded towers of William Randolph Hearst's castle, so if you're thinking of visiting while your dog is with you, forget it. He'll have to wait in the car for at least three hours while you tour the castle, and that's a very bad idea.

But that doesn't mean you have to forgo this spectacular attraction. The Tail Wag's Inn, about nine miles south in Cambria, will board your dog for as long as your tour takes. With all the frills the inn provides your pet, she may come back thinking she should be living in Hearst Castle.

Unfortunately, dogs are no longer allowed to amble on San Simeon State Beach (although you can still camp there), so your romping room here is rather limited. But if you stay at the wonderful Best Western Cavalier Oceanfront Resort (see below), you'll be staying at the only beach around here where dogs are allowed. They have to wear leashes, but at least they get to enjoy themselves. (You can get to the beach even if you don't stay there, but it's sure nice to stay at a place where you can play on the beach.)

PLACES TO EAT

San Simeon Beach Bar and Grill: The panoramic ocean views from the outdoor tables (where dogs are allowed) make this a real destination restaurant for hungry dogs and their people. It can get windy here, though. Enjoy clam chowder, pizzas, and good grilled grub. 9520 Castillo Drive; 805/927-4604.

PLACES TO STAY

Best Western Cavalier Oceanfront Resort: This is San Simeon's only oceanfront hotel, and it's one of the most attractive and well-run Best Westerns we've ever checked out. (But don't let its brochure get your hopes up: The picture on the cover is not of the Best Western. It's Hearst Castle.) Many of the 90 rooms have a wood-burning fireplace, a stocked minibar, close-up ocean views, and a private patio. There's even room service, so you and your dog can dine together in the comfort of your own seaside abode. The humans in your party can keep in shape in the fitness room or at the two outdoor pools here (with ocean views to drool for). And if you stay here, you and your leashed pooch will have easy access to the long beach that backs up to the lodging. This is a huge deal right now, because no other beach in the area permits pooches.

Sunny Dog, a canine reader from Dayton, Ohio, had his person, Peggy, describe what they love most about their visits here: "It is quite delightful to sit on your patio and drink in that fabulous ocean view. The firepits (surrounded by chairs) are lit at sunset and left burning through the night for those folks that want to enjoy the fire, the sound of the ocean, and the distant light from the Piedras Blancas Lighthouse." Nice writing, Sunny.

Many people are tempted to leave their dogs in their rooms when they go explore magnificent Hearst Castle, but this is a big no-no. The Cavalier makes it easy for you to do the right thing: It provides numbers for dog-sitters and for a wonderful kennel (see the Cambria section for kennel info). Be forewarned, though: At busy times, you need to make dog-care reservations well ahead of your visit.

Rates are $119–279. 9415 Hearst Drive 93452; 805/927-4688 or 800/826-8168; www.cavalierresort.com.

Motel 6: A Motel 6 in the same town as Hearst Castle? Go figure. This one started as a Holiday Inn, so it's a cut above many other Motel 6s. Rates are $38–47 for one adult, $6 for the second adult. The size limit of the past is history: "Just no horses," says a manager. 9070 Castillo Drive 93452; 805/927-8691.

San Simeon State Park camping: Dogs can no longer enjoy a romp on the sand at the beach here, nor on the trails, but they're allowed to camp. Sites are $12–16. The campground is about six miles south of Hearst Castle, along Highway 1. For reservations, phone 800/444-7275.

Silver Surf Motel: The cover of the brochure for the Silver Surf has a picture of a magnificent mansionlike building with a cherub statue pointing to it. "Stay at Silver Surf Motel" it declares. And you thought Hearst Castle was gorgeous. Oh, wait, that *is* Hearst Castle on the cover. Ohhh, the brochure also says, "Visit Hearst Castle." Alas. The Silver Surf isn't exactly Hearst Castle, but then again, what is? This motel is pretty darned decent, with 72 rooms in a peaceful garden setting with plenty of trees to sniff, and a really attractive indoor pool and spa. Some rooms even have ocean views and fireplaces. Not bad for a motel, eh? Rates are $39–139. Dogs are $10 extra. 9390 Castillo Drive 93452; 805/927-4661 or 800/621-3999; www .silversurfmotel.com.

Cambria

A stroll through this charming village can be fun for you and your dog, but Cambria serves a more important purpose: It's the home of the Tail Wag's Inn, a quality kennel where you can board your dog for part of a day while you visit Hearst Castle about nine miles north in San Simeon.

Laura, the owner of this kennel, heard of too many dogs who had been left unattended in sweltering cars as their caretakers sauntered around the magnificent castle for hours. So she created a relatively inexpensive, yet luxurious package to encourage people not to risk the lives of their dogs. For $11 (she has upped the price only $1 in 14 years), your kenneled dog gets a "continental breakfast" of dog treats, takes at least two good walks, and drinks Crystal

Springs bottled water. Hey, what the heck, if you're spending the day among opulence, why shouldn't your pup? And the walks aren't just to the corner and back. Laura takes the dogs' needs to heart and strolls them to a nearby grassy area with a creek, trees, "and god knows, lots of smells," she says.

The **Tail Wag's Inn** is a boarding kennel (overnight boarding is the mainstay), but it's the kind of kennel a dog doesn't seem to mind. One regular boarder escaped from her house during a thunderstorm and her owner was frantically looking everywhere for her. Where did she run? To the Tail Wag's Inn, in fact, to the kennel she normally uses. "She was just there barking at her kennel as if to say, 'OK, let me in, and where's my blanket and some food?'" says Laura.

Day-boarding dogs can arrive 8 A.M.–1 P.M. and have to leave by 5 P.M. Reservations are required. This is important, because some folks have thought they could just drive here and drop off their pooches. They've been mighty disappointed when they've had to forgo their trip to Hearst Castle because there was no room at the inn. In addition, your dog's shot record is also required. The kennel is at the Village Service Center, 2419-A Village Lane. Call 805/927-1589 for reservations or more information.

Bad news for dogs who like sand and surf: We've had to eliminate two terrific beaches from the book this time around, thanks to the snowy plover. Moonstone Beach and Shamel County Park's beach no longer permit pooches. Fortunately the boardwalk at Moonstone does. It's a very pleasant little 1.5-mile jaunt each way. There are even poop bags along the way (for your dog, in case you were wondering).

PARKS, BEACHES, AND RECREATION AREAS

See the intro to the Cambria section for a tip on where you can take your dog for a decent stroll overlooking the ocean. The pickings are slim here these days, so dogs tend to take what they can get and not complain.

PLACES TO EAT

Main Street Grill: Your dog is sure to love the smells emanating from the barbecue here. It's a meaty place, with decadent fries to boot. The Grill doesn't have outdoor tables, but there's plenty of grass outside for your picnic-style dining pleasure. We've seen many dog folks sharing their meal with their pooches on the grass. (Do you really have any choice other than to share your barbecued meat with your hungry dog when eating it at dog's-mouth level? We think not.) 603 Main Street; 805/927-3194.

Mustache Pete's: Two dogs wrote to tell us about this fun eatery's covered patio area (which is heated when it gets chilly). Charlie Dog says he felt very welcomed because he got a biscuit upon arrival. And Copper Dog really lucked out: The server gave him a prime rib bone while his person, Kim, enjoyed her spaghetti. "I doubt Copper will ever be the same again after this gourmet snack," writes Kim. There's always a big bowl of water here, too. The gourmet pizzas are delectable, but Terry and Belle (Charlie's people) recommend the meatloaf. 4090 Burton Drive; 805/927-8589.

Pasta Factory: The homemade pastas here are delicious. Dine alfresco with your dog at the breezy patio tables. 1316 Tamsen Street; 805/927-5882.

PLACES TO STAY

Cambria Pines Lodge: You and your dog get to stay at one of nine cabins here that permit pooches. The 25-acre property comes with oodles of Monterey pines for your dog's perusal. Your stay here comes with a full breakfast in the lodge. The cabins are $109–149. Dogs are $25 extra. 2905 Burton Drive 93428; 805/927-4200 or 800/445-6868; www.cambriapineslodge.com.

Cambria Shores Inn: This charming and very dog-friendly little inn is just a bone's throw from the dog-friendly boardwalk at beautiful Moonstone Beach. Literally. You could throw a bone (OK, a tennis ball) from your room, and if you have a good arm, it will cross the street and end up down on the beach. Of course, this won't work if you don't have an ocean-view room, but with three-quarters of the rooms here blessed with ocean views, your chances for a water landing are pretty good.

The innkeepers welcome dogs with open arms and with a VIP dog basket! The basket includes a beach towel (these can be replenished), a matching green sheet to cover the bed if your dog sleeps there (it matches the decor of the room, too), and dog treats (these are not green). "Dogs are our niche," explains a friendly innkeeper. "We like to make them feel right at home." If only home were like this. Upon check-in, humans get homemade chocolate chip cookies. At "hors d'oeuvres hour" in the late afternoon, guests can relax after a long day of fun and eat all kinds of tasty treats, and in the future, drink a little wine. (The inn will be going through a remodel soon. After it's done, the owners will go for a liquor license.) A scrumptious continental breakfast, consisting of fresh fruit, croissants with chocolate nut butter, bagels with cream cheese, a carafe of orange juice, and a dog biscuit (for the Very Important Pooch in your party), is delivered to your room in the morning. If you prefer, you can pick up your breakfast in the lobby.

Rates are $95–180. Dogs are $10 extra, with a maximum of two dogs per room. 6276 Moonstone Beach Drive 93428; 805/927-8644 or 800/433-9179; www.cambriashores.com.

Fogcatcher Inn: If your dog has a look of panic on his face while reading this over your shoulder, reassure him you're not taking him to the Dogcatcher Inn. (This is how I first read the sign, and I figure if I can make that mistake, dogs can too.) In fact, this is one of the most relaxing and lovely places you could stay with a dog in these parts. The inn has a lovely English country style, with vaulted ceilings and gardens that are to drool for almost all year-round. The rooms are spacious and well appointed, and each has a fireplace, microwave, and fridge. The heated outdoor pool has a decent ocean view, and a free hot breakfast buffet comes with your stay here. (No beasts at the buffet, please. We know how literally dogs take the phrase "all you can eat.")

What dogs like best is that they get a dog biscuit or two or three upon check-in. As for size limits, don't worry: "Last weekend we had a big German shepherd and a little Pekingese," says Mike, who loves doggy guests. "We take any good dog." Two rooms allow pets. Rates are $119–320. Dogs are $25 extra. 6400 Moonstone Beach Drive 93428; 805/927-1400 or 800/425-4121; www.fogcatcherinn.com.

Mariner's Inn: The owners here like dogs; they have a 132-pound English mastiff who's the sweetest thing around. Some of the rooms have ocean views. Rates are $55–210. Dogs are $10 extra. 6180 Moonstone Beach Drive 93428; 805/927-4624 or 800/344-0407; www.marinersinncambria.com.

Atascadero

PARKS, BEACHES, AND RECREATION AREAS

🐾 Atascadero Lake Park

🐾🐾 (See San Luis Obispo County map on page 654)

Great blue herons, ducks of every shape, bluebirds, and even red-tailed hawks are just a few of the birds you may see during a visit to this large city park. Dogs have to be on leash to explore the lake and surrounding lawns and picnic areas, but they seem to enjoy themselves despite the constraints.

This is the place to take your dog in Atascadero. While they aren't allowed to swim or rent a paddleboat, they revel in life's simple pleasures, such as sniffing each other end to end.

The Charles Paddock Zoo is next door. Instead of those typical zoo odors, this place smells like fresh jasmine when you walk by. It's good if you're trying to fool your dog into thinking you just dropped off the kids at some botanical garden and not at the home of wild and smelly animals.

From U.S. 101, take Santa Rosa Road west for three long blocks. The park is on your right, between Mountain View Drive and Morro Road. For the best parking, turn right on Morro Road and make another right into the park. 805/461-5000.

PLACES TO STAY

Motel 6: Rates are $44 for one adult, $7 for the second adult. 9400 El Camino Real 93422; 805/466-6701.

Cayucos

A funkier coastal community would be hard to find. Cayucos, about eight miles north of Morro Bay, provides a great escape from summer crowds. Even on holiday weekends, the place doesn't get packed. The Old West stores and saloons are a real find, but if you'd rather fish than shop and drink, try the old pier on Cayucos State Beach. It was built in 1875, and those in charge figure a few dogs aren't going to hurt it now. Besides, the fishing is great, and what dog wouldn't enjoy watching you reel in a mackerel or a salmon?

PARKS, BEACHES, AND RECREATION AREAS

❸ Cayucos State Beach

🐾🐾🐾🐾 (See San Luis Obispo County map on page 654)

This beach is wide and wonderful, and dogs are actually allowed here on a leash! This is a big contrast to other state beaches in the area. Since the county actually runs the beach, and since there aren't big environmental issues at this one, dogs are still OK.

A couple of good greasy-spoon joints lurk nearby. We like to order lunch and bring it to the beach, where dogs pray hard that you'll drop a french fry in the sand.

The south end of the beach has fewer people and more seaweed—the stuff of fine dog outings. From Highway 1, go southwest on Cayucos Drive and turn left at Ocean Drive. You can enter almost anywhere between Cayucos Road and E Street, west of Ocean Drive. 805/781-5930.

PLACES TO STAY

Cayucos Beach Inn: This attractive, upscale, very dog-friendly motel is one block from the ocean, with easy beach access. Dogs love this. And they really love how they're treated here. Upon arrival, dogs get a Pet Package with dog treats, white towels (decorated with paw prints) for use after beach romps, a dog blanket, and temporary pet ID tags (when in stock). The inn is so well set up for dogs that there's even a special hose outside for rinsing off wet, sandy dogs. Dogs don't like this, but it helps keep the place clean.

Room amenities for humans include fridges, microwaves, a wet bar, very comfy pillow-top beds, and a delicious continental breakfast. Many rooms have ocean views. Rates are $85–125. Dogs are $10 for the first night, $5 thereafter. That fee is good for up to three dogs! And it's not a per-pooch fee, but a per-stay fee. That's a doggone good deal, considering what they get. 333 South Ocean Avenue 93430; 805/995-2828 or 800/482-0555; www.cayucosbeachinn.com.

Dolphin Inn: Frankly, I'd stay here just for the name, but the inn has other attractive features, such as its proximity to the water and a continental breakfast that comes with your room. Rates are $59–169. Dogs pay a flat fee of $10. 399 South Ocean Avenue 93430; 805/995-3810 or 800/540-4276; www.thedolphininn.com.

Estero Bay Motel: Just a half block from the ocean, this U-shaped motel is a fine place to spend the night with your dog. We like the owner's explanation for the motel's dog-friendly policy: "There are a lot of nice older women who have dogs they just can't part with. We want to help them stay together." *Awwww.* Rates are $59–129. Dogs are $10 extra. 25 South Ocean Avenue 93430; 805/995-3614 or 800/736-1292; www.esterobaymotel.com.

Shoreline Inn: If your dog longs for sand between his toes, stay here. This attractive inn is a few long steps from the beach, where leashed pooches are allowed. All rooms have a view of the strand, surf, and ocean. The rooms are typical motel-style, but the suites are really lovely. They're light and airy, and all feature private balconies and TVs with extended cable channels. Our favorite two suites have fridges and fireplaces. All rooms and suites come with VCRs, which is a real plus when traveling with kids. Rates are $80–140. Dogs pay a flat $10 fee. 1 North Ocean Avenue 93430; 805/995-3681 or 800/549-2244; www.cayucosshorelineinn.com.

Morro Bay

The landmark Morro Rock draws more visitors to this seaside community than its beaches and quaint stores. This 576-foot-tall, 50-acre-wide extinct volcano peak juts into the Pacific and beckons anyone who gets a glimpse. In fact, in 1512 it attracted explorer Juan Rodríguez Cabrillo, who named the rock, which has become a landmark for ocean navigators and tourists. Dogs are no longer allowed to visit the rock, since it's part of the whole rotten deal with state beaches in the area. But they can come mighty close by visiting Coleman City Park.

PARKS, BEACHES, AND RECREATION AREAS

🐾 Coleman City Park

🐾🐾 (See San Luis Obispo County map on page 654)

This is the park to visit if you forgot your sunscreen. At the right time of day, the shadow of Morro Rock will loom over you and protect you from those wrinkling rays. Walking through the dunes here while under the spell of the volcanic mound can be a hypnotic experience. Don't let the otherworldly quality of it all make you forget that your dog is supposed to be leashed.

There's a little area just north of the rock where dogs are allowed to wet their paws, since it's not state land. Water dogs, and any dog who is running a little warm, really appreciate this. The park is to the north of Morro Rock. For easy access, park in the Morro Rock lot, after Embarcadero turns into Coleman Drive. There's another lot for the park on the north side of Coleman Drive just before the rock. 805/772-6200.

PLACES TO EAT

Dorn's Original Breakers Cafe: The specials here include clam chowder, fresh seafood, and New York steaks. Dogs are welcome at the patio in back. 801 Market Avenue; 805/772-4415.

PLACES TO STAY

Adventure Inn: This place faces the waterfront and has terrific views of Morro Rock, a view the Adventure Inn claims is the best view in Morro Bay. The rooms are small, but there's a pool and an attractive sunning area with a hot tub. Rooms have fridges and come with a continental breakfast. Rates are $59–139. Dogs are $10 extra. 1150 Embarcadero 93442; 805/772-5607 or 800/799-5607; www.adventureinn.net.

Best Western El Rancho: Rates are $69–99. Dogs pay a $10 fee for the length of their stay, up to seven days. 2460 Main Street 93442; 805/772-2212; www.bestwestern.com.

Keystone Inn/Sandpiper Motel: Medium and smaller dogs can stay at this 1960s-era motel. It's bright white with aqua doors—a real throwback to the glory days of motels. The rooms are small but not cramped. The smaller room size is one reason big dogs can't stay here. The other: fur. "It adheres to everything, and the bigger dogs have more of it," says innkeeper Priscilla. "It even clings to the plants outside the room doors." Bring a lint roller if you really want to make her happy. She's a nice woman, and she likes her plants. An empty lot across the street is decent for a pit stop, as long as you scoop the poop. Rates are $49–$99. Dogs are $10 extra. 540 Main Street 93442; 805/772-7503 or 888/900-3692; www.keystoneinn.com.

Morro Bay State Park: This verdant state park overlooking Morro Bay has 135 campsites set in pine woodlands. Dogs are banned from the park's trails and from every other natural wonder. Campsites and paved roads are their only stomping grounds. At press time, the campground was under construction and scheduled to reopen in mid-2005. Fees were not available. Take Highway 1 to the south end of Morro Bay and follow the signs to the park. This campground gets crowded, so call 800/444-7275 for reservations.

Morro Dunes Travel Trailer Park and Resort Campground: I'm not sure the name of this place is long enough. Anyway, there's plenty of space for recreational vehicles and tents here, and the view of Morro Rock is pretty good from some areas. But what dogs like best is that Morro Dunes has its very own little dog run in back for dogs who need to exercise off leash. It makes it worth staying here, even if you're a tenter who balks at life among the trailers. Rates are $15–20. 1700 Embarcadero 93442; 805/772-2722; www.morrodunes.com.

Morro Strand State Beach: The beach gets much less use than many others around here, and it used to be heavenly for dogs. But now dogs are allowed only at the 104-site campground. The campground is nothing fancy or rustic. It's actually a converted parking lot. But it's right over the beach, so if sounds of crashing surf send you to sleep, you'll get your eight hours here. Camping costs $21–30. The beach/campground is west of Highway 1 between Atascadero Road and Yerba Buena Avenue. For camping reservations, call 800/444-7275.

Motel 6: Rates are $70–81 for one adult, $6 for the second adult. 298 Atascadero Road 93442; 805/772-5641.

San Luis Obispo

This city is the big jewel of the Central Coast. Some of the smaller gems such as Pismo Beach and Morro Bay can be more lustrous for dogs, but there's so much history here, and so much to do, that you're both bound to enjoy your visit.

If the past interests you at all, be sure to stop at the Chamber of Commerce and pick up a Heritage Walks pamphlet showing the fascinating buildings where much of California's history was shaped. Dogs may yawn as they trot by some of the ice cream–colored Victorians and whitewashed adobes, but when they arrive at Mission Plaza, the good times roll.

The plaza is the heart of the city and the home of Mission San Luis Obispo de Tolosa, built in 1772. Dogs aren't allowed inside, but it's the world outside that will interest them more anyway. That's where the beautiful Mission Plaza tantalizes with scents and sounds dogs love. A brick path follows a cool stream nestled in conifers full of songbirds and takes you by a few delicious-smelling restaurants with tables on the wood patios overlooking the stream.

But beware: The reason dogs like it here so much isn't necessarily for the food or ambience. They're wild about all the four-legged creatures who slink around here meowing for handouts of food and attention. If you have a cat-crazed canine, either avoid this area or keep a very tight hold on her leash.

PARKS, BEACHES, AND RECREATION AREAS

🐾 El Chorro Regional Park

🐾🐾🐾🐾 (See San Luis Obispo County map on page 654)

For some reason, not that many people visit this 1,730-acre park, except on holidays and some summer weekends. You'll rarely find others on the four miles of trail here, but you may well run into deer, so keep your dog leashed. (The exception: the fairly new dog park within the boundaries of the park. See below for details.)

It's not even that common to see people using the many group picnic areas. There are 45 developed campsites, all with full hookups. Sites are $16–25. On weekends and holidays April–September, there's a $2 fee for dogs to get into the park, as well as a $2 per-vehicle fee. Driving south on U.S. 101, take the

---

DIVERSION

Catch a Fur Flick: The **Sunset Drive-In Theater** allows quiet dogs for no extra charge. Some pooches really enjoy a movie starring a dog, so be sure to bring your best friend if you notice one playing. Rates are $6 per human adult. Kids under 11 are free. 255 Elks Lane, San Luis Obispo; 805/544-4475.

Santa Rosa Street/Highway 1 exit. Turn left on Santa Rosa (which turns into Highway 1 after Highland Drive). Continue about five miles. The park is on your right across from Cuesta College. 805/781-5930.

6 El Chorro Regional Park Dog Park

🐾🐾🐾🐾🐕 (See San Luis Obispo County map on page 654)

How many dog parks have a big, working barbecue pit in them? The fenced-in dog park at El Chorro Regional Park is a hot dog place, in more than one sense: It's a very popular dog park, and it really does have a huge barbecue pit in it. (It's about three feet by 10 feet. That's 30 square feet of dog heaven.) Cooking juicy burgers, hot dogs, and chicken in the center of a bunch of dogs who have worked up big appetites seems like an invitation to trouble, but apparently it's never been a problem here. (Then again, Jake has never been here during a cookout.)

Small and large dogs have separate areas (the grill is in the large-dog section). There's fresh water, and plenty of trees, picnic tables, and tennis balls. Gus the Dog, who visits the park almost every day, wrote to tell us that he adores the wood chips that cover the ground here. "It makes for great digging and chewing on sticks!" he wrote, via his translator, Erin.

The dog park is in the rear of El Chorro Regional Park (see previous listing for directions), within the Lupine group picnic area. There are signs once you're in the park entrance. On weekends April–September and on holidays, there's a $2 fee for dogs to get into the park, as well as a $1.50 per-vehicle fee. 805/781-5930.

7 Laguna Lake Park

🐾🐾🐾 (See San Luis Obispo County map on page 654)

Early morning is the best time to visit this beautiful, large city park shaded by willows, pines, and eucalyptuses. That's when it's the coolest and most peaceful. The moist morning air and the smell of pine, clean earth, and fresh lake water intermingle and make for a relaxing outing for you and your fine furry friend.

During days when the park is a little crowded (it rarely gets this way), there are still plenty of spots for you and your dog to escape from the masses. If you follow the Fitness Trail and bear right after Fitness Stop Number 8, you'll come to secluded fields abutting a marshy part of the lake. If you're not doing the Fitness Trail, you'll find this quiet area by walking to the other side of the long line of eucalyptus trees past the gazebo. In addition, there's a wonderful boon here for dogs, but a park ranger swore me to not give away the details in print yet. My lips are sealed.

From U.S. 101, take the Los Osos Valley Road exit northwest for several blocks and turn right on Madonna Road. In a few blocks, go left on Dalido Drive and park at any of the several lots in the park. 805/781-5930 or 805/781-7300.

PLACES TO EAT

Country Yogurt Culture: Enter from the Mission Plaza side, where you and your dog can enjoy creekside tables and eight flavors of award-winning yogurt. The friendly service makes dogs feel right at home. 746 Higuera Street; 805/544-9007.

Mo's Smokehouse: Even the most effete dogs drool when they smell this place. It's meaty, it's smoky, it harks back to primitive days (except for the cole slaw). Thirsty dogs get a bowl of water. Dine outside at the umbrella-topped tables. 970 Higuera Street; 805/544-6193.

Rudolph's Coffee and Tea Company: Enjoy a spot of tea, coffee, or hot chocolate while your dog guards your muffin for you. 670 Higuera Street; 805/543-4902.

San Luis Fish and Barbeque: If you and Tex feel like good ol' barbecued anything, this is the place to get it. Slurp it down at the tables out front. 474 Marsh Street; 805/541-4191.

Uptown Espresso: Sip yours with a fresh bagel and your dog at your side on the large patio. You can even buy a pooch biscuit for a quarter. 1065 Higuera Street; 805/783-1300.

PLACES TO STAY

Best Western Royal Oak Motor Hotel: This is a terrific place to stay if your dog wants to stretch his legs. It's a quick walk to beautiful Laguna Lake Park (see above). When you're done walking, you can wash your sweaty clothes at the motel's laundry facility. Rates are $79–129. Dogs are $10 for the length of their stay. 214 Madonna Road 93405; 805/544-4410; www.royaloakhotel.com.

Days Inn San Luis Obispo: This newly remodeled Days Inn rates "5 Sunbursts," which is Days Inn lingo for super-duper. The rooms are big and airy, with furnishings that are a cut above those of most Days Inns. You'll get a fresh and fruity breakfast here. You'll also have access to a heated outdoor pool, hot tub, and exercise room. Your dog will have access to a nearby green strip. Everyone will be happy. Rates are $69–149. Dogs are $10 extra, and the management likes to keep them under 50 pounds, but that doesn't always happen. 2050 Garfield Street 93401; 800/544-7250.

El Chorro Regional Park: See El Chorro Regional Park, above, for camping information.

Heritage Inn Bed and Breakfast: Very well behaved dogs who promise not to rile the owner's cat can stay with you on weekdays at this lovely, antique-furnished Victorian house. Advance arrangements are essential. The owner is careful about which dogs get to stay here. Joe would definitely not have been a welcome guest because of his tendency to try to make cats into eats. Dogs who get to stay are lucky indeed. The inn, while not in a rural area, is in a natural creekside setting. Pooches who do the dog paddle love it. Rates are $85–150 and include a full breakfast and a wine and cheese hour in the afternoon. Dogs pay a $35 flat fee. 978 Olive Street 93405; 805/544-7440; www.heritageinnslo.com.

Holiday Inn Express: Stay here and you can swim in the heated outdoor pool and have a free continental breakfast. Your dog can't, but don't feel bad: He's not paying the bill. Rates are $89–109. Dogs are $25 extra for the length of their stay. 1800 Monterey Street 93401; 805/544-8600.

Motel 6: There's a big field in back where dogs are allowed, at least for now. Rates are $50–72 for one adult, $6 for the second adult. 1625 Calle Joaquin 93401; 805/541-6992.

Sands Suites and Motel: The Sands is a good place to stay if you need to do your laundry (or your dog's) after a few days on the road. It's got a little laundry facility if you've got the quarters. Rates (for rooms, not laundry) are $79–169. Dogs pay a $10 flat fee. 1930 Monterey Street 93401; 805/544-0500 or 800/441-4657; www.sandssuites.com.

Vagabond Inn: Rates are $69–145. Dogs are $10 extra. 210 Madonna Road 93401; 805/544-4710 or 800/522-1555.

Santa Margarita

PARKS, BEACHES, AND RECREATION AREAS

🐾 Santa Margarita Recreation Area

🐾🐾🐾 (See San Luis Obispo County map on page 654)

You and your dog don't have to like swimming or fishing to enjoy this park centered around Santa Margarita Lake. If hiking is more your style, try the 10 miles of trails that weave through the area. Keep your dog leashed and watch out for horses.

For the rest of the family, there are playgrounds, horseshoe pits, and a swimming pool. And if you just can't help throwing a line in the water, you may well land supper.

The entry fee is $6 per car and $2 per dog. But there's plenty of parking just outside the park if you want to avoid the vehicle fee. The park even has camping, for $16 per site. (Dogs also pay $2 for camping.) From U.S. 101, take the Highway 58 exit and drive east about four miles. Follow the signs the rest of the way. 805/788-2397.

PLACES TO STAY

KOA at Santa Margarita Lake: You and your dog can camp at the 110 sites a quarter mile from the lake, and then fish for catfish, trout, bass, or crappie (CROP-py, in case angling isn't your cup of fish). Rates are $29–65. Dogs aren't allowed in the Kamping Kabins here. 4765 Santa Margarita Lake Road, Santa Margarita, CA 93453; 805/438-5618.

Santa Margarita Recreation Area: See Santa Margarita Recreation Area, above, for camping information.

Avila Beach

This small coastal community is about the farthest north you'll find the Southern California beach lifestyle. And if you hear three siren blasts, prepare to have the beaches to yourself—the Diablo Canyon Nuclear Plant, which sits on a fault six miles north of town, just may have had a little boo-boo.

PARKS, BEACHES, AND RECREATION AREAS

🐾 Olde Port Beach

😺😺😺 (See San Luis Obispo County map on page 654)

Dogs, get your hankies ready. This used to be the only off-leash beach in this part of California. But leashes are now the law. (Sniff, honk.) That's a shame, because the beach is secluded, with nary a soul around.

It's still a much better beach for dogs than Avila Beach (see below) and most state beaches in the county (which no longer even permit pooches). The name itself is picturesque, and so is the beach, looking out as it does on fishing boats moored offshore. If you have any salt in your blood, you'll enjoy the view from here. The occasional rider of personal watercraft can mar the tranquility, but if you visit in the cooler months, they are usually off doing more quiet activities.

From Highway 1/U.S. 101, take the Avila Beach exit west. Once in town, continue west, on Harford Drive. The beach is on your left. If you reach the Port San Luis Pier (not the modern, very long Union Oil Pier you'll come to first, but the woody old one in the harbor), you've gone too far. It's not so bad, though. You can either turn right around and find the beach or hang out at the pier and harbor area for a while. Dogs are fond of those fishy breezes and you'll enjoy looking at the old boats. 805/595-5400.

🔟 Avila Beach

☙☙ (See San Luis Obispo County map on page 654)

If you have images of strolling down the beach paw-in-hand with your dog all day long, change that image. Or at least change the hours. Dogs are permitted here, but only before 10 A.M. and after 5 P.M. You can understand the restrictions if you come here in the summer, when the place looks like Son of Jones Beach.

Dogs must be leashed. The beach runs along Front Street in the main part of Avila Beach. 805/595-5400.

PLACES TO STAY

Avila Hot Springs Spa and RV Resort: If you want to treat yourself like a king or queen, and you have an RV, stay here. You won't be able to sleep at the spa's luxurious suites or rooms because you're traveling with your pooch, but you may camp here. RVs are welcome, as are the dogs who stay in them. Granted, it's not very regal to stay in a traveling tin box, but that's OK, because the real royal treatment here is given in the spa. The massages and mineral baths are out of this world. Avila Hot Springs is famous for its spa treatments. Take turns with your human friend walking your dog friend around the beautiful grounds (on leash) so you can each get massages without having to leave your pooch alone. Sorry, but no dog massages are given. There are also a swimming pool and a hot mineral pool here, but dogs aren't allowed in those either.

Camping is $30–40. Call for spa prices—they're reasonable. 250 Avila Beach Drive; 805/595-2359 or 800/332-2359; www.avilahotsprings.com.

Pismo Beach

The Chumash Indians, who lived here for at least 9,000 years, referred to this area as the place to find *pismu,* or tar. History has changed this once-pristine land to a busy seaside community, but your dog might show you that there's one thing that hasn't changed: This is still the place to find tar. Joe found it all over his paws when he was exploring one of the beaches. Later, despite cleaning his feet, I found it all over the inside of the truck. Even the dry cleaner found it—he found it amusing that the jacket I'd left inside the truck was covered with indelible paw prints.

This never happened again, and it has never happened to any other dogs we talked to on the beaches, so fear not. Pismo Beach is a good place for you and your dog to share some quality time. Most of the beaches here allow leashed dogs, who can be champion partners in clamming for the famous Pismo clams. They don't need a fishing license, but you will.

Pismo Beach is usually cool and foggy. It's ideal if you have a dog who melts in the heat. When we drive to Southern California, this is a must-stop area for whatever dog we're chauffeuring. Although there are no leash-free areas, they always appreciate land that is naturally air-conditioned.

PARKS, BEACHES, AND RECREATION AREAS

City parks here don't allow dogs. The 1,250-foot pier in the middle of the beach area also bans them. But there are a couple of beaches that more than make up for these places.

11 Oceano Dunes/Pismo State Beach

🐾🐾🐾🐾 (See San Luis Obispo County map on page 654)

It's hard to tell what dogs enjoy more here—exploring the long, wide beach or wandering through the great dunes above. Your leashed dog can get all the exercise he needs by trotting down the miles of trails on the unspoiled dunes. If he likes cold ocean spray, take him down to the beach for a romp among the gulls. (Dogs are allowed at both of these state beaches. This is a huge relief when you've come from the dog-verboten state beaches to the north.)

Camping is available at a couple of sections of the beach. Fees are $10 for the on-beach camping area south of the Grand Avenue entrance (four-wheel-drive vehicles are recommended) and $20–29 for camping among the trees at the Pismo State Beach North Beach Campground. There are a total of 185 campsites. For more info, call 805/489-1869. Call for reservations: 800/444-7275.

To avoid the $6 day-use fee at the Grand Avenue entrance, drive west from Highway 1 and park on Grand Avenue before the ranger kiosk. Once at the beach, head north. Walking south will put you in the middle of a busy off-highway vehicle area—not the best place for a dog. 805/473-7230.

12 Pismo Beach City Beach

🐾🐾🐾 (See San Luis Obispo County map on page 654)

Does your dog like watching people in bathing suits play volleyball? Does she enjoy sniffing at bodies slathered with coconut oil? If so, this beach is for her. It's rarely so crowded that it's uncomfortable, but it's rarely so uncrowded that it's a bore for a social butterfly dog.

The farther north you walk, the fewer people you'll encounter. Dogs have to be leashed everywhere, though. But this shouldn't stop the digging breeds from helping you uncover prize Pismo clams (fishing licenses are required for the human half of the team). We once saw a dog who would thrust his entire snout into the wet sand and come up with a clam every time. His owner didn't even have to use his clam fork.

One of the many access points is west of Highway 1, at the foot of Main Avenue near the recreation pier. 805/773-4658.

PLACES TO EAT

Old West Cinnamon Rolls: This little café has some of the best cinnamon rolls we've ever laid teeth on. They're hot, sticky, and absolutely decadent. Enjoy them at the front bench with your pooch at your side. 861 Dolliver Street; 805/773-1428.

The Scoop Ice Cream Parlor: When you say "The Scoop" to most dog people, they tend to think of the plastic bags, newspapers, or little shovels they use for scooping the, well, you get the picture. But this ice-cream parlor is so good that "The Scoop" might hold a whole new meaning to you after you visit with your pooch. Hang out, cone in hand, canine at feet, at the outdoor seating. 607 Dolliver Street; 805/773-4253.

PLACES TO STAY

Cottage Inn by the Sea: Stay here and you get a very attractive, spacious, country-style room with a gas fireplace, a fridge, and a microwave. You also get a deluxe continental breakfast. About the only thing you don't get is an ocean view. People without dogs can get the ocean views, but people with dogs have to settle for looking at the Pacific from the terrific pool and spa, which is on a bluff over the ocean. (Pooches can peep at the Pacific only from the beach itself, since they need to stay away from the pool area.) The best part for dogs is that the pet-friendly rooms are on the ground level, and each has a fenced area in back. This makes dogs smile. So do the biscuits they get at check-in. Rates are $99–179. Dogs are $10 extra. 2351 Price Street 93449; 805/773-4617 or 888/440-8400; www.cottage-inn.com.

Motel 6: Rates are $35–62 for one adult and $4 for the second adult. 860 4th Street 93449; 805/773-2665.

Oceano Dunes/Pismo State Beach: See Oceano Dunes/Pismo State Beach, above, for camping information.

Oxford Suites: From the attractive lobby with the tiled fountain and big fireplace to the guest suites, which include a work table (should you actually want to work while in Pismo Beach), sofa, microwave, and fridge, this place is a comfy home away from home. It's ideal for traveling with a dog, because you can do some kind of cooking here. Oxford Suites looks motelish from the outside, but once you're inside it doesn't really feel that way. Your stay here includes a full breakfast buffet and an evening reception with beverages and light hors d'oeuvres. There's even a year-round pool, but dogs have to keep their paws on terra firma. Rates are $89–149. Dogs are $5 extra, and they pay a $5 cleaning fee. 651 Five Cities Drive 93449; 805/773-3773 or 800/982-7848; www.pismobeachoxfordsuites.com.

Sandcastle Inn: This one's comfortable, attractive, and on the beach. Even dogs enjoy an ocean view. Rates are $139–269. Dogs are $10 extra. 100 Stimson Avenue 93449; 805/773-2422; www.sandcastleinn.com.

Sea Gypsy Motel: If you're looking for a reasonably priced room or studio apartment on the beach, pull your caravan over to the Sea Gypsy Motel. It's conveniently situated a couple of blocks from "downtown" Pismo Beach, and it has a heated pool in case the ocean is a little too clammy for you. Rates are $45–145. Dogs are $15 extra. 1020 Cypress Street 93449; 805/773-1801 or 800/592-5923; www.seagypsymotel.com.

Spyglass Inn: This is a great place for the family, from the breakfast to the pool to the miniature golf course. Many of the rooms have ocean views. The managers don't like gigantic dogs as guests, but they're pretty generous about the size of the pooches they'll accept. Dogs are allowed only in the downstairs rooms. Rates are $149–279. Dogs are $10 extra. 2705 Spyglass Drive 93449; 805/773-4855 or 800/824-2612; www.spyglassinn.com.

Arroyo Grande

PARKS, BEACHES, AND RECREATION AREAS

🐾 Lopez Lake Recreation Area

🐾🐾 (See San Luis Obispo County map on page 654)

The rules at this county-run park are just like those at state parks: Dogs are not allowed anywhere but at campsites and paved areas. It's a restrictive, frustrating place for dogs. All the trailheads are marked by something that looks like a horse with a slash through it. Rangers swear it's a dog, though a big one. But if you sneak your dog onto a trail and get caught, don't try the old

"I thought it meant 'No Great Danes'" excuse. They've heard it before and it didn't work then either.

The 940-acre lake is off-limits to dogs, unless they fish in your boat with you. In fact, most of the 4,200-acre park bans dogs. Plenty of dogs do camp here, though, at any of the 359 sites set in oak woodlands. Reservations are recommended. Leashes are mandatory, and dogs are supposed to sleep in your tent or camper at night. A bear is resident here, as are plenty of deer.

The entrance fee is $6 per car, $2 per dog. Campsites are $16–25. Call for reservations. As always, be prepared with proof of your dog's rabies vaccination. You'll probably need it here. Exit U.S. 101 at Grand Avenue and travel northeast, following the signs to Lopez Lake. 805/781-5930.

PLACES TO STAY

Lopez Lake Recreation Area: See Lopez Lake Recreation Area, above, for camping information.

Nipomo

PARKS, BEACHES, AND RECREATION AREAS

14 Nipomo Regional Park Dog Park

🐾🐾🐾🐕 (See San Luis Obispo County map on page 654)

Tree-loving dogs enjoy sniffing out the scents of a few big pines here and even the woodchip ground cover. Jake tends to think the chips are bones, and he parades them around with a big grin on his snout as if to say, "Hey! Look what

I got! Yup, and you don't!" to his dog pals. The dog park has the usual amenities, including poop bags and picnic tables. It's within the larger regional park, so if you want to take your dog around to watch a ball game or just stroll past picnickers (temptations to quiver for, for some dogs), you can do that too.

It costs $2 per dog and $1.50 per vehicle to enter the regional park on weekends April–September and on holidays. From U.S. 101, take the West Tefft Street exit and drive west. The park entrance is on the right, just past the Nipomo Library. The dog park area is on the West Tefft Street side, near the Pine day-use area. 805/781-5930.

CHAPTER 49

Kern County

This large southern San Joaquin Valley county is a diverse land o' plenty. There are plenty o' farms, plenty o' deserts, plenty o' mountains, and plenty o' windmills—5,000 to be exact, enough to make Don Quixote quiver.

The county also has plenty of fertilizer, and that fact will jump right out at you as you cruise down certain roads during certain fertilizer seasons. Bring a gas mask or forever hold your breath. When we drove through one fine October afternoon, the humans in the car turned green from the extra-ripe cow-patty smell. The dogs just sat there mesmerized, with big smiles on their snouts.

NATIONAL FORESTS

The National Forests and Wilderness Areas resource at the back of this book has important information and safety tips on visiting national forests with your dog and has more information on the national forests listed below.

PICK OF THE LITTER—KERN COUNTY

BEST LEASH-FREE HIKE
Kern National Wildlife Refuge, Delano (page 680)

MOST INTERESTING USE OF DRAINAGE BASINS/SUMPS
City of Bakersfield dog parks (page 684)

GOOD, CLEAN FUN
20 Mule Team Museum, Boron (page 689)

Los Padres National Forest

A sliver of this huge national forest pokes into the southwest edge of Kern County.

Sequoia National Forest

Only little segments of this grand forest dribble into Kern County from Tulare County.

Delano

PARKS, BEACHES, AND RECREATION AREAS

1 Kern National Wildlife Refuge
😾😾😾😾 🐾 (See Kern County map on page 678)

If your dog hunts waterfowl, she'll find this 10,618-acre refuge a four-paw destination. If your dog isn't a hunter, as long as she doesn't chase or harass wildlife, she's welcome, too. (Just be careful during the hunting seasons.)

There's a great auto tour route that goes around the natural valley grasslands and marsh areas. Wildlife-watching is excellent. There are at least 200 species of birds here during the year, along with all sorts of other critters. You may see snowy egrets, ring-billed gulls, warblers, peregrine falcons, endangered San Joaquin kit foxes, and leopard lizards. If you're walking around the refuge, be sure your dog is leashed when near the wildlife. In more open spaces, dogs under voice control can be leashless. Dogs aren't allowed in the water certain times of year. If you have a water dog, phone first to find out so she won't be crying on your shoulder all the way home.

From I-5 around the town of Lost Hills, take Highway 46 five miles east to Corcoran Road and turn north. Drive 10.6 miles and you'll be at the refuge. 661/725-2767.

Alta Sierra

PARKS, BEACHES, AND RECREATION AREAS

❷ Greenhorn Mountain County Park
🐾🐾🐾 (See Kern County map on page 678)

This rugged park is surrounded by extraordinary Sequoia National Forest land. While the park itself is a speck compared with the forest, it resembles the wooded wonderland in every other way except one: Dogs must be leashed. Jake likes the place, but it's really easy to drive down the road a bit and start on a real wilderness hike in the national forest.

Greenhorn is slightly more civilized, if that's what your dog prefers. It's got a playground and a picnic area. But most of the undeveloped forest areas at Greenhorn are as wild as the surrounding national forest land. Its 160 acres are set at 6,000 feet. Trails run through thick cedar and white fir forests.

The park is on Highway 155, about six miles west of Lake Isabella. 661/868-7000.

Lake Isabella

PARKS, BEACHES, AND RECREATION AREAS

❸ Lake Isabella
🐾🐾🐾 (See Kern County map on page 678)

If what you want is a long hike with your leash-free dog, don't expect to find it right here. The land is surrounded by Sequoia National Forest, but there really aren't any trails around the lake. Just a short drive up the road, you'll find all the nude dog hiking you could imagine. Ask a ranger for directions to the national forest trails.

You can walk around some of the lake with your dog, but he must be leashed. With 38 miles of shoreline, this is the largest freshwater lake in Southern California, and it's worth taking a look around. The bird-watching is hot here, and so is the fishing for such goodies as largemouth bass.

There are nearly 800 campsites. Some sites are available on a first-come, first-served basis. Reservations are recommended for holiday weekends; call 877/444-6777. Campsites are $17; there are four no-fee primitive sites available. Some offer blissful seclusion. The lake is at Highways 155 and 178. From Bakersfield, head east on Highway 178 for about 30 miles. Call the ranger office for directions to your particular destination within the lake area. 760/379-5646.

PLACES TO STAY

Lake Isabella: See Lake Isabella, above, for camping information.

Inyokern

Friends who visited from New York could only call this town "Inyoface." It was amusing for at least a few seconds the first time they said it. But dogs find high amusement at the Chimney Peak Recreation Area, which lets them run around off leash and get rid of all that pent-up canine energy.

PARKS, BEACHES, AND RECREATION AREAS

🄴 Chimney Peak Recreation Area

🐾🐾🐾🐾 (See Kern County map on page 678)

This 13,600-acre swath of land is not the Mojave Desert and it's not the Sierra Nevada. It's somewhere in between—a transition zone with less severe temperatures and an unusual mix of vegetation.

You and your well-mannered mutt will enjoy hiking through pinyon and juniper woodlands, foothill pines, sage, and desert needlegrass. In the spring, wildflowers explode with color and the place comes to life.

Speaking of coming to life, a brochure produced by the Bureau of Land Management describes another aspect of nature here: "Highlighting the wildlife attractions of the area are mule deer, black bear, mountain lion, bobcat...." These are just a few of the reasons leashes are now the law here.

The trails join with the surrounding dog-friendly national forest land, making this piece of dog heaven seem utterly vast. While there's plenty of good BLM turf in Kern County, the best section of the Chimney Peak Recreation Area is in Tulare County to the north. You can get there by taking Highway

178 to Canebrake Road and heading north. You may stop on the Kern side of the border if you wish, but the Tulare side has the good campgrounds and trails. 661/391-6000.

Wasco

PARKS, BEACHES, AND RECREATION AREAS

5 Westside Park

😾😾 (See Kern County map on page 678)

Park staff labored hard to get some little hills built into this 17-acre park. "We didn't want it to be flat and boring like the rest of the landscape," a city worker told me. In addition to some contours, the park has many different adolescent trees, including rose hill ashes, elms, oaks, and even some redwoods.

The park is in the west end of town, just west of Beckes Street, at Parkside Drive. 661/758-3081.

Oildale

If you like oil (the dark, inedible kind), you'll love this town. Grasshopper-like oil derricks are everywhere. Tanks, too. It's an interesting place to visit if you happen to be sick of forests and other forms of pristine landscapes.

PARKS, BEACHES, AND RECREATION AREAS

6 Standard Park

🐾 (See Kern County map on page 678)

Old railroad cars and oil tanks clutter the area just to the east of the park. There's no mistaking where you are: You're in Oildale, land of much oil and many places named after the oil companies that have a stake in the town.

Standard Park is a flat 15-acre park edged with trees. If your leashed dog needs to get out of the car, it's a tolerable place for a little stretching and a few leg lifts. The park is a block south of Norris Road, just east of North Chester Avenue. 661/392-2000.

Bakersfield

This is the country music capital of California. You'll know it when you turn on your car radio. Find yourself a good country station, and as you cruise past oil derricks and the surrounding agricultural land, you'll feel right at home.

Bakersfield also happens to be the hub of the southern San Joaquin Valley. It doesn't draw many tourists, but whether you live here or just do business here (with your pooch, of course), you'll find enough decently dog-friendly parks to make your friendly dog happy.

PARKS, BEACHES, AND RECREATION AREAS

Bakersfield has gone to the dogs of late: There are now four grassy areas within larger city parks where dogs can run around without leashes, and that number was likely to increase soon. But don't call these fenced-in areas "dog parks." They're not strictly devoted to dogs. Soccer players and other park users can hang out in these areas. At this point it's kind of a first-come, first-served situation. So far, the easygoing policy has worked well. "If someone's there first and someone else wants to use it, they work it out," says friendly, helpful park supervisor Joe Gonzalez.

The dog areas have no amenities other than poop stations and double gates. Their real purpose, and the reason they're fenced and gated, is that they're actually drainage basins. When it rains, excess rainwater has to go somewhere. It comes here. The areas can get pretty sumpy at times and often close for a few days after it rains. But being Bakersfield, as opposed to a soggier place such as Seattle, the areas dry out fairly quickly and are usually back in action within a few days of a heavy rain. The dogs of Bakersfield do lots of wagging when they see those gates unlock again.

7 Centennial Park Dog Area

🐾🐾🐾🐕 (See Kern County map on page 678)

This is the largest of the city's four leash-free dog areas. Dogs here get to whiz around on nearly four acres. It's big enough so that even humans can get good exercise if they choose to go for a walk, rather than hang out and talk. (Please see the intro to Parks, Beaches, and Recreation Areas for details on the city's four bare-bones off-leash areas.) This one is within Centennial Park, at Montclair Street and Marella Way. 661/326-3117.

8 Panorama Park

🦮 (See Kern County map on page 678)

If a park is going to have the guts to call itself "Panorama" Park, it had better supply a pretty decent view. Not so here. There's a view, all right, but it's not the kind you photograph, enlarge, and hang on your living room wall as evidence of your enviable summer vacation.

The vista includes oil tanks, a refinery, smokestacks, and freeways. Somehow, the few pastured horses by the river lose their rustic charm amid these surroundings.

The park is fairly narrow and follows the road closely. About all you and your leashed dog can do here is walk down the paved path, sit on the benches, and admire the industrial scenery. The park is set along Panorama Drive from Union Avenue to Bucknell Street. The best parking is at the foot of River Boulevard. 661/868-7000.

9 University Park Dog Area

😺 😺 🐕 (See Kern County map on page 678)

It's relatively small (1.5 acres), and it's bare, but it's a place to run off-leash. (Please see the intro to Parks, Beaches, and Recreation Areas for details on the city's four bare-bones off-leash areas.) This one's within University Park, at University Avenue between Camden and Mission Hills streets. 661/326-3117.

10 Hart Park/Kern River County Park

😺 😺 😺 (See Kern County map on page 678)

Hart Park and Lake Ming make up the bulk of this 1,400-acre park. Hart Park, in a setting that's part golf course and part lunar landscape, is by far the better one for dogs. The bare rock mountain on one edge of the park gives way to huge green meadows, with shaded paths running throughout. And if you're a food hound, you'll be happy to know that you and your leashed dog are never more than a one-minute walk from a picnic table.

Down the road a bit is a huge soccer area. When no one's around, it's a terrific place to trot about with your pooch.

The easternmost section of the park is Lake Ming, a 100-acre lake with tolerable fishing in the cooler months and nothing in summer. At last look, only two tiny sections were open to anglers. Because of a parasite that can cause swimmer's itch, swimming and wading are often banned here. In all, it's not exactly a water dog's dream.

The 57 first-come, first-served campsites here are set in a remote, lush section of the Lake Ming area. Unlike the dry, dusty feel of most of the lake's shoreline, the camping here is a riparian escape. Sites are $15. Dogs are $3 extra.

From Panorama Drive in north Bakersfield, drive east to Alfred Harrell Highway and follow it as it curves by the Kern River. Eventually the road will lead you through the gates of the park. Follow the signs to the areas that most interest you and your dog. 661/868-7000.

11 Kroll Park Dog Area

😺 😺 🐕 (See Kern County map on page 678)

Dogs can throw their leashes to the wind in this 2.5-acre grassy fenced area. (Please see the intro to Parks, Beaches, and Recreation Areas for details on the city's four bare-bones off-leash areas.) This one is at Kroll Way and Montalvo Drive, within Kroll Park. 661/326-3117.

12 Wilson Park Dog Area

😺 😺 🐕 (See Kern County map on page 678)

At two fenced acres, this is the second-smallest of the off-leash areas in Bakersfield. But it's also the most heavily used. (Please see the intro to Parks, Beaches, and Recreation Areas for details on the city's four bare-bones off-leash areas.) This one is at Wilson Road and Hughes Lane, within Wilson Park. 661/326-3117.

PLACES TO STAY

Bakersfield has so many dog-friendly lodgings that it puts many larger cities to shame. We'll mention just a fistful of them here.

Best Western Hill House: "Not too big" dogs are welcome, says the manager. Rates are $59–99. Dogs are $10 extra. 700 Truxton Avenue 93301; 661/327-4064.

Doubletree Hotel: This is one of the better Bakersfield accommodations, with large, attractive rooms, a pool, spa, and exercise area. Rates are $104–149. Dogs are $15 extra. 3100 Camino del Rio Court 93308; 661/323-7111; www.doubletree.com.

Kern River County Park: See Kern River County Park, above, for camping information.

La Quinta Motor Inn: Dogs under 35 pounds may sleep here. Rates are $69–81. 3232 Riverside Drive 93308; 661/325-7400.

Motel 6: There are five Motel 6s in Bakersfield. This is an amazing per capita number. Rates are $36–52. Call the national reservations number at 800/466-8356 for the location nearest your destination.

Residence Inn by Marriott: This is a convenient place to stay when traveling with a pooch. The rooms are all suites and apartments, and they all have full kitchens, so you don't have to worry about finding a pooch-friendly restaurant in these parts. The inn even provides dogs with their own poop bags and dog dish. Rates are $134–199. The long-term rate is less. You'll pay $6 extra for one pooch, $3 for each additional pet. There's also a pooch deposit of $40–60. 4241 Chester Lane 93309; 661/321-9800; www.residenceinn.com.

California City

PARKS, BEACHES, AND RECREATION AREAS

No California City park permits pooches, and the Bureau of Land Management would sure appreciate it if you wouldn't take your dog to the Desert Tortoise Natural Area here. Even leashed dogs can pose a threat to the tortoise population.

13 Red Rock Canyon State Park

🐾🐾🐾 (See Kern County map on page 678)

This magnificent park is known as "the Grand Canyon of the West," and it lives up to the hype. The best time to be at this 10,384-acre park is at sunrise or at sunset. The low-lying sun dances with the red and white cliffs, and the results are magical. Dogs aren't permitted on the trails, but they can go along the small roads and seek out some of the stunning paleontological sites with you. Leashes are a must.

If you like borax, you'll be happy to know that this was a watering hole for the 20-mule team freight wagons on their grueling journey hauling the stuff.

The day-use fee is $3. There are 50 very primitive camping sites available on a first-come, first-served basis for $9 per night. The park is 25 miles northeast of the town of Mojave, on Highway 14. 661/942-0662.

PLACES TO STAY

Red Rock Canyon State Park: See Red Rock Canyon State Park, above, for camping information.

Tehachapi

The Tehachapi area is home to thousands of windmills that supply more than one billion kilowatt-hours of electricity per year. Next time you're driving through some of the back roads with your dog, pull over and turn off your engine for a minute. The humming turbines provide an eerie contrast to the silence of the surrounding desert. Joe Dog loved the strange noises and would tilt his head every which way to try to figure out who was making them. When he ruled out the other passengers and the nearby rocks, he'd stare at me with an accusing look on his furrowed brow.

PARKS, BEACHES, AND RECREATION AREAS

🐾 Tehachapi Mountain Park

🐾🐾🐾🐾 (See Kern County map on page 678)

We love coming to this 490-acre park in late autumn, when there's a little nip in the pure, pine-scented air. With elevations of up to 7,000 feet and dozens of types of pines, firs, and oaks, this park provides a stunning contrast to the desert surroundings.

Bill and Joe slid around on their butts when we visited, because there was a good layer of slick snow in the upper reaches of the park. They had a great time slipping, sliding, and sniffing the mountain sage that was poking out of the snow. Leashes are the law here, but you can still have a terrific time exploring this beautiful park via the trails that run throughout. And you may never run into another soul.

The camping is some of the best we've seen in any county park. Many of the 61 sites are 200 feet away from each other. Tall trees add a little more privacy. Sites are $8–10 and are available on a first-come, first-served basis. Pooches are $2 extra.

From Highway 58, exit onto Highway 202 and drive south, continuing straight onto Tucker Road when Highway 202 veers west. In about another mile, at Highline Road, turn right, drive about 1.5 miles to Water Canyon Road, and turn left. The park is another 2.2 miles. 661/868-7000.

PLACES TO STAY

Best Western Mountain Inn: Rates are $59–65, and the inn asks for notice if you're coming with a pooch. 416 West Tehachapi Boulevard 93561; 661/822-5591.

Tehachapi Mountain Park: See Tehachapi Mountain Park, above, for camping information.

Boron

Don't be surprised if your dog starts looking inquisitively at the empty sky here. Chances are that within a few moments the sky won't look so empty. This is the home of Edwards Air Force Base, and it flies some mighty odd-looking experimental aircraft up yonder. Dogs usually seem to notice well before their people. (See the Diversion Call Out the 20-Mule Team for one heckuva fun outing.)

DIVERSION

Call Out the 20-Mule Team: If your dog has fond memories of those puppyhood days when you sprinkled 20 Mule Team Borax on the rug almost daily to get out those "oops" odors, a trip to the **20 Mule Team Museum** will be a journey down olfactory memory lane.

The town of Boron is the home of U.S. Borax, whose open pit mine is one of the major sources of borate in the world. The museum pays homage to the days when 20-mule teams hauled 36-ton wagonloads of borax across 180 miles of desert to waiting railroad cars in Mojave. On the museum's grounds, you'll find the oldest house in Death Valley, built in 1883 by a borax miner. Other features of the rather small museum include an early Boron beauty shop and tons of mining equipment. Dogs can't enter the museum, but that's OK because there's plenty to see outside. (Be sure not to let your dog do leg lifts on the displays. It's probably a good idea to take him for a walk before you get here.)

There's no fee, just a requested donation. From Highway 58, take the Boron Avenue off-ramp and drive south about 1.5 miles. 760/762-5810.

Frazier Park

The dusty little streets of this community near the interstate hide a fairly dog-friendly park. If your dog is crossing his legs on a long journey down the highway, it's not a bad place to stop.

PARKS, BEACHES, AND RECREATION AREAS

🔟 Frazier Mountain Park

🐾 🐾 🐾 (See Kern County map on page 678)

This 26-acre park is almost entirely fenced, but dogs are supposed to be leashed anyway. In addition to a grassy picnic area and a little pond, sections of the park have shrubs, shady oaks, and scrubby fields. Dogs love the fact that it's not a perfectly manicured work of art.

Exit I-5 at the Frazier Park exit and drive east about 3.5 miles. Turn left at the post office (Monterey Trail) and make an immediate right onto Park Trail Drive. Park on the street. 661/868-7000.

Lebec

PARKS, BEACHES, AND RECREATION AREAS

16 Fort Tejon State Historic Park

🐾🐾🐾 (See Kern County map on page 678)

The U.S. Army's First Dragoons established a camp here in 1854. Their mission was to protect white settlers and Native Americans in the Tejon Reservation from raids by other Native American groups, including the Paiutes, Chemehuevi, and Mojave.

The buildings here are all restored versions of structures that were the backbone of the fort back then. There's even a miniature museum to get you up to date with the past.

Dogs like it here, but their pleasure has little to do with the buildings and lots to do with the land. There's plenty of land to peruse, on leash of course. If you get away from the main features of the fort and walk toward the backcountry (past the outhouses), you're in for a treat. Large valley oaks, blue oaks, black willows, and cottonwoods are plentiful here, and critters such as deer, rabbits, quail, and several kinds of hummingbirds call the park home.

Admission is $2 for adults. Kids and dogs get in free. Exit I-5 at the Fort Tejon exit and follow the signs. It's just west of the freeway. 661/248-6692.

SOUTH COAST COUNTIES

CHAPTER 50

Santa Barbara County

If you're like most folks, when you hear the words "Santa Barbara," you probably think of a sun-drenched vacation paradise on the central California coast. Images of whitewashed, Spanish-style buildings, palm-lined beaches, and big green resorts representing big green bucks may flash through your head. You can almost smell the suntan lotion and feel the warm sand caressing your body.

On the other hand, if you're a dog, when you think of Santa Barbara County, you'll likely think of a leash that barely comes off on beaches that are to drool for. Images of "No Dogs" signs on the most glorious beaches will flash through your furry head. You may even try to convey to your owner, "Hey, I've got a great idea. Let's go to Carmel!"

Well, at least there are lots of great restaurants with outdoor tables dogs can go to in Santa Barbara County, right? Well, yes and no: A few years ago, the Santa Barbara County health department decided to no longer allow dogs at the county's myriad restaurants with outdoor tables. It's a long and complicated story that I won't get into here. (Just know that it had nothing to do

PICK OF THE LITTER—SANTA BARBARA COUNTY

BEST DOG PARK
WOOF PAC Park, Santa Maria (page 695)

BEST OFF-LEASH ROMPS
Douglas Family Preserve, Santa Barbara (page 701)
Elings Park, Santa Barbara (page 702)

BEST LEASH-FREE BEACH
Hendry's Beach/Arroyo Burro Beach, Santa Barbara
(page 703)

MOST DOG-FRIENDLY PLACES TO STAY
Meadowlark Inn, Solvang (page 698)
Fess Parker's DoubleTree Resort, Santa Barbara (page 706)
Four Seasons Biltmore, Santa Barbara (page 706)
San Ysidro Ranch, Montecito (page 708)

BEST PLACE TO STAY IN A COVERED WAGON
Rancho Oso Guest Ranch and Stables, Santa Barbara
(page 707)

BEST PLACE TO BE A POODLE
Bastille Day Parade, Santa Barbara (page 701)

with health hazards at all). This means dogs are officially not allowed at any restaurants with outdoor tables in the county. Restaurant owners can end up in court if they're too dog-friendly, and this can be costly.

We've heard the enforcement is difficult, but after long consideration we've decided to exclude all Santa Barbara County restaurants from this edition, since to leave them in could be inviting legal trouble for them. Your dog will probably still be welcome at the outdoor tables of dozens of restaurants throughout the county, but we'd rather err on the side of caution and let you find them as you explore the area. (Putting them in the book is kind of like pointing a big flashing arrow at them for health officials.)

A very active group called Dog PAC of Santa Barbara, which is dedicated to the promotion and preservation of dog owners' rights and to responsible dog ownership, is working on dealing with this problem, as well as on getting more doggy access to parks here. Check out Dog PAC at its website, www.dogpacsb.org. Or call 805/967-3949. The group recently won a huge battle over off-leash use of a magnificent park (see Douglas Family Preserve in the Santa Barbara section), and it's behind a pilot off-leash program at a half-dozen parks around the county. Some of these off-leash parks have been switched since the pilot program's inception, and much more could change by the time you read this book, so we won't go into detail here. We don't want to get your dog's hopes up about something that may not exist anymore. For updates, check Dog PAC's website. We hope to be able to bring you news of several permanent new off-leash dog parks in the next edition.

NATIONAL FORESTS

The National Forests and Wilderness Areas resource at the back of this book has important information and safety tips on visiting national forests with your dog and has more information on the Los Padres National Forest.

Los Padres National Forest

Sections of the forest are near the Santa Barbara coast. The off-leash trails provide a much-needed breather from the strict leash rules around this county.

Santa Maria

PARKS, BEACHES, AND RECREATION AREAS

1 Preisker Park

(See Santa Barbara County map on page 692)

If you're traveling south on U.S. 101 and you've promised your pooch that you'd stop at the very first park you find when you cross the border from San Luis Obispo County into Santa Barbara County, this is it.

This park is right on the border. It's flat, with lush grass and plenty of places to barbecue those burgers you've been keeping in your cooler. (Jake Dog asked me to say that last part.) It can get crowded with locals who sometimes hang out here all day, but since dogs must be leashed anyway, there's little danger of your dog's crashing someone else's picnic.

Driving south from the northern edge of the county, exit U.S. 101 at Highway 135. Drive southwest and take your first right, Preisker Lane. You'll be at the park within a few blocks. 805/925-0951.

2 WOOF PAC Park

(See Santa Barbara County map on page 692)

This three-acre fenced-in off-leash dog park is in the back of Waller County Park. (Which is a real gem itself.) It's a little hard to find, but once you see the entrance, you'll know you're in the right place: It looks like a giant red dog-house. Big dogs and bitty dogs have separate areas here, and there's plenty of water and poop bags. A fire hydrant graces each section. The grassy ground cover can turn to mud, but dogs don't mind a bit.

After your dog has had her leash-free fun inside the dog park, pop on a leash and stroll around the rest of Waller County Park. It's a beautiful 153-acre park with two duck ponds, quiet picnic spots, loads of trees, and sprawling lawn area.

From Highway 135, go west on Goodwin Road and follow it to the park. 805/934-6145; for more info, www.woofpac.org.

PLACES TO STAY

Best Value Inn: Rates are $50–100. Dogs are $10 extra. 839 East Main Street 93450; 805/925-2551 or 800/315-2378; www.bestvalue.com.

Lompoc

It may be the home of a notorious federal penitentiary, but because of a few pooch-permitting parks, dogs don't feel imprisoned here.

PARKS, BEACHES, AND RECREATION AREAS

🔳 La Purisima Mission State Historic Park

🐾🐾🐾🐾 (See Santa Barbara County map on page 692)

This is a truly amazing place to bring dogs. Not only can they hike with you along 14 miles of trails here, but they're actually allowed inside the restored mission. They have to promise not to do leg lifts, bark, throw up, or any of those other activities that are not suited to the indoors. And they have to be on a leash at all times.

The original La Purisima Mission was founded in 1787, but an earthquake destroyed it in 1812. The mission was eventually picked up and moved across the Santa Ynez River to its present spot. During the 1930s, many of the mission's adobe buildings were restored. It was the largest mission restoration in California.

It's a treat to be able to take a dog inside such a historic place. But frankly, most dogs would rather be outside exploring this 967-acre park in their own doggy fashion.

The entrance fee is $4 per vehicle and it's good for up to nine people (and a dog). From Highway 1 in Lompoc, turn east on Purisima Road. The park entrance will be on your left in a couple of miles. 805/733-3713.

◢ Jalama Beach Park

🐾🐾🐾🐾 (See Santa Barbara County map on page 692)

The park may be only 24 acres, but there are so many ways to enjoy nature here that it seems much larger. Bring your binoculars and you won't regret it. Gray whale–watching is excellent February–March and September–November. Bird-watching is hot year-round, but springtime attracts many rare birds.

Joe Dog's favorite activity was rockhounding, but he probably just liked the name. The beachcombing is great here, and since the park is within the Pacific Missile Range of the Vandenberg Air Force Base, you never know what you'll find. Wildlife-watching and surf fishing are also first-rate. As long as your dog is on a leash and not harming the environment, she can accompany you anywhere here.

There's also camping at 110 campsites, some right by the beach. Sites are $15–20. Dogs are $1 extra. All sites are first-come, first-served. The beach is 15 miles off Highway 1, at the end of Jalama Road. The Jalama Road exit is about four miles south of the main part of Lompoc. 805/934-6123.

PLACES TO STAY

Best Value Inn: Rates are $50–100. Medium dogs and smaller are welcome, and their fee is $10 for one dog, $25 for two. (There is no bulk discount here.) 1200 North H Street 93436; 805/735-3737 or 888/315-2378; www.bestvalueinn.com.

Jalama Beach Park: See Jalama Beach Park, above, for camping information.

Quality Inn and Executive Suites: If you want a view of the Lompoc Airport, you've got it from the parking lot here. Joy of joys! Rates are $64–109. Dogs pay a $25 fee for the length of their stay. 1621 North H Street 93436; 805/735-8555 or 800/224-6530; qualitysuiteslompoc.com.

Super 8 Motel: There's a nice little grassy area on the premises. Rates are $50–159. (Who knew Super 8s could command such a price?) Dogs are $10 extra for up to two pooches. 1020 East Ocean Avenue 93436; 805/735-6444.

Solvang

Solvang is a sweet Danish village, with architecture as authentically Danish as its baked goods. The place was settled in 1911 by Danish folks who missed their homeland. They bought property and perpetuated all the Danish customs they could.

After an article about the small community appeared in the *Saturday Evening Post* in 1947, entrepreneurs rushed in from all over the country and created something of a Danish theme park atmosphere here. Still, the town retains its core of true Danish charm.

PARKS, BEACHES, AND RECREATION AREAS

5 Hans Christian Andersen Park

🐾🐾🐾 (See Santa Barbara County map on page 692)

When you tell a dog that he's going to get to visit a park that's half developed and half rough, you know which half he's going to want to explore. This 52-acre park has a good undeveloped section for dogs who couldn't care less about refinement.

The area is full of brush, but there are enough trees and navigable walking areas for any dog to have a good time, even on the mandatory leash. If some human in your group insists on hanging out at the developed section of the park, your dog will get along just fine.

From Highway 246, take Atterdag Road north. The arched gateway to the park is about three blocks on the left. 805/568-2461.

6 Nojoqui Falls County Park

🐾🐾🐾 (See Santa Barbara County map on page 692)

In nondrought springtimes, you'll be wowed by the Nojoqui (NAH-ho-wee) Waterfall, which plunges 100 feet. The rest of the year, you and your dog will still be in awe.

People often compare this 88-acre park with Yosemite National Park. It's kind of a miniature version, complete with thick forests and minimountains (also known as hills). Unlike in Yosemite, dogs are allowed to really explore the area. They have to be on leash, but they don't seem to mind.

From Solvang, go south on Alisal Road about 10 miles. After about six miles, the road will veer sharply to the right. Follow it for four more miles, and the park will be on your left. If you're on U.S. 101 south of Buellton, you can exit at the signed marker for the park and follow the signs for about two miles. The park will be on your right. 805/568-2461.

PLACES TO EAT

Please see the introduction to this chapter for the reason we haven't included any of Solvang's very dog-friendly outdoor eateries in this edition.

PLACES TO STAY

Meadowlark Inn: Good dogs are welcome at this lovely inn, which bills itself as a "wine country inn." Stay here and you get a comfy room and a small pool. Your dog gets big oaks and redwoods and two large lawns in front. Equally as appealing for dogs: They now get dog treats when they stay here. Rates are $120–195. Dogs are $15 extra. 2644 Mission Drive 93463; 805/688-4631; www.meadowlarkinnsolvang.com.

Royal Copenhagen Inn: The rooms here are spacious and somewhat Danish in their decor. The exterior looks so much like a Danish village that it will leave you wondering if you're really in California anymore. You'll want to take a few photos here with your dog. It's the next best thing to visiting Copenhagen, and you don't have those cramped airplane seats to contend with. Guests get a free breakfast as well as an afternoon wine tasting. Rates are $79–155. 1579 Mission Drive 93463; 800/624-6604; www.royalcopenhageninn.com.

Viking Motel: Rates are $49–120. Dogs are $10 extra. 1506 Mission Drive 93463; 805/688-1337 or 800/695-8284.

Goleta

PARKS, BEACHES, AND RECREATION AREAS

7 Lake Los Carneros County Park

😾😾😾 (See Santa Barbara County map on page 692)

A beautiful lake is at the center of this wonderful county park and nature preserve. To protect the lake, no one except fish, birds, and little bugs are allowed to swim in it. But you and your leashed dog can explore the area on miles of trails (both dirt and paved). You'll likely see rabbits, squirrels, turtles, ducks, and geese. Please note: The name "Los Carneros" may or may not have its origin in *carne,* the Spanish word for meat, but please be sure your dog realizes the critters around here are not for his dining pleasure. If your dog is a chaser and you see this wildlife, keep a tight hold of that leash.

The park has a few picnic tables near the historic Stow House and even a minitrain ride for kids. (Open by special arrangement.) The area is undeveloped, with only one chemical toilet. But dogs don't care about that. They've got two mutt-mitt stations, and if you use them, pooches will continue to be welcomed here.

Take Los Carneros Road north off Highway 101, cross over Calle Real, and you'll see the vehicle entrance to this park next to a county fire station on your right. If you're hiking to get here, you'll also have access to this park from Covington Way and La Patera Lane. 805/568-2461.

8 Girsh Park

😾😾😾 (See Santa Barbara County map on page 692)

This lovely 12-acre park is an oasis in development-crazy Goleta. Leashes are a must, but it's still a dog-friendly place: Girsh is host to obedience trials, dog fairs, and pooch agility groups. This makes for lots of interesting doggy scents for your furry friend to investigate. The park is at 7050 Phelps Road, off Storke Road; 805/968-2773.

⑨ Goleta Beach County Park

🐾🐾🐾 (See Santa Barbara County map on page 692)

Leashed dogs enjoy strolling down the beach at this county park. You and your pooch can enjoy a relaxing picnic under pine and palm trees in the small park area, and then go get your paws wet as you saunter down the beach together. We prefer the section of beach near the Goleta Slough, which is wilder and more primitive.

From U.S. 101, go west on Highway 217. Just before you get to the University of California, turn left onto Sandspit Road and follow it to the beach. 805/568-2461 or 805/967-1300.

Santa Barbara

The fur has been flying in this exquisite community for years, but in 2004, dogs won a major battle to continue being allowed off leash at the Douglas Family Preserve. (See below.) As a wonderful bonus, well-behaved dogs now have a stretch of leash-free beach to enjoy. (See Hendry's Beach/Arroyo Burro Beach, below.) Dog tails are wagging so hard around here that I'd swear it's been breezier the last few times we visited.

Dogs can also stroll very close to the beach on a wonderful walkway that runs the entire beach length along Cabrillo Boulevard. On Sunday and holidays, the Santa Barbara Arts and Crafts Show makes its home under the grand palm trees here. It's a great opportunity to go shopping and take your dog along for advice on issues such as which scarf would look best on Aunt Edna.

DIVERSION

The Big Dog Is a Big Deal: The Santa Barbara–based casual clothing company, **Big Dogs Sportswear,** has a large factory outlet store right in town. Are dogs allowed? "Oh, by all means," a dog-loving manager told us. After all, the Big Dogs logo—a black-and-white Saint Bernard with a big smile and red tongue—is on every piece of clothing here. So what's another dog in the store? (Just don't let your own dog leave his own logo on any clothes, if you know what I mean.) 6 East Yanonali Street; 805/963-8728.

For more fun with the Big Dog, check out the chain's website, www.bigdogs.com. You can join the Big Dogs Club (no membership fee) and submit your dog's photo to be featured on the web page, send Big Dogs e-cards, play Big Dogs computer games (Jake's favorite is Chasing the Bone), or help with the Big Dogs Foundation's many worthwhile causes. And if you like discounts, you're barking up the right tree: The website offers Big Dogs members deals that are worth sniffing out.

DOG-EAR YOUR CALENDAR

If you're in Santa Barbara during the summer, keep your ears peeled for two delightful parades. **The Big Dog Parade,** which features at least 1,000 dogs (many in costume) and 10,000 spectators, is held the first Saturday of June. Check out www.bigdogs .com for more info, or phone 805/963-8727. And in mid-July, oodles of poodles and pseudopoodles take to the streets to celebrate **Bastille Day.** Keep your eyes peeled for Molly, a springer spaniel who gives us marvelous travel tips. She was planning to don black tights and black pompoms next Bastille Day in an effort to fit in with the poodles. For more information on Bastille Day, check out www.frenchfestival.com/poodle.html.

An interesting way to spend a dog day is to walk around the historic sections of the city. While pooches aren't permitted inside buildings such as Mission Santa Barbara or the city's historic adobes, they love having their pictures taken outside so their friends at home can envy their worldly ways.

PARKS, BEACHES, AND RECREATION AREAS

10 Alice Keck Park Memorial Gardens

😺😺 (See Santa Barbara County map on page 692)

There's an abundance of natural sniffables here for dogs and their human friends. This one-square-block park is a fragrant, voluptuous garden, complete with flowering trees, a pond, a gazebo, and a stunning procession of brilliant flowers. Leashed dogs like it here, but most would rather be able to inspect a good, fresh cow patty than a dahlia.

The park is at Arrellaga Street and Carmelita Avenue, four blocks away from the courthouse. 805/564-5433.

11 Douglas Family Preserve

😺😺😺😺🐕 (See Santa Barbara County map on page 692)

This is one terrific chunk of leash-free land, and thanks to the very hard-working members of the Dog PAC of Santa Barbara, and hundreds of dogged volunteers, it looks as if it's going to stay that way. In spring 2004, the Santa Barbara City Council voted unanimously to let dogs be their doggy selves and continue to enjoy this big park naked. (Lest any lewd images of dogs not wearing clothes cross your mind, this is dog park parlance for leash-free.)

The preserve is about 70 acres, and it's on a magnificent bluff overlooking the Pacific. Dogs drool over this place, and rightly so. The ocean breeze is cool, relaxing, and must contain some pretty fascinating scents, judging by

DIVERSION

Got Mud?: Want your dog to return to your house or hotel as clean as when she left? Visit the self-service pet wash at **TJ Paws** in Santa Barbara. Rates are $8–12, depending on your dog's size. (The staff will wash or groom your pet for you, if you prefer. It'll just cost you more.) 2601 De La Vina Street; 805/687-8772.

the looks on dogs' faces as they sniff it in rapture. The park has great unpaved trails for perusing the preserve. It also has quite a few oaks, cypresses, and pines. To the north of the park is oak woodland, to the south is coastal sage scrub. An estuary and wetlands are below. Way below. Two hundred feet down the bluff, to be exact. Dogs have to stay away from there, because that's where some protected species hang out. There's really no access anyway, so it's almost a moot point.

There's still a bone of contention between the preserve's neighbors and the park patrons with dogs, and some buffer-zone issues had yet to be resolved. Dog PAC cofounder Mary Anne Morrison implores dogs and their people to "Please be considerate of the neighbors. We want everyone to be happy with this arrangement." Keep leashes on until you're well within the preserve. For an update, phone the parks department at 805/564-5433, or contact Dog PAC at 805/967-3949 or www.dogpacsb.org.

From northbound or southbound U.S. 101, take Cabrillo Boulevard in the direction that's away from the mountains. Turn right on Cliff Drive. You'll come to two stoplights within a block of each other. Turn left onto Mesa Lane (the second light) and then turn right onto Borton Drive. Turn left onto Linda Road and follow it to the end. There is on-street parking. (You can enter the park at Medcliff Drive, Borton Drive, or Mesa School Lane.)

12 Elings Park

🐾🐾🐾🐾🐕 (See Santa Barbara County map on page 692)

Read no further if you aren't a Santa Barbara County resident, or if you are a resident but don't feel like paying $52 a year for the privilege of letting your dog run free. This 230-acre wonderland is now a privately run nonprofit, and it bans all dogs except for a lucky 550 for whom permits have been set aside. To get a coveted permit, a dog's owner must be a county resident, pay $52 yearly, and pay strict attention to the rules here. Dogs must be under voice control and licensed.

To find out how to obtain a permit, phone the park at 805/569-5611. Elings also has an active dog organization, Elings Park Dog Owners Group (EPDOG) that's working on accessibility and responsibility issues. For information on EPDOG, email epdog@cox.net or phone 805/687-9709. You can click onto the EPDOG link from the park's website, www.elingspark.org. (You can even download a permit application from the EPDOG site.) The park is at Las Positas Road and Jerry Harwin Parkway.

13 Hendry's Beach/Arroyo Burro Beach

🐾🐾🐾🐾🐾 (See Santa Barbara County map on page 692)

You can throw your good dog's leash to the wind here (don't forget to pick it up, though; they're not cheap these days) and take a little stroll on a sandy, crescent-shaped beach together. It's the only beach in the county that allows leash-free dogs, so enjoy! Along your way you'll see surfers, joggers, and loads of other happy dogs. What you won't see—at least if the beach's current leash-free status remains—is a ranger approaching you with ticket book in hand. (This is too common a sight at most beaches around here.)

But be careful where you tread: If you go in the wrong direction once you hit the sand, you could be in for a $75 ticket. Here's how you get to the right place: The beach (signs will call it Arroyo Burro) is on Cliff Drive, just west of Las Positas Road. Park in the lot, walk to the beach, and turn left—*not* right! (You'll see the fun beachside restaurant, the Brown Pelican. Go to the left of it. You should also see a sign that points dogs in the right—that is, left—direction.) Dogs who are under voice control can shed their leashes east of the slough. The off-leash section starts there and goes almost to the steps at Mesa Lane.

The off-leash program here could change at any time, so be sure to check on its status. The city likes to say this is a county beach, and the county likes to say this is a city beach. The leash-free part appears to be a city-controlled section of a county beach. The city parks department number (where some people who answer the phone will tell you dogs aren't even allowed at the beach) is 805/564-5433, or check the website www.dogpacsb.org for updates.

DIVERSION

Hi Ho, Surrey, Away!: Get your canine companion to hop up into your lap or onto the seat beside you and drive away in your very own surrey with the fringe on the top. Don't you hurry, though, because there are plenty of dog-friendly spots where you can rent one of these pedal-powered vehicles.

One of our favorites is **Beach Rentals,** at 8 West Cabrillo Avenue, Santa Barbara. The folks here want you to hang on to your dog, and for good reason: Cats and hamburgers are common sights on the oceanfront paths you're likely to use. Small surreys (for three adults and two small kids/one hefty dog) are $24 an hour. Large surreys are $34. 805/966-2282.

DIVERSION

Take Her to a Bark Bar: The **Three Dog Bakery** is the only Santa Barbara eatery where you know you can bring your dog and not break the law these days. What's especially fun about the bakery is that since it's exclusively a pet place, your dog can eat inside at a doggy bar, bench, or counter. Now you'll know how your dog feels watching you chow down on your eats at a human restaurant, because chances are you'll be watching him with hungry eyes. (Some of the dog cookies can begin to look pretty good to humans around lunchtime.) The bakery also offers fun events throughout the year. Check the schedule for pet psychics, pooch parties, and other interesting happenings. 727 State Street; 805/962-8220.

14 Santa Barbara Botanic Garden

🐾🐾🐾 (See Santa Barbara County map on page 692)

As soon as you park your car, you'll be enveloped in the magical scents of lush vegetation and fresh earth. Dogs prefer to smell the compost heaps here, but what else would you expect?

This botanic wonderland is a rarity. Places such as this usually exclude dogs without a second thought. But the folks here actually like dogs. In fact, there's even a philanthropic doggy donor, a poodle named Sophie. This environmentally conscious gal has a bouffant hairdo and the distinction of being the garden's only canine member.

You and your leashed dog are welcome to explore this 65-acre garden on the 5.5 miles of trails that take you through the meadows, canyons, and ridges here. The garden features more than 1,000 species of rare and indigenous California plants. The entry fee for adults is $6.

Exit U.S. 101 at Mission Street and drive northeast. The road curves to the left after about 10 blocks (its name becomes Mission Canyon Road). Continue to Foothill Road, bear right, and then take a quick left on the continuation of Mission Canyon Road. The park will be on your left in about a half mile. The address is 1212 Mission Canyon Road. 805/563-2521.

15 Shoreline Park

🐾🐾 (See Santa Barbara County map on page 692)

Lots of dogs come here for their daily walks. Leashed dogs are allowed on the green area (not the beach). They walk the path, roll on the grass, and smell the ocean and the scent of the offshore oil rigs that dot the coast.

The park is on Shoreline Drive, between San Clemente Street and San Rafael Avenue, just south of Leadbetter Beach. 805/564-5433.

PLACES TO EAT

Many Santa Barbara restaurants have outdoor tables and, at least in the past, welcomed dogs. But for their sakes, we can't include them in this edition. Please see the chapter's introduction for the rotten reason why. (If you've just got to bring your dog to an eatery for a treat, and *you're* not hungry, stop by the Three Dog Bakery; see the Diversion Take Her to a Bark Bar.)

PLACES TO STAY

Bacara: Not many dogs who read this are under 25 pounds, so we won't spend much time describing this understated but very luxurious resort. (Eighty-five-pound Jake wanted to keep it out of the book entirely, but in deference to his Chihuahua friend, Baby, he'll let it stay.) Suffice it to say that it's big yet intimate, and casual yet about as upscale as it gets. You can get any number of exquisite spa treatments here, and of course your room comes with the finest linens and softest robes. Rates are $450 to more than $2,600. Dogs need to weigh less than 25 pounds to stay here, and they pay $150 for the length of their stay. 8301 Hollister Avenue 93117; 805/968-0100 or 877/422-4245; www.bacararesort.com.

Best Western Beachside Inn: This clean, inviting hotel is across the street from the beach, but don't get your tail wagging too fast: It's a typical Santa Barbara beach—beautiful, warm, sandy, and dog-banning. Well, it doesn't hurt to look, anyway. Stay here and you get to use the cute little pool and indulge in the hotel's decent continental breakfast. Rates are $125–189. Dogs are $20 extra. 336 West Cabrillo Boulevard 93101; 805/965-6556 or 800/932-6556; www.beachsideinn.com.

Cachuma Lake Campgrounds: Although Cachuma Lake has 42 miles of shoreline and numerous trails, dogs who visit here are stuck in the campgrounds. Dogs are banned from trails, and pooches and people aren't permitted to swim in the lake. Dogs can't be within 50 feet of the lake, and they're not even allowed to accompany their people on a boat here. Bummerooo, say the dogs. Fortunately, there are plenty of campsites here—500 to be exact. You won't be roughing it, but at least you'll be with your dog. Sites are $18–22. Dogs are $3 extra. All are available on a first-come, first-served basis. The day-use fee is $5. Dogs require proof of rabies vaccination. From Santa Barbara, take the San Marcos Pass exit (Highway 154) off U.S. 101 and drive about 20 miles to the entrance. 805/688-4658.

Casa del Mar: Guests at this small Spanish-style inn get treated well for a decent price (at least decent for these parts). Stay here and you can partake in an extended continental breakfast in the morning, and a relaxing wine and cheese social hour in the evening. The inn is clean, quiet, and attractive, with a lush little garden, a sundeck with whirlpool tub, and cozy rooms. It's just a half block from the beach and two blocks from State Street. If you really want a home away from home, you can stay in a suite with a full kitchen and fireplace. Rates are $99–204. (Most regular rooms fall in the lower price range.) Dogs are $10 extra. 18 Bath Street 93101; 805/963-4418 or 800/433-3097; www.casadelmar.com.

Fess Parker's DoubleTree Resort: At first glance, the name "Fess Parker" and the word "luxury" make strange bedfellows. After all, Fess was the actor who brought American frontiersman Davy Crockett and Daniel Boone into millions of homes in the 1950s and '60s. But while Fess Parker's characters are synonymous with sweat and grit, the real Fess Parker, a longtime Santa Barbara County resident, is known for his good taste and good business sense. (He also owns a respected winery in the county.)

Fess, who hails from Texas, likes things big. The seaside resort has 337 luxurious guest rooms. It's set on a sprawling 24 acres. Standard rooms are a spacious 450 square feet. He also likes things first-class. The rooms are attractive and comfortable, with feather pillows (unless you're allergic), high-quality bath products, evening turndown service, and excellent views. Suites are especially spacious and attractive. The resort even has its own spa, billed as a "French sea spa."

We think Fess must also like dogs, because dogs get the royal treatment here. Fess Parker's dog guests don't have to watch hungrily as you chow down on your tasty room-service meal: They can order their own. The in-room pooch dining menu includes premium ground sirloin, a quality brand wet dog food, and gourmet dog cookies. And if you really want to treat your dog, canine massages are available. For $65, your dog can get a 40-minute in-room massage from a dog-knowledgeable massage therapist from the resort's spa. The massage is supposed to be especially good for arthritic dogs.

Although the resort is across from the beach, it's a beach you can't visit with your dog friend. Try the path that runs along the beach's edge, if being near the water is your wish. Otherwise, the 24-acre resort has ample room for romping with your leashed friend. Be sure to clean up after your dog.

Rates are $269–349. 633 East Cabrillo Boulevard 93103; 805/564-4333 or 800/222-8733; www.fpdtr.com.

Four Seasons Biltmore: This elegant oceanfront resort is renowned for its impeccable style, and its gracious, dog-friendly policy is the epitome of that style. Upon check-in, dogs get two dog bowls, a toy, tasty snacks, and their very own pooch menu. Dog-walking is available, but who'd want someone else to walk his or her dog with nearby parks and the beautiful grounds of the Biltmore beckoning? Dog-sitting is also available. The Biltmore is made up of a gorgeous, top-drawer hotel surrounded by 30 private cottage rooms that are to die for. People with pooches have to stay at the cottages. If your budget is plump, it's well worth the stay. The standard cottage rates are $545–750. Super-deluxe ones go up to $2,750. 1260 Channel Drive 93108; 805/969-2261; www.fourseasons.com/santabarbara.

Motel 6: Rates are $65 for the first adult, $6 for the second. 3505 State Street 93108; 805/687-5400.

Pacifica Suites: If you and your dog need more room than just a room, check out the luxurious Pacifica Suites. The Pacifica is an all-suites hotel, so no matter which room you stay in, you'll have a bedroom and a living room. Each room has a phone and a TV (this is convenient if *Lassie* is on at the same time as *Survivor*). Suites also have stereo-cassette players, VCRs, fridges, and microwaves. These extras make a real difference when traveling with a dog.

A full breakfast comes with the room, so don't worry about cooking your eggs in the nuker. People love the pool and spa, and leashed dogs dig walking around the Pacifica's grounds. The hotel is nestled in a peaceful grove of exotic plants and trees and century-old gardens. Sniff out the area via a meandering pathway. The hotel is right next to the Sexton House, a beautifully restored architectural landmark from the 1880s.

Dogs who smoke are in luck; pooches are relegated to the first-floor smoking suites. Rates are $179–189. 5490 Hollister Avenue 93111; 805/683-6722 or 800/338-6722; www.pacificasuites.com.

Rancho Oso Guest Ranch and Stables: Dogs and people who enjoy the Old West love staying at Rancho Oso. It's not historic, but it looks that way. You can stay in one of five rustic one-room cabins with knotty pine walls and bunk beds. Or if you really hanker for your pooch to be a "dawgie," try one of the 10 covered wagons here. You bring the sleeping bag, the ranch provides the army cots. They're loads of fun to stay in, and they make for great photo backdrops.

The ranch is on 310 acres of hills with enough trees for decent shade in the summer. You can walk your dog on the many trails, but keep her on a leash, because a lot of horses jog on the trails too. In fact, if you want to ride a horse yourself, you can set that up back at the ranch office. Guided trail rides are offered year-round. (Lots of folks come here to camp with their horses, but that's through a members-only camping organization, and that's a horse of a different color so we won't go into detail.)

Rates are $79–89 for cabins, $54 for wagons. Dogs are $5 extra. 3750 Paradise Road 93105; 805/683-5692; www.rancho-oso.com.

Secret Garden Inn and Cottages: Six of the nine pretty cottages and rooms here allow dogs. Since the dog ambience doesn't necessarily mix with the flowery romantic feel many guests come here for, dogs are asked not to peruse the pretty gardens and public areas around the inn and cottages. A great choice for a night or two is the Garden Room, which has French doors that open to a private little garden. It's your own little Secret Garden, with no nuzzling couples to annoy.

If you like to eat in a cozy setting, you'll never want to leave the inn. You get a full hot gourmet breakfast in the morning, a light snack with wine and cheese in the afternoon, and homemade brownies, cider, and tea in the evening.

Rates for the dog rooms are $160–231. Dogs require a $50 deposit. 1908 Bath Street 93101; 805/687-2300; www.secretgarden.com.

Montecito

PARKS, BEACHES, AND RECREATION AREAS

16 Manning County Park

❄️❄️❄️ (See Santa Barbara County map on page 692)

It's beautiful here—lush and heavenly. This isn't a huge park, but with its narrow, ivy-covered walkways and ultragreen lawns and foliage, you may want to make a day of it. Bring your leashed dog, a picnic, and a book, and enjoy this verdant wonderland to its fullest. A heads-up: The ranger lives on the premises. If you're going to break a leash law, don't do it here.

Exit U.S. 101 at San Ysidro Road and drive north for almost a mile. The park will be just after the school, on your left. 805/568-2461.

PLACES TO STAY

San Ysidro Ranch: A word to the pooches who plan to come here: You lucky dogs! This top-notch 540-acre resort (where Laurence Olivier and Vivien Leigh wed and Jackie and John F. Kennedy honeymooned) is treat enough. But dogs who stay here get the truly royal treatment, also known as the Privileged Pet Program. The Ranch has been offering the program to pooches for more than a century. Here's how it goes:

Upon registering at the Pet Register and wolfing down some tasty peanut butter biscuits, the guest dog goes to his cottage and finds his name and his accompanying human's name on a sign outside his cottage door. Inside, he'll be greeted by a basketful of VIP goodies, including a bowl filled with squeak toys, rawhides, tennis balls, cookies, and a two-liter bottle of Pawier water. His bed is soft and cedar-stuffed.

A room-service pet menu offers several dining items, including biscuits, ravioli, cheeseburgers, canned dog food, and even New York steak. If we could afford to stay here, Jake would surely check off every item on the list, vacuum it down, and wait patiently at the door for room service to deliver the next course.

Pooches who stay here can also get a luxury most people would drool for: a professional massage. A "slow and gentle" massage is said to increase circulation, help aches and pains, and soothe away fears. A half-hour massage costs $65. (Really.)

Dogs must stay in one of the Ranch's 21 freestanding cottages. Rates are $399–4,100. There's a $100 fee for the length of your dog's stay. Dog menu items are extra. You must let the staff know ahead of time that you'll be coming with your pooch so appropriate arrangements can be made. 900 San Ysidro Lane 93108; 805/969-5046; www.sanysidroranch.com.

Carpinteria

PARKS, BEACHES, AND RECREATION AREAS

The part of the city beach where dogs are permitted is fairly difficult to reach, and it pretty much bans dogs during the harbor seal birthing season in the spring. It's much easier to go to the Rincon Beach County Park (see below), but if you really want to hit the small strip of city beach that permits dogs, call 805/684-5405 and find out its status.

17 Rincon Beach County Park

🐾🐾🐾 (See Santa Barbara County map on page 692)

A wooden stairway takes you from a green blufftop picnic area down to the sandy beach. It's not a huge beach, but the Beach Boys sang about it and surfer dudes love it.

The bluff provides an excellent view of the ocean. Even though nude bathing is illegal, naked people flock here. Just cover your dog's eyes as you pass by the fleshy masses. (The nudists really appreciate it if your dog obeys the leash law.)

The park is at Bates Road and U.S. 101, at the south end of Carpinteria. 805/684-5405.

PLACES TO EAT

Please see the introduction to this chapter for the reason we're not including the dog-friendly restaurants of Carpinteria in this edition. (An amazing coffee café we'd love to include provides a water bowl, doggy treats, and dog bagels. But I won't mention the name because I don't want to bring the most dog-friendly eatery in the county to the attention of the authorities.)

PLACES TO STAY

Carpinteria State Beach: Camp along the Pacific Ocean at one of the 261 beachfront sites here. Dogs love it, but don't let them get any ideas about running around on the beach. They're banned. Sites are $14–20. From U.S. 101, take the Casitas Pass exit and drive west about a mile to the campground. Call 805/684-2811 for information, or call 800/444-7275 for reservations.

Holiday Inn Express: This one's cozy, clean, and conveniently situated. You get a pool, whirlpool, exercise room, and big continental breakfast when you stay here. Your dog gets, well…your dog gets to stay here. Rates are $89–209. Dogs are $10 extra. 5606 Carpinteria Avenue 93013; 805/566-9949.

CHAPTER 51

Ventura County

This diverse coastal county is not a place to bring a dog who is seriously obsessed with swimming. All but a handful of beaches along the 42 miles of coastline here ban dogs, although a few allow them in their camping or picnicking areas.

Even the big and bassy Lake Casitas makes sure dogs stay more than 50 feet from the lake's edge. We've seen water dogs tremble with genetic anticipation as they try to pull their owners close enough to dip a paw. A ranger told us about a dog who got so frustrated at not being able to swim that when he got back to the motel that night, he ran straight past the manager and into the swimming pool.

Try not to let your dog visit Dog Hell here. You enter Dog Hell when you drive miles and miles to get to a county park, only to find Sir Ranger shaking his head at you, hands on hips, ready to do battle. County parks ban dogs from every inch of their terrain except campgrounds, which are generally not the most scenic spots in the world.

PICK OF THE LITTER—VENTURA COUNTY

COOLEST TRAIL
Ojai Valley Trail, Ojai (page 713)

BEST DOG PARK
Arroyo Verde Dog Park, Ventura (page 715)

BEST PARK FOR BOB HOPE FANS
Rocky Peak Park/Runkle Ranch, Simi Valley (page 718)

BEST PARK FOR WESTERN FANS
Corriganville Park, Simi Valley (page 719)

MOST DIVERSE HIKE POSSIBILITIES
Happy Camp Canyon Regional Park, Moorpark (page 718)

BEST BEACHES
Hollywood Beach, Oxnard (page 723)
Sycamore Cove Beach, Port Hueneme (page 725)

COOLEST RESTAURANT
Deer Lodge, Ojai (page 714)

BEST RIDE
Channel Islands Water Taxi, Oxnard (page 722)

FRIENDLIEST DOG CLUB
Star Canine Social Club, Oxnard (page 724)

Fortunately, between the Santa Monica Mountains National Recreation Area and the Santa Monica Mountains Conservancy, there's plenty of terrific land to explore. (For specific parks in Ventura County run by these entities, see below. For more details on these park entities themselves, see the Los Angeles County chapter.)

NATIONAL FORESTS

The National Forests and Wilderness Areas resource at the back of this book has important information and safety tips on visiting national forests with your dog and has more information on Los Padres National Forest.

Los Padres National Forest

Ojai

PARKS, BEACHES, AND RECREATION AREAS

❶ Ojai Valley Trail

🐾🐾🐾 (See Ventura County map on page 710)

You and your leashed dog may have to share this 9.5-mile trail with a few fast bicycles and sweet-smelling horses, but don't let that stop you. It's a great way to get from Ojai to Ventura. Although most people start at the southern end and work their way northeast, it's an uphill climb that can get mighty toasty certain times of year. We recommend starting from Ojai. As they say, Go Southwest, young dog! (You can always meet a friend at the end who will drive you home.)

The trail is a "rails-to-trails" conversion of a more than 100-year-old railroad line that hauled oranges and other goodies from local orchards to far-flung markets. It takes you and your leashed dog through little forested areas and quiet neighborhoods, past rolling hills and Christmas tree farms. Views of the surrounding mountains at times are to drool for. For the fair of paw, there are plenty of shaded, tranquil resting spots along the way. About midway there's a market and some fast-food–type restaurants—nothing you'd normally care to see on a nature hike, but a welcome oasis if you've worked up an appetite or if you're crossing your legs for a pit stop. (There are no public restroom facilities on the trail at this point.)

Even if you walk only one segment of the trail, it's worth the trip. When the trail first opened, dogs were banned (it's a county parks thing), but the rule was so difficult to enforce that eventually pooches were given the OK. Take advantage of this! Rejoice! Take a hike!

The trail runs parallel to Highway 33. Its easternmost end just brushes Soule Park, but it's not well marked or as easy to get to as it is just a few blocks to the west, on Fox Street, east of Libbey Park. You can park at the Park and Ride lot at East Ojai Avenue and Fox Street and walk down Fox to the trail. You'll also find limited parking on residential streets. 805/654-3951.

PLACES TO EAT

Deer Lodge: This wood and stone landmark restaurant is one of the most cool, fun eateries where you can bring a doggy. You feel as if you're at an Old West outpost, albeit a most civilized and attractive one, when you dine here. Deer figure prominently on the signage, decor (heads on old wooden walls), and the menu. You can get a venison salad, venison barley soup, or go for broke and try the "World Famous Deer Lodge Game Plate," which can include a selection of deer, wild boar, elk, antelope, kangaroo (oh god, no, say it's not true! Not cousins of Kanga and little Roo!), alligator, and pheasant. Your dog wants you to order this plate. Your dog is getting your car keys right now.

For those whose palates prefer animals of the more farmy variety, the apricot cashew chicken, Buffalo Bill burger, or cowboy's tri-tip offer less wild alternatives. Vegetarians can even make a meal here, with a hearty salad, some slowly roasted garlic, and a big plate of deer-free pasta.

Best of all, the cowboy-hat–clad waitresses are mighty dog-friendly, and dogs and their people have a choice of two patios. We prefer the lower patio, which is bigger, prettier, bamboo-covered, and warmed on cool evenings by an outdoor fireplace. 2261 Maricopa Highway; 805/646-4256.

Ventura

This seaside community has always had a wealth of parks for leashed dogs to sniff out. But thanks to some hard-working dog people, it's now home to two parks where dogs can throw their leashes to the wind. It's also home to the ninth—and last—mission founded by Father Junipero Serra. Dogs can't go inside, but they're more than happy to smile at the camera for an exterior shot.

PARKS, BEACHES, AND RECREATION AREAS

🐾 Lake Casitas Recreation Area

🐾🐾🐾 (See Ventura County map on page 710)

Don't bring a water dog here. She'll just stare at the water and weep. Dogs have to be kept 50 feet away from the lake, meaning they can't even go on a boat with you. With 50,000 people who rely on this lake for water, it's understandable that they wouldn't want a bunch of flea-bitten beasts floating around in their drink. But that's a hard one to explain to a quivering, frothing Labrador retriever. Actually, people aren't permitted to swim here either, but that news probably won't do much to console your dog-paddling pooch.

Once you enter this 6,200-acre park, your best bet is to bear to the right and follow the road to a dense, lush, oaky campground. Park wherever you can and walk with your leashed dog as far back as possible. You'll find some short trails winding through this part of the park and some excellent places to relax and get away from the bulk of the people who visit here. (They're all at the water, like most normal folks.)

The day-use fee is $6.50. Dogs are $1. Sites at the 480 campsites are $16. Camping dogs cost $2. Reservations are not necessary. From the heart of Ventura, drive 11 miles north on Highway 33. Turn left on Highway 150 and drive about four miles to the main entrance. 805/649-2233.

3 Ojai Valley Trail

🐾🐾🐾 (See Ventura County map on page 710)

Please see the listing in the Ojai section for details about this 9.5-mile trail that goes from Ojai to Ventura. In case you want to go from Ventura to Ojai (if you like a vigorous uphill hike that leads you away from the ocean), Foster County Park Campground (see Places to Stay, below) is the trail's staging area. But keep in mind that dogs are allowed at that park only at the trailhead and the campsites. Exit Highway 33 at Casitas Vista Road and follow the signs. As you head northeast on the trail, you can also get to it from points such as San Antonio Creek, Santa Ana Boulevard, Barbara Street, and Baldwin Avenue. 805/654-3951.

4 Arroyo Verde Dog Park

🐾🐾🐾🐾 ✦ (See Ventura County map on page 710)

Early-rising canines have it good here: They've got eight acres of grassy, shady land to frisk about on without leashes in the early morning. The dog area is unfenced, full of trees, and features a drinking fountain for dogs and their people, mutt mitts, and restrooms (for people—dogs can use the grass).

I've been told three different things by three different park department employees about the hours and days the park is open to off-leash dogs. The schedule has been in flux for a while because of some conflicts between dog people and other park users, so be sure to check the signs at the park before you set your dog free, or call before you visit. The hours given me by the park supervisor who probably knows the most and latest about the situation: The dog area is open for off-leash fun Tuesday–Friday 6–9 A.M., Saturday 6–8 A.M., and Sunday 6–9 A.M. It's closed Monday for maintenance, and it's also closed on city holidays and for special events.

The dog area is right at the entrance of the rugged 129-acre Arroyo Verde Park. It's clearly marked. Most of the park is pretty much impassable by anyone except creatures of nature, but you and your leashed dog can take a short trail or two that get you a little closer to the wilds.

There's a $1 fee per vehicle on Sundays and holidays. (You probably won't be coming here on a holiday, being that you can't bring your leash-free dog.) Be sure to leash up from the parking lot to the off-leash area. Exit U.S. 101 at Victoria Avenue and drive north on Victoria for about two miles. Where it ends, turn left on Foothill Road. In about two-thirds of a mile, the park will be on your right, at the corner of Foothill and Day Roads. 805/652-4550.

5 Grant Memorial Park

🐾🐾🐾 (See Ventura County map on page 710)

In 1782, Father Junipero Serra raised a wooden cross on the mountain overlooking his newly built Mission San Buenaventura. That mountain is now part of this 107-acre park. A cross still sticks out of the top of the park, and if you go anywhere near it, you'll find wonderful views of the city, the Pacific, and the Channel Islands.

Surrounding the cross is a little grassy area where you can unwind, take in the views, or eat a picnic. But if you want to be kind to your dog, before you sit down to ooh and ahh at the scenery, turn around. On the other side of the parking lot you'll see a dirt trail heading up the adjacent hill. It's not shady, so your leashed dog won't be able to ooh and ahh at the trees, but it's a great way for you to get away from the park's never-ending trickle of visitors.

From Cedar Street (two blocks east of Ventura Avenue), turn east on Ferro Drive and follow it to the top of the park. 805/652-4550.

6 Annie Dransfeldt Dog Park

🐾🐾🐾🐕 (See Ventura County map on page 710)

Annie Dransfeldt is a real person and a great local dog advocate. So great, in fact, that they named this terrific little park after her. It's about two fenced grassy acres, with trees, double gates, a separate area for small dogs, a drinking fountain for dogs and their humans, and poop bags. Since the park is named after her, she asks people to please scoop the poop. (You could even pick up an "orphan" poop while you're at it. Apparently there have been too many of these little lovelies hanging around.)

The park is within Camino Real Park, a 38-acre complex with lots of playing fields and courts and a refreshingly eucalyptus smell. It's closed on city holidays. Unlike the other city dog park, this one's open 6 A.M.–dusk every day except Wednesday, when it opens at 9 A.M. because of park maintenance. It's at Dean Drive and Varsity Street. 805/652-4550.

PLACES TO EAT

Ventura restaurants are generous with doggy water bowls. As one server recently told us, "A dog can't order food. The least we can do is give them a free drink."

The Coastal Cone Company: Dine on frosty treats at one of three patio tables. Thirsty dogs can get water on request. 1583 Spinnaker Drive; 805/658-2837.

Duke's Griddle 'n' Grill: Your dog just might get a special treat from a waiter while you dine on the good grilled grub served at the outdoor tables here. At the very least, she'll get a bowl of water if she asks for one. 1124 South Seaward Avenue; 805/653-0707.

Top Hat Burger Palace: You don't have to be of royal blood to enjoy this fast-food palace. All of the seating is outdoors; you just go to an order window to get your food and then dine in leisure with your mutt. Thirsty dogs can order a bowl of water. 299 East Main Street; 805/643-9696.

PLACES TO STAY

For a city of this size, there's a disappointing dearth of decent doggy digs. We don't even list the one upscale hotel, the Marriott Ventura Beach Hotel, because only dogs under 15 pounds can stay, and we don't want to disappoint dogs whose only crime is that they're bigger than cats.

Foster County Park Campground: Some of the sites here are near oaks, but that's about the best thing we can say about this place, except that the park is the local staging area for the Ojai Valley Trail (see above). Dogs are banned from the day-use area of the park. The 48 sites here are $22–35. 805/654-3951.

Hobson County Park Campground: You're so close to the water here (you're actually at the ocean's edge), yet so very far away. Dogs aren't allowed on the beach, and that can be a bummer with a capital B. This is not beach camping at its most peaceful. In fact, before you come, open a can of sardines to get an idea of how tight the campers, RVs, and tents can be packed. The campground is small, and it has 31 oceanside sites. Rates are $22–35. Dogs are $1 extra. From Ventura, drive northwest on U.S. 101 and exit at the State Beaches exit. Drive north on West Pacific Highway for five miles. The campground is on the left. For park info or campsite reservations, call 805/654-3951.

Lake Casitas Recreation Area: See Lake Casitas Recreation Area, above, for camping information.

La Quinta Inn: This inn has had all sorts of nonhuman visitors—even birds and rabbits. Dogs are welcome here, as long as they're under 40 pounds and they stay out of the outdoor pool and whirlpool. Rates are $83–103. 5818 Valentine Road 93003; 805/658-6200.

McGrath State Beach Campsites: Your dog can't go on the beach with you here, but the camping area is pretty enough that it's not such a bad fate to hang out here together and read a good book. There are 174 sites. Rates are $10–12. From U.S. 101, take the Seaward Avenue/Harbor Boulevard exit and drive four miles west on Harbor Boulevard to the beach. For reservations, phone 800/444-7275. For park info, call 805/968-1033.

Motel 6: Rates are $48–70 for the first adult, $6 for the second. 2145 East Harbor Boulevard 93001; 805/643-5100.

Vagabond Inn: There's a decent grassy area on the premises dogs like to sniff out. This is where many Kennel Club Fair attendees stay with their humans when in town. Rates are $69–99. (That's a hefty price for vagabonds.) Dogs are $5 extra. 756 East Thompson Boulevard 93001; 805/648-5371.

Moorpark

PARKS, BEACHES, AND RECREATION AREAS

7 Happy Camp Canyon Regional Park

☻☻☻☻ (See Ventura County map on page 710)

This 3,000-acre wonderland of lush forests, colorful shale outcroppings, and wide-open grasslands is a great place for a dog to bring a human. People love the splendid geological formations and the seasonal wildflowers. Dogs adore the variety of hiking possibilities in this vast wilderness area. The park has more than 12 miles of trails, but only some permit pooches. Signs will let you know what's OK and what's not. Dogs need to be on leash here; the park is home to sensitive wildlife habitats.

The address is 14105 Broadway. Exit U.S. 101 at Highway 23 and drive north to New Los Angeles Avenue. Go left (west) and at the third signal, Moorpark Avenue, turn right. Drive 2.6 miles (Moorpark Avenue will turn into Walnut Canyon Road) past the railroad crossing. You'll see a sharp 30-mph left curve at that point, but do not go left; continue straight and you'll almost immediately come to Broadway Avenue, where you'll make a right. Continue to the park, where there's plenty of parking. 310/589-3200.

Simi Valley

PARKS, BEACHES, AND RECREATION AREAS

8 Rocky Peak Park

☻☻☻☻ (See Ventura County map on page 710)

If you and your dog want to pay homage to Bob Hope, watch some of his road flicks one evening, and the next morning, venture out to this sprawling 4,815-acre park. Hope once owned 4,400 acres of this land. Back then it was known as Runkle Ranch. Today it's known as an amazing place to hike through wide-open grasslands, oak savannahs, and gigantic sandstone boulder formations. If you visit in the spring, you'll be wowed by the wildflowers here. There's abundant wildlife here, and mountain bikes and equestrians, so leashes are the law.

Several trails that start at various points on the park's perimeter take you to vastly different parts of this huge park. Go to www.smmc.ca.gov if you want to make hiking plans before going, or just check out the trail map near the park entrance when you get here. A trail leading to a couple of popular trails starts here. The park entrance is across Highway 118 from Corriganville Park (see below). From the east, exit Highway 118 at Rocky Peak Road. The park is on the north side of the off-ramp. From the west, exit Highway 118 at Kuehner Drive. Turn right and follow it to the top of the pass (it will become Santa Susana Pass Road) and to the park entrance. 310/589-3200.

⑨ Corriganville Park

🐾🐾🐾🐾 (See Ventura County map on page 710)

If you're a fan of old Westerns, stop your stagecoach right here, pardner. And if you have a penchant for old jungle flicks, you also need to swing into this big park, which is named after actor and stuntman Ray "Crash" Corrigan, who bought the property in the 1930s.

Hundreds of movies were shot here from the 1930s and into the 1960s. Back then, the property was as large as 2,000 acres, but now it's 220. That's OK. There's still plenty of room for you and your leashed little doggy (or big doggy) to git along and see some fun old movie backdrops. A few of the films that were shot here: *Fort Apache, Trail of the Vigilante, Mule Train, Rogues of Sherwood Forest, Escape from Fort Bravo, Skipalong Rosenbloom, Tarzan Escapes,* and even *The Inspector General.*

A stream cuts through an empty concrete-lined pool that was filled during Corriganville's movie days. It has windows in the side where cameramen were stationed to get underwater shots of the good guys fighting the bad guys in the "lake," or in the case of the Jungle Jim movies (also shot here), wrestling an alligator.

If you're interested in more information about Corriganville, there's a marvelous website about Corriganville, with a biography of its colorful namesake, information on all the former sets and present sites, and tons of old photos. The site name is a long and clunky one, with lots of slashes, so it's easier to just type "Corriganville" into a search engine. It will come up immediately. One piece of news it won't tell you is that the park has poop-bag dispensers; this is something that dogs with forgetful humans (the kind who leave the poop bags at home) like to know.

(A huge thank-you to Sheryl Smith, and her dear English springer spaniel Gracie—who is now galloping around leash-free in Dog Heaven—for their heads-up about Corriganville and for their contribution to our description of this wonderful park.)

From I-5 or I-405, head west on Highway 118 (the Ronald Reagan/Simi Valley Freeway), exit at Kuehner Drive (you'll be coming down out of the Santa Susana Mountains), and turn left. In about a mile, turn left at the signal at Smith Road. The entrance to Corriganville Park is at the end of the street. (Shortly before that entrance on the left you'll see the original entrance to the property.) 805/584-4400.

10 Sage Ranch Park
🐾 🐾 🐾 🐾 (See Ventura County map on page 710)

The 652 acres of wild parkland at Sage Ranch have the kind of diversity most parks can only dream of. Coastal sage scrub, the park's namesake, dominates, but along the park's 2.6-mile loop trail you'll also find grasslands, wildflowers (in spring), oak woodlands, an old orange grove, and a riparian area with sycamores, walnut trees, and ferns. The ferny fauna isn't far from some rocky outcroppings that look as if they belong in an old Western flick. The contrast of environments makes for intriguing hikes. Even dogs seem to dig the varying scenery.

The address is 1 Black Canyon Road. Exit U.S. 101 at Valley Circle Drive/Mulholland Drive. Drive north on Valley Circle Drive for about six miles. You'll come to a three-way stop at Woolsey Canyon Road. Go left and follow Woolsey Canyon Road to the end, where you'll head right on Black Canyon Road. The entrance to the park is about 200 yards north of the intersection. 818/999-3753 or 310/589-3200.

11 Ahmanson Ranch/Upper Las Virgenes Canyon Open Space Preserve
🐾 🐾 🐾 🐾 (See Ventura County map on page 710)

Every acre of this spectacular 3,000-acre park is in Ventura County. But the only access is from Los Angeles County, so that chapter is where you'll find its description in this book.

PLACES TO EAT

Pasta and Salads Company: You'll enjoy eating healthful foods at the outdoor tables with your pooch at your side. 464 Madera Road; 805/520-4649.

PLACES TO STAY

Motel 6: Rates are $60–70 for the first adult, $6 for the second. 2566 North Erringer Road 93065; 805/526-3533.

Oak County Park Campground: This county campground is directly below some railroad tracks in what looks like a dirt parking lot with a few trees. It's not what you'd call a hot spot for getting back to nature, but it is popular with Scout troops and their ilk, so there's definitely some habitat worth sniffing out.

There are 55 sites. Rates are $5 per adult for tent sites, $2 per child, and $1 per dog. (The minimum charge for tent sites is $10, so if it's just you and your dog, you'll still have to fork over a tenner.) RV sites start at $25 per RV. Dogs are $1 extra, and more than two humans will cost you a little extra, too. This being a county park, dogs are not allowed on the park's trails or anywhere but the campground.

About halfway between Moorpark and Simi Valley on Highway 118, exit onto Los Angeles Avenue and drive southeast about 1.5 miles. The park entrance will be on your left, directly across from a really big, ugly contractor's storage facility. The address is 901 Quimisa Drive. 805/654-3644.

Oxnard

What this city lacks in the appealing name department (you just can't say "Oxnard" so it sounds like anything remotely attractive), it makes up for with a couple of beaches that allow dogs and a twice-monthly dog gathering that's a real gas (see the Diversion Run, Spot, Run!).

PARKS, BEACHES, AND RECREATION AREAS

I once had a scintillating conversation with a parks department employee about the subject of dog doo-doo. He quoted from the scriptures (city code): "It says right here—'No person shall permit any dog to defecate on public property...without the consent of the person owning it.' That's the law."

"OK, so you have to fax the park commissioners, tell them your dog ate a whopper of a supper last night, and that you might be needing the use of their parks the next morning?" asked I. It took him a few minutes before he figured out that maybe there was more to this law than meets the eye. "Oh, right here it says that if you clean it up right away, you don't have to get permission," said he. "Whew!" said I. "Whew!" breathed Joe Dog.

Another city law says that you must always carry a pooper-scooper when

DIVERSION

Be Harbor Hounds: The best way to see the sights of Channel Islands Harbor is from the water, and thanks to the **Channel Islands Water Taxi,** you don't have to be rich or an angler to do the boat thing. You and your salty dog can hitch a ride on this 22-foot enclosed boat that motors to five stops around the harbor, and it will barely make a dent in your dog food budget. The cost: $6 for a round-trip cruise (about 40 minutes), or $1–2 per hop. Dogs ride free. During summer, the taxi runs most days noon–6 P.M. or 7 P.M. During the off-season, the taxi usually sets sail on weekends only. If you want to rent the boat for a private to-do, it will cost you $100 an hour, and you can bring up to 22 guests. (The captain is included with the fee.)

Our favorite place to catch the water cab is at Fisherman's Wharf in Oxnard. The wharf is at 2741 South Victoria Avenue. (That's also where you'll find the Channel Islands Visitors Center, where you can pick up water taxi schedules and fun info about the area.) For other stops or more information, call 805/985-4677 or 805/985-4852.

with your dog. If you don't have one on hand, you could be fined. But what if your dog already did his business and you threw it out? "You'd better carry a spare just for show," another city employee told me.

The biggest park in the city, College Park, doesn't permit pooches because it's actually a county park. (And we know how dog-friendly those are.) Fortunately, there are two beaches dogs can visit on leash and a terrific free dog club that welcomes any decent dog to cavort around leash-free every couple of weeks. (Please see the Diversion Run, Spot, Run!)

12 Oxnard Beach Park

😸 😸 😸 (See Ventura County map on page 710)

This is a state park, but don't let that scare you off: It's run by the city of Oxnard, and dogs are welcome on leash. The park is less developed than many other beaches in the area. It covers about 62 acres and features dune trails and a picnic area. The beach is an extra-wide one, and dogs really dig it here, even though they have to be attached to people.

The parking fee is $5 for the day. The beach is west of Harbor Boulevard, between Beach Way and Falkirk Avenue. 805/385-7950.

13 Hollywood Beach

🐾🐾🐾 (See Ventura County map on page 710)

You may not see silver-screen stars at Hollywood Beach, but your dog will still be dazzled as she joins you on a leashed walk on this beautiful chunk of sand and sea. Many dogs drag their humans here for a walk, and you may find some naked ones (sans leash) running around, but leashes are the rule. It's off Harbor Boulevard, at the corner of La Brea Street and Ocean Drive. 805/382-3007.

PLACES TO EAT

Buon Appetito: The food here is *delicioso,* the atmosphere charming. The cuisine leans heavily toward Italian, but you can also get some great seafood dishes. (After all, it *is* Fisherman's Wharf—see below.) We've heard the salmon in puff pastry is delectable, but we were more in the mood for a giant, drippy calzone when we visited. Dine with your dog at the 10 attractive patio tables. If you bring your pooch's water bowl, someone will be happy to pour her some fresh water. 2721 South Victoria; 805/984-8437.

Fisherman's Wharf: This is a thoroughly charming, dog-friendly collection of old-fashioned shops and good restaurants. Little benches abound, but many of the restaurants have their own outdoor seating. We see at least a couple of dogs here each time we visit, and we figure they're dogs of the nautical persuasion. They're in great shape, but their leashes seem to be boating line and their owners have tan, leathery skin and a hint of salt on the hair. The wharf is at 2721 South Victoria Avenue.

PLACES TO STAY

Best Western Oxnard Inn: The rooms here are comfortable and attractive, and the expanded continental breakfast will fill you up for a day of exploring the area. You'll have use of a pool, a whirlpool tub, and a little exercise room, too. Sounds great, but hold the phone if you have a large dog. "We prefer dogs to be under 35 pounds," a front-desk person said sweetly when I checked out the place. She didn't say firmly that "Dogs *must* be under 35 pounds," so maybe there's some leverage for larger beasts. Rates are $90–129. Dogs are $20 extra. 1156 South Oxnard Boulevard 93030; 805/483-9581.

Residence Inn by Marriott: This is a convenient place to park it when traveling with a pooch. All the rooms are studios or apartments and all come with full kitchens. Rates are $119–159 and include a full breakfast and afternoon beverages. The staff is experienced in the world of dog travel here: If you forgot your dog's bowl or leash, you can get a loaner. Here's the long list of dog fees: Dogs pay a $100 fee for the length of their stay (dogs usually stay a while here to make it worth their money), and they're $5 extra per night. In

DIVERSION

Run, Spot, Run!: The **Star Canine Social Club** has to be the most fun, relaxed dog club in California. Any well-behaved dog can attend its lively off-leash gatherings in Oxnard two Saturday afternoons a month. Nothing is breed-specific, as is the case in most dog clubs. "If it vaguely resembles a dog, it's welcome here," says Becky, who is a vertebra in the club's backbone. There are no competitions, no membership fees. "We're a nonprofit organization," she says. "Extremely nonprofitable." (Donations will be accepted, but they are not solicited.)

Socialization and leash-free running on six areas of totally fenced open space are the biggest draws, but the gatherings offer much more, including: agility equipment, Frisbees, tennis balls, sticks, toys, a doggy pool, refreshing sprinkler, and fun events such as egg-on-spoon walks for dogs, bobbing for hot dogs, obedience practice, and birthday parties. Small and timid dogs get their own fenced area. (The group will even work with dogs who have social problems, but you have to make arrangements.)

For location and schedule, phone 805/389-6149 or check out the club's funny website at www.i-love-dogs.com/dog/hamlet.

addition, there's a $250 deposit. 2101 West Vineyard Avenue 93030; 805/278-2200; www.residenceinn.com.

Vagabond Inn: There's a decent little neighborhood park across the street, should your dog want to stretch her legs upon arrival. Room rates are $81–84. Dogs are $5 extra. 1245 North Oxnard Boulevard 93030; 805/983-0251.

Port Hueneme

PARKS, BEACHES, AND RECREATION AREAS

Dogs are not allowed at this Navy city's beaches, but they can peruse the parks here and one terrific beach down the coast just a bit in Point Mugu State Park territory. (See Sycamore Cove Beach.)

14 Moranda/Bubbling Springs Park

🐾🐾 (See Ventura County map on page 710)

A stream runs through much of this park, and in the summer dogs love to dip their hot little toes in it to cool off. The park is actually two connected parks. Most of the Bubbling Springs Park, to the north, is a greenbelt area. Moranda Park is a chunk of green with trees, green grass, shaded picnic areas, and playgrounds.

Many people and their leashed dogs hike from one end of the adjoining parks to the other. Going north to south (toward the beach), you can begin your walk at Bard Road and Park Avenue and follow the park as it winds south, crossing a few streets along the way. Your hike will end around Seawind Way. 805/986-6542.

15 Sycamore Cove Beach

🐾🐾🐾🐾 (See Ventura County map on page 710)

This big, beautiful beach welcomes leashed dogs to stroll on the sand, wade in the surf, and sniff around a grassy picnic area. It's the most dog-friendly part of the 15,000-acre Point Mugu State Park, which bans dogs from trails. You can even camp here; across the highway is a 55-site campground. (See Places to Stay for more details on camping at Point Mugu.)

The day-use fee is a steep $10 per vehicle. The beach is about 11 miles south of Port Hueneme (about six miles north of the Los Angeles County line) on Highway 1/Pacific Coast Highway. 818/880-0350.

PLACES TO STAY

Point Mugu State Park Campgrounds: Dogs aren't permitted on the magical trails in this spectacular park, even with a leash. "They're a hazard to wildlife and other park visitors," a young ranger told me in a monotone, robotic voice. Creepy! But there are a few paved roads you can walk them on, if tar's your cup of tea. At least dogs are allowed to help you pitch a tent at one of the 131 camp-sites. One of our favorite camping areas is at Thornhill Broome Beach. Dogs love camping beachside. (They can't visit the beach here, though, but they're welcome at Point Mugu's Sycamore Cove Beach, above.) Rates are $20. The park is about nine miles south of Port Hueneme Road, on Highway 1. For park info, call 818/880-0350. Call 800/444-7275 to reserve a site.

Camarillo

PARKS, BEACHES, AND RECREATION AREAS

16 Camarillo Dog Park

🐾🐾🐾🐕 (See Ventura County map on page 710)

If only dogs could see in color (and maybe they can, but that's another story): The fire hydrant and drinking fountain in this one-acre, fenced dog park are so dazzling you almost need sunglasses to look at them. The hydrant is a bright fire-engine red, the fountain is a brilliant green. They look especially colorful when surrounded by white dogs, black dogs, and Dalmatians.

The park has plenty of trees, which provide welcome shade in the warmer months. Dogs and their humans also have water fountains, benches, and a picnic table. It's a fun place to visit for a little relaxation and a lot of leash-free dog fun.

The dog park is in Camarillo Grove Park. There's a $3 fee to enter this park, but if you have a dog with you, it's free. (Dogs are like a bulky coupon.) You're relegated to the dog park, so don't go wandering off anywhere else once you're in. Exit U.S. 101 at Camarillo Springs Road. If you're coming from the north, go left at the stop sign at the bottom of the off-ramp and continue to the park. If you're coming from the south, keep heading straight from the off-ramp and you'll hit the park. The park is off Camarillo Springs Road at the base of the Conejo grade. 805/482-1996.

Thousand Oaks

PARKS, BEACHES, AND RECREATION AREAS

Zounds! The Thousand Oaks area is home to 13,000 acres of open space you can peruse with a leashed dog. Most of these areas are difficult to get to, but if you can find them, they're well worth the visit. We describe a couple of open-space areas below. The Conejo Open Space Conservation Agency, which oversees these areas, can provide you a general map and directions to other open-space parks. 805/495-6471.

The city now even has its very own dog park. Waverly Dog Park has proven very popular with the pooch set.

The Thousand Oaks area is also home to some of the Santa Monica Mountains National Recreation Area (see the National Forests section of the Los Angeles County chapter). Dogs dig Thousand Oaks. As one very helpful local reader, Carolyn Greene, put it: "Although I enjoy living here myself, it's even better for dogs." Her beautiful 85-pound German shepherd, Jasmine, couldn't agree more.

17 Conejo Creek Dog Park

😺😺😺🐕 (See Ventura County map on page 710)

Dogs who like to socialize dig this park. Every afternoon, dogs of all shapes, sizes, and backgrounds gather to sniff and chase around the three grassy acres here. (It's grassy in part because the park closes whenever it rains.) The dog park is divided into two sections: a smaller section for small or shy dogs and a bigger chunk for everyone else. There are three drinking fountains for dogs and their people, mutt mitt stations galore, and a few double-gated entries. But there's not much as far as trees: Lots of horses have to pass very close to the dog park to reach popular trails, and trees could obscure their ability to see the dogs, which could lead to a startled horse and an injured rider. That said, all's not lost for dogs who like shade: By the time you read this, hot dogs (of the furry variety) and their humans should have some shade structures to hide out under.

The dog park is across the street from Waverly Park, a nice little community park, at 1350 Avenida de las Flores. 805/495-6471. A hot line for the dog park will tell you whether it's open or closed because of maintenance or mud. 805/381-1299.

18 Wildwood Park

😺😺😺😺 (See Ventura County map on page 710)

It's not every day you and your dog get to hike to a 60-foot waterfall, so take advantage of this amazing 1,700-acre park, run by the Conejo Open Space Conservation Agency. Joe Dog liked to walk to the waterfall and stand there in awe that such waterworks can actually exist in what is otherwise dry land.

Several trails wind through the coastal sage and xeric scrub–covered hills that make up most of the park. In the spring, the wildflowers go wild in a burst of intoxicating color and scent.

You'll have to keep your dog leashed as you hike the many miles of trails. The wildlife appreciates it. After all, there's not much habitat around here for these animals anymore. If you need more convincing, see the plea made by a park official in the description (below) of Los Robles Open Space.

From U.S. 101, exit at Thousand Oaks Freeway/Highway 23 and drive north about 2.5 miles to Avenida de los Arboles. Turn left and follow the road all the way to the end (about three miles). The parking area is on the left, next to the entry kiosk that holds maps and brochures of the park. 805/495-6471.

🔟 Los Robles Open Space

🐾🐾🐾 (See Ventura County map on page 710)

If it's trails you want, it's trails you'll get at this terrific swatch of open space land run by the Conejo Open Space Conservation Agency (COSCA). The total trail system here is 15 miles! That's a lot of trail for you and your leashed, outdoors-loving pooch to peruse. Some of the trails are killer, with very steep grades, so avoid these for the sake of your dog's paws. The trail system is going to be a real wonder one day—there are plans to join the trails in Los Robles with trails in the Santa Monica Mountains National Recreation Area (see the National Recreation Areas section of the Los Angeles County chapter) to form a 40-mile trail system from Malibu to Point Mugu.

I promised COSCA coordinator Mark Towne that I'd make a plea for dogs to be leashed here. So before I continue, and since he said it so well, I'll put it in his words:

> We have a lot of problems with dogs off leash. It impacts the wildlife, and it could impact the dogs, too.… We've had dogs chasing rabbits, ground squirrels, and other wildlife. For a dog's sake, leashes are important because there are rattlesnakes and ticks.

Got it? It's tempting, but leashes are the law here, and apparently for good reason.

The trails at Los Robles are actually wide fire-access roads, winding through chaparral country and coast live oaks. They're very well marked. If you start at the parking area at the end of Moorpark Road, you can connect to the Los Robles Trail. Take the trail west to the Spring Canyon Trail and follow it to Lynn Oaks Park and back for an easy three-mile round-trip hike. If you're in the mood for food, pack a lunch and take the Los Robles Trail due south (from Moorpark) for about a mile. You'll come to a pleasant little picnic area where you and your leashed beast can have a feast. If you continue on that trail, it gets extremely steep, with lots of switchbacks and mountain bikes careening blindly down. The views become splendid, but it's not worth it unless you're very tough of paw.

Dogs who like nature love the half-mile Oak Creek Canyon Loop. This is a self-serve nature trail detailing the area's indigenous plant life. You can get here by hiking from the Moorpark entrance, but you can also drive to this trail by following Green Meadow Avenue to the end.

JoAnna Downey, and her gorgeous George Dog, checked out this park for me on a recent visit and provided me with great info on the park. I don't usually rely on others to visit parks for me, but JoAnna and George are highly qualified dog-park explorers: They're the coauthors of the wonderful *Dog Lover's Companion to New England*.

From U.S. 101, take Moorpark Road south to the end (about a mile). The parking lot is on the right. 805/495-6471.

PLACES TO EAT

Jamba Juice: You and your thirsty dog can down all kinds of tasty, healthful concoctions here. (Jake recommends avoiding the green ones, though.) Share your fruit shake at one of many tables at the plaza. (Jamba Juice shares its tables with the likes of Starbucks and Noah's Bagels, so there's something for every taste here.) 33 North Moorpark Road; 805/449-1300.

PLACES TO STAY

Motel 6: Rates are $40–$45. 1516 Newbury Road 91320; 805/499-0711.

Thousand Oaks Inn: Stay here and you're next to Borders Books, which is great for literary dogs. You'll also get use of the hotel's free video library, which is great for couch-potato dogs. Your room comes with use of the hotel's heated pool and whirlpool bath, passes to a local workout joint, and a continental breakfast. Rates are $130–250. There's a $75 pooch fee per visit. 75 West Thousand Oaks Boulevard; 805/497-3701 or 800/600-6878; www.thousandoaksinn.com.

CHAPTER 52
Los Angeles County

Slowly but surely, Los Angeles County is going to the dogs, in the best sense of the phrase. This is a wonderful development if you're a dog or just someone who knows a dog.

When I wrote this book's first edition, there were only a couple of leash-free areas in the whole county. Today, there are 21 and counting. Most are fenced dog parks, but one is a spectacular 1,500-acre swatch of wilderness. (See Westridge-Canyonback Wilderness Park in the Encino section.) Go ahead, dogs: Wag your tails, pant, let it all hang out. Look for the running dog symbol 🐕 in the pages that follow, and take your humans to a dog-gone great park.

Of course, there needs to be a much larger number of leash-free areas if Los Angeles County's estimated 300,000 dogs are going to get the running room they deserve. If dogs had opposable fingers, they'd be crossing them hard for more places where they could just be their good old doggy selves and trot around naked. Many cities and park departments are working hand in paw with dogs and their people to help accomplish this mission. Jake and

I hope we'll be sniffing out many more leash-free havens for the book's next edition.

The Los Angeles County Parks system is a good one, with dozens of large parks dotting the county. Most allow leashed pooches. So do most of the huge, wonderful parklands within the Santa Monica Mountains National Recreation Area (see below), and dogs are allowed on just about every inch of land operated by the Santa Monica Mountains Conservancy.

But not everything is to a dog's liking here. Dogs are still banned from all beaches except one in the Malibu area and one in Long Beach. (Dogs can run leash-free at the Long Beach one, but it's only in the testing stages; nothing is set in stone yet.) The rest of the county's 74 miles of shoreline are off-limits, verboten, badlands. But that may soon come to an end if a couple of active dog groups get their way: A group called Unleash the Beach is working to get a chunk of Santa Monica Beach approved for off-leash use, and the long-entrenched group Freeplay is striving for the same thing at El Segundo's Dockweiler Beach. Jake and I applaud both groups for going beyond setting their sights only on leashed use. See www.unleashthebeach .org and www.freeplay.org.

One of the best deals going for L.A.'s well-behaved dogs is the Sierra Club's K-9 Hiking Section, which encourages dogs on outings. Its stated purpose is "to explore and enjoy the trails and remote areas of the great outdoors with our canine friends and promote responsible dog ownership and behavior in pursuit of these goals." Outings include hikes in pristine national forest land, camping trips, and full-moon doggy hikes. "It's admirable to see a Pomeranian do a 10- to 12-mile hike cross-country, agilely dodging chollas (most of the time), fending off ticks, bounding over boulders in order to contemplate the fantastic views from the summit," a K-9 Committee chair wrote me. For information on the K-9 Hiking Committee and its entertaining newsletter, "Waggin' Trails," contact the Angeles chapter of the Sierra Club at 213/387-4287; www.angeles.sierraclub.org/k9.

Another terrific group to consider joining for awe-inspiring (and sometimes sweat-inspiring) hikes is the California Canine Hikers (CCH). These fun folks hold about 50 hikes per year. For more information or an online application, see their website: www.caninehikers.com.

Back in civilization, you can take a train ride with your dog at Griffith Park and even take your extremely well-behaved poochum-woochums shopping at certain exclusive Beverly Hills stores. You can spend the night at some of the world's finest hotels with your dog, or take him to some super-dog-friendly eateries around town.

Dogs can compare paw prints with the prints of Hollywood's biggest stars at Mann's Chinese Theatre. If you want a little exercise with your stargazing, pick up a map of the stars' homes and take a little walk around town. It's an extremely hackneyed, sometimes rude pastime, but most of the homes on

LOS ANGELES COUNTY

PICK OF THE LITTER—LOS ANGELES COUNTY

BEST BACKDROP
The Paramount Ranch, Agoura Hills (page 743)

BIGGEST VICTORY FOR NATURE
Ahmanson Ranch/Upper Las Virgenes Canyon Open Space Preserve, Calabasas (page 744)

MOST SURPRISING OFF-LEASH HIKE
Westridge-Canyonback Wilderness Park, Encino (page 747)

BIGGEST DOG PARK
Laurel Canyon Park, Studio City (page 753)

BEST LEASH-FREE BEACH (ONLY LEASH-FREE BEACH)
Dog Beach Zone, Long Beach (page 792)

BEST ARCHITECTURAL KITSCH
Tail O' the Pup, West Hollywood (page 757)

MOST DOG-FRIENDLY PLACES TO EAT
All India Cafe, Pasadena (page 779)
Java Man, Hermosa Beach (page 784)
Fleur de Lis, Long Beach (page 794)

MOST DOG-FRIENDLY PLACES TO STAY
Loews Santa Monica Beach Hotel, Santa Monica (page 752)
Sheraton Universal Hotel, Universal City (page 755)
L'Ermitage, Beverly Hills (page 765)
W Los Angeles, Westwood (page 786)

COOLEST CANINE CAMP
Iron Dogs Training Camp, Malibu (page 740)

BEST RIDES
Griffith Park's miniature trains, Los Angeles (page 773)
Catalina Express **ferry,** mainland–Catalina Island (page 799)

these tours have long since changed hands, so you're often just staring at a home where the star lived many moons ago. Anyway, it's a great excuse to walk your dog.

Anthony Shipp, a Beverly Hills veterinarian to the stars, says celebrities often feel that their dogs are the only ones who really love them for who they are. "So many people like them only for what they can get from them, or for the dazzle," says Shipp, who has ministered to the dogs of Frank Sinatra, Kirk Douglas, Pierce Brosnan, and Richard Simmons, to drop a few names. (He recounts how, many years ago, he helped Sinatra's and Douglas's disinterested dogs to mate, but the dogs would do it only after they put on a tape of the crooner's hits. "It seems even dogs get romantic to Sinatra's voice," he says.)

Ah, doggy love.... But we must move on to the practical—the nuts and bolts of this section. This chapter separates some of the districts in the city of Los Angeles into their own sections. For instance, instead of listing Hollywood under "Los Angeles," it has its own heading. The city is too huge to lump all its districts together. Now git along little doggy, and start sniffing out the tens of thousands of acres of urban and wild parks that welcome you and your ilk.

NATIONAL FORESTS

The National Forests and Wilderness Areas resource at the back of this book has important information and safety tips on visiting national forests with your dog and has more information on the Angeles National Forest.

Angeles National Forest
🐾🐾🐾🐾🦮

NATIONAL RECREATION AREAS

Santa Monica Mountains National Recreation Area
🐾🐾🐾🐾

Attention, smog-coated dogs and city-weary people: You can breathe a sigh of relief. Nature is only a stick's throw away from the crowded freeways and urban sprawl of one of the largest cities in the world.

Contrary to what some local dog people have heard, leashed dogs really are allowed to explore sections of this 65,000-acre wonderland of mountains, canyons, woods, and fern glens. This national recreation area is a patchwork of county, state, and federal lands throughout the Santa Monica Mountains. While dogs are banned from trails on all state park lands and from most beaches within the recreation area, the majority of the recreation area's parks and open spaces welcome leashed dogs. Dogs need to wear a leash no longer than six feet (if it's retractable, measure carefully!) and be under control. (It seems to be a redundant rule, but apparently the parks have had their share of out-of-control leashed dogs.) The most dog-friendly of the national recreation area's lands are managed by the Santa Monica Mountains Conservancy. (We describe many of these gems throughout this chapter and in the Ventura County chapter.)

The Mountain Parks Information Service provides a free map showing all the parks, delineating which permit dogs. You can also get free brochures of many of the dog-friendly parks, which show trailheads and give descriptions and directions. They're essential for planning any enchanting back-to-nature outing with your dog. Call 800/533-PARK (800/533-7275) to get your maps and brochures. For a map of the entire recreation area, go to www.nps.org/samo. In a hard-to-navigate-to page within that site (www.nps.gov/samo/brochure/dogleash.htm), you'll also find a list of parks within the recreation area that allow dogs and the detailed dog rules. The people at the National Park Service Visitor Center can be very helpful in answering questions about the recreation area. You can reach them at 805/370-2301.

Spring is a terrific time to explore these lands. Wildflowers blossom white, yellow, orange, blue, red, and every other color your dog might not be able to see if he's as color-blind as scientists claim. Birds sing their hearts out. The grass-lands, normally a dead tan-brown color, become as green as green gets.

But watch out in the warmer months: "A lot of people bring their dogs hiking in the 90° heat and don't give them as much water as they need," says Walt Young, chief ranger for the Santa Monica Mountains Conservancy. "The dogs get heat stroke and we have to be called in to help out." Take his advice and leave your dog at home if it's hot. If you must take your dog during the hot months, bring only a fit, nonsenior-citizen dog, and be sure to offer her water very frequently, even if she recently turned down a snootful.

Castaic

PARKS, BEACHES, AND RECREATION AREAS

🔳 Castaic Lake

🐾🐾🐾 (See Los Angeles County map on pages 732–733)

At 9,000 acres, this is the largest of Los Angeles County's recreation areas. But before your dog starts drooling with excitement, you should be warned that there's not much for a dog to do around here.

Hiking trails are virtually nonexistent. Dogs must be leashed everywhere. They're never allowed in either the large Castaic Lake or the 180-acre After-bay Lagoon, no matter how many trout or bass they see. (But humans can once again go swimming at the lake now that a bacteria problem is gone.)

Because there are no trails around Castaic Lake, it's pretty much impossible to hike its perimeter. The Afterbay Lagoon is a good sight easier for a dog jaunt, since it's developed. It has plenty of grassy areas, some trees, picnic tables, and a couple of playgrounds.

If you and your dog aren't anglers, but you're with someone who is, it's a fine place to spend the day. But it's not the kind of destination you'd want to visit just to walk your dog.

There's a $10 fee per car in summer, $8 in winter. Boat-launching is an additional $8. The lake's 60 campsites cost $15–18 nightly. From I-5, exit at Lake Hughes Road and follow it to the lake. 661/257-4050.

PLACES TO STAY

Castaic Lake: See Castaic Lake, above, for camping information.

Comfort Inn: The lake is down the road a bit. Rates are $50–110. Dogs can stay only in smoking rooms. Dogs under 25 pounds are $5 extra. Over that size, they're $10. 31558 Castaic Road 91384; 661/295-1100 or 800/228-5150.

Saugus

PARKS, BEACHES, AND RECREATION AREAS

🔲 Vasquez Rocks Natural Area Park

🐾🐾🐾 (See Los Angeles County map on pages 732–733)

This is Los Angeles County? It looks more like another planet. The slanted, jagged rocks and hidden caves are among the state's most famous geological wonders. They're so unusually beautiful that film crews routinely use them as a backdrop. When you call the park, chances are the answering machine will tell you how to get permission to make movies here. It's probably not the kind of information you and your dog need to know, but that's entertainment.

This smog-free 745-acre park in the high desert near Agua Dulce also features Tataviam Indian archaeological sites. Many trails branch off through chaparral and riparian plant communities. Make sure you bring drinking water; there's none in the park and you can work up a mighty thirst.

Dogs must be leashed, but back in the days of the bandit Tiburicio Vasquez, there were no such rules. If there had been, Vasquez, the park's namesake, would have found a way to break them. In the mid-1800s, Vasquez was a sort of Robin Hood character, robbing from the wealthy and giving the money to poor Mexicans. He used the caves and rocks as a hideaway from the sheriff's posses and vigilantes who were always on his trail. When you visit the park, stop at the entry kiosk and read about Vasquez's dramatic final days here. Then take your dog for a hike on the very trails Vasquez may have fled on, and let your imagination take you back to the days of the Wild West.

Exit Highway 14 at Agua Dulce Canyon Road and follow the signs to the park. 661/268-0840.

Newhall

PARKS, BEACHES, AND RECREATION AREAS

❸ Mentryville

☺☺☺ (See Los Angeles County map on pages 732–733)

Once upon a time, there was oil in these hills. Mentryville was home to what's claimed to be the longest continually operating oil well in the world, running from the 1880s until 1990. The little town housed more than 100 families from its inception to about 1930, and some of it has been preserved and turned into a very cool park. You can see a handful of historic buildings and landmarks here, including a one-room schoolhouse, an old barn, the site of the famed oil well, and founder Charles Mentry's big old mansion.

Dogs can't go in the buildings, but they can check them out with you from the outside, as long as they're leashed. If this disappoints your dog, tell her that there's something even better for visiting pooches: They can join you on a wonderful hike through Pico Canyon, in the north end of Santa Clarita Woodlands Park. The trail takes you from Mentryville through chaparral-covered slopes and into a shaded, lush riparian area near the headwaters of Pico Canyon and the Santa Susana Mountains. The trail continues but gets very rugged, so be prepared to turn around when your dog is tired. This isn't a loop trail.

From the San Fernando Valley, go north on I-5 and take the Lyons Road/ Pico Canyon Road exit. Turn left at the off-ramp's stop sign (this will be Pico Canyon Road), cross over the freeway, and continue straight until you come to a Y intersection near the end of the road. Go left at the Y and continue to the end of that road, where you'll find a parking lot. The physical address is 27201 Pico Canyon Road; 310/589-3200.

❹ William S. Hart Regional Park

☺☺☺ (See Los Angeles County map on pages 732–733)

If you and your dog are fans of the Old West, you must amble on down here. Coming to this park is like getting a personal invitation to the house and ranch of the silent Western movie hero William S. Hart. Unfortunately, Hart isn't around anymore to give you a personal tour, but feel free to peruse the property via a couple of trails. If you get a hankering to check out his hacienda, you can leave your dog at the shaded picnic area with your traveling pardner and take a guided tour.

Dogs have to be leashed at the park. Hart, a cowboy himself, might not have liked that rule, but it's a small price to pay to enjoy the hospitality of the ghost of these here hills. Besides, the property houses a little zoo with farm animals and a compost demonstration site. You don't want your pooch meddling with either.

Exit Highway 14 at San Fernando Road and follow the signs west to the park. 661/259-0855.

Malibu

This mountainous oceanfront community is L.A.'s final frontier. Too remote for some, too expensive for others, it's one of the more natural and untouched areas in the county. Malibu's combined incorporated and unincorporated areas cover about 45,000 acres and are 27 miles long and up to eight miles wide. Only 28,000 people live here. Compared with the typical Los Angeles ratio of people to acres, this seems like the countryside. Here you'll find a few magnificent parks where you and your happy pooch won't believe you could be within a bone's throw of one of the world's largest cities.

PARKS, BEACHES, AND RECREATION AREAS

Many of the Santa Monica Mountains National Recreation Area parks are found here. Malibu is also home to the only beach in L.A. County where pooches are permitted. (See the Long Beach section for info on a leash-free beach pilot program, Dog Beach Zone.)

5 Leo Carrillo State Beach

🐾🐾🐾 (See Los Angeles County map on pages 732–733)

Leashed dogs are allowed to trot around a section of this 6,600-foot-long beach that straddles Los Angeles and Ventura Counties. Dogs can sniff around the beach north of Lifeguard Tower 1 and south of Lifeguard Tower 3. Ask a ranger about where this area is when you park.

Dogs may also camp at one of the 136 sites here. Dogs prefer the campsites by the beach, but they go fast, so make reservations. Sites are $20. Call 800/444-7275 for reservations; 805/488-1827 for beach info. The beach entrance is on the 36000 block of Pacific Coast Highway, just south of the county border.

6 Charmlee Wilderness Park

🐾🐾🐾🐾 (See Los Angeles County map on pages 732–733)

If you and your dog don't like to sweat when you hike, but do like being rewarded with great ocean views on the trail, leash up and head to this 560-acre park. The Meadow Trail starts at a point high enough that you can see the Pacific from your very first steps. It's easy, often breezy terrain, and since the trail is actually a fire road, it's wide enough to accommodate you and your furry friend and any passing mountain bikes or horses. It's great for beginners or anyone not needing a big challenge. (It's a good choice for dogs getting on in years but still up for tackling something more than the corner hydrant.) You can loop around and come back for a bite to eat at the park's picnic tables. The park has a nature center (sorry, no dogs inside) and an informative native plant display. Come February–April and you'll be agog with all the wildflowers here.

DIVERSION

Pack Off to Canine Camp: If images of overnight camps from your childhood still haunt you (oh, the food; oh, the homesickness; oh, the mandatory weaving of multicolor potholders), it's time to get over it. And what better way to do this than to go to camp with your dog? The **Iron Dogs Training Camp** is a three-day, two-night weekend for people to learn about dogs and dogs to have a ball and learn a few things themselves. You can choose from all kinds of activities, including flyball, agility, and the ever-ridiculous "musical mats" party game. You can also learn about things such as clicker training, canine first aid, and doggy massage.

Cabins in the scenic Malibu canyons house between two and 20 people on bunks, and an even greater number of dogs on the ground. (Bring earplugs if the sound of many dogs licking themselves or scratching or gnawing or snoring in unison would keep you awake.)

The fee is $299 and includes training, food, and lodging for one person with up to two dogs. See the camp's website, www.iron-dogs.com, for more information, or phone 818/335-9889.

There's a $3 fee per car. The park is at 2577 South Encinal Canyon Road. From Highway 1/Pacific Coast Highway in the Zuma Beach area, take Encinal Canyon Road north for four miles to the park. Turn left at the entrance and drive about a half mile to the parking area. 310/457-7247.

7 Corral Canyon Park

🐾🐾🐾🐾 (See Los Angeles County map on pages 732–733)

We love this 340-acre park because it has such a variety of habitat, plus terrific views. You and your leashed dog can take a 2.5-mile loop trail that takes you through pristine wilderness, ancient marine terrace, sage scrub, coastal salt marsh, and a lush creek area with alders, oaks, sycamores, willows, and other trees that make boy dogs happy. At the top, you'll have terrific views of the Pacific and surrounding mountains.

The trailhead is conveniently situated at 25623 Pacific Coast Highway, between Malibu Canyon Road and Kanan Dume Road. It's a civilized place to start a hike, with water, restrooms, picnic benches, and yes, even parking. (Note: Although a trail from here leads to Dan Blocker State Beach, dogs aren't allowed there, so don't even try it.) 310/589-3200.

PLACES TO EAT

Coogie's Beach Cafe: Enjoy gussied-up diner-style food with a few twists, including dishes such as Italian-style eggrolls and charbroiled garlic turkey salad. Dine with doggy at several outdoor tables. Palm plants try to shield you from the traffic at this fairly new shopping area. Coogie's is at Malibu Colony Plaza, 23750 Pacific Coast Highway; 310/317-1444.

Johnnie's New York Pizza: Small dogs are preferred here, but if you've got an angelic larger pooch, you can bring him to eat with you at the outdoor tables if it's not too crowded and it's OK with your neighbors. 22333 West Pacific Coast Highway; 310/456-1717.

Malibu Kitchen and Gourmet Country Market: The extra-good sandwiches and salads make this place a hit with dogs and their people. Sandwiches vary from the sublimely vegetarian (warm seasonal roasted veggies with balsamic vinaigrette, goat cheese, and mixed greens) to the sublimely meaty. The "Better than Mom's Meat Loaf" sandwich, with ketchup, on homemade rustic bread, is a huge hit with dogs whose people tend to drop bits of food while eating. Dine at the seven outdoor tables. It's in the heart of Malibu, at 3900 Cross Creek Road; 310/456-7845.

PLACES TO STAY

Leo Carrillo State Beach: See Leo Carrillo State Beach, above, for camping information.

Topanga Ranch Motel: Stay at these cute, simple motel-style cottages from the 1920s if you want to be close to the only beach for many, many miles that officially allows dogs. (See Leo Carillo State Beach, above.) They're white with red trim, and they have little white fencing around their rosebushes. (This makes them sound more charming than they really are. They're fine, but nothing storybook-like.) All 30 units have a fridge, and about half have private patios. The canyon is your backyard. Rates are $75–105—very affordable for this pricey area. 18711 West Pacific Coast Highway 90265; 310/456-5486; www.topangaranchmotel.com.

Topanga

PARKS, BEACHES, AND RECREATION AREAS

8 Red Rock Canyon Park

😺😺😺 (See Los Angeles County map on pages 732–733)

There's a bone of contention about the old notion that dogs see only in black and white. Let's hope they don't, because if they see in color, they'll be wowed by the giant sandstone rock outcroppings here. They're red, as you may have guessed by the park's name. And because the rocks provide homes to various teeny forms of life, they can also be tan, white, and even purpleish.

Contrasting with the sandstone gorge is a fairly lush, cool riparian area with trees whose trunks boy dog noses love to explore. A fire road and trail take you and your leashed dog through these different habitats. At some points, you'll come to incredible views of the surrounding mountains. Mountain bikes like it here, so keep your eyes peeled.

The park's address is 23601 West Red Rock Road. From Highway 1/Pacific Coast Highway, go north on Topanga Canyon Boulevard. At Old Topanga Canyon Road, turn left. Drive 1.7 miles to Red Rock Road. You can park at this intersection and walk nearly a mile to the park entrance, or you can drive all the way to the park entrance, but keep in mind that .2 mile of this road is an unimproved dirt road. You can also get to the park from U.S. 101, but you'll still end up dealing with the dirt road. 310/589-3200.

Chatsworth

PARKS, BEACHES, AND RECREATION AREAS

🐾 Garden of the Gods

🐾🐾🐾 (See Los Angeles County map on pages 732–733)

The huge sandstone rock formations at this 23-acre park have provided a dramatic background for many an old film. The Garden of the Gods is one of the last undeveloped remnants of the once thriving Iverson Movie Ranch, used by dozens of directors during its reign from the earliest days of film in 1912 all the way up through 1976. Movies and shows shot at the ranch include *Stagecoach, The Lone Ranger, Bonanza, Superman, Batman and Robin, Tarzan the Ape Man, Little Big Horn,* and *The Fighting Seabees.* Even Laurel and Hardy and Shirley Temple filmed some scenes here.

If your dog's nose is very keen, he just might be able to sniff out where Rin Tin Tin once performed some scenes. We're not sure if the famous dog ever actually ventured to the Garden of the Gods during his time at Iverson, but he was definitely nearby.

A short trail takes you to some jaw-dropping rock formations. Exit Highway 118 at Topanga Canyon Boulevard and in less than a half mile make a right at Santa Susana Pass Road. In about another half mile you'll come to Redmesa Drive. Go right and follow it a few hundred feet to the park's entrance. (Redmesa bisects the park.) 310/589-3200.

PLACES TO STAY

Summerfield Suites Hotel: The suites are big and their fireplaces are awfully inviting. Rates are $159–189. You'd better plan on staying for a few nights, because the dog fees aren't cheap. You'll pay $150–200 for the length of their stay, depending on the room size. If your dog is staying only one night, it's the same price as dressing him in a human disguise and getting him his own room! 21902 Lassen Street 91311; 818/773-0707 or 800/238-8000; www.summerfieldsuites.com.

Agoura Hills

PARKS, BEACHES, AND RECREATION AREAS

🔟 The Paramount Ranch

🐾🐾🐾🐾 (See Los Angeles County map on pages 732–733)

Want to take your dog around the United States without leaving California? A visit to this 436-acre ranch could fool your dog into thinking he's in Tombstone, Dodge City, New Mexico, the Ozarks, Colorado's Royal Gorge, or colonial Salem. The Paramount Ranch has been a convincing backdrop for hundreds of films since the 1920s. Among the stars who made movies here are John Wayne, Gary Cooper, Cary Grant, Basil Rathbone, Roy Rogers, Lucille Ball, Kirk Douglas, Jane Russell, and Cornel Wilde. Your dog may not be able to sniff out their scents anymore, but if he has a keen nose, he can probably still track down Jane Seymour, whose popular series *Dr. Quinn, Medicine Woman* was filmed here for several years in the 1990s. (The ranch is still a working set, and it works pretty hard, judging by a look at a recent filming schedule.)

But chances are that your dog will be thrilled just to be allowed to join you at this fun park. The ranch is much smaller than it was in its heyday, but there's still plenty to see here, including an old Western town set complete with a saloon, a sheriff's office, and various stores. Several short trails, including the aptly named Backdrop Trail, take you past landscapes that will probably look very familiar thanks to their frequent use in films and TV shows.

Exit U.S. 101 at Kanan Road and follow it south for about three-quarters of a mile. Turn left on Cornell Road and drive about 2.5 miles to Paramount Ranch Road. Turn right and follow the road to the ranch. 818/597-9192.

1️⃣1️⃣ Peter Strauss Ranch

🐾🐾🐾 (See Los Angeles County map on pages 732–733)

This beautiful 65-acre property was once the home of actor and producer Peter Strauss, most noted for his role in the TV miniseries *Rich Man, Poor Man*. He needed a place for his myriad collection of cacti and other succulent plants (he'd had hundreds of them on his apartment roof), and what better locale than this oak woodland? Although he moved on (and protected the property from development by selling it to the Santa Monica Mountains Conservancy), some of his plants can still be seen in the cactus garden here.

A few remnants of Strauss's predecessor, a resort and amusement park known as Lake Enchanto, also remain. In the 1930s and '40s, the property had many amusement rides and the largest swimming pool in the West, with a capacity of up to 3,000 people. You can still see the circular pool from the lush lawn here. (The pool is empty, but try to imagine it in its heyday.) You and your leashed dog can also sniff out the lovely imported Italian terrazzo tile dance floor near the lawn.

The ranch is a fine place to bring a dog, especially if you have a child in tow. Although the rides are gone, there's a sweet playground (for human kids, not dog kids) overlooking the remains of Lake Enchanto's dam. The Peter Strauss Trail is less than a mile long, and it's an easy, pretty hike. It's shaded by coast live oaks, and ferns are everywhere. (There's a little poison oak here, which we mention only because it's not something you'd expect at such a well-groomed place.) A shallow creek runs through the property and along the trail at times, making the setting even more tranquil.

Exit U.S. 101 at Kanan Road and drive south for 2.8 miles. Turn left on Troutdale Road and at the end of the road, the park will be in front of you. To reach the entrance, go left on Mulholland Highway, cross the creek, and bear right into the ranch's parking lot. 805/370-2301.

Calabasas

PARKS, BEACHES, AND RECREATION AREAS

🐾🐾 Ahmanson Ranch/Upper Las Virgenes Canyon Open Space Preserve

🐾🐾🐾🐾 (See Los Angeles County map on pages 732–733)

Parts of *Gone with the Wind* were filmed on this stunning 2,983-acre wildland. But the land itself could have been gone with the wind starting as early as 2003 if Washington Mutual had been able to proceed unimpeded: The corporation had planned a 3,050-home development here. Fortunately, the development was so contentious that the state ended up being able to buy the Ahmanson Ranch land from Washington Mutual and will keep it as an undeveloped wildlife refuge and park.

This is great news for the environment and excellent news for people and pooches who like to hike on oak-studded rolling hills, wide-open mesas, and cool canyon bottoms shaded by sycamores. A few trails are already up and running, with many more planned. (A big bonus, if you aren't fond of itching: There's no poison oak here.) Some endangered species that helped save the land from development live here, so leashes are the law.

Although the property lies entirely in Ventura County, we list it here because Los Angeles County provides the only access. Access from the Simi Valley area is likely at some time, but for now, this is the way to get here: Exit U.S. 101 at Las Virgenes Road and follow it north all the way to the end. At press time, the Santa Monica Mountains Conservancy was trying to get the OK for a large parking lot at the end of Victory Boulevard. 310/589-3200.

13 Calabasas Bark Park

😾 😾 😾 😾 🐕 (See Los Angeles County map on pages 732–733)

This is the first dog park we've heard of that has a separate gated area not for small dogs, but for children! It's actually a good idea, because some children feel overwhelmed by big dogs running around. Apparently the area isn't used much. Most kids prefer to be with parents and canine siblings. But it's nice to know it's there. I know a few parents whose children would love to have their space separate from swirling dogs.

The park is two fenced acres of grass, with some shade trees, benches, poop bags, lights, and a dog drinking fountain. The park is at 4232 Las Virgenes Road, south of the Las Virgenes Municipal Water District. 818/878-4225 or 818/880-6461.

Pacific Palisades

PARKS, BEACHES, AND RECREATION AREAS

14 Will Rogers State Historic Park

😾 😾 😾 (See Los Angeles County map on pages 732–733)

"It's great to be great, but it's greater to be human," said humorist and actor Will Rogers, who made his home here during the 1920s and 1930s. Dogs may not exactly agree with this sentiment, but they do appreciate being able to peruse this 186-acre park.

Leashed dogs may explore along the trails that wind past a polo field, a roping ring, and Rogers's ranch house. Dogs can't go into the ranch house and should stay away from the stables and from the polo fields on weekends, when polo matches are held.

A major warning: Heed the leash law. Rattlesnakes abound in the far reaches of the park, and nosy dogs who are allowed to romp off leash find them fairly frequently. Rangers here say that about one dog a month gets bitten in the summer. Half survive it. Half don't. The trail here is wide, and if you stay toward the middle, you'll have no problems.

There's a $5 parking fee. The park is at 1501 Will Rogers State Park Road, off Sunset Boulevard. 310/454-8212.

PLACES TO EAT

A La Tarte Bistrot: Want a ménage à trois? You can order one right off the menu. After all, this is a French place! (The ménage is actually just a three-part salad. Sorry.) This chic French bistro has some delectable food. Dine at several shaded outdoor tables with your dear doggy at your side. (After all, this is a French place!) 1037 Swarthmore Avenue; 310/459-6635.

Jacopo's: My favorite pizza here is Max's Big Apple. It's about as close to real New York pizza as you and your dog will get in these parts, and you won't have to deal with airline hassles. But if Jake could choose, he'd probably pick the barbecue pork pizza. It has smoky pork, barbecue sauce, corn, and cilantro. (It's enough to make the stomach turn, isn't it?) 15414 Sunset Boulevard; 310/454-8494.

Palisades Bakery: Choose from a variety of foods here, from burgers to Chinese food to Indian specialties. Eat at umbrella-covered tables with your pooch. 15231 ½ La Cruz Drive; 310/459-6160.

Brentwood

PARKS, BEACHES, AND RECREATION AREAS

15 Barrington Dog Park

🐾🐾🐾🐾 (See Los Angeles County map on pages 732–733)

This oddly shaped park (it looks kind of like a bow tie) features a separate area for small dogs and is a couple of acres of grass and wood chips, with poop bags, water, tennis balls galore, and trees that offer pleasant shade for humans and pleasant leg-lift spots for boy dogs. People can rest their laurels on aluminum benches. (The folks here, the Friends of Barrington Dog Park, don't rest on their laurels long—they're always striving to make some kind of improvement in this fairly new park.)

The park is closed for maintenance Tuesday 6–10 A.M. It's at 333 South Barrington Avenue. Since it's close to I-405, here are directions from the freeway: Take the Sunset Boulevard exit and head west to Barrington Place. Go left on Barrington Place and drive past the entrance to Brentwood School. Go left immediately after the post office. The park is behind the post office. 310/840-2187. The Friends of Barrington Dog Park has a fun website: www.fobdp.org.

PLACES TO EAT

Belwood Bakery: You and your pooch can dine on tasty baked goods and sandwiches at the three outdoor tables here. 11625 Barrington Court; 310/471-6855.

Encino

PARKS, BEACHES, AND RECREATION AREAS

🔟 Westridge-Canyonback Wilderness Park

🐾🐾🐾🐾🐕 (See Los Angeles County map on pages 732–733)

Yes, that little running dog you see above really does belong there. It's not a typo—it's a miracle.

This is the only huge park (besides national forests and BLM lands) in the greater L.A. area where dogs under voice control are allowed off leash. Around these parts, dogs are usually relegated to fenced-in dog parks if they want to run around in the buff (sans leash). But thanks to the dog-friendly Santa Monica Mountains Conservancy, well-behaved dogs can be their doggy selves here and not be stopped by a fence in the face or a ranger with a citation book.

This 1,500-acre open space (and we're talking open—not much shade here, so bring lots of water for you and your dog) offers great views of the Pacific Ocean on clear days. The fire road along the north-south ridgeline is a popular hiking area, but it's also big with mountain bikers, so be careful with your off-leash pal.

At one point, the property had been slated for a 500-home development. It was also approved as a landfill (dump). Now that it's in the hands of the conservancy, it won't have to face those terrible fates again.

From I-405, take Mulholland Drive west 2.7 miles to the 17000 block. You can park in a 20-car roadside parking area and walk 10 minutes to the park entrance and the trail. 310/589-3200.

🔟 Sepulveda Basin Off-Leash Dog Park

🐾🐾🐾🐾🐕 (See Los Angeles County map on pages 732–733)

It's big, it's fairly grassy, and it has four boy dog toilets (OK, fire hydrants). What more could a dog want? Water? It's here at four mud-free drinking stations. Shade? There are enough small shade trees for comfort during the summer. If those won't do, there are plenty of picnic tables. Dog friends? Yup. A section for small dogs? Yap! Sirloin strip? OK, the park doesn't have everything.

This is a heavenly place to visit if you're a dog who longs to be off leash, or if you're a dog person who longs to see your dog off leash. "It's been successful beyond our wildest dreams," says Ken Novak, a manager with the city of Los Angeles Recreation and Parks Department. Even the fencing is terrific here: It's green, so it matches the park. Ivy has been planted at its base, and it's starting to creep up toward its goal of becoming a wall of ivy. Outside the fence, there's a little more acreage for leashed dogs who want to lounge around on the grass and/or have a picnic with their people pals.

The park is at the corner of White Oak Avenue and Victory Boulevard; 818/756-8616 or 818/756-8191. For info on dog events at the park, phone 818/343-0013.

Van Nuys

PARKS, BEACHES, AND RECREATION AREAS

18 Woodley Park

🐾🐾🐾 (See Los Angeles County map on pages 732–733)

If you like your parks big and grassy, check out this one. Dogs really enjoy it here. You'll find ample shade, plenty of picnic areas, and a fitness course to keep you and the pooch in good condition. Unfortunately, there's also an unattractive water reclamation plant on the north side of the park, but they have to go somewhere.

The park is between I-405 and U.S. 101. Take the Burbank Boulevard exit from I-405 and drive west into the park. Turn right on Woodley Avenue and drive past signs for the Japanese garden. The meadow area will be on your right. 818/756-8891.

Lakeview Terrace

PARKS, BEACHES, AND RECREATION AREAS

19 Hansen Dam Recreation Area

🐾🐾🐾 (See Los Angeles County map on pages 732–733)

This is 1,400 acres of hills, trees, shrubs, and grassy meadows. And the good news is that once again it has a lake as its centerpiece. The lake disappeared for a few years during a long process of reclamation, but it's here to stay. Dogs enjoy sniffing around its perimeter, and they especially appreciate the horse trails here. They smell good to pooches, who may find an occasional munchie along the way (but try as your dog might, don't let him nibble these morsels).

From I-210, exit at Osborne Street and follow the signs for a couple of blocks. 626/899-4537.

Sherman Oaks

PARKS, BEACHES, AND RECREATION AREAS

20 Dixie Canyon Park

🐾🐾 (See Los Angeles County map on pages 732–733)

If you like your urban walks on the wild side, take a hike at Dixie Canyon. This 20-acre park, donated to the Santa Monica Mountains Conservancy by Warren Beatty, is a pretty decent place to take a leashed dog. There's lots of shade from the California black walnut trees and coast live oaks, and the park's trail takes you by a year-round stream in the middle of the canyon. Watch out for poison oak: It's very thick on the canyon's east side. You should be OK if you stay on the trail.

From the intersection of Ventura Boulevard and Dixie Canyon Avenue, go south on Dixie Canyon Avenue for .8 mile and then turn left on Dixie Canyon Place. You'll quickly come to the end of the road (actually, a cul-de-sac). Park, and take the stairs to the park's entrance. 310/589-3200.

PLACES TO STAY

Best Western Carriage Inn: Rates are $99–189. 5525 Sepulveda Boulevard 91411; 818/717-2300.

North Hollywood

PARKS, BEACHES, AND RECREATION AREAS

21 Whitnall Off-Leash Dog Park

🐾🐾🐾🐕 (See Los Angeles County map on pages 732–733)

Before this park became a dog park, it had really gone to the dogs: It was a haven for drug dealing, gang activity, and illegal dumping. Then along came the dog park in 2002 and now it's clean as a whistle (a stray dog poop or two notwithstanding). Three cheers for the dogs and their people! (And for Three-Dog Dave and Tamar Love Grande for giving us the heads-up about this place.)

The park is a couple of grassy acres. It's got all the usual dog-park amenities, including drinking fountains, shade umbrellas, benches, poop bags, double gates, and trees. Small dogs have a 100- by 200-foot section to call their own. Not bad for bitsy beagles. At the corner of Cahuenga Boulevard and Whitnall Highway; 818/756-8060.

Santa Monica

Even though tourist dogs don't have many places to run around off leash (dogs must be licensed Santa Monicans to use the two off-leash areas here), Santa Monica is a great place to be a dog. It's laid-back, upscale, and down to earth. Dog-friendly eateries abound, and the city is home to some of the most dog-friendly hotels on earth. Soon, there may even be a leash-free beach, if the dogs of Santa Monica win over the hearts of decision-makers. (See below.)

PARKS, BEACHES, AND RECREATION AREAS

A note to dogs who like to run leash-free at beaches (in other words, 99.999 percent of dogs): At press time a movement was apaw to open a section of Santa Monica Beach to naked (leashless) dogs. This would be a major boon to the Santa Monica area's 5,000 dog people and their praying pooches. See www.unleashthebeach.org for updates or info on how you can help.

Leashed dogs are permitted in all city parks. (You must have a poop bag–type implement showing, or you could get a ticket. It's best to carry an extra, in case a cop comes after your dog goes.) The two dog parks allow only licensed Santa Monica dogs. It's not great if you're just in town for the day, but it's good for local dogs anyway.

🐾 Joslyn Park Dog Park

🐾🐾🐾🐾 (See Los Angeles County map on pages 732–733)

The park may be small, but it's beautiful. It's set on a grassy hill with a few trees and has great views of the city. It's completely enclosed, so those lucky pooches who get to go leashless are safe from traffic. It has poop bags, lighting, and a separate area for small dogs.

Licensed Santa Monica dogs may run leashless 7:30 A.M.–8:30 P.M. on weekdays, and 8:30 A.M.–8:30 P.M. on weekends. They must stay away from the playground and recreation area. All other dogs must be leashed, so it's best to keep them out of the dog run and explore other parts of the park. The park is at 7th Street and Kensington Road. 310/458-8974.

🐾 Pacific Park Dog Park

🐾🐾🐾 (See Los Angeles County map on pages 732–733)

This small, fenced dog park, right next to a kennel, won't provide your pooch with endless miles of leash-free exercise, but it will provide her with endless leash-free socializing. If your dog is a social pooch, she'll probably get all the exercise she needs here while engaging in faux wrestling matches and chase games. The park has everything a dog needs, including water, a little shade, occasional grass, and benches to chase each other under.

Licensed Santa Monica dogs may run leashless in the enclosed section west of the tennis courts 7:30 A.M.–8:30 P.M. on weekdays, and 8:30 A.M.–8:30 P.M. on weekends and holidays. All other pooches have to be leashed, so it's best to stay outside the doggy area. The park is at Pacific and Main streets. 310/458-8974.

PLACES TO EAT

Some of Santa Monica's most unusual and trendy restaurants are on the **3rd Street Promenade** between Wilshire and Broadway, and most have outdoor areas. That doesn't necessarily mean your dog is welcome at all of them, but your chances are better than walking down a row of restaurants in Tahoe in January. You may want to watch your food, though, because a few of the homeless have been known to sneak up and grab it out from under you. Restaurants along Santa Monica's **Main Street** are in a quieter setting than the restaurants in the 3rd Street Promenade. Unfortunately, we've found that most of the more upscale eateries won't allow dogs to dine with you outside.

If we listed all, or even most, of the restaurants in these popular eating parts of Santa Monica, we'd run out of pages in the book. So here we'll mention just a few.

Acadie Hand Crafted French Crepes: The crepes here are out of this world, with down-to-earth prices. My favorite is the Cevenol, with chestnut puree and crème Chantilly. Jake's favorite is anything that drops on the ground. The outside eating area houses several functional steel tables with plenty of room for pooches. 213 Arizona Avenue (at the 3rd Street Promenade); 310/395-1120.

Café Dana: We've been welcomed at this café's wonderful brick courtyard before and even offered a bowl of water (Jake has, I haven't), but we're now told dogs may have to be relegated to the sidewalk tables. Be sure to ask before you bring your dog to the enchanting courtyard. The house specials lean toward Greek food, but there's a wide variety of dishes here. If you like thing English, try the afternoon tea, which comes with all the fixin's you'd get at a teahouse. 1211 Montana Avenue; 310/394-0815.

Joe's Diner: Joe Dog liked this one. He thought the name was in good taste, but he thought the good old-fashioned American cuisine was even tastier. Eat at one of two outdoor tables. 2917 Main Street; 310/392-5804.

Newsroom Espresso Cafe: Dine with your dog at the many umbrella-topped outdoor tables here. A must-try dish, even if you're not a vegetarian, is the Ultimate Maui Veggie Burger. 530 Wilshire Boulevard; 310/319-9100.

Peet's Coffee: There's a big water bowl right by the front door here. Dogs can lap while you latte. 800 14th Street (at Montana). 310/394-8555.

Starbucks Coffee Company: Sip a cup of java at the tables out front while your dog gets that Maxwell House expression on his face. You'll recognize it. It's that "Ahh-I'm-so-content-with-the-world-because-I'm-smelling-good-coffee" look. 2671 Main Street; 310/392-3559.

Sunset Bar and Grill: Eat continental cuisine on the happening patio with your happy pooch. Actually, your happy pooch has to be tied to the other side of the rail, but she'll still be well within petting (and mooching) distance. 1240 3rd Street; 310/395-7012.

PLACES TO STAY

Some of the most posh, dog-friendly hotels in California call Santa Monica home. The more affordable lodgings, such as the local Best Westerns and Comfort Inns, don't allow dogs. If you want to stay in this beautiful coastal city, be prepared to dig deep in your wallet.

The Fairmont Miramar Hotel Santa Monica: You and your smallish dog (under 30 pounds) can live in California-style casual elegance when you stay at this sprawling, lovely hotel. You can sleep in a 10-story tower, a bungalow surrounded by beautiful gardens with little waterfalls, or a gorgeous six-story wing of the hotel. Rates are $300–1,200. 101 Wilshire Boulevard 90401; 310/576-7777; www.fairmont.com/santamonica.

Le Merigot: This opulent oceanfront gem has been described as "reminiscent of the fine hotels on France's Côte d'Azur" and also as "blending European elegance with the vibrant lifestyle of Southern California." *Brides* magazine describes the hotel as "Zen meets the millennium." You get the idea. It's cool, it's sleek, it's to drool for. Even the luxury spa here has won coveted awards. The rooms' ultracushy "Cloud Nine" beds—festooned with Frette linens, down duvets, and feather pillows—should win an award for comfort.

"Yada, yada, yada," your dog might be saying right about now. "But what's in it for me?" Well, doggy, Le Merigot has a marvelous program called "Club Meg," which allows dogs up to 100 pounds to be pampered guests at the hotel. (The brochure for the program features a dog who's the spitting image of Jake. Jake as the mascot for a luxury hotel pooch program is a funny thought, indeed.)

Dogs get pooch cookies, a dog magazine, and some other doggy amenities. They can also order dog-food room service. The kibble isn't as appealing as Loews' dog cuisine (see below), but it's nothing to quibble about. There's also a grassy dog-walk area next to the hotel.

Rates are $250–460. Dogs require a $150 deposit and are $35 extra for the length of your stay. 1740 Ocean Avenue 90401; 310/395-9700; www.lemerigothotel.com.

Loews Santa Monica Beach Hotel: Everything about this elegant beachside resort is first-rate, from the gorgeous rooms to the sumptuous spa and health club. The lobby is to die for, too. It's also a great place to have a cocktail with your dog. Karen Dawn, founder of Dawn Watch, an animal rights media-watch organization, stayed at the hotel with her two dogs and significant other when they first moved to Los Angeles. "We'd come into the lobby's lounge area and order cocktails, and they'd put a little mat down for Paula and Buster and give them a bowl of water," she says. "They're incredibly dog-friendly." Paula, a pit bull rescued from the Bronx, is still dumbfounded by the whole experience. (So is Buster, Karen's big mutt who trotted to the edge of the pool one day, leaned a little too far in to sniff at a ball, and tipped right in, much to his consternation.)

Loews is, indeed, dog-friendly. The "Loews Loves Pets" program considers all pet visitors VIPs (Very Important Pets) and starts their visit with a personal welcoming note from the hotel's general manager. Attached to the letter is a listing of pet-friendly places in the area. Dogs get a bag of biscuits, a toy, special placemats, and food and water bowls. If you want to borrow a doggy bed, that's no problem—the hotel has got them for every size of pooch. Loews offers dogs gourmet room service with items such as grilled lamb with rice and even a vegetarian alternative should your dog be so inclined. Dog-walking or pet-sitting is available, too.

Rates are $275–625. Dogs cost nothing extra, but they do have to pay for room service, pet-sitting, other bonus services. 1700 Ocean Avenue 90401; 310/458-6700 or 800/235-6397; www.loewshotels.com.

Studio City

PARKS, BEACHES, AND RECREATION AREAS

24 Wilacre Park

🐾🐾🐾 (See Los Angeles County map on pages 732–733)

This scrubby, shrubby 128-acre park is the former estate of silent-movie star Will Acres. It's in the middle of one of Studio City's more posh neighborhoods, but once you're hiking, you'll feel as if you're in the middle of nowhere. Dogs are welcome here, but so are horses and bikes, so be sure to leash. For a really fun hike, take the 2.7-mile loop trail to the very dog-friendly Coldwater Canyon Park (see the Beverly Hills section), headquarters of the forest-friendly organization TreePeople. If you hike up toward TreePeople's main building, you'll find a doggy drinking fountain along the way.

If it's toasty out, sniff out a narrow road at Wilacre that takes you to a shady canyon thick with big oak and eucalyptus trees. It's a popular spot for filming, so if you see a crew, you'll have to head back. The park is at the intersection of Laurel Canyon Boulevard and Fryman Canyon Road. The address is 3431 Fryman Canyon Road; 310/589-3200.

25 Laurel Canyon Park

🐾🐾🐾🐾 ✖ (See Los Angeles County map on pages 732–733)

Yee haw! Dogs, throw off your leashes and come here to be all the dog you can be! This is the biggest of the off-leash dog runs in Los Angeles County, and many consider it the best. It's nearly 20 acres, and there are sufficient trees and picnic tables to make everyone comfortable.

If you and your dog like to socialize, you couldn't ask for a better place. Canine rush hour (around 5 P.M., depending on the time of year) is a real scene. On a typical dog-day afternoon, you'll find more than 100 dogs running like mad, sniffing each other in unmentionable places, and pushing their noses to the ground in search of unusual odors. Their owners, meanwhile, chitchat about this and that (often, "this" being their dog and "that" being your dog).

People flock here from all over Los Angeles and the San Fernando Valley. They find plenty of water, plenty of poop bags, plenty of fence, and, most important, plenty of good dog fun. And for people who like to watch the stars, we hear that celebrities sometimes frequent the place on weekends.

(Note: Since the last edition of this book, we've heard about some aggressive dogs who have attacked other dogs here, and about their people who have given false contact information to avoid taking responsibility for their dogs' behavior. These are rare problems, but since I heard from more than one person about this, I'd be negligent not to mention it. Fortunately, most dogs here never even hear a cross word from other dogs, much less feel their teeth.)

Get here early so you can nab a parking space. The park is on Mulholland Drive, about a quarter mile west of Laurel Canyon Boulevard. From Laurel Canyon Boulevard, go west on Mulholland and take the first left. The road winds down a hill and into the parking lot. 818/756-8189.

PLACES TO EAT

Jumpin' Java: Don't let the name fool you. There's more than just coffee for your canine here. You can get breakfast, lunch, and dinner, too. The Mediterranean-style cuisine makes for tasty, light eating. Dine with your dog at the covered patio with six tables. 11919 Ventura Boulevard; 818/980-4249.

Studio Yogurt: If the cool, creamy, refreshing frozen yogurt served here is beyond your caloric capacity, order one of the fat-free or sugar-free treats. They taste every bit as good. Your dog won't complain either. Dip your spoon with your dog at the covered patio. 12050 Ventura Boulevard; 818/508-7811.

Universal City

If you go to the exciting Universal Studios tour/theme park here, your pooch will be pleased to know that she can accompany you at least part of the way.

Universal Studios has a kennel, which dogs of visitors get to use for free. Bring a blanket and her favorite toy, and she'll rest in comfort while you get jostled around a bit by King Kong or get the wits scared out of you at the Revenge of the Mummy ride. (Your dog should actually be glad she's not allowed on the rides.) The climate-controlled kennel is unattended, but it's locked. Water is supplied. You can visit your dog any time by getting a key-bearing information-booth employee to accompany you. A nearby bushy and grassy area serves as the squat spot.

To use the kennel, bring your leashed dog to the information booth just before the main entrance. 818/622-3801 or 800/UNIVERSAL (800/864-8377); www.universalstudios.com.

PARKS, BEACHES, AND RECREATION AREAS

26 South Weddington Park

🐾🐾 (See Los Angeles County map on pages 732–733)

Golf, anyone? This park is so green and trim that you can't help but think of Arnold Palmer. Joe Dog liked it because of its proximity to Universal Studios—it's right across the street. He enjoyed the kennels there (see above for details), because he knew a cat could end up spending the day just down the row from him.

The park is bordered by a couple of small side roads, so it's fairly safe from traffic. But since dogs are supposed to be leashed, that's not something you have to worry about.

Heading south on Lankershim Boulevard, go right on Bluffside Drive (directly across from the north gate of Universal Studios). 818/756-8188 or 323/923-7390.

PLACES TO STAY

Sheraton Universal Hotel: How often do you get to sleep on the back lot of a major motion picture studio with your dog? Stay here, and you will actually be on a back lot of Universal Studios together. (It's as close as your dog will come to Universal, except for being in the kennel there.) And what a fun, imaginatively designed, attractive hotel this is. It's big, with cushy, well-appointed rooms. Some of the rooms and suites are theme rooms, embellished with Universal characters and movie decor. Our favorite is the Shrek Suite, with its pine log furniture and large pictures of Shrek and his cohorts. You'll feel as if you're in his living room. Dogs feel right at home here.

Dogs love staying at any room here: As part of their stay, they get to use a comfy dog bed (the Sheraton Sweet Sleeper Dog Bed, the smaller cousin of the Sheraton Sweet Sleeper Bed for humans) and get bowls for their food and water. Dogs need to weigh less than 80 pounds (Jake could get in by sucking in his belly) and you can have only one per room. Rates are $149–199. Suites start at $269. 333 Universal Hollywood Drive 91608; 818/980-1212; www.starwood.com/sheraton.

West Hollywood

Dogs love hanging around West Hollywood. It's an eclectic place with what seems to be a higher-than-normal percentage of dog lovers. Jake simply loves all the attention lavished on him and others of his ilk here.

PARKS, BEACHES, AND RECREATION AREAS

27 William S. Hart Park

🐾🐾🐾🐕 (See Los Angeles County map on pages 732–733)

A Parisian pooch named Boo had his Parisian person Birgit write to tell me about this dear little park. "It isn't much bigger than an oversized handkerchief, but the dogs love it anyway," they wrote. And indeed they do. Lots of off-leash pooches trot around here with big smiles on their snoots. It's a very pretty little fenced park with trees and a doggy water fountain. Maintenance crews try to keep the park green, but with up to 100 thundering paws at a time, it's an onerous task.

It's easy to confuse this park with the big William S. Hart Regional Park in Newhall. (See the Newhall section.) They're both named for the same Old West movie star, but that's where the similarities end. While the Hart Park in Newhall is his 200-plus–acre former ranch, this Hart Park is essentially the yard of his former West Hollywood home. It's fitting that dogs are allowed to romp on both his country and his city property. He was a cowboy through and through, and he'd have liked this.

Dogs can visit on leash any time, but they can run around naked only 7–9 A.M. and 5–7 P.M. daily. (This is an ongoing test program, so please check hours before letting your dog loose.) The park is at 8341 De Longpre Avenue, just off North Sweetzer Avenue, one block south of West Sunset Boulevard. 323/848-6400.

PLACES TO EAT

Basix: Every meal here is a joy. For breakfast, try the "Croissant Very French Toast." It's served with real-deal maple syrup. The blackened chicken pasta is a hit with the lunch crowd. (And the dog crowd.) Your dog may join you at the covered patio area. 8333 Santa Monica Boulevard; 213/848-2460.

Comedy Store: Have a drink and an appetizer on a Friday or Saturday night with your best bud at the comedy palace of Los Angeles. As you sip your screwdriver and eat your little pizzas at the outdoor patio bar, you and your pooch can watch for your favorite comic. Sometimes comics do a little warm-up act on the patio. Your dog will be howling. 8433 West Sunset Boulevard; 323/656-6225.

Irv's Burgers: You and your dog can dine on great, meaty burgers and some healthier cuisine at this beloved eatery across from city hall. You sit on a stool at the counter while your dog looks on from below. 8289 Santa Monica Boulevard; 323/650-2456.

Joey's Cafe: Dine with your doggy at one of six shaded sidewalk tables here. The omelets are droolworthy. Jake and I suggest the oven-roasted sun-dried tomato omelet with basil, spinach, and goat cheese. 8301 Santa Monica Boulevard; 323/822-0671.

Mel's Drive-In: This isn't a real drive-in, but you and your dog can park yourselves at the many umbrella-topped tables out front. Enjoy classically good burgers, fries, and shakes here. With all this decadent food floating around, the doggy drool can flow. Sneak yours a little bite of something and watch your dog smile. 8585 Sunset Boulevard; 310/854-7200.

Rage: It's all the rage to eat the continental cuisine with your dog at the shaded tables out front. 8911 Santa Monica Boulevard; 310/652-7055.

Tail O' the Pup: This is one of the last examples of architectural kitsch in Los Angeles. The counter where you order food is encased in a giant hot dog, complete with mustard and bun. Jake the Dog looked utterly bewildered when he first laid his hungry eyes on it. I could just see his thought process: "It smells like a hot dog, but there's something weird about it." More than one million hot dogs have been served here since it opened in 1945. (It may be tacky, but it's beloved.) Burgers and the like are also popular here. Dine with your dog (furry, not hot, although that works too) at the large outdoor seating area. Thirsty dogs get water. 329 North San Vicente Boulevard; 310/652-4517.

Tango Grill: Chicken and steak are the specialties here, and they're pretty tasty, too. Dine outside with the dog of your choice. Your dog will get water if she asks for it. 8807 Santa Monica Boulevard; 310/659-3663.

PLACES TO STAY

The Grafton Balboa: The rooms at this gracious, first-rate hotel have a "feng shui reverential decor," according to the friendly manager. I think this means you and your dog will find it a peaceful place, but that could have more to do with the comfy beds and lovely furnishings than the fact that mirrors aren't facing the door. You'll adore the large, beautiful courtyard pool and Mediter-ranean gardens, but dogs need to keep their paws dry at the pool and down at the gardens (if ya know what I mean). Rates are $119–300. Dogs pay a $100 fee for the length of their visit. The hotel is on the Sunset Strip, at 8462 West Hollywood Boulevard 90069; 323/654-4600; www.graftononsunset.com.

Le Montrose Suite Hotel/Hotel Gran Luxe: This attractive French-influ-enced hotel is homey, cozy, and nestled in a lovely neighborhood. You'll get fresh fruit and mineral water upon check-in and homemade cookies when you leave. (Dogs will want to leave again and again.) Pooches get a bowl of water upon request. All rooms have fireplaces and some have kitchenettes. Rates are $145–950. Dogs pay a $100 fee for their stay. 900 Hammond Street 90069; 310/855-1115 or 800/776-0666; www.lemontrose.com.

Le Parc Suite Hotel: Stay at this all-suite hotel and you'll get twice-daily maid service, a robe, and even slippers, which some dogs find quite fetching. All rooms at this quiet, out-of-the-way hotel have kitchenettes and separate living/dining areas. Some even come with a fireplace. While the hotel boasts that it has beautiful balconies, it doesn't matter to dogs, who need to stay in the first-floor (smoking) rooms during their visit. Rates are $155–300. There's a $75 fee for the length of your dog's stay. 733 North West Knoll Drive 90069; 310/855-8888 or 800/578-4837; www.leparcsuites.com.

Hollywood

Tinseltown just isn't what it used to be. The wealth of art deco architecture and grandiose theaters has faded. The half-mile Hollywood Walk of Fame is home to the homeless (although there are plans in the works to improve the area). But it's still worth visiting, for the myth and lure of Hollywood will never completely fade. (If you visit toward dusk, you may be glad you brought your dog.) Meanwhile, if you can foot the bill, a stay in the fabulous Chateau Marmont (below) might restore a little of the old glow of Hollywood for you and your dog.

PARKS, BEACHES, AND RECREATION AREAS

28 Trebek Open Space

🐾🐾🐾 (See Los Angeles County map on pages 732–733)

The category: Generous Gentlemen.

The answer: A 62-acre parcel of wilderness with fire roads for leashed dogs, mountain bikers, equestrians, and hikers was donated by this game show host who's always looking for life's questions, not answers. (Be sure to phrase your response in the form of a question.)

If you answered "Who is Alex Trebek?" you're right! (If you said only "Alex Trebek," your dog wins.) The popular, longtime *Jeopardy!* host donated this rugged, hilly area to the Santa Monica Mountains Conservancy, and even dogs who don't know a thing about his show are game for a vigorous romp here. It's adjacent to the leash-free Runyon Canyon Park (see below), should your dog hanker to throw his leash to the wind and trot around naked. (Runyon is easier to find and easier to park at, should that be a consideration.)

Exit U.S. 101 at Hollywood Boulevard, and drive west for about two miles. Go right (north) onto Nichols Canyon Road. Roadside parking will be on your right in a little less than a mile. It's signed, but poorly signed, so keep your eyes peeled. 310/589-3200.

DIVERSION

Compare Paw Prints: On a visit to the forecourt of **Mann's Chinese Theatre,** Joe the Dog found out his paws were as big as the heels of Gene Autry's boots. Since he was an old Western movie buff (we'd caught him watching Westerns on TV), it was doubtless a thrill for him to see that he could, if necessary, walk a mile in Autry's boots. You and your dog can spend part of a fun-filled Hollywood afternoon measuring your feet and paws against the footprints of the stars. Be sure to bring a camera. Everyone else will have one, and your dog is likely to have his mug snapped more than once. The theater itself is at 6925 Hollywood Boulevard; 323/461-3331 or 323/464-6266.

When you're done comparing shoe sizes with the stars, take your feet for a stroll down the **Hollywood Walk of Fame.** It's on Hollywood Boulevard, between Gower Street and La Brea Avenue, and along Vine Street, from Sunset Boulevard to Yucca Street. More than 2,500 celebs are immortalized with stars planted into the sidewalk featuring their names. Your dog might be especially interested in seeing the stars for Rin Tin Tin and Lassie. The walk is free, but be prepared for a barrage of homeless people and scam artists with their paws out. For a list of the stars and their locations, go to www.hollywoodchamber.net.

29 Runyon Canyon Park

🐾🐾🐾🐾 🐕 (See Los Angeles County map on pages 732–733)

Dogs are actually allowed to be their leash-free selves at this 125-acre undeveloped park. It's full of overgrown weeds and brush, but dogs don't care. In fact, they like it this way. Besides, there are plenty of trees to keep their interest while they walk up and down the hilly paths here.

And although it happened a long time ago, Jake thought you might want to know a little Hollywood lore a park ranger told us: This is the very same park where Errol Flynn was caught with a minor, causing a major public scandal. (Was this at the same time he was making the film *Assault of the Rebel Girls*?)

The park is on Fuller Avenue, north of Franklin Place. 323/666-5046.

PLACES TO STAY

Best Western Hollywood Hills Hotel: Rates are $100–190. Dogs are $25 for the length of their stay. 6141 Franklin Avenue 90028; 323/464-5181 or 800/287-1700.

Chateau Marmont Hotel: This is that grand, white, castlelike building that makes you do a double take as you're driving on Sunset. Yes, dogs really are allowed to stay in this legendary Hollywood hideaway. Joe Dog was on his best behavior when we checked it out, walking rather regally and not even stopping to scratch his ears.

The chateau, which opened in 1929, is modeled after an elegant Loire Valley castle. You'll hear a lot of French around here. Actually, the staffers speak several languages, including "discreet." That last language has helped make the Marmont very popular with Hollywood's icons through the decades.

Huge suites and romantic bungalows offer privacy, and many are set among lush, peaceful gardens. There's something for nearly every robust budget, from a 400-square-foot room to a two-bedroom penthouse suite with two bathrooms, a dressing area, a large living room with hardwood floor and working fireplace, a full kitchen, a formal dining room, and a 1,250-square-foot private terrace with great views of Hollywood. I think that's the room Joe Dog once wanted, but we ended up elsewhere. (The Motel 6 in Long Beach, to be exact. Hey, you can't tell one place from the other when the lights are out. Well, not when there's no moon and you're sleeping. Deeply.)

If you and a human friend want to go out for a night on the town sans pooch, the concierge can help hook you up with a pet-sitter. Room and suite rates are $295–2,000. Dogs pay $100 extra per visit. 8221 Sunset Boulevard 90046; 323/656-1010 or 800/242-8328; www.chateaumarmont.com.

Burbank

PARKS, BEACHES, AND RECREATION AREAS

30 Johnny Carson Park

🐾🐾 (See Los Angeles County map on pages 732–733)

Remember all of Johnny Carson's lines about "beautiful downtown Burbank"? Since the former *Tonight Show* host did his best to put Burbank on the map, the city decided to do the same for him. Just across from the NBC studios where he hosted his show year after year, there's a decent little park named after him.

The park, which used to be called Buena Vista Park, is a great place to visit with your dog if you're dropping off a friend at NBC or at the nearby Disney studios. It's well shaded and has many picnic tables and a footbridge that leads you to a fitness course. With Highway 134 roaring so close, it's not quiet, but who comes to this part of Burbank for tranquility?

A word of warning: Don't let your male dog lift his leg on the stone "sign" with Johnny Carson's mug engraved on it. We met a man who apparently sits on the grass all day watching for such indiscretions. He came running up to Joe after the dog did a quick leg lift. I thought perhaps he knew Joe or was running up to say Joe was a fine dog, but something about the way he was screaming, "No, no pee on this! Bad dog!" led me to believe he had another mission.

Exit I-5 at Alameda Avenue and drive southwest for about 20 blocks. At Bob Hope Drive, turn left. The park will be on your left in about a block. 818/238-5378.

31 Wildwood Canyon Park

🐾🐾🐾 (See Los Angeles County map on pages 732–733)

The only way Jake would like this big park better than he already does would be if he could go leashless. It's beautifully manicured and surrounded by miles of forest. If he's in the mood to roll on the grass and enjoy a picnic near regal stone archways, we stay in the developed part of the park. If he's raring to explore nature and admire trees in his unique way, we take the myriad trails leading from various points around the park.

His favorite kind of day involves a long hike through the hills, followed by a a leisurely picnic at the serene, secluded, shaded picnic spots that dot the main area. You can't help but feel pampered in this lush park: It's run with such class that even the portable toilets are disguised to look distinguished.

Coming north on I-5, take the Olive Avenue exit and head northeast. Turn left at Sunset Canyon Drive. In six blocks, turn right on Harvard Drive, which will take you into the park. Make sure you bear right once you come to a fork in the road, or you'll end up on the adjacent golf course. 818/238-5378.

PLACES TO EAT

Chez Nous: If you like California-continental cuisine, you'll enjoy dining under the canopies with your pooch. 10550 Riverside Drive; 818/760-0288.

Priscilla's: If you and your pooch want to feel really welcome at a restaurant, come here. "We love dogs and would let them inside if we were allowed," says a manager. "We give them water, a little milk, whatever they want." You'll like the relaxed atmosphere on the patio with umbrella-shaded tables, as well as the gourmet coffees and tasty light fare. 4150 Riverside Drive; 818/843-5707.

Toluca Garden: This is a good Chinese restaurant where you and the dog can dine at umbrella-topped outdoor tables. 10000 Riverside Drive; 818/980-3492.

PLACES TO STAY

Coast Anabelle Hotel: Business travelers enjoy staying here. It's somewhat upscale but not very (cotton terry robes come with your room, but so do typical motel-style beds and bedding), and the pool and fitness center make even a long stay here a little more relaxing. Some rooms come with a full kitchen. Rates are $129–169. Dogs have to offer a $200 deposit (credit card is fine; you won't feel a thing if your dog doesn't do any damage) and sign a pet agreement. 2011 West Olive Avenue 91506; 818/845-7800 or 800/663-1144; www.coastanabelle.com.

Hilton Burbank: This large Hilton across from the Burbank airport recently underwent a huge renovation. The rooms, spa, pool, and fitness center are now to drool for, especially for dogs used to the typical business-style hotel. Rates are $129–250. Dogs are $25 extra and need to weigh about 50 pounds or less. There's a grassy area on the grounds for little walkies. 2500 Hollywood Way 91505; 818/843-6000; www.hilton.com.

Holiday Inn: Rates are $110–135. Dogs are $10, and they need to be under 50 pounds. 150 East Angeleno Avenue 91510; 818/841-4770; www.holidayinn.com.

Safari Inn: Dogs who dig colorful retro chic love staying at the Safari Inn. This is a fully restored and renovated classic from the 1950s, complete with an ultraretro 1960s neon sign announcing the motel to the world. The rooms here are bright, cheery, and well appointed—a few steps up from a typical motel. (How many motels offer room service from their very own decent restaurant?) You can even get a "groovy martini" at the inn's restaurant/lounge if you really want to stroll (stumble?) down memory lane. Relax in the pool under a few tall palms and the bright lights of the neon sign. Rates are $92–129. Dogs require only a $200 deposit (a credit-card deposit will do) and a signature on a pet policy. 1911 West Olive Avenue 91506; www.safariburbank.com.

Beverly Hills

This golden city offers dogs first-class treatment. "I never felt so at home as when I visited Beverly Hills," reports Shelby, a large chocolate Lab mix, via his translator, Heidi. "I got to go shopping and eating and everyone was giving me pats on the head." Shelby writes that his best time was at Loews Beverly Hills Hotel. (See below.) It's a four-paw experience you shouldn't miss, and the price is startlingly affordable. (Relatively speaking.)

PARKS, BEACHES, AND RECREATION AREAS

Dogs aren't allowed in the stunningly beautiful Greystone Park. But then again, neither are cameras or picnics, so canines shouldn't feel too offended.

As for the rest of the parks, a woman at the parks department here had to double-check the dog rules with a supervisor when we called to update the book. When she came back to the phone, she had this answer: "I'm told we prefer the wind-up type, but we'll take the live ones." We give four paws for self-effacing humor in the land of 90210. If you want to sniff out a little wilderness in the land of opulence, Franklin Canyon Park and Coldwater Canyon Park offer big, wild chunks of dog heaven.

32 Coldwater Canyon Park

🐾🐾🐾🐾 (See Los Angeles County map on pages 732–733)

Los Angeles Magazine touted this 45-acre park as "one of the 300 best reasons to stay in Los Angeles," and dogs couldn't agree more. Although it's not one of

DIVERSION

Charge It with Your Wee Doggy: If you can easily carry your well-behaved pooch under your arm, many top **Beverly Hills shops** will welcome your business (but not your dog's business, if you know what I mean—walk your dog first).

Several small boutiques also allow the occasional pooch, but they asked not to be mentioned for fear of being besieged with giant dogs and dogs with bad bathroom habits.

One place you'll have to avoid with your dog is Neiman Marcus. A dog in another Neiman store once bit a customer, and the Beverly Hills store has had to go along with a company policy banning all dogs. Try **Saks Fifth Avenue** instead. 9600 Wilshire Boulevard; 310/275-4211. (Should you feel like taking a little drive, the Saks in Pasadena allows well-behaved dogs of "just about any size." 35 North DeLacey Avenue; 626/396-7100.)

the bigger Santa Monica Mountains Conservancy lands, it's one of the better ones for dogs who like a little socializing on their jaunts: It's rare to come here and not see several other people out hiking with their happy leashed dogs.

Boy dogs are especially tickled when they visit, because the park is headquarters for TreePeople, a grassroots group helping to keep trees in L.A., educating nontree-people about the importance of urban forests, and planting oodles of arbors around Los Angeles. There are plenty of trees along some of the trails here, and there's a trail for every hiking ability. The park is part of a 1,000-acre cross-mountain park, so you're not relegated to Coldwater property. Good trail maps can help you and your dog figure out where you want to hike. Before you head for the hills, top off your dog's tank with a swig from the doggy water fountain, near the TreePeople headquarters. (And as always when hiking in this region, don't forget to pack along plenty of water for you and your dog.) If you want to treat your dog to an extra-special treat, take him on a full-moon hike here. They're out of this world. (See the Diversion Give Your Dog the Moon.)

The park is at Mulholland Drive and Coldwater Canyon Avenue. The actual address is 12601 Mulholland Drive. 818/753-4600.

33 Franklin Canyon Park

🐾🐾🐾🐾 (See Los Angeles County map on pages 732–733)

Dogs dig this 605-acre park. It has everything dogs love, from lakes to woodlands to hilly grasslands. Most of all, it has space—a hot commodity in these parts. Dogs need to be leashed, but they still love sniffing around the park and trotting down the various trails. Jake's favorite is the Hastain Trail, a

DIVERSION

Give Your Dog the Moon: You and your dog will have a howl of a good time at the popular **full-moon walks** at Coldwater Canyon Park in Beverly Hills. **TreePeople** (see the Coldwater Canyon description for more on this great group) welcomes your good dog to accompany you on its fun, one-hour hikes. You can choose from two or three hiking levels and topics of discussion. (The guides here aren't silent: You're going to learn something about insects or trees or the moon on their walks. Even your dog may come back more knowledgeable.)

The walks are given on the night of the full moon April–October. They start at sundown or, more precisely, moon-up. They're free to members of TreePeople, and $5 for plain old people. Dogs are free. For details and schedules, check out www.treepeople.org or phone 818/753-4600.

fairly arduous 2.3-mile round-trip that leads to an overlook with great views of the area. On a clear day, you can't see forever, but you can allegedly see the Pacific. (We couldn't; the smog was rather thick when we checked it out.)

The park is home to dozens of species of birds in the Pacific flyway, so bring your field glasses if you and your dog like bird-watching. It's also home to a nature center, amphitheater, and auditorium, but dogs need to steer clear of all these. The park's address is 2600 Franklin Canyon Drive. The best way to get there from U.S. 101 is to take the Coldwater Canyon Boulevard exit and drive south to the intersection of Coldwater Canyon and Mulholland Drive. Make a 90-degree turn onto Franklin Canyon Drive. (Note: There's no signage for the street.) At press time, there was also no signage for the park, but when you see a sign that says "Road Closed 800 Feet" and "Sunrise to Sunset," you're at the park entrance. You can park in the north end of the park near the nature center, or keep driving south to get to other areas to park and explore. 310/858-7272.

🐾 Will Rogers Memorial Park

 (See Los Angeles County map on pages 732–733)

Dogs and their elegantly clad people come to this lush park to lounge the afternoon away. Dogs have to be leashed here, and it's not a large park, but it is verdant and rich with the colorful sights and sounds of Beverly Hills. When Joe, Bill, and I visited, we witnessed a tiny bit of a dog being led out of a Rolls by a chauffeur who had the same air of noble servitude as if he were escorting the queen of England. He walked the little thing around once and said, "Now,

Emily." The dog did her little business on command. The chauffeur scooped and they sped off, no doubt to more pressing engagements.

The Will Rogers Memorial Park is a triangular chunk of fine real estate at the corner of Canon and Beverly Drives and Sunset Boulevard, right across from the Beverly Hills Hotel. 310/285-2537.

PLACES TO EAT

The eateries listed on Beverly Drive are all near a free two-hour parking lot.

California Pizza Kitchen: Your dog can dine outside with you here, but she has to be tied up on the other side of the wrought-iron fence. 207 South Beverly Drive; 310/275-1101.

Champagne French Bakery: If your dog doesn't mind being tied up on the other side of the railing (right next to you, though) this is a fine place to come for some tasty food and some sun. Thirsty dogs get water upon request. 200 South Beverly Drive; 310/271-4556.

Frida Mexican Cuisine: This is some of our favorite Mexican food. Try the *pollo pipian* (chicken simmered in a ground pumpkin-seed sauce) or the *torta vegetariana* (grilled cactus with tomato, avocado, beans, and other yummies). Dine with your doggy at the neat little row of four white-tablecloth–festooned sidewalk tables. If your dog is thirsty, she can get a bowl of water. 236 South Beverly Drive; 310/278-7666.

Il Tramezzino: The eggplant parmesan here is *delicioso.* Eat it at one of the umbrella-topped tables. 460 North Canon Drive; 310/273-0501.

Jacopo's Pizzeria: Besides pizza, you can get chicken, seafood, and pasta at the outdoor tables here. Got a thirsty dog? Just ask for a bowl of water. 490 North Beverly Drive; 310/858-6446.

Sansai Japanese Grill: Enjoy good, fast Japanese with your dog at this local chain's two sidewalk tables. 281 South Beverly Drive; 310/274-2070.

Subway: Yes, Virginia, there is a Subway in Beverly Hills. Dine with doggy at the outside tables. 279 South Beverly Drive; 310/278-7827.

PLACES TO STAY

Beverly Hilton: This elegant hotel has gone from allowing even the biggest moose of a dog to permitting pooches only if they're under 25 pounds. Even these wee dogs must sign a damage waiver. Rates are $199–399. Dogs are $25 extra. 9876 Wilshire Boulevard 90210; 310/274-7777; www.hilton.com.

L'Ermitage: If you can afford the first-class European elegance of this exclusive and very private hotel, you won't regret a night or two here. You and your medium to small dog (40 pounds or less) will be pampered beyond belief. A chauffeur comes with your stay, so you and the pooch, who will be treated like anything but a pooch, can hitch a ride to nearby locales. A wonderful array of goodies awaits you daily and nightly in your suite. The marble bathrooms alone come complete with a steam room, phones, a TV, and a plush robe.

Dogs get a doggy bowl, a pooch bed, and a menu upon check-in. It's the most fascinatingly expensive and fancy pet room-service menu I've ever seen. Some of the items: grilled fillet of beef with organic rice and brown gravy ($28), poached salmon belly in frothed milk (for kitties, I imagine; $23), and the pièce de résistance, beluga caviar with a hard poached egg ($155; again, it must be a rich cat thing—I've never spent that much on a dinner for four, much less on an appetizer for a pet).

Room rates are $295–895 ($3,000 for a suite that's to drool for). Dogs are charged a $150 fee for the length of their stay. 9291 Burton Way 90210; 310/278-3344; www.lermitagehotel.com.

Loews Beverly Hills Hotel: If you want vintage-style glamour with super dog-friendly service, you'll find it at the delectable Loews Beverly Hills Hotel. From the palm tree-lined entrance to the stylish lobby to your sumptuous room (complete with an amazingly comfortable TempurPedic bed), this place is all about seemingly effortless class and luxury.

Unlike many other hotels of this genre, Loews welcomes dogs of any size. Thanks to the popular "Loews Loves Pets" program, dogs get the VIP treatment here. Upon their arrival, they receive a note from the hotel's manager welcoming them and giving them tips about nearby dog-friendly places. They also get some treats, a toy, food and water bowls, and can have use of a dog bed if they need one. In addition, gourmet room service awaits them. "The chefs prepare meals for dogs just like they do for our other guests," says the friendly concierge. Well, the menu may be different, but the prices and quality are right up there with those of the human meals.

The concierge can arrange for in-room pet-sitting or for dog-walking, should you be otherwise occupied in the heated outdoor pool or on Rodeo Drive. In fact, the hotel will lend you a "puppy pager" in case of a pooch emergency while you're elsewhere.

The rates are fairly reasonable here, considering the locale and amenities. They start at $149, and the normal room rates go up to about $200. Large suites can run up into the four-figure arena. It costs nothing to bring a dog. You'll pay only for the extras, such as room service and pet-sitting. What a deal! 1224 South Beverwil Drive 90035; 310/277-2800; www.loewshotels.com.

Regent Beverly Wilshire: This hotel puts the "E" in elegance and the "L" in luxury. Unfortunately, it also puts the kibosh on dogs who are barely larger than most cats. There's a 20-pound weight limit. Don't read any further if you don't want your larger dog to get tears all over your shoulder. Normally I wouldn't write much about a place that has such a restrictive weight limit, but the Beverly Wilshire deserves the full treatment, despite its rather archaic pooch size limit.

Upon arrival, your tiny pooch will be presented a silver tray containing two ceramic bowls. One has Milk-Bones and is accented by a sprig of fresh mint, the other bowl is for the bottle of Evian water your dog gets. Also on the tray are two white linen napkins, a rubber squeeze toy, and a vase with a long-stemmed rose. Your dog will also get a special pillow for napping. And all this is free! In addition, for a fee, the hotel provides dog-sitting and dog-walking. It'll even arrange for a vet or a groomer to come to your room, should you need one. Special gourmet meat selections are also at your dog's pawtips.

Oh yeah, the hotel. Well, it's in the heart of Beverly Hills, at Wilshire Boulevard and Rodeo Drive, and it's exquisite. It's a historic hotel, built in 1928, and has 275 luxurious guest rooms, including 69 suites. All the rooms have a marble bathroom with deep-soaking bathtub, fully stocked private bars with fridges, fresh flowers, terry robes, a private safe, foam and down pillows, 100 percent cotton linens, an in-room fax, twice-daily maid service, and so on. You get the picture. There's even a heated outdoor pool, but no dog-paddling pooches, please.

The hotel is probably best known in recent years as the setting for the hit movie *Pretty Woman*. The more intimate scenes between Richard Gere and Julia Roberts took place in the hotel's Presidential Suite. For a mere $5,000 per night, you and your dog (and your human guests) can stay here, too. For the price, you get 4,000 square feet of space with gobs of rooms, two fireplaces, and lots of special touches (not the kind of touches in *Pretty Woman*, though). Some notables who really stayed in the Presidential Suite are Elvis Presley, the Dalai Lama, King Hussein and Queen Noor, Prince Andrew, Andrew Lloyd Webber, Elton John, and Mick Jagger.

If you want something a little simpler (cheaper), you can stay in a gorgeous room for as little as $365. The average room rate runs about $450. There's a $125 deposit for dogs. 9500 Wilshire Boulevard 90212; 310/275-5200 or 800/241-4354; www.regenthotels.com.

Glendale

PARKS, BEACHES, AND RECREATION AREAS

35 Brand Park

🐾🐾🐾 (See Los Angeles County map on pages 732–733)

If you feel as if you're on the estate of William Randolph Hearst when visiting this green and verdant park, you're not far off. It's actually the former property of the late real-estate tycoon Leslie C. Brand, aka "The Father of Glendale."

Upon entering the park, you'll be greeted by a great white Moorish/Indian-style mansion. The mansion is now a library, surrounded by lush, shaded land. You and your leashed dog can pass an afternoon in perfect serenity here. Go ahead, pretend it's your estate. Relax, read, sniff the flowers, and have a little picnic.

If you prefer a little exercise with your lounging, there's a fire road that takes you through the park and up to a ridge with a great view. This hike is not for the fair of foot: It's almost a six-mile round-trip and, to put it mildly, it's not flat. But it's one of the more enjoyable hikes we found in the Los Angeles area. And if you want to keep going, there are ways to reach the thousands of acres of open space that lie outside the park's perimeter. Unfortunately, the leash law applies in this area, too.

Exit I-5 on Western Avenue and go northeast about 1.5 miles. The road will take you to the park's magnificent library entrance. 818/548-2000.

36 George Deukmejian Wilderness Park

🐾🐾 (See Los Angeles County map on pages 732–733)

When we first heard the name of this park, we thought someone was making a joke. The words "George Deukmejian" and the word "wilderness" were often used in the same sentence when he was governor, but more like: "That George Deukmejian, he should have been more concerned about wilderness."

A couple of locals told us that back in the late 1980s, the Duke was actually against setting aside this large parcel of land for a park. But he was finally sold on it when a clever environmentalist came up with the idea to name the park after him. Whether this is true or just a semiurban myth, dogs can be grateful to the governor for making room for this 700-acre square of land.

This isn't what you'd call a breathtaking park. It can be very dry and dusty, with only an occasional tree to provide relief from the sun in these chaparral-covered hills. But the dogs we've seen cavorting around the park really love it here. They seem to smile as they accompany their leashed people up and down the canyon.

Maybe they're smiling because of the lack of people or the abundance of singing birds. Maybe it's the scents of strange fauna on the couple of miles of dirt road here. Or perhaps they know that if they walk far enough, they'll be in Angeles National Forest, where they can run around in leashless ecstasy. (It will be 100 percent easier to get there once some trails connecting the two areas are completed.) Whatever the case, this is a park that you might not find aesthetically pleasing, but your dog will.

Exit U.S. 101 on Pennsylvania Avenue. Go north a few blocks and turn left at Foothill Boulevard. Drive northwest about six blocks, then turn right on Dunsmore Avenue. The road will lead you into the park in about a mile, where you'll bear right after the sign for the park and drive up a narrow paved road to a dirt parking lot next to a horse corral. The wide, gated road just above the lot is where you'll start your hike. 818/548-2000.

PLACES TO EAT

Hot Wings Cafe: This little restaurant has a shaded outdoor area and a loyal following of dog-toting patrons. 314 North Brand Boulevard; 818/247-4445.

La Fontana Italian Kitchen: You and your dog will be surrounded by an impressive wrought-iron fence as you dine at one of the umbrella-topped tables. 933 North Brand Boulevard; 818/247-6256.

PLACES TO STAY

Days Inn: Rates are $83–104. Dogs require a $50 deposit and must stay in smoking rooms. 450 West Pioneer Street 91203; 818/956-0202; www.daysinn.com.

Vagabond Inn: Rates are $89–99. Dogs are $10 extra and are relegated to smoking rooms. 120 West Colorado Street 91204; 818/240-1700.

Venice

Looking around Venice these days, you can see barely a hint of the dream of Abbot Kinney, the city's founder. In 1900, he began creating a city that was a near-duplicate of Italy's Venice, complete with canals, Italian architecture, and imported singing gondoliers. He had hoped to create a cultural renaissance in America.

If he could see the scantily clad roller skaters, the punkers with metal in every conceivable body part, the homeless, and the body builders and religious zealots in action, old Mr. Kinney would shudder. But despite the wayward ways of those inhabiting his dream, the place has a wild charm, a playland quality. And what really counts is that dogs think Venice is cool.

There are plenty of dogs here. As of this writing, they're not allowed on the beach, but there's a big battle being waged about that. A terrific group, Freeplay, is working hard to get beach access and more off-leash parks. Freeplay started as an acronym standing for Friendly, Responsible, Environmentally Evolved Pet Lover's Alliance—Yes. (Not short, but the resulting acronym was worth it.) www.freeplay.org.

PARKS, BEACHES, AND RECREATION AREAS

🐾 Westminster Dog Park

😺😺😺😺🐕 (See Los Angeles County map on pages 732–733)

Since Freeplay helped open this fenced-in park a few years back, beach-area dogs have joyously awaited their daily or weekly jaunts here. The park is more than an acre within very tiny Westminster Park, with plenty of shade and a few benches.

Small dogs have a choice of running with the big boys or playing in their very own smaller fenced-in dog-run area. Most tiny canines we know would opt for the chance to be as big as they feel and not be set apart as a little dog. But it's a great feature for dogs in need of some protection from giant paws.

The park is at Pacific and Westminster Avenues. The regional park office phone is 310/837-8116.

DIVERSION

Do It All at the Dogromat: All the Milk-Bones your dog can eat and a bath to boot. That's the way life is at the **Dogromat,** one of the most engaging self-service "dog laundromats" in the West.

Even dogs who hate baths don't mind coming here. Something in the air says, "It's OK. Thousands of dogs before you have been bathed here and survived, and you're next, and you won't die." Plus, as one of the owners freely admits, "We're notorious for feeding treats." Humans like it even better than dogs. It's much easier to bathe a dog here than at home because the tubs are waist high and everything you need is at your fingertips. Other benefits include ready advice from the staff (which is made up of grooming professionals), socializing in a dog-friendly atmosphere, and letting flea carcasses wash down someone else's drain.

The *Los Angeles Times* wrote that "What Chuck E. Cheese is to children, this place is to dogs." And your dog won't have greasy pizza drippings all over his clothes when he leaves. Dogromat rates are based on the size and hair type of your pooch. The average is $12. You'll find Dogromat at 12926 Venice Boulevard in Venice; 310/306-8885.

PLACES TO EAT

In addition to these restaurants, little eateries abound along Ocean Front Walk. Just grab a chair and table from the communal sidewalk restaurant furniture and enjoy one of the most scenic and unusual lunches you've ever experienced. (See the restaurant listings in the Marina del Rey section for more super-close eateries.)

Abbot's Habit: Your dog will want to make a habit of visiting this laid-back hangout, especially after he's offered a bowl of fresh water and you've bought him some of the crunchy dog treats sold here. Everyone from surfers to artists (often one and the same) comes here for the delectable baked goods and rich coffees. The sidewalk tables, where dogs are allowed, offer great people-watching opportunities. 1401 Abbot Kinney Boulevard; 310/399-1171.

Figtree's Cafe: The food here is fantastic and eclectic. You may eat at the patio as long as you tie your dog to the other side of the rail. She'll still be at your side, but there will be a couple of bars between you. A water bowl is available if your dog is thirsty. 429 Ocean Front Walk; 310/392-4937.

Pasta Factory: The pasta and breads are made fresh right here every day. You'll give your crunch-boxed pastas at home the evil eye after you taste the difference. The pizzas and seafood are tasty, too. Dine with your dog at the outdoor tables. 425 Washington Boulevard; 310/823-9838.

DIVERSION

Stroll to a Different Drummer: Since Venice's parks are so tiny, most people like to take their dogs for a jaunt along **Ocean Front Walk,** between Rose Avenue and Venice Boulevard. It's about as close to the beach as dogs are allowed, and for many, it's close enough. This is where you can consult a psychic; have your cards read by a tarot dealer; listen to street musicians; buy incense, T-shirts, or sunglasses; and watch skaters skate and lovers love.

If you like to check out bikini-clad babes—apparently one of Jake the Dog's favorite pastimes—this is a hot spot. Jake smiles pantingly as cuties skate or jog or saunter by. Sometimes he even steps out into their path, urging them to stop with his big brown eyes. They often do, and they lavish him with pats and cuddles. On a recent visit, a human dood saw the lovin' Jake was getting and asked if he could borrow him "just for 15 minutes." He said, "Your dog gets more attention in five minutes than I got all week here." Jake wanted to tell him that losing the nose ring and the nipple rings and covering his very hairy chest might help, but he remained politely silent.

You never know what you'll run into here. One day Joe the Dog, Jake's predecessor, was trotting merrily along sniffing the air for all the great, cheap places to eat along the walk, when suddenly a hand appeared on the path before him. It wouldn't have been a big deal, except the hand wasn't attached to a body. It was writhing and doing sickening somersaults. Joe trembled and ran backward right into a juggler. He stood there wrapped around the juggler's leg until the hand crawled away, back to the pile of motionless rubber hands from which it had strayed. He gave a shudder, unwrapped himself, and marched onward, never glancing back.

Marina Del Rey

PARKS, BEACHES, AND RECREATION AREAS

🐾🐾 Burton Chace Park

🐾🐾 (See Los Angeles County map on pages 732–733)

Water dogs love this 10-acre park, because it's on a spit surrounded by water on three sides. But unless you visit via a boat (guest docks are available for a reasonable fee), dogs don't really get access to the water here. It's Dock City here.

Leashed dogs of all ilks enjoy sniffing the salty breeze from this lovely, well-groomed park. The lawn can be golf-course green, and the pathways are immaculate. This is a popular spot for weddings and group picnics, which you'll need to steer clear of, even if your dog loves parties. 13650 Mindanao Way; 310/305-9595.

PLACES TO EAT

The Cow's End: This is a fun coffeehouse where you can sip your stuff under a canopy. They're so doggone friendly here that your dog may even be offered a tasty dog biscuit if he plays his cards right. 34 Washington Boulevard; 310/574-1080.

Mercedes' Cuban Grill: The Cuban-Caribbean creations here are spicy and exotic. The ambience inside is cozy and creative, and outside, where dogs are allowed, it's pure fun in the sun. (Or in the moon, if you choose to have dinner here.) If you're thirsty for a unique drink, try the banana *mojitos*. Dogs get only a bowl of water if they're thirsty, but that's OK, because who wants a dog with banana breath? 14 Washington Boulevard; 310/827-6209.

Los Angeles

Many communities and districts within the city have their own headings. Check individual headings if you don't find the area you need here.

PARKS, BEACHES, AND RECREATION AREAS

The dogs of Los Angeles are keeping their paws crossed for more off-leash spaces. Several different dog groups are working hard to find leash-free park areas. At press time, a group of Northeast Los Angelenos were within a bone's throw of getting approval for a nice chunk of leash-free land at Hermon Park in the Montecito Heights area. For more info, or to support their efforts, check out www.montecitohts.org/dogpark.

39 Elysian Park

🐾🐾🐾 (See Los Angeles County map on pages 732–733)

The views of Dodger Stadium and downtown Los Angeles don't get much better than from this 585-acre park. The hills here often rise above the smog, and the Los Angeles skyline actually looks attractive from a couple of high-altitude picnic spots.

Angel's Point is a must-see for leashed dogs and baseball fans. Dogs like the breezes that blow in from the different sections of the city. Ball fans enjoy being able to peer into a little segment of Dodger Stadium. The park is conveniently nestled between I-5, U.S. 101, and I-110. To get to Angel's Point and the many roads and trails beyond, exit I-5 at Stadium Way and follow the signs to the park. Once you're in the park, take your first left, Elysian Park Drive. If you're on your way to drop off friends at a Dodger game and your dog needs a quick walk, take your first right after you enter the park. It's a very green, tree-laden area that won't take you far off track from your destination. 213/485-5054.

40 Griffith Park/Griffith Park Dog Park

🐾🐾🐾🐾🐕 (See Los Angeles County map on pages 732–733)

This 4,017-acre park has something for dogs of every stripe (and spot), from dogs who need to run off leash to dogs who want to check out the famous "Hollywood" sign.

Since most dogs enjoy the leash-free life, we'll start with the dog park. It's a fenced-in park, with double-gated entries and a separate section for little or shy dogs. It's half grass, half dirt; not one of the prettier dog parks in the area, but it does the trick. To get to the Griffith Park Dog Park, exit Highway 134 at Zoo Drive and follow Zoo Drive into the park. The dog park is next to the John Ferrar soccer field, on the right side of the road. (The freeway is on the left side.)

Anywhere else in this giant park, dogs must be leashed. Much of the acreage is taken up by such nondog attractions as the city zoo, an observatory and planetarium, a bird sanctuary, an outdoor theater, an equestrian center, golf courses, tennis courts, a swimming pool, a transportation museum, and a Western heritage museum. But fortunately, two-thirds of the park is wild and wonderful, straddling the eastern end of the Santa Monica Mountains. You can explore the undeveloped sections of the park via more than 57 miles of trails! This is the largest municipal park in the United States, and it can be quite an attractive place considering it's in the middle of three major freeways in the city that puts the "M" in Metropolis. About 100 tree species thrive here, including oaks, pines, and even redwoods. Birds are abundant, which makes sense when you consider their alternatives in the urban realities beyond the park's perimeter.

DIVERSION

Choo on This: From your seat aboard one of **Griffith Park's miniature trains,** you and your dog will see goats, horses, llamas, pigs, and a little Native American town. Your dog's ears will flap with wonder as the open-air train chugs gently along. The ride lasts only about eight minutes, but the price is right: Dogs go for free. ("Dogs can't hold down a job, so they shouldn't have to pay," a funny train lady told us.) Humans are $2, be they of the adult or child variety. The train departs from the section of L.A.'s Griffith Park around Los Feliz Boulevard and Riverside Drive. Call 323/664-6788 for more information.

With all the trails here (few are very developed), you have myriad choices about what kind of hiking you and your dog can do. Here are two suggestions to get you started:

1) Get a map before you arrive, so you'll have time to plan your trek. Call the number below and the rangers will send you a free map showing all the trails.

2) Be careful. Because of the remoteness of some of the trail areas, they've become dumping grounds for bodies. And we're not talking bodies of literature, bodies of evidence, or even pigeon and squirrel bodies. Even with your dog at your side, you may not want to venture too far by yourself.

One fun hike you can take is the one that winds you as close as is legally possible to the infamous "HOLLYWOOD" sign. From central Hollywood (Franklin Avenue and Beachwood Drive), go north on Beachwood Drive about 1.5 miles. At the street's northernmost end, it will come together with Hollyridge Drive. Park around here, and after walking about a block, you'll come to a wide trail on your left. It's not marked, but it will take you about 1.5 miles up Mt. Lee, where you'll be stopped by an ungracious fence. The fence is there at least in part because of the radio tower at the hilltop. (Maybe the powers that be also don't want dogs doing leg lifts on this oft-molested sign.)

One of the most entertaining activities you and your dog can share at Griffith Park is a train ride (see the Diversion Choo on This). U.S. 101, I-5, and Highway 134 surround the park. A popular entry is off I-5 at Los Feliz Boulevard. 323/913-4688.

🐾 Hancock Park

🐾🐾 (See Los Angeles County map on pages 732–733)

Take your dog to a tar pit that once trapped scads of Ice Age animals! What fun! The tar still bubbles up from its pondlike setting, but fear not: It's well fenced, so even the most ardent water dogs will be safe from the alluring mire. You can see how animals were drawn here thinking it was a place to splash around and guzzle some liquid refreshments. A few replicas of mammoths charging into the tar pit add a prehistoric air to the park.

The park itself has enough green grass for a pleasant stroll, but it's not big enough for a major exercise experience. There's a snack bar near the tar pit, but hanging around here probably won't give you an appetite, since on a hot day, it can smell like roofing tar.

Hancock Park is alongside the George C. Page Museum, which houses skeletons and re-creations of formidable prehistoric animals trapped in the Rancho La Brea Tar Pits during the Ice Age. The Los Angeles County Museum of Art flanks the park's other side, so the park is convenient if you have to drop off a culturally minded friend.

The park is between 6th Street and Wilshire Boulevard and Curson Avenue and Ogden Drive. Your best bet for free parking is along 6th Street. The park is "owned" by one government entity and operated by another, and no one seems to want to take phone calls for it. In fact, last time we talked to the officials, no one even knew the park existed. Scary! Well, here's the number for the museum. Whoever answers the phone will have information on the park. 323/857-6311.

42 Kenneth Hahn State Recreation Area

😊 😊 😊 (See Los Angeles County map on pages 732–733)

Here's a Los Angeles–area park where the birds singing in the trees are actually louder than the drone of the freeways! The hilly section of this large park is a fascinating place to visit. Not only can you and your leashed dog do some intense hiking, but you can also experience the world-uniting feel of the Olympics.

In 1932, the area was the site of the 10th Olympics. Then in 1984, Los Angeles again hosted the Olympics, drawing athletes from 140 nations. To serve as a continual (and growing) reminder of the events, 140 trees have been planted together on the hills where the 1932 events occurred. Each tree represents a nation that took part in the 23rd Olympics.

Watching their young leaves blowing in the breeze is enough to send patriotic shivers up your spine. It's also enough to make most male dogs stretch their leashes to pay their kind of homage to these saplings. But they can't. The trees are fenced in until they are big enough to withstand such assaults.

But there are many other trees to sniff in this large park. Several trails branch out from the parking lot at the Olympic Forest. Most take you up the hill, but you can also hike down by the lake and stream in the adjoining section of park.

Fees are $4 per vehicle on weekends and holidays. As you drive north on La Cienega Boulevard in the Ladera Heights neighborhood north of Inglewood, you'll pass an oil drilling site and then come to signs for the park. Although it's a state park, it's operated by Los Angeles County. 323/298-3660.

43 Silver Lake Park Dog Park

😊 😊 😊 🐕 (See Los Angeles County map on pages 732–733)

It's hard to believe, but right in the middle of what has traditionally been the Land o' Leashes (that is, in the metro region of the city rec and parks department) lies this small, fenced, leash-free mecca.

The trees here are relatively wee, but dogs still are relatively happy weeing on them. Someday when the trees get big and strong, they won't mind so much. The park also has water for pooches and people. The benches here make for more comfy human visits and also make a great place to sit down and talk to a new human acquaintance. (The park draws lots of singles from the surrounding community. We've heard there have been some matches made in heaven here.)

The park is on Silver Lake Boulevard, just south of Silver Lake and a bit north of Sunset Boulevard. 323/644-3946.

PLACES TO EAT

This is just a sampling of the eateries in Los Angeles proper. Some of the best dog-friendly restaurants are in surrounding areas. (See listings for other communities/areas for doggy dining details.)

Melrose Baking Company: If you want great baked goods at a fun outdoor setting, don't skip this place. 7356 Melrose Avenue; 323/651-3165.

Sante LaBrea: This is among our favorite California restaurants. The outdoor area is lovely, the folks here like dogs, and the food is healthful and very delicious. 345 North La Brea Avenue; 323/857-0412.

Stir Crazy: The staff loves dogs at this coffee shop. "We don't discriminate against anyone," one of the managers told us. 6917 Melrose Avenue; 323/934-4656.

Trattoria Farfalla: The people-watching at this Los Feliz eatery is fun, and the food here is tasty. Jake Dog apparently loves the lamb chops, but the closest he came to them was when he decided to visit a neighboring table—ostensibly at the invitation of the couple sitting there—and ended up with his snout resting firmly on their table, dangerously, pleadingly, close to the meaty dish. (I was eating one of the signature ultrathin-crust pizzas.) Dine with doggy at the sidewalk tables. Thirsty dogs get water here. 1978 Hillhurst Avenue; 323/661-7365.

PLACES TO STAY

Please see other cities and communities (such as Beverly Hills, Westwood, or West Hollywood) for nearby hotels.

Beverly Laurel Motor Hotel: You'll get a decent room for a decent price here. And it's in a great location, three blocks from CBS, and near the farmer's market. Cool off with a dip in the pool after a long day of exploring. The motel was built in 1964, and it looks it. Rates are $94–110. Dogs are $25 extra. 8018 Beverly Boulevard 90048; 323/651-2441.

Four Points Hotel Sheraton L.A. Airport: This one's near the airport, which is convenient for traveling pooches. Rates are $119–175. There's a $50 deposit for dogs, who also have to pay $10 extra nightly. 9750 Airport Boulevard 90045; 310/645-4600 or 800/529-4683.

Holiday Inn Brentwood-Bel Air: This is that funky old cylindrical tower you see right off the 405 when stuck in traffic. Dogs under 40 pounds can stay here. Rates are $99–129. 170 North Church Lane 90049; 310/476-6411.

Hotel Sofitel Los Angeles: "We love dogs here," more than one doghappy manager has told us. This big, attractive, upscale hotel is near the best of Beverly Hills. Rates are $189–329. 8555 Beverly Boulevard 90048; 310/278-5444; www.sofitel.com.

Le Meridien at Beverly Hills: You'll get contemporary European-style digs at this beautiful hotel. The rooms aren't chichi, but they're delightfully comfortable in a clean, spacious, overstuffed kind of way. Amenities include a robe and slippers, a deep-soak tub, and a free nightly shoeshine. (Don't wear tennis shoes here if you want to get your money's worth.) Rates are $179–235. Your dog can stay for up to four nights for $100 extra. (So one night will be $100, as will four nights.) After four nights, it's $25 nightly. 465 South La Cienega Boulevard 90048; 310/247-0400; www.lemeridien.com.

The St. Regis Los Angeles: It's elegant. It's sophisticated. It's expensive. But if you have some extra change jingling around your pockets, and you like sleek, modern luxury accommodations, it's worth a visit. The staff is super-dog-friendly here: Dogs get St. Regis's own brand of dog biscuits, a "silver" (read stainless steel) bowl, and use of a doggy bed. And the hotel isn't just for fluffy-wuffy dogs. "As long as your dog isn't the size of a wildebeest, it's OK," says a manager. (I'm not sure exactly what the average wildebeest weighs, but I think most dogs could safely make a reservation here. If not, it's gnus to me.) Rates are $369–469. (Well, at least your dog doesn't cost extra.) 2055 Avenue of the Stars 90067; 310/277-6111.

TraveLodge Hotel at LAX: Rates are $64–109. Dogs are $10 extra. 5447 West Century Boulevard 90045; 310/649-4000 or 800/421-3939.

Vagabond Inn Figueroa: Rates are $89–109. Dogs are $10 extra. 3101 South Figueroa Street 90007; 213/746-1531.

Westin Hotels and Resorts: There are three Westins within city limits, but we'd run out of space if we went into the detail each deserves. Suffice it to say they're all luxurious (the Westin Century Plaza has hosted presidents), stylish, and very welcoming for medium-sized or smaller dogs: Each offers the doggy version of the chain's ultracomfy beds for people. "Dogs love the Heavenly Dog Beds," says one concierge. "I would do if I were a dog." One offers bowls, another treats. **The Westin Century Plaza Hotel and Spa** (2025 Avenue of the Stars 90067; 310/277-2000) is the most pricey, with standard rooms $259–325. Dogs must be 35 pounds or under. **The Westin Bonaventure Hotel and Suites** (404 South Figueroa Street 90071; 213/624-1000) will run you $109–259 and allows dogs under 40 pounds. **The Westin Los Angeles Airport** (5400 West Century Boulevard 90045; 310/216-5858) is the least expensive, with rooms $104–180, and allows the biggest dogs, up to 50 pounds. You can get more details on all the hotels by checking out www.starwood.com/westin.

Pasadena

PARKS, BEACHES, AND RECREATION AREAS

Pasadena residents have been fighting to get a much-needed off-leash park or dog-run area for years. At press time, construction was about to start on what promises to be an incredible dog park on Pasadena's east side, within Eaton Wash Park. The Alice Kennedy Frost Dog Park will be two acres, with tunnels, hills, and all kinds of fun dog doohickeys. It was scheduled to open during summer 2005. For an update, see www.pasadenapooch.org, or phone the parks department at 626/744-4321.

44 Brookside Park
🐾🐾🐾🐕 (for restricted training purposes)
(See Los Angeles County map on pages 732–733)

Brookside Park, home of the Rose Bowl, is a beautiful place, with roses hither and thither. The park has a playground, ball fields, trees, and acres of green grass. When there are no major games going on, it's a quiet park. There's even a trail you and your leashed pooch can take to get farther away from the madding crowd, in case you happen to be accompanying someone who has only one Rose Bowl ticket.

Dogs are allowed off leash here only for training purposes, and only at a designated area near the Rose Bowl. The hours for this training are 6 A.M.–10 P.M. weekdays, and 6–10 A.M. weekends. (A word about training: We're not talking about training your dog to hike off leash or chase tennis balls. The training clause is for specific feats that don't cover a lot of ground, such as teaching your dog to come when called, to stay, and to heel. Be careful out there; park rangers know the difference between truly training your dog and walking around the park reading the newspaper with your dog.)

Exit I-210 at Seco Street and follow the signs to the Rose Bowl. As you approach the Rose Bowl stadium, look for a big green meadow on your left. It's part of this large park complex. 626/744-4321.

45 Central Park
🐾🐾 (See Los Angeles County map on pages 732–733)

Visiting Old Town Pasadena? Bring your leashed dog here for a little siesta between your café-hopping adventures. The park has several tall old trees that boy dogs are wild about, and plenty of other good dog amenities such as big grassy areas, a shaded paved path, and lawn bowling. (OK, they can't bowl, but they enjoy watching for a few seconds.) The park is at Del Mar Boulevard and Fair Oaks Avenue. 626/744-4321.

46 Eaton Canyon Park
🐾🐾🐾 (See Los Angeles County map on pages 732–733)

This wild and beautiful 184-acre park can be a little too enticing for dog folks: Half of the users allow their dogs off leash, according to rangers. This is something the rangers consider a big no-no, in part because of the wildlife here (many a deer has been chased, they say), in part because of the horses who share the trails (many a horse has been spooked, they say), and in part because of the rattlesnakes and poison oak here (many a dog has encountered both, the former with nasty results for the dog, the latter with nasty results for the dog's human).

Rangers here say dogs may be banned if people continue to disobey the leash law. "They're hanging on by the skin of their teeth," says one. If you don't want to lose this park, use your leash. And use your poop bags. If you don't have one, the park has mutt mitt dispensers.

Traveling east on I-210, exit at Altadena Drive and go north on Altadena. Drive 1.6 miles. The main park entrance is on the right. Follow the winding road to the park's nature center, where you can pick up a map and get your bearings. 626/398-5420.

PLACES TO EAT

All India Cafe: The food here is utterly delicious. It seems every time you sneeze, it gets lavished with yet another "best Indian cuisine"-type honor. Vegetarians and meat-eaters alike love the delectable cuisine. Dogs would be content to laze at the sidewalk tables in the shade of an awning, but as a bonus they get their own doggy delight: cool water and a treat! 39 South Fair Oaks Avenue; 626/440-0309.

Crocodile Cafe: You can't get crocodiles here, but you can get a terrific barbecued chicken pizza or a tiger shrimp salad. "Our food is swell," says a friendly waiter. Dine with your dog at the umbrella-topped tables out front. 88 West Colorado Boulevard; 626/568-9310.

Jake's: Jake the Dog loves visiting this Old Town Pasadena eatery and smelling the big burgers, chicken strips, and chunky fries. Humans can wash it all down with one of many brands of brews, and dogs get a bowl of water if they're thirsty. Dogs and their people can sit at several well-shaded outdoor tables. 38 West Colorado Boulevard; 626/568-1602.

Mi Piace: In Italian, the name of this restaurant means, "I like it." And I do. The Italian food has a light and healthy California bent. Try the chicken Mi Piace, which is white-meat chicken sautéed with mushrooms in a garlicky-herby white-wine concoction. (A menu writer I'm not.) The little pizzas are zippy. Eat with your dog under the sidewalk awning. Dogs get fresh water if thirsty. In Old Town Pasadena, at 25 East Colorado Boulevard; 626/795-3131.

Three Dog Bakery: Dogs take comfort in knowing that there's one place that always allows dogs inside in Old Town Pasadena. Pooches get to nose around and choose from dozens of fresh-baked treats and dog pastries while their people eye (and buy) fun dog gift items. Watch your dog dine at the one little table here. (Now you know how it feels when your dog watches you dine.) The bakery is in 24 Smith Alley; 626/440-0443.

Trattoria Farfalla: Dine on tasty pastas and pizzas at the sidewalk tables here. Dogs dig the mellow atmosphere and the water they'll get if thirsty. 43 East Colorado Boulevard; 626/564-8696.

PLACES TO STAY

Millard Campground: This tiny five-tent site is the perfect getaway just north of town. Since it's in Angeles National Forest, your dog is welcome. And outside the campground, he can go off leash on the many first-rate trails here. The beauties of this camping area are that you don't have to make a reservation and coming here is free. Exit I-210 at Lake Avenue and drive north to Loma Alta Drive. Go left on Loma Alta Drive. Follow the signs to the campground. 626/574-5200.

Quality Inn Pasadena: Rates are $59–79. Dogs are $10 extra and need to stay in a smoking room. 3221 East Colorado Boulevard 91107; 626/796-9291.

The Ritz-Carlton, Huntington Hotel and Spa: Remember all those times you've stayed at other hotels and shrugged off the postage stamp–sized towels or the paper-thin walls with a "Well, it ain't exactly The Ritz"? Well, this is exactly the Ritz. Only lucky little dogs (under 30 pounds) get to experience this gorgeous, crème de la crème hotel. It's set on 23 acres of gardens with every luxury amenity imaginable. I won't go into more detail since most dogs are too big or too budget-conscious to stay here and it would break their hearts. Rates are $200–320. (Suites can cost more than $3,000.) 1401 South Oak Knoll 91106; 626/568-3900; www.ritzcarlton.com/hotels/huntington.

Vagabond Inn: Rates are $89–99. Dogs are $10 extra. 1203 East Colorado Boulevard 91106; 626/449-3170.

The Westin Pasadena: If your dog is 40 pounds or under, he'll feel like a small human at this lovely hotel: Humans get the luxurious Heavenly Bed, dogs get the luxurious Heavenly Dog Bed. Humans get a fitness center, dogs get, well, free poop bags and some grass to peruse outside. Rates are $169–219. 191 North Los Robles 91101; 626/792-2727; www.starwood.com/westin.

Sierra Madre

PARKS, BEACHES, AND RECREATION AREAS

47 Sierra Madre Dog Park

🐾🐾🐾🐾 (See Los Angeles County map on pages 732–733)

To visit this little dog park, you need to attend a tag sale of sorts. Dogs who come here need to wear a tag issued by the city. The tag is $25 for the calendar year, but the fee is prorated depending on the time of year you buy the tag. If you want to just check out the park for an afternoon, you're supposed to buy a daily pass for $5.

The park isn't even an acre, but it's got a separate fenced area for small or shy dogs, wheelchair access, lights, water, benches, and lots of dogs who are really fun to play with. It's within Sierra Vista Park, which has restrooms, should you need to heed nature's call after your dog does.

The park is at 611 East Sierra Madre Boulevard, south of the tennis courts in Sierra Vista Park. Call 626/836-8468 for park info. You can buy tags at the city building at 232 West Sierra Madre Boulevard. The phone number there is 626/355-7135.

El Segundo

Are you near the airport and looking for a place to run your dog off-leash? Be sure to sniff out El Segundo's little off-leash gem. And if the dogs of L.A. County get their way, there could be an off-leash beach at Dockweiler Beach by the next edition of this book. The terrific group, Freeplay, is trying hard to make this happen. See www.freeplay.org for updates and info. For now, dogs have to be content only to camp there in an RV, on leash, and away from the water. (See Places to Stay.)

PARKS, BEACHES, AND RECREATION AREAS

48 El Segundo Dog Park

😽😽😽 🐾 (See Los Angeles County map on pages 732–733)

Like plane spotting? Bring your furry pal to this dog park. It's set on a grassy bluff that has views of nearby LAX, and you can watch the planes take off and land all day if you like. But chances are that your off-leash dog will have more important things to do at this long, 1.5-acre park, such as sniff trees, sniff other dogs, run around a lot, and sniff more dogs. The park has water, benches, poop bags, double gates, and a separate section for small dogs.

It's on East Imperial Avenue between McCarthy Court and Sheldon Street, across from Imperial Avenue School. 310/524-2700.

PLACES TO STAY

Dockweiler Beach RV Park: Got an RV and an urge to cozy up to the ocean? Stay at one of the 118 sites here for a couple of nights. Pets must be leashed, and they can't officially go to the nearby beach. Rates are $25–32. From I-405 about 12 miles south of Santa Monica, exit at Imperial West Highway and drive four miles west to Vista del Mar. That's where you'll find the park. Call for reservations. 310/322-7036.

Summerfield Suites by Windham: You and your dog never have to leave your suite (except for the occasional potty break at the hotel's little dog-walk area...uh, for your dog) when you stay at this clean, comfortable lodging that's a favorite among people doing business near the airport. The suites all have a full kitchen, cozy living room, nice bedroom, and business-oriented services features such as high-speed Internet and a large, attractive working area. If you want your groceries delivered, that can be arranged for no extra fee (except for the groceries).

Of course, you'll want to leave your suite so your dog can get some well-deserved off-leash exercise. And what better place than the El Segundo Dog Park, which is a quick car ride away? (See above.)

Dogs need to be under 60 pounds to stay here. Rates for suites are $129–189. There's a $150 fee per visit for dogs in the one-bedroom suites, and a $200 fee per visit for dogs in the two-bedroom suites. 810 South Douglas Street 90245; 310/725-0100; www.wyndham.com.

Manhattan Beach

Dogs and people usually take an automatic liking to this seaside town. It's a friendly place, with people who stop you in the street to talk about how much they like your dog. This is not that common in these parts, so enjoy it. Unfortunately, the friendly attitude doesn't extend to the city's beaches or parks. Only one allows pooches.

PARKS, BEACHES, AND RECREATION AREAS

49 Manhattan Beach Parkway Park

🐾🐾 (See Los Angeles County map on pages 732–733)

This is a jolly green continuation of Hermosa Beach's Hermosa Valley Greenbelt. It's skinny, dozens of blocks long, and it's the only public green in town that allows dogs. Leashes are a must, and don't even think about going on the beach with your pooch. Sorry, water dogs.

The park runs along Ardmore Valley Avenue for much of its length. 310/545-5621.

PLACES TO EAT

El Sombrero: The folks here make a mean burrito. Try one at the sidewalk benches. 1005 Manhattan Avenue; 310/374-1366.

Hennessey's: Dogs can dine with you at the sidewalk tables here, but not the patio tables. Try the granola French toast. Yum!! 313 Manhattan Beach Boulevard; 310/546-4813.

Local Yolk: If you want a great breakfast, this place is just killer. (And this is not a reference to the cholesterol-raising dishes here.) A photo inside shows a man with a dog outside the restaurant. It says, "A safe place for dogs" (or something like that). And it is. Dogs are welcome to dine with you at the outdoor tables here. 3414 Highland Avenue; 310/546-1407.

Sloopy's Beach Cafe: Inside this is a very funky place. It looks like a jungle or forest with tons of plants and tree-trunk tables. Outside there are just a few little tree-trunk tables with plastic chairs. Dogs can dine with you on tasty breakfast food and California lunch fare.

Uncle Bill's Pancake House: This is one of the more dog-friendly eateries around. "We love dogs!" says a manager. Uncle Bill's has been hailed as "the king of the South Bay breakfast eateries." Try the cheddar and bacon waffle. You'll be drooling as much as your dog. (Thirsty dogs get a bowl of water.) Dine with your furry friend at any of several tables out front. 1305 Highland Avenue; 310/545-5177.

PLACES TO STAY

Residence Inn by Marriott: You and your dog can get a roomy apartment-style suite here. Some come with fireplaces, and all come with a kitchen, which is a mighty convenient feature when traveling with a pooch. Rates are $139–199. There's a $75 deposit and a $100 cleaning fee for the length of your stay when you visit with a dog. 1700 North Sepulveda Boulevard 90266; 310/546-7627 or 800/321-2211.

Hermosa Beach

PARKS, BEACHES, AND RECREATION AREAS

Dogs aren't allowed at any of Hermosa Beach's beaches.

50 Hermosa Valley Greenbelt

🐾🐾 (See Los Angeles County map on pages 732–733)

This long, narrow strip of green runs 30 blocks—the entire length of the city. It's got a pleasant soft dirt/chipped bark path down the middle, which leashed dogs really enjoy treading on. It's shaded in parts and can be fairly quiet, considering that it's sandwiched by two roads. But it's quite narrow, not ideal for a dog who likes to do heavy-duty exploring.

You can enter the park almost anywhere along Ardmore Avenue or Valley Street. The park continues north into Manhattan Beach (see Manhattan Beach Parkway Park in the Manhattan Beach section). 310/318-0280.

PLACES TO EAT

As if to make up for the lack of poochy beach access, dog-friendly eateries abound here.

Good Stuff: This delightful eatery is right by the strand and the beach. Dine on everything from traditional (really yummy) breakfast dishes to burgers, to wraps, to pretty darn good Mexican food. Dogs can join their people at the many outdoor tables. If it's busy, you have to sit at the side tables with your dog. 1286 The Strand; 310/374-2334.

Hennessey's: Hennessey's outdoor area is a hit with the dog set: Water bowls are always out and almost always filled with fresh water. People like the big heaping plates of food that's not necessarily the healthiest in the world (burgers, corned beef hash, beer-battered onion rings, and the like), and dogs like to sit around and wait for food to fall to the ground. If it's busy, dogs are relegated to the other side of the patio fence, but they can still be right beside you. 8 Pier Avenue; 310/372-5759.

Java Man: Dogs enjoy this old, funky sandwich/coffee/soup place. It's on a busy part of the street, but dogs don't seem to mind: The folks here give dogs treats and water, and the dogs don't notice the traffic passing by. 157 Pier Avenue; 310/379-7209.

Le Petite Cafe: "We are very happy to tell you we are very dog-friendly," announced the manager when last we spoke. Dogs can join you at the outdoor eating bar, where you can get a great omelette or a beefy burger. 190 Hermosa Avenue; 310/379-1400.

Martha's 22nd Street Grill: They'll often let your dog sit beside you at the outside tables here, but if it's crowded, you'll be asked to tie your dog up to one of the poles on the side. The food is really good—and good for you, too. The menu includes apple pancakes, Monte Cristo sandwiches, and veggie burgers. Your dog can get a bowl of water if his whistle needs wetting. 25 22nd Street; 310/376-7786.

Redondo Beach

PARKS, BEACHES, AND RECREATION AREAS

Dogs are banned from all city parks, beaches, and open-space lands, with one very special exception. When you're done getting down and dirty at the dog park, take a trip to the Ushampooch, a fun, clean self-serve dog wash just one block from the park, at 1218A Beryl Street; 310/798-7300; www.ushampooch.com.

🐾 Redondo Beach Dog Park

🐾🐾🐾🐾🐕 (See Los Angeles County map on pages 732–733)

A few years ago, dogs were thrilled to have a 2.5-acre leash-free, fenced park to call their very own, even though there was no shade and much of the park ran under big power lines. After all, before that, dogs couldn't even set paw in any local parks. But now that the park has been expanded and gussied up a bit, dogs are positively ecstatic.

The park is now six big acres. It's divided into three parts—two big parks that switch off being open to give the grass a chance to grow, and one smaller park for small dogs. The park also has about 30 fairly new trees. The trees are still too small to give shade, but at least they give hope for shade in the near future.

The power lines over a swatch of the park don't do much for the place aesthetically, but dogs don't care. There's doggy drinking water, cool green grass, good sniffs, and lots of other dogs to pal around with. In fact, a survey shows that the dog park is the busiest park in the city, with about 1,500 visitors on some of the busy weekends.

The park is at Flagler Lane and 190th Street. Driving north on the Highway 1/Pacific Coast Highway, go right on Beryl Street. In about 10 blocks you'll come to Flagler Lane. Go left on Flagler. Parking is on the right, before the stop sign on the top of the hill. 310/318-0610; www.rbdogpark.com.

PLACES TO EAT

Catalina Coffee Company: The folks here roast their own beans, and it smells divine. Have a sandwich and a café drink with your dog at your side at the spacious, shaded outdoor area. Thirsty dogs can get a bowl of water. 126 North Catalina Avenue; 310/318-2499.

Coffee Cartel: Buy books and a cuppa joe at this older, fun place with a literary bent. Coffee Cartel sponsors everything from poetry readings to bluegrass bands. Dogs can join you at the outdoor tables. 1820 South Catalina Avenue; 310/316-6554.

Petit Casino: Who says food at a minimall has been chain-restauranted to death? The food's not fancy, but it's not cookie-cutter, either. Dine at the outdoor tables with your dog. 1767 South Elena Avenue; 310/543-5585.

Redondo Beach Brewing Company: The grilled food is great, and the ales are all that. For something different, try the Greek tacos or the scrumptious chicken adobo sandwich. Drink and dine with your dog at the shaded tables out front. 1814 South Catalina Avenue; 310/316-8477.

Zazou: This terrific restaurant offers a fun mix of California-Provençale cuisine. The dishes are flavorful, and for the most part, healthful. (Dogs long for the braised rabbit, but the butternut squash and ginger raviolini are truly droolworthy.) You can eat at the tables out front with your dog, but you can't drink alcohol out here. (Neither can your dog, if that makes you feel better.) 4810 South Catalina Avenue; 310/540-4884.

PLACES TO STAY

Best Western Redondo Beach Inn: Rates at this attractive Best Western, which features a pool and spa, are $89–109. Dogs are $50 extra for the length of their stay. 1850 South Pacific Coast Highway 90277; 310/540-3700.

Westwood

This lively University of California community is a fun place to have a dog. People around here genuinely like them.

PARKS, BEACHES, AND RECREATION AREAS

52 Westwood Park

🐾🐾 (See Los Angeles County map on pages 732–733)

For a flat, squarish park, this isn't a bad place for a leashed dog. Long dirt paths wind their way through very green grass, past modern sculptures and many shaded picnic tables.

From I-405 take the Wilshire exit heading toward Westwood. Take your first right (on Veteran Avenue). The park will be on your right shortly after the federal building. Another section of the park is on Sepulveda Boulevard, just north of Ohio Avenue. 310/473-3610.

PLACES TO EAT

Stan's Corner Donut Shop: Lots of local cops hang out here, so it's got to be good. If you're in the mood for Indian food or a hot dog, Stan's serves this, too. Stan says, "I love dogs. I have a little French blood in me!" And dogs love the outdoor tables on this sunny corner and the water they'll get if thirsty. 10948 Weyburn Avenue; 310/208-8660.

PLACES TO STAY

The official mailing address of these two hotels is Los Angeles, but they're true Westwood glories.

Beverly Hills Plaza Hotel: This is a gorgeous hotel, upscale from the ground floor up. (It's only four stories tall, but still....) There used to be a 30-pound size limit, but management is smart and now permits any size well-behaved pooch. There's a $200 cleaning fee for dogs and a $500 deposit, so bring the bankroll or the credit card if you decide to stay here. Rates are $185–525. 10300 Wilshire Boulevard, Los Angeles 90024; 310/275-5575 or 800/800-1234; www.beverlyhillsplaza.com.

W Los Angeles: Dogs really dig this luxurious, peaceful, ultracomfortable and super-dog-friendly hotel. The beds have featherbed toppers and goosedown comforters and pillows. (Not that your dog should go on the bed or anything.) It's an all-suites hotel, so you can relax in your lush terry robe (hotel-supplied) on your cushy sofa in your roomy suite with your faithful, happy, furry friend at your side. The doggy details are just as splendid: Visiting pooches will get a cozy pillow bed, bowl, food, treats, and a leash. The W gives new meaning to the phrase, "It's a dog's life." The suites are $300. 930 Hilgard Avenue, Los Angeles 90024; 310/208-8765; www.starwood.com/whotels.

City of Commerce

What a quaint, cozy name for a city. *Not.* Well, at least if you need to do business here, and you're lucky enough to have your dog with you, you'll have one great place to stay.

PLACES TO STAY

Ramada Inn: "We're very pet-friendly," boasted one of the managers of this hotel. At a typical Ramada, that usually means dogs are allowed. Period. But at this Ramada, it means dogs are as welcome as their humans. Dogs get their very own doggy bed and enough rawhide chews to make their jaws look like Arnold Schwarzenegger's biceps. (This was originally written years before he became the Governator, but it still holds true.) This is wonderful news for dogs on the go. Speaking of dogs on the go, there's even a dog-exercise area for leashed pooches in the back of the hotel. The hotel asks that only small- to medium-sized dogs stay here, but we're told the rule can be bent for some big dogs. Rates are $59–85. 7272 Gage Avenue 90040; 562/806-4777 or 800/272-6232; www.ramadainn.com.

Palos Verdes Estates

PARKS, BEACHES, AND RECREATION AREAS

53 Malaga Park

 (See Los Angeles County map on pages 732–733)

We mention this tiny park only because it's so close to a really lovely European-style part of this luxurious city. You and your leashed dog can catch a refreshing ocean breeze at Malaga Park, since it's high on a hill. Dogs like to relax on the small plot of lush grass and contemplate what it would be like if their backyard looked like this. People enjoy sitting on the stone benches and contemplating the same thing. In the spring, a little garden comes alive with color. Make sure your leashed dog doesn't think the park is larger than it is and accidentally wander into the flower beds.

From Palos Verdes Drive going west, go right on Via Corta. Park on the street. The park is immediately on your left. Don't blink or you'll miss it. 310/378-0383.

PLACES TO EAT

Rive Gauche: Elegance is the operative word at this four-star French restaurant. Yet the managers gladly permit pooches to dine with you at the patio tables. "We're very dog-friendly here," they say. Some patrons have been bringing their dogs here for years, much as they would if this restaurant were in France. One regular told us that sometimes her dog manages to mooch a little something from her waiter. But I don't think that's the norm here. Still, maybe your dog will get lucky. There's a canopy over the patio, so you and your *chien* can dine without the sun's smacking you in the eyeballs. 320 Tejon Place; 310/378-0267.

Torrance

PARKS, BEACHES, AND RECREATION AREAS

54 Miramar Park

☘ (See Los Angeles County map on pages 732–733)

Is your dog thirsty? This tiny, grassy park overlooking the ocean provides the best dog-watering hole in the county. Fido Fountain was built in 1990 because dogs were drinking from the human water fountain and many humans were complaining. "The large dogs jump up as their masters turn on the water for them," wrote one resident. "Very upsetting to me, and others, if they knew they were drinking after dogs. I myself love my dog, but I do not eat or drink after my own dog."

Fortunately, City Hall didn't allow such letters to result in more regulations against dogs. The city just went ahead and built a dog-sized fountain right beside the other drinking fountain. Then the tables were turned: Sand-covered humans started rinsing off their feet in the Fido Fountain. So the city built a miniature headstone reading: "Fido Fountain—Dogs only, please." It did the trick. Now human feet and dog lips rarely come together at Miramar Park.

The park is at the northern border of the city, just south of Redondo Beach on Paseo de La Playa. 310/618-2930.

South El Monte

PARKS, BEACHES, AND RECREATION AREAS

55 Whittier Narrows Regional Park

☘☘☘ (See Los Angeles County map on pages 732–733)

Is your pooch picky about parks? This one is bound to please: There's something for almost every dog in this very large chunk of county land. For dogs who like to hang out near lakes, the park is home to the Legg Lakes. These are actually three connected ponds. The fishing for trout is about as good as it gets in the middle of a major metropolitan area. The section of the park with the lake also has a long path around it for dogs who prefer not to get grass on their paws.

For dogs who like to explore nature, try the self-guiding nature trail at the Whittier Narrows Nature Center. Starting at the visitor center, get a pamphlet explaining the various phenomena you might encounter on the half-mile nature trail. Make sure your leashed dog doesn't disturb this precious little piece of nature. A chicken sometimes runs around the parking lot, so beware in case your dog plans to be self-sufficient for dinner.

And for chow hounds, a very big area east of Santa Anita Boulevard is devoted almost entirely to picnic tables. When it's not crowded, it's a great place to run around with your dog. Although dogs are supposed to be leashed, it's nice to know that two sides of this large section are fenced.

There's actually a small segment of the park where dogs are allowed off leash for sport training. Call the park to find out the details.

From Highway 60, exit at Rosemead Boulevard, go south to Durfee Boulevard, and turn left. The Legg Lakes part of the park is in about three-quarters of a mile, and the parking lot is on the left. On summer weekends there can be a $4 fee per car, but there's plenty of free street parking if you drive a little farther and go left on Santa Anita Avenue. This is also the place to park if you want to take your dog to the very large picnic section of the park. For the nature trail, continue on Durfee past Santa Anita Avenue and follow the signs to the visitor center. The park also extends north of Highway 60, both to the east and west of Rosemead Boulevard. 626/575-5526.

Irwindale

PARKS, BEACHES, AND RECREATION AREAS

56 Santa Fe Dam Recreation Area

🐾🐾🐾 (See Los Angeles County map on pages 732–733)

When you're approaching this large county park, you'll find it hard to believe anything but industry could exist here. The area is utterly fraught with unsightly evidence of rampant "progress."

But in the middle of it all is a big patch of green doing its best to fend off the onslaught of civilization. It's not the most attractive park in the world, but it's a commendable attempt.

The park's Santa Fe Reservoir is a decent place to share a picnic with your dog. You can also fish for trout or launch a boat here for a relaxing morning on the water. You won't exactly feel as if you're in the middle of Wisconsin, but it's better than some water holes we've seen down here.

The best time you can have with your dog at this park is if you take a hike on the nature trail. Signs and pamphlets point out the flora and fauna you'll come across in the 1,000-acre nature area. The trail provides a good hike, but it's not without its sad side: As if the surrounding scenery were not enough of a reminder, signs tell you how humans have destroyed the habitat. Do your part to protect it, and make sure your dog is leashed and doesn't disturb the birds and beasts here.

There's a $8 fee per vehicle, which you can avoid by parking on a nearby street. (If you have the $8, keep in mind that the county park system is financially devastated and can use every penny to keep parks running.) Exit I-210 at Irwindale Avenue and go south about 1.5 miles. Turn right at Arrow Highway, and within a few blocks turn right again at the signs for the park. To get to the nature trail, bear to the right after the entry kiosk and follow the signs. 626/334-1065.

San Pedro

Stick close to the waterfront here and you'll have a great time. Los Angeles Harbor is a working harbor where you can see tankers, container vessels, cruise ships, and pleasure craft going about their business.

San Pedro is a point of embarkation for one of the ferry lines to Catalina. It's a fun excursion to take with a sea-loving pooch. (See the description of the various ferry services to the island in the Santa Catalina Island section.) For more on fun things to do in this town, check out www.sanpedro .com. The folks who run this site are very helpful and have a couple of dogs themselves.

PARKS, BEACHES, AND RECREATION AREAS

57 Knoll Hill Dog Park

🐾🐾🐾🐾🐾 (See Los Angeles County map on pages 732–733)

This three-acre dog park has everything a dog could ask for, and something a dog would never think of asking for: great views of the Port of Los Angeles. Set on a hilltop above the hustle and bustle of the city, the park is a wonderful place to visit if your dog needs to burn off steam while you take a breather on one of the park's chairs or benches.

The park is divided into two sections: a two-acre section for all dogs, and a one-acre section for small dogs. The parks have water stations, poop-bag dispensers, multiple fire hydrants, and some trees. Parking is ample here, which is reason alone to visit in these parts.

This pooch paradise is on top of Knoll Hill—which announces itself in big white letters against the hillside—just north of the Vincent Thomas Bridge. Exit I-110 at Highway 47 and drive east. In less than a mile you'll come to the Harbor Boulevard exit, just before the bridge. Follow it north (it will actually be signed as Front Street once you exit) and make a left at the second Knoll Drive (the first Knoll Drive is a one-way street away from the hill) and head up the hill. At press time, the park was being managed and maintained by its users. They're hopeful that the city will take over one of these days. Meanwhile, if you have questions or want to contribute or help with upkeep, contact Peninsula Dog Parks at 310/514-0338; www.dogparks.org.

PLACES TO EAT

Sacred Grounds: In case you end up downtown, here's one dog-friendly downtown eatery. Desserts, pastries, and robust coffees are the specialties. Eat, drink, and be merry with your good dog at the sidewalk tables. 399 West 6th Street; 310/514-0800.

PLACES TO STAY

Holiday Inn San Pedro—LA Harbor: Rates are $95–125. Dogs pay a $25 fee for the length of their stay. 111 South Gaffey Street 90731; 310/514-1414.

Vagabond Inn: Rates are $70–80. Dogs are $8 extra. 215 South Gaffey Street 90731; 310/831-8911.

Long Beach

After 36 years of a strict no-dog policy on the beach, dogs are being given their day in the sun. Depending on how things turn out, it could end up being a long, sunny day or a short chilly one. Please see Dog Beach Zone, below, for more on this long-term pilot program.

No matter how it turns out, you and your pooch can at least have your day on a ferry. Long Beach is where you can board a fast (about 75 minutes) ferry to beautiful Catalina. (See the Santa Catalina Island section for details about the ferry service.)

DOG-EAR YOUR CALENDAR

If you like Easter, and if your dog has a sense of humor, put the **Haute Dog Easter Parade** in Long Beach on your must-do list. Leashed pooch participants trot down the street in their Sunday best. Prize categories include best Easter hat/bonnet, best Easter attire, most whimsical outfit, best kissin' canine, longest ears, shortest tail, dog-person lookalike, and best dog legs. The parade takes place in a very dog-friendly section of town, and it benefits local charities. For details and this year's dates, log on to www.hautedog.org. You'll also find info there on other terrific dog events, including the Haute Dog Howl'oween Parade and an interfaith blessing of the animals. In addition, the lively and beautifully designed site features info on the Dog Beach Zone, a leash-free (at least for now) section of beach that Haute Dog has been behind all the way.

PARKS, BEACHES, AND RECREATION AREAS

58 Dog Beach Zone

🐾🐾🐾🐾🐕 (See Los Angeles County map on pages 732–733)

This three-acre chunk of sand and surf is the only beach in Los Angeles County that allows off-leash dogs. We're hoping that by the time you read this, it has permanent off-leash status. But a parks department coordinator tells me that unless more people start following the rules during the beach's extended pilot program, doggy days here could be numbered. So here's a message to dogs: Tell your people to heed the rules. They need to scoop your poop, keep you in the off-leash section, come during the appointed hours, and not bother nondog people.

Before heading to this 235-yard-long stretch of beach, you'll need to head to your computer or phone and contact the park district (www.lbparks.org; 562/570-3100) to see if dogs are even allowed on the beach anymore. You can also check the website of Haute Dogs (www.hautedogs.org), the high-energy organization that started the off-leash movement here. (While you're at the Haute Dogs site, be sure to check out the schedule for some of its fun events.)

Originally, Dog Beach Zone hours were limited to the early morning and the evening. At press time, the beach was open to dogs 6 A.M.–6 P.M. Be sure to check the hours before you set paw on the beach.

Even if the pilot program doesn't end up peachy for pooches, all may not be totally lost: "No matter what, we're hoping we can continue, at least in some manner," says Geoff Hall, of the city parks department. One scenario entails dramatically limited doggy days here—more than Haute Dogs had started with on its once-a-month permit basis, but nothing like the pilot program. "We want this to work for everyone, and we'll keep working together on this," says Geoff.

The pilot off-leash section is approximately between Roycroft and Argonne Avenues. You'll see the signs. (Or you won't, if dogs aren't allowed any more.) Parking at the metered beachfront lot (enter off Bennett Avenue) is $.25 per 25 minutes. You don't pay a cent after 6 P.M., though, but that's kind of a moot point with the current off-leash hours. There's also free parking along Ocean Boulevard.

A final note: If your pooch works up a powerful thirst during her escapades at the beach, be sure to visit the nearby Fountain of Woof, next to the restrooms at the end of Granada Avenue. Even if dogs no longer have their day at the beach, they'll always have their fountain by the restrooms.

59 El Dorado Regional Park

🐾🐾🐾 (See Los Angeles County map on pages 732–733)

You and your dog can fish in the lakes here, watch dozens of ducks waddle around, stroll down shaded winding paths, or frolic together on the park's numerous huge fields of green.

Pooches have to be leashed, so it's not quite as dog heavenly as it could be. But you don't find too many 450-acre parks in these parts, so your pooch will be pleased as punch to visit here.

Fees are $3 per vehicle on weekdays, $5 on weekends and holidays, but free street parking is available on some of the side streets. Exit I-605 at Spring Street and drive west about a quarter mile to the park's entrance, which will be on your right. The nature study area of the park, where dogs aren't allowed, will be on your left. 562/570-3100.

60 Recreation Park Dog Park

🐾🐾🐾🐾🐕 (See Los Angeles County map on pages 732–733)

Pooches passing through or living in Long Beach are extremely lucky dogs. This is an incredibly fun, attractive park for leashless dogs and their people.

The fenced park is about two acres with a few big old shade trees, 20 benches, several picnic tables, poop bags, doggy water fountains, and a small fenced area for small or shy dogs. Dogs tremble with excitement as they approach. It's wonderful to watch their joy as they bound from one end of the park to the other, somersaulting and crashing into each other with gleeful abandon.

The park is also very human-friendly, with bathrooms and a water fountain for people. It's not cheap to keep up a park like this, so if you feel like donating to the cause, please put some spare change in the parking meter at the park's gate to help keep the park in good working order.

Exit I-405 at Bellflower Boulevard and drive south about two miles to 7th Street. Turn right and drive about another mile to the sign for the park's maintenance yard and dog park. Turn right again and park in the lot next to the dog run. Dogs are allowed in other parts of Recreation Park, but they must be leashed. 562/570-3100.

PLACES TO EAT

Dogs are banned from the charming Shoreline Village shops and restaurants. Too bad, because it's the perfect atmosphere for well-behaved pooches and their people. But here are a few places that will make you forget about Shoreline's lack of doggy dining.

Fleur de Lis: Your dog will think he's in pooch paradise when dining at this lovely café's shaded outdoor tables on its lower terrace. From here, you get wonderful bay views. Dogs love this, because there's just something about big bodies of water that sets a dog's nose aquiver. But that's not the half of it. The Fleur de Lis staff makes sure dogs feel welcome by giving them tasty dog biscuits and big bowls of water. That puts the "wow" in bow-wow.

The food here is scrumptious. Among the mouthwatering menu items: warm brie with tomato and basil, portabella and grilled eggplant sandwich (complete with all kinds of roasted veggies), and a salad consisting of tangy grilled chicken breast, apples, caramelized walnuts, and blue cheese, on a bed of spring lettuce tossed in a raspberry vinaigrette dressing. (Forgive me, I'm drooling.) The café is near Recreation Park and a couple of popular dog-walking areas. Open for breakfast and lunch. 335 Nieto Avenue; 562/494-4668.

Johnny Rockets: If you and your dog are fans of the '50s, you'll feel right at home at the outside tables here. Try the chocolate malted. It's really decadent. 245 Pine Avenue; 562/983-1332.

Polly's Gourmet Coffee: Sip fresh coffee and chow down on house-baked muffins and pastries at this café's patio with umbrella-topped tables. Polly's actually shares the patio with a couple of other restaurants (including Z Pizza, below), so your dog can smell everything from pizza to fried chicken while accompanying you for your meal. 4606 East 2nd Street; 562/433-2996.

Rubio's Baja Grill: The fresh Mexican food here is delicious and reasonably priced. If you're a seafood hound, try the lobster tacos. Dine with your dog at the restaurant's brick patio. Got a thirsty dog? The friendly servers will provide him a bowl of water. 4702 East 2nd Street. 562/439-8317.

Z Pizza: This pizzeria may be the last one in the phone book, but it's tops with dogs. You can get every kind of pizza imaginable here. Dine at the patio Z Pizza shares with a couple of other restaurants, including Polly's Gourmet Coffee. (Or if you're staying in a nearby hotel, Z will deliver, by bicycle.) 4612 East 2nd Street; 562/987-4500.

PLACES TO STAY

It's not easy being a medium to large dog who needs to stay in Long Beach. Only a couple of accommodations are accommodating. The rest are for the small-dog set.

Days Inn: Ooh, your dog has to be itsy-bitsy to stay here. Fifteen pounds is the limit. At that rate, Jake Dog couldn't even get a beefy leg in the door. Rates are $70–90. Your tiny canine will cost you $10 for your entire visit. 1500 East Pacific Coast Highway 90802; 562/591-0088; www.daysinn.com.

GuestHouse Hotel: This one's close to California State University, Long Beach. Humans enjoy the outdoor "tropical" pool and attractive decor. Your stay includes a continental breakfast and passes to a health club nearby. Got kids? Try the bunk-bed rooms. Rates are $89 –129. Dogs are $10 for the length of their stay. 5325 East Pacific Coast Highway 90804; 562/597-1341 or 800/990-9991; www.guesthouselb.com.

Hilton Long Beach Hotel: This used to be called the Long Beach Hilton at the World Trade Center, but 9/11 put an end to that. This is a beautiful hotel in a jazzy location. There's a big fitness center, too, in case walking your dog isn't enough exercise. (Then you can use the steam room or the pool for that spa feel.) Unfortunately, only small dogs (under 25 pounds) can stay here. Those little guys need a $100 deposit. Rates are $90–245. 701 West Ocean Boulevard 90831; 562/983-3400 or 800/445-8667; www.hilton.com.

Holiday Inn—Long Beach Airport: Rates at this retro round tower are $79–139. Dogs are $25 extra and require a $150 deposit. The only size limit: "No St. Bernard–sized dogs," says management. 2640 Lakewood Boulevard 90815; 562/597-4401.

Residence Inn by Marriott: You and your small to semimedium-sized dog (pooches must be under 35 pounds) can have a very comfortable stay at this all-suite lodging. Condos and townhouses are also available. The hotel welcomes many dogs every week. It's a good place to stay if you're in town for a while, because your suite comes with many of the comforts of home, including a little kitchen area and a living room. Most rooms come with VCRs, and a few even have fireplaces. Guests get a hot breakfast every day. Once a week the hotel hosts a fun barbecue by the pool. It's a great way to mix and mingle with other guests. The property even has two outdoor areas designated for leashed dogs to walk and do their thing. (Don't forget to scoop.) Rates are $113–189. Dogs are $6 ($5 after 10 days), and require a $40–60 fee for the length of their stay. (The fee depends on the size of your suite.) The manager can work out a simple and fair doggy fee if you stay a while. 4111 East Willow Street 90815; 562/595-0909; www.residenceinn.com.

San Dimas

PARKS, BEACHES, AND RECREATION AREAS

🐾 Frank G. Bonelli Regional Park

🐾🐾🐾 (See Los Angeles County map on pages 732–733)

The good rating we're giving this park has nothing to do with friendliness. Park officials (the ones in the office, not out and about in the park) were so rude that we almost decided not to include this place in the book. If you can avoid it, don't go to the visitor center. At least don't go there and let them know you have a dog.

After they let us into the park ($6 at the time, $8 now), we drove past the entry kiosk and a tree immediately came crashing down. It would have landed right on the car, but I was able to swerve. The dogs ended up squished together in the corner, but at least they weren't squished to the floor by a lumberjack's mistake.

When we were done dealing with the humans here, it became obvious that this really is a great place to take a dog. About 14 miles of trails can easily make you forget about any churlish people you may have encountered earlier. The trails are rugged and geared toward equestrians, so be sure to keep that leash on your dog. You can hike up grassy hills and scrubby, weedy areas to majestic views of the region. The best spot we found to start one of these hikes was right across from the entrance to the east picnic valley. It's perfect; after a rigorous hike, you can hang out at a shaded picnic table and enjoy a little wine/water and cheese with your dog.

Puddingstone Reservoir is the centerpiece of the park, and the bass and trout fishing here is rumored to be pretty hot. But dogs aren't allowed to swim in it. Too bad, because it covers a whopping 250 acres when full. When we visited, even humans weren't allowed to swim in the lake because of bacteria. But you can still pull a bunch of fish out and eat them for dinner.

The park is right next to the Raging Waters park, so it's a convenient place to take your dog if you don't feel like going home after you've dropped off the kids at that exhilarating attraction. From I-210, exit at Raging Waters Drive/Via Verde and follow the signs east into the park. 909/599-8411.

Claremont

Claremont is a very dog-friendly place to be. Not only is there a fairly new leash-free dog park (Pooch Park), but now there's also a huge park where leashed dogs love to roam (the Claremont Hills Wilderness Park). All this, and Claremont is the home of famed rapper Snoop Doggy Dog. Just thought your own doggy dog would like to know.

PARKS, BEACHES, AND RECREATION AREAS

62 Claremont Hills Wilderness Park
🐾🐾🐾🐾 (See Los Angeles County map on pages 732–733)

The city obtained a beautiful 1,200-acre chunk of land and turned it into a beautiful 1,200-acre chunk of park. Pooches can peruse this delightful acquisition, as long as they're on leash.

Claremont Hills is a hilly park (duh), with several miles of trails and fire roads leading through open land dotted with oaks and scrub. A creek runs through it during nondrought years. The park has cool, shaded canyons as well as terrific vistas of the surrounding valleys. All this makes it prime turf for mudslides. During rainy season, the entire park can close. Enter at the very south end of Mills Avenue. 909/399-5490.

63 Claremont Dog Park/Pooch Park

🐾🐾🐾🦴 (See Los Angeles County map on pages 732–733)

Dogs are so happy to come here you can sometimes hear them baying from blocks away. It's the most popular park in Claremont, at least according to Ralph Dog and Zippity Dog, who are frequent visitors and can be trusted implicitly.

This 1.25-acre park is completely fenced, so dogs can run around to their heart's delight. It's a long park, which is great for dogs who want to work up a full head of steam before having to turn around and run in another direction.

Pooches love the green grass and the old trees that grace a couple of sides of the park. There are benches galore for people, and a water fountain for pooches and their people. Two fire hydrants sit in the middle of the park and garner adulation from male dogs. Pooch Park is within College Park, on College Avenue, just south of 1st Street and the Metrolink station. 909/399-5490.

PLACES TO EAT

Walter's Restaurant: Walters has been a Claremont landmark restaurant since 1957, which is pretty much ancient history in these parts. You and your dog will lick your lips at the combination of California and French-style cuisine using foods from around the world. "We have no boundaries," is how one manager describes the wonderful fusion foods. You'll find lots of terrific kabob dishes and menu items influenced by cultures from Afghanistan to India to Italy to Spain to Zaire. (Yes, that's A to Z.) Dogs are allowed at the sidewalk patio area but need to sit on the other side of the fence. (They can be pretty much at the feet of their humans; it's just that there's a little fence-y thing between you.) 308 Yale Avenue; 909/624-4914.

PLACES TO STAY

Ramada Inn and Tennis Club: This motel is so dog-friendly that it even hosts dog shows. At times, all 121 rooms are taken up by dogs of the well-bred (literally) variety. The grounds have plenty of room for roaming with a leashed dog: The grassy courtyard alone is 31,000 square feet.

Every room comes with a fridge and a continental breakfast. Work it off in the pool or at the motel's eight tennis courts. Rates are $69–99. 840 South Indian Hill Boulevard 91711; 909/621-4831.

Pomona

PARKS, BEACHES, AND RECREATION AREAS

64 Ganesha Park

🐾🐾🐾 (See Los Angeles County map on pages 732–733)

If you don't feel like paying $6 to get into the nearby Frank G. Bonelli Regional Park (see the San Dimas section), try this fee-free park. It's a popular place, but most visitors congregate around the swimming pool, tennis courts, and playground. Leashed dogs can zip around the rest of the park without much fear of crashing into hordes of people. The grassy, rolling hills and flat meadows are perfect for a good romp.

The park is at White Avenue, just north of I-10 and south of the Los Angeles County Fairplex. 909/620-2321.

PLACES TO STAY

Motel 6: There's a decent grassy area on the grounds. Rates are $48–60 for one adult, $6 for the second adult. 2470 South Garey Avenue 91766; 909/591-1871.

Sheraton Suites Fairplex: "The bigger the dog, the better," a staffer here told us. That's the attitude we like to see. If you and your dog are going to be spending some time at the adjacent Fairplex Exhibition Center, this might be the place to stay. It's pretty exotic for this area. Rates are $100–299. 600 West McKinley Avenue 91768; 909/622-2220.

Shilo Inn Hotel: Rates are $102–117. Dogs are $10 extra. 3200 Temple Avenue 91768; 909/598-0073 or 800/222-2244.

Santa Catalina Island

Catalina is slowly becoming an easier place to vacation with your dog. Getting here with a dog has never been a problem, thanks to the ferries being so dog-friendly (see the Diversion Nautical Dog!). It used to be that once you arrived on the island, there was no place to spend the night with your dog. But now two hotels permit pooches! And to add to a dog's vacation pleasure, by the time you read this, there will even be a very small dog park in the charming seaport village of Avalon—the only city on the island.

Neva Jennings, the personable former longtime president of the Avalon Humane Society, is the force behind the little leash-free area. "I've been yapping and carrying on for two years to try to get this little space," she says. The park, which was an unused patch of grass behind a skate park, will be in the middle of town—an easy walk from the ferries. Don't be expecting your typical two-acre dog park: This one will be no bigger than a very modest backyard and will have only the most basic amenities. But compared to the off-leash opportunities that existed before, it's heavenly. For info on its status, phone

DIVERSION

Nautical Dog!: Unless you have your own boat, you're going to have to rely on passenger ships to take you to Santa Catalina Island. Although dogs must be leashed and muzzled, most seem to enjoy the scenes, smells, and sounds they experience aboard these big boats. (Muzzles can be of the lightweight nylon and Velcro variety. Many dogs barely notice them.)

The *Catalina Express* is the fastest passenger boat to the island's only real town, Avalon. The excursion takes a little more than an hour. If it's foggy, however, the trip can last a long time, so the short cruise time is not a guarantee. Our last excursion to Catalina on this line took well over two hours because of the drippy September morning fog. Trips leaving from San Pedro and Long Beach cost $47.50 round-trip per adult, and a little less for seniors and children. Trips leaving from Dana Point take a little longer and cost a bit more. Although you'll pay $6 to bring a bike, surfboard, or stroller on either excursion, dogs still go for free! Reservations are highly recommended. 310/519-1212; www.catalinaexpress.com.

the city at 310/510-0220. (Neva hopes the park will be named Bark Park. Jake and I think it should be named the Neva Jennings Bark Park—not just because she helped win this little patch of land for dogs, but also because of her 21 years as president of the humane society here.)

As far as stretching your dog's legs elsewhere, it's pretty restrictive. With the exception of the magnificent and wild Santa Catalina Island Conservancy lands (see below), and a 10- by 10-foot patch of dog-dedicated dirt on the way from the ferry to town, dogs are not allowed at any parks, beaches, or along most of Avalon's main oceanfront drag, Crescent Avenue. Be sure to carry a poop bag and some spares with you any time you're with your dog: If you're walking with your dog and you get caught without a cleanup bag in your possession (regardless of whether you've already used it and won't be needing another one), you can be fined.

If there's no room at the two dog-friendly hotels, or if you just want a little time to explore Avalon with the human you came with, Neva Jennings can help you here, too. In addition to all her other work on behalf of dogs, she runs the Avalon Boarding Service. This is no kennel: This is Neva's own home. Happy dogs who stay with her get to make her home their home. Neva knows dogs, loves dogs, and will treat your pooch kindly and warmly. Even the most skittish dogs tend to feel content at her side.

Neva says she's "very elastic" about pick-up and drop-off times, and she'll meet you somewhere other than her home if it's easier for you. She'll even just board your pooch for the day, if that's all you need. Dog-boarding starts at $15 for 24 hours, which includes high-quality pooch food and some exercise. You can phone her at 310/510-0852, or write her at P.O. Box 701, Avalon, CA 90704.

PARKS, BEACHES, AND RECREATION AREAS

If you don't know where to go, this place can be hell for a dog. It seems that every time you find a decent spot of green or beach, you also spot a "No Dogs Allowed" sign or a ranger with his hands on his hips and a frown on his lips.

But by the time you read this there will be a small off-leash area in the middle of Avalon (see above). And lucky local water dogs know of a couple of spots where pooches can do the dog paddle: Casino Point and Pebbly Beach. These are not public beaches but decent little swimming holes. We've been implored not to include directions to these unofficial dog patches in our book, because last time we did there was a backlash against dogs' using them. But any local can tell you where to find them.

The bulk of the island is undeveloped. Dogs are permitted on these natural lands if they have a permit and wear a leash. (See below for details.)

65 Catalina Island Conservancy land

🐾 🐾 🐾 (See Los Angeles County map on pages 732–733)

Catalina Island is 76 square miles. A whopping 85 percent of this land is maintained by the county and by the Santa Catalina Island Conservancy, whose mission is to keep this beautiful terrain in its natural state.

Dogs are allowed to join you on the trails here. Leashes are the law, and for good reason: Conservancy lands truly are where the buffalo roam, and the deer and the antelope play. (To be more precise, it's where the American bison roam and the mule deer and black buck antelope play. But let's not get carried away with details.) It's also home to the endangered island fox, and some shrews, bats, and snakes who are considered a California Species of Concern—a few steps below threatened or endangered, but nothing you want your dog trying to chase down anyway. Rattlesnakes also slither about, although you'll be unlikely to see any if you stay on the trails. And poison oak is among the 600 or so plant species here, and it's quite common in the canyons and creek beds. Keep your eyes peeled and your dog leashed and you'll enjoy a terrific hike on any of several trails that loop around the island's wild lands. There's a trail for just about every level of hiker.

Dogs aren't allowed to stay at developed campgrounds, but if you have your own boat, you'll be happy to know that your dog can join you in the primitive boat-in campsites. (Primitive as in there's no water, no bathroom, and hooray!: no tourists thronging about. You must bring your own water and your boat's portable toilet if you plan to go to the bathroom during your stay.) Rates are $12 per adult, $6 per child. Dogs are free, but must be leashed or on a lead at all times. (This is a service not only to the delicate wildlife, but to your dog. You might get a visit from some wild boars, and not of the crashingly-so variety.) See www.campingcatalina.com for more important boat-in camping information. Phone 310/510-3577 for reservations.

You'll need a permit to hike anywhere but Avalon. The permits are free and can be obtained at the Conservancy office in Avalon, at 125 Clarissa Avenue; 310/510-2595. Two other locales on the island also offer permits. See www.catalinaconservancy.com for details. Or phone 310/510-1421. You can get a free hiking map by sending a self-addressed stamped envelope to the Catalina Island Conservancy, Attention Visitor's Services—Hiking Map, P.O. Box 2379, Avalon, CA 90704.

PLACES TO EAT

Casino Dock Cafe: This is the only restaurant on the island that openly welcomes dogs! Dine outside, overlooking Avalon Bay, at the base of the casino. The cuisine is of the burger-seafood-chicken variety. Thirsty dogs get a bowl of water. 2 Casino Way; 310/510-2755.

PLACES TO STAY

Best Western Catalina Canyon Resort: This 72-room hotel permits pooches under 40 pounds. It has a pool, a day spa, and a hot tub. Nice for humans, but dogs don't care that they can't get massaged or soak their paws. They're just happy to be here. It's more than a half mile to the water, and there's no ocean view, but dogs don't care about that either. A restaurant is on the premises, but no pooches there, please. We think dogs do care about this, but you can always get a doggy bag. Rates are $195–300. Dogs are $50 for the length of their stay. 888 Country Club Road, Avalon, CA 90704; 310/510-0325; www.bestwestern.com.

Catalina Island Conservancy Boat-In Camping: Please see Catalina Island Conservancy land, above, for camping information.

Edgewater Beachfront Hotel: Any size dog is welcome to stay at this fun and funky harborside hotel. Carlton, a very cute cocker spaniel mix, is the official hotel greeter, and he can be found hanging out in the lobby most afternoons. There's nothing that makes you feel more at ease about bringing your dog to a hotel than having a friendly resident dog on hand. "It was like he was saying, 'It's OK, come on in, we love dogs here!' when we visited," writes Jeannie, whose terrier, Smurfboy, felt utterly at home during his stay. The rooms are all different. Our favorite has a brick wall and a nautical theme, but there are big suites with whirlpool tubs and several other rooms to choose from. All rooms include dual-headed shower tubs, minifridges, microwaves, and "electric" fireplaces. (This just means there's no wood, but there is a flame.) The ocean view rooms are worth the extra price, if you don't get to view much ocean where you're from. Rates are $79–300. Dogs are $50 for the length of their stay. 415 Crescent Avenue, Avalon, CA 90704; 310/510-0347; www.edgewaterbeachfronthotel.com.

Brea
90
57
1 2
Fullerton
91
91
3-5
Anaheim
6 7
72
Orange
405
22
Santa Ana
Fountain 8
Valley 9
39
5
11
Costa
Irvine
10
Mesa 55
19
Huntington
20
Beach 12-13
73
133
14
21 22
Newport Beach
Corona del Mar
23
Mission Viejo
15-18
24
Balboa
Laguna
Island 25
Niguel
26
74
Laguna 27-29
Beach
1
31
Pacific
San Juan
Ocean
Capistrano
Dana
30 32 33 34
Point
San Clemente

CLEVELAND
NAT'L
FOR.

N
W—E
S

CHAPTER 53
Orange County

This is the amusement capital of America, and that's not an amusing thought to dogs. They're banned from such first-rate attractions as Disneyland and Knott's Berry Farm. But the county is also home to some dog-friendly places that just might put a grin on your pooch's rubbery lips and make a stay well worth his time.

The scent of money is unmistakable here—the land is some of the most expensive in the country. That ends up being a boon for dogs, since the communities can afford to support hundreds of parks.

Dogs are allowed at all county-run parks except wilderness parks. The only beaches that permit pooches are those of Huntington Beach, Newport Beach, and Laguna Beach, and dogs are very restricted as far as times they can visit the parks or sections they can use.

If you and your dog are salty sea dogs, make a beeline to Newport Beach's Balboa Pavilion. You can sail away with a few companies here. You won't go far—the shorter trip lasts three minutes, while the longer trip goes around the harbor for a couple of hours. But you will have a splashingly smashing good time.

PICK OF THE LITTER—ORANGE COUNTY

BEST LEASH-FREE BEACH
Dog Beach, Huntington Beach (page 811)

BEST DOG PARKS
Best Friend Dog Park, Huntington Beach (page 812)
Bark Park, Costa Mesa (page 814)
Central Bark, Irvine (page 820)

MOST SNOUT-LICKING-GOOD DOG MENU
Park Bench Cafe, Huntington Beach (page 813)

BEST FREE DOG BAGELS
Bruegger's Bagel Bakery, Newport Beach (page 819)

MOST DOG-FRIENDLY PLACES TO STAY
Westin South Coast Plaza Hotel, Costa Mesa (page 816)
Four Seasons Hotel Newport Beach, Newport Beach
(page 820)
Casa Laguna Inn, Laguna Beach (page 825)
St. Regis Monarch Beach Resort and Spa, Dana Point
(page 828)

BEST WATER ADVENTURES
Ferries and cruises, Newport Beach (page 818)

SWINGIN'EST POOCH POOL PARTY
Three Dog Bakery, Newport Beach (page 819)

NATIONAL FORESTS

The National Forests and Wilderness Areas resource at the back of this book
has important information and safety tips on visiting national forests with
your dog and has more information on the Cleveland National Forest.

Cleveland National Forest
🐾🐾🐾🐾🦴

Fullerton

PARKS, BEACHES, AND RECREATION AREAS

◼ Brea Dam Recreation Area

🐾🐾🐾 (See Orange County map on page 802)

Dogs love to cool their heels in the stream that winds through this 250-acre park. While there are plenty of trails throughout the park, not one runs by the stream for any significant length. But it's fairly open land with only occasional thick brush, so it's not too tough to get around.

For dogs who like trees (and what canine isn't an arborist at heart?), you'll find oaks and California bay laurel galore. When Joe Dog used to visit, he liked to picnic under a shady oak and sleep on his back, all four legs pointed straight up to the sky.

Enter at the Fullerton Tennis Center area, at Harbor Boulevard and Valencia Mesa Drive. 714/738-6300.

◻ Craig Regional Park

🐾🐾🐾 (See Orange County map on page 802)

This natural haven's undulating tiers of green slopes create an island of tranquility right next to the bordering Highway 57. A nature trail leads for 2.2 miles through the hills and flats of the park. Pick up a brochure at the ranger kiosk and learn about the multitude of plant and animal life that hides from civilization here.

For the humans in your crew, there are facilities for basketball, softball, volleyball, and racquetball. You can picnic with your pooch or have your dog help you watch your kids at the playground.

The parking fee is $2 per car on weekdays, $4 on weekends, $5 on major holidays. The entrance is on State College Boulevard, just south of Highway 90. 714/990-0271.

PLACES TO STAY

Fullerton Marriott Hotel: If you and your pooch need to stay near California State University, Fullerton, this is the place for you. Rates are $99–159. Dogs pay a $35 cleaning fee for the length of their stay, plus a $100 deposit. 2701 East Nutwood Avenue 92631; 714/738-7800.

Anaheim

Anaheim is the home of Disneyland and just a few miles from Knott's Berry Farm, Movieland Wax Museum, Medieval Times Dinner Tournament, and Wild Bill's Western Dinner Extravaganza.

These attractions may be fun and laughs for humans, but they don't exactly make a dog howl with joy. "Who cares?" say the dogs. If humans were banned, you'd feel the same way.

If someone in your party is sick of Disneyland and has just come along for the ride, he can take the dog around while you play. There are several parks that make life a little easier for the canines among us.

Otherwise, if you go to Disneyland and don't have a dog-sitter, you can bring your dog to the Disneyland Kennel Club for the day. Rates are $10 per day (no dogs overnight). Bring your dog's favorite toy or blanket. (The Kennel Club supplies food and water, but you can bring your own food if you prefer.) You can take a break from Fantasyland, Tomorrowland, or any of the other incredible lands and take your pooch for a leashed walk in the kennel's tiny exercise area whenever you want. For details, call 714/781-7662 or 714/781-7290.

PARKS, BEACHES, AND RECREATION AREAS

3 Boysen Park

🐾🐾 (See Orange County map on page 802)

Not only is this park attractive and green, it's also fairly close to Disneyland. Leashed dogs enjoy romping in the short grass, lounging under a big shade tree, and watching the kids ride in the faux rockets in the creative playground here.

From Harbor Boulevard around Disneyland, go north several blocks and turn right on Vermont Avenue. The park will be on your right in about 1.5 miles. You can park on the street, or turn right on State College Boulevard and make a quick right onto Wagner Avenue, which will take you to the parking lot. 714/765-5191.

4 Pearson Park

🐾🐾 (See Orange County map on page 802)

This park is a straight shot north from Disneyland. Besides all the recreational facilities, which include tennis courts and a pool, there are plenty of trees and a ducky little pond. Leashed dogs like walking in the green, grassy fields here.

From Disneyland, continue north on Harbor Boulevard for a little more than 1.5 miles. The park will be on your right, at Cypress Street. If it's too crowded here, drive up the street another six blocks and take your dog to La Palma Park, a triangular park with a winding path and palm trees. 714/765-5191.

5 Yorba Regional Park

🐾🐾🐾 (See Orange County map on page 802)

If you like suburban-style parks, this one's for you. There are tot lots, ball fields, and plenty of picnic areas in this 166-acre park. You can also fish at the little lakes and connecting streams or ride your bike or hike around the trails here.

The park can get very crowded, so try to visit on a weekday. Dogs must be leashed. The parking fee is $3 per car weekdays, $5 weekends, $7–10 on major holidays. From Highway 91 in the far east reaches of Anaheim, exit at Weir Canyon Road/Yorba Linda Boulevard, drive north to La Palma Avenue, and follow the signs. 714/973-6615.

PLACES TO STAY

Many of Anaheim's zillion or so hotels now permit pooches. Don't be tempted to leave your dog in your room when you go out to play for the day. It's not good for your dog, your room, or any unsuspecting housekeepers. Disneyland's kennel is a decent option and a good deal if you're doing the Disney scene. (See above.)

We don't go into much detail on the hotels here because there are so many and we'd rather give you a wide selection in this area, since rooms here can be scarce at busy times. Every hotel below has a pool, which is nice for humans but makes water dogs ache with desire.

Anaheim Marriott Hotel: Rates are $129–159. Dogs are $50 extra for the length of their stay. 700 West Convention Way 92802; 714/750-8000 or 800/228-9290.

Anaheim Plaza Hotel and Suites: Rates are $59–139. Dogs require a $50 deposit and must stay in a smoking room. 1700 South Harbor Boulevard 92802; 714/772-5900 or 800/622-6415.

Anaheim Quality Inn: Dogs must be under 50 pounds to stay here, and they pay $25 extra per visit. Rates are $70–115. 2200 South Harbor Boulevard 92802; 714/750-5211.

Canyon RV Park: This is a really attractive park, with 700 acres of wilderness and 117 campsites. But you and your dog can come to the park only if you camp. Observe the leash law here, as folks here have lost a couple of dogs to coyotes in the past. Sites are $27–30. Dogs are $1 extra. Reservations are required mid-May–October. From Highway 91 in the eastern part of Anaheim, exit at Gypsum Canyon Road and follow the signs to the park. Since it borders the highway, it's just a couple of minutes until you're there. To reserve a campsite, call 714/637-0210.

Clarion Anaheim Resort: Dogs need to be under 60 pounds to stay here. Rates are $90–209. Dogs pay $25 for the length of their stay. 616 Convention Way 92802; 714/750-3131; www.choicehotels.com.

Coast Anaheim Hotel: This one rates high with our dog readers, whose people love the pool and the dog fee. (There is no fee.) Dogs must stay on the first floor and can peruse a grassy area on hotel grounds. Rate are $89–149. 1855 South Harbor Boulevard 92802; 714/750-1811.

Embassy Suites Hotel Anaheim North: This is one of the more attractive place to stay with a dog. The hotel's gardens, complete with waterfalls and koi pond, are a welcome relief to all the plasticized perfection of Disneyland.

Rates are $119–159. Dogs are $50 extra per stay. 3100 East Frontera Street 92806; 714/632-1221.

Hilton Anaheim: This luxurious hotel will allow your dog, as long as you sign (and follow) a pet agreement. Dogs must be under 85 pounds. Rates are $79–399. Dogs require a $25 deposit. 777 Convention Way 92802; 714/750-4321 or 800/916-2221.

La Quinta Inn Anaheim: Rates are $90–140. 1752 South Clementine Street 92802; 714/635-5000.

Residence Inn by Marriott: You'll feel right at home in the comfy suites here. (And you won't be stuck eating Mickey Mouse–shaped pancakes. Each suite has a kitchen.) Rates are $109–139. Dogs pay a $60 fee plus $10 per day. 1700 South Clementine Street 92802; 714/533-3555.

Sheraton Anaheim Hotel: If your dog has a long face because she can't go to Snow White's Castle in Disneyland, then stay here: This big, sprawling hotel on 13 acres has a castlelike look to it. (The lobby even features a huge stone fireplace.) Rates are $110–230. Dogs are $25 extra. 900 South Disneyland Drive 92802; 714/778-1700; www.sheratonanaheim.com.

Staybridge Suites by Holiday Inn—Anaheim Resort: All the suites at this attractive hotel have kitchens. You get a breakfast buffet with your stay, too. Rates are $110–235. Dogs are $150 for the length of their stay. 1915 South Manchester Avenue 92802; 714/748-7777; www.hianaheimresort.com.

Orange

PARKS, BEACHES, AND RECREATION AREAS

No dogs are permitted in any City of Orange parks.

6 Santiago Oaks Regional Park

😺😺😺😺 (See Orange County map on page 802)

This 350-acre wildlife reserve is dominated by majestic coast live oaks and California sycamores. Santiago Creek, the main tributary of the Santa Ana River in Orange County, runs through much of this park.

Dogs love it here, but they have to be leashed. Boy dogs seem to have a special fondness for the park, no doubt because there are thousands of ornamental trees on the north side of the creek.

Bring your binoculars. The wildlife-watching is terrific. More than 130 species of birds have been observed here. Coyotes, bobcats, and mountain lions have also been known to frequent the park. If you need any extra inspiration to keep your dog leashed, that should do the trick.

The parking fee is $3 per car on weekdays, $5 on weekends, $7–10 on major holidays. From Highway 55, take the Katella Avenue exit east about 4.5 miles to Windes Drive (Katella Avenue eventually becomes Santiago Canyon Road). Turn left on Windes Drive and follow its angular turns as it leads you north to the park entrance. 714/973-6620.

7 Irvine Regional Park

😺😺😺😺 (See Orange County map on page 802)

This 447-acre park is home to the Orange County Zoo, but since dogs aren't allowed at the zoo, they don't care much for it. They prefer to hike along the miles of equestrian and nature trails that run through the chaparral and forests of huge oaks and sycamores.

There's something for everyone here. You can rent a horse, a pony, a bicycle, or a paddleboat. You can walk by the creek, eat lunch at shaded picnic tables, play softball, throw horseshoes, or just do nothing and take a snooze with your dog under a big old tree. Dogs usually opt for the hike, the snooze, or both.

The parking fee is $3 per car weekdays, $5 on weekends, $7–10 on major holidays. If you walk in, there is no fee. From Highway 55, take the Chapman exit and head east for about five miles to the park entrance. 714/973-6835.

PLACES TO EAT

Pickle's: This deli serves great sandwiches and fries at its outdoor tables. 312 South Main Street; 714/978-6071.

Santa Ana

It's refreshing to see that a few farm fields still thrive in the midst of this governmental center of Orange County. The downtown area is a charmer, but there's not much for a dog to do, unless he feels like soaking up history on a walking tour of the renovated district. Call the Orange County Historical Society at 714/543-8282 for information.

PARKS, BEACHES, AND RECREATION AREAS

🟦 Prentice Park

🐾🐾🐾 (See Orange County map on page 802)

While your kids are visiting the adjacent Santa Ana Zoo, you and your leashed dog are free to wander around the attractive parkland surrounding it. Dogs like the grass and picnic tables, but they're often so intoxicated by the ripe animal odors emanating from the zoo that they notice little else.

Exit I-5 at the 1st/4th Avenue exit and follow the signs to the zoo. It's at Chestnut Avenue, a few blocks east of Grand Avenue. 714/571-4200.

🟦 Centennial Regional Park

🐾🐾🐾 (See Orange County map on page 802)

If you want a real treat, get here early on a cool morning and watch the steam from the park's lake rising through the surrounding willows. As the sun's rays turn the vapors a golden-orange hue, you'll swear you've never seen such a beautiful sight.

The sign on the lake says "No Swimming," but the ducks just don't listen. You and your leashed dog should stay high and dry, though, no matter how tempting a little wade would be on a hot summer afternoon.

The park has many big green fields, most of which are sports fields. But if you visit during a nonathletic time, you'll just about have the whole place to yourself. Walkways run throughout the park, so you and your dog can cover lots of ground with ease.

The park's main entrance is at Centennial Park and Mohawk Drives. 714/571-4200.

PLACES TO STAY

Motel 6: Rates are $40–48 for the first adult, $6 for the second. 1623 East 1st Street 92701; 714/558-0500.

Red Roof Inn: Rates are $55–70. 2600 North Main Street 92701; 714/542-0311.

Huntington Beach

Hey, dog dude! This is the surfing capital of the Orange coast. And you're allowed off leash here! (See below.) Dogabunga!

PARKS, BEACHES, AND RECREATION AREAS

10 Dog Beach

🐾🐾🐾🐾 🐕 (See Orange County map on page 802)

It was a tough fight, but Dog Beach has finally gone to the dogs! In the end, the courts made the final decision: A .75-mile strip of beach here is now off-leash heaven! Your dog needs to be in the water or on wet sand (the courts said that this territory is federal land, and that the city—which was not being terribly cooperative—didn't have jurisdiction), but there's always enough room for a great walk. You'll have a wider berth if you visit during an outgoing tide, but as Stu Black, information director for Huntington Dog Beach told us, "There is plenty of room for lots of dogs on the wet sand at all times."

Dog Beach is on the Pacific Coast Highway between 21st Street and Seaport Street. You'll recognize it by all the blissed-out dogs running around the golden sand and jumping into the surf. Be sure to bring plenty of quarters, because the parking here is all meters. At a quarter for 10 minutes, an hour here will cost you $1.50. The hours here are 5 A.M.–8 P.M. every day. Be forewarned: If you stay at the parking lot past 8 P.M., you are very likely to get a ticket. The phone number for more beach info is 714/536-5281.

Until relatively recently, dogs had been in danger of losing even their leashed-pooch privileges here, because too many owners seemed to think their dogs had poop privileges. The poop on the beach was getting out of hand. The problem was actually that it was never getting *into* hand, or at least into poop bags. When the city made noises about banning dogs here, a group of responsible, energetic dog people got together and formed the Preservation Society of Huntington Dog Beach. Their motto: "To preserve, protect and pick up."

Their clean-up rallies and increased signage, as well as casual spot patrols for scofflaws, started bringing dogs back into good graces with the city. At various rallies, hundreds of people came to help scoop the poop. Newspapers and TV stations got the scoop and gave the group lots of coverage. "All my life I've done important things and haven't had a lot of public notice," says society chairman Martin Senat, a dapper English gent. "All of a sudden I'm picking up dog feces and the world is watching."

The graces weren't quite good enough to convince the city, so the courts ended up making the final—and wonderful—decision. To find out what you can do to help with Dog Beach, call 714/841-8644 or check out the Dog Beach website at www.dogbeach.org. This is a very active group, with fund-raisers and fun items for sale to benefit beach maintenance. Dogs around California wish to thank Martin Senat and the rest of the crew for a job very well done. Three arfs for you all!

⓫ Best Friend Dog Park

🐾🐾🐾🐾🐾 (See Orange County map on page 802)

Pooches here can let down their hair and run around like the dogs they were meant to be—happy and leash-free, sniffing anywhere they want to sniff without their people getting embarrassed. The dog park is two acres, with mulch ground cover (for mud-free romping), fledgling trees, running water, benches for people, poop-bag dispensers (they go through more than 52,000 bags a year!), and even an ocean breeze. You can see the ocean from parts of the park.

Small dogs love it here, because they have their own little fenced area. Of course, most small dogs think they're really huge dogs, so they don't need their own park. But for the more timid tiny pooch, this "park within a park within a park" offers a feeling of security.

There's even a **Doggy Walk of Fame** here. The sidewalk from the parking lot to the park's front gate is covered with more than 800 12-inch-squares of concrete on which dogs have impressed their own paw prints and people have written something about their dogs. Kind of a Mann's Chinese Theatre of the canine world.

The dog park is in the west side of the park, on Edwards Street, a little north of Ellis Avenue and south of Slater Avenue. Call the Best Friend Park hot line for info on dog-park activities: 714/536-5672.

Best Friend Park is set in the beautiful 350-acre Central Park. Unless you visit the park on a sunny weekend day, it isn't hard to find a peaceful place where you can be away from people and just have a restful picnic with your favorite person, your favorite book, and your favorite dog. There are lots of trees, rolling hills, and all the natural kinds of settings dogs dig.

Central Park is divided in half by Golden West Road. It's almost as if there are two separate parks. Each half even has a truly wonderful restaurant chock-full of outdoor tables (read about and then visit Alice's Breakfast in the Park and the amazing Park Bench Cafe, a must-visit for dogs). You can enter the east half of the park by heading east on the entry road, just across from Rio Vista Drive. The west half is accessible by driving west on Ellis Avenue. The dog park is on Edwards Street, at Talbert. 714/848-0690.

PLACES TO EAT

Alice's Breakfast in the Park: Many folks bring their dogs to this enchanting restaurant during a Sunday morning stroll. It's in the western half of Central Park and has plenty of outdoor tables. The cinnamon rolls are great. 6622 Lakeview Drive; 714/848-0690.

Ibiza Bistro: You can eat tasty Mexican cuisine here at the patio dining area with your pooch at your side. Thirsty dogs can order a bowl of fresh, cool water. 209 Main Street; 714/536-7887.

Park Bench Cafe: This extremely dog-friendly eatery warrants a write-up in the *Los Angeles Times.* It deserves to be featured on NBC *Nightly News.* The BBC could even do a nice piece on it. In fact, these news organizations and many others have been drooling over this place since owner Mike Bartusick created a dog menu and added some picnic tables just for dogs and their people in 1994.

Now dogs can drool just like the media, thanks to some snout-watering culinary treats for dogs only. The motto here is "Every Dog Has His Day at the Park Bench Cafe." On weekends, the place is jammed with dogs having their days. "It's crazy busy," says Bartusick. "I love it." With Central Park's leash-free pooch park just a bone's throw away, this place is almost always hopping.

The Canine Cuisine menu items include the Hot Diggity Dog (a plain all-beef hot dog, sans bun, cut up in doggy bite sizes), the Wrangler Roundup (a juicy lean turkey burger patty, again bun-free), and Anabelle's Treat (four chopped strips of bacon). As you can see, the dog menu is much like the human menu, only with the focus more on meat, less on accessories. All pooch items are served on disposable dishes, so don't worry about finding dog slobber on your plate when you're downing your own food here.

The Park Bench Cafe, which sits in the shade of pine trees at the edge of Central Park, has been a dog-friendly eatery for years. Thirsty canine cruisers were invariably offered a big bowl of water when their people stopped by for a bite during a long walk through this beautiful park. Bartusick saw that many of the people were also ordering food items for their pooches. "Eventually I thought, why not have a menu where dogs are as welcome as people?" he says. "It's very California, but hey, what's wrong with that?"

The café is conveniently situated at the entrance to the east side of Central Park. 17732 Golden West Street; 714/842-0775.

PLACES TO STAY

Unless you're a very tiny dog, you'll have to find your overnight digs elsewhere. The only dog-friendly hotel is the Hilton Waterfront Beach Resort, and all dog guests must weigh less than 10 pounds. Yipes and yips! Meanwhile, if you feel like camping, try this one:

Bolsa Chica State Beach: Your dog can come mighty close to the beach here if she joins you for a night of camping at one of the 60 sites. Fees are $25–39. The camping area turns into a parking lot by day, so don't be expecting to lounge around. There's a small paved trail where you and your dog can go for a stroll. Sorry, pooches, but you can't set a paw on the beach itself. Fortunately, just down the sand a bit is Huntington's Dog Beach. The state beach is on Highway 1, about three miles north of the main section of Huntington Beach. For information, call 714/846-3460. For reservations, phone 800/444-7275.

Costa Mesa

PARKS, BEACHES, AND RECREATION AREAS

🖸🖻 Bark Park/TeWinkle Park Dog Run

🐾🐾🐾🐾🐾 (See Orange County map on page 802)

I met a woman who has trained her dog, Nadine, to go to the bathroom on command. The magic word is "Tinkle." It's not dignified, but it works just about every time. When she first took her dog to TeWinkle Park, a few people were talking about "TeWinkle," and sure enough, Nadine went tinkle just about every time.

Dogs can tinkle in TeWinkle, but they can also do plenty of other fun things. Now that this 50-acre park has three acres fenced for dogs, they can cavort about the dog run sans leash for hours on end. After a heated battle with the city over whether to cover the park with 12–18 inches of mulch (making life for small dogs rather difficult) or replant grass, the park users won out, and green grass is everywhere. The park is at Arlington Drive and Newport Boulevard. 714/754-5300.

🖸🖼 Fairview Park

🐾🐾🐾 (See Orange County map on page 802)

The poop bags here are handsome, and the city offers them free to all dog owners. But if you need a better reason to visit the park with your pooch, try this one: It's a big, mostly undeveloped park, with dirt trails that wind through grassy, weedy areas. Your dog will have a good time sniffing around. The farther back you go, the less likely you are to run into other people.

If you are traveling north on Placentia Avenue, the entry road is on your left. 714/754-5300.

PLACES TO EAT

Diedrich Coffee: This is a happening place for dogs. "We get lots of good dogs. They're the best," one server said. On pleasant days, the big windows here are wide-open, so if you don't want to find an outdoor seat for you and your pooch, you (the human) can sit inside by a window and pat your outside dog on the head. (It helps if you order him a really buttery pastry.) 474 East 17th Street; 949/646-0323.

Gypsy Den Café: At the wonderfully different Lab Anti-Mall, the Gypsy Den serves some great veggie food as well as "light carnivorous cuisine," as

DIVERSION

Take Your Lab to The Lab: Dogs are welcome to cruise around with you as you peruse **The Lab Anti-Mall.** The Lab is kind of the flipside of malls. It's mellow. It's artsy. It's cutting edge. It's a dog's kind of place. "You're never going to see as many people with tattoos and pierced body parts as you'll see here," says Mary Bavry, who has frequented The Lab for years with her sweet dogs. "But dogs sure do feel welcome."

The stores are not what you'd find at the Fashion Island mall. The Lab has hipster and progressive clothing stores, edgy gift stores, and Dr. Freeclouds, a popular underground electronic music store. Many stores will let your pooch inside to shop with you. The **Gypsy Den** café permits pooches at its outside table.

The Lab is at 2930 North Bristol Street in Costa Mesa. 714/966-6660; www.thelab.com.

one employee puts it. Dine with your dog at the many outdoor tables, which come with heat lamps when needed. 2930 North Bristol Street; 714/549-7012.

Side Street Cafe: Want to dine on decadent, delectable food with your dear dog? Come to this café's four umbrella-topped tables for breakfast and order the stuffed French toast. "Cheapskates welcome," says a server. The prices are indeed good for what you get. 1799 Newport Boulevard; 949/650-1986.

PLACES TO STAY

Best Western Newport Mesa Inn: Rates are $160–180. Dogs are $25 extra. 2642 Newport Boulevard 92627; 949/650-3020 or 800/554-2378.

La Quinta Motor Inn: Dogs must be under 25 pounds to stay here. Rates are $91–111. 1515 South Coast Drive 92626; 714/957-5841.

Ramada Inn: Stay here with your little dog (25 pounds and under only) and you get a continental breakfast, a *USA Today* (my alma mater), a heated pool and spa, a fitness room, and a pleasant guest room. This is all fine and dandy with your dog (at least the muffins at breakfast are of some interest), but what dogs really enjoy about this place is that there's a Trader Joe's adjacent to it. If you can't figure out why your dog might be pawing you to go in Trader Joe's direction, I'll give you a hint: Dog treats are delicious and plentiful at TJ's, and inexpensive too. Grab a bag of rawhides or a box of peanut butter biscuits, and your stay at this hotel will be one your dog will look back on fondly. Rates are $79–129. 1680 Superior Avenue 92627; 949/645-2221 or 800/272-6232; www.ramadalimitednewport.com.

Vagabond Inn: Rates are $59–80. Dogs are $5 extra. 3205 Harbor Boulevard 92626; 714/557-8360.

Westin South Coast Plaza Hotel: The rooms are spacious and well-appointed, the beds are heavenly (truly: the Heavenly Bed is the cornerstone of the hotel's luxury comfort reputation), and the luxury amenities are top-rate. But what small-to-midsized model dogs (40 pounds or less is the rule here) dig most is that they get the royal treatment: Guest dogs receive treats upon check-in, plus use of dog bowls and the pooch equivalent of the Heavenly Bed: the Heavenly Dog Bed. After a restful night on the king of dog beds, your dog can stretch his gams at a park across the street. Rates are $109–209. 686 Anton Boulevard 92626; 714/540-2500; www.westin.com.

Newport Beach and Corona Del Mar

If your dog enjoys the water-dog lifestyle, he's sure to love Newport Beach. Between the beaches, bays, and boats, many watery adventures await any dog who doesn't get seasick while watching you fill the bathtub.

The city encompasses several communities, including Balboa Island, Corona del Mar, and Mariners Mile. (Balboa Island has its own section in this chapter.)

PARKS, BEACHES, AND RECREATION AREAS

14 Upper Newport Bay Regional Park

🐾🐾🐾 (See Orange County map on page 802)

The Upper Newport Bay is surrounded by shopping centers and suburban sprawl. But fortunately, this large park preserves the remaining sanctity of the once-pristine bayside.

The myriad dirt trails in this open, hilly area provide you and your leashed dog a great way to get around. Dog footprints are embedded in the trails—evidence of happy pooches on muddy days.

The park is made up of tall grasses and twiggy weeds. No trees get in the way of the bird-watching here. Bring your binoculars and try to ignore the tall office buildings in the distance.

You can also do some excellent, up-close bird-watching from Back Bay Road, on the east side of the bay. But it's easier to get to the regional park section, and it's less stressful for the birds if you keep your dog far from them. The poor birds have enough on their minds with the onward march of malls and suburban subdivisions.

If you're traveling north on Irvine Avenue, turn right on University Drive. About the equivalent of a block down the road, turn around and park on the other side of the street (there's no parking on the south side) and walk back across the street and to the park entrance. 949/644-3151.

DIVERSION

Go Island Shopping: Dogs are a normal part of the scene at **Fashion Island,** Newport Beach's huge open-air shopping mall. There's plenty of walking room and even some grassy areas where your dog can rest her weary paws. Some of the mall's 200 stores permit pooches inside, but since they do it on a case-by-case basis, we'll let you explore for yourself. (FYI, should you be looking for lingerie, Victoria's Secret allows any well-behaved dog. "We've had our share of mishaps, but we still welcome dogs here," says a manager.)

Be sure to stop by the concierge desk with your dog. Most concierge employees love dogs and will supply your dog with a treat. As an added bonus, the mall is just a bone's throw away from Upper Newport Bay Regional Park, a great place to drop after you shop. Fashion Island is on the Pacific Coast Highway (Highway 1), between Jamboree Road and MacArthur Boulevard (Veterans Memorial Highway). 949/721-2000.

15 Balboa Beach

😾😾😾 (See Orange County map on page 802)

Balboa Beach is wide and sandy enough for a dog to forget that it's a dog's life. The only reminders here are the mandatory leash attire and the restricted dog-access hours. Dogs are permitted 6–9 A.M. and after 5 P.M. year-round these days (a big improvement over the previous ban on dogs in summer).

The beach runs from around Main Street to the west jetty area. You can enter the beach at the ends of many of the streets here. 949/644-3047.

16 Corona del Mar State Beach

😾😾😾 (See Orange County map on page 802)

Fear not! Although this is a state beach, dogs are permitted to peruse the place. That's because the city of Newport Beach maintains it and makes most of the rules. Dogs can sample the sandy life 6–9 A.M. and after 5 P.M. daily.

If you happen to be east of the eastern jetty at the entrance to Newport Harbor, you'll be happy to know that this large and popular beach also permits leashed pooches. The beach starts at the eastern jetty at the entrance to Newport Harbor. 949/644-3047.

17 Newport Beach

😾😾😾 (See Orange County map on page 802)

This beach starts out quite narrow at the northern border of Newport Beach and widens as it continues south to around Main Street. You'll have fun watching the surfers surf and the sun worshippers sizzle to a golden brown.

DIVERSION

A Three-Minute Tour: The historic **Balboa Pavilion/Balboa Fun Zone** is where you and your dog can embark on nautical adventures on two unique boat lines. This is one of our favorite places to go with pooches because they're so welcome on these vessels. It's easy for your dog to feel like one of the family here. Best of all, pooches go for free on both excursions.

The smaller of these boats is the **Balboa Island Ferry,** which is open-hulled and fits only three cars and a few passengers at a time. The trip from Newport Beach to lovely Balboa Island takes only a few minutes, but it's a good way to test if your dog is up for a longer journey on the other dog-friendly boat line here. Fees range from $.35 for a walk-on passenger to $1 for a car and passenger. The ferries run every few minutes during daylight hours.

Dogs with a more nautical bent can join you for a howling good time on a cruise of Newport Harbor—one of the nation's finest yacht harbors. The **Fun Zone Boat Company** offers a couple of grand tours. On one, you'll see the homes and yachts of celebrities and learn the history of the area. On the other tour, you'll cruise up to the haunts of the vocal, local sea lions. "The sea lions are fascinated by the dogs, and the dogs are fascinated by the sea lions," says Captain Mike. "It's quite a sight." Each tour is 45 minutes long and costs $7 per adult and $2 per child. Or take a 90-minute tour that combines both of the shorter jaunts. It costs $9 per adult and $2 per child. Call 949/673-0240.

The only problem is that during the times when dogs are allowed, there's not a whole lot of sun to worship. Dogs, who must be leashed, can enjoy the beach 6–9 A.M. and after 5 P.M. daily.

Many dogs, including Jake, enjoy hanging out by the pier area and grabbing a bite from the nearby restaurants. Your dog will, too. (Jake asked me to write that on behalf of his pooch friends in the area.) 949/644-3047.

18 Peninsula Park

 (See Orange County map on page 802)

What? It's summer, you're near the beach, and your leashed dog needs to go for a walk? If she can't hold it until fall, when the beaches here permit pooches, a visit to this square-block park is a tolerable solution.

The park is west of Ocean Front Avenue, just south of the Balboa Pier. It's flat and grassy, with a band shell, baseball diamonds, a playground, and picnic tables. There's not much shade, but the ocean breeze usually cools things off enough. 949/644-3047.

DIVERSION

Swimwear Optional: Visit the **Three Dog Bakery,** and you may find dogs in bathing suits (or naked—gasp!). Or they may be wearing board shorts. Or wacky Halloween costumes. Anything is possible. The bakery's owner, Sandy, and her Labs, Storm and Jag, think up all kinds of fun events for their dog customers. Pool parties (three wading pools in the parking lot, a pet psychic, and a toenail-painting groomer were among the attractions at a recent pool party attended by 200 dogs), luaus, and various seasonal parties are the norm here. And now, once a month, the bakery is home to a pet-adoption fair. On the best day so far, 21 lucky dogs and cats and an iguana found new homes.

The fresh-baked dog goodies at this bakery are so good, and the service so doggone dog-friendly (read: they get a free treat), that dogs have been known to tear into here, leaving their people scratching their own heads about the location of their canines. They always sniff them out, though. And once your dog enters, you may be hard-pressed to get her to leave. Sandy says that sometimes a dog's people have to bribe the stubborn (and smart) pooch out with dog delicacies.

The bakery is in Newport Beach's upscale Corona del Mar Plaza, at 924 Avocado Street; 949/760-3647.

PLACES TO EAT

Alta Coffee: The large gazebo outside the restaurant is a terrific place for you and your pooch to sip the great coffee and dine on the café's tasty soups, pastas, and pastries. In fact, the gazebo is packed with lucky dogs every weekend, according to a manager. We've also heard it's a great place to sniff out potential romance (with your dog first introducing you to someone else's dog, and then, of course, the dog's person). If your dog is thirsting for something more quenching than love, a bowl of water will be provided on request. 506 31st Street; 949/675-0233.

Bruegger's Bagel Bakery: If you don't have a dog, you may feel positively naked here. This terrific bagelry is so doggone dog-friendly that on weekends, you can find up to a couple of dozen dogs at a time hanging out on and around Bruegger's wraparound porch. Dogs love it here, not only because they get to chat with each other and socialize with other humans, but because Bruegger's treats dogs like kings: Dogs who visit get a free bagel! And not even a day-old bagel—a fresh one. The bagels are delicious, so your dog will be a lucky dog indeed if he gets to accompany you here. George Dog and his person, JoAnna Downey, told us about this place. A big thanks to them! (George Dog is the one with the poppy seeds stuck between his teeth.) Dogs also get fresh water.

This is a four-paw, must-visit destination. 2743 East Pacific Coast Highway; 949/723-4485.

Sabatino's Sicilian Restaurant: The Sicilian cuisine here is *fantastico*. Jake highly recommends the sausages, although the lasagna is to drool for, too. Dogs get to dine very close to you, but they have to be tied on the other side of the shrubbery "railing." Plus they can't join you for dinner because of the crowds. But the lunches here are *delicioso*. If your dog's snout looks dry, the folks here will likely offer him a bowl of cool water. 251 Shipyard Way; 949/723-0621.

PLACES TO STAY

Your dog has to be a wee one to stay at the only two dog-friendly hotels here. The hotels are lovely, but if you have a medium or large dog, sniff around somewhere else for your lodgings.

Four Seasons Hotel Newport Beach: This glorious five-diamond hotel rolls out the plush red carpet for dog guests, who must be under 25 pounds: They get a little welcome card when they arrive, and they receive doggy biscuits and even doggy dishes with their names on them. This sumptuous hotel is a breathtakingly luxurious urban oasis for humans, but since the dog size limit rules out most dogs reading this book, we won't devote more space to the details. You can find out more at www.fourseasons.com/newportbeach. 690 Newport Center Drive 92660; 949/759-0808.

The Sutton Place Hotel: Dogs must be under 25 pounds to stay at this large hotel, and they pay $50 extra for the length of their stay. Rates are $135–180. 4500 MacArthur Boulevard 92660; 949/476-2001; www.suttonplace.com.

Irvine

PARKS, BEACHES, AND RECREATION AREAS

19 Central Bark

🐾🐾🐾🐾🐕 (See Orange County map on page 802)

With a whopping three acres of off-leash romping room, Central Bark is one of the largest dog parks in Southern California. It's a big fenced field with a smaller fenced area for small or shy dogs. There's not much in the way of trees here, but in the summer people bring a tarp and canopies for shade.

Central Bark is a very popular spot, and it includes all the dog-park accoutrements, including doggy fountains, lights, poop bags, and even faux fire hydrants. If your dog isn't the only one who has to lift a leg while you're at the park, you'll be happy to know that restrooms are available for humans, too.

The park is open every day except for Wednesday, when it's closed for maintenance. It can get mucky and muddy here in the rainy months, and if it's bad enough, the park will close for the day or a few days. If in doubt, phone 949/724-MUDD (949/724-6833) for updates on park closures. The park is at 6405 Oak Canyon, one driveway past the Irvine Animal Care Center. 949/724-7740.

20 William R. Mason Regional Park

🐾🐾🐾 (See Orange County map on page 802)

If you're a local University of California dog and you need to get away from campus for a few hours, tell your owner about this county park. Three miles of hiking and biking trails wind through the park's eastern wilderness. It's a great escape from the urban realities lurking just outside the park's perimeters.

The park has the usual human recreational facilities and one unusual one: a Frisbee golf course. It's a good thing dogs have to be leashed, or it would be pure, unbridled, ecstatic mayhem among the retrieving pooches here.

The parking fee is $3 per car on weekdays, $5 on weekends, $7–10 on major holidays. You don't have to pay a thing if you walk in. The park is at University and Culver Drives. 949/923-2220.

PLACES TO STAY

Candlewood Suites: If your dog needs plenty of room, the spacious suites here will fill the bill. There's even a walking trail around the hotel's property. Rates are $80–150. Dogs must be under 70 pounds and are $75 extra for a stay of up to two weeks; they're $150 extra for more than two weeks. 16150 Sand Canyon Avenue 92618; 949/788-0500 or 800/946-6200; www.candlewood-suites.com.

Hilton Irvine/Orange County Airport: Rates at this attractive hotel are $149–219. Dogs are $50 extra per visit. 18800 MacArthur Boulevard 92612; 949/833-9999.

Irvine Marriott Hotel: This fancy hotel permits pups of every poundage. Rates are $80–160. 18000 Von Karman Avenue 92715; 949/553-0100.

La Quinta Inn: Some of the rooms here are architecturally fascinating—one of the buildings used to be a lima bean silo! Really. You must see this place for yourself. Rates are $89–99. 14972 Sand Canyon Avenue 92718; 949/551-0909.

Residence Inn Irving Spectrum: Stay in a suite and you can cook for yourself and your dog in a nice little kitchen. Rates are $140–200. Dogs pay $60–80 per stay plus $10 extra daily. 10 Morgan Street 92618; 949/380-3000.

Mission Viejo

PARKS, BEACHES, AND RECREATION AREAS

🐾 Wilderness Glen Park

🐾🐾🐾 (See Orange County map on page 802)

At certain times of year, a creek rushes through this narrow, two-mile-long wooded park and provides a refreshing escape from the surrounding suburbs. This is a hidden, unmarked park that most people just drive past without realizing it's there. It's in a narrow canyon, surrounded by lush foliage. A trail follows the creek, so you and your leashed dog can have a waterside sojourn. You can even dip all your feet in the water to cool off on a warm afternoon.

The park is bordered by Los Alisos Boulevard on the east side. You can enter the park at many points by turning left on any street that runs into the park. Our favorite is Via Noveno. Park around Atomo Drive and walk down the wooden stairs into the park. 949/470-3000.

🐾 O'Neill Regional Park

🐾🐾🐾🐾 (See Orange County map on page 802)

So close to suburbia, and yet so far, this is the paws-down favorite Orange County park for dogs who like wilderness. Dogs are not permitted in the county's true wilderness parks, but for some reason, this 1,700-acre piece of lush land doesn't fall into that category.

Dogs love to hike along the 6.5 miles of trails that go past streamside oak and sycamore woodlands. They have to be leashed, which is something the mountain lions here don't appreciate. Besides the woodlands, you can peruse grassy meadows and shrub-covered hillsides. And if you're in a hungry mood, the area near the entryway has plenty of picnic tables. You supply the food and the park will supply the ambience.

Camping is available along the creek and in the higher-elevation Mesa Camp area. There are 90 campsites, all first-come, first-served. Fees are $15–17. Camping pooches are $2 extra. If you're just here for the day, you'll be charged a parking fee of $3 per car on weekdays, $5 on weekends, $7–10 on major holidays.

Follow El Toro Road (in the city's northernmost reaches) northeast. It eventually turns into Live Oak Canyon Road and veers to the south. About three miles past where the road changes names, you'll come to the park's main entrance. It's just south of the Rama Krishna Monastery, on the right side of the road. 949/949/923-2260.

PLACES TO STAY

O'Neill Regional Park: See O'Neill Regional Park, above, for camping information.

Balboa Island

This small Newport Harbor island is a bayfront wonderland. You can drive here from the mainland, but dogs prefer to take the ferry from Newport Beach. The island isn't exactly replete with big parks, but dogs enjoy strolling down Bayfront to the Grand Canal and back. When you've worked up a big hunger, head for the dog-friendly Park Avenue Cafe, not far away.

PLACES TO EAT

Park Avenue Cafe: Dogs are welcome to dine at one of the two tree-shaded patios with you, and boy, do they like it here. It may have something to do with the thick steaks, steaming racks of lamb, and other assorted goodies. (Just a hunch.) 501 Park Avenue; 949/673-3830.

Laguna Woods

PARKS, BEACHES, AND RECREATION AREAS

2.3 Laguna Woods Dog Park

🐾 🐾 🐾 🐕 (See Orange County map on page 802)

This is a pretty little dog park with some shade trees (hey, it's Laguna Woods, after all) that provide welcome relief from the summer sun. Dogs are provided water and poop bags. The list of rules on the park's website says that dog tags must be "worm and visible," which I hope is a typo.

If your big dog is a morning dog, you'll have to take her elsewhere for her early constitutional: The park is open only to small dogs 8 A.M.–1 P.M. Small and large dogs can run about here 1–7 P.M. The park is on Ridge Route between Moulton Parkway and Avenida de Carlotta. 949/452-0600.

Laguna Beach

Exclusive but friendly, Laguna Beach has an unmistakable Mediterranean feel, thanks to the mild seaside climate and all the fine art galleries and outdoor cafés. Dogs are happy here, especially because of a fine off-leash dog run. (See Bark Park, below.)

PARKS, BEACHES, AND RECREATION AREAS

24 Bark Park/Laguna Beach Dog Run

🐾🐾🐾🐾🐾 (See Orange County map on page 802)

People come from many miles away to take their dogs to this fenced-in dog-exercise area in the canyon. During dog rush hour, it's not uncommon to see dozens of leashless, grinning dogs running and tumbling around in great joy.

Although there's no shade, there's plenty of doggy drinking water. Picnic tables add a dimension of comfort for the park's humans.

The park has to close periodically because of the danger of mudslides, so if you're traveling a long way to get here, you may want to call the city first to check on the situation. In addition, we've heard that there was quite the problem with poop. The city had to come in and haul it out in huge barrels. Park people have apparently been doing a better job of scooping since that ugly day.

From Highway 1, go north on Broadway/Laguna Canyon Road. The park will be on your right in 2.6 miles, just before the GTE building. 949/497-0706.

25 Heisler Park

🐾🐾 (See Orange County map on page 802)

The landscaping is lovely and the view is just as good. This small, palm-filled park sits on a bluff just above Picnic Beach. Dogs must be leashed, but they enjoy cruising around here during the times they're restricted from the beaches.

The park runs from Canyon Drive to Broadway/Laguna Canyon Road, just west of Cliff Drive. 949/497-0706.

26 Laguna Beach Beaches

😺😺😺 (See Orange County map on page 802)

Leashed dogs can peruse the beaches, but their visiting times are limited. Pooches aren't allowed on the beach 8 A.M.–6 P.M. June 1–mid-September.

Main Beach is a long, sandy beach that has a playground and basketball courts. A good entry point is just south of the Heisler Park area (see above). If you want to get away from people, you may be better off at any of the pocket beaches that dot the city's coast. There are also several small, rocky pocket beaches you can reach via walkways off Cliff Drive. 949/497-0706.

PLACES TO EAT

A La Carte: You and your dog are welcome to dine on the patio of this pink restaurant. With its 16 different entrées (not to mention numerous salads and desserts), it's likely that no one will go away hungry. And your dog surely won't go away thirsty, because if she asks for a bowl of water, someone will be happy to bring her one. 1915 South Coast Highway; 949/497-4927.

Cafe Zinc: This place is just one outdoor table after another. At times, reports café regular Mary Bavry, "there's a dog at every table." Don't trip, and try the apple spice muffins. (Thirsty dogs can get a big bowl of fresh water here.) 350 Ocean Avenue; 949/494-6302.

Cottage Restaurant: As long as you and the pooch sit on the outer rim of the patio, the folks here will be happy to see you. 308 North Coast Highway; 949/494-3023.

Subway: There are plenty of benches for you and the hungry pooch. 1350 South Coast Highway; 949/376-1995.

PLACES TO STAY

Carriage House: Only the most well-behaved dogs are welcome here, and only if you call ahead of time and get the OK. After all, it's not every day a dog gets to stay in a 1920s bed-and-breakfast that's a historic landmark. You'll get a carafe of wine, some fresh fruit, and other taste treats when you check in. The courtyard here is lovely and relaxing, but no leg lifts, please. Rates are $140–175. Dogs are $10 extra. The friendly folks here will help you arrange a pet-sitter if you find yourself in need of some pooch-free time. 1322 Catalina Street 92651; 949/494-8945 or 888/335-8945; www.carriagehouse.com.

Casa Laguna Inn: The Casa Laguna is an enchanting, romantic Spanish-style bed-and-breakfast that overlooks the mighty Pacific Ocean. Its 15 rooms, four suites, Mission House, and charming cottage are set on a terraced hillside. Surrounding the lodgings are luscious tropical gardens that include such goodies as banana and avocado trees and bougainvillea. Well-behaved dogs and their people love to relax on the aviary patio, beneath a family of glorious queen palms. There are many little nooks and gardens to discover at the Casa Laguna, and your dog will enjoy helping you find them all. As the day ends, watch the sun set over Catalina Island. Dog guests feel very welcome here: Upon check-in they get a doggy food bowl and a water bowl, some pooch treats, and a list of nearby dog-friendly parks. Rates are $130–350 and include an extensive buffet breakfast and afternoon wine with hors d'oeuvres. Dogs are $25 extra. 2510 South Coast Highway 92651; 949/494-2996 or 800/233-0449; www.casalaguna.com.

Vacation Village: Dogs love staying at this vacation oasis, because they're allowed on the beach, which is right behind the hotel. Leashed pooches can peruse the beach here anytime it's open to dogs (see Laguna Beach beaches, above, for dog-OK times). Humans like the fact that there's full beach service, complete with towels and lounge chairs. Usually, however, sunbathing and dogs don't mix. The hotel's restricted dog times (they're not allowed in from the last week of June through Labor Day) certainly decrease the temptation to get tan with your dog. If you (the human in your party) want to swim but find the surf a bit rough, the hotel has two pools for your paddling pleasure. Rates are $85–349. There's a $10 pooch fee per visit. 647 South Coast Highway 92651; 949/494-8566 or 800/843-6895; www.vacationvillage.com.

Laguna Niguel

PARKS, BEACHES, AND RECREATION AREAS

🐾🐾 Aliso/Wood Canyons Regional Park

🐾🐾 (See Orange County map on page 802)

Since dogs aren't permitted in county wilderness areas, they're banned from the Wood Canyon section of this 2,500-acre park. But because Aliso Canyon isn't considered wilderness, leashed dogs are welcome. The good news is that about two-thirds of the acreage is in Aliso Canyon. The 13-mile-long Aliso Creek Trail takes you and your pooch through some very scenic areas, but unless you're both in extraordinary shape, you won't want to tackle the whole thing.

The "eh" news is that Aliso Canyon is brushy and scrubby, with none of the wonderful trees that grace Wood Canyon. One school of thought behind the contrasting landscapes is that back around 1776, when Father Junipero Serra was building missions, his men may have denuded this canyon to create the San Juan Capistrano Mission. The county is considering reforesting the canyon, but it's an expensive task.

The parking fee is $3 per car on weekdays, $5 on weekends, $7–10 on major holidays. There's an entrance to the park off Alicia Parkway, just west of town. Call 949/923-2240 for directions to specific parts of the park.

28 Crown Valley Community Park

🐾🐾🐾 (See Orange County map on page 802)

It's so peaceful here that it's hard to believe you're in a community park. The park is fairly large, with green hills, lots of trees, and trails that wind through all this splendor. You and your leashed dog will enjoy the tranquility here.

The park is on the west side of Crown Valley Parkway, just north of Niguel Road. 949/362-4350.

29 Pooch Park

🐾🐾🐾🐕 (See Orange County map on page 802)

It's only a bit over one acre, and it has only three small trees, but to dogs who long to run unfettered by a leash, this fenced park is poochy paradise.

Pooch Park is gobs of fun for dogs on the go. It's at the top of a canyon, and it's got the coolest dog-watering area yet. If your dog is Lassie, or a Lassie wanna-be, she can press a lever with her paw and drink the water as it streams several inches into the air. Or she can let the water fill a strategically placed water bowl. Of course, if she's like Joe Dog was, she can accidentally step on the paw-activated fountain, get splashed in the face, and have the heebie-jee-bies for the rest of the afternoon.

No longer grassy, the park is filled with wood chips. It can be a little tough on tender paws, but it's easier to maintain than grass, and it's not as splintery as it sounds. Humans enjoy the shaded sitting areas under attractive canopies and sun umbrellas on hot days. Dogs do too.

The park is on the west side of Street of the Golden Lantern, between Beacon Hill Way and Chapparosa Park Road (closer to Beacon Hill Way). My faithful correspondent "Three-Dog-Dave" Hepperly tells me there are now signs stating "Dog Park Parking," which make the entrance easier to find than it used to be. 949/362-4350.

Dana Point

PARKS, BEACHES, AND RECREATION AREAS

Dogs are not allowed on any beaches here or at any Dana Point city park. The city's adventure-loving namesake, Richard Henry Dana Jr., who wrote the high-seas novel *Two Years Before the Mast*, probably wouldn't have liked Dana Point's attitude. But he's been dead for more than a century, so there's little he can do about it.

30 Lantern Bay Park

🐾🐾🐾 (See Orange County map on page 802)

Since this is a county park, pooches are permitted. It's a beautiful stretch of grass and trees set high above the ocean. Paved walkways meander throughout and there are picnic tables galore. Leashed dogs love to sniff the sea breezes and watch the gulls.

From Highway 1, turn toward the beach on Harbor Drive and make a right onto Lantern Street. 949/248-3530.

PLACES TO STAY

Doheny State Beach: Dogs can't go on the long sandy beach here, but if you camp with them at one of the 122 sites, they can hang out on the grassy area of the park. They can pay a whopping day-use fee of $10 (per vehicle) to explore for a few hours, but it's better to make a real vacation of it and camp here. Some campsites border the beach. Rates are $21–31. From Highway 1, turn toward the beach on Harbor Drive and make a left onto Lantern Street. Call 949/496-6171 for information, or call 800/444-7275 for reservations.

Laguna Cliffs Marriott Resort and Spa: The rooms at this spectacular hotel are very attractively appointed, with a fresh, colorful decor that even an artful dog could appreciate. Some overlook the shining Pacific. (Even if your room doesn't, the two pools do.) You can bring any size dog here "as long as it isn't noisy or yappy," says a front desk employee. Rates are $250–415. Dogs are $75 extra per stay. 25135 Park Lantern 92629; 949/661-5000.

St. Regis Monarch Beach Resort and Spa: Oh, to drool for! This five-diamond ultraluxury resort hotel has everything you could want in a sumptuous seaside vacation, from to-die-for rooms to a private beach club to pampering spa treatments. There's no size limit for humans, but alas, dog guests here are limited to 30 pounds. Little dogs get treated well here and are provided with a doggy bed, cute little dishes, and bone treats. A stay here is not cheap, with rooms starting at $410. Dogs are $75 for the length of their stay. One Monarch Beach Resort 92629; 949/234-3200 or 800/722-1543; www.stregismb.com.

San Juan Capistrano

The rebuilt version of the mission that was constructed by Father Junipero Serra in 1776 attracts 300,000 visitors annually. Around March 19 every year, the swallows arrive from Argentina to nest in the valley. They used to flock to the mission, but with recent noisy renovations and hordes of visitors, they've taken to other parts of the valley. "They've gone to the suburbs, just like humans," says one docent.

Dogs aren't allowed on the grounds of the mission, but you can watch this annual migration from just about anywhere in town. It's not as dramatic as

Alfred Hitchcock's *The Birds,* but it's still a great way to pass a lazy afternoon in one of the parks here.

PARKS, BEACHES, AND RECREATION AREAS

图 C. Russell Cook Park

🐾🐾🐾 (See Orange County map on page 802)

Big old trees line the perimeter of this park, where you and your leashed dog may choose to amble along the shaded path near the creek bed.

If your dogs likes his paws to hit green grass with every step, you can hang out on the greenbelt area. You'll find ball fields and playgrounds here, but you'll also find some open areas where you can get away from other folks.

The park is on Calle Arroyo and stretches for several blocks between Calle del Campo and Avenida Siega. 949/493-5911.

图 Acu Park

🐾🐾 (See Orange County map on page 802)

This park is about 11 blocks long but only a couple of blocks wide. When the park isn't packed with people, you and your leashed pooch can cruise through the soccer fields, play in the open areas, or picnic at the many tables here. Trees surround the park, but there's not much shade in the heart of the park.

The park is between Connemara Drive and Camino Las Ramblas and Kinkerry and Pescador Lanes. 949/493-5911.

PLACES TO EAT

Cedar Creek Inn: You and your history-loving dog can dine at the lovely, big, tree-shaded patio that faces Mission San Juan Capistrano. The fresh fish is delicious, as are the house-made desserts. 26860 Ortega Highway; 949/240-2229.

PLACES TO STAY

Best Western Capistrano Inn: "Smallish" dogs only, please. The hotel offers breakfast to humans on weekdays. (Actually, it's a breakfast voucher for Denny's.) Rates are $70–130. Dogs are $25 extra. 27174 Ortega Highway 92675; 949/493-5661.

San Clemente

San Clemente has become a very dog-friendly place since the last edition of this book. Dogs now have an off-leash park to call their own. And they can also set paw in three city parks (Calasia Park, Mira Costa Park, and Verde Park)—a feat their feet had never known. At press time, city park decision-makers were considering allowing leashed dogs in all parks. Call 949/361-8264 for updates on this great development.

PARKS, BEACHES, AND RECREATION AREAS

33 Rancho San Clemente Ridgeline Trail

🐾🐾🐾 (See Orange County map on page 802)

The views from this three-mile trail are to drool for: At certain points you and your leashed dog can see the mighty Pacific, Catalina, and even some parts of San Diego. If you venture to the highest parts of the park (a 700-foot elevation), you can even see Los Angeles County in all its smoggy splendor. You'll hike through brush and grass, with not much in the way of shade trees. Bring plenty of water.

Mountain bikes share the trail, so keep your eyes peeled and your leash ready to reel in your dog. There are several entrance points, including one at Avenida Salvador, from Avenida Presidio or East Avenida San Juan, and one at Calle Cordillera, off Calle Amanecer. If you happen to be going to the dog park (see below) and want to get a little exercise yourself, you can start at a fire road behind the dog park. 949/361-8278.

34 San Clemente Dog Park

🐾🐾🐾🐕 (See Orange County map on page 802)

When it first opened, this fenced dog park got a lot of publicity about being a park for canine senior citizens. Everyone from national radio stations to the *Los Angeles Times* called it a "gerontological dog park," where 80-year-old dogs could sniff around and not have to roughhouse.

Well, it's kind of true, but it's really a media-induced exaggeration of something many of the new breed of dog parks have: a separate section for small dogs or dogs who just don't want to race around with the big ones. The main part of the park is for any good dog, the smaller is for little, shy, or older dogs.

The park is a terrific little gem with all the good dog-park amenities, including benches, some shade, water, and poop bags. It's not terribly big, but dogs—young and old—have a great time here. It's at Calle Extremo and Avenida La Pata; 949/361-8278.

PLACES TO EAT

Beach Garden Cafe: The views from the outdoor tables are gorgeous, and the breakfast and lunch fare is just as delectable. 618 1/2 Avenida Victoria; 949/498-8145.

PLACES TO STAY

Holiday Inn San Clemente: If you're lucky, you might get a room with an ocean view here. Rates are $159–225. Dogs are $10 extra. 111 South Avenida de Estrella 92672; 949/361-3000.

ANZA-
BORREGO
DESERT
STATE
PARK

CLEVELAND
NAT'L
FOR.

CLEVELAND
NAT'L
FOR.

Escondido

San
Marcos

Rancho
Santa Fe

Poway

Santee

El Cajon

La
Mesa

Oceanside

Carlsbad

Encinitas

Solana Beach

Del Mar

La Jolla

San Diego

Coronado

Pacific
Ocean

N
E
S
W

CHAPTER 54

San Diego County

Look at a map of the county and you'll see green blotches everywhere. But don't be fooled. Most of these verdant expanses are golf courses. Golf is the game of choice here, and since dogs don't play golf very well (their hair gets in their eyes), you can ignore all those areas.

But fear not. San Diego County isn't such a tough place for dogs. Most county-run parks permit them, although they're banned from trails at camping parks. And there are now several beaches and parks where dogs are allowed to run in leash-free ecstasy. In fact, in San Diego alone, seven new leash-free parks have sprung up since the last edition of the book. (And more diminutive Encinitas is home to a whopping five new leash-free areas!)

The historic mining town of Julian, about 50 miles northeast of San Diego, is a great place to vacation with a pooch. If your dog is fond of apples, or if you're big on apple pie, visit during the fall: In October, more than 10,000 apple pies a week are baked here. If you don't visit, who's going to eat them? (It's a crusty problem.)

PICK OF THE LITTER—SAN DIEGO COUNTY

BEST LEASH-FREE HIKING
Elfin Forest Recreational Reserve, San Marcos (page 838)

BEST DOG BEACHES
Dog Beach, San Diego (page 856)
Fiesta Island, San Diego (page 857)

MOST DOG-FRIENDLY PLACES TO EAT
Stratford Court Cafe, Del Mar (page 844)
Froglander's Yogurt, La Jolla (page 846)
Terra, San Diego (page 863)
Cafe 1134, Coronado (page 868)

MOST DOG-FRIENDLY PLACES TO STAY
Julian Flat Top Mountain Retreat, Julian (page 850)
Pine Haven, Julian (page 851)
Westin Horton Plaza, San Diego (page 866)
Crown City Inn, Coronado (page 869)
Loews Coronado Bay Resort, Coronado (page 869)

The majority of the eastern half of the county is taken up by Anza-Borrego Desert State Park and Cleveland National Forest. The forest is heavenly for dogs. The 600,000-acre desert park, on the other hand, is a doggy drag. Pooches are permitted only in campgrounds and on roads. Granted, there are some dirt roads that aren't used much, but it's just not the same as hiking the trails here. And dogs are banned from walking on the desert itself.

Speaking of deserts, the coastal area from Oceanside all the way down to Cardiff is a virtual desert for dogs. They don't get to go near the water at all because beaches in this stretch ban the beasts.

Fortunately, once you get down to the Del Mar area, little bits of dog heaven pop up fairly frequently. You'll really hit paydirt (paysand?) when you venture onto San Diego's Dog Beach. Many adventures await you.

NATIONAL FORESTS

The National Forests and Wilderness Areas resource at the back of this book has important information and safety tips on visiting national forests with your dog and has more information on the Cleveland National Forest.

Cleveland National Forest

San Onofre

PARKS, BEACHES, AND RECREATION AREAS

1 San Onofre State Beach

(See San Diego County map on page 832)

This is one of the more dog-friendly state beaches we've come across. It can afford to be dog-friendly because it isn't exactly a coveted beach destination for most people: It's right next to the giant San Onofre Nuclear Power Plant. Ahhh, there's nothing like basking in some rays.... You just have to hope they're from the sun. Seriously, it's safe here, but it's not exactly Shangri-La. More on that later.

Unlike most state parks, this one actually allows dogs on a couple of trails. These wide trails lead from the 90-foot-high bluffs (where the campsites are) to the beach. Trail 1 and Trail 6, which book-end the three-mile-long campground, are the dog-friendly trails. Dogs must be leashed, but that's OK. They enjoy the adventure.

You'd probably find yourself using the trails only if you happen to be camping here. My ace correspondent "Three-Dog-Dave" Hepperly reports that camping here was a most interesting experience, and it wasn't exactly crowded. "There is a reason for this," he writes. "1) People don't like to camp next to nuclear reactors. 2) The San Diego mainline Amtrak is about 100 feet away from the campsites, and 10 to 15 trains a day go by at 70 mph. 3) I-5 is about 200 to 300 feet away and there is a constant roar of big rigs. 4) Helicopters guarding the nuclear reactor fly by day and night." Still, Dave says he'll come back again and again because his dogs love the beach. (He dearly loves his dogs, if you can't tell.)

About 500 feet of this beach is clothing-optional, by the way. (No wonder the Camp Pendleton choppers fly over so regularly.) The nude section is not far from the dog area, so watch out lest your dog end up sniffing out more than you bargained for.

Rates for all this glory aren't cheap: Camping is $21–30. Call 800/444-7275 for reservations. Bring your own water, should you want to drink any. The day-use fee is just $3 per vehicle. Exit I-5 at Basilone Road and turn south toward the ocean. Drive three miles, past the nuclear power plant. Basilone ends at the park entrance. For park info, phone 949/492-4872. If you're of the technical mindset and want to learn more about the nearby nuclear plant, go to www.nucleartourist.com and do a search for San Onofre.

Oceanside

PARKS, BEACHES, AND RECREATION AREAS

Dogs are banned from the city's beaches, as well as from the Oceanside Pier. Bummer, doggy surfer dudes. But you'll have the last laugh: By the time you read this, you'll probably have your very own dog park. See www.oceansidedogpark.com or phone the city parks department at 760/435-5041 for updates and location.

❷ Guajome Regional Park

🐾🐾🐾 (See San Diego County map on page 832)

Bring your binoculars and settle in for a day of bird-watching and hiking in one of the richest riparian areas in the county. Spring-fed lakes and a marsh are the centerpieces of this 569-acre park.

It's a little tricky to get around this place with a dog, because while there are miles of hiking trails, dogs aren't allowed on any of them. That's the general rule in San Diego County's camping parks and it's a doggy drag. But you can fish with your dog or picnic in the grassy hilltops here.

Humans like visiting the historic 22-room adobe ranch house on the park's eastern boundary. About 150 years ago, when this land was part of a vast Mexican land grant and the hub of the area's cultural life, the ranch house was the centerpiece of social activity.

Thirty-five campsites are available at $12–18 per site. Dogs are $1 extra. From I-5, take Mission Avenue east seven miles to Guajome Lakes Road, then south to the park's entrance. Call 858/565-3600 or toll-free 877/565-3600 for camping reservations. For park info, phone 858/694-3049.

❸ Buddy Todd Memorial Park

🐾🐾🐾 (See San Diego County map on page 832)

This is a really green, fairly quiet park that's far enough off the beaten path to dissuade most visitors. Dogs should be happy here—they're allowed to have 24 additional inches on their leashes, making for a grand total of eight feet!

There are plenty of pines here, plus fun little trails on the hilly part of the park. Kids love it, too, because the playgrounds have a train theme.

From I-5, exit at Highway 76 and drive east about 1.5 miles to Butler Street. Go right and follow it as it curves; then turn left onto Barnwell, left again on Mesa, and then left into the park. 760/435-5041.

PLACES TO EAT

Beach Break Cafe: You and your dog can enjoy each other's company at the tables outside this daytime café. You can buy a doggy bone here, and your hungry pal will be less inclined to drool over your food. 1902 South Hill Street; 760/439-6355.

PLACES TO STAY

Guajome Regional Park: See Guajome Regional Park, above, for camping information.

Carlsbad

It used to be that dogs weren't allowed in any city parks. Unfortunately, it's still that way, with one exception: a little off-leash park. If it were a little bigger, it would help put the "good" in Carlsbad. But for now, we'll have to just call it "CarlsOK." Some progressive new management in the parks department might end up loosening up the dog ban at other parks. Keep your paws crossed, doggies. Alga Norte Community Park, 33-acre park that was set to open in 2006, will have a two-acre pooch park if all goes as planned. Between this and a lifting of the no-dogs rule at city parks, dogs could soon end up calling this place "Carlsgood." You can phone 760/434-2826 for updates.

PARKS, BEACHES, AND RECREATION AREAS

🖢 Carlsbad Dog Park

🐾🐾 (See San Diego County map on page 832)

This half-acre park is the only parkland dogs can visit in all of Carlsbad, since all other city parks ban poochies. So it's a pretty popular park, despite its size, and it smells decent for a dog park: The mulchy wood-chip ground cover is made from local eucalyptus trees, and it seems to absorb much of the dog-doo aroma. The park has some benches, scoop dispensers, water, and a little parking. It's in the northeast part of Carlsbad, on Carlsbad Village Drive, just east of El Camino. 760/434-2826.

PLACES TO EAT

Jay's Gourmet Restaurant: The locals know about this place and drool over it, and now you know, too. So drool! The pastas, pizzas, and Italian-style seafood are delicious. The attitude here is dog-friendly, with pooches who dine at the four outdoor tables getting lots of oohs and ahhhs and bowls of water from the staff. 2975 Carlsbad Boulevard; 760/720-9688.

La Costa Coffee Roasting Company: As long as they don't go hopping onto the furniture, dogs are fine here. The staff will even give your dog a "glass" of water. And since the patio is in a mall, you could go shopping if you have a pooch-sitter along with you. 6965 El Camino Real; 760/438-8160.

Spirito's: If you're in the mood for Italian food, this patio is for you (and your dog). It even has handmade ravioli. If pasta makes your pooch thirsty, the servers will happily pour him a bowl of water. 300 Carlsbad Village Drive; 760/720-1132.

PLACES TO STAY

Inns of America: This place overlooks the freeway, but the price is right. Rates are $69–139. Dogs are $5 extra. 751 Raintree Drive 92009; 760/931-1185; www.innsofamerica.com.

South Carlsbad State Beach: Dogs aren't allowed on the beach here, but they're welcome to camp with you, even at the oceanside campground. There are 224 sites, with nightly fees of $16–36. For reservations, call 800/444-7275. For campground information, call 760/438-3143.

San Marcos

PARKS, BEACHES, AND RECREATION AREAS

5 Elfin Forest Recreational Reserve

🐾🐾🐾🐾🐾 🐕 (See San Diego County map on page 832)

This 750-acre park is pure heaven for dogs and their people. If your dog is truly under voice control, you can let her off leash to explore this riparian forest area, with 10 miles of trails (more were to be restored soon!), a gorgeous babbling brook, and incredible vista points. Please, *please* don't allow your dog to be off leash if she isn't well trained. A few bad incidents (chasing horses, for instance) can end up getting all dogs leashed. In fact, park officials are monitoring bikes and dogs to see if new regulations are needed.

Several trails offer different levels of hikes. If you can get to the ridge, you'll see many wonderful trail options branching out before you. Although there's plenty of forest area, the park is mostly wide-open, and it can get pretty toasty in the hot months. There's water on some of the trails. There's even a watering area for dogs at the middle of where the trails converge! But bring plenty of your own, just in case. Since bikes are also free to use most trails here, it's best to ask a ranger which trails may be the most bike-free.

Dogs need to be leashed in staging areas and picnic areas. As always, be sure to scoop your dog's poop. We promise you won't have to carry it for long. Plenty of trash cans await your dog's doings.

The park is nestled between the communities of San Marcos, Del Dios, Escondido, and Carlsbad. Exit I-5 at Leucadia Boulevard, and drive east. It will turn into Rancho Santa Fe Road. Drive until you get to San Elijo, and go right. Go right again at Elfin Forest Road, which becomes Harmony Grove Road. Drive until you're between Mile Markers 6 and 6.5, and you'll be at the reserve. The Olivehain Municipal Water District, which manages this area, has a very helpful feature on its website to help you figure out how to get here from your departure destination. It's kind of like a MapQuest just for Elfin.

Go to www.olivehain.com/parks.html and click on the directions/driving tab. 760/753-6466.

Escondido

Dogs are banned from this city's parks. The only exception is an undeveloped service road in a section of Kit Carson Park, but it's generally just used by very local neighbors. Even the large Dixon Lake Recreation Area bans dogs, since it's operated by Escondido. Fortunately, the city finally has a place for dogs to romp, other than Escondido sidewalks: They have their very own park. (See below.)

PARKS, BEACHES, AND RECREATION AREAS

🖸 Mayflower Dog Park/Escondido Dog Park

🐾🐾🐾🐾 (See San Diego County map on page 832)

At last, Escondido dogs have a park they can set paw in! And it's an off-leash one at that. Dogs love coming to this 1.5-acre grassy park. It has water, benches, fire hydrants, poop stations, night lighting, and plenty of parking. It even has three different sections, so when one section gets worn down from the stampeding, it can take a breather while dogs gallop around another area. The third area is an agility course, should you have a dog who hankers for this kind of fun. A big thanks to Target and Marley, two marvelous English bulldogs, for sniffing out this park for us.

The park's address is 3420 Valley Center Road. It's between Washington Avenue and Lake Wohlford Road. 760/839-4691.

PLACES TO EAT

Metaphor: Thirsty dog? This pooch-friendly café comes complete with water bowls for pooches who need quenching. You can also order anything from pastries to pasta. Dine at the outdoor benches here. 258 East 2nd Avenue; 760/489-8890.

PLACES TO STAY

All Seasons RV Park and Campground: If you get lucky, you can stay at a lakeside RV site with your pooch. Tent campers can set up camp in a separate area with grass and shade. If fishing is your angle, you'll be happy here; there's free fishing in a stocked, five-acre lake. But you won't be having a fish fry with your dog, because the fishing's all catch-and-release. They just keep getting bigger that way. (The fish, not the dogs.) Rates are $18–34. 30012 Highway 395 92026; 760/749-2982.

Castle Creek Inn Resort and Spa: This former Bavarian retreat has a cozy, quaint Hansel and Gretel feel—minus the cannibalistic witch. You and your dog can stay in one of 30 attractive suites here and you (the human, not the dog; sorry pooch) can use the resort's tennis courts, pools, hot tub, sauna, and relax while luxuriating in one of many spa treatments. There's plenty of room to roam around the beautifully landscaped grounds with a leashed dog. Rates are $79–249. The higher price is for the inn's spacious three-bedroom villa. Dogs require a $100 deposit and are $35 extra. 29850 Circle R Way 92026; 760/751-8787 or 800/253-5341; www.castlecreekinn.com.

Borrego Springs

PLACES TO STAY

Borrego Valley Inn: The surrounding Anza-Borrego Desert State Park may not be the most dog-friendly place in the world, but this gorgeous inn makes the trek out here worth it. The inn, set on 10 acres, has a wonderful, upscale, Southwestern/Mexican feel. The rooms are spacious, and graced by cool tile floors and elegantly simple decor. You'll get a tasty breakfast, cookies at bedtime, and best of all (especially in the hotter months) use of the inn's two outdoor pools and two hot tubs. The pools have fabulous views of the nearby mountains, and they're open until midnight, meaning you can float around under the stars with the sweet desert air enveloping you. It's a blissful experience.

If you'd like to really feel one with nature while enjoying a splash, one of the pools is clothing-optional. (This would be the pool for dogs, but their fur clogs up the drains, so they have to be content to lounge poolside.) Speaking of nature, the innkeepers will point you and your dog to a pooch-friendly trail nearby, so you won't have to contend with the state park.

The inn is open on weekends only during summer. Sometimes it even closes completely in the hot months. That's fine, because you don't want to be bringing your dog to the desert then anyway. Rates are $135–250. Dogs are $25 for the length of their stay. 405 Palm Canyon Drive 92004; 760/767-0311 or 800/333-5810; www.borregovalleyinn.com.

Encinitas

Although this is the home of Paramahansa Yogananda's gold-domed Self Realization Fellowship Center, dogs are banned from Swami's Beach and all other municipal beaches. The beach that does allow dogs is a state beach in the charming Cardiff-by-the-Sea district of Encinitas.

Fortunately, most of the city's parks allow dogs. And best of all, there's now a leash-free dog park in Encinitas, a leash-free area, and three parks with limited leash-free hours. It's enough to make a dog howl with happiness. (And some dogs truly do. Check it out sometime when there's a hound around.)

PARKS, BEACHES, AND RECREATION AREAS

The city has recently really gone to the dogs—in the best sense of the phrase. Not only is there one dedicated dog park, a dog-walk area, and three parks with off-leash hours, but the city was also strongly considering other pooch-park areas. Way to go, Encinitas! For info on the local dog park access group, People and Dog Zones, go to www.padz.org.

🐾 Cricket's Corner/Rancho Coastal Humane Society Dog Park

🐾🐾🐾🐕 (See San Diego County map on page 832)

It's unusual to find such a green dog park. Somehow despite the park's popularity, its gorgeous grass keeps growing. (This can change at any time, of course, so don't be disappointed if you come here and find a big dirt lot.) Dogs have a little less than an acre of off-leash running room here. Small dogs get their own park within a park so they can stay away from the thundering paws of the big guys, but they're welcome in the big section. The park has water, trees, benches, and even a soda machine. (The latter is an odd amenity, but welcome on hot days.)

The park is on the property of the Rancho Coastal Humane Society, and is open only when the society is open, 11 A.M.–5 P.M. (On Mondays, it opens at 11:30 A.M.) The address is 389 Requeza Street. From southbound I-5, take the Encinitas Boulevard exit and turn left onto Encinitas Boulevard. Go right on Westlake Street. At the stop sign turn right on Requeza Street. At the bottom of the hill go left into the driveway for the Rancho Coastal Humane Society. 760/753-6413.

🐾 Encinitas View Park

🐾🐾🐾🐕 (See San Diego County map on page 832)

Dogs may be off leash in the lower part of the park (not the upper part with the great views) 6–7:30 A.M. and 4–6 P.M. Monday, Wednesday, and Friday. It's about 2.5 acres, and it's not fenced. Dogs love to run around on the grass, but keep 'em out of the tot lot. The park is at Cornish Drive and D Street. 760/633-2740.

🐾 Orpheus Park

🐾🐾🐾🐕 (See San Diego County map on page 832)

Dogs love to sniff around this 2.5-acre park, but they're not looking for Eurydice. They're joyously checking out the grass, the trees, and the eau du dog that's everywhere. This is a pretty hillside park with a decent ocean view. Dogs may be off leash 6–7:30 A.M. and 4–6 P.M. Monday, Wednesday, and Friday. 482 Orpheus Avenue. 760/633-2740.

🔟 Sun Vista Park

😺😺😺 🐾 (See San Diego County map on page 832)

Dogs must be very cognizant of where they go during the limited off-leash hours at this young four-acre park. They're allowed only on the east side of the creek/creekbed. The west side is the part where human kids cavort about. Signs warn against going over to the other side of the creek, but most dogs can't read, so keep an eye peeled.

Dogs may be off leash 6–7:30 A.M. and 4–6 P.M. Monday, Wednesday, and Friday. 2011 Avenida la Posta, at Rancho Santa Fe Road. 760/633-2740.

1️⃣1️⃣ Village Park Trail & Off-Leash Area

😺😺 🐾 (See San Diego County map on page 832)

This leash-free area is located right under the power lines, but if you don't look up, it's a pretty cool place. It's about a quarter mile long by 200 feet wide and has a trail that winds through it. But this is no grassy park. This is all natural, with dirt, chaparral, cactus, and other plant life of its ilk. It's only partially fenced, so if your dog isn't under voice control, you may not feel comfortable letting her off leash. But once you're away from the roads and the entrances, it's a pretty safe haven for most off-leash pooches.

This area permits unleashed dogs every day, without the limited hours mandated at three other city parks. The park parallels Village Run West and runs from Mountain Vista Drive south to Encinitas Boulevard. There are four access points, but our favorites for easy access are on the south side, at either Encintas Boulevard (although this spot has no parking) or where Village Run East turns north and becomes Village Run North. There's a helpful map at www.padz.org/sdge.html; 760/633-2740.

1️⃣2️⃣ Pacific Scene Recreation Trail

😺😺😺 (See San Diego County map on page 832)

You and your leashed dog can walk almost two miles one-way on this rugged trail. The trail goes through both chaparral land and a lush riparian creekside area. Escondido Creek runs the entire length of the trail.

City officials are hopeful that eventually the trail will be connected with another trail, so the round-trip won't entail turning around and walking the same path back. You may encounter some horses on the trail, but they're generally not going to be going very fast on this terrain.

Enter at Lone Jack Road and Camino del Rancho. 760/633-2740.

1️⃣3️⃣ Cardiff State Beach

😺😺😺 (See San Diego County map on page 832)

A while back, Joe Dog and I visited here during the highest tide of the year. Joe looked at me as if I were crazy for bringing him to a beach that was all ocean and no sand. He slowly shook his head, glared at me, and pulled me back to the car.

But normally there really *is* sand here, and quite a bit of it, too. It's a good place to bring a leashed dog, especially since it's the last beach area that allows dogs for many, many miles as you drive north.

If you're going to park your car here, it's $6. But you can walk in for free. The beach is on Old Highway 101, directly west of the San Elijo Lagoon, in Cardiff-by-the-Sea. 760/753-5091.

PLACES TO STAY

Best Western Encinitas Inn and Suites and Moonlight Beach: Rates are $120–150. Dogs are $50 extra for the length of their stay. 85 Encinitas Boulevard 92024; 760/942-7455.

San Elijo State Beach Campgrounds: Dogs are banned from all but a smidgen of the cobblestoned beach here, but they can camp right above it on the bluffs. There are 171 sites, and they cost $16–25. The part of the beach that permits leashed pooches is at the south end, south of lifeguard tower 7. It's only about 50 feet of running room, but it's better than nothing. The entrance is on Old Highway 101, north of Chesterfield Drive, in Cardiff-by-the-Sea. For campsite reservations, call 800/444-7275. For beach information, call 760/753-5091.

Rancho Santa Fe

PLACES TO STAY

Inn at Rancho Santa Fe: Dogs and their people love it at "the inn," as everyone seems to call it. Set on 22 acres of lawns, gardens, and tree-dotted expanses, this is a very peaceful place to stay with a pooch. The inn consists of 104 rooms, most of them in the form of cottages. Half have wood-burning fireplaces, most have private patios or balconies, and some come with kitchens. Most of the cottages have four rooms, which is a comfortable size when you're traveling with a pooch. Rates are $210–750. 5951 Linea del Cielo 92067; you have your choice of phone numbers: 858/756-1131 or 800/843-4661; www.rsf.com.

Del Mar

This stylish but sweet coastal community is mighty friendly to dogs. Within a few blocks, Jake got stopped and talked to by seven different pedestrians. One dapper old gent carried a Ziploc bag filled with gourmet dog treats in his coat pocket. Jake fell in love, not wanting to leave his side, and looking back longingly as we parted company.

PARKS, BEACHES, AND RECREATION AREAS

🐾 Dog Beach/Del Mar City Beach

🐾🐾🐾🐾🐕 (See San Diego County map on page 832)

OK, dogs, get out your calendars and you can figure out when you can take off your leashes at this great beach. It gets a little confusing, so you might want to have your person help you figure it out.

Different segments of the beach have different rules regarding beach access and off-leash use. Here's a breakdown of the rules:

• The part of the beach most dogs like to know about is the north section. Dogs congregate at the northernmost end, near the bluffs. It's not a long segment, but it's wide and very far from the road. Dogs have so much fun here that they usually collapse in ecstatic exhaustion when they get back to the car.

Leashes are the law June 16–September 14, but the rest of the year, your well-behaved dog can go sans leash! The entire off-leash area runs from 29th Street north to the Solano border. The best way to reach it from I-5 is to exit at Via de la Valle and drive west to Camino del Mar, where you'll go south for just about a block before you should start looking for street parking. It's across from the Del Mar Racetrack.

• The middle section of the beach, from 29th Street down to Powerhouse Park/17th Street, prohibits dogs June 1–September 30. During the rest of the year, they can visit with a leash.

• Dogs who visit the south part of the beach, from 6th Street up to Powerhouse Park/17th Street, can visit year-round, as long as they wear a leash.

A current dog license is required. And because too few people are cleaning up after their dogs, it may soon become mandatory to carry a poop bag in plain view. That way, you're telling the world (and any poop patrol police who pass by), "My dog doesn't need a toilet. He has *me*." 858/755-1556.

PLACES TO EAT

En Fuego Cantina and Grill: "We are the hottest place in San Diego. We're *en fuego!* On fire!" exclaimed an enthusiastic host. "We like dogs, too!" Dogs get a bowl of water while their humans dine on tasty Mexican food at the attractive patio. 1342 Camino del Mar; 858/792-6551.

Stratford Court Cafe: This place is a real charmer—a feast for the eyes and for your beast. You can eat your scrumptious food in a beautiful garden setting, next to the 1915 Cape Cod–style café. (Try the Californian salad, with its caramelized walnuts and smoked gouda.) And your happy dog will be offered a big bowl of water and even tasty dog biscuits made by Steve, the café's chef/owner. (The biscuits are $.25 each. They're worth it.) 1307 Stratford Court 92014; 858/792-7433.

La Jolla

Back in the 1950s, Raymond Chandler wrote that La Jolla is "a nice place… for old people and their parents." He could have added two more categories to his description and it would have been more accurate. Something such as: La Jolla is "a nice place for old people, their parents, young people, and dogs."

Dogs, young folks, old folks, and older folks adore strolling along the seven miles of cliff-lined seacoast here. And they all equally love the impressive restaurant scene.

Unfortunately, your pooch won't be able to visit the parks and beaches of this stunning coastline 9 A.M.–6 P.M., but few dogs mind a nighttime stroll above the pounding Pacific. Luckily, cool cafés and elegant eateries abound. Many of them allow dogs to hang out with you as you dine at their outdoor tables.

La jolla means "the jewel" in Spanish. The name couldn't be more appropriate for this pristine, sparkling village. That's why, although it's actually part of the city of San Diego, it's being given its own listing here. It's like Monaco—a ravishing principality unto itself.

PARKS, BEACHES, AND RECREATION AREAS

15 Mount Soledad Park

😛 (See San Diego County map on page 832)

If you've never been to La Jolla, this is the ideal starting place for your visit. Unlike other city parks, this one allows dogs during daylight hours, so get on up here and take a gander. The views of San Diego and the La Jolla coast are phenomenal. Spending a few minutes at the top of the hill is a great way to get your bearings.

That's about all you can do at the top of the hill. The park looks quite large on the map, but most of the land is made up of impassable cliffs. The flat, walkable area on the hilltop is actually rather small. Unless you own a teacup poodle, your leashed dog won't feel exercised after a visit to this park. But boy, will he know his geography.

From the south part of the La Jolla coast, take Nautilus Street east about two miles to South Street. Turn left and then make a right onto Soledad Road, in a couple of blocks. You'll know you're here when you see the large white cross that is visible from many areas of San Diego. It's a memorial to the war dead, and every Easter it's the site of a magical sunrise service. 858/552-1658.

🐾16 La Jolla Shores Beach

🐾🐾🐾 (See San Diego County map on page 832)

Just down the road from the famous Scripps Institution of Oceanography, this beach provides some breathtaking views of the La Jolla coast. But if you're visiting in the dark winter months, you might not get to see the views if you're with a dog. Dogs are banned 9 A.M.–6 P.M. year-round. During their visiting hours, they must wear the mandatory leash.

The beach here is wide and lined with palms. Since you can't come here before 6 P.M. anyway, try to visit at sunset, when the gulls circle the bright gold sky and the orange waves crash on the distant cliffs. It's a stunning sight.

The beach is just west of Camino del Oro in the northern part of La Jolla. 619/235-1100.

🐾17 Point La Jolla Cliffs and Beaches

🐾🐾🐾 (See San Diego County map on page 832)

This is another one of those 9-to-6ers famous in the San Diego area. Dogs can visit the cliffs and beaches here only before 9 A.M. or after 6 P.M. Get out those infrared goggles and have a great time with your leashed pooch. OK, a flashlight would be more appropriate, but the goggles would make a better statement.

What's great about this area is that there's access to the beach via stairs that take you down the cliffs, and there's also a grassy little park at the top of the cliffs. It's extremely beautiful and dramatic here. During the right tides, tide-pooling is magnificent. Just make sure your dog doesn't stick his snout in the tidepools. The critters who call them home need all the peace they can get.

Enter on Coast Boulevard around Girard Avenue, and when you're done, go grab a bite to eat in any of the nearby mouthwatering restaurants. 619/235-1100.

PLACES TO EAT

La Jolla is a terrific place to grab a bite to eat with your dog. Many restaurants have lovely outdoor areas, and most of those happily permit pooches.

Froglander's Yogurt: The dog-loving owner here will gladly give your canine companion a free yogurt sample. 915 Pearl Street; 858/459-3764.

Girard Gourmet: Enjoy the beautiful blue skies while Girard's serves you gourmet food at the outdoor tables. 7837 Girard Avenue; 858/454-3321.

La Vache: Trees and grass surround you and your dog as you dine on fine French food on the patio tables. Bringing a good dog here feels so right, so French! 8008 Girard Avenue; 858/459-9750.

The Living Room: Dogs can accompany you at the tables on the sidewalk. Enjoy soups, sandwiches, salads, and pastries. 1010 Prospect Street; 858/459-1187.

Sammy's California Woodfired Pizza: The folks here love dogs, and dogs love the folks here, so everyone's happy. You'll drool for the incredible pizzas. Try the barbecued chicken pizza. It's out of this world, if you can stomach the idea of something other than pepperoni on your pizza. Dine at the outdoor tables with your favorite doggy. 702 Pearl Street; 858/456-5222.

PLACES TO STAY

Andrea Villa Inn: Many rooms here come with kitchenettes, and there are a heated pool and spa, a continental breakfast, and fresh-baked cookies every afternoon. I've heard mixed reviews of this motel, so you may want to check an Internet hotel review site (such as www.tripadvisor.com) for the latest before making reservations. (How bad could it be with homemade cookies?) Rates are $119–175. Dogs are $25 extra for the length of their stay. 2402 Torrey Pines Road 92037; 858/459-3311; www.andreavilla.com.

La Jolla Village Lodge: If you like to eat, stay at this 1950s-era motel. Not only does your room come with a fridge and microwave, but you get continental breakfast, and snacks are available all day. (It's not a great place for dieters.) Rates are $70–140. Dogs are $20 extra for the length of their stay. 1141 Silverado Street 92037; 858/551-2001; www.lajollavillagelodge.com.

La Valencia Hotel: It's exquisite, it's upscale, it's expensive, and it's for dogs who are less than 30 pounds. (Stop reading now if you have anything larger or a budget that matches your little dog's size.) Some rooms overlook the beautiful gardens, others have views of the ocean or La Jolla's village. You can also stay at a super-attractive villa here. This European-style hotel has been charming visitors and their dogs since 1926. Rates are $275–665. Dogs are $75 extra nightly. Whoo, that's a lotta doggy dough. 1132 Prospect Street 92037; 858/454-0771 or 800/451-0772; www.lavalencia.com.

Residence Inn La Jolla: This is a lovely place for humans and their hairy sidekicks. Stay at studios or penthouse suites. All rooms come with kitchens and range $149–279. Dogs are $25 extra for the length of your stay. 8901 Gilman Drive 92037; 858/587-1770; www.residenceinn.com.

San Diego Marriott La Jolla: It's surprising to find such a large hotel in this little community, but it fits in fairly well with its lovely pools and nice landscaping. Rates are $159–189. Dogs are $75 extra for the length of their stay. 4240 La Jolla Village Drive 92037; 858/587-1414.

Poway

PARKS, BEACHES, AND RECREATION AREAS

18 Poway Dog Park

🐾🐾🐾🐾 🐕 (See San Diego County map on page 832)

A visit to Poway Dog Park is like a stint on Let's Make a Deal. Dogs get to choose between Door Number One, Door Number Two, or Door Number

Three. But unlike the old Monty Hall game show, no matter which door your dog chooses, she'll always be a winner. (No booby prizes of canned spinach here.) Poway Dog Park has three separate fenced areas for leash-free dogs, and they're all doggone great. Your dog can visit any or all of them in a given day. If the sniffs are boring in one area, try another. If there's a cute dog your pooch wants to meet in another fenced area, open the door for her mystery date and let the good times roll.

Each section of this nearly two-acre park is a poochie wonderland, with dog water fountains and even a fire hydrant for your dog's pee-rusal. There's some shade, but on hot days dogs could use a little more.

Exit I-15 at Poway Road and drive east about four miles. Turn right on Bowron Road. Park in the lot at the end of the road. Walk past the soccer and baseball fields to the pooch park, which is behind the swimming pool and baseball fields in Poway Community Park. 858/679-4342.

PLACES TO EAT

Chicken Pie Diner: This is a great '50s-style diner that boasts of "serving classic comfort food at family prices." Dogs dig it here, because even though they need to eat at the seven umbrella-topped tables outside, they still get the ambience of the place because the '50s jukebox music is piped out to this area. A big thank-you to Dyson Dog for letting us know about this place. 14727 Pomerado Road; 858/748-2445.

Julian

This entire old gold-mining town is a Designated Historic District. It's full of nifty old storefronts and dog-friendly folks. It's also full of tourists, especially if you visit during October, which is apple month in these parts. People here bake more than 10,000 apple pies a week in October—a fun time to visit if you like autumn leaves and crispy apples. Julian is recovering from the terrible wildfires of 2002 and 2003. The more touristy parts of Julian survived, but businesses could use your business; come and play. Your dog will thank you.

PLACES TO EAT

The Julian Grille: You and your dog can dine on tasty burgers, pastas, steaks, and salads at the restaurant's 15-table patio area. 2224 Main Street; 760/765-0173.

Romano's Dodge House: The Italian food here is *benissimo.* Dine with your dog at the six outdoor tables. 2718 B Street; 760/765-1003.

DIVERSION

Pick a Peck of Apples: What Peter Piper did with pickled peppers, you and your dog can do with apples, thanks to the dog-friendly folks at **Calico Ranch orchards** in Julian. From about mid-September through Thanksgiving, you and your leashed, cleaned-up-after dog can sniff out your favorite apples at the orchard's 30 acres of trees. Then take them home to make a to-drool-for apple pie or two. (Or 10.) 4200 Highway 78; 858/586-0392.

PLACES TO STAY

This mountain town has some doggone terrific lodgings for lucky dogs and their people.

Angel's Landing: Angel's Landing is an appropriate name for this 53-acre chunk of pine-covered paradise. It's beautiful here and so secluded you won't even hear any traffic. The owners are some of the most animal-friendly people you'll ever encounter. They love dogs and even have an animal-rescue area on the property, with adopted chickens, bunnies, pigs, goats, and horses.

The Old Butterfield Stage Coach Route runs through the property and makes for a terrific hike with your leashed dog. (Leashes are a necessity here, because the place is also heaven for many deer and wild turkeys.) If it's a very clear day, you might be able to see the ocean from the meadows above Angel's Landing.

The rooms and suites at the lodge and smaller buildings are clean and pretty. The rates are $49–149. Dogs are $10 extra on weekends; otherwise there's no doggy fee. 2323 Farmer Road 92036; 888/253-7747; www.angelsresort.com.

Eaglenest Bed and Breakfast: It's rare to find a bed-and-breakfast that allows pets, but, as Eaglenest owner Julie says, "How can we not allow dogs? We're lucky enough to have four ourselves!" The quartet of beautiful golden retrievers—Lucy, Rick, Luke, and Leah—live in the adjacent house with Julie and her husband, Jim, and their cats. You'll see the friendly goldens plenty during your stay here ("They're free-range," says Julie), but the felines pretty much steer clear of visiting dogs.

Eaglenest is a Victorian-style inn just a block away from the main part of town. It features attractive bedroom suites—each with a fireplace—and a wonderful pool and hot tub set in a big redwood deck. You can really relax here; there's even an apple tree–shaded hammock. In fall you can pick a sweet fruit and munch it while reading a book below. The breakfasts here are scrumptious, but just as much in demand are Jim's homemade chocolate chip cookies. If there aren't any around during your stay, try a dog trick: Beg. (They're that good.)

Any size dog is welcome to stay during weekdays, but because weekends

DIVERSION

Get Carriaged Away: Ah! There's nothing like the smell of horse heinie to put a smile on a dog's face. Lucky dogs get to experience this olfactory bliss up close when they join you on a **Country Carriages buggy ride.** The carriage rides take you down quiet country roads around beautiful Julian. It can be romantic, but with your dog involved, it's just fun. Owner Wayne says some dogs are oblivious to the equines until partway through the ride. "Then it's like they go 'Hey! There's a horse in front of me!' and they let out a bark or two. The owners are embarrassed and try to make the dog be quiet. It's never been a problem," he says.

A half-hour ride is $25 for a couple with a couple of kids and/or a dog. The more people and the longer the ride, the more it costs. Wayne will even pick you up at your lodging, if it's not too far away, but he also picks up rides in front of the Julian Drug Store at Washington and Main Streets. Reservations are strongly recommended, especially during weekends. 760/765-1471.

can get very busy here, they ask that only small dogs be weekend guests. Rates are $145–185, with a number of midweek deals available. Dogs are $25 extra per stay. 2609 D Street 92036; 760/765-1252 or 888/345-6378; www.eaglenestbandb.com.

Julian Flat Top Mountain Retreat: This beautiful three-bedroom vacation home on eight acres is very private and secluded, which comes in handy with all the huge windows here. (Your dog can walk around in the buff and no one will care.) And yet it's only 1.6 miles to town.

The house has a wood-burning stove, three wonderful decks with great views, and a loft bedroom that also sports killer views. (If you like seeing stars while you sleep, stake out that room.) But best of all for dogs is that outside they have their very own 32- by 24-foot dog run enclosed by a four-foot-high wooden fence. Dogs can gallop around leash-free to their hearts' content.

Owner Mary adores dogs and their people. "The dog lovers have been the nicest guests," she says. Being a dog person herself, she knows how to make dogs feel welcome at the house: Dogs get a little variety of biscuits in a little bag tied with a red ribbon upon their arrival. Between this and the dog run, your dog may never want to leave.

Rates are $200–210. Specials are often available. When you make reservations, you'll get the address. 858/454-6733 or 800/810-1170; www.julianflattop.com.

Little Acorn Cabin: Many dogs have vacationed at this decent little housekeeping cabin. If you like to barbecue, you'll enjoy the cabin's grill and little picnic area. Rates are $85–125. 2142 Whispering Pines Drive 92036; 760/765-1611.

Pine Haven: This sweet, cozy cabin is one of the most pooch-friendly cabins we've come across. The entire 1.25-acre property is completely and securely fenced, so it's one big doggy playground! Not only that, but scattered around the tiered property are hidden "treasures" dogs revel in finding. (They're actually dog toys and tennis balls; no gold bullion or anything. "The dogs love running around and suddenly finding a toy," says cabin owner Teresa, who adores dogs and is very involved with dog-rescue groups.) In addition, dogs get a basket of toys they can play with and a doggy treat of their own. Plus, they can use the cabin's doggy beds and have a choice of two types of "tables" they can dine on. Jake loves slurping water and munching food from these raised bowl platforms. (He has made me promise to buy him his own.) It really doesn't get more dog-friendly than this.

With all these dog amenities, it's easy to brush over the cabin itself, but it's got loads of appeal. The living room is especially wonderful, with a floor-to-ceiling stone fireplace and views of a beautiful meadow. The cabin is on a small lane four miles from town and offers plenty of privacy. Rates are $160–180. Dogs are $30 extra for the length of their stay for the first dog, $10 for the second. You'll get the address when you make your reservation. 760/726-9888; the adorable dog-focused website is www.pinehavencabin.com.

El Cajon

PARKS, BEACHES, AND RECREATION AREAS

🔟 Louis A. Stelzer Regional Park

🐾🐾🐾 (See San Diego County map on page 832)

You and your favorite leashed pooch can walk in dreamy seclusion on most winter weekdays in this 314-acre park. A series of small meadows and a mile-long stretch of riparian woodland beg to be visited. If you hike up to Stelzer Ridge, you'll get spectacular views of the surrounding land.

If civilization is more your style, you can picnic under big, shady trees while the kids frolic at the two playgrounds. Louis A. Stelzer, who donated his ranch to create this park, specified in his will that he wanted the park to be developed for disadvantaged and disabled children. The results are commendable.

From Highway 67, exit at Mapleview Street and drive east about a half mile to Ashwood Street. Turn left and follow it for a couple of miles as it changes its name to Wildcat Canyon Road and leads you into the park. 858/694-3049.

San Diego

San Diego is both laid-back and exciting. You and your dog can stroll through the old Gaslamp quarter, eating up the local history as well as the good food served at a few dog-friendly eateries. You can visit La Jolla's pristine shores (see the La Jolla section, above) for breathtaking scenery and clean-breathing air. You can even walk on historic land where California actually started (at the Presidio Park). If that's not stimulating enough, you can stroll down action-packed beaches together at sunset (on Mission Beach/Pacific Beach).

San Diego has one of the best dog beaches in the state. And now it's also home to more dog parks than any other city in California. (There are 11 leash-free areas in the city, and that number was to increase soon.) No wonder so many dogs here look so doggone happy.

PARKS, BEACHES, AND RECREATION AREAS

San Diego has seven more leash-free areas since the book's last edition. It's an absolutely terrific development, but it presents a bit of a problem for this book: Space to write about them all! There's a severe lack of it this time 'round,

DIVERSION

Hail a Cab with Your Lab: Need to get from your home or hotel to the groomer, the beach, or the airport? If you don't have your own wheels, what are you going to do? Buses in San Diego don't take doggies, and many taxis don't either. But if you phone the folks at **PETCAB Pet Taxi Service,** you'll be able to get from Point A to Point B in comfort, style, and safety. And the cab driver won't keep glancing back and giving your dog the evil eye, warning you not to "let that dog ruin my cab!" (This has happened to me, if you can tell. To add to our enjoyment, the driver sprayed alarmingly awful air freshener toward the back seat every few minutes. I'd just given Jake a bath, so maybe the spray was meant for me.) The drivers at PETCAB are licensed pet-sitters who adore dogs.

The cab is actually an attractive white and gold Chrysler Town and Country LXi minivan that super-nice owner Jesse Ouwens, an industrial engineer by day, has modified with all kinds of pet- and people-oriented extras such as rear air-conditioning, additional passenger handles, leash hooks, floor tie-downs, and stain-free carpeting. Your dog can ride with you on the seat, or lie on the floor, which is very roomy. Oh, and the cab comes with treats and water, too.

Rates are very reasonable. Phone 858/829-3071 or check out www.petcabtaxi.com for more info.

thanks to the tremendous growth in dog-friendly places in the state. Rather than go into depth about each park, I'll save the longer descriptions for the more spectacular ones, and keep the typical dog park descriptions brief.

The number of dog parks is likely to continue growing as the parks department here tries to navigate the fine line between dog users and nondog users. There's a tremendous push from dog people for more parks. At press time, a leash-free dog park next to Rancho Bernardo Community Park was in the works. Located at 18448 West Bernardo Drive, the 2.5-acre park is scheduled to open in 2005. Call 619/525-8239 to check on its status.

20 Cadman Community Park

🐾🐾🐾🐕 (See San Diego County map on page 832)

If your dog's theme song is "Don't Fence Me In," she'll be happy here: The park's leash-free dog area—marked by signs—has no fences. But it does have grass, trees, park benches, and mutt-mitt dispensers. It also has limited hours: It's open to off-leash dogs 7:30–10 A.M. and 4:30–7 P.M. during the school year. It's open 7–9:30 A.M. and 5–7:30 P.M. in summer. Leashes are mandatory on July Fourth, and on Saturdays March 1–June 15. 4280 Avati Drive, at Moraga Court. 619/525-8239.

21 Capehart Park Dog Park

🐾🐾🐾🐕 (See San Diego County map on page 832)

Small dogs who are worried about big dogs can take refuge in this fenced park's separate area for wee dogs. The entire park is about an acre, so there's not gobs of room to roam, but dogs enjoy it anyway. The park has water, picnic tables, and benches. It's at the corner of Felspar and Soledad Mountain Roads. 619/525-8239.

22 Doyle Community Park Dog Park

🐾🐾🐾🐕 (See San Diego County map on page 832)

You won't find trees here, but in the warmer months you will find awnings where warm humans and hot dogs (the furry kind) take refuge. The fenced one-acre park has water, benches, and a separate section for small dogs. Doyle Park is at 8175 Regents Road, but the dog area is toward the back of the park, on Cargill Avenue south of Nobel Drive. 619/525-8239.

23 Dusty Rhodes Park Dog Park

🐾🐾🐕 (See San Diego County map on page 832)

At press time, this one-acre fenced park had no water, so be sure to bring your own. It's mostly grass, with some mulch ground cover. There's talk (among dog people) about expanding the park to five acres, which could make it a four-paw wonder. It's on Sunset Cliffs Boulevard between Nimitz and West

DIVERSION

Whatever Floats Your Boat: If you and your salty dog want to explore beautiful **San Diego Bay** by water, a couple of boat-rental companies are happy to accommodate you. You'll have your choice of sailing or motoring around the bay. The sailboats range 14 feet–27 feet, with a price range of about $30–100 per hour. Powerboats come in a variety of sizes and horsepowers, with an hourly rate of $65–150.

Note: If your dog isn't a decent dog paddler, you should bring a doggy life jacket for her. Even if she's Esther Williams, it's not a bad idea. The smaller the sailboat, the better the chance you'll end up in the drink. Plus it can get busy in the bay, with Navy-type ships crossing here and there to make things interesting.

Seaforth Boat Rentals is on the San Diego waterfront at 333 West Harbor Drive (it shares the address with the San Diego Marriott Hotel and Marina, should you be looking for a place to stay on the water); 619/239-BOAT (619/239-2628). Action Sport Rentals is in Coronado and right next to the magnificent Loews Coronado Bay Resort, at 4000 Coronado Bay Road; 619/424-4466.

Point Loma Boulevards, across Sunset from the wonderful Mission Bay Park (see below). 619/525-8239.

24 Kearny Mesa Community Park Dog Park

😊 😊 🐕 (See San Diego County map on page 832)

Jake gives this park only two paws because even though it's a decent off-leash fenced area, there's no water, and parking can be problematic. If you want to fetch your dog a drink, you'll have to go to the adjacent restroom's drinking fountain, fill up a container (there are usually gallon milk containers at the park), and then pour it into a bowl you'll find here. Park users are hoping for a real doggy and human water fountain one of these days. Kearny Mesa Park is at 3170 Armstrong Street, at Mesa College Drive; you'll have to drive to the back of the park, past the pool and playing fields, to get to the dog area. 619/525-8239.

25 Maddox Park Dog Park

😊 😊 😊 🐕 (See San Diego County map on page 832)

Maddox Park is a small park surrounded by a residential area, so try to keep the barking to a dull roar. The fenced park within Maddox has about an acre of grass, with a picnic table and drinking fountain. It's at 7815 Flanders Drive, at Dabney Drive. 619/525-8239.

26 Torrey Highlands Park Dog Park

🐾🐾🐾🐕 (See San Diego County map on page 832)

Dogs enjoy romping leash-free at this one-acre fenced dog park in the Carmel Valley area. The park has decent-sized trees along one side, and benches, water, and an adjacent restroom for humans. The ground cover is grassy with some mulch, and fairly easy on the paws. It's on Lansdale Drive off Del Mar Heights Road. 619/525-8239.

27 Balboa Park

🐾🐾🐾🐾🐕 (See San Diego County map on page 832)

This luxuriant semitropical park is one of California's best urban parks for people. Attractions include the San Diego Zoo, an enormous planetarium, several theaters, and a few world-class museums. But with the recent addition of three off-leash areas for dogs, Balboa Park is now one of the best urban parks for pooches, too.

Dogs used to be relegated to the lush, green center and the dirt paths on the east and west sides of this 1,200-acre park. Leashes were—and still are—a necessity in those areas. Dogs who wanted more freedom were out of luck until a kindly park official thought it might be nice to give them a chance to cavort about sans leash in a small area. The dogs all thought this was a mighty good idea, and they've been so well behaved that the park doubled their stomping grounds.

The two dog runs aren't fenced, but they're well marked with signs. The more popular dog area is Morley Field, which is the smaller of the two. It's lined by a grove of eucalyptus trees, so there's plenty of shade on hot days. You'll almost always find gaggles of pooches gallivanting about in high spirits. You can get to Morley Field from Morley Field Drive, off Florida Drive, in the north-central part of the park (northwest of the tennis courts). The second and larger of the areas is Nate's Point, on the northwest side of the park off Balboa Drive, just south of the Laurel Street Bridge. It's a picturesque place (nice for pooches with a sense of aesthetic beauty), with views of the famous old California Tower, Coronado, and even part of Mexico. It's about 1.5 acres, and like Morley Field, it's unfenced, so keep an eye peeled for signs for its boundaries.

To get to the park from I-5, exit at Park Boulevard and head north. Call the Balboa Park Visitors Center for more information and maps. 619/239-0512.

28 Black Mountain Open Space

🐾🐾🐾 (See San Diego County map on page 832)

It's utterly quiet here. So quiet you can hear your dog breathe when he's sitting still. So quiet you'll swear you hear his fleas gnashing their teeth. And except when people are shooting bullets through the signs that say "No Liquor and No Firearms," it's almost always this silent.

A few miles of trails run through this mountainous, shrubby, completely undeveloped 200-acre park. It's not exactly Mt. Whitney, but from the top of Black Mountain (elevation 1,552 feet), you can get some good views of the surrounding hills and peaks.

The trek here looks complicated, but it's not bad. Exit I-15 at Rancho Peñasquitos Boulevard/Mountain Road and drive west about two miles to Black Mountain Road. Turn right and drive north about 2.5 miles, where the road will come to an abrupt end. Just before it does, turn right on the dirt road there. Follow the winding road up the mountain and eventually you'll come to a sharp right, where the road becomes paved. The road ends in a small parking lot. From here, you can see the start of the trail. 858/538-8082.

29 Dog Beach

🐾🐾🐾🐾🐾 🐕 (See San Diego County map on page 832)

"Welcome to Dog Beach!" the sign announces at just about the same place that your dog charges out of the car to meet all his best buddies. Dogs truly do feel welcome here. They're free to run off leash and to get down to the business of being a dog. As long as they listen when you call and don't get into trouble, they can hang out leashless all day. Many dog people bring a folding chair so they can relax while their dog experiences heaven on earth.

We've seen several folks visit here because, although they don't have a dog, they get great joy out of watching the footloose creatures tearing around. "They have such innocent happiness when they run about and play so gleefully," said dogless dog lover Maxine Chambers one gray morning. "It makes my day."

There are more dog footprints in the sand than human footprints, and not just because dogs have more feet. People come from many miles around, sometimes bringing their friends' dogs and their neighbors' dogs to participate in the whirlwind of excitement.

Dogs are allowed off leash at the north end of the beach, which is wide enough to be very safe from traffic. It's marked by signs. If you wander onto the other part of the beach, make sure you do so before 9 A.M. or after 6 P.M., and be sure to leash your dog.

Exit I-5 at I-8. Drive west and follow the signs to Sunset Cliffs Boulevard. After several blocks, bear right at Voltaire Street. Follow Voltaire Street to its end and the entrance to Dog Beach. 619/235-1100.

30 Embarcadero Marina Park

🐾🐾🐾 (See San Diego County map on page 832)

This park is like a big green thumb jutting into the San Diego Bay. It's a terrific place for a little walk with your leashed dog. Dogs and their people enjoy watching the seabirds glide around the fresh air over impressive views of the city and Coronado.

DIVERSION

Wash That Sand Right Outta His Hair: After a long jaunt on Dog Beach, come to the **Dog Beach Dog Wash,** a wonderful place to keep your pooch looking as if he just strolled out of a dog-food commercial. If location is everything, this business has it all. It's only two blocks from Dog Beach. The owners say that some folks bring their dogs here almost every time they visit the beach. It's a great way to get rid of all that sand and dog slobber before getting back in your car. It's at 4933 Voltaire Street, Suite C, San Diego; 619/523-1700.

If you're nearer the Grape Street Dog Park with a dirty dog, be sure to check out the wonderful **South Bark Dog Wash.** It has a spalike ambience and very reasonable prices for what you get. It's at 2037 30th Street, San Diego; 619/232-7387; www.southbark.com.

Baths at both places cost $8, with blow dryers and medicated shampoos costing extra.

The big bummer here is that dogs are not allowed to visit Seaport Village, a major dining and shopping attraction right next to the park. Hey, who needs to spend money anyway? Take Kettner Boulevard (it runs parallel to Pacific Highway, one block to the east) to its southernmost end. 619/686-6200.

🐾 Fiesta Island

🐾🐾🐾🐾 ✍ (See San Diego County map on page 832)

Hey, dogs! You're going to find out just why they call this 1.5-mile-long island Fiesta Island. You can have a fabulous fiesta, then take a soothing siesta—and you can do it all off leash.

Yes, pooches, you can meet friends, swim in the bay, chase your shadow, and catch a stick without ever wearing that pesky old leash. As long as you listen to your people and don't cause any problems, this island is all yours. There's no development (as of this printing, anyway, although there's plenty of talk about it)—just dirt and sand and a little grass.

If you aren't very good at listening to your owners, ask them to take you to the far side of the island, where fewer cars cruise by. The perimeter of the island is a beach, and unfortunately, the road runs right behind the beach. It doesn't give water dogs a whole lot of room to run around, but it's enough for most.

If you choose to stay on the beach, you can avoid annoying little personal watercraft by staying away from the watercraft recreation sections of water, which are clearly marked. The interior of the island is made up of fields of dirt. Since this is a bigger area, you'll be farther from traffic here.

The views of downtown San Diego and Mission Bay Park are really spectacular from the south side of the island. Cameras come in mighty handy here. (Fiesta Island is actually part of Mission Bay Park, but the rules are so different that I prefer to discuss them separately. See the Mission Bay Park listing, below, for more information.)

From I-5, take the Sea World Drive/Tecolote Road exit southeast to Fiesta Island Road, which is your first right. The road will take you onto the island. 619/235-1100.

3 2 Grape Street Park

🐾🐾🐾🐾 🐕 (See San Diego County map on page 832)

Dogs love running on this attractive, grassy, unfenced five-acre area near downtown San Diego. There's shade, water, restrooms (for humans; dogs just use the trees), benches, and lights—everything you could want in a pooch park. There's talk about either fencing in a dog park here or making this unfenced area a full-time leash-free zone. For now, the hours dogs can run around without leashes: 7:30–10 A.M. and 4–9 P.M. Monday–Friday; 9–11 A.M. and 4–9 P.M. weekends and holidays. Leashed dogs can visit any time. The park is at Grape Street and Granada Avenue. 619/235-1100.

3 3 Kate O. Sessions Park

🐾🐾🐾 (See San Diego County map on page 832)

This is another of those San Diego parks that looks so much like a golf course that it fools people. In fact, this park even has a sign: "Golf practice prohibited!" The other major rule up here is that dogs must be leashed.

Kate O. Sessions Park is very green, very hilly, very peaceful, and very charming. Not that dogs care, but the views of the city are terrific from up here.

The park is between Pacific Beach and the Muirlands districts of town, on Soledad Road at Park Drive. 858/581-9961.

3 4 Mission Bay Park

🐾🐾🐾🐾 (See San Diego County map on page 832)

Dogs are not allowed at this spectacular, huge park 9 A.M.–6 P.M., making for some rather tight daylight hours in the winter. But when it's light enough to see, you can't help but enjoy yourself here. This is one of the nation's largest and most beautiful aquatic parks.

It's so big (4,600 acres, including the bay), with so many more entry points than signs, that you may make the same mistake many others have when seeing the park for the first time: "I thought it was a bloody golf course! Gawd! OK, Ginger, let's go for a walk," said Henry Miles, a British chap in his 70s. He was walking Ginger for his sister, who had told him about Mission Bay Park and how to get there. But when he saw the perfect grass, the gently rolling hills, and the sand, he figured he'd gotten the directions wrong. "They've got a lot of golf courses here, you know. Gawd, even their parks look like them. Ginger looks relieved, eh?"

I ran into Miles at the section of park near the San Diego Visitor Information Center. That section is particularly reminiscent of a golf course—in fact, it's just around the bend from a golf course that's a dead ringer for the park.

If you're on I-5 and your pooch wants to exercise while you get tourist information, exit at the Clairemont Drive/Visitor Center turnoff and follow the signs to the visitor center. Keep in mind that the visitor center and the pooch-walking hours rarely coincide, so it helps if you have a friend who can get the necessary tourist information while you walk your dog. You can park in the parking lot for only an hour, so if you're planning on a longer stay, there's street parking a little farther south.

The zillions of other access points are north of the San Diego River and south of Pacific Beach Drive. The east-west boundaries are East Mission Bay Drive (which parallels I-5) and Mission Boulevard (which runs a block east of the Pacific). You can also visit dog-friendly Fiesta Island, which is actually part of this park's territory (but listed separately, above). 619/235-1100, or to speak with a ranger, 858/581-7603.

35 Mission Beach/Pacific Beach

🐾🐾🐾🐾 (See San Diego County map on page 832)

The great thing about strolling down these two contiguous beaches with a dog is that no one seems to care if you don't have bulging biceps or a bikini-perfect body. Having a dog eliminates the need for physical prowess here. And on beaches that have built a worldwide reputation on how dazzling its bathers look, that's a mighty big plus.

On the downside, dogs are allowed to accompany you here only before 9 A.M. and after 6 P.M. The same hours hold for the paved promenade that runs behind the beaches. It's an understandable law during crowded summer days, but it would be a real boon for dogs if that rule could be eliminated during the winter. Since the poor pooches have to be leashed anyway, what's the harm? (Joe made me write that.)

To make the best of these restricted hours, try a visit to beautiful Belmont Park. The big attraction at this old-style amusement park is a restored 1925 roller coaster, the Giant Dipper. In addition, there's a quaint old carousel and a historic indoor swimming pool. Dogs are required to be leashed and remain with all four feet planted firmly on the ground, but they can still have a good time watching the kids have fun. The park area is also home to dozens of shops and restaurants. It's at West Mission Bay Drive and Mission Boulevard. Its back faces Mission Beach. Call 619/491-2988 for Belmont Park hours and information.

Pacific Beach is north of Mission Beach. It starts around Tourmaline Street. The beach hooks up with Mission Beach and is one long, never-ending strip all the way down to the Mission Bay Channel. 619/235-1100.

36 Mission Trails Regional Park

🐾🐾🐾 (See San Diego County map on page 832)

This is a really big chunk of green—5,109 acres, to be exact. Actually, it's a good deal greener on a map than it is in reality. Several miles of dirt trails wind through low brush and boulders, all in a rather desolate setting. Because this park is managed by the city (although owned by the county), dogs are permitted on the trails.

They love to bound up and down hill after hill with you tagging along behind them. There's a leash law here, so make sure that if they're bounding, you're bounding, too.

One good destination for your leaps and bounds is the Old Mission Dam Historical Site. Native Americans built it many decades back and it's still in good working order.

Good news for pooches: Dog-friendly rangers lead informative guided nature hikes for dogs and their people every other month. The hikes are not for the soft of paw or the fair of foot, but they're not usually terribly difficult, and we hear they're great fun. Call 619/668-3275 for more information.

Exit I-8 at Mission Gorge Road (one of the exits for the San Diego-Jack Murphy Stadium) and drive northeast past all the gas stations and fast-food marts. In about four miles, turn left on Father Junipero Serra Trail and you're in the park. Or if you want, you can park on Mission Gorge Road, at the trailhead off Jackson Road, just before you get to Father Junipero Serra Trail. 619/668-3275.

🟦37 Presidio Park

😺😺😺 (See San Diego County map on page 832)

This is where California began. The hill here is known as the "Plymouth Rock of the West." Dogs are stepping on very historic land when they walk here. Back in 1769, Father Junipero Serra dedicated his first of many California missions on this very same hill.

The mission has since moved, but a fascinating museum is a major draw here. Dogs don't have great interest in the Spanish furniture and historic documents in the museum, though, and they're not permitted inside anyway. They prefer the many wide dirt trails that run around the hill.

The trails are on rolling hills, shaded by plenty of trees. The views from here are incredible. On a clear day, you can see all of the city. Someone marching with a telescope said he could check out the beach scene from here, but I didn't confirm that.

From I-8, take the Taylor Street exit west. Go left at Presidio Drive, which will take you up to the park. You can park at the museum and get a map of the park. There's also a lower parking lot that has easy trail access. Call 619/297-3258 for the history of the area and general park information.

🟦38 Tecolote Canyon Natural Park

😺😺😺 (See San Diego County map on page 832)

There's a nine-acre nature center just as you enter one end of this huge canyon. Dogs love looking at the whale skeleton that was found here, and they even seem to like listening to rangers chat about the geologic wonders and natural history of the place. But they'd give it all up to go on a hike down this rugged eight-mile canyon.

The trails don't go all the way through the canyon in one neat sweep. If you dare to do the entire hike, you'll have to negotiate a golf course, some fairly rough terrain, and a couple of roads. But once you reach the northern Clairemont area of the park, you're in for some real beauty. Tecolote Creek is particularly refreshing here, and the scrub doesn't look as scrubby as it does elsewhere. There are even some shaded little ponds where you still might be able to find some crawdads.

A word of warning: Rangers are supposed to take photographs of people with off-leash dogs. The photos can be used as evidence against you if you try to argue with the ranger's word.

From I-5, take the Sea World Drive/Tecolote Drive exit (just north of the intersection with I-5) and drive east. You'll be dumped off almost immediately into the recreation center/nature center area. 858/581-9952.

PLACES TO EAT

Boardwalk Bistro: If you and your dog find your tummies rumbling when you're walking around Mission Bay, come here and dine together at one of 16 outdoor tables in a scenic garden setting. Try the "low-tide special." 370 Mission Boulevard; 858/488-9484.

Cheese Shop: "We're one of the cool shops," says one waiter. And he's right—while dining with your dog under umbrella-topped tables outside, the two of you can enjoy mouthwatering cheese samplers and delicious sandwiches. If your dog is a cheese nut, she'll find it an ecstatic experience just to sit and sniff the brie. 401 G Street; 619/232-2303.

K-9 Country Club: This is a doggone fun, casual place to take a pooch. The name alone beckons, but since the owner loves dogs, this deli/café has pictures of dogs and sells all kinds of hot dogs, further adding to the poochy ambience. You and your dog can get sandwiches, gourmet coffees, and, of course, hot dogs. Dine together at the outdoor tables. 202 C Street; 619/239-0304.

The Original Paw Pleasers: Dogs and other four-legged critters are welcome to dine inside (yes, *inside*) at least one restaurant around here. The Original Paw Pleasers is a beautiful little pets-only restaurant with gorgeous murals of a park scene of happy dogs and cats. It's a cozy, uplifting place, with oak cabinets and even a "tree." (OK, it's a post disguised as a tree, but it looks enough like a tree that your boy dog might be tempted…Don't let him!) And the food is to die for—if you're a pet. If you're a human, you can use coupons this place has in conjunction with eateries nearby and grab yourself a bite to bring here so you can eat beside your dog. Some of the more popular items are "dogolate" chip cookies and "bark-la-va." There's also frozen (lactose-free) yogurt with doggy toppings such as liver (this won't cross over to human ice creameries, I'm quite sure), and a doggy Sunday brunch. Owner Loree will even custom-make birthday cakes for your dog.

I rarely mention cats in this book (it's a four-letter word to some dogs), but this is too good to ignore. Cats can come here and get a chicken or calamari cake with faux cream frosting, or a tuna muffin with a delicious nondairy whipped topping. Mmm, good! By the way, if your dog thinks cats are part of the menu, make sure there are none inside before you venture in. The restaurant also sells lots of gift items for pets and their people. It's in an upscale shopping center in the Hillcrest area of San Diego. This is a must-visit on any dog's list. 1220 Cleveland Avenue; 619/293-7297; www.pawpleasers.com.

Point Loma Seafood: You want a dog-friendly restaurant? Romp on over to Point Loma Seafood, where the dog-loving attitude is as yummy as the seafood. You and your dog can share a bayside table and the stuff memories are made of (that is, french fries). While you dine on such goodies as a shrimp sandwich or crab Louie, your dog will be eating and drinking his own restaurant food: free biscuits and fresh water. The only thing Joe Dog winced at here was the pickled squid cocktail. As it passed by our table, en route to some less fortunate soul, he sniffed the air and backed up as far as his leash would allow. That boy always had good taste. 2805 Emerson Street; 619/223-1109.

Seven-17: Dogs can dine with you at the shaded patio tables at this California cuisine–slanted steak and seafood restaurant. 717 4th Avenue; 619/232-4440.

Terra: This warm, sophisticated restaurant in the heart of beautiful Hillcrest serves some simply mouthwatering dishes. To name a few we found in the autumn, pumpkin ravioli (with toasted hazelnuts and roasted corn cream), wasabi-crusted portabella mushroom (over rice noodles with tomato-ginger broth), and honey-roasted chicken (on pearl barley risotto). If you're more into your meat, try the filet mignon or the braised lamb shank (with Chilean red wine sauce and root vegetable purée). This upscale restaurant doesn't forget your canine companion. Indeed not. In fact, Terra has teamed up with the Original Paw Pleasers pet bakery to provide dogs some lip-licking choices from their very own menu. You may want to try the Puppy Pizza, followed by a carob-dipped pig's ear (advertised as "same great taste, no hair or veins!"). Dogs can dine alfresco at the lovely patio. (At night, you wouldn't even see the veins anyway.) 3900 Vermont Street; 619/293-7088.

Trattoria La Strada: Enjoy a delicious meal outside with your pooch at this classy Gaslamp Quarter restaurant. If you like northern Italian cuisine, or just plain pizza, you'll love it here. 702 5th Avenue; 619/239-3400.

PLACES TO STAY

Beach Haven Inn: Dogs have to be itsy-bitsy angels on their best behavior to stay here—25 pounds is the limit and they have to be "well behaved and well trained." Plus they can't stay here June 15–September 15. Cheez! This picky hotel is in the Pacific Beach area. Rates are $85–130. Dogs are $10 extra. 4740 Mission Boulevard 92109; 858/272-3812 or 800/831-6323.

Best Western Lamplighter Inn and Suites: If you and the pooch like your lodgings peaceful and palmy with plenty of flowering plants and trees, the Lamplighter is for you. The rooms are attractive, too. Suites have a breakfast bar and full kitchen. Some have a separate living area. Rates are $69–165. Dogs are $10 extra. (The dog-friendly folks here call it "pet rent.") 6474 El Cajon Boulevard 92115; 619/582-3088 or 800/545-0778; www.lamplighter-inn.com.

The Bristol Hotel: This is one of the cooler hotels to bring a canine in San Diego. It's contemporary, it's hip, it's a happenin' place. The lobby is jazzy, and the rooms are sleek, colorful, and comfortable. Stay here and you get use of a fluffy terry robe. Your dog will have to be content with her coat. Rates are $190–280. Dogs are restricted to 50 pounds or under, and cost $50 for the length of your stay. (If you have the max-sized dog, that's a buck a pound.)

1055 1st Avenue 92101; 619/232-6141; 800/662-4477; www.thebristolsandiego.com.

Campland on the Bay: This is a popular place: Reservations can be made up to two years ahead of time! And if you want a coveted waterfront site, you'd better reserve early or hope for a cancellation. Up to three well-behaved dogs who are not pit bulls or rotties (sorry guys) can stay at any site. Well-bred mutts like the "Super Site," an enclosed beachfront site with its own whirlpool tub, barbecue, phone, washer and dryer, and lots of other amenities you'd never think of having to yourself at a campground. Site rates range from $35 for basic tent and RV sites to $120 for bayfront sites with all the fixin's. Dogs are $3 extra. 2211 Pacific Beach Drive 92109; 858/581-4260 or 800/422-9386; www.campland.com.

Casitas del Mar: This large, attractive duplex vacation rental is a quick two-minute walk to Pacific Beach in the north part of San Diego, bordering La Jolla. The size limit for dogs here is 50 pounds, so if you have a bigger pooch and want to stay in the neighborhood, try the Hohe House (see below). Casitas del Mar has separate upstairs and downstairs units, each with two bedrooms and two baths. If you like sunsets over the ocean, choose the upstairs unit, "El Cielo." Rates are $1,900–2,600 weekly, with seasonal specials available. Dogs are $100 extra. You'll get the address once you make the reservation. 619/200-1242; www.casitasdelmar.com.

Crown Point View Suite-Hotel: If you want to feel right at home while staying in a dog-friendly part of town, try the apartments/hotel rooms here. Crown Point is a mere five-minute walk from Mission Bay Park. Rates are $125–205. Dogs are $75 extra for the duration of their stay. 4088 Crown Point Drive 92109; 858/272-0676 or 800/338-3331; www.crownpoint-view.com.

Doubletree Hotel San Diego/Mission Valley: Dogs need to stay on the hotel's third or fourth floor. At least you won't be paying for a penthouse. Rates are $109–230. Dogs are $50 for the length of their stay. 7450 Hazard Center Drive 92108; 619/297-5466.

The Hohe House: This two-bedroom, two-bath oceanview vacation rental (Hoy, not Hoe-Hee, as I was saying until Steven Hohe himself informed me of my errant ways) comes with everything you need for a fun beachside vacation, including bikes, boogey boards, beach chairs, beach towels, beach umbrellas, and coolers. It's a two-minute walk to Pacific Beach and a bone's throw from La Jolla. Dogs are welcome here as long as they're under 80 pounds. The well-appointed house is usually rented by the week, for $1,275–1,875. There's a $350 security deposit and an $85 cleaning fee. Dogs are $10 extra daily. Off-season there's a four-night minimum at $200 nightly. Next to the house itself is a very cozy little studio efficiency, where only tiny dogs—20 pounds maximum—are allowed. The Hohe Guest Studio rents for $110–130 a night, with a two-night minimum. You'll get the Hohe address when you make your reservation; 858/273-0324; www.10kvacationrentals.com/hohe/hohehouse.

Holiday Inn on the Bay: As long as you're willing to sign a contract stating that you will accept responsibility for any damage your dog may do and that you won't leave him alone in your room, you and your dog are welcome here. (Oh, and you have to pay a one-time $25 dog fee and a $100 deposit.) But don't try to sneak off and leave the pooch alone—the hotel will call the pound folks, who will arrive pretty quickly since they're just across the street. How convenient. Rates are $159–209. 1355 North Harbor Drive 92101; 619/232-3861.

Horton Grand Hotel: Oh, this grand, exquisite, 1880s-era Gaslamp Quarter hotel is as gorgeous and sumptuous as they come. But since it allows only the most itsy-bitsy of dogs (under 15 pounds), I'm not going to go into more detail here. (Horse-sized Jake won't let me.) Rates are $119–209. Dog-ettes are $100 for the length of their stay. 311 Island Avenue 92101; 619/544-1886 or 800/542-1886; www.hortongrand.com.

Ocean Villa Inn: Here's a dog's dream come true: The adored, famed, revered, worshipped Dog Beach is right next door to this motel! It doesn't get any more convenient than this. Rates are $69–159. Dogs are $25 extra (for up to two pets) for the length of their stay, and require a $100 deposit. 5142 West Point Loma Boulevard 92107; 619/224-3481 or 800/759-0012; www.oceanvillainn.com.

Old Town Inn: The rooms at this Spanish-style motel are spacious but standard issue. The palms surrounding the inn make for a pretty picture. Rates are $60–145. Dogs are $10 extra. 4444 Pacific Highway 92110; 619/260-8024 or 800/643-3025.

Residence Inn San Diego Central: Stay at studios, apartments, or penthouse suites at this attractive lodging designed for travelers who want more than a bed in their hotel room. All rooms come with kitchens. Rate are $109–189. Extended stays get discounted rates. Dogs are $75 for the length of their stay. 5400 Kearny Mesa Road 92111; 858/552-9100; www.residenceinn.com.

San Diego Marriott Hotel and Marina: The people who work at this lovely waterfront Marriott have a great attitude about large dogs. Not only do they tolerate them, but they're happy to see them. "The size doesn't matter. It's often the small ones that bark a lot anyway," says one hotelier. (Smart man.) This Marriott is on the water, right next to the dog-unfriendly Seaport Village. At least the views of the bay are to bark about—er, to write home about. The humans in your party can enjoy the heated outdoor pools, and the sauna, whirlpool, and exercise room. If you like the boating life, you and your dog can rent a boat from a boat-rental company on the property and have a great day on San Diego Bay. (See the Diversion Whatever Floats Your Boat.) It's one of the more expensive Marriotts we've come across. Rates are $350–390. 333 West Harbor Drive 92101; 619/234-1500.

San Diego Marriott Mission Valley: This one's just a ball's throw from San Diego's Jack Murphy Stadium, not that it matters to your dog. Rates are $129–189. There's a $200 dog deposit, and a $50 nonrefundable postdog-visit room-cleaning fee. 8757 Rio San Diego Drive 92108; 619/692-3800; www .marriott.com.

Staybridge Suites by Holiday Inn: Rates are $95–205. Dogs cost $75 for the length of your stay. 6639 Mira Mesa Boulevard 92121; 858/453-5343.

Vagabond Inn: This one's in the Mission Valley area. Rates are $69–99. Dogs are $10 extra. 625 Hotel Circle South 92108; 619/297-1691.

Westin Horton Plaza: It's modern, it's chic, it's a cool place to stay with a dog who's not too big. (Dogs need to be under 40 pounds.) Lucky dog guests will get use of a Heavenly Dog Bed (a smaller version of the Heavenly Bed human guests rave about) and bowls for water and food. "We like to see dog guests come in," says a friendly front-desk worker. "They are so much fun." This large, upscale hotel is downtown, right next to the famed Horton Plaza shopping center. Rates are $165–225. 910 Broadway Circle 92101; www.starwood.com/westin; 619/239-2200.

La Mesa

PARKS, BEACHES, AND RECREATION AREAS

39 Harry Griffen Park

😺😺😺 (See San Diego County map on page 832)

This grassy, 53-acre park is home to a pleasant little reservoir and some good fields for a leashed dog's enjoyment. For even better exercise, try the jogging path here. Dogs like it almost as much as they like the shaded picnic area.

The park is in the easternmost section of the city, on the border of El Cajon. The main entrance is on Milden Street, in back of Grossmont High School. 858/463-6611.

Coronado

Folks traveling with dogs aren't allowed to take the ferry to this islandlike destination across the San Diego Bay. But a graceful 2.2-mile bridge will get you there just as fast—which is the speed your dog will want to go when she learns she can run off leash at one of the beaches here.

PARKS, BEACHES, AND RECREATION AREAS

40 Coronado City Beach/Dog Beach

😺😺😺😺🐾 (See San Diego County map on page 832)

The westernmost part of this beach is a nude beach for dogs, where they can strip off their leashes and revel in their birthday furs. And since few people know about it, even the shyest dog will feel at home running around flaunting her more natural self.

DIVERSION

Venice, Shmenice: When you and your dog share a private gondola that takes you through Coronado Cays's scenic canals and waterways, you'll feel almost as if you've been transported to Italy's famed land of canals. The only difference is that instead of your gondolier singing, he'll use a CD player for the Italian tunes. Oh, and there's no ancient architecture. And no magnificent old-world charm. OK, it may not be just like Italy, but it's still a wonderful excursion, and the gondolas—which are very sizeable and water-way-worthy—are pretty much guaranteed not to tip over, even if your dog gets a case of the wiggles.

The **Gondola Company** can arrange all kinds of special cruises, some featuring a brunch or dinner excursion. The most popular, the basic Passport Cruise, lasts one hour, and includes an hors d'oeuvre or dessert plate. Bring your own vino or bubbly; the gondolier provides the wine glasses and an ice bucket. You'll also get use of a blanket. The Passport Cruise is $70 for two people and a dog. (You can invite your friends for $15 extra each. The boat can hold up to six passengers.) Cruises are offered 11 A.M.–midnight. The Gondola Company is right next to the ultra dog-friendly Loews Coronado Bay Resort, at 4000 Coronado Bay Road; 619/429-6317; www.gondolacompany.com.

As long as your dog is under voice control, she can be leashless at a small segment of this little beach. Your dog has only a few hundred feet of shoreline to run along, but the area between the beach border and the water is fairly wide.

The off-leash section is marked by signs and runs along Ocean Boulevard from around the foot of Sunset Park (on Ocean Drive) to the border of the U.S. Naval Station. You'll see the doggy litter bags. (Not far down the street is a hose-off station, should you not want to go home with sandy paws.) From the bridge, continue straight. In a few blocks, turn left on Orange Avenue and drive through town all the way down to the traffic circle. Go around the circle to Loma Avenue and follow it south about a block to Ocean Boulevard. Drive northwest a few blocks and park on the street around Sunset Park. 619/522-7380.

41 Coronado Tidelands Regional Park

🐾🐾🐾 (See San Diego County map on page 832)

Situated on San Diego Bay just north of the toll plaza, this is the largest of Coronado's parks and it's got a little of everything. From manicured golf course–like lawns to playing fields, walking paths, and terrific views of San

Diego, the park suits the needs of just about any dog. There's even a small beach here. Dogs must be leashed, though, so there's no swimming back to San Diego!

After crossing the bridge, take your first right onto Glorietta Boulevard. Go right again into the park on Mullinix Drive. 619/686-6225.

PLACES TO EAT

Bay Books Cafe: Besides coffees, teas, and pastries, this place sells books. Make sure you have a pooch-sitter along to hang out at the outdoor tables with your dog while you scope out the selections inside. 1029 Orange Avenue; 619/435-0070.

Cafe 1134: Pooches who keep you company at these outdoor tables while you dine on sandwiches and coffee are lucky dogs indeed: The staff here provides dog biscuits and a water bowl for your fine furry friend. 1134 Orange Avenue; 619/437-1134.

Coronado Bakery: Besides the usual cakes and muffins, this place serves cappuccino and other specialty coffee drinks. You and your dog are welcome to partake in these treats at the outdoor seating. 1206 Orange Avenue; 619/435-9272.

Crown Bistro: The breakfasts here have won "best breakfast"–type awards many years in a row. It's a mighty convenient place to dine if you're staying at the Crown City Inn (below), since it's part of the inn's property. Dine with your very good doggy on scrumptious California-style food at the bistro's six small shaded patio tables. This is an intimate place, and at times when it's busy, you may be asked to come back with your dog when there's a little more space. The folks here are really friendly to dogs, and they even provide water to thirsty pooches, but the space is small enough that the owners ask patrons with pooches to call ahead to see if it's a good time to come. Any size well-behaved dog is welcome, pending adequate space. Regulars here include a 170-pound rottweiler and a 15-pound miniature dachshund. 520 Orange Avenue; 619/435-3678.

Deli by the Bay: Stop and smell the cool ocean breezes with your dog as you eat on the patio. The deli has tasty soups, sandwiches, and salads. 1201 1st Street; 619/437-1006.

Rhinoceros Cafe and Grill: It's tables galore at the shaded sidewalk area here. That means you and the pooch will have plenty of places to choose from when dining on fresh fish, chicken, steak, and pasta dishes. 1166 Orange Avenue; 619/435-2121.

Viva Nova: The folks at this restaurant love dogs. The vegetarian cuisine includes hot soups and chili, which you can eat at the outdoor tables. There's also a juice bar and a health-food store that stocks all-natural pet supplies. 1138 Orange Avenue; 619/435-2124.

PLACES TO STAY

Coronado Victorian House: In this gorgeous 1894 Victorian, all the beds in the seven bedrooms are from the 1800s and are topped with featherbed mattresses. You'll feel as though you're sleeping on a very elegant cloud. The rooms at this bed-and-breakfast all have private bathrooms (some with claw-foot tubs) and are beautifully furnished, reflecting the tastes of Bonni Marie, the inn's dog-loving owner. Bonni Marie will proudly tell you about her three "monkeys," her trio of rescued Cairn terriers. She's a most friendly innkeeper. She may even get you out on the dance floor. It's not what you think; Bonni Marie is a dance instructor. Many guests here opt for couples dance lessons in her large dance studio here. Dance lessons come in mighty handy for burning off at least part of the inn's bountiful breakfast.

Sadly for dogs who weigh more than a large bag of dog food, 40 pounds is the size limit for pooches here. Don't be surprised when Bonni Marie also inquires about your dog's temperament when you call for reservations. "I just want to make sure everyone will be happy," she says.

Rates are $250–500 nightly, with a two-night minimum stay. Dogs are $25 for the length of their stay. An important piece of information to know when you make your reservation: Your reservation is noncancelable, and your fee is nonrefundable. Ouch! 619/435-2200 or 888/299-2822; www.coronadovictorianhouse.com.

Crown City Inn: This sweet little hotel is as welcoming for dogs as it is for humans. People get free use of bicycles, and iced tea/hot chocolate and cookies every afternoon. Dogs get a food mat, water bowl, a treat bag with a toy, and info on pet sitters and dog-friendly parks and eateries. Everyone who comes here is happy. Your room comes with a fridge and microwave, but with the Crown Bistro restaurant (see above) so close to your room, you may want to give your kitchenette skills a break. Rates are $100–240. Dogs are $8–25. 520 Orange Avenue 92118; 619/435-3116; www.crowncityinn.com.

Loews Coronado Bay Resort: Prepare to be impressed. This modern, luxurious hotel presides over a 15-acre peninsula, with the Pacific on one side and San Diego Bay on the other. The rooms are crisp and clean, yet super-comfy, with great waterfront views. The gardens are gorgeous, and the palm-lined three-pool area is to drool for (although no drool or dogs are allowed in the pools; pooches can take their dog paddle to the nearby Coronado City Beach/Dog Beach). If you like the sporting life, you can play tennis at the hotel's three lighted courts or rent a boat and set sail on the bay, with your dog as first mate. (See the Diversion Whatever Floats Your Boat in the San Diego section.) Or you and your dog can hire a gondola for an enchanting cruise through the Coronado Cays. (See the Diversion Venice, Shmenice.)

Speaking of dogs, the treatment they get here is nothing short of Red Carpet, thanks to Loews' Very Important Pet Program. Your dog will be welcome with a note from the hotel's general manager. It includes a list of nearby dog-friendly locales, as well as groomers, pet shops, and vets. In your room you'll find food and water bowls, treats, and toys. A doggy room-service menu is also available, with items that sound so good you might be tempted to share them. If you forgot a leash or your pet's bed, you can borrow these from the concierge's "Did You Forget" closet. Dog-walking and pet-sitting can be arranged if the staff isn't too busy. If you opt for a pet-sitter, you'll get a Puppy Pager, which allows hotel staff to contact you in case of emergency.

Rates are $199–515. 4000 Coronado Bay Road 92118; 619/424-4000; www.loewshotels.com.

SOUTH INLAND COUNTIES

872

GULP!

CHAPTER 55

Inyo County

The elevation: As low as 282 feet below sea level. Some of the hot spots to visit: Funeral Mountains. Chloride City. Death Valley. Furnace Creek.

It may sound like pure hell, but a visit to this county during the cooler months of the year actually might be one of the most interesting adventures you and your dog share in California.

Inyo County has an incredible variety of landscapes. The desert contains the lowest land in the United States, at 282 feet below sea level. The adjacent Sierra Nevada and the silver, knifelike pinnacles of towering Mt. Whitney make a strong contrast. In fact, Mt. Whitney, with its peak at 14,494 feet, is the highest point in the contiguous United States. Because its sheer eastern wall rises out of the low desert landscape of the Owens Valley, the effect is especially dramatic.

But Mt. Whitney is a place you just want to observe with your dog. First of all, while many areas of Inyo National Forest are enchanting places to take a dog, this climb is very difficult, and no pooch should be asked to perform such feats. But even more important, dogs aren't allowed anywhere near the mountain's peak. It happens to be in Sequoia National Park, which pretty

PICK OF THE LITTER—INYO COUNTY

BEST HUGE PARK
Death Valley National Park (page 875)

PARK WITH OLDEST LIVING THINGS ON EARTH
Ancient Bristlecone Pine Forest, Big Pine (page 878)

BEST PLACE TO PRETEND YOU'RE IN A WESTERN
Alabama Hills, Lone Pine (page 879)

BEST PLACES TO STAY
Glacier Lodge, Big Pine (page 878)
Stove Pipe Wells Village, Death Valley (page 879)

BEST PLACE TO WATCH A WESTERN
Lone Pine Film Festival, Lone Pine (page 880)

much bans dogs. Rangers tell me that a few avid, sicko climbers have left their dogs behind (tied up) at the national forest border when they discovered no dogs were allowed at the peak. Stick with the lower elevations here.

In spring, wildflowers are everywhere. The sight of towering mountains against flowering desert makes dogs sniff the air in heavenly awe.

The canine and human folks who inhabit these areas are every bit as colorful as the desert springtime. During my research, I received a letter from Martha Watkins of the Death Valley Chamber of Commerce. It could have been from Mark Twain.

She wrote, "The only mayors of Shoshone and Tecopa have been dogs. B. J. was the mayor of Tecopa for many years. He was a small wirehaired terrier mix who really had a way with (human) women. I had the dubious distinction of running him over. My name was mud for a long time. No dog since B. J. has reached his stature.

"Shoshone's mayor is a small wiener-and-Doberman mix named Lifter. You can guess where his name came from. He's very macho."

Watkins still occasionally gets the evil eye from women who were seduced by B. J.'s scruffy looks. She told me that the late mayor lived with one of "our very hard-rock miners. Talk about a big wheel. B. J. would get up in the morning and sit by the side of the road until someone gave him a ride into town. He'd hang out at the bar all day. If he saw a girl with bare shoulders sitting in a booth by herself, he'd jump in the adjoining booth and start kissing her shoulders."

B. J.'s charms won him the unofficial vote as mayor of this small Death Valley town. Alas, he met Death Valley face-to-face under Watkins's tire on his barhopping rounds one fateful day. But his spirit lives on in this dog-lovin' land.

Warning: Don't bring your dog to the desert areas of the county in the summer or early fall. Dogs who aren't accustomed to the heat may not survive the average daily temperatures of 116°F, not to mention the perilously hot ground. It's not much fun for most humans, either.

NATIONAL FORESTS

The National Forests and Wilderness Areas resource at the back of this book has important information and safety tips on visiting national forests with your dog and has more information on the Inyo National Forest.

Inyo National Forest
😺😺😺😺🐾

Dogs love the 28,000-acre Ancient Bristlecone Pine Forest, part of this national forest northeast of Big Pine. The gnarled pines that look like living driftwood are thought to be the world's oldest living trees—and are probably the oldest living things on Earth! Tell your boy dog to be respectful of these aged arboreal wonders. Temperatures here are cooler than in much of the surrounding area because of the 10,000-foot elevation.

NATIONAL PARKS

Death Valley National Park
😺😺😺😺

What's in a name? When I first thought about taking Joe to Death Valley, I pictured him ending up as a pile of bones in the sand while coyotes bayed and vultures licked their beaks. Taking a dog to Death Valley seemed like something rather, well, mean.

But not so! As long as you stay away during the grueling months before, during, and after summer (April–September), you and your dog could have some of your best adventures ever. Dogs must be leashed, but it's for their own good. There are some hungry coyotes here, and the heat of the sun can surprise you even during the cooler months. It's best to have your pooch close at hand.

This 3.2-million-acre park is new in name only. It encompasses the former Death Valley National Monument, Eureka Sand Dunes National Natural Landmark, and several other federally run natural areas. In 1994, the Desert Protection Act merged these areas into one big, full-fledged national park. In most areas, that doesn't affect dog rules. But where dogs were once permitted to run around off leash at Bureau of Land Management lands here, they have to obey the new leash rules. And sadly, at the Eureka Sand Dunes area, whose centerpiece is a 700-foot-high mountain of sand, dogs can no longer cavort about on the dunes at all. It's a howling shame.

Fortunately, although dogs aren't permitted on trails at Death Valley, there are so few trails that it won't matter to you. What matters is that they're allowed to hike at your side on the more than 500 miles of roadway that stretch from one landscape to another within Death Valley. Most of these roads are unpaved and barely get used by vehicles, so chances are you can get plenty of pure desert solitude with pure desert air.

Keep in mind that dogs also aren't supposed to wander far off the road into backcountry. About 100 yards is the limit. Remember that with air as clean and land as flat as this, rangers are omniscient. Watch yourselves, because they are sure to be watching as well.

You'll see some of the most fascinating geologic formations on Earth here. Of course, most of the time it won't look like you're even on Earth, but don't let that bother you. The park's otherworldly nature is one of its charms. Much of the park is below sea level. The lowest point in the United States is here, in Badwater Basin. Within the park are elevations from 282 feet below sea level to 11,049 feet above sea level. Betwixt and between, you'll find vast salt flats, endless sand ridges, huge rocks, and twisting mountainsides.

When you get to the visitor center, pick up brochures on the history and geology of the place and decide which parts of Death Valley you and your dog would enjoy most. The park has nine campgrounds, six of which are open all year. There are more than 1,500 campsites available on a first-come, first-served basis. Fees range from free to $16.

The entry fee for the park is $10 per carload, good for visits of up to a week. Being that the park is bigger than the state of Connecticut, there are many spots where you can enter it. To get to the main visitor center from U.S. 395, take either Highway 136 or Highway 190 east. Highway 136 will join Highway 190. From U.S. 395, the drive is a little more than 100 miles. Follow Highway 190 through all its confusing turns and you can't miss it. Even in the cooler months of the year, it's a good idea to bring extra water, just in case you break down and the temperature decides to do one of its soaring routines. 760/786-2331.

Bishop

Set between the state's two highest mountain ranges, Bishop has become the hub of this recreational wonderland. It's a small, laid-back town with only one thing that peeves pooches: Dogs are banned from the only city park here.

PARKS, BEACHES, AND RECREATION AREAS

■ Pleasant Valley County Park

😾 😾 😾 (See Inyo County map on page 872)

This park has the long, narrow Pleasant Valley Reservoir as its centerpiece. The reservoir is created by the Owens River, and fishing here is pretty hot (thanks in part to planted trout). Leashed dogs are allowed to cheer at your side as you catch supper from shore.

For dogs who aren't fishing fans, try the hiking trail on the reservoir's east side. The big rocky bluffs here are interesting, but the surrounding mountains topped with snow year-round are really impressive. However, dogs don't seem to care much for the visuals. Something about this place keeps their flaring nostrils pressed firmly to the ground. Since leashes are the law, you may feel some tugging when your dog decides to try to track one of these enticing smells.

There are 200 campsites, but they're pretty far from the lake. Sites are $10. Reservations are not necessary. Take U.S. 395 about seven miles north of Bishop, and then turn north on Pleasant Valley Road and drive about 1.5 miles to the lake. 760/878-0272.

PLACES TO EAT

Manor Market: This grocery store is home to some pretty good grub, including hot chicken and soup. There are a few outdoor tables in the warmer months. 3100 West Line Street; 760/873-4296.

PLACES TO STAY

Comfort Inn: This isn't just your average Comfort Inn. It's a mighty dog-friendly Comfort Inn. Hannah Dog (a husky-shepherd mix) and her folks were nice enough to write to let me know that the owner adores dogs, and that she "cheerfully takes dogs of all sizes." I called the owner to confirm, and indeed she's a doggy person. "Sure, we take all good dogs," she said. "We've even had Saint Bernards." The place even has a fish-cleaning station. I guess the owner likes fish, too. Rates are $64–109. Dogs are $5 extra. 805 North Main Street 93514; 760/873-4284 or 800/576-4080.

Millpond Recreation Area: Dogs with human children in the family enjoy spending the night here, because little humans are allowed in the adjacent park. (Dogs aren't allowed there, though.) There's a playground, sports fields, tennis courts, a pond, and horseshoe pits. The campground itself is comfortable but not too exciting. There are 60 sites available. Dogs must be leashed. Fees are $16–19. From U.S. 395 about six miles north of town, take Ed Powers Road south. Go the equivalent of about three city blocks, and turn west on Sawmill Road. In about a half mile, you'll be at the park. The campground is open March–November. 760/873-5342.

Pleasant Valley County Park: See Pleasant Valley County Park, above, for camping information.

Rodeway Inn: Rates are $55–80. Dogs are $5 extra. 150 East Elm Street 93514; 760/873-3564.

Super 8 Motel: Rates are $60–150. Dogs are $10 extra. 535 South Main Street 93514; 760/872-1386.

Thunderbird Motel: Rates are $40–80. Dogs are $5 extra. 190 West Pine Street 93514; 760/873-4215.

Vagabond Inn: This one comes with its own fish-cleaning facilities and a freezer. If you and your dog have a successful day angling, this might be the place for you. Rates are $90–110. Pooches are $5 extra. 1030 North Main Street 93514; 760/873-6351.

Big Pine

PARKS, BEACHES, AND RECREATION AREAS

2 Ancient Bristlecone Pine Forest

🐾🐾🐾 (See Inyo County map on page 872)

This remarkable area is in Inyo National Forest (see the National Forest section at the beginning of the chapter for details), about 25 miles northeast of Big Pine.

There's no fee for campsites. Winter usually makes the access roads impassable, but the forest is accessible early June–late October. From U.S. 395 in Big Pine, take Highway 168 east about 15 miles to White Mountain Road. Turn left, and in another 10 miles you'll come to the south end of the forest. 760/873-2400.

PLACES TO STAY

Ancient Bristlecone Pine Forest: See Ancient Bristlecone Pine Forest, above, for camping information.

Big Pine Motel: Your dog can't weigh more than 35 pounds if he's going to stay here. Rates are $35–75. Dogs are $4 extra. 370 South Main Street 93513; 760/938-2282.

Glacier Lodge: The main lodge here, built in 1917, burned down a few years ago. It will soon be rebuilt, and when it is, it's going to be an intriguing modern building, with fascinating architectural touches such as sleeping windows that are deep enough for a sleeping bag to fit into. Meanwhile, dogs and their people are welcome to stay at the mountain lodge's 10 rustic housekeeping cabins. You're surrounded by all kinds of recreational opportunities here, from fishing to hiking miles and miles of trails with your furry friend. Rates are $80–95. Dogs are $15 extra. The lodge is 11 miles west of Highway 395. The mailing address (there's really no street address) is P.O. Box 370 93513; 760/938-2837; www.sonic.net/~kwofford/glacier-lodge.

Death Valley

PLACES TO STAY

Stove Pipe Wells Village: Set on 100 acres of Death Valley National Park, this sprawling, rustic resort is mighty dog-friendly. Maggie the Wonder Dog, the canine companion of San Francisco's Kim Wonderly, wrote to us to tell us she gives it two paws up. You and your leashed dog are free to peruse the village's 100 acres and beyond. The lodging is a mere 10-minute walk from the most-photographed sand dunes in the world—if you love *Lawrence of Arabia*, you can pull a Peter O'Toole here and run around in your white robe. Rates for the hotel/motel are $59–99. Dogs require a $20 deposit, and your room may be checked for doggy damage before you leave. There's no street address. For information, write Stove Pipe Wells Village 92328; 760/786-2387; www.stovepipewells.com.

Lone Pine

This is a one-stoplight town—the gateway to Mt. Whitney. As Marilyn, an enthusiastic native who works at the Chamber of Commerce, put it: "We've got a real pretty town, real Western."

And real Westerns are what they've been shooting here for decades. See the Alabama Hills description below for details on the showbiz history of this area. This place is a must-visit location for dogs and their people.

PARKS, BEACHES, AND RECREATION AREAS

🖪 Alabama Hills

😃😃😃😃🐾 (See Inyo County map on page 872)

Pardner, if you like Western films and TV shows, you're gonna love this place. For more than 70 years, Hollywood has used Lone Pine's unique scenery in almost 300 films and countless TV shows.

This is where the *Lone Ranger* ambush was first filmed, where Roy Rogers found Trigger, and *Bonanza* became a bonanza. Giants such as Gene Autry, Roy Rogers, Hopalong Cassidy, Humphrey Bogart, Cary Grant, Gregory Peck, Spencer Tracy, and Clint Eastwood did their big scenes here. In fact, this is where Roy Rogers and Robert Mitchum filmed their first features.

Put a bandanna on your four-legged varmint and have a rip-roaring time exploring the rock formations, canyons, and barren flats that are the real stars here. Some photo markers are placed in the area showing which famous scenes were shot where. It's a real education for you and your dog. Be really careful where and if you allow your dog to be leashless, because dogs and the cars that wind around the park don't mix.

DOG-EAR YOUR CALENDAR

Leashed dogs are welcome to attend all the outdoor segments of the three-day **Lone Pine Film Festival** celebrating the myriad Western flicks shot in the nearby Alabama Hills. Some of the most famous old cowboys and cowgals gather during this three-day festival, which is held on the second weekend of October, to talk with fans and even reenact a scene or two. If your dog is lucky, maybe he'll get to shake paws with one of the greats. See www.lonepinefilmfestival.org or call 760/876-9103 for information on this year's event.

From U.S. 395, take the Whitney Portal Road about 2.5 miles west of Lone Pine and you'll find yourself on Movie Road. That's where your trek through movieland begins. Don't forget to bring a camera. 760/872-5000.

4 Diaz Lake

🐾🐾🐾 (See Inyo County map on page 872)

This small lake is set under the watchful eye of the Sierra Nevada and Mt. Whitney, and it really bustles in the summer. Leashed dogs can hike around the 86-acre lake with you and hang out while you catch bass, bluegill, or trout.

Camping here costs $8. It's a convenient place to spend the night, since it's just off U.S. 395, two miles south of Lone Pine. 760/878-0272.

PLACES TO STAY

Diaz Lake: See Diaz Lake, above, for camping information.

Dow Villa Motel: Dogs can stay in smoking rooms only, but the managers like dogs and will make them feel at home. Rates are $82–113. Dogs require a $50 deposit against dog deposits, if ya know what I mean. 310 South Main Street 93545; 760/876-5521; www.dowvillamotel.com.

National 9 Trails Motel: Small pets only, please. Rates are $39–99. Dogs are $10 extra. 633 South Main Street 93545; 760/876-5555.

Little Lake

PARKS, BEACHES, AND RECREATION AREAS

5 Fossil Falls

🐾🐾🐾 (See Inyo County map on page 872)

Pick up a brochure and you'll learn all about the intriguing history and geology behind what caused the fossilized falls to form. Dogs don't usually give a hoot for such subjects, but they do seem interested in the bumpy lava covering the ground on your way from the parking lot to the falls. Joe tried to dig at it, but we discouraged this terrier behavior. It's not every day a volcano leaves behind such amazing tracks. Beware of sharp rocks underfoot. Your shoes may not mind, but your dog's paws may.

From about three miles north of Little Lake on U.S. 395, turn east onto Cinder Cone Road (watch for the cinder cone) and follow it to the park. The parking lot is about 1.5 miles from the highway. Your drive will take you through a large volcanic field, which is almost as interesting as the fossilized falls themselves. 760/384-5400.

Tecopa

The population is 99 as of a recent census. The neighboring community of Shoshone has a whopping 106 residents. These are fairly big numbers when you get this deep into the desert. (See the introduction of this chapter for the tale of the mutty mayors of these tiny towns.)

PARKS, BEACHES, AND RECREATION AREAS

⑥ Tecopa Hot Springs County Park

🐾🐾🐾 (See Inyo County map on page 872)

The Paiute Indians used to bring their lame and sick ancestors to bathe in the hot mineral springs here, and now people from all over the world come for a soak. The 107°F waters are supposed to help alleviate the pain of arthritis, rheumatism, and other bodily woes.

While dogs can't take a dip, they are allowed to roam the 40-acre park with you. Switch off hanging out with the dog with a friend as you take turns rejuvenating yourselves in the baths.

Most of the park is taken up by a large, 250-site campground. Sites are $10–14. Many are available on a first-come, first-served basis, but you can also make reservations if that makes you feel better about driving all the way out here. The bathing is free. Make sure you don't come with your dog in the hot months. The temperature can climb to 118°F in some summer months, and that's hotter than the mineral baths.

From Death Valley Junction (Highways 190 and 127), follow the road about 36 miles to the park. 760/852-4264.

PLACES TO STAY

Tecopa Hot Springs County Park: See Tecopa Hot Springs County Park, above, for camping information.

CHAPTER 56

San Bernardino County

This is the Texas of California. It's just plain big. In fact, it's the biggest county in the nation, weighing in at more than 20,000 square miles.

That means you'll find a lot of variety here. This is where dogs can do just about everything they ever imagined a dog could do. They can ride the rails through a ghost town, roam around off leash on millions of acres of land, herd goats in Chino, take a horse-and-buggy ride in Big Bear, ride a rented boat around Big Bear Lake, and stay in some of the most wonderful cabins and resorts this side of the Rockies.

Try to visit the San Bernardino Mountains at sunset, when occasionally they play an optical trick. A few of the mountains will turn purplish pink, while others stay the same sandy brown and forest green. Then everything fades into a surreal orange mist. For people, it's a stunning sight. If dogs really do have black-and-white vision, they're probably not quite so thrilled.

PICK OF THE LITTER—SAN BERNARDINO COUNTY

BEST OFF-LEASH HIKING
San Bernardino National Forest (page 884)
Rainbow Basin Natural Area, Barstow (page 886)
Stoddard Valley Open Area, Barstow (page 887)

BEST DOG PARK
Wildwood Dog Park, San Bernardino (page 902)

MOST DOG-FRIENDLY PLACES TO STAY
Cienaga Creek Ranch Mountain Cottages, Big Bear Lake (page 897)
Eagle's Nest Bed and Breakfast Lodge, Big Bear Lake (page 898)
Arrowhead Tree Top Lodge, Lake Arrowhead (page 903)
Rimrock Ranch Cabins, Pioneertown (page 911)

MOST WELCOMING STORE
Big Dogs Sportswear, Lake Arrowhead (page 904)

BEST LIVE "THEATER"
Pioneertown Posse's Old West skits, Pioneertown (page 910)

NATIONAL FORESTS

The National Forests and Wilderness Areas resource at the back of this book has important information and safety tips on visiting national forests with your dog and has more information on the San Bernardino National Forest.

San Bernardino National Forest

Much of the southwest corner of San Bernardino County is San Bernardino National Forest land. So far, dogs are allowed off leash in most parts of the forest, except for several times when they meet up with state parks. (Dogs aren't allowed there even *on* leash.) Unfortunately, local national forest rangers are facing the question of whether off-leash rules are appropriate in the forest. Complaints about dogs running up to frightened humans or fighting with each other have led to this state of affairs. So make absolutely certain your dog is Mr., Mrs., or Ms. Obedience before taking off that leash.

On the way up to Big Bear Lake via Highway 38, you'll find numerous forest trailheads and picnic areas that make great rest stops on a long journey. (See the Big Bear Lake section in this chapter for more on this popular resort area.)

NATIONAL PARKS

Joshua Tree National Park

Although most of this 794,000-acre park is in Riverside County, Twentynine Palms is where you'll find the visitor center and the gateways to some of the most beautiful areas in the park.

This is amazing land, with striking granite formations rising around dramatic desert plants and wildlife. In spring, it becomes a showcase of brilliant wildflowers. The giant Joshua tree plants are in the higher western half, and they're definitely worth a visit.

Dogs can be walked on paved and dirt roads, but not on hiking trails. They're permitted to wander on leash up to 100 yards from the road, and there are plenty of small dirt roads where you'll be far from most traffic. Leashes are the law here, but they're also a very good idea because of critters such as mountain lions and bobcats. A bigger danger than those cats is actually the cactus. Dogs sometimes rub up against the prickly plants or try to bite them and end up with a major problem. One last warning: The ground here can get really toasty—sometimes too toasty for your dog's paws. If you wouldn't want to walk barefoot here, neither would your dog. Rangers report several cases of paw pad injury each year because of the hot ground. Come when it's cooler and you'll be better off.

There's a $10 entrance fee, and if you want to camp without water, it's $5. Otherwise, sites are $8–10. There are 492 sites available on a first-come, first-served basis. However, the 100 sites at Black Rock Canyon require reservations. Always bring lots of water on your hikes here, and make sure your dog gets her fill. It doesn't usually get nearly as hot as in other parts of the desert, but you don't want to take a chance. From I-10, exit at Highway 62 and drive northeast for about 39 miles to the town of Twentynine Palms. The visitor center is on Utah Trail, just south of the highway about a mile east of town. 760/367-5500.

Barstow

This is a mighty dog-friendly town. In fact, it's just the place for a bruised canine ego to go after stepping on one too many threadbare doggy welcome mats. The folks here generally like dogs at least as much as they like people.

PARKS, BEACHES, AND RECREATION AREAS

1 Rainbow Basin Natural Area

🐾🐾🐾🐾 🦮 (See San Bernardino County map on page 882)

If you or your dog like bones, faults, sediment deposits, or leash-free walks, don't miss this geological and anthropological wonder. Fossils of ancient animals are everywhere in the colorful sedimentary layers of the canyon walls (once a lake). Mastodons, camels, three-toed horses, rhinos, and dog-bears are among the animals whose remains have been discovered here. As you hike around, you'll be able to see insect fossils that are among the best-preserved in the world. You and your dog need to keep your paws off these fossils so they remain undisturbed for others to enjoy them.

The geology of the place is also fascinating. Rainbow Basin's sediment deposits are textbook examples of folds, faults, and other disturbances of the earth's crust. If you're studying geology in school, this is the place to visit if you want to get the big picture.

DIVERSION

Go West, Young Pup: How many dogs can say they watched an Old West shootout on a dusty saloon-packed street? How many can brag they rode aboard a train through a ghost town?

Your leashed dog can be that lucky dog, if you take her to **Calico Ghost Town.** Calico thrived during the 1880s silver boom, and you can still roam around silver mines and stroll along wooden sidewalks on Main Street.

If you're a fan of this era, spend the night. Camping costs $18–22. There are about 260 campsites available here. Reservations are recommended in spring and fall. Or rent one of the six cabins in town. They're not haunted, but the price is so low you'll howl for joy: $28 for up to four people. A $25 deposit is required.

Admission to Calico Ghost Town Regional Park is $6, $3 for children ages 6–15. Train rides are $2.50, $1.25 for children. Dawgs are a buck. From Barstow, drive about six miles east on I-15, and exit at Calico Ghost Town/Ghost Town Road. Drive north for three miles. When you see a yellow wagon, you'll know you're there. 760/254-2122; www.calico.com.

Unfortunately, your dog probably doesn't give a hoot about bones she can't eat and sediment she can't wallow in. She knows what's important—being able to be at your side, off leash, while you peruse the area. The Bureau of Land Management, which operates the park, has some of the most lenient, dog-friendly rules in the state for obedient pooches.

The best place to take an off-leash dog is any flat area where she won't have much chance of disturbing this national natural landmark. There are no developed paths or trails, but since the place is nearly devoid of trees and thick underbrush, it's easy to navigate a course almost anywhere here. Be aware that you may run across desert kit foxes and bobcats. If you can't control your dog with critters such as these around, keep her leashed. And make sure she goes nowhere near desert tortoises, the California state reptile (bet your dog didn't know that). Tortoises are easily traumatized, and contact with people or dogs could lead to their deaths.

For your pet's sake, don't visit in the summer. Our favorite time to hike here is in late autumn, when it's crisp but not freezing. Leashed dogs are allowed to camp with you at the 22-site Owl Canyon Campground (no hookups). The fee is $4 per vehicle. No reservations are necessary.

From Highway 58 in Barstow, drive 5.5 miles north on Fort Irwin Road and turn left on Fossil Bed Road. It's a rough dirt road, and it will seem like an eternity of bouncing before you reach your destination, but it's actually just three miles. 760/252-6060.

❷ Stoddard Valley Open Area

🐾🐾🐾🐾🐕 (See San Bernardino County map on page 882)

Is your dog tired of those five-acre parks where leashes are a must? Does she long for wide-open desert ranges where she can tear around without a care in the world (except rattlesnakes and their friends)?

This 52,000-acre parcel of land just southeast of Barstow could be the answer to her poochie prayers. Not only are there mountains and endless open areas, there are also plenty of fascinating rock formations for you and your dog to explore.

To enter at the northern end, where there's a campground, exit I-15 at Sidewinder Road and drive the only way the road takes you. The campground has no developed sites, and no reservations or permits are required. The public land here is interspersed with private land, but Bureau of Land Management folks say that unless an area is fenced off, posted, or developed, it's probably OK for hiking. 760/252-6060.

PLACES TO EAT

Foster's Freeze: 1580 West Main Street; 760/256-8842.

PLACES TO STAY

There's no shortage of dog-friendly lodgings in Barstow.

Best Motel: Rates are $30–40. 1281 East Main Street 92311; 760/256-6836.

Econo Lodge: Rates are $35–55. Dogs are $5 extra. 1230 East Main Street 92311; 760/256-2133.

Executive Inn: Rates are $27–35. Dogs are $5 extra. 1261 East Main Street 92311; 760/256-7581.

Gateway Motel: Rates are $36–55. Dogs are $10 extra. 1630 East Main Street 92311; 760/256-8931.

Quality Inn: The folks here really like dogs. But because of guests' allergies, you'll have to stay in a room designated for smokers. Rates are $50–110. 1520 East Main Street 92311; 760/256-6891.

Rainbow Basin Natural Area: See Rainbow Basin Natural Area, above, for camping information.

Stoddard Valley Open Area: See Stoddard Valley Open Area, above, for camping information.

Afton

PARKS, BEACHES, AND RECREATION AREAS

❸ Afton Canyon Natural Area

🐾🐾🐾🐾 (See San Bernardino County map on page 882)

Wow! Woof! How does 42,000 acres of land sound to you and your canine companion? If you don't demand lush green meadows to be part of your elysian ideal, this can be heaven on Earth.

Afton Canyon is one of only three places where the Mojave River flows above ground year-round, so not only has it attracted visitors throughout history, it's also a water dog's delight. If you don't expect fine fishing here, no one will be disappointed.

Keep in mind that hundreds of bird, mammal, and reptile species call Afton Canyon their home, or at least their migratory hotel. It's a great place for wildlife-watching, and you need to keep leashed.

Camping here isn't the prettiest, but it's comforting to know you're just a stone's throw from another day of off-leash adventures. Sites (there are no hookups) are $6. There are 22 sites available on a first-come, first-served basis.

Afton is about 40 miles east of Barstow. From I-15, exit at Afton Canyon Road and drive three miles south to the park. 760/252-6060.

PLACES TO STAY

Afton Canyon Natural Area: See Afton Canyon Natural Area, above, for camping information.

Needles

Named for the sharp peaks at the southern end of the valley, this Colorado River town is surrounded by some of the most fascinating desert landscapes in the world.

If all the wide-open territory near Needles makes you and your dog feel like insignificant specks in the universe, try a side trip to London Bridge, just down the road a bit in Lake Havasu City, Arizona. This is the same London Bridge that was sinking into the Thames River in 1962, until developers of this town bought it for $2.5 million and shipped it to the United States—granite block by granite block. Your dog can go back home and tell all his buddies that he visited London Bridge, and they'll be impressed (most of them think it's still in London). English springer spaniels get a misty, faraway look when they come here.

PARKS, BEACHES, AND RECREATION AREAS

🐾 Mojave National Preserve

🐾🐾🐾🐾 (See San Bernardino County map on page 882)

The next time your dog gives you one of those sideways glances that says, "I gotta get outta the city," you might want to consider spending a few days exploring a desert environment that seems to go on forever. It actually does go on forever, or at least for 1.5 million acres to the west and north of Needles, whichever comes first.

Within this gigantic swath of land are volcanic cinder cones, booming sand dunes, old mines, new mines, mysterious petroglyphs, and dramatic cliffs. If you're a newcomer to desert life, you'll find the wildflowers, cacti, and yucca fascinating.

Dogs must be leashed here, now that the once leash-free land has been transferred from the dog-loving Bureau of Land Management to the National Park Service. Fortunately, the Park Service designated it as a preserve rather than a park, so dogs are still allowed in many areas. They can join you for a jaunt along any of the many miles of old mining roads, but they're not permitted on the trails. And they're not allowed in the designated wilderness area unless they're hunting with you, and then they may hunt off leash. (Hunting just doesn't work well with leashes.)

Keep in mind that nearly 300 species of animals live here, including coyotes and Mojave green rattlesnakes. Since these rattlers are more aggressive than most other rattlers, and since dogs have been known to be a coyote delicacy, it's extra inspiration to keep your dog close at paw.

Camping ranges from no cost for wilderness camping to $12 for regular sites. Dogs must be leashed at the campgrounds. There are 65 campsites available on a first-come, first-served basis. The preserve can be entered at several points along I-40, and at several points along I-15. Call 760/733-4040 to find out which entrance would best suit your travel plans.

5 Moabi Regional Park/Park Moabi

🐾🐾🐾 (See San Bernardino County map on page 882)

If your dog likes the water, tell her that the Colorado River runs through this park. If she's a landlubber, let her know that most of the park is lawns and desert land. There's something for most tastes at this 1,025-acre county park, but it's not always the quietest place in the world. Anglers can become frustrated with all the personal watercraft and fast boats that cruise around here. To have the run of the lake, you can try renting a houseboat from the park's marina. It's loads of fun, and all your dog has to do to go for a swim is hop out the back door.

There's a $6-per-vehicle day-use fee. Camping at the 130 sites is $12–25 (the pricier sites are on the river). Dogs are $1 extra. The park is at the intersection of I-40 and Park Moabi Road. 760/326-3831.

PLACES TO EAT

Burger Hut: Sure, you can get traditional beef burgers, but vegetarians will be happy to know that the folks here also serve a mean veggie burger. 701 Broadway; 760/326-2342.

Jack-in-the-Box: It's so refreshing to find a dog-friendly link in a restaurant chain. This one allows pooches to dine at the 12 outdoor tables, and the staff will even supply your dog with water if you tell them he's thirsty. 221 J Street; 760/326-4746.

PLACES TO STAY

Best Western Colorado River Inn: Enjoy the hotel's heated indoor pool, and the sauna and small exercise room (without your dog, of course). Dogs have to stay in the smoking rooms here, which is convenient if your dog smokes. Rates are $63–70. Pooches pay a $25 deposit. 2271 West Broadway 92363; 760/326-4552.

Moabi Regional Park: See Moabi Regional Park, above, for camping information.

Mojave National Preserve: See Mojave National Preserve, above, for camping information.

River Valley Motor Lodge: If your dog is small and has short hair, the management here will be mighty accommodating. Otherwise, you'll find there's no room at the inn. Rates are $25–40. Dogs are $5 extra. 1707 West Broadway 92363; 760/326-3839.

Victorville

PARKS, BEACHES, AND RECREATION AREAS

6 Center Street Park

😾😾 (See San Bernardino County map on page 882)

While it's only a couple of blocks long, this park is Victorville's most attractive municipal park. It's full of trees, so there's plenty of shade and plenty of places for your leashed dog to sniff. And it's usually quiet, except when there's a ball game going on at one of the playing fields here.

Exit I-15 at Mojave Drive and go east a little more than a mile to Hesperia Road. The park is on your right. 760/955-5257.

7 Mojave Narrows Regional Park

😾😾😾 (See San Bernardino County map on page 882)

This 840-acre park is by far the largest park in the area. It's kind of triangular, bordered on the left by railroad tracks and on the right by the Mojave River. The rangers tell that to people hiking with dogs, lest they get a little lost in their eagerness to get back to nature.

There are plenty of fields here, but the best place for walking around with your leashed dog is the more forested part of the park. If you're an angler with a dog who likes to cheer you on as you cast for supper, you'll be happy to know there's fishing year-round for $3 per day.

Camping costs $10–17. Dogs are $1 extra. There are approximately 65 campsites available. Reservations are recommended, and there's a $2 reservation fee. The park's day-use fee is $3 per vehicle, $1 per dog. From I-15, take the Bear Valley Cutoff exit and drive east for five miles. When you come to the railroad track overpass, turn left at Ridgecrest Road. Drive three miles north to the park. 760/245-2226.

PLACES TO STAY

Mojave Narrows Regional Park: See Mojave Narrows Regional Park, above, for camping information.

Ramada Inn: The Ramada website says that this big Ramada is the only full-service hotel "in the High Dessert" with indoor corridors. Yum, I've always wanted to spend a night or two in a dessert. But I suppose that "desert" is the real word, alas. The rooms are standard motel/hotel fare, but the outdoor pool is a real plus, as is the free continental breakfast. Rates are $75–90. Dogs are $20 extra. 15494 Palmdale Road 92392; 760/245-6565.

Red Roof Inn: This motel is conveniently close to Mojave Narrows Regional Park. Rates are $55–79. 13409 Mariposa Road 92392; 760/241-1577.

Lucerne Valley

PARKS, BEACHES, AND RECREATION AREAS

🐾 Johnson Valley Open Area

🐾🐾🐾🐾🐕 (See San Bernardino County map on page 882)

If city life has your dog tied in knots, a visit to the Johnson Valley Open Area is bound to unkink him. There's nothing like 250,000 acres of leashless terrain—including mountains, scrubby desert, dry lakes, sand dunes, and rock formations—to take the "d" out of "doldrums" and put it back in "dog."

While you may not run into any other people during your visit, keep in mind that much of this land is OK for off-highway vehicles to cruise. If you hear one of these loud beasts coming, make sure your dog is close by. Some dog owners like to put something bright orange on their dog just in case. You'll also want to be aware that coyotes are not unheard of around here. Don't let your dog wander far from you.

There are many access points to this huge acreage. One good bet is to exit Highway 247 at Bessemer Mine Road and drive north a few miles. Big signs will show you the way. The public land here is interspersed with private land, but Bureau of Land Management folks say that unless an area is fenced off, posted, or developed, it's probably OK for hiking. 760/252-6000.

Hesperia

PARKS, BEACHES, AND RECREATION AREAS

🐾 Hesperia Lake Park

🐾🐾🐾 (See San Bernardino County map on page 882)

Most people visit this 200-acre park to nab a trout or catfish out of the seven-acre lake. But since dogs aren't allowed on the lake bank, or in the lake, it's probably not the activity of choice if you're looking for something you can do with your pooch at your side.

The park has plenty of trees for shade and leg lifts, plus sports fields and playgrounds for the humans in the family. Look for the small waterfall, which feeds a meandering rock-lined stream that eventually leads to the lake. It's a great spot to stop for a picnic.

While there's no day-use fee, you'll be charged $10 to fish. Camping is $20–25, and dogs are $2 extra. The 58 campsites are set near the lake. The campsites can be reserved, but are available on a first-come, first-served basis. Although there's a sign for this park from the Bear Valley Cutoff exit of I-15, don't be fooled into thinking it's just off the highway, especially if your dog is getting that glazed look that tells you he can wait no longer. The park is actually several miles southeast of the exit. The route is complicated, but the signage is excellent, so follow the brown signs all the way. 760/244-5951.

🐾 Silverwood Lake State Recreation Area

🐾🐾🐾🐾 (See San Bernardino County map on page 882)

Got a water dog? This is a fine place for a little dog paddle. The park used to ban dogs from being in the water, even on a boat. But now pooches can swim, or join you on your boat while you fish or putter around the 1,000-acre lake. They're supposed to be leashed, but at least they can get their paws wet.

Landlubbing dogs are happy to know that the 2,500-acre park has 13 miles of paved hiking/biking trails. You'll go through high chaparral country here, with all the bushes and trees a boy dog could ever dream of claiming for himself. And if that's not enough, you can head over to the national forest land on the lake's east side and hike forever.

Dogs must be leashed at Silverwood Lake. There are coyotes and bobcats and bears, oh my. Camping costs $20 a night. There are 131 sites available on a first-come, first-served basis. (Reservations are required in the summer.) Call 800/444-7275 for reservations. The day-use fee for the park is $8 per vehicle. From the Crestline area, 10 miles north of San Bernardino, take I-15 to Highway 138 and drive east about 11 miles on Highway 138 to the park. 760/389-2281 or 760/389-2303.

PLACES TO STAY

Days Inn Suites—Hesperia/Victorville: Fill your belly at the extended continental breakfast and out you go for a day of adventuring with poochface. Rates are $65–110. Dogs are $7 extra. 14865 Bear Valley Road 92345; 760/948-0600.

Hesperia Lake Park: See Hesperia Lake Park, above, for camping information.

Mojave River Forks Regional Park: This 1,100-acre patch of high desert land has 80 campsites and five group areas available. Sites are $8–15. Dogs are $1 extra. If you camp here, you can hike, explore the often-dry Mojave River, and have access to the nearby Pacific Crest Trail. Be sure not to miss the Santa Fe Mormon Trail, complete with ruins. The park is on Highway 173 between Silverwood Lake and Hesperia; 760/389-2322.

Silverwood Lake State Recreation Area: See Silverwood Lake State Recreation Area, above, for camping information.

Big Bear Lake

This lakeside mountain resort community isn't exactly Lake Tahoe, but that's part of its charm. It's generally more rustic, more natural, and far less crowded. The crisp, clean alpine air is a godsend any time of year.

The town's old-fashioned honesty and lack of smooth public relations pros is evident as soon as you approach the old village section. There, you'll see a road sign for skiing, with an arrow pointing to the left. Immediately below that is a sign for the hospital, with an arrow pointing to the right. It's not a joke.

This is a very dog-friendly community, complete with incomparable off-leash hikes, great restaurants, and charming lodgings where dogs are as welcome as their chauffeurs. Check out the old Big Bear Lake village. It gives a new meaning to old-style charm.

PARKS, BEACHES, AND RECREATION AREAS

Although this book doesn't normally go into detail on specific trails in national forests, we're mentioning a few here because they're so integral to your pooch's having a doggone good time in the Big Bear Lake area. (Sadly, these used to be off leash, but leashes are now the law.)

11 Cougar Crest Trail

🐾🐾🐾🐾 (See San Bernardino County map on page 882)

This two-mile trail goes through a mixed conifer section of San Bernardino National Forest. It's full of juniper, Jeffrey pine, and pinyon. Obedient dogs used to be able to go leash-free, but no more.

DIVERSION

Whatever Floats Your Boat: A great way to explore **Big Bear Lake** with your dog is to do it by boat. A couple of marinas will rent you and your dog a variety of boats, with the proviso that you try not to let your dog have any little accidents on board. (Take frequent land breaks if your dog has a small bladder or has just eaten.) Pontoon boats are probably the most fun for dogs, because they're big, slow, and stable. Aluminum fishing boats are an option for fairly calm dogs who won't wriggle themselves into the drink with excitement when you land a big one. Very mellow dogs can even find out the answer to the age-old question: Can you canoe? (If your dog isn't a swimmer, she should wear a doggy life jacket on any boat. Even if she is a swimmer, it's not a bad idea, and especially on a tippy canoe ride.)

Holloway's Marina (398 Edgemoor Road, Big Bear Lake; 909/866-5706 or 800/448-5335; www.bigbearboating.com) rents fishing and pontoon boats. Big Bear Marina (500 Paine Road, Big Bear Lake; 909/866-3218; www.bigbearmarina.com) rents fishing boats, pontoon boats, pedal boats, and canoes. You could also rent a wave runner with your dog, but don't.

We like it best here in late autumn, when a dusting of snow rests on the pine needles and the air is crisp. We've never run into another person on the trail during this time of year. Cougar Crest Trail eventually connects with the Pacific Crest Trail, which traverses 39 miles of the Big Bear area. The scenery here is outstanding.

From the Big Bear Lake village, cross the lake at the Stanfield Cutoff and turn left on Highway 38. As you drive west, the trail is just over a half mile west of the ranger station, on the right side of the road. There's plenty of parking. 909/866-3437.

12 Pedal Path

🐾🐾🐾🐾 (See San Bernardino County map on page 882)

Here's one way to hike the Big Bear Lake area without roughing it too much. This six-mile paved path allows you and your leashed, lake-loving dog to hike along the scenic north shore of Big Bear Lake.

Sometimes bikers think they own the trail (it is called Pedal Path, not Four-Paw Path, after all), so make sure your dog is close to you. The trail starts at the north end of the Stanfield Cutoff. 909/866-3437.

DIVERSION

Get Hitched, with Your Dog's Help: The Big Bear **Hitching Post Wedding Chapel** is a dog's kind of marriage sanctuary. It's got a mountain/Western theme and no overly frilly froufrou.

Owners John and TraCee Green have played host to canine ring bearers, canine bridesmaids, and canine best men. A former owner said he once even helped a dog sign a marriage certificate (not the license, though). "We just put his paw on the ink pad, then stamped the certificate. He was a smart dog, but his penmanship wasn't good enough to sign his name," he said.

The Greens ask that dogs attend only midweek weddings. On busy days such as Saturday, they don't have enough time to vacuum up dog hairs, and a few people visiting after dogs participated have complained about their allergies flaring up.

The fee for getting hitched here is $95 and includes the chapel and a donation for the minister. Licenses are extra. For more information, call 909/584-1030 or 800/828-4433, or write them at P.O. Box 1583, Big Bear Lake, CA 92314; www.bigbearweddings.com.

DIVERSION

Catch a Stagecoach: If you and your little varmint have a han-kerin' to be part of the Old West, hanker no longer! Michael Homan and his trusty **Bear Valley Stage Lines** in Big Bear Lake will take you and your dog and up to 12 other people on a 15-minute ride around town in a stagecoach so genuine it looks as if John Wayne ought to be at the reins. Dogs will want to sit up front with Homan, who wears Western clothes. But it's not Homan they want to be near. It's the horses. Actually, the horses' rears, to be exact.

Enough of that. Adults are $8, children are $4. Dogs don't pay a cent. Homan says you'll need to be able to lift your dog 3.5 feet to get him inside the stagecoach (it's a high entrance). The stagecoach stand is on Village Drive across from Chad's Place. No reservations needed. Homan also can hitch a beautiful carriage to some beauti-ful horses, should you care to go on a more elegant, intimate ride. You'll need to make special arrangements for that, but dogs are also welcome. 909/584-2277; www.stagelines.com.

13 Woodland Trail

🐾🐾🐾🐾 (See San Bernardino County map on page 882)

This 1.5-mile nature trail in San Bernardino National Forest has 20 stops where you and your well-behaved, leashed dog may learn about the flora and fauna of this mountainous region. It's especially glorious in an early-morning mist.

The trail rarely gets crowded, so it's a sure escape from the madding crowd. From the Big Bear Lake village, cross the lake at the Stanfield Cutoff and turn left on Highway 38. Shortly after you turn, the trail will be on your right. 909/866-3437.

PLACES TO EAT

Most of the restaurants listed below are in the old-style alpine village in the heart of Big Bear Lake. Whenever you visit here, you'll feel as if it's Christmas.

The Log Cabin: You can eat on the deck here, which is three feet above the lawn, where your dog has to be tied. You can tie your dog securely under a shady tree and hover above her as you eat the German-American food here or sip any of the 10 beers on tap. 39976 Big Bear Boulevard; 909/866-3667.

Mozart's Restaurant: This place looks like a huge alpine cottage, with a big wooden deck where dogs may watch their people dine. 40701 Village Drive; 909/866-9497.

Pine Knot Coffee House and Bakery: Mmm. Come here on a cool autumn afternoon and try the hot pot pies or mulligan stew while sitting on the small deck. 535 Pine Knot Avenue; 909/866-3537.

PLACES TO STAY

Big Bear Lake is one of the best places in the entire state to spend the night with your dog. There are so many lodgings that accept dogs that you'll have a hard time choosing.

Bear Claw Cabins: These homey cabins are a quarter of a mile from the lake and skiing. Rates are $99–129, and dogs can stay in all rooms except the ones with whirlpool tubs. 586 Main Street 92315; 909/866-7633.

Big Bear Frontier Cabins and Hotel: If your dog wants to splash around the lake, this is a great place to stay. Most of the 33 cabins and 22 motel rooms are on the lakefront or just across the street. Dogs and humans can wet their paws at the private beach here, and humans (sorry, dogs) can also enjoy the lodging's heated pool and large hot tub. The lodgings are cozy, and even the motel rooms have beautiful wood paneling that's so shiny you could practically ice skate on it if gravity weren't an issue. All but a couple have wood-burning fireplaces. It sounds far off the beaten track, but Big Bear Frontier is just one block from the dog-friendly village of Big Bear Lake. Rates are $70–300. Dogs are $15 extra. (As for pet rates, the website also mentions that "birds fly free. Call about mules or horses." I asked if the place really gets mules and horses, and a front-desk clerk cheerfully told me, "No, but we love animals, so maybe we could work something out.") 40472 Big Bear Boulevard 92315; 800/457-6401; www.big-bear-cabins.com.

Big Pine Flats Campground: This is one of the more out-of-the-way campgrounds in the Big Bear area. You and your dog can hike around the area and be fully enveloped by ravishing Mama Nature. Or you can drive a few miles and be in the heart of Big Bear Lake. There are 19 sites available on a first-come, first-served basis. The campground closes in winter. Sites are $16. From Fawnskin, follow Rim of the World Drive (its name will change) for seven miles to Big Pine Flat Station. The campground is on your right. 909/866-3437.

Black Forest Lodge: Everything here is Swiss chalet–style, from the cute motel to the cabins to the real chalets. A few of the cabins date from 1895! These log beauties have been gutted and a couple of the old ones even have whirlpool baths inside. Many accommodations are graced by fireplaces, and all are clean and attractive. The lodge's property has lots of trees for your pooch's perusal. Rates are $45–150. (And up to $225 for a chalet that sleeps 10.) Dogs pay a $25 flat fee. 41121 Big Bear Boulevard 92315; 909/866-2166 or 800/255-4378; www.blackforestlodge.com.

Cienaga Creek Ranch Mountain Cottages: The five upscale-yet-rustic cottages here are set on 50 acres of forest where well-behaved dogs can say *sayonara* to their leashes. As if that's not enough, this tranquil acreage is surrounded by thousands of acres of dog-friendly national forest land. It's enough to make a grown dog cry with joy. And the giant pines, firs, and junipers that blanket the land are another dream come true for many boy dogs. Combine this with some pet treats at the beginning of your visit, and you'll surely have a dog who thinks he's found canine heaven on earth.

It's pretty heavenly for people, too. Everything is solar-powered, so ubiquitous utility lines don't mar the landscape. The cottages combine the rustic (log beds, log trim, wood wainscoting) with the divine (featherbeds, artisan tile, and marble in the spacious kitchen and bathroom). All have fireplaces, and some have whirlpool spas. They're 100–200 feet away from each other, so there's plenty of privacy, too. And the little extras, including high-end toiletries and super plush towels and robes, help guests feel extra-pampered in the wilderness. Rates are $119–299. Dogs are $10 extra. There's no street address. P.O. Box 2773 92314; 888/336-2891; www.mountaincottage.com.

Cozy Hollow Lodge: This lodge deserves its name, since the simple cabins here have fireplaces and are definitely on the cozy side. It's a great place to stay after a long day on the slopes. In summer, a stream runs through the woods behind the lodge. Rates are $59–159. There's a $100 deposit for dogs and an additional $10 fee for each pooch. 40409 Big Bear Boulevard 92315; 909/866-8886; www.cozyhollowlodge.com.

Eagle's Nest Bed and Breakfast Lodge: Dogs are warmly welcomed here with a pet basket full of goodies, including treats, a doggy toy, food and water bowls, and a towel for drying off wet paws. (The latter two are loaners.) They can stay at a charming two-room cottage suite with a fireplace or in the Highland Cabin, an absolutely wonderful, cozy, two-bedroom cabin with a wood-burning fireplace and even a deer head on the wall. (Jake is scared of it. This is embarrassing.) The cabin is rustic yet beautifully appointed. The exterior looks as if it's straight out of a fairy tale in some woodland setting.

But dogs don't care about the decor or the storybook charm. What they want to know is: 1) Where can I go sniff out some nature and check out some trees? 2) What do I do while the humans are just sitting around reading and talking and watching TV? The answers will put a wag in any dog's tail: 1) The dog-friendly San Bernardino National Forest surrounds the cabin, and 2) You can curl up by the wood-burning fireplace or hang out in your completely fenced backyard. And don't forget to eat the treats. Rates are $99–165. Dogs are $10 extra. 41675 Big Bear Boulevard 92315; 909/866-6465 or 888/866-6466; www.eaglesnestlodgebigbear.com.

Golden Bear Cottages: There's an unmistakable bear theme going here. Most of the 28 cabins sport bear names. (Little Bear, Honey Pot, Snuggle Bear Manor, and Grizzly's Den are but a few of the cabins.) The paw prints on the lodging's literature seem like dog-paw prints at first glance (at least to the dog-oriented among us), but they are actually bear prints. You and your dog will have a beary good time at the interesting assortment of rustic cabins strewn over five acres. The prices are quite bearable, too. Rates are $79–229. Dogs are $10. 39367 Big Bear Boulevard, Highway 18 92315; 909/866-2010 or 800/461-1023; www.goldenbear.net.

Grey Squirrel Resort: These charming cottages are a half block from the lake, on 4.5 acres. Several of the cottages have fireplaces. For those achy muscles fraught with postskiing stress disorder, the resort has a heated pool, which is enclosed in the winter (but pooches can't paddle here). Rates are $85–170. There's a $100 deposit for pets and an additional $10 fee per pooch. The cabins are on Highway 18, just west of town at 39372 Big Bear Boulevard 92315; 909/866-4335 or 800/381-5569; www.greysquirrel.com.

Pine Knot Guest Ranch: Love llamas? Bonkers for bunnies? Stay at the comfy housekeeping cabins at Pine Knot and you can interact with animals other than your traveling companion (the one with dog breath). The two-plus-acre property is home to llamas you can join for a stroll or bunnies whose huge cage you can enter for a close encounter of the rabbit kind. It's also home to eight cabins, five of which allow dogs. All but one cabin has a wood-burning fireplace, and they all feature spa tubs for two. They're great to come back to after a long day on the slopes or on the lake. Rates are $139–299. The people who run the ranch also have six vacation home rentals not far away. Call to inquire about these. 908 Pine Knot Avenue 92315; 909/866-6500 or 800/866-3446; www.pineknotguestranch.com.

Quail Cove: "Pets are always welcome!" exclaims the lodge's brochure. The six cottages here are in a wooded, parklike setting by the water. All have wood-burning fireplaces, knotty-pine paneling, and full kitchens. Rates are $79–229. Dogs are $15 extra and require a $100 deposit. 39117 North Shore Drive 92315; 909/866-5957 or 800/595-2683; www.quailcove.com.

Serrano Campground: If you like rustic campsites and good hot showers, this San Bernardino National Forest campground is worth the $24–34 fee. The 132 sites are close to Big Bear Lake and the solar observatory (which is open to the public during certain days in the summer). The campground is on the north side of the lake, about two miles east of Fawnskin. It's very close to the Cougar Crest Trail. Call 909/866-3437 for more information or 877/444-6777 for reservations. The campground is closed in the winter.

Shore Acres Lodge: Does your dog love to swim and hike? If so, Shore Acres is a great place to stay, because it has lake access and is near some fun trails. This two-acre property has 11 comfortable housekeeping cabins, each with a fireplace, sundeck, and barbecue grill. Humans who enjoy outdoor recreation can also swim in the pool during warmer months, fish from the lodge's property, or embark on a boat trip from the lodge's own dock. Little humans enjoy the playground here. Soak in the year-round hot tub at the end of a long day of fun. Rates are $105–245. Dogs are $10 extra. 40090 Lakeview Drive 92315; 800/524-6600; www.bigbearvacations.com/lodge.htm.

Timberline Lodge: Like woods? You're in a little foresty area here. Like being close to the village? Stay here and you will be. How about lake views from cozy housekeeping cabins? The views are terrific. And the active life? The lodge has a seasonal heated outdoor pool, a children's playground, and volleyball, basketball, horseshoes, and tetherball (for humans only). The folks behind the front desk can tell you about some fun nearby hikes with your dog. "We love our puppy dogs up here!" says friendly manager Dave. Dogs dig Dave, too. Rates are $79–200. Dogs are $10 extra. 39921 Big Bear Boulevard 92315; 909/866-4141; www.thetimberlinelodge.com.

Wildwood Resort: When we inquired whether dogs could stay at this wonderful four-acre resort, we were immediately and enthusiastically told, "Oh yes!" The woman we spoke with belongs to a Newfoundland dog club (actually, her dogs do), and she said that when the resort played host to the club's 50 Newfies, not a single pile of poop remained after their visit. It's stories like this that give dog people a good name and make dogs more welcome at other lodgings.

The resort has 25 sweet cabins that permit pooches. All have full kitchens, and most have fireplaces. You'll like it here. Rates are $100–205. Dogs are $10 extra. 40210 Big Bear Boulevard 92315; 909/878-2178 or 888/294-5396; www.wildwoodresort.com.

Twin Peaks

PLACES TO STAY

Arrowhead Pine Rose Cabins: This five-acre property is three miles from Lake Arrowhead. Dogs like the fact that they can walk around the spacious land here and check out all the sweet-smelling pines. About half of the 17 cabins permit pooches. Some cabins have back patios where your dog can relax in a quasioutdoor atmosphere without escaping. Pet blankets are provided. If your dog makes himself at home on human furniture, please cover it with the blanket. Rates are $59–450. Anything above $200 is in the three-bedroom-plus category, so you probably won't need to worry about that price. Dogs are $10 extra, and there's a $100 pooch deposit. 25994 Highway 189 92391; 909/337-2341 or 800/429-PINE (800/429-7463); www.lakearrowheadcabins.com.

Upland

PARKS, BEACHES, AND RECREATION AREAS

14 Baldy View Dog Park/Upland Dog Park

🐾🐾🐾🐾🐕 (See San Bernardino County map on page 882)

This fenced dog park is five grassy acres of fun, with lots of trees for your pooch's perusal. Small dogs have their own little area. Humans get to repose on benches. It's the de rigueur dog spot in Upland.

The people here know how to party. If they're not entering their dogs in the local Christmas parade, they're partaking in Valentine's festivities with their furry friends, or hosting a "spring fling" party for them. You can get an idea of some of the events by checking out www.uplanddogpark.com.

The park is on 11th Street between San Antonio and Mountain Avenues. 909/931-4280.

Rancho Cucamonga

PARKS, BEACHES, AND RECREATION AREAS

15 Rancho Cucamonga Dog Park

🐾🐾🐾🐾🐕 (See San Bernardino County map on page 882)

This is one of the more attractive fenced dog parks we've come across. The park is about 30,000 square feet of grass, with great views of the San Gabriel Mountains. It's shaded here and there by beautiful jacaranda trees. When they bloom, their purple flowers are stunning. Bring a camera, and see if you can get your pooch to hold still long enough to get a photo of her under a canopy of purple blossoms.

The park has all the usual dog-park amenities, including water and benches. There's a separate area for shy or tiny dogs (or both rolled into one) to get away from it all. Many more amenities, including a dog wash, were in the offing. Dogs are not necessarily smiling about this last addition.

We're going to give you directions from the freeway, since this park is so close to a major freeway that traveling dogs routinely find themselves on. Exit I-15 at Baseline Avenue and immediately take the option for heading north on East Avenue. The park, which is in Etiwanda Creek Community Park, will be on your right within a few blocks, at the corner of Banyan Street and East Avenue. 909/477-2700.

San Bernardino

PARKS, BEACHES, AND RECREATION AREAS

16 Glen Helen Regional Park

🐾🐾🐾🐾 (See San Bernardino County map on page 882)

This 1,425-acre park features two lakes that are regularly stocked with such goodies as trout and catfish. But if your leashed dog doesn't like to fish, she's sure to enjoy such goodies as the ecology trail and the grassy little hills that await her happy paws.

Rangers tell us that some dogs seem to get a kick out of watching kids zoom down the 300-foot, two-part water slide at the swim complex in the park's southeast corner. Dogs aren't allowed there, but the park has plenty of viewing spots for pooches and their people.

With all these activities, Glen Helen Regional Park is a great place for your dog to take the family. You can even camp here. There are 50 sites available on a first-come, first-served basis. The fee is $10, and dogs are $1 extra.

The day-use fee here is $5, plus $1 per dog. Fishing is $5 per person over six years old. Exit I-215 at Devore Road (just south of the I-15/215 junction) and follow the signs about 1.5 miles to the park. 909/887-7540.

17 Wildwood Dog Park

🐾🐾🐾🐾🐾🐕 (See San Bernardino County map on page 882)

The grass is always greener on the other side of the fence here. That's because dogs use one side of this lush 3.5-acre park some days, and when the turf starts getting a little worn down, they switch to the other half to let the trampled half recover. It keeps it attractive and mud-free.

This is a super dog park in many ways. Small dogs have their own area, there are restrooms, benches, poop bags, drinking fountains, lights, and even a building used for vaccination clinics. Enough trees provide shade to make some parts of the park more tolerable in summer.

The dog park is within the 24-acre Wildwood Park, at East 40th Street and Waterman Avenue. If you feel as if it's just your dog who gets exercise at the dog park (let's face it, it's not as if humans get in great shape standing around talking and occasionally lobbing a tennis ball), you can pop on your dog's leash and head to the main park, where you can breeze along a fitness trail. 909/384-5233.

18 Perris Hill Park

🐾🐾🐾 (See San Bernardino County map on page 882)

This park makes dogs happy, in part because there's dense shade almost everywhere. The trees providing this comfort are generally very big and very old. Although dogs must be leashed, they have smiles on their snouts when they gather during dog rush hour, around 5 P.M. or so.

The park is at Highland and Valencia Avenues. 909/384-5233.

PLACES TO STAY

Dog lodgings aren't exactly abundant here.

Glen Helen Regional Park: See Glen Helen Regional Park, above, for camping information.

La Quinta Motor Inn: Dogs are allowed to stay in this motel's smoking rooms. Fortunately, there's a little grassy area outside where they can get some fresh air. Rates are $69–85. 205 East Hospitality Lane 92408; 909/888-7571.

Motel 6: There are two of these pooch-friendly motels in town. Rates are $38–49 for the first adult, $6 for the second. In northern San Bernardino: 1960 Ostrems Way 92407; 909/887-8191. The other location is 111 West Redlands Boulevard 92408; 909/825-6666.

Lake Arrowhead

This attractive resort village in the mountains of the San Bernardino National Forest has plenty for a dog to do. Dogs can lounge in lodges. They can hike the hillsides.

The Arrowhead district of the national forest has some terrific trails varying in elevation 3,000–7,000 feet. Pooches are welcome to join you on a day hike or an overnighter. Contact the ranger station at 909/337-2444 for trail maps and advice on which hikes and campsites are better suited for your skill level and the time of year you'll be visiting. We've listed two of the more popular trails and campgrounds below, but there are plenty of smaller hike-in sites as well.

The lake itself is managed by an exclusive homeowners association, so public lake access is rather limited.

PLACES TO STAY

Arrowhead Tree Top Lodge: "We love dogs," says a kindly employee who also works for the local humane society. In fact, dogs get treats upon arrival. Some of the rooms at this attractive lodge have kitchens and fireplaces, for that homey touch. The lodge is on five acres with a nature trail and creeks. Dogs dig that. It's a short walk to the village and to the lake from here. Rates

DIVERSION

Sniff Out Some Cool Clothes: A clothing store with the name **Big Dogs Sportswear** that has a giant St. Bernard as its logo can't help but allow clean, well-behaved dogs to shop with their people. Most stores in the chain are dog-friendly, but the folks at the Lake Arrowhead store go the extra mile and keep a bowl of fresh water handy for thirsty dogs, and they even give biscuits to their canine customers. 28200 Highway 189; 909/336-1998.

are $69–179. Dogs are $8 extra. 27992 Rainbow Drive 92352; 909/337-2311 or 800/358-TREE (800/358-8733); www.arrowheadtreetop.com.

Dogwood Campground: This isn't one of the more secluded or rustic campgrounds in the area, but I mention it here because it's conveniently situated one mile from the lake, and because my dog friends insist I list it because of its name. Dogwood is a privately operated national forest campground with 93 sites and all the amenities a camper could need, and then some ("then some" refers to things such as laundry facilities). The camp is set along the lake's outlet. The campground is open May–mid-October. Sites are $24–29. Dogwood is at Highway 18's Blue Jay turnoff. For information, call 909/337-2444. For reservations, call 877/444-6777.

Prophets' Paradise Bed and Breakfast: This bed-and-breakfast is a real charmer. You and your dog will drool over the cozy antique-filled living room, which is especially inviting in winter when the fireplace is roaring. Take a dog here at Christmas for the best present you could give him. (And speaking of Christmas, the "Prophet" in Prophets' Paradise is the last name of the innkeepers, not anything prophetic.) The bed-and-breakfast is a five-level, 5,000-square-foot house on a hillside. Each room has its own floor. It's wonderfully private for a bed-and-breakfast. The pet rooms have decks and outside entrances. Rates are $120–185. 26845 Modoc Lane 92352; 909/336-1969 or 800/987-2231; www.prophetsparadise.com.

Saddleback Inn: Howard Hughes frequented this enchanting historic inn (although it wasn't quite so historic then, having been built in 1919), as did Charles Lindbergh and countless Hollywood icons, including Mae West.

In keeping with Mae West's famous line, now your dog can "Come up and see me sometime" at the Saddleback Inn. Many of the lovely cottages in back of the three-story inn welcome dogs. They're decorated in kind of a country-mountain cabin style, and most have gas-log fireplaces and whirlpool tubs. All come with a little fridge and microwave, should your dog hanker for a midnight snack. There's a fun restaurant on the premises, but your dog will have to be content with leftovers, as there's no outdoor dining. What dogs and their people usually like best about Saddleback is the gorgeous setting over-looking Lake Arrowhead, in the midst of big pines and cedars. The cottages are surrounded by these arbors, and that puts a smile on any dog's face.

Rates are $109–218. Dogs are $8 extra. 300 South State Highway 173 92352; 909/336-3571; www.saddlebackinn.com.

Crestline

PARKS, BEACHES, AND RECREATION AREAS

19 Lake Gregory

🐾🐾🐾 (See San Bernardino County map on page 882)

Here's a county park the way we like to see them: free. It's rare, but it happens. Lake Gregory is an 86-acre lake in a park that has only about 20 acres of dry land. But the land is lush and forested, with ponderosa pines, sugar pines, and cedars everywhere.

A 2.75-mile path (complete with fitness stops) takes you around the lake, but alas, dogs aren't allowed in the water. They must be leashed at all times. At one point you'll come to a section of the park that's popular with the pooch set. It's so green that signs warn "No Golf." It's also very popular with the ball-playing set, so keep away during game time.

From Highway 18, take the Crestline exit, which turns into Lake Drive. Follow the road into the park. For the hiking path, start at the south shore. The golf-green entrance to the park is at 24646 San Moritz Drive. The Rim of the World Recreation and Park District runs that area: 909/337-7275. San Bernardino County Regional Parks is in charge of the rest: 909/338-2233.

Ontario

PARKS, BEACHES, AND RECREATION AREAS

20 John Galvin Park

🐾🐾 (See San Bernardino County map on page 882)

Lazy leashed dogs like this park. The big old trees seem as if they were made for shading dogs whose main focus is sleeping. For a perfectly lazy afternoon outing, bring a book, lean against a tree, and revel in the sound of your snoring pooch. An open field in one section of this municipal park provides just enough room to roam should your mellow dog choose not to snooze.

Leashed dogs are permitted in all of Ontario's parks, should you care to check out some others. For John Galvin, exit I-10 at 4th Street and go west a couple of blocks. The park will be on your left. 909/395-2020.

PLACES TO EAT

Casa Corona: Dogs can eat at the four outdoor tables next to some trees out front. Try the enchiladas. They're really tasty. Thirsty *perros* get a bowl of water. 401 North Euclid Avenue; 909/986-5200.

PLACES TO STAY

Country Inn and Suites: Stay here at this all-suites hotel, and you'll get breakfast and can take part in a social hour. Rates are $79–144. Dogs are $50 extra for the length of their stay. 231 North Vineyard Avenue 91764; 909/937-6000; www.countryinns.com.

Holiday Inn Hotel and Suites Airport: This is the best hotel for dogs who have to stay near the airport. Not only do you get a continental breakfast, but all the rooms are actually suites, complete with kitchenettes. And guess what else? Fire hydrants are pretty prominent outside the hotel. It's a boy dog's dream. People prefer the whirlpool baths, which grace half the rooms. Rates are $112–142. Dogs pay a $25 fee for their stay, in addition to a $50 deposit. 3400 Shelby Street 91764; 909/466-9600.

Residence Inn by Marriott: Staying at the one- and two-bedroom suites here is like staying at home, except here you get regular maid service. It's a great place to stay if you like having a kitchen when you travel, and a living room with a fireplace, and access to a swimming pool (heated outdoor), whirlpool, and exercise room. The suites are comfortable, attractive, and across from the Ontario Convention Center, which is convenient if your dog has an important convention to attend. Rates are $135–$185. Dogs pay a $100 "sanitation fee" per stay for a smaller suite, $150 for a larger suite, plus $10 extra each night, so try to stay for a few nights to make it worth your while. (Or at least eat a lot at the continental breakfast buffet.) 2025 Convention Center Way 91764; 909/937-6788.

Chino

PARKS, BEACHES, AND RECREATION AREAS

🐾 Prado Regional Park/Prado Recreation

🐾🐾🐾🐾🐾 🐕 (See San Bernardino County map on page 882)

This 2,200-acre park is actually in two sections. There's the regular old regional park, with lakes, huge manicured fields, and playgrounds, and the dog park, with 1,100 acres of land for dogs to go leashless.

The regular old park charges $5 per vehicle, and $1 per dog. Dogs must be on leash. A day here makes for a pleasant family outing. Camping can be fun, too. Sites are $16–20. If you want to fish, it'll cost you $2–7, depending on your age.

The dog-training park will cost you $10 per person or per couple per day (up to two dogs are included in the fee). Camping anywhere on the 1,100 acres costs $6. But don't get the idea that this place is just a heavenly area where your dog can run like a crazy California canine. This is a dog-training area, and we're generally not talking about the old sit-stay stuff. We're talking hunting and herding. We're talking dogs who work for a living.

Prado Recreation is not for vegetarians or antihunting folks. Chances are good that you'll see some dead birds here. You'll even see people shooting and the dogs retrieving what they've shot. (If your dog spooks at gunshots, this is not a good place to take him.) As we drove through, we saw Labs and springers everywhere obeying hand signals in ponds and fields where there were bound to be birds.

People laughed at poor old Joe Airedale as we cruised through. "Ha ha ha" was all we could hear as they pointed at his dumbfounded, curly head. Somehow they could tell that his retrieval instincts stop where his nose starts. He was embarrassed, but he continued to stick his head out the window anyway. Mr. Yellow Lab, Jake, has not yet visited, but he'll fit right in here, even though the only hand signal he obeys is: "Look, I've got a treat! Come sit down and you'll get it!"

Dogs who herd really can go to town here. On a mist-shrouded field, we saw an elderly gent walking with a long wooden staff. He would quietly whistle or give subtle hand signals to two very intense border collies who were keeping a couple of big goats in line. It was as if we'd been transported across the Atlantic. Aye, rarely have we seen a more lovely dog scene.

You'll need to bring along proof of your pooch's rabies vaccine to either part of the park. The regular section of Prado Regional Park is about seven miles south of Highway 60, on the left side of Euclid Avenue. Call 909/597-4260 for information or camping reservations. To get to the dog-training section, take the first left after Prado Regional Park. You'll be on a very bumpy dirt road for what may seem like a long time, but eventually you'll come to the park's office. Call the Prado Kennel at 909/597-6366 for more information.

PLACES TO STAY

Prado Regional Park: See Prado Regional Park, above, for camping information.

Redlands

Parts of this lush, resortlike town provide a breath of fresh air from smog-ridden and traffic-filled Southern California.

PARKS, BEACHES, AND RECREATION AREAS

22 Prospect Park

🐾🐾🐾 (See San Bernardino County map on page 882)

You'll be surrounded by exquisite views, towering palms, multitudes of orange trees, and flowers everywhere at this enchanting, verdant park. Prospect Park is out of a fairy tale. It's one big hill, with delicate wooden seats overlooking the surrounding orchards. At the top, you'll find an open-air theater, some peacocks, and a resident cat, so be sure to follow the rules and leash your dog.

This one's well worth the short trek from I-10. For the most scenic ride, exit the freeway at Orange Street and drive south, through the quaint downtown area. In about seven blocks, bear right at Cajon Street. The park is on your right in about one mile. Park on Cajon Street just after Highland Avenue (just past the orange grove and before the picnic area on your right). Walk back several feet to the wide paved path and embark on your wondrous journey. 909/798-7509.

PLACES TO EAT

Cafe Society: Dogs are welcome to help you dine on good sandwiches and tasty bakery items at the sidewalk and patio tables. 308 West State Street, #1A; 909/798-5578.

Yucaipa

PARKS, BEACHES, AND RECREATION AREAS

23 Yucaipa Regional Park

🐾🐾🐾🐾 (See San Bernardino County map on page 882)

This picturesque park is surrounded by the San Bernardino Mountains and Mt. San Gorgonio. But dogs who visit here have more important things on their minds than pretty scenery. First of all, they're not relegated to the usual six-foot leash—their leashes can be 10 feet long! Joy of joys. Then there's the size of this park—it's 885 acres, with enough grassy fields to tire even the friskiest hound dog.

Water-loving dogs enjoy accompanying their people to the three trout-stocked lakes, and water-loving kids get a kick out of the 350-foot water slides at the swim lagoon (no dogs allowed on the slides because they'd make the slides too hairy). Several campsites are available near the lake, so if you're in the mood for a little camping with your angling, you couldn't ask for a more convenient location. Sites are $13–22. There are about 35 campsites here. Reservations are recommended.

The day-use fee is $5 per vehicle. On major holidays, it's $7 per vehicle. Dogs are $1 extra. Fishing permits are $5 daily for anyone over eight years old, $2 for the little-kid set.

From I-10, take the Yucaipa exit and follow the brown signs for "Regional Park." It's about five miles from the freeway. 909/790-3127.

PLACES TO STAY

Yucaipa Regional Park: See Yucaipa Regional Park, above, for camping information.

Angelus Oaks

PLACES TO STAY

The Lodge at Angelus Oaks: One day I got a letter written in silver ink and very big, childish handwriting, signed with paw prints by Jake Dog (not my Jake the dog; this was before he was even a twinkle in his mother's eye) and Sadie Dog. They were writing to tell me about this wonderful place, which they call "a hidden secret."

Jake and Sadie are very smart dogs, indeed, because the Lodge is one terrific place to stay with a dog. The Lodge is made up of several homey wooden cabins and is set on some prime acreage in the San Bernardino National Forest. It was built in the early 1900s as a stagecoach stop for pooped-out travelers,

DIVERSION

Woof for the Good Guys: Dogs can boo the bad guys, cheer for the good guys, and laugh at the drunken guys as they watch some amusing **Old West skits** with you on Pioneertown's scenic "Mane Street." (The good guys always win.) A dozen or so members of a local Western reenactment ensemble perform these lively sketches in this seemingly historic old movie town at 2:30 P.M. Sunday April–November. The cost: free. You might even get to see some rope tricks and hear cowboy poetry. And you'll surely hear some loud gunfire (blanks, but loud; the opposite of silent-but-deadly). If your four-legged varmint is skittish of loud noises, it may be best to keep your distance. Afterward you and your dog can have your photo taken with a gunslinger. For more information, phone the Pioneertown Posse at 760/228-0494 or check out www.pioneertown.com.

and it really hasn't changed much since. Each of the 12 cabins has a kitchen, bathroom with shower, and one or two bedrooms. The main lodge/office is very cozy, with a stone fireplace, a library, and an antique billiards table. But what dogs dig most about the Lodge is that it has lots of fun things to do outside. There's a snow play area (in winter) and a horseshoe pit and other fun nonsnow recreational opportunities. Best of all, the San Bernardino National Forest is everywhere. Some prime trails start just a short car ride away.

Rates are $70–95. Dogs are $5 extra. 37825 Highway 38 92305; 909/794-9523.

Pioneertown

Everything on this town's "Mane Street" looked 100 years old from the moment it came to life in 1947. Pioneertown was built with two purposes in mind: as an Old West–style getaway for folks in the film business and a location for Hollywood westerns. If it looks familiar, you may have seen it as a backdrop in a few Gene Autry films, including *On Top of Old Smokey* and *Whirlwind*. If you're a real buff of the genre, you may know it from lesser-known B-grade films such as *The Gay Amigo* and *The Daring Caballero*. (Gotta love those names.)

What separates this from your typical movie backlot is that it's a real town (albeit a tiny one). The false fronts aren't just propped up with lumber: They're the fronts of real working buildings, including the local post office.

P-town is a very cool place to visit with your dog, because dogs, like horses, fit in beautifully. Mane Street is unpaved and as casual as it gets. In fact, dogs who don't mind the sound of guns (shooting blanks) can watch some Old West skits here on Sundays. (See the Diversion Woof for the Good

Guys.) For lots more details on this great, out-of-the-way place, check out www.pioneertown.com.

PLACES TO EAT

Pappy and Harriet's: What used to be a biker hangout (Harleys, not Schwinns) is now one happening restaurant and saloon. Its look fits right in with the Old West theme of Pioneertown, and so does the food (salads and veggie burgers notwithstanding). The steaks, chicken, and ribs are smoked and grilled over an outdoor mesquite fire, giving them a taste that will make your dog drool puddles. Dogs can join you at the picnic tables in the outdoor beer garden. "Horses, dogs, they're all fine with us," says friendly co-owner Robin. 53688 Pioneertown Road; 760/365-5956; www.pappyandharriets.com.

PLACES TO STAY

Rimrock Ranch Cabins: Like everything else in this pseudo–Old West town, the four cozy, spotless housekeeping cabins here were born in the 1940s as a place where the directors and stars of Western movies could kick off their boots and relax. Gene Autry and Roy Rogers were probably among the guests, say the owners, who are researching the history of the ranch. The cabins have a wonderfully funky charm, each with original knotty-pine paneling, attractive antique/Western decor, artisan tile floors, a well-equipped kitchen, and a private patio with outdoor fireplace. Guests get use of the wonderful mineral-water swimming pool here, too. It's a delightful treat and seems to do wonders for skin and hair.

What dogs love is that the cabins are on 35 acres, and that this acreage is backed by hundreds of acres of fairly new wilderness preserve. This is beautiful, pristine land with lots of fun hiking. (Keep it pristine and bring your poop bags.)

Dogs come here and never want to leave. "We're very dog-friendly," says Szu (pronounced Sue) Wakeman, who owns the cabins with her Texas-born husband, Dusty. (Great name for these parts.) Dogs get tasty biscuits when they check in, and they also get a doggy bed and food and water bowls during their stay. You'll be greeted at the gate by Yellow Dog, a canine you'll never forget. He's a sweet, shaggy dog with piercing ice-blue eyes. "People come here and want to take him home. He's our canine ambassador," says Szu. He's been in hundreds of guest photos (they send them to Szu) and he apparently endears himself to guests so much that some even end up letting him sleep on their bed. (Not that he's pushy; just cushy.)

Rates are $103–157, with a 20 percent discount in summer. Dogs are $10 extra. The mailing address is P.O. Box 313, 92268; 760/228-1297; www.rimrockranchcabins.com.

Joshua Tree

An entry point into Joshua Tree National Park (see the National Parks section at the beginning of the chapter for details) is just down the road from here.

PLACES TO STAY

Joshua Tree Highlands House: You'll feel as if Joshua Tree National Park is your very own backyard when you stay at this roomy, attractive vacation home on 10 acres. (The park is actually three short minutes away, but it looks as if it's right here.) Dogs who like contemporary-yet-retro decor will brag to their furry friends about this clean, cool, sleek two-bedroom, two-bath home with a whirlpool tub, steam shower, full kitchen, and enclosed deck.

By day you get a jaw-dropping 360-degree view of the beautiful surrounding desert from this remote locale, and at night you get amazing stargazing. There's nothing like breathing in the sweet scent of desert night air while lying in your comfortable lounger looking up at Orion with your own down-to-earth Canis Major at your side.

The house's owners, Frederick and Jimmy, love dogs. In fact they have three of their own, and one regularly visits a children's ward at an Los Angeles–area hospital to give the kids a boost.

Rates for the house are $750 for a week, and $350 for a weekend. Nightly rates are available. (A smaller, less expensive home is available as well, and it's just a bone's throw away.) Dogs are $35 extra. They don't give out the address until you reserve, but you can phone them to make arrangements at 760/366-3636 or 310/827-5144; www.joshuatreehighlandshouse.com.

Twentynine Palms

PARKS, BEACHES, AND RECREATION AREAS

24 Joshua Tree National Park

🐾🐾🐾 🐕 (See San Bernardino County map on page 882)

This town houses the headquarters and a good-sized swatch of this stunning park. (See the National Parks section at the beginning of the chapter for details.)

PLACES TO EAT

Foster's Freeze: Eating the cold, creamy treats here is the perfect way to end a day of exploring Joshua Tree National Park. Your dog will be indebted if you happen to drop a tad of vanilla on the ground. 73629 Two Mile Road; 760/367-9303.

PLACES TO STAY

29 Palms Inn: Set on 70 acres of beautiful desert, this rustic resort is just what the vet ordered for you and your pooch. It's a stress-free environment, with a peaceful spring-fed shaded pond for toe-dipping, a pool (with a cute little bar) and hot tubs for lounging, hammocks galore, phone-free bungalows and adobe cottages, and a view of the heavens you don't want to miss. You can get a massage in your room, on your sun patio, or even in the great outdoors. The cooks at the delightful restaurant here can pack a picnic lunch that you and your dog will drool for. Take it on a hike in Joshua Tree National Park, which is just down the road.

The cottage and cabins are unique, with a down-home, Old West, nouvelle-desert feel. Some have a fireplace and a kitchen. They all have evaporative coolers for hot summer days and heaters for cool winter nights. They also have cable TV, but the TVs are small and most are black and white. The resort's brochure says this is to help guests focus on more important things, but Jake Dog thinks it's because televisions are expensive. I love the lack of big Sonys, though, and I believe the brochure. Besides, snazzy new TVs just wouldn't fit in.

Rates are $75–245. There's a $35 dog fee per visit. 73950 Inn Avenue 92277; 760/367-3505; www.29palmsinn.com.

CHAPTER 57

Riverside County

Dogs are dancing with happiness in Riverside County these days, because they now have seven dog parks to call their very own, and at least three more were in the works. Dogs are no longer going to have to take to the desert to have a good time around here.

Actually, a trip to the desert during the more temperate months isn't a bad idea at all. In fact, dogs think it's a four-paws notion. But if it's hot or even warm outside, please forget it. The sand can be scorching even if the air isn't, and it can poach a pooch's paws.

Palm Springs has become quite the doggy destination of late. If you're in the mood for delectable desert oasis life, you'll find this resort town most amenable to dogs and their people.

The Bureau of Land Management (BLM) oversees millions of acres of desert and mountain land out in Riverside County, and dogs applaud the great job the agency does. On almost all the BLM land (except places such as nature preserves), pooches are permitted to go leashless.

PICK OF THE LITTER—RIVERSIDE COUNTY

BEST DOG PARKS
Pat Merritt Dog Park, Riverside (page 917)
Palm Springs Dog Park, Palm Springs (page 930)

MOST JUICY PARK
California Citrus State Historic Park, Riverside (page 918)

MOST DOG-FRIENDLY PLACE TO STAY
Caliente Tropics Resort, Palm Springs (page 931)

FRANK CAPRA'S MUSE
La Quinta Resort and Club, La Quinta (page 939)

BEST HOMAGE TO MAN'S BEST FRIEND
March Air Field's War Dog Memorial, Riverside (page 920)

BEST RIDE
Orange Empire Railway Museum trains, Perris (page 924)

Our favorite BLM land in Riverside County is the Santa Rosa Mountains National Scenic Area. It's rugged, desolate, and utterly pristine. It's also so sweeping that giving general directions is futile. It spans much of the area of the central county from I-10 south to the north border of the Anza-Borrego State Desert. Call the BLM's Palm Springs district office at 760/251-4800 for specifics.

County parks welcome leashed dogs, but be forewarned: Most of these parks charge $2 for adults, $2 for dogs, and $1 for kids. (I think this price structure means your dog had better act like an adult, not a child.)

NATIONAL FORESTS

The National Forests and Wilderness Areas resource at the back of this book has important information and safety tips on visiting national forests with your dog and has more information on the national forests listed below.

Cleveland National Forest

San Bernardino National Forest

NATIONAL PARKS

Joshua Tree National Park

Although the bulk of this huge desert park is in Riverside County, the large visitor center area with easily accessible hikes is north of the county border. (Please see the national parks section of the San Bernardino County chapter for details.)

Riverside

If your dog loves trees (Jake's ears just perked up), a jaunt along beautiful Victoria Avenue is a must. The seven-mile-long historic avenue is lined with more than 4,000 trees of 95 species. Male dogs think they've died and gone to heaven when they stroll down the avenue's walking path, past tree after tree after tree. To get a brochure that will help you identify the trees you and your dog admire here, call the visitor center at 951/684-INFO (951/684-4636).

PARKS, BEACHES, AND RECREATION AREAS

❶ Pat Merritt Dog Park

(See Riverside County map on page 914)

Dogs are ecstatic when they see this lush, green park—even if they can see only in black and white. The park is two terrific acres with great mountain views, and it's full of very happy dogs and their super-friendly people. The trees are merely glorified sticks at this point, but they'll grow. The fencing—something I don't usually mention except to note that a park is fenced—is some of the most attractive dog-park fencing I've seen. Chain-link be damned! Stylish black wrought iron is what you'll see here. (The Palm Springs Dog Park fencing beats it out, but that's Palm Springs. What else can I say?) The park features two sections: One for all dogs, one for small or timid dogs. It has all the usual amenities, including benches and picnic tables (sleek and modern), water, poop bags, and lights. A huge thanks to my intrepid correspondent "Three-Dog-Dave" Hepperly for the heads up (and photos) of this terrific park.

The park is at Limonite Frontage Road and Emery Street, about a half-mile north of the Santa Ana River. 951/955-1151.

DIVERSION

Take Your Dog Out on a Date: Going to the **Van Buren Drive-In Theatre** in Riverside is a great way to catch a first-run movie and spare yourself the guilt of leaving your dog home alone. And it's cheap: Adults are $5 each, and kids 11 and under are free, as are dogs of any age. Of course, if your dog is like Jake, he'll want you to keep getting out of the car and going to the snack bar for one greasy item after another—and this gets expensive. During Jake's drive-in stints, he's been so busy staring at the floor in hopes of runaway popcorn that he hasn't even realized a movie's going on.

Drive-in theaters are a dying breed. Catch a flick here while you can. (Note: Dogs need to be walked before the movie, because management prefers that they stay in the cars. And no barkers allowed.) 3035 Van Buren Boulevard; 909/688-2360.

🐾 California Citrus State Historic Park

🐾🐾🐾🐾 (See Riverside County map on page 914)

Do you ogle oranges? Go ga-ga for grapefruit? Lust for lemons? If you're even remotely a citrus fan, this is a must-see park for you and your leashed dog. Dogs may not be as interested in citrus, but they love coming here anyway.

The park is a huge 377 acres, with a whopping 125 varieties of citrus trees. The citrus-curious (and their canines) can learn more about these delights on a ranger-led tour or a self-guided tour around the huge groves. Many of the trails here are lined with palm trees, which add another level of that California Experience feel. In addition, there are miles of lush, landscaped trails and more rugged terrain. You'll learn so much about the history of oranges and their brethren that you'll never look at orange juice the same way again.

The people behind the park have big plans. They were building a 6,000-square-foot visitor center, which will tell the story of California's earliest orange encounters. (The arrival of the orange in Southern California was like the gold rush in Northern California. These fruity beginnings led to the state's image as the Golden State—land of sunshine, opportunity, and plenty of sun-kissed eats.) The next phase of development involves the re-creation of a citrus-producing community circa 1880–1935. This was to include an operating packing house, a workers' camp, a wealthy grower's home (which may serve as a restaurant), and an early citrus settlement with all kinds of neat old buildings.

Regular visitor Wendy and her dog, Molly, say they adore this park, and they inform us that dogs are not the only critters who visit here. "I have seen pet raccoons and pot-bellied pigs bring their owners to the park," says Wendy.

Those animals have good taste! And unlike most dogs, they're not averse to a little citrus.

Bring a picnic and enjoy lounging on the park's large grassy lawn (complete with barbecue grills). Now orange you glad you took the time to read this? (Joe Dog made me write that.) The entry fee is $4 per vehicle. The park is in the heart of Riverside, one mile east of Highway 91, at Dufferin Avenue and Van Buren Boulevard. 951/780-6222.

🔒 Carlson Dog Park

😺😺😺🐾 (See Riverside County map on page 914)

This one-acre pooch park is in a really pretty spot, at the base of Mt. Rubidoux along the Santa Ana River. The dog park is fenced, with green grass, big shady trees, water fountains at human lip level and dog-slurping level, and poop mitts.

My wonderful correspondent "Three-Dog-Dave" Hepperly keeps me up to date on the goings-on of this pooch park and other parks in the region, where he adventures with his dogs. Since the last edition of this book, he tells me, there have been some problems with less-than-savory types drifting to the park's parking lot after they're kicked out of the adjacent Fairmount Park at night. The park folks were working on a remedy, but in the meantime Dave and I wanted to let you know that nighttime may not be the right time for a visit until things get cleaned up.

The park is one mile west of downtown Riverside, on the east bank of the Santa Ana River, at Mission Inn Avenue near the bridge. 951/826-2000.

🔒 Mount Rubidoux

😺😺😺 (See Riverside County map on page 914)

The views from the top of this isolated granite outcrop are well worth the hike to get here. From its 1,364-foot elevation, you and your dog will see the surrounding mountains, the Santa Ana River, the city of Riverside, and probably a few other happy, peppy, leashed pooches.

There's not a lot of shade on the way up, so make sure you go when it's not hot. You and your dog should be in good shape to make this hike. If you have any doubts, go to Carlson Park (see above) and let your dog off leash to romp at a more leisurely pace.

A bit of history, courtesy of Patty Tambe of the city's parks department: In 1907, one of the park's founders put a cross at the hill's summit. The first Easter sunrise service here was held two years later, and that service is said to have inspired a cycle of outdoor Easter services across the country. Apparently, this was the granddaddy of these Easter events. So now you know. It's kind of fun to think about while you're at the summit.

The most convenient entrance to Mt. Rubidoux is at the small parking lot at Carlson Park. (See above for directions.) 951/826-2000.

DIVERSION

Pay Tribute to War Dogs, and See Planes Too: Back in the Vietnam War, thousands of specially trained dogs accompanied troops to the front lines in South Vietnam. Because their acute senses could detect danger in the form of ambushes, hidden trip wires, and explosives, and because of their dedication to their handlers, these amazing dogs are attributed with saving the lives of 10,000 soldiers. Nearly 300 dogs were killed in combat, and tragically, the rest were euthanized after the war because the military thought they'd be too dangerous to return to civilian life.

These dogs are gone, but far from forgotten, at least by the veterans who accompanied them on their one-way trip. On a rainy afternoon in February 2000, some 2,000 people, many of whom were veterans from across the United States, attended a dedication of the **War Dog Memorial** outside the **March Air Field Museum** near Riverside. Tearful veterans patted and hugged the bronze German shepherd depicted with his soldier in the striking 18-foot statue. The vets referred to their dogs as "America's forgotten heroes." They placed dozens of flowers at the statue's base.

Now you and your civilian dog can pay homage to these war dogs. Since the statue is outside (in the museum's front courtyard, to be exact), the folks at the March Air Field Museum say it's perfectly OK to bring your dog with you to visit. (Bringing a dog has provided at least one visitor with a convenient excuse about being a bit misty-eyed here: "I told my date sometimes I'm allergic to my dog," says the man, who was a hair too young for the war. "I don't think she bought it.") To find out more about the War Dogs association, call 877/WAR-DOGS (877/927-3647); www.war-dogs.com.

While you're at March Air Field, you can have a more uplifting experience if you expand your visit to include the outdoor section of the museum's aircraft exhibit. About 40 historic aircraft are "parked" outside, and leashed dogs can accompany your exploration. You'll see everything from the Lockheed SR-71 Blackbird to the B-17 Flying Fortress and the B-25 Mitchell bomber. If you're an airplane buff, put this place on your must-see list. It's a good idea to take your dog for a thorough walk before your visit, because you really don't want him making his mark anywhere here.

If you're visiting with another human, you can switch off between being outside with the pooch and going inside to see more fascinating aircraft and related artifacts. The museum is a nonprofit organization, and a $5 donation is requested. It's just off I-215 at the Van Buren exit. Its orange and white checkerboard roof is visible as you approach from the freeway. 22550 Van Buren Boulevard; 951/697-6600; www.march-field.org. (A special thanks to my invaluable correspondent "Three-Dog-Dave" Hepperly for helping me sniff out this wonderful place.)

🔢 Rancho Jurupa Regional Park

🐾🐾🐾🐾 (See Riverside County map on page 914)

This huge county park encompasses a few others, including the Hidden Valley Wildlife Area. Stretching east to west for almost 10 miles, it more than makes up for all those smaller city parks that say "no way" to dogs.

Depending on which section you visit, you and your leashed dog can see lots of wildlife, fish for your supper, hike through fields and woods, or relax on the manicured grass of a shaded picnic area. Since our tastes are sometimes dictated by money, we like to go where we can avoid driving in and paying the $2 per person and $2 per pooch fee—especially if we just need to stretch our legs. We've found a wonderful spot next to the park's nature center, where many interesting hikes originate.

To reach this fee-free area, exit Highway 60 at Rubidoux Boulevard, drive southwest a few blocks, and turn right on Mission Boulevard. In about six blocks, turn left on Riverview Drive/Limonite Avenue. In just a little more than a half mile, there should be a sign for a county park. That's where Riverview Drive veers to the left (Limonite will continue straight). Follow Riverview for about another 1.5 miles. It will be smaller and more rural than the previous road. The park will be on your left. Park in the lot near the nature center. Look for a trail and have yourselves a great hike.

If camping is your bag, you'll have to go to the fee area at Rancho Jurupa. From Highway 60, exit at Rubidoux Boulevard and drive south to Mission Boulevard. Turn left and drive about a half mile to Crestmore Boulevard. Follow Crestmore as it curves around the north side of the park. In about 1.5 miles, you'll be at the gate. Sites are $18. Dogs are $2 extra. There are approximately 70 sites available. For camping information, call Rancho Jurupa at 951/684-7032. For camping reservations, call 877/444-6777.

PLACES TO EAT

Check out the attractive pedestrian mall along Main Street for some doggone friendly eateries and some interesting history. These restaurants are a bone's throw from the Mission Inn, the city's premier historic and architectural landmark, at 3696 Main Street. You can't go inside with your dog, but you can gawk from the outside.

42nd Street Bagels: "We're dog-friendly here," one of the servers told us. "We really like dogs." Dogs do feel welcome. The people are friendly, but I think it's the cream cheese that makes dogs feel particularly at home. Slather a bagel with shmear and share it with your dog at the outdoor tables. 3737 Main Street; 951/274-9445.

Mission Inn Coffee Company: The coffee here is delicious, as are the tasty pastries and the sandwiches. Dine at the outdoor tables with your favorite dog. 3600 Main Street; 951/341-6789.

Simple Simon's: This bakery and café in the old mission district is a great place to lunch with your pooch. There's plenty of outdoor seating. 3639 Main Street; 951/369-6030.

PLACES TO STAY

The county seat is not flush with places to stay, especially places of the dog-friendly variety. Here are your choices, should you need to bunk here overnight.

Best Western of Riverside: Rates are $75–150. Dogs are $10 extra, and can't be "too huge." 10518 Magnolia Avenue 92505; 951/359-0770.

Dynasty Suites Riverside: Here are two hoops your dog must jump through to be allowed to stay here: 1) He needs to weigh less than 25 pounds, and 2) "It has to be a AAA member," says a front desk clerk. I hope she meant that the dog's people must be members of AAA, because I don't know too many card-carrying canine members of this auto club. Rates are $60–80. Dogs are $10 extra. 3735 Iowa Avenue 92507; 951/369-8200.

Motel 6: Rates are $39–53 for the first person, $6 extra for the second person. 1260 University Avenue 92507; 951/784-2131.

Rancho Jurupa Regional Park: See Rancho Jurupa Regional Park, above, for camping information.

Desert Hot Springs

This little community is known for its naturally hot mineral water—and it doesn't smell like rotten eggs! Folks with aches and pains come to soak in pools and tubs full of the stuff, and they swear by it. Dogs do some swearing of their own around here, but for a different reason: Pooches aren't permitted in any city parks.

PLACES TO STAY

Sky Valley Resort: If you have an RV and a hankering to soak in water that's good for you, come here. Sky Valley Park has nine naturally heated mineral whirlpool baths, as well as four large swimming pools. The RV resort is set on 160 acres, with eight fishing ponds and lots of grassy areas and palm trees for leashed pooches to sniff out. It's also surrounded by the desert, so you can get a taste of the area's natural environment, too. If you're bored traveling around in your RV, the park also offers 10 shuffleboard courts, horseshoes, a huge clubhouse, tennis courts, and a hobby court with lapidary, stained glass, and ceramic equipment. Sky Valley Park has a sister RV park where only seniors are permitted, but all ages are welcome here. Rates are $37–38. 74-711 Dillon Road 92241; 800/800-9218; www.skyvalleyresort.com.

Corona

PARKS, BEACHES, AND RECREATION AREAS

6 Butterfield Dog Park

🐾🐾🐾🐕 (See Riverside County map on page 914)

The dog people here worked hard for almost five years to make this fenced park a reality. The park's size, under an acre, is nothing to bark home about. But with its big old shade trees, cool green turf, benches, poop-bag dispensers, and friendly people and dogs, it's been a smash hit with dogs who dig the leash-free life. It's at 1886 Butterfield Drive. Exit Highway 91 at North Maple Street and follow it as it parallels the tracks for the Atchison, Topeka and Santa Fe (the railroad, not the song). Maple dead-ends into North Smith Street. Turn left on Smith, and go about three blocks to Butterfield Drive, where you'll go left again. The park is on your right, within the Butterfield Stage Trail Park. 951/736-2241.

PLACES TO STAY

Dynasty Suites Corona: Dogs need to be under 25 pounds to stay at this motel, and they're $25 extra. Rates are $65–79. 1805 West 6th Street 91720; 951/371-7185.

Motel 6: Rates are $40–46 for one adult, $6 extra for the second. 200 North Lincoln Avenue 92882; 951/735-6408.

Perris

Dogs love Perris in the springtime. Dogs love Perris in the fall. Dogs love Perris in the winter, when it drizzles. Dogs don't love Perris in the summer, when it sizzles. Other than summertime, Perris is a favorite place for dogs. Not, as with the Paris song, because their love is near, but because the Orange Empire Railway Museum is here.

PARKS, BEACHES, AND RECREATION AREAS

7 Lake Perris State Recreation Area

🐾🐾🐾 (See Riverside County map on page 914)

When people talk about this park, they generally focus on the lake. Comments I got when I asked friends about the park included the following: "You can catch some world-class fish there." "We had a great time swimming at the beach." And "I like to stand on the edge and watch for birds."

Great. Well, dogs, if you're into any of the above activities, forget it. You can't go near the lake, much less in it or on it. In fact, pooches have to stay at

DIVERSION

Chug It Out with Your Dog: Dogs and railroads go together like love and marriage—or maybe even better. The **Orange Empire Railway Museum** is a great place to take a pooch. Jake Dog and I want to thank reader Marsden Chew MacRae for opening our eyes to this fun place. "On one memorable day, my golden retriever and I rode every single running exhibit, including the steam engine," writes Marsden Chew MacRae. (I use his three names again because he has such a great name.) "I also noted a rail fan with an attending German shepherd, who was much better trained than my dog and could actually get on and off without being lifted! Many dogs find the steps confusing and can't or won't navigate them, so bringing a dog small enough to lift might be important." That's some good advice from a man who knows his railroads. (He's traveled to many of the state's railroads with his faithful pooch.)

Leashed, well-behaved dogs can visit the museum's collection of streetcars, trolleys, a steam engine, and several diesels. They're not allowed in the buildings, but that's OK because the trains are much cooler. Speaking of cooler, it can get really hot here in summer, and this place can roast, so it's a good idea to bring your pooch here during other times of year.

Trolleys and trains operate 11 A.M.–5 P.M. Saturday and Sunday and major holidays. Special events are held throughout the year. An all-day ride pass is $8 for adults, $6 for children 5–11. Dogs and little kids don't pay a penny. Call or write for details. 2201 South A Street, P.O. Box 548, Perris, CA 92572-0548; 951/657-2605 or 951/943-3020; www.oerm.org.

least 50 feet from the lake's edge. But fortunately, you are allowed to wear a leash and hike the trails here. You'll be in sage scrub countryside, and there's not much shade, so go somewhere else if it's a hot day.

The day-use fee is $8 per vehicle. Camping costs $15–28. There are 167 tent-only sites and 265 RV sites. To reserve, phone 800/444-7275. From Highway 60, exit at Moreno Beach Drive and drive south a little more than three miles to the park. 951/657-0676.

PLACES TO STAY

Lake Perris State Recreation Area: See Lake Perris State Recreation Area, above, for camping information.

Idyllwild

This sweet, year-round mile-high resort is great for dogs on the go or for dogs who just like to sniff around artsy shops. Outdoorsy dogs can check out some marvelous hiking and cross-country skiing opportunities at the nearby San Bernardino National Forest (see the National Forests section at the beginning of the chapter). Indoorsy dogs can putter around the quaint alpine community's lovely village area.

With its myriad art galleries, visual art events, and music, dance, and theater productions, Idyllwild has been named as one of the 100 Best Small Art Towns in America. Dogs are invited into some galleries and little shops on a case-by-case basis, so we won't go into specifics here. Just let your terribly cute and well-behaved dog sniff toward the door of one of these establishments, and she may well get an invitation to come in and help you select some merchandise.

If you and your pooch want to experience small-town types of events in this quaint alpine community, there's plenty to keep you busy. Dogs and their well-behaved people are invited to everything from outdoor pancake feasts (always benefiting a good local cause) to the July Fourth parade (complete with a greyhound contingent). The Idyllwild Chamber of Commerce website lists these and other to-do's: www.idyllwildchamber.com; 951/659-3259.

PARKS, BEACHES, AND RECREATION AREAS

8 Idyllwild County Park

🐾🐾🐾 (See Riverside County map on page 914)

In the morning, the cool mountain air is delicately scented with fresh pines, and you may find yourself so invigorated that you actually want to get out of your tent and start the day early.

This is an attractive park, with scenic self-guided nature trails for you and your leashed pooch to peruse. Better yet, there's easy access to the wonderful, off-leash trails of San Bernardino National Forest. But you must check with a ranger before venturing out, because you could easily find yourself in the middle of Mt. San Jacinto State Park—a major no-no for four-legged beasts of the domestic persuasion.

The day-use fee is $2 for adults, $2 for dogs, $1 for kids. Campsites cost $15, with dogs being charged the usual $2 county fee. Reservations are accepted for the 96 sites April 1–October 24. The rest of the year they're available on a first-come, first-served basis. The park is one mile north of Idyllwild, at the end of County Park Road; 951/659-2656. For reservations call 800/234-PARK (800/234-7275).

PLACES TO EAT

Cafe Aroma: Your schnozzle may not be as sensitive as your dog's, but come anywhere near here and you'll find that the Cafe Aroma really lives up to its name. The place smells simply *mahvelous!* The cuisine is a mixture of coffee-house and Italian. Cafe Aroma is famous around here for its morning scones and coffee. Later in the day, the café is full of wonderful garlicky, saucy, rich smells. Evening diners get to eat on white tablecloth–covered tables. It's lovely but a bit perilous for the life of the tablecloth when you're downing your penne in spicy red sauce or your meatball pie! Dogs can join their people on the deck. (That sound you may hear is just your dog fervently praying for you to drop a chunk of that meatball pie.) 3596 North Circle Drive; 951/659-5212.

Oma's European Bakery and Restaurant: The salmon mousse, veggie sandwiches, and soups are tasty, but if you're hankering for something really different, try Oma's Famous Wurst Platter, a heavy-duty dish with three "European links," red cabbage or sauerkraut, and German potatoes. Get a soft pretzel on the side, and you'll be doing the polka all the way home. Dine with your drooling dog under the magnificent pines at Oma's big outdoor section. Thirsty dogs get water. 54241 Ridgeview; 951/659-2979.

PLACES TO STAY

Fireside Inn: The seven duplex cottages here are oh-so-cozy. (Please don't let "duplex" conjure images of ugly 1970s-style housing units. The wood cottages here are just partnered together, but they're not cheap-looking. Of course, even if they were, your dog wouldn't care.) Each cottage has its own fireplace, a private bath with shower, a sitting room, and color cable TV complete with VCR. Real wood, stained in a warm golden hue, flanks cabin walls. Most cabins have kitchenettes, and a few have patios. All are nonsmoking. Rates are $65–135. Dogs pay a $20 flat fee. 54540 North Circle Drive, P.O. Box 313 92549; 951/659-2966 or 877/797-3473; www.thefireside-inn.com.

Idyllwild County Park: See Idyllwild County Park, above, for camping information.

Knotty Pine Cabins: Dogs are welcome to stay at three of the eight wonderfully cozy, unique, well-appointed cabins here. (If you didn't already guess by the name, knotty pine figures heavily into the design schemes.) The cabins back up to a hill that's a fun place to give your dog some exercise. Although the cabins are within walking distance of Idyllwild village, this is a peaceful place to vacation with your dog. In addition to the usual pines, oaks, and other flora, the grounds are blessed with lilac bushes! The scent of these glorious flowers is well worth planning a spring vacation around. Rates are $59–135. Dogs are $20 extra for the length of your stay. 54340 Pine Crest 92549; 951/659-2933; www.idyllwild.com/knotty.

Tahquitz Inn: Here's a dog rule you don't hear every day: No peeing on the totem pole! The eagle-topped totem pole here is a tempting target for many a boy dog, so steer clear. There's plenty of room on the grounds for a good walk, and plenty of trees for dogs who want to lift a leg. Most of the 16 cabins that make up the inn are attached in sort of a stepped pattern. This arrangement looks very much like a giant shallow staircase that winds around the inn's small pool. The cabins are pretty basic and somewhat motelly inside, but they all have kitchens, and most have kind of funky fireplaces, so it's not so bad. The inn is 400 yards from Idyllwild's village. Rates are $85–110. Dogs are $10 extra. 25840 Highway 243 92549; 951/659-4554; www.tahquitzinn.com.

Mountain Center

While in town, stop by the Living Free animal sanctuary and see just how beautiful and livable an animal-rescue facility can be. Living Free occupies 160 acres of scenic mountain country at the edge of the San Bernardino National Forest. You and your dog can visit together, and while you're on tour finding out about the many wonderful programs here, your dog will be cared for in a special pen. Your dog is guaranteed tender loving care while you learn about ways to help other animals get the same kind of love. For more information, call 951/659-4684.

🐾 Hurkey Creek Park

🐾🐾🐾🐾 (See Riverside County map on page 914)

At an elevation of about 4,500 feet and surrounded by 7,000-foot peaks, this meadowlike park stays cool even in the summer. Hurkey Creek flows through here, attracting lots of critters, so be sure your dog is leashed.

There are a couple of hiking trails here and dogs love them. They'd really like to be able to sneak into the adjacent San Jacinto Wilderness, but it's one of the few national forest wilderness areas that doesn't permit pooches (because of its intermingling with a state park that bans dogs).

The day-use fee is $2 for adults, $2 for dogs, $1 for kids. Camping is $15, with dogs paying $2 for the privilege. The park is four miles south of Mountain Center off Highway 74. There are 130 campsites available. The park phone number is 951/659-2050. For camping reservations, call 800/234-PARK (800/234-7275).

PLACES TO STAY

Hurkey Creek Park: See Hurkey Creek Park, above, for camping information.

Palm Springs

First, the warning, straight from Esther M. W. Petersen, of the Palm Springs Animal Shelter: "Our area can be quite warm (HOT!!!!) all year-round, so please, please, please be sure to warn travelers about the dangers.... Our visitors don't seem to realize how hot it is. With our low humidity, it doesn't feel as hot as it really is, and pets can't handle the hot cement sidewalks, hot desert sand, and hot asphalt without getting burned pads."

DOG-EAR YOUR CALENDAR

The Caliente Tropics Resort, one of the most dog-friendly lodgings in California, is home to one of the most fun pet-charity events around: the **Bow-Wow Hukilau.** Among the events at this Polynesian-themed party (which goes hand-in-paw with the lodging's decor) is a Polynesian Water Sacrifice Ceremony, where local celebs get dunked in the pool in the name of charity. A pet psychic or two will do free readings even if your pet is not at the event. (If the psychic is good, here's what she'd hear from Jake the Dog: "Hmm. I wonder how hard it would be to get to the cookie jar off the counter again." Or more likely: "Zzzzzz, it's so nice sleeping on the couch. I hope Maria stays at that party for a long time.")

This is the time when famous pets and/or their famous people get inducted into the brand-new Pet Star Walk of Fame. Anna Nicole Smith and her Prozac-popping puppy Sugar Pie have their star embedded here. Most recently, Marcel, the black capuchin monkey who stole the show on *Friends* for a while, dipped his hands in the concrete. The Walk of Fame area gets lots of everyday use from happy dogs: It's in a wonderful, fenced, grassy area where dogs can walk around leash-free. (See the listing for the hotel for more on the dog perks here.)

The event, which is held in early September, also features cool dog events, pet adoptions, and scrumptious food. The ticket price is $25. Children under 12 get in free, as do dogs of any age. Phone 800/592-0157 for reservations. Walk-ins are invited too. 411 East Palm Canyon Drive, Palm Springs; www.calientetropics.com.

Petersen knows her stuff. She has seen too many dogs whimper their last breaths because of heatstroke and other heat-related horrors. The municipal code forbids dogs to be left unattended in enclosed vehicles, no matter what time of year. The law is a good one. Since it was enacted in 1988, not a single pet has been lost to this disastrous practice.

Believe it or not, the entire posh desert playground city of Palm Springs is a wildlife preserve. You can routinely spot coyotes, bobcats, raccoons, snakes, lizards, and migratory birds around town. Occasionally, mountain lions and badgers have been sighted. Make sure your dog is leashed and that you hold the leash securely at all times.

For many, many years, dogs were not allowed to set paw in any of the city's parks. But tails are wagging fast and furiously around here these days, because dogs now have a spectacular park of their own. (See Palm Springs Dog Park, below.) Palm Springs is also home to a few natural areas around

DIVERSION

Make Tracks to Saks: Need a frock for that special occasion and just can't bear to leave your furry friend behind? Good news! If she's clean, flea-free, well-behaved, leashed, and promises not to leave puddles, you can bring her with you to shop at **Saks Fifth Avenue.** The woman we spoke with at Saks says that "maybe you wouldn't want to bring a St. Bernard here." If you do bring a fairly decent-sized dog, please be sure to ask an employee if it's OK before starting your shopping spree. 201 North Palm Canyon Drive, Palm Springs; 760/327-4126.

town where you can take your pooch for a good walk. In addition, you can also take your dog to some fun, if *un*natural, places.

Several spectacular lodgings (and several not-quite-so-spectacular ones) welcome well-behaved dogs. Many Palm Springs restaurants permit dogs to dine outside with you. And many of the shops on Palm Canyon Drive let pets shop with their people. If you want your dog's opinion on a new bangle or beaded dress, you can even bring him to Saks Fifth Avenue. Just make sure he doesn't do a leg lift on the merchandise.

PARKS, BEACHES, AND RECREATION AREAS

If you want to feel the desert in your paws when you and your dog go out for a walk, you'll be happy to know that Palm Springs is surrounded by land run by the Bureau of Land Management. Call 760/251-4800 for information on fun places to hike during the cooler months.

Dog owners in town frequently use the many local "wash" areas (dry streambeds) to run on leash with their dogs. You'll see them on the outskirts of town and beyond, but with the new park's opening, you might not see them as much as you used to.

You can also take your leashed pooch to a nearby hiking area for an interesting desert romp. The Carl Lykken Hiking Trail starts at the extreme west end of Ramon Road. Don't forget your water. (There's some talk about banning dogs from the trail, so don't be surprised if you see one of those horrible signs with a slash through a dog silhouette during a future walk.) Unfortunately, our other favorite area for dogs, the 27,000-acre Indian Canyons, no longer allows dogs because of some very bad incidents with pit bulls and their people.

DIVERSION

Who Needs Hollywood?: You and your dog can sniff out the sidewalk-embedded stars of more than 70 celebrities who have "lived, loved, and played" in Palm Springs. The **Palm Springs Walk of Stars** includes stars for Ralph Bellamy, Elizabeth Taylor, Frank Sinatra, Bob Hope, Ginger Rogers, Marilyn Monroe, and Marlene Dietrich. The Walk is on Palm Canyon Drive in the beautiful central village. You can get a complete list of stars and their locations on the Walk by visiting www.palmsprings.com/stars.

10 Palm Springs Dog Park

🐾🐾🐾🐾🦮 (See Riverside County map on page 914)

Dogs of Palm Springs are panting, but not because of the heat (they all live in air-conditioned quarters, after all). They're panting with joy, because their dog park is so wonderful. This isn't just any ordinary dog park. Lest you've forgotten, this is Palm Springs, after all.

This 1.6-acre park is a real work of art, complete with an iron fence and double gates designed by sculptor Phil Evans. (How many dog-park fences have dog paws and faces carved into them?) It's big compared to many dog parks, and it has everything a dog could want—and a lot more: It's grassy, with some trees, awnings for extra shade, a separate fenced area for pups or tiny dogs who are overwhelmed by the big dogs running around the main area, drinking fountains that have two levels so humans and their pooches can slurp together, picnic tables, lights at night, and plenty of poop bags. For your boy dog's aiming pleasure, the park also features *11* fire hydrants. Of course, these aren't your run-of-the-mill hydrants. These hydrants are of the beautiful antique variety. Your dog will do leg lifts in style.

The park is directly behind City Hall, at 222 Civic Drive North; 760/322-8362.

PLACES TO EAT

Palm Springs is full of fine restaurants with outdoor areas where dogs are welcome.

Blue Coyote Grill: You and your dog can't exactly eat together here, since she must remain tied up just outside the railing while you sit just inside it. But she'll still be close enough to drool over the Southwestern delights on your dish. 445 North Palm Canyon Drive; 760/327-1196.

Hair of the Dog: As long as you don't find anything resembling this English pub's name floating in your appetizers or your beer, you'll enjoy it here. People can sit at a half-dozen outdoor tables with their pooches. 238 North Palm Canyon Drive; 760/323-9890.

DIVERSION

My Fair Laddy: Well-behaved, leashed pooches may accompany you 7–10 P.M. Thursday evenings to Palm Springs's glamorous Palm Canyon Drive, where an old-fashioned **street fair** will charm the spots off your dog. Musicians, food, arts and crafts vendors, and a certified farmer's market make this street even more charming than it normally is. The fair takes place between Tahquitz Canyon Drive and Baristo Road. Parking is best behind the Desert Inn Fashion Plaza. Call 800/34-SPRINGS (800/347-7746) for more information.

Native Foods: "A most outrageous vegetarian restaurant" is how regular diners Hannah the Human and her dogs Gracie and Petey describe this comfortable and dog-friendly restaurant. "It's the best place of all for your book." It's certainly right up there, especially if you're a vegetarian or vegan. Native Foods offers all kinds of tasty dishes—so tasty, in fact, that even avid omnivores enjoy plowing through the menu's offerings. Co-owner Tanya Petrovna is a dog lover through and through. She makes sure canine guests get a big bowl of water. (This distracts doggies, who are then less likely to beg for your delectable veggie wrap or cheesecake—at least for a minute.) Native Foods has one of Palm Spring's more pleasant patio areas for pooches and their people. Misters keep things cool, or at least tolerable. We're talking mister, as in a device that provides a cool mist, not mister as in Mister Rogers. (Although come to think of it, he always kept things cool too.) 1775 East Palm Canyon Drive; 760/416-0070.

Peabody's: You won't find Mr. Peabody here, but all other dogs, brainy or not, are welcome to dine with you on the patio. 134 South Palm Canyon Drive; 760/322-1877.

Spencer's at the Mountain: Dogs go ga-ga when you order the delicious pecan-crusted chicken, but the drool really flows when they sniff out the steak and lobster dishes Spencer's is known for. (The liver and bacon sets their noses aflutter too, but that combo sounds too much like canned dog-food varieties for us.) Dine next to the trees at one of two patios here. Thirsty dogs get a bowl of water. 701 West Baristo Road; 760/327-3446.

PLACES TO STAY

Palm Springs has oodles of quality canine accommodations. It used to be that they allowed only the itsy-bitsy-est of dog-ettes. Now most welcome any size good dog.

Caliente Tropics Resort: If you like campy, retro, fun, attractive, super-dog-friendly accommodations, look no further than this fully renovated 1960s

Polynesian-style motel. The rooms are tiki-boutique-y, tiki torches flank the pool and the grounds, and the signage is delectably 1964.

You and your dog can sniff out tiki god statues and other Polynesian artifacts throughout the resort. There's a tall, cylindrical, angry-looking god head outside that can scare the daylights out of more sensitive dogs. One pooch wrote to tell me he had a little accident when he sniffed it out, thinking it was a tree at first until he saw its glowering eyes and fierce mouth. He fluffed up, cowered two steps back, and "suddenly my owners found themselves wishing they had a pooper-scooper." This dog asked that I not use his name because he is embarrassed about this incident. Poor Frank. (Oops! Sorry, Frank.)

With the exception of a few rare incidents such as Frank's, dogs absolutely adore this place. It's one of the more dog-friendly lodgings in this book. Dogs who come here get gourmet treats shaped like tiki heads, water and food dishes, blankets, poop bags, and cushy dog beds. Best of all, there's a fenced grassy area by the pool where well-behaved dogs are welcome to trot around leash-free. In fact, there's even a fledgling Pet Star Walk of Fame right there. The stars will be dedicated annually at a really fun fund-raiser called the Bow-Wow Hukilau. (For more on this, see Dog-Ear Your Calendar.)

In case you or your dog are interested in a little celeb history, you should know that long ago the Caliente had a private underground supper club where Elvis, the Rat Pack, and other big celebs could relax in peace. It was beautiful, with the popular colors of the time—purple and white—on the leather banquettes, white tablecloths, and a stage. Alas, a former owner concerned about earthquake-proofing filled it with concrete.

Room rates are $65–225. Dogs are $20 extra. 411 East Palm Canyon Drive 92264; 760/327-1391 or 866/HOT-9595 (866/468-9595); www.calientetropics.com.

Casa Cody Country Inn: Dogs love this quaint, quiet historic country inn almost as much as their peace-seeking people do. Past canine visitors have caused some problems because irresponsible owners have left them alone in the room. Don't even think of doing this. Rates are $49–199. Dogs are $10 extra for the length of your stay. 175 South Cahuilla Road 92262; 760/320-9346; www.casacody.com.

Doral Resort: This attractive hotel is set on a golf course. Some of the rooms have great views. Dogs up to 50 pounds can stay here. Rates are $69–219. Dogs pay a $50 flat fee. 67-967 Vista Chino 92234; 760/322-7000; www.doralpalmsprings.com.

Hilton Palm Springs Resort: "We are delighted to have dogs as guests. They find it very entertaining here," a vivacious, dog-loving staffer tells us. "That's why all the rooms have balconies. Dogs like to look out and see what's going on." From one side of this very comfortable, attractive hotel, dogs can look out at the mountains. From the other, they can look down at the swimming pool. Ask the concierge about nearby places to walk with your dog. "Lots of folks bring their pets here, and we've got some great places for them to walk," another staffer said. Rates are $130–400. Dogs require a $100 deposit, and they pay a $20 flat fee. 400 East Tahquitz 92262; 760/320-6868 or 800/522-6900; www.hiltonpalmsprings.com.

Motel 6: There are three of these motels in Palm Springs. Rates are $40–58 for one adult, $6 extra for a second adult. Phone 800/466-8356 for information and reservations.

Musicland Hotel: "Any pooch under 200 pounds is OK," says a dog-friendly staffer. Rates are $33–99. Dogs are $5 extra. 1342 South Palm Canyon Drive 92264; 760/325-1326.

Palm Springs Riviera Resort and Racquet Club: If you like recreation, you'll love this large, gorgeous resort. The Riviera boasts Palm Springs's biggest pool, plus an 18-hole lighted putting course and several lighted tennis courts. (It's home of the Billie Jean King World Team Tennis Finals, if that tells you how nice the courts are.) You can also play basketball and volleyball here, and the workout room is more than adequate.

Dogs don't care about all this, because they can't do much other than lounge in the room and stroll the palm-festooned grounds with you. But the rooms are beautifully appointed in relaxing earthy hues, and the grounds are 24 acres of fun (no golf-course jaunts with dogs, please), so there's plenty to keep a pooch happy here. If you want to live it up, stay at one of the poolside suites. They're exquisite. Rates are $79–349. Dogs are $20 extra and require a $200 deposit. 1600 North Indian Canyon Drive 92262; 760/327-8311; www.psriviera.com.

A Place in the Sun: This is a fun place to stay if you like your immaculate room or larger bungalow surrounded by greenery and palms and backed by mountains. The two-bedroom bungalows (the largest accommodations) have a patio and fireplace, as well as a full kitchen. The pool and whirlpool tub are blissfully chorine-free! They're actually filled with mild salt water (advertised as being only half as salty as your own teardrops). And yahoo! There's no longer the former size limit of 20 pounds. Any size good dog can stay here. Rates are $79–309. Dogs are $15 extra. 754 San Lorenzo Road 92264; 760/325-0254 or 800/779-2254; www.aplaceinthesunhotel.com.

Quality Inn Resort: Rates are $49–189. 1269 East Palm Canyon Drive 92264; 760/323-2775 or 800/221-2222.

7 Springs Inn and Suites: Dogs and their people adore staying at this charming, affordable boutique hotel. The 50 rooms and suites are relaxing and beautifully designed, with tranquil earth tones, 500-thread-count sheets (the last motel we stayed at seemed to have 25-thread-count sheets; ouch!), goose-down pillows, marble floors, granite countertops, and views of the inn's little pool and garden area. Rates are $69–259. Dogs are $15 extra. 950 North Indian Canyon Drive 92262; 760/320-9110 or 800/883-0417; www.7springs.info.

Super 8 Lodge: If you're traveling with more than one dog, this is a good place to bunk for the night: You can have up to three dogs per room, and the cost is only $10 extra per room. Room rates are $45–85. 1900 North Palm Canyon Drive 92262; 760/322-3757.

Villa Rosa Inn: It's trees, trees everywhere at this lovely motel/inn, where all six accommodations are poolside. Dogs love the trees, and they enjoy the spacious southwest-meets-Pier-1-Imports–style rooms and suites. Especially comforting to hot dogs are the cool terracotta tile floors. Built in 1948, this inn is just as immaculate and crisp as the day it was born. (Except the flowers and arbors are a lot bigger now.) Rates are $89–169. Dogs are $20 extra, and shouldn't be too big. "We try to keep them not major size," says an innkeeper. 1577 South Indian Trail 92264; 760/327-5915; www.villaroseinn.com.

Palm Desert

This desert resort town's motto, "Where the sun shines a little brighter," could use an addendum these days. We think it should read, "Where the sun shines a little brighter and dogs smile a little wider." See why below.

PARKS, BEACHES AND RECREATION AREAS

You may think nothing grows in the desert, but two dog parks have recently popped right out of the ground like miraculous desert flowers. Actually, it was a lot more work than just popping out of the ground. But the success of these dog parks has paved the path for more in the future. A city councilman told the *Desert Sun* newspaper that he doesn't foresee any parks being built in Palm Desert without having some kind of dog park. Oh, what a wonderful place to be a dog!

🔢 Civic Center Park Dog Park

🐾🐾🐾🐕 (See Riverside County map on page 914)

This luscious canine oasis is grassy, with trees, shaded seating, double gates, a beautiful iron fence, a separate area for small dogs who would rather not mess with the big guys, poop bags, and a big fire hydrant. The hydrant is so popular we've even heard about dogs lining up to make their mark.

The park is less than an acre, but dogs take advantage of their leashless freedom. They run and run, drink some water, run and run, sniff a newcomer, run and run, head for the hydrant, and run and run some more. Meanwhile, the people here have a grand old time socializing with each other. The park is set within the attractive Civic Center Park, where there's a nice playground and lovely landscaping. It's at Fred Waring Drive and San Pablo Avenue, near College of the Desert. 760/346-0611.

🔢 Country Club Dog Park

🐾🐾🐕 (See Riverside County map on page 914)

No, you won't see dogs clad in white golf outfits showing off their pedigrees here. Any breed or mutt is welcome at Country Club Dog Park, and they can be stark naked, too. They don't even have to wear leashes at this fenced park. The reason for the exclusive-sounding name is because the park is in the Palm Desert Country Club neighborhood.

The park is less than half the size of the Civic Center dog park, but it has many of the same amenities, including grass, benches, water, poop bags, shade cover, and even a fire hydrant. It's set in a new community park (which also has "country club" in it) at Avenue of the States and California Avenue. 760/346-0611.

PLACES TO STAY

Desert Patch Inn: Dogs who dig quiet digs will enjoy this small inn. The rooms are spacious, and while not super-stylish, they're clean and have fridges and microwaves. The grounds are lovely, with palms, a pool, and loads of greenery. An extensive continental breakfast comes with your stay. Rates are $47–130. 73-758 Shadow Mountain Drive 92260; 760/346-9161 or 800/350-9758; www.desertpatch.com.

The Inn at Deep Canyon: You and your dog can feast your eyes on the motel's palms, garden, pool, and hydrotherapy spa from most rooms here. You'll get a continental breakfast, too. Rates are $47–261. Dogs are $10 extra. 74-470 Abronia Trail 92260; 760/346-8061 or 800/253-0004; www.inn-adc.com.

Indio

It may look flat and boring, but this dry old town has the distinction of being the king of the only region in the United States that grows dates. And we're not talking a few trees—we're talking 4,000 acres' worth, making a semioasis out of an otherwise blah, depressing area.

PARKS, BEACHES, AND RECREATION AREAS

🔢 Miles Avenue Park

😾 😾 (See Riverside County map on page 914)

If you're dropping someone off at the adjacent Coachella Valley Museum and Cultural Center, your dog might appreciate a little pause at this grassy, meadowy park. It looks like a golf course, but miraculously enough in this golf-inundated land, it's not. There are some deciduous trees, as well as palms, for the benefit of the boy dogs in the crowd.

The park is on Deglet Noor Street and Miles Avenue, about three blocks north of Highway 111. 760/342-6580.

PLACES TO EAT

Andy's Restaurant: The outdoor seating area is not huge, but that won't make your dog drool any less over the burgers, pastrami, and hot dogs you can eat here. Breakfast is also available. 83-699 Indio Boulevard; 760/347-1794.

PLACES TO STAY

Best Western Date Tree Motor Hotel: Rates are $60–120. Pooches are $10 extra. 81-909 Indio Boulevard 92201; 760/347-3421; www.datetree.com.

Palm Shadow Inn: This motel is truly a desert oasis. Its three acres of green grounds are ripe with flowers and date trees. There are a pool and hot tub too. Not much here says "desert" except the sweet, dry air. Some of the rooms come with kitchens, which can make life easier when traveling with a pooch. Rates are $84–129. Dogs are $5 extra. 80-761 Highway 111 92201; 760/347-3476 or 800/700-8071; www.palmshadowinn.com.

Royal Plaza Inn: You'll get a heated pool and a spa when you stay here, but no pooches in the *agua,* please. Rates are $44–129. Dogs are $10 extra. 82-347 Highway 111 92201; 760/347-0911.

Blythe

If you're traveling from the east on I-10 and vow that you'll stop in the first California town you hit, get ready to brake. Blythe isn't an exciting town, but it's a welcome sight if you've traveled across the country with the Golden State as your goal.

PARKS, BEACHES, AND RECREATION AREAS

14 Mayflower Park

🐾🐾🐾 (See Riverside County map on page 914)

This park covers only 24 acres, but because it backs up on the refreshing Colorado River, it seems much bigger. The folks here are pretty laid-back about dogs when it's not crowded. Pooches should be leashed, but you can still let them do a little wading in the water. Just watch out for those pesky boats.

Mayflower Park is an excellent place to stop if you've been driving all day and feel like fishing for stripers or catfish, cooking your catch for dinner, and then camping by the river.

The day-use fee is $2 for adults, $2 for dogs, $1 for kids. Camping costs $15–16, with dogs costing $2 extra. There are 180 sites available. The park is six miles northeast of Blythe, just north of 6th Avenue and Colorado River Road. Sites are first-come, first-served. For park info, call 760/922-4665.

PLACES TO STAY

Best Western Sahara Motel: Rates are $59–109. 825 West Hobson Way 92225; 760/922-7105.

Hidden Beaches: This is one of the many camping resorts along the Colorado River. Sites are $22–27 per day, and pooches cost $2 extra. There are 92 sites available. Reservations are recommended in the summer. 6951 6th Avenue 92225; 760/922-7276.

Legacy Inn: Rates are $45–62. Small pooches are preferred, and they need to stay in smoking rooms. 903 West Hobson Way 92225; 760/922-4146.

Mayflower Park: See Mayflower Park, above, for camping information.

McIntyre Park: Dogs can stay here only in the winter (November–March). The camping fee is $20–25 per car or RV. There are sites to accommodate approximately 700 people. We're not exactly talking an intimate camping experience. Call for RV or riverfront reservations. Others are available on a first-come, first-served basis. 8750 East 26th Avenue 92225; 760/922-8205.

Temecula

If cruising around the area makes you and your dog think it's all just one big subdivision after another, you need a visit to Old Town Temecula, with its attractive storefronts, antique shops, eateries, and host of fun events. While you're at it, take a trip to the area's wine country. You can drive while your dog drinks. Wait, your dog can drive while you drink. Hmm. Well, I'm sure you'll work it out between you. (See the Diversion Whine Not!)

PARKS, BEACHES, AND RECREATION AREAS

Some people here drive 80 miles round-trip to use Escondido's dog park—one of the closest around at this point. Locals have been working toward getting their own dog park for years, and at press time it looks as if they were finally going to get their wish: In 2005, if all goes as planned, there will be a fenced dog park at the Temecula Community Recreation Center, at 30875 Rancho Vista Road. Call 951/694-6410 for updates.

15 Lake Skinner County Park

😺😺😺😺 (See Riverside County map on page 914)

So what if your dog can't swim in the lake or even hang out in your boat with you? Of the 6,040 acres of park, the lake makes up only about 1,200 acres. That means several thousand acres of hilly chaparral country are all yours. Leashed pooches are permitted to peruse the trails and run around the open turf areas.

During the rainy season, the trails may be closed. Call before you visit. The day-use fee is $2 per adult and $1 per child. Campsites are $12–18. Dogs are $2 extra. There are approximately 265 campsites. From I-15, take the Rancho California Avenue exit northeast and drive about nine miles to the park. For park information, call 951/926-1541. Call 800/234-PARK (800/234-7275) for reservations.

DIVERSION

Whine Not!: You can visit Temecula's fine wineries with your dogs, so there's no need to cry into your beer. Most of the 18 wineries here allow dogs to join you at their outdoor picnic areas. One of the humans in your party can go inside, do some tasting and touring, and perhaps bring out a bottle fresh from the cellars for your little picnic.

A very dog-friendly winery is **Bella Vista Cilurzo Vineyard and Winery,** at 41220 Calle Contento; 909/676-5250. "We love dogs!" says a winery rep who has a dog of her own. Equally dog-friendly is **Keyways Vineyard and Winery,** at 37338 DePortola Road; 909/302-7888. "We allow horses," says a Keyways vintner. "Every week about 20 riders come up, park their horses, drink some wine, and ride away." (Now that's a new twist on drinking and driving.) "So of course we'll allow dogs." **Wilson Creek Winery** also welcomes pooches at its picnic tables. It's at 35960 Rancho California Road; 909/699-9463.

You'll find a helpful list and map of all of Temecula's wineries, their websites, and basic info at www.temeculawines.com.

PLACES TO STAY

Lake Skinner County Park: See Lake Skinner County Park, above, for camping information.

Motel 6: Rates are $45–67 for the first adult, $6 for the second. 41900 Moreno Drive 92590; 951/676-7199.

La Quinta

PLACES TO STAY

La Quinta Resort and Club: First, for all of you who have stayed at the La Quinta motel chain with your dog, this isn't one of those motels. Not by a long shot. This La Quinta is the mother of all La Quintas. This internationally famous resort is probably the most legendary of all the posh getaways in the Palm Springs area. The town of La Quinta was named after it, if that tells you anything. Built in 1926, it's the area's oldest resort. It quickly became a favorite retreat for the stars of the Golden Era of Hollywood. (Frank Capra wrote *It Happened One Night* in a casita here, and after its success, he declared it his good-luck charm and returned frequently to write other screenplays.)

Before you read on, you should know that if your dog is more than 25 pounds, he can't accompany you here. Jake Dog cried in his kibble when he heard about this rule. I thought I'd spare you and yours the same disappointment and tell you up front, and not down below. Actually, according to some unidentified sources, bigger dogs have been known to be allowed here. It may be worth a try, if your heart is set on this wonderland and your dog weighs more than his bag of dog food.

Everything here is top-drawer. The 804 guest casitas, each a Spanish-style cottage, are beautifully furnished and offer real privacy and peace. Many have wood-burning fireplaces. The landscaping is lush, with gorgeous flowers and palms everywhere. The restaurants are magnificent (some allow doggies at their patios) and the shops at La Quinta's plaza are some of the finest around. Even the beauty parlor is special—a fun art deco style. For humans, there are 41 swimming pools, 34 spas, 23 tennis courts, and 90 famous holes of championship golf. You can get a massage in the sun, work out in the fitness center, and do a zillion other wonderful things. For dogs, there are a few little areas to ramble leash-free on the surrounding 45 acres, but you'll have to ask about those because we're not supposed to tell you where they are.

Dogs are relegated to the cottages with enclosed private patios. Rates for these are $225–445. Dogs pay a $100 fee for the length of their stay. 49-499 Eisenhower Drive, P.O. Box 69 92253; 760/564-4111 or 800/598-3828; www.laquintaresort.com.

Mecca

PARKS, BEACHES, AND RECREATION AREAS

🐾6 Salton Sea State Recreation Area

🐾🐾🐾 (See Riverside County map on page 914)

If you ever wanted to explore the Salton Sea (see the introduction to the Imperial County chapter for information on this strange and wonderful body of water), this is a great place to start your observations. The park has 16 miles of shoreline, including five beaches. Dogs must wear the mandatory leash attire, but they manage to have a fabulous time anyway.

Unfortunately, dogs are not allowed on the trails that connect a couple of these areas together, but you can transport your pooch from one area to another by car. You should try to spend at least one night. Three of the beaches are primitive and they have campsites right at the seaside. While dogs must be leashed, they still love dunking their paws in the very buoyant water.

The day-use fee is $4. Camping costs $10–14. There are 149 developed sites available on a first-come, first-served basis. Dogs generally prefer the cheaper, more primitive sites. About half of the park is in Imperial County. If you're approaching the lake from the southeast side, see the listing in the

Imperial County chapter for directions. Otherwise, take Highway 111 southeast of Mecca about 10 miles, and you'll find the park headquarters and visitor center on the west side of the highway. 760/393-3059.

PLACES TO STAY

Salton Sea State Recreation Area: See the Salton Sea State Recreation Area, above, for camping information.

CHAPTER 58
Imperial County

Although this county is home to the Imperial Valley, one of the richest farming areas in the world, it's much more than just an agricultural wonderland. In fact, when you wander into the most dog-friendly areas, you'll wonder how land around here could be used for anything but sandboxes.

About 1.5 million acres of desert here is run by the Bureau of Land Management—those dog-friendly folks who rarely demand a leash. The dune areas are fascinating, and your dog will love racing up and down the sandy expanses.

Nearby is the strange and salty Salton Sea. At 36 miles long and 15 miles wide, it's one of the world's largest inland bodies of salt water. Although officially considered a lake, it's got most of the qualities of a sea, including the fact that from most of its shoreline, you can look across and see vast, astounding nothingness.

PICK OF THE LITTER—IMPERIAL COUNTY

MOST MOONLIKE PARK
Red Hill Marina County Park, Calipatria (page 946)

BIGGEST LEASH-FREE SANDY PLAYGROUND
Imperial Sand Dunes, Brawley (page 947)

The sea is situated at 234 feet below sea level (the "normal" sea level, that is), directly atop the San Andreas Fault. Millions of years ago, the valley region here was filled with lakes and streams. But the lakes dried up as seismic activity caused the mountains to the west to grow, cutting off the moist, cool air from the ocean.

Then in 1905, the Colorado River flooded in Mexico and caused a two-year flood through the brand-new Imperial Valley irrigation system. It sparked the rebirth of the lake known as the Salton Sea.

Mixed with minerals left by earlier seas, as well as present-day evaporation and fertilizer runoff, the water is 10 percent saltier than an ocean. Dogs like to float around in it, but watch out for their eyes.

And if you smell a really foul stench while you're here, you may be tempted to drive away as fast as your four wheels will take you. The occasionally malodorous air is caused by an algae bloom and resulting fish die-off, and the operative expression here is *"Peeuuuw!"* But before you zip away, stop for a moment and let your dog take a few good, deep breaths of this wretched stink. She'll be on an olfactory high for the rest of the day.

Salton City

If you happen to have the *Twilight Zone* theme in your car, pop it in as you approach this land that time forgot.

After you notice the bright blue Salton Sea in the background, you'll become aware of lots and lots of lots. Empty ones. Many miles of curved, suburban-style roads wind in and out of this flat waterfront community, but no one is home. There should be thousands of houses on these paved grids, but there are only a smattering. It's as if Rod Serling went all out and made one of his eerie dollhouse-scale sets life-sized.

What actually happened was an optimistic real estate sellout in the 1950s and 1960s. An extensive road system was developed and 20,000 lots were sold. But the folks who bought them generally just kept their investment without plopping down so much as a mobile home. So the roads essentially lead to nowhere. When you get lost on them, don't panic. Just remember that Rod Serling isn't around anymore, so this really couldn't be as strange as it seems, and you really couldn't be in the *Twilight Zone.* Could you?

PARKS, BEACHES, AND RECREATION AREAS

🟥 Martin Flora Park

🐾 (See Imperial County map on page 942)

Although the Salton City area is full of empty shoreline, community-service folks ask that you stick to the public parks with your dog. This isn't such a bad place to take a leashed pooch. It looks a little like a gravel parking lot, but never mind that. The Salton Sea is right here and so are plenty of picnic tables. The park is an unusual place to stop for lunch.

From Highway 86, turn northeast on North Marina Drive and follow it past all the empty streets. As the road approaches the sea, it will curve to the right. In a few blocks, you'll come to Sea Port Avenue. Go left, and follow it a few more blocks to the park. Make sure you can figure out how to get back to Highway 86 before you leave, because many people have become mighty lost here, and there aren't many homes where you can stop and ask for help. And this park doesn't have any sort of a phone number we can refer you to. We talked to eight people at different entities, and they all know vaguely about the park, but no one has any idea who would be the contact. Perhaps the Twilight Zone isn't as far away as we think....

Bombay Beach

PARKS, BEACHES, AND RECREATION AREAS

🟥 Salton Sea State Recreation Area

🐾🐾🐾 (See Imperial County map on page 942)

Since most people visit the north end of this 16-mile-long park that sits on the northeast section of the Salton Sea, you'll find its description in the Mecca section of the Riverside County chapter. But if you have a hankering to discover the Imperial County section of the park, take Highway 111 to any of several entrances, including the popular Bombay Beach area. 760/393-3052.

PLACES TO STAY

Salton Sea State Recreation Area: See the Mecca section of the Riverside County chapter for camping information.

Palo Verde

PARKS, BEACHES, AND RECREATION AREAS

❸ Palo Verde County Park

🐾🐾 (See Imperial County map on page 942)

While this is only a 10-acre park, its location at the border of Arizona directly off Highway 78 makes it a popular stopping point for dogs and their human chauffeurs.

The park is set on a backwater of the Colorado River. It's a refreshing place to spend an hour, a day, or a night. Camping and day-use fees are nonexistent and no permits are required. The fishing's pretty decent, too, in case you're hankering to angle.

From I-10 in the Blythe area (Riverside County), exit at Highway 78 and drive south, following the occasional westward jogs in the highway. After about 18 miles, you'll cross into Imperial County. The park is another 2.5 miles down the road, just off the highway. 760/482-4384.

PLACES TO STAY

Palo Verde County Park: See Palo Verde County Park, above, for camping information.

Calipatria

PARKS, BEACHES, AND RECREATION AREAS

❹ Red Hill Marina County Park

🐾🐾🐾🐾 (See Imperial County map on page 942)

This peninsular park jutting into the southeast corner of the Salton Sea feels more like an island. The terrain is early moonscape and the 240-acre park is pretty much one big hill. You and your dog can see all the way to the Mexican border from here!

Dogs must be leashed, but at least they're allowed. They're banned from the neighboring Salton Sea National Wildlife Refuge.

The day-use fee is $2. Campsites are $7–12. There are 400 campsites available. No reservations are necessary. From Highway 111 just north of Calipatria, go west on Schrimpf Road, which is a graded dirt road. In about five miles, you'll be at the park. 760/482-4384.

PLACES TO STAY

Red Hill Marina County Park: See Red Hill Marina County Park, above, for camping information.

Brawley

PARKS, BEACHES, AND RECREATION AREAS

🔟 Imperial Sand Dunes

🐾🐾🐾🐾🦮 (See Imperial County map on page 942)

Before going on about how enthralling this enormous, off-leash desert sandbox is, I want to play back something local Bureau of Land Management staffer Roseann Madrigal told me.

"Too often we get calls from someone who starts out crying, and when we ask what's wrong, they say they lost their poor dog in the desert," she said. "We hate those kind of calls. It's so sad. People let their pets wander too far sometimes, and they get disoriented and lost. Out here, there's not a good chance for survival, even when it's not extremely hot. We try to help them find their dog, but this is a big place. You feel so helpless.

"Please tell your readers not to let their dog go far, and always have an eye on him. If they can't, then just keep him leashed," she said.

Got it? This applies to any off-leash area discussed in this book, but out here in the desert, follow Madrigal's words like the gospel. She's fielded many of these distraught phone calls, and she knows what she's talking about.

Now the good stuff. The Bureau of Land Management oversees 1.5 million acres in Imperial County. Much of the acreage is within this vast dune system, full of wind-sculpted crests and ripples that extend for more than 40 miles. The Imperial Dunes (also known as the Algodones Dunes) rise to 300 feet, and they're great fun to hike on or around with your leash-free pooch.

Two-thirds of the dune area north of Highway 78 is closed to vehicles, so it's an ideal place for a dog hike. This is also where you may spot all sorts of desert wildflowers. An added bonus: You can set up your tent just about anywhere in the area, and there's no fee.

The BLM ranger station is a good place to start your adventure. No permit is necessary. From central Brawley, drive east on Highway 78 about 19 miles to Gecko Road. Turn right, and the ranger station is about a mile down the road. 760/337-4400.

PLACES TO STAY

Imperial Sand Dunes: See Imperial Sand Dunes, above, for camping information.

Town House Lodge: All rooms come with a microwave and a refrigerator, so if you and your dog want to eat in, this is a good choice. Rates are $49–65. Dogs are $5–10 extra. 135 Main Street 92227; 760/344-5120.

Imperial

PARKS, BEACHES, AND RECREATION AREAS

6 Eager Park

🐾 (See Imperial County map on page 942)

Stop here if your dog is longing to get out of the car or house and doesn't mind visiting a postage stamp–sized park. There are a few small trees and a small playground. Maybe the park should be reserved for Chihuahuas and Pekinese pooches, or at least dogs with small expectations. Dogs must be leashed.

From Highway 86, go west on 10th Street and left on H Street. 760/355-4371.

El Centro

PARKS, BEACHES, AND RECREATION AREAS

7 Sunbeam Lake County Park

🐾🐾🐾 (See Imperial County map on page 942)

This county park is filled with big old eucalyptus trees. That's not normally a selling point, but boy dogs who are tired of lifting their legs on desert boulders around this area seem to appreciate any kind of tree.

Sunbeam Lake itself is a fun fishing and swimming hole. Dogs must be leashed, so swimming is a bit restricted. The trails in this 140-acre park provide a fun walk for you and the leashed pooch.

It'll cost you $2 to use this park during the day. The park has an RV campground, and it's privately run. The 309 RV-only sites are $25–35. The park is seven miles west of El Centro. Exit I-8 at Drew Road and drive about a half mile north. 760/337-4557.

8 Bucklin Park

🐾🐾 (See Imperial County map on page 942)

It's like a golf course here, complete with ultragreen, ultrashort turf, the occasional palm tree, and a little pond. It's a lovely place to take a Sunday afternoon stroll with your favorite leashed pooch.

The park is at 8th Street and Ross Avenue. 760/352-2111.

PLACES TO STAY

Brunner's Inn and Suites: Rates are $50–75. 215 North Imperial Avenue 92243; 760/352-6431.

Ramada Inn El Centro: It's comfortable and clean here, and you get use of a heated outdoor pool and a small exercise room. Rates are $72–$90. Dogs are $10 extra. 1455 Ocotillo Drive 92243; 760/352-5152.

Sunbeam Lake County Park: See Sunbeam Lake County Park, above, for camping information.

RESOURCES

National Forests and Wilderness Areas

Dogs of California, rejoice! If you really want to stretch those gams, the U.S. Department of Agriculture's Forest Service has a real treat for you. Instead of a walk in your friendly neighborhood park, how does an exhilarating, off-leash hike sound? You'll have your choice of 20 million acres of national forests (an astounding 20 percent of California) spread over a fascinating variety of terrain.

Most dogs call the forests "dog heaven." Those who don't speak English just pant with joy. There's something for every dog's tastes in national forests. Desert dogs are as happy as dogs who like dank redwood forests. Most national forests have no entry fees, few leash rules, and plenty of free camping. And they all have some of the most beautiful land in California.

If your dog is obedient enough to come when she's called, and you trust her not to wander off in pursuit of deer or other wildlife, she's more than welcome to be off leash in most of the forest areas. Be aware that the frontline personnel at the forests might tell you that dogs must be on leash, but they're not always right. Ask for a supervisor or ranger if you have reason to think the leash laws are more lax. (There are definitely areas where dogs must be on leash. There's good reason for this, so make sure you follow these rules where they do exist.)

Always carry a leash with you. It's a good idea to leash your dog on the trail when you see other hikers, or at least to pull your dog to the side so they can pass by. "Believe it or not, not everyone loves dogs," says Matt Mathes, a dog-loving, very helpful representative of the USDA Forest Service. Dogs must be leashed in developed campgrounds (which usually charge a small fee) and in developed recreation areas. But most areas of the forests are set up so that you can plop down a tent just about anywhere you please (for free). When you find that perfect, cool stream with a flat, soft area on the bank, your dog doesn't have to be leashed. But it's a bad idea to leave your dog leashless and outside your tent at night. The best place for a backpacking dog to sleep at night is in the tent with her people.

The Forest Service's California website, www.fs.fed.us/r5, offers excellent guides to every National Forest in the state. Maps of specific national forests and wilderness areas are available for $6–10 each via the website or at local forest headquarters, or you can buy them at many outdoor stores (but they'll be more expensive). It's always a good idea to contact the forest rangers in the area you'll be visiting and ask if there are any exceptions to the leash-free policy where you're planning to hike, or if your forest destination is charging a small fee for use. Only a few forest areas are charging fees at this point (and they're nominal), and at least 80 percent of the fee goes back into upkeep and improvements of those forests.

Now for the obligatory poop paragraph. As far as bathroom etiquette goes, it's not necessary to pack out the poop. If you don't mind it squishing along in your backpack, that's great. But if you bury it, as you should bury your own, that's OK. Leave the forest as you found it. And please don't let your dog go to the bathroom near a stream. It can be a health hazard to anyone drinking the water later.

And dogs, if you come to really love your national forests, tell your people that because of severely reduced budgets, trail maintenance is suffering. Tell them that the trails could sure use a hand. Tell them that rangers would be thrilled to have teams of dog owners working together to help keep up the trails they use. Your people can contact a ranger to see how they can volunteer.

What follows is a very brief description of each forest. For excellent information about each forest, be sure to visit www.fs.fed.us/r5.

ANGELES NATIONAL FOREST

This 693,000-acre forest with more than 620 miles of trails covers about one-quarter of Los Angeles County and most of the San Gabriel Mountains. Forest Headquarters, 701 North Santa Anita Avenue, Arcadia, CA 91006; 626/574-5200.

CLEVELAND NATIONAL FOREST

This 566,000-acre chaparral- and conifer-covered land has 331 miles of trails, including a section of the Pacific Crest Trail that runs between the Anza-Borrego Desert and Mexico. Forest Headquarters, 10845 Rancho Bernardo Road, Suite 200, Rancho Bernardo, CA 92127-2107; 858/673-6180.

ELDORADO NATIONAL FOREST

Alpine meadows, rivers, streams, and glacial lakes are among the refreshing landscapes you'll come across in this forest, which encompasses 884,000 acres. This one's getting more "leashy," so talk to a ranger to get the scoop if you want leash-free hiking. Forest Headquarters, 100 Forni Road, Placerville, CA 95667; 530/622-5061.

INYO NATIONAL FOREST

This 1.8 million-acre forest stretches 165 miles from eerie, salty Mono Lake south past Owens Lake. It borders Mt. Whitney, the highest peak in the lower 48 states, and is home to hundreds of waterfalls and glacial lakes. Forest Headquarters, 351 Pacu Lane, Suite 200, Bishop, CA 93514; 760/873-2400.

KLAMATH NATIONAL FOREST

Tired of traffic, loud neighbors, and people snarling at your dog? Come here! (But don't tell anyone else about it.) This lovely 1.7 million-acre forest with 1,160 miles of trails is one of the least-used of California's national forests. Forest Headquarters, 1312 Fairlane Road, Yreka, CA 96097; 530/842-6131.

LAKE TAHOE BASIN MANAGEMENT UNIT

The bulk of this 205,000-acre unit of national forest is on the southern half of beautiful Lake Tahoe. Because it gets such heavy use, dogs are required to be leashed at all times. Forest Headquarters, 35 College Drive, South Lake Tahoe, CA 96150; 530/573-2600.

LASSEN NATIONAL FOREST

Wherever you and your dog tread at this 1.4 million-acre forest with 300 miles of trails is breathtaking. Volcanic craters and fascinating geologic features abound. Forest Headquarters, 2550 Riverside Drive, Susanville, CA 96130; 530/257-2151.

LOS PADRES NATIONAL FOREST

Ranging in elevations from sea level at Big Sur to nearly 9,000 feet at the crest of Mount Pinos, this spectacular forest is one of the most rugged and beautiful in the West. At 1.9 million acres, it's also one of the largest forests in the state. Forest Headquarters, 6755 Hollister Avenue, Suite 150, Goleta, CA 93117; 805/968-6640.

MENDOCINO NATIONAL FOREST

Many Bay Area residents come to this million-acre forest for quick day or weekend trips. This is the only one of California's national forests that is not crossed by a paved road or highway, so if you're looking to escape the world of wheels, you'll find your peace here. Forest Headquarters, 825 North Humboldt Avenue, Willows, CA 95998; 530/934-3316.

MODOC NATIONAL FOREST

This 1.9 million-acre forest in the far northeast reaches of the state is where the wild horses and the antelope play. The spartan chaparral- and juniper-covered Modoc Plateau and the surrounding evergreen lands are home to more than 300 species of wildlife. Forest Headquarters, 800 West 12th Street, Alturas, CA 96101; 530/233-5811.

PLUMAS NATIONAL FOREST

Canine hikers and other outdoors enthusiasts are attracted year-round to this 1.2 million-acre magical forest's streams, lakes, deep canyons, and lush mountain valleys. The forest has more than 1,000 miles of sparkling rivers and streams, along with about 100 lakes. Forest Headquarters, 159 Lawrence Street, Quincy, CA 95971; 530/283-2050.

SAN BERNARDINO NATIONAL FOREST

This forest is home to famed Big Bear Lake and Lake Arrowhead, popular Southern California resorts. It comprises 810,000 acres of land that vary from thick pine woods to rocky, cactus-filled desert. Forest Headquarters, 1824 Commercenter Circle, San Bernardino, CA 92408; 909/382-2600.

SEQUOIA NATIONAL FOREST

Giant sequoias, among the world's largest trees, grow in more than 35 magnificent groves on Sequoia National Forest's lower slopes. The park encompasses 1.1 million acres and has 830 miles of trails. Forest Headquarters, 900 West Grand Avenue, Porterville, CA 93257; 559/784-1500.

SHASTA-TRINITY NATIONAL FOREST

Magnificent, massive Mt. Shasta is the most striking of many visual highlights within this 2.1 million-acre forest (the largest national forest in the state). Dogs can explore the less steep parts of this 17-mile-wide, 14,162-foot-high mountain, but the forest has a whopping 1,500 miles of other, more appropriate trails to try. Forest Headquarters, 3644 Artech Parkway, Redding, CA 96002; 530/226-2500.

SIERRA NATIONAL FOREST

Surrounded by big, popular, restrictive-to-dogs national parks such as Yosemite, the 1.3-million-acre Sierra National Forest is a joy for dogs. Forest Headquarters, 1600 Tollhouse Road, Clovis, CA 93612; 559/297-0706.

SIX RIVERS NATIONAL FOREST

Six major rivers (surprise!) are among the 1,500 miles of water in the forest. This long, narrow forest encompasses one million acres of Douglas firs, incense cedars, ponderosa pines, and dozens of other types of trees. Forest Headquarters, 1330 Bayshore Way, Eureka, CA 95501; 707/442-1721.

STANISLAUS NATIONAL FOREST

You and your dog can hike on 660 miles of trails that take you over volcanic ridges, through lush alpine meadows, and under tall pines and cedars in this million-acre forest. Forest Headquarters, 19777 Greenley Road, Sonora, CA 95370; 209/532-3671.

TAHOE NATIONAL FOREST

Lake Tahoe, the blue jewel of the Sierra, makes up this forest's southeast boundary. A hike on even a small part of the forest's 600 miles of trail will take you and your dog through a vast variety of vegetation, including mountain chaparral, mixed conifers, alpine plants, lodgepole pine, and pinyon juniper. Forest Headquarters, 631 Coyote Street, Nevada City, CA 95959; 530/265-4531.

TOIYABE NATIONAL FOREST

Although most of this 3.5 million-acre forest (the largest national forest in the lower 48) is spread throughout Nevada, a relatively small section of it crosses into California. You and your dog can peruse thundering waterfalls, clear streams, glacial lakes, and alpine meadows. Forest Headquarters, 1200 Franklin Way, Sparks, NV 89431; 775/331-6444.

INDEXES

Accommodations Index

For general accommodations information, see pages 14–16.

T

UV

WXYZ

Camping

Restaurant Index

For general restaurant information see pages 13–14.

General Index

QR

XYZ

Acknowledgments

Many tailwags to…

My crackerjack fact-checkers, especially my four-paw hubby, Craig Hanson (who once again came through in a pinch), Denise Selleck (so did she), Nellie Fong (ditto), Kristi Grier, and Nathan Arbuckle.

The intrepid "Three-Dog-Dave" Hepperly and his ever-traveling canine crew for their innumerable and invaluable tips and photos.

Sheryl Smith and her dear dog, Molly, for her continued suggestions of dog-gone great places.

Johanna Lack and Alec Brewster, for helping me sniff out dog-friendly restaurants.

The legions of terrific California dogs who had their humans write to tell me about their wonderful dog-friendly finds around the state. Wherever possible, I've noted you in the text, doggies.

My editor, Kathryn Ettinger, who handled some tricky issues with grace and intelligence.

And to Auntie Silly and Christina Ketchum, for being there for the human child in our family while I slaved away doggedly on this edition.

Keeping Current

Note to All Dog Lovers:
While our information is as current as possible, changes to fees, regulations, parks, roads, and trails sometimes are made after we go to press. Businesses can close, change their ownership, or change their rules. Earthquakes, fires, rainstorms, and other natural phenomena can radically change the condition of parks, hiking trails, and wilderness areas. Before you and your dog begin your travels, please be certain to call the phone numbers for each listing for updated information.

Attention Dogs of California:
Our readers mean everything to us. We explore California so that you and your people can spend true quality time together. Your input to this book is very important. In the last few years, we've heard from many wonderful dogs and their humans about new dog-friendly places, or old dog-friendly places we didn't know about. If we've missed your favorite park, beach, outdoor restaurant, hotel, or dog-friendly activity, please let us know. We'll check out the tip and if it turns out to be a good one, include it in the next edition, giving a thank-you to the dog and/or person who sent in the suggestion. Please write us—we always welcome comments and suggestions.

The Dog Lover's Companion to California
Avalon Travel Publishing
1400 65th Street, Suite 250
Emeryville, CA 94608, USA
email: atpfeedback@avalonpub.com

OGHORN OUTDOORS®

YOUR ADVENTURE STARTS HERE

Foghorn authors are recreation gurus who have hiked and biked the trails, fished the rivers, and pitched their tents to provide readers with the most up-to-date information on enjoying the outdoors. **www.foghorn.com**

ROAD TRIP USA

OPEN ROAD. ENDLESS POSSIBILITIES.

See what the interstates have left behind. **ROAD TRIP USA** takes you off the beaten path, onto classic blacktop, and into the soul of America. **www.roadtripusa.com**

THE DOG LOVER'S COMPANION

The Inside Scoop on Where to Take Your Dog

A special breed of guidebook for travelers and residents who don't want to leave their canine pals behind.

WWW.DOGLOVERSCOMPANION.COM

LIVING ABROAD

DREAM. PLAN. MAKE IT HAPPEN.

With authors who have made the move themselves, these guides show readers how to make their dream of living in another country a reality. www.livingabroadin.com